ISBN 978-1-331-95480-4
PIBN 10259219

This book is a reproduction of an important historical work. Forgotten Books uses
state-of-the-art technology to digitally reconstruct the work, preserving the original format
whilst repairing imperfections present in the aged copy. In rare cases, an imperfection in
the original, such as a blemish or missing page, may be replicated in our edition. We do,
however, repair the vast majority of imperfections successfully; any imperfections that
remain are intentionally left to preserve the state of such historical works.

1 MONTH OF
FREE
READING

at

www.ForgottenBooks.com

By purchasing this book you are eligible for one month membership to ForgottenBooks.com, giving you unlimited access to our entire collection of over 700,000 titles via our web site and mobile apps.

To claim your free month visit:

www.forgottenbooks.com/free259219

Similar Books Are Available from
www.forgottenbooks.com

THE DESCENDANTS

OF

ANDREW WARNER

COMPILED BY

LUCIEN C. WARNER, M.D., LL.D.

AND

MRS. JOSEPHINE GENUNG NICHOLS

THE TUTTLE, MOREHOUSE & TAYLOR CO.
NEW HAVEN, CONN.
1919

TABLE OF CONTENTS

LIST OF ILLUSTRATIONS

FOREWORD

For many years I have desired that some one should prepare a genealogy of the descendants of Andrew Warner, but I felt that my own time was so fully occupied with other duties that I could not consider it. Finally, as no one else seemed likely to undertake the task, in 1914, after completing the publication of my "Personal Memoirs," I decided to commence work on the genealogy. I was fortunate at the outset in securing the assistance of Mrs. Josephine G. Nichols (Mrs. L. Nelson Nichols), a genealogist of large experience and skill. For the past four years she has given almost her entire time to this work and it is largely to her painstaking labor and ability that the genealogy has been carried through with such eminent success.

In first planning the work, I expected to give to it a large amount of my own time, but the extra duties thrown upon me by the great world war has made this impossible. Almost the only direct contributions I have made to the genealogy are the two chapters on "The Warners in Europe" and "Andrew Warner in America." I am especially gratified that I have been able to get together so full an account of our first American ancestor. The numerous data collected from many sources at first seemed like dull statistics, but by being brought together and carefully studied, they take on life and character and bring before us a vivid portrait of the sturdy pioneer, the devoted Christian, the loyal and public-spirited citizen, and the aggressive leader in every important enterprise. Every descendant of Andrew Warner can read this record with a feeling of pride that we have as our first American ancestor a man of such ability and character, and one so worthy to be an example to all succeeding generations of the Warner family.

In gathering the material for this work, help has been received from many sources. As a foundation we had a small volume of fifty pages prepared by Andrew Ferdinando[8] Warner, Jr., and later published by J. J. Warner. Mr. J. R. Hutchinson, a genealogist of London, has made extensive examinations of the records of Essex County in England, and has carried back the record of Andrew Warner from his parents, John and Mary Warner of Hatfield Broad Oak, to his grandfather, John Warner of Great Waltham, and probably also to his great-grandfather, Thomas Warner. Mrs. Selah Raymond of Hartford has also collected for me important facts connected with the history of Andrew Warner, and also of many of his descendants, especially the descendants of Joseph[4]. Special acknowledgment should also be made to Frank F. Starr of Middletown, Conn., who has published a sketch of Andrew Warner based on a careful examination of the original records; also to Henry E. Warner, Ernest N. Warner, Rev. Edgar Haga Warner, Mrs. Erastus S. Warner, S. M. Alvord, Moses M. Warner, and to numerous other members of the Warner family, who are represented in this genealogy. Without their assistance, the facts could not have been secured.

The record has been made as complete as possible with the data which we have been able to collect. There are many breaks in the different lines which we have not been able to fill out. In many cases we have only been able to secure the names and dates of birth, marriage and death, with no incident to give life or individuality to the possessor, but wherever possible, we have inserted some act or circumstance which should reveal the personality of the individual.

As the years go by, records of this kind become increasingly valuable. The history of the Warner family in its earlier generations is largely a New England history. As such the Warners have contributed their full share in developing this continent, and shaping the character of its people. It is for us to see that the contribution of the present and future generations shall be not less honorable and useful than that of our forefathers.

Lucien C. Warner.

New York, October 1st, 1918.

THE WARNERS OF ENGLAND

Several explanations have been suggested as to the origin of the name "Warner". It was used in England in early times as a personal name and occurs in the Domesday Book. In the reign of Henry III of England, mention is made of "Henri le Warn", and in 1302 the annals of Crokerdon Abbey contain the name of "Ythel le Warner". An early English record speaks of "Jacke le Warner", and Langland, the poet, writes of "Watte the Warner". Some authorities give the derivation from *Wern,* in the sense of nationality, combined with *Hari,* warrior, making the Old High German form *Warender,* from which come the English Warner and Warrener, meaning hero-warrior. Others have considered the name as springing from the office or occupation: Warner, one who issues summons in a law court; or, game-warden, who warns away intruders from his lord's domains. These trace the derivation to Anglo-Saxon *Warian,* the "ware" of alarm shouts in England, like the "gare" of France, the latter syllable of beware and aware, and the *wehrer* of Germany.

Andrew Warner, the American ancestor of the Warners described in this book, was descended from the Warners of Essex County, England. The first of his ancestors of whom we have direct proof is John Warner, the father of John² Warner and the grandfather of Andrew. He resided in Great Waltham, or, as it is called in some wills, "Much Waltham," Essex County, England. In his will, dated May 23d, 1584, and proved the 9th of the following September, he bequeaths the lease of his farm in Much Waltham to his wife Margaret. He mentions nine children: Thomas, John, Edward, Andrew, a daughter unnamed (probably Mary who married Emmaston), Margery, Elisabeth, Margaret and Joan, each of whom received bequests, either of money or other property. He calls himself a "husbandman" and his gifts would indicate that he was a man of thrift and of considerable prominence in the community.

Some writers have believed that Great Waltham was the earliest home of the Warners in England. John Philiputt's writing in 1629 gives the pedigree of the early Warner families with their coats of arms, and adds, "All these families with this surname now in existence were surely descended or derived from the Warners of Great Waltham." He does not, however, give proof of this statement that can be accepted as conclusive.

A study of the coats of arms of the different Warner families in England reveals at least six quite different types among the twenty-eight noted in Burke's General Armory (London, 1883, pp. 1076, 7). The simplest and probably the oldest are the arms of the Warners of Great Waltham in Essex County, which were emblazoned on their shields and carved in several parts of the ceiling of the south aisle of the church. They were: Or, a bend engrailed between six roses or cinquefoils three and three gules barbed vert. As our branch of the Warner family resided in Great Waltham, there is strong presumption that this is the shield used by our early ancestors.

ARMS OF WARNER OF GREAT WALTHAM

Eleven Warner crests are described in Fairbairn's Book of Crests (London 1905, pp. 576, 7). The Great Waltham family used a man's head couped below the shoulders, habited chequy or and azure, wreathed about the temples gold and gules, on the head a cap argent. In these heraldic descriptions or denotes gold; gules, red; vert, green; argent, white or silver; sable, black; azure, blue. No motto is quoted for this family but "Spero" is the motto of the Warners of Walthamstow whose arms are almost the same.

Another ancient and simple design was that of John Warner, Esq., High Sheriff of Kent: Argent, a chevron gules between three mulletts pierced sable. The arms of John Warner, Sheriff and Alderman of London, were similar to the above, except that boars' heads took the place of the mullets.

The coat of arms of John Warner of Norfolk (1374) was: Vert, a cross engrailed argent, ermines. This is very similar to the arms engraved on the silver of Captain Augustine Warner, who settled in Virginia in 1628, except that the ermines are omitted.

Still another type is seen in the arms of Sir Edward Warner of Norfolk: Per bend indented sable and argent, azure a fleur-de-lis or. John Warner, Bishop of Rochester from 1637 to 1666, adopted a coat of arms very similar to that of Sir Edward Warner of Norfolk.

The arms of the Warners of Middlesex were: Azure fesse argent with five ermine above and three fleur-de-lis below.

The records of the Great Waltham Warner families go back to the fourteenth century, and from them are traced Warners who

ARMS
CAPTAIN AUGUSTINE
WARNER

resided in the counties of Essex, Suffolk, Hants, Leicestershire, Norfolk, Kent, Middlesex and London. The most noted of the Essex family was Edmund Warner, Esq., who had an estate as early as 1360 in the eastern part of Essex County between Great Waltham and Dunmow, known as "Warner Hall" or "Warner Manor." Edmund was succeeded in 1372 by his son, John Warner, who added largely to the estate through his marriage to Jane, the sister and heir of John Walden. This property, consisting of 418 acres, descended to successive Warner heirs until 1556, when the direct line become extinct, and it was purchased by Richard Lord Rich.

It is quite probable that our ancestor, John Warner, and the Warners of Warner Manor were derived from a common ancestry, though the evidence is not complete. Among the wills recorded in the Archdeacons Court of Essex, is one of William Briggs of Waltham, dated 21 April 1553, which is witnessed by Thomas Warner. The date of this will and the fact that Thomas was the name of both a son and grandson of John Warner who died in 1584, makes it probable that this Thomas Warner was the father of John.

Another of these Essex wills reveals the maternal grandfather of our ancestor, Andrew Warner. John Purchas, in his will dated 27 March, 1585, makes the following bequest: "And the other £10 I give to Mary, my daughter, wife of John Warnerd. I give to either of the two children of the said Mary, my daughter, namely: to Thomas Warner and Mary Warnore, 6 shillings, 8 pence apiece at the age of 18, or the day of marriage." The John here mentioned is the father of Andrew Warner, and Thomas and Mary were two of his brothers and sisters. This will, therefore, connects our ancestors directly with the Purchas family, one of the most distinguished of the Essex families. Samuel Purchas, born in 1577 at Thaxted, less than ten miles from Hatfield, was a noted clergyman and author. His best known work, "Purchas, his Pilgrimage," is still read because of its great literary and historic value.

It is evident from all the above facts that the ancestors of Andrew Warner had been residents of Essex County for several generations, at least, and were connected with the prominent families of the county. It is quite probable, therefore, that further research will reveal a common ancestry of our family and the Warners of Warner Manor.

John[2] Warner, the father of Andrew, was a legatee under and a witness to the will of his brother Thomas, made in 1613. In 1609 he had evidently settled in Hatfield Broad Oak, about ten miles from Great Waltham, as the "Lay Subsidies" or personal taxes for Essex showed that John Warner of Hatfield Broad Oak in that year paid a tax on £3 of household goods, but there is no record of a tax on land. Five years later, on March 10th, the "Feet of Fines," corresponding to our record of deeds, shows that he bought thirty-five acres of freehold land consisting of garden, meadow and pasture, for which he paid forty-one pounds sterling.

Hatfield Broad Oak was formerly known as Hatfield Regis, or Kings' Hatfield, because the manor of Hatfield was a royal manor and was owned by the Kings of England, and to distinguish it from several other Hatfields in the kingdom. It has been associated with many names familiar in English History, and is the supposed burial place of Harold, last of the Saxon Kings. The later name of Hatfield Broad Oak probably originated from the great oak which stood in the forest near the village. It is a pretty, quaint old English village, and not much change has taken place in the number of its inhabitants during the past three hundred years. It still preserves its ancient appearance, notwithstanding some modern innovations. It is situated on an eminence commanding an extended view of the country to the south and west, and is located about twenty-five miles north of London.

In the will of John[2] Warner made a few months after purchasing this land at Hatfield Broad Oak, he calls himself a "Yeoman," that is, one who owns and works his own land as distinguished from the tenant farmer on the one hand and the wealthy landlord on the other. This land usually consisted of several detached pieces; one for a homestead, another for pasture and others for the cultivation of crops. He evidently belonged to the class of small freeholders, or what is now termed the middle-class.

We have little positive knowledge of the members of the family, with the exception of the son, Andrew Warner, and the daughter, Rose Sanford, three of whose sons came to America and settled near Andrew Warner in Hartford. We know that Andrew was born in about the year 1595, the exact date, however, being unknown, and that he remained in England until about his thirty-fifth year. It is probable that he was born in Great Waltham, and that there he passed his earlier years, removing with his parents to Hatfield Broad Oak when he was twelve years old. From his surroundings, and the circumstances of the family, we can infer with some certainty the nature of his early life. During that period he received some education, and was undoubtedly employed in assisting his father and perhaps others in the tillage of the soil. It is probable that he accumulated some property while still in England, for soon after reaching America he became a landowner.

It may be of interest to describe the circumstances which led to the discovery of the will of John Warner of Hatfield Broad Oak, and through it the identity of the father and mother of Andrew Warner. In searching the early history of Hartford, Conn., a record was found of a Court Order on December 5th, 1678, in the settlement of the estate of Zachary Sanford, late of Saybrook, Conn., giving letters of administration to John Durrant and John Loomy of Hadley, as the representatives of Miles Clay of Braintree, England. Miles Clay was one of the heirs of the estate of Zachary Sanford, and it was known that three of the Sanfords, Thomas, Robert and Andrew, were nephews of Andrew Warner and either came to America with him or followed soon after and settled in or near Hartford. This clue led to a search of the records of towns in the vicinity of Braintree, England, and to the discovery of the wills of John and Mary Warner of Hatfield Broad Oak in Essex County.

The will of John Warner of Hatfield Broad Oak, dated July 16th, 1614, mentions six children: Thomas, John, Andrew, Edward, Elizabeth and Rose; also four grand-children, Thomas Warner and Thomas, John and Elizabeth Sanford, who were the children of his daughter Rose. The will of Mary Warner, made thirteen years later, mentions nineteen grand-children. Among these were "The two children of Andrew my sonne." Diligent search has been made to find a record of the birth or baptism of the children of Andrew Warner, who were born in England, but without success. Records were found of an Andrew Warner and his wife, Mary, who bought land in Waltham Holy Cross, Essex County, in 1627, which they sold in 1636. Between 1630 and 1635 there is a record of the baptism of their five children, three of whom were named John, and died within a few days of their baptism. The two who survived were Mary, baptized June 20, 1630, and Francis, baptized November 1, 1635. Four of the dates here given are after the arrival of our Andrew Warner in America, as is shown by the records of Cambridge, Mass. We must conclude, therefore, that the records of Waltham Holy Cross refer to some other Andrew Warner, perhaps a cousin, as there was an uncle of Andrew Warner bearing the same name, and the name Andrew Warner occurred in England after 1700.

We append herewith complete copies of the wills of John Warner of Great Waltham, and of John and Mary Warner of Hatfield Broad Oak, also that of John Purchas. It will be observed that each will is signed with a mark, showing that they could not write, or, what is more probable, that they were too feeble to sign their names. One of the witnesses of the will of John[2] Warner was his son-in-law, Ezekial Sanford. The will of John Warner is dated in the year of the reign of His Sovereign and not in the year of our Lord, as is now customary in giving dates. The wording of these wills is a fine example of the quaint English of three hundred years ago.

The early colonial records show that there were five immigrants of the name of Warner who came to America in or before 1639. The first was Andrew Warner, who was residing in Cambridge in 1632. Another was John Warner, who came on the ship *Increase* in 1635, and settled in Providence, R. I., in or before 1637, at which time he signed a "Compact" in that place. Later he went back to England with his family, but his son John returned to

Rhode Island in 1655 where he afterwards resided. In 1676 he was married to Ann Gorton.

The third was William Warner, who came from England in 1637 accompanied by his two sons, John and David, and settled in Ipswich, Mass. This family has a large number of descendants residing in New England and scattered throughout the states.

The fourth was John Warner, who appears among the original proprietors of Hartford in 1639 and later was one of the original settlers of the town of Farmington. He died in 1679, when he was planning to remove to Waterbury. Colonel Seth Warner of Revolutionary fame is descended from the line of John[1] Warner of Farmington, Conn.; John[2] of Waterbury, Conn.; Doctor Ebenezer[3] and Martha (Galpin) of Woodbury, Conn.; Doctor Benjamin[4] and Silence (Hurd) of Woodbury and Arlington, Vt. Colonel Seth[5], born May 6, 1743, died December 26, 1784, married Hester Hurd. Colonel Seth Warner was third in command of the forces at the taking of Ticonderoga by Colonel Ethan Allen, May 10, 1777, was in the battle of Bennington, August 16, 1777, and was in command at the taking of Crown Point. A monument has been erected to him in his native town, Roxbury, Conn., and another is in Bennington, Vt.

The fifth was Captain Augustine Warner, who came to Virginia about 1628 and settled in York County. Later, in 1656, he removed to Gloucester County, where he acquired a large estate and was prominent in the affairs of the colony. His son, Colonel Augustine, was educated in England and succeeded to his father's estate and influence in the colony. He married Mildred, the daughter of George Reade, and their daughter, Mildred, married Lawrence Washington the grandfather of General George Washington.

No direct relationship has been traced between any of these families, but the fact that the John Warner who settled in Hartford was a fellow townsman of Andrew Warner in both Hartford and Farmington makes it probable that he was connected with the Hatfield Broad Oak family, perhaps a brother or cousin of Andrew Warner. This probability is strengthened by the names of his four children: John, Daniel, Thomas and Sarah, as John and Thomas were the names of two of the children of John Warner of Great Waltham and also of his son John[2] Warner of Hatfield Broad Oak, while John and Daniel were the names of two of the children of Andrew Warner.

WARNER WILLS

In the Name of God Amen the xxiijth Daye of Maye and in the yeare of our lord god 1584 I JOHN WARNER of Much Waltham in the countye of Essex husbandman being sicke in bodye and troubled with Disease but perfect in remembraunce thanks be to Allmightie god for it and waighinge the vncertantye of my life doe ordaine and make this my present testament and last will in manner and forme followinge That is to saye firste and moste principallie I humblie recomend and bequeath my Soule into the hands of Allmightie god my maker steadfastlye beleving that I shalbe saued by Jhesus Christe my savior and redemer and by the marcye of god and by no other meanes merritts or diserts of·myne owne or any others and my bodye to be buried in the Churchyard of Much Waltham aforesaide wth such coste of funeralls as shalbe thought most meete by my executrix Item I giue vnto Margarett my wyfe the lease of my ffarme with the stocke and Cattells as it is nowe and yf it shall happen that Margaret my wyfe do marrye againe before thend and terme of the Indenture or lease of my ffarme as it dothe appeare in the same then I will that the lease of my ffarme remaine vnto my two sonnes Edward and Andrewe payeing the Legacye yf there be any to paye Also I giue vnto them foure of my best horses and the one halfe of my moueable goods to be parted betwixt my fyve daughters and my foure sonnes equallye Deuided Item I giue vnto Thomas my sonne the least shott of Barley in Stonecrofte and two seame of wheate and the ploughinge of half the ground he hathe this year and the next Item I giue and bequeath vnto Edward my· sonne fyve pounds to be paide within fyve yeares after my decease Item I giue and bequeath vnto Andrew my sonne fyve poundes to be paide within sixe years after my decease and yf it shall happen either Edward or Andrewe to departe this worlde then the one of them to be thothers heire Item I giue vnto Margerye my daughter Sixe poundes thirteene shillings foure pence to be paid at the Daye of her marriadge or at the age of xxvj yeares w^{ch}soever shall first happen Item I giue vnto my daughter Elizabeth three poundes to be paid at the age of xxvj yeares or at the Daye of her marriadge w^{ch}soever shall first happen Item I giue vnto Margarett my daughter three pounds to be paid at thage of one and twentye yeares or at the daye of her marriadge wch shall firste happen Item I giue vnto Johan my Daughter three poundes and one wennell calfe to be brought vpp vntill it be wth calfe and yf it shall happen the said Elizabeth Margarett and Johan to departe this worlde before the portion be paid then it allwayes prouided thone to be thothers heire I giue vnto Thomas Saward iij^s iiij^d to be paid imediatlye after my decease Item I giue vnto Xpian Casse iij^s iiij^d to be paide ymediately after my decease Item I giue vnto Thomas Warner the sonne of John Warner my sonne one quarter of Barley or so much money as shall buye one quarter of Barley to be deliuered vnto him when he shall accomplishe the age of tenne yeares Item I giue to three of the children of my daughter Emmerston x^s viz iij^s iiij^d to Vrsula iij^s iiij^d to John iij^s iiij^d to Agnes The residue of all my goode vnbequeathed aswell moveables as vnmoveable in this present will and testament not deuised giuen or bequeathed my Debts paid my necessarye funeralls discharged and this my present will performed accordinge to the true meaning thereof I giue and bequeath vnto Margarett my welbeloued wyfe w^{he} said Margarett my·wyfe I ordaine and make my full and sole Executrix of this my present testament and last will hoping that she will be good vnto her children and myne according to the truste I reposse in her And I clearlye renounce all bequeasts guiftes and Deuises whatsoever heretofore by me made or done and doe ordaine and make .this to be my true and last will In witnes whereof I haue putt my hand and seale the daye and yeare aboue written Sealed and Deliuered in the presence of Richard Pond Thomas Blower John Warner junior The marke of John Warner. *Probatum fuit hujusmodi testamentum nono die mensis Septembris Anno Domini 1584 jurata relicte et executrice.*

Memorandum that THOMAS WARNER of Much Waltham, co. Essex, husbandman, deceased, did on xxvij May, 1613, declare his last will nuncupative in manner and form following:—Unto his daughter Margerie Warner iij^{li}. To Sarah Warner iij^{li}. To Marie Warner iij^{li}. To Elizabeth Belsted, wife of William Belsted, xl^s. All the rest of his goods he gave to Thomas Warner his son, whom he made sole executor, in presence of John Warner, Nicholas Hutt and Andrew Warner. Proved 1 July, 1613, by the executor named. (Arch: Essex, 1613, Filed Will No. 66.)

WILL OF JOHN PURCHAS

27 March, 1585, I John Purchas of Much Waltham, co. Essex, tanner, being grown in age and trobled with disease, do ordain this to be my testament and last will:—First I commend my body to be buried in the churchyard of Much Waltham with such costs as shalbe thought mete by myne executor and my wief. I give to ten of the poorest householders 5s. on the day of my burial. I give to Margaret my wief one-half of my moveable goods within the houses and £13-6-8. To John Purchas my eldest son £6-8-4, and to his three children John, William and Alice 6s.8d. each at 21 or marriage. To George Porcas my youngest son £40, and if it happen to him to depart the world ere he receive it, then John my younger son shall have £20 of his portion, Thomas my son £10, and the other £10 I give to *Mary my daughter, wife of John Warnard. I give to either of the two children of the said Mary my daughter, namely, to Thomas Warnar and Mary Warnare,* 6s.8d. apiece at the age of 18 or the day of marriage. To the daughter of Thomas my son 10s. *To Mary my daughter, wife of John Warner,* £5. To my sister's daughter Joan Downham 10s. at 23 or marriage. To my sister Sandford's daughter Mary 5s. All the rest of my goods I give unto John Purchas my youngest son, to do his will and best withal; which said John my youngest son I ordain and make my full and whole executor, and Thomas my son overseer. Witnesses: Thomas Edwards, Richard Pond the writer of the same. Proved 11 October, 1585, by John Purcas the younger son and executor. (Arch: Essex, Draper, 85.)

WILL OF JOHN WARNER

Commissary Court of London (Essex and Herts). Will filed July, 1614.

In the name of God amen The Sixtenth daie of July in the yeares of the Reigne of our soueraigne Lord James by the grace of god of England Scotland Praunce and Ireland Kinge Defender of the faith that is to say of

England Fraunce and Ireland the twelvth & of Scotland the seaven and
forteth I John Warner of Hatfield Broadoke alias Hatfeild Kinges in the
county of Essex yeoman not sicke in bodie but whole and sound of mynde
and memory, thankes be geven to almightie god doe make and ordeyne this
my last will and testament in mannor and forme followinge First I comitt
and comend my soule into the handes of Almightie god my maker and to
Jesus christ his only sonne my saviour and redemer hoping thorowe his
merittes death and passion to be made partaker of lief euerlastinge and my
bodie to be buried at the discretion of my executor Item I geve and bequeath
unto Mary my wief during her lief all those my freehould landes and tenements with their appurtenances scituate and beinge in Hatfield aforesaid
conteyninge by estimacion five and thirty acres be it more or lesse upon
Condicion that the said Mary my wief shall well and truly paie or cause to
be paid unto Elizabeth Warner my daughter tenne poundes a yeare duringe
the terme of Sixe yeares next and imediately ensuinge after my decease yf
the said Mary shall soe longe live at the two feastes or termes of the yeare
that is to say the feast of the birth of our lord and saviour christ and St.
John the baptist by even and equall porcions, The first payment thereof to
begin and be made at the first of the said two feastes that shall first happen
after my decease & to Thomas John and Ezechiell thre of the sonnes of
Ezechiell Sandford my sonne in lawe the some of thre poundes sixe shillinges
and eight pence a peece as they shall come to be of the age of xxi yeares the
same to be paid by my said wief to some honest man whom my wief shall
thinke well of to the use of the said thre Children that shall pay them the
same at the time of their said seuerall ages of xxi yeares and after the said
time & terme of Sixe yeares my will & mynde is that the said Mary my wief
or hir assignes shall duringe hir lief paie or cause to be paide to Andrewe
Warner and Edward Warner my tw sonnes the some of Fyftie shillinges a peece
yearly at the two feasts or termes of the yeare aforesaid And after the decease
of the said said Mary my wief I geve and bequeath all those my frehould landes
and tenements in Hatfeild aforesaid with their appurtenances unto the said
Andrewe Warner and Edward Warner and to their heires and assignes for
euer upon Condicion that they the said Andrewe and Edward their heires or
assignes shall pay or cause to be paid to Thomas Warner my grandchild the
some of twentie poundes of lawfull englishe money within one month after
he shalbe of the age of xxi yeeres Prouided alwaies that yf Mary my wief
shall dye and departe this lief within the said time and terme of Sixe yeares
next after my decease wherby the said Elizabeth my daughter shalbe unpaid
the porcion that I have geven hir by this my will then my will & mynde is
that the said Andrewe & Edward my said sonnes their heires or assignes shall
pay the same yearly to the said Elizabeth at the feasts aforsaid for &
duringe such time of the said sixe yeares as the same shall be unpaid at the
time of the death of the said Mary & alsoe yf the said Mary doe dye before
said sixe yeares be expired then the said Andrewe & Edward or their heires
shall pay the said sum of iij^{li} vj^s viij^d a peece to the three sonnes of my
said sonne in lawe at the time aforesaid And further if my said wief shall
die before the said sixe yeares shalbe expired then my will and mynde is
that the overseers of this my will herafter named shall have the disposinge
& lettinge of my said frehould landes to the use of the said Andrewe &
Edward untill the said sixe yeers be accomplished & then John my sonne
to have one yeares Rent or profitt thereof Item I geve to said Mary my wief
the lease of a meade called the further mead next Hatfeild duringe the time
I have in the same & thre Milch hease the best she can choose two gelt

horse a cart sadle & harnes fitt for them a load cart a dongue cart & thre load
of wheat strawe yearly to be brought to hir & deliuered by Thomas my sonne
duringe the time of Sixe yeares after my decease yf she liue soe longe alsoe
I geve to the said Mary my wief the one halfe of all my Lynnen thre of my
best beddes with all that belonge to them halfe my brasse half my pewter the
Coubert in the hall the longe table in the hall the Table in the parlour thre
of the best Chestes save one and fower small wooden vessells as tubbes &
keelers & such thinges two hogges of the biggest sort excepting sowes thre
store pigges tenne ewes my executor to choose one and she another; thre
seame of wheat to be paid hir by Thomas my sonne betwene Bartholmewetide
and midsomer next as she shall need the same   Item I geve to John my sonne
the some of one hundred and fortie poundes of lawfull money of England to
be paid him by Thomas my sonne in manner and forme followinge that is
to say fower score poundes therof within one yeare after my decease & thre-
score poundes beinge the residue therof within thre yeares after my decease
Item I geve to the said John my sonne one bed in the chamber wher the
folkes lye called Thomas his bedd with all thinges belonginge to it Item I
geve to Thomas my sonne my lead as it now standes my great brassepot Item
I geve to Rose my daughter the best chest save one   Item I geve to th said
Thomas my sonne thre bedds in the folkes chamber with all that belonge
unto them & my will & mynde is that all other my goodes within my house
not geven nor bequeathed shall be equally devided betwene John Andrewe &
Edward my sonnes & Elizabeth my daughter parte & parte alike The residue
of all my goodes and chattells not geven nor bequeathed (my debts paid &
funerall discharged I geve and bequeath it wholly to Thomas my sonne whom
I make my executor charginge him as he shall answere before god to per-
forme it accordinge to the true meaninge therof And I desire Christofer
Wilkyn & Abraham Purcas to be my ouerseers therof & I geve them for their
paines xx s. In witnes wherof I the said John Warner have herunto sett my
hand and seale the day & yeare abousaid

mark

John   D   Warner

his

(No entry of probate act.)

Sealed and delivered in the presence of

mark

Ezeakell Sanford   Christofor Wilkin   Rober^d   ‡   Howe

his

WILL OF MARY WARNER

Commissary Court of London (Essex and Herts) 1627 No. 148.

In the name of God Amen The Tweleth day of may 1627 and in the third
yeare of the Raygne of our Soveraygne Lord Charles by the grace of God
of England Scotland France and Ireland Kinge defendor of the fayth &c I
Mary Warner of Hatfeild Broadoke alias Hatfeild Regis in the Countie of
Essex widow do Ordayne and make this my last will and Testament in
manner and forme followinge viz. First I bequeath my soule into the handes
of God my Savior and my body to be buried in Christian Buriall.
Item I give unto Thomas Warner my eldest sonne the somme of Twentie
shillinges and also my brewing Leade and unto his wife Joane my best
Gowne except one and one band.

Item I give unto John Warner my sonne the somme of foure poundes of good and lawfull money of England to be payd unto him within one month after my decease.

Item I give unto John my sonne the somme of Twentie shillinges to be payd unto him within one yeare after my decease and also I give unto him one Gowne and one peticoate.

Item I give unto Rose my daughter my worst blackgowne and one peticoate one fetherbed one bolster one Covering one pillow wheron I now ly and three payer of sheetes in her Chest.

Item I give unto my daughter Elizabeth One Chest with linnen Ready layd up and my best gowne and one peticoate.

Item I give unto Rose my daughter the somme of Twentie shillinges to be paid unto her within one yeare after my decease.

Item I give unto Elizabeth my daughter the some of Twentie shillinges to be paid unto her within one yeare after my decease.

Item I give unto Thomas Warner my Grandchild the somme of Tenn shillinges And also I give unto him One Covering One Chest and one pewter platter to be payd and delivered unto him when he shall Come to the Age of One and Twentie Yeares.

Item I give unto Thomas Sanford my Grandchild one Chest one pewter platter one Kettle and one Covering to be delivered unto him when he shall Come to the Age of One and Twentie yeares.

Item I give unto the Two children of my daughter Elizabeth the somme of Twentie shillinges to either of them Tenn shillinges to be payd unto them when they shall Come to the Age of One and Twentie yeares.

Item I give unto Mary Warner the daughter of my son John the somme of Tenn shillinges and also one box with linnen and other thinges layd up in it.

Item I give unto the Two Children of Thomas Warner the somme of Ten shillinges to be equally devyded betweene them and payd unto them when they shall Come to Age of one and Twentie yeares.

Item I give unto the other Two Children of my sonne John the somme of Tenn shillinges to be equally devyded and payd unto them when they shall Come to the Age of one and Twentie yeares.

Item I give unto Mary Sandford the daughter of my daughter Rose the somme of Tenn shillinges.

Item I give unto the other Seven Children of my daughter Rose to every one of them the somme of five shillinges to be payd unto them when they shall severally Come to the Age of One and Twentie yeares.

Item I give unto the Two Children of Andrew my sonne the somme of Twentie shillinges to be Equally devided and payd unto them.

Item I give unto Andrew Warner my sonne the greatest Chest and greatest Ketle and also all other my moveable goodes or Chattells whatsoever to discharge my Legacies and pay such Charges as shall Arise for my buriall And I do Ordayne and make him the sole Executor of this my present last will and Testament in writeing. In witnesse hereof I have putte my hand and seale the day and yeare first above written.

sigum
Mary δ Warner

Sealed and subscribed in the presence of us

sigum
Peter P Linzell & Jonathan Ince

Proved at Stortford 17 July 1627.

ANDREW WARNER IN AMERICA

The first direct mention of Andrew Warner in America is an entry in the town records of Cambridge, Mass., then known as "Newtowne." On January 7th, 1632-3, there are recorded several votes regarding the erection of houses in the town and the division of the pale or fence to enclose the common, with the number of rods each settler was to build. This was the first entry made in the records of the town, except for a single item on December 24th calling a monthly meeting. Forty-two names were given in two columns, and the eleventh line in the first column reads:

"Andrew Warner, 20 Rod"

Twenty-four of the forty-two settlers built less than ten rods each, while only eleven built as much as twenty rods. This would indicate that Andrew Warner was already a resident of Cambridge and was among the more prominent and wealthy members of the new colony. Among the other names was that of John Steel, who afterwards married Mary, the oldest daughter of Andrew Warner.

The same record shows that on November 4th, 1633, Andrew Warner received one "Acker" of land in an award of "Lotts for Cowyards." In January 1634, he bought one piece of "swampe ground by the 'ould feild'" and a little later another piece of three acres in the division of planting ground in the Neck.

On February 3d, 1634, Andrew Warner was appointed on a committee of five to survey the Towne lands and enter them in a book. The constable was head of the committee and "itt is further ordered that these 5 men meet every first Monday in the month at the Constables house....at the Ringing of the bell."

In April 1634, a law was passed by the General Court of Massachusetts Bay Colony, requiring the inhabitants of each town to choose four or more men who, with the constable of the town, should make a record or survey of the lands of each of the inhabitants and send a report of the same to the colonial officials. Andrew Warner was chosen by the inhabitants of Cambridge or Newtowne as one of the four to act for that town.

On May 14th, 1634, Andrew Warner was made a freeman of the Massachusetts Bay Colony.

On November 23d, 1635, Andrew Warner was the third of nine persons "Chossen to order bussines of the whole Towne for the year following and untell new bee Chossen in their rooms,....wch nyne are to haue the power of the whole Towne as those formerly Chossen hadd." This record shows that "commission government" is not altogether a modern invention, but was practiced in the early New England colonies.

The above records show that as early as 1632-3 Andrew Warner was residing in America and was a member of the Cambridge colony. He was born about 1595, so he was at this time thirty-seven years old—in the full vigor of early manhood. The reason for his removal to America we can only know by inference. It was during the reign of Queen Elizabeth that Protestantism was restored to England, and it was also during her reign that Puritanism appeared. Towards the close of her life, the persecutions of the Puritans, who were non-conformists to the established church, became severe, and under her successor, James I, matters became decidedly worse for them both in civil and religious affairs.

In 1625, Charles I ascended the throne of England. He at once assumed all the power of Church and State and commenced a pitiless warfare against Puritanism. His chief instrument for that purpose was the infamous Archbishop Laud. The ministers of that religion were driven from their livings, or into exile, and the laymen were tortured and forced from their homes. Thousands of the best blood in old England sought a home or refuge in the new world.

Among those who dared to oppose this policy was the brilliant preacher, Rev. Thomas Hooker. He was "silenced" as a minister of the church by Bishop Laud in 1626, but he continued to speak as a "lecturer" in Chelmsford, Essex County, until 1629, when the persecution became so strong that he left Chelmsford and the following year fled to Holland.

Hooker had a powerful influence in all that part of England where he lived, and after his escape to Holland, a large number of his followers emigrated to America. These were known as the "Hooker Company" and also as the "Braintree Company" from Braintree, which was the chief town in that part of Essex County from which they came. In 1633 Mr. Hooker left Holland and came to America, where he arrived September 4th, 1633, on the Griffin, to become the pastor of the church at Cambridge, made up very largely of his former followers.

John Warner, the father of Andrew, moved to Hatfield Broad Oak in Essex County, England, in 1609, where he lived until the time of his death in 1614. Hatfield is only twenty miles from Braintree, and only sixteen miles from Chelmsford where Hooker lectured from 1626-29. Andrew Warner must have lived in or near Hatfield at this time, for in 1627 his mother died at Hatfield and Andrew was the executor of her estate.

We see, therefore, that Andrew Warner was a member of the community in England which was so profoundly stirred by the teaching of Hooker and that he came to America at the same time as the large emigration of Hooker's followers. We also learn that later he followed Hooker to Hartford and was a deacon in his church. In view of all these facts, it seems altogether probable that Andrew Warner was one of Hooker's adherents while in England; that he left England to avoid persecution, and that he came to America to find that freedom in religious worship which was denied to him in his own country.

It is interesting to note that Andrew Warner came to America near the beginning of that great tide of emigration which started in 1629. Up to that time Plymouth and Salem had been settled, but the total English population of New England was hardly more than eight hundred. In 1629 Charles I dissolved Parliament and began his active crusade against all dissenting forms of religion. In April, 1630, Winthrop left for America, followed later in the year by seventeen ships and over one thousand people. By 1634 the annual emigration had increased to four thousand. In 1640 the Long Parliament met, the power of the King was checked and the active flood of emigration ceased, but at this time the population of New England had increased to 26,000.

The first of the Braintree Companies settled at Mount Wallaston, afterwards called "Quincy." Governor Winthrop's history of New England makes the following reference to this colony under date of August 14th, 1632. "The Braintree Company (which had begun to sit down at Mount Wallaston) by order of Court, removed to Newtowne. These were Mr. Hooker's company." There is a tradition in the Warner family that Andrew Warner was at Mount Wallaston with this early Braintree Company and it is quite probable that this is true, but no positive evidence has been discovered. The reason for removal to Newtowne or Cambridge was for the greater safety of the people, as Newtowne had been fixed on as the site of a fortified town, by order of the General Court December 30th, 1630.

Before the advent of the Braintree Company, Mount Wallaston passed through a unique and unsavory experience for a New England town. A trading settlement was established there about 1625, by Captain Wallaston, who soon went away to Virginia leaving affairs in the hands of Thos. Morton. He gathered about him a boisterous crowd of adventurers, quite non-Puritan in their conduct. The Plymouth colony was so outraged by their behavior that Governor Bradford in his history of Plymouth Plantation devoted eight pages to their unholy doings. Hawthorne's "May-pole of Merry-Mount" is based on the stories of this band.

The following records are an additional evidence of the prominence of Andrew Warner in the town of Cambridge, as well as an illustration of the early methods of doing town business. These early records show that spelling was not an exact science three hundred years ago.

"The 4th January 1635"

"It is furthered ordered that the burryinge place shalbee palled in: whereof John Taylcot is to doe 2 Rodd, Georg Steele 3 Rod and Agate Thomas Hosmer 3 Rod, Mathew Allen 1 Rodd and Andrew Warner appointed to get the Remainder done at A publik Charge & he is to have iii A Rodd"

The homestead occupied by Andrew Warner is thus described in the "Proprietor's records of the town of Cambridge":

"June The 4th (1635)"

"Andrew Warner In the Towne one Howse and about one Roode for a Backside and garden, Marsh Lane on the south west, Creeke Lane on the northwest, Will Kellsey northeast, Mathew Allen on the southeast."

According to Page's History of Cambridge, Marsh Lane corresponds to the present Elliot Street, and Creek Lane to Brattle Square. This places Andrew Warner's early home within a few rods of Harvard University, in the very heart of Cambridge. Besides this home lot he also owned six other parcels of land in Cambridge; one acre in the West End, eighteen acres in the Neck, fifteen acres in the Great Marsh, two lots of one-half acre each in Ox Marsh and twelve and one-half acres in Old Field.

William Wood, writing about this time of Cambridge, describes it as follows:—

"One of the neatest and best compacted towns in New England, having many fair structures with many handsome contrived streets. The inhabitants are most of them very rich and well stored with cattle of all sorts, having many hundred acres of ground paled in with one general fence, which is about a mile and a half long which secures all their weaker cattle from the wild beasts."

"The 4th of Aprill 1636"

"Andrew Warner and Joseph Cooke to make a rate for the devision of the Aylwifs"

"The 23d Aprill 1636"

"Agreed with Andrew Warner to fetch home the Aylwifs from the weir and he is to have a Thowsan and load them himselfe for Caredge and to have power to take anny man to help him he payeinge of him for his woorke."

The significance of hauling Aylwifs will be made clear by the following quotation from "Johnson's 'Wonder-Working Providence' " ·

"But the Lord is pleased to provide for them great store of Fish in the springtime, and especially Alewives about the bignesse of a Herring, many thousands of these they used to put under their Indian Corne, which they plant in Hills five foote asunder, and assuredly when the Lord created this Corne hee had a speciall eye to supply these his peoples wants with it, for ordinarily five or six graines doth produce six hundred."

On December 20th, 1636, Andrew Warner sold to Capt. George Cook his dwelling house, and all his other lands in the town of Cambridge, and either before or soon after this time, he removed to Hartford, Conn. After the coming of Hooker and his colony to Cambridge, the people began to question the desirability of their location and in May, 1634, complained to the General Court of straitness for want of land, especially meadow, and asked leave to look out either for enlargement or removal. Their request was at first refused, but in September of the same year, after a fuller statement of their needs had been presented to the General Court, they were granted more territory. The people having heard glowing accounts of the fertility of the soil of the Connecticut Valley from some of their number who had been there, and not being fully satisfied with the new arrangement, petitioned the General Court for permission to remove to Connecticut, stating that it was not desirable that this territory should fall into the possession of the Dutch who had settled in New York. It is also probable that Mr. Hooker was restive under the theocratic form of government which had been established in the Massachusetts Bay Colony, for "religious liberty" meant to them that the right to vote and hold office should be limited to the members of the Congregational Church. Mr. Hooker was probably the earliest man in America to advocate true democracy, or the rights of all the people, and under his leadership a new and much broader policy was adopted in the Hartford Colony. ‾

Seeing the "strong bent" of the people to remove to Connecticut, the General Court held at Newtowne, March 3rd, 1635-6,* granted their petition. At the same time a commission was appointed to govern said plantation, to hear and determine in a judicial way all

* Up to 1751 England and her colonies adhered to the old calendar in which the year began on March 26th instead of January 1st. Accordingly in most of the dates before that year we find the old year with a new year affixed to it in giving dates between January 1st and March 25th. This was not a uniform practice and leads to some confusion of dates.

differences that might arise among the people, and in case of mis
demeanor to fine and levy the same or inflict corporal punishment
as might seem best, to make and decree such orders as might seem
necessary for the public good and military discipline. This commission was composed of eight members, one of whom was Andrew
Warner. He had already served on a similar commission in charge
of the affairs of Newtowne, and it is proof of his able and faithful
service that he was, within less than a year, appointed on the new
commission for Hartford.

A few of the Newtowne company removed to Hartford in
October, 1635, but the majority did not leave until May 31st, 1636.
Mr. Benjamin Trumbull gives the following description of the
journey in the History of Conn., pub. 1797, p. 55:

"About the beginning of June, Mr. Hooker, Mr. Stone and about a hundred men, women and children took their departure from Cambridge and
travelled more than a hundred miles, through a hideous and trackless
wilderness to Hartford. They had no guide but their compass; made
their way over mountains, thro' swamps, thickets and rivers, which were
not passable, but with great difficulty. They had no cover but the heavens,
nor any lodgings but those which simple nature afforded them. They drove
with them a hundred and sixty head of cattle, and by the way, subsisted
on the milk of their cows. Mrs. Hooker was borne through the wilderness
upon a litter. The people generally carried their packs, arms and some
utensils. They were nearly a fortnight on their journey."

Arriving at their destination, this little company laid the foundation of Hartford, Conn. They proceeded at once to obtain title
to the land and purchased the same in 1636 from the Indians.
The portion, now covering the older settled part of the city, was
parcelled out to each, the home lots consisting of about two acres
of land.

The first mention of Andrew Warner in the records of Hartford
is a description of his home-lot entered in February, 1639:

"One parcell on which his dwellings house now standeth with other out
houses, yards, or gardens therein beinge, Containinge by Estimacon two acres,
more or lesse, abuttinge on the high way lyinge on the South side of the
little river on the North, and on the high way Leadinge from George Steels
to the South meadow on the South and on Samuell Wakemans Land on the
East, and on Nathaniell Wards Land on the West."

According to this description, his residence was on the north side
of the present Charter Oak Avenue a little east of Main Street. In
addition to the home lot, the records show Andrew Warner to have
owned four other parcels of land located in different parts of the
town, aggregating in all about 80 acres.

In speaking of him as the owner of the "home lot" described

above he is called "Andrew Warner, Deacon to the Church of
Christ there." There is no direct proof of the time when he was
made deacon, but most of the writers have thought it was before
his removal from Cambridge.

The records of Hartford, like those of Cambridge, give evidence
of the abundant activities of Andrew Warner in the new town. In
later years a monument has been erected to the Founders of Hartford in the burying ground back of the First Church, and tenth of
the names inscribed on this monument is that of Andrew Warner.
The following items are for the most part published in the Public
Records of Connecticut and in the Conn. Hist. Soc. Publications and
are also given in the careful accounts compiled by Frank F. Starr
in his work on the Ancestral Lines of Judge Goodwin.

In 1639-40, there were entered on the Town Records

"The names of such Inhabitants as have Right in undivided Lands."

The fifteenth name in the list is that of Andrew Warner.

January 3d, 1639-40, the inhabitants of Hartford entered into
an agreement as to the proportion each resident should receive in
the division of common lands, evidently based on their financial
rating.

The largest apportionment, that of one hundred and sixty acres,
went to John Haynes, Esq. The smallest division was three acres.
Only eight persons had larger shares than Andrew Warner's allotment of eighty-four acres. It is interesting to note that his prosperity was well maintained, for seven years later, on the tax list of
1657, Andrew Warner stood fifth from the highest.

At a town meeting held January 11, 1640 (1639-40), a committee
of ten men, including Andrew Warner, was appointed to survey
and divide the lands on the east side of the Great River.

In January, 1639, and again in 1647, he was chosen a Surveyor
of Highways, and in January, 1640, he with two others were
appointed to lay'out highways in the South Meadow and the Forty
Acres and highways leading to the swamps, and to arrange with
the owners satisfaction for the land taken for such highways.

At this time his abilities were recognized by the General Court of
Connecticut, for on the 8th of February, 1640-1, he was appointed
on a committee of six, consisting of two men from each of the towns
of Hartford, Wethersfield and Windsor:

"For the prventing of differences that may arise betwixt the Plantations
from trespasses of Cattle wch are ofte necessitated by reson of their border-
ing on agᵗ another—they shall take into their serious consideration how the
grownd belonging to the seuerall Plantations may be best imprued, so as to

sute ech others conuenience, whereby their Corne may be prserued and their Cattle keepte wth lest chardge of fencing or herding, as may most conduce to the common good".

A few days later, Feb. 18th, 1640-1, the town appointed him on a committee to arrange for the equable division of lands on both sides of the Great River.

"At a Ginerall Toune metting" held in Hartford, Jan. 27th, 1647-8, he with four others was appointed to survey the common lands and fences.

The name of Andrew Warner does not occur in the Hartford records from January, 1647-8 to April, 1650. With others he had become interested in the adjoining plantation of Farmington, and it is probable that he resided in Farmington during this time. The Farmington records show that Andrew Warner in March, 1648, owned four pieces of land in that town. The five acres "on which his dwelling house now standeth" was bounded north on the common, south on the highway, east on land of William Lewis, and west on land of Matthew Webster." The second volume of the Memorial History of Hartford County contains an old map of Farmington which locates this home lot on the north side of the highway facing Main Street. This is now the property of the Country Club. Andrew Warner also owned ten acres in the "Slipe," twenty-two acres in the Lower Meadow and one-hundred acres in the Great Meadow.

Andrew Warner must have returned to Hartford in 1649-50, for in February, 1650, his home lot in Farmington is recorded as the property of William Lewis.

In the records of the Particular Court of Hartford, for the term beginning March 7th, 1649, is this interesting entry :—

"This Courte Adiudges Natha: warde and Andrew warner to pay Thomas Lord for Curing the eare of the Indian Squaw which theire doggs bitt off, and to pay the squaw 2 bush of Indian Corne, which Corne, the next Indian or Indians that Shall any way by clapping hands or throwing stones at any dogg or doggs, provoke them, shall pay to the said warde againe."

At a town meeting held April 15, 1650, power was given to Andrew Warner and five others

"to set in order the worke of the high wayes belonginge to both sides of the Towne & to establish the same."

At the same meeting, he and John White agreed with the town

"to make a fence crosse the riuerett & to Indeavor keepe the same for seauen yeares. for the keepinge of cattell & swine out of the meadowes that they shall haue for their Labor ffowerty shillings by the yeare to be payd them wth in the yeare in euery of the sayd seauen yeares."

Andrew Warner was chairman of a coroner's jury, Dec. 2, 1652, which decided that, "Wee doe finde that the sd partye, going against his master's Comand with his master's cannoe into a place of danger, or that is to the milldam, is guilty of his own death, being drowned—" (Hartford Court records, p. 38).

In May, 1657, Mr. Clarke and John Allen were asked to present at the next session of the Court " a list of them that desire to bee troopers   which said Court is to approve of them they see meet." This list contains fourteen Hartford men, of whom Andrew Warner was one. As Andrew Warner was at this time over sixty years of age, it is possible that this record refers to the son Andrew, and not to the father.

Upon the death in 1647 of the Reverend Thomas Hooker, the latter's associate, Samuel Stone, was in charge of the church as teacher, but not as pastor. In a few years differences arose between Mr. Stone and many of the congregation. This controversy, at first local, regarding matters of church membership, discipline, and baptism, spread to neighboring churches and was felt throughout New England. It led not only to the establishment of the Second Church of Hartford, but to the settlement of Hadley by colonists from Hartford, Wethersfield and neighboring churches, and greatly disturbed the peace of the town and colony.

Attempts were made by the General Court and various advisory bodies to end the quarrel. Warner belonged to the anti-Stone party and with twenty others signed a letter dated March 12th, 1655-56, in which they stated their inability to accept the suggestions of the other side and asked for

"an Able and Indifferent Councell".

The letter is so characteristic of our early New England ancestors that we give it entire.

Dear Brethren,—We have as seriously and sadly as the Lord hath helped vs considered and weighed what hath beene p^rsented to vs in the papers receiued from Mr. Stōne and seuerall brethren, and doe solemnly profess wee have laboured wth all o^r might according to o^r Abilities and Light, to receiue satisfaction in those things wee have p^rsented to you for help in, but cannott meete wth that in yor Answ^rs wch wee hoped and looked for, and therefore, doe declare o^rselves that o^r doubts and difficulties yet remaine wth vs, and in some of them they are rather increased than remoued, and therfore to the great greife of o^r hearts must say, that as the case now stands wth this Church wee cannott wthout sin till wee receiue other Light joine wth you in any office acts put forth by Mr. Stone, for hee hath as much as in him lyes laide downe his place, hath acted since accordingly, and the church hath done that wch wee conceive holds forth their acceptance; neither has Mr. Stone in his Answer to those questions that concernes the same held forth satisfying and convincing Light to vs to the contrary: Wee doe therfore humbly desire that you would forbear doing that wch will put vs oppon doing that wch you shall Judge offensiue or otherwise expose vs to temptations to act wth you doubtingly, to the great offence of God and hazard (if not wounding) o^r inward peace, vntill wee can haue helpe from an able and Indifferent Councell mutually chosen wch wee desire may bee indeauored and attended wth as much speed as may bee.

The following extract from Hull's Diary (p. 183) sheds a little side light on the controversy:

"The breach at Hartford again renewed; God leaving Mr. Stone their officer, to some indiscretion, as to neglect the Church's desire in the celebration of the Lord's supper, and to proceed to some acts of discipline towards the formerly dissenting brethren; and Satan taking occasion also by Mr. Stone's absence some weeks from them, and neglecting of the use of all means to cherish and to look unto their newly set bones and joints, they easily brake again."

George Leon Walker, D.D., pastor and historian of the First Church, Hartford, after reviewing this controversy concludes that

"On the whole, respecting the controversy itself which turmoiled the Church so long, the impartial verdict of history must be, that spite of many irregularities and doubtless a good deal of ill-temper on both sides, the general weight of right and justice was with the defeated and emigrating minority."

In this view, Doctor Edwin Pond Parker, historian of the Second Church, Hartford, concurs.

Finding all attempts at reconciliation impossible, a number of the residents of Hartford with some of their friends from Wethersfield and Windsor entered into the following agreement which resulted in the founding of Hadley, Mass.

"At A meting at Goodman Wards house in Hartford Aprill 18th, 1659, the Company there mete Ingaged themselves (under their owne hands or by their Deputies whom they had Chosen) to remove themselves and their ffamilies out of the Jurisdiction of Connecticut Into the Jurisdiction of the Mattatusets as may Apeare in A paper Dated the day and yeare Abovesaid: the Names of the Ingagers are these:"

Then follow fifty-nine names, of which Andrew Warner was one. At the end of the names is the following addition: "Not fully under this Ingagement Danniell Warner A house lot."

On April 25th, 1659, at another meeting, a committee of five was appointed to go to the new territory which they had selected on the east side of the Connecticut River opposite Northampton and to lay out home lots for the new settlers. Andrew Warner at this time was about 65 years old. He had been a resident of Hartford for over twenty years, and had seen it grow from a few huts in the wilderness to an organized and prosperous town, but now for the third time in his life he left an established home to settle as a pioneer in the unbroken wilderness.

Andrew Warner sold his Hartford homestead on November 17th, 1659, to William Loveridge of Hartford for £130,

"to be payd one-third part In wheat, the other third part in peas, both at the price Currant and the other third part in suteable Hatts the corn to be payd in at the Comon landing place or any House in Hartford as the sayd Andrew or his assigne shall appoynt, the corn to be sweet & every way well Conditioned & the hats to be two shillings in the pownd cheaper than I sell thos sorts By retayle".

The manner of payment for this property suggests that Andrew Warner may have been engaged in the mercantile business. In any case he must have been very much of a trader to have taken one-third of his pay for this land in hats.

Another piece of his Hartford property was sold to Jonathan Gilbert, for in Gilbert's will, September 10th, 1679, he speaks of the "pasture I bought of Andrew Warner."

We do not know just when Andrew Warner removed to his new home, but it was before October 8th, 1660, for on that date there was "a Towne meeteing at Andrew werner's House" at which action was taken regarding the admission of inhabitants. The votes passed at this meeting were signed by twenty-eight men, including Andrew Warner. It is probable that these twenty-eight were all the settlers who at that date had taken possession of their land. Some of the original signers of the agreement did not remove to Hadley and others selected lots on the west side of the river at Hatfield. The village of Hadley, as finally laid out, consisted of forty-seven lots, nearly all of eight acres each, laid out on each side of a street running north and south, 330 feet wide and about one mile in length. These lots were situated in a bend of the river so that the street led directly to the river at both the north and south ends. Andrew Warner's homestead was on the west side of the street, the twelfth lot from the north end. The present highway and street car line from Amherst to Northampton runs immediately to the south of Andrew Warner's former lot.

In addition to the home lot, Andrew Warner later became the owner of eight other pieces of property in or near Hadley, aggregating in all forty-two acres. It seems to have been the custom of the early New England settlers to have their land scattered in several parcels rather than united in one or two holdings. As we have shown, Andrew Warner was the owner of seven pieces of land in Cambridge, at least four in Hartford, and four in Farmington.

The records of Hadley show the active part that Andrew Warner continued to take in public affairs. He was three times elected Townsman, or Selectman, as it was afterwards called, in 1660, 1667 and 1673.

Rev. Samuel Hooker, the son of their Hartford pastor, was at this time preaching at Springfield. On December 17th, 1660, Andrew Warner was one of a committee "chosen to meet and Confere together to send Some propositions to Mr. Hooker About his Removell to us." Mr. Hooker did not accept the invitation to Hadley, but he became the pastor of the church in Farmington, where he died.

On December 12th, 1661, the town voted to build a meeting house in the common street and "Goodman Warner" was appointed one of the committee to take charge of the work.

In March, 1662-3, he served on a committee to treat with the town of Northampton about the lay-out of the highway through the meadows of that town.

February 13, 1664, he was chosen on a committee

"to view the way to the mouth of Chickopay River & to the Falls in the Great River, to see if it is a feasible way for transporting goods & to confer with Springfield & Northampton men about it".

In August, 1663, November, 1664, and September, 1665, he was one of a committee appointed to view and report concerning lands which certain inhabitants of the town had desired to have set out to them.

July 11th, 1666, he was appointed one of a committee to lay out some land given by the town for the benefit of the Grammar school. In the following March he was one of a new committee to let out the land.

In February, 1667, he was one of a committee of five to "provide a Boate ffor the fferrye who shall have power to call out all men that are willing to worke aboute the same rather than to pay their proportion in corne as allsoe to call out any they Judge most meete ffor the worke."

In March, 1661, and September, 1663, he served on the jury of the Hampshire County Court.

In March, 1665, suit was brought against Andrew Warner by the legatees of John Barnard, a former resident of Hadley, for damages caused by the burning of a malt house he was using which belonged to Barnard's estate. The case did not come to trial, but was settled by agreement.

The evidence that Andrew Warner was a maltster is further

shown by the following entry on an account book of John Pynchon, the leading citizen and merchant of Springfield:

"Goodm: Warner of Hadley, ye Maulster Dr."

The credit side, covering a period from February 28, 1671, to September, 1674, reads thus:

"By 7 bush. of Malt 1672 at 4^{s}3^d 01–09–09
July 5, 1673, By 33 bush & ½ Malt at 4^{s}6^d 07–10–09
Sept. 1674 By 30 bush of Malt at 4^s 06–00–00
                                                     ————————
                                                     15–00–06"

It is very probable that Andrew Warner learned the brewing business at his childhood home, for in his mother's will is recorded this item ·

"I give unto Thomas Warner my eldest sonne, the somme of Twentie shillinges and also my brewing Leade."

Judd, in his History of Hadley, makes the following statement of Andrew Warner's still: "Andrew Warner was the owner of a small still, valued at 10 shillings." That this was of small size is shown by the valuations of other stills in the settlement, notably that of Dr. Hastings of Hatfield, whose still was valued at 40s. Most of them ranged from 15 to 45s. The small stills were used for distilling cordials, sweet waters and medicinal waters from herbs, flowers, spices, etc. Judd also states that the malting business established by Andrew Warner was continued for 130 years by three generations of his descendants, Jacob,[2] Jacob,[3] Jr., and Orange.[4]

Under date of March 29th, 1670, the Hampshire County Records contain the following entry:

"Andrew Warner of Hadley is free frō military exercise with the company there."

As he was at this time about seventy-five years old, he might well be excused from further military service.

In October, 1678, the General Court passed an act that

"all his majestjes subjects within this jurisdiction that are of sixteene yeares of age and upwards"

should take the oath of allegiance. Among those who took the oath from Hadley were "Andrew Warner, Isaac Werner and Jacob Werner." Among the Hatfield names was "Daniel Werner."

Of the first wife of Andrew Warner we have not been able to

discover a single record. The family tradition is that her name was Mary, but we find no positive proof. Not far from the time of Andrew Warner's removal to Hadley, he was married to Esther or Hester Wakeman Selden, baptized June 15, 1617, died in Hadley in 1693, daughter of Francis Wakeman of Bewdley, Worcestershire, England, and his wife, Anne Goode. Her first husband was Thomas Selden who died in 1655. They had eight children, Thomas, John, Mary, Esther (1), Joseph, Hannah, Esther (2), and Sarah. The first mention of Esther Selden in connection with Andrew Warner is a record of the Connecticut Probate Court, December 3d, 1663, in which complaint is entered against Andrew Warner because he had not given proper security to the Court for the payment of the legacies due from the estate of Thomas Selden to his children. The children were not of age, and Andrew Warner evidently had the custody of the money. The matter was adjusted as is shown by the court records for the following March. Later records show that in 1673 Andrew Warner conveyed to Joseph Selden certain lands for £60, of which £40 was the legacy due from his father and £20 was for labor. In 1678-9 a similar deed was given to Hannah Selden for her share of the legacy from her father. It is probable that the settlements were made at about the time the children became of age.

In the original volume of "Births, Burials & Marriages of Families" of Hadley on folio 20 is this entry:

"Andrew Warner died jenewary 1684"

This entry does not give the exact date and probably was made some time after his death, for in the inventory of his estate taken December 23, 1684, it states "who dyed december 18, 1684, aged about 90 years." This latter statement may therefore be accepted as the date of his death, and also as authority for his age.

The life of Andrew Warner was remarkable because of the time in which he lived, as well as because of the many important incidents connected with his own distinguished career. Born in the reign of Queen Elizabeth, he outlived the reign of two kings, the Protectorate of Oliver Cromwell and saw the restoration to the throne of Charles II. His life thus covers the entire period of the religious persecution in England, and the great flood of emigration which settled and gave character to the American colonies.

We cannot but admire the record of the life of this sturdy Puritan, and the spirit which caused him, for the sake of a greater religious freedom, to give up the comforts of civilization in old England, for an unknown destiny in a far distant and unexplored

country; which impelled him to take up a life of self denial, priva-
tion, hardship and danger in the depths of the New England
wilderness, that he might be independent, and might worship God
in the manner dictated by his conscience.

He saw, at the dawn of the early settlement of this country,
history in the making, and for fifty years was a part thereof; and,
at last, after a long period of devotion to his Church, of which he
was a pillar, and to the new State, of which he was a founder, he
laid himself down to sleep in the last home he had made in the
lovely valley of the Connecticut. In the quaint language of his day,
he "rested from his labors." No monument marks his grave in
Hadley, but Mount Warner, nearby, standing through the ages, is
a sufficient and enduring monument to his memory. Time may
erase the name, and destroy the stone, but the mountain will remain
forever.

On March 31st, 1685, the will of Andrew Warner was presented
to the Hampshire County Court by his son Daniel Warner, an
inventory of the estate was filed, and the property was distributed
as directed by the will. There is so much of interest connected
with the life of Andrew Warner on the part of all of his descendants, that we give his will in full.

Immediately following the will is an inventory of the property
which consists of real estate, clothing, household goods, grain and
stock of a total value of £365–11–4. The real estate consisted of
nine parcels as follows:

"4 acres Ld in Hoccanum at 20^l £020–00–00
2 acres & a rood at ye burieing yard 5^l house & homestead 65^l 070–00–00
6 acres in ye great meadow On the South side of ye Midle
    way at 030–00–00
4 acres in ye Swamp at 8^l 4 acres in s^d Meadow at 24^l 056–00–00
4½ acres in Hoccanum at 20^l One piece of skirts there at 2^l 022–00–00
12 acres of Land Over ye River at 55^l .... 055–00–00"

The will of Andrew Warner mentioned nine children, each of
whom received legacies. Five of the number receive only ten
shillings each, probably for the reason that they had been provided
for by earlier gifts. The widow, Esther, received £100 which was
over one-fourth of the estate, besides annual payments during her
life of eighty shillings, the use of one-half of the dwelling house
and lot, ten loads of wood and other supplies. The only gift not
to his immediate family was five pounds to Mary Taylor, the
daughter of his wife Esther by her first marriage. It is probable
that she came into the family with her mother as a little girl, and
this gift was a special token of his affection for her.

It has generally been considered that Jacob, the youngest child of Andrew Warner, was the son of his second wife Esther, though the reasons for this view are not entirely conclusive. Andrew Warner in his will directs Jacob to pay "forty shillings annually or yearly to his mother, Easter Werner"; but in the next paragraph he uses the same language in reference to Daniel who was a young man at the time of his father's removal to Hadley and one of the signers of the Hadley agreement. A stronger proof is found in the fact that after the death of Esther Werner, in March, 1693, a bond was filed in the settlement of her estate by Thomas Selden, Joseph Selden and Jacob Warner, "Sons to Easter Werner alias Selding of Hadly deceased." On the other hand, Jacob did not receive any of Esther Warner's estate, but it was divided between four of her children by her first marriage, Joseph Selden the eldest receiving £36 and the others £18 each.

No record of the birth of any of the children of Andrew Warner has been found so that our knowledge of them is not accurate. In the will of Mary Warner, the mother of Andrew Warner, made May 12, 1627, she gives twenty shillings to "the Two Children of Andrew my sonne," showing that Andrew then had two children, and as he was made the sole executor of the will, he must have been living in England at that time. In the will of Andrew Warner he mentions "My daughter Pratt." This is believed to be Hannah Warner, the wife of Daniel Pratt of Hartford. In the graveyard of the First Church of Hartford is a tombstone to the memory of Hannah, wife of Daniel Pratt, who died September 3d, 1682, aged about 50 years. This would indicate that she was born in 1632 at the time Andrew was living in Cambridge, Mass. The term "about 50" is, however, rather elastic, and it is possible that she may have been born one or two years earlier or later. It is probable that the two children mentioned in the will of Mary Warner were Mary and Andrew, and it is quite probable that the next two sons, Robert and John, were also born before the removal to America. The date and place of Daniel's birth are altogether uncertain. If Hannah's age and date of death are correctly given on the tombstone, it is probable that Daniel is younger than Hannah instead of older, as has been heretofore assumed.

Children of Andrew Warner, probable order

2 *Mary Warner*, m. (1) John Steel, Jr.; (2) William Hills.
3 *Andrew Warner*, m. Rebecca Fletcher.
4 *Robert Warner*, m. (1) Elizabeth Grant; (2) Deliverance (Bissell) Rockwell.
5 *John Warner*, m. Anna ————.
6 *Hannah Warner*, m. Daniel Pratt.

7 *Daniel Warner,* m. (1) Mary ———; (2) Martha Boltwood.
8 *Isaac Warner,* m. Sarah Boltwood.
9 *Ruth Warner,* m. John Kellogg (?).
10 *Jacob Warner,* m. (1) Rebecca ———; (2) Elizabeth Goodman.

WILL OF ANDREW WARNER

(Hampshire County, Mass., Probate records, volume 1, page 248)

"I Andrew Werner of Hadley in the Countie of Hampshire in New England being through ye mercy of God Sound in mynde & Memory doe make & Ordeine this as my last Will & Testiment in Manner & fforme ffollowing .

"Imp^r I Comitt my self Soule & Body into the hands of almightie God my havenly ffather & into ye Armes of the Lord Jesus x^t my Only Redeemer & Saviour On whome On whome I desire Ever to repose & Stedfastly to beleive & my Body I leave it to bee interred with Christian & Comely buriall in Assured hope of a blessed Resurrection through the mercy of God Unto Eternall life at the Glorious appeareing of the Lord Jesus christ at the Last day, And ffor that Outward Estate the Lord hath Blessed me with all My Will is that after my just debts are payd & funerall Expences discharged as ffollowes

"It I give to my Loveing Wife Easter Werner according to a former agreem^t Signed Under my hand One hundered Pounds to bee payd Out of my Moveable Estate Viz household Goods & Chattells & in case the s^d Moveables amounts not to ye Sum afores^d then to be made up in Other Estate & this to be at her free & absolute dispose to her & to her heir^rs for Ever

"I give to my Wife ye One half of my Now dwelling house to be for her use & improvement dureing the tyme of her Natureall life as alsoe the use of half the Garden plot ajoyneing to the sayd house as alsoe the use of half the Ortchard with the fruites thereon & the use of half the Yards ajoyneing to ye house all these to be for her use dureing the tyme of her Natureall life

"I give to my Son Jacob Werner ye One half of my dwelling house and ye whole of the s^d house at his mothers decease with the house-lot Containeing Eight acres with all Edifices & buildings thereon to be to him & his heir^rs for Ever

"I give to my Son Jacob Werner alsoe ten acres of Meadow land lyeing in ye great meadow belonging to Hadley Viz my Six acre Lot of plowing Land & four acres of grass Land lyeing in the Swamp or Aquevitie Comonly Soe called to be to him & his heir^rs for Ever, That is the heir^rs begotten by ye body of the sayd Jacob Werner, provided alsoe & withall that the s^d Jacob Werner hee his heir^rs Executo^rs & Assignes truely pay fortie shillings Anuallie or yearelie to his Mother Easter Werner dureing the tyme of her Natureall Life as alsoe to Cowes for his s^d Mother & to keepe & provide winter meate for them & all this dureing the Term of her Natureall life as alsoe anualy to bring home to his sayd Mother ten Loads of Wood dureing her life

"I give to my Son Dan^ll Werner all my Land lyeing Over the great River in great ponset & litle ponset being twelve acres more or Less to be to him & to his heir^rs for Ever he paying within a Yeare after my decease ten pounds to his sister Ruth Werner & alsoe fortie shillings.

Anuallie to his Mother Easter Werner dureing the tyme of her Natureall Life

"I give to my Son Isaack Werner the One half of my alotment in Hoccanum to be to him & his heir^rs for Ever

"I give to my Daughter Ruth Werner fowr acres of Meadow in the great Meadow abutting against the Middle high way to be to her & to her heir^rs for Ever,

"I give to my Son Andrew Werner ten shillings

"I give to my Son Robert Werner ten shillings

"I give to my Son John Werner ten shillings

"I give to my Daughter Hills ten shillings & to my Daughter Pratt I give ten shillings

"And my Will is that if my Moveables make not up ye hundered pound above Expressed to bee payd to my Wife it shall bee made up Out of the Other half of my Land in Hoccanum & of that two acres & One fowrth ajoyneing to the burieing place the Rest of what Remaynes of s^d p^rsells I Leave to my Executo^rs Only paying Out five Pounds which I give to Mary Taylo^r the wife of John Taylo^r

"And of this My p^rsent Testiment, I make & Ordaine my deere Wife Easter Werner and my Loveing Son Dan^{ll} Werner as mine Executo^rs Revokeing & adnulling all & any Other Testiments, Wills, Legacies, bequeasts, Executo^rs by me in any Wise before this tyme made, Named, Willed & bequeathed as Witness my hand & Seale this Eighteenth day of June Anno domini One Thousand Six hundered Eightie One

"Sealed & delivered & Subscribed   Andrew Werner
in ye p^rsence & Witness of   To wch Instruem^t was a Seale afix^t"

Marke Werner

Peter Tilton"

SECOND GENERATION

2 **MARY[2] WARNER,** daughter of Andrew[1] Warner, was doubtless born in England before the removal of the family to this country. Her name has appeared as Mercy in some of the records. Owing to the peculiarities of the writing of some of the early scribes, the two names are easily confused, Mercy often being spelled Marcy.

She was first married in Hartford, Conn., January 22, 1645-6, to **JOHN STEEL, JR.,** who died in 1653, in Farmington, Conn. "John Steel was maryed To Maryy Warner on the Twenty & Two of Jenru[r] one Thousand Six hundred forty & five." (Conn. Hist. Soc., vol. 14, 606.) He was son of John Steel, who married at Fairstead, near Braintree, England, Rachel Talcott, daughter of John and Anne (Skinner) Talcott, and sister of John Talcott, Jr., one of the early proprietors of Hartford. John Steel, Sr., was one of the original proprietors of Hartford and was secretary of the colony from 1634 to 1639. For a complete record see "A Genealogical history of John and George Steele, settlers of Hartford"; Albany, 1862.

Mary Warner married (2) **WILLIAM HILLS,** who was born in England, came in the ship Lyon, arriving in Boston, September, 1632, and died July, 1683, probably in Hartford, as his will was probated there December 6, 1683. He married (1) Phillis Lyman, (2) after 1648, Mrs. Richard Risley, the date of whose death is not known, (3) Mary Warner. He had children: William, b. 1646; John, b. 1648; Joseph, b. 1650; Benjamin; Susannah, b. 1651; Mary, b. 1654; Lieutenant Jonathan, b. in Hartford, about 1665, d. there Sept. 29, 1727; Hannah, and Sarah. It is possible that some of these were by Mary Warner. The will of William Hills, Sr., of Hoccanum, within the township of Hartford, dated February 21, 1680-1, mentions his wife Mary, sons William, Jonathan, Joseph, and Benjamin, and daughters Mary Hills, Sarah Ward, and Susannah Kilbourn. (Manwaring's Early Conn. Probate, vol. 1, p. 321.) See also Hills Family in America, N. Y., 1906, p. 2, etc.

Children of John and Mary (Warner) Steel (order not known)

Benoni Steel, d. in Farmington; no children.
Henry Steel, d. in infancy.
Daniel Steel, b. April 29, 1645; d. 1646.
Mary Steel, b. Nov. 20, 1646; m. Oct. 24, 1670, John Thompson. Chil-

dren: i. John, b. Dec. 29, 1671. ii. Thomas, b. June or Jan. 30, 1674.
iii. Samuel, b. Dec. 29, 1676. iv. Joseph, b. March 25, 1679. v. James,
b. May 30, 1680.

John Steel, b. Nov. 5, 1647; d. Aug. 26, 1737; was made freeman May
10, 1677; lieutenant; m. Ruth Judd, daughter of Deacon Thomas
Judd of Farmington. Children: i. Lieutenant John, bapt. March 7,
1685-6; d. April 2, 1751; resided in Farmington and, after 1736, in
Bethlehem Society, Woodbury; m. Dec. 17, 1716, Mary Newell,
daughter of Samuel Newell, and had ten children. ii. Ebenezer, b.
1697; d. young. iii. Mary, m. (1) Joseph Bird, Jr.; (2) ——— Hart;
settled in Northington, Conn.; had four children by the first husband.
iv. Ruth, d. 1751; m. June 8, 1724, John Thompson. v. Elizabeth,
bapt. March 28, 1677-8; d. young. vi. Sarah, bapt. Nov. 25, 1683;
d. 1751. vii. Rachel, bapt. June 2, 1689; d. June, 1773; resided in
Farmington; not married.

Samuel Steel, b. March 15, 1652; d. 1710; resided in Hartford; m.
Sept. 16, 1680, Mercy Bradford, b. Sept. 2, 1660; d. 1720; daughter
of Deputy Governor William and Alice (Richards) Bradford, and
granddaughter of William Bradford, who came in the Mayflower,
and his second wife, Mrs. Alice (Reynor) Southworth. Children of
Samuel and Mercy (Bradford) Steel: i. Thomas, b. Sept. 9, 1681; d.
1757; resided in West Hartford; m. May 10, 1709, Susannah[4] Webster, b. April 25, 1686, d. Nov. 27, 1757, daughter of Deacon Jonathan[3] and Dorcas (Hopkins) Webster (Robert[2], John[1]), and had
eight children. ii. Samuel, b. Feb. 15, 1684-5; d. 1710; not married.
iii. Jerusha (twin with Samuel), b. Feb. 15, 1684-5; m. ——— Smith
and resided in Hartford. iv. William, b. Feb. 20, 1687; d. in Hart-
ford, 1713; not married. v. Abiel, b. Oct. 8, 1693; m. Dec. 25, 1712,
John Webster, who resided in Southington, Conn. vi. Daniel, b.
April 3, 1697; d. May 28, 1770, in West Hartford; m. 1725, Mary
Hopkins, and had six children. vii. Eliphalet, b. June 23, 1700; d.
July, 1773; m. Catharine Marshfield, who died in West Hartford,
June 7, 1788, and had eleven children. Fourth of these eleven was
Mercy Steel, bapt. Oct. 8, 1727, who married Noah[5] Webster, b. 1722
(Daniel[4], John[3], Robert[2], Governor John[1] of Hartford, b. in War-
wickshire, England). Noah[5] and Mercy (Steel) Webster were parents
of the more celebrated Noah[6] Webster, and among their descendants
of the present generation are Paul Leicester Ford, Worthington C.
Ford, Gordon L. Ford, and Mrs. Roswell Skeel, Jr.

Data regarding the foregoing will be found in the following:
A Genealogical history of John and George Steele, settlers of
Hartford, Albany, 1862; Stiles' Ancient Windsor, 2:60; Bliss
Genealogy, 183; Porter Genealogy, 116; Ancestry of William
F. J. Boardman, 200; History of Seymour, Conn., 1:204; His-
tory and genealogy of the Governor John Webster family of
Connecticut, Rochester, 1915.

3 ANDREW[2] WARNER, son of Andrew[1] Warner, may
have been born in England before his father's removal to
America, but no record of the date of his birth has been found.

His marriage occurred in 1653, thus indicating 1625-30 as the, approximate date of his birth. He died in Middletown, Conn., January 26, 1681-2. At the time of his marriage he was called of Hartford and his name is among the list of troopers from Hartford under Major John Mason, March 11, 1657-8. (Public records of Conn., 1:309.) Later he settled in Middletown and was a land-holder there as early as 1666. With his brothers, Robert and John, and their wives, Andrew and his wife Rebecca signed the covenant, "the 4th of the 9th mo 1668," the date of the beginning of the records of the Middletown Church. According to the old-time system of reckoning this would be November 4, 1668. The wives of Andrew Warner and Robert Warner were admitted to full membership in the church, March 18, 1669.

Some of Andrew Warner's property was described as situated in the district "commonly called Wongum." The inventory of his estate February 20, 1681, amounted to £329, 05, 03, a considerable sum for that time. Administration papers were granted on March 2d to the widow Rebecca, John Warner and Robert Warner, and the estate was divided on April 2d, 1684, the eldest son receiving £86, the others smaller amounts. The list of heirs, as given in 1681, was: Andrew, aged 19; John, 11; Joseph, 9; Abigail, 21; Mary, 17; Hannah, 15; Rebeckah, 6. (Manwaring's Probate Records of Conn., 1:374.)

It is probable that Andrew Warner's death was untimely or unexpected, as his executrix was empowered after his death to complete the sale of lands for which he had arranged but had not yet signed the deeds. The widow was instructed to give a deed, May, 1683, to David Sage, for property sold him by Andrew Warner before his death; again, May, 1684, a deed to John Hollybutt, for property in Wongum sold him in the same way.

"Rebecca, widow of Andrew Warner, sen., of Middletown, Testified that at her husband's request, some time before his decease, she had written a deed of gift of a parcel of meadow and swamp to his son-in-law, John Wetmore, but that he died before executing it." The instrument was later signed by his administrators. (Public records of Conn., 1:109, 120, 140.)

Andrew[2] Warner was married, Oct. 10, 1653, to **REBECCA FLETCHER**, who died in Hartford, June or January 25, 1715, aged 76 or 77. "Andrew Warner of Hartford was married to Rebecca ffletcher dau. of John ffletcher of Milford, Oct. 10, 1653, before me William ffowler, Majistrate". She was the daughter of John and Mary (Clark) Fowler and married (2) Jeremy

Adams who came from England with Thomas Hooker's com_
pany and resided in Cambridge, later in Hartford. His first
wife was Rebecca, widow of Samuel Greenhill, by whom he had
children, John, Ann, Hannah, Samuel, Hester, and Sarah.

Children of Andrew and Rebecca (Fletcher) Warner, b. in Middletown,
Conn.

Samuel Warner, b. Aug., 1659; d. Dec., 1659.

11 *Abigail Warner,* b. Dec. 3, 1660; m. John Wetmore.

Andrew Warner, b. Mar., 1662; d. Apr. 9, 1726, in Middletown, buried
in old North Cemetery. He was a wheelwright by trade. In May,
1717, he was appointed lieutenant of the trainband or military company on the south side of the ferry in the town of Middletown. He
married Hannah ———, who died Aug., 1726. They probably had
no children as his property was left to his sister Hannah. A copy
of his will appears further.

Mary Warner, b. April, 1664; d. in Middletown; m. ——— Bartlett.
Her children received a share of her brother Joseph's estate, 1745.

John (1) Warner, b. Sept., 1667; d. Sept., 1667.

Hannah Warner, b. Nov. 14, 1668; d. Dec. 6, 1730, not married; buried
in old North Cemetery. Administration upon her estate was granted
to John Warner, Dec. 9, 1730, and the inventory included also the
estate of her brother Lieutenant Andrew Warner, that had been
given to her. (Middletown probate records.)

12 *John (2) Warner,* b. April 8, 1671; m. Anna Ward.

Joseph Warner, b. Feb. 20, 1672; d. June 8, 1745, in East Middletown
or Chatham, now Portland, Conn.; buried in the old "Quarry Yard."
He moved to the east side of the river in Middletown among the
early settlers there and seems to have been a man of influence with
extensive land holdings. In October, 1720, he was one of a committee of three to arrange about the tax rates on the east side of
the river. He married in Middletown, June 16, 1703, Sarah Hurlbut, b. Nov. 5, 1676, in Middletown; d. Jan. 4, 1765, daughter of
John and Mary (Deming) Hurlbut. She was buried in the old
"Quarry Yard" in Portland. They had no children. By his will,
dated March 21, 1745, he bequeathed an estate valued at £700, as follows: one third to widow Sarah for life; to niece Mary Churchill,
daughter of John (or Nathaniel), who lived with him, £200; to
children of his sister Mary Bartlett, children of his sister Rebecca,
the wife of John Hurlbut, Jr., and children of Daniel Hurlbut, decd.,
son of his brother-in-law John Hurlbut, Jr., fourteen in all, £205;
to the church in Chatham, £5; balance to nephew David Sage, who
was also executor. (Conn. probate records, etc.)

13 *Rebecca Warner,* b. July 2 or 1, 1675; bapt. July 2, 1675; m. John
Hurlbut.

WILL of Lieutenant ANDREW³ WARNER of Middletown.

I, Andrew Warner of Middletown, in the county of Hartford & colony
of Connecticut in New England being sick and weak in body but of perfect
mind and memory, thanks be given to God .   Imprimis—I give and
bequeath to my loving sister Hannah Warner, the use of all my dwelling

house and barn and all my Homelot and the meadow bought of Thomas
How and the Land we call Adams Lot and my Indian Hill Lott—the use
of the whole of these *till my nephew Andrew Warner who dwells with me,*
shall come of age and then to assign one half of the barn and house and
one half of all the above lands to him, and to keep the use of the other
half during her natural life. Also I give to her, after my just debts and
funeral charges are paid and the legacy . . . to the Church and that to
John Barns; the use of all my household stuff, money, stock, husbandry,
utensils, and moveables of all kinds during her natural life, then to be
equally divided between my brethren and sisters.

Item—I give to my Cousin Andrew Warner who now lives with me, my
house and my Lott at Indian Hill. All the above I give to him and his heirs
forever to have use of the one half when he shall arrive at the age of 21
years and the other half at the decease of his aunt Hannah.

Item—To my brothers John and Joseph and my sisters Mary and Rebecca
I give all my other land excepting what is given to John Barns, to be equally
divided among them, and also what shall be left of my . . . flock at
my sister Hannah's decease to be equally divided among them and their
heirs. '

Item—I give to the Church in this place £10 to be delivered to the pastor
and deacons, to be laid out in a piece of plate for the sd. church's use.

Item—I give to John Barnes all my wheelwright tools . . . , also I
appoint my sister Hannah with my brothers John and Joseph my executors
to this will.

Signed, sealed, and published and declared the names of us
Also William Russell and   William Luffer
Deacon Rockwell to be overseers   Joseph Rockwell
to this my last will and Testament   Robert Warner
        Andrew Warner

In addition to what is written on the other side this Paper and Explanation
my will is that if my Cousin Andrew Warner should die without issue then
what I have here given him shall be divided equally between my brothers
and sisters and their heirs . . . . .

(Recorded in Middletown.)

4 ROBERT[2] WARNER, son of Andrew[1] Warner, died in
Middletown, Conn., April 10, 1690. The time and place of his
birth have not been found on any record, but he was probably
born not far from the time of his father's coming to America,
and may have been brought to this country as a baby. The
earliest records of him are those of his marriage and the births
of his children entered upon the Middletown records, 1654 and
following. In 1665 David Sage pre-empted the town pound of
12 square rods, and it was ordered "that Robert Warner shall
forthwith see what the town hath suffered by David Sage's
pulling down the   and so to get the town rited for soon
as may be in that case." (Middletown town records.) He was
made freeman, May 21, 1657; was a Deputy to the General
Court, October 12, 1665; held land, as recorded at Middletown,
January 10, 1665; was on the list of proprietors of Middletown,

March 22, 1670; was again Deputy, January 26, 1686, October 14, 1686, March 30, 1686-7, May 12, 1687, June 15, 1687, and September, 1689. March 31, 1687, Robert Warner sold 42 acres of land on the east side of the Connecticut River, which had been laid out to Seth Grant, his father-in-law. The inventory of his property, taken June 5, 1690, shows him to have been a man of means, with a valuation of over four hundred pounds. The property was distributed to his heirs: Seth, aged 32; John, 28; Samuel, 7; Elizabeth, 30; Mary, 26; Sarah, 20; Mehitable, 17; Ruth, 15; Bethiah, 10. The widow and eldest son Seth, with Francis Wetmore and Sargt. John Warner, were overseers. (Hartford probate records, 5 :62.)

Robert Warner married (1) February, 1654, **ELIZABETH GRANT,** who died December 26, 1673. She was the daughter of Seth Grant who came from England in the ship "Lion" in 1632, was. one of the original proprietors of Hartford and lived later in Windsor. She and her husband signed the covenant, November 4, 1668, when the records of the church in Middletown were commenced. She was admitted to full communion in the church, March 18, 1669.

Robert Warner married (2) February 2, 1674, **DELIVERANCE (BISSELL) ROCKWELL,** who died June 12, 1718. "Robard warrenak of Mideltown & deliuranc Rockwell wido that had bin wife to John Rockwell of Windsor ware married by m^r wolcott—febuy-2-74." (From entry in Hartford land records, folio 46.) She was admitted to the church in Middletown, July 30, 1681, and, with her daughter Ruth Warner Bissell, she was dismissed from the First Church of Middletown to the Scantic Church in Windsor, August 22, 1708.

Children of Robert and Elizabeth (Grant) Warner, recorded in Middletown

> *Samuel* (1) *Warner,* b. Sept., 1656; d. "in the beginning of November, 1662" (Middletown records).

14 *Seth Warner,* b. March 1, 1658; m. Mary Ward.

> *Elizabeth Warner,* b. "in the 1 March 1660"; was living at the time of her father's death. The records given under Elizabeth[3] (John[2]) may refer to this Elizabeth.

ꜰ *John Warner,* b. Feb. 1, 1662; d. Dec. 2, 1711, not married. An inventory of his estate was taken on May 3, 1712, and his brother Seth was made administrator. "John Warner aforesaid is indebted to Seth Warner for his. keeping etc. about 20 years, more than £100," an amount exceeding the value of the estate.

15 *Mary Warner,* b. Sept., 1664; m. Abraham Bartlett.

> *Sarah Warner,* b. March 5, 1669-70; m. (1) Sergeant John Clark, son of John Clark of Farmington. He was elected hayward, Dec. 17, 1694, and the same day received a grant of land from the town. He

died intestate, Oct. 6, 1709, and the property was distributed April 9, 1712. They probably had no children. His widow probably married (2) Oct. 25 or 11, 1711, Captain Job Ellsworth, as his second wife, and was living at the time of his will, Sept. 5, 1750. He was born April 13, 1674, and died Sept. 29, 1759, son of Sergeant Josias and Elizabeth (Holcomb) Ellsworth. His first wife was Mary Trumbull. They were married in 1695 and had six children. (Stiles' Ancient Windsor; Clark Genealogy.)
Mehitabel Warner, b. Nov. 21, 1673.

Children of Robert and Deliverance (Bissell) Warner

16 *Ruth Warner*, b. Nov., 1675; m. David Bissell.
17 *Bethia Warner*, b. Oct. 8, 1680; m. Nathaniel Grant.
18 *Samuel (2) Warner*, b. May 19, 1683; m. Susannah Hall.

5 JOHN² WARNER, son of Andrew¹ Warner, died in Middletown, Conn., June 24, 1700. The date and place of his birth are unknown but he was probably born in England before the removal of the family to America. According to the records of Connecticut, October 8, 1663, he was to be made a freeman on the following day. There is no record of his early life in America but he settled early in Middletown, Conn. His name is one of those on a granite and bronze memorial unveiled in 1905 to Middletown's "Founders, Fathers and Patriots," as one of the founders of the period from 1650 to 1680. With his wife and his brothers, Robert and Andrew, and their wives, he signed the covenant of the Middletown Church, Nov. 4, 1668, the date of the beginning of the church records. The list of proprietors of Middletown, March 22, 1670, gives John Warner, with a valuation of £96, slightly larger than that of his two brothers of the same town. His lot was on the west bank of the Connecticut River, next south of Thomas Ranney's and the middle one of five lots between the roads. He seems to have spent the remainder of his life as a farmer there. His will, made March 19, 1700, mentions the following: eldest son John; John North, guardian to his two children by Mary Warner, Anna and Mary North. Distribution of the property was made to John Warner, the eldest son, Jonathan Warner, Hannah Warner, Elizabeth Warner, John North's children by his first wife, and to Ebenezer Ranney in right of his wife.

Married ANNA ————. Her name is given as Anna Norton in Nash's Fifty Puritan Settlers, p. 62, but this may be an error, for John Warner, the early settler of Farmington, married Anna Norton. The Middletown Church records have the following entry: "May 23, 1669, Goodman John Warner & his yoke fellow Anna Warner & the wife of David Sage in full com-

munion. . . . May 30, 1669 (baptized) child[n] of Brother
Warner; viz.: Hannah, John, Jonathan, Mary, Elizabeth, our
sister Sage herself likewise and her 3 children namely, David,
John, Elizabeth in ʸ seale."—John Warner Sen[r] and Anna Warner Sen[r] were among the signers of the covenant at the Middle
town Church, "the 4th of the 9th mo 1668."

*Children, order not known but inferred from record of their baptism
in Middletown in 1669*

Hannah Warner, mentioned in the distribution of her father's property, 1700, probably not married.

19   *John Warner*, b. about 1657; m. Mrs. Silence Hand Wilcox.

Mary Warner, died March 1, 1694-5. Married, as his first wife, John
North, who died April 20, 1745, son of Samuel and Hannah (Norton)
North of Farmington and grandson of John and Hannah (Bird)
Norton who came to Boston in the Susan and Ellen in 1635. He
was made guardian for his two children Anna and Mary North, who
were minors at the time of their grandfather's death. Anna North,
b. about 1694; m. June 28, 1716, Thomas Wilcox, b. July 5, 1687, d.
Jan. 20, 1726, son of Israel and Sarah (Savage) Wilcox, and had
children, Hannah, Thomas, who m. Freelove Bradley, Jonathan and
Hannah. Further records of this family will be found in Nash's
Fifty Puritan Ancestors, p. 63.

Elizabeth Warner, received part of her father's property in 1700. It is
not clear if the following record refers to this Elizabeth or to her
cousin, Elizabeth, daughter of Robert Warner. In October, 1703, the
court of Middletown ordered that land of Elizabeth Warner be sold,
"as much as may be needfull for the defraying of the necessary
charges that have been or shall be expended for the keeping and
maintenance of the said Elizabeth, she being a distracted person and
now in close custodie to prevent her doing mischieff." One Elizabeth
Warner married Nov. 22, 1709, Samuel Pease (Hadley Town Records), but she may be a descendant of William of Ipswich.

Jonathan Warner, b. 1660; d. Nov. 4, 1733, in East Middletown (Port-
land) to which place he had removed about 1710; buried in old
Quarry burying ground, Portland. He was a farmer and died leaving
a substantial property to his wife by a will of May 22, 1733. After
her death, it was distributed, Jan. 3, 1758, to Ebenezer Ranney,
Richard Coleman and Jabez Warner. Jonathan Warner married in
Middletown, Aug. 4, 1698, Elizabeth Ranney, b. in Middletown Upper
Houses, Apr. 12, 1668; d. Feb. (or Sept.) 11, 1757; buried in old
Quarry burying ground, Portland. She was the daughter of Thomas
and Mary (Hubbard) Ranney, and a sister of Ebenezer Ranney who
married Sarah Warner (see below). She was received into full communion of the Middletown Church, July 28, 1695, was an original
member of the North Society, Jan. 5, 1714-5, and an original member
of the Third Church at East Middletown, which was organized in
1721. Children, b. and d. in Middletown: i. Jonathan, Jr., b. July
2, 1699-1700; d. July 6, 1699-1700. ii. John, b. Aug. 16, 1701; d. Sept.
19, 1701.

20   *Sarah Warner*, b. Mar. 5, 1669; m. Ebenezer Ranney.

6 HANNAH² WARNER, daughter of Andrew¹ Warner. In the will of Andrew Warner he mentions his daughter Pratt. This is believed to be Hannah, wife of Daniel Pratt of Hartford, Conn. In the graveyard of the First Church of Hartford is a tombstone to the memory of Hannah, wife of Daniel Pratt, who died September 3, 1682, aged about 50 years. As this designation of her age is somewhat indefinite, it is hardly possible to state that she was born in 1632 at the time when her father was living in Cambridge, or a year or two earlier or later.

Married **DANIEL PRATT,** born in Hartford about 1639, son of John and Elizabeth (   ) Pratt. He was made freeman, February 26, 1656; was a Trooper, March 11, 1657-8; appointed "to order the affaires of the town," February 11, 1657; held the offices of fence-viewer, constable, collector and other local offices for many years; was proposed for deacon in the First Church in Hartford, March 11, 1686, but was not elected. He was buried April 24, 1691. His will, dated April 19, 1680, probated April 29, 1691, "at present under weakness of body & know not how soon the Lord may put an end to my days," mentions his son Daniel and seven daughters. Several of these daughters have already received their portions and are not named, only Hannah, "daughter Goodwin," and Mary Sanford being designated. (Manwaring's Early Connecticut Probate, vol. 1, p. 499.) For further records of this family, see "The Ancestry and descendants of John Pratt of Hartford, Conn.," Hartford, 1900, by Charles B. Whittlesey.

Children

Daniel Pratt, b. in Hartford, 1670; d. January, 1703; m. in Hartford, March 10, 1691, Elizabeth Lea, who m. (2) John Sheldon, son of Isaac Sheldon of Northampton, Mass. Children, b. in Hartford: i. Elizabeth, b. Aug. 19, 1693; m. Feb. 29, 1716, Isaac Sheldon, son of Isaac and Sarah³ (Warner) Sheldon, see number 22. ii. Hannah, b. June 29, 1695; d. Apr. 8, 1696. iii. Daniel, b. Feb. 17, 1696; d. in infancy. iv. Rebecca, b. Aug. 27, 1699; m. Daniel Sexton. v. Elisha, b. Apr. 12, 1702; m. Dec̄. 7, 1726, Susan Burnham, daughter of Captain William Burnham of Hartford, and had nine children, baptized at East Hartford.

Hannah Pratt, married 1678, Daniel Clark, bapt. Apr. 10, 1654; moved to Colchester about 1710. Children, b. in Hartford: i. Daniel, b. 1679. ii. Moses, b. 1683. iii. John, b. 1685. iv. Aaron, b. Nov. 13, 1687. v. Abraham, b. March 26, 1693. vi. Noah. (See Goodwin's Genealogical Notes; Stiles' Ancient Windsor, 2:153; Marsh Genealogy.)

Elizabeth Pratt, bapt. Aug. 20, 1693; d. after July, 1724; m. as second wife, Nathaniel Goodwin, b. about 1637, d. Jan. 8, 1714. Children: i. Samuel, b. Aug. 22, 1682; m. Mary Steele. ii. Hannah, b. Dec. 6,

1685; d. Jan., 1693. iii. Ozias, b. June 26, 1689; m. Martha Williamson. iv. Mary, b. 1690. v. Elizabeth, b. Oct. 14, 1691; m. John Cole. (See Goodwin's Genealogical Notes.)

Sarah Pratt, perhaps m. as second wife Timothy Phelps, b. 1692, son of Samuel Phelps of Windsor, Conn. There was another Sarah Pratt contemporary.

Rachel Pratt, b. 1671; d. Aug. 17, 1748; m. Feb. 22, 1693, John Skinner, b. March 1, 1666, d. Oct. 27, 1743. Children: i. Rachel, b. Feb. 2, 1694; d. Jan. 18, 1787; m. May 19, 1726, Ebenezer Welles, b. Oct. 5, 1694; d. Dec. 27, 1737 (See Tuttle Genealogy). ii. John, b. July 1, 1697; m. Dec. 24, 1724, Mary Turner (See Loomis Genealogy). iii. Daniel, b. Jan. 19, 1699; d. Jan. 15, 1701. iv. Timothy, b. Feb. 8, 1701; m. May 1738, Ruth Colton of Hartford. v. Mary, b. May 28, 1704. vi. Hannah, b. June 27, 1707; d. Oct. 23, 1709.

Mary Pratt, m. ―――― Sanford.

(Daughter.)

Esther Pratt, died Oct. 7, 1702; left a will in which she mentioned her brother Daniel and five sisters.

7 DANIEL² WARNER, son of Andrew¹ Warner, was probably born after his parents came to America. His birth record has never been found and the year is uncertain, although the evidence would be in favor of a date between 1632 and 1635. He died in Hatfield, Mass., April 30, 1692. He went in 1659 with his father from Hartford, Conn., to Hadley, and settled in the part of town that was set off as Hatfield in 1670. Dani: Warner, freeman, Hatfield, May 7, 1673 (Mass. Bay Records, vol. 4, pt. 2, 587). Daniel Warner was appointed ensign to the foot company in Hadley, Oct. 7, 1674, and returned a bill for caring for soldiers, May 30, 1679 (Mass. Bay Records, vol. 5, 239, 336, etc.). He is designated in early records as Lieutenant Daniel Warner. He was a grantee of Northfield in 1682 and was there at the Second Settlement (History of Northfield). With seven others from Hadley he signed a letter to the General Court, sent from Hadley April 29, 1676, regarding the nearness of the enemy (N. E. Reg., 41:202). This was during the French and Indian War.

The settlers on the two sides of the river at Hadley were obliged to do many things separately on account of the treacherous swiftness of the water at the point of crossing. The church was on the east side of the river and the ninety residents of the west side found great difficulty in attending services. In May, 1667, Daniel Warner was one of those who sent a petition to the General Court asking to be set off as a separate parish or society. They had lived on the west side for six years and found it difficult and dangerous to cross. "Our vessels tossed up and down so that our women and children do screech, and are so affrighted that they are made unfit for ordinances, and cannot hear so as to profit by them by reason of their anguish of spirit."—"When we do go over the river we leave our relatives and estates lying on the outside of the colony, joining to the wilderness, to be a prey to the heathen when they see their opportunity." Thrilling tales were told of the canoes filling with water, or of the worshippers breaking through the ice. (History of Hadley.)

"Here ffolloweth an Inventory of ye estate of Lt Dan^{ll} Werner of Hatfield who dyed Intestate Aprill 30 1692 taken May 6 1692 by Sarjt John Hubbird Deacon Church & Sam^{ll} Partrigg . . . .

To 1 Leather Suite 12 s One Coate & Wascoate 12s One p Searge britches 5 s	01–09–00
To 1 great Coate 10s One great Coat 3 s 1 p^r New Stockins 5s 2 p^r Stockins 4s	02–09–00
To 1 Remnant Cloath 2s hat 5s 3 shirts 16s one chest 4s Rapier 10s Carbine 20s	02–13–00
To 1 Gun 25s 2 belts pouch & bullets 3s Boots 7s 5 Bar——3s 2 Neckcloths 2s	02–00–00
To 3 handcherchers 3s New cloath 2s table 2s One handchercher 1s 6 chairs 12s	01–00–00
To 12 cotten napkins 26s 15 napkins 22s 2 large table cloaths 10s a small dito 6s	03–04–00
To 9 pillowbeers 2s 8 towels 10s one p^r of sheets 15s 1 p^r sheets 10s 1 p^r sheets 15s	03–08–00
To 1 p^r sheets 18s 1 p^r sheets 2s 1 p^r sheets 10s 1 sheet 8s 1 sheet 10s 1 p^r sheets 18s	04–00–00
To 1 p^r sheets 20s chest 4s box 1s litle wheel 3s 10 yds Searge at 5s a yd	03–19–00
To 3 yds½ of Lining Cloath at 3s & 4 yds of Linsewoolen at 4s & chest 5s	01–11–06
To 1 Warmeing pan 6s one sheet at 8s one great bed at 6£ 10s & trondle bed 40s	09–04–00
To 4 Blankets at 20s 2 pees hooks 5s Bullits & Lead 2s powder & pouches 3s	01–10–00
To a tin Candlestick 2s sheep shears 2s horn 1s 3 sickels 3s broad ax 10s saw 5s	02–01–00
To 1 meale Sive 1s childbed Lining & blankets 20s 1 feather pillow 2/6 Cradle 3s	02–06–06
To thread 2s & to Lining yarn 16s Oatmeale 1s dyed wool 2s Seed peck 2s table 7s	02–08–00
To 1 p^r Cobirons 20s great wheel 4s ham^r 2s great auger 2s old iron 5s 1 p^r gloves 2s	02–05–00
To 1 powder bagg 2s 1 greatKettell 20s old Kettell 4s iron Kittell 6s litle pot 3s	01–14–00
To a small Kittell & skillitt 5s great pot & hooks 20s tramel & chaine 6s	02–00–00
To 1 payle 18s 18 pieces of wooden ware 12s 3 pewter plates 16s pint cup 3s	01–12–00
To 1 brass cup 4s 2 glasses 2s books 7s tubs meate, bar^l, churn, tallo, sope, 35s	02–07–00

To fire shovel & tongs at 5s wort sive 2s half bush^{ll}18s a bagg & nayles 4s brush 6s	00–12–00
To 1 p^r bellows 2s a bridle & sadle& male pillian 16s 1 shave 2s 7 baggs at 4s	02–07–00
To 2 baggs with tow 5s 6 hemp 3s fork 18s 26 flax 12s wool 2s hopps & bagg 2s	01–03–00
To a rope 5s bayle for a payle 2s sith & sneath 7s old sith & sneath 2s	00–16–00
To 1 bush^{ll} &½ of Indian meale at 2s & 1 bush^{ll} malt 2s pees 2s 3 bush^{ll} malt 3s	00–15–00
To a melting Ladle2s 5 hoes 14s tosting iron 2s 2 felling axes 8s shovel 18s	02–05–06
To 1 payle 2s spade 2s Chees tub 2/6 tub 2s tub 2s 20 bush^{ll} Indian at 2s	02–08–06
To 8 bush^{ll}wheate, at 3/3s 3 bush^{ll} oats at 4/6 basket tow 2s ½ bush^{ll} salt 3s	02–15–06
To 1 bed & furniture 40s 13 bush^{ll} of Indian corne at 2s & cart wheel irons 55s	06–01–00
To 1 plow 25s Chaine 8s harrow 12s slead 5s 1 p^r horse chains braces 2̇ collers & hames 20s	03–20–00
To 2 oxen 20£ horse 6£ 3 cows 3£/20s Yoke of Steers 5£ heifer 2£/20s	34–00–00
To 23 sheep & lambs 20 s 5 hoggs 20s 3 piggs 8 2 mares & a colt 5£	20–08–00
To a ffann 5s fork 2s Raks 3s house & homestead in Hatfeild at 140£	148–08–00
To 7 acres of Land in ye south meadow at 5£ & 2 acres ½ in ye Indian hollow at 12 £ 20s	47–10–00
To 12 acres Land at 5 £ litle Ponset 14 acres of Land in ye great meadow at 4 £	116–00–00
To 8 acres of Land in ye Mill Swamp 8 £ Comons 2 £ wool 2s testiment 1s	10–03–00
To 1 rugg 3s 2 baskets 2s break 2/6 Compasses 2s hemp 8s Chest in ye barn 5s	01–01–06
To 1 Lathe 5s yoke & irons 5s 1 p^r shoes 3s 1 p^r shoes 4s Hetchell 5s	01–02–00
To a debt due from Sam^{ll} Boltwood 10 £/20s Cropp at 20 £	30–20–00
	476–06–06
To debts and other necessary expenses at about	50–00–00
	426–06–06

The Court appointed the widow Martha and Samuel Partridge as administrators on September 30th, 1692, and ordered the "property to be devided amongst ye children of the deceased which are fowrteen, the eldest son named Dan^{ll} Werner a double portion, 2d son Andrew, Sarah Shelding, Anna Hubbirt, Mary Warner, Hannah Worner, John, Abram, Samuel, Ebenezer, Mahitabell, Elizabeth, Hester, Nathaniel." (Northampton Probate Records, 3 :1.)

Daniel[2] Warner married (1) **MARY** ————, who died September 29 (or 19), 1672.

.Married (2) April 1, 1674, **MARTHA BOLTWOOD**, who died September 22, 1710, daughter of Robert and Mary ( ) Boltwood of Northfield.

Robert[1] Boltwood, a native of Essex County, England, came to America before 1648, when his name first appears in the Connecticut records. He settled in the east part of Wethersfield, in the part now included in Glastonbury, and received a grant of a pond with a quantity of land adjacent thereto, which he purchased from the Indian chief, Peckharen. He was made freeman May 20, 1658, and the following year was one of the "engagers" who removed to Hadley, Massachusetts, and became one of the original proprietors of that settlement. His home lot of eight acres was located on the west side of Main Street of Hadley, the fourth in order from the north limits of the settlement. He died in Hadley April 6, 1684, and his wife Mary, whose parentage is unknown, died there May 14, 1687. In Hadley Robert Boltwood was a sergeant in the militia, held many civil offices, was a farmer and ran the corn mill from 1677 until his death. Robert[1] and Mary Boltwood had five children: Samuel[2]; Sarah[2], m. (1) Isaac[2] Warner of Hatfield (see number 8); Lydia[2], m. April 2, 1674, John Warner of Springfield; Martha[2], m. Daniel[2] Warner; and Mary[2], m. October 24, 1667, James Beebe. Samuel[2] Boltwood was a soldier stationed at Deerfield at the time of the fearful Indian attack upon the settlement, February 29, 1704, and was killed in the encounter. When the news of the attack reached Hadley, his sons, Samuel, Robert, and Eleazer, knowing that their father was involved, joined the troop and rode rapidly to the relief of Deerfield. The father and three sons were all engaged in the desperate fight on Deerfield meadows for the recovery of the captive inhabitants. In the same band were four other grandsons of Robert Boltwood, John[3], Ebenezer[3], and Samuel[3] Warner (sons of Daniel[2] and Martha (Boltwood) Warner), and Daniel[3] (son of Isaac[2] and Sarah (Boltwood) Warner).

· Robert Boltwood of Hadley, in his will dated 19 Jan. 1682, proved at Springfield 30 Sept. 1684, provides as follows (among other items) ·

"Item I give & bequeath to my daughter Sarah wife to Isaac Warner ten pounds. Item I give & bequeath to my daughter Martha wife to Danll Warner fifteene pounds. Item I give & bequeath to my daughter Lydia wife to John Warner fifteen pounds Item I do give & bequeath to my daughter Mary deceased her three children five pounds apiece. Item— to

my loveing son Sam^u Boltwood—five pounds. Item—al the rest—I bequeath
to my Loveing wife. Son Samuel Boltwood Executor."

(Hampshire Probate, Northampton, 2:18.)

Children of Daniel² and Mary (   ) Warner

Mary (1) Warner, b. Feb. 24, 1662 (Hadley town recs., I:61).

21   Daniel Warner, b. 1666; m. (1) Mary Hubbard, (2) Thankful Billings.
22   Sarah Warner, m. Isaac Sheldon.
23   Andrew Warner, b. June 24, 1667 (Hadley town records, I:61); m.
       (1) Ruth Clark, (2) Mrs. Hannah Stannard.
24   Anna, b. Nov. 17' 1669 (Hadley town records, I:61); m. Isaac Hub-
       bard.
     Mary (2) Warner, b. Sept. 19, 1672; probably m. Samuel Sheldon.

Children of Daniel² and Martha (Boltwood) Warner

     Hannah Warner, b. Jan. 24, 1675 (History of Hadley, History of North-
       field); d. June 28, 1699; m. Oct. 14, 1696 (Hadley town records),
       Samuel Ingram of Northfield, b. Oct. 8, 1670, son of John and Eliza
       beth (Gardner) Ingram. He probably resided in Hadley until after
       1703, then removed to Hatfield. He was mentioned in his father's
       will, 1722.
25   John Warner, b. April, 1677, in Hatfield; m. Mehitabel Chapman-
       Richardson.
     Abraham Warner, b. Dec. 20, 1678, in Hatfield; resided in Hartford,
       Conn., for some years. Josiah Dewey, Senr of Lebanon, Conn., and
       William Clarke of the same place sold to Abraham Warner of
       Hartford for £5-00, 200 acres at "Lebanon Village," Dec. 15, 1701
       (Lebanon Deeds, I:304). July 17, 1705, Abraham Warner of Hart-
       ford sold to Thomas Fletcher of Lebanon, 200 acres, "in that part
       of town called ye villiage," consideration £18 (Lebanon Deeds, II:5).
26   Samuel Warner, b. April 13, 1680, in Hatfield; m. (1) Hannah Sackett,
       (2) Elizabeth Morton.
27   Ebenezer Warner, b. Nov. 5, 1681; m. (1) Ruth Ely, (2) Mrs. Mary
       Bellows.
28   Mehitabel Warner, b. Oct. 1, 1683; m. Preserved Clapp.
     Elizabeth Warner, b. 168–; m. Dec. 26, 1705, Thomas Wells of Had
       dam, Conn.
29   Hester Warner, b. Dec. 15, 1686; m. Samuel Harvey.
     Martha Warner, b. April 3, 1688; d. Nov. 25, 1689.
     Nathaniel Warner, b. Oct. 11, 1690, in Hatfield. He is perhaps the
       Nathaniel Warner of Suffield who married Thankful Taylor of Had-
       ley, May 1, 1710 (Hadley town records).

8 ISAAC² WARNER, son of Andrew¹ Warner, died in
Deerfield, Mass., 1691. No records of the date and place of his
birth have yet been found, although some have conjectured that
he was born in Hartford, Conn., about 1645. As one of the
inhabitants of Hadley, Mass., to which place he had doubtless
removed with his father in 1659, he signed a petition against
imposts, February 19, 1668. He was one of the engagers for
Northfield in 1683 and was there at the Second Settlement. He

became a man of influence in the new plantation, but when the settlement was deserted after King William's War, he removed to Deerfield where he died.

Inventory of his property was made March 26, 1692 (Springfield probate, A:8). The Judd MSS. in the Forbes Library, Northampton (2:159) gives the following note:

"Court at Northampton March 31, 1691
Isaac Warner of Deerfield Deceased—Sarah relict, presented Inventory 59£ free—Land in Northfield & Hadley not prized. Inventory taken by Thos Wells & Jos. Barnard."

The widow Sarah Warner was appointed administrator and asked that her son Isaac and brother Ltt. Daniell Warner and Jacob Warner be also appointed. The widow Sarah, "relict of Isaac of Deerfield," made a deed November 4, 1692, to Abigail, "relict of Thomas Croffts sometime of Hadley." (Springfield records, A:12, 124.)

In Book A, land records at Springfield, page 8 at the back of the book, among other entries regarding estates, is the following entry:

"Sarah the relict of Isaack Warner deceased late of Derefld who dyed intestate presented to this Court an Inventory of the Estate of her late Husband to which she made oath it was a true Inventory soe farr as she knew & if more estate doe appear she will make discovery of it."

Powers of administration were granted to the widow Sarah and Lieutenant Wells and they were under bond for two hundred dollars. The inventory was taken by Lieutenant Thomas Wells and Joseph Barnard, March 26th, 1692.

To a feather bed 1£–20s & 2 coverlets 24s bed & bolster 20s blankets
    6s 2 bedds 2 bolsters 2 coverlits 2 pillows at 2 £ 11s   05–15
To 1 yd new Cloath 3s 3 iron pots 30s 2 pᵣ of pot hooks 3s   01–16
To 1 iron skillet 4s 4 putar dishes 12 s 1 putar cup 1/6   00–18
To 1 candlestick & warmeing pann 5s puddings 2s poringᵣ 1s botle 1s   00–20
To 1 powdering tub with pork in it 30s sope 5s   01–15
To wooden ware 10s stone jugg 1s 1 box iron 3s knives 6s   00–14
To tubs & old barˡ 10s chest 4s box 4s box 3s   01–01
To 2 spinning wheels 6s yarn 9s satt 5s tackling for a loome 20s   01–18
To wool at 2s Armes & Amunition 17s Indian Corne & barly 12s   01–11
To a sadle & bridle 12s sive 1/6 cards 3s chars 3s cart & wheels 25s   02–04
To a plow & irons 15s horse tackling 20s broadhoes 6s stubing hoe
    5s axe 4s   02–00
To 1 plow chaine 10s flax 10s hopps 3s fish nets 4s rope 2s 2 oxen 9£   10–19
To 4 cows 12 £ one mare & colt 3£ one horse 4 £ 8 sheep 4£ 2
    swine 30s   24–10
To 2 baggs 4s   00–04

To house & homestead in Northfd with 36 acres of ld with some
other lumber   (valuation cut off edge)
To debts due yᵉ estate   19–00

                                                                    74-16
Due from yᵉ Country in Expony   Debts due from yᵉ estate at   15–00
at Northfd & g—ing of Soldeary   ——
given in to Majoʳ Pynchon   Free. estate   59–16
There is also an alotmt at Springfd & 14 acres of land in fortieacre——
at Hadley &c

Hampshire Probate (Northampton, Mass.) 4:30, files 153:50,
contain

"An additional Inventory of ye Estate of Isaac Warner of Northfield
Deceased taken this 5th of February 1713/14 as followeth—
To his accommodation of Meadow Upland of Right to him & may grow
        to be of right within the precincts of ye Township of Northfield
                                                               at 15″
To his homelot in said place at   5″

Apprized by Deacon Jno. White, Joseph Smith& Westwood Cook having first
taken ye apprizers oath to which they have subscribed this day of the date
abovesd.   John White
                                                   Joseph Smith
                                                   Westwood Cooke

As to a Setlement of the abovesd Estate the totall sum it being twenty
pounds their being twelve children & Isaack Warner the eldest son he
to have a double portion viz.   3– 1-6

to Andrew Warner	1–10–9	to Ebenezer Warner	1–10–9
to Sam'll Warner	1–10–9	to Ichebod Warner	1–10–9
to Sarah Frentch	1–10–9	to Lydia Brooks	1–10–9
to Mercy Gilbirt	1–10–9	to Thankfull Loomas	1–10–9
to Mehitabell Hitchcock	1–10–9	to Dan'll Warners hers	1–10–9
to Mary Crowfoots hers	1–10–9		
			10–15–3
	———		
	9– 4-6	Totall	19–19–9

The abovsd Setlemᵗ was Considered & allowed of this
10th of March 1719/20 by me   Sam'll Partridge   Judge of Probate"

Isaac² Warner married May 31, 1666 (or May 30, Hadley
town records), **SARAH BOLTWOOD,** who died July 14, 1726,
daughter of Robert and Mary (   ) Boltwood of Northfield.
She married (2) Deacon John Loomis of Windsor, Conn., son
of Deacon John² (Joseph¹) and Elizabeth (Scott) Loomis of
Windsor and Lebanon, Conn. Sarah Boltwood's sister Martha
married Daniel² Warner, and a more complete account of the
Boltwoods will be found on page 43.

Children of Isaac and Sarah (Boltwood) Warner, first four recorded at Hadley

30 *Sarah Warner,* b. May 2, 1668; m. Jonathan French.
31 *Isaac Warner,* Jr., b. Jan. 13, 1669-70; m. Hope Nash.
32 *Mary Warner,* b. Jan. 6, 1671-2; m. Samuel Crowfoot.
33 *Andrew Warner,* b. Feb. 24, 1672-3; m. Deborah (Leffingwell) Crow.
     Hannah Warner, b. Nov. 14, 1674; probably was the Hannah Warner
     who m. Eleazer Williams, son of Rev. John Williams of Deerfield,
     Mass., who was ordained first pastor of the church in Mansfield. She
     must have died before 1713-4, leaving no children, as she does not
     appear in the list of her father's heirs at that date.
34 *Ebenezer Warner,* b. Feb. 25, 1676; m. Waitstill Smead.
35 *Daniel Warner,* b. Feb. 25, 1677; m. Sarah Golden or Goulding.
36 *Samuel Warner,* b. Mar. 14, 1681; m. Sarah Field.
     Ruth Warner, b. Oct. 18, 1682; probably d. young as no further men-
     tion is found.
37 *Ichabod Warner,* b. about 1684; m. Mary Metcalf.
38 *Mercy Warner,* b. Sept. 25, 1685; m. Samuel Gilbert.
39 *Lydia Warner,* m. Joseph Brooks.
40 *Thankful Warner,* m. Josiah Loomis.
41 *Mehitabel Warner,* m. (1) Samuel Hitchcock, (2) Joshua Austin.

9 RUTH[2] WARNER, daughter of Andrew[1] Warner, was
probably one of the younger children and born in this country.
The only definite information we have of her is in a Hadley
court record of 1677 that well illustrates the times and puritanical conditions under which the family lived. An ordinance had
been passed forbidding women to wear silk, unless their fathers
or husbands were worth a certain stated amount, endeavoring
to prevent by law what is best left to those most deeply interested. Ruth Warner defied this old blue law and openly
appeared in public apparelled in silk. She and two others, who
had likewise offended, were, as expressed in the court record,
"presented at court." They were charged with "wearing silk
contrary to law," and two of them for "wearing it in a flaunting
manner to the offense of sober people." Ruth was admonished
by the court and her father was ordered to pay the clerk's fees
and witnesses. Andrew Warner was worth £356, a large
amount for this period, and one cannot but admire the spirit of
Ruth Warner who thus asserted her inherent and inalienable
right to adorn herself in such manner as she saw fit.

The name of her husband has been variously reported as John
or Daniel Pratt, ——— Caley, or ——— Kellogg. The Pratt is
doubtless an error for her sister Hannah's marriage. The
name Caley does not appear among the early colonists. Of the
early Kelloggs but one is recorded as having a wife Ruth.
John[4] Kellogg, son of Lieutenant Joseph[3] Kellogg, bapt. in

Farmington, Conn., Dec. 29, 1656, m. (1) in Hadley, Dec. 23, 1680, Sarah Moody, b. 1660, d. 1689, m. (2) Ruth ———; who died after 1732. He died between 1723 and 1728. By this second marriage he had six children, born between 1693 and 1701, Ruth, Joanna, Esther, Abigail, John and James. (Kelloggs in the old world and new, p. 35.)

10 JACOB² WARNER, son of Andrew¹ Warner, died in Hadley, Mass., Nov. 8, 1711 (tombstone record) or November 29, 1711 (Hadley town record). He was a freeman in Hadley, May 30, 1690. The date and place of his birth are unknown. There have been some who think he was the son of Andrew by his second wife, Esther Selden, but the facts on which they base their claim are not sufficient, in the absence of more conclusive evidence, to substantiate the claim. From the dates of birth of his children, it is evident that he must have been one of the younger children, at any rate. His grave in Hadley is next to Meadow Road. He was one of the early settlers on Plot 10, Hadley, the tenants of which were: Andrew Warner, 1663; Andrew and Jacob, 1682; Widow Andrew Warner and Jacob, 1690; Widow Elizabeth Warner and Jacob, 1720 (the son); Jacob, 1731; Orange, Elihu, and Oliver, 1770; 1821 and later, other family names. (Grafton Magazine, vol. 1.) Letters of administration on the estate of Jacob Warner were issued to his widow Elizabeth and son Jacob, May 18, 1711. The inventory was taken February 7, 1711-12, and listed housing and homestead, land in Aqua Vitae and at ye Great Meadow, together with an extensive list of articles, the whole valued at £359, 5, 4. The son Jacob, as eldest, received a double portion, and the other five children, portions of £29, 11, each. (Northampton probate records, 3:255, 267, etc.)

Married (1) REBECCA ———, who died April 10, 1687 (Hadley town record). No children are recorded by this marriage.

Married (2) ELIZABETH GOODMAN, daughter of Richard Goodman and his wife, Mary Terry, daughter of Stephen Terry of Windsor. Richard Goodman was killed by the Indians April, 1676, at the age of 67. He was of Cambridge, 1632; Hartford, 1639; Hadley, 1659. Another of his daughters married John Noble, first settler of New Milford, Conn., where many of this branch of the Warner family later settled. Mrs. Elizabeth Warner probably married (2) ——— Picket.

Children of Jacob and Elizabeth (Goodman) Warner, b. in Hadley

Jacob (1) *Warner,* b. Nov. 5, 1687; d. July, 1687 (dates as in Hadley
town records).

Rebecca Warner, b. March 13, 1690, "March ye last" under 1690
Hadley records.

42 *Jacob* (2) *Warner,* b. Sept. 27, 1691 (Hadley town records); m.
Mary ———.

43 *Mary Warner,* b. July 22, 1694; m. Benjamin Graves.

Elizabeth Warner, b. March 20, 1696 (Hadley town records); d. young.

John (1) *Warner,* b. June 10, 1698; d. 1698.

44 *John* (2) *Warner,* b. March 10, 1701; m. Mercy Curtis.

45 *Joseph Warner,* b. April 2 or 30, 1707; m. Sarah Bartlett.

David Warner, b. June 4, 1710; d. in Hadley after 1794, leaving no
children. He had land holdings in New Milford, Conn., near those
of his brothers John and Joseph; bought land Jan., 1732-3; sold
land to John, Feb. 12, 1733-4; David of Hadley sold land to John
of New Milford, Feb. 15, 1748. He received an annuity of $30.00 by
the will of his nephew Oliver in 1779. (New Milford public records.)

THIRD GENERATION

11 ABIGAIL³ WARNER, daughter of Andrew² and Rebecca (Fletcher) Warner, born in Middletown, Conn., 1660; died May 5, 1685.

Married December 30, 1680, JOHN WETMORE or WHIT-MORE, bapt. at Hartford, Conn., Sept. 6, 1646; died Sept. 1, 1696, son of Thomas and Sarah (Hall) Whitmore. He married (2) April 1, 1686, Mary Savage, daughter of John Savage, Sen., of Middletown, by whom he had children, Elizabeth, Mary, John and Ebenezer. After his death she married Obadiah Allen. John Wetmore's name, variously spelled, is found on the land records of Middletown as early as 1668. The executors of the estate of Thomas Whitmore and the administrators of Andrew Warner's estate in 1682 gave him deeds to property. "Rebecca, widow of Andrew Warner, sen., of Middletown, Testified that at her husband's request some time before his decease, she had written a deed of gift of a parcel of meadow and swamp to his son-in-law, John Wetmore, but that he died before executing it. Catherine, widow of Thomas Wetmore, testified that her husband intended to perfect a deed of gift, written but not signed, to his son John Wetmore . . ."

The will of John Whitmore of Middletown was made August 6, 1689. The inventory showed an estate of about £267. He left six minor children, the last four being children of his present wife, Mary Savage: Thomas, to whom was given the home in Middletown; Abigail; Elizabeth, aged 9; Mary, aged 5; Ebenezer, aged 3 months. He mentioned land given him by his father Thomas Whetmore, and signed himself John Wettmore. "I give to my daughter Abigail Wetmore one peice of Meadow Land at Wangonque containing about two acres, with the pond adjoyning to it, as it is specified in Father Andrew Warner's Deed of Guift to me." His wife Mary Savage was executor, and his two brothers, Beriah and Joseph Wetmore, and his brother-in-law Andrew Warner, overseers.

Children of John and Abigail (Warner) Wetmore

Thomas Wetmore, was under 21 at the making of his father's will in 1689. There is no record of his marriage but the name appears among some fifty heads of families belonging to the Middlefield Society in 1744.

Abigail Wetmore, b. in Middletown, May 2, 1685; d. Apr. 2 or 9, 1738. Married June 21, 1733, Ebenezer Clark and had two children: i. Abigail, b. Apr. 1, 1734; ii. Jedediah, b. Jan. 16, 1738. Ebenezer Clark married (2) Anna⁴ Warner, b. Apr. 12, 1716; see number 50.

12 JOHN³ WARNER, son of Andrew² and Rebecca (Fletcher) Warner, born in Middletown, Conn., April 8, 1671; died in Upper Middletown, Aug. 5, 1743. His tombstone may still be seen in Riverside Cemetery. He was a farmer, a weaver by trade and a man of influence in his town. As early as 1698 he received a grant of land in Upper Middletown; in 1712 he was Deputy to the General Court; in 1716 he was appointed ensign of the north company or trainband of Middletown, lieutenant in 1719, and captain in 1725.

Records of Middletown contain many references to John Warner, and it is not always clear if the record pertains to John, son of Andrew², or John, son of John². It is probable that this John is the one who took an active interest in the school question and was treasurer, receiving "for his trouble about the school, 6s., 1d." He was on a committee to hire a school master in 1714-5 and the following year was one of a "comity to look after the school and to hire a school master or school dame as they shal think fit and most for ye Society's advantage." A Mrs. Smith, who had a husband and three children to care for, kept the school for three months in this year for £5.

His commission as captain and account books from 1698 to 1743 are carefully preserved by some of his descendants. There are several accounts showing that he received for his weaving about a shilling a yard. His account with the Rev. Joseph Smith extends over a period of years and is particularly interesting. He did weaving in exchange for his church rates at times, or in exchange for 3 pounds of sugar, at 2 shillings, or a quart of rum, at one shilling, and so on down to 1736, when the account ended with the charge for digging the grave of the minister. These accounts show dealings with nearly every family in Middletown, and often show the trade of the people. They were of great value in preparing the history of the town. Many references to the Warners are found in Charles Collard Adams' "Middletown Upper Houses."

The inventory of his property was taken June 2, 1743, and amounted to about £160. Letters of administration upon "the estate of Captain John Warner, late of Middletown, were granted unto Jabez Warner of Middletown, son of the late dec'd." (Early Connecticut Probate Records.) His homestead was deeded to his son Jabez, who later sold it and removed to Washington, Conn.

Married in Middletown, December 14, 1699, ANNA WARD, born March 20, 1670, died March 8, 1737-8, daughter of Ensign William and Phoebe (   ) Ward.

Children, births recorded in Middletown

Anna (1) *Warner*, b. June 19, 1702; d. June 19, 1709.
46 Abigail *Warner*, b. Nov. 18, 1704; m. Joseph Ranney.
47 *John Warner*, b. Mar. 31, 1706-7; m. Mary Wilcox.
48 *Jabez Warner*, b. Mar. 30, 1710; m. Hannah[4] Warner.
49 *Andrew Warner*, b. Sept. 14, 1713; m. Martha Wilcox.
50 Anna (2) *Warner*, b. Apr. 12, 1716; m. Ebenezer Clark.
51 *Mary Warner*, b. Nov. 14, 1720; m. Timothy Sage, 2d.

13 REBECCA[3] WARNER, daughter of Andrew[2] and Rebecca (Fletcher) Warner, born in Middletown, Conn., July 2 or 1, 1675; died before 1752. About 1730 she, with her brother and sister, signed an agreement releasing land to her brother Joseph Warner.

Married July 8, 1698, JOHN HURLBUT, JR., son of John and Mary (Deming) Hurlbut, born in Middletown, December 8, 1671; died after 1752. He was a farmer and occupied the house and land in Middletown given him by his father. His will, made March 14, 1752, was probated September 1, 1753. An account of his family will be found in the Hurlbut Genealogy, page 25, etc.

Children, born in Middletown

John Hurlbut, 3d, b. Oct. 14, 1701; d. Mar. 24, 1775. He was a Lieutenant and lived in Middletown. Married June 11, 1724, Elizabeth Sage, b. Mar. 9, 1701, daughter of John Sage of Middletown Upper Houses. Children, born in Middletown: i. Jemima, b. May 17, 1725. ii. Hezekiah, b. June 2, 1727; m. Anna Hall. iii. Mary, b. Nov. 12, 1729; d. before Mar. 13, 1756. iv. Elizabeth (1), b. Mar. 16, 1732; d. Aug. 22, 1732. v. Elizabeth (2), bapt. Oct. 21, 1733; m. Elisha Doane. vi. Daniel, bapt. June 6, 1736; d. before Mar. 13, 1756. vii. John, 4th, bapt. July 16, 1738. viii. Rebecca, bapt. Mar. 22, 1741; m. as his second wife, Elisha Colton, Sr.

Rebecca Hurlbut, b. July 17, 1703; m. July 31, 1735, Capt. John Whitmore. Children: i. Jacob, b. May 6, 1736. ii. Rebecca, b. Oct. 17, 1740; d. Aug. 22, 1742. iii. Mary, b. Aug. 2, 1742.

Mary Hurlbut, b. Jan. 25, 1706; d. young.

Daniel Hurlbut, b. Mar. 7, 1709; lost at sea, Dec. 15, 1736. Married Nov. 19, 1729, Esther Hamlin, b. Jan. 14, 1711, daughter of William Hamlin of Middletown. Children: i. Susannah, b. Jan. 30, 1730; m. and had children. ii. Hannah, b. Oct. 3, 1731; m. and had children. iii. Esther, b. Feb. 6, 1734.

14 SETH[3] **WARNER**, son of Robert[2] and Elizabeth (Grant), Warner, born in Middletown, Conn., March 1, 1658; died there November 28, 1713 (date as given in Middletown vital records). The inventory of his property was taken January 29, 1713-4, by John Bacon, John Warner, and Joseph Rockwell, and the whole value was given as £321-09-09. The widow Mary and the eldest son Robert were appointed administrators. The property was distributed February 7, 1714-5, to the heirs, Mrs. Mary Warner, Robert, Samuel, Seth and Mary.

Married in Middletown, December 25, 1686, **MARY WARD**, who died July 17, 1729, daughter of Samuel Ward. There is on file in Middletown (land records, 5:135) an agreement between Mary Warner and Abigail Ward, daughters of Samuel Ward, and Capt. Jno. Warner of Middletown with Ann his wife, daughter of said Samuel Ward, dated August 15, 1726. The inventory of Mrs. Mary Warner was taken on August 12, 1729, and amounted to £24-14-06. Her son Robert was appointed administrator.

Children, b. in Middletown

52 *Mary Warner*, b. Dec., 1687; m. Joseph Whitmore.
53 *Robert Warner*, b. June 22, 1692; m. Isabella Whitmore.
54 *Samuel Warner*, b. Feb. 6, 1694-5; m. (1) Dorothy Williams, (2) Mehitabel ———.
     Seth Warner, Jr., b. July 29, 1705; d. in Middletown, 1729; not married. His will dated July 8, 1729, left property to his brothers Robert and Samuel and sister Mary Whitmore. The inventory was taken Nov. 28, 1729, and amounted to £529-11-10.

15 MARY[3] **WARNER**, daughter of Robert[2] and Elizabeth (Grant) Warner, born September, 1664, probably in Middletown, Conn.; died May 28, 1738.

Married June 11, 1693, **ABRAHAM BARTLETT** of Guilford, Conn., born February 19, 1667, died February 20, 1731, son of Deacon George and Mary (Cruttenden) Bartlett. He is recorded as owning four and one-half acres of hassocky meadow lying beyond the East Creek and thirty-four acres of upland. An account of this family will be found in the N. E. Historical and Genealogical Register, vol. 56, p. 156.

Children

Mary Bartlett, b. May 18, 1694; d. June 4, 1755.
Abraham Bartlett, Jr., b. Mar. 4, 1697; d. Jan. 13, 1764. Resided in Durham, Conn. Married Lydia ———. Children: i. Abraham. ii. Isaac, m. in 1758, Susannah ——— and lived in Granville, Mass.
Joseph Bartlett, b. Oct. 24, 1699; d. Aug. 29, 1769. Resided in Guilford and Durham. Deacon in the Fourth Church after 1768. Married

Jan. 9, 1726, Mindwell Cruttenden who died Sept. 24, 1769. Children: i. Joseph, m. and had children. ii. Mindwell, m. Samuel Chittenden. iii. Abraham, m. and had children. iv. Ruth, m. Miles Griswold. v. Samuel, m. and had children.

Timothy Bartlett, b. Mar. 13, 1702; d. Dec. 1, 1773. Married (1) 1728, Susanna Cruttenden who died Sept. 15, 1751; (2) Thankful Chitten. den, daughter of Joseph Chittenden, who died July 9, 1780. Children by first wife: i. Lucy, m. Reuben Leete. ii. Timothy, m. and had children. iii. Ruth, d. young. iv. Sarah, m. Gilbert Dudley.

Ebenezer Bartlett, b. Nov. 17, 1704; d. Oct. 19, 1777, not married. Lived on Clapboard Hill, Guilford.

16   RUTH³ WARNER, daughter of Robert² and Elizabeth (Grant) Warner, born November, 1675, in Middletown, Conn., bapt. there November 14, 1675; died in East Windsor, March 1, 1733. She and her mother were dismissed from the First Church in Middletown to the church in Scantic, Windsor, August 22, 1708.

Married February 24, 1703, **D A V I D   B I S S E L L,** son of Nathaniel and Mindwell (Moore) Bissell, born in East Windsor, November 18, 1681, died there October 20, 1733. He was known as Lieutenant. Further records of this family will be found in Stiles' History of Ancient Windsor.

Children, born in East Windsor

Nathaniel Bissell, b. Jan. 20, 1705; d. June 16, 1734.

David Bissell, b. Apr. 3, 1708-9. He was known as Ensign David. Married (1) Sept. 30, 1730, Sarah Grant, b. at Windsor, July 17, 1710, d. at East Windsor, June 12, 1753, daughter of Matthew and Hannah (Chapman) Grant; m. (2) Sarah Burt-Williston, who died June 27, 1756, in her 39th year. Children by first wife: i. Archippus. ii. David. iii. Sarah, m. —— Grant. iv. Noadiah, d. young. v. Lucy, m. Samuel Webster. vi. Daniel. vii. Elisha. viii. Rachel, d. young. ix. Rufus, d. young.

Hezekiah Bissell, b. Jan. 30, 1710. He was pastor of Wintonbury Parish, Windsor. Married Nov. 20, 1740, Mrs. Mary Woodbridge of Groton, Conn. Children: i. Hezekiah (1), d. young. ii. Hezekiah (2). iii. Mary, d. young. iv. Wealthy Ann, d. young.

Ruth Bissell, b. Nov. 20, 1713.

Noah Bissell, b. June 26, 1716; d. Aug. 22, 1776. He was called "Landlord Bissell." Married Dec. 2, 1741, Silence Burt of Springfield, who died July 22, 1761, in her 41st year. Resided at East Windsor. Children: i. Sibil (1), d. young. ii. Silence. iii. Noah (1), d. young. iv. Nathan, d. young. v. Sibil (2), d. young. vi. Noah (2), m. Eunice Olcott and had children. vii. Roxy, m. Elisha Bissell.

Noadiah Bissell, b. Nov. 3, 1720; d. Aug. 29, 1722.

17   BETHIA³ WARNER, daughter of Robert² and Elizabeth (Grant) Warner, born October 8, 1680, probably in Middletown, Conn.

Married in Windsor, May 16, or October 12, 1699, NATHAN-, **IEL GRANT,** born in Windsor, April 14, 1672, son of Samuel and Mary (Porter) Grant. Nathaniel and Bethia owned the covenant at East Windsor, August 25, 1700. They probably removed to Tolland about 1713, and about 1723-4 to Ellington, where they were among the earliest settlers. He was hayward, collector and tythingman. Records of this family are found in the Grant and Porter Genealogies and in Stiles' History of Ancient Windsor.

Children, first seven born in Windsor

Bethia Grant, b. Jan. 17, 1699-1700; bapt. at East Windsor, Aug. 25, 1700.

Ruth Grant, b. Feb. 26, 1702-3; m. ——— Booth.

Nathaniel Grant, b. Oct. 18, 1705, settled at Ellington as early as 1734 and had three children who died there before 1740. He held the offices of fence-viewer and surveyor. He was perhaps the Nathaniel Grant who was a member of the Congregational Church at Lyme, N. H., in 1782.

Benjamin Grant, b. July 8, 1708; d. in Lyme, N. H., Apr. 17, 1795. Married Feb. 10, 1736-7, Anne Wood of Enfield, b. Nov. 16, 1713, d. Nov. 12, 1783. She was sister of Daniel Wood and widow of Joseph Hunt of Somers. Benjamin Grant removed with his father to Ellington before 1734, and lived later in Bolton, after 1768 in Lyme, N. H. While in Ellington he served as fence-viewer, tythingman, lister and constable; he was first on the list of organizers of the Congregational Church in Lyme in 1771; was on the alarm list of a militia company in 1776; built the first mill in Lyme. Children: i. Benjamin. ii. Anne. iii. Deliverance, m. Dr. Samuel Cary, a physician in East Windsor, Conn., and Lyme, N. H. iv. Peters, m. Ann ———. v. Dorcas, m. Col. Ebenezer Green. vi. Miriam, m. Samuel Root. vii. Esther, m. Timothy Bartholomew.

Esther Grant, b. Oct. 31, 1710; d. 1804. Married June 12, 1739, Joseph Hayden, b. Nov. 17, 1711; d. Feb. 26, 1781-2, son of Samuel and Anna ( ) Hayden. He settled at Harwinton, as early as 1737.

Jonathan (1) *Grant,* b. Aug. 18, 1713; d. Sept. 10, 1713.

Jonathan (2) *Grant,* b. about 1714. As a resident of Ellington he was petitioning to be freed from taxes in 1734. He served as fence-viewer, hayward, tythingman, collector and grand juror. Married July 9, 1741, Mary Ladd of Tolland, daughter of Jonathan and Susannah (Kingsbury) Ladd. Children: i. Mary. ii. Susannah. iii. Phebe. iv. Rhoda, m. ——— Goodale. v. Keturah. vi. Prudence. vii. Grace, m. Asahel Green. viii. Ann, m. ——— Gustin. ix. Rachel, m. Rufus (?) Crane. (Two children died young in Ellington, and a third was buried in East Windsor, Aug. 4, 1724.)

Hannah Grant, b. in Ellington about 1721; d. Aug. 25, 1759. Married Oct. 19, 1743, Benjamin Brown, b. at Windsor, Aug. 11, 1711, son of Peter and Mary (Barber) Brown. He married (2) Mrs. Mary Brown of West Hartford by whom he had two children. Benjamin and Hannah (Grant) Brown had seven children.

18 SAMUEL³ WARNER, son of Robert² and Deliverance (Bissell-Rockwell) Warner, born in Middletown, Conn., May 19, 1683; died in East Middletown (Portland), May 6, 1732, buried in old Quarry Cemetery, Portland. The inventory of his property at the time of his death shows that he was a man of considerable means, but the public records have left little trace of his life.

Married in Middletown, November 13, 1712, **SUSANNAH HALL**. She survived her husband, and her name is found in land transactions of Middletown. With other heirs of Giles Hall, she signed a deed on March 14, 1754: Experience Cotton, a widow; Phebe Cromwell, a widow; John, Richard and Jabez Hall. Eleazer Gaylord, on February 10, 1736-7, transferred property to Susanna Warner, widow of Samuel, and her two youngest children, Deliverance and Phebe. On May 12, 1737, there was recorded a deed by which Deliverance Warner and Mary Gaylord received equal shares, and their sister Phebe is mentioned. This land was on the east side of the Connecticut River.

Children, recorded in Middletown

Samuel Warner, Jr., b. Nov. 27, 1713; d. Dec. 27, 1713.
Mary Warner, b. July 27, 1715; m. Ebenezer Gaylord. She is mentioned in land records of Middletown, see above.
Susanna Warner, b. May 29, 1717; m. John Gains.
Deliverance Warner, b. Jan. 26, 1719-20, in East Middletown (Portland), Conn.; d. there Sept. 17 or 29, 1751, buried in old Quarry Cemetery, Portland. He held lands on the east side of the river in Middletown in 1737; had property adjacent to that of John Gains in 1744; took inventories in 1745, 1746, and 1749. He was married and had a son, Deliverance, who died in 1792.
Phebe Warner, b. 1727; noted as one of the two youngest children, and had a share in her father's property. She is perhaps the Phebe Warner who married, Mar. 9, 1758, Wait Wooster, son of Abraham Wooster, Jr., who resided at Quaker's Farm, Oxford Parish. Their children were: i. Moses and ii. Hinman (twins), b. Dec. 21, 1758. iii. Mary, b. Dec. 31, 1760. iv. Benjamin, b. Oct. 29, 1762. v. Wait, b. Oct. 28, 1764. vi. Abraham, b. July 28, 1770.

19 JOHN³ WARNER, JR., son of John² Warner. The date of his birth has been variously stated, 1654, 1657, and 1659. His will, dated June 29, 1736, probated Sept. 2, 1741, says "I, John Warner, sen., of Middletown in the County of Hartford, being advanced to the age of 77 years, do make this my last will and testament." This places the date of birth as 1659. He was a farmer and died at Middletown Upper Houses. To his son

John he left his dwelling and homelot, seven acres of pasture at Siding Hill, a three-acre piece of land at Pistol Point, and land at Wongunk, "as well what is my own proper inheritance as also what right I have in any lands there or that did belong to my brother Jonathan Warner deceased." He also left property to the heirs of his daughter Mary Wilcock, deceased, and to his daughter Hannah; son John, sole executor. The will is recorded as Capt. John Warner's.

There is some danger of confusion between records of John³, b. 1671, son of Andrew², and John³, b. 1659, son of John², as they were living in Middletown and active at the same period, and both names occur frequently on the land, town and vital records.

There is found in the land records of Middletown a receipt given by John Warner, May 11, 1726. "These are to signify that I have Recev⁴ the whole part of the estate that belounged to my wife who is deceast who was the widow of Epram Willcock and of her children and therefore I do acquit James Willcock administrators from all molestation from me or my children. John Warner."

Married (1) ————.

Married (2) July, 1715, **Mrs. SILENCE HAND WILCOX**, born March, 1678-9 (or November 12, 1679), probably in Guilford, Conn.; died before 1726. She was the daughter of Joseph Hand (son of John of Easthampton, L. I.), who settled in the eastern part of the town of Guilford after 1660 and married in 1664, Jane Wright, daughter of Benjamin Wright. Joseph Hand was a Representative to the General Court in 1720, and seems to have been one of the substantial men of the town, serving on various committees. Silence Hand first married, October 23, 1698, Ephraim Wilcox of Middletown, who died January 4, 1711. They had children: Esther; James; Mary, m. John⁴ Warner (John³, Andrew², Andrew¹); Jane; Ephraim · John.

Child of John Warner by first wife

Mary Warner, b. 1688, probably in Middletown, Conn.; d. Apr. 23, 1735; m. in Middletown, Apr. 12, 1710, John Wilcox, b. July 5, 1682, d. May 12, 1751. He was the son of Israel and Sarah (Savage) Wilcox of Middletown, and was a deacon in the Congregational Church. Children, recorded in Middletown: i. Mary, b. Jan. 25, 1710-11. ii. John, b. Feb. 13, 1712-3, "the same John abovesaid departed this life by death suddenly, Apr. 15, 1713." iii. Joseph, b. Aug. 14, 1714; d. Feb. 11, 1736-7. iv. Sarah, b. Oct. 1, 1716. v. Ebenezer, b. Sept. 10, 1718, d. Apr. 15, 1741. vi. Esther, b. Dec. 3, 1720. vii. Jemima, b. July 1, 1723. viii. Huldah, b. Jan. 21, 1725-6. ix. Moses, b. July 31, 1728. x. Ozias, b. Sept. 16, 1730.

Children of John Warner by second wife, recorded in Middletown

Hannah Warner, b. Sept. 10, 1716; d. in Washington, Conn., 1811; m. Jabez⁴ Warner, son of John³ and Anna (Ward) Warner; see number 48.

55 *John Warner, 3d,* b. Mar. 14, 1718-9; m. Rachel Burlison.

20 SARAH³ WARNER, daughter of John² Warner, born March 6, 1669, probably in Middletown, Conn.; died there October 4, 1741. Resided in Middletown on a farm adjacent to that of her father. A fuller record of her family will be found in the account of the Ranney family as given in Middletown Upper Houses, by Charles Collard Adams.

Married in Middletown, August 4, 1698, EBENEZER RANNEY, born in Middletown Upper Houses, died there May 8, 1754. He was the son of Thomas and Mary (Hubbard) Ranney and inherited his father's homestead, which he, in turn, willed to his son Ebenezer. The inventory of his property shows him to have been a man of some means, and active in the life of the community.

Children, born in Middletown

Sarah Ranney, b. Jan. 15, 1699; d. Sept. 4, 1742.

Hannah Ranney, b. Mar. 25, 1702; d. 1748; not married.

Ebenezer Ranney, Jr., b. Nov. 22. 1704; d. Dec. 22, 1783; m. Nov. 25, 1742, Margaret Ranney, b. Aug. 21, 1708, d. July 28, 1783, daughter of Thomas and Rebecca (Willett) Ranney. Children: i. Sarah, b. 1743; d. Sept. 23, 1786; m. Apr. 2, 1766, Nathaniel Smith. ii. George, d. young. iii. Ebenezer, b. 1748; d. Oct. 7, 1822; was a Revolutionary soldier; m. Nov. 30, 1769, Lois Blinn, b. May 13, 1745, in Wethersfield, Conn., d. Oct. 24, 1831; had seven children. iv. Lucy, b. 1748-9; m. Aug. 16, 1772, Reuben Sage, and had eleven children.

Ruth Ranney, b. Apr. 6, 1707; m. Apr. 13, 1738, Theophilus Moss, b. Oct. 24, 1704, son of Samuel and Susannah (Hall) Moss of Wallingford, Conn. Children: i. Ebenezer, b. Nov. 25, 1740; m. ·Apr. 27, 1764, Esther Preston. ii. Esther, b. June 10, 1744; d. Aug. 25, 1744. iii. Ruth, b. Apr. 17, 1746.

Esther, b. Mar. 17, 1710; d. Oct. 7. 1741.

21 DANIEL³ WARNER, JR., son of Lieut. Daniel² and Mary (   ) Warner, born in Hadley, Mass., 1666; died in Hardwick, Mass., March 12, 1754, aged 88; buried in the old cemetery in Hardwick. He resided at Hatfield, and at Sunderland for a time about 1722, and finally removed to Hardwick, where some of his children were already settled.

Married (1) December 12, 1688, MARY HUBBARD, born April 10, 1669, daughter of John and Mary (Merriam?) Hubbard who came from Wethersfield to Hadley about 1660. John was the son of George Hubbard who was born in England about 1600, settled first in Watertown, and in 1635, in Wethersfield. He was a member of the first General Court in 1638 and in later years removed to Milford in 1644 and to Guilford in 1648. His wife was Mary Bishop, daughter of John and Anna ( ) Bishop of Wethersfield and Guilford. John[2] Hubbard, b. 1630, removed to Hadley in 1660, and in 1683 to Hatfield, where he died in 1702. He was one of the first proprietors of Hadley and married Mary Merriam, who was probably the sister of Robert Merriam. John Hubbard was selectman and Lieutenant of the Hatfield Militia Company.

Married (2) August 4, 1714, THANKFUL BILLINGS, who died June 13, 1716.

Children, by first wife

Mary (1) *Warner*, b. Aug. 31, 1689; d. Feb. 24, 1692, in Hatfield.
56 *Daniel Warner, 3d*, b. March 1, 1693; m. Elizabeth Adams.
57 *Mary* (2) *Warner*, b. Aug. 17, 1694; m. Joseph Wait.
58 *Hannah Warner*, b. 1700; m. Samuel Billings.
59 *Jonathan Warner*, b. 1704; m. Bathsheba Allis.
Sarah Warner, b. Oct. 11, 1707.
60 *Joseph Warner*, b. June 18, 1710; m. Mary Hubbard.

Child, by second wife

Thankful Warner, b. June 8, 1716. One Thankful Warner m. as first wife Nathan Dickinson, son of Ebenezer and Hannah (Frary) Dickinson, b. May 30, 1712, d. Aug. 7, 1796. The History of Amherst Church calls her Thankful, daughter of Daniel[4], which is possible, although this one seems more likely. They had four children: i. Nathan, b. 1735. ii. Ebenezer, b. 1741. iii. Irene, b. 1743. iv. Enos, b. 1746. He m. (2) Joanna Leonard, (3) Judith Hosmer, had eight children by the second wife and two by the third.

22 SARAH[3] WARNER, daughter of Lieut. Daniel[2] and Mary ( ) Warner, born probably in Hatfield, or Hadley, Mass. The date of her birth has been given in published records as June 21, and January 24, 1667, but this is doubtless an error, as June 24, 1667, was the birth date of her brother Andrew (Hadley town records, I :61).

Married (recorded in Northampton, Mass.) Nov. 25, 1685, ISAAC SHELDON, JR., of Northampton, born September 4, 1656, died March 29, 1712, son of Isaac and Mary (Woodford) Sheldon. He succeeded to his father's homestead at Northampton and the births of his children are recorded there.

Children

Isaac Sheldon, 3d, b. Aug. 26, 1686; m. Feb. 29, 1716, Elizabeth Pratt of Hartford, daughter of Daniel and Elizabeth (Lea) Pratt; see number 6.

Sarah Sheldon, b. July 16, 1688; m. June 22, 1710, Josiah Parsons of Northampton.

Mary Sheldon, b. Sept. 18, 1690; d. Aug. 6, 1767; m. Feb. 2, 1709-10, Increase Clark of Northampton, son of Deacon John and Mary (Strong) Clark of Northampton. He was born April 8, 1684, d. Aug. 27, 1775. Children: i. Mary, b. Jan. 7, 1710; m. Jerijah Strong, Jr. (See Strong Genealogy.) ii. Daniel, b. March 3, 1713; d. Dec. 26, 1804; m. (1) Experience Allen, (2) Mary Field. iii. Eunice, b. Dec. 18, 1714; d. Jan., 1715. iv. Moses, b. June 7, 1716; m. four times and had in all fourteen children. v. Lois, b. Sept. 5, 1718; m. as 2d wife, Nov. 29, 1764, Bela Strong of Northampton. vi. Deacon Simeon, b. Oct. 19, 1720; was one of the founders of Amherst; m. Rebecca Strong and had twelve children. vii. Rachel, b. Sept. 5, 1725; d. Aug. 28, 1745. viii. Jemima, b. Sept. 5, 1728; m. Aaron Baker, b. 1726, son of Captain John and Rebecca (Clark) Baker. ix. Deacon Elijah, m. Experience Field and had eight children. The Strong Genealogy contains further records of many of these.

Mindwell Sheldon, b. March 22, 1692-3; d. May 23, 1780; m. Dec. 18, 1712, Capt. Moses Lyman, Jr., b. Feb. 27, 1689, son of Moses and Ann (   ) Lyman. Children: i. Moses, b. Oct. 3, 1713; m. March 24, 1742, Sarah Hayden, b. Sept. 17, 1716, daughter of Samuel and Anna (Holcomb) Hayden, and the father of Colonel Moses Lyman, of Revolutionary fame, who m. Ruth Collins. ii. Phebe, b. Aug. 20, 1717, m. Lieut. Caleb Strong and had son Caleb who became governor of Massachusetts.

Daniel Sheldon, b. April 4, 1696; d. 1703.

Thankful Sheldon, b. June 6, 1698; d. Feb. 20, 1774; m. Dec. 23, 1719, Deacon Josiah Clark, b. June 11, 1697, d. April 7, 1789, son of Deacon John and Mary (Strong) Clark of Northampton. Children: i. Josiah, b. May 6, 1721; d. Nov. 16, 1808; m. Dec. 10, 1747, Mary Baker, b. about 1725, d. March 3, 1797, daughter of John and Rebecca (Clark) Baker of Northampton. ii. Enoch, b. May 4, 1726. iii. Thankful, b. July 1, 1731; m. 1769, Nathan Frary of Deerfield. iv. Isaac, b. Oct. 2, 1732; d. Nov. 21, 1732.

Hannah Sheldon, b. Oct. 30, 1701; m. John Miller of Northampton.

23 ANDREW[3] WARNER, son of Lieut. Daniel[2] and Mary (   ) Warner, born in Hadley, Mass., June 24, 1667; was a large land-holder in Hadley and removed to Saybrook, Conn., about 1696, where, in partnership with Joseph Selden and John Church, he purchased Twelve Mile Island Farm, situated on both banks of the Connecticut River in the towns of Lyme and Saybrook. A deed of John Leverett of Boston, dated February, 1695, conveyed this land to Joseph Selden, who on June 22, 1697, deeded the Saybrook part to Andrew Warner. Part of the land is still owned by the family. The early dwelling house stood

about one quarter mile northeast of where the Middlesex Turn
pike crosses the Warner's Ferry Road, or from the present homestead.

Married (1) **RUTH CLARK**, who died in 1704 or 5.

Married (2) April 4, 1706, **Mrs. HANNAH STANNARD.**

Children, recorded in the L'Hommedieu transcript of Saybrook records
(Conn. State Library) with the note, "which three children said
Andrew had by his first wife Ruth Clark"

Ruth Warner, b. Nov. 27, 1701.

61 *Andrew Warner, Jr.*, b. Jan. 25, 1703; m. Sarah Graves.

62 *Ichabod Warner*, b. July 8, 1704; m. ————.

24 ANNA³ **WARNER**, daughter of Lieut. Daniel² and Mary
( ) Warner, born in Hatfield, Mass., Nov. 17, 1669; died
June 26, 1750, in Sunderland, Mass.

Married **ISAAC HUBBARD**, born January 16, 1667, died in
Sunderland, August 7, 1750, son of John and Mary (Merriam)
Hubbard of Wethersfield, Hadley and Hatfield. He removed to
Sunderland, Mass., in 1714 and was one of the first forty settlers
there, holding as his home lot No. 8, west side. He was one
of the first deacons of the Sunderland Church and was a member
of the council that installed the Rev. Jonathan Edwards at
Northampton. (History of Sunderland.)

Children, born in Hatfield

John Hubbard, b. Apr. 20, 1693; m. Hannah Cowles of East Hartford,
Conn.; d. Aug. 25, 1778.

Isaac Hubbard, b. Jan. 14, 1695; m. (1) July 4, 1723, Christian Gunn,
who died Feb. 5, 1744, daughter of Samuel Gunn, (2) Jan. 24, 1745,
Mrs. Abigail (Kellogg) Atherton, who died Apr. 22, 1774, daughter
of John and Sarah (Moody) Kellogg of Hadley and widow of
Jonathan Atherton. Children of Isaac Hubbard: Israel; Hannah;
Isaac; Elijah; Christian; Anna; Giles.

Mary Hubbard, b. Feb. 25, 1697.

Daniel Hubbard, b. Apr. 30, 1699; d. May 30, 1779. Married Nov. 16,
1732, Mary Gunn, who died Jan. 14, 1790, daughter of Samuel Gunn.
Children: Mary; Daniel; Martha (1); Martha (2).

Hannah Hubbard, b. Sept. 7, 1701; m. Sept. 18, 1727, Nathaniel Mattoon; d. Apr. 16, 1797.

Jonathan Hubbard, b. Dec. 29, 1703; d. July 6, 1795. He was graduated
at Yale in 1724, and became pastor at Sheffield, Mass. Married
Rachel Ely, b. Nov. 11, 1716, d. Mar. 28, 1796, daughter of Deacon
John and Mary (Bliss) Ely of West Springfield. Children: John
(1), d. young; John (2); Moses and Aaron (twins); Timothy;
Noah Ely.

Joseph Hubbard, b. Apr. 8, 1708; d. about 1783. Married Nov. 4,
1737, Joanna Porter, who died Dec. 12, 1766, daughter of Samuel
and Anna (Colton) Porter. Children: i. Susannah, b. Nov. 4, 1737;

m. Wilder Willard. ii. William, b. July 6, 1739. iii. Anna, b. Aug. 7, 1742. iv. Joanna, b. 1744. They resided at Sheffield, Mass.
David Hubbard, b. Mar. 11, 1711; d. Feb. 3, 1787. Married Mar. 10, 1743, Miriam Cooley, who died Feb. 24, 1804, daughter of Simon Cooley. Children: Moses; David; Gideon; William; Elijah; Miriam.

25 JOHN³ WARNER, son of Lieut. Daniel² and Martha (Boltwood) Warner, born in Hatfield, Mass., April, 1677; died March 17, 1750. "Sarg* John Warner died March 17, 1750" (East Haddam records). Both he and his wife are buried in the old cemetery near the residence of George Rose, in Hadlyme, Conn., about three miles southeast of Chapman's Ferry. He went from Hatfield to Sunderland, Mass., at an early date and from there to East Haddam, and received a grant of land there in 1735-6. There have been published various records of this John Warner which cannot be proved correct: Judd's History of Hadley says he removed to Wethersfield and died in 1714, aged 38, and this has been quoted in later works; the History of Northfield says he removed to Westfield and died in 1714.

Field's Haddam, p. 48, says: "John Warner from Sunderland, Mass., was the father of John, Daniel, Nathaniel, Jabez, Abraham, Noadiah, a clergyman, and Joseph." In 1744 there was recorded in East Haddam, "John Warner his mark for his creatures is a hole in the near ear and a half penny the upper side of the of ear. . .   March first 1798 this mark is Recorded to John Warner . . . the now 2d." Between 1740 and 1746 John and Mehitabel made several deeds to their sons: to John, 30 acres with a barn on the east side of their lands between lands of Jabez Chapman and Samuel Richardson; to Daniel, 30 acres with house, bounded on the east by the Great Highway, north on highway, west on land of Lieut. Jabez Chapman and south by land bought of the widow Ann Selden and Robert and Joseph Selden; to Nathaniel, 60 acres, of the eighth division of land in East Haddam, commonly called parsonage land.

The record of the family is found on the fly leaf of volume 1 of East Haddam land records: "John Warner and Mahittable Richardson ware Joyned in marage March ye 21ˢᵗ 1716." Dates of the births of the children there recorded are exactly as given below.

His will was probated January 17, 1748, and mentioned wife Mehitabel and children, John, Daniel, Nathaniel, Jabez, Abraham, Noadiah, Joseph, and Elizabeth. (Colchester probate records, 2:88.)

John Warner married in East Haddam March 21, 1716, **MEHITABEL CHAPMAN RICHARDSON,** born 1690, died March 10, 1776, aged 86, daughter of Captain John Chapman of East Haddam and widow of Lemuel Richardson. According to one account her mother was the widow of Lemuel Richardson and married John Chapman, and the daughter was called by both names. She is buried by her husband in Hadlyme. She and her husband were among the heirs of her sister Lydia Chapman of East Haddam, August, 1838.

Children, births recorded in East Haddam

63 *John Warner, Jr.,* b. Dec. 19, 1716; m. Mary Taylor.
64 *Daniel Warner,* b. May 6, 1717; m. Elizabeth Clark.
    Nathaniel Warner, b. Dec. 25, 1718. He bought several pieces of land in East Haddam in 1753, and 1779. In 1788, Nathaniel Warner of Colchester, New London County, sold land to Joseph Warner, Jr., of East Haddam. He was a member of the Hadlyme Congregational Church about 1770. No record of his family has been found. "Becoming pecuniarily embarrassed he removed to New York State after the Revolution." (One of the Warner family.)
65 *Jabez Warner,* b. Nov. 25, 1720; m. Hannah Brainerd.
    Judah Warner, baptized June 24, 1722 (Selden Warner notebook, not recorded in East Haddam births).
    Elizabeth Warner, b. Jan. (or July) 25, 1724; m. as second wife, James Cone, b. in East Haddam, Aug. 24, 1698, died in Millington, Conn., April 3, 1774, son of Nathaniel and Grace (Hungerford) Cone. He married (1) Grace Spencer, who died in 1767. He was appointed Lieutenant in the Colonial troops in 1738 and served in the war of 1745 under Sir William Pepperill; was a member of legislature of the colony in 1747-8-9; belonged to the ecclesiastical society of Millington in 1733 and was its first clerk; held many positions of trust and responsibility. By his first wife he had children, Elizabeth, Mehitable, Huldah, Sylvanus, Rufus, Esther, and James. For further records see the Cone Genealogy.
    Abraham Warner, b. Feb. 13, 1725-6; d. Apr. 5, 1791. He resided in the lower part of the town of East Haddam, received a deed of land from his father, and sold land in 1755 and 1782. Married Thankful Beebe, daughter of Jonathan Beebe, 2d, who sold land in Millington Parish, East-Haddam, Apr. 27, 1780, to his daughters Thankful, wife of Abraham Warner, and Rachel, wife of Samuel Dean. They had no children, and were recorded in the Census of 1790 as living alone.
66 *Noadiah Warner,* b. Jan. 12, 1728-9; m. Elizabeth De Forest.
67 *Joseph Warner,* b. Jan. 13, 1731; m. Elizabeth Cone.

26 SAMUEL[3] WARNER, son of Lieut. Daniel[2] and Martha (Boltwood) Warner, born April 13, 1680, in Hatfield, Mass.; died in 1746. The will of Samuel Warner of Hatfield, yeoman, was dated September 25, 1742, probated December 7, 1746. It names his wife Elizabeth, sons Jesse, Nathan and Samuel and daughter Rebecca, and refers to other children. The inventory, dated December 19, 1746, gives a long list of clothing and utensils, with seventy acres of land, valuation, $480. In February, 1747, guardians were chosen for his children: Ebenezer Morton for David, over 14; Deacon John Hubbard of Hatfield, for Joshua, over 14, and for Hannah, Elizabeth, Abraham and Sarah, under 14.

Married (1) May 1, 1715, HANNAH SACKETT, born June, 1692, in Westfield, Mass.

Married (2) October 27, 1731, ELIZABETH MORTON, daughter of Joseph Morton.

Children of Samuel[5] Warner, two, at least, by second wife ·

Rebecca Warner, b. May 6, 1716; m. April 1, 1737, John Perry (Hadley town records).

68 *Jesse Warner*, b. May 6, 1718; m. (1) Miriam Smith; (2) Mrs. Mary (Cooley) Ven Horn.

Samuel Warner, Jr., b. Oct. 27, 1722.

Nathan Warner, was possibly the Nathan of Harvard, Mass., who m. Jan. 17, 1737, Dorothy Goodnow, and had a child, Lucy, b. 1742, m. David Sampson.

David Warner, b. Feb. 15, 1732.

69 *Joshua Warner*, b. Dec. 12, 1733; m. (1) Mary ————, (2) Hannah ————.

Hannah Warner, d. in infancy.

Elizabeth Warner, m. Israel Chapin.

Abraham Warner, was lost at sea.

Sarah Warner, m. Elijah Wait.

Samuel Warner's first wife, Hannah[4] Sackett (William[3], John[2], Simon[1]), was a descendant of Simon[1] Sackett who sailed from Bristol, England, December 1, 1630, in the ship Lyon, arriving at Boston, February 5, 1631, after a severe mid-winter voyage. He was in Newtown in the spring of 1631, and was settled there in 1632, when, on January 7, he was given six rods of the pale or fence to build. He resided on the north side of what is now Winthrop Street, between Holyoke and Dunster Streets. The trials of the voyage were said to have undermined his health, and caused his early death, at Newtown, October, 1635. In 1636 his wife Isabel and her children accompanied the Hooker party to Hartford, Connecticut. Their son, John[2] Sackett, was born in 1632, the first white child born in Newtown; resided in Springfield, Mass., 1653-9; in Northampton, 1659-65; after that in Westfield, where he was selectman in 1672 and for many years thereafter; died October 8, 1719. On October 27, 1675, his house and barn were burned by the Indians, who drove off his cattle and also destroyed a large amount of other property. He married November 23, 1659, Abigail[2] Hannum, daughter of William[1] and Honor (Capen) Hannum. She was baptized November 22, 1640; died in Westfield, October 9, 1690. Their son, William[3] Sackett, was born April 20, 1662; married, 1689, Hannah Graves, daughter of Isaac and Hannah (Church) Graves of Hatfield; was drowned March 28, 1700, in the Connecticut River near Deerfield, while returning from a wedding with a party of relatives and friends.

William Hannum, one of the first settlers in Dorchester, removed to Windsor, Conn., and, in 1655, to Northampton, Mass., where he died June 1, 1677. His wife Honor died 1680. She was the daughter of Bernard Capen, a native of Dorchester, England, who came in 1633 to Dorchester, Mass., with his wife Joan, and daughter Honor. Bernard Capen was born about 1562 and married on Monday of Whitsun week in 1596, Joan, daughter of Oliver Purchase. He received grants of land in Dorchester, Mass., 1633; was by trade a shoemaker; was made freeman in 1636; died in Dorchester, November 8, 1638. His wife Joan died March 26, 1653, aged 75 years. The original stone erected over their graves is now in the possession of the New England Historical and Genealogical Society, the inscription partially destroyed by time.

Isaac Graves, mentioned above, was born in England, probably as early as 1620, and came to America with his parents, Thomas and Sarah, locating a few miles inland from Boston before 1632. They later removed to Hartford, and in 1661 to Hadley, settling in the part that was later Hatfield, where Thomas died in 1662, and his widow Sarah, in 1666. Isaac was a prominent man in Hatfield; was one of the committee in 1663 to build the church; went to Boston, May, 1668, as the representative of Hatfield settlers in the proceeding for the separation from Hadley; was a sergeant in the colonial militia and a member of the Council of War held to provide means of defence against the Indians. During King Philip's War he and his brother John were surprised by the Indians, September 19, 1677, while shingling a roof in Hatfield, and were killed with several others.

Hannah Church, wife of Isaac Graves, born November 2, 1632, died June 9, 1695, was the daughter of Richard and Anne (Marsh) Church of Braintree, England, Hartford, Conn., and Hatfield, Mass., and granddaughter of Richard and Alice Church, and of Edward Marsh. The Church ancestors have been traced back

in a direct line for eight generations in England, to Great Parn-
don Parish, manor of Geround, County of Essex. (From MSS.
of Henry E. Warner.)

27 EBENEZER³ WARNER, son of Lieut. Daniel² and
Martha (Boltwood) Warner, born November 5, 1681, in Hatfield, Mass.; died August 25, 1749. He removed from Hatfield
to Belchertown probably among the early settlers of that place
and was on a list of valuations there as early as 1743, with lands
valued at £30, housing, £4, and personal estate, £12, s.15. The
territory now known as Belchertown was first called "Equivalent lands," because of their having been given by Massachusetts to Connecticut in exchange for Suffield and Enfield, which
had been at first controlled by Connecticut. At that time these
"Equivalent Lands" were not settled. They were later, in 1727,
sold in six divisions to parties from Boston, who induced three
families from Northampton and two from Hatfield to locate
there in 1731. The settlement was called Cold Spring until
1761 when the name was changed to Belchertown in honor of
one of the Boston owners.

Ebenezer Warner married (1) December 15, 1709, **RUTH
ELY,** born in Springfield, Mass., about 1688, died in Belchertown, Mass., about 1747. She was the youngest of the sixteen
children of Samuel and Mary (Day) Ely and was a granddaughter of Nathaniel Ely and Robert Day, the emigrants.

Ebenezer Warner of Cold Spring married (2) July 5, 1748,
Mrs. MARY BELLOWS of Hadley (Descendants of Nathaniel
Ely, p. 14), or Sarah Bellows (Hadley town records).

Children of Ebenezer and Ruth (Ely) Warner

Ruth Warner, b. Dec. 13, 1712; d. Dec. 11, 1730 (as in histories of
   Hadley and Hatfield, or b. July 31, 1712, d. Dec. 17, 1730, according
   to Descendants of Nathaniel Ely).
Martha Warner, b. June 27, 1715 or 1716; m. Oct. 2, 1736 or 1738,
   Abner Smith, b. Sept. 10, 1712, in Hatfield, d. in Springfield, Nov.
   19, 1766, son of John and Elizabeth (Hovey) Smith.
70 *Moses Warner,* b. May 13, or June 27, 1717; m. Sarah Porter.
Lydia Warner, b. Feb. 15, 1720; d. in Belchertown, 1812.
Eli Warner, b. Aug. 14, 1722; d. in Belchertown, Aug. 25, 1747.
John Warner, b. Jan. 28, 1727; no further record.
71 *Ebenezer Warner,* b. July 26 or 29, 1729; m. Dinah Phelps.

28 MEHITABEL³ WARNER, daughter of Lieut. Daniel²
and Martha (Boltwood) Warner, born in Hatfield, Mass., October 1, 1683; died October 1, 1767.

Married January 21, 1703, **PRESERVED CLAPP**, born in Northampton, Mass., April 29, 1675, died October 11, 1759, son of Preserved and Sarah (Newberry) Clapp, and grandson of the famous Roger Clapp, author of the well-known "Memoirs" reprinted in Young's Chronicles of Massachusetts. Roger Clapp was born in Salcombe Regis, Devon, England, came to America in the "Mary and John" in 1630, was lieutenant and captain of an artillery company, and representative from 1652 to 1673.

Children

Mehitabel Clapp.
Preserved Clapp.
John Clapp, b. 1708; m. Feb. 10, 1732, Eunice Parsons, perhaps the daughter of Daniel Parsons of Northampton and his wife, Abigail Cooley of Springfield. Children: Eunice; Mehitabel; John; Martha; Daniel; Solomon; Elihu; Susan; Eleanor; Sarah.
Eliphaz Clapp.
Ezra Clapp.

29 HESTER[3] or **ESTHER WARNER**, daughter of Lieut. Daniel[2] and Martha (Boltwood) Warner, born December 15, 1686.

Married in Hatfield, Mass., June 26, 1707, **SAMUEL HARVEY**, who died in Montague, Mass., 1764. His name is given in the History of Hadley as Samuel Henry, but this is doubtless an error. Samuel Harvey was one of the first forty settlers in Sunderland, Mass., in 1714, on lot 40, west side. He came from Taunton to Hatfield in 1706; was among the earliest settlers at Hunting Hill; later removed to Montague, where he died.

Children

Samuel Harvey, Jr., b. March 23, 1709; m. Dec. 2, 1736, Lydia Bodman, daughter of Joseph Bodman of Hatfield. They settled in Montague, Mass. Children: i. Experience, b. Sept. 17, 1737. ii. Medad, b. March 30, 1739. iii. Philip, b. April 25, 1741. iv. Simeon, b. July 20, 1743; was a blacksmith; m. Mary Arms, daughter of Daniel Arms, and had several children. v. Samuel, 3d, b. Feb. 4, 1746. vi. Jonathan, b. June 3, 1749. vii. Ephraim, bapt. Aug. 25, 1751. Perhaps others.
Daniel Harvey, d. before Aug. 10, 1762; m. Oct. 9, 1760, Mrs. Anna Bodman, widow of Manoah Bodman. Child: Esther.
Nathan Harvey, b. July 12, 1716; m. Elizabeth ————. Children: i. Ruth. ii. Nathan.
Elisha Harvey, b. March 9, 1719.
John Harvey, b. April 14, 1721.
Moses Harvey, b. July 20, 1723; d. Jan. 17, 1795. He was a Captain, served in the fifth Indian War and in the Revolution; was representative from Montague; m. Esther ————. Children: i. Pearlis. ii. Frances. iii. Moses. iv. Elihu. v. Anna. vi. Loyal.
Nathaniel Harvey, b. Sept. 26, 1725; resided at Northfield.

Ebenezer Harvey, b. Feb. 25, 1728; d. in Chesterfield, N. H., 1810; m. (1) Feb. 28, 1759, Sarah Janes, who d. Nov. 12, 1764, aged 25, daughter of Jonathan Janes; (2) Feb. 25, 1768, Lucy Wright, daughter of Azariah Wright. Children: i. Electa. ii. Osea (1). iii. Rufus. iv. Sarah. v. Lucy. vi. Osea (2). vii. Ebenezer.
Esther Harvey, b. March 21, 1730.

30 SARAH[3] WARNER, daughter of Isaac[2] and Sarah (Boltwood) Warner, born in Hadley, Mass., May 28, 1668; died after 1724.

Married about 1692, JONATHAN FRENCH, born at Ipswich, Mass., July 30, 1667, died in Northampton, Mass., February 17, 1714, son of John and Freedom (Kingsley) French

"The inventory of the estate of Jonathan french of Northampton, taken March 19, 1714 by Ebenezer Strong, John Kingsley, and Ebenezer Wright, amounted to £107:4:8, and was presented to court May 6, 1714 by Sarah the Relict of Jon. Frentch of Northampton deceased. An account of the debts of the estate was given in by widdow Sarah French administratrix, Jan. 28, 1724-5. Aprizement of the Estate of Lands of Jonathan French presented Jan. 28, 1724, total £103-10-00; In moveable goods at 32-7-5; ffees at 12-0; Totall 134-15-5. As to a settlement of the estate of Jon[th] Frentch deceased the total sum of 134-15-5 which is devided to Jon[th] Frentch 29-10-00 for his double portion; to Eben[r] Frentch 14-19-6; to Sam[ll] Frentch 14-19-6; to John Frentch 14-19-6; to Sarah Frentch alias Coss 14-19-6; to Hannah Frentch alias Edwards 14-19-6; to Mary Frentch alias Edwards 14-19-6; to Elizabeth Frentch alias Bascomb 14-19-6. This estate being mostly in land and it will not be broken without damage, therefore the whole estate is disposed to Jonathan Frentch; he is to pay out . . . to his brothers and sisters as above distributed to them and this settlement was to the satisfaction of the wido Sarah Frentch the mother of them all; this is allowed as a settlement of said estate Jan. 28, 1824-5." [Hampshire Probate, 58:27.]

Children of Jonathan and Sarah (Warner) French, born in Northampton
Jonathan French, b. Aug. 28, 1693; d. Feb. 5, 1696-7.
Sarah French, b. March 1, 1694-5; d. Jan. 4, 1768 [Judd MS.] (June 11, 1768, according to Sheldon's Deerfield) ; m. Nov. 2, 1715, Northampton, Sergt. Ebenezer Corse, b. April 7, 1692, d. Southampton, Mass., May 3, 1776 [Judd MS.] (May 14, 1776, Sheldon), son of James and Elizabeth (Catlin) Corse. Ebenezer Corse was of Northampton 1717; a first settler at Southampton, where he had a house May 25, 1730. By his will, dated Nov. 1753, not proved, he gave his property to his wife Sarah and his six daughters; Reuben, the only son, was given only twenty shillings. Children [Judd MSS. 4:182] : i. Sarah, b. Nov. 25, 1716; m. Nov. 3, 1751 (Coventry, Conn., record), Eleazer Gillet of Lebanon, Conn. ii. Reuben, b. Sept. 24, 1718; d. in the army, Jan., 1760; m. Sarah ————. iii. Elizabeth, b. Aug. 24, 1720; m. 1752, Jonathan Wait. iv. Dinah, b. Sept. 21, 1723; m. as his second wife, int. pub. Southampton, July 25, 1778, Obadiah Frary, b. May 20, 1717, d. Southampton, Aug. 20, 1804, son of Nathaniel Frary of Deerfield. v. Mehetabel, b. March 24, 1725; perhaps m. Ebenezer

Coleman of Coventry, Conn. vi. Lemuel (1), b. Dec. 2, 1727. vii. Tryphena, b. Jan. 28, 1730. viii. Lemuel (2), b. April 19, 1732. ix. Benoni, b. Sept. 17, 1734; d. Sept. 9, 1748. x. Abilene, b. Sept. 27, 1736; was of Chester in 1767; m. John Smith of Westhampton.

Hannah French, b. March 4, 1697; d. Aug. 31, 1761; m. (1) Sept. 3, 1719, Northampton, Nathaniel Edwards, 2d, b. Oct. 21, 1685, d. Aug. 26, 1724, slain by Indians, son of Samuel and Sarah (Boykin) Edwards; m. (2) about 1728, Nehemiah Strong, b. 1694, d. Amherst, Mass., Feb. 28, 1772, aged 78, son of Samuel and Esther (Clapp) Strong. Children of Nathaniel and Hannah Edwards: i. Jonathan (1), b. May 10, 1720; d. May 16, 1720. ii. Hannah, b. May 7, 1721; living in 1739. iii. Jonathan (2), b. Dec., 1722; d. about 1798; m. Sept. 6, 1748, Rebecca, dau. of Samuel Smith of Sunderland. (The will of Jonathan Edwards of Amherst, dated Nov. 8, 1794, was proved March 6, 1798; ten children, given in Judd's Hadley). iv. Silence, b. Dec. 25, 1724; d. before 1739, when her father's estate was settled. Children of Nehemiah and Hannah Strong: i. Nehemiah, b. Feb. 24, 1730; d. Bridgeport, Conn., Aug. 12, 1807; was graduated at Yale in 1755; tutor there 1757-60; was settled as pastor at Granby, Conn., Jan. 21, 1761-68; in Dec., 1770, he became professor of mathematics and natural philosophy at Yale; resigned in 1781; studied law but practised little. ii. Mary, b. Feb. 21, 1732; d. Aug. 1, 1814; m. Aug. 29, 1751, her second cousin, Lieut. Solomon Boltwood of Amherst, b. Dec. 26, 1727, d. May 17, 1777, son of Solomon and Mary (Norton) (Pantry) Boltwood; had ten children (Strong Genealogy, p. 1317). iii. Simeon Strong, b. March 6, 1735-6; d. Dec. 14, 1805; was graduated at Yale in 1756; studied theology and preached several years, though declining settlement on account of pulmonary complaints; studied law and was sworn in as an attorney in 1761, becoming an eminent lawyer at Amherst; representative to the General Court, 1767-9; state senator, 1793; justice of the Supreme Court of Mass., 1800-05; m. (1) Jan. 12, 1763, Sarah Wright, b. Feb. 24, 1739-40, d. Dec. 3, 1783, dau. of Stephen and Esther (Cook) Wright of Northampton; m. (2) in 1787, Mary (Whiting) Barron, who d. West Springfield, Mass., Feb. 12, 1808, aged 65, wid. of William Barron; had seven children (Strong Gen., p. 1334).

Mary French, probably b. 1698-9, but unrecorded; d. Coventry, Conn., Oct., 1767, as "wife of Denis Maraugh"; m. (1) Northampton, Dec. 3, 1719, Joseph Edwards, b. about 1698, d. Coventry, Dec. 16, 1750, in his 53d year, son of Benjamin and Thankful (Sheldon) Edwards; she appears to have married (2) a Sprague (perhaps Ephraim Sprague of Lebanon, whose will, sworn to by the witnesses John, Eliakim, and Susannah Sprague at Coventry, Dec. 2, 1754, left to his wife Mary so long as she should remain his widow all the eastward part of his dwelling house, etc.); for as Mary Sprague of Coventry she married Dec. 29, 1763 (as his second wife), Denis Maraugh, who died in Coventry, Dec. 1, 1767, in his 79th year, probably son of Denis and Jaen [sic] Marroh of Norwich, 1711. Benjamin Edwards of Northampton in his will of Oct. 30, 1724, the day before his death, gave to his son Joseph the homelot on the other side of Mill River and the house, and made him co-executor with his eldest son Benjamin, but provided that "if Joseph removes without paying the legacies he is to have only the lot over the river." Joseph Edwards sold his Northampton lands to his brother Benjamin in 1725, and removed to Coventry, where, as Joseph Edwards of Northampton, he had purchased 72 acres from Ezekiel Herrick of Coventry, Nov. 4, 1724. Joseph Edwards of Coventry, by his will dated Nov. 20, 1749, sworn to by the witnesses Dec. 25, 1750, and proved April 29, 1751, gave all his property to his wife Mary, except twenty shillings to his brother Ebenezer Edwards. The will of Mary Meraw, wife to Mr. Denis Meraw of Coventry, dated July 18, 1767, recites "The estate now in my possession is estate given to me by my former husband Joseph Edwards late of Coventry which I have a lawful right to dispose of."; she therefore bequeaths "unto John Waite, to Ebenezer French, and to the widow Hannah Star relict of Thomas Star, all of Northampton, all my stock and cattle . . . to my Brother Eben^r. French abovesaid my grate Bible; to the children of my Brother Jonathan French late of Windham deceased, and to the female heirs of my sister Elizabeth the wife of Daniel ˙Bascom late of Lebanon, and to Sarah wife of Eleazer Gillet of Lebanon" . . . ; other bequests are made to Mehitabel Colman wife of Eben^r. Colman of Coventry, to Sarah wife of Ebenezer Wintworth Junr. of Coventry, to Joseph Phelps son to Benjamin Phelps deceased and to his sister Eunice the wife of John Robinson, grandchildren to William Phelps of Northampton; Ebenezer Colman of Coventry is appointed executor. Distribution of the estate was made Dec. 11, 1767. Children of Joseph and Mary (French) Edwards (all probably dying early): i. Joseph, b. Northampton, Nov. 23, 1722. ii. Samuel, b. Coventry, July 11, 1732. iii. Eunice, b. Nov. 12, 1734.

Elizabeth French, b. Nov. 15, 1700; d. Lebanon, Conn., Jan. 15, 1749-50; m. Northampton, Feb. 27, 1723, Ensign Daniel Bascom, b. there Feb. 13, 1703, d. Lebanon, March 17 or 18, 1761, son of John and Thankful (Webster) Bascom. Children, born in Lebanon: i. Abigail, b. April 4, 1726; m. April 6, 1749, Ephraim Wilcox, and had six children. ii. Daniel, b. Feb. 13, 1727-8; d. Stafford, Conn., 1790; m. Elizabeth Ward, b. Union, Conn., Oct. 29, 1738, d. Belchertown, Mass., 1810; four children (Bascom Genealogy). iii. Elizabeth, b. Aug. 26, 1729; m. Feb. 18 or 19, 1746, David Bartlett of Northampton, and had three children. iv. Thankful, b. April 20, 1731; m. March 13, 1764 (as his second wife), John Strong, Jr., of Hebron, Conn., b. about 1726, d. Thetford, Vt., about 1796, son of John Strong of Colchester. v. Sarah, b. April 17, 1733; m. Sept. 11, 1766, Elijah Root, b. Hebron, March 1, 1730, son of Jonathan and Sarah (Tarbox) Root; three children (Root Genealogy). vi. Mary, b. Feb. 12, 1734-5; m. Nov. 21, 1754, Samuel Allen. vii. John, b. Dec. 9, 1736; m. Jan. 9, 1763, Sarah Burley, b. March 22, 1740, dau. of John and Miriam (Fuller) Burley of Union; he removed from Union to the western part of Connecticut; six children (Burley Genealogy and History of Union). viii. Elihu, b. Jan. 13, 1738-9; d. in Springfield, Vt.; m. in Northampton, Mass., Sept. 21, 1762, his second cousin, Elizabeth Bascom, b. Deerfield, Mass., Nov. 1 or 7, 1741, d. Greenfield, Mass., March 30, 1783, dau. of Jacob and Hannah (Rider) Bascom; nine children. ix. Jonathan, b. Sept. 14, 1740; d. Orleans, Mass., Nov. 18, 1807; was graduated at Yale in 1764, and was ordained pastor of the Congregational Church at Orleans in 1772; m. (1) Dec. 23, 1766, Temperance Knowles, who died Orleans, April 8, 1782, aged 34, dau.

of Col. Willard Knowles of Eastham; m. (2) Aug. 16, 1782, Phebe (Taylor) Sears, who died Aug. 16, 1784, aged 37, widow of David Sears and dau. of John Taylor of Orleans; m. (3) Feb. 10, 1785, Betty Freeman of Orleans; eight children. x. Bille [William], b. Oct. 3, 1742, died in Lebanon; m. Mary Williams and had eight children. xi. Abiel, b. Oct. 13, 1753; d. Lebanon, Jan. 8, 1834; m. Sybil Roberts, who died Feb. 8, 1847; ten children (Bascom Genealogy). xii. Olive, b. Oct. 1, 1755; m. Thomas Howes. xiii. Rachel, b. Jan. 22, 1758; m. Ebenezer Northam.

Jonathan French, b. 1702; d. Windham, Conn., 1743; m. there Dec. 15, 1725, Sarah Walcut, who survived her husband. Ralph Wheelock of Windham sold a tract of 50 acres to Jonathan French, July 21, 1725. The inventory of the estate of Jonathan French late of Windham was taken by Nathaniel Skiff, Joseph Hebard Jun., and Joseph Warner, Dec. 1, 1743; administration was granted to Capt. Samuel Murdoch, who gave bonds with Mrs. Sarah French, Dec. 14, 1743. Distribution was made March 1, 1744, to the widow Sarah French and the children, Jonathan, Sarah, Rachel, and Miriam French. Children, recorded in Windham: i. Jonathan, b. Jan. 19, 1726-7; shared in the distribution of the estate of his aunt Mary Marough, 1767; probably m. Mary ————, for Amos French, son of Jonathan French and Mary his wife, born Aug. 30, 1748, appears on Windham town records. ii. Sarah, b. June 13, 1729, is perhaps the Sarah Lyman, wife of Benjamin Lyman, mentioned next after Miriam, wife of Recompence Tifuny, in the distribution of Mrs. Mary Marough's estate. iii. Rachel, b. Feb. 19, 1730-1; m. Jan. 9, 1755, Walter Woodworth [Lebanon, Conn., church record]. iv. Miriam, b. March 22, 1735; m. Feb. 5, 1756, Lebanon, Recompence Tiffany, son of Isaiah and Elizabeth (Smith) Tiffany, b. Woodstock, Conn., June 19, 1731, died childless, Lebanon, Dec., 1800.

Ebenezer French, b. Nov., 1705; d. Southampton, Mass., April 29, 1776; m. Northampton, Oct. 25, 1727, Mary Edwards, b. Northampton, Oct. 26, 1707, dau. of Benjamin and Mary (Clark) Edwards. By his will, dated March 7, 1776, proved Aug. 6, 1776, Ebenezer French left his property to his wife Mary and his three sons and eight daughters, the four youngest being then unmarried. Children: i. Ebenezer (1), b. Northampton, Aug. 20, 1728; d. Sept. 8, 1728. ii. Ebenezer (2), b. Feb. 10, 1731; m. Rachel (Carpenter) Boynton, b. Coventry, Conn., March 29, 1729, dau. of Amos and Deborah (Long) Carpenter, widow of Joshua Boynton (who d. Oct. 16, 1752). (Children, born in Southampton: Rachel, b. March 12, 1762; Asenath, b. April 12, 1764; Scrible, b. April 27, 1766; Joshua Boynton, b. Jan. 20, 1768; Widow Anna French was appointed administratrix of the estate of Joshua Boynton French of Westhampton, Nov. 30, 1802; he left minor children; Byanton French of Westhampton and Susanna Bartlett of Southampton published intention of marriage Jan. 11, 1789. Amariah, b. April 17, 1776). iii. Silence, b. 1733; d. Southampton, Oct., 1811, aged 78; m. about 1750, Joseph Torrey, who d. Sept. 23, 1794, in his 71st year. (Children, born in Southampton: Joseph, b. Dec. 17, 1750; Silence, b. Jan. 15, 1754; Deborah, b. Jan. 16, 1757.) iv. Sarah, bapt. May 25, 1735; mentioned in her father's will as Sarah Sprague, she is probably the Sarah French who married at Lebanon, Conn., March 13, 1755, Ephraim Sprague,

Jr., who died Sandisfield, Mass., June, 1764, son of Ephraim and Abigail (Woodward) Sprague; his will mentions wife Sarah and children Oliver, Sarah, and Damaris; the widow Sarah is said to have died in 1775 [Sprague Gen., p. 36]. But a Widow Sarah Sprague d. at Southampton, April 17, 1804, aged 72 [town record]. v. Mary, d. before 1776; m. 1755, Capt. Abner Pomeroy, b. Southampton, Sept. 7, 1734, son of Caleb and Thankful (Phelps) Pomeroy; eleven children (Pomeroy Genealogy, p. 250). vi. Lois, and vii. Eunice, bapt. Dec. 17, 1739. viii. Samuel, m. (pub. int. Oct. 24, 1772, Southampton) Huldah Kingsley, b. Southampton, March 27, 1746, dau. of Ebenezer and Mary Kingsley; had child, Jarrid, b. Oct. 31, 1773. ix. Hannah, b. about 1741; d. July 31, 1819, in her 79th year; m. 1766, Solomon Ferry, b. Feb. 22, 1744, d. Feb., 1810, son of Ebenezer and Mary (Phelps) Ferry. (Children: Hannah, bapt. March 12, 1769, d. Oct. 23, 1771; Mary, bapt. Dec. 2, 1770; Solomon, bapt. April 5, 1772; Ebenezer, bapt. Nov. 17, 1776; Asa, bapt. July 26, 1778, and Hannah, bapt. May 5, 1782.) x. Benjamin, bapt. Nov. 3, 1745; m. (int. Feb. 19, 1769) Hannah Clark, b. 1744, dau. of Selah and Eunice (Wright) Clark of Southampton. (Children, born there: Ephraim Sprague, b. Oct. 28, 1770; Ezra, b. Aug. 8, 1772; Marcy; b. Feb. 4, 1774, and Asenath, b. April 16, 1776.) xi. Kezia, bapt. March 27, 1748; m. (int. May 6, 1781) Timothy Alvord of Southampton.

Samuel French, b. 1708; living Jan. 28, 1724-5; no further record.

John French, b. Aug. 21, 1710; m. Coventry, Conn., May 20, 1736, Mehitable Root, b. Feb. 11, 1713, dau. of Thomas and Thankful Root. March 30, 1733, John ffrench of Coventry conveys for £30 to "my brother Jonathan french of Windham . . . ten acres in Windham, that I bought of s'd Jon^{n}. french, bounded southerly on s'd Jon^{n}. ffrench land where he now lives and northerly on . . . Ebenezer Wright and westerly on . . . Ralph Wheelock and easterly on Ralph Wheelock." Children, born in Coventry: i. Sarah (1), b. May 3, 1737; d. May 24, 1737. ii. Sarah (2), b. April 6, 1739; d. March, 1827, Hinsdale, Mass.; m. Nov. 11, 1762, Ebenezer Wentworth, Jr., b. Norwich, Conn., June 26, 1741, d. Hinsdale, March, 1813, aged 72, son of Ebenezer and Ann (Haskin) Wentworth; he bought a farm in the northwest part of Coventry in 1774; five children (Wentworth Gen., 1:406). iii. Selah, b. Aug. 30, 1741. iv. Stephen, b. July 12, 1743. v. Samuel, b. Nov. 8, 1746. vi. John, b. Sept. 27, 1748. vii. Ichabod, b. Nov. 27, 1750.

(French family records compiled by Dr. Tracy E. Hazen.)

31 ISAAC^3 WARNER, son of Isaac^2 and Sarah (Boltwood) Warner, born in Hadley, Mass., January 13, 1669-70; died in Northfield, Mass., September 8, 1854. He doubtless removed with his father to Northfield about 1686 and when the settlement was deserted on account of the Indian raids, he may have gone back to Hadley for a time. He was a resident of Northfield at the Third Settlement and was selectman there in 1718.

Married in Hadley, January 24, 1693-4, **HOPE NASH,** born in Hadley, November 26, 1670, died in Northfield, daughter of Lieutenant Timothy and Rebeckah (Stone) Nash. Timothy was the youngest child of Thomas Nash, the immigrant, and was born in England or in Leyden, in 1626. Thomas Nash was a gunsmith by trade, became a blacksmith, came to Boston first, then went to New Haven (then Quinnipiac), landing March, 1638. Timothy Nash was a blacksmith, came from Hartford, Conn., to Hadley in 1663, and died in 1699, aged 73. His wife, Rebeckah, was the daughter of Rev. Samuel Stone of Hartford.

Children of Isaac and Hope (Nash) Warner, recorded in Hadley
Isaac Warner, Jr., b. Nov. 12, 1694; d. Feb. 18, 1711-2.
Daniel Warner, b. Oct. 10, 1697; d. Apr. 7, 1698, date as in Hadley
town record.
Sarah Warner, b. Apr. 13, 1699, date as in Hadley town record.
Rebecca Warner, b. Sept. 5, 1701.
Israel Warner, b. Dec. 1, 1703; d. in Northfield, Nov. 12, 1772, aged
68; not married (History of Northfield). He was a soldier in 1758.
Ruth (1) *Warner,* b. Feb. 14, 1705-6.
72 *Ebenezer Warner,* b. Jan. 26, 1709; m. Lydia Brooks.
Ruth (2) *Warner,* b. July 13, 1713.

32 **MARY³ WARNER,** daughter of Isaac² and Sarah (Bolt-wood) Warner, born in Hadley, Mass., January 6, 1671-2; died April 9, 1702.

Married **SAMUEL CROWFOOT,** who died February 10, 1733, aged 71. He was probably the son of Joseph Crowfoot of Springfield, who mentions a son Samuel in his will (S. M. Alvord), although the History of Hadley said he was probably son of Samuel of Hadley.

Children of Samuel and Mary (Warner) Crowfoot
Samuel Crowfoot, b. Jan. 21, 1694.
Stephen Crowfoot, b. Apr. 13, 1695.
Mary Crowfoot, b. Apr. 6, 1697; m. 1719, Peter Domo.
Joseph Crowfoot, b. July 3, 1699.
Daniel Crowfoot, b. June 5, 1700.
Ebenezer Crowfoot, b. Apr. 3, 1702.
Sarah Crowfoot, b. May 26, 1706.

33 **ANDREW³ WARNER,** son of Isaac² and Sarah Bolt-wood) Warner, born February 24, 1672-3, in Hadley, Mass.; died between January 31 and June 9, 1732, in Mansfield, Conn.

Married in 1696-7, **DEBORAH (LEFFINGWELL) CROW,** daughter of Lieut. Thomas Leffingwell of Norwich, Conn., widow of Nathaniel Crow (who died July 30, 1695, East Hartford, Conn. [Mem. Hist. Hartford Co. 1.235]). The widow Deborah Crow was appointed administratrix of the estate of Nathaniel Crow, September, 1695; February 6, 1709-10, Andrew Warner

DEED OF LIEUT. THOMAS LEFFINGWELL OF NORWICH TO ANDREW AND
DEBORAH WARNER.
WINDHAM DEEDS, D:45.

late of Hartford, now of Windham, and Deborah his wife, administrators on the estate of Nathaniel Crow, presented an account; Andrew and Deborah Warner were awarded one third of the real estate. [Manwaring, Early Conn. Prob. Rec., 1:435, 7:121.] That Andrew Warner's wife was an unrecorded daughter of Thomas Leffingwell[1] is proved by his deed recorded in Windham [Book D:45]: "I Thomas Leffingwell of Norwich in consideration of the love good will and fatherly affection that I have and bear to my well beloved daughter Deborah Warner, give . . . unto my son-in-law Andrew Warner of Hartford Conn. all my right in 100 acres of land, mentioned in the within deed given to me from Abimelech; June 21, 1704." Samuel Whiting of Windham conveyed to Andrew Warner of Hartford for £6, 50 acres on the southeast side of Auquebatuck abuting northerly on s'd Andrew Warner's land, March 2, 1708; witnesses, John ffitch, Joshua Lassell. Samuel Whiting also sold to Andrew Warner of Windham for £5, ten acres of meadow on the southwest side of Shautucket River, August 1, 1711. January 15, 1714, Andrew Warner of Windham conveyed to Ens[n]. Thomas Leffingwell of Norwich 58 acres on the southwest side of Shautucket River, which he had purchased of Samuel Whiting. [Windham Deeds D:72, 211, 413.] Andrew Warner of Windham sold to Samuel Hutchinson of Lebanon "one acre on the south part of my farm in Windham and adjoining to s'd Hutchinson's land," March 5, 1711 [D:205]. February 6, 1729-30, Andrew Warner of Mansfield conveyed to his son Joseph Warner of Windham for £50 the "tract I purchased of Whiting on the southwest side of Shautucket River in Windham (ten acres)." [Windham Deeds 8:98.] January 21, 1731-2, Andrew Warner of Mansfield, farmer, for natural affection, love and good will, conveys to "my well beloved son Joseph Warner of Windham" 88 acres on the west side of Windham River. [G (7):424.] January 25, 1731-2, Andrew Warner of Mansfield conveys to his son Thomas Warner of Mansfield land in Windham on the west side of Windham River; witnesses Elisha Warner, Richard Abbe. [9:27.] Andrew Warner and Deborah Warner his wife of Mansfield sold land there to Thomas Fitch of Boston, October 18, 1723; Nathaniel Bassett and wife Joanna of Mansfield sold land to Andrew Warner of Mansfield, November 26, 1723. [Mansfield Deeds 2:295, 290.] No later deeds are found in Mansfield, although Andrew Warner calls himself of that town in his will dated 31 Jan. 1731-2.

The children of Andrew and Deborah Warner were recorded all together in Windham as late as 1726; and a comparison of the records of baptism in the Second Church of Hartford [pages 307, 309] indicates that a mistake of one year was made in the case of the first two children.

The will of Andrew Warner[3] (Isaac[2], Andrew[1]), Windham Probate, I :450:

In the name of God Amen ye 31st Day of January In ye year of our Lord 1731/2 I Andrew Warner of Mansfield In The County of Wendham In ye Coloney of Connectticut In New England yeoman, being weak and sick in body but of perfict mind and memory Thanks be given to God Tharefor Caling to mind ye mortality of my body and knowing that It is appointed for men once to dye doe make and ordain this my last will and Testement

That is to say princeply and first of all I give and Recomend my soul into ye hands of God that gave it hopeing through The merits Death and passion of my Saviour Jesus Christ to have full and free pardon and for Givenes of all my sins and to In herit ever lasting life: and my body I comit to ye Earth to be decently buried at ye discretion of my Executor Hear after named nothing doubting that at ye General Resurrection I shall Receive ye same again by ye mighty power of God: and as touching such worldly estate wherewith it hath pleased God to bless me In this Life I Give demise and dispose of ye same In ye following maner and form That is to say—

First I will that all Those Debt and Deuties as I owe In Right or Conciance to any maner of person or persons whatsoever shall be well and truly contented and paide or ordained to be paide In covenant time after my deceas by my Executor Heareafter named

Item I give and bequeath unto Debaroh my dearly beloved Wife ye use and Improvement of such moveables within doars as she shall stand in need of for her comfort so long as she lives or Continues my widow and also to be maintained and supported Honourably so long as she lives or Continues to be my Widow by my son or sons as may more fuly apear In the following part of my will

Item I give to my well beloved son Joseph Warner a tract and Parsel of land lying in Windham wch land he has a Deed of Gift as may more fuly apear by sd Ded wch I estem to Be his portion ye sd land is part of my farm lying In wendham and Is ye north∙ side or north west side of sd farm and further It is my will that my son Joseph shall Pay or cause to be paid to my well beloved wife ye sume of five pounds yearly If she Removes from my son Elisha's Home. I give to my well beloved son Thomas Warner a tract and parcel of land lying In wendham wch land he has a deed of gift of as may more fuly apear by sd deed which I estem to be his portion ye sd land Is part of my farm lying and being In wendham afore sd and Is ye south or southerly part of sd farm and farther It is my will that my Son Thomas shall pay or cause to be paide to my wellbe loved Wife ye sume of three pounds yearly If she Remains [sic] From my son Elishas—

Item I give to my well beloved son Elisha Warner ye Remainder and Resedeu of my farm lying in wendham It being ye midle part of sd farm and als all my moveabls with doars and with out together with all bonds Bills &c ye sd Elisha for to take care of and Honourable Provide for' his mother Deborah my well beloved wife both in Sickness and In Health during her natural life or so long as she shall continue my widow further it is my will that If my sd wife shall of her own will and Pleasur Goe from my sd son Elishas and live with eithar of my other sons or Daughtars hear-after mentioned Then my sd son Elisha shall yearly and every year pay or cause to be paid to his Hon^r. Mother ye sume of Ten pounds of Good and currant money so long as she lives or continues my widow and also It Is my Will that my son Elisha pay to his two sistars These Particular sums of money that are bequeathed them In this will farther also I Do constitute make and ordain my sd son Elisha my only and solè executor of this my last will and Testement

Item I give to my well beloved daughtar Thankfull Huntington ye sume of Thirty pounds to be paid Hur by my son Elisha within five year after my decease—

Item I give to my well beloved Daughtar Mary Stoars ye som of thirty pounds money to be paide her by my son Elisha within five years after my deceas Furthar It is my will and True Intent That ye sd sixty pounds money wch I Give to my Daughtars so much of It shall be paide that may Remain to make up thirty Pounds money a peace that they may not have Received of me In my life Time Towards ye sixty Pounds that I Give Them In this present will besides what they have already Recieved as part of Their por-tion so that what money I Have paid them since ye makeing of this Will shall be looked upon as part of ye sixty pounds that Is willed them To be paide them by my son Elissha Finaly I do hereby uttarly disalow Revoak and disan Null all and every othar formar Testements will legases bequests executors by me In any way before this time Named willed and bequeathed Ratifieing and confirming this and no othar To be my last will and Teste-ment In witnes whereof I have hearunto set my hand and seall ye day and year above writen

Signed Sealed Published Pronounced and
declared by ye sd Andrew Warner as his   Andrew Warner   [SEAL]
last will and Testement In ye presents
of us ye subscribers (viz)
     Eleazar Williams
     Ebenezer Abbe
     Joshua Abbe

Mansfield June ye 9th 1732— Then ye Reverend Mr Eleazar Williams Ebenezar Abbe and Joshua Abbe all apeared and made Solemn oath that they were present together with Andrew Warnar at his Publishing Ratie-fieing and signing this his last will and Testement and that thay then see him sign and herd him declare this and no othar to be his last will and that thay did Judg him To be composed In mind and of Good understand-ing and memory and sutable Capasaty when he signed and Declared It and that thay ware Caled and did sign thare to as witness.

       Before me Tho^ms Huntonton   Justis of peace

A Court of Probate held In Wendham June ye 30th 1732 Present Temothy Peirce Esqr Judg The last Will and Testement of Mr Andrew Warnar of mansfield Deceased was exhibited Into sd Court by ye executor named in sd will (who excepted of that Trust In sd Court) The witneses to sd Will being sworn In maner accustomed wch will Is by sd Court proved approved alowed of and ordered to be Recorded and kept on File

       Test   John Crery   Clark of probate

A True Inventory of all and singulear ye goods chattles and credits of Mr Andrue Warnar Decd Prised at mansfield Octobar ye 30 1732: by us Thomas Stoars and John Slapp

[amount not added up in record]

Mansfield June 29, 1732

. . . These are to Sertifie to your Hon^r that I am well satisfied with ye last will and Testament of my late Deceased Husband (viz) Andrew Warner and also I do desier that your Honour woold allow and approve of ye sd will wch will bars date Jan. 31, 1731-2

Signed In Presents of
    Ebenezer Abbe
    Joshua Abbe
                                 Deborah Warner

                                 (Windham Probate, 2:88.)

Children of Andrew³ and Deborah (Leffingwell-Crow) Warner

73 *Thankful Warner*, bapt. May 2, 1697; m. John Huntington.
74 *Joseph Warner*, bapt. Apr. 28, 1700; m. Elizabeth Allen.
75 *Mary Warner*, b. Apr., 1703; m. Captain Samuel Storrs, Jr.
76 *Thomas Warner*, b. Apr., 1705; m. (1) Delight Metcalf (2) Mrs. Elizabeth Ladd.
77 *Elisha Warner*, b. Apr., 1707; m. Elizabeth Babcock.

FAMILY RECORD OF ANDREW³ WARNER.

Windham town records

34 EBENEZER[3] WARNER, son of Isaac[2] and Sarah (Boltwood) Warner, born probably in Hadley, Mass., February 25,
1676. He was a resident of Deerfield, Mass., at the time of
the memorable attack upon the settlement by a band of some
three hundred French and Indians during Queen Anne's War.
In the dead of night on February 29, 1704, the stealthy invaders
attacked the little town, overpowered the faithless guard, and
assisted by the crust on the snow that had carelessly been
allowed to drift against the palisades, they effected an easy and
noiseless entrance just before daybreak. The inhabitants roused
from sleep were practically all either killed in the fighting there
or were taken prisoners, and their dwellings set on fire. The
captives were almost immediately started under guard for Canada. The story of this terrible journey in the middle of winter
with the snow up to the knees is vividly described by the Reverend John Williams, the aged pastor of Deerfield, in "The
Redeemed Captive," first published in Boston, 1707, but in many
subsequent editions. An appendix by his son Samuel Williams
gives the names of the captives and their fate, in cases where
that was known. The minister with his family was captured
and started on the march. His wife was unable to keep up with
the rest and he was compelled by his savage captors to leave
her behind. Her death at the hands of one of the enemy was
soon reported to him. He was later redeemed and returned to
the settlements. In a few cases children were carried by the
Indians, but most of them were killed when they could no longer
keep up the pace set by the band, and their elders were sub-
jected to all kinds of tortures.

Among the captives was Ebenezer Warner with his wife and
two little ones. His wife was killed on the march to Canada
but Ebenezer and his daughter Sarah were redeemed by the
party from the nearby settlement of Hadley which rushed to
their relief. The daughter Waitstill was among those who
never returned and whose fate was unknown. The relief party
from Hadley contained several of their relatives. See under
number 7.

The desolated town of Deerfield was at once made a military
post and strongly garrisoned. The men were pressed into service and those not able to fight were sent to the towns below.
Persistent efforts were made to recover the captives. Ensign
Sheldon was sent to Canada three times on this errand. One
by one, and against great odds, the most of the men and women
were recovered, but a large proportion of the children remained
in Canada. Many of their descendants have been traced and

among them are some of the most distinguished men and women of Canadian history. Miss C. Alice Baker has published an interesting account of these in "True Stories of New England Captives."

A petition to the General Court, under date of May, 1743, regarding John Smead, contains the following deposition by Ebenezer Warner:

"I was in Dearfield Meadow fight . . . and I see the said Smead kill an indian, & some of the souldiers tock off this Indians scalp & secured it, & I see the said John Smead shoot at another Indian, which he gave a mortal wound & yᵉ Indian died in a short time at the place where he received yᵉ wound or very near the place.

    (Signed)   Ebenezer Warner"   (Mass. Archives.)

Ebenezer Warner also did service with the Thomas Baker Scout, in April, 1712.

Married January 5, 1689-9, **WAITSTILL SMEAD**, daughter of William Smead. She was captured by the Indians at the Deerfield massacre and was killed on the subsequent march into Canada.

Children

Sarah Warner, b. Nov. 29, 1699; was captured by the Indians, Feb. 29, 1704, but was redeemed.

Waitstill Warner, b. Nov. 6, 1701; was captured by the Indians, Feb. 29, 1704, and was never returned.

35 **DANIEL³ WARNER**, son of Isaac² and Sarah (Boltwood) Warner, born probably in Hadley, Mass., February 25, 1677; died December 21, 1711 (Hadley town record). He was of Deerfield in 1702. The inventory of his estate gave a valuation of two hundred pounds.

Married April 13, 1704, **SARAH GOLDEN** or **GOULDING**, daughter of Peter Golden or Goulding of Hadley. She married (2) July 6, 1714, Thomas Horton.

Children, recorded in Hadley

78 Martha Warner, b. Oct. 25, 1706; m. William White.

79 Daniel Warner, Jr., b. Mar. 22, 1709. Through some oversight the name of this son has not appeared in previous printed records of the Warner family, but the entry is on the Hadley records. It is most probable that he is the Daniel Warner who married Jerusha Hitchcock and resided in Wilbraham. See further.

Comfort Warner, b. Dec. 1, 1711; d. Jan. 28, 1728.

36 **SAMUEL³ WARNER**, son of Isaac² and Sarah (Boltwood) Warner, born March 14, 1681, probably in Hadley, Mass ;

he was a joiner and lived in Springfield, Mass. There is'·
recorded in Springfield (Land records, T:348) a transfer of
property from Samuel Warner of Springfield, yeoman, to Jabez
Hendricks of Union, Windham County, husbandman and joyner,
land in the lower division of the outward common on the east
side of the river, September 6, 1751, to which Zechariah Warner
was a witness. He also sold land to Ebenezer Warner in 1754.
His will was dated May 14, 1756, probated August 31, 1758
(Northampton probate records, 9:25). The heirs were his wife
Sarah, children Zechariah, Sarah Morgan, Mary Mirick, Desire
Ely, and Catherine Morgan, and grandchild Abigail Chapin,
daughter of his deceased son Samuel.

Married November 18, 1702, **SARAH FIELD**, born June 30,
1683, probably in Northfield, Mass., daughter of Samuel and
Sarah (Gilbert) Field. Samuel Field settled in Hatfield, was
sergeant under Captain Turner in the Falls Fight and was killed
by the Indians, June 24, 1697. The Springfield records contain
the record of the intention of marriage: "October 10th 1702
Samuel Warner of Springfeild doth enter his intention of
mariage with Sarah Feild of Hatfeild & were published the
same day."

Children, births recorded in Springfield

Samuel Warner, b. Mar. 18, 1703-4; d. 1726. Administration on his
estate was granted Nov. 3, 1726, to his widow Abigail and Ebenezer
Warriner of Springfield. Married May 7, 1723 (Hadley town records), Abigail Church, b. Oct. 12, 1705, d. Dec. 9, 1763, daughter of
Ensign Ebenezer Church. She m. (2) Aug. 28, 1733, Abraham Pease
of Enfield, by whom she had ten children. Child of Samuel and
Abigail (Church) Warner: Abigail, m. ——— Chapin, and received
a share of her grandfather's estate in 1758.

Zechariah (1) *Warner*, b. July 23, 1707; d. July 12, 1712.

Sarah Warner, record of birth not found on Springfield records; was
mentioned among her father's heirs, 1756 and 1758; m. in Springfield, June 20, 1737, Ebenezer Morgan, son of Nathaniel and Hannah
(Bird) Morgan, and grandson of Miles and Elizabeth (Bliss) Morgan. He married (1) in 1719, Mary Horton; no record of children
by this marriage. Children of Ebenezer and Sarah (Warner) Morgan, recorded in Springfield: i. Ebenezer, b. June 12, 1738; m. Feb.,
1766, Miriam Kilbourn, and had Lucius, Philip, Lucretia, Ebenezer,
Zelotes, Abiram, Jonathan and Miriam (Morgan Genealogy). ii.
Samuel, b. Feb. 2, 1739-40; m. Nov., 1766, Abigail Cooley, had Amos,
Phyllis, Prudence, Ruth, Elizabeth, Phoebe, Abigail, Eunice and
Maria. iii. Sarah, b. Nov. 7, 1742; m. Titus Morgan, 2d. iv. Katherine, b. Dec. 31, 1744; m. (1) Moses Cooley, (2) James Melvin.
v. Chloe, b. Oct. 14, 1747; m. May 10, 1782, John Burt. vi. Mary,
b. Feb. 10, 1749.

Mary Warner, b. Jan. 31, 1713-4; d. June, 1813, in her one hundredth
year; m. May 15, 1738, as his second wife, Thomas Merrick, b. in

6

Springfield, Jan. 13, 1703-4, d. Feb., 1785, son of John and Mary (Day) Merrick. He m. (1) Eunice Stebbins by whom he had one child. They resided in Wilbraham. Children of Thomas and Mary (Warner) Merrick, recorded in Springfield: i. Timothy, b. May 24, 1739; was bitten by a rattlesnake and d. Aug. 7, 1761. ii. Eunice, b. May 8, 1742; d. Dec., 1808; m. Jan., 1771, Deacon Gideon Burt. iii. Lucy, b. Nov. 11, 1746; d. Oct. 15, 1752. iv. Mary, b. Sept. 9, 1751; m. Lieut. Jonathan Merrick, a wealthy farmer and officer in the Revolution, b. in Wilbraham, Mar. 21, 1747, d. Mar., 1812, had children, Mary, m. ——— Lyman; David, d. young; John; Thomas; Laura (1), d. young; Laura (2), m. L. Brewer (Merrick Genealogy).

Desire Warner, b. Sept. 8, 1716; m. (intentions published in Springfield, June 4, 1744) Abner Ely. Children: Desiah and Thankfull.

80 *Zechariah* (2) *Warner*, b. Apr. 11, 1719; m. Mary Cooley.

Ebenezer Warner, b. July 13, 1723, twin with Catherine.

Catherine Warner, b. July 13, 1723; m. Apr. 27, 1741, Jonathan Morgan of Springfield. Children, recorded in Springfield: i. Jonathan, b. July 5, 1750; d. Aug. 2, 1756. ii. Gideon, b. Aug. 8, 1754. iii. Delight, b. Mar. 28, 1756.

37 ICHABOD³ WARNER, son of Isaac² and Sarah (Boltwood) Warner, born about 1684, probably in Northfield, Mass., as his father was an engager in that settlement in 1685, and his birth is not recorded with those of his older brothers and sisters in Hadley, Mass.; died in Windham, Conn., January 18, 1767, in his 83d year.

Ichabod Warner probably went to Lebanon, Conn., with his mother and her second husband, Deacon John Loomis. Deacon John Loomis received a grant from the proprietors of Lebanon in 1700 and settled there as early as 1703-4.

"I, John Mason of Lebanon   .   for & in consideration of three years & eight months service allready served by Ichabod Warner of Lebanon . . . have granted   unto him ye s'd Ichabod Warner . . . one hundred acres of Land . . . in Lebanon in yt tract of land commonly called & knowne by ye name Mr. ffitches Mile & also to alow the s'd Warner two suits of appariell & the breaking up of two acres of land the land above mentioned . . . Lying on the southwestwardly side of peases Brook . . . ," dated Oct. 26, 1705. (Lebanon Deeds, 2:4.)

In 1714 Samuel Hutchinson deeded to Andrew Warner, land adjacent to that of Ichabod Warner, lying south from Aquebatuck, part in Lebanon and part in Windham. November 2, 1714, Ichabod conveyed to his brother Ebenezer of Lebanon, 20 acres of the farm he bought of John Mason. January 10, 1714-15, Andrew Warner conveyed to his "brother Ichabod Warner of Lebanon", eight acres of the land he had bought of Samuel Hutchinson, and adjacent to Ichabod's holdings. (Lebanon Deeds, 1:116.)

Ichabod Warner of Lebanon bought land in Windham of James Babcock, June 29, 1721. James Babcock of Coventry sold to Ichabod Warner land partly in Lebanon and partly in Windham, November 25, 1728. Ichabod Warner exchanged land with William Allen of Windham, January 26, 1729. Ichabod Warner of Lebanon bought from Joseph and Caleb Downer of Norwich, the mill and property which said Downers bought of Ephraim Sawyer, July 7, 1734. Ichabod sold part of this mill to his son Ichabod, August 6, 1735. Ichabod of Windham and Ichabod of Lebanon sold their farm to Nathan Bushnell of Norwich, January 6, 1735-6, land partly in Windham and Lebanon. (Weaver's MSS. in Conn. Hist. Soc. Library.)

An early mention of Ichabod Warner in the public records of Connecticut is February 21, 1711-2, £9-4-7, wages due, probably for his services on the expedition to Canada the preceding summer. In May, 1725, he was appointed ensign of a trainband in the town of Lebanon. The records of Windham show that permission was given to Ichabod Warner to build a dam across Pigeon Swamp Brook in 1727. A meeting at Lebanon, October 18, 1731, considered "the great difficulty the east farmers some of them are under, namely Benjamin Seabury John Johnson Thomas Bishop and Ichabod Warner to come to the sd Town street of Lebanon, Having no Highway thither." Perhaps the condition of the highways may have been the reason for Ichabod and his wife Mary belonging to the church in Windham in 1726. In May, 1732, a memorial was issued by Thomas Badcock, Ichabod Warner, John Johnson, Benj. Seabery and Stephen Bingham, all of Lebanon, regarding "Needful Highwais yn Lebanon for them to travill yn to ye Publick Worshyp of god in ye sd Lebanon." On May 8th Ichabod Warner was one of those residing in the township of Lebanon, adjoining Windham, who asked to be relieved of their rates in Lebanon and worship in Windham, or given a road. (Conn. State Library, Travel, I :36, 38a, 39, 44b.)

The following records from Windham Probate Records 7 :232, 234, 344, 508, give valuable information about him and his family·

The Inventory of the Estate of Ichabod Warner Late of Windham Deceased Taken by us the Subscribers under oath is as Followeth viz. March 23d 1767   (List of personal property) . . .

The above moveables to the amount of 33 :4 :3 are delivered to Sarah Warner ye widow which is the full of what was due to her out of the estate.

About 90 acres of land with half the house with the mill malt house and barn and the utensills belonging to the mill and malt house £ 370 :00 :00

One half of an 8 acre Lott in Mansfield Plain	I :00 :00
One half of an 11 acre Lott	4 :00 :00
One half of a Lott near 6 acres at the Cedar Swamp	0 :15 :00
Lands	375 :15
Moveables	38 :11 :11
	414: 6 :11

20 acres of Land Lying in Lebanon which was given by Ichabod Warner
Deceased to his son Ichabod   80:
59 acres of Land Lying in Canterbury which sd Ichabod Warner gave to
his son Dan¹.   73:
Windham March 23, 1767   Samuel Murdock ⎰
Additional inventory 3 Nov. 1767   Nath¹ Holbrook ⎱ apprizers
          £252 :5 :8

Feb. 4, 1767 Rec'd of Nathl. Warner of Windham adm. to the est. of the
within mentioned Ichabod Warner . . . the full . . .

her
Sarah 6 Warner
mark

Distribution of the estate of Ichabod Warner was made to Ichabod War-
ner eldest son . . . ; Isaac Warner; Daniel Warner; Ebenezer War-
ner; Nathaniel Warner; heirs of Dr. Timothy Warner, and grandchildren
of Ichabod, Jared, Hannah and Irene Warner; Ruth Bingham, daughter
of sd. deceased. Feb. 16, 1768, Nathl. Holbrook, Isaac Robinson and Silas
Phelps, distributors.

The original receipts of the heirs are on file, with their auto-
graphs. These were signed by Isaac Warner, dated "Liver-
pool, Nov. 17, 1768" (copied Windham); John Warner of
Windham; Gideon Bingham and Ruth Bingham of Windham;
Nathan Hebberd of Windham, guardian to Hannah Warner;
William Ripley of Windham, guardian to Irene Warner; David
Ripley of Pomfret, guardian to Jared Warner; Daniel Warner
of Dutchess County, New York; Ebenezer Warner of South
Hamton, Province of New York.

The family of Ichabod's son Daniel have within recent years,
as least, been the possessors of his family Bible and an old coat
which he is said to have worn. One of his descendants wrote
a description of the coat about 1890.

"About fifteen years ago the coat was in the posession of Joshua Warner,
the great, great, great, grandson of Ichabod. Jonas Warner and his wife
saw this coat and handled it, the former put on the coat and he says it
hung to the floor. It was the longest coat he ever saw and must have
belonged to an exceedingly tall and slender man. It was made of some
kind of thin cloth of a grayish blue color, was a sort of sack coat without
many seams and had nine silver-colored buttons."

Ichabod Warner married (1) in Lebanon, March 5, 1711-2, **MARY METCALF**, who died April 26, 1747 (recorded in Windham). She was the daughter of Jonathan and Hannah (Kenric) Metcalf and was first married to John Pratt (**N. E.** Register, 6:175). She was a member of the church in Windham.

Ichabod Warner married (2) February 4, 1748, **SARAH PHELPS** of Lebanon (Connecticut marriages, 2:44), who survived him and is probably the widow Sarah Warner who died June 2, 1783, aged 78 (Abington Congregational Church records). She joined the church in Windham in 1748. There were probably no children by this marriage.

The cemetery in Windham contains the gravestones of Ensign Ichabod and his wife Mary, inscribed as follows:

Here lies yᵉ body — of Ens. Ichabod — Warner who
died Jan yᵉ 18th— 1767 in yᵉ 83rd— year of his age
Mrs. Mary wife of Ens. Ichabod — Warner died April yᵉ 20th 1747
in yᵉ 57th year — of her age.

Children of Ichabod and Mary (Metcalf) Warner, dates of birth recorded in Lebanon and also in family record, which varies from the town record slightly, as noted

81 *Ichabod Warner, Jr.,* b. Dec. 10, 1712 (family record); bapt. July 16, 1712 (Lebanon, 1st Church record); m. Mrs. Mary Mapes Goldsmith.

82 *Daniel Warner,* b. July 10 (or 11), 1714, bapt. Aug. 8, 1713-4 (Lebanon 1st Church record); m. Bethiah Gining.

83 *Isaac Warner,* b. Jan. 4, 1716-17 (or Jan. 11, 1716); m. Ann Davison.

Ebenezer Warner, b. Mar. 20, 1719; owned the covenant in the Windham Church in 1741; signed receipt for property from his father's estate in 1769 as of "South Hamton, province of New York."

84 *Nathaniel Warner,* b. Feb. 18, 1721-2; m. Elizabeth Webb.

85 *Timothy Warner,* b. Dec. 1, 1724; m. Irena Ripley.

Samuel Warner, b. Aug. 21, 1726 (or Aug. 12); d. June 21, 1747, recorded in Windham.

Mary (1) Warner, baptized 1729; probably died young.

Mary (2) Warner (twin), b. Sept. 13, 1730; bapt. 1732; d. Jan. 29, 1747, recorded in Windham.

Hannah Warner (twin), b. Sept. 13, 1730; d. Sept. 28, 1750, recorded in Windham.

86 *Ruth Warner,* b. Oct. 17, 1732; m. Gideon Bingham.

87 *John Warner,* b. May 22, 1734; m. Priscilla Wood.

38 MERCY³ WARNER, daughter of Isaac² and Sarah (Boltwood) Warner, born September 25, 1685, at Deerfield, Mass.; died October 31 or 13, 1759, in Hebron, Conn., buried in ~~Gilead~~ Cemetery.

Some of the published records have given her marriage to Samuel Gillette but an original deed and records of Hadley prove conclusively that she married **SAMUEL GILBERT**, born

Salem

in Hartford, Conn., February 5, 1687-8; died May 1, 1760, in
Hebron, buried in ~~Gilead~~. He was the son of Captain Samuel
and Mary (Rogers) Gilbert. He probably resided early at Colchester; December 11, 1718, he made his first purchase of land
in Hebron. His will, made September 20, 1754, probated June
16, 1760, mentions 5 sons and 5 daughters. The first children
were probably born at Colchester, others were recorded at Lebanon, and the last five in Hebron. Records of this family are
found in "One of the Gilberts in New England," and the Carter
Genealogy.

Children of Samuel and Mercy (Warner) Gilbert, 1-3 recorded in
Lebanon, Conn., 5-10 in Hebron

Abilena Gilbert, b. Mar. 10, 1710; d. before 1793; m. ——— Saxton
(perhaps James Saxton of Westfield and Sheffield, Mass., b. Nov. 9,
1702, d. Sheffield, Oct. 31, 1756; settled in Sheffield about 1743).
[See C. E. Booth, One Branch of the Booth Family, p. 40.]

Sarah Gilbert, b. Mar. 10, 1710; d. Warren, Conn., July 12, 1796; m.
Dec. 9, 1730 (as his second wife), Thomas Carter, b. Woburn, Mass.,
June 13, 1686, d. Warren, Nov. 18, 1772, son of Thomas and Margaret (Whittemore) Carter. Eight children in the Carter Genealogy, p. 27.

Samuel Gilbert, b. May 1, 1712; d. Lyme, N. H., Oct. 16, 1774. He
removed to Lyme about 1771, and was buried on his farm on the
bank of the Connecticut River; the inscription on the headstone is
gone, but the footstone still shows "Honorable Colonel Samuel Gilbert Esquire." During the French and Indian War he was captain
of the 7th Company in the 3d Regiment, raised for the expedition
against Crown Point. In his will, dated at Hebron May 1, 1773, and
a codicil, dated at "Lime," N. H., Sept. 28, 1774, he mentions his wife
Susannah and her brother Lawrence Grosse, his sons Samuel, John,
Silvester, Gardner, and Thomas, his daughter Elizabeth Sumner,
and son-in-law Rev. Samuel Peters; to John Gilbert he gives the
"Tillotson farm" (now owned by F. P. Bissell); to his son Silvester Gilbert "my house and barn and the lott of land lying in
the first society in Hebron near the Meeting House"; to his son
Samuel Gilbert the "Polly house so-called and the Warner lott";
to his son Thomas Gilbert "all my lands lying in the Township of
Lyme in the Province of New Hampshire, being about 1500 acres,
also one wright of land in the Township of Thetford in the Province
of New York" [Thetford, Vt.]; "my wife Susannah, Lydia Morrison and her daughter Susannah Morrison also their household goods
shall be transported to Hebron." The original will, proved Dec. 6,
1774, is on file with the East Haddam probate records in the Connecticut State Library, Hartford. He m. (1) Hebron, Feb. 7, 1732,
Elizabeth Curtice, b. there Jan. 31, 1707-8, d. June 25, 1739, dau. of
Samuel and Mary Curtice of Southold, L. I., and Hebron; m. (2)
May 22, 1740, Abigail Rowley, b. Hebron, Feb. 13, 1716, d. Oct., 1764,
dau. of Samuel and Elizabeth (Fuller) Rowley; m. (3) Jan. 27,
1765, Susannah (Gross) (Morris) Phelps, widow of Lieut. Joseph

Phelps of Hebron and formerly of Dr. Roderick Morris of Hartᵣ
ford. Children, born in Hebron, by the first wife: i. Samuel, b.
June 3, 1734; d. Apr. 24, 1818, Gilead, Hebron; m. (1) May 29,
1760, Lydia Post, b. May 12, 1734, d. Feb. 8, 1775, dau. of Gideon
and Mary (Chase) Post; m. (2) Gilead, Sept. 3, 1775, Deborah
Champion, b. Westchester, Conn., May 3, 1753, d. Gilead, Nov.
20, 1845, dau. of Col. Henry and Deborah (Brainard) Champion.
He was a member of the 15th Company, 12th Regiment, Conn.
Militia, May, 1773, and a lieutenant in 1775; he was deputy from
Hebron to the General Assembly 1775-79, 1790, 1792, 1793, 1799;
presiding judge of the Court of Common Pleas of Tolland County
for twenty-one years. Several descendants are members of the
D. A. R., citing the service of Col. Henry Champion, and of his
daughter Deborah, who carried despatches from New London to
headquarters at Cambridge [see Champion Genealogy]. ii. Elizabeth, b. Aug. 19, 1736-7; d. Swanzey, N. H., May 19, 1818; m.
Hebron, Apr. 15, 1759, Rev. Clement Sumner, b. Hebron, July 15,
1731, d. Keene, N. H., Mar. 29, 1795, son of Dr. William and Hannah
(Hunt) Sumner, was pastor at Keene, 1761-72, at Thetford, Vt.,
1773-77, and afterwards lived at Swanzey; eleven children (Sumner
Genealogy). iii. Anne (1), b. May 24, 1739; d. Sept. 30, 1743. Chil-
dren by the second wife: i. Thomas, b. Sept. 15, 1743; m. Jan. 19,
1763, Lydia Lathrop, b. Aug. 15, 1742, dau. of Benjamin and Mercy ·
(Baker) Lathrop of Windham. ii. Anne (2), b. Sept. 19, 1745; d.
Apr. 10, 1748. iii. John, b. Feb. 12, 1749; m. Mar. 18, 1769, Millicent
Goodrich (probably dau. of Samuel and Elizabeth (Whiting) Good-
rich, b. Nov. 29, 1752). iv. Abigail, b. Jan. 31, 1752; d. Hebron,
July 14, 1769; m. June 25, 1769 (as his second wife), Rev. Samuel
Peters, b. Hebron, Dec. 1, 1735, d. New York, Apr. 19, 1826, son of
John and Mary (Marks) Peters; he was buried at St. Peter's
Church, Hebron, where he was for several years rector. v. Syl-
vester, b. Oct. 20, 1755; d. Hebron, Jan. 2, 1846; m. Hebron, Oct.
25, 1774, Patience Barber, b. Hebron, Apr. 27, 1757, d. May 14, 1838,
dau. of Capt. David and Abigail (Newcomb) Barber; was a lawyer,
chief judge of the county court, judge of probate, member of the 15th
Congress, deacon; had fifteen children. vi. Gardiner, b. Apr. 15,
1758; living in 1774.

John Gilbert, bapt. Lebanon, Nov. 21, 1713-14; d. Hebron, Jan. 19, 1794,
aged 80; m. Hebron, Nov. 11, 1736, Abigail Carter, b. Reading, Mass.,
1717, d. Hebron, Aug. 15, 1796, dau. of Thomas and Abigail (Locke)
Carter. The will of Lieut. John Gilbert, dated Jan. 17, 1793, probated Feb. 6, 1794, recorded at Andover, supplied the names of his
five sisters, who had been mentioned in his father's will as his five
daughters: Sarah Carter, Mercy Dart, Abilena Saxton deceased,
Mary Curtis deceased, Hannah Mann deceased; he bequeathed to
the Gilead Society in Hebron, where he lived, £200 toward the support of a regular gospel minister for the parish.

Elisha Gilbert, b. Dec. 10, 1717; bapt. Feb. 16, 1716-17 (Lebanon record) ;
d. New Lebanon, N. Y., July 23, 1796; m. (1) Hebron, Feb. 7, 1732-3,
Abigail Curtice (probably b. Hebron, Apr. 1, 1714, dau. of Richard
Curtice); m. (2) after 1739, Hannah Adams, b. Colchester, Conn.,
July 4, 1722, d. New Lebanon, July 31, 1806, dau. of Thomas and
Sarah (Collins) Adams. He settled in Bolton, Conn., about 1742,

and in 1749-50 removed to New York. Children: i. Joseph, b. Hebron, Dec. 30, 1739. ii. John, b. Bolton, May 14, 1743; d. young. iii. Abigail, b. Bolton, Sept. 14, 1744; d. Jan. 25, 1748-9. iv. Elisha, b. Feb. 20, 1745-6; d. New Lebanon, Jan. 12, 1823; m. Oct. 24, 1749, Sarah Wheeler, who died at New Lebanon, Mar. 8, 1825; was a captain in New York troops in the Revolution. v. Hannah, b. Aug. 14, 1748. vi. Abigail, b. Mar. 19, 1749. vii. Samuel, b. New Lebanon about 1750; d. Jan. 1, 1816. viii. John, b. Oblong, N. Y., Dec., 1759; d. in Upper Canada. ix. Benjamin, b. in New Canaan, N. Y. ix. Lydia. xi. Polly.

Mary Gilbert, b. Aug. 24, 1719; d. before 1793; m. Hebron, Aug. 31, 1737, Hosea Curtice, b. Hebron, Jan. 25, 1716-17, son of Samuel Curtice, who came from Southold, L. I., about 1702, and died in Hebron, Mar. 24, 1740, and his wife Mary, who died Dec. 14, 1724. Children, born in Hebron: i. Mary, b. Mar. 14, 1738. ii. Hosea, b. July 24, 1739. iii. Samuel, b. Apr. 28, 1741. iv. Joel, b. May 16, 1743. v. Abigail, b. Feb. 13, 1745-6. vi. Rachel, b. May 17, 1748. vii. Reuben, b. Apr. 10, 1750; d. July 21, 1752.

Hannah Gilbert, b. Apr. 8, 1722; d. Hebron, Aug. 15, 1777; m. Hebron, Nov. 27, 1740 (as his second wife), Joseph Mann, b. Lebanon or Hebron, Apr. 5, 1713, d. probably in Hebron, son of Nathaniel and Mary (Root) Man. Children, born in Hebron: i. Joel (1), b. Sept. 4, 1741; d. young. ii. Joel (2), b. Oct. 1, 1743; d. Milton, Saratoga Co., N. Y., Nov. 24, 1824; m. Oct. 16, 1768, his cousin, Mercy Mann, b. Hebron, Mar. 5 or 16, 1749, d. May 17, 1820, dau. of John and Margaret (Peters) Mann; seven children (Mann Genealogy). iii. Hannah (1), b. Nov. 17, 1745; d. young. iv. Hannah (2), b. July 4, 1747; m. John Weed of Malta, N. Y. v. Frances, b. Aug. 21, 1749; m. Solomon Bailey. vi. Joseph, b. Nov. 12, 1751; d. Oct. 21, 1758. vii. Abilena, b. May 31, 1754; d. Hebron, Dec. 27, 1823; m. Hebron, Nov. 29, 1774, Levi Bissell, b. Hebron, Mar. 22, 1747, d. there, Dec. 10, 1828, son of James and Elizabeth (Sawyer) Bissell; ten children. viii. Deborah, b. Sept. 30, 1756; d. Lenox, Mass., July 6, 1810; m. (as his second wife) Eleazer Phelps, b. Hebron, May 13 or 18, 1756, d. Lenox, July 12, 1823, son of Lieut. Nathaniel and Rachel (Sawyer) Phelps; ten children (Phelps Genealogy). ix. Zadock, b. Feb. 7, 1759; d. East Plymouth, Ohio, Sept. 29, 1846; m. (1) at Ashtabula, Ohio, Sept. 18, 1780, Esther Warner of Waterbury, Conn., who died July 9, 1825, aged 66; m. (2) Hannah Williams, who died Jan. 24, 1846, aged 76; six children (Mann Genealogy). x. Joseph, b. Oct. 25, 1761; d. July 29, 1843; m. Patience Barber, b. Jan. 12, 1767, d. Hebron, Aug. 5, 1837, aged 70, dau. of Oliver and Mary Barber. (In his will he left his real estate to two of his wife's nieces, and a yearly stipend to St. Peter's Church.) xi. Candis, b. Jan. 4, 1764; m. Ezekiel Brown of Hebron, who died in 1843. xii. James, b. Feb. 24, 1768; d. Ballston, N. Y., Mar. 21, 1856; m. in Hebron, about 1790, Tryphena Tarbox, b. Hebron, Dec. 27, 1765, d. Nov. 1, 1850, dau. of Solomon and Asenath (Phelps) Tarbox; removed to Ballston about 1791; seven children. xiii. John, d. young [Mann Genealogy].

Ezra Gilbert, b. May 23, 1726; m. Hebron, Mar. 28, 1750, Hannah Rust (perhaps the daughter of Nathaniel and Hannah (Hatch) Rust, b. Coventry, Conn., Mar. 25, 1732).

Mercy Gilbert, b. Nov. 17, 1728; m. June 7, 1752 (Bolton, Conn., record), Daniel Dart, Jr., b. Bolton, Jan. 26, 1725-6, son of Daniel and Jemima (Shayler) Dart. Children, born in Bolton: i. Daniel Gilbert, b. Mar. 16, 1753; d. April 21, 1753. ii. Anna, b. Aug. 23, 1754; d. Nov. 1, 1763. iii. Marcy, b. Apr. 24, 1756. iv. Abigail, b. Dec. 6, 1757. v. Rockeylaney, b. Sept. 8, 1760. vi. Daniel Gilbert, b. Dec. 10, 1762; d. Aug. 24, 1765. vii. Daniel, b. Dec. 20, 1767; d. Dec. 29, 1767.

Ebenezer Gilbert, b. Apr. 9, 1732; m. Hebron, Aug. 6, 1753, Anne Phelps, b. Hebron, Feb. 1, 1730, dau. of Noah and Anna (Dyer) Phelps. Children, born in Hebron: i. Rosannah, b. June 10, 1754. ii. Ebenezer, b. Aug. 23, 1756. iii. Keziah, b. Dec. 5, 1757. iv. Asahel, b. Dec. 15, 1760. v. Anna, b. July 9, 1762. vi. Mercy, b. Mar. 8, 1764. vii. Lucy, b. Oct. 30, 1767. viii. Abigail, b. Jan. 9, 1769. ix. Mary, b. July 14, 1771. x. Hannah, b. Jan. 10, 1774.

39 LYDIA[3] WARNER, daughter of Isaac[2] and Sarah (Boltwood) Warner, born probably in Northfield or Deerfield, Mass.; resided later in Northfield.

Married December 8 (or 29), 1698, **JOSEPH[2] BROOKS,** born in Springfield, Mass., October 17, 1667; died in Northfield, 1743. He was the son of William[1] and Mary (Burt) Brooks of London, Springfield and Deerfield. He was at Deerfield in 1692; was a participant in the Meadow Fight in 1704, and was recorded as a resident of Northfield in 1737. The N. E. Hist. and Gen. Reg. for April, 1918, has an article on the Brooks family.

Children of Joseph and Lydia (Warner) Brooks, born probably in Deerfield

Silence Brooks, b. Sept. 7, 1701; m. June 7, 1720, Edmund Grandy.

Mary Brooks, b. Feb. 14, 1704; d. in Northfield, June 10, 1775; not married.

Lydia Brooks, b. Nov. 25, 1706; d. Sept. 25, 1793; m. Ebenezer[4] Warner, son of Isaac[3], Jr., and Hope (Nash) Warner. See number 72.

Abigail Brooks, b. Oct. 15, 1708.

Hannah Brooks, b. July 15, 1710.

Joseph Brooks, b. Feb. 3, 1713-4; m. Dec. 22, 1748, Miriam Wright. Children: i. Tirza, b. Feb. 10, 1754. ii. David, b. Feb. 10, 1758; d. Mar. 2, 1758. iii. Uri, b. July 8, 1759. iv. Miriam, b. Feb. 9, 1761; m. Apr. 2, 1779, John Moseley.

Sarah Brooks, b. Mar. 4, 1715-6; m. Mar. 27, 1754, John Beaman.

Benjamin Brooks, b. Feb. 26, 1717-8; d. at Northfield, June 15, 1786; was a soldier in the French and Indian War; m. Mary Miller, dau. of Benjamin Miller of Northfield. Children, b. probably at Northfield: i. Lydia, b. Nov. 11, 1750. ii. Benjamin, b. July 12, 1752. iii. Mary, b. Mar. 2, 1754; m. June 1, 1775, Joseph Fuller. iv. Cephas, b. Jan. 10, 1755; a Revolutionary soldier. v. Thaddeus, b. Sept. 16, 1756; a Revolutionary soldier, was at Burgoyne's surrender in 1777 and at West Point in 1780. vi. Alpheus, b. May 18, 1758; was a

Revolutionary soldier with his brother Thaddeus. vii. Ruth, b. Jan. 6, 1760; m. Oct. 30, 1774, Enos Denio. viii. Annis, b. Nov. 28, 1760. ix. Lebbeus, b. May 2, 1762. x. Jerusha, b. Feb. 16, 1765. xi. Persis, b. Oct. 22, 1766. xii. Joseph, b. July 13, 1769. xiii. Elnathan, bapt. July 19, 1774; d. Aug., 1774.

Ruth Brooks, b. June 20, 1720-1; d. Apr. 10, 1721.

Daniel Brooks, b. Mar. 25, 1722; m. Sept. 19, 1754, Mary Wright. Children: i. Euselia, b. 1755; d. 1756. ii. Submit, m. Ebenezer Roberts. iii. Daniel, b. 1759; m. at Northfield, Aug. 27, 1789, Lavina Morgan of Northfield.

40 **THANKFUL³ WARNER,** daughter of Isaac² and Sarah (Boltwood) Warner, born probably at Northfield or Deerfield, Mass., about 1690; died 1751.

Married, as his second wife, **JOSIAH LOOMIS,** born January 23, 1687-8, died in Lebanon, Conn., 1739, son of Josiah and Mary (Rockwell) Loomis of East Windsor and Lebanon. He married (1) October 15, 1718, Esther ————, of Lebanon, by whom he had a son, Benoni. For further records, see Descendants of Joseph Loomis in America, p. 150.

Children of Josiah and Thankful (Warner) Loomis

————, d. young.

Esther Loomis, m. in Hebron, Conn., June 5, 1746, John Polly.

Rachel Loomis, bapt. July 29, 1722; d. after 1797; m. in Hebron, Aug. 20, 1746, Daniel Polly. He had children by a former wife, Daniel, b. Nov. 11, 1742, Rachel, b. Oct. 5, 1744, and Sarah, b. July 26, 1746. Children of Daniel and Rachel (Loomis) Polly: i. Freedom, b. Oct. 7, 1749. ii. Elizabeth, b. Aug. 17, 1751. iii. Abigail, b. Aug. 14, 1753. iv. Hannah (1), b. Aug. 27, 1755; d. May 1, 1759. v. Ann, b. Oct. 5, 1757; d. May 12, 1759. vi. Daniel, b. Mar. 29, 1760. vii. Thomas, b. Dec. 4, 1765. viii. Hannah (2), b. Nov. 5, 1762; d. Feb. 20, 1767. The dates of all these are recorded in Hebron, Conn., 1:83, 85, 87; 2:222, 223, 224, 226, 230, 231, 337, 338.

Daniel Loomis.

Elijah Loomis, lived in Hebron in 1794; m. Jan. 21, 1750-1, Deborah Dunham, recorded in Hebron. She was born in Hebron, Mar. 16, 1729, dau. of Nathaniel, Jr., and Margaret (Shattuck) Dunham. Child: Elijah, b. Mar. 22, 1753, recorded in Lebanon.

Thankful Loomis, bapt. 1726; d. after 1797; m. (1) Josiah Rockwell, (2) Daniel Reed.

Jerusha Loomis, m. Samuel Bacon.

Ebenezer Loomis, b. June 26, 1730, in Lebanon; lived there in 1797; m. July 15, 1756, Mary Huntington, who d. Feb. 5, 1799, aged 65. Children, born in Lebanon: William; Sarah; Philomela; Josiah and Gamaliel (twins); Ebenezer; Mary; Hannah; Lydia.

Sarah, d. aged 7.

41 **MEHITABEL³ WARNER,** daughter of Isaac² and Sarah (Boltwood) Warner, born probably in Deerfield, Mass.; died December 9, 1760.

Married (1) May 13, 1715, **SAMUEL HITCHCOCK** of Springfield, Mass., born March 7, 1678, in East Haven, Conn., died there 1732, son of Eliakim and Sarah (Merrick) Hitchcock, and grandson of Matthias and Elizabeth (Nicholls) Hitchcock (see Hitchcock Genealogy).
Married (2) 1732, **JOSHUA AUSTIN.**

Children of Samuel and Mehitabel (Warner) Hitchcock

Samuel (1) *Hitchcock, Jr.,* b. Apr. 12, 1716; d. Apr. 20, 1716, at Springfield.

Sarah Hitchcock, b. Mar. 27, 1717, at Springfield.

Thomas Hitchcock, b. Nov. 19, 1718, at Springfield; d. in Bethlehem, Conn., Jan. 16, 1801; m. Dec. 24, 1741, Abigail Downs, daughter of Daniel Downs of West Haven and Milford, Conn. Children, b. in Milford: i. Sarah, b. Dec. 2, 1742; d. in Bethlehem, Jan. 20, 1810; m. Mar. 10, 1793, Enos Hinman. ii. Daniel, b. May 10, 1745, "was twin with David born next day" (Milford town records). iii. David, b. May 11, 1745; d. before 1790; m. in Bethlehem, Nov. 7, 1769, Lydia Parmlee, who d. in Bethlehem, Mar. 28, 1824, aged 80; had six children of whom were David, Daniel, Abel, Jared, and Sally. iv. Abel, b. May 2, 1751. v. Mary, b. Sept. 14, 1753. vi. Jared, b. June 14, 1759; d. Nov. 17, 1836, in Franklin, N. Y.; m. and had ten children, b. in Bethlehem, Conn. David Hitchcock, Jr., was the author of several religious works and his family was distinguished for its religious workers, among whom were: his son Harvey Rexford Hitchcock, a missionary at Molokai, Hawaii, and his son H. R. Hitchcock, principal of the first high school or seminary carried on by missionaries for the benefit of the natives; Edmund Rogers, husband of Elizabeth M. Hitchcock, a missionary printer in Hawaii; George B. and Allen B. Hitchcock, home missionaries. Abel and Jared Hitchcock, mentioned above, were Continental soldiers, 1777.

Samuel (2) *Hitchcock,* b. about 1722, in Oxford, Conn.; d. in Watertown, N. Y., June 3, 1793; m. Abigail ———, b. in 1730, in West Haven, Conn., d. Mar. 1, 1813. Children: i. John, b. 1765; d. Apr. 12, 1835, in Augusta, N. Y.; m. Mamre ——— who d. Aug. 27, 1845. ii. Samuel, b. 1767; d. June 25, 1826; m. Hannah ——— who d. Mar. 7, 1813. iii. Amos, b. Aug. 29, 1771, in Oxford, Conn.; d. in Augusta, N. Y., July 28, 1854; m. Roxy Miller, b. May 1, 1774, in Brimfield, Mass., d. June 13, 1843, in Norwich, N. Y., and had eleven children. iv. Grace, d. in Harpersfield, N. Y., Feb. 17, 1854; m. Abel Dalin. v. Sally, d. Feb. 24, 1860; m. Ezra Munson, who d. in Augusta, N. Y., June 12, 1827. vi. Ann. vii. Thomas. viii. Mary. ix. Mehitabel. x. Abigail.

Child of Joshua and Mehitabel (Warner) Austin

Joshua Austin, Jr., b. Sept. 17, 1733; m. May 6, 1756, Abigail Hitchcock, b. Apr. 25, 1734, d. Aug. 29, 1764, daughter of Daniel and Abigail (Chedsey) Hitchcock of East Haven, Conn. Her Hitchcock line is Matthias[1], Nathaniel[2], Nathaniel[3], Daniel[4], Abigail[5].

42 JACOB³ WARNER, JR., son of Jacob² and Elizabeth (Goodman) Warner, born in Hadley, Mass., November 5, 1691; died there October 3, 1747. He received a double portion of his father's estate as eldest son, and resided on the plot in Hadley where his father and grandfather had lived. He continued the malting business of his father and his name occurs frequently in the town records as a land-holder.

Married **MARY** ————, who died in Hadley, March 20, 1756.

Children, born in Hadley

88 *Moses Warner*, b. Sept. 30, 1715; m. Mary Field.
89 *Jacob Warner*, b. Nov., 1716; m. Ann Fowler.
90 *Aaron Warner*, b. Mar., 1717; m. Ruth Selden.
91 *Jonathan Warner*, b. July 10, 1718; m. Mary Graves.
92 *Orange Warner*, b. Oct. 5, 1720; m. (1) Elizabeth Graves, (2) Mrs. Lydia Wait or Coleman.
93 *Gideon Warner*, b. May 15, 1722 (or 1721); m. (1) Mary Punderson or Parsons; (2) Mrs. Freelove Stow.
   Oliver Warner, b. Aug. 10, 1723; d. in Hadley, May 15, 1780. Judd's History of Hadley says he m. Ann ————, who d. Mar. 3, 1778, leaving no children. The following record seems more likely to be correct: m. (1) 1754, Hannah Jones of Stockbridge; m. (2) Nov. 28, 1771, Eunice Church (intentions published in Springfield, Oct. 15, 1771), b. May 24, 1741, d. Aug. 8, 1822, daughter of Deacon Jonathan Church of Springfield. She married (2) Dr. Seth Coleman, deacon and physician in Amherst, b. in Hartford, Mar. 17, 1740, d. Sept. 9, 1816, whose first wife was Sarah Beecher, the mother of eight children. Oliver Warner of Hadley, "gentleman," left a will dated Nov. 27, 1779, probated July 7, 1780, in which he mentioned his wife Eunice; uncle David Warner; "to wife of Timothy Kellogg of Egremont a suit of green curtains which were her sister's, my first wife's"; "to Olive Warner, daughter of my brother Gideon, a case of Drawers which were my honored mother's"; "to Gideon Warner, son of my brother Gideon, my gun and bayonet"; to nephews Lemuel and Elihu, each one half right in a new saw mill in Hadley. In case of the death or re-marriage of his wife, the property was to go to his five brothers, Jacob, Aaron, Jonathan, Orange, and Gideon and their heirs, and the heirs of his brother Moses, deceased. His wife Eunice and kinsman Noadiah Warner were executors.
   Noadiah Warner, b. Nov. 3, 1726; was a student at Yale in the class of 1748, and died in New Haven, Conn., Sept. 24, 1748.
   Mary Warner, b. Jan. 21, 1730-1; d. young.

43 MARY³ WARNER, daughter of Jacob² and Elizabeth (Goodman) Warner, born July 22, 1694, at Hadley, Mass.; died October 10, 1779, at Hadley.

Married April 1 or 17, 1720, **BENJAMIN GRAVES**, born August 12, 1689, died October 1, 1756, son of John and Sarah (Banks) Graves of Hatfield. He was one of the first 40 settlers in Sunderland, Mass., where his home lot was No. 16 on the west side. An account of this family is found in the "History of Sunderland."

Children

Mary Graves, b. Dec. 23, 1720; m. June 20, 1745, Jonathan⁴ Warner; see number 91.

Elizabeth Graves, b. Aug. 17, 1723; m. Dec. 21, 1749, Orange⁴ Warner; see number 92.

Sarah Graves, b. Sept. 16, 1726; m. Sept. 22, 1748, Moses Montague of Hadley; d. Oct. 17, 1810.

Daniel Graves, b. Nov. 5, 1728; d. Feb. 26, 1793. Married (1) Miriam ———— who died Apr. 8, 1760, in her 29th year, (2) Apr. 30, 1761, Maria Mattoon, daughter of Isaac Mattoon of Northfield. She died July 15, 1823, aged 90. Children: i. Martha (1), d. young. ii. Cotton, m. Mrs. Huldah (Hubbard) Graves. iii. Miriam, m. John Russell. iv. Martha (2), m. James Stratton.

Benjamin Graves, b. Feb. 29 (?), 1734; d. Aug. 17, 1777; Revolutionary soldier, died at Pittsfield on his return from the army. Married Sept. 15, 1757, Thankful Field who died Apr. 11, 1794, daughter of Deacon Joseph Field. Children: i. Rufus, b. Sept. 27, 1758; was an agent for Amherst College in its infancy and contributed largely to its success; m. Experience Graves, his cousin. ii. Benjamin, b. Oct. 4, 1760; m. Abigail Graves, his cousin. iii. Thankful, m. Nathaniel Smith. iv. Timothy (twin with Thankful), d. young. v. Electa, m. Daniel Montague.

Moses Graves (twin), b. Oct. 10, 1736; d. Apr. 30, 1803. He was a deacon, and removed to Leverett, Mass. Married (1) Jan. 12, 1758, Sarah Clary, who died Oct. 23, 1767, aged 29, daughter of Joseph Clary, (2) Jan. 12, 1768, Experience Oaks, b. Mar. 17, 1742, d. Aug. 15, 1824, daughter of John Oaks. Children: i. Enos, m. Sibyl Kellogg. ii. Mary, m. Sylvanus Clark. iii. Sarah, m. Roswell Field. iv. Naomi, m. Daniel Abbott. v. Achsah, m. Elisha Hubbard. vi. Lucy, m. ———— Willard. vii. Experience, m. her cousin, Col. Rufus Graves; see above. viii. Martha, m. ———— Bannister. ix. Moses, d. young. x. Elihu, d. unmarried.

Aaron Graves (twin), b. Oct. 10, 1736; probably died young.

Eunice Graves, b. Jan. 25, 1741; m. Oct. 23, 1760, Seth Lyman of Northfield.

44 JOHN³ WARNER, son of Jacob² and Elizabeth (Goodman) Warner, born in Hadley, Mass., March 10, 1701; settled in New Milford, Conn., and died there December 9, 1762. He was one of the first settlers at the South Farms, so called, in New Milford, about 1725, and became one of the large landholders and a man of influence in the community, in town, ecclesiastical and military affairs. The births of his first two children were recorded in New Milford, January 28, 1731-2, but it was not until February 27, 1742-3, that he was admitted to the church. He was a member of the Second Military Company, organized 1744, captain of the company in 1751, lieutenant of the 5th Company in the 6th Regiment of the Colony in 1754, and captain of the same in 1756. He was interested in the Iron Works and petitioned the town for the privilege of utilizing the ore in 1758. His house, erected in 1735, was a pretentious one for the period, with a fireplace sixteen feet in width and intended to burn wood from ten to twelve feet long. "On each side of the fire stood a large block of wood on which one could sit on wintry evenings, and through the enormous opening, one could, if inclined to the study of astronomy, get a pretty good view of the firmament."

To each of his seven sons he gave a farm, and built, or helped to build, a house. His heirs, June 15, 1763, were: Oliver, Lemuel, Martin, Eliezer, John, Asa, Orange, Prudence Bostwick, and Mercy Warner. The name is often spelled "Walner" on the New Milford records.

Married July 3, 1727 (attested by the Rev^d Mr. Wm. Burnham and recorded in New Milford, August 24, 1727), **MERCY CURTIS** of Farmington, who died in her 52d year at the South Farms, buried in Gallows Hill Cemetery, New Milford. She was the daughter of Thomas Curtis.

Children, born in New Milford

Honor Warner, bapt. May 21, 1728 (New Milford Church records); probably d. young.
94 *Oliver Warner,* b. Oct. 12, 1729; m. Lois Ruggles.
95 *Lemuel Warner,* b. Sept. 6, 1731; m. Sarah Gaylord.
96 *Prudence Warner,* b. Dec. 3, 1733; m. Isaac Bostwick.
97 *Martin Warner,* b. Jan. 11, 1735; m. Mary Ruggles.
98 *Elizur Warner,* b. Dec. 17, 1737; m. Mary Welch.
99 *John Warner, Jr.,* b. Oct. 27, 1739; m. (1) Hannah Westover, (2) Eunice Waller.
Solomon Warner, b. Oct. 13, 1741; d. Sept. 20, 1760, "at Montreal in the English Camp."
100 *Asa Warner,* b. Oct. 1, 1743; m. Eunice Camp.
101 *Orange Warner,* b. Jan. 18, 1745-6; m. Abigail Prindle.
102 *Mercy Warner,* b. Dec. 25, 1747; m. John Merwin.

45 **JOSEPH³ WARNER,** son of Jacob² and Elizabeth (Goodman) Warner, born April 2, 1707, in Hadley, Mass.; died ———— 21, 1743, in New Milford, Conn. He settled in New Milford in 1728, and received his first grant of land, May 25, 1728, west of the half-way falls adjacent or near to that of his brother John Warner. This property was probably at the "Iron Works," then called Newbury, and a part of New Milford. He was a cooper by trade. June 18, 1738, he united with the church at New Milford and the children were baptized there.

On October 8, 1738, there was "baptized a son of John Dean' of New Fairfield, called Ebenezer, whom Joseph Walner took charge of and baptized upon his own account." The name is most frequently spelled Walner in the early New Milford records.

Married December 25, 1729, recorded in Hadley, Mass., **SARAH BARTLETT**, who survived him, and who, with his brother John, settled his estate and made deeds in 1744-5.

Children, births recorded in New Milford

Thankful Warner, b. Aug. 26, 1730.

Rhoda Warner, b. Aug. 25, 1732; m. in New Milford, Jan. 10, 1753 (Church records), John Lake of Newtown.

Christian Warner, b. Feb. 2, 1734-5; m. in New Milford, Nov. 16, 1757 (Church records), Jonathan Hitchcock, Jr., born in New Milford, Oct. 16, 1727, son of Jonathan Hitchcock and Miriam Mallery (Hitchcock Gen.) or Mary Brownson (History of New Milford). He may have married (2) Mary ————, who was admitted to the New Milford Church by letter from the church at Newbury, Jan., 1777. Children, recorded at New Milford: i. Mary, b. Nov. 12, 1766. ii. Jonathan, b. Aug. 25, 1770. iii. Lucy, bapt. July 27, 1777, was probably a child of the second wife.

Sarah Warner, b. Mar. 22, 1736-7. She is probably the Sarah who married May 29, 1750 (New Milford Church records), Moses Knap of Danbury or New Fairfield, who died Sept. 17, 1751. Child: Gilead, b. May 25, 1751.

103 *Elizabeth Warner,* b. July 28, 1739; m. Israel Baldwin.

Joseph Warner, b. Sept. 12, 1741. The only further record of him is in the New Milford Town Records, "laid out 5 acres for the son of Jos. Warner decd. upon the east side of the Great River and upon the west side of Rocky Mountain."

Mary Warner, b. Dec. 10, 1743, brought for baptism by her widowed mother, Jan. 15, 1743-4; m. May 5, 1761, recorded in New Milford, Domini Douglas. Children, recorded in New Milford: i. Sarah, b. Oct. 7, 1761. ii. Joseph, b. Oct. 9, 1763.

FOURTH GENERATION

46 ABIGAIL⁴ WARNER, daughter of John³ and Anna (Ward) Warner, born in Middletown, Conn., Upper Houses, November 18, 1704; died there February 14, 1777.

Married in Middletown, July 21, 1725, Captain **JOSEPH RANNEY,** born in Middletown, Upper Houses, April 11, 1699; died there October 18, 1783. He was the son of Joseph and Mary (Starr) Ranney and grandson of Thomas and Mary (Hubbard) Ranney. Thomas Ranney was one of the early settlers of Middletown and probably came from Scotland. An interesting account of this family will be found in "Middletown Upper Houses" by Charles Collard Adams. Joseph Ranney was given the eight-acre lot on the east side of the upper green which had been given to his father by his grandfather. A row of sycamore trees which he set out about 1725 is still standing. Before his death he built a house for his son Fletcher that stood until 1903. His son Hezekiah received the homestead.

Children, born in Middletown Upper Houses

Fletcher Ranney, b. Apr. 29, 1726; d. Dec. 14, 1772; m. Elizabeth Powell of Hartford, who died Jan. 14, 1785. She was descended through her mother from Governor Thomas Welles. Fletcher Ranney was a carpenter and always lived in Middletown Upper Houses. Children: i. Joseph, m. (1) Ruth White, (2) Lucy Edwards; had eight children, one of whom, Mary, m. Luther Smith and was the mother of Mary Smith who married John Warburton, the wealthy philanthropist, who built Warburton Chapel. ii. Caroline, m. John Hamlin, a Revolutionary soldier. iii. Rebecca, d. young. iv. Elizabeth Welles, m. Epaphras Sage, a Revolutionary soldier. v. Simeon, m. Mary Sage and had Simon and Martin. vi. Lois, m. Daniel Arnold. vii. William, m. (1) Olive Hamlin, (2) Sarah Clark; was a deacon in the Baptist Church and his home was known as the "Minister's tavern"; had nine children. viii. Sarah, d. aged 20.

Joseph Ranney, b. June 3, 1728.

Stephen Ranney, b. Sept. 19, 1730; m. Nov. 27, 1752, Patience Ward, b. Mar. 25, 1733, daughter of Samuel and Lucy (Rogers) Ward. He was a ship-builder and resided in Lower Middletown.

Lois Ranney, b. Aug. 2, 1733; m. May 11, 1756, Robert Stevens and had a daughter Grace.

Hezekiah (1) *Ranney,* b. Apr. 1, 1736; d. Nov. 8, 1741.

Rhoda Ranney, b. June 27, 1738; m. Feb. 23, 1775, Edward Little.

Hezekiah (2) *Ranney,* b. Sept. 1, 1742; d. 1826; m. (1) Feb. 28, 1765, Lucretia Hartshorn, daughter of Jacob and Martha (———) Hartshorn, (2) Martha (Edwards) Stocking, (3) Ann (Wright) Sage. He resided on the homestead in Upper Middletown.

Abigail Ranney, b. Apr. 18, 1745; m. Dec. 1, 1766, Elisha Wilcox.

Huldah Ranney, bapt. July 24, 1748; m. Dec. 24, 1772, Captain Nathan Sage, a noted ship-builder and captain of merchant ships. During the Revolution he had command of the Hunter and the Middletown, and captured a British powder vessel. After 1795, he went to New York State, was judge for thirty years, then collector of customs at Oswego, N. Y., where both he and his wife are buried. Their two sons died young and are buried in Middletown; the daughter, Huldah, m. (1) Normand Knox, (2) Russell Bunce, both of Hartford.

47 JOHN[4] WARNER, JR., son of John[3] and Anna (Ward) Warner, born in Middletown, Conn., March 31, 1706-7; died February 12, 1761, in the Westfield Society district of Middletown. He was a farmer with extensive land holdings in Westfield Society. He probably held a commission as officer of one of the trainbands, as he was called Captain. His will was made February 7, 1761, and probated March 2, 1761. In it are mentioned his wife Mary, son Hezekiah, and daughters, Mary, Bethiah, Ruth and Lucy.

Married, as recorded in Middletown, January 15, 1735-6, MARY WILCOX, who died August 21, 1761.

Children, births recorded in Middletown

104 *Hezekiah Warner,* b. Dec. 24, 1736; m. Loiza Penfield.

Mary Warner, b. Mar. 2, 1738-9.

Ebenezer Warner, b. Aug. 4, 1741; d. in Middletown, Aug. 17, 1741.

Bethia Warner, b. 1742.

Rachel Warner (twin), b. Mar. 29, 1746; d. in Middletown, May 29, 1746.

Ruth Warner (twin), b. Mar. 29, 1746; perhaps m. Jan. 7, 1768, in Middletown, Timothy Clark (Conn. marriages, 6:96).

Lucy (or *Lois*) *Warner,* b. Aug. 17, 1750; d. 1814; m. (1) in Chatham, Conn., Nov. 22, 1772 (Conn. marriages, 2:97), Captain Joseph Kellogg, b. in Suffield, Conn., Oct. 14, 1742, d. Nov., 1795, son of Ensign Jonathan and Lucy (Kent) Kellogg. He served in Connecticut and Rhode Island as Second Lieutenant in 1776-7; turned out in 1779 to repel the enemy at New Haven; was a captain under Washington; was present at Cornwallis' surrender; studied law, but carried on a mercantile business at the time of his death. Details of his family are given in "Kelloggs in the old world and new." Lucy Warner m. (2) Hezekiah Goodrich of Chatham. Children of Joseph and Lucy (Warner) Kellogg: i. Joseph (1), b. Aug. 26, 1773; d. in infancy. ii. Lucy (1), b. Feb. 8, 1775; d. in infancy. iii. Lucy (2), b. Jan. 21, 1777, in Chatham; m. Nov. 2, 1794, Stephen Sexton of Somers, b. Mar. 23, 1771, son of Stephen and Mehitabel (Kibbe) Sexton, and had children, Lorin, Horace, Fanny, Kellogg, Lester, Stephen, Lucy, George, and William O. iv. Joseph (2), b. Apr. 3, 1779; d. in New York, 1810; m. there Margaret Stickler (who m. (2) ——— Lintz); had one son, Joseph, b. Nov. 6, 1808, m. (1) Rachel Ann Jacques, (2) Mary Jane Worrell, (3) Anna Huyler. v. Martin M., b. Nov. 21, 1780; d. Nov. 14, 1825; resided in

Barre, Vt., m. —— Willard of Barre; had one son, Martin M., b. July 24, 1817, m. Fanny M. Hubbard and their property was the foundation of the Kellogg-Hubbard Library of Montpelier, Vt. vi. Horace, b. Aug. 31, 1783; left no children. vii. Jonathan Dwight, b. in Chatham, Sept. 11, 1785; d. in Northampton, Mass., Sept. 5, 1882; m. Experience Day, and had eight children, b. in Northampton, Lucy Ann, Joseph Martin, (daughter), Caroline Experience, Jonathan Dwight, George William, Lucy Warner, and Mary Josephine. viii. Daniel, b. Oct. 31, 1787; d. in Suffield, 1835; not married. ix. William, b. Nov., 1790; d. in Chatham, 1824; not married. x. Samuel, b. Dec., 1795; d. about 1797.

48 JABEZ[4] **WARNER,** son of John[3] and Anna (Ward) Warner, born in Middletown, Conn., March 30, 1710; died in Judea parish, Woodbury, Conn., June, 1787. It was through an old account book in his possession that the name of John Warner as father of Andrew[1] Warner was first known to some of his descendants. Jabez Warner removed to Judea, which was later known as Washington, about 1754. In 1767 he was appointed guardian to his nephew Deliverance Warner of Middletown.

Married in Middletown, July 14, 1737, HANNAH[4] **WARNER,** daughter of John[3] and Silence (Hand) Warner, see number 19.

Children, births recorded in Middletown, but last three born in Parish of Judea, Woodbury

Hannah Warner, b. Nov. 5, 1737; d. in Judea or Washington, 1823.

Joseph Warner, b. Mar. 11, 1739-40; d. 1818 in Roxbury or Washington, Conn. He went with his father to Judea in 1754. Married Rhoda Gillett and had one son who died in infancy.

105 Eliphaz Warner, b. Sept. 1, 1742; m. Mercy Drinkwater.

Lucina Warner, b. Jan. 22, 1745; d. 1831, in Jericho, Vt.

Jabez Warner, Jr., b. Apr. 15, 1747; d. July 9, 1748.

Sylva Warner, b. May 23, 1749; d. 1824, in Judea.

Mary Warner, b. Oct. 30, 1751; d. 1837, in Jericho, Vt.

Abigail Warner, b. Aug. 18, 1754, in Judea; d. 1837, in Avon, Ohio; m. Ezra Gun.

Ann Warner, b. Jan. 24, 1757, in Judea, recorded in Woodbury; d. there Nov. 24, 1760.

106 Jabez Ichabod Warner, b. May 17, 1761; m. (1) Ann Wakely, (2) Mary Youngs.

49 ANDREW[4] **WARNER,** son of John[3] and Anna (Ward) Warner, born in Middletown, Conn., September 14, 1713; died in Upper Middletown, 1761. He resided when a boy with his uncle Andrew Warner.

Married in Cromwell, Conn., October 19, 1738, **MARTHA WILCOX,** who died in 1759. She was the daughter of Thomas Wilcox and Anna North. Thomas[3] Wilcox was a descendant of John[1] and Katherine (Stoughton) Wilcox, Israel[2] and Sarah (Savage) Wilcox. Sarah Savage was the daughter of John and Elizabeth (Dubbin) Savage. Anna[4] North was descended from John[1] and Hannah (Bird) North, Samuel[2] and Hannah (Norton) North, John[3] and Mary (Warner) North. This Mary Warner was the daughter of John Warner, an original proprietor of Farmington, Conn., and a soldier in the Pequot War, and his wife Anna Norton, daughter of Thomas and Grace (————) Norton. No connection has yet been ascertained between the above John Warner and Andrew, although the evidence would point to a relationship in England. He came to America at a later date, and settled in Farmington, where Andrew also owned property and may have resided for a few years.

Children of Andrew[4] and Martha (Wilcox) Warner, born in Middletown, Conn.

Andrew Warner, Jr., b. Apr. 28, 1739; d. 1758, in Middletown.
Ann Warner, b. Oct. 31, 1740; d. 1758, in Middletown.
Rebecca Warner, b. Sept. 3, 1742; d. in 1747, in Middletown.
Sarah Warner, b. Oct. 14, 1745; d. 1752, in Middletown.
107 *Deliverance Warner,* b. Nov. 22, 1747; m. Esther Karr.
John Warner, b. Nov. 30, 1751; is said to have died in Norfolk, Conn.; m. Hepzibah Treat, daughter of Samuel and Mehitabel (————) Treat. Children: i. John. ii. Treat.
Martha Warner, name is given on one chart of the family, not recorded in Middletown.

50 **ANNA[4] WARNER,** daughter of John[3] and Anna (Ward) Warner, born in Middletown, Conn., April 12, 1716; died March 3, 1795, in Washington, Conn.

Married, as his second wife, in Middletown, September 20, 1739, Deacon **EBENEZER CLARK,** born July 12, 1711, in Middletown, son of John and Sarah (Goodwin) Clark, died April 5, 1800, in Washington, Conn. About 1753 he removed with his young family from Middletown to Washington (then a part of Woodbury) and there remained until his death. His first wife was Abigail Whitmore, daughter of John and Abigail[3] (Warner) Whitmore (see number 11), and had children, Abigail and Jedediah. Records of this family are found in "Descendants of William Clark of Haddam," by Salter S. Clark, and Cothren's History of Woodbury.

Children of Ebenezer and Anna (Warner) Clark

Tabitha Clark, b. June 18, 1740; d. Nov. 23, 1796; m. in Washington, Dec. 28, 1768, Dr. John Calhoun of Washington.

Ebenezer Clark, Jr., b. Feb. 28, 1742; d. Mar. 14, 1813, in Washington; m. there Sept. 16, 1762 (Judea Church records), Hannah Tenney, b. Apr. 24, 1743, in Norwich (West Farms), Conn., d. Feb. 13, 1823, in Washington, daughter of Joseph and Abigail (Wood) Tenney. They had ten children.

Ann Clark, b. Mar. 1, 1744; d. Nov. 16, 1839, in Washington; m. there, Sept. 18, 1765, Abner Moseley, b. May 17, 1738, in Norwich, Conn., d. Feb. 22, 1812, in Washington, son of Increase and Deborah (Tracy) Moseley. They had four children.

Rebecca Clark, b. Dec. 28, 1745; d. Nov. 11, 1755.

Susannah Clark, b. Apr. 23, 1748.

Joseph Clark, b. May 30, 1750; d. Feb. 24, 1832; m. in Washington, Dec. 4, 1783, Mabel Bartholomew.

Jerusha Clark, b. Apr. 24, 1752; d. July 14, 1808, in Washington; m. ˙ about 1776, Thomas Parker.

Sarah Clark, b. Mar. 3, 1755; d. June 30, 1776, not married.

Moses Clark, b. Mar. 4, 1757; d. Mar. 4, 1757.

51   **MARY[4] WARNER**, daughter of John[3] and Anna (Ward) Warner, born in Middletown, Conn., November 14, 1720; died there September 25, 1752. Brief accounts of her family will be found in the Genealogy of David Sage of Middletown, and Commemorative biographical record of Middlesex County, Conn. By the will of Abigail Ward of Middletown, November, 1741, Mrs. Mary Sage, "my well-beloved cousin," received one half the wearing apparel, one third of the linen, one half the house hold stuff and one half the residue money.

Married, as recorded in Middletown, May 24, 1739, **TIMOTHY SAGE, 2d**, born February 26, 1714, son of Timothy and Margaret (Hollibert or Hurlburt) Sage.

Children, first four recorded in Middletown

Abigail Sage, b. May 9, 1741.

Timothy Sage, 3d, b. Sept. 28, 1743; m. and had children: i. Asa, b. 1768; m. Sarah Eels and had a son Henry. ii. Abigail, b. 1775; m. ——— Kirby. iii. Mary, b. 1784; m. Calvin Ranney and had only one son, Asa Sage. iv. Timothy, 4th, b. 1785.

Mary (1) *Sage*, b. May 4, 1746; d. young.

Loudiah (1) *Sage*, a son, b. Mar. 12, 1748-9; d. young.

Loudiah (2) *Sage*, b. 1754.

Epaphras Sage, b. 1757; served in the Revolution, and was captain of a training band; was an extensive farmer and took a prominent part in the management of financial affairs, appraisals and settlement of estates. Lived at the Nooks in Cromwell. Married Elizabeth Ranney. Children: i. Elizabeth, b. 1780; m. ——— Beckwith. ii. Justus, b. 1782; was a captain in West India trade; d. in Cromwell, Conn.;

m. Mary Kirby; had three sons and two daughters. iii. Betsey, b. 1784. iv. Sarah, b. 1789; m. Allen Butler, resided in Cromwell. v. Caroline, b. 1791, never married. vi. Epaphras, Jr., b. 1793; d. 1853; m. Salome Goodrich, daughter of Alpheus Goodrich, b. 1804, d. 1874; had three sons, Charles Parks, who was a prominent resident of Cromwell, representative in State Legislature, 1884-5, Henry Lewis and John Luther, and one daughter, who died young. vii. Ann, b. 1796; m. Luther Sage of Portland. viii. Maria, b. 1798; m. Charles Parks, lived in Springfield, Mass.

Mary (2) Sage, b. 1759.

52 MARY⁴ WARNER, daughter of Seth³ and Mary (Ward) Warner, born December, 1687, in Middletown, Conn.; died there May 2, 1722. She received property from her father's estate.

Married in Middletown, May 16, 1709, **JOSEPH WHITMORE,** born in Middletown, August 1, 1687; died in Lyme, Conn., April 29, 17-7. They resided in Middletown. He was the son of Francis and Hannah (Harris) Whitmore. See "Record of the descendants of Francis Whitmore," by W. H. Whitmore, Boston, 1855.

Children

Mary Whitmore, b. Apr. 15, 1710; m. Jan. 11, 1733, Joseph Savage.
Joseph Whitmore (twin), b. Mar. 26, 1713; d. Jan. 1, 1714.
Abigail Whitmore (twin), b. Mar. 26, 1713.
Hannah Whitmore, b. Dec. 25, 1715; m., as his second wife, Judge Seth Wetmore.
Seth Whitmore, b. Apr. 24, 1717; m. May 28, 1745, Elizabeth Hall.
Martha Whitmore, b. June 11, 1719; d. at Judea (Washington), Conn., Dec. 20, 1767; m. Jan. 1, 1740-1, Thomas Savage, son of Thomas and Mary (Goodwin) Savage, b. at Middletown, Dec. 15, 1714, removed to Hartford, Vt., 1774, and died there, Oct. 11, 1798. They had sons, Seth, Thomas and Francis, and three daughters.
Francis (1) Whitmore, b. Aug. 3, 1721; d. Mar. 8, 172–.
Samuel Whitmore, b. Jan. 10, 1723-4.
Francis (2) Whitmore, b. Apr. 8, 1725; m. Nov. 15, 1750, Elizabeth Hale; resided in Middletown. Child: Samuel, b. Dec. 26, 1751.
Jedediah Whitmore, b. June 29, 1728; d. Feb. 1, 1730.

53 ROBERT⁴ WARNER, son of Seth³ and Mary (Ward) Warner, born in Middletown, Conn., June 22, 1692; died there August 18, 1732, buried in old North burying ground. He was appointed Lieutenant of the trainband of the town, October, 1728. With five other men of Middletown he "cleared a place for fishing in the great river near the mouth of the little river" and the partners asked the town for the sole use and improvement of that place for ten years. This request was granted October, 1730. His will was made August 15, 1732, and was witnessed by Samuel Warner and others. The inventory of his property was taken November 10, 1732, and showed a valuation of £996-2-3.

Married June 24, 1714, **ISABELLA WHITMORE**, b. 1694, daughter of Francis and Hannah (Harris) Whitmore of Middletown, granddaughter of Francis and Isabella (Parke) Whitmore, of Cambridge.

Children, born in Middletown ·

(Son), b. Apr. 24, 1715; d. the same evening.

Robert Warner, Jr., b. Dec. 4, 1716; d. in Middletown, May 5, 1744, buried in Middletown, old North burying ground.· His brother Daniel was appointed administrator of his estate, June 3, 1746, and the inventory, taken June 27, 1746, amounted to £50-16. Married Betsey or Betty Doan, who died Apr. 23, 1744, in her 24th year, buried in Middletown, old North burying ground. Children: i. Phebe, b. 1742. ii. Robert, b. 1744; d. 1744, in Middletown.

108   *Daniel Warner*, b. Oct. 4, 1718; m. Lucy or Lucia Stow.

109   *Stephen Warner*, b. July 11, 1722 or 1721; m. Mary Starr.

110   *Joseph Warner*, b. Feb. 4, 1724-5; m. Alice Ward.

Mary Warner, b. Jan. 26, 1730-1.

54 SAMUEL⁴ WARNER, son of Seth³ and Mary (Ward) Warner, born in Middletown, Conn., February 6, 1694-5; died in 1773. This is probably the Samuel Warner who was lieutenant of a company or trainband at Three Mile Hill in the town of Middletown, October, 1740, and captain of the 16th company, 6th regiment, May, 1749. He was administrator of the estate of his brother Lieutenant Robert Warner and was empowered by the court to sell lands, May, 1737. His will dated June 29, 1773, was probated September 20, 1773. Heirs were his wife Mehitabel; son Samuel; Timothy and Anne Miller, children of his deceased daughter Ann Miller; son Williams John. The inventory amounted to £495. There is in Middletown a deed by which Samuel, Jr., conveyed to his brother Williams John, property received from their mother Dorothy and the four heirs of Robert Warner, deceased.

Married (1) December 6, 1725, **DOROTHY WILLIAMS**.

Married (2) **MEHITABEL** ————

Children, all by first wife, born in Middletown

Samuel Warner, Jr., b. Nov. 2 (or 6), 1727; m. Oct. 24 or Nov. 6, 1751, in Middletown, Mary Hubbard. Children, b. in Middletown: i. Seth, b. Feb. 20 or 28, 1753; d. Mar. 13, 1753. ii. Sarah, b. Mar. 3, 1754, is perhaps the Sarah Warner who m. in Middletown, Apr. 29, 1773, Enoch Johnson. iii. John.

Ann Warner, b. May 8, 1731; d. in Middletown, 1772; m. Timothy Miller. Children: i. Timothy. ii. Anne. They were mentioned in their grandfather's will.

Seth Warner, b. Jan. 19, 1733-4; d. in Fairfield, Conn., Apr. 14, 1769.
He was graduated from Yale, studied medicine and practiced in
Fairfield; m. there Dec. 13, 1764, Mrs. Sarah (Hanford) Wakeman,
widow of Ebenezer Wakeman who died 1762. She died Nov. 27,
1769, in her 41st year. His inventory amounted to £273 and included
a library of thirty volumes. Some authorities have wrongly said he
was an officer in the Revolution and died unmarried, but the data
here given shows the error of that statement.
Sarah Warner, b. Oct. 25, 1734; d. in Middletown, May 6, 1740.
Williams John Warner, b. July 13, 1741, name usually spelled in this
way on the deeds found in Middletown. He served from Apr. 12,
1761, to Dec. 2, 1761, in the 6th Company, 1st Regiment, under Captain
Herlihy of Middletown. (Volume 10, French and Indian War Rolls,
Campaigns of 1758-64.)

55 JOHN[4] WARNER, 3d, son of John[3] Warner, Jr., and his
second wife, Silence (Hand) Wilcox, born in Upper Middletown,
Conn., March 14, 1718-9, recorded in Middletown; died in Middletown, 1751. His will is found in Hartford probate records
(16:187). It bears the date, November 14, 1751, and was probated January 7, 1752. He calls himself "John Warner the second of Middletown, sick in body," and mentions his wife
Rachel, gives equal portions to his sons John, David, and Jonathan, not of age, also bequests to his daughters Elizabeth, Temperance and Rachel. Captain Joseph Ranney and "brother"
Jabez Warner were executors. The inventory shows a large
estate of about £4500.

Married in Cromwell, Conn., April 14, 1741, RACHEL BUR-
LISON, who married (2) John Fuller of Simsbury, Conn., and
died in Pittsford, Vt., aged 86. She was appointed administrator for John Warner's estate, January 4, 1764, and the following
November was made guardian for their son Jonathan. She
deeded property to her sons David and Jonathan, March 23,
1771. August 5, 1769, Elijah Wilcox received a deed of land in
Middletown, from David, Jonathan, Rachel, Jr., and Temperance
Warner of Middletown, and Edward Prouty and Elizabeth his
wife, of Simsbury, Conn., land that had belonged to their
mother Rachel.

Children, first four recorded in Middletown

iii *Rachel Warner*, b. July 15, 1741; m. Elnathan Strong.
    Elizabeth Warner, b. May 3, 1743; d. in Susquehanna, Pa.; m. in
    Cromwell, Conn., Sept. 27, 1762, Edward Prouty of Pennsylvania.
    They were of Simsbury, Conn., in 1769.
    Temperance Warner, b. Jan. 3, 1745; d. in Middletown, 1770, not
    married.
    John Warner, 4th, b. in Upper Middletown, Oct. 4, 1746; d. 1762, in

Havana. He was a youth of great bodily strength; at 15 years was able to withstand in a scuffle any three young men of 18 that could be found in the town. He enlisted as a soldier under the command of General Lyman and died of dysentery in Havana, at the age of 16.

David Warner, b. 1748; d. in Vermont, aged about 45. Aug. 6, 1763, he chose Ezekiel Kellogg of Wethersfield as his guardian. He moved to Vermont and was a farmer there. He was a Sergeant in the Green Mountain Boys. "Vermont Revolutionary Soldiers" gives the following service under David Warner: Oct. 17-21, 1777, in Capt. Abraham Salisbury's Company, on Otter Creek, raised in Clarendon; sergeant in same company, 12 days service, 1781; in Capt. Ichabod Robinson's Militia Co., Clarendon, 1781, 2 days; in list of Capt. Salisbury's Scouts, Oct. 17-21, 1777, at Pittsford. He married Rebecca Smith and had a large family. The boys all died in infancy, and the four girls married and went west.

112 *Jonathan Warner*, b. Mar. 17, 1750; m. Mary Griffin.

56 **DANIEL⁴ WARNER, 3d**, son of Daniel³ and Mary (Hubbard) Warner, born in Hatfield, Mass., March 1, 1693; died in East Haddam, Conn., January 1, 1770. He was one of the forty first settlers of Sunderland, Mass., having home lot number 15, west side. He removed to East Haddam before 1736, as in 1736-7 he sold property there. In 1739 his ear-mark was recorded in East Haddam, "Daniel Warner his mark for his creatures is a half crop the upper side of each ear, April 12." This mark was recorded to Roswell Rogers in 1802.

Married December 29, 1719, **ELIZABETH ADAMS**, born August 16, 1686, in Suffield, Conn., daughter of Jacob² Adams, son of Robert¹ Adams, and his wife Anna Allen. She died in East Haddam, January 3, 1778, aged 90 ((town record), or 88 (tombstone). The inscription in the River View Cemetery, East Haddam, reads, "Mrs. Elizabeth wife of Mr. Daniel War nor d. Jan.3.1778 in 88th yr."

Children

Jonathan Warner. "One of the Warner family," published 1892, says he was born and died in Hardwick, Mass., and left a family. Probably this was confused with another Jonathan Warner who was living in Hardwick. Nothing further is definitely known of this Jonathan.

113 *Elizabeth Warner*, b. Oct. 17, 1721, probably in Sunderland, Mass.; m. Bezaleel Brainerd.

114 *Martha Warner*, b. May 15, 1725, in Sunderland; m. Matthew Sears.

Mary Warner, b. Nov. 20, 1728; d. Aug. 8, 1746.

115 *Anna Warner*, b. Nov. 17, 1731; m. Thomas Cone.

57 **MARY⁴ WARNER**, daughter of Daniel³ and Mary (Hubbard) Warner, born probably in Hatfield, Mass., August 17,

1694; died at Whately, Mass., August 18, 1792. It has been said that she was 99 years, 9 months old at the time of her death, so this date given for her birth may be a baptismal date. In her extreme age her mental faculties almost entirely failed her, and she became like a child up to about a week before she passed away, when her mind suddenly brightened and she repeated the whole of the Assembly's shorter catechism, questions and answers and proof texts. She was residing with her daughter Mary in Whately at the time of her death. She left 6 children, 45 grandchildren, 98 great-grandchildren, and 1 great-great-grandchild.

Married September 22, 1720, **JOSEPH WAITE**, born at Hatfield, November 11, 1688, son of Sergeant Benjamin and Martha (Leonard) Waite. He married (1) Hannah Billings, by whom he had two children, Moses and Hannah. Sergeant Benjamin Waite was well versed in Indian warfare and was a brave and fearless guide and leader of scouts, in this way of much service to the colonists. He was killed February 29, 1704, while driving the enemy across the meadow in Deerfield, during the memorable attack on the town. His son Joseph was also much occupied with military affairs and often led bands of scouts. In 1710 he led a band nearly to Canada, their purpose being to reach Canada and destroy the enemy at the beginning of hostilities. They went up the river 120 miles, then struck off for the French River, then to Lake Champlain, where they met two canoes loaded with Indians and a battle ensued. One Indian was killed and scalped; then, being discovered, they started homeward.

Children of Joseph and Mary (Warner) Waite, born in Hatfield

Rhoda Waite, b. Aug. 21, 1721; m. Noah Morton of Athol.

David Waite, b. Dec. 7, 1722; m. Martha Bardwell of Hatfield.

Martha Waite, b. Oct. 7, 1724.

Lucy Waite, b. Sept. 27, 1727; d. Apr. 1, 1814; m. (1) Reuben Bardwell of Deerfield, who died three months after marriage, (2) Feb. 22, 1750, Asahel Wright of Deerfield, who died Dec. 4, 1816. They had nine children, the oldest being Lucy, who married Deacon Thomas Sanderson of Whately. The story is handed down in the family that Asahel Wright's mother had been anxious for him to marry and settle down in life. The Sunday after Lucy's marriage to Reuben Bardwell, she attended church in Deerfield, and Asahel told his mother that if he could find a girl just like her, he would not hesitate to marry at once. The death of her husband in a few months made the way clear for him to find such a wife, and as soon as her period of mourning had elapsed, he courted and won the fair Lucy.

Mary Waite, b. Oct. 17, 1730; resided in Whately; m. Captain Salmon Wright.

58 HANNAH[4] **WARNER,** daughter of Daniel[3], Jr., and Mary (Hubbard) Warner, born 1700; died March 5, 1767. She resided in Hardwick, Mass.

Married **SAMUEL BILLINGS** (name also printed in some records as Belding), who died January or May, 1778. He was the son of Samuel Billings and married (2) November 26, 1767, Mrs. Sarah Crosley. He was one of the forty first settlers of Sunderland, Mass., on home lot number 18, west side; removed later to Hardwick, where he died.

Children, born in Sunderland

Hannah Billings.
Elisha Billings.
Sarah Billings.
Daniel Billings, b. Nov. 21, 1731; d. Dec. 20, 1798; was a farmer, lieu-tenant of militia, and selectman of Hardwick; m. Feb. 23, 1758, Mary Ruggles, b. May 7, 1738, d. June 8, 1835, daughter of Captain Benjamin and Alice (Merrick) Ruggles. Children: i. Gideon, b. Jan. 9, 1759. ii. Polly Mary, b. Apr. 12, 1761; d. young. iii. Eunice, b. July 7, 1763; d. Mar., 1843; m. Dec. 26, 1784, Robert Dean. iv. Daniel, b. July 6, 1765; d. 1808, in the Island of Trinidad; not mar-ried. v. Barnabas, b. Apr. 16, 1769. vi. Mary, b. Sept. 25, 1771; d. Mar. 11, 1847, in Bangor, Me.; m. (1) Oct. 8, 1797, Barnabas Hinck-ley, an ensign in the militia, (2) Luther Paige. vii. Timothy, b. July 3, 1774, became major of militia; d. Nov. 19, 1822. viii. Samuel, b. June 4, 1779.
Nathan Billings.
Rebecca Billings.
Asahel Billings.
Samuel Billings.

59 JONATHAN[4] **WARNER,** son of Daniel[3], Jr., and Mary (Hubbard) Warner, born 1704, probably in Hatfield, Mass.; died in Hardwick, Mass., May 28, 1763, aged 59, buried in the old Cemetery in Hardwick, where his tombstone is one of the oldest. He removed early from Hatfield to Hardwick and resided a few years in the south part of the town. ·In 1743 he bought a large farm adjoining the Common, land which was in the family for many years. He was an energetic and thrifty farmer and also kept the store and tavern at the south end of the Common. He was selectman for five years from 1738, and town treasurer for nineteen years from 1744 to 1762.

Married August 8, 1733, BATHSHEBA ALLIS, daughter of Ichabod and Mary (Belding) Allis of Hatfield, granddaughter of Captain John and Mary (Meekins-Clark) Allis, and great-grand-daughter of William Allis who came from England. He took the freemen's oath at Braintree in 1630, removed to Hatfield in

1662, where he was lieutenant and a prominent citizen. Bathsheba Allis Warner married (2) August 19, 1765; John Burt,
born April 13, 1712, died September 14, 1794, son of Captain John
and Abigail (Rix) Burt of Springfield. His first wife was
Sarah Stebbins.

Children

116 *Daniel Warner*, b. Dec. 22, 1734; m. Mary Wright.
117 *Mary Warner*, b. Feb. 23, 1736-7; m. (1) Zurishaddai Doty, (2) Peter
       Harwood.
       Bathsheba (1) *Warner*, b. Oct. 7, or Nov., 1738; d. Dec. 5, 1740.
118 *Lydia Warner*, b. Nov. 3, 1740; m. (1) Dr. Challis Safford, (2) Dr.
       Jonas Fay.
119 *Sarah Warner*, b. Nov. 1, 1742; m. (1) Thomas Wheeler, (2) Captain
       Elijah Warner.
120 *Jonathan Warner*, b. July 14, 1744; m. Hannah Mandell.
121 *Bathsheba* (2) *Warner*, b. July 24, 1746; m. Eliakim Spooner.
       Lucy Warner, b. May 10, 1748; m. Jan. 23, 1766, in Hardwick, Mass.,
       Asa Hatch.
       Rhoda (1) *Warner*, b. Mar. 3, 1752; d. Sept. 15, 1753.
       Rhoda (2) *Warner*, b. Nov. 11, or 17, 1754; m. (1) Nov. 26, 1772, in
       Hardwick, Robert McIntyre, who died Aug. 29, 1775, is buried in the
       old Hardwick Cemetery; m. (2) April 26, 1778, Jonathan Lynde of
       Petersham. Children of Robert McIntyre: i. Fanny, d. Aug. 28,
       1775, buried in the same grave with her father. ii. William, d. Sept.
       11, ——, buried in old Cemetery at Hardwick, the lower part of the
       stone so buried as to be indecipherable.

60 **JOSEPH[4] WARNER**, son of Daniel[3], Jr., and Mary
(Hubbard) Warner, born in Hatfield, Mass., June 18, 1710; died
in Cummington, Mass., April 20, 1794. Some time before 1747
he removed from Hatfield to Hardwick, and resided on a farm on
the road from Hardwick to Enfield, a mile or more from the
Hardwick Common. He took an active part in the life of the
neighborhood, as is shown by the frequent appearance of his
name in the town, church and military records that have been
preserved.

Captain Joseph Warner led a company in Col. Timothy Ruggles' Regiment to the relief of Fort William Henry, August 9,
1757, during the French and Indian War. In 1761, as Captain
of the 2d Hardwick Company, Col. John Murray's Regiment, he
enlisted for the invasion of Canada.

Slavery, even in the Colonial period, was never regarded with
general favor in Massachusetts, yet it was allowed by law, and
negroes brought from the Barbadoes and other British colonies
were occasionally sold to the colonists for about twenty pounds
each. Joseph Warner was one of the few slave-holders of Hardwick, as, on July 27, 1755, Rev. Mr. White baptized one Zebulon,

the son of Philip and Bathsheba, man and maid servant of Joseph Warner. Zebulon is probably the young colored man who enlisted with the Revolutionary army in May, 1781, at the age of 21, the very year that slavery was abolished in Massa-chusetts.

In 1762 Captain Joseph Warner and several others received temporary licenses to act as innholders during the fair held in the town in May and October.   In 1770 he was elected selectman and assessor of the town.

Shortly after this he must have removed to Cummington, for Capt. Joseph Warner was moderator of the first meeting of the proprietors of that town, July 19, 1771, and also at a meeting August 21, 1771, was on a committee "to see about hiring a preacher and to listen to the report in regard to a meeting house cite."   It was not until September 4, 1774, that he was dismissed from the church in Hardwick and recommended to the church in Lot No. 5, the town later known as Cummington.   On February 3, 1773, he was on the committee to supply the town with preaching.

After the Second Continental Congress, held at Philadelphia September 5, 1774, Committees of Correspondence were appointed, for the purpose of spreading as quickly as possible through the colonies any news regarding the actions of Great Britain.   The proprietors of Cummington voted, at a meeting September 29, 1774, that their Committee of Correspondence be composed of Capt. Daniel Reed, Ensign Peter Harwood, and Capt. Joseph Warner.   This committee continued until March 4, 1777.   The town also voted the purchase of a barrel of powder and half a hundred of lead, for a town store of ammunition. ·

About this time there was a fad for persons or whole families to segregate themselves and inoculate for smallpox, hoping by this means to avoid the usual serious effects of the disease as it often occurred in epidemic form.   On May 25, 1774, the town ordered a hospital for the inoculation of smallpox set up on the southwest corner of Capt. Joseph Warner's lot in Cummington.

All during the war there were frequent meetings of the proprietors, called for the discussion of ways and means of providing clothing and other necessities.   Capt. Warner was a contributor financially, as is shown by entries on the records. He was on a committee chosen to make remarks upon the new constitution, May 22, 1780, but the record failed to note whether the remarks were made or not.

By 1790 his family had doubtless all married and left home, as the Census of that year records him and his wife only.

His will, made December 21, 1783, was probated August 5, 1794, and is recorded in Northampton. Mention is made of his wife Rebecca, who was a widow at the time of her marriage to him. To his son Elijah, besides the lands already given him, he left all his land in Greenwich, and one-fourth of his lands on the Susquehanna. Land was also given to his sons Moses, Joseph, and Stephen, and household furniture and smaller bequests to his daughters, Anna Page, Hannah Bradish, Huldah Warner, Mary Clark, Persis Mitchell, and a grandson Timothy Moore.

Joseph Warner married (1) June 19, 1738, **MARY HUBBARD**, born July 28, 1719, died March 2, 1779. She was the daughter of John and Hannah (Cowles) Hubbard of Hatfield, granddaughter of Timothy and Hannah (Pitkin) Cowles of East Hartford, and great-granddaughter of John Cowles who came to Massachusetts about 1635, and of William Pitkin. The latter came to Hartford in 1659, was appointed attorney for the Colony in 1664, and was a member of the General Court much of the time from 1670 to 1690. William Pitkin married the daughter of Ozias Goodwin, the progenitor of the large and influential Goodwin family of Connecticut, and his wife Mary Woodward, daughter of Robert Woodward of Braintree, Essex County, England. Of this family was Martha Pitkin, who married Simon Wolcott, and became the ancestress of seven governors, one of them, Oliver Wolcott, the signer of the Declaration of Independence

Joseph Warner married (2) November 12, 1781, **Mrs. REBECCA SPOONER**, born May 12, 1718, died January, 1812, widow of Thomas Spooner of New London, Conn., and daughter of Judah and Alice (Alden) Paddock. She was granddaughter of John and Mary (Southworth) Alden and great-granddaughter of John and Priscilla (Mullins) Alden, of Mayflower fame.

Children of Joseph[4] and Mary (Hubbard) Warner

122 *Elijah Warner*, b. Dec. 14, 1738; m. Submit Wells.

Mary Warner, b. Apr. 3, 1741; m. (1) in Hardwick, May 26, 1768, Timothy Moore, one of the earliest settlers of Cummington and a proprietor of the town; (2) —— Clark. By her first husband she had a son Timothy who was mentioned in his grandfather's will.

123 *Joseph Warner, Jr.*, b. July 2, 1743; m. Mary Whipple.

124 *Stephen Warner*, b. 1744; m. (1) Lois Goss, (2) Mary (Norton) Porter.

125 *Anna Warner*, b. May 2, 1750; m. James Paige.

126 *Hannah Warner*, b. Oct. 7, 1752; m. Col. John Bradish, Jr.

John Warner, b. Apr. 2, 1755; d. in Cummington, Mass., Jan. 2, 1776.

Persis Warner, b. Oct. 22, 1757; d. in Bridgewater, Mass., 1799; m.

Sept. 22, 1782, Lieutenant Bradford Mitchell, b. 1752, a descendant of Francis Cook and Governor William Bradford, two signers of the Mayflower compact. They resided in Cummington for a short time, then removed to Bridgewater. Children: i. Nahum, m. (1) ——— Deane, who d. in Raynham, Mass., daughter of Josiah Deane, (2) Chloe (Pratt) Crossman, widow of Alvan Crossman, and daughter of Nathaniel Pratt. ii. Lucretia, m. 1820, Josiah Bassett.

127 *Moses Warner*, b. Apr. 4, 1760; m. (1) Molly Ward, (2) Abigail Colton.

Huldah Warner, b. July 12, 1762; d. July 25, 1796; m. Dec. 28, 1786, Joseph Knowlton of Templeton, Mass., who died Oct. 7, 1839. He was a soldier in the Revolution, served over a year in Captain Ezekiel Knowlton's Company, Col. Dyer's regiment. They resided in Phillipston, Mass. Children, b. in Phillipston: i. ———, d. young. ii. Polly, b. Aug. 13, 1793; m. Nov. 7, 1816, Artemas Mann, had children, Harrison, Henry, Joseph, and Rosanna.

61 ANDREW[4] WARNER, Jr., son of Andrew[3] and Ruth (Clark) Warner, born in Saybrook, Conn., January 25, 1703; died September 23, 1751. He was a farmer and is said to have been a lieutenant of a militia company. Both he and his wife are buried in the Old Chester Cemetery.

Married SARAH GRAVES, who died February 10, 1756.

Children, order not known, probably born in Saybrook or Chester, Conn.

128 *Ruth Warner*, m. Charles Deming before 1750.
129 *Jonathan Warner*, b. Oct. 1, 1728; m. Elizabeth Selden.
130 *David Warner*, b. Aug. 7, 1730; m. (1) Sarah Ward, (2) Eunice Prout.
     Sarah Warner, b. 1732; d. 1811.
131 *Eleazer Warner*, b. 1733; m. Elizabeth Kirtland.
132 *James Warner*, b. 1736; m. Abigail (or Elizabeth) Bates.
     Andrew Warner, b. 1738; d. in Chester, 1757.
133 *Seth Warner*, b. Jan. 28, 1743; m. Mrs. Hannah Le Moyne De Angelis.
     Prudence Warner, d. in Chester, 1765.
     Deborah Warner, d. in Chester, Feb. 1, 1813; m. John Lewis.
     Lucy Warner, m. in Saybrook, Nov. 11, 1762, Samuel Watrous (or Waterhouse).
     Thankful Warner, m. ——— Shepard.

62 ICHABOD[4] WARNER, son of Andrew[3] and Ruth (Clark) Warner, born in Saybrook, Conn., July 8, 1704.

Married ———

Child

134 *John Warner*, m. ———

63 JOHN[4] WARNER, JR., son of John[3] and Mehitabel (Chapman-Richardson) Warner, born in East Haddam, Conn., December 19, 1716; died there August 11, 1797. He was

recorded in the 1790 Census, two males over 16, three females in the family.

Married in East Haddam, February 20, 1751, MARY TAY LOR, who died August 21, 1791.

Children

Mary Warner, b. Jan. 15, 1752; d. in East Haddam, June 15, 1827, not married. She left property to her brother John as heir, by her will of Aug. 24, 1825 (Colchester probate records, 9:314; inventory, p. 317).

John Warner, 3d, b. June 18, 1754; d. in East Haddam, May 17, 1827, not married. He was one of the founders of the East Haddam Episcopal Church.

64   DANIEL[4] WARNER, son of John[3] and Mehitabel (Chapman-Richardson) Warner, born May 6, 1717, perhaps in Hatfield or Sunderland, Mass.; died in East Haddam, Conn., March 18, 1801.

Married in East Haddam, July 28, 1769, ELIZABETH CLARK, who died March 27, 1816.

Family records and the published account of the Warner family, "One of the Warner family," 1892, have said that Daniel who married Elizabeth Clark and resided in East Haddam was the son of John and Mehitabel (Richardson) Warner, but the present compiler feels that there has been lost a record of an intervening generation. In the record of the marriage, 1769, he is called Daniel, Jr., and he would be 52 years old at that time. No other definite proofs have been discovered, and no record of the older Daniel's family. The older Daniel may have spent most of his life in Sunderland, and had only the one son.

Daniel Warner is recorded in the 1790 Census of East Haddam, one male over 16, one under 16, six females. In 1800, we find him with three males and four females residing in his family He was one of the founders of the Episcopal Church in East Haddam on April 26, 1791.

Children of Daniel and Elizabeth (Clark) Warner, recorded in East Haddam

Elizabeth Warner, b. Mar. 27, 1772.
135 *Anna Warner,* b. Apr. 21, 1774; m. Pardon Winslow.
136 *Daniel Warner,* b. July 9, 1776; m. Nancy Brainerd.
Phebe Warner, b. July 27, 1782; d. Feb. 14, 1794.
Prudence Warner, b. Apr. 21, 1785; d. Mar. 25, 1839 (Records of the rector of St. Stephen's Church, East Haddam).
Charity Warner, b. May 26, 1788.

65 JABEZ[4] **WARNER,** son of John[3] and Mehitabel (Chapman-Richardson) Warner, born in East Haddam, Conn., November 25 or 5, 1720; died about December 17, 1816, aged nearly a hundred years. He was a farmer and resided a little north of the East Haddam line, near Hadlyme. The ear-mark for his cattle was recorded in East Haddam in 1750, "a crop off the end of the off ear, and a half penny the uper side of the same ear." This mark was recorded next to Halsey Brainerd in 1831. In the Census of 1790, Jabez Warner was recorded in the town of East Haddam, two males over 16, three females in the family.

Before his death he made several deeds to his heirs: to Lucinda Willis, wife of Richard Willis of East Haddam, "a certain part of the house in which I now live, viz. the kitchin or northeast room in sd house also the east half of the middle room at the north eand of the house adjoining sd kitchin also the chambers over sd rooms also the one half of the barn standing near sd house it being the west end of sd barn," March 19, 1814; to "dutiful daughter Mehitabel," grant of a "bedroom and ½ little room adjoining and ½ east part of the barn" and certain privileges, December 23, 1811; to Sarah Warner of East Haddam, "guardian to Jabez Warner, eldest son to Jabez Warner, 2d, decd., also guardian to Lucy, fifth daughter to sd decd also guardian to Asa H., 2d son to sd decd, and also as guardian to Mary, 6th daughter to sd decd," August 16, 1814.

Jabez[4] Warner married May 9, 1749, HANNAH **BRAINERD,** born in East Haddam, April 17, 1729; died in the fall of 1811. She was the youngest daughter of Daniel[3] (Daniel[2], Daniel[1], of East Haddam in 1649), and his wife Hannah Selden, who was the daughter of Joseph[2] and Rebecca (Church) Selden, and granddaughter of Thomas Selden, the emigrant. Rebecca Church was the daughter of Ensign John and Elizabeth (Olmstead) Church and granddaughter of Edward Church of Hatfield, Mass. Elizabeth Olmstead was the daughter of Samuel and Mary (————) Olmstead and granddaughter of Captain Nicholas Olmstead of Hartford.

Richard Willys was appointed administrator of Hannah Warner's estate, March 18, 1818, inventory was made July 7, 1818, and the property was distributed to the heirs: daughters Susannah Banning, Hannah Phelps, Elizabeth Graves, Mehitabel Warner, Sarah Clark, Lucinda Willys; sons Selden and Jabez Warner (Colchester probate records, 8:94, 109, 132, 139).

Children, born in East Haddam

137   *Jabez Warner, Jr.,* b. Aug. 19, 1750; m. Sarah Harvey.
138   *Susannah Warner,* b. Apr. 9, 1753; m. Joseph Banning.

Hannah Warner, b. Nov. 21, 1755; m. in East Haddam, June 17, 1784, Samuel Phelps of East Haddam. Children, recorded in East Haddam: i. Hannah Brainerd, b. Apr. 16, 1785; d. Aug. 11, 1794. ii. Chine (a daughter), b. Mar. 17, 1787; d. Sept. 6, 1794. iii. Samuel, b. June 19, 1789. iv. Rebekah, b. Mar. 20, 1791; d. Aug. 13, 1794. v. John, b. Mar. 3, 1793.

Elizabeth Warner, b. May 18, 1758; m. in East Haddam, Mar. 27, 1783, Elijah Graves.

139 *Selden Warner,* b. Dec. 8, 1760; m. Betsy Brockway.

Mehitabel Warner, b. Aug. 31, 1763. The Brainerd Genealogy says she m. (1) James Ranney, (2) Joseph Gates. This is perhaps an error, as Mehitabel was not married in 1811, when her father made a deed to her, and she is also called Mehitabel Warner in the distribution of her mother's property in 1818.

Daniel Warner, b. June 22, 1766; d. in East Haddam.

Sarah Warner, b. Mar. 6, 1769; d. July 5, 1855; m. in East Haddam, Oct. 29, 1788, Sterling Clark of East Haddam. Children, b. in East Haddam: i. Mary, b. Apr. 19, 1789. ii. Sterling, b. July 17, 1790. iii. Jabez, b. Apr. 27, 1792.

Lucinda Warner, b. Mar. 29, 1773; m. Richard Willis; was granted a part of her father's house for a residence, 1814.

66 NOADIAH[4] WARNER, son of John[3] and Mehitabel (Chapman-Richardson) Warner, born in East Haddam, Conn., January 12, 1728-9; died in Newtown, Conn., February 2, 1794, aged 66. He was a graduate of Yale College, 1759, and the Divinity School. He became a Congregational preacher and was settled as pastor in Danbury in 1762, later preached in Hoosac and Trumbull, Conn. In 1781 when the church he was preaching in was taken to store rebel provisions, he bought a farm in Newtown, Conn., and passed the remainder of his life there.

One of his descendants sends a copy of a paper found among the papers of Harvey De Forest Warner, probably written in the hand of Noadiah himself:

Noadiah Warner — Elizabeth Deforrefst was married September —
  17— 1761
Grifsel Warner Borne Aug. 6, 1762
Noadiah Warner Borne Apr. 24, 1764
Loraina Warner Borne Feb. 16, 1766
Bemon Peet Warner Borne Aug. 31, 1767
Harvey Deforest Warner Born Aug. 1, 1769
Elizabeth Betsy Warner Born Aug. 29, 1772
Augustus & Abby Warner Born June 25, 1774
Polly Warner Borne Dec. 22, 1778.

Noadiah Warner married September 17, 1761, ELIZABETH DE FOREST, who died September, 1812, aged 75. She was of Huguenot descent from Jesse De Forest, born 1575, who removed

from France to Holland in 1615, and was one of the leaders of
the Huguenot colony that settled in New York in 1623. She
was also descended from John Peet who came from Duffield,
England to Stratford, Conn., in 1635

Children

Grisel Warner, b. Aug. 6, 1762; resided in Derby, Conn., and Hunting
ton, Conn., where she died aged 82; m. David Judson. Child:
Donald, m. —— Sheldon, and had a son David who m. ——
De Forest and resided in New Haven.

140 *Noadiah Warner, Jr.*, b. Apr. 24, 1764; m. (1) Polly Curtis, (2)
Harriet Miles.

Loranda or *Loraina Warner*, b. Feb. 16, 1766; d. in Danbury, Conn.;
m. Alexander Mc Lean. Children: i. Hugh, m. and had sons, was
in California in gold-seeking times. ii. Alexander, m. and had
children. iii. Mary, m. —— Smith. iv. Deborah, m. —— Lake;
had two sons. v. Elisabeth, m. late in life, had no children. vi.
Laura, m. and had children.

Bemon Peet Warner, b. Aug. 31, 1767; removed to Sutton, Lower
Canada, and died in Canada. He was on the tax list of South Britain, Conn., in 1801. Married and had two daughters.

141 *Harvey De Forest Warner*, b. Aug. 1, 1769; m. (1) Elizabeth Clark,
(2) Mrs. Climena Howe.

Elizabeth Warner, b. Aug. 29, 1772; m. Abijah Beardsley; no children.

142 *Augustus Warner* (twin), b. June 25, 1774; m. Maria Cande.

Abigail Warner (twin), b. June 25, 1774; m. Gamaliel Benham. Children: i. Elizabeth, m. Henry Curtis and lost her only child when
young. ii. Donald S., died the day he was to have been married.

Polly Warner, b. Dec. 22, 1778; d. in New Milford, Conn.; m. as
second wife, Sept. 13, 1815, Russell Leavenworth, b. in Woodbury,
Conn., Jan. 18, 1777, d. Apr. 17, 1865, son of John and Abigail (Peck)
Leavenworth. He m. (1) Althea De Forest who d. in 1814, leaving
children, John D., Abigail, Emeline and Mark. He was a mechanic,
removed about 1824 to Newtown, Conn., resided on a farm in New
Milford in 1827, and in Bridgewater in 1830. Child of Russell and
Polly (Warner) Leavenworth: Lorenzo W., b. in Woodbury, July 2,
1821, was a teacher, later a merchant in New Milford and Bridgeport;
m. in Monroe, Jan. 18, 1843, Sarah E. Tyrrel, b. in Monroe, Apr. 28,
1821, daughter of Squire Tyrrel; had children, Mark R., b. Jan. 19,
1846, hardware dealer in Bridgeport, Theodore D., b. Mar. 19, 1850,
bookkeeper in Bridgeport, LeRoy W., b. Sept. 15, 1851, hardware
dealer in Bridgeport, and Eliza Jane, b. May 8, 1856.

67 JOSEPH[4] WARNER, son of John[3] and Mehitabel (Chapman-Richardson) Warner, born in East Haddam, Conn., January 13, 1731; died there December 27, 1792. He was a farmer
in the town of East Haddam, and was recorded in the census of
1790, three males over 16 and one female in the family. The
earmark for his cattle was recorded in East Haddam in 1772,

two holes in the off ear and one hole in the near ear. This mark was again recorded to Lieutenant Oliver Warner, July 13, 1803, and to Orren Warner, March 5, 1828.

Married in East Haddam, January 24, 1760, **ELIZABETH CONE**, baptized in East Haddam, February 21, 1730, died December 18, 1811. She was the daughter of Ebenezer and Elizabeth (Willey) Cone.

Children, births recorded in East Haddam

143 *Joseph Warner*, b. Feb. 6, 1761; m. Sarah Osborne.
144 *Oliver Warner*, b. April 30 or 13, 1765; m. Charity Brainerd.
145 *Ephraim Warner*, b. Apr. 19, 1767; m. (1) Elizabeth Brainerd, (2) Elizabeth Gardner.

68 **JESSE⁴ WARNER**, son of Samuel³ and Hannah (Sackett) Warner, born May 6, 1718, in Hatfield, Mass.; died in Hinsdale, Mass., May 10, 1793. He was a resident of Belchertown, Longmeadow and Dalton, Mass. In 1743 he appears upon the Belchertown records assessed for taxes. In 1755 was called "yeoman" and sold property to Alexander Smith of Hadley, a farm of ninety-four acres in the Turkey Hill district of Cold Spring (Belchertown). Jesse of Dalton, County of Berkshire, deeded property to his son Jesse of Conway, County of Hampshire, April 14, 1784, land in Longmeadow. (Springfield deeds, 23: 326.) May 5, 1789, he was one of the members at the organization of the Baptist Church of Whately, which was made up of those who had withdrawn from the Congregational Church and settled in the western part of the town. Administration upon the estate of Jesse Warner was granted to David Warner of Warrensburg, N. Y., Nathan Warner of Dalton and Thomas Hubbard acting as his bondsmen. An allowance was made to his wife Mary. This was dated January 31, 1794, and the estate was found to be insolvent. (Berkshire County probate records at Pittsfield.)⁻

Jesse Warner married (1) October 30, 1739, **M I R I A M SMITH**, born October 30, 1718, daughter of John and Elizabeth (Hovey) Smith of Belchertown, Mass.

Married (2) in Longmeadow, Mass., August 29, 1753, as her second husband, **Mrs. MARY (COOLEY) VEN HORN**, widow of Dyrick Ven Horn, and daughter of Samuel and Mary (Clark) Cooley of Longmeadow. She was born in Longmeadow, April 5, 1724, and died in Hinsdale, Mass., October 19, 1801. This marriage is recorded in Springfield, Jesse of Cold Spring, and his wife of Springfield.

Children by first wife, born at Belchertown

Elisha Warner, b. Apr. 1, 1740.

Hannah Warner, b. Aug. 28, 1741.

Miriam Warner, b. July 21, 1743. It is suggested that this is the "Mary" Warner who m. Lieut. Alexander Oliver in Conway, Mass., in 1770, and had children: Mary, Lucretia, Lancelot, Elizabeth, Sarah, Lucinda, John, Alexander, Electa, Mahala, and David. Alexander Oliver, Jr., had a son Jesse Warner.

Rebecca Warner, b. Sept. 16, 1745.

146 *Jesse Warner, Jr.,* b. Feb. 1, 1747; m. Sarah Warriner.

Philotheta Warner, b. Feb. 21, 1749; d. 1771; m. Nov. 15, 1770, Elijah Howe, b. about 1745, d. 1826 (Belchertown Cong. Chh. records).

Mary Warner (?), see above notes under Miriam. Mary may have been born near the time of her mother's death.

Children by second wife

147 *Nathan Warner,* m. (1) Jerusha Webb, (2) Mrs. Amy (Wetter) Cook, (3) Mrs. Kimball.

147a *David Warner,* b. at Longmeadow or Springfield, July 12, 1758 (Springfield town records) ; moved to Phelps, Orleans County, N. Y., before his brother Jesse, then to Wayne County, N. Y., and is said to have removed later to Michigan. In 1794 he was called of Warrensburg, N. Y. (Warren County). Married Mary Russell.

Submit Warner, bapt. Mar. 29, 1763, at Longmeadow.

Elihu Warner, b. in Springfield or Longmeadow, May 17, 1764 (Springfield town records).

(According to records of one branch of the family there was also a son John and the married names of three of the daughters were Wells, Tracy and Church.)

Miriam Smith, first wife of Jesse[4] Warner, traces back to the following colonial ancestors: Joseph[1] Smith, Sergeant Joseph[2], Deacon John[3], Miriam[4]; Rev. Ephraim[1] Huit, Lydia[2], m. Joseph[1] Smith; Nathaniel[1] Dickinson, Sergeant John[2], Rebecca[3], m. Joseph[2] Smith; Nathaniel[1] Foote, Frances[2], m. John[2] Dickinson; Richard[1] Hovey, Daniel[2], Thomas[3], Elizabeth[4], m. John[3] Smith; Robert[1] Andrews, Abigail[2], m. Daniel Hovey; Aaron[1] Cooke, Captain Aaron[2], Sarah[3], m. Thomas[3] Hovey; Thomas[1] Ford, Mary[2], m. Aaron[1] Cooke; William[1] Westwood, Sarah[2], m. Aaron[2] Cooke.

Joseph[1] Smith was first recorded in Hartford; freeman, 1657; had three brothers, Christopher, Simon and William, who settled in the Connecticut Valley after 1640; died in Hartford, January, 1690. His wife Lydia Huit was the daughter of Rev. Ephraim and Elizabeth Huit or Hewett, pastor of Wraxall, near Kenilworth, Warwickshire, England, who was prosecuted by the Bishop of Worcester for non-conformity in 1638, and removed to America, where he became teacher of the church in Windsor.

In 1644 he published a book of 358 pages on the prophecies of Daniel.

Joseph[2] Smith was born in Hartford, March, 1657, eldest of fifteen children; died October 1, 1733; removed about 1680 to Hadley where he was cooper and inn-keeper in 1696, selectman in 1707 and 1710; sergeant of militia; took charge in 1687 of the grist mill in Hadley which was located in a lonely spot three miles north of Hadley and had been given up by others. With his three sons he attended this mill most of the time during the Indian wars and until his death, but for some reason he was not molested by the Indians. He married February 11, 1681, Rebecca[3] Dickinson of Hadley, born about 1658, died February 16, 1731, daughter of John[2] and Frances (Foote) Dickinson, and granddaughter of Nathaniel[1] and Anna (Gull) Dickinson, and of Nathaniel and Elizabeth (Deming) Foote, the latter of whom came from Colchester, England, to Watertown, Mass., then to Wethersfield, Conn., where he was one of the first ten "Adventurers" to settle the place, became one of its richest men, was Deputy to the General Court at Hartford, 1641-4, and held many offices of trust.

Nathaniel[1] Dickinson was born in 1600, son of William and Sarah (Stacey) Dickinson of Ely, Cambridge, England; married in 1630 at East Bergholat, Suffolk, Anna, widow of William Gull; came to America in 1634, settling at Watertown, Mass.; removed in 1636 to Wethersfield, Conn., where he was appointed Town Clerk in 1645, and was Deputy to the General Court of Connecticut from 1646 to 1656. In 1659, with his sons John, Thomas, and Nathaniel, Jr., he joined the Hartford band in their removal to Hadley, and he was chosen one of the delegates to lay out the new plantation. He was also present at the town meeting held at the home of Andrew Warner, October, 1660, at which the laws for the government of the new settlement were promulgated. At Hadley he was Town Clerk, assessor, magistrate, a member of the Hampshire Troop under Captain Pyncheon, one of the founders and first trustees of Hopkins Academy, and a deacon in the church, as he had been at Wethersfield. He removed to Hatfield for a time but returned to Hadley and died there June 16, 1676. His son Sergeant John[2] Dickinson went with his father to Hadley and was killed by the Indians in the (Turners) "Falls Fight," in King Philip's War, May 19, 1676. Two of Nathaniel Dickinson's sons had been slain by Indians the year before and another son was taken captive and carried to Canada, but returned the following year.

In the "Ancestry of Nathaniel Dickinson," the line is carried

back for fourteen generations to Walter de Caen (or de Kenson),
who accompanied William the Conqueror in 1066, and from
there back to Ivor, a soldier of fortune who appeared at the court
of the King of Norway in about 700, became commander of the
king's army and in 1725 married Eurittia, daughter of King
Halfdan of Norway.

Daniel Hovey was the son of Richard, born at Waltham
Abbey, Essex, England, 1618, came to Ipswich, Mass., before
1635, was surveyor and town officer there, removed to Brookfield, then to Hadley, and returned to Ipswich where he died in
1692. Abigail Andrews, Daniel's wife, was the daughter of
Robert and Elizabeth (Franklin) Andrews, who came to America
as captain, owner and master of the ship "Angel Gabriel," which
was cast away at Tammaquid, Maine, during a terrible storm
on August 15, 1635. He settled at Ipswich and kept an inn for
many years.

Their son Lieut. Thomas Hovey died in Hadley and his monument is in the old cemetery there. His wife, Sarah[3] Cooke, was
daughter of Captain Aaron[2] Cooke of Hadley, a justice for thirty
years and captain for thirty-five years, and his wife Sarah Westwood, daughter of William and Bridget (————) Westwood.
William Westwood was one of the six members of the commission appointed to govern affairs at Hartford, one of its founders,
and later one of the committee to lay out the settlement of
Hadley. Captain Aaron Cooke was the son of Major Aaron
Cooke, an original proprietor of Windsor, Conn., of Northampton, Mass., in 1661, and of Westfield in 1667-8, a popular figure
in all the communities in which he lived. (From data collected
by Henry E. Warner.)

69 JOSHUA[4] WARNER, son of Samuel[3] and Elizabeth
(Morton) Warner, born December 12, 1733, in Hatfield, Mass.;
died about 1820; settled in Williamsburg, near the Hatfield line.
The following records probably refer to Joshua, son of Samuel.
He made several deeds, recorded in 1773, 1789, 1791, 1792, etc.,
in some of which he is styled "gentleman"; in 1789 he is called
of Newport, Cheshire County, N. H., but in 1791, of Hatfield.
His will, made September 23, 1816, was probated September 5,
1820. His land was located partly in Hatfield and partly in
Williamsburg, and the administrators were Aaron Cleveland
and Elisha Hubbard, Jr. His will mentions the following:
wife Hannah; daughters, Naomi Cleveland, Catherine Curtis,
Lois Smith, Judith Kingsley; grandchildren, the sons and
daughters of his son Solomon, deceased; sons Samuel, Guy

Carleton, and Obadiah, to whom he bequeathed the lands and buildings in Williamsburg.

Married (1) **MARY** ———.

Married (2) HANNAH ———

Children, births recorded in Williamsburg

Naomi Warner, b. July 23, 1758; m. Aaron (?) Cleveland.

Catherine Warner, b. Mar. 26, 1760; m. ——— Curtis.

Solomon Warner, b. Feb. 22, 1762; d. before Sept. 23, 1816, leaving sons and daughters mentioned in their grandfather's will.

Lois Warner, b. June 2, 1766; m. in Williamsburg, Feb. 10, 1791, Benjamin Smith, Esq., of Hatfield.

Judith Warner, b. Oct. 10, 1768; m. in Williamsburg, June 7, 1796, Supply Kingsley.

Samuel Warner, b. Nov. 29, 1771; m. in Williamsburg, Feb. 9, 1797, ——— Kingsley, daughter of Geneva and Rhoda (———) Kingsley.

David Warner, b. and d. Jan. 5, 1774.

Guy Carlton Warner, b. Nov. 18, 1775; m. July 1, 1795, Irena Brewster. Child: David, b. Nov. 23, 1795, in Williamsburg.

148 *Obadiah Warner,* b. July 10, 1778; m. Jane ———

70 **MOSES⁴ WARNER,** son of Ebenezer³ and Ruth (Ely) Warner, born May 13, 1717 (Hatfield records), or June 27, 1717, probably in Hatfield, Mass.; died January 9, 1759, in Belchertown, Mass. He settled in Belchertown, then known as Cold Spring, before 1743, and perhaps immediately after his marriage in 1739. The first mention of him as a land owner in Belchertown is on a list of 1743, when he owned land valued at £7, housing, £1, 10s., personal estate, £9, 8s. On December 7, 1747, he was appointed one of three who are to cut and draw firewood for the pastor. October 12, 1750, he appears as a member of the church and one of the town committee. January 22, 1753, he was appointed one of a committee of three, "to take care of disorderly persons on the Sabbath." In 1755 and later, he was officially paid from two to three shillings a night for keeping the council's horses over night, and after February 16, 1756, he was called Sergeant· Moses Warner, although no special service or appointment to this office is noted. Late in the year 1756 he was on a committee to oversee the mending of the "great rode through the town from Hadley to Brookfield."

There is on record in Springfield, Mass., a deed by which Eli Warner of Hatfield, laborer, Moses Warner of Hatfield, laborer, Jonathan Warner of Belchertown, joiner, and Submit Warner of Belchertown, convey to their brother Seth Warner of Belchertown, land which they had received from their father Moses

Warner of Belchertown, and which "our said Honored father deceased owned and held by virtue of deeds from his honored father Ebenezer Warner of Cold Spring formerly now Belchertown long since deceased and of his brother Ebenezer Warner of said Belchertown and which our grandfather Ebenezer Warner held by deed from Ebenezer Marsh of Hadley." The land was located in Belchertown and the deed was signed November 24, 1780, by Jonathan, Submit (mark), and Ely Warner. In other deeds of 1747 and 1757, the father Moses is described as a husbandman of Cold Spring.

James Porter of Hatfield was appointed administrator of his estate and guardian to the older children, Seth, Phinehas and Martha, April 3, 1759. His brother Ebenezer was appointed guardian, November 11, 1762, to his children, Jonathan, Sarah, Moses, Submit and Ichabod, minors under the age of 14. Eli, aged over 14, on November 3, 1767, chose Moses Hannum as his guardian. The estate was settled April 5, 1768, when £375, 5s. were equally divided between Seth, Eli, Jonathan, Moses, Ichabod, Martha, Sarah and Submit, "saving that Seth Warner the eldest son is to have a double share."

The inventory in 1759 showed an estate as follows:

The farm on which the deceased lived,	£362-0-0
The house in which the deceased lived	9-0-0
The other house £7 The new barn £20	27-0-0
The old ditto £2 One cyder mill 9s	2-9-0
The farm lying by £62-10s, the house £3-10s	66-0-0
Personal property about £120.	

Later, debts due the estate were reported as about £64 and debts due from the estate, about £126.

Moses Warner married in Hatfield, January 24, 1737 (or 1739), **SARAH PORTER**, born in Hadley, November 2, 1718, died in Belchertown, October 10, 1757, daughter of Ichabod and Dorcas (Marsh) Porter.

Children, first probably born in Hatfield, others in Belchertown

149 *Seth Warner*, b. Oct. 28, 1739; m. Mary Clark.

Phinehas Warner, b. Mar. 29, 1742; probably d. between 1759 and 1768, as he was not mentioned as one of the heirs at the final division of his father's property.

Martha Warner, b. Jan. 17, 1743; m. Sylvanus Howe, who d. 1829, aged 79, brother of Dr. Estes Howe, first physician in Belchertown. Children, recorded in Belchertown: i. Phinehas, b. Apr. 27, 1770. ii. Sally, b. Jan. 13, 1772. iii. Mary, b. Oct. 30, 1773. iv. Sylvanus, Jr., b. Aug. 21, 1775; m. —— Joslin and had three children, Sumner, b. Sept. 28, 1807, George Williams, b. Aug. 2, 1810, and Eliza Jane, b. Nov. 17, 1812.

Eli or *Ely Warner*, b. Dec. 17, 1745. On Nov. 3, 1767, he chose Moses Hannum as his guardian. In 1780 he signed a deed transferring to his brother Seth property received from their father. In this deed he is described as a laborer of Hatfield.

150 *Jonathan Warner*, b. 1751; m. Mary ————.

Sarah Warner, b. about 1753. Her uncle Ebenezer Warner was appointed her guardian in 1762 and she received a share of her father's property in 1768.

Submit Warner, b. Oct. 24, 1756; m. 1783, Samuel Clark, son of Colonel Caleb Clark who came from Northampton to Belchertown. Their children, Samuel and Caleb, removed to Pelham, Mass.

151 *Moses Warner, Jr.*, b. 1758; m. Mary King.

Ichabod Warner, received a share of his father's property in 1768.

71 **EBENEZER⁴ WARNER**, son of Ebenezer³ and Ruth (Ely) Warner, born in Hatfield, Mass., July 29, 1729, Old Style; died in Belchertown, Mass., in 1812, aged 83. He doubtless removed early with his father to Belchertown before 1743, and his name is found frequently on the town records in various capacities. He was an inn-keeper; was elected fence-viewer at the first town meeting, September 30, 1761; was first selectman, 1788-9, second selectman, 1791. The Census of 1790 notes him with one male over 16, one under 16, three females in the family. In 1800 he is listed with a family of four. He died within twenty-four hours of the death of his wife, and the death of the wife of his son Elisha, with whom these parents lived, occurred the same day. His will was made August 21, 1806, probated April 14, 1812. The inventory showed an estate of over $2700. The property was left to his wife, Dinah, daughters Jerusha, Molly, Miriam, sons Elisha and Phineas.

Married August 22, 1751, recorded in Belchertown, **DINAH** (or **DIANA**) **PHELPS**, born June 16, 1732, in Northampton, Mass., died in Belchertown, 1812, daughter of Joseph and Hannah (————) Phelps.

Children, recorded in Belchertown

Elisha Warner, b. Apr. 27, 1752; d. in Belchertown, 1829, aged 77. He was a member of the Belchertown Congregational Church, was town clerk in 1799, and kept a tavern in what was known as Federal Street. He was called captain. Married (1) in Belchertown, Feb. 15, 1776, Sarah Scott, who joined the church in 1785, and died in 1812, aged 62. He married (2) in Belchertown, Oct. 18, 1812, Mrs. Rachel Vanhorn of Springfield, Mass., who survived him and was administratrix of his estate. There were no children by either marriage.

Josiah Warner, b. Nov. 29, 1753; d. in Belchertown, Mar. 30, 1782, aged 28. He joined the Congregational Church in 1777.

Jerusha Warner, b. Aug. 5, 1755; was mentioned in her father's will in 1806.

Elihu Warner, b. June 7, 1757; d. in Belchertown, Mar. 4, 1798, aged 40. The name is wrongly given in Belchertown Church records as Stephen. His father was appointed administrator for his estate. One of the items of the inventory was a debt of $83.00 to Dr. Philip Paddleford for medicine and attendance in his last sickness. "Paid Phineas Warner $5 for his journey and expenses to Taunton to settle with Dr. Paddleford." Elihu Warner joined the church at Belchertown in 1785.

Huldah Warner, b. June 20, 1759; d. in Belchertown, Dec. 31, 1783; m. in Belchertown, 1781, Captain Simeon Bardwell, son of Captain Jonathan and Violet (————) Bardwell. She joined the Belchertown Congregational Church in 1781.

Esther Warner, b. May 22, 1761; d. June 10, 1784, in Belchertown; m. Artemas Green.

152   *Phineas Warner,* b. Mar. 7, 1764; m. (1) Sally Rich, (2) Mary Huntington Abbey.

Rhoda Warner, b. Feb. 5, 1766; d. Aug. 22, 1788, in Belchertown.

Molly Warner, b. Dec. 9, 1768, recorded in Belchertown town records.

Miriam Warner, b. Apr. 28, 1770, "their tenth child and sixth daughter"; m. (1) Nov. 26, 1801 (Belchertown town records), Captain Jonathan Towne, b. in Belchertown, Dec. 24, 1756, d. 1824, son of Israel and Naomi (Stebbins) Towne. His first wife was Mary Holbrook. Miriam Warner m. (2) May 4, 1826, recorded in Belchertown, James Whitcomb of Williamsburg and removed to that place.

72   **EBENEZER[4] WARNER,** son of Isaac[3] and Hope (Nash) Warner, born in Hadley, Mass., January 26, 1709; died in Northfield, Mass., October 20, 1768, buried in Northfield. The inscription on his tombstone reads:

Here lies buried the) Body of Mr. Ebenezer) Warner who) Decd) Octobr ye 20 1768) In the 59 year of His Age. (History of Northfield, p. 590.)

Married **LYDIA BROOKS,** born November 25, 1706, probably in Deerfield, Mass., died September 25, 1793, aged 87, daughter of Joseph and Lydia[3] (Warner) Brooks; see number 39.

Children, four, according to the Nash Genealogy

Lydia Warner, b. Feb. 21, 1742-3; m. Nov. 9, 1775, Amaziah Roberts (Robberts or Robbarts), son of Amaziah of Winchester, b. about 1748, and resided in Northfield from 1769 to 1781.

Ebenezer Warner, Jr., b. Dec. 7, 1744.

Samuel Warner, b. July 6, 1748; removed from Northfield to Greenfield but was on the polling list of Northfield in 1771; m. Aug. 19, 1775, Abigail Field, b. probably in Northfield, Aug. 7, 1754, daughter of Pedajah and Hannah (————) Field. Children, bapt. in Northfield: i. Ebenezer, bapt. Nov. 17, 1776; prob. m. Achsah Parsons (?) and had children, Lucretia, d. Jan. 8, 1823, aged 1 year, 8 months, buried in Northfield (Cemetery records), and Charles, who d. Jan., 1887, m. Mary Augusta Allen, daughter of Albert Winslow, resided

in Troy (Winslow Memorial, p. 89). ii. Samuel, bapt. Aug. 9, 1778.
iii. Lydia, bapt. July 23, 1780. iv. and v. Sarah and Mary, twins,
bapt. July 3, 1785. vi. Electa, bapt. Mar. 7, 1788. vii. Phila, bapt.
Feb. 9, 1791. viii. Amaziah, bapt. July 28, 1793.

73 THANKFUL[4] WARNER, daughter of Andrew[3] and
Deborah (Leffingwell) Warner, born probably in Hartford,
Conn., baptized at Second Church, Hartford, May 2, 1697,
although the date of her birth is recorded in Windham, Conn.,
as May 1, 1698 (town record). This birth record was not
recorded until as late as 1726. She died in Tolland, Conn., July
14, 1739.
Married April 16, 1723, JOHN HUNTINGTON, born in Norwich, Conn., July 4, 1691, died in Tolland, June 2, 1737, son of
John and Abigail (Lathrop) Huntington. He removed to Tolland early in that settlement; was ensign of the trainband,
October, 1722; lieutenant, May, 1725; on a committee to fix the
meeting-house, May, 1725. An account of his family will be
found in the Huntington Genealogy, and the Porter Genealogy.

Children, born in Tolland

John Huntington, Jr., b. Feb. 22, 1726; was killed in an accident, Mar.
22, 1774; m. Mar. 23, 1748, Mehitable Steele, b. June 6, 1733, daughter
of Rev. Stephen and Ruth (Porter) Steele. He was a farmer in
Tolland. Children: i. John, b. May 11, 1749; m. Rebecca Newell and
had seven children. ii. Mehitabel, b. Jan. 17, 1752; m. Hezekiah
Betts. iii. Elisha, b. Oct. 17, 1754; m. Esther Ladd, had nine children. iv. William, b. Sept. 19, 1757; m. Prescendia Lathrop; had
seven children. v. Hezekiah, b. Dec. 30, 1759; m. Susan Kent;
had seven children. vi. Deborah, b. Nov. 14, 1762; m. Gamaliel
Kent; had five children. vii. Samuel, b. Mar. 23, 1765; m. Sally
Howard. viii. Abigail, b. Mar. 19, 1767; m. H. Farnsworth. ix.
Ruth, b. May 12, 1769; m. Ab. Malvoisin. x. Thankful, b. Oct. 3,
1771; m. Jonathan Hartshorne.
Thankful Huntington, b. Mar. 16, 1727; d. July 14, 1739.
Samuel Huntington, b. July 14, 1728; d. during the French War; m.
and had one child.
Andrew Huntington, b. Sept. 17, 1730; d. young.
Abigail Huntington, b. Oct. 1, 1732; d. Jan. 6, 1769; m. as first wife,
Jan. 24, 1754, James Steele, son of Rev. Stephen and Ruth (Porter)
Steele. He was b. Feb. 6, 1737, probably in Hartford, and was an
officer in the Revolution. Children: i. Aaron, b. Oct. 19, 1754; was
killed in the Revolution. ii. James, b. Oct. 20, 1756; was in the
Revolution; m. Jemima Wolcott. iii. Zadock, b. Dec. 17, 1758; was
in the Revolution; m. Hannah Shurtleff. iv. Samuel, b. May 10,
1761; m. Sarah Shurtleff; was in the Revolution. v. Andrew, b.
Dec. 25, 1763; m. Elizabeth Lathrop. vi. Abigail, d. young. vii.
Deborah, b. Dec. 31, 1768; m. Dr. Philip Lyon. (Huntington Genealogical Memoir, 1915, p. 414.)
Deborah Huntington, b. May 21, 1736.

74 JOSEPH⁴ WARNER, son of Andrew³ and Deborah (Leffingwell) Warner, born April 27, 1701 (Windham town record), baptized April 28, 1700 (Hartford church record); died in Windham, Conn., September 13, 1767, in his 66th year (tombstone record). He united with the church in Windham before 1726; was lieutenant of the 1st Company, 5th Regiment, October, 1747 (Conn. Col. Records, vol. 9). His will bears the date of August 22, 1767, was proved October 7, 1767; gave bequests to his sons Joseph and William; to his daughter Elizabeth Tracy, and his daughters, Mary, Naomi and Lydia Warner (Windham probate record, 7:309).

Married in Windham, June 4, 1722, **ELIZABETH ALLEN**, born February 18, 1697-8, in Salem, Mass., died February 26, 1767, daughter of William and Elizabeth (Small) Allen of Salem and Windham. She was a member of the Windham Church before 1726.

Children, born in Windham, baptized in Windham First Church

Joseph Warner, Jr., b. Apr. 2, 1724; m. in Windham, Dec. 31, 1754, Anna Lathrop, who joined the church in Windham in 1755 and died in 1761. She was perhaps the daughter of John and Ann (————) Lathrop, and b. Mar. 10, 1730, in Tolland, Conn. (Lathrop Memorial, p. 92.) Child: Anna, b. Oct. 5, 1755, d. Oct. 29, 1755 (Windham records). It is possible that there is some error about the dates of death of the mother and daughter, for there was an Anna Warner who m. June 21, 1775, Joseph Johnson, and died June 19, 1777, having a daughter Elizabeth, b. Apr. 21, 1777, d. June 19, 1777 (Windham records).

Andrew (1) Warner, b. Nov. 25, 1725; d. Dec. 23, 1726. (Bapt. Feb. 13, 1726, church records.)

153 *Elizabeth Warner*, bapt. Nov. 12, 1727; m. Lieut. Thomas Tracy.
154 *William Warner*, b. Apr. 7, 1729; m. (1) Lydia Murdock, (2) Mary Williams.

Andrew (2) Warner, b. March 29, 1731; bapt. Feb. 13, 1732; d. Nov. 24, 1753, in his 21st year (tombstone records), not married. He joined the Windham Church in 1753.

Mary Warner, b. Apr. 7, 1733; bapt. May 5, 1734; m. Joseph Hutchinson of Lebanon, Conn.

Naomi Warner, b. July 6, 1736; bapt. Aug. 1, 1736; d. May 12, 1780, not married, buried in Windham, tombstone inscribed "Mrs. Naomi Warner, daughter of Lieut. Joseph and Elizabeth Warner." She joined the Windham Church in 1765.

Lydia Warner, b. 1738; bapt. July 15, 1739; d. Jan. 27, 1772, not married, buried in Windham beside her sister Naomi, as "Mrs. Lydia Warner, daughter of Leut. Joseph and Elizabeth Warner." She joined the Windham Church in 1764.

Will of Joseph Warner⁴ (Andrew³, Isaac², Andrew¹) Windham Probate, 7:309.

In the Name of God Amen I Joseph Warner of Windham in the County of Windham being now indisposed as to my bodily health but of sound &

disposing mind & memory calling to mind that it is appointed unto all men
once to die Do make this my last will & Testament, in the Following maner
that is to say first & above all things I recomend my soul To God through
the meritts of Christ & my body I comit to the Dust to have a decent
Christian burial at the discretion of my executor hereafter named, nothing
Doubting the Resurrection of my body to life again at the great & Last day
and as to what worldly estate it hath pleased God to bless me with, my will
that the same be disposed of the Following manner that is to say after my
just debts & funarel charges are paid— Imprimis— I give & bequeath unto
my beloved son Joseph Warner all my wearing apparel & that meadow or
lott of Land lying on the east side of Shatucket river & bounding easterly
on land belonging to Nathl Wales Junr & northerly on Isaac Cranes land
& westerly & southerly on the highway and also I give him out of my other
estate fifteen pounds lawful mony to be paid to him by my executor hereafter named to be paid in one year after my decease all which I give to my
sd son Joseph his heirs & assigns forever.

Item— I give and bequeath to my well beloved son William Warner all
my other lands lying in the Towns of Windham & Lebanon In sd County
with all the buildings thereon & privileges & appurtenances thereunto belonging as the same are bounded & described in my deed thereof on Record and
also I give & bequeath to him the one half of all my stock & cattle horse
kind, sheep & swine for Quantity & Quality & the one half of all my Farming
utencels & all my black smith Tools & utencels of every kind, which land &c
I give To him & to his heirs & assigns forever he paying the aforesaid
Legacie of Fifteen pounds & the Legaceys hereafter to be mentioned to my
Four daughters as hereafter expressed To be paid by him as my Executor,
also I give &c to my sd son William the one halfe of all my corn & grain
hay & oats for Quantity & Quality— Item— I give & bequeath to my
beloved Daughter Elisebeth Tracy fourteen pounds lawful mony to be paid
by my sd Executor out of my estate given to sd W^m as aforesd to be paid
in one year after my decease — Item— I give & bequeath to my beloved
Daughters Mary, Naomi, & Lydia twenty pounds Lawful mony each to be
paid to them out of the estate given to my sd son William as aforesd to be
paid by him as my executor in one year after my decease; and also Liberty
of Covenant room for their use for them to dwell in my new Dwelling
house during the time they shall live single before marriage— Item—I
give & bequeath unto my sd Four Daughters To be equally divided between
them all my household utencels & their mother's wearing appariel & the
other halfe of my stock & cattle horse kind, swine sheep hay & grain of all
sorts to be equally divided between them & their Brother William to whom
the other halfe is given as aforesaid— Item—all my outstanding Debts due
to me & any & all other estate to me in any wise belonging not before in
this will disposed of I give &c to my sd son William his heirs &c—

And my will is that if my executor my sd son William can not pay the
aforesd Legacies viz fifteen pounds to my son Joseph fourteen pounds to
my daughter Elizebeth & Twenty pounds to each of my other Three daughters as aforesd that is if he cant pay sd Legacies without selling lands that
then he may if he judge it best for him Cause to be sett of to each of sd
Legatees so much of sd Lands given to him as shall be worth the sum of
such legacie so to be paid to each or all of them to be apprized by Indeferant
persons mutually chosen by my sd son & such Legatee or Legatees who are
to receive the same— or my sd executor may pay sd Legacies in chattles to
be sett out by apprizement in the same manner as the Land may be sett of
by this will—

And I do by these Presents ordain appointe and constitute my sd son William my sole Executor of this my last will and Testament to execute the same according To the True intent & meaning thereof hereby declaring this & no other to be my last will & Testament revoking all others In witness whereof I have hereunto sett my hand & seal this Twenty second day of August A. D. 1767

Declared to be my last
will & Testament In presence
of us

Nath¹ Wales Junʳ
Stephen Payn
Daniel Edwards

his
Joseph + Warner
mark

The above will was proved October 7, 1767.

The inventory taken November 20, 1767, amounted to £676–16–10.

75 **MARY⁴ WARNER**, daughter of Andrew³ and Deborah (Leffingwell) Warner, born April, 1703 (Windham, Conn., town record); died in Mansfield, Conn., October 23, 1782, in her 80th year.

Married May 27, 1726 (Mansfield town records), Captain **SAMUEL STORRS, Jr.**, born in Mansfield, August 22, 1701, died there October 28, 1786, son of Samuel and Martha (Burge) Storrs. The Storrs Genealogy compiled by Charles Storrs, 1886, gives an account of their family.

The inscriptions on their tombstones are here given:

"This monument is erected to the memory of the well-beloved and Godly man, Capt. Samuel Storrs, who we trust fell asleep in Jesus May 27, A. D. 1786, in ye 85th year of his age.
Death overcomes us all."

"In honor to the memory of Mrs. Mary Storrs, ye amiable and virtuous consort of Capt. Samuel Storrs, who departed this life Oct. 23, 1782, in ye 80th year of her age. A shining example of conjugal affection, maternal tenderness and a faithful servant of Jesus Christ."

Children, born in Mansfield

Deborah (1) *Storrs*, b. Mar. 13, 1726-7; d. Apr. 3, 1727.

Martha Storrs, b. Apr. 28, 1728; m. Nov. 7, 1745, Nathaniel Hall, b. Feb. 8, 1723, son of Theophilus and Ruth (Sargeant) Hall of Mansfield. Children, b. in Mansfield: i. Nathaniel, b. Aug. 3, 1746. ii. Deborah, b. June 5, 1748. iii. Ruth, b. Mar. 27, 1751. iv. Olive, b. June 25, 1753. v. Martha, b. June 14, 1755. vi. Andrew, b. Feb. 9, 1758. vii. Azariah, b. Dec. 1, 1760. viii. Richard, b. Apr. 21, 1762. ix. Aaron, b. Aug. 22, 1764. x. Asahael, b. Aug. 20, 1766. xi. Mary, b. Jan. 3, 1769.

Samuel Storrs, b. Mar. 6, 1729-30; m. May 7, 1752, Huldah Snow, daughter of Jabez Snow. He was also known as Captain Storrs and

died before his father, Oct. 28, 1776. Children, b. in Mansfield: i.
Deborah, b. Jan. 31, 1753; d. Aug. 15, 1773. ii. Elisabeth, b. Mar. 24,
1755; d. Oct. 17, 1772. iii. Mary, b. Apr. 27, 1757; m. Sept. 29, 1774,
James Bennett of Mansfield; had eleven children. .iv. Jehiel, b. Sept.
29, 1759; m. Rachel McCall; settled in Middlebury, Vt., later in Canton, N. Y.; had four children. v. Lydia, b. July 16, 1761; m. Jesse
Swift of Mansfield. vi. Huldah, b. July 17, 1763; m. Feb., 1784,
Thomas Turner; had a child, Ruth, b. in Mansfield. vii. Achsah,
b. Oct. 22, 1765; m. June 3, 1787, Jonathan Dimmock of Mansfield;
had nine children. viii. Jabez, b. Mar. 12, 1768. ix. Andrew (1),
b. Nov. 10, 1770; d. Sept. 15, 1772. x. Andrew (2), b. 1772; d. July,
1773. xi. Ruth, b. 1774; d. Oct. 26, 1776.

Deborah (2) *Storrs,* b. Apr. 20, 1733.

Andrew Storrs, b. Dec. 20, 1735; d. 1785; was graduated from Yale,
1760; A.M., Harvard, 1765; ordained pastor at Northbury, Conn.,
1765. His widow m., 1786, Dr. Joseph Bellamy of Bethlehem, Conn.,
whom she survived many years.

Richard Storrs, b. Oct. 7, 1746.

76 THOMAS[4] WARNER, son of Andrew[3] and Deborah
(Leffingwell) Warner, born April, 1705, probably in Hartford,
Conn., although his birth is recorded with his father's family in
the Windham town records; died in Ashford, Conn., about 1756.
He removed from Windham to Mansfield (where he was living
in 1731), and in 1750 to Ashford where he remained until his
death. His name occurs frequently on the land records of those
towns, beginning with a deed from his father, Andrew of Mansfield, in 1731, "in consideration of natural affection, love and
good will to Thomas Warner, his son, of town, county and colony aforesaid." By the will of his father, January 31, 1731, he
received property. In a deed of January 30, 1734, to Daniel
Allen, he is described as of the town of Windham. In a mortgage transaction of 1738-41, he is also of Windham, but in a
deed of 1742, he is called of Mansfield. Again in 1747, Joseph
Warner of Windham deeds property to Thomas of the same
place. The papers pertaining to the settlement of his estate are
recorded in Pomfret, Conn. William Warner of Windham was
the administrator and the final division was made May 3, 1760,
upon motion of Eleazer Warner, eldest son of Thomas.

"To Eleazer eldest surviving son of the.deceased Thomas Warner, equal
shares with the remainder of the heirs, viz. (House and 14 acres
described) . . .
And to Abigail Warner, daughter 20 acres (described) . . .
And to Sarah, one of the heirs, 11 acres (described) . . .
And to Eless Warner, 6 acres with barn (described) . . .
And to Delight Warner, 11 acres (described) . . .
And to Elisha Warner, youngest son of the deceased, 14 acres (described).

Thomas Warner married (1) in Mansfield, Conn., June 7, 1737, **DELIGHT METCALF**, born about 1717-8, daughter of Rev. Joseph and Abiel (Adams) Metcalf of Falmouth, Mass. Abiel Adams was the daughter of Rev. William[3] Adams (William[2] and Elizabeth Stacy, William[1], of Cambridge in 1635, later of Ipswich). Abiel Adams' mother was Alice Bradford, daughter of William Bradford, 2d, and granddaughter of William Bradford of Plymouth Colony and of Mayflower fame. Joseph Metcalf was born April 11, 1682, was graduated with honors from Harvard in 1703, became pastor of the Falmouth church in 1707, where he preached until his death in 1723. (Some Descendants of William Adams of Ipswich, by William Sumner Appleton, Boston, 1881, gives further Adams data).

Thomas Warner married (2) **Mrs. ELIZABETH LADD,** widow of Nathaniel Ladd of Coventry, Conn.

Children of Thomas and Delight (Metcalf) Warner; first four dates recorded in Mansfield (town record)

155 *Eleazer Warner,* b. Feb. 8, 1738; m. (1) Joanna Hale, (2) Elizabeth ————.

156 *Sarah Warner,* b. May 9, 1740; m. David Strong.
157 *Elis* or *Alice Warner,* b. Aug. 11, 1742; m. Peter Cross.
     Eliphalet Warner, b. Feb. 11, 1743-4, in Mansfield; bapt. Apr. 15, 1744; d. young, as he was not mentioned among his father's heirs.
     Abigail Warner, bapt. Dec. 21, 1746, in Mansfield.
158 *Delight Warner,* b. in Willington, Conn., June 9 or 10, 1749; m. Dr. Thomas Sadd.

Children of Thomas and Elizabeth (————) Warner

Thomas Warner, b. Jan. 16, 1753, in Ashford, Conn.; d. before 1760, as he was not mentioned in distribution of his father's property.
Elisha Warner, b. May 30, 1756; received a share of his father's estate in 1760.

77 **ELISHA[4] WARNER,** son of Andrew[3] and Deborah (Leffingwell) Warner, born April, 1707, recorded in Windham, Conn.; died August 21, 1751, in Mansfield, Conn. He was ensign in the 1st Company of Mansfield, 1745, and lieutenant, 2d Company, 5th Regiment, October, 1750 (Conn. Col. Records, 9:107, 554). June 24, 1752, Captain Samuel Storrs of Mansfield was appointed guardian for Elisha, Samuel, and Josiah, minor children of the late Elisha Warner, while his widow, Mrs. Elizabeth Warner, was appointed guardian for Elizabeth, Mary and Zerviah. These two were appointed administrators, September 25, 1752. (Windham Probate, Orders and Decrees, 2:282, 352.)

Married June 21, 1730, recorded in Mansfield, **ELIZABETH**

BABCOCK, born in Coventry, Conn., July 8, 1716, daughter of James and Mary (———) Babcock.

Children, recorded in Mansfield

159 *Elizabeth Warner*, b. Apr. 17, 1738; m. Jonathan Bingham.
   Zerviah Warner, b. July 8, 1741 (bapt. Sept. 14, 1740, Mansfield records, p. 368); m. Nov. 30, 1757, Ebenezer Russ (Mansfield town record). Child: Ebenezer, b. Aug. 23, 1761.
   Elisha Warner, b. Apr. 19, 1743 (bapt. as "Elijah," July 10, 1743); d. in Mansfield, Nov. 6, 1755. (Mansfield records, p. 371.)
160 *Josiah Warner*, b. Aug. 7, 1745; m. Deborah Hall.
   Samuel Warner, b. Dec. 25, 1747, in Mansfield; bapt. there Jan. 10, 1748. The following records may pertain to this Samuel: m. in Cheshire, Conn., Feb. 10, 1773, Abigail Matthews (Early Connecticut marriages, vol. 3); ensign, 8th Company, 15th Regiment, 1779 (Conn. State Recs., vol. 2:299).
   Mary Warner, b. Sept. 26, 1751.

78 **MARTHA[4] WARNER**, daughter of Daniel[3] and Sarah (Golden or Goulding) Warner, born in Hadley, Mass., October 25, 1706; died October 3, 1787.

Married in Hadley, as second wife, June 2, 1737, **WILLIAM WHITE** of Hadley (town records), born August 15, 1698, died May 30, 1774, son of Nathaniel and Elizabeth (Savage) White. His first wife was Mrs. Mary (Selden) Taylor, daughter of John Selden and widow of John Taylor. She died in 1735, leaving children, Mary, Sarah and William.

Children of William and Martha (Warner) White

Daniel (1) *White*, d. young.
Nathaniel White, b. Nov. 12, 1738.
Daniel (2) *White*, b. Sept. 1, 1740; d. Nov. 11, 1815; m. Sarah Goodrich, who died 1837. Children: i. Zenas, b. Oct. 10, 1772; d. 1844, not married. ii. Judith, b. May 17, 1775; m. Eli Graves. iii. Bethene, b. Feb. 14, 1777; m. Eli Graves. iv. Sarah G., b. Jan. 26, 1779; m. John Cooke. v. Pamela, b. Nov. 2, 1780; m. Roswell Welles. vi. Grace G., b. Oct. 18, 1782; m. Nov. 28, 1802, Stephen Montague, b. Sept. 4, 1779; d. in Hadley, 1851 (had children, Sarah G., d. not m., Sophronia, d. not m., Mary, Daniel, m. Mary Peirce, Henry, m. Abigail Kingsley, Susan, m. Elijah Ayres, Stephen S., m. Mary C. Kellogg, Harriet M., m. Edward Bartlett, and Sabra W.). vii. Sylvia, b. Apr. 20, 1785; m. John Baker. viii. Daniel, b. Nov. 6, 1789. For further details see Porter Genealogy, p. 343.
Martha White, b. Aug. 3, 1742; d. Oct. 14, 1816; m. Apr. 26, 1770, William Cooke.
Ebenezer White, b. May 16, 1744; d. May 15, 1794; m. Mar. 13, 1766, Abigail Porter, daughter of Abraham and Mary (Edgerton) Porter of Hartford, Conn. They settled in Pittsfield, Mass. Children: i. Esther, b. Apr. 24, 1767; m. Josiah Wait. ii. William Porter, b. May 24, 1769; m. Elizabeth Allen; resided in Buenos Ayres; had

two children. iii. Lydia, b. May 24, 1772; m. Butler Goodrich; had
eleven children. iv. Enoch, b. Mar. 19, 1775; m. Sarah Lanckton;
had seven children. v. David, b. Apr. 19, 1780, d. in South America.
vi. Polly, b. Nov. 20, 1782; d. 1847, not married. See Porter Genealogy, p. 383.

John White, b. Mar. 28, 1746; d. May 22, 1819 (or 1814), not married.
David White, b. Feb. 18, 1748; m. Roxelana⁵ Warner, daughter of
Gideon⁴; see number 183.

79 ˙ DANIEL⁴ WARNER, son of Daniel³ and Sarah (Golden
or Goulding) Warner, born in Hadley, Mass., March 22, 1709,
birth recorded on town records, although it has not appeared in
previous published records of the family. It seems most probable that the following records of a Daniel Warner who settled in
Wilbraham, Mass., are of this Daniel⁴. Daniel Warner of Wilbraham died in 1774, aged 66. (Centennial of Wilbraham, p.
310.) Administration on his estate was granted August 2, 1774,
to his son Jesse Warner.

Married June 9, 1731, (as in Hitchcock Genealogy) JERUSHA
HITCHCOCK, daughter of Ensign John³ Hitchcock (John²,
Luke¹) and his wife Mary Ball, of Springfield and Bernardston.
She was born February 23, 1709, died December 2, 1797.

Children

Comfort Warner, b. Mar. 15, 1731-2 (as in Wilbraham record), first
     birth recorded in the town of Wilbraham; d. July 14, 1757.
Daniel (1) *Warner*, b. Dec. 26, 1735; d. July 22, 1748.
161 *Jesse Warner*, b. Oct. 15, 1738; m. Hannah Colton.
Jerusha Warner, b. Aug. 17, 1741; d. Nov. 1, 1749.
David Warner, b. Apr. 11, 1746; d. Apr. 12, 1766.
Daniel (2) *Warner*, b. July 22, 1748.

80 ZECHARIAH⁴ WARNER, son of Samuel³ and ˙ Sarah
(Field) Warner, born in Springfield, Mass., April 11, 1719.
There is recorded in Springfield (land records, T:549), the deed
from Zachariah Warner, yeoman, of Springfield, to George Pynchon, of six acres of land in Springfield on the east side of the
great river, May 18, 1754. He received a share of his father's
property in 1756. He and his wife were members of the First
Congregational Church of Springfield, April 19, 1741.

Married (intentions published in Springfield, May 9, 1740),
MARY COOLEY of Springfield.

Children, births recorded in Springfield

Zechariah Warner, Jr., birth date not given in Springfield records, but
     received property from his parents Zechariah and Mary, land in

Springfield, Apr. 7, 1764; was recorded in the 1790 Census of Spring-field; d. Dec. 17, 1813; m. there Apr. 29, 1762, Dorcas Cooley, daughter of Jacob and Abigail (Chapman) Cooley. She died Aug. 19, 1833. Children, recorded in Springfield: i. Beulah, b. Aug. 22, 1762; d. Aug. 12, 1764. ii. ————, d. in infancy, Apr. 30, 1764. iii. James, b. Mar. 28, 1765; was recorded in the 1790 Census of Springfield; m. (intentions published Apr. 9, 1785), Achsah Sanderson of Springfield, who was a member of First Congregational Church, Springfield, 1795; had a child, Dorcas, b. Mar. 9, 1791. iv. Peter, b. Apr. 2, 1767; m. (intentions published, June 19, 1790) Mrs. Eunice Shepard of Springfield. v. John, b. May 7, 1769; m. the widow Achsah Warner (of his brother James) in 1802. vi. Dorcas, b. Dec. 13, 1771; d. Mar. 11, 1772. vii. ————, d. in infancy, Apr. 14, 1775. viii. Zachariah, 3d, bapt. Mar. 2, 1779 (First Church records). ix. Jacob Cooley, b. Jan. 2, 1781. (Springfield town and First Church records.)

Samuel (1) *Warner,* b. Oct. 23, 1743; d. young.

Samuel (2) *Warner* (twin), b. Feb. 23, 1745.

Mary Warner (twin), b. Feb. 23, 1745.

Ebenezer (1) *Warner,* b. July 2, 1748; d. July 2, 1748.

Jemima Warner, b. June 7, 1749; m. Sept. 14, 1770, George Bates of Springfield.

Beulah Warner, b. Sept. 17, 1752; d. Jan. 26, 1759.

Ebenezer (2) *Warner,* b. Oct. 20, 1754.

Noah Warner, b. Aug. 8, 1760; was probably the Noah of West Springfield (1790 Census).

81 ICHABOD[4] WARNER, JR., son of Ichabod[3] and Mary (Metcalf) Warner, born December 10, 1712, recorded in Lebanon, Conn., baptized First Church, Lebanon, July 16, 1712 (1712-3?); died in Windham, Conn. He received land lying between Windham and Lebanon by deed from his father in 1734, also a share in mill property. As his wife is said to have been of a Long Island family, the following records of Brookhaven, Long Island, must be of this Ichabod: 1741, town assessment, Icobud Warner, 1s., 5½ d.; Samuel D'Honneur of Brookhaven in will of March 5, 1844-5, mentions "land I bought of Ickabud Warner" (Abstract of Brookhaven Wills). He was not assessed there in 1749, so probably returned to Windham before that date. He may have been the proprietor of the ferry across the Connecticut in 1769 (Acts and laws of Connecticut, 4th revision, 2d edition, 1769, p. 345).

"An Act for Stating the fare of the Ferry called Warner's Ferry, on Connecticut River. Be it enacted by the Governor, Council and Representatives, in General Court assembled, and by the Authority of the same, That the Fare of the said Ferry shall be for a Man and Horse, Three Pence, for a Footman, One Penny, for a lead Horse, One Penny Halfpenny, for an Ox or other Neat Kine, Two Pence, for Sheep, Hogs and Goats, one Half-Penny per Head. 1769."

Ichabod Warner married March 12, 1737, **Mrs. MARY (MAPES) GOLDSMITH**, widow of Joseph Goldsmith, probably from Long Island.

Child

162 *Ichabod Warner, 3d,* b. Mar. 1, 1738; m. Mary Lazell. Some of his descendants have said he was born in Southold, Long Island.

82 DANIEL[4] WARNER, son of Ichabod[3] and Mary (Metcalf) Warner, born July 10, 1714, recorded in Windham, Conn., (town records), or in Lebanon (Moravian Church records). He joined the Congregational Church at Windham in 1729 or 1731, and after his marriage resided for a time in Windham, where his first five children's births were recorded, and later in Hebron. He removed with his family to Dutchess County, New York, about 1755, as his son Samuel was born in the Oblong in 1756. They became members of the Moravian settlement known as the Sichem Moravian Congregation, near the border line of Connecticut. According to the catalogue of 1769, the membership consisted for the greater part of the two large families of Warner and Edmonds, living on rented farms. On the expiration of their leases they were attracted by the favorable offers of land on the Mahoning in Pennsylvania, and, after a tour of inspection made in July, 1770, Daniel Warner, his wife and six children, moved to Gnadenhütten, Northampton Co., Pennsylvania, and took up temporary quarters in the old Fort Allen. In February, 1771, they were followed by his son Nathan with his wife and three children, and in October their old neighbors, the family of Edmund Edmonds, joined them. The two Warner families completed their houses in Gnadenhütten in January, 1772, and moved from the fort across the river.

During the Revolution the family remained true to their belief as Moravians, that they should not take part in army service. On September 24, 1777, "Brother Warner's oxen and horse were taken to Allentown," where, to redeem them, he had to pay his son John's fine of £50. On December 12th of the same year, "the married Brethren Nathan and Daniel Warner, both heads of large families, were forcibly taken to Allentown, and, being unwilling to serve in the militia for two months, and unable to pay £108 ransom, they were forced to cut fifty cords of wood each, in the neighborhood of Allentown, for the use of the soldiery." Their task was duly completed and in February of the following year they returned to their homes with the promise of four pence per cord as pay for their services. `

Daniel Warner was a cooper by trade. Tradition says that in

later life he became insane and died in that condition. His spirit was said to have returned to his former cabin, and he was known as "Spookin' Dan'l." The date of his death has not been found, but the necrologies of the Moravian Church during the incumbency of Schmidt include "several of the older members of the church, viz. Daniel Warner, his wife Bethia" and others. He was probably buried in Gnadenhütten.

The will of Daniel Warner, of Gnadenhuetten on the Manony Creek, mentioned his wife Bethia, deceased, children, Samuel, Ezra, Massa (the executor), Hannah, Daniel, John, Mary (wife of Elisha Smith). Boaz Walton and Peter Edmunds were witnesses (Northampton Co., Pa., probate record).

Daniel Warner married December 8, 1739 (Windham, Conn., town records), BETHIAH **GINING (JENNINGS?)**, born in Windham, March, 1720; died in Gnadenhütten, Pa., before her husband.

Children, first five recorded in Windham, next two in Hebron, Conn., dates of others from family record. The dates of the family record are given Old Style, while the town records are New Style, thus accounting for the discrepancy in dates

> *Daniel Warner, Jr.,* b. Aug. 15 or 26, 1740. He may be the Daniel Warner who married in Hebron, Oct., 1775, Hannah Sumner (Records of Gilead Church, Conn. Hist Soc. Library). He doubtless removed with his father and brothers to Pennsylvania, as there was a Daniel Warner taxed in Penn township, Northampton Co., 1780-8, owner of a considerable tract of land. In 1777 he was one of the Moravian Church at Gnadenhütten, Pa., and with his brother Nathan, both heads of large families, was compelled to cut wood for the soldiers at Allentown in place of doing military service which was contrary to their religious principles.
>
> *Jonathan Warner,* b. Aug. 25 or Sept. 5, 1742. He went to Gnadenhütten, Ohio, from Pennsylvania, Nov. 6, 1799, and with his wife Sarah and six children, settled as a lessee on the Gnadenhütten tract west of the Tuscarawas river. It is recorded in the records of the Beersheba Moravian Church that, during September and October of 1805, Jonathan Warner filled in the chinks of the new building that was erected that year and stood one mile west of Gnadenhütten. He was married in Gnadenhütten, Pa., Sept. 18, 1774, to Sarah Everit. The new chapel was dedicated on Sept. 17, 1774, and the following day in the new chapel "was performed the marriage ceremony of the single brother Jonathan Warner with the single sister Sarah Everit." No list of their children has been found, but at least six were born before 1799.

163 *Nathan Warner,* b. June 6, 1744 (Windham records), or June 17 (family record); m. Mary Silbernagel or Silvernail.

> *Bethiah Warner,* b. Mar. 18, 1745; d. Apr. 19, 1746 (Windham record).
> *Mary Warner,* b. May 4, 1747; m. Elisha Smith.
> *Hannah Warner,* b. Mar. 22, 1751, recorded in Hebron; m. in Bethlehem, Pa., Jan. 12, 1792, Nils Tillofson.

164 *Massah Warner*, b. June 3 (2, family record), 1754; m. Maria Dorothea Miksch.
Samuel Warner, b. at Oblong, N. Y., Jan. 1, 1756 (Moravian Church record); died at Gnadenhütten, or Bethlehem, Pa., Nov. 19, 1816, not married. He was taxed as a single freeman in Penn township, Northampton Co., Pa., in 1786. He worked at Christiansbrunn on the farm and in Bethlehem as a tanner.
John Warner, b. Aug. 5, 1758, in Sichem, Dutchess Co., N. Y.; d. in Bethlehem, Pa., 1797. He learned the carpenter's trade and worked at Gnadenhütten, Pa., and at Bethlehem.
165 *Ezra Warner*, b. Sept. 2, 1762; m. Maria Magdalena Laner.

83 ISAAC[4] WARNER, son of Ichabod[3] and Mary (Metcalf) Warner, born January 4, 1717 (Lebanon town record), or January 11, 1716 (family record). He resided in Windham, was a tavern-keeper and a man of some prominence as is shown by these records from Connecticut Colonial Records (10; 176, 463).

"Upon the memorial of Isaac Warner of Windham showing that on or about the 12th of November 1752 he had 3. £ 3 bills new tenor of this Colony and about forty sh. new tenor bills more, and that his pocket-book, in which were said bills, by accident fell into the fire and said bills were all consumed and burnt up" . . . The Assembly ordered the Treasurer of the Colony to pay him £ 11 in bills of this Colony new tenor.
"Isaac Warner declares that 3 men of Windham are suspected of having counterfeit bills in their possession & he is apptd. to pursue them and search for counterfeit money at the expense of Colony," February, 1756. The following May he returns a bill for £ 9 for his services.

Married October 11, 1739, recorded in Windham, **ANN DAVISON**. In 1760 she was granted a license to keep a tavern in Windham.

Children, recorded in Windham

Anne Warner, b. Jan. 19, 1741-2; d. Nov. 14, 1760.
166 *Matthew Warner*, b. June 28, 1743; m. Eunice Stoel.
Lucy Warner, b. June 12, 1748; m. in Windham, July 9, 1770, James Sawyer.
Isaac Warner, Jr., b. Apr. 20, 1750; joined the Windham Church in 1773.
Roswell Warner, b. Sept. 18, 1753; d. Apr. 15, 1754.
167 *Eunice Warner*, b. Nov. 3, 1756; m. John Bingham.
Andrew Warner, b. Oct. 6, 1758; died Jan. 20, 1778. He was a Corporal in the Connecticut Line, enlisted Feb. 17, 1777, 7th regiment, under Col. Elderkin of Windham, for three years. He had a powder horn that had been made for him and was handed down to the family of his nephew Andrew Warner, who was a teamster in the War of 1812. The horn was engraved with the words, "Andrew Warner His horn made at Cambridge Nov. 24. A. D. 1775." It bore a picture of the liberty pole and flag at Prospect Hill, a fort, gunboats, British and American soldiers, birds, flags and other emblems.

84 NATHANIEL⁴ WARNER, son of Ichabod³ and Mary (Metcalf) Warner, born February 18, 1722, recorded in Lebanon, Conn.; died April 12, 1807, recorded in Windham, Conn. He was recorded in the 1790 Census of Windham with a family of two males over 16, two males under 16, and seven females. He and his wife joined the church at Windham in 1750 or 1751. The family record is in the possession of George D. Wells of Windham, a descendant.

His will is on file in Windham, dated April 2, 1807, in which he called himself "stricken in years." To beloved wife Elizabeth improvement of one-half the real estate; to son Elnathan, all real estate with buildings; to daughter Elizabeth, wife of Eleazer Hibbard £50; to five children of daughter Huldah Fitch, £10; to two daughters Azubah and Tryphena, £10 each; son Elnathan, executor; witnesses, Zachariah Howes, David Howes, and Hezekiah Manning. The will was sworn to by the first two witnesses April 17, 1807, probated April 22, 1807. Receipts were signed by the following heirs: Elizabeth Warner, widow, Windham, July 3, 1807; Eleazer Hibbard and Elizabeth Hibbard, Windham, June 24, 1807, with Sarah Warner and Lydia Warner, jun\., witnesses; Tryphena Young, Windham, March 30, 1808; Azuba Maxwell, Windham, March 19, 1808; grandchild, Nath\ Fitch of Verona, N. Y., January 29, 1810; grandchild, Jesse Fitch Jun\. January 11, 1810 (no place given); grandchild, William Fitch, Windham, May 4, 1809, Lucy Warner witness; grandchild, Daniel Fitch, Windham, April 2, 1811. (Windham probate, 15:292, 551.)

Nathaniel Warner married in Windham, June 19, 1749, **ELIZABETH WEBB,** who died in Windham, November 27, 1812, in her 90th year.

Children, recorded in Windham

Samuel Warner, b. May 6, 1750; d. Nov. 6, 1754, buried in the Windham Cemetery.

Elizabeth Warner, b. Dec. 29, 1751; m. Eleazer Hebard or Hibbard of Windham.

168 *Elnathan Warner,* b. Nov. 1, 1753; m. (1) Lydia Beaumont, (2) Philena Dunham.

Huldah Warner, b. Aug. 28, 1756; m. in Windham, Apr. 29, 1779, Jesse Fitch. Children: Nathaniel, b. Apr. 14, 1780, in Windham, resided in Verona, N. Y., 1807; Jesse, Jr.; William; Daniel; Betsey.

Azubah Warner, b. July 27, 1758; m. in Windham, Apr. 15, 1779, Joshua Maxwell.

(Son), b. and d. June 1, 1761.

Tryphena Warner, b. Sept. 10, 1768; m. —— Young.

85 DR. TIMOTHY⁴ WARNER, son of Ichabod³ and Marv (Metcalf) Warner, born December 21, 1724, recorded in Lebanon, Conn.; died April 8, 1760, recorded in Windham, Conn., buried in old Cemetery in Scotland, Conn., where the following inscription is found on his tombstone:

> Here lies yᵉ Body
> of Dʳ Timothy
> Warner who died
> Suddenly by a Fall
> From a horse April
> 8ᵗʰ 1760 in yᵉ 36 Year
> of his Age.
> The Benevolence of
> his Temper his un
> wearied Application
> to Business & Exten
> five Ufefulnefs as a
> Phyfician Rendered
> his Perfon Amiable
> his life very benefici
> al & his death Great
> ly lamented.

He was appointed physician to the "army gone to Crown Point, October, 1755" (Conn. Col. Records, 10:444).

Documents pertaining to the settlement of his estate are found in the Windham Probate Records, 6:162, 7:117, 118. He owned buildings near the meeting house of the third society of Windham.

The inventory was taken May 9, 1760, by John and Hezekiah Manning, and Ichabod Warner, junʳ, and showed a valuation of £633–14–11, which was finally divided among the widow and heirs in 1766. Jonathan Rudd, John and Hezekiah Manning were the distributors, and property was set out to Mrs. Ireny Hibberd the widow and Relict of the aforesaid Deceasᵈ; to Jared, eldest son; to Hannah, eldest daughter; to daughter Ireney. David Ripley, William Ripley, and Nathan Hibberd signed as guardians of the last three respectively.

Dr. Timothy Warner married January 11, 1749-50, recorded in Windham, **IRENA RIPLEY,** born February 11, 1729, died February 24, 1804, daughter of David and Lydia (Carey) Ripley of Scotland, Conn. She was a descendant of William Ripley, the emigrant, of John² and Elizabeth (Hobart) Ripley, and of Joshua³ Ripley who married Hannah Bradford, the daughter of Deputy Governor William Bradford and the granddaughter of

Governor William Bradford. Irena Warner was received as a member of the Scotland Church in 1750; was administrator of her husband's estate, and married (2) as his second wife, December 4, 1764, Nathan Hebard, by whom she had three children, Timothy Warner, Elizabeth and Lydia. She married (3) Rev. James Cogswell, D.D., pastor of the Congregational Church in Scotland.

Children of Dr. Timothy and Irena (Ripley) Warner, births recorded in Windham

Hannah Warner, b. Nov. 23, 1751; m. in Windham, Nov. 5, 1772, Ensign Darius[6] Peck (descended from Henry[1] Peck, settler in New Haven, 1638, Benjamin[2] and Mary (Sperry) Peck, Benjamin[3] and Mary (———) Peck, Jonathan[4] and Bethia (Bingham) Peck. Darius Peck was born Mar. 14, 1749-50; d. 1804; m. (2) in Franklin, 1793, Mary Frances by whom he had a daughter Lucy, who m. Alfred A. Young. Children of Darius and Hannah (Warner) Peck, recorded in Norwich vital records: i. Bradford, b. Nov. 5, 1773. ii. Darius, Jr., b. Oct. 11, 1775. iii. John, b. May 6, 1778. iv. Joseph, b. Jan. 21, 1782.

Irena Warner, b. Nov. 30, 1753; m. Mar. 5, 1772, John Fitch of Norwich. Children, births recorded in Norwich: i. Rebeckah, b. Jan. 26, 1773. ii. John, b. Mar. 7, 1775. iii. Benjamin, b. June 10, 1777.

Jared (1) *Warner*, b. Sept. 10, 1754; d. Oct. 15, 1755, buried in the old cemetery in Scotland.

> "Jared son of Doctor Timothy Warner
> & Mrs. Ireney his wife he died
> Oct. ye 15 1755 ae 13 mo: 5 d."

169 *Jared* (2) *Warner*, b. Sept. 17, 1756; m. Mary Ripley.

Lydia Warner, b. Mar. 1, 1759; d. Dec. 6, 1764, buried in the old cemetery in Scotland.

> "Mrs. Lydia, dau.of Doct.Timothy
> Warner & Mrs.Ireney his wife
> She died Dec.6.1764 in 6th yr."

86 **RUTH[4] WARNER**, daughter of Ichabod[3] and Mary (Metcalf) Warner, born October 17, 1732, recorded in Lebanon, Conn.; died April 21, 1817.

Married in Windham, Nov. 15, 1761, **GIDEON BINGHAM**, born December 2, 1735, in Windham, died there March 19, 1791, son of Gideon and Mary (Cary) Bingham, and grandson of Deacon Eleazer Cary of Windham. He resided at what was later called Bingham's Mills, which he had purchased from his father-in-law who owned it as early as 1735. The mill and farm descended to his son Roger Bingham. The Bingham Genealogy contains an account of this family.

Children, recorded in Windham

(*Son*), b. and d. Oct. 7, 1762.

Oliver Bingham, b. Dec. 28, 1763; was a miller, resided at the Hollow in Mansfield, Conn.; m. Nov. 13, 1783, Lucy Moulton, daughter of James Moulton. She died Feb. 23, 1827. Children: i. James, b. in Windham, Nov. 28, 1784; d. Oct. 29, 1813. ii. Jesse, b. Apr. 15, 1786; resided in Mansfield; m. Maria W. (Barrows) Stowell, daughter of Stephen Barrows and widow of Warner Stowell. iii. Lucy, b. Jan. 13, 1788. iv. Polly, b. May 14, 1790; m. Joshua P. Barrows and had a family. v. Nabby, b. Dec. 30, 1792; m. Charles Arnold of Mansfield and had a family. vi. Ora (a son), b. Nov. 17, 1795; d. May 16, 1820.

Mary Bingham, b. Mar. 13, 1765; d. Mar. 3, 1776.

Hannah Bingham, b. Mar. 19, 1767; d. Aug. 1, 1855, not married.

Roger Bingham, b. June 23, 1768, in Windham; d. there Jan. 17, 1836. He owned and resided at his father's homestead known as Bingham's Mills. He was ordained as a Christian minister of a sect of reformed Abbe-ites and often preached in Windham and the vicinity. He married Sept. 1, 1814, Nancy Waldo, b. Oct. 7, 1784, d. Apr. 19, 1862, daughter of Zacheus and Esther (Stevens) Waldo (Waldo Genealogy). Children: i. Gideon, b. Sept. 20, 1815; d. in New Orleans, Dec. 13, 1850, not married; was graduated from Yale in 1842 and became a book-seller. ii. Waldo, b. May 3, 1817; m. (1) Mary Perkins, (2) Elizabeth Hartshorn Ladd, and had by the first wife, Josephine, who resided at Windham, not married, and Mary West, who d. young. iii. Samuel, b. Dec. 21, 1818; d. Jan. 5, 1887; resided at Windham Center and was cashier of the Windham Bank; m. Ann Robinson Cushman, and had children, Agnes, Annette, Herbert Cushman, May Louisa, Willie H., Wallace, Edward and Robert; the last two d. young. iv. Nancy Maria, b. Oct. 17, 1821, resided in Owego, N. Y.; m. Henry McCollum and had children. v. Lucy, b. Nov. 17, 1824; m. John M. Colcord of Boston and had children. vi. Sarah Jane, b. Dec. 22, 1826; m. George Lathrop; resided in Windham Center; had no children.

Lydia Bingham, b. Apr. 13, 1771; d. Nov. 15, 1842; m. as second wife, John Staniford, Jr. No children.

Eunice Bingham, b. Feb. 4, 1773; died at an advanced age, not married.

Lucy Bingham, b. Oct. 15, 1774; m. Captain Eliphalet Young.

Salomy Bingham, b. June 3, 1778; d. Aug. 11, 1809.

87 **JOHN[4] WARNER,** son of Ichabod[3] and Mary (Metcalf) Warner, born May 22, 1734, recorded in Lebanon, Conn., and also in Scotland parish records; baptized May 26, 1734 (Lebanon Church records); died June 7, 1773, aged 39 years, buried in old Cemetery, Scotland, Conn.

Married February 28, 1762 (Windham record, he of Windham), **PRISCILLA WOOD** of Sharon, Conn., who died December 20, 1833, aged about 92. She joined the Scotland Church in 1774, and was noted on the tax list of Scotland in 1781 with a small tax.

Children, first two births recorded in Windham, others from family records and from papers of Miss Ellen Learned in Conn. State Library

> *Timothy Warner*, b. Nov. 13, 1763; d. between Feb. 13, 1844, and June 14, 1856; resided in 1844 in Oppenheim, Fulton Co., N. Y. He was a Revolutionary soldier and the pension application gave the following data: Served 1 month in 1780 as private in Connecticut, names of officers not remembered; 5 months, 15 days, in 1781, under Capt. Vaughan; enlisted in Windham, Conn.; application made Feb. 13, 1844, but rejected for lack of proof of six months service as required by law then in force. On June 14, 1856, his son John stated that his father was dead. John Warner with his wife Nancy appears on the land records of Fulton County, N. Y., as making deeds in 1840 and 1842 to Arphaxed Loomis, Bingham Warner and John Robinson. Bingham Warner and wife Pamelia made deeds in the same county 1841-4. Timothy may also have had a daughter who m. ——— Deuslar.

170 *Mary Warner*, b. June 8, 1765; m. Elijah Barber.
171 *William Warner*, b. Jan. 13, 1768; m. Mary Trowbridge.
172 *Ichabod Warner*, b. Oct. 17, 1769; m. Hannah Collins.
173 *Rosamond Warner*, b. March 27, 1773; m. Ira Loomis.

> *John Warner*, said to have been a brother of William and b. after his father's death.

88 MOSES[4] WARNER, son of Jacob[3] and Mary (———) Warner, born in Hadley, Mass., September 30 or April, 1715; died in Amherst, Mass., May 3, 1772. He was one of the non-commissioned officers under Capt. Nathaniel Dwight of Belchertown on the expedition to Crown Point, 1755. With his brother Aaron he removed early to Amherst, among the first settlers there. He owned several pieces of land in Amherst and his name occurs frequently on the town records. He kept an inn for many years, as early as 1757, and as late as 1772. The introduction to the 1884 edition of the Amherst records by J. F. Jameson has this to say:

"The 'Inhabitants' are very amusing in the preference they exhibit for the schoolhouse near Landlord Warner's tavern as the place to which to adjourn their meetings. Doubtless the meeting-house was cold; and doubtless Landlord Warner knew how to warm the chilled voters."

Both he and his son were on record as opposed to the establishment of the Second Church of Amherst in 1773. His widow and brother Oliver were administrators of his estate, 1774, and April 12, 1797, his estate was divided between his widow, the children of Moses Warner, the younger, and Mary, wife of David Smith.

Married May 18, 1738(?) **MARY FIELD** of Hadley, born June 18, 1715, died 1796, daughter of John and Sarah (Coleman) Field,

according to one account, or the daughter of Zachariah and
Sarah (Clark) Field (History of the First Church of Amherst,
p. 107). John Field was a soldier in the Indian Wars. His wife
Sarah Coleman was one of the captives in Ashelon's raid in September, 1677, and was redeemed by Wait and Jennings in 1678.
A shoe worn on her homeward trip from Canada in 1678 is one
of the treasures of Deerfield Memorial Hall.

Children

Mary Warner, baptized May 18, 1738; m. David Smith. The date of
    her baptism is in History of Hadley the same as date of her parents'
    wedding; the error is probably in the former date.
174 *Moses Warner*, m. Sarah Selden.

89 JACOB[4] WARNER, 3d, son of Jacob[3] and Mary (———)
Warner, born in Hadley, Mass., November, 1716; died 1795.
He went to Amherst from Hadley after his brothers Moses and
Aaron, some time after 1745; was appointed on a committee to
issue warrants for precinct meetings, 1752, and was one of the
incorporators of the Second Parish in Amherst. He was surveyor in 1754, and at the first meeting of the district of Amherst,
March 19, 1759, was elected fence-viewer. Frequent mention of
his name occurs on the records of Amherst for the next few
years, and in 1788 he was on the list of land owners.

Married July 29, 1742, **ANN FOWLER.** The New Milford
Church record, p. 25, has this record, "Jacob Warner of Deerfield married Ann Fowler, July 29, 1742."

Children (given in Judd's History of Hadley)

Wareham Warner, records are rather uncertain, as there was a Ware-
    ham Warner living in the same locality who was a descendant of
    William Warner of Ipswich, Mass., an entirely different line. The
    following probably refer to this Wareham: served in the Revolu-
    tion 18 days in 1775 and three months in 1777, was one of the minute
    men at Ticonderoga; bought land from Jacob Warner, Jr., in
    Amherst, April 18, 1791; was in the 1790 census of Amherst with
    wife and one other in the family.
Jacob Warner, 4th, bapt. Dec. 15, 1745; was probably the Jacob of
    Amherst, who served in the Revolution; together with other young
    men was appointed hog reeve in 1772; was one of the incorporators
    of the Second Church in Amherst in 1773; sold land in Amherst to
    Wareham Warner in 1791; was mentioned in the 1800 Census of
    Amherst, one male and one female over 45, two females between 16
    and 26, and two females between 10 and 16. Married ——— Hulet
    of Belchertown.
Anna Warner, bapt. Feb. 23, 1752.

Abigail Warner, bapt. Oct. 13, 1754.
Esther Warner, bapt. June 1, 1760.
Reuben Warner, m. in Amherst, Nov. 18, 1787, Olive Payne.
Sarah Warner.

90 AARON[4] WARNER, son of Jacob[3], Jr., and Mary
(————) Warner, born in Hadley, Mass., March, 1717; died
in Amherst, Mass., about 1787. He was a blacksmith by trade
and settled in the third precinct of Hadley which was later the
town of Amherst. His name occurs frequently on the records
of the town beginning with his purchase of land in 1741. March
25, 1743, the town voted "to give Aaron Worner thirty shillings
to sweep the meeting Hous and to give a Signe when to go to
Meeting." Other town records show that the customary way
to give the sign in those days was to 'blow ye Kunk," and this
was doubtless Aaron Warner's method. He was on a committee
to give out warrants for precinct meetings, March 19, 1745, and
March 18, 1746; with his brother Moses was appointed to help
build the pound, November 3, 1746; was tithing man in 1766;
received a grant of land in 1770; signed a petition against the
building of a second church in 1773. His inventory was taken
December 6, 1787. His son David was administrator, and sons
Aaron, Noadiah and Jonathan, deceased, are mentioned.

Married (1) May 20, 1741 (Hadley town records), RUTH
SELDEN.

Married (2) ESTHER ————. In the Amherst town records of Lucy and Hannah, they are called daughters of Aaron
and Esther Warner.

Children, first two in Hadley town records

175 *Meribah Warner,* b. Feb. 23, 1742; m. Eli Colton.
    Ruth Warner, b. May 23, 1745.
    Aaron Warner, Jr., bapt. Jan. 10, 1748, in Hadley; Captain Aaron War-
    ner, Jr., d. Oct. 14, 1774, in his 27th year (tombstone in Amherst)
    or d. Oct. 12, 1776, aged 26 (History of Hadley); m. in Amherst,
    Hannah Dickinson, b. in Amherst, Jan. 22, 1749, daughter of Gideon
    and Hannah (Edwards) Dickinson. His heirs were mentioned as
    holders of a lot in Amherst in 1788, but no names are known.
    Lucy Warner, bapt. 1749, in Hadley; m. in Amherst, May 21, 1778, John
    (or Jesse, according to Amherst town records) Emerson of Wendell.
    They went to New Connecticut, Ohio, and he died in Ohio.
    Noadiah Warner, bapt. 1751, in Hadley.
    David (1) Warner, bapt. May 27, 1753; d. July 18, 1753.
176 *Hannah Warner,* bapt. June 30, 1754; m. Jeremiah Cady.
177 *David (2) Warner,* bapt. Sept., 1756; m. Mrs. Lucy Orchard.
178 *Jonathan Warner,* m. Margaret Elizabeth Sewall.

Elisha Warner, bapt. 1761, in Hadley; d. in Amherst, Dec. 10, 1823, buried in Amherst. He was a Revolutionary soldier. By his will of Mar. 16, 1815, probated Apr. 13, 1824, he left his property to his wife Sarah and to Sally Tilden, eldest daughter of Elisha Tilden. Married Sarah Peck, who died Sept. 13, 1825, aged 72, buried in Amherst, daughter of Major Nathaniel and Mary (Mitchel) Peck. They were recorded in the 1800 census of Amherst, a man and a woman between 26 and 45, and a boy between 10 and 16 in the family. They had no children.

91 JONATHAN[4] WARNER, son of Jacob[3], Jr., and Mary (——————) Warner, born in Hadley, Mass., July 10, 1718; died December 23, 1791, in Hadley. In 1770 one Jonathan Warner was a tenant of plot 45, Hadley, formerly belonging to the Dickinson family. His son Noadiah was administrator of his estate, March 19, 1792.

Married June 20, 1745, **MARY GRAVES,** born December 23, 1720, daughter of Benjamin and Mary[3] (Warner) Graves of Sunderland, Mass.; see number 43.

Children

William Warner, name given in list of children in History of Hadley but not in the list in History of Sunderland. One William P. Warner was a tenant of plot 45, Hadley, in 1807.
179 *Lemuel Warner,* b. about 1747; m. (1) Dorothy Phelps, (2) Mrs. Elizabeth Stone, (3) Martha H. Allen.
180 *Noadiah Warner,* b. 1749; m. Martha Hunt.
     (Daughter), b. Jan. 29, 1752; d. Aug. 16, 1752.
     Lucy Warner, b. July 4, 1754; d. May 14, 1778, in Hadley.

92 ORANGE[4] WARNER, son of Jacob[3] and Mary (——————) Warner, born in Hadley, Mass., October 5, 1720; died there July 7, 1809, buried in Hadley. He was a maltster and occupied the property of his great-grandfather Andrew Warner, which descended to a grandson named Seymour. His family is noted in the Census of 1790 and that of 1800, and his name is found on deeds of 1776 to 1800. In 1795 he gave property to his children, Elizabeth Seymour, Martha Crafts, and Elihu Warner.

Married (1) about 1749, **ELIZABETH GRAVES** of Sunderland, Mass., daughter of Benjamin and Mary[3] (Warner) Graves; see number 43. She died February 25, 1795, in her 72d year, buried in Hadley.

Married (2) November 18, 1795 (Hadley records) **Mrs. LYDIA COLEMAN** of Whately. Other records have given her as Lydia Wait of South Hadley. She died November 23, 1804, aged 76 years, buried in Hadley.

Children by first wife, born in Hadley

William Warner, b. Oct. 9, 1750; d. Apr. 24, 1751.

(Daughter), b. and d. Sept. 25, 1752 (or Sept. 16, Hadley records).

Elizabeth Warner, b. Dec. 29, 1753; m. in Hadley, Apr. 27, 1780, Nathaniel Seymour. In 1795 her father gave her the homelot on which she was then residing. Children, b. in Hadley: i. Mary, b. Nov. 11, 1780. ii. William, b. Aug. 19, 1782. iii. Samuel, b. Feb. 3, 1785. iv. Horace, b. Jan. 22, 1787. v. Fanny, b. July 17, 1789. vi. Nathan, b. Mar. 31, 1792. vii. Henry, b. Mar. 25, 1797.

181 *Martha Warner,* b. Sept. 17 or 11, 1756; m. John Crafts.

182 *Elihu Warner,* b. Oct. 29, 1758; m. Elizabeth Freeman.

93 GIDEON[4] **WARNER,** son of Jacob[3], Jr., and Mary (———) Warner, born in Hadley, Mass., May 15, 1721; died there about 1789. He settled in Haddam, Conn., about 1752, resided also in Durham, Conn., for a time and owned property in East Haddam which he sold August 7, 1771, styling himself Gideon of Hadley. His estate was inventoried by Lemuel Warner, January 14, 1789, in Hadley, was found insolvent and settled on the basis of five-eights to the pound.

Married (1) 1748, **MARY PUNDERSON** or **PARSONS** of Durham.

Probably married (2) in 1760, **Mrs. FREELOVE STOW,** who joined the church in Durham, September 5, 1762.

Children, probably all by first wife

183 *Roxelana Warner;* m. (1) David White, (2) Joseph Crafts.

Olive Warner, was mentioned in the will of her uncle Oliver Warner.

Gideon Warner, Jr., bapt. in Durham, Conn., Dec. 1, 1754; was mentioned in the will of his uncle Oliver in 1779; is said to have removed to Windsor, Vt.

94 OLIVER[4] **WARNER,** son of John[3] and Mercy (Curtis) Warner, born in New Milford, Conn., October 12, 1729; died there December 21, 1814, buried in Gallows Hill Cemetery. He settled on the farm given him by his father on Wood Creek Hill in the southern part of the town of New Milford, and was a man of influence and a successful farmer. With his wife he owned the covenant at the New Milford Church, December 17, 1752; in 1772 was on a committee to arrange for draining land so as to prevent the overflow of Wood Creek; in 1776 was on the Committee of Inspection and Correspondence; was Deputy for New Milford in May, 1777; was noted in the Census of 1790, and on church and town records at frequent intervals. His will, dated November 29, 1800, was probated April 6, 1814. The heirs were: son Reuben; daughter Lucy Dirkee, deceased, and her heirs, **Anna** and Sally Bostwick (or Brockway), also her last husband, Nathaniel Dirkee, and children by him; daughters Tryphena Mygatt, Mabel Carrington, Prudence Couch, and Tamar Beach. Property was distributed November 23, 1818, to the heirs of Tryphena and Mabel Carrington.

Married in New Milford, October 16, 1751, **LOIS RUGGLES,** born in New Haven, Conn., April 2, 1727, died October 14, 1781, daughter of Joseph and Rachel (Toll or Tolls) Ruggles, who later resided in New Milford and Brookfield, Conn. Joseph Ruggles was a Deacon of the Separate Congregational Church of New Haven, and later of the Congregational Church of Brookfield. He was son of the Rev. Benjamin and Mercy (————) Ruggles of Suffield; was a member of the Committee of Inspection; fifer in the Connecticut militia; captain.

Children, recorded in New Milford

Lucy Warner, b. Sept. 17, 1752; d. Aug. 22, 1799; m. (1) Feb. 26, 1771, Ichabod Bostwick, b. in New Milford, Dec. 13, 1741, d. in the Provincial Army at Kingsbridge, New York, Sept. 15, 1776, son of Nathaniel and Esther (Hitchcock) Bostwick; m. (2) Nathaniel Dirkee, by whom she had children, mentioned, but not by name, in her father's will of 1800. By her first husband, Ichabod Bostwick, she had children: i. Lois Ann, b. Jan. 9, 1772. ii. Sally, b. Oct. 12, 1773; d. Oct. 27, 1841; m. June 13, 1790, Beman Brockway, b. Jan. 23, 1763, in Lyme, Conn., son of Gideon and Lois (Beman) Brockway, d. 1814, in Lysander, N. Y., where he had settled, had three children, Augustus Frederick, b. May 11, 1791, d. Oct. 3, 1793, Sally M., b. Sept. 15, 1793, d. July 2, 1794, and Beman Bostwick, b. Sept. 22, 1797, d. Oct. 15, 1807. iii. Oliver, b. Feb. 17, 1776; d. Feb. 18, 1776.

Tryphena Warner, b. Dec. 14, 1753; d. in Danbury, Conn., June 16, 1815, buried there; m. (1) Apr. 5, 1775, Benjamin Starr Mygatt, b. 1746, d. in New Milford, Feb. 6, 1794, buried in old Bridgewater Cemetery, son of Joseph, 3d, and Elizabeth (Starr) Mygatt; m. (2) July 19, 1802, Dr. Daniel Noble Carrington, b. March 8, 1759, d. June 5, 1835, buried in Danbury, son of Dr. John and Susannah (Noble) Carrington of Danbury. He was a physician in Danbury, and had married (1) Tryphena's sister Mabel; see below. He m. (3) Olive Cook, widow of Dr. Joseph Trowbridge. Children of Benjamin S. and Tryphena (Warner) Mygatt: i. Augustin, b. April 6, 1776; m. Fanny Dickerson of New Milford, and had two children, George W., b. Jan. 15, 1805, was an architect in Milwaukee, and Mary Rebecca, b. Feb. 15, 1807, m. Edwin Palmer of Painesville, Ohio. ii. Rebecca (1), b. Dec. 22, 1777; d. of smallpox, March 15, 1778. iii. Sarah, b. May 16, 1779; m. Isaac Hayes of Unadilla, N. Y. iv. Rebecca (2), b. May 7, 1787, m. Curtis Clark of Danbury.

Mabel Warner, b. Sept. 30, 1756; d. May 3, 1801; m. Oct. 4, 1781, Dr. Daniel Noble Carrington, who m. (2) her sister Tryphena; see above. Children: Polly; John Warner; James Morton; Lucy; Mabel. All these children were baptized June 13, 1802 (New Milford Church records).

184 *Reuben Warner,* b. May 23, 1759; m. Eunice Carrington.
Prudence Warner, b. Aug. 28, 1761; m. before 1800, —— Couch.
Tamar Warner, b. July 20, 1764; m. before 1800 —— Beach.

95 LEMUEL⁴ WARNER, son of John³ and Mercy (Curtis) Warner, born in New Milford, Conn., September 6, 1731; died there February 20, 1814, buried in Gallows Hill Cemetery. He settled on Wood Creek Hill on the farm given him by his father. In May, 1772, he was one of five Commissioners of sewers to arrange for the draining of land in New Milford to prevent the overflow of Wood Creek (Conn. Public Records, vol. 13, 661). He was recorded in the 1790 Census of New Milford and is also mentioned in church records. His son-in-law Joshua Knapp was appointed his administrator, March 14, 1814, and the heirs were: Lodemia Knapp, a daughter; David, Charles H. and Lemuel W. Ruggles, sons of his daughter Mercy Ruggles; Phebe, wife of Rev. Peter Starr (New Milford probate records, vol. 7, p. 115).

Married February 15, 1758, in New Milford, **SARAH GAYLORD,** born September 13, 1733, died December 23, 1810, daughter of Aaron and Phebe (Smith) Gaylord. She is buried in Gallows Hill Cemetery.

Children, born in New Milford

Phebe Warner, b. Nov. 14, 1758; d. Mar. 3, 1832; m. (1) May 13, 1781, Rev. John Stevens; m. (2) Oct. 24, 1810, Rev. Peter Starr, b. in Ridgefield, Conn., Sept., 1744, son of Samuel and Abigail (Dibble) Starr. He was a graduate of Yale College in 1764 and became a member of the Yale Corporation. He was pastor of the church in Warren, Litchfield County, Conn., for 57 years. His first wife was Sarah Robbins, who died July 17, 1807, and his children were by this first wife.

Mercy Warner, b. Sept. 22, 1761; d. before Mar. 14, 1814; m. Joseph Ruggles, a judge in New Milford. Children: i. David, b. 1783. ii. Charles Hermon, b. Jan., 1789. iii. Lemuel W., d. young. These children were mentioned in the distribution of their grandfather Warner's estate.

Lodemia Warner, b. July 27, 1765; d. in Cherokee, Ohio, May 28, 1845; m. in New Milford, Conn., Oct. 26, 1785, Joshua Knapp, Jr., b. in Danbury Conn., May 6, 1762, d. in Sherburne, N. Y., 1829. Children: i. Archesa Warner, b. Sept. 10, 1786, m. Betsey —— and had a child who d. in New Milford, Apr. 22, 1812, aged one year. ii. Levi Philetus, b. Mar. 10, 1789; m. Aug. 25, 1808, Ellis Brooks. iii. Edwin Gavin, b. Aug. 24, 1795; m. Nov. 29, 1815, Marietta Ferris and had children, b. in Cairo, N. Y., Edwin Joshua, b. Dec. 22, 1817, and Urania Cordelia, b. Apr. 18, 1820. iv. Sally Julia, b. Dec. 31, 1800; m. Mar. 25, 1818, Samuel Horace⁶ Warner, b. 1795, son of Orange⁵ Warner; see number 330.

10

96 PRUDENCE[4] WARNER, daughter of John[3] and Mercy (Curtis) Warner, born in New Milford, Conn., December 3, 1733; died in Hinesburgh, Vt., October 4, 1801.

Married in New Milford, Nov. 27, 1754, ISAAC BOSTWICK, born in New Milford, September 6, 1730, died in Hinesburgh, Vt., April 21, 1808, son of Lemuel and Ann (Jackson) Bostwick. He was appointed ensign in the Second or "South End" Company of Militia in New Milford, May, 1769, and became captain in 1770. This company became the 7th Company, 7th Regiment of Connecticut in the Revolution and he was commissioned captain, July 6, 1775. The regiment assisted in fortifying New York City and was at the battles of White Plains and Trenton. Captain Bostwick was one of the advance guard who crossed the Delaware on Christmas night, 1776, and received honorable discharge, December 31, 1776. He also served as captain of a company in the Danbury alarm, April, 1777. He was part owner in a mill property in Lanesville on the Great Falls and was an influential man in the town. He was town treasurer and state collector of taxes in New Milford. He joined his children in Hinesburgh, Vt., late in life. A more complete account of this family is found in the Bostwick Genealogy.

Children, born in New Milford

Lemuel (1) *Bostwick,* b. Aug. 27, 1755; d. Sept. 12, 1757.

Reuben Bostwick (twin), b. May 21, 1757; d. in Burlington, Vt., Oct. 14, 1842; was a Revolutionary soldier; m. in New Milford, Oct. 18, 1780, Mary B. Allen, who d. in 1826. Children: i. James, b. May 7, 1781; m. three times and had three children by the first wife. ii. Betsey, b. 1782; d. 1863, not married. iii. (Daughter), d. in infancy.

Prudence (1) *Bostwick* (twin), b. May 21, 1757; d. young.

Lemuel (2) *Bostwick,* b. Dec. 27, 1758; d. Oct. 17, 1819; removed to Hinesburgh, Vt., in 1787, later to Mechanicsville and Pine Brook, Vt., and in 1816, to New York State; was town clerk and representative from Hinesburgh; m. in New Milford, Conn., June 27, 1784, Polly Trail, who was born July 10, 1764. Children: i. Sally Maria, b. Mar. 23, 1786; m. (1) Avery Huntington, (2) ————. ii. George Trail, b. July 13, 1792; m. Charlotte Hamilton and had children. iii. Isaac Henry, b. Aug. 27, 1796; d. not married. iv. Prudence, b. July 15, 1799; m. Gideon Newton. v. Polly, b. Jan. 27, 1803; m. ———— Kellogg.

Solomon Bostwick, b. Aug. 8, 1762; d. at sea, 1797 or 8; m. at New Milford, 1793, Mary Smith, b. in Amherst, Mass., d. in Bernardstown, Mass., 1827. Child: Solomon, Jr., b. Dec. 30, 1795; m. (1) June 11, 1821, Minnie G. Colony, (2) Oct. 12, 1823, Sallie C. Thurber.

Prudence (2) *Bostwick,* b. Nov. 30, 1764; d. in New Milford, Nov. 22, 1841; m. in New Milford, 1784, Benoni Stebbins Sanford, b. in New Milford, Mar. 5, 1762, d. there Oct. 24, 1846, son of Zechariah and Rachel (Gould) Sanford. Children: i. Isaac, b. Feb. 9, 1785; m. Sept. 11, 1806, Betsey Northrop. ii. Gould, b. Oct. 31, 1786; m. ———— Sheldon. iii. Sarah, b. Mar. 21, 1788; m. July 19, 1812, Elijah Bennett.

97 **MARTIN**[4] **WARNER**, son of John[3] and Mercy (Curtis) Warner, born in New Milford, Conn., January 11, 1735; died in Brookfield, July 15, 1807, buried in Gallows Hill Cemetery, New Milford. Martin Warner gave to each of his sons a hundred acres of land and built each one a house. To each of his daughters he gave fifty acres of land. The house which he built for himself still stands on the road leading from the upper Longmeadow road to the Housatonic River, in Brookfield, Conn. The south part of the house was the original home and the north part was added as a home for his son Lemuel. Lemuel's son Solomon lived and died in this house. Benjamin Ruggles Warner's house stood on the same road near the river and Clarissa Warner Wildman's house was in sight of that.

Martin Warner was a private in the 10th Company of Col. David Wooster's 3d Regiment, Connecticut Levy, in 1759, also did military service in 1751, at Fort William Henry, and in 1758. He was ensign in a battalion raised in the state, May, 1777, and ensign of the alarm list, 10th Company, 16th Regiment, May, 1777 (Conn. State Records, vol. 1, 256, 276). His name occurs frequently in town proceedings and also in land records. In 1780 he was selectman of New Milford and on March 13, 1780, he was appointed on the Committee of Inspection for provisions in the War of the Revolution. He was on a committee to fix a place for and the dimensions of the schoolhouse, December 24, 1787. He was a farmer and was known as "Lieutenant," when he was first selectman elected at the first town meeting of the newly formed town of Brookfield, June 9, 1788.

Married **MARY RUGGLES**, born about 1730; died December 16, 1819, in her 89th year, buried in Gallows Hill Cemetery.

Children of Martin and Mary (Ruggles) Warner

185 *Solomon Warner*, b. about 1761; m. Rachel Ruggles.
186 *Benjamin Ruggles Warner*, b. Sept. 28, 1766; m. (1) Mercy Ruggles, (2) Hannah Nichols.
     Martin Warner, Jr., is said to have removed to Wood County, Ohio. He may be the Martin Warner who resided in Rose, N. Y., for a time and was an elder in the Presbyterian Church. Married Sally Landers, daughter of Joseph and Zeruiah[6] (Warner) Landers; see number 185.
     Philena Warner, m. ———— Somers.
     Mary Warner, m. ———— Brooks, son of the first minister in Brookfield, Conn.
     Clarissa Warner, m. Ar Wildman or Wellman.
187 *Lemuel Warner*, m. Martha Baldwin.

98 **ELIZUR**[4] **WARNER**, son of John[3] and Mercy (Curtis) Warner, born in New Milford, Conn., December 17, 1737; died

there July 23, 1806, buried in Gallows Hill Cemetery. With his wife, he owned the covenant at the New Milford Church September 7, 1764; in 1772 he was one of the committee appointed by the Congregational Church to converse with those who had withdrawn to form an Episcopal Church and to learn their reasons; was on committee to assist the pastor in examining persons wishing to renew their covenant with the church, 1779; was a deacon of the Congregational Church after 1792; in 1797 was one of the seven New Milford signers of a paper upholding the preaching of the Rev. Stanley Griswold, at the time of his trial, "not at that time seven men in New Milford more capable of judging in such matters as these; all of them advanced in years." He was early a member of a militia company; was lieutenant in the 2d New Milford company, May, 1770, and also in a company that served from February 1, 1776, for two months and twenty-three days; captain in 8th Company, 3d Regiment, May, 1776; captain in the 7th Connecticut Regiment, January, 1777, and resigned September 1, 1777; was on the committee of inspection and correspondence, 1778; on committee of inspection of provisions, March 13, 1780. He settled in New Milford on the farm given him by his father, just below the homestead farm. See also many references in Orcutt's History of New Milford regarding this family.

Married in New Milford, October 26, 1762, **MARY WELCH,** born 1740, died October 21, 1815, aged 75, buried in Gallows Hill Cemetery.

Children

188 *Amaryllis* (or *Amanda S.*) *Warner,* b. Aug. 8, 1763; m. Homer Boardman.

Elizur Warner, Jr., b. Mar. 10, 1770, in New Milford; d. there May 6, 1842, buried in Gallows Hill Cemetery. He was made Captain in the 37th Regiment of Infantry, Apr. 30, 1813, honorably discharged, June 15, 1815 (Journal of the Executive Proceedings of the U. S. Senate, 1813, p. 413). After the war he received an appointment under the government for several years at the armory in Springfield, Mass. The administration of his estate was in 1837, showed a valuation of $1,500, which was divided among the following: sister Amaryllis Boardman; nephew, Rev. Charles A. Boardman of Hudson, Ohio; nieces, Orinda H. Vanderburgh of New York, Laura A. Lane, wife of Rev. Aaron D. Lane of Waterloo, N. Y., and Harriet M. Swift of Phelps, N. Y., wife of Reuben Swift, Esq.

Oliver Warner, b. July 18, 1774; d. in Albany, N. Y., June 4, 1796.

99 **JOHN⁴ WARNER, JR.,** son of John³ and Mercy (Curtis) Warner, born in New Milford, Conn., October 27, 1739; died there March 11, 1800, buried in Gallows Hill Cemetery. He

inherited the homestead farm of his father in New Milford. He and his wife owned the covenant at the church there in July, 1765, and she was baptized at that time. His will, made March 14, 1799, was probated March 22, 1800, mentions his wife Eunice, son John, Jr., daughters Annice Stevens, Lucina Keeler, Anne Bostwick, Hannah Stevens, and Lois Bostwick. Annice was to receive a larger share than the other daughters "on account of her long continuance in my service." His son John was executor and Elizur Warner and Reuben Warner, Jr., were witnesses. The inventory shows a long list of furniture and clothing valued at about £125, and real estate valued at £475. (New Milford probate records, vol. 3, p. 474.) The family is listed in the Census of 1790 in New Milford.

Married (1) in New Milford, July 6, 1763, HANNAH WESTOVER, born 1739, died in New Milford, January 10, 1775, in her 36th year, buried in Gallows Hill Cemetery.

Married (2) May 20, 1778, EUNICE WALLER of New Milford, who died May 5, 1799, in her 62d year, buried in Gallows Hill Cemetery.

Children, born in New Milford

189 *John Warner, 3d*, b. Apr. 10 or 18, 1764; m. Abigail Stevens.
190 *Annice Warner*, b. Nov., 1766; m. Aden Stevens.
191 *Lucina Warner*, b. 1767; m. Elisha Keeler.
    Amy or *Anne Warner*, m. Reuben Bostwick. She is mentioned in her father's will.
192 *Hannah Warner*, b. 1770; m. Nathan Stevens.
193 *Lois Warner*, m. Esbon Bostwick.

100 ASA[4] WARNER, son of John[3] and Mercy (Curtis) Warner, born in New Milford, Conn., October 1, 1743; died there December 13, 1819, buried in Gallows Hill Cemetery. He settled on a farm given him by his father, just below his own homestead. He was killed in an accident caused by his horses running away, the pole fell and threw him out of the wagon. His will, dated May 5' 1813, was presented for probate December 20, 1819, by Captain Elizur Warner. It mentioned his wife Eunice; children of his deceased eldest daughter, Anna Picket; children of his deceased daughters, Thalia Blackney and Tryphena Merwin; other daughters. Distribution was made to the following: Apphia Ruggles, wife of John Ruggles; Urania Merwin, wife of Samuel Merwin; Huldah Wheeler; children of Anna Picket, wife of Daniel A. Picket; children of Thalia Blackney, wife of Clark Blackney; children of Tryphena Merwin, wife of Orange Merwin.

Married in New Milford, December 29, 1768, **EUNICE CAMP,** born 1749, died February 12, 1818, aged 69, buried in Gallows Hill Cemetery. She was an early member of the church in New Milford, and, with her husband, owned the covenant March 11, 1770.

Children, born in New Milford

Anna Warner, b. Oct. 20, 1769; d. before May 5, 1813; m. Daniel A. Picket. Children: Oliver; Asa.

Thalia Warner, b. Mar. 24, 1772; d. before May 5, 1813; m. Oct. 10, 1793, Clark Blackney. Had children.

Apphia Warner, b. May 21, 1774; m. Sept., 1792, in New Milford, John Ruggles.

Urania Warner, bapt. May 19, 1776; m. Samuel Merwin.

Huldah Warner, m. ———— Wheeler; resided near Trumbull, Conn.

Tryphena Warner, b. May 18, 1778; d. May 13, 1808; m. in New Milford, Apr. 7, 1800, Orange Merwin, b. Apr. 7, 1777, d. Sept. 4, 1853, buried in New Milford, son of David and Tamesin (Comstock) Merwin. He was a farmer, settled in Merryall; was member of Congress, 1825-9; "by his public popular influence did his native town much honor"; m. (2) Lydia S. Bostwick, by whom he had three children, Harriet, d. young, Charlotte, and Horace. Children of Tryphena Warner: i. Caroline, b. 1801; d. Jan. 20, 1824. ii. Henry, b. July 3, 1803; d. Apr. 3, 1880. iii. Tryphena, b. 1805.

101   ORANGE[4] WARNER, son of John[3] and Mercy (Curtis) Warner, born in New Milford, Conn., January 18, 1745-6; died March 10, 1831, buried in Gallows Hill Cemetery. He settled in New Milford, on a farm given him by his father, now known as the Wright Place. With his wife he owned the covenant February 15th, 1767.

Married in New Milford, December 5, 1765, **A B I G A I L PRINDLE,** born 1745, died March 31, 1830, aged 86, buried in Gallows Hill Cemetery, daughter of Samuel Prindle of Sharon, Conn.

Children, born in New Milford

194   *Curtis Warner,* b. July 14, 1766; m. Eunice Hull.

195   *David Warner,* b. Jan. 7, 1768; m. Annis Noble.

196   *Orange Warner, Jr.,* b. Apr. 13, 1770; m. Lucy Sanford.

197   *Cyrus Warner,* b. Jan. 6, 1773; m. (1) Polly Weller, (2) Hannah Peck.

Chloe Warner, b. June 25, 1774; d. not married.

Abigail Warner, b. Nov. 9, 1778; m. in New Milford, Jan. 9, 1797, Isaac Briggs. Children: i. Harmon, m. a daughter of Peter Nichols; moved to Pennsylvania; had several children. ii. Homer, m. ———— Hollister; had four sons and three daughters. iii. Henry Prince, m. Polly[6] Warner, daughter of Orange[5] Warner, Jr. (see number 196); had one child who d. in infancy. iv. Sally, m. Martin Lee; had two sons and two daughters. v. Charles, m. Minerva Baldwin; had no children. vi. Garry, settled in Dexter, Mich., m. and had one child. vii. James, m. and d. while still a young man; had one son.

102 **MERCY⁴ WARNER,** daughter of John³ and Mercy (Curtis) Warner, born in New Milford, Conn., December 25, 1747; died November 7, 1776.

Married in New Milford, November 6, 1766, **JOHN MER-WIN,** born in New Milford, August 24, 1744, died May 22, 1826, son of David and Mary (Noble) Merwin. He married (2) December 31, 1777, Mrs. Ruth Gaylord (by whom he had children, Jonathan, Hannah, Betsey, Lois, Daniel and Homer) and married (3) March 2, 1818, Mrs. Sarah Dibble.

Children of John and Mercy (Warner) Merwin, born in New Milford

Mercy Merwin, b. Aug. 9, 1767.
Clarina Merwin, b. Feb. 17, 1769.
Onor Merwin, b. June 16, 1771; m. Truman Stone, Aug. 8, 1799 (Orcutt's History of New Milford), but New Milford town records say, "and the s^d Onor was married to Truman Stone—Deceased on ye 8th day of August 1799."
Mary Merwin, b. Dec. 12, 1772; d. Oct., 1776.
John Warner Merwin, b. Sept. 16, 1774; m. Feb. 18, 1796, Esther Gaylord.
Ichabod Merwin, b. July, 1776; d. of smallpox, Mar., 1778.

103 **ELIZABETH⁴ WARNER,** daughter of Joseph³ and Sarah (Bartlett) Warner, born in New Milford, Conn., July 28, 1739; died in Hinesburgh, Vt., March 13, 1811.

Married in New Milford, February 25, 1761, **ISRAEL BALD-WIN,** born in New Milford, March 19, 1736-7, died March 16, 1778, "of small pox and is buried in one corner of the cemetery by himself as if his grave was infectious." He was the son of Captain Theophilus and Jerusha (Beecher) Baldwin. His father was appointed captain of the company or trainband in New Milford by the Assembly in 1738 and was member of the Assembly from 1735 to 1741. Israel Baldwin is said to have been in the Revolution, and was probably the Lieutenant of Col. Silliman's Regiment, appointed June 14, '1776' to be marched directly to New York and join the Continental Army. Israel and Elizabeth Baldwin joined the church in New Milford, July 4, 1762. Further records of this family will be found in the Baldwin Genealogy.

Children, births recorded in New Milford

Pamelia (1) *Baldwin,* b. Oct. 4, 1761; d. July 6, 1762.
Daniel (1) *Baldwin,* b. Apr. 18, 1763; d. Sept. 15, 1766.
Esmond Baldwin, b. July 9 (?), 1765; d. Sept. 28, 1766.
Pamelia (2) *Baldwin,* b. July 2, 1767; d. Sept. 28, 1867; m. (1) May 14, 1787, Reuben Gillett and settled in Nicholsville, N. Y.; (2) Joseph

Stearns of Nicholsville. Children, by first husband: Elizabeth War-
ner; Daniel Baldwin; Luthena Hart; Rhoda Merrill; Ursula Clark;
Peramah Baldwin; Sally Maria; Israel Jackson; Annah Morinda;
Aminta Annise; Chidelsa Silva.

Daniel (2) Baldwin, b. Nov. 8, 1769; d. 1781.

Annis Baldwin, b. Apr. 22, 1772; d. May 3, 1824; resided in Bristol,
Conn., and, after about 1790, in Hinesburgh, Vt.; m. Nov. 24, 1791,
Milton Clark, b. Mar. 14, 1767, d. Aug. 1, 1822. Children: Edmund
Baldwin; Orange Baldwin; Jude; Apphia; Ralsey; Aurilla M.

Edmond Baldwin, b. July 6, 1774; removed to Hinesburgh, Vt., where
he was justice of the peace and representative from 1814 to 1816;
m. Mar. 10, 1795, Susannah Howe of New Milford. Children: i.
Laura, m. Truman Hall. ii. Frederick Warner, m. (1) Amanda
Bostwick, (2) Lucy E. Stanley, (3) Sarah B. Bostwick. iii. Anny
or Amy, b. Dec. 12, 1799; d. in Coldwater, Mich., Mar. 12, 1870; m.
Burr D. Gray. iv. William Stone, m. Sophia Bartlet. v. Harley
McEwen, m. Eliza Sherman. vi. Edmond, m. Polly Ann Alden. vii.
Milton Alonzo. viii. Orlo Judson, m. Polly Ann Sherman. ix.
(Daughter), d. young.

Orange Baldwin, b. Nov. 15, 1776; removed to Hinesburgh, Vt.; m.
Betsey A. Gorham of New Milford, b. Nov. 7, 1776. Children: i.
Israel, m. Harriet ———. ii. Daniel G. iii. Parmelia, m. Charles
Hall. iv. Horace, m. Sarah J. Heath. v. George, m. Almira J. Keith.

FIFTH GENERATION

104 HEZEKIAH[5] WARNER, son of John[4], Jr., and Mary (Wilcox) Warner, born in Middletown, Conn., December 24, 1736; died there September 25, 1773, buried in Westfield. He was a farmer and owned property in Westfield Society, Middletown (Middletown deeds, 36:117, etc.). He was appointed lieutenant of the 10th Company, 6th Regiment or trainband, October, 1770 (Connecticut public records, 13:378). The inventory of his estate amounted to over a thousand pounds and the distribution was made April 6, 1775, to the following heirs: widow Lois; oldest son, John; second son, Hezekiah; sons Ebenezer and Junia; eldest daughter, Huldah, a minor, to whom Timothy Clark was appointed guardian, October 3, 1774; second daughter, Mary; daughters Submit and Lois. The widow was appointed guardian to Ebenezer, Hezekiah, Junia, Submit and Lois, May 8, 1775. John Warner was appointed guardian to Hezekiah, 1783. (Middletown probate records, 3:159, etc.)

Married February 8, 1759 (Wallingford-Meriden records), LOIS (or LOIZA) PENFIELD of Wallingford, who died before July 31, 1815. Her name is found on the probate records of Middletown at the settlement of her husband's estate, and in connection with a settlement made by her children after her second marriage to John Higby of Ballstown. On November 17, 1814, they guaranteed to pay her $35.00 a year during her lifetime. This agreement was signed by Huldah Clark, Mary Tryon, Lois Wilcox, Hezekiah, Ebenezer and Junia Warner, and representatives of John Warner and Submit Bartlett, deceased. (Middletown deeds, 42:405.) Her estate was distributed July 31, 1815, to the following: Huldah Clark, wife of Michael Clark; heirs of John Warner, deceased; Mary Tryon, wife of Josiah Tryon; heirs of Submit Bartlett, deceased, wife of John Bartlett; Lois Wilcox, wife of Elijah Wilcox.

Children of Hezekiah and Lois (Penfield) Warner, births recorded in Middletown, Conn.

Huldah Warner, b. Nov. 9, 1759; was living in 1815; m. Apr. 1, 1781, Michael Clark. Children: i. Mary, b. July 20, 1782. ii. Rebekah, b. Apr. 3, 1784. The births of these two children are recorded in Middletown.

198 *John Warner*, b. Apr. 17, 1761; m. (1) Patience Hall, (2) Polly Plumb, (3) Lament ———

Mary Warner, b. Jan. 30, 1763; was living in 1815; m. Josiah Tryon.

199 *Lois Warner*, b. Nov. 9, 1764; m. Elijah Wilcox.
200 *Hezekiah Warner, Jr.*, b. Aug. 25, 1766; m. Lucy Stocking.
201 *Ebenezer Warner*, b. July 4, 1768; m. (1) Mary Gaylord, (2) Katherine Denison.
      Submit Warner, b. Nov. 15, 1770; m. John Bartlett and died before 1815, leaving heirs.
202 *Junia Warner*, b. Feb. 1, 1773; m. (1) Elizabeth Wilcox, (2) Mrs. Parthenia (Raymond) Merry.

105 ELIPHAZ[5] WARNER, son of Jabez[4] and Hannah[4] (Warner) Warner, born in Middletown, Conn., September 1, 1742 (town records); died in Sandgate, Vt., March 12, 1816. He removed with his father to Judea, Conn., 1754, and to Sandgate, Vt., 1776. He was a soldier in Col. G. Warren's Regiment, Capt. Gideon Ormsby, June 5 to July 6, 1778; Capt. Lemuel Bradley's Company, August 6 to 9, 1781; Capt. Richard Hurd's Company, Col. Ira Allen's Regiment, October 20, 21, 1781.
Married **MERCY DRINKWATER.**

Children

203 *William Warner*, b. Nov. 12, 1770; m. (1) Lucy Coan, (2) ————— (3) —————.
204 *John Warner*, b. Dec., 1772; m. Mary De Witt.
      Ann Warner, b. 1774; d. 1834, not married.
      Elizabeth Warner, b. 1777; d. 1845; m. Joel Bassett of Salem, Washington Co., N. Y. Children: i. James, went west when a young man to assist in the exploration of Michigan Territory, was never heard from and was supposed to have been killed by Indians. ii. Eliza, married and lived in the vicinity of Sandgate, Vt. iii. Esther. Esther Bassett was never married, lived in Salem, N. Y., in a house where her mother died, was a tailoress for years and, after her health failed, did light sewing. She was an invalid for years and a very lovely character. It is said she always had a word of cheer for people who were in trouble. She died some time after 1890.
      Hannah Warner, b. 1783; d. 1818, not married.
      James Warner, b. 1785; d. 1813, in Jericho, Vt., not married. He was a physician.

106 JABEZ ICHABOD[5] WARNER, son of Jabez[4] and Hannah[4] (Warner) Warner, born May 17, 1761, in Judea Parish, Woodbury, Conn., recorded there and also in Middletown, as of Judea Society; died January 14, 1849, in Jericho, Chittenden County, Vt. He was a soldier in the Revolution. Service is noted of one Jabez Warner, town of Washington, in Col. Canfield's Militia, 1781, and also one in Vermont, for 26 days, July 26, 1781, Captain Parmalee's Company. He received a pension by the act of 1832. He was said to have had an unusually good memory, and lived to vote at every presidential election from the formation of the government to the election of Polk. His children were all born in Connecticut and the two oldest sons never lived in Vermont.

Married (1) April 5, 1784, ANN WAKELEY, baptized in Woodbury, Conn., May 3, 1761, daughter of Abner and Sarah (————) Wakeley. She died in Washington, Conn., June 7, 1794, in her 34th year.

Married (2) May 27, 1796, MARY YOUNG, born 1767, died in Jericho, Vt., June 4, 1853, aged 86. She was of Scotch descent.

Children by first wife, born in Washington, Conn.

205 *John Warner*, b. June 6, 1785; m. Abby Ackley.
206 *Abner Warner*, b. 1787; m. Eliza Spicer.
   Jabez Warner, b. Feb. 1, 1791; moved to Plymouth, Mich., before 1830; married. Children: i. Betsey Maria, b. 1829; d. 1830. ii. Wakeley Winthrop, b. 1831; d. 1836. iii. Betsey M. Wakeley, b. 1837. iv. Margaret J., b. 1840.

Children by second wife, born in Washington, Conn.

   Ann Warner, b. Feb. 19, 1797; d. in Jericho, Vt., Aug. 24, 1838; was a teacher and worked at the tailor's trade in Jericho; not married.
   Betsey Warner, b. June 10, 1799; d. May 25, 1822, in Jericho; not married.
   Silence Margaret Warner, b. Feb. 27, 1802; d. Aug. 4, 1857, not married. She was a teacher and resided in Jericho.
207 *Andrew Warner*, b. March 25, 1806; m. Emily Graves.
   Nancy Janet Warner, b. June 6, 1808; m. Nov. 18, 1862, Joseph W. Geer, and moved to Michigan.

107 DELIVERANCE[5] WARNER, son of Andrew[4] and Martha (Wilcox) Warner, born in Middletown, Conn., November 22, 1747; died in Chatham, Conn., May 22, 1813, buried in Portland Cemetery. His uncle Jabez Warner of Woodbury was appointed his guardian, October 5, 1767 (Middletown probate records, II, 132). He enlisted in 1776 in Captain Jonathan Hale's Company which occupied Boston after the evacuation. His family is noted in the 1790 Census in the town of Chatham, and in that of 1800 in Glastonbury. The births of his children Rebeckah, Esther, Andrew, Anna and Sally are found in East Hampton town records (I, 131), others are from family records.

Married in Chatham-Portland, Conn., ESTHER KARR, born March 8, 1747-8, died October 5, 1842, one of twin daughters of John and Dorothy (Hale) Karr. Dorothy[4] Hale was descended from Samuel[1] Hale, the settler, and a soldier in the Pequot War, and his wife Mary, John[2] and Hannah (Nott) Hale, Ebenezer[3] and Ruth (Curtis) Hale. Hannah Nott was the daughter of John Nott, a prominent man in the history of early Wethersfield, and his wife **Ann**. Stiles' History of Ancient Wethersfield gives much information about this family. Ruth Curtis, mentioned above, was the daughter of Samuel and Sarah Curtis, and granddaughter of Thomas and Elizabeth Curtis.

Children of Deliverance⁵ and Esther (Karr) Warner

Rebecca Warner, b. July 3, 1768, recorded in East Hampton, Conn.; m. Asa Fuller; lived and died at Fort Edwards.

Esther Warner, b. Nov. 10, 1769, recorded at East Hampton, Conn.; m. Dec. 25, 1791, at Chatham-Portland, Conn., Isaac Hodge, b. Jan. 24, 1768, son of John and Sarah (Taylor) Hodge of Glastonbury.

208   *Andrew Warner*, b. Nov. 9, 1771; m. Gillet or Jeanette Goodale.

Deliverance Warner, b. 1773; d. Nov. 30, 1773, in Chatham, Conn.

Anna Warner, b. April 2, 1776; m. —— Fox; lived and died in Rome, N. Y.

209   *Sarah Warner*, b. June 9, 1778; m. (1) William Pelton, (2) John Pelton.

Mary Warner, b. Aug. 13, 1780; resided in Chatham; never married.

210   *Martha Warner*, b. June 28, 1782; m. Silas Hewitt.

John Warner, b. Mar. 29, 1784; m. Mrs. Crane of Great Barrington, Mass. One John Warner died in Chatham, Conn., Feb., 1822, but Middletown probate records, 10:75, state that Anna Warner was appointed guardian to John and David, sons of John Warner, late of Chatham, on Mar. 29, 1813, a record that seems to refer to this John Warner. Children: i. John, lived and died in Otsego Co., N. Y. ii. David, lived in Otsego Co., N. Y.

Oliver Warner, b. Apr. 3, 1786, in Chatham; was living at Haddam Landing in Middletown about 1850; m. (1) Feb. 4, 1808, Betsey Ann Markham, daughter of John Markham, Jr., a Revolutionary soldier of Middle Haddam, and his wife, Asenath Smith; m. (2) —— Child by first wife: Betsey, b. 1809; d. in Chatham, 1831.

Lucy Warner, b. June 13, 1788; d. Dec. 19 or 20, 1804, buried in Portland, Conn.

Orren Warner, b. June 2, 1790, in Chatham; resided in Portland; m. Mary Burnham of East Haddam, who was born in Chatham, and died May, 1848. Child: William, b. about 1813; d. in Portland, Conn., Apr. 25, 1887, aged 74. This is probably the William Warner who m. Oct. 10, 1836, Louisa Ann Arnold, who d. Apr. 29, 1901, aged 87, daughter of Chauncey Arnold, buried in Farm Hill Cemetery.

108 DANIEL⁵ WARNER, son of Robert⁴ and Isabella (Whitmore) Warner, born in Middletown, Conn., October 4, 1718; was a sea captain and was lost at sea, September 14, 1753. As administrator of his estate, his widow Lucy was empowered to sell land, October, 1754. She was appointed guardian for her son Robert, March 2, 1761. Robert, William, Sibel, Lucy, and Esther Warner, heirs of Daniel, gave a quit-claim to Mary and

Lucretia Warner, heirs of their father Stephen Warner, late of Middletown, deceased, on April 22, 1767. The witnesses were Joseph, Allis and Robert Warner, Abigail Shaler, and Rebecca Hulbert. (Middletown probate records, 2:29; Middletown deeds, 23:220; Connecticut public records, 10:303.)

Married in Cromwell, Conn., February 28, 1744-5, **LUCY** or **LUCIA STOW**, born August 31, 1723, died February 21, 1806, daughter of Samuel and Esther (Mould) Stow of Middletown. Her father was deacon of the church in Middletown. She married (2) Moses Bush of Chatham, Conn.

Children of Daniel and Lucy (Stow) Warner, born in Middletown

211 *Robert Warner*, b. Dec. 30, 1745; m. Lucy Tuels.
212 *William Warner*, b. Apr. 1, 1747; m. (1) Isabel Warner, (2) Sarah Dow.
Sibil Warner, b. July 24, 1749.
Lucy or *Lucia Warner*, b. Aug. 31, 1751.
Esther Warner, b. Aug. 28, 1753; m. Apr. 21 or 22, 1770, Jonathan Bush (Chatham-Portland records). Children: i. Moses, b. Jan. 4, 1772. ii. Jonathan, Jr., b. May 5, 1775.

109 STEPHEN[5] **WARNER**, son of Robert[4] and Isabella (Whitmore) Warner, born July 11, 1722 or 1721, in Middletown, Conn.; died in the Bay of Honduras, August 3, 1752. He was a sea captain. The Middletown record contains this statement: "Departed this life Aug. 3, 1752, at the Bay of Honduras as per account from Capt. Giles Hall." The inventory of his estate was taken by Joseph Starr, 2d, and William Rockwell, March 29, 1752-3, and consisted mainly of household goods, expensive clothing and fine linens. On January 2, 1786, Mr. John Scott, one of the heirs, asked for a distribution, and this was done by Comfort Sage, Benjamin Henshaw, and Asher Miller, April 21, 1787. Heirs were: the widow Mary; Lucretia Scott, widow of the late John Scott, deceased; Mary Starr, wife of Josiah Starr.

Married in Middletown, February 9, 1748-9, **MARY STARR**, born August (or October) 20, 1728, daughter of Samuel and Elizabeth (De Jersey or Farrie) Starr, died May 30, 1811. She married (2) in Cromwell, Conn., October 8, 1761, Stephen Van Overwyke or Van Overwight of Middletown, who died June 6, 1764, leaving a child, Sally, b. May 27, 1763.

Children of Stephen and Mary (Starr) Warner

213 *Mary Warner*, b. Apr. 10, 1751; m. Josiah Starr.
214 *Lucretia Warner*, b. Sept. 23, 1752; m. (1) John Scott, (2) Seth Wetmore, Jr.

110 **JOSEPH**[5] **WARNER,** son of Robert[4] and Isabella
(Whitmore) Warner, born in Middletown, Conn., February 4,
1724-5; died July 14, 1779, buried in Middletown, old North Cemetery. He was a sea captain. His estate was inventoried
August 4, 1779, valued at £458-10-3. Distribution was made
August 7, 1780, to the heirs: Chloe, late wife of William Miller,
Jr., of Middletown; heir or heirs of Isabella, late wife of William
Warner of Middletown; Abigail Warner; Lucy Warner; Sarah
Warner.

Married October 3, 1751, **ALICE WARD,** who was buried
July 19, 1776 (Middletown records).

Children, born in Middletown

Chloe Warner, b. May 28, 1752; m. William Miller.
Isabel Warner, b. July 4, 1754; d. before Aug. 7, 1780; m. William[6]
   Warner, b. Apr. 1, 1747, son of Daniel[5] and Lucy (Stow) Warner, see
   number 212. They had a son William who died Feb. 19, 1800. His
   father was appointed his guardian, Sept. 20, 1780.
Abigail Warner, b. Dec. 4, 1759.
Sarah Warner, b. May 26, 1762.
Lucy Warner, b. Oct. 3, 1763.
(Infant), buried Nov. 8, 1766.
(Infant), buried Nov. 26, 1770.
(Infant), buried Apr. 11, 1774.

111 **RACHEL**[5] **WARNER,** daughter of John[4], 3d, and
Rachel (Burlison) Warner, born July 15, 1741, recorded in Middletown, Conn.; died October 9, 1789. A fuller account of her
family will be found in the Strong Genealogy.

Married 176–, **ELNATHAN STRONG,** born September 23,
1736; died December 16, 1806. He was the son of Capt. Joseph
and Elizabeth (Strong) Strong of Coventry, Conn., and married
(2) Mary Marsh. He was a farmer at Granby, Conn., and
deacon of the Congregational Church.

Children

Rachel Strong, b. 1768; d. Dec. 3, 1838; m. Elihu Hayes, b. 1763,
   d. Oct. 9, 1821, son of Andrew Hayes, a farmer in Granby. Children:
   i. Justin, b. Jan. 9, 1799; m. Lucretia Case, and had children. ii.
   Clarissa, b. Aug., 1800; m. Sylvester Case and had children. iii.
   Elihu, Jr., b. Jan. 9, 1803; m. (1) Theodosia Wright, (2) Helen Lane,
   (3) Mabel (Bradley) Olds, and had children by each wife. iv. Silas,
   b. Jan. 17, 1806; m. Eliza Roby and had children. v. Orrin, b.
   Mar., 1811; d. 1838, not married.
   ——— Strong.
Elnathan Strong, Jr., b. Apr. 11, 1775; d. Dec. 4, 1842; m. Jan. 6, 1806,
   Annis Higley, b. Nov. 8, 1781, d. Nov. 17, 1842. Children: i. Annis

Elizabeth, b. Nov. 19, 1816; m. John Burwell and had children. ii. Julia, b. Apr. 10, 1821; d. Feb. 16, 1822.

——— Strong.

Asa Strong.

Nathan Strong, b. May, 1780; d. May 10, 1858; m. Theodosia Higley, b. 1781, daughter of Asa and Eunice (———) Higley, d. Oct. 9, 1853. He was a farmer in Granby, Conn., and had no children.

Joseph Strong, b. Oct. 24, 1781; d. Mar. 6, 1836; m. Sept. 12, 1814, Rhoda Climena Gates, b. June 25, 1792, d. at Owatoma, Minn., Feb. 16, 1867. She was the daughter of Jesse Gates of Simsbury and Rhoda Reed, and married (2) Thomas Smart. Children of Joseph Strong: i. Elizabeth Rachel, b. Apr. 17, 1816; m. Deacon Erastus Graves. ii. Rev. John Cotton, b. May 12, 1818; was graduated from Williams College and East Windsor Theological Seminary, became a missionary to the Choctaws at Mt. Pleasant under the A. B. C. F. M., and later was pastor of Congregational Churches at Chain Lake Centre, Minn., and elsewhere; m. (1) Celia Semantha Wright, (2) Mrs. Cynthia Rosetta (Newton) Hamlin, widow of Chapin Hamlin, and had children. iii. Tabitha Emily, b. Sept. 12, 1820; d. Nov. 8, 1825. iv. Joseph Dwight, b. June 5, 1823; was graduated from Williams College and East Windsor Theological Seminary, pastor in Congregational and Presbyterian churches in Westport, Conn., Honolulu (1855-8), Oakland and San Francisco, superintendent of public schools of Alameda Co., editor of the Hesperian and Pacific Monthly, author of "Children of Many Lands"; m. Margaret Dewing Bixby and had children. v. Julia Adelia, b. Aug. 14, 1825; m. Oliver Nash and had children. vi. Minerva Lewis, b. June 1, 1828; m. Dr. Foster Bodle and had a child. vii. Charles Asa, b. Dec. 31, 1831; m. Nancy Jane Carr and had children. viii. Emily, b. Apr. 9, 1834; m. Hon. Nicholas Mills Donaldson and had a child.

112 JONATHAN⁵ WARNER, son of John⁴, 3d, and Rachel (Burlison) Warner, born March 17, 1750, probably in Middletown, Conn.; died in Pittsford, Vt., March 20, 1810. He lived in Wintonbury from the age of 6 to 14, in Middletown until 18, then went to Vermont. He purchased, in 1772, land in Pittsford, Vt., a part of which remained in the family, at least until recent years. The following year he began improvements on his place, made a clearing and, in 1774, built a log house. The following year he married and intended to make Pittsford his home but the outbreak of the war altered his plans and he entered the service of his country. He was in the battle of Brooklyn, was with Washington on his retreat through New Jersey, and was in the battles of Trenton and Princeton.

It is said that upon arriving at the Delaware River the night before the former battle, Washington wished to obtain a boat from the opposite shore, and called upon someone to swim the stream to get it. Warner volunteered and obtained the boat. Patting him on the shoulder, Washington exclaimed, "Brave fellow," and sent him for a dry suit of clothes. His term of enlistment expired in the fall of 1779, when he was discharged and took his pay in continental money, which, on account of its great depreciation, went but a short way toward procuring an outfit for housekeeping. He paid $60 for a small kettle and other things in proportion.

In the spring of 1780, he went to Pittsford and occupied the house he had built some years before. After a short residence there his house was burned while he was on a visit to his old friends in Connecticut, and on his return he built another house on an adjacent site, which was used until 1795, when he built the home later occupied by his grandson. "No blemish is left to sully his character."

Jonathan Warner married in Connecticut, January 1, 1775, **MARY GRIFFIN** of Simsbury

> *Children, eight; two were born before their removal to Pittsford, and five died young*
>
> *Mary Warner,* b. June 27, 1776; d. Mar. 5, 1793 (Pittsford town record).
>
> 215 *Jonathan Warner, Jr.,* b. Aug. 27, 1778; m. Anna Ripley.
>
> *Olive Warner,* d. young.
>
> *Mariam* or *Miriam Warner,* d. about 1848; m. —— Wood.
>
> *John Warner,* b. Aug. 10, 1788 (Pittsford record); d. young.
>
> 216 *Levi Warner* (twin), b. Sept. 11, 1795; m. Mrs. Martha (Bailey) Winters.
>
> *Judith* or *Judah Warner* (twin), b. Sept. 11, 1795; d. June, 1796.

113 ELIZABETH[5] WARNER, daughter of Daniel[4], 3d, and Elizabeth (Adams) Warner, born October 17, 1721, in Sunderland, Mass.; died October 5, 1746, in East Haddam, Conn.

Married June 17, 1744, as his second wife, **BEZALEEL BRAINERD,** born in East Haddam, April 17, 1701, died there October 9, 1749, son of Daniel, Jr., and Susannah (Ventres) Brainerd. The Warner Genealogy published in 1892 says he married Elizabeth, daughter of John and Mehitabel (Richardson) Warner, born January 25, 1724-5, and a cousin of this Elizabeth. The Brainerd Genealogy gives the record of this marriage and, as the data is more complete, this is probably the right Elizabeth.

Bezaleel Brainerd was a farmer and lived about a mile north of East Haddam Landing. He was appointed Captain of the South Company or trainband in the town of East Haddam. "As he took command of the military company, his soldiers, wishing to honor him on his promotion, fired a salute, which, by an accidental discharge of the gun, wounded him in one of the legs, causing his death. He died while making his will and before he had signed it. The will was accepted, however, and is now filed at Colchester." He married (1) Mary or Hannah Gates, by whom he had seven children, and (3) Phebe (Smith) Almany or Almang, by whom he had one child. See the Brainerd Genealogy for a fuller account of the family.

Child of Bezaleel and Elizabeth (Warner) Brainerd

Daniel Brainerd, b. Mar. 17, 1746, in East Haddam. He was a farmer, and town clerk of East Haddam from 1769 to 1777. Married (1) Apr. 16, 1768, Ann Marsh, b. May 15, 1748, in Quincy, Mass., daughter of John Marsh, d. Jan. 31, 1772, or Dec. 31, 1771; m. (2) Dec. 31, 1773, Dorcas (Dimmock) Gilbert, daughter of Samuel and Hannah (Davis) Dimmock and widow of William Gilbert. Children by first wife: i. Anna Marsh, b. Feb. 7, 1770; m. Darius Gates; had no children. ii. Daniel Adams, b. Dec. 31, 1771; resided in East Hamilton, N. Y.; m. Irena Brainerd and had eight children. Children by second wife: i. Robert, b. about 1775; probably died not married. ii. Samuel Dimmick, b. Dec. 26, 1777; resided in Weybridge and New Haven, Vt.; m. (1) Tamar Lawrence, by whom he had three children, and (2) Electa (Chalker) Hoisington, by whom he had two children.

114 MARTHA⁵ WARNER, daughter of Daniel⁴, 3d, and Elizabeth (Adams) Warner, born May 15, 1725, probably in Sunderland, Mass.; died in East Haddam, Conn., March 17, 1797, buried in River View Cemetery, East Haddam.

Married March 13, 1746, recorded in East Haddam land record, book 3, p. 510, **MATTHEW SAYRE** or **SEARS** (Seyers, in early records), born about 1717; died in East Haddam, February 25, 1796, in his 79th year, buried in River View Cemetery. He was the son of Nathan and Mary (————) Sayre of Middletown, Conn., whose family changed the name to Sears. He removed to Bashan in East Haddam. He bought land in East Haddam from Daniel Warner, Jr., in 1758. He settled near the Landing where he had a grist mill and cloth works. He was by trade a cloth dresser. The family record is found in the Sears Genealogy, p. 629.

Children, born in East Haddam

Mary Sears, b. July 1, 1747.

Elizabeth (1) *Sears*, b. Feb. 12, 1748-9; d. Mar. 10, 1756.

Lucy Sears, b. Oct. 1, 1752; m. Nov. 21, 1776, John Wright, b. in Colchester, May 27, 1745, d. June 6, 1826, son of Timothy and Mehitabel (Brainerd) Wright. Children: i. Lucy b. Sept. 4, 1777; d. Mar. 22, 1803. ii. Timothy, b. Nov. 18, 1779; d. Apr. 3, 1846. iii. Ann S., b. Feb. 15, 1782; d. Sept. 14, 1814. iv. John, b. Nov. 25, 1783; d. in Chicago, Sept. 20, 1840. v. Amasa, b. Jan. 6, 1787; d. Apr. 30, 1861;

m. Nancy Curtis, b. Jan. 16, 1796, and had Lucy Ann (1), d. young, and Lucy Ann (2), b. Nov. 25, 1816, d. Apr. 20, 1843, m. Rollin Sanford of Brooklyn, N. Y., whose daughter Carolyn is Mrs. Henry F Foster of Brooklyn.

Matthew Sears, b. Nov. 25, 1754; d. May 8, 1777, in his 23d year, buried in River View Cemetery, East Haddam.

Elizabeth (2) Sears, b. Oct. 27, 1757.

Jane or *Asenath Sears,* b. July 11, 1760. In the East Haddam record of birth of the children (land record, 3:510) the name is given Jane; but the New York Genealogical and Biographical Record, 2:135, gives the name "Scena," born on this date, d. Mar. 7, 1846, m. July, 1781, William Gelston, and the Sears Genealogy says Asenath Sears m. William Gelston, b. Sept. 3, 1756, d. June 24, 1840, son of Maltby and Mary (————) Gelston of Bridgehampton, L. I. He was a farmer in East Haddam. Children: i. Abigail, m. Joseph Sluman Brainerd; no children. ii. Matilda, m. Timothy Wright; no children. iii. Larissa, m. ———— Welles; no children. iv. William, m. Lucy Bigelow, and had children. v. Hugh (1), d. young. vi. Hugh (2), m. Rebecca Durham. vii. Maltby, probably d. not married. viii. Richard D., m. Carile D. Palmer. ix. Henry, m. Ann M. Howell, and had children. x. George Sears, m. ———— Minell.

Annie Sears, b. Mar. 10, 1763; d. Oct. 8, 1779, in her 17th year, buried in River View Cemetery, East Haddam.

Martha Sears, b. Oct. 13, 1765.

115 ANNA[5] WARNER, daughter of Daniel[4] and Elizabeth (Adams) Warner, born November 17, 1731, probably in Sunderland, Mass.; died July 20, 1789, in East Hartland, Hartford Co., Conn., where they had removed soon after the Revolution. She and her husband were both active members of the churches in East Haddam and East Hartland.

Married in East Haddam, November 23, 1752, **THOMAS CONE,** 2d, born in East Haddam, February 22, 1729, died in East Hartland, May 1, 1808, son of Stephen and Abigail (Barnes) Cone of East Haddam. For a more complete account of this family, see the Cone Genealogy, p. 104, etc.

Children, born in East Haddam

Lucy Cone, bapt. May 6, 1759; d. in Kinsman, Ohio, Jan. 17, 1834; m. Sept. 26, 1781, John Andrews, who d. in East Haddam, Oct. 24, 1809, son of Richard and Rachel (Ackley) Andrews. Children: i. John, b. July 9, 1782; d. Jan. 24, 1864; m. Harriet Reeves. ii. Marquis, b. Sept. 21, 1786; d. Nov. 11, 1838; m. Hannah Crosby. iii. Calvin, b. Jan. 16, 1791; d. Feb. 20, 1864; m. Elizabeth Crosby. iv. Lucy, b. Feb. 1, 1793; d. Aug. 18, 1825; m. William Jones.

Vicee Cone, bapt. Sept. 15, 1765; d. in Hartland, Ohio.

Calvin Cone, b. June 19, 1768; d. in Hartland, Ohio, Sept. 5, 1845; m. (1) Sally Brockway, who d. in East Hartland, Conn., June 30, 1796, aged 29, (2) Mary Bushnell, daughter of Alexander Bushnell, (3) Mrs. Hannah Hutchings. He was representative for the town of

Barkhamstead, in the Connecticut Legislature in 1801; was a high degree Mason; went to Ohio in 1804, as State Agent for the sale of Connecticut lands; resided in Hartland after 1816. Children: i. Anna, b. Oct. 15, 1788; d. Oct. 14, 1854; m. John Brainard. ii. Lester, b. Aug. 29, 1789; d. Oct. 23, 1835; m. (1) Phebe Bidwell, (2) Estella Humphrey. iii. Rolzalmon, d. in South Carolina, not married. iv. Louisa, d. young. v. Sally, b. Nov. 9, 1798; d. Aug. 13, 1884; m. Wayne Bidwell. vi. Lucy, b. Dec. 6, 1803; d. Feb. 6, 1850; m. Daniel J. Mattocks. vii. Julia, b. May 1, 1808; d. Sept. 10, 1855; m. Cornelius Silliman. viii. Sylvester, b. Mar. 18, 1810; d. Apr. 4, 1833; m. Caroline Howe. ix. Erastus, b. May 13, 1812; m. Candace Green.

Anna Cone, b. Sept. 9, 1770; d. not married.

116 DANIEL[5] WARNER, son of Jonathan[4] and Bathsheba (Allis) Warner, born December 22, 1734, probably in Hardwick, Mass., where he spent most of his life; died in Putnam, Ohio, 1823, aged 89. He resided near Gilbertsville until about 1807 when he removed to Ohio. He was a soldier in the French and Indian and later wars, and captain of militia; a member of the Committee of Safety and Correspondence for five years; selectman for six years; assessor for ten years.

Married in Hardwick, May 31, 1758, **MARY WRIGHT.**

Children, born in Hardwick

217 *Lydia Warner,* b. Aug. 12, 1759; m. Samuel French.

Daniel Warner, Jr., b. July 28, 1761. No further record of him has been found, although he may be the Daniel recorded in the 1810 Census at Hardwick, Vt., or the Daniel who m. Patty ——— and resided at Dummerston, Vt., with these children: i. Lyman, b. Apr. 24, 1786. ii. Sally, b. Apr. 1, 1788. iii. Harriet, b. Oct. 25, 1795. iv. Willard, b. Jan. 24, 1797. v. George, b. May 26, 1799. vi. Calvin, b. Apr. 29, 1801. vii. Daniel, b. Mar. 15, 1808 (Dummerston town records).

218 *Jonathan Warner,* b. Sept. 13, 1763; m. (1) Sally Paige, (2) Mrs. Annis Marsh.

Mary Warner, b. Oct. 19, 1765; d. Oct. 30, 1820, at Hardwick, Vt.; m. (intentions published) Oct. 12, 1788, Rev. Solomon Aiken, b. July 15, 1758, d. June 1, 1833, son of John and Jerusha (Atwood) Aiken. He was graduated at Dartmouth in 1784, was pastor in Dracut from 1788 to 1812, when he was dismissed to enter the army as a chaplain. Before entering college he served two years in the Revolution. In 1818 he removed to Hardwick, Vt., and was Representative, 1821-2. They had four sons and five daughters living in 1853. One of the daughters was Selina, m. George Henry Cook, and had a son, Edward Burbeck Cook of Portland, Maine.

Justus Warner, b. May 22, 1768; d. May 17, 1793, buried in old Hardwick Cemetery; m. Dec. 29, 1791, Catherine Hall of New Braintree. Child: William Augustus, b. Nov., 1792; d. Feb. 25 or 26, aged three months, buried in old Hardwick Cemetery.

219 *Alpha Warner,* b. Dec. 8, 1770; m. (1) Lydia Cobb, (2) Mrs. Anna Burton.

Wright Warner, b. Sept. 11, 1773. He resided at Hardwick, Newbury, Vt., and Amherst, Mass., and in 1812 removed to Coshocton, Ohio. He was a practicing lawyer in Tuscarawas County in 1818 and prosecuting attorney from 1820 to 1825. Married (1) Jan. 19, 1804, in Franklin, Vt., Anna Baxter (Vermont town records), (2) in Amherst, Mass., Jan. 28, 1806, Esther Cutler, b. in Pelham, Mass., June 11, 1775, d. in Steubenville, Ohio, daughter of Dr. Robert and Esther (Pomeroy) Cutler. Wright Warner is said to have had a son and two daughters, one of whom was Eliza Whipple, b. in Amherst, Mass.

Charles Lee Warner, b. Nov. 30, 1776; m. and resided in Hardwick, Vt., where his son, George W., was born Aug. 14, 1800 (town records).

Betsey Warner, bapt. Apr. 23, 1780; m. Aug. 21, 1803, Levi Whipple.

Patience Warner, b. Dec. 2, 1782; m. John Leavens. A granddaughter is Mrs. Eliza Lewis Potwine, a member of the D. A. R.

117 **MARY[5] WARNER**, daughter of Jonathan[4] and Bathsheba (Allis) Warner, born in Hardwick, Mass., February 23, 1737; died in Bennington, Vt., October 27, 1810. The Doty Genealogy contains a most interesting account of her, written by one who remembered her, as well as a record of her descendants. She was a woman of considerable talent, greatly respected and beloved by all who knew her.

Married (1) in Hardwick, December 4, 1755, **ZURISHADDAI DOTY**, born in Rochester, Mass., November 19, 1731, son of Edward and Mary (Andrews) Doty; died in Wilmington, Vt., about 1793. He emigrated about 1752 to Hardwick and at the close of the war, to Wilmington. He was a blacksmith by trade and during the war was employed by the government as blacksmith in the army. He served in the Revolution in the same company in which his brother-in-law, Dr. Challis Safford, was surgeon. He was a witness to the will of James Alexander of Perth, now Salem, Washington Co., N. Y., July 16, 1783, and probably lived there at the time, as his brother Theodorus was then residing there.

Mary Warner married (2) June 10, 1794, **PETER HARWOOD**, born in Concord, Mass., July 14, 1735, son of Benjamin and Bridget (Brown) Harwood; died in Bennington, Vt., July 12, 1815. He married (1) in Colerain, Mass., June 9, 1759, Margaret Clark, who died February 16, 1794, and by her he had a large family.

Children of Zurishaddai and Mary (Warner) Doty; births recorded in Hardwick, Mass.

John Doty, b. Sept. 12, 1756; d. aged over 70. He was surveyor of highways in Hardwick in 1789, later removed to Westminster, Mass., where he kept a tavern. Married in Hardwick, Sept. 19, 1779, Mary Mandell, b. in Hardwick, Oct. 30, 1759, daughter of Paul and Susanna (Ruggles) Mandell. Children, born at Hardwick: i. Chauncey, m. Isabella Hinckley. ii. Susan, m. and d. leaving no children. iii. Philotheta, m. —— Pierce; no children. iv. Timothy Ruggles, m. Susan Cowee. v. Martha Woodbridge, m. Abram Wood; no children. vi. Lucia, d. young. vii. Mary Warner, m. (1) Rev. Joseph Wood, who died in Tuscaloosa, Ala.; (2) Thomas Buchanan of Tuscaloosa.

Moses Doty, b. July 2, 1758; d. in Hamilton, Madison Co., N. Y., June 4, 1823. He was a soldier in the Continental Army, lived later in Wardsburg, Mass., Wilmington, Vt., Williamstown, Mass., about 1800 in Troy, N. Y., where he kept a famous tavern, "The Red Lion," Chenango Co., and Madison Co., N. Y. Married (1) in Hardwick, 1781, Betsey Webster, b. Oct., 1761, d. May 15, 1812; (2) about 1813, probably in Norwich, N. Y., Mrs. Elizabeth (Pike) Dorrance, widow of George Dorrance. She married (2) Elijah Owen and died in Sherburne, 1867. Children of Moses and Betsey (Webster) Doty: i. Theodosia, d. young. ii. Ellis, m. Ruth Pierce; had six children. iii. Nancy, m. Thomas Evans; no children. iv. Sophia, m. v. Barbara, m. John A. Collier. vi. Martin B., d. not married. vii. Betsey, m. James Birdsall; no children. viii. Marcia Louisa, m. Virgil Whitney. Children of Moses and Elizabeth (Pike) Doty: i. Mary Jane, m. Zebulon Willoughby. ii. Ellen Sophia, m. Dr. Edward Maynard. iii. John Henry Hobart, m. Mary Jane Graves.

Ezra Doty, b. Sept. 28, 1760; d. in Lockport, N. Y. Served seven years in the Revolution, lived later in Wilmington and Bennington, Vt., Adams, Mass., Choconut, Pa., and Lockport, N. Y. Married (1) in Wilmington, Jan. 17, 1786, Ann Mellen, b. in Framingham, Mass., Aug. 4, 1797, d. in Choconut, Pa., May 26, 1813, daughter of William Mellen; (2) Jan. 30, 1815, Mrs. Eunice (Longworth) Bishop, b. Apr. 9, 1772. Children: i. Asa, m. and had children. ii. Achsah, m. Ezra Conant. iii. Almira, m. Sylvester Stewart; had children. iv. William Mellen, m. Priscilla Faxon; had children. v. Sabra, m. Hiram F. Faxon; had children. vi. Nathan, m. Joanna Faxon; had children. vii. Ezra (1), d. young. viii. Ezra (2), d. young. ix. Charles, d. young. x. Zuri Shaddai, m. and had children.

Ellis Doty, b. Oct. 20, 1762. Lived in Wilmington, Vt., and Chautauqua Co., N. Y. Married Huldah Kilby. Children: Warner; Kilby.

Asa Doty, b. Sept. 9, 1765; d. in Parkman, Ohio, Jan. 12, 1843. Sea captain, made several voyages to China, lived in Williamstown, Mass., and in Ohio. Married Lorana Coffin, b. in Nantucket, Mass., Aug. 18, 1771, d. in Cleveland, Ohio, daughter of Charles Coffin. Children: i. Ezra, m. Edna Fuller; nine children. ii. Charles Coffin, m., and had children. iii. John, m. Jane Greer. iv. Anna, m. James Noles. v. Sophia, m. William Henry Stillman. vi. Asa, m. Nancy Moody; four children. vii. Lorana Mary, m. Capt. H. R. Case. viii. Sarah Marilla, m. John Davis Stillman. ix. Benjamin Howard.

Jonathan Doty, b. July 27, 1767; d. 1856, in Mechanicsburg, Ohio; m. Mar. 7, 1792, Cynthia Merrill, b. Mar. 7, 1771, d. July 31, 1834. Children: i. William, d. not married. ii. Polly, d. not married. iii. James, m. Nancy Carpenter; no children. iv. Sarah, d. not married. v. Hiram, m. Elizabeth McCorkle. vi. Ellis, m. Jane Scott.

Molly Doty, b. July 12, 1769; lived in Braintree, Mass., and died there aged 80. Married ——— Thompson; had five children.

Betsey Doty, b. May 23, 1773; d. in Enosburg, Vt., aged about 80. Married in Bennington, Vt., Nov. 1, 1796, Challis Safford, b. in Hardwick, Apr. 15, 1771, d. in Enosburg, Vt., Aug. 22, 1841, son of Dr. Challis and Lydia (Warner) Safford. Removed to Enosburg in 1800. Child: W. D., lived in Enosburg. See number 118.

Horatio Gates Doty, b. Aug. 28, 1779; d. in Saratoga Co., N. Y., about 1860, probably had a family.

118 LYDIA⁵ WARNER, daughter of Jonathan⁴ and Bathsheba (Allis) Warner, born in Hardwick, Mass., November 3, 1740; died probably in Vermont.

Married (1) in Hardwick, February 8, 1760, Dr. **CHALLIS SAFFORD,** baptized September 9, 1733; died about 1771. He was the son of Joseph and Mary (Challis) Safford, who resided in Ipswich, Sutton, and, after 1751, in Hardwick. He was first married in 1755 to Rebecca Winslow, at which time he was called of Rutland, probably the Rutland District, now Barre. He seems to have become a resident of Hardwick immediately after his marriage and lived at the north end of the Common. He was a physician, served in the French War two campaigns in Col. Ruggles' regiment; surgeon, 1757, and surgeon's mate in 1759. The date of his death is not known, but his inventory was taken June 21, 1771.

Lydia Warner married (2) November 20, 1777, **Dr. JONAS FAY,** born January 28, 1737, in Hardwick, son of Stephen and Ruth (Child) Fay; died in Bennington, March 6, 1818. By his first wife, Sarah Fassett, daughter of Captain John Fassett, he had seven children. During the campaign at Fort Edward and Lake George in 1756, Jonas Fay was clerk of Capt. Samuel Robinson's company, and was described as cordwainer. In 1761 he was noted on the town records as ensign. He studied medicine and practiced in Hardwick, Mass., for several years, and also taught school. About 1768 he removed to Bennington, Vt., where he became distinguished as a physician and politician. In 1772 he and his father were among the agents sent to Gov. Tryon of New York to explain the grounds of complaint of the Vermont settlers. In 1774 he was clerk to the convention that resolved to defend by force, Ethan Allen, Seth Warner, and others who were threatened as outlaws by the New York Assembly, and, as clerk, he certified their proceedings for publication. He served as surgeon in the expedition under Ethan

Allen at the capture of Ticonderoga, and held the position under the Committee of the Massachusetts Congress who were sent to the Lake in July, 1775, also appointed to muster the troops as they arrived for the defence of that port. He was also surgeon in Col. Warner's regiment for a time. In January, 1776, he was clerk to the Convention at Dorset that petitioned to be allowed to serve the country as inhabitants of the New Hampshire Grants and not under New York; he was a member of the Westminster Convention of 1777 that declared Vermont a separate state; secretary of the Convention that formed the Constitution of the State in July, 1777; one of the Council of Safety then appointed; member of the State Council, 1778-1785; judge of Supreme Court in 1782; judge of probate, 1782-7; attended Continental Congress at Philadelphia as agent of Vermont, 1777, 1779, 1781, and 1782. He was able to draw with skill and ability the public papers of the day, and was the reputed author of many of them. In 1780, in collaboration with Ethan Allen, he prepared and published a pamphlet on the New Hampshire and New York controversy. Dr. Fay resided in Bennington except for a few years after 1800, which he spent in Charlotte and Pawlet.

Children of Challis and Lydia (Warner) Safford

Anna Safford, b. Feb. 22, 1761.

Jonas Safford, b. July 23, 1763.

Jonathan Safford, b. Feb. 27, 1766; d. 1821. He went with his mother to Bennington in 1777; studied medicine with his step-father, Dr. Jonas Fay; settled at Pawlet, Vt., in 1793, and was a successful and popular practitioner until his death.

Robert Safford, b. July 17, 1768.

Challis Safford, Jr., b. Apr. 15, 1771; d. Aug. 22, 1841. Accompanied his mother to Bennington in 1777. Married Nov. 1, 1796, Betsey Doty (see number 117) and removed in 1800 to Enosburg, Vt., where he was a farmer. He was elected deacon in 1833. "He won the confidence and friendship of his fellow-citizens to a remarkable degree, and it was not known that he had an enemy in the world."

Children of Dr. Jonas and Lydia (Warner) Fay

Ethan Allen Fay (twin), b. Jan. 12, 1779. He kept a hotel in Charlotte, Vt., and died at Queensburg (Fort Ann), N. Y.

Heman Allen (twin), b. Jan. 12, 1779. He was graduated from West Point in 1808; was appointed Lieutenant in the army; served through the War of 1812; soon afterwards became keeper of military stores in Albany, holding the office for several years, then returned to Bennington.

Lydia Fay, m. Uriah Edgerton.

Sarah Fay, m. Henry Hopkins.

119 SARAH⁵ WARNER, daughter of Jonathan⁴ and Bath sheba (Allis) Warner, born in Hardwick, Mass., November 1, 1742; died in Greenwich, December, 1837.

Married (1) in Hardwick, September 8, 1762, **THOMAS WHEELER,** son of Thomas and Mary (Brooks) Wheeler, born at Acton, Mass., March 22, 1788-9; died at Hardwick, July 10, 1804. He was a farmer and resided at Hardwick all his life except from 1770 to 1777 when he was at Brookfield. The Massachusetts "Spy" of July 18, 1804, says, "while giving instructions to his hired men respecting his hay, he felt himself faint, fell into their arms, and instantly expired."

Sarah Warner married (2) December 30, 1807, as his third wife, her cousin, Captain **ELIJAH⁵ WARNER,** son of Joseph⁴ and Mary (Hubbard) Warner, born in Hatfield, December 14, 1738; died there January 24, 1819; see number 122. She had no children by this marriage.

A more complete account of the Wheeler family will be found in the Wheeler Genealogy, although Sarah's name is recorded Anna by error.

Children of Thomas and Sarah (Warner) Wheeler, born in Hardwick

Charles Wheeler, b. Oct. 13, 1763; d. Nov. 11, 1805, not married.

Thomas Wheeler, b. Mar. 3, 1767; d. in Worcester, Apr. 26, 1851, buried in Hardwick. He was an iron-founder at Hardwick and removed to Ticonderoga, N. Y. He was captain of a military company in 1801, major in 1811, and colonel in 1813. He was married four times but the names of his last two wives are not known. Married (1) June 3, 1790, Anna Dexter, daughter of Lieut. Job Dexter, b. Jan. 22, 1770, d. Mar. 20, 1804; (2) Feb. 14, 1805, Mary Paige, daughter of Timothy Paige, d. at Ticonderoga, Sept. 18, 1828, aged 47. Children by first wife: i. Charles, b. Mar. 26, 1791, at Hardwick; d. Sept. 30, 1818, at Ticonderoga, where he was an iron-worker; m. Luthera Bangs, daughter of Elijah Bangs, and had two children. ii. ———, d. May 2, 1793. iii. Sarah, b. Apr. 28, 1794; d. June 26, 1864; m. Daniel Wheeler, son of John and Mary (Paige) Wheeler, and had ten children. iv. ———, d. young. v. William Augustus, b. Mar. 31, 1798; d. Feb. 16, 1873; was an iron-founder at Worcester; m. Almira Warner Allen, daughter of Moses and Anna (Paige) Allen, and had nine children. vi. ———, d. young. vii. ———, d. young. viii. Ann Dexter, d. young. ix. ———, d. young. x. Thomas Alonzo, d. young. xi. Charlotte Sophia, b. May 8, 1811; lived in Lawrence, Mich.; m. (1) William Burnett Cooper, (2) Ashley Cooper Bennett. xii. Mary Emeline, b. June 21, 1813; d. Feb. 20, 1843; m. Thomas R. Green of Belchertown. xiii. Rebecca Ann, b. Mar. 6, 1816; d. June 10, 1853, at Dunkirk, N. Y.; m. Lyman Burrill. xiv. Eliza Jane, b. Apr. 15, 1819; d. Mar. 4, 1848; m. Rev. Stephen Lovell, and had two children. xv. Juliet Elvira, b. Sept. 10, 1821; d. June 19, 1840, not married.

Moses Wheeler, b. May 26, 1769, at Hardwick; d. there Aug. 14, 1828.
He resided in Randolph, Vt., from 1790 to 1803, then returned to
Hardwick. Married 1798, Mehitabel Pearson, who died Aug. 13,
1854, at Brewer, Me. Children, first three b. at Randolph, others at
Hardwick: i. Sophia, b. Dec. 11, 1799; m. John Wheeler. ii. Daniel,
b. July 10, 1801; d. at Bangor, Me., July 13, 1886; m. (1) Mary
Hinckley, daughter of Barnabas Hinckley, (2) Mrs. Mary Gay; had
four children. iii. Amanda, b. Dec. 6, 1802; m. Alanson Johnson.
iv. Sarah Warner, b. Dec. 2, 1804; m. Artemas Wheeler. v. Moses,
b. Sept. 2, 1806; drowned June 8, 1819. vi. Hilly, b. May 24, 1808.
vii. Henry Parsons, b. Aug. 27, 1810; d. Mar. 15, 1816. viii. Harriet, b. July 24, 1812; m. John Holyoke of Bangor, Me.

Daniel Wheeler, b. about 1771; d. Oct. 8, 1798, not married.

Sally Wheeler, b. 1774; d. July 5, 1793, not married.

120 JONATHAN[5] WARNER, son of Jonathan[4] and Bath
sheba (Allis) Warner, born in Hardwick, Mass., July 14, 1744;
died January 7, 1803, at Craftsbury, Vt., where he had gone on a
matter of business. He inherited his father's homestead in
Hardwick, cultivated the large farm and managed the store and
tavern. At the beginning of the Revolution he was Lieutenant
of the South Company. September 22, 1774, he was elected
Captain of that company and Captain also of the company of
minute men that was organized that day. The following October he was elected Colonel, and was promoted to the office of
Brigadier-General, February 13, 1776. Upon the reorganization
of the militia in 1781, after the adoption of the Constitution, he
was elected Major-General, to which office he was re-commis-
sioned, April 3, 1786, under the new arrangement. He faithfully
performed the arduous duties of his office during the Revolution
and Shays' Insurrection and was honorably discharged upon
his voluntary resignation, December, 1789.

General Warner was also active in civic affairs; a member of
the Committee of Correspondence for three years; selectman,
three years; representative, five years; senator, nine years;
member of the Council, two years. His name occurs frequently
on the annals of Colonial history. His will, made December 9,
1802, probated January 10, 1803, in Orleans Co., Vt., mentions
his wife, and surviving children: Susanna Howe; Bathsheba
Brown; Hannah Hitchcock; Frances Parker; Harriet, Alma,
Mary White, Louisa and William Augustus Warner, all under
21; Jonathan Warner, to whom is given the home farm at Hardwick. Land in Craftsbury is mentioned.

Jonathan Warner married in Hardwick, February 5, 1766,
HANNAH MANDELL, daughter of Paul and Susannah (Ruggles) Mandell. She died in Enfield, Conn., August 3, 1839, aged

91. She resided at the homestead until late in life, when she entered the home of her youngest daughter in Enfield.

The Ruggles pedigree is as follows: Thomas[1], from Nazing, Essex Co., England, of Roxbury, Mass., 1637, wife Mary; Captain Samuel[2] and wife Ann Bright; Captain Samuel[3] and wife Martha Woodbridge, a descendant of Governor Thomas Dudley; Rev. Timothy[4] and Mary White of Rochester, Mass.; Susanna[5]; who married Paul Mandell. Paul Mandell was a merchant of New Bedford, Mass., and is said to have left the town because his aristocratic nature could not brook the idea that an apprentice should presume to compete with him in trade in the same town. He removed to Hardwick, Mass., thereby placing his family where educational advantages were few, and throwing upon himself and his wife the task of educating their children. For this duty they were, fortunately, both well qualified, as Mrs. Mandell had been educated with her brothers, at least one of whom, Brig.-Gen. Timothy Ruggles, was a graduate of Harvard College. Consequently Mrs. Hannah (Mandell) Warner was never a student at any school.

Children, born in Hardwick, Mass.

220   *Susanna Warner*, b. July 10, 1767; m. (1) Artemas Howe, (2) Moses Robinson.
221   *Bathsheba Warner*, b. Mar. 25, 1769; m. Luke Brown.
        Hannah Warner, b. Feb. 20, 1771; m. July 17, 1791, Peletiah Hitchcock, son of Capt. David and Martha (Keyes) Hitchcock. He was born Feb. 19, 1765, in West Brookfield, Mass.; was graduated at Harvard, 1785; became a lawyer and practiced at Hardwick before 1791; moved to West Brookfield and died Apr. 25, 1851. Children: i. George Augustus, b. Apr. 28, 1792; removed to Virginia and was living there in 1858; was a general. ii. Eliza Augusta, d. 1796, aged 19 months. iii. Henry, b. May 7, 1800; d. Oct. 30, 1880; lived at Jamaica Plain and was a successful merchant in Boston.
        Betsey Warner, b. Mar. 22, 1773; d. Aug. 18, 1778, buried in Hardwick, old cemetery.
        Joseph Warren Warner, b. July 13, 1775; d. Aug. 9, 1777, buried in Hardwick, old cemetery, tombstone sunken so low in the ground as to obscure the date.
        Fanny Warner, b. Sept. 14, 1778; m. Feb. 23, 1801, John A. Parker of Roxbury.
        Jonathan Warner, b. June 13, 1781. He inherited his father's homestead at Hardwick.
222   *Harriet Warner*, b. Jan. 15, 1783; m. Alexander Holton.
        Alma Warner, b. May 15, 1785.
        Mary White Warner, b. Mar. 7, 1787; m. Joseph Chittenden Bradley. A descendant was Mrs. Isaac H. Arthur, a member of the D. A. R.
        Louisa Warner, bapt. May 30, 1790; d. at Springfield, Mar. 2, 1872; m. (intentions) Aug. 21, 1825, Eliphaz Jones of Enfield, Conn. She resided in Enfield and in Springfield, Mass.

William Augustus Warner, b. May 26, 1795; d. in Boston, Dec. 23, 1830. He was a lawyer of high reputation in Boston. He was graduated at Harvard in 1815, and delivered an oration upon "Imagination as affecting Individual Happiness." His oration for the Master's degree in 1818, upon "the Condition and Prospects of the American People," is said to have "afforded universal satisfaction," according to the journal of one who heard it.

121 BATHSHEBA[5] WARNER, daughter of Jonathan[4] and Bathsheba (Allis) Warner, born in Hardwick, Mass., July 24, 1746; died January 29, 1831.

Married September 2, 1764, ELIAKIM SPOONER, born April 7, 1740, in Petersham, Mass., son of Deacon Daniel and Elizabeth (Ruggles) Spooner; died January 3, 1820. He resided in Worcester, Mass., until 1780 and was prominent in public life, holding town and county offices. He enlisted in the colonial service in 1757 and again in 1775. In 1780 he removed to Vermont to the New Hampshire Grants, later to Westminster, and spent his last years in Woodstock, Vt. He frequently represented his town in the Vermont Legislature and was for seven years a member of the Executive Council of the state.

Children

Eliakim Spooner, b. Aug. 25, 1770; d. Aug. 21, 1776.

Alfred Spooner, b. Nov. 24, 1780, in Petersham; d. about 1834. He resided in Westminster, Vt., and kept a hotel there until his wife's death, when he sold out, and, leaving his children with their grand parents, went south. Married Dec. 15, 1800, Hannah Harlow, daughter of Eleazer and Rhoda (Alexander) Harlow, b. Aug. 10, 1778, d. Aug. 3, 1816. Children: i. Frances Julia, b. 1801. ii. Eliakim Ruggles, b. 1802. iii. Bathsheba Alice, b. 1804; d. 1804. iv. Jonathan Warner (called only Warner), b. 1805. v. Bathsheba, b. 1806. vi. Rhoda Ann, b. 1808. vii. Hannah Neckayah, b. 1810. viii. Alfred Rassales, b. 1812. ix. Nancy Adeline, b. 1814.

122 ELIJAH[5] WARNER, son of Joseph[4] and Mary (Hubbard) Warner, born in Hatfield, Mass., December 14, 1738; died in Hardwick, Mass., January 24, 1819. He accompanied his father's family to Hardwick when he was a boy and later settled in that town on a farm on the road to Enfield, three and a half miles from the Common. When he was but nineteen he joined his father's company which was ordered to the relief of Fort William Henry in the French and Indian War. Again in 1774, at the outbreak of the Revolution, he was called to military duty. At a meeting held in Hardwick, September 22, 1774, to make provision for those who were to serve as minute men, the members

of the earlier organized military companies of the town resigned and two new companies were formed, known as the North and South Companies. Of these, Elijah Warner was appointed ensign of the South Company. On May 14, 1776, he was elected lieutenant of Captain Josiah Locke's 10th Company, from Hardwick, 4th Worcester County Regiment, Mass., militia, under Col. James Converse, and was commissioned by order of the Council, May 31, 1776. He served the town as selectman in 1777, 1780, and again from 1793 to 1795. In 1781, after the adoption of the constitution of Massachusetts, the militia was re-organized and, on the roster of the newly appointed officers, was the name of Elijah Warner, commissioned as captain,. May 23, 1783. This was four months before the definite treaty of peace was signed and six months before the British evacuated New York.

The Census of 1790 in Hardwick gives him with a family of three males over 16, one under 16, and nine females. Again in 1810, the Census notes his family of one male and one female over 45, one female between 26 and 45, three males and three females between 16 and 26, two males and two females under 10. His will was made January 2, 1810, and mentioned his thirteen children then living. There are many references to this family in Paige's History of Hardwick.

Elijah Warner married (1) in Hardwick, Mass., January 14, 1762, SUBMIT WELLS, daughter of John and Martha (Allis) Wells of Hardwick, and granddaughter of Ichabod Allis.

Married (2) May 15, 1786, RACHEL SAMPSON, of Templeton, who died May 16, 1807.

Married (3) December 30, 1807, his cousin SARAH[5] WARNER, daughter of Jonathan[4] and Bathsheba (Allis) Warner, born November 1, 1742, died in Greenwich, Mass., December, 1837. Her first husband was Thomas Wheeler, by whom she had several children. See number 119.

Children of Elijah and Submit (Wells) Warner, born in Hardwick

223   *Abel Warner*, b. Apr. 29, 1763; m. Sarah Cook.
224   *David Warner*, b. Mar. 10, 1765; m. (1) Martha (Cottle) White, (2) Ruth (Rogers) Porter, (3) Dulcena (Carpenter) Stetson.
225   *Elijah Warner*, b. June 10, 1767; m. Betsey Mitchell.
      Lydia (1) Warner, b. Aug. 18, 1769; d. young.
226   *Giles Warner*, b. Dec. 3, 1771; m. (1) Betsey Sampson, (2) Mary Staples.
      Lydia Warner, bapt. June 19, 1774; m. (intention dated Feb. 25, 1796) Charles Gilbert of Chester, son of Timothy and Martha (Rogers) Gilbert of Hardwick.

227 *Electa Warner*, bapt. Sept. 15, 1776; m. Simeon White.

Charles Warner, bapt. Feb. 5, 1780. He is said to have gone west. His father's will indicates that he had received his portion of the estate before that date, 1810.

Polly Warner, bapt. July 21, 1782; probably d. young. One account gives this date as Patty's birth.

228 *Persis Warner*, b. Aug. 17, 1784; m. Noah Joy.

Olive Warner, m. Oct. 27, 1807, as his second wife, Pyam Mitchell of Cummington, son of William Mitchell. They had five children, "none of whom are living."

229 *Patty Warner* (according to one record, b. July 21, 1782); m. Isaac Durfee.

Children of Elijah and Rachel (Sampson) Warner

230 *Rachel Warner*, b. Oct. 6, 1787; m. Joseph Robinson.

John Whitcomb Warner, bapt. Oct. 2, 1791; was killed at a sham fight in Hardwick, Oct. 2, 1811, during a military parade. The iron ramrod had been left in the weapon by mistake and he was shot through the head.

Submit Wells Warner, bapt. Dec. 7, 1794; died Sept. 9, 1828.

123 **JOSEPH⁵ WARNER, JR.**, son of Captain Joseph⁴ and Mary (Hubbard) Warner, born in Hatfield, Mass., July 2, 1743; died in Cummington, Mass., June 8, 1818. A deed of September 5, 1771, gives his residence as "Hardwick in the province of Massachusetts Bay," but he later joined his father and brother Stephen in Cummington. In 1774 he was chosen lieutenant of the company of minute-men pledged to take the field at a minute's notice, raised by the town in anticipation of the approaching conflict with the mother country. When news of the battle of Lexington was brought to the town, this company, under command of Lieutenant Joseph Warner, marched to Lexington, stopping at Williamsburg for recruits and leaving the latter place on April 21st. After a service of seven days the company enlisted in Capt. Abel Thayer's Company, Col. John Fellows' Regiment, and Joseph Warner, Jr., was commissioned lieutenant of the company. March 22, 1776, he was commissioned captain of the 15th Company, 2d Hampshire County Regiment, and August 16, 1777, captain of Col. Benjamin Ruggles' Woodbridge Regiment; served at the battle of Saratoga. Besides his actual service on the field, he loaned the town money to pay its soldiers. (Massachusetts soldiers and sailors in the Revolution; Massachusetts State Revolutionary Archives, certified copy; Proprietors' records, Cummington.)

He held various town offices and was also interested in the affairs of the church. He was chosen to attend to the "seatingof the pews," and paid for his own pew the sum of thirty-three dollars, an amount considerably above the average. His will was probated August 11, 1818, and mentions land in Palmyra, N. Y., and Marlborough, Vt., a mill site in Cummington on West-field River and Swift River, dwelling house, homestead and other property. The heirs were his children: John, Paul, Susannah French, Sally Norton, Molly Warner, Rhoda Robinson, Cynthia Warner, and Joseph Warner, the last of whom was executor.

Captain Joseph Warner married November 14, 1764, **MARY WHIPPLE**, born February 19, 1745, died March 24, 1813,

JOSEPH WARNER HOMESTEAD IN CUMMINGTON, MASS.

daughter of Joseph and Mary (Whipple) Whipple, and a lineal descendant of Matthew Whipple, one of the early settlers of Ipswich, Mass.

Children, first three born in Hardwick, but all recorded in Cummington, Mass.

Susannah Warner, b. Dec. 18, 1765; m. Dec. 22, 1788, Stephen French. Children: i. Charles, b. Sept. 12, 1789. ii. Erastus, b. Oct. 11, 1793. iii. Susanna, b. Feb. 11, 1796. iv. Stephen, b. Oct. 8, 1799; m. and had three children, Ellen, who m. —— Porter of Cummington, Jennie, who m. —— Welch and lived in Waterbury, and Charles, who d. in youth. v. Otis, b. Nov. 30, 1801.

Paul Warner, b. Nov. 20, 1767; d. Jan. 17, 1806, not married. He was a farmer and held various town offices.

Sally Warner, b. Oct. 4, 1769; d. Nov. 4, 1849; m. Nov. 4, 1792, Bela

Norton. Children: i. Nancy, b. Sept. 18, 1793. ii. John, b. June 30, 1796. iii. Sally, b. Aug. 24, 1801. iv. Eliza, b. Sept. 26, 1803.

Mary (Molly) Warner, b. Oct. 23, 1771; d. Dec. 22, 1863, in Cummington, aged 92 years and 2 months; not married.

Rhoda Warner, b. Jan. 10, 1774; d. June 19, 1853; m. Oct. 19, 1797, Clark Robinson of Cummington. Children: i. Lydia, b. Oct. 21, 1798. ii. James, b. July 22, 1800. iii. Czarina, b. June 6, 1802. iv. Lucius Clark, b. Apr. 20, 1805.

John Warner, b. Jan. 4, 1777; d. Feb. 20, 1847, not married; was for a number of years a merchant in Canajoharie, N. Y.

Lydia Warner, b. Nov. 25, 1780; d. May 21, 1796.

Joseph (1) *Warner,* b. Jan. 12, 1783; d. Aug. 16, 1785.

Cynthia Warner, b. May 11, 1786; d. Sept. 10, 1850 (or 1849, Reed Genealogy); m. Oct. 20, 1814, Daniel Reed, b. Nov. 5, 1786, d. Nov. 29, 1854, in Cummington, son of Noah and Abigail (Rice) Reed of Cummington. Children: i. Noah Warner, b. Nov. 25, 1815; m. Nancy ———— and had six children, Mary Jane, b. June 17, 1839, Cynthia W., b. Mar. 20, 1841, John S., b. Mar. 31, 1843, Nancy E., b. Oct. 18, 1848, (son), b. Oct. 19, 1850, and Horace E., b. May, 1855. ii. Daniel Edwin, b. Mar. 17, 1818. iii. John Clark, b. July 4, 1820, resided in Cummington; m. Sarah ———— and had a son, b. Mar., 1854, and Mary A., b. Jan. 9, 1856. iv. Paul Dwight, b. Feb. 24, 1823. v. Lucius Franklin, b. Sept. 24, 1826.

231 *Joseph* (2) *Warner,* b. Sept. 29, 1788; m. Olive Holbrook.

124 STEPHEN⁵ WARNER, son of Joseph⁴ and Mary (Hubbard) Warner, born in Hardwick, Mass., 1744; died in Cummington, Mass., December 12, 1812. He was an early settler and proprietor of Cummington, Lot No. 5. He was a farmer, and operated a clover mill, and is frequently mentioned in the records of the town for his public services. He enlisted on July 19, 1777, Lieutenant in Capt. Nathaniel Harwood's Company, Col. John Dickenson's Regiment, marching on the alarm to Manchester under the command of his cousin, Col. Jonathan Warner. He was commissioned Lieutenant, July 6, 1778, in a company of the 2d Hampshire County Regiment, under Col. Israel Chapin, and also served as one of the Committee of Correspondence during the last years of the war. (Mass. Archives, vol. 19, p. 220; vol. 28, p. 45.) The first town meeting, or meeting of the proprietors of Cummington, was held at the house of Stephen Warner, June 19, 1771. This was later known as the Deacon Rogers Place. The Proprietors' Records are full of allusions to the various activities in which he took part, as tithing-man, fence-viewer, warden, constable, collector, selectman, surveyor of lumber, roads, and bridges, inspector of corn and flax, etc. Lieutenant Warner was on the committee to survey the line between Cummington and Windsor, January 17, 1780; was on a committee chosen, May 22, 1780, "to make remarks upon the Constitution"; was on the committee to hire four soldiers, June 15, 1780, when the town voted the money to hire and pay such soldiers; was chosen to "perfix" the site where the two pounds were to be built; was one of a committee to hire laborers to work on the roads, who were to be paid by the town at the rate of 37 cents a day; with Andrew Packard was appointed to build the bridge across the Westfield River. Stephen Warner was on the committee to divide the school and ministerial lands, and was a delegate to the convention held at Hatfield, March 27, 1781, to consider ways of remedying grievances arising from the late war and to establish a new form of government. He was appointed to instruct Deacon Barnabas Packard, who was a delegate to a convention held at Hatfield for the same purpose, August 22, 1786. In 1800 he represented the towns of Plainfield and Cummington in the General Court at Boston.

His interest in church matters was no less keen than his attention to public duties. He was one of the organizers of the Cummington Church and one of the first eight to sign its covenant. He assisted in selecting the site for the church and building it. Later, in 1806, he was one to arrange "to paint the meeting-house anew and to paint it white." Not long before his death he wrote a farewell letter of advice to his children and step-children, some copies of which have been preserved.

His will, made May 4, 1812, bequeaths lands in Palmyra, N. Y., to his son Jonathan; his farms in Cummington and Windsor, Mass., to his son Stephen; lands in Onondaga Co., N. Y., to his daughters, Betsey Baldwin, Lois Warner, Rosamond White, and to his grandchildren, Aurelia, Cordelia, Celina, and Philena, children of his daughter, Nancy Fobes.

In the 1800 Census, his family consisted of one man and two women over 45, two boys and a girl between 16 and 26, two girls between 10 and 16. In 1790 he was recorded with three males over 16, one under 16, and five females in the family.

Stephen Warner married (1) in Hardwick, Mass., LOIS GOSS. The date of this marriage is given as May 26, 1768, in Early Massachusetts Marriages, vol. 1, p. 118, the same date as the marriage of Mary Warner and Timothy Moore. There is doubtless an error here and the marriage of Stephen Warner was earlier.

Married (2) MARY (NORTON) PORTER, daughter of William Norton of Abington, Mass. She died in Westmoreland, N. Y., in 1826. She was first married in Abington, February 2, 1766, to Noah Porter, by whom she had children: i. Noah, Jr.,

b. April 17, 1767 (see No. 224) ; ii. Mary, b. May 18, 1769, m. Dr. Pomroy, and d. in Burlington, Vt., Oct. 2, 1846; iii. Norton, b. 1771 ; iv. William, b. Aug., 1773.

Children of Stephen and Lois (Goss) Warner

Jonathan Warner, b. Mar. 1, 1768; went to Palmyra, N. Y., with Webb Harwood, near the close of the year 1789. He was elected assessor of Palmyra in 1796. In his father's letter of farewell to his children, he is called a farmer.

232 Elizabeth or Betsey Warner, b. June 11, 1769; m. Jonas Cutler Baldwin.

Children of Stephen and Mary (Norton-Porter) Warner

233 Stephen Warner, b. Apr. 18, 1778; m. Clarissa Mitchell.
234 Nancy Warner, b. Oct. 16, 1781; m. Philander Fobes.
Lois Warner, b. Aug. 12, 1783; m. Sept. 6, 1812, Benjamin Frisbie. Child: Mary, m. —— Parrish, a lawyer, who lived in Sandusky, Ohio, and had two children, Mary and Sarah. Mr. Parrish is said to have been interested in the underground railway in the days of slavery.
235 Rosamond Warner, b. Aug. 12, 1786; m. James White, M.D.

125 ANNA[5] WARNER, daughter of Joseph[4] and Mary (Hubbard) Warner, born in Hardwick, Mass., May 2, 1750; died there, January 5, 1814. Her family is recorded in Paige's History of Hardwick.

Married in Hardwick, October 25, 1770, JAMES PAIGE, born May 12, 1735; died January 18, 1817. He was the son of John and Rebecca (Wheeler) Paige, grandson of Nathaniel Paige, and had married (1) Mary Stone, by whom he had a daughter Polly. He was a cordwainer, removed from Bedford to Framingham before October 21, 1762, on which date he bought a farm in Hardwick and doubtless removed there at once. He resided on the Petersham Road in Hardwick. Both John Paige and his father Nathaniel were cornets in the militia.

Children, born in Hardwick

Luther Paige, b. Nov. 5, 1772; d. Jan. 18, 1843; m. (1) Aug. 22, 1802, Sarah Bangs, who died Apr. 21, 1816, aged 34, daughter of Elijah Bangs; (2) Sept. 4, 1816, Mrs. Mary Hinkley, widow of Barnabas Hinkley. She died at Bangor, Me., Mar. 11, 1849. He was a farmer on the Paige homestead at Hardwick. Children: i. Erastus Warner, b. July 1, 1803; m. (1) Lucinda Lawrence, (2) Emeline M. Paige; was a farmer; selectman for six years; had five children. ii. John Adams, b. Feb. 12, 1805; d. Jan. 5, 1864; was a mason in Boston. iii. Bela Bangs, b. July 13, 1807; m. Nov. 28, 1844, Rhoda Ann Clark, daughter of Stillman Clark, resided in Boston and Hardwick. iv. Rosamond, d. young. v. Sarah Ann, b. Mar. 16, 1813; d. Sept. 23,

12

1861; m. Mar. 31, 1833, Captain John Raymond. vi. Fanny, d. young.

Anna (1) *Paige*, b. Apr. 1, 1775; d. Aug. 11, 1777.

James (1) *Paige*, b. Jan. 13, 1777; d. Oct. 4, 1777.

Anna (2) *Paige*, b. Oct. 18, 1778; d. June 7, 1824; m. June 26, 1802, Captain Moses Allen.

James (2) *Paige*, b. Jan. 2, 1781; d. Nov. 2, 1846. He was a mason in Boston and wrote the name Page. Married July 8, 1810, Thirza Hopkins of Petersham. Children: i. Henry A., b. July 20, 1811. ii. Ely, b. Nov. 5, 1821; m. July 5, 1843, Andrew J. Richardson.

Calvin Paige (twin), b. May 8, 1784; d. July 7, 1850. He was a mason in Boston, and wrote the name Page. Married (1) Nov. 12, 1815, Martha Ruggles, who died Aug. 5, 1816; (2) Sept. 19, 1819, Philinda Gates, who died Oct. 23, 1867. Children: i. Silvanus Gates, d. young. ii. Calvin Gates, b. July 3, 1829; m. Susan Haskell Keep and was the father of Hollis Bowman Page, b. in Boston, Oct. 27, 1859, d. Aug. 4, 1901, an artist who was interested in experiments in color harmony.

Fanny Paige (twin), b. May 8, 1784; d. in Boston, Feb. 15, 1873; m. (1) Stephen Rice, Jr., who died Aug. 16, 1821; (2) intentions published May 7, 1825, Captain Moses Allen, who had first married her sister. After his death she removed to Boston. Child: Eliza Ann, b. Jan. 13, 1814; m. Feb. 18, 1835, John P. Robinson of Brookfield and removed to Boston.

126 HANNAH[5] WARNER, daughter of Joseph[4] and Mary (Hubbard) Warner, born October 7, 1752, in Hardwick, Mass.; died 1828.

Married in Hardwick, March 4, 1773, Col. **JOHN BRADISH, JR.,** who died 1825. He was the son of Deacon John and Mary (Green) Bradish of Hardwick. Among descendants of this family may be mentioned: Miss Julia Gavit of New York City; George Eltweed Pomeroy of Toledo, Ohio; George S. Tiffany of Tecumseh, Mich.; Zim Rhoda Bradish of Adrian, Mich.

Children

Calvin Bradish, b. Dec. 26, 1773.

Chloe Bradish, b. Apr. 29, 1775.

Rowena Bradish, b. Sept. 30, 1776, in Cummington, Mass.; d. Feb. 8, 1870, in Raisin township, Michigan; m. 1801, John Comstock, b. 1774, in Adams, Mass., d. in Raisin Valley, Mich., June, 1851, son of Nathan and Mary (Staple) Comstock. He was a lawyer for many years in Ontario County and Lockport, N. Y., removed to Michigan about 1830. Child: Warner M., b. Sept. 8, 1802, in Palmyra, N. Y.; d. Nov. 2, 1882, in Raisin, Mich.; was for many years a merchant at Adrian, Mich., and Postmaster under Fillmore; m. (1) Feb. 7, 1826, Mary M. Perry, b. July 28, 1805; d. Jan. 14, 1876; m. (2) June 3, 1877, Alice Sheldon. Warner M. Comstock had children, b. in Lockport, N. Y.: i. Horace Warner, b. Dec. 19, 1826; d. in Adrian, Mich., Feb. 17, 1897; m. (1) May 1, 1855, Louise Kinsley, (2) Oct. 19, 1863,

Fannie C. Comstock, daughter of Jared and Catherine (Hall) Comstock, and had children, Harriet Virginia, b. July 18, 1857, a teacher in Cleveland, and Albert, d. in infancy. ii. Miriam B., b. Sept. 28, 1829; d. Nov. 11, 1857; m. Sept. 24, 1848, Jerome B. Chaffee, b. Apr. 17, 1825, near Lockport, d. Mar. 10, 1886, in Salem Centre, Westchester County, N. Y., resided for some years in Denver, Colo., and was U. S. Senator 1865 and 1876. Jerome and Miriam (Comstock) Chaffee had children: i. Horace Jerome, b. Aug. 27, 1849; d. Sept. 4, 1850. ii. Nellie Virginia, b. April 27, 1853; d. Aug. 12, 1861. iii. Edward Fenton, b. Dec. 4, 1855; d. Dec., 1855. iv. Fannie Josephine, b. in Adrian, Mich., Jan. 16, 1857; m. Nov. 1, 1880, Ulysses S. Grant, Jr., and had children, Miriam, b. Sept. 26, 1881, Chaffee, b. Sept. 28, 1883, Julia Dent, b. Apr. 15, 1885, Fannie, b. Aug. 11, 1889, and Ulysses, 3d, b. May 23, 1893.

Charles Bradish, b. April 20, 1778.

Sarah Bradish, b. Sept. 25, 1781; d. at Palmyra, N. Y., Sept. 23, 1853; m. Bartlett Robinson.

Luther Bradish, b. 1783; was graduated from Williams College in 1804, became a lawyer and was lieutenant-governor of New York State, 1839-43. He was at one time president of the New York Historical Society.

127 **MOSES⁵ WARNER,** son of Joseph⁴ and Mary (Hubbard) Warner, born in Hardwick, Mass., April 4, 1760; died July 11, 1837, in Cummington, Mass. He was a farmer in Cummington and his farm is still owned by his descendants. When a boy of 11, he removed with his family to Cummington, and was entrusted with the driving of the two yokes of oxen that drew the family's possessions. In August, 1777, he was a private in Capt. William·Ward's Company, Col. Ezra May's Regiment, on the expedition to Bennington, Vt. Later in the same year he served in Capt. Christopher Bannister's Company of the same regiment on an expedition to Stillwater and Saratoga. In 1779 he served in Capt. Benjamin Bonney's Company, Col. Elisha Porter's Hampshire County Regiment, at New London, Conn. For his Revolutionary service, he was granted a pension in 1832. He appears in the 1790 Census at Cummington with two males over 16 and three females in the family. In the 1800 Census of the same town, he is recorded with one female over 45, one male and one female between 26 and 45, one female 16 to 26, one between 10 and 16, and a boy and two girls under 10.

Above Swift River Village on the Westfield River was a grist mill and a sawmill owned in early times by Moses Warner. He was surveyor of highways in 1795 and 1803; tithingman in 1797; superintendent of the surveyors of highways in 1800; served on the committees on roads and bridges at various times from 1795 to 1800. His will was dated March 18, 1825.

Moses Warner married (1) May 4, 1785, **MARY (MOLLY) WARD**, daughter of Capt. William and Sarah (Trowbridge) Ward of Worthington, Mass. She was born in Cummington, August 25, 1766, and died there August 29, 1795.

Married (2) October 17, 1796, **ABIGAIL COLTON**, born March 1, 1764, recorded at Springfield, Mass., died August 23, 1829. She was the daughter of Gideon and Deidemia (Purchase) Colton.

Children by first wife

Minerva (1) *Warner*, d. Sept. 17, 1788.

Minerva (2) *Warner*, b. in Cummington, Nov. 26, 1788; d. Apr. 25, 1826; married May 22, 1816, Jonathan Brewster, Jr., of Worthington, Mass. Children: i. Jonathan, b. Apr. 19, 1817. ii. Marshal, b. July 4, 1818. iii. Moses Warner, b. Aug. 10, 1820. iv. Lois, b. Aug. 21, 1822. v. Chester, b. Aug. 12, 1824.

236   *Orrin Warner*, b. July 3, 1791; m. (1) Lucinda Starks, (2) Delia McLouth, (3) Mary Davenport.

Children by second wife

Polly Warner, b. Sept. 16, 1797; m. Nov. 28, 1824, Jonathan Farrar (Parrow, in Colton Genealogy) of Cummington, Mass. They resided in Cummington, later in Agawam, Mass. Children: i. Pretania Anna. ii. Jonathan Warner, m. Dec. 31, 1857, Lydia M. Bodurtha, and had children, Flora Ellen, b. July 5, 1860, Nellie Jane, b. Apr. 30, 1862, and Howard Augustine, b. Oct. 27, 1870, d. Jan. 3, 1871. iii. Egbert. iv. Mary Aspasia. v. Eugene, b. in Agawam.

Persis Warner, b. June 20, 1799; d. Jan. 14, 1865, not married.

237   *Norman Warner*, b. Apr. 4, 1801; m. Elvira Hartwell.

Ambrose Warner, b. Feb. 28, 1804; d. Dec. 2, 1824, not married.

William Warner, b. Sept. 1, 1808; d. Aug. 23, 1811.

128   RUTH[5] WARNER, daughter of Andrew[4], Jr., and Sarah (Graves) Warner, born probably in Saybrook, Conn.; died in Cambridge, N. Y. ·

Married **CHARLES DEMING**, born June 26, 1714, in Wethersfield, Conn.; died in 1780. He was the son of Jonathan and Abigail (Tyler) Deming. In 1737 he made several transfers of property in which he styles himself as of Wethersfield, and he probably removed to Saybrook in 1738. In 1739 he deeded to his brother Daniel land in Wethersfield which he had received from their father Jonathan. His will, probated in Guilford, March 7, 1780, mentions his wife Ruth and nine children, Stephen having died earlier. The Deming Genealogy gives an account of descendants of this family.

Children, probably all born in Saybrook

Stephen Deming, d., not married.

Daniel Deming, b. Apr. 11, 1751; d. May 15, ——, in Sharon, Conn.; m. Jan. 24, 1780, Cynthia Hunt, b. May 11, 1762, d. Apr. 4, 1850, in Sharon. He was a' shoemaker by trade, removed from Saybrook to Torrington in 1782. He owned a tannery in the vicinity of Sharon. His wife joined the church at Sharon in 1792 and the first four children were baptized there. Children, first born at Saybrook, others at Sharon: i. Stephen, b. Dec. 19, 1780; d. June 24, 1867, in Litchfield, where he settled after his marriage; kept a hotel in Litchfield and was sheriff of the county; m. (1) Fanny Beecher, (2) Sarah Buel; had eight children by the second wife. ii. James, b. Oct. 13, 1782; d. Nov. 17, 1782. iii. Erastus, b. Oct. 3, 1783; d. Oct. 24, 1821, not married. iv. Laura, b. June 15, 1787; d. Feb. 14, 1873, not married. v. Betsey, b. Mar. 12, 1789; d. June 5, 1852; m. (1) Sept., 1806, Henry Winchester of Amenia, N. Y., (2) Abram Pratt. vi. Julia, b. Nov. 24, 1790; d. May 10, 1791. vii. Adelia, b. Mar. 22, 1795; d. Mar. 10, 1842; m. Dec. 20, 1814, Robert Ranson Beaslin of Adrian, Mich. viii. Ralph, b. Oct. 19, 1798; d. July 21, 1871; was graduated from Yale, 1824; honorary M.D., Yale, 1857; was a physician in Sharon; member of State Legislature for 14 terms and of the Senate for one; warden of the Episcopal Church for twenty years; m. Mary T. Cornwall and had four children. ix. Harriet, b. May 13, 1801; d. Oct. 1, 1829; m. Feb. 3, 1819, Hezekiah Goodwin of Lime Rock. x. Daniel Hunt, b. Sept. 25, 1804; d. Apr. 7, 1871, in Wales, Mich.; m. Apr. 22, 1840, Mary Jane Bailey, and had three children; was a farmer, supervisor of the town for nine years, member of state legislature; moved from Dover, Mich., to Rome, Mich., 1860.

Samuel Deming, b. Nov. 20, 1755; d. Dec. 11, 1803; m. in Cambridge, N. Y., Dec. 20, 1781, Huldah Dewey, b. Mar. 9, 1761, in Canterbury, Conn., d. Dec., 1840, daughter of Josiah and Huldah (Frost) Dewey. He was a farmer of means and owned slaves, resided in Center White Creek, N. Y., where he left many descendants. He enlisted July 10, 1775, and served at various times during the war; was at the battle of Bennington; at the close of the war was promoted to the rank of captain and placed in command of a company. Children: i. Anna, b. Feb. 20, 1783; m. Dec. 19, 1805, Nahum Dunham. ii. Ruth, b. Oct. 6, 1784; m. Aug. 22, 1815, Daniel H. Pratt. iii. Mary, b. July 30, 1786; m. Oct. 13, 1807, Russell Norton. iv. Elizabeth, b. Sept. 29, 1788; d. Mar. 29, 1789. v. Huldah, b. Feb. 23, 1790; d. Mar. 3, 1872; m. May 7, 1833, Gardner Cleveland. vi. Cynthia, b. July 16, 1792; m. Jan. 25, 1810, John Hamlin. vii. Olympia, b. Jan. 28, 1795; m. May 28, 1825, Wait S. Pratt. viii. Sarah, b. June 24, 1797; m. Wait S. Pratt. ix. Mehitable, b. Mar. 11, 1800; m. Nov. 18, 1823, John Dalee.

James Deming, d. not married.

Lydia Deming, b. Sept. 22, 1760; d. June 20, 1835; m. (1) —— Crampton, (2) 1784, Isaac Bartholomew.

Charles Deming, Jr., b. Aug. 28, 1768; m. (1) Hannah⁶ Warner, daughter of Seth⁶ and Hannah Le Moyne (De Angelis) Warner, (2) Judith Boardman, (3) Clarissa Brundage. See number 253.

Elizabeth Deming, m. —— Hinsdale.

Anna Deming, m. —— Hopkins.

Abigail Deming, m. (1) Solomon Hodges, (2) Benjamin Wyman.

Sarah Deming, m. Daniel Holbrook.

129 JONATHAN⁵ WARNER, son of Andrew⁴ and Sarah
(Graves) Warner, born in Saybrook, now Chester, Conn.,
October 1, 1728; died in Hadlyme, February 22, 1810, buried
in the South Burying Ground at Hadlyme. He was a farmer
and took an active part in civil and military affairs. He is
probably the Jonathan Warner who had the following military
record: Ensign, 9th Company, 6th Regiment, May, 1752; Lieutenant, same, 1759; Captain, 9th Company, 3d Regiment, Oct.,
1764; Ensign, 5th Company, Lyme, May, 1773; Lieutenant,
same, Jan., 1774. With other inhabitants of Lyme and Saybrook he signed a petition for the establishment of a ferry, April

WARNER HOUSE IN CHESTER, CONN.

25, 1760. A petition of Jonathan and Eliza Warner, Samuel
Selden and others, object not stated, was refused by the
Assembly, October, 1766. In May, 1769, there was recorded a
permit for Jonathan Warner to run a ferry from Fort Hill, parish
of Chester in Saybrook, to Lyme. The fares were as follows:
man and horse, 3 pence; footman, one penny; a led horse, 1
penny half penny; an ox or other neat kine, 2 pence; sheep,
hogs and goats, ½ penny per head. In May, 1787, he was noted
as the proprietor of Warner's Ferry. (Conn. State Library,
Travel: 292; Conn. Public Records, 10:82, 11:265, 12:301, 538.)
    Jonathan Warner was on a committee for supplying the Con-
tinental soldiers during the Revolutionary War. He was
recorded as a resident of Saybrook town in the 1790 Census. In

1798 he built the house in Chester which has been handed down by inheritance to the present owner, Andrew E.[8] Warner. The frame and most of the timber of which it is constructed is oak, hewn from trees which grew on the farm, but the clapboards and boards with which the interior is finished, are of pine which came from Maine in rafts. There are in existence the bills of cost of building, amounting to £1616–11– . An old building in the rear of the house is still designated as the "Chaise house."

Jonathan Warner married in Hadlyme, in 1751, **ELIZABETH SELDEN,** born November 27, 1722, died June 17, 1804, buried in the South Burying Ground in Hadlyme. She was the daughter of Joseph Selden of Hadlyme.

238 *Lovice Warner,* b. Dec. 26, 1751; m. Robert Hungerford, Jr.
239 *Jonathan Warner, Jr.,* b. June 17, 1756; m. Hepsibah Ely.
240 *Selden Warner,* b. Oct. 20, 1760; m. Dorothy Selden.
241 *Chapman Warner,* b. May 19, 1764; m. Sarah Comstock.

130 D A V I D [5] W A R N E R, son of Andrew[4] and Sarah (Graves) Warner, born in Saybrook, Conn., August 7, 1730; died November 6, 1800, in Saybrook (Chester). The 1800 Census records him as of Saybrook; one male over 45; one male and one female, 26 to 45,; one male 16 to 26,; one female, 10 to 16 in his family. He was a Revolutionary soldier; served from May 8 to December 18, 1775, in the 9th Company, 6th Regiment, Connecticut State Troops; in Major Skinner's Troop, Regiment of Light Horse, State Troops, from June 10, to August 13, 1776; as seaman on the galley "Trumbull" of the Lake Champlain flotilla, discharged November 25, 1776. His will mentions wife Eunice; sons Phineas and William; daughter Sally Ely; grandchildren, Thomas, William, Samuel, Anne, and Lydia Silliman.

Married (1) 1748, **SARAH WARD** of Saybrook, who died February 20, 1793.

Married (2) in Middletown, Conn., March 27, 1794, **EUNICE PROUT,** who died 1819, aged 74. She joined the Congregational Church at Chester May 2, 1802, as the widow of David Warner.

Children by first wife

242 *Phineas Warner,* b. 1749; m. Eunice Church.
243 *Lydia Warner,* m. Thomas Silliman.
244 *William Warner,* m. Rhoda Silliman.
    Sarah Warner, d. in Chester, Conn., 1838; m. Oct. 25, 1795, Marsh Ely of Lyme, Conn., b. 1761, d. 1835, son of Samuel and Hannah (Marsh) Ely. No children.

131 ELEAZER⁵ WARNER, son of Andrew⁴, Jr., and Sarah (Graves) Warner, born in Saybrook (now Chester), Conn., 1733; died in Cambridge, Washington County, N. Y., October 26, 1817, aged 85, buried in Cambridge. According to his tombstone and a record in the Public Library in Cambridge, he was a Revolutionary soldier. It is said in the family that he or possibly his son Eleazer was one of the guard over Major André the night before his execution. Eleazer Warner removed to Washington County among the first settlers there and his name is found among the quit-rents, 125 acres, on lot 11 (Cambridge town clerk's book, 1787). He and his wife were among the founders of the First United Presbyterian Church in Cambridge.

Married January 14, 1762, **ELIZABETH KIRTLAND,** born May 23, 1740, died March 29, 1804, buried in Cambridge, daughter of Captain Philip and Lydia (Marvin) Kirtland. She united with the First United Presbyterian Church in Cambridge, November 22, 1795.

Children, probably all born in Saybrook, now Chester, Conn.

245 *Andrew Warner,* b. Nov. 15, 1762; m. Rachel Crocker.
246 *Eleazer Warner, Jr.,* b. April 2, 1764; m. Elizabeth ———
247 *Philip Warner,* b. Feb. 16, 1766; m. Sarah Woods.
248 *Sylvester Warner,* b. Feb. 21, 1768; m. Elizabeth Reed.
249 *Kirtland Warner,* b. Feb. 8, 1770; m. (1) Elizabeth ———, (2) Sarah Trumbull.
     Nathan Warner, b. Mar. 23, 1772.
     Betsey Warner, b. Apr. 4, 1775; d. in Cambridge, N. Y., 1819; m. John W. Fisher. Children: i. Solomon, left no children. ii. Adinarum.
     Lydia Warner, b. Feb. 14, 1777; d. 1814 or 1816; m. Joseph Greenleaf, b. Feb. 28, 1779, d. Feb., 1842, son of Stephen and Eunice (Fairbanks) Greenleaf. He m. (2) Mrs. Ruth (Perry) Cooper. He had six children.
     Ann Warner, birth not recorded in Saybrook records with other children's births. She married Nathaniel Simpson and died in Canada in 1820.

132 JAMES⁵ WARNER, son of Andrew⁴, Jr., and Sarah (Graves) Warner, born 1736, in Saybrook, now Chester, Conn.; died December 11, 1812, aged 77, buried in Cambridge, N. Y. With his two brothers he was among the first settlers in 1780 of Washington County, New York, on the Cambridge Patent, from which Jackson was largely made up. They moved their effects through the wilderness with an ox-team, finding their way by means of marked trees. The town clerk's book of 1787, Cambridge, has the following entries regarding him: quit-rents on lot number 11, 300 acres, land taken or damaged during the Revolution; mark of the stock, a slit in the end of each ear. In 1791 a petition was entered for a road to run east along James Warner's land on the south side through to the Annaquasicoke road. His tombstone notes him as a Revolutionary soldier.

Married (1) ABIGAIL ————, who died October 12, 1807, aged 66, buried in Cambridge.

Married (2) ELIZABETH BATES, who died June 12, 1809, aged 65.

Children

(*Infant*), b. and d. in Chester, Conn., 1766.

250 *James Warner, Jr.*, b. 1767; perhaps m. Rebecca Hatch.

Graves Warner, b. 1770, in Saybrook; was a subscriber to the Cambridge Washington Academy, Cambridge, N. Y., in 1814; resided later in Silver Creek, N. Y. Graves and Polly Warner made a deed in Chenango Co., N. Y., in 1830.

251 *Arnold Warner*, b. 1772; m. Polly Cutter.

Abigail Warner, b. 1774; d. June 18, 1794, was the first person buried in the cemetery of the First United Presbyterian Church in Cambridge, N. Y.; m. Seth Rising.

Joseph Warner, b. in Saybrook; d. Jan. 6, 1813, aged 37, buried in Cambridge, N. Y.; m. ————. Children: i. Joseph, Jr. (perhaps had son James, b. in Jackson, N. Y., Aug. 7, 1833; m. Charlotte B. Townsend; removed to Sandwich, Ill., in 1855, where he was a teacher and later a merchant; had a son James Leroy, b. in Sandwich, May 19, 1863, a merchant of Sandwich). ii. James. iii. Tilla. iv. Frances.

Prudence Warner, b. 1777, in Saybrook; resided in Rome, N. Y.; m. Clark Putnam.

252 *Solomon Warner*, b. 1778; m. Elizabeth Woodworth.

Ezra Warner, b. 1782, in Cambridge, N. Y.; resided in Florence, Oneida Co., N. Y., where he died Nov. 7, 1807 or 1817; m. Cynthia Carpenter, b. Dec. 3, 1783, d. Aug. 24, 1839. Children: Lucy, Harriett. His widow married (2) Adnah Abbott of Tolland and Cambridge, N. Y., who moved to Hartford, Washington County, in 1832.

Sally Warner, resided in Cambridge, N. Y.; m. William More or Moore.

Polly Warner, m. Edward Wells.

133 SETH[5] (or SETH ANDREW) WARNER, son of Andrew[4], Jr., and Sarah (Graves) Warner, born in Saybrook, Conn., January 28, 1743; was lost at sea, April 9, 1790. His home was in Saybrook. He was a sea captain and was for many years captain of a vessel engaged in the West India trade. In the Revolution he rendered valuable aid to the colonies by raising a crew of forty seamen for service on the lakes. An order for £180 was made out to him on August 13, 1776. The men were to receive a bounty of five pounds for enlisting; for finding

themselves blankets, twelve shillings; guns, six shillings; cartouch-box, belt, and knapsack, two shillings; and one month's wages of forty-eight shillings advanced.

Married in Newport, R. I., December 19, 1773, **Mrs. HANNAH LE MOYNE DE ANGELIS,** born in Boston, January 29, 1742, died August 16, 1804, in Saybrook. She was the daughter of Captain Charles Le Moyne and granddaughter of the Sieur Charles Le Moyne, a native of Sables-d'Olonne, near Rochelle, France, one of the distinguished Le Moyne family that furnished a governor of Montreal, one of Rochefort, one of Cayenne, and two governors of Louisiana. Her first husband was Pascal Constant Petit De Angelis, of Italian ancestry, a resident of the Island of St. Eustatia, West Indies. While in feeble health he engaged passage for himself and family on one of Captain Seth Warner's return voyages, and died on the journey. His widow later married the captain, who adopted her son, Pascal Charles Joseph De Angelis, born on St. Eustatia, 1763, and gave him as liberal an education as the times afforded.

Children of Seth Warner

253 *Hannah Warner,* b. Aug. 26, 1775; m. Charles Deming.
  Sarah Warner, b. Feb. 26, 1778; d. Nov. 16, 1807; m. ———— Atkins.
  Mary Warner, b. Aug. 4, 1780, in Saybrook; d. Dec. 31, 1865 (or Jan. 17, 1840, in Ingham Co., Mich.); m. Apr. 3, 1803, William Smith. Child: Le Moyne M. S., who has been editor of the Grand Haven (Mich.) Record.
254 *Melinda Warner,* m. Harry Smith.
255 *Seth Andrew Le Moyne Warner,* b. Feb. 12, 1786; m. (1) Sally Wixom, (2) Emma Palmer.

134 JOHN[5] WARNER, son of Ichabod[4] and ———— Warner, born in Saybrook, Conn.; resided for some years in East Haddam, Conn., then removed with his sons to New York State, where he died in Herkimer County about 1813. His will, recorded in Herkimer, was probated March 16, 1813, and states his residence as Litchfield. The heirs were: daughters Ann, Mehitabel Spencer and Lucy Hadley; Halsey Spencer, oldest son* of his daughter Mehitabel; other children, John, Samuel, Ichabod, Darius, Lydia, Sarah, and Susannah. He may be the John Warner who was recorded with his family in East Haddam, Census of 1790, two males over 16, one under 16, and six females in the family. There is a deed of 1802 by which he received property in Litchfield from Abner Rising, Henry Watrous, and Ezra Mallory.

Married. The name of his wife has nowhere been found.

Children

Ann Warner.
Mehitabel Warner; m. —— Spencer and had a son Halsey, b. before
     1813.
256 *Lucy Maria Warner*, m. William Hadley.
Samuel Warner, m. —— Parker.
Ichabod Warner. With his brother Darius he bought land in East
     Haddam, Conn., 1791.
Darius Warner. Bought land in East Haddam, 1791; land in Lyme,
     Conn., near Warner's Ferry, 1794; bought and sold land in Lyme,
     1794-1801; was described as of Lyme in 1797; probably removed to
     New York State with his father. One Darius Warner "of some
     Eastern state" was living in Newburgh, near Cleveland, Ohio, in
     1801 and had children, Darius, Lydia and Esther.
Susannah Warner.
John Warner.
Lydia Warner.
Sarah Warner.

135 ANNA[5] WARNER, daughter of Daniel[4] and Elizabeth
(Clark) Warner, born in East Haddam, Conn., April 21, 1774;
died in East Hartford, December 10, 1834. Her family is more
fully recorded in the Winslow Memorial.

Married in East Haddam, September 6, 1795, PARDON
WINSLOW, born in Freetown, Mass., September 26, 1773, died
in Hockanum, Conn., February 17, 1855, son of Jonathan and
Sibyl (Potter) Winslow. He married (2) about 1842, Mary
Parmalee. He removed from near Charlton, Mass., to East
Haddam about 1794, to Wethersfield, 1797; went to South
America to get live oak lumber for ship building; was a sea-
faring man until April, 1806, when he moved from Wethersfield
to a farm in East Hartford (Hockanum), Conn. He was a
trustee of the Methodist Church for about fifteen years and was
one of its most active supporters.

Children

Charles Winslow, b. Mar. 16, 1796, in East Haddam; d. in Hockanum,
     1856; m. in Wethersfield, May, 1823, Hannah Rhodes of Wethers-
     field, daughter of Selah Rhodes of Glastonbury. No children.
Ann Winslow, b. Sept. 15, 1799; d. in Hockanum, Mar. 14, 1854; m.
     Ralph Risley of Hockanum, who died before 1851. Children: i.
     Ralph, Jr., resided in Hockanum, 1872. ii. Charles, U. S. soldier.
     iii. Elisha, U. S. soldier. iv. Amanda. v. Anna.
Daniel Winslow, b. Mar. 17, 1801, in Wethersfield; d. May 17, 1873, in
     East Hartford; m. in East Hartford, June 16, 1822, Marinda Keeney
     of Manchester, b. Feb. 4, 1803, daughter of Ashbel and Sarah (Hills)
     Keeney of East Hartford. He was selectman and member of the
     Legislature from East Hartford; a farmer. Children: i. Sarah
     Ann, b. Jan. 26, 1824; m. Willis S. Bronson of Hartford and had

four children. ii. Nelson, b. May 8, 1826; m. June 29, 1855, Altresta Keeney of Manchester; resided in East Hartford, East Haddam, and Hartford; had four children. iii. Ellen, b. Apr. 19, 1838; m. Apr. 19, 1856, Hector Chapman, b. in Glastonbury, son of Aziel and Altresta (House) Chapman; resided in Hartford and had two children.

Eliza Winslow, b. Jan. 15, 1806, in Wethersfield; m. in East Hartford, Jan. 22, 1826, Austin Lester, b. in East Hartford, Feb. 4, 1801, son of Isaac and Comfort (Risley) Lester, d. Oct. 3, 1851. Children, b. in East Hartford: i. Newell, b. Jan. 21, 1827; m. Oct. 15, 1851, Lydia Maria Hills, b. Apr. 15, 1832, daughter of Horace Hubbard and Miranda (Porter) Hills; resided in Hartford and had four children. ii. Martin Kellogg, b. Dec. 24, 1828. iii. Lawrence Varranes, b. Apr. 11, 1834; resided in Hartford; m. in East Hartford, June 8, 1859, Maria Theresa Larrabee, ,b. Sept. 9, 1840, in East Hartford, daughter of William W. and Amelia (Roberts) Larrabee; had three children. iv. Charles Edward Winslow, b. Oct. 6, 1846; lives in Hartford.

136 DANIEL⁵ WARNER, JR., son of Daniel⁴ and Elizabeth (Clark) Warner, born July 9, 1776; resided in East Haddam, Conn., where he died September 24 (14, town records), 1865. He was a farmer and after middle life was engaged in the ship lumber trade at Haddam Landing. He resided in the South School District, and was a member of St. Stephen's Episcopal Church.

Married in East Haddam, December 25, 1801, N A N C Y BRAINERD, born in East Haddam, June 30, 1776, died October, 1860, daughter of John and Anna (Smith) Brainerd of East Haddam. John Brainerd was one of the founders of St. Stephen's Church at East Haddam. For further data of the Brainerd family, see the Brainerd Genealogy.

Children, born in East Haddam

Phebe Ann Warner, b. Nov. 9, 1802; d. Sept. 19, 1889, not married; buried in River View Cemetery on Main Street, East Haddam.

Catherine Gennette Warner, b. May 27, 1804; d. Sept. 29, 1806, buried in East Haddam.

Floretta Warner, b. Jan. 16, 1806; d. Oct. 23, 1809.

257 *Daniel Brainerd Warner*, b. March 24, 1807; m. Mary Anna Green.

Elijah Clark Warner, b. Dec. 12, 1809; d. in East Haddam, Nov. 8, 1890, buried in Riverview Cemetery there. He was a farmer, never married, but resided with his sister Phebe at the old homestead southeast of East Haddam Landing.

Elizabeth Floretta Warner, b. Feb. 13, 1812; d. Aug. 17, 1845; m. George Collins and had a daughter Jenette Brainerd (Brainerd Genealogy). Elijah C. Warner was appointed administrator of his sister's estate, Dec. 15, 1845 (Moodus probate rceords).

Amanda Melvina Warner, b. Sept. 11, 1814; m. George Collins of East

Haddam. Children: i. Henry, d. Dec., 1872. ii. Lillie, resides in Ithaca, N. Y., not married.

John Chapman Warner, b. June 27, 1817; d. in East Haddam, Apr. 11, 1866; a farmer; not married.

Nancy Catherine Warner, b. Jan. 24, 1818; resided in Longmeadow, Mass., and died Mar., 1897; m. Sept. 27, 1848, by the rector of St. Stephen's Church, East Haddam, Sylvester Bliss, b. Sept. 7, 1820, son of James and Eunice (Chandler) Bliss. Children: i. Hannah Brainerd, b. July 17, 1849; resided in Westfield, Mass.; m. ——— Fisher. ii. Marilla Chandler, b. May 6, 1853; d. June, 1897; resided at Naugatuck; m. Arthur Hayden Dayton; had a son Bliss. iii. James, b. May 29, 1857; was educated at Harvard; d. Jan. 1, 1896. iv. Hattie, Maria, b. Mar. 22, 1862; resided with her sister, Mrs. Dayton, in Naugatuck.

137 JABEZ⁵ WARNER, JR., son of Jabez⁴ and Hannah (Brainerd) Warner, born in East Haddam, August 19, 1750; died there February 8, 1812. The ear-mark for his cattle was recorded in East Haddam in 1780, "a crop off the end of each ear, and a slit in the end of the right." He was recorded in the 1790 Census, one male over 16, one male under 16, three females in the family; in 1800, one male and two females over 45, three females between 26 and 45, one female between 10 and 16, and one male under 10. On March 11, 1812, Sarah Warner and Julius Andrews were appointed administrators of his estate (Colchester probate records, 7:592, 602, 604).

Married December 25, 1786, **SARAH HARVEY** of East Haddam. She was appointed guardian for minor children in 1814, Jabez, Lucy, Asa H., and Mary.

Children

Huldah Warner, b. Apr. 29, 1788, recorded in East Haddam.
Hannah Warner, b. Apr. 26, 1790, recorded in East Haddam; m. Abijah Andrews of East Haddam. Her father deeded property to his "daughter Hannah, wife of Abijah Andrews," land in East Haddam, Jan. 11, 1810.
Sarah Warner, b. May 29, 1792, recorded in East Haddam.
Jabez Warner, 3d.
Asa H. Warner.
Lucy Warner.
Mary Warner.

138 SUSANNAH⁵ WARNER, daughter of Jabez⁴ and Hannah (Brainerd) Warner, born in East Haddam, Conn., April 9, 1753. An extended account of her family is included here, on account of the numerous intermarriages of her descendants with Warners.

Married JOSEPH BANNING, born May 9, 1749, son of John, Jr., and Margaret (De Wolf) Banning, and grandson of John Banning who came to Lyme, Conn., about 1700.

Children, order not known

Marvin Banning.
Brainerd Banning, m. (1) ——— Pratt, (2) Laura Whipple.
Philemon Banning, m. ——— Maitland.
Susanna Banning.
Selden Warner Banning, b. in the town of East Haddam, Conn., 1778; d. there 1864; farmer and ship carpenter at East Haddam; m. (1) at Colchester, Conn., Alice Ransom, who d. aged 33; m. (2) at Colchester, Fannie Keeney. Children, b. in East Haddam, first four, at least, by first wife: i. Abigail, m. her cousin George W. Lay, and d. soon after. ii. Mary or Jane, m. (1) her cousin Erastus Samuel Lay, (2) ——— Albee, and has many living descendants. iii. Sophia, d. not married. iv. George Ransom, b. Feb. 19, 1824; d. Feb. 17, 1899; m. Oct. 27, 1851, Celinda Keeney of Colchester, had three sons and six daughters, of whom one d. in childhood, the others m. and all but one had families (Frederick E. Banning of Hadlyme is one of the sons). v. Selden, d. aged 14. vi. Susan, d. aged 18, not married.
Joseph Banning, b. Mar. 2, 1780, in East Haddam; is ancestor of the Deep River Banning family; m. Oct. 24, 1805, Azuba Clark, daughter of Beamont and Hannah (Bull) Clark. Children: i. Joseph L., b. Nov. 14, 1807; m. Sylvia M. Post of Westbrook. ii. Henry S., b. Jan. 27, 1810; m. Nancy M. Robinson of Coventry. iii. Arba H., b. Sept. 13, 1817; m. Hannah M. Moore, and was the father of Judge Joseph Beamont Banning, Louisa Camilla Banning who m. Jabez Southworth, Hannah Moore Banning who m. J. Ely Beebe of Grassy Hill, Lyme, Conn., and Mary Pritchard Banning who m. Charles E. Alling of Waterbury. (See Conn. Biog. Rec. Middlesex Co., Conn., p. 158.)
Nancy Banning, b. 1790; d. Dec. 1, 1871; m. (1) 1808 or 1809, Erastus Lay of Essex, Conn., b. 1787, d. Feb. 27, 1839, a descendant of Robert Lay of Lynn and East Saybrook and his wife Sarah Buckingham; m. (2) Ebenezer Brockway[6] Warner, see number 259. Children by first husband: i. Sarah Buckingham, b. July 17, 1810; d. May 14, 1893; m. (1) Thomas Jefferson[6] Warner, see number 261, (2) Jonathan La Place. ii. Robert, b. Oct. 21, 1813; d. of smallpox in Savannah, Ga., Feb. 13, 1848. iii. Erastus Samuel, b. Mar. 21, 1816; d. Jan. 1, 1884; m. his cousin Jane Banning, daughter of Selden Warner Banning, see above. iv. George W., b. Dec. 21, 1819; d. June 18, 1907; m. (1) his cousin Abigail Banning, daughter of Selden Warner Banning, (2) Sarah Wilbur, who is living aged 91 (Aug., 1916). v. Carlos, b. Nov. 21, 1821; m. (1) ——— Rogers, and had a son Israel, (2) Mary Avery, and had a daughter Addie who m. Forrest Leffingwell. vi. Nancy Elizabeth, b. Jan. 21, 1825; d. Feb. 26, 1910; resided in Joshuatown; m. Mar. 28, 1847, Robert Henry La Place, b. Dec. 20, 1819, d. May 20, 1902, son of Frank and Abigail (Wood) La Place (for descendants see below). vii. Julius W., b. May 31, 1827; d. Oct. 31, 1844. viii. Mary Melissa, b. June 27, 1830; d. Apr. 13, 1907. ix. Lemira A., b. Apr., 1833; d. May 16, 1834.

Benjamin Banning, b. in Hadlyme, Conn., July 30, 1793; d. in Millington, Conn., July 19, 1861; m. Theodosia Bramble, b. Mar. 30, 1802, in East Haddam, Conn., d. there June 19, 1876. They had twenty-one children, of whom seventeen lived past infancy: i. Benjamin, b. Nov. 6, 1819; m. Mary Green. ii. Joseph, b. Oct. 1, 1821; d. unmarried. iii. Rosetta, b. Dec. 15, 1822; m. Jonathan Stevens. iv. Charlotte, b. Mar. 13, 1824; m. Phineas David, who d. in Libby Prison. v. William Warner, b. Sept. 1, 1825; d. July 7, 1907; m. Dec. 7, 1847, Mary A. Flood, and had a son William S., b. in East Hampton, Conn., Feb. 13, 1851, a real estate dealer and builder in Springfield, Mass. vi. Jabez Warner, b. Mar. 15, 1828; d. 1870; m. Mary Emily Brown. vii. Samuel, b. Jan. 15, 1829; m. (1) Katherine Banta, (2) Eliza Fox. viii. Clarissa, b. Apr. 21, 1831; d. young. ix. Betsy E., b. Nov. 5, 1832; m. Nathan Stark. x. Calvin, b. Apr. 4, 1834; d. young. xi. Matilda, b. Oct. 29, 1835; m. ———— Brown. xii. Simon M., b. Jan. 1, 1837; d. Sept. 2, 1915; m. Lydia A. Knight. xiii. Laura, b. Feb. 11, 1838; m. Nelson Bramble. xiv. Mary, b. Apr. 10, 1839; m. Henry Derby. xv. Rachel, b. Dec. 13, 1840; m. Elisha Brown. xvi. Almira, b. Apr. 5, 1842; m. Theron Markham. xvii. Clarissa, b. Mar. 31, 1845; m. Lorin Lewis.

Lucinda M. Banning, b. 1795; d. Dec. 4, 1867; m. Ebenezer Brockway[6] Warner, see number 259.

Nancy Elizabeth Lay, sixth child of Erastus and Nancy (Banning) Lay, see above, and grandchild of Joseph and Susannah[5] (Warner) Banning, m. Robert La Place, and had children: i. Robert, b. Jan. 15, 1848; d. 1848. ii. Morgianna, b. July 18, 1850; m. Feb. 9, 1871, Lodowick Bill Brockway, b. Oct. 8, 1845; resides in Lyme; has sons, Charles Linus, b. June 28, 1875, d. in New Britain, Conn., Oct., 1918, and Clarence, b. Apr. 28, 1882. iii. Georgianna M., b. Apr. 22, 1853; d. Mar., 1897; m. Jan. 31, 1872, Oliver Sterling, b. Nov. 5, 1843; no children. iv. Henry C., b. Oct. 23, 1857; d. Nov. 23, 1915; m. Oct. 12, 1886, Minnie Anderson, b. Nov. 21, 1865, daughter of John and Augusta (————) Anderson of Boston. Henry C. La Place has children: i. Robert, b. Dec. 26, 1887. ii. George, b. Dec. 14, 1889; m. Aug. 26, 1914, Selma Brucellius and has a child, Ida E., b. Feb. 18, 1916. iii. Augusta, b. Nov. 24, 1894; m. Aug. 26, 1914, Ellsworth Gay; has a child, Beatrice, b. Aug. 13, 1915. iv. Oliver b. Nov. 5, 1901. v. Cecil, b. June, 1903 or 1904.

139 SELDEN[5] WARNER, son of Jabez[4] and Hannah (Brainerd) Warner, born in East Haddam, Conn., December 8, 1760; died in Lyme, August 31, 1844. He was recorded in the Census of 1790 in East Haddam with his wife and one child. In 1800 he had a family of eleven persons living with him. He was a farmer. In 1793 the ear-mark of Nathaniel Ackley was recorded to Selden Warner, "a crop off the end of the near ear and a half-penny in the under side of the off ear."

Married June 30, 1785, or June 29, 1784, **BETSY BROCKWAY** of Lyme, born 1764, died October, 1832, daughter of Ebenezer and Mary (Butler) Brockway. Ebenezer Brockway's line is Wolstan[1], William[2], John[3], Ebenezer[4]. Mary Butler was the daughter of Zebulon Butler of Lynn, Mass., and Lyme, Conn., the man of Wyoming fame.

Children, born in East Haddam

258 *Selden Jewett Warner*, b. Sept. 9, 1787; m. Mary Brockway.
259 *Ebenezer Brockway Warner*, b. Feb. 8, 1791; m. (1) Lucinda M. Banning, (2) Nancy (Banning) Lay.
     Clarissa B. Warner, b. May 8, 1793; d. Jan. 29, 1852.
     George Warner, b. Nov. 2, 1795; d. Oct., 1818.
260 *David Warner*, b. Mar. 7, 1798; m. Elizabeth Parker Johnson.
     Don Carlos Warner, b. Apr. 19, 1800; d. Nov., 1821.
     Elizabeth Warner, b. Nov. 10, 1802; d. Apr., 1816.
261 *Thomas Jefferson Warner*, b. Jan. 17, 1805; m. Sarah Buckingham Lay.
     Caroline L. Warner, b. Feb. 5, 1807; d. Mar. 26 or 30, 1853, in Hebron, Conn.; m. Rev. Walter Wilkie. Child: Walter.
     Lemira M. Warner, b. Mar. 26, 1809; d. Oct. 12, 1883; m. John Cleaveland, who died Oct. 24, 1859, aged 58. No children.

140 NOADIAH[5] WARNER, son of Noadiah[4] and Elizabeth (De Forest) Warner, born April 24, 1764, probably in Danbury, Conn.; died in South Britain, Conn., January 16, 1839, buried in Warner Cemetery there. He resided about a quarter of a mile southeast of Bennett's Bridge in the town of Southbury, and was on the tax list of that town in 1787.

Married (1) November 27, 1785, **POLLY CURTIS**, born 1762, died November 29, 1832, daughter of Samuel and Currence (————) Curtis of South Britain, who are buried in the Warner Cemetery. The marriage is recorded in Woodbury, South Britain, and Southbury.

Married (2) October 10, 1833, **HARRIET MILES**.

Children by first wife

Curtis Warner, b. Jan. 24, 1787; d. in Winchester, Conn., Apr. 18, 1813, not married. He was a graduate of Yale College, 1804, was of eminent scholarship in college and delivered the salutatory oration. In 1810 he took charge of a grammar school in Winchester, which he conducted until his death. He was a member of the Methodist Church in South Britain.
262 *Agur Warner*, b. Mar. 23, 1789; m. Polly Bassett.
     Currence Warner, b. Nov. 26, 1794; d. in Southbury, Feb. 16, 1796.
     Harriet Warner, b. Jan. 16, 1798; d. Nov. 17, 1838, aged 40 years, 10 months (Bible record); m. Charles Edmunds (as in Bible record) or Edmond (tombstone inscription). Child: Theodore, d. Apr. 10, 1829, aged 7, buried in Warner Cemetery.
     (Infant), b. and d. Dec. 29, 1804.

141 **HARVEY DE FOREST⁵ WARNER**, son of Noadiah⁴ and Elizabeth (De Forest) Warner, born in Danbury, Conn., August 1, 1769; died in Salisbury, Conn., March 30, 1859, buried in Town Hill Cemetery, Salisbury. He was a farmer and owner of an iron ore mine. He resided at Ore Hill in Salisbury. It is said of his family that "the Warner brothers were all great jokers and story-tellers." He was a man of moderate circumstances as his father had lost his estate during the Revolution.

Married (1) December 10, 1796, **ELIZABETH CLARK**, born September 4, 1778, daughter of Nathaniel Carey and Sarah (Judson?) Clark of Salisbury, granddaughter of Gamaliel Clark of Milford and his wife, Elizabeth Carey of Bristol, R. I., a Mayflower line. She died in Woodbury, Conn., June 2, 1821, buried in Town Hill Cemetery, Salisbury.

Married (2) **Mrs. CLIMENA HOWE**, born August 3, 1785, died September 22, 1883, buried in Town Hill Cemetery, Salisbury

Children by first wife

263 *Judson Warner*, b. in Southbury, Feb. 28, 1798; m. Abigail Leavenworth.

Allen C. Warner, b. in Southbury, Oct. 18, 1799; was a merchant in New York City, later in Paterson, N. J.; m. Phebe Verdon, daughter of Abram Verdon, of an old New York family. Children: i. Allen, d. in childhood. ii. Augustus, lived to old age in Paterson, was not married. iii. Emma Louise.

Augustus Warner, was a merchant in Akron, Ohio; m. Mary Howell (?); no children.

Charles Warner, resided in Paterson, N. J.; m. and "had two children, names forgotten, both dead, childless and unmarried" writes a relative.

264 *Noadiah Warner*, b. Dec. 12, 1809; m. Adaline Jones.

John Warner, b. about 1812; d. of yellow fever in Louisville, Ky., 1831, aged 19. "My father, youngest of the family, had great reverence for the memory of his brother John as very chivalrous and noble in appearance," writes the daughter of Donald Warner.

Darwin Warner, resided in Westport, N. Y.; m. (1) Eliza Sherman, daughter of Isaac and Maria (Burroughs) Sherman; (2) Maria Peet of Salisbury. Child: Arthur, d. in infancy.

265 *Jennette Warner*, b. July 15, 1817; m. James Elisha Kellogg.

266 *Donald Judson Warner*, b. Sept. 15, 1819; m. Lois Camp Ball Ticknor.

142 **AUGUSTUS⁵ WARNER**, son of Noadiah⁴ and Elizabeth (De Forest) Warner, born June 25, 1774, in Danbury, Conn.; died of lockjaw, October 14, 1829, in Southbury, New Haven County, Conn.; buried in the Warner Cemetery, South Britain, Conn. He belonged to the Coast Guard in the War of 1812.

13

Both he and his wife were members of the Methodist Church of South Britain. They resided on a farm in Southbury.

Married in Southbury, March 21, 1813, **MARIA CANDE**, born in Oxford, Conn., May 15, 1787; died in Otego, N. Y., April 18, 1841. She was the daughter of Dr. Enos and Nabba (Hatch) Cande, and was educated at the Hartford Female Seminary.

Children, all born at the home farm in Southbury

267 *Deforest Warner*, b. Feb. 27, 1814; m. Lovicy Curtis.
268 *Emeline Warner*, b. Nov. 20, 1816; m. Salmon Beers Curtis.
269 *De Luzon Warner*, b. July 4, 1824; m. Susan Sherman.
270 *Clarinda Maria Warner*, b. Feb. 1, 1828; m. John J. Curtis.
      (Infant son), buried in Warner Cemetery, South Britain.

143 JOSEPH[5] **WARNER**, son of Joseph[4] and Elizabeth (Cone) Warner, born in East Haddam, February 6, 1761; died there in 1838. He was a farmer and blacksmith and was recorded in the 1790 Census of East Haddam as Joseph Warner, 2d, two males over 16, two males under 16 and two females in his family. In 1800 he had one male and one female over 45, two males and one female between 26 and 45, one male between 10 and 16, and a girl under 10. His will was made March 10, 1832, and probated August 27, 1838. It mentions his wife Sarah, son Charles, who was made executor, daughters Arispa Howell and Sarah Warner. Oren and Matilda A. Warner were witnesses. The estate consisted of land and blacksmith shop as well as personal property.

Married in East Haddam, April, 1783, **SARAH OSBORNE** of Long Island, who died after January 31, 1855.

Children

George Warner, d. young.
Joseph O. Warner, d. in East Haddam, 1812.
271 Charles Warner, m. Fannie Comstock.
Arispa Warner, m. before 1832, —— Howell.
Sarah Warner, was not married at the time of her father's will, 1832.

144 OLIVER[5] **WARNER**, son of Joseph[4] and Elizabeth (Cone) Warner, born in East Haddam, Conn., April 30 or 13, 1765; died there April 30 or 13, 1828. He was a farmer in East Haddam, and the Census of 1790 recorded him with his family of three males over 16 and one female. In 1800, the census noted a family of seven. He was one of the founders of the Episcopal Church in East Haddam, April 26, 1791. He was called Lieutenant Oliver Warner on town records of 1803, when his father's ear-mark was transferred to him. He was Noble Grand of the I. O. O. F.

Married at First Church, East Haddam, June 6, 1790, **CHARITY BRAINERD,** daughter of Joshua and Susannah (Chapman) Brainerd, born in East Haddam, August 4, 1767, died April 13, 1839. She was descended from Daniel Brainerd, one of the original settlers of East Haddam.

Children, born at the Warner homestead in East Haddam
Elizabeth Warner, b. Apr. 6, 1791; d. Sept. 16, 1842; m. about Oct. 7, 1817, Thomas Moseley, son of Dr. Jonathan Ogden and Gertrude (Van Voorhis) Moseley, b. Sept. 26, 1787, d. July 3, 1860, in East Haddam. Dr. Jonathan Moseley, b. 1762, was a surgeon in the Revolution, a graduate of Yale, and member of Congress for twenty years. He delivered the oration in East Haddam at the time of Washington's death. Children: i. Charity W., b. Sept. 20, 1822; d. May 23, 1902; buried in East Haddam, First Ecclesiastical Society Cemetery; m. Sept. 6, 1842, Hiram Willey, b. in East Haddam, May 23, 1818 (see further). ii. Gertrude E., b. May 21, 1824; d. before Sept. 22, 1902; m. Dr. Leonard G. Warner of Albany, N. Y., who died in 1868. iii. William Oliver, b. Dec. 21, 1825; d. Jan. 7, 1892. iv. Phoebe E., b. Apr. 2, 1830; m. Nov. 12, 1856, Frederick W. Warner, see number 272.
Charity Warner, b. Mar. 20, 1793; d. June 7, 1821.
272 *Oliver Warner,* b. Sept. 26, 1795; m. Elizabeth Ann Blakesley.
Electa Warner, b. Jan. 23, 1798; d. Apr. 24, 1824; m. May 25, 1820, Abner Comstock Smith, b. Mar. 29, 1796, d. Mar. 5, 1876, son of Jeremiah and Temperance (Comstock) Smith. He m. (2) Hope Marshall and had ten children.
(Son), b. Nov. 11, 1800; d. Nov. 13, 1800.
Abby Warner, b. Apr. 20, 1802; d. Jan. 14, 1892, buried in First Congregational Church Cemetery, East Haddam; not married. She was a communicant of St. Stephen's Church in 1855.
273 *Orren Warner,* b. Sept. 3, 1805; m. Matilda Ann Willey.
Clarissa Warner, b. Sept. 28, 1808; d. in East Haddam, Dec. 21, 1889, buried in First Congregational Church Cemetery, East Haddam; not married. She was a communicant of St. Stephen's Church in 1855.

Hiram[7] Willey-(see above) was the son of Ethan Allen[6] and Mary (Brockway) Willey (Abraham[5], Allen[4], John[3], John[2], Isaac[1]). He was one of the first graduates of Wesleyan University of Middletown; studied law and became State's Attorney; was a member of the Legislature and State Senate; Mayor of New London; Judge of Probate Court and of the Court of Common Pleas; returned to Hadlyme to reside in 1875; was lay reader in the P. E. Church of Hadlyme; member of F. and A. M.; First Grand Commander of the Encampment in New London. Children of Hiram and Charity (Moseley) Willey were: i. Thomas Moseley, b. July 5, 1846; was a graduate of West Point and served ten years in the regular army. ii. Allen, b. Jan. 28, 1858; was a graduate of the New London High School and was for ten years proprietor and publisher of the Hartford Globe. (See Commemorative Biographical Record, Middlesex County, Conn.)

145 ·EPHRAIM⁵ WARNER, son of Joseph⁴ and Elizabeth (Cone) Warner, born in East Haddam, Conn., April 19, 1767; died there 1844. He was a farmer and resided in Millington. The 1800 Census of East Haddam recorded him with his family of seven. He was one of those who signed a petition for the establishment of an Episcopal Church in East Haddam. The church was founded April 26, 1871.

Married (1) March 31, 1791, ELIZABETH BRAINERD, born in East Haddam, August 18, 1770, died July 21, 1807, daughter of Lieutenant Amasa Brainerd, who was vestryman and one of the founders of the Episcopal Church, and his wife, Jedidah Osborne.

Married (2) ELIZABETH GARDINER.

Children by first wife

274 *Ephraim Warner*, bapt. July 5, 1795; m. Mary Spencer Miner.
 Amasa E. Warner, bapt. at the Episcopal Church in East Haddam with his brother Ephraim, July 5, 1795; settled at first in Kentucky but died in Georgia; not married.
 George Warner, bapt. June 26, 1796; d. in Philadelphia or Middletown, Conn. (Brainerd Genealogy); m. Diana Burrell of Madison, Conn., and had three sons, George, Albert, and ———.
 Dyer Warner, was murdered in Pennsylvania.
 Ansel Warner, b. in East Haddam; lived in Haddam and died there May 17, 1838, aged 37; m. in Middletown, Conn., April 13, 1825, Mary Ann Clark, who died in Haddam, 1866, aged 59, daughter of Noah Clark. She joined the Haddam Congregational Church in 1824, and her children were baptized there. She m. (2) Benjamin Kelsey. Children of Ansel Warner: i. Philo Ives, bapt. May 4, 1828, lived in Chicago. ii. George O., bapt. May 2, 1830; lived in East Haddam. iii. Ansel Gardner, bapt. July 1, 1832. iv. John Austin, bapt. May 17, 1838.
275 *William Warner*, b. June 25, 1800; m. Lydia Ray.
276 *Betsey Ann Warner*, b. May 31, 1805; m. Guy Davenport.
 (Son), d. July 20, 1807, buried with his mother.

Children by second wife

 Joseph Warner.
 Nicholas Gardiner Warner. "One of the Warner family" gives a son Noadiah, d. in Philadelphia. There is no Noadiah in MSS. record of the family in Connecticut Historical Society and perhaps this is the same.
 Mary Warner.
 Orpha Warner.

146 JESSE⁵ WARNER, JR., son of Jesse⁴ and Miriam (Smith) Warner, born February 1, 1747, in Belchertown, Mass.; died August 14, 1834, in Orleans, Ontario County, N. Y. He resided in Belchertown and he and his wife were members of the church there; he removed to the town of Conway, Mass., in

the latter part of the year 1773, and became one of the early settlers of that town. He took up his residence on Poplar Hill in the extreme southern portion of the town. Here he remained until 1796, when there was an exodus of many families from Conway and vicinity to Ontario County, N. Y. In that year, Jesse, with his family, made the long journey to the town of Phelps, Ontario County, and settled on what was afterwards known as "Warner Hill," just above and a little to the east of the village of Orleans. He left a rocky, barren farm in Conway, and came into a country which was covered with heavy timber, but which when cleared was found to be very fertile land. He purchased several hundred acres of such land, and, with the aid of his sons, cleared it up. He gave a farm to each of his sons. Jesse built a log tavern over what developed to be an old Indian burial ground. This building was situated on the southwest of the four corners on Warner Hill. His son John located on the northwest corner on said hill. Another son, Elijah, settled on the farm north of John's, where Dwight Severance now resides. Another son, Lewis, was located on the farm south and adjoining that of his father's, while Oliver, another son, settled a short distance west of the village of Orleans in the town of Hopewell. In the early days of his residence in this new country, Jesse had many experiences with the Indians, who found it convenient to call when journeying through the wilderness.

He no doubt served in the Revolution but there are at least four of the same name, so his services cannot be defined. One Jesse Warner, with the rank of corporal, served in Capt. Abel Dinsmore's Company of Conway, Col. David Field's Regiment, August 17 to 19, 1777. They marched northward at the request of Gen. Horatio Gates and were dismissed by order of Gen. Lincoln. Jesse Warner of Conway was appointed on a committee to go to Northampton "to attend upon the Superior Court," and to form a convention with reference to the controversies which led to Shays' rebellion, 1782.

Jesse Warner was one of the prominent men of his community and acted in many official capacities in town affairs. He was a rigid Baptist and a deacon in the church. He was a most positive character, fond of theological argument, a hardy pioneer and a man of great physical strength. During an epidemic of fever throughout the country, he was so near death that his son Lewis measured him and went to Geneva, the nearest town, for a shroud. Upon his return the father was out of danger, but the son was stricken with the same disease and the shroud was soon used for him. Jesse Warner died in the town of Phelps, August 14, 1834, at the ripe old age of 87 years and 6 months, and was buried with his wife at Orleans.

Jesse Warner married in Springfield, Mass., May 11, 1769, SARAH[5] WARRINER (Ebenezer[4], Ebenezer[3], James[2], William[1]), born in Longmeadow, Mass., September 14, 1745, died in Orleans County, N. Y., 1826. See below.

Children of Jesse and Sarah (Warriner) Warner, first two probably born in Longmeadow, six in Conway, and the last in Orleans, N. Y.

277 *Elijah Warner*, b. Feb. 25, 1770; m. Relief Marble.
278 *Lewis Warner*, b. Nov. 11, 1772; m. Mercy Rice.
279 *Rufus Warner*, b. Feb. 25, 1775; m. Hazel Elponi Rice.
      Jesse (1) Warner, bapt. Aug. 31, 1777; d. Jan. 14, 1778.
280 *John Warner*, b. Jan. 2, 1781; m. Susan Ann Post.
281 *Oliver Warner*, b. Dec. 28, 1782; m. Lucinda Rice.
282 *Jesse (2) Warner*, b. Dec. 23, 1786; m. Margaret Hutchison.
      James Warner, removed to Ohio.
283 *Lucinda Warner*, b. Nov. 21, 1796; m. Elisha Peck.

Sarah Warriner's ancestry has been traced in the following lines: William[1] Warriner, James[2] and Elizabeth[2] (Baldwin), Ebenezer[3] and Joanna[3] (Dickinson), Ebenezer[4], Jr., and Sarah (Chapin), Sarah[5]; Joseph[1] and Hannah (————) Baldwin, Elizabeth[2]; Nathaniel[1] and Anna (Gull) Dickinson, Hezekiah[2] and Abigail (Blakeman), Joanna[3]; Rev. Adam[1] and Jane (Wheeler) Blakeman, Samuel[2] and Elizabeth (Wheeler) Blakeman, Abigail[3] m. Hezekiah Dickinson; Samuel[1] and Cicely (————) Chapin, Henry[2] and Bethia[2] (Cooley), Deacon Benjamin[3] and Hannah (Colton) of Longmeadow and Chicopee, Sarah[4] m. Ebenezer Warriner; Ensign Benjamin[1] and Sarah (————) Cooley, early settler of Longmeadow in 1642, selectman and held other offices, d. in 1684, Bethia[2] m. Henry[2] Chapin; George[1] and Deborah (Gardner) Colton (who emigrated from Sutton-Coldfield, Warwick, England, to Windsor, Conn., and in 1644 to Springfield, located in Longmeadow, was selectman, freeman in 1665, "Quarter-master," representative in General Court, 1669), Isaac[2] m. Mary[2] Cooper, Hannah[3] m. Benjamin Chapin; Lieutenant Thomas[1] Cooper, Mary[2].

William[1] Warriner was made a freeman in Springfield in 1638 and held various offices after that time; held a home lot near the present site of the old court house; married (1) in England, (2) in 1639, Joanna Scant of Springfield, who died 1660, (3) Mrs. Elizabeth Hitchcock, widow of Luke of Wethersfield; died 1676. His son James[2], born November 21, 1640, died May 14,

1727, was a soldier in King Philip's War and deacon in Springfield Congregational Church.

Joseph[1] Baldwin was son of Richard of Cholesbury, Bucks, England, born about 1610, came to Milford, Conn., in 1639 among first settlers; removed to Hadley, 1660; was made freeman, 1666. See Baldwin Genealogy

Rev. Adam[1] Blakeman, born in Staffordshire, England, about 1598, was educated at Christ's College, Oxford, and was pastor for many years in Leicestershire and Derbyshire before coming to America in 1638. He was one of the first settlers and first minister at Stratford, Conn., "a man of great learning, prudence and fervent piety, and greatly beloved by his people." He married Jane Wheeler, probably sister of Moses Wheeler (who came from County Kent to New Haven, 1643, and Stratford, 1648, died 1698, married Miriam Hawley). Samuel[2] Blakeman, born probably in England, died 1668, married Elizabeth Wheeler and had a daughter Abigail, born December 11, 1663, married Hezekiah Dickinson of Stratford, Hatfield, Hadley and Springfield. She was the mother of the famous Jonathan Dickinson, president of New Jersey College. See also under number 68.

Samuel[1] Chapin came from England to Roxbury, Mass., about 1635 with his wife Cicely and children, and removed later to Springfield, where he died in 1675. He was freeman at Springfield, 1644, selectman, 1644-52; deacon, magistrate, and on the commission to rule the affairs of the town. His son Henry is said to have been master of a merchant ship, then resided in Boston, and after 1659, in Springfield and Chicopee.

Lieutenant Thomas Cooper, born in England about 1617, came to Boston in the ship Christian about 1635, was early in Windsor and removed to Springfield about 1641; was a farmer and carpenter, bonesetter and surveyor, practicing attorney before the County Court, Deputy at General Court, one of the principal Indian traders, and invaluable in dealing with the Indians. His daughter Mary married Isaac Colton of Springfield. See also Green's History of Springfield. (From data compiled by Henry E. Warner.)

147 NATHAN[5] WARNER, son of Jesse[4] Warner and Mary (Cooley) Ven Horn, born in Hinsdale, Mass., 1755; died in Lexington, Ky., February 17, 1829. His father sold him land in the "Ashuelot equivalent" in 1780 (Berkshire Co., Mass., deeds, B :270). He moved to Unionville, Ohio, in 1811, took up five hundred acres of land, endured the hardships of frontier life and did considerable fighting in the War of 1812.

Married (1) JERUSHA WEBB, who died September 25, 1794, in her 32d year, buried in Hinsdale, Mass.
Married (2) Mrs. AMY (WETTER) COOK. Intentions of the marriage of Lieut. Nathan Warner of Dalton and Mrs. Amy Cook were published May 25, 1795. She was living in Geauga County, Ohio, in 1812, as there is a record of her signing off her dower interest in the farm on Warner Hill when it was sold in 1812.
Married (3) Mrs. KIMBALL. No children.

Children by first wife, born in Hinsdale, Mass.

284 *Nathan Warner, Jr.*, b. Jan. 31, 1785; m. Sarah (Sally) Cook.
  Elijah Warner, settled and lived in Kentucky; married. Children: i. William, liberated his slaves at the beginning of the Civil War, and was a Colonel with the Union forces; m. a daughter of Major-General Coombs of the Mexican War (?). ii. Almira, m. —— Van Swearingen, a rabid Confederate.
  Jerusha Warner.
  Anson Warner, lived and died in Kentucky.
  Philothete Warner, m. —— Eames.

Children by second wife

  Otis Warner, lived and died at Leroy, Ohio.
  Oliver Warner, lived and died on his home farm in Unionville, Ohio.
  Alfred Warner, moved first to Lexington, Ky., then to Monroe City, Mo.

147a DAVID[5] or DAVID C. WARNER, son of Jesse[4] and Mary (Cooley-VenHorn) Warner, born July 12, 1758, recorded in Springfield, Mass., although the family may have lived in Longmeadow. He removed to the western part of New York State and then to Michigan, where many of his descendants are living in the vicinity of Coldwater and Albion.
Married MARY RUSSELL.

Children

  Lucinda Warner, m. Enos Pembrook.
  Polly Warner, m. Asa Adams.
284a *David Warner*, m. Olive Rawson.
  Lucretia Warner, d. young.
  Anna Warner, m. Richard Church. Mrs. Brownlee of Morgan Park, Ill., and Mrs. Edw. Howe of Kalamazoo are descendants.
  Russell Warner, m. Ora Phelps.
  Stephen Warner, m. Betsey Rice.
  Betsey Warner, d. 1857; m. David Johnson.
  Harriet Warner, d. in Coldwater township, Branch Co., Mich., Jan. 11, 1863; m. Sylvester Rice, who d. in Homer, Mich., Sept., 1875. They removed with their sons and daughters from Wayne County, N. Y.,

to Michigan in 1844, settled in Homer, Calhoun County, for two years, then removed to Coldwater township, Branch County. Four sons purchased farms in Coldwater. Children: i. Philetus, d. in Coldwater township. ii. David, d. in Toledo, Ohio. iii. Lucinda, m. —— Smith, d. in Giraud township. iv. Eber, d. in Giraud township. v. Samuel W., b. in Wayne County, N. Y., Jan. 12, 1823; m. Nov. 6, 1873, Lavonia Kilborn, b. in Sherwood, Mich., daughter of David and Clarinda (Hawley) Kilborn; had two children, Hattie, b. Mar. 3, 1875, m. Nov. 21, 1900, Charles Culp, resides in Coldwater township (has two children, Frances Josephine and Walton), and William, b. Jan. 26, 1879, m. Effa Irene Bennett and is a successful farmer in Coldwater, m. ——— Atwater. vii. Emma Jane, resided in Coldwater. viii. Russell, d. in Coldwater. ix. Sylvester, d. in Giraud township. (See History of Branch Co., Mich., 1906, p. 353.)

Elihu Warner, removed with his family to New York State at the age of six years, then to Calhoun County, Mich., and in 1842, to Hillsdale County. Married Lucina Clarke, daughter of Enoch and Anna (Hutchinson) Clarke. They had nine children, four sons and five daughters, the eldest of whom died young. The youngest, C. D. Warner, b. in Calhoun County, Dec. 17, 1840, was educated at Hillsdale College and business school, entered the Union Army in 1861, Company G, Michigan Cavalry, was honorably discharged for physical disability and resumed his studies; went to the copper mines and was engaged in a contracting business for about ten years, after which he began the manufacture of White Wine of Tar and other remedies. He settled in Coldwater in 1889, retaining his farms in Reading and mining interests in Mexico. He married (1) Julia St. John, (2) Josephine M. Brown. Children: i. Donna, m. B. L. Van Auken, resides in Coldwater and has a daughter Lucille. ii. Hiram E., owns the homestead at Reading and is engaged in selling his father's remedies in the states of Ohio and Indiana. (History of Branch County, p. 615.)

John Warner, m. Hannah Brown.

Luther Warner, m. Pamilla Stanton.

284b *Warham Warner,* b. about 1801; married.

148 OBADIAH[5] **WARNER,** son of Joshua[4] Warner, born in Williamsburg, Mass., July 10, 1778; received land and buildings in the town of Williamsburg by his father's will of 1816.
Married JANE ———

Children, recorded in Williamsburg

Hiram Warner, b. Oct. 29, 1802.
Eliza Ann Warner, b. Sept. 3, 1804; d. July 9, 1808.
Theron Warner, b. July 26, 1806; d. about 1889; will dated Dec. 16, 1885, probated Dec. 3, 1889; m. (1) intentions dated June 26, 1830, Almira Nash, daughter of Thomas and Naomi (Warner) Nash of Williamsburg, (2) Julia ———, who had a son Justus A. Wright by a former marriage. Children of Theron Warner: i. Jenet, b. Mar. 17, 1832; m. Rollin Montague. ii. William Henry, b. Nov. 8,

1833; was on October 1, 1889, appointed guardian for his father who was at that time insane (Northampton records). iii. Harriet, b. Dec. 27, 1835; m. George King. iv. Almira, b. Aug., 1840. v. Ann Eliza, mentioned in her father's will, but birth not recorded in Williamsburg, m. Walter Barton. vi. Thomas Nash, mentioned in his father's will, but birth not recorded in Williamsburg.

Rodolphus Warner, b. June 8, 1811; d. Aug. 10, 1831, in Williamsburg.

Obadiah Warner, Jr., b. Dec. 23, 1812.

Eliza Warner (twin), b. May 3, 1815.

Miranda Warner (twin), b. May 3, 1815.

William Henry Warner, b. Mar. 16, 1817; d. Oct. 8, 1831, in Williamsburg.

Charles Howard Warner, b. May 26, 1822.

149 SETH[5] WARNER, son of Moses[4] and Sarah (Porter) Warner, born October 28, 1739, in Hatfield, Mass., or possibly in Belchertown; died in Belchertown, 1822, aged 83. He was a resident of Belchertown, in the "Middle of the Town District," and in his early life took a prominent part in public life, so that his name occurs frequently on the town records. His father died when he was but twenty, and his uncle James Porter of Hatfield became his guardian. On March 3, 1762, the town voted that Josiah Lyman and Seth Warner be "Dear reves." From 1763 to 1766 he was buying his home farm, a part of which he received from his father's estate, and he also purchased his sister's share of that estate. March 2, 1763, he was one of the four appointed surveyor of highways, but for some reason he was not sworn. December 20, 1764, the town "voted Seth Warner to be a constable to serve in the Room of Stephen Crowfoot that is moved away, to serve with Phinehas Hannum." March 17, 1766, the town chose Caleb Clark for constable in the year ensuing and Caleb Clark hired Seth Warner to serve in his stead, the town accepting him by a vote. December 8, 1766, it was voted that one-half the town shall get the wood for the pastor, Rev. Mr. Forward, this year, and the other half the next. Seth Warner's side is to get it this year.

In a list of January 26, 1784, he is listed in the "Middle of the Town District," and a few years later his name is found in a list of some forty or more, "concerned in the late rebellion . . . lived in Belchertown and took and subscribed to the oath of allegiance." This is in reference to Shays' Rebellion. He is listed in the 1790 Census with two males over 16 and two females in the family, and in that of 1800 with one male and one female over 40. He purchased a piece of property in Belchertown in 1795. The appraisal of his estate noted about a hundred acres of land, a grist mill on Batchelor Brook with its privileges, and two pews in the Congregational meeting house, one in the gallery. It is interesting to note that the pew in the Church and the grist mill had the same value, $103.00, and both were considered real estate. His personal property included the following items: 1 horse, $.50 (fifty cents); 1 cow, $14; 5 sheep, $6.67; 85 gal. cider brandy, $28.05; 7 bbls. cider liquor only, $5.25; 1 bed, $2.00; 2 coverlets, $2.00; 2 blankets, $1.50; 3 woolen sheets, $1.00; 2 looking glasses, $.20; 1 bible, $2.00; 1 inkstand, $.17; 1 pr. spectacles, $.25; 3 hats, $.2.50; 2 old coats, $1.00; 2 vests, $.25; 3 pr. pantaloons, $.50. His son having died, the estate was divided among his grandchildren, Alonzo, Fanny, Park, Mary, Seth Porter, and George Warner.

Seth Warner married **MARY CLARK** of Northampton, daughter of Samuel Clark, born about 1740, died in Belchertown in 1819, aged 79. Both Seth and Mary Warner joined the Belchertown Congregational Church in 1779.

Child

285   *Titus Warner*, b. Jan. 26, 1767; m. Mary or Polly Baggs.

150 JONATHAN[5] **WARNER**, son of Moses[4] and Sarah (Porter) Warner, born 1751, probably in Belchertown, Mass., where he died in 1782, aged 31. Little is known of him except the record of his joining the Congregational Church at Belchertown in 1774. His estate was divided November 28, 1796, between the widow, son Jonathan, daughters Sally and Lucretia. Jonathan Porter was guardian to Lucretia, aged 20, Sally, aged 17, and Jonathan C., aged 14.

Married **MARY** ————, who married (2), before December 5, 1798, Phineas B. Clark.

Children of Jonathan and Mary (————) Warner

286   *Lucretia Warner*, b. 1774; m. Theodore Bridgeman.
        Sarah Warner, b. about 1777; probably m. (intentions, Nov. 3, 1799) Justus Williams, Jr., of Belchertown, son of Justus and Abigail (Pomeroy) Williams. He died in Amherst, and his parents are buried there.
287   *Jonathan Coleman Warner*, b. about 1780; m. Achsah Dickinson.

151 MOSES[5] **WARNER**, son of Moses[4] and Sarah (Porter) Warner, born in Belchertown, Mass., in 1758; died in Hatfield, Mass., August 1, 1828. He served in the Revolution from Hatfield and was a deacon in the church there. The History of Hatfield has many references to him and his family, p. 276, etc. Deacon Warner was a man held in high esteem by the whole community. His will, recorded in Northampton, was dated April 17, 1822, with a codicil of May 6, 1823, and was probated September 2, 1828. The heirs were: his wife Mary; sons Moses and Elisha; son John, who received the homestead in Hatfield; daughter Sarah; daughter Mercy, to whom the codicil bequeathes "the mansion house in which I now live," as her husband was in embarrassed circumstances and unable to provide for Mercy and her children. (Northampton probate records, 37:274.)

Married June 4, 1779, **MARY KING** of Hatfield who died November 30, 1831.. She was the daughter of Elisha King.

Children, born in Hatfield

288 *John Warner,* b. Nov. 7, 1781; m. Caroline Whiton.

Elisha Warner, b. Feb. 14, 1786; d. in Hatfield, Sept. 26, 1831; m. Apr. 8, 1824, Hannah Field, b. Dec. 2, 1789, d. Mar. 16, 1836, daughter of Medad and Martha (Morton) Field of Whately, Mass. They had no children. She left a will giving property to her brothers Elijah and Moses Field and her sister Editha Graves, the land being situated on the "Pantry Road." (Northampton probate records, 40:557.)

Sarah Warner, b. May 17, 1788; d. Feb. 8, 1868; m. Samuel King Morgan, bapt. in Northfield, Mass., Dec. 16, 1766, son of Noah and Mary (King) Morgan. He was a dyer and farmer of Hatfield. His first wife, Sarah Beale Kellogg, died May 8, 1823, leaving three children, Stillman, Samuel and Sarah. There were no children by the second marriage.

Mercy Warner, b. Aug. 16, 1790; d. Feb. 5, 1868, probably in Hatfield; m. Oct. 22, 1812, Henry Hubbard of Charlemont, who died at Reading, Pa., in 1826, aged 40. Children: i. George W., b. Feb. 26, 1818; d. Apr. 28, 1888; m. Mar. 8, 1843, Philura T. Dickinson of Hatfield. ii. William Henry, b. July 28, 1821; d. Jan. 11, 1877; m. July 4, 1850, Anna Hinds.

Moses Warner, 3d, b. Sept. 14, 1793; d. Feb. 26, 1868, not married. About 1830 there were many mulberry trees set out in .Hatfield. Moses Warner was one of the three largest growers and set out several hundred. It proved to be an unprofitable and short-lived industry.

152 **PHINEAS⁵ WARNER**, son of Ebenezer⁴ and Dinah (Phelps) Warner, born March 7, 1764, in Belchertown, Mass.; died there April 9, 1849. He is doubtless the Phineas Warner mentioned in the 1790 and 1800 censuses as a resident of Belchertown. His will (Northampton probate records) was made November 26, 1838, probated June 5, 1849. He mentions his wife Mary H., heirs of his daughter Henrietta, lately the wife of Joseph Kennedy, sons Theron, Ebenezer, Jairus R., and John Ely, and the wife of his son Theron, who had no children at that time.

Married (1) November 27, 1788, **SALLY RICH**, who died in Belchertown, August 25, 1831, aged 62.

Married (2) in Belchertown, November 29, 1831, **MARY HUNTINGTON ABBEY**, born March 4, 1791, died April 17, 1864, daughter of Mason and Sarah (Frissell) Abbey. Her line is from John[1] Abbey of Salem and Wenham, Mass., John[2], John[3], Richard[4] and Mary Huntington; see Abbe Genealogy, page 64. There were no children by this marriage.

Children of Phineas and Sally (Rich) Warner, born and died in Belchertown

Esther Warner, b. Mar. 13, 1791; d. June 14, 1791.

Henrietta Warner, b. June 11, 1792; d. 1831, aged 38; m. as second wife, 1821, Joseph Kennedy of Belchertown, who died 1834, aged 54. They had children as referred to in Phineas Warner's will, but no names given.

Jairus Parkman Warner, b. Dec. 23, 1793; d. June 23, 1803.

Almira Warner, b. Apr. 20, 1796; d. Jan. 30, 1808.

Josiah R. Warner, b. July 11, 1798; probably d. young. This child is recorded in Belchertown records as Sarah R.

Theron A. Warner, b. Aug. 20, 1800; joined the Congregational Church in Belchertown in 1819; was a physician and resided in Mexico, Oswego Co., N. Y., in 1854, when he made deed to his brother Ebenezer of Belchertown for some property in Belchertown, formerly owned by Phineas Warner. Married Angeline T. ———— No children in 1838.

Ebenezer Warner, b. Nov. 21, 1802; joined the Belchertown Congregational Church in 1819; was representative from Belchertown in 1855. There are on file deeds of 1854 and 1855, conveying land from Theron to Ebenezer, and relating to a sale of land in which Ebenezer reserved rights of his "mother-in-law, Mary H. Warner." There has been no record of his marriage found, but the Mary Warner who married Samuel Bascom, Jr., Aug. 28, 1843, may have been his daughter.

Sarah Rich Warner, b. Aug. 8, 1805; d. Mar. 24, 1828, in Monson, Mass.; m. in Belchertown, Dec. 27, 1826, Lucius Freeman Newton, b. in Monson, Aug. 15, 1795, d. there Apr. 23, 1879, son of Stephen and Susannah (Davison) Newton. He m. (2) Maria Dunham (by whom he had children, George Henry, Sarah Warner, and Frederick Dunham, d. young), and m. (3) Zerviah Miller, and had Frederick Dunham, David Lucius, and Abbie Maria. No children by the first marriage. Mr. Newton was a carpenter and later a merchant. With his brothers he settled near his father's homestead, making a little colony of Newton families, known as "Newton's Corner."

John Ely (1) Warner, b. Nov. 17, 1807; d. Mar. 1, 1809.

Marietta Warner, b. Apr. 9, 1810; probably d. young.

John Ely (2) Warner, b. Sept. 27, 1813.

Jairus R. Warner, b. Dec. 21, 1815.

153 ELIZABETH[5] WARNER, daughter of Lieut. Joseph[4] and Elizabeth (Allen) Warner, baptized in Windham, Conn.,

November 12, 1727; died March 25, 1801, aged 73, in Hartford, Vt.

Married in Windham, October 28, 1751, Lieut. **THOMAS TRACY**, born August 19, 1725, in Windham, died in Hartford, January 28, 1821, son of Stephen and Deborah (Bingham) Tracy. Thomas Tracy was one of the charter proprietors of the town of Hartford, where he settled with his family in 1778-9. He was a large land owner, and took a prominent part in the affairs of the town. During the Revolution he was active in the frontier service of the militia: the names of Thomas Tracy and Sergt. Tracy appear on a pay roll of Capt. Edmund Hodges' Company for service done at Fort Fortitude by the order of Col. Joseph Safford, from the towns of Pomfret and Hartford in October, 1780; the names of Thomas Tracy, James Tracy, and Sergt. Andrew Tracy on a pay roll of Capt. Joshua Hazen's Company in Col. Wood's Regiment that marched to Brookfield in the alarm, October, 1780; also on a pay roll of the same company who marched to Piermont, upon Gen. Bailey's request, March 9, 1781, in the alarm at Peacham [Vt. Rev. Rolls, pp. 201, 283, 355] The title of lieutenant which appears on his tombstone was doubtless received after the Revolution.

Children, born in Windham, Conn.

Mary Tracy, b. Nov. 12, 1752; d. unmarried.

Andrew Tracy, b. Aug. 1, 1754; d. in Hartford, Vt., Aug. 26, 1802. He was register of deeds several years, and held other town offices. He married Dec. 2, 1784, Sarah Bliss, b. Oct. 19, 1763, d. Sept. 29, 1814, dau. of David and Polly (Porter) Bliss.

Deborah Tracy, b. Mar. 10, 1756; d. in Barnard, Vt., Nov. 15, 1818; m. Gen. Joseph Foster, b. in Ware, Mass., Sept. 10, 1759, d. in Barnard, Dec. 27, 1839, son of Joseph and Susannah (Roberts) Foster; Gen. Foster m. 2d, Oct. 20, 1819, Dolly Parmenter. He served in the Revolution; enlisting from Ware, he was a private in Capt. John Thompson's Company, Col. Leonard's (Hampshire Co.) Regiment, from May 7, 1777, to July 8, 1777; he was a lieutenant in Capt. William Brakenridge's Company, Col. Porter's Regiment, from July 9 to July 29, 1777; he was in Capt. Benjamin Cox's Company of Militia scouting in Barnard in 1780, and in Lieut. and Capt. Beriah Green's Company of Rangers in 1781 and 1782; he applied for a pension, Aug. 9, 1832. He was a brigadier general of the Vermont Militia after the Revolution. He represented Barnard in the Legislature, 1788-89, and was a selectman in Barnard, 1790-1801; overseer of the poor, 1808-15, 1817-21. No issue.

Susannah Tracy, b. July 2, 1758; d. in Hartford, Nov. 30, 1820; m. there Dec. 7, 1780, Capt. Asa Hazen, b. in Woodbury, Conn., Nov. 5, 1749, d. in Hartford, Mar. 12, 1819, son of Thomas and Ann (Tenney) Hazen. Asa Hazen was a constable in Hartford in 1776, a lister in 1778, and town clerk in 1780. In Aug., 1778, he served in

a scouting party sent out by Capt. Joshua Hazen; he served as a
sergeant in Capt. Joshua Hazen's Company in 1780 and 1781; also
lieutenant in Capt. William Bramble's Company which marched to
Bethel, Aug., 1781. He was appointed captain of the 1st Company in
the 2d Regiment, 3d Brigade, Militia of Vermont, Oct. 2, 1787.

James Tracy, b. Jan. 28, 1760; d. in Hartford, Sept. 19, 1834. He was
clerk of the charter proprietors, 1800 to 1809, treasurer of the town,
1802-1828. He married Oct. 22, 1795, Mercy Richmond, b. in Taunton, Mass., June 15, 1772, d. in Hartford, Oct. 19, 1859, dau. of Sergt.
Ebenezer and Mercy (Paull) Richmond of Barnard.

Thomas Tracy, b. Sept. 4, 1761, drowned, unmarried.

Joseph Tracy, b. July 18, 1763; d. in Hartford, Mar. 10, 1829; m. in
Hartford, Ruth Carter, b. in Fryeburg, Me., Dec. 7, 1772, d. in Hudson, Ohio, Feb. 20, 1845, dau. of Ezra (?) and Mary (Fifield) Carter.

Elizabeth Tracy, b. Apr. 15, 1765; d. in Hartford, June 2, 1800; m. there
Jan. 14, 1790, Capt. Josiah Tilden, b. in Lebanon, Conn., Apr. 19, 1760,
d. in Hartford, 1849, son of Stephen and Abigail (Richardson) Tilden.
Capt. Tilden was a farmer and hotel keeper. He was a private in
Capt. Joshua Hazen's Company in 1780 and 1781. [Further records
of this family may be found in Tucker's History of Hartford, Vt.]

154 WILLIAM[5] WARNER, son of Joseph[4] and Elizabeth
(Allen) Warner, born in Windham, Conn., April 7, 1729, baptized
May 3, 1730; died July 10, 1799; buried in Windham, Conn.,
tombstone inscribed Captain William Warner. He joined the
Windham Church in 1766; was tithing man about 1755; was
ensign of the 1st Company, 5th Regiment, May, 1771; lieutenant, same, October, 1772; captain, same, May, 1773; with
other residents of Windham petitioned for a bridge, 1771; was
administrator of the estate of Thomas Warner of Ashford, 1759;
and was recorded in the 1790 Census of Windham. (Conn. Col.
Records, vol. 11, 13, 14, etc.) His will bears the date of December 29, 1797.

Married (1) November 1, 1769 (Windham town record),
LYDIA MURDOCK, who died August 8, 1770, in her 26th year,
buried in Windham. She joined the Windham Church in 1764.

Married (2) in Lebanon, Conn., May 17, 1774 (Conn. marriages, 2:49), **MARY WILLIAMS,** who died June 31, 1793, in
her 53d year, buried in Windham. She joined the Windham
Church in 1775.

Child of William and Lydia (Murdock) Warner

Lydia Warner, b. Aug. 4, 1770 (Windham town record); d. in Windham; m. Thomas Sluman Smith.

Child of William and Mary (Williams) Warner

William Warner, b. Oct. 18, 1777 (Windham town record).

155 ELEAZER[5] WARNER, son of Thomas[4] and Delight (Metcalf) Warner, born in Ashford, Conn., February 8, 1738; died in New Lisbon, Otsego County, N. Y., June 2, 1821 (or 1826). He resided in Ashford and Mansfield, Conn., and Garrettsville, N. Y. On March 4, 1770, Eleazer Warner and his wife were received into the Congregational Church at Ashford and he was dismissed to the Second Church at Mansfield, July 3, 1791. He had purchased land in Mansfield as early as 1769, but did not remove until 1785-90. He was residing in Otsego County, N. Y., as early as 1813, as is shown by deeds recorded in Cooperstown, N. Y.

During the Revolution he rendered the following service: April, 1775, Lexington Alarm, marched from Ashford for the relief of Boston, junior ensign, served 8 days; commissioned captain, January 1, 1777, 7th Regiment, Connecticut line, resigned September 1, 1777, or retired because of ill-health, November 1, 1777; was one of the short levies, June 27, 1780, to December 13, 1780, under Col. Heman Swift, 7th Regiment.

Eleazer Warner married (1) in Ashford, Conn., April 29, 1762, JOANNA HALE, born in Ashford, August 24, 1740, probably died there about 1791. She was the daughter of James[4], Jr., and Elizabeth (Bucknell) Hale and her line of ancestry is as follows: Robert[1] Hale, arrived in Boston, 1632, was one of those who were set off from the first church in Boston to the first church in Charleston, became a deacon in that church, married Jane ————; Rev. John[2] Hale, b. 1636, was graduated from Harvard in 1657, was the first minister in Beverly, Mass., m. (1) Rebecca Byles, m. (2) 1684, Mrs. Sarah Noyes; Rev. James[3] Hale, b. 1685, d. 1742, first minister settled in Ashford, Conn.; James[4] Hale, Jr., b. 1716. Capt. Nathan Hale, the martyr-hero of the Revolution, was descended from Samuel[3] (next younger brother of Rev. James[3]), Richard[4], Nathan[5]. See also Life of Captain Nathan Hale, by Isaac William Stuart, Hartford, 1856, pp. 185-9; In Memoriam, Clement Edson Warner, Madison, Wis., 1917, pp. 67-9.

Eleazer Warner married (2) **ELIZABETH** ————, who died at New Lisbon, N. Y., November 16, 1817. So far as known there were no children by this marriage.

Children of Eleazer and Joanna (Hale) Warner, born in Ashford, Conn.

    Elizabeth Warner, b. Feb. 19, 1763; bapt. Mar. 7, 1770.
289 *Thomas Warner*, b. Feb. 28, 1764; m. Rhoda Hopkins.
    Abigail (1) *Warner*, b. Dec. 27, 1765; d. young.
    Eleazer (1) *Warner*, b. Sept. 27, 1767; d. young.

290 *Samuel Warner,* b. Jan. 26 (or Dec. 6), 1769; m. Irene Allen.
    Eliphalet Warner, b. Apr. 29, 1771; bapt. May 29, 1771.
    Joanna (1) *Warner,* b. Sept., 1772; bapt. Nov. 15, 1772; d. young.
    James Warner, b. Nov. 5, 1773.
    Delight (1) *Warner,* bapt. Aug. 13, 1775; d. young.
    Eleazer (2) *Warner,* bapt. Mar. 26, 1777.
291 *Zachariah Warner,* bapt. Dec. 3, 1778; m. (1) Laura Hale, (2) Nancy
    Storrs.
    Joanna (2) *Warner,* b. July 30, 1784; bapt. July 20, 1791; m. Elijah
    Chamberlain. Children: i. Henry, d. before 1891, leaving two sons.
    ii. (Son), d. before 1891.
    Abigail (2) *Warner,* b. Apr. 5 (or Sept. 4), 1787; bapt. July 20, 1791;
    d. in Norwich, N. Y.; m. Frederick Hale, who died in Norwich, and
    had a large family.
    Delight (2) *Warner,* b. Mar. 24, 1789; bapt. July 20, 1791; m. Lester
    Royce or Rice and lived in Cortland Co., N. Y.

(These last three baptisms are noted on the church records of Ashford "children of Eleazer Warner at his house." Perhaps it was at the time of their mother's death.)

156 SARAH[5] WARNER, daughter of Thomas[4] and Delight (Metcalf) Warner, born in Mansfield, Conn., May 9, 1740. There is on file at Ashford a receipt for property sold to her brother. "Know ye that I David Strong and Sarah Strong my wife formerly Sarah Warner of Ashford now of Stafford County of Hartford and Colony of Connecticut in New England, for and in consideration of 33 lbs. lawful money received to our full satisfaction of our loving brother Elezer Warner of Ashford . . . being that part of land set off to my wife Sarah Warner, now Sarah Strong etc."

Married in Union, Conn., November 27, 1760, Capt. DAVID STRONG, a farmer of Stafford, Conn., born June 4, 1736, son of Samuel, Jr., and Martha (Stoughton) Strong. He was a captain in the Revolution. He married (2) Jane Groves of Brimfield, Mass. See also Strong Genealogy.

Children of David and Sarah (Warner) Strong

Eliphalet Strong, b. Aug. 20, 1761; d. Jan. 15, 1847; m. Dec. 11, 1794, Marcia Groves of Monson, b. July 4, 1771, d. Jan. 21, 1831, daughter of Nicholas and Mary (Hubbard) Groves. He was a farmer at Stafford. Children: i. Lyman, m. and lived in Strongsville, Ohio. ii. Retire Groves, lived in Strongsville. iii. Eliphalet, was graduated from Amherst, became a minister, was finally a farmer in Milton, Ill. iv. Mercia, m. Horatio Amidon. v. David, resided in Somers, Wis. vi. Sarah, twin with David, d. in infancy. vii. Lurancy, d. not married. viii. Alvin, resided in Somers, Wis. ix. Delight, m. Samuel Morse of Sturbridge. x. Samuel Sanford, d. young while at school in Amherst.

14

Sally Strong, b. 1763; m. Nathaniel Hyde, b. Mar. 7, 1757, d. 1825, an iron founder in Stafford. Children: i. Alvin, m. Sarah Pinney. ii. Nathaniel. iii. Sarah, m. Asahel Johnson. iv. Lavinia, m. David Rockwell. v. Martha, m. Joseph Phelps Pinney.

Hannah Strong, b. about 1766; m. Josiah Wheeler of Stafford. Children: Clarissa; Laura; Martha; Ira; Hannah.

John Stoughton Strong, b. July 19, 1771; d. Feb. 23, 1863; m. June, 1795, Tamar Whitney, b. July 9, 1779, d. Aug. 2, 1856, daughter of Jonas and Tamar (Houghton) Whitney. He was a farmer and merchant in Strongsville, Ohio, after 1818, kept hotel, and bought and sold cattle, driving them through from Ohio and Kentucky to Boston and New York. Children: i. Emory. ii. Renda, m. Dr. Benjamin Olds. iii. Stoughton, d. young. iv. Warner, a merchant in Strongsville. v. Franklin. vi. Clark Ross. vii. Lavina (1), d. young. viii. Lavina (2), m. Jabez Lyman Burrell. ix. John Chipman. x. Lyman Whitney. xi. John Stoughton.

Delight Strong, b. about 1774; d. Mar. 22, 1855; m. Jasper Hyde, b. Dec., 1769, d. Aug. 4, 1848, son of Ephraim and Martha (Giddings) Hyde. He was an iron manufacturer in Stafford.

David Strong (twin), b. 1778; m. Abigail Pinney; was a farmer in Marlboro, Vt.

Abigail Strong (twin), b. 1778; d. Aug. 2, 1837; m. Thurston Carpenter, a farmer of Stafford, b. Oct. 2, 1766, son of Deacon John Carpenter. Children: i. Samuel, a physician. ii. Abigail, m. Wyllys Ellis. iii. Calista. iv. Azubah, m. Daniel Pinney. v. George Loomis. vi. Lucy, d. young. vii. John Oscar (1), d. young. viii. John Oscar (2) and ix. Calista (twins). x. Thomas, d. young. xi. Calvin.

Eunice Strong, b. about 1781; m. Jehiel Cross of Mansfield; see number 157.

Samuel Strong, m. Rebecca Cross of Mansfield; no children.

Mary Strong, b. Sept. 10, 1787; d. May 31, 1829; m. May 23, 1804, Eliakim Lyon, b. in Woodstock, Conn., Nov. 3, 1781, d. June 17, 1856, son of Lyman Lyon. He was a farmer in Stafford, Conn., until 1818, then in Strongsville, Ohio. Children: i. Danforth Strong. ii. Jane Groves, m. Captain Harpin Johnson. iii. Martha. iv. Lydia, m. Theron Goodwin. v. Mary, m. William Goodwin. vi. Samuel Strong. vii. Eliakim L. viii. Nancy Ann, d. young. ix. Charles Carlos. x. Clark Strong. xi. Reuda L., m. Leonard F. Burgess.

Azubah Strong, m. Deacon Samuel Lyon, a farmer of Stafford.

157 ELIS[5] or **ALICE[5] WARNER**, daughter of Thomas[4] and Delight (Metcalf) Warner, born August 11, 1742, in Mansfield, Conn.

Married November 20, 1766, **PETER CROSS**, son of Wade and Rebecca (————) Cross of Mansfield. The marriage is recorded in Mansfield although she was given as a resident of Ashford and they were probably married there.

Children, born in Mansfield

Jehiel Cross, b. Apr. 20, 1767; m. (1) Dec. 26, 1790, Hannah Sessions, who d. Apr. 4, 1804, daughter of John Sessions of Union; m. (2)

Apr. 4, 1805, Eunice Strong of Stafford, see number 156. Children by first wife: i. Mary, b. Aug. 7, 1791. ii. Alice, b. June 13, 1793. iii. Oril, a daughter, b. May 19, 1795. iv. Jehiel Warner, b. Aug. 8, 1797. v. Hannah, b. Apr. 1, 1804. Child by second wife: Austin, b. Sept. 27, 1806.

Reuben Cross, b. Dec. 30, 1768; d. in Manlius, N. Y.; m. Apr. 9, 1789, in Mansfield, Marilla Hanks, who died in Mansfield. Children, first four born in Mansfield: i. Angelina, b. Oct. 22, 1790. ii. Harriet, b. Oct. 15, 1795. iii. Maria, b. Jan. 7, 1797. iv. Marilla, b. May 11, 1799. v. Jefferson, b. in Lisle, N. Y., Dec. 5, 1802; d. in Morrisville, N. Y., Mar. 28, 1850; m. in Hartford, Mar. 14, 1826, Elizabeth Leffingwell Cooke, b. July 15, 1807, d. Dec. 20, 1876, daughter of John and Nancy[4] (Steele) Cooke (Thomas[3] Steele, Daniel[2], Samuel[1], who m. Mercy[3] Bradford, daughter of William Bradford, Jr.).

Wade Cross, b. Apr. 19, 1771.

Alice Cross, b. June 13, 1773.

Rebeckah Cross, b. May 26, 1775.

Peter Cross, b. Jan. 6, 1778; m. Polly Dimock, daughter of Eliphalet Dimock.

Eleazer Cross, b. Sept. 4, 1783; m. Hannah Williams.

Eleanor Cross, b. June 5, 1786; d. 1860, not married.

158 DELIGHT[5] WARNER, daughter of Thomas[4] and Delight (Metcalf) Warner, born June 9 or 10, 1749, in Willington, Conn.; died June 27, 1825.

Married **Dr. THOMAS SADD,** born March 29, 1748, in Wapping (South Windsor), Conn., son of Deacon Thomas and Waitstill (Rockwell) Sadd. Records of the family may be found in Stiles' Ancient Windsor, and in the Grant Genealogy.

Children, born in Wapping

Noah Sadd, b. June 20, 1774; d. Apr. 11, 1825; resided in Wapping; m. Apr. 15, 1797, Irene Strong, daughter of Elijah Strong of Coventry, Conn., b. July 21, 1778, d. Feb. 11, 1855. Children: i. Betsey, m. George Foster. ii. Eunice, d. young. iii. Lucina, m. Benoni O. King. iv. Joseph Lyman, m. Mary Rockwell. v. Frederick H., d. young. vi. Amanda, m. Joseph Sadd. vii. Mary, d. not married. viii. William Warner, m. Emily Chapin. ix. Frederick Henry, m. Hannah Collins. x. Ralzaman Thomas, d. young. xi. Cornelia, d. young. xii. Harriet, m. Horace Skinner.

Harvey Sadd, b. Oct. 5, 1776; d. Oct. 11, 1840, at Austinburgh, Ohio; m. Jan. 20, 1801, Lydia Merrill, b. Apr. 3, 1777, d. Oct. 2, 1843. Children: i. Joseph Merrill, was a missionary in several of the central western states, and for the last ten years of his life, city missionary in Louisville, Ky.; m. his cousin, Corinne Gilmore Sadd. ii. Elizabeth Parnal, m. Lewis Austin. iii. Cornelia Flower, m. Rev. Charles Danforth. iv. Mary Harvey, m. (1) John Mills, (2) —— Chapman, (3) —— Weston. v. Julia Warner, m. George Hawley. vi. Harvey, m. Clarinda Austin. vii. Sylvia, m. (1) Wolcott P. Marsh, (2) —— Strong, (3) —— Bates. viii. George Franklin, m. (1) Jane R. Strong, his cousin (see further), (2) Mary M. Kingsbury.

Chauncey Sadd (twin), b. June 1, 1779; removed to Sheldon, N. Y.; m.
  Cynthia Barber, b. in Canton, N. Y., Mar. 11, 1779, d. Jan. 5, 1844, in
  Peru, Ind., daughter of John and Elizabeth (Case) Barber. Children:
  i. Maria, m. Jerot Sutherland. ii. William Chauncey, d. not married.
  iii. Julia Warner, m. Rev. Asa Johnson. iv. Corinne Gilmore, m.
  Rev. Joseph Sadd, see above. v. George Franklin, m. Laura H. Arm-
  strong.
Betsey Sadd (twin), b. June 1, 1779; d. Mar. 18, 1821; resided in New
  Hartford; m. Elijah Strong of New Hartford. Children: i. Irene, m.
  George Hubbell. ii. Edward. iii. Thomas. iv. Elizabeth, m. ———
  Strong. v. Mary, m. Samuel E. Judd. vi. Julia, m. Jehiel Hunt.
  vii. Jane R., m. George Franklin Sadd.
Sally Sadd, b. May 18, 1782; d. Mar. 9, 1851; m. (1) Alfred Grant, (2)
  Dec. 11, 1827, Ebenezer Gibbs.
Hepsibah Sadd, b. June 3, 1786; d. Dec. 18, 1828; m. Jan. 6, 1831, John
  Stoughton, b. Aug. 29, 1786, d. July 7, 1861, son of John and Bridget
  (Fitch) Stoughton.

159 ELIZABETH⁵ WARNER, daughter of Elisha⁴ and
Elizabeth (Babcock) Warner, born in Mansfield, Conn., April 17,
1738; baptized there April 30, 1738.

Married in Mansfield, April 12, 1764, **JONATHAN BING-
HAM, JR.**, born February 20, 1735, son of Jonathan and Mary⁴
(Abbe) Bingham. Mary Abbe was descended from Ebenezer³
and Mary (Allen) Abbe, Samuel² and Mary (Knowlton) Abbe,
John¹ Abbe of Wenham, Mass., 1637. There are said to be
numerous Bingham descendants in New Hampshire and Vermont.

Children

Elisha Bingham, b. at Mansfield, Mar. 23, 1765.
Erastus Bingham, b. Apr. 17, 1767, at Mansfield; removed to Cornish,
  Cheshire Co., N. H. Children: Frederick and Amy.

160 JOSIAH⁵ WARNER, son of Elisha⁴ and Elizabeth
(Babcock) Warner, born in Mansfield, Conn., August 7, 1745;
baptized there August 18, 1745. He removed to Amherst,
Mass.; was on the Committee of Correspondence in Amherst,
1777-9; tithingman, 1781; an officer in the Revolution; listed
in the Census of 1800 in Amherst, two males and one female
over 45, one male between 16 and 26, one male and one female
between 10 and 16. (Mansfield records, Amherst town records
and History of Amherst, History of Hadley, p. 419.)

Married in Mansfield, March 24, 1768, **DEBORAH HALL**,
born in Mansfield, June 5, 1748, daughter of Captain Nathaniel
and Martha (Storrs) Hall.

Children

Parthena Warner, b. in Mansfield, Dec. 19, 1768; m. in Amherst, Mass., Feb. 11, 1788, Ezra Roods (Amherst town records).

Thirza Warner, b. in Mansfield, Jan. 24, 1771; m. in Amherst, Mass., Sept. 28, 1789, William Dickinson, b. Feb. 6, 1767, in Amherst, d. there Nov. 4, 1824, son of Ebenezer and Ruth (Eastman) Dickinson. Children, bapt. in Amherst: i. Anna, bapt. Jan. 25, 1795; m. Ira Kellogg. ii. Armanda, bapt. Jan. 25, 1795; m. in Amherst, Mar. 23, 1812, Amos Bigelow. iii. Ebenezer, bapt. Jan. 25, 1795. iv. Josiah Warner, bapt. July 24, 1796; m. Elenor ———— and had three children, bapt. in Amherst, William, bapt. Feb. 9, 1817, Elvira, bapt. Nov. 22, 1818, and Maria Chapin, bapt. May 6, 1821, m. in Amherst, May 3, 1841, E. Chandler Hayward, son of Amasa and Betsey (————) Hayward. v. Deborah, bapt. Nov. 14, 1802. (History of Amherst, and town records.)

Lothrop Warner, b. Mar. 15, 1773, in Amherst (town record).

Jeremy D. Warner, b. in Amherst, date not given in record.

Sarah A. Warner, b. in Amherst, date not given in record.

Deborah Warner, m. in Amherst, Nov. 24, 1797 or 1799, John Cowles, b. Dec. 29, 1779, d. in New Haven, Vt. He was the son of Eleazer and Hannah (Dickinson) Cowles, and was descended from John Cole who came from the west of England to Farmington, Conn., about 1640. Children, bapt. in Amherst: i. Mary, bapt. Apr. 26, 1801. ii. Martin, bapt. Aug. 28, 1803. (Amherst town records.)

Augusta Warner, m. in Amherst, Sept. 21, 1795, Chester Hawley, b. in Amherst, July, 1773, d. in Hadley (Plainville), Mass. He was the son of Zechariah and Rebecca (Edwards) Hawley and m. (2) Mrs. Josiah Ayres, the daughter of Timothy Green of Amherst. Children of Chester and Augusta (Warner) Hawley, bapt. in Amherst: i. Isaac (1), bapt. Feb. 22, 1801. ii. Lucy, bapt. Sept. 22, 1805. iii. Isaac (2), bapt. Feb. 25, 1810, moved to Plainville, Hadley. iv. Augusta, bapt. Jan. 5, 1812. v. Susan, bapt. June 12, 1814. (Amherst town records.)

292 *Josiah Warner, Jr.,* b. June 18, 1784; m. Achsah Eastman.

161 JESSE⁵ WARNER, son of Daniel⁴ and Jerusha (Hitchcock) Warner, born in Wilbraham, Mass., October 15, 1738, and resided there. (Centennial of Wilbraham.)

Married December 3, 1761, HANNAH COLTON, born in Springfield, Mass., October 27, 1740, daughter of Benjamin and Elizabeth (Pynchon) Colton (Colton Genealogy).

Children

Jesse (1) *Warner,* b. Sept. 11, 1762; d. Sept. 18, 1764.

Jerusha Warner, b. Jan. 15, 1764.

Jesse (2) *Warner,* b. Sept. 15, 1765; m. Mary ————. Children: i. Polly, b. May 17, 1787; d. Oct. 21, 1799. ii. Nathan, b. Sept. 22, 1789. iii. David. iv. Clarissa, b. Mar. 7, 1794. v. Thomas, b. July 18, 1796. vi. Jesse, b. Nov. 25, 1798. vii. Pynchon, b. Apr. 8, 1801. viii. John.

Daniel Warner, b. July 14, 1767; was drowned in the Chicopee River, Feb. 20, 1807. Left a wife Sarah and a minor son Daniel (Springfield, administrations, 25:10).

Clarissa (1) *Warner*, b. June 5, 1769; died.

Ichabod Warner, b. Aug. 22, 1771. He is perhaps the "Ichabod Warner, a soldier of Massachusetts," who m. Ruth Howard of Cohansey, N. J., at the First Baptist Church of Philadelphia, Pa., June 18, 1795 (Pennsylvania marriage licenses).

David (1) *Warner*, b. Nov. 26, 1773; d. June 6, 1775.

David (2) *Warner*, b. Aug. 22, 1775; m. Sarah Lyon. Children: 1. Daniel, b. Aug. 7, 1792. ii. William Colton, b. Apr. 21, 1801. iii. Philip Lyon, b. Dec. 11, 1803.

Noah (1) *Warner*, b. June 29, 1777; d. Oct. 8, 1778.

Clarissa (2) *Warner*, b. Jan. 10, 1780.

Noah (2) *Warner*, b. Aug. 8, 1783.

162 ICHABOD[5] WARNER, 3d, son of Ichabod[4] Warner, Jr., and Mary (Mapes) Goldsmith, born March 1, 1738, at Southold, L. I., N. Y.; died in Bolton, Conn., November 16, 1815. Dr. Ichabod Warner went from Scotland, Conn., to Bolton, about 1761. He and his wife were admitted to the church in Bolton, September 27, 1761. He was the best known and most highly respected physician of his time in the territory now occupied by Bolton, Andover, Coventry, Hebron, Glastonbury, Manchester, East Hartford and Vernon. For many years he was justice of the peace and was a member of the convention in Connecticut that ratified the United States Constitution. He was one of the charter members of the Connecticut State Medical Association. Physically he was a man of unusual size and strength. His first home in Bolton was on West Street, about a mile and a quarter from Bolton Center. After the marriage of his son, he gave this place to him and moved to Bolton Center on the place now owned by his great-great-grandson, Samuel M. Alvord. Dr. Warner died on this place.

Married July 17, 1760, recorded in Scotland Church records, MARY LAZELL, born April 5, 1737, in Hingham, Mass., daughter of Joshua and Martha (Harris) Lazell. She died in Bolton, June 30, 1820.

Children, born in Bolton, Conn.

293 *Martha Warner*, b. Jan. 24, 1761; m. David Post.
294 *Mary Warner*, b. Sept. 7, 1762; m. Benjamin Welles, Jr.
295 *Lucy Warner*, b. May 11, 1764; m. Levi Strong.
     Pamelia (1) *Warner*, b. Nov. 21, 1765; d. Dec. 24, 1765.
     (*Infant*), b. and d. Feb. 10, 1767.
296 *Pamelia* (2) *Warner*, b. Feb. 26, 1768; m. Isaac Birge.
297 *Ichabod Mape Warner*, b. Feb. 14, 1770; m. Mary Talcott.

298 *Jerusha Warner*, b. Feb. 18, 1772; m. Judah Strong.
    Elijah (1) Warner, b. Jan. 21, 1774; d. Feb. 10, 1774.
299 *Sarah Warner*, b. Apr. 28, 1775; m. Jonathan Birge.
    Octa or *Octavia Warner*, b. Apr. 21, 1777; d. June 3, 1777.
    Elijah (2) Warner, b. Nov. 28, 1779; d. Nov. 29, 1779.
    Hannah Warner, b. Feb. 16, 1781; d. Mar. 10, 1781.

163 NATHAN[5] WARNER, son of Daniel[4] and Bethia (Gining) Warner, born June 6, 1744 (Windham, Conn., town record), or June 17 (family record); died in Gnadenhütten, Northampton Co., Pa., August 26, 1802. He removed with his family from Connecticut to the Moravian settlement in Dutchess County, New York, known as Sichem, and from there to the Moravian settlement at Gnadenhütten, Northampton Co., Pa., about 1766. With others of his family and of that religious body, he suffered more or less persecution in Revolutionary times for refusing to serve in the army. On December 12, 1777, he and his brother Daniel, "both heads of large families, were forcibly taken to Allentown, and, being unwilling to serve in the militia for two months, and unable to pay £108 ransom, they were forced to cut fifty cords of wood each in the neighborhood of Allentown, for the use of the soldiery." They completed their task and returned to their homes in February with the promise of four pence per cord for their services. Nathan Warner's family is recorded in the 1790 Census of Penn township, Northampton County, two males over 16, one under 16, four females.

Married, probably in Hopewell, Dutchess Co., N. Y., MARY SILVERNAIL or SILBERNAGEL, born March 13, 1746; died June, 1817, in Ohio, whither she had removed to join her children about a year after her husband's death, arriving at Gnadenhütten, Ohio, October 19, 1803. After her son Daniel came to Ohio, she resided with him until her death at the age of 71 years.

WILL OF NATHAN WARNER

In the name of God, Amen,

I, Nathan Warner of Gnadenhutten, Penn township, County of Northampton and State of Pensylvania, yeoman; being at present in a weekly state of body but in sound mind and memory, thanks be to God for the same; but calling to mind the certain dissolution from my body and the uncertain hour when, I do hereby for peace and good order's sake make and ordain my last will and testament in manner following:

First I resign my soul into the merciful hands of my dear Savior and Redeemer Jesus Christ, who through his holy offering and blood-shedding purchased and procured grace for me and all mankind, and—

Next my body to be buried in a decent and orderly manner as my executrix and executors shall think fit.

And, after my just debts and funeral expenses be duly paid out of my personal estate I do ordain that after my death my estate and all what belongs thereto shall be praized by two judicious men and be sold or disposed of, and then the half of the amount of that sum of my estate and yearly property what it may amount to I bequeath the interest thereof to my dearly beloved wife, Mary Warner, born Silbernagel, during her natural life, and after her death I bequeath then the capital to my then living children, and that in equal divided sums.

The other half of the amount of my property I bequeath in the following manner :— I first bequeath to my two sons Nathan Warner and Peter Warner: both of them now living on the Muskingum at Gnadenhutten: each of them two hundred dollars, or £75; out of which sum their due to me must be deducted; and then the remaining part of the half sum of my property I ordain to my children, and that it be divided to them by my executrix and executors in equal sums.

And, lastly, I do hereby nominate, constitute, and appoint, to my executrix and executors my beloved wife Mary Warner, and my dear, beloved brother-in-law Nils Tilloson and my beloved, confidential friend Joseph Rhoads of this my last will and testament, hereby disannulling all former will and testaments by me made, and gratifying and confirming this to be my last.

In witness whereof I have hereunto put my hand and seal this twenty-first day of August, one thousand eight hundred and two.

Nathan Warner (seal)

Witnesses: William Carny
            Mary (her mark) Ackerman.

(Copied by M. F. Warner, Ashland, Ohio, Aug. 11, 1883.)

The following letter was written by Mary (Silvernail) Warner to her children on the Muskingum before coming herself. This letter was written in the spring after her husband's death.

My dear children: Nathan, Peter, and Catherine: the latter now Walton:

Gnadenhutten on the Mahony, May 3d—1803.

As I understand from my brother and sister-in-law N. and Hannah Tilleson that there is now next week an opportunity to convey letters to you, I cannot omit to write you some lines how your now widow mother do. First of all, I with my other executors have had a great deal of pleasure, and also great deal of trouble. The pleasure we have had consists in this: that we act with one another in love and harmony and seek to do the best for you and the other heirs, without seeking our own interests, and this shall be no concern till all things shall be settled. (Details of settlement of estate, selling the property, etc.)   I will if it please our Savior come to you and live with you next autumn; and I wish that one of you would come and help me on my journey, or perhaps Assa Walton. I have been spoken with one man who intends to pay a visit on the Muskingum but I would not like to go with him alone. I long much for to see you, and will be glad when that once shall be the case. I live now in the school-house near my br. and sister Tilloson's, your uncle and aunt's who loves you most tenderly, and sends their kind love to you, to Ezra's family, to Jonathan's, to your minister and his wife, to Heckewalder's and Peter's. Give our love to all. We, I and your uncle and aunt desire to give our love to brother and sister Mortimer. Be you all my tender children tenderly saluted from your most affectionate mother.

Mary Warner

P.S. Young Boaz Walton has yesterday bought Joseph Rakestraw's place which contains 150 acres for 450 pounds and he pays 70 punds cash and then the other in terms. Where Nathan lived formerly that place is gone through many hands, at present one Martin Wagner lives on it who bought it for five weeks ago. There is here now great call for land. Be pleased to write as soon as possible. Br. & sister Tilloson wonder much that Ezra and Lenel [Magdalena] do not write, neither do Jonathan. They speak often of them.

Haste:

On the outside of the letter was the following:

Bethlehem, May 8th, 1803.
   To Nathan Warner
       at
          Gnadenhutten
             on the Muskingum

To the care of the Revd
T. Gebhardcunno (?)
  in Bethlehem   To the Post-Office
Care of John Heckewelder Esq.
             Brook Court House,
Gnadenhutten Muskingum
              Ohio

Children of Nathan⁵ and Mary (Silvernail) Warner

300 *Nathan Warner*, b. Oct. 31, 1765, in Hopewell, N. Y.; m. Ann Adelia Davis.

301 *Peter Warner*, b. July 26, 1767, in Northampton Co., Pa.; m. Grace ———.

302 *Ebenezer Warner*, b. Sept. 2, 1769; m. ——— Davis.
     Hannah Warner, b. Nov. 25, 1772 (?); d. 1805 (?); m. Rev. ——— Longbolle, a missionary to South America.
     John Warner, b. about 1774; d. about 1780, aged 6 years.

303 *Mary Ann Warner* (or *Anna Mary*), b. Apr. 30, 1776; d. Sept. 3, 1832; m. Rev. Charles Gottlieb Bleck.
     Elizabeth Warner, b. Feb. 6, 1778, in Gnadenhütten, Pa.; d. 1848 in the Sisters' House in Bethlehem, Pa., not married.

304 *Catherine Warner*, b. Mar. 10, 1780; m. Asa Walton.

305 *Daniel Warner*, b. Nov. 6, 1782; m. Mary Simmers.
     John Warner, b. Jan. 8, 1785.

164 MASSAH⁵ WARNER, son of Daniel⁴ and Bethiah (Gining) Warner, born in Hebron, Conn., June 3, 1754; died in Bethlehem, Pa., May 24, 1824. He removed at an early age with his father's family to Dutchess County, New York, and thence to

the Moravian settlement at Gnadenhütten, Pa. He was taxed
in lower Saucon township, Northumberland County, Pa., in 1786;
in 1790 was noted as the ferryman in Bethlehem, Pa. He was
also a carpenter and conducted the saw mill. The ancient ferry
at Bethlehem was a rope ferry so contrived and fastened on
both banks of the river, that a flatboat, large enough to hold a
team of six horses, could be conveyed across the river backwards
and forwards by the mere force of the stream, the flatboat
always being put in an oblique direction with its foremost end
verging towards the line described by the rope. After this was
replaced by a bridge, Massah Warner was the toll-keeper.

Married May 31, 1781, **MARIA DOROTHEA MIKSCH,** born
October 10, 1755, in Gnadenthal, near Nazareth, Pa., died August
20, 1826, in Bethlehem, Pa., daughter of Michael Miksch, born
in Kunewalde, Moravia, 1710, married 1741, Johanna Rosina
Kuhn. Both she and her husband are buried in the old Moravian Cemetery in Bethlehem. She left three sons and three
daughters at her death, and fifteen grandchildren.

Children

John Christian Warner, was probably one of these children. He was
born in Bethlehem, Pa., in 1786; died June 30, 1858; married in 1810,
Martha McGilton or McJilton of Philadelphia, b. 1794, d. 1854. They
joined the church in Philadelphia in 1812; removed to Christianspring
in 1836 and to Bethlehem in 1850. They had five sons and five
daughters, one son and three daughters surviving her. One of the
daughters was Maria Dorothea, b. in Philadelphia, Feb. 5, 1818, d.
in Nazareth, Pa., Apr. 24, 1837, not married. She removed to Bethlehem in her 6th year; was confirmed April 4, 1833, was assistant
teacher of small girls in Bethlehem until, on account of illness and
melancholy, she was obliged to go to her parents in Christianspring.
(Moravian records.)

Catharine Warner, b. Apr. 15, 1789, in Bethlehem, Pa., d. there Apr.
25, 1855. She was for a number of years engaged in the Sisters'
House in Bethlehem as kitchen and waiting maid in the Old Boarding School dining hall; then served as sick nurse to the inmates of
the Sisters' House for twenty years. During the summer of 1842
she visited her relatives in Ohio, and in 1850, her friends in Salem,
N. C. (From Church Books of the Moravian Congregation at Bethlehem, Pa.)

David Warner, b. Aug. 17, 1791, in Bethlehem, Pa.; d. Aug. 27, 1881;
m. Apr. 5, 1818, Esther Miller, who died Jan. 8, 1882, daughter of G.
and Salome (————) Miller. They removed to Nazareth in 1832
and resided there for forty-eight years. Their married life together
was of sixty-three years. They had three children, all of whom died
in childhood: James N., b. in Bethlehem, 1828, d. there 1831; and a
child b. and d. 1832. (Moravian Historical Society publications.)

306 *Benjamin Warner,* b. Nov. 6, 1794; m. Anna Louisa Stotz.

165 EZRA[5] WARNER, son of Daniel[4] and Bethiah (Gining) Warner, born September 2, 1762, probably in the Moravian settlement in Dutchess Co., N. Y., where his family had lived a few years previous. He resided for a time in Gnadenhütten, Pa., on the Mahoning River but removed from there May 29, 1799, and became one of the first permanent white settlers in Clay township, Tuscarawas Co., Ohio. He cleared a few acres of land west of the river opposite Gnadenhütten and returned to Pennsylvania for his family in the autumn of the same year. With his wife and four children he reached his future home on the Tuscarawas, November 15, 1799. He was a Moravian, was mentioned among communicants in Gnadenhütten, July 13, 1799, and later was steward for the west side of the river. Although he attended the Methodist meetings there is no record of his joining the society.

Married **MARIA MAGDALENA LANER.**

Children, probably born in Pennsylvania

Lydia Warner, b. Nov. 14, 1792; d. 1841; joined the Methodist Church in 1808; m. Nov. 5, 1812, Daniel Noggle, both of Wayne County, Ohio, the first marriage recorded in the county. (History of Wayne County.)

Ruth Warner, b. July 18, 1795; d. 1862; joined the Methodist Church in 1808.

Sarah Warner, b. Sept. 15, 1797.

307 Samuel Ettwine Warner, b. May 10, 1799; m. Mary Warner (?).

Mary Warner, b. Feb. 12, 1802; d. 1846.

Hannah Warner, b. May 3, 1806; d. 1834.

166 MATTHEW[5] WARNER, son of Isaac[4] and Ann (Davison) Warner, born June 28, 1743, recorded in Windham, Conn.; died April 4, 1823 or 1824, in his 80th year, in Worthington, Mass. From the records found of his family, he seems to have resided in Windham until about 1772, then the next child was baptized in Williamsburg, Mass., but those born from 1774 to 1780 are recorded in Mansfield, Conn. His will, filed in Northampton, describes him as of Worthington, and owning land there. The will was made April 11, 1821, probated May 13, 1823. Heirs were his wife Eunice; son Bela; daughter Fanny Burr; son Stoel; daughter Nabby Cotterill; son Andrew; Henry Warner and Harriet Marble, children of his deceased son Millen. (Northampton probate records, 34:304.)

Married April 10, 1769, **EUNICE STOEL,** who died in Worthington, Mass., November 21, 1837, aged 91.

Children

308 *Milan Warner,* b. Feb. 8, 1770, at Windham; m. Polly Watt.
309 *Bela Warner,* b. Oct. 25, 1771, at Windham; m. Sally Kingman.
     Eunice Warner, bapt. in Williamsburg, Mass., July 1, 1772, recorded in
       Worthington.
310 *Stoel Warner,* b. Mar. 7, 1774, in Mansfield, Conn.; m. Anna Crandall.
     Fanny Warner, b. June 2, 1776, in Mansfield; received land in Worth-
       ington by her father's will; m. in Worthington, Apr. 18, 1814, Calvin
       Burr. She had at least one daughter, who m. Elkanah Ring, and
       settled in Norwich, Mass.
311 *Andrew Warner,* b. July 16, 1778, in Mansfield; m. Chloe Fairman.
     Nabby Warner, b. Dec. 17, 1780, in Mansfield; received land in Worth-
       ington, Mass., by her father's will; settled in Covington, Mass.; m.
       June 24, 1806, Nicholas Cotterill or Cottrel of Cummington. Chil-
       dren: Warner; Fanny; Addison; Achsa; Wealthy; Norma; Eunice.

167 EUNICE[5] WARNER, daughter of Isaac[4] and Ann
(Davison) Warner, born November 3, 1756, recorded in Windham, Conn.

Married in Windham, May 1, 1777, JOHN BINGHAM, born
November 26, 1755, died February 21, 1808, son of Gideon and
Mary (Cary) Bingham. He resided in the old Bingham house
on the hill in Willimantic and ran the grist mill at the "State."
The Bingham Genealogy contains a more extended account of
this family.

Children, recorded in Windham

George Bingham, b. July 11, 1781; was a carpenter by trade, attended
  the mill for several years, then went to western New York to live;
  m. Oct. 22, 1809, Mercy Denison. Children: i. Julia, b. Aug. 16, 1810.
  ii. Henry Laurens, b. Apr. 1, 1814.
Polly Bingham, b. Aug. 4, 1784; went west.
Julia Bingham, b. Apr. 6, 1787; d. May 15, 1789.
Eunice Bingham, b. May 16, 1789; was a teacher and went west.
John Bingham, b. Dec. 27, 1793; was a jeweller and an ingenious
  mechanic; resided in Willimantic; m. July 4, 1830, Julia Ann Ingra
  ham, who resided in Willimantic after his death, with two or three
  children.
Laura Bingham, b. Nov. 24, 1795; m. Elijah Safford and went west.

168 ELNATHAN[5] WARNER, son of Nathaniel[4] and Eliza-
beth (Webb) Warner, born November 1, 1753, recorded in
Windham, Conn.; died August 2, 1827, buried in Windham.
He served in the Revolution eight days during the Lexington
Alarm, from the town of Windham, and was a corporal in
Capt. Clarke's Company, Col. Johnson's Regiment, 1778. The
Census of 1800 recorded his family consisting of two males and
one female over 45, one female between 26 and 45, one male and

one female between 16 and 26, two girls between 10 and 16, and a boy and a girl under 10.

The inventory of his estate was taken by Amos D. Allen and Jesse Spafford, October 12, 1827, 113 acres of land and dwelling house valued at $1,813.10, with 15 acres on the east side of the Shetucket River, valued at $105.00. The distribution was made March 17, 1828, to the heirs: heirs of Elizabeth Eells, deceased; Sarah Warner; Lucy Segur; Charlotte Warner; Lydia Burchard; Huldah Warner; Charles Warner. (Windham probate records, 19:114-6, 169.)

Married (1) May 9, 1781, LYDIA BEAUMONT, probably born at Lebanon, May 23, 1757, daughter of William and Sarah (Everet) Beaumont; joined the church at Windham in 1783; died February 28, 1814.

Married (2) February 5, 1815, PHILENA DUNHAM, who joined the church at Windham in 1799, and died March 12, 1823, in her 51st year, buried in Windham Cemetery. Probably no children by this marriage.

Children of Elnathan and Lydia (Beaumont) Warner, recorded in Windham

312 *Elizabeth Warner*, b. Apr. 9, 1782; m. Joseph Eells.

Nathaniel Warner, b. Sept. 26, 1784; d. Dec. 21, 1784.

Sarah Warner, b. Oct. 10, 1785; d. Apr. 26, 1837, not married; buried in Windham Cemetery.

Lucy Warner, b. Mar. 26, 1788; d. in Lebanon, June 15, 1859; m. (1) Nov. 3, 1812, Samuel H. Potter, b. Sept. 27, 1780, d. Nov. 29, 1820, resided in Lebanon; m. (2) Apr. 1, 1827, Benjamin Segar of Lebanon, b. about 1770, d. Mar. 21, 1851, aged 81. Children by first husband: i. Lucy A., b. Aug. 11, 1813; d. Apr. 17, 1860. ii. Lydia M., b. May 1, 1815; d. Jan. 27, 1882; m. Joseph Potter. iii. Samuel W., b. Aug. 16, 1817; d. Apr. 21, 1845. iv. Abby, b. Mar. 17, 1820; d. Dec. 20, 1849; m. (1) Dan C. Scovill, (2) Jasper Murdock. Child of Benjamin and Lucy (Warner) Segar: Mary T., b. Mar. 15, 1828; d. Feb. 8, 1850. (From Kingsley's record, Lebanon.)

Erastus Warner, b. Mar. 23, 1790; d. July 24, 1800; buried in Windham Cemetery.

Lydia Warner, b. Feb. 19, 1792; d. in Woodstock, Conn.; m. ―――― Burchard.

Harry Warner, b. Feb. 23, 1794; d. Aug. 17, 1794.

Huldah Warner, b. Dec. 29, 1795; d. Oct. 26, 1877; joined the church in Windham in 1830. She married as his second wife, Jan. 3, 1836 (Windham town records), Nathaniel Lincoln, b. in North Windham, Feb. 1, 1771, d. there Dec. 27, 1864, only son and child of Captain Nathaniel Lincoln, who died at the age of 105, and his wife, Agnes Austin, grandson of Samuel Lincoln, 2d, of Windham, who died at the age of 101. He was first married in 1792, to Anna Stowell, by whom he had a son, Sumner Lee.

313 *Charles Warner*, b. Aug. 2, 1798; m. Margaret W. Hall.

Charlotte Warner, b. Dec. 4, 1801; m. as second wife, Mar. 7, 1832

(Windham town records), Captain George Loomis, b. in Lebanon, Conn., Aug., 1786, d. Jan. 13, 1837, son of Benoni and Grace (Parsons) Loomis. He resided in Columbia and m. (1) Louise Bliss, by whom he had children, George A. and Louisa M.; probably none by the second wife.

169 JARED[5] WARNER, son of Dr. Timothy[4] and Irena (Ripley) Warner, born in Scotland, Conn., September 17, 1756; died in Pomfret, Conn., May 23, 1802. The tax lists of Scotland contained his name in 1782, 1785, 1786, as a resident of "Lower Scotland" in 1785. He purchased land in Pomfret with house and barn in 1785, was a physician in the Abington district of Pomfret for many years and was highly respected. Dr. Warner was a man of great size, six feet seven inches tall. He was stricken with typhoid fever during an epidemic and was carried on a litter to the bedside of his patients until he died from exhaustion. His epitaph at Abington reads as follows:

"Stop ye, my friends and weep, for Warner's gone.
See here, his glass of time doth cease to run.
No more his liberal hand shall help the poor,
Relieve distress, and scatter joy no more.
While he from death did others seek to save,
Death threw a dart and plunged him in the grave!"

Dr. Warner was a member of the Masonic Lodge organized in Canterbury in 1790, which was composed of the leading men of Windham County.

Jared Warner married in Pomfret, December 28, 1784, MARY RIPLEY, born August 23, 1763, died January 28, 1826, daughter of Rev. David Ripley, first pastor of the Congregational Church of Abington, and Betsey Eliot, granddaughter of John Eliot, the apostle to the Indians.

Children, births recorded in Pomfret town records

David Ripley Warner, b. Jan. 24, 1786; d. Mar. 28, 1822, records of Abington Congregational Church.

Augustus Warner, b. Dec. 4, 1787; d. Feb. 11, 1857, not married.

314 Maria Warner (*Muriel* on town records), b. Oct. 1, 1789; m. Samuel Huntington Lyon.

Eliot Warner, b. Dec. 1, 1792; d. Dec. 4, 1794, Dec. 8 in Church records.

Albigence Waldo Warner, b. Aug. 18, 1794; d. Aug. 28, 1794.

315 Jared Eliot Warner, b. Mar. 31, 1796; m. (1) Alathea R. Lord, (2) Julia W. James, (3) Jane Helen Ryley.

170 MARY[5] WARNER, daughter of John[4] and Priscilla (Wood) Warner, born June 8, 1765, recorded in Windham,

Conn.; died January 29, 1839. She resided in Pomfret at the time of her marriage, and later in Windsor, Conn.

Married January 18, 1795, **ELIJAH BARBER**, born October 24, 1769, died July 19, 1812, son of Elijah and Abigail (Wood) Barber of Windsor, and descended from Thomas Barber of Windsor.

Children, born in Windsor

Maria Barber, b. Oct. 12, 1795; d. in Longmeadow, Mass., Sept. 16, 1854; m. the Rev. Mr. Hunt, a Baptist minister, who died 1854.

John Warner Barber, b. Feb. 2, 1798; m. (1) Harriet ————, who d. Mar. 17, 1826; m. (2) Ruth Green, who d. Nov. 18, 1851. See below for account of him and his family.

Guy Barber, b. May 24, 1800; resided in Hamden, Conn.; m. Oct. 24, 1824, Maria Jewett who d. Mar. 10, 1878. Children: i. James, b. May 25, 1826; d. in Hamden, Oct. 31, 1865; m. Julia Bradley, who d. 1863; had one child. ii. Maria, b. June 9, 1831; not married. iii. Charlotte, b. Sept. 12, 1833; not married. iv. Edmund, b. July 8, 1835; m. and went to Manitoba. v. Jennett, b. Dec. 6, 1837; resided in New Haven; not married.

Douglas Barber, b. May 29, 1805; d. Oct. 21, 1827, in Hartford.

Edmund L. Barber, b. Nov. 18, 1808; d. in San Francisco, Cal., Jan. 9, 1870, not married.

Charlotte Barber, b. Aug. 15, 1811; d. 1904; m. Rev. Lewis C. Gunn, who died in Berlin, Conn., in 1877. Children: i. Mary, b. 1848. ii. Lillie, b. 1850.

John Warner Barber, son of Elijah and Mary (Warner) Barber, resided in New Haven. In early life he learned the engraver's trade, later turned his attention to literature, and produced many historical books which he illustrated with wood cuts of his own engraving. Among these are: History and antiquities of New Haven, 1831; Historical collections of Connecticut, 1839; History and antiquities of New England, New York and New Jersey, 1841; Elements of general history, 1844; Incidents in American history, 1847; Religious emblems and allegories, 1848; European historical collections, 1855; Our whole country, history and description, 1861. With Henry Howe he published: Historical collections of New York, 1841; of New Jersey, 1844; of Virginia, 1844; of Ohio, 1847. With his daughter Elizabeth: Historical, poetic, and pictorial American scenes, 1853. By the first marriage he had two children: i. Mary, b. Aug. 30, 1823; m. Lieut. Kirby S. Woodward of the U. S. Revenue Cutter Service, who was drowned in California, Nov. 9, 1850, leaving two children, Kate, b. 1844, d. Feb. 19, 1857, and Arthur, b. 1847, resides in San Francisco. ii. David Brainard, b. Mar. 9, 1826; d. Aug. 7, 1826. By the second marriage he had five children: i. Elizabeth G., b. Nov. 20, 1827; collaborated with her father and also wrote poems, a volume of which was published after her death; m. Apr. 8, 1861, Capt. Charles H. Barrett (Yale, 1852), and d. on board her husband's ship in the China Sea, July 19, 1863, leaving a child, Ruth Louise, b. Jan. 25, 1862, d. Nov. 5, 1863. ii. Caroline T., b. May 23, 1829; resides in Ithaca, N. Y. (1918); m. Aug. 11, 1862, George W. Jones, a graduate of Yale, 1859, and for many years a member of the mathematical faculty of Cornell University and author of mathematical works. iii. John, b. Nov. 5, 1830; resided in New Haven; m. Mar. 7, 1854, Sarah E. Barnes; had two children, Charles, b. Jan. 27, 1855, d. July 9, 1877, and Walter, b. May 19, 1862. iv. James, b. Nov. 5, 1830; resided in Hamden, Conn.; m. and had a daughter Cornelia, b. 1857. v. Harriet, b. Feb. 27, 1835; d. June 24, 1862.

171 WILLIAM[5] WARNER, son of John[4] and Priscilla (Wood) Warner, born January 13, 1768, probably in or near Windham, Conn.; died December 31, 1804, in Hartford, Conn., buried in Center Church Yard, Hartford. He was a man respected by all; was called "artisan" and made swords for the army in Revolutionary times. A house built by him was said to be standing on Main Street, on the Windsor Road, Hartford, in 1900. The original copy of Center Church records in the Connecticut Historical Society Library corrects the mistake in his age as it appears in the published records of the Church, by the following entry·

December 31 the
Town of Hartford D[r] #
aged 37 to diging a grav for
Wilam Warner   0–10–0

Married February 23, 1791, **MARY TROWBRIDGE,** born February 8, 1771, in Abingdon Parish, Pomfret, Conn., daughter of Daniel and Mary (Pearl) Trowbridge.

Children

316   *George Trowbridge Warner,* b. Mar. 5, 1802; m. Tamzen Smith Rogers.
      Pamelia Warner, lived and died in Hampton, Conn.; m. James Fuller, a farmer and soldier in the War of 1812. Their daughter Dora, d. Mar., 1917, aged 93, m. —— Skinner, and had a daughter Alice, who m. Judge John Doyle and resides in Toledo, Ohio.
      Laura Warner, d. aged 16.
      John Warner, b. after his father's death.

172 ICHABOD[5] WARNER, son of John[4] and Priscilla (Wood) Warner, born October 17, 1769, probably in the town of Windham, Conn., although not recorded on town records there; died August 4, 1854, buried in old cemetery, Scotland, Conn. He was a shoemaker by trade and was recorded in the Census of 1800 and 1810 in Windham. On January 13, 1836, he sold his dwelling house in Scotland Society on the south side of Scotland Green to William L. Warner of Brooklyn (Windham deeds, 32: 131).

Married April 2, 1798 (Windham records), HANNAH COL
LINS, who died May 10, 1843, aged 63 years, buried in old cemetery, Scotland, Conn.

Chldren, births recorded in Windham

Betsey Warner, b. Feb. 9, 1799; m. June 30, 1822 (Windham town
record), Thomas Winship, who was a deacon in Dr. Bushnell's
Church in Hartford, where they resided for many years.

WARNER HOUSE SCOTLAND, CONN. BUILT BY
ICHABOD WARNER, 1769–1854

Roxanna Warner, b. Feb. 17, 1801; d. May 17, 1802, buried in old
cemetery, Scotland.
Lucia Warner, b. Aug. 25, 1803; lived to old age.
317 *Earl Warner,* b. Aug. 15, 1806; m. (1) Harriet S. Gilbert, (2) Adeline
Lester, (3) Mary Eliza Fitch.
Emily Warner, b. June 25, 1809.
George Warner, b. Nov. 29, 1811; d. young.
William L. Warner, b. May 17, 1814; was called of Brooklyn in 1836
when he purchased his father's house in Scotland.
Maria W. Warner, b. June 29, 1816.
John Warner, b. Feb. 12, 1819
George Erastus Warner, b. July 7, 1823.

173 ROSAMOND⁵ WARNER, daughter of John⁴ and Priscilla (Wood) Warner, born probably in Scotland, Conn.; died

15

January 9, 1849. She was of Scotland at the time of her marriage and lived later in Windsor, Conn.

Married March 5, 1798, **IRA LOOMIS**, born February 13, 1770, died January 9, 1842, son of Serajah and Sibyl (Loomis) Loomis. (Conn. marriages, 3:51, Stiles' History of Windsor, 444).

Children

Gurdon Loomis, b. Dec. 14, 1799, was living in 1894; m. in Windsor, Jan. 21, 1830, Miriam Warner. Children: i. Charlotte Ann, b. Feb. 1, 1831; m. Nov. 25, 1857, James Henry Harvey. ii. Lucy W., b. Aug. 21, 1833; m. Oct. 20, 1856, Ebenezer Gates. iii. John E., b. July 19, 1835; m. June 8, 1864, Maria Root.

Ira Loomis, b. May 2, 1802; was a farmer and mechanic in Windsor; m. Feb. 12, 1834, Eliza Sheldon of Suffield. Children: i. Newton Sheldon, b. Jan. 17, 1835; m. June 4, 1863, Susan Caswell and had Barton Samuel, b. Nov. 10, 1868. ii. Edmund Walton, b. May 13, 1837; m. Feb. 18, 1863, Susan A. Camp, and had Edmund Howard, b. Mar. 16, 1864, and George Arthur, b. July 13, 1867. iii. Mary Angeline, b. May 30, 1844.

Wealthy P. Loomis, b. Jan. 29, 1806; d. Aug. 26, 1826.

Ruth P. Loomis, b. Apr. 19, 1815; m. Noah Griswold.

174 MOSES⁵ WARNER, JR., son of Moses⁴ and Mary (Field) Warner, born probably in Belchertown, Mass.; died before 1790, when his wife was appointed administratrix of his estate. His name does not appear on the town records except when as a boy he was appointed one of the hog-reeves.

Married in Amherst in 1767, **SARAH SELDEN** or **SELLON**, who died in Amherst, March 29, 1812, in her 64th year. She was appointed guardian for her two minor children, Mary Field and John, February 16, 1795.

Children, births recorded in Amherst

Mary Warner, b. May 28, 1773; d. young.
318   *Mary Field Warner*, b. June 17, 1779; m. David Dickinson.
John Warner, b. June 19, 1787.

175 MERIBAH⁵ WARNER, daughter of Aaron⁴ Warner, born in Hadley (Amherst precinct), Mass., February 23, 1742; died in Rowe, Mass., July 29, 1809. Her name has also been recorded as Maribee and Marilla. Meribah is according to the Amherst town records. For fuller records of her family see the Colton Genealogy.

Married in Amherst, Mass., August 27, 1761, **ELI COLTON**, born in Longmeadow, Mass., January 17, 1837, died in Rowe, January 16, 1800, son of Ephraim and Sarah (Burt) Colton. He removed from Longmeadow to Conway, Mass., thence to Rowe. He was a soldier in the French and Indian War.

Children

Gideon Colton, b. Aug. 28, 1761; bapt. in Amherst, Jan. 11, 1767; d. Sept. 10, 1832, in Borodino, Onondaga Co., N. Y.; m. Rhoda Fowler of Borodino, who died there Sept. 9, 1842. He was a farmer. Children: i. Harriet, b. Dec. 2, 1811; m. Henry Ide of Borodino, and had children. ii. Alanson E., b. Oct. 13, 1813; m. Charity Ide.

Eli Colton, Jr., b. 1763; d. Oct. 19, 1798; m. in Rowe, 1795, Lovisa Warner, who m. (2) in Rowe, Mar. 30, 1801, John Williams. Children: i. Zebina, b. Mar. 17, 1796. ii. Clarissa, b. Apr. 23, 1798; d. Jan. 16, 1803.

Eunice Colton, b. Apr. 25, 1764; bapt. in Amherst, Jan. 11, 1767; d. in Rupert, Vt., Nov. 6, 1842; m. Henry Wilson, who died in Sherburne, Vt. They had eleven children.

Aaron Colton, b. 1766; was drowned in the Deerfield River, aged about 21.

Silas Colton, b. Apr. 23, 1768; d. in Sherburne, Vt., Mar. 24, 1826; m. Nov., 1796, Mary Hines, who died in Rowe, Mass., Apr. 16, 1818. Children, b. in Rowe: i. Nancy. ii. Silas. iii. Hiram. iv. Gideon. v. Dorcas. vi. Aaron. vii. Polly, d. young. viii. Eli, d. young. ix. David, d. not married. x. Elisha W. xi. Jonathan. xii. Mary.

Hannah Colton, b. 1770; d. not married.

176 HANNAH[5] WARNER, daughter of Aaron[4] and Esther (————) Warner, baptized at Amherst, Mass., June 30, 1754; died about 1829.

Married November 12, 1772, **JEREMIAH CADY,** born in Killingly, Conn., July 17, 1752, died in Hadley, Mass., June 4, 1848. He was the son of Samuel and Elizabeth (Winter) Cady, and a descendant of Nicholas Cady, who was an early settler in Watertown, and of John Winter, who came to Watertown in 1633. Samuel Cady removed his family from Killingly to Shutesbury, Mass., in 1764. At the age of 21, Jeremiah Cady made a visit to Boston and chanced to attend the memorable meeting held in Old South Church in December, 1773. He accepted the invitation to attend the immortal tea-party on the night of December 16, 1773. In later years he often recited the story of the party, and, although his name does not occur in the imperfect published list of participants, his character was such that his story was to be believed, and his name was doubtless concealed, like many others, for political reasons.

On one occasion when the Cadys, among others, had erected a liberty pole in Shutesbury, the Tory minister of the town ordered the rebels to disperse. They, in turn, ordered him to go home, and upon his refusal, young Jeremiah Cady, who had the strength of a giant, seized him and threw him a rod or so on his way, whereupon he prudently obeyed the order. Jeremiah was early enlisted in the defense of his country and was at the battle of Bunker Hill.

About 1800 he removed with his family to Friendship, Allegany County, N. Y., and later to Henrietta, Monroe County. After their log house had been erected, Mrs. Cady, who with her husband was deeply religious, suggested to the neighbors holding services there on Sunday. This was done, and, with Mr. and Mrs. Cady as leaders, the custom was continued until the Congregational Church was organized in 1818, with them among its members. They later removed to Cuba, to live with one of the children, but after his wife's death he returned to Massachusetts to live with his daughter in Hadley. A full account of his family is found in the Cady Genealogy (1910) by Orrin Peer Allen.

Children, born in Shutesbury, Mass.

Clark Cady, b. June 3, 1774; d. May 23, 1783.

Hannah Cady, b. Jan. 10, 1776; d. Sept. 28, 1791.

Salome Cady, b. Jan. 1, 1779; d. Jan., 1853, in Hadley, Mass.; m. Nov. 23, 1799, David White Cook, b. in Hadley July 26, 1779, d. in Belchertown, Jan. 29, 1854, a lineal descendant of Captain Aaron Cook and Elder John White, early settlers of Hadley. Children: i. Hannah, m. Asa Brown. ii. Justin. iii. Salome, m. Elisha H. Osborn. iv. Mary, d. young. v. David William. vi. Martha Mary, m. James Beaman. vii. Jeremiah, m. Harriet Butterfield. viii. Dorothy, m. Luther Hooker. ix. Sophia, m. Harrison Dunbar Dwight. x. Aaron, m. Clara Clark.

Samuel Cady, b. Nov. 26, 1780; d. about 1805, not married.

Polly (1) *Cady,* b. Feb. 10, 1782; d. young.

Sophia Cady, b. Mar. 5, 1784; d. May 2, 1795.

Stephen Cady, b. Feb. 26, 1786; d. in Cambridge, Ill., July 29, 1863; m. Dec. 16, 1810, Cynthia Robinson, b. in Williamstown, Vt., June 18, 1793, d. in Cambridge, Sept. 13, 1869. Children: i. Polly, m. James Bribner Vincent. ii. Stephen Willard, d. young. iii. Lucy Melissa, m. Alexander H. Showers. iv. Cynthia, m. Norman Malcolm. v. Levia Willard. vi. Stephen Cromwell. vii. Nancy, m. (1) Joseph Showers, (2) William Mealmans. viii. Lyman Spaulding, m. Anna Marshall. ix. Luther Henry, m. Sarah Stephens. x. Samuel Perkins, m. Letitia Grant. xi. Alzina Maria, m. John S. Buckles.

Polly (2) *Cady,* b. May 24, 1788; lived in New York; m. ——— Williams.

Dorothy Cady, b. Dec. 17, 1791; d. near Buffalo, N. Y., about 1872; m. Walter Perkins, b. in Canterbury, Conn., d. about 1877. Resided in Henrietta, N. Y., and at Falls Church, Va. Children: i. Leonard Brewster (1), d. young. ii. Leonard Brewster (2). iii. Emma S., m. John Bartlett. iv. Emily S., m. Clinton Squares. v. Samuel C., m. Almira Love. vi. Seth W., m. Mary Jane Smith.

Joanna Cady, b. Mar. 2, 1795; d. Mar. 12, 1795.

Chester Cady, b. Apr. 11, 1796; d. about 1862, in Cambridge, Ill.; m. near Cuba, N. Y.; removed about 1850 to Wheeling, Va., thence to Cambridge. His wife died before 1862. Children: i. Warren (1), d. young. ii. Homer. iii. Warren (2). iv. Stephen. v. Jane. vi. Mary. vii. Angeline, m. ——— Davis.

177 DAVID⁵ WARNER, son of Aaron⁴ Warner, born in Amherst, Mass., 1756, baptized September, 1756; died December 10, 1828, in Amherst, aged 72 (town records) or 71 (tombstone). He was of Amherst at the time of his marriage and was living in Amherst in 1800 when, with his wife, son and daughter, he was recorded in the Census.

Married in Chatham-Portland, Conn., February 12, 1783, **Mrs. LUCY ORCHARD**, who died May 30, 1819, buried in Amherst.

Children

Phineas Warner, b. in Amherst, Apr. 28, 1786; d. there July 19, 1855 (Amherst town records); lived and died on the farm that had been allotted to his great-grandfather Jacob Warner in the laying out of Amherst; m. Octavia Dewey, bapt. at Bolton, Conn., June 22, 1788, d. in Amherst, Feb. 14, 1865, aged 77 years, 1 month, 4 days, daughter of Solomon and Christiana (Cone) Dewey. Children: i. and ii. David S. and a twin brother who died young. David S. Warner was b. in Amherst, Feb. 2, 1815; was a farmer and d. there Mar. 17, 1886; m. June 22, 1857, Mary Jane Thayer, b. in Amherst, or Lanesboro, about 1835, d. Sept. 19, 1904, aged 69 years, 5 months, 7 days, daughter of Lyman K. and Mary T. (Smith) Thayer of Plainfield. David S. Warner had four children, recorded in Amherst: i. Mary L., b. July 26, 1859. ii. Effa G., b. Nov. 1, 1863; d. Nov. 28, 1863. iii. Etta Octavia, b. Feb. 10, 1865. iv. David, b. Jan. 23, 1867; d. Feb. 25, 1867.
Polly Warner, d. Nov. 27, 1807, in her 20th year, buried in Amherst.

178 JONATHAN⁵ WARNER, son of Aaron⁴ Warner, born probably in Amherst, Mass., and resided there. Made several deeds in 1807 and 1808. With his wife Margaret Elizabeth he sold to his sons Aaron and Jonathan his home farm and also land in Hadley "on Mount Hollock so-called."

Married December 2, 1779, **MARGARET ELIZABETH SEWALL (or JEWELL)**.

Children, baptisms recorded in Amherst

Jonathan Warner, Jr., baptism and birth not recorded. His father sold property to him in 1808, and with his brother Aaron he bought land in Amherst, 1807-8.
319 *Aaron Warner,* bapt. Oct. 2, 1783, probably b. 1781; m. Rebecca Smith.
Francis P. Warner, bapt. Oct. 26, 1783.
Alexander Warner, bapt. Aug. 6, 1786; m. Lucy Russell.

Elijah Warner, bapt. Aug. 10, 1788.
Elisha Warner, bapt. July 25, 1790; resided in Rutland, Vt., in 1850 (Census of 1850); farmer; m. Gezier ———, who was born in Vermont about 1792. Children: i. Lucius O. P., b. in Vermont about 1828; was a farmer in Rutland, with his father in 1850. ii.(?) Rufus, b. in Vermont about 1832; was a printer residing in the family of George A. Tuttle of Rutland, in 1850. iii. John P., b. in Vermont about 1833; was a laborer in Rutland in 1850. iv. Charles Smith, b. in Vermont about 1844.
Robert P. Warner, bapt. Jan. 9, 1793.
Margaret E. Warner, bapt. Nov. 1, 1795.
Jane Warner, bapt. Mar. 6, 1798.
Rufus Warner, bapt. Apr. 20, 1800.
Lucius Warner, bapt. Nov. 7, 1802.

179 LEMUEL⁵ WARNER, son of Jonathan⁴ and Mary (Graves) Warner, born in Hadley, Mass., about 1747; died there August 11, 1829, in his 82d year. His uncle Oliver Warner conveyed to him half interest in a new sawmill in Hadley by his will of 1779; he was recorded in the 1800 Census of Hadley; in 1807 was one of the tenants of plot 45, Hadley; left will dated May 9, 1824, probated September 1, 1829, in which he mentioned his wife Martha, sons Oliver and Jonathan, daughter Dorothy, the wife of Deacon William Dickinson, and two children of his deceased daughter Polly, the wife of Sylvester Smith.

Married (1) July 9, 1772 (Hadley town records), **DOROTHY PHELPS,** born in Lyme, Conn., died in Hadley, Mass., August 23, 1804, in her 55th year, buried in Hadley, daughter of Zuriah and Dorothy (———) Phelps.

Married (2) intentions recorded at Hadley, September 29, 1805, **Mrs. ELIZABETH STONE.** The stone in Hadley cemetery bears this inscription:

"Elizabeth, wife of Lemuel Warner and formerly wife of John Stone of Chesterfield, died Sept. 20, 1807, aged 50. This monument is erected by direction of her daughter Aurelia Stone who now rests in her grave in Rochester, N. Y."

Married (3) April 28, 1808, **MARTHA H. ALLEN** of Greenfield, Mass., born November 25, 1758, died January 27, 1836, daughter of Amos and Jemima (Root) Allen.

Children by first wife, recorded in Hadley

Jonathan Warner, b. Dec. 16, 1773; resided in Hadley (1800 Census); m. June 22, 1796 (Hadley town records), Sally Shipman. Children baptized in Hadley: i. Elizabeth (1), d. young. ii. Emily, bapt. Nov. 5, 1797. iii. Charles, bapt. Feb. 3, 1799. iv. Elizabeth (2), bapt. Jan. 18, 1801. v. Dorothy, bapt. 1803. vi. Sally Shipman, bapt.

June 2, 1805. vii. Henry Phelps (1), bapt. June 28, 1806. viii.
Henry Phelps (2), bapt. Sept. 18, 1808. ix. Mary, d. Sept. 23, 1836,
aged 26, buried in Hadley.
320 *Dorothy Warner,* b. Mar. 19, 1777; m. William Dickinson.
321 *Oliver Warner,* b. June 27, 1789; m. Jemima Severance.
       Pòlly (2) *Warner,* b. Sept. 29, 1792; d. Aug. 19, 1817; m. Jan. 1, 1812,
       Sylvester Smith, and left two children, mentionèd in her father's
       will, 1824.

180 NOADIAH[5] WARNER, son of Jonathan[4] and Mary
(Graves) Warner, born in Hadley, Mass., 1749; died there about
1825. He was tenant of plot 45 in Hadley in 1807, and was on
the Census of Hadley in 1800. The administrators of his estate,
February 1, 1825, were Moses Porter, and the husbands of his
two daughters, Abel Warner and Giles C. Kellogg. An interesting light on the expenses of the day is shown in two of the
items of the inventory: for digging the grave, $1.50; for coffin,
$3.00.

Married September 8, 1783, **MARTHA HUNT,** born July 17,
1750, died October 25, 1787, buried in Hadley, daughter of Samuel and Anna (Elsworth) Hunt of Northfield, later of Guilford
and Hertford, Vt.

Children, born in Hadley

Lucy Warner, b. Nov. 15, 1784; d. there Apr. 20, 1868. She may have
       married (1) Robert Cook, (2) Abel[6] Warner, son of Elihu[5] and Eliza-
       beth (Freeman) Warner, see number 182. History of Hadley records
       her sister, Patty Hunt Warner, as the wife first of Robert Cook and
       then of Abel Warner, but it is quite certain that she married Giles
       C. Kellogg, see below. Lucy Warner, wife of Abel Warner of Had-
       ley, bought land in 1825 from the heirs of Arad Hunt (Northamp-
       ton deeds, 52:620). This land was adjoining land of Lemuel Warner.
322 *Martha Hunt Warner,* b. Oct. 9, 1787; m. Giles Crouch Kellogg.

181 MARTHA[5] WARNER, daughter of Orange[4] and Elizabeth (Graves) Warner, born in Hadley, Mass., September 11 or
17, 1756; died in Whately, Mass., March 21, 1830. Her father
deeded her his own home in Hadley, in 1795, calling her "of
Whately."

Married, as his second wife, **JOHN CRAFTS,** born in Hatfield, Mass., January, 1743, died May 3, 1826, son of Thomas[5] and
Sarah (Graves) Crafts (John[4], Thomas[3], John[2], Lieutenant
Griffin[1] Crafts). He married (1) Thankful Adkins, who died
in 1786, leaving one child, Thankful. John Crafts served in
Capt. Israel Chapin's Company, Col. John Fellows' Regiment,
marching April 20, 1775, at the Lexington alarm, and was in
several other campaigns. At the outbreak of the war, the

authority of the King was ignored and taxes could not be collected. The town chose a committee of ten, among whom was
John Crafts, to "encourage the collector in the faithful discharge
of his duties." He owned a large farm in Whately and kept a
hotel for many years. Records of the family are found in "The
Crafts Family."

Children of John and Martha (Warner) Crafts, all born in Whately

Orange Crafts, b. Feb. 12, 1796; d. Feb. 5, 1801.

Emily Crafts, b. Feb. 13, 1798; d. June 29, 1836; m. Jan. 3, 1822, John
Russell, Jr., of Hadley, b. Apr. 13, 1797, d. at Greenfield. Children,
born in North Hadley: i. Orange Matoon, b. Feb. 2, 1823; d. Feb. 22,
1829. ii. Sarah, b. Dec. 22, 1824; d. Apr. 24, 1842. iii. Christopher,
b. 1827; d. Mar. 14, 1831. iv. Martha, b. 1829; d. Feb. 12, 1831. v.
Lydia Hibbard, b. July 18, 1831; d. Oct. 30, 1876; m. Feb. 5, 1857,
Orsamus Cutler of West Brookfield, son of Thomas Browne and
Harriet S. (Judd) Cutler of Northampton, b. Dec. 1, 1813, d. Oct.
30, 1876, the same day as his wife, leaving a daughter, Abbie Eliza-
beth, who married Warren Tyler and lived in West Brookfield. vi.
Emily A., b. June 4, 1833; m. May 26, 1852, Dexter B. Bruce of
Belchertown, and had two children, Charles R. and George H. vii.
Mary Jane, b. Dec., 1835; d. June 14, 1839.

Lydia Crafts, b. Aug. 10, 1800; d. Aug. 1, 1875; m. Aug. 25, 1829, Elias
Hibbard, son of John and Irene (Belden) Hibbard, b. Feb. 7, 1794,
d. Feb. 2, 1856, in Troy, Wis. They moved from North Hadley to
Troy, Wis., in 1842. In both places he was a prominent farmer and
manufacturer of brooms. Children: i. Elias Worcester, b. June 30,
1830; m. June 30, 1856, Loraine Warren, daughter of Hinkley Warren
of Stoughton, Wis., moved to Missouri Valley, Iowa, where he was
in the lumber and coal business and sold agricultural implements,
had two daughters, Cora Jane and Carrie Loraine. ii. Phila Elizabeth, b. Dec. 9, 1832; m. June 1, 1852, Andrew Jackson Bliss, son of
Gideon and Prudence (————) Bliss of Troy, Wis., b. Sept. 28,
1830, was a farmer in Troy and had seven children, Arthur De Wayne,
Alice Luella, Martha L., Emily Adaline, Jennie Hibbard, Dwight
Jackson, and Henry Ward. iii. Rufus Pomeroy, b. Oct. 7, 1834; m.
and lives in Denison, Grayson Co., Texas. iv. Emily Jane, b. Apr.
29, 1836; d. in Grand Rapids, Mich., Sept. 11, 1873; m. Jan., 1864,
George Augustus Gould, son of Eli Gould, formerly of Greenfield,
Mass., a manufacturer of brooms in Grand Rapids. v. Henry Harrison, b. June 6, 1840; d. June 5, 1874, in Missouri Valley, Iowa, where
he was in the lumber and grain business and sold agricultural implements. vi. John De Wayne, b. Oct. 1, 1843; d. Mar. 9, 1848.

182. ELIHU[5] WARNER, son of Orange[4] and Elizabeth
(Graves) Warner, born in Hadley, Mass., October 29, 1758; died
there January 14, 1851. He was a farmer; received one-half
interest in the new sawmill in Hadley by the will of his uncle
Oliver in 1779; received by deed from his father in 1795, property in Hadley on the south side of his homelot, which, combined

with what he had previously given him, made the equivalent of half a homelot, also a lot in "Partridge Swamp," and two wood-lots on Mount Warner. His family is recorded in the Census of 1790 and later ones.

Married October 31, 1784, **ELIZABETH FREEMAN**, who died July 25, 1834, in her 68th year (aged 68, Hadley town records).

Children, all but last two recorded in Hadley

Abigail Warner, b. Dec. 20, 1785; m. Samuel Wood.
(Daughter), b. and d. Oct. 21, 1787.
Hannah Warner, b. May 1, 1789; m. John H. Jones.
John (1) *Warner*, b. Aug. 5, 1791; d. Oct. 21, 1801.
323 *Harriet Warner*, b. July 2, 1793; m. Jonathan Marsh.
Elizabeth Warner, b. Aug. 16, 1795; d. in Hadley, Aug. 25, 1850, not married.
William Freeman Warner, b. Apr. 1, 1797; d. July 6, 1846, not married. He was a farmer living in Hadley.
Abel Warner, b. Feb. 28, 1799; d. June or July 19, 1831; m. probably as second husband, Lucy⁶ Warner, daughter of Noadiah⁵ and Martha (Hunt) Warner, see number 180. They had no children.
John (2) *Warner*, b. Jan. 1, 1802; d. Jan. 11, 1822, while a member of the junior class at Dartmouth College.
Giles Warner, b. Sept. 24, 1803; d. Sept. 15, 1804.
Lydia W. Warner, b. Nov. 17, 1805; d. Jan. 4, 1841, not married.
Sophia Warner, b. Aug. 22, 1807; d. Dec. 30, 1809.

183 ROXELANA⁵ or **ROXCELLANA WARNER**, daughter of Gideon⁴ and Mary (Punderson or Parsons) Warner, born probably in Hadley, Mass.; died in Whately, 1830.

Married (1) in Hadley, December 17, 1772, **DAVID WHITE**, born February 18, 1748, died about 1778, son of William and Martha⁴ (Warner) White; see number 78. He was a lieutenant in the expedition to Canada early in 1776.

Married (2) in Hadley, May 20, 1779, **JOSEPH CRAFTS** of Whately, born in Hatfield, November 6, 1745, died October 18, 1815, son of Thomas and Sarah (Graves) Crafts, and sixth in descent from Lieut. Griffin Crafts. He was a soldier in the Revolution in Capt. Israel Chapin's Company, Col. John Fellows' Regiment at the Lexington alarm, and was also in several later campaigns. He lived in Whately on the road running from Whately Center to the Baptist Meeting-House, around the southerly end of Mt. Esther. He is remembered as a great walker. His last walk, at the age of 70, was one of 98 miles from Boston to Whately on his return from a trip to sell cattle. A more complete account of this family may be found in "The Crafts Family."

Children of David and Roxelana (Warner) White, born in Hadley

Cotton White, bapt. July 10, 1774.

Luther White, bapt. Sept. 10, 1775; married and went South.

Children of Joseph and Roxelana (Warner-White) Crafts, born in Whately

Mary Paulina Crafts, b. Jan. 8, 1780; m. 1806, Curtis Root; resided in Columbia, Me., with her sister, then in Sandy Creek, Oswego Co., N. Y. Children: Roxelana and others.

Lucretia Crafts, b. Dec. 9, 1781; d. in Whately, Sept. 30, 1811; m. Dec. 29, 1801, Joseph Wait, b. July 17, 1782, son of Jeremiah and Rachel (Bement) Wait of Whately. They resided in Columbia, Me., where two children were born, Warner and Albert, then returned to Whately. After Lucretia's death, he removed to Pennsylvania.

Chester Crafts, b. Dec. 9, 1783; d. Sept. 27, 1827; was a farmer and resided for some years at South Deerfield; m. Mar. 16, 1809, Phila Jewett, b. Jan. 25, 1791, in South Deerfield, d. July 2, 1880, in Northampton, daughter of Reuben and Electa (Allis) Jewett. Children: i. Josephus, m. Roxa D. Cross; was a banker in Northampton and had seven children. ii. Chester, m. (1) Martha Graves Morgan, (2) Sarah Wright Knight, (3) Olive Louisa Day, lived in Ireland Parish of West Springfield, later in Holyoke, kept a store and hotel and ran a farm, later was postmaster and bank director, had eight children. iii. Mary Ann, m. Capt. Enos Persons of Northampton and had five children. iv. Parthena, m. Elihu S. Stall. v. Sylvia, m. Alvan Field and had two children. vi. David White, m. Wealthy White; was connected with the Northampton Gas Light Company; had three children. vii. Roswell Parsons, m. Delia Charlotte Jones; was in mercantile and real estate business in Holyoke and has been mayor; had one child. viii. Albert William, was a merchant in Goshen and Whately; m. Statira Ann Bardwell; had ten children. ix. Phila Amelia, m. Henry J. Walker; lived in Northampton; had two children.

Sabra Crafts, b. 1785; d. in Boston, Feb. 26, 1814, not married.

Ansel Crafts, b. 1787; d. Oct. 15, 1805 or 1809 (Hatfield records), his death being caused by a fall from the roof of a church at Westfield upon which he was working.

David Crafts, b. Oct. 15, 1790; d. in Whately, Aug. 31, 1844' not married. He was a wheelwright by trade, for a time in Pittsfield, then travelled all over the western states.

Roxelana Crafts, b. Mar. 8, 1793; d. Apr. 8, 1793.

Roswell Crafts, b. 1794; d. Sept. 25, 1827, at South Deerfield, not married. Resided at Mill River, Mass.

Parsons Crafts, b. 1796; d. 1839, in Rome, Peoria Co., Ill. He was a blacksmith and maker of agricultural implements in Deerfield, then in Pennsylvania, Ohio, Michigan, and Illinois. Married at Georgetown, Beaver Co., Pa., Mrs. Judith (Chase) Dudley. Children, who became widely scattered after their parents' death: i. Olive. ii. Lydia. iii. Pamelia. iv. Sophronia. v. Josephus, m. Agnes Smith; was a woolen manufacturer in Burton, Ohio, and Athens, Ala.; had eight children. vi. James, m. Melvina Simpton; was a minister at Delphos, Ohio; d. of smallpox in the Civil War, leaving two children. vii. Mary. viii. David King, m. Phoebe Ann Rodebeck; lived in Ingersoll, Utah; a Mormon, but opposed to polygamy; had ten children.

Josephus Crafts, b. 1798; d. Dec. 15, 1805.

184 REUBEN[5] WARNER, son of Oliver[4] and Lois (Ruggles) Warner, born in New Milford, Conn., May 23, 1759; died there November 14, 1825, buried in Gallows Hill Cemetery. He is called Reuben Warner, Jr. or 2d, in New Milford records, doubtless to distinguish him from another Reuben Warner of the same date, who was descended from an entirely different line of Warners. He attained considerable military distinction and held the post of colonel. He was justice of the peace for many years. Mr. Stanley L. Warner has his old account book with lists of the marriages he performed. The usual fee was a dollar, although occasionally a man gave a dollar and a half, thinking, as Mr. Warner says, the wife was worth the extra amount. His children, John Carrington, Oliver, Harriet, Sally Maria, Cornelia and Horace, were all baptized February 5, 1798 (New Milford Church records).

Married January 1, 1781, **EUNICE CARRINGTON** of Danbury, born in New Milford, about 1762, died February 5, 1839, aged 76, buried in Gallows Hill Cemetery. She was the daughter of Dr. John and Susannah (Noble) Carrington.

Children, born in New Milford

John Carrington Warner, b. Feb. 18, 1782; d. Feb. 17, 1829; was graduated from Yale, 1804, M.A., 1808; studied medicine at Columbia and was admitted to the Medical Society of the City and County of New York, Mar., 1808; settled in practice in Wilmington, Del.; probably removed about 1811 or 1812 to Philadelphia, and thence to a farm called "Deer Park," in Haddonfield, N. J., on a tract of land originally taken up by his wife's grandfather, Mordecai Howell. Here he practiced for the rest of his life, mixing his own medicines, among which was one of some note, called "Warner's Gout Cordial." He died at Deer Park and is buried in the Friends' Burying Ground at Haddonfield. Married May 17, 1809, Elizabeth Howell, who died Aug. 16, 1867, daughter of Samuel Howell of Philadelphia. They had four daughters and two sons, who died in infancy.

Loria Warner, b. Dec. 25, 1783.

Oliver Warner, b. Mar. 3, 1786.

Harriet Warner, b. June 29, 1788; resided in Stamford, Conn.; m. Isaac Scofield; probably had no children of their own, as they brought up her brother William's daughter Charlotte.

Sally Maria or *Maria Warner*, bapt. with other children, Feb. 5, 1798; m. Comfort Knapp of Danbury and brought up a daughter of her brother William. They probably had children of their own also.

Cornelia Warner, bapt. with other children, Feb. 5, 1798.
324 *Horace Warner,* b. Aug. 29, 1790; m. Emeline Stevens.
   William Reuben Warner, bapt. June 13, 1802; d. Nov. 3 or 7, 1853, aged
   54, buried in Gallows Hill Cemetery; m. Dec. 23, 1823, in New Milford, Laura Brownson or Bronson. Children: i. Charlotte, was
   brought up by her aunt Harriet, m. —— Lockwood and resided in
   Stamford, Conn. ii. (Daughter), was brought up by her aunt Maria
   in Danbury. iii. Helen E., b. 1835; d. Mar. 1, 1845, aged 10 years,
   buried in Gallows Hill Cemetery. Probably sons also.

185 SOLOMON⁵ WARNER, son of Martin⁴ and Mary
(Ruggles) Warner, born about 1761, in New Milford or Brookfield, Conn.; died in Bainbridge, Chenango Co., N. Y., August 9
or 10, 1839, aged 78. He was a Revolutionary soldier from New
Milford; removed to Bainbridge about 1802-3 and settled on a
farm where he remained until his sons were grown up. He
gave this homestead to his sons Robert and Lemuel and
removed to another farm. With his wife Rachel he made deeds
in Chenango County in 1812, 1820, 1829, and 1830. In 1812 he
is described as of Inico, Chenango County. Solomon Warner
was one of the organizers of St. Peter's Church, Bainbridge, in
1825, and in 1827 bought a pew and was one of the two church
wardens. His will mentioned his children: Athelia Warner;
Sally Newell, deceased; Mercy, wife of Arad Stowell; Zerµiah,
wife of Joseph Landers; Cornelia, wife of Ezra Hutchinson;
Asa; Robert B.; Lemuel; Solomon, Jr. (Norwich, N. Y., probate records, D:311.)
Married **RACHEL RUGGLES,** who died February 25, 1834,
aged 70.

Children

Athelia Warner, d. in Allegany County, N. Y., 1879; m. William Cole-
   man; no children.
Sally Warner, d. before 1839; m. Lewis Newell. He was an early
   and prominent merchant in Bainbridge, and was also a blacksmith.
   He resided in Bainbridge in 1814, but later removed to Oneonta. Chil-
   dren: Mary; Emily; Elizabeth; Charles.
Mercy Warner, d. in 1858; m. Arad Stowell. Children, all died before
   1917: i. Dorr, b. 1807; m. Mary ————; had seven children. ii.
   Abel, b. 1809; m. Betsey Poole, and had two children, one of whom,
   Mary, m. Gaylord Hull and resides in Afton. iii. Hannah, b. 1811; m.
   Charles Bixby; had four children. iv. Rachel, b. 1813; m. Calvin P.
   Smith; had four children. v. Asa, b. 1815; d. in youth. vi. Elijah,
   b. 1817; m. Louisa Sherman; no children. vii. Solomon, b. 1819;
   m. Austania Pratt; no children. viii. Isaac, b. 1821; m. Harriet
   Decker; had five children. ix. Cornelia, b. 1823; m. E. Ogden
   Beach; had six children. x. Nathan, b. 1825; m. Charlotte Patrick;
   no children. xi. Lepha, b. 1826; m. George O. Smith; had four

children. xii. Genette or Janet, b. 1828; m. Henry Jones; no children.

Zeruiah Warner, m. Joseph Landers, b. in Afton, N. Y., July 6, 1790, son of Ebenezer and Olive (Osborn) Landers. Children, mentioned in the citation to attend the reading of their grandfather's will: i. Esther. ii. Polly. iii. Sally, m. Martin Warner. iv. Athelia. v. Harriet. vi. Solomon Warner.

Cornelia Warner, m. Ezra Hutchinson. Children: Ezra, Jr.; Solomon; Jane or Janet.

Asa Warner, d. Dec. 31, 1867, or Dec. 30, 1866; resided in Bainbridge, N. Y. He is said to have been married five times. His wife Hannah Redfield, b. Dec. 26, 1804, d. Sept. 2, 1842, daughter of Russell and Elizabeth (Bixby) Redfield of Bainbridge, with him signed a deed to his brothers Lemuel and Solomon, Jr., in 1830. One of his wives was Amy Pearsall, daughter of Thomas Pearsall of Bainbridge. A granddaughter is Mrs. Bion E. Smith of Sidney, N. Y. Children of Hannah Redfield: i. Amy Antoinette, b. 1830-1, at Bainbridge; d. at Unadilla,- N. Y., 1892; not married. ii. Emma Sophia, b. June, 1835, at Bainbridge; d. at Unadilla, 1898; m. 1860, Alexander Benedict. iii. Lawrence, b. 1837, at Guilford, N. Y.; d. during the Civil War. iv. De Witt Clinton, b. 1839, at Guilford; m. 1870 (?); resided in Rockdale, N. Y. v. Herbert Alvah, b. 1839, at Guilford; m. about 1869-70; resided at Rockdale. The last two served in the Civil War.

Robert Bostwick Warner, called Bostwick, b. Apr. 22, 1796, near Meriden, Conn.; d. June 8, 1865, at Bainbridge, N. Y.; m. Jan., 1825, Priscilla Bixby, b. Aug. 22, 1800, at Bainbridge, daughter of Asahel and Clarina (Smith) Bixby. She died there, Nov. 2, 1876. Children, born at Bainbridge: i. George Washington, b. Nov. 13, 1826; d. Dec. 1, 1902, at Emporium, Pa.; m. Dec., 1859 (or 1861), Julia Frances Earle, had a son Robert Bostwick, b. June, 1862, at Emporium, resides there, m. about 1896, Myra Watkins, and has three children, George W., Robert A., and Lois Clarine, b. July 20, 1903. ii. Adeline, b. Feb. 14, 1829; d. Apr. 6, 1865, at Bainbridge; m. there, Dec. 6, 1864, Darwin Thompson of Wellsboro, Pa.; no children. iii. Clarina, b. Aug. 26, 1831; resided at Bainbridge; not married. iv. Robert Bostwick, b. Feb. 10, 1834; served three months in a volunteer regiment in the Civil War; was drowned May 2, 1867. v. Mercy Ellida, b. Feb. 4, 1836; d. Dec. 21, 1900, at Bainbridge; not married. vi. Lois Emeline, b. Sept. 15, 1839; d. at Bainbridge, Oct. 7, 1917; not married. vii. Caroline Priscilla, b. Jan. 21, 1842; m. at Bainbridge, Sept., 1875, Daniel T. Banner, had a child who died the same day as born, and a daughter Priscilla, b. June, 1878, d. Jan., 1879. (From data compiled for Bixby Genealogy by Willard G. Bixby.)

Lemuel Warner, b. 1800; resided in Bainbridge about 1829 and 1830, when he made deeds there; removed about 1839 to Braintrim township, Wyoming County, Pa.; m. Louisa Chapman, b. about 1810. Children: i. Oliver, b. 1829. ii. Orrin, b. 1831. iii. Austin, b. 1833. iv. Charles, b. 1835; was a soldier in the Civil War. v. Clark, b. 1839; was a soldier in the Civil War. vi. Sarah, b. 1842. vii. Lois, b. 1847. viii. Oscar, b. 1849. ix. Jane, b. 1851. x. Edgar, b. 1853.

Solomon Warner, Jr., resided in Bainbridge, and, in 1839, in Smithboro, Tioga County, N. Y.

186 BENJAMIN RUGGLES[5] WARNER, son of Martin[4] and Mary (Ruggles) Warner, born September 28, 1766, prob-ably in New Milford Conn.; died May 24, 1848. He was a farmer and resided in Brookfield, where his father gave him a hundred acres of land and built a house for him. He was recorded in the town of New Milford, 1790 Census. When an old man he burned the King's grant of land given to Captain John Warner, because he feared that some of his descendants might try to claim land that by that time had gone out of the family's possession. His granddaughter Sarah Jane Warner Gillette, recalled having seen the document when she was a little girl.   •

Married (1) **MERCY RUGGLES**, his cousin, born August 28, 1769; died December 3, 1800.

Married (2) November 5, 1801, HANNAH NICHOLS, born November 17, 1777; died November 12, 1857.

Children by first wife

325 *Debby Aurelia Warner*, b. Feb. 10, 1789; m. William Agur Hawley.
Polly Minerva Warner, b. Sept. 10, 1790; m. Edmund Bostwick, and removed to Ohio.
Flora Warner, b. Apr. 26, 1792; d. Apr. 7, 1874; m. Apr. 6, 1824, Amos Stevens, b. Aug. 27, 1796, d. Dec. 9, 1871. Children: i. Susan, b. Mar. 28, 1828; d. May 4, 1870; m. H. C. Jenkins. ii. Almon, b. Apr. 8, 1830. iii. Flora, b. July 22, 1832; d. Apr. 7, 1875; m. Sept. 26, 1851, J. D. Clark. A great-granddaughter is Lillian M. Cole of Ben-nington, Vt.

326 *Ashbel Ruggles Warner*, b. Mar. 20, 1794; m. Avis Eliza Woodworth.
Hiram Warner, b. Nov. 28, 1795; m. Sophia Bliss. Children: i. Beza-leel; m. Clara Williams, and had William, Frank, Grace, and Richard. ii. Elizabeth Mercy. They adopted Amelia D. Warner, daughter of his brother Daniel Nichols Warner. She died in New York, Jan. 5, 1845, aged 4 years, 1 month, 6 days, buried in Gallows Hill Ceme-tery, New Milford, Conn.
Almon Warner, b. May 31, 1798; d. Oct. 23, 1818.

Children by second wife

327 *Daniel Nichols Warner*, b. Aug. 8, 1803; m. (1) Dorothy Baker, (2) Amy Keeler, (3) Betsey Fry.
Benjamin Elizur Warner, b. Jan. 28, 1810; m. (1) in Hinsdale, Mass., Sept. 26, 1837, Rebecca W. Parsons, who died Sept., 1865, aged 49; m. (2) Cynthia Parsons, who died May, 1872, aged 61. Benjamin and Rebecca received letters of dismissal from the Hinsdale Church in 1856; Cynthia, in 1867. Children by first wife, bapt. in Hinsdale: i. Wallace Parsons, b. Mar. 27, 1840. ii. Almon Nichols, b. Oct. 27, 1842. iii. Charles Benjamin, b. Aug. 27, 1844. iv. (Daughter), b. Nov. 10, 1849.

187   LEMUEL[5] WARNER, son of Martin[4] and Mary (Ruggles) Warner, born probably in Brookfield, Conn., where he later resided in the house built by his father.

Married MARTHA BALDWIN, born June 26, 1780, daughter of Thaddeus and Sarah (————) Baldwin of Newbury Society, New Milford.

Children

Solomon B. Warner, b. 1809; resided in Brookfield in 1874; lived and died at the homestead of his father and grandfather; m. Apr. 10, 1850, Mary Julia Crane, b. July 11, 1818, daughter of Stephen and Chloe (Averill) Crane; no children.

Luzon Warner, removed to Ohio; married and had two children, Chelsea and a daughter, b. before 1858, and mentioned in the will of their uncle Elmer Warner.

Elmer Warner, b. 1815, in Brookfield; d. Apr. 23, 1858, in New Milford, Conn. He was a farmer, owned property in Brookfield and was twice married. His will, dated Mar. 18, 1858, probated May 6, 1858, is filed in New Milford (17:505). It mentions his wife, Cornelia Eliza Warner, brothers Solomon B. and Luzon Warner, "Chelsea Warner and a little girl whose name I do not know, the reputed children of my brother Luzon," and his own son, Elmore B., not yet 21, who shall "have a good education and to be qualified to do almost any kind of business and to teach school but not a college education." Sherman Minor of Roxbury was appointed guardian of the son, Elmore B.

188   AMARYLLIS[5] WARNER, daughter of Elizur[4] and Mary (Welch) Warner, born August 8, 1763, in New Milford, Conn.; died September 26, 1839, buried in old Bridgewater Cemetery, the name "Amanda S." on the tombstone. More complete accounts of her family will be found in the Boardman and Bostwick Genealogies.

Married in New Milford, November 14, 1787, Hon. HOMER BOARDMAN, born October 10, 1764, died May 27, 1851, son of Sherman and Sarah (Bostwick) Boardman. He was a farmer at the Boardman Homestead at Boardman's Bridge in New Milford, all his life; "a man of remarkably noble personal appearance and one of the finest appearing men of whom New Milford could ever boast—of intellectual qualities of unusual symmetry and proportion"; was Representative and State Senator; Presidential Elector in 1824.

Children

Charles Adolphus Boardman, b. Nov. 19, 1788; was a minister in Hudson, New Preston and New Haven, Ohio; m. Sophia Hine. Children: i. Homer, d. not married. ii. Sarah, m. George H. King. iii. Orinda, m. J. Baxter McEwen. iv. Laura V., m. Dr. Armstrong.

Esther Orinda Boardman, b. Jan. 9, 1792; m. Dr. Federal Vanderburgh. Children: i. Mary, m. John B. James of Albany, and d. in New York City leaving ·a son and daughter. ii. Charlotte, m. Robert McKim of Baltimore; had a son and three daughters. iii. Laura, d. aged 4.

Harriet Maria Boardman, b. Jan. 1, 1795; m. Dr. William H. Taylor. In the will of her uncle Elizur Warner she is called wife of Reuben Swift of Phelps, N. Y.

Sarah Boardman, b. Jan. 5, 1798; d. Jan. 13, 1798, buried in old Bridgewater Cemetery.

Oliver Warner Boardman, b. Sept. 14, 1799; d.¯Oct. 30, 1815, buried in old Bridgewater Cemetery.

Daniel Homer Boardman, b. May. 21, 1803; d. Oct. 15, 1834, in New Orleans, La.; was a physician.

Laura Amaryllis Boardman, b. Mar. 27, 1806; m. Rev. Aaron David Lane of Waterloo, N. Y.; had a son and two daughters.

189 JOHN[5] WARNER, 3d, son of John[4], Jr., and Hannah (Westover) Warner, born in New Milford, Conn., April 18, 1764; died there September 8, 1850, buried in Gallows Hill Cemetery. He inherited the homestead of his father and grandfather. His family is recorded in the 1790 Census of New Milford, one male over 16, one under 16, two females. He died intestate and there are several papers relating to the settlement of his estate in the New Milford probate records. At the distribution of the estate, January 15, 1853, the heirs were: son Elizur of New Milford; son Harmon of Pike, Bradford Co., Pa.; Hannah Smith; John Roberts, son of Anna Roberts, deceased; Lois Osborn; Susan Warner; Caroline Hoag; Samuel Warner; Eunice A. Knowles; Laura Osborn. Objections to this were filed February 14, 1853, and in this were mentioned the following heirs: Elizur and Harmon Warner; Hannah Smith; Lois Osborn; Almira Marsh; Samuel Hays; Nelson and Eunice A. Knowles; Susan Warner and her guardian, Isaac Northrup; John Osborn and wife Laura (all these of New Milford); Hannah, wife of Charles Smith of Monroe township, Knox Co., Ohio, daughter of John Warner; Lois, wife of Isaac Osborn of Texas, Crawford Co., Ohio, daughter of John Warner; Almira Marsh, wife of Elliott Marsh of Pike, Bradford Co., Pa., a daughter of Anna Roberts, deceased, who was a daughter of John Warner. (New Milford probate records, vol. 14, p. 405; 15, p. 3, etc.)

John Warner married **ABIGAIL STEVENS**, born 1765, died December 29, 1851, aged 86, buried in Gallows Hill Cemetery. She was the daughter of Peter Stevens, two of whose sons married sisters of John Warner.

Children, born in New Milford

Samuel Warner, went to Pennsylvania and died in Pike township, Bradford County; m. in Connecticut, Susanna Porter.

328 *Harmon Warner,* b. July 2, 1798; m. Sally Maroxa Joyce.
329 *Elizur Warner,* b. Mar. 6, 1807; m. Lyra Ann Totman.

Eunice A. Warner, resided at Lanesville, Conn.; m. Nelson Knowles, b. Aug. 15, 1806, son of Elizur and Johannah (Hill) Knowles. Children: i. George Henry, resided in New Fairfield, Conn.; m. (1) Mrs. Eliza Bogardus, (2) Wealthy Pulling; had children, William Henry and Harriet. ii. Mary Ann, m. Lyman Jennings, Jr. iii. John Elizur, lived in Maryland; m. Sarah Jane Morehouse. iv. David Watson, was a physician, and lives at Still River, Conn.; m. Sarah Jane Nichols, and has children, William Sheridan, George Wendell and Clara Louise. v. Susan Abigail. vi. Charles Wesley, m. (1) Harriet Bard, (2) Maria Nichols, lived at Norwalk, Conn.; had sons, Frederick and Edward. vii. Martha Eliza, m. Edmund Atwood. viii. James Nelson, lived in Maryland; m. Emily Booth; had six children. ix. Caroline Elizabeth, m. Henry S. Hurlbut of Roxbury; had four children. x. William Andrew, lived in California; m. Jennie Lloyd. xi. Abraham Jay, m. Jennie Nearing. xii. Eveline Maria.

Laura Warner, m. John Osborn, and lived in New Milford in 1853.

Lois Warner, m. Isaac Osborn; lived in Texas township, Crawford Co., Ohio, in 1853.

Hannah Warner, m. Charles Smith, and lived in Herricksville, Ohio.

Anna Warner, d. in Leraysville, Pa., before 1853; m. in Connecticut, Timothy Roberts. Children: i. Joshua. ii. Almira, m. Elliott Marsh b. New Milford, Nov. 14, 1802, d. in Pike, Pa., 1853, son of William and Rachel (Nichols) Marsh.

John Warner, Jr., d. before 1852; resided in New Milford and was a fox hunter; m. (1) Feb. 10, 1825, by the pastor of the First Church in New Milford, Orilla Smith of New Milford; m. (2) Polly Wheeler. Child by first wife: Caroline, m. Nehemiah Hoag, and was mentioned among her grandfather's heirs. Child by second wife: Susan Rebecca, b. Nov. 2, 1837, in New Milford; ˉchose Isaac Northrup as guardian, Dec. 6, 1852; d. Sept. 27, 1913, not married.

190 **ANNICE⁵ WARNER**, daughter of John⁴ and Hannah (Westover) Warner, born in New Milford, Conn., November, 1766; died in Stevensville, Pa., February 6, 1814.

Married in New Milford, November 13, 1796, **A D·E N STEVENS**, born April 20, 1770; died July 28, 1858. He was the son of Peter Stevens, a Revolutionary soldier who was wounded at the capture of Danbury, did not fully recover and died about a year later in 1779, at the age of 48. Five of his sons settled in Pike, Bradford County, Pa. One son, Nathan, married Hannah Warner, sister of Annice, and settled in Stevensville with Aden. Another son, Samuel, was a tanner, shoemaker and currier, and was the first to carry on the manufacture of leather on the Wyalusing.

Nathan and Aden Stevens reached the present site of Stevensville in the spring of 1794 and purchased a farm. Nathan returned to New Milford for his family while Aden chopped a fallow and put in a piece of grain. For the first two winters Aden returned to Connecticut and taught school, returning in the spring to work on the new clearing. After his marriage he settled in Pennsylvania, and in 1809 built a framed house on the property. The early years were full of excitement and trials due to the wild conditions by which they were surrounded. Aden Stevens was commissioned on September 9, 1805, as colonel of the 129th Regiment, Pennsylvania militia, 2d Brigade, 9th Division, composed of companies from Northumberland, Lycoming and Luzerne. During the War of 1812 he was ordered to Northumberland, but peace was declared before he took part in any engagement. He was a member of the Presbyterian Church for over fifty years and was a deacon in that church.

His second wife was Rebecca Purda Somers, by whom he had children, Philena, m. Elisha Lewis; Louis, d. in infancy; Peter, d. in Kansas.

Numerous references to this family and the active part they have taken in the life of Bradford County are found in the History of Bradford County.

Children of Aden and Annice (Warner) Stevens

Oliver W. Stevens, went to Ohio in 1819 and was a merchant in Cincinnati and engaged in steamboating. About 1850 he went to California and remained there until his death. He was a banker and a successful business man.

Hiram Stevens, was a successful farmer in Stevensville and died before 1890.

Cyrus Stevens, remained on the homestead farm in Stevensville and died Feb. 12, 1890, in his 87th year. He held many public offices, was first postmaster of Stevensville in 1837, and captain in the militia, also wrote and published many articles. He married, in 1830, Lydia Ann Lacey, daughter of Ebenezer and Zeruah (Northrup) Lacey. Children: i. Oliver W., b. Jan. 15, 1831; was a teacher and farmer, county surveyor and holder of other town and county offices; married and had five children. ii. Lucretia, d. young. iii. Maria, d. young. iv. Lydia Philena, m. (1) Charles Ingram, (2) Ellicott 'A. Ingram; resided in Iowa. v. Ebenezer Lacey, b. Apr. 4, 1843, resided on the homestead farm in Stevensville, was a merchant, elder in the Presbyterian Church; m. Oct. 8, 1868, Abbie Burchard, daughter of John and Mary (Griswold) Birchard, and has three children. vi. Zeruah, m. James Avery. vii. Louisa, m. Dr. Frank Taylor, son of Rev. Covington E. and Emeline Elmira' (Warner) Taylor (see number 518). viii. Cyrus Lee, was a physician in Asia Minor, Turkey, for a few years, then in New York City and later in Athens, Pa.; m. in 1880, Nettie J. Keeney; is an elder in the Presbyterian Church and prominent in medical circles.

Ann Stevens, m. Abel Bolles.

Sally Stevens, m. Elkanah Bolles.

191 LUCINA[5] WARNER, daughter of John[4] and Hannah
(Westover) Warner, born in New Milford, Conn., 1767; died
March 6, 1834.

Married 1786, ELISHA KEELER, born at Milton, Conn.,
1764, died November 12, 1814, son of John Keeler, a Revolutionary soldier, and his wife, Abigail Copley. In the spring of
1793, Elisha Keeler, with his wife and three children and his
aged father, left Brookfield, Conn., and went to Wilkesbarre, Pa.,
from which settlement they traveled by canoe up the Wyalusing
to the territory that is now the southern part of Pike County.
On this part of the journey their canoe upset, drenching all their
goods, but after drying them out they proceeded to the property
they, with others, had arranged to purchase, and some of the
family have remained on the original farm for generations.

The old Bible of John Keeler was one of the articles that was
immersed in the river, but he was a tailor by trade and carefully
ironed it out leaf by leaf on his goose. It is still in the family,
a highly prized memento of the hardships of the pioneers in the
wild country, covered by a tangled and unbroken forest.

Elisha Keeler was not a man of robust constitution and could
not do the heavy work of clearing heavily timbered land. He
had learned the tailor's trade from his father, but it was a profession little needed here, so in 1804 he purchased a stock of
goods and for a few years conducted a store in his house. He
later purchased, with a partner, the first wool-carding machine
in that section of the country and continued in that business
until his death, drawing customers from all parts of the country.

Many references to this family will be found in the History
of Bradford County, Pa., and many of the descendants reside in
Pike, Wyalusing, Herrick and Warren, in that county.

Children of Elisha and Lucina (Warner) Keeler

Arabella Keeler, b. July 30, 1786, in Connecticut; m. Wells Loomis.
Charles W. Keeler, b. May 12, 1789, in Connecticut; m. Lucy Nichols.
Marietta Keeler, b. June 21, 1791, in Connecticut; d. 1864; m. 1816,
  John Elliott, b. 1791, d. 1876. Their granddaughter is Mrs. Susie
  Dodge Hallock, of Wyalusing, Pa., a member of the D. A. R.
Polly Keeler, b. Nov. 25, 1793, in Pennsylvania; m. Dec. 3, 1812, Justus
  Lewis, b. in Wyalusing, Pa., Aug. 24, 1787, d. May 10, 1874, son of
  Thomas Lewis, a Revolutionary soldier, and his wife, Mary Turrell.
  He was a farmer and lumberman. They were members of the Pres-
  byterian Church in Wyalusing and were actively engaged in temper-
  ance and anti-slavery work. They had five sons and two daughters.
Elisha Keeler, b. Dec. 15, 1796, in Pennsylvania; m. Mary Lovett.
Lucy Keeler, b. Mar. 16, 1798, in Stevensville, Pa.; d. June 28, 1862;
  m. Jan. 17, 1832, Roswell Lee Coburn, b. June 24, 1804, d. June 5,

1862, son of Deacon Reuben and Hannah (Flint) Coburn of Dracut, Mass. They resided in Warren, Pa. Children: i. Matthias. ii. Lewis Justus, m. Lucinda C. Cleveland. iii. Theodore, m. (1) Cornelia E. Chaffee, (2) Amanda J. Overton. iv. Charles. v. Jennie, m. Joseph Gaskell. vi. Lucina.

John Keeler, b. Dec. 17, 1800, in Pennsylvania; m. Elizabeth Gregory; resided in Wyalusing.

192   HANNAH[5] WARNER, daughter of John[4] and Hannah (Westover) Warner, born in New Milford, Conn., 1770; died September 25, 1847, in Stevensville, Pa.

Married in New Milford, **NATHAN STEVENS**, who died April 6, 1854, aged 86. He was the son of Peter Stevens, a Revolutionary soldier, and was the brother of Aden Stevens, who married Hannah's sister, Annice Warner. Nathan and Aden first went to the present town of Stevensville in the spring of 1794, and bought a farm there. Nathan returned to Connecticut and brought back his wife and three children in the fall. For three months they had no flour in the house; cornmeal, ground at home in a mortar, was the only meal for bread. Various interesting tales of the hardships of their early life in the new country are told in the History of Bradford County. After the first year the brothers divided the farm and each worked his own part. Nathan built a new log house in 1800.

Child

Myron Stevens, m. Susan Bosworth, daughter of Reed Bosworth. They had eight children, the youngest of whom was Elmer F., b. in Stevensville, May 12, 1850, is a manufacturer of lumber, lath and shingles, m. Sept. 11, 1870, Clara B. Easterbrook.

193   LOIS[5] WARNER, daughter of John[4] and Hannah (Westover) Warner, born in New Milford, Conn.

Married in New Milford, February 12, 1794, **ESBON BOSTWICK**, born in New Milford, March 19, 1768, died in Ohio, July 25, 1826, son of Edmund and Nancy (Ruggles) Bostwick. A more complete account of this family will be found in the Bostwick Genealogy.

Children

George Bostwick, b. in Vermont, April 28, 1798; d. in Fort Madison, Iowa, Jan. 13, 1848; m. in Newton Falls, Ohio, Laura Lane, daughter of John and Electa (Bostwick) Lane, b. in Dutchess Co., N. Y., June 14, 1798, d. in Newton Falls, Ohio, Nov. 3, 1851. Children: i. John, b. June, 1820; d. Sept. 5, 1863, not married. ii. Electa, d. young. iii. Emmogene, d. young. iv. Elizabeth, b. in Newton Falls, Aug. 3, 1825; d. in Kearney, Neb., Aug. 16, 1893; m. in Fort Madison, Iowa,

Jan. 8, 1844, John Milton Finch, b. in Montrose, Pa., Sept. 30, 1815, d. in Kearney, Neb., Dec. 13, 1888, and had eight children. v. John, d. young. vi. Frederick, d. young. vii. Marietta, b. in Newton Falls, May 5, 1830; m. in Dallas City, Ill., Feb. 1, 1855, William Henry Rolloson, b. in Williamsburg, Va., Jan. 8, 1820; d. in Dallas City, Oct. 9, 1864; had five children.

Electa Bostwick, b. Apr. 12, 1800.

Charles H. Bostwick, b. Mar. 12, 1802; m. Lydia ————, and died without children.

Marietta Bostwick.

William Bostwick, b. Aug. 6, 1808; m. and had no children.

194 CURTIS⁵ WARNER, son of Orange⁴ and Abigail (Prindle) Warner, born in New Milford, Conn., July 14, 1766; died there October 11, 1818, buried in Gallows Hill Cemetery.

Married in New Milford, November 4, 1792, **EUNICE HULL**, who removed to Dexter, Mich., with her son William in 1826.

Children, born in New Milford

Charles Warner, b. Dec. 27, 1793; d. not married.

Henry Warner, b. Oct. 14, 1795; resided in Dexter, Mich., where he was a prominent farmer and breeder of Durham cattle. He was an early settler in Section 9, Lima township. He married, probably in New Haven, Conn., and rather late in life, Melinda Goodyear, who died in Dexter, Mich., daughter of Alonzo Goodyear. They had no children.

Deborah Warner, b. Sept. 20, 1797; d. not married.

Laura Warner, b. Sept. 14, 1799; d. not married.

Hull Warner, b. May 20, 1801; left home in early life and the family never knew what became of him.

Sally Caroline Warner, b. Feb. 23, 1803; d. not married.

William Warner, b. May 5, 1806; removed to western New York, then to Lima township, Washtenaw County, near Dexter, Mich., in 1826, where he was known as one of the prominent farmers of the community. He settled on Sections 4 and 9. His children probably went to Minnesota. Married March 18, 1846, Helen Ann Holmes, b. May 20, 1821, daughter of Rosencrans Holmes of Northville, Mich. Children: i. Eva, m. Nicholas Macken of Minnesota. ii. Anna L. iii. Mary H., d. before 1881. iv. William H., d. before 1881.

George Warner, b. Feb. 27, 1808; was a merchant in Dexter, Mich.; m. and had a daughter.

Frederick Warner, was an early settler in Section 4, Lima township, Washtenaw County, Mich.; m. and had a daughter or a son. Perhaps Eunice Louisa Warner of Dexter, Mich., whose guardian he was in a matter of property in New Milford, 1868, was the daughter.

195 DAVID⁵ WARNER, son of Orange⁴ and Abigail (Prindle) Warner, born in New Milford, Conn., January 7, 1768; died January 25, 1846, in Pike, Pa. He was a farmer and a

maker of weaver's reeds, settled first in New Milford, then
resided in Brookfield, New Fairfield, Essex (New York), again
in New Milford, and finally removed to Pennsylvania.

Married about 1793, **ANNIS NOBLE**, born in New Milford,
November 23, 1773, died in Pike, Bradford County, Pa., May 7,
1848, daughter of Elisha and Sally (Crane) Noble.

Children

Harriet Warner, b. Dec. 26, 1795, probably in New Milford; d. in
Jessup, Susquehanna County, Pa., May, 1858, aged 62; m. about 1815,
Asa Fairchild, a farmer who resided in New Milford, and later in
Pike and Jessup, Pa.

Sally Warner, b. Sept. 17, 1797, in Ferrisburgh, Vt. A relative thinks
her name was Anna or Annis. Married Oct. 22, 1817, Jonathan
Nichols, a cabinet maker. They resided in 1876 in Camptown, Wyalusing township, Bradford County, Pa.

Belden Noble Warner, b. Dec. 28, 1805, in Essex, N. Y.; resided in
Brushville, town of Pike, Bradford County, Pa., in 1876; m. May 20,
1832, Polly Ann Pulford, b. May 4, 1803, in New Milford, Conn.

196 ORANGE⁵ WARNER, JR., son of Orange⁴ and Abigail
(Prindle) Warner, born in New Milford, April 13, 1770; died
there, April 17, 1863. He was a farmer in New Milford.

Married in New Milford, November 10, 1793, **LUCY SAN-
FORD**, born about 1772, died in New Milford, July 8, 1830,
buried in Gallows Hill Cemetery, daughter of Samuel and Sarah
(Olmstead) Sanford.

Children, born in New Milford

330 *Samuel Horace Warner,* b. 1795; m. Sally Julia Knapp.
331 *Henry* (called *Harry*) *Sanford Warner,* b. 1796; m. Eliza Ann Hill.
Polly W. Warner, m. Henry Prince Briggs, son of Isaac and Abigail⁵
(Warner) Briggs, see number 101. One child, d. in infancy.
Hiram Warner, d. young.
Sally M. Warner, b. 1803; d. Sept. 28, 1824, aged 21, buried in Gallows
Hill Cemetery, New Milford.
Minerva Elizabeth Warner, b. 1811; d. Nov. 20, 1829, aged 18, buried in
Gallows Hill Cemetery, New Milford.

197 CYRUS⁵ WARNER, son of Orange⁴ and Abigail
(Prindle) Warner, born in New Milford, Conn., January 6, 1773;
died there, February 28, 1858.

Married (1) October 30, 1794 (New Milford Church records),
POLLY WELLER. She was a member of the Church in New
Milford, January 6, 1828.

Married (2) **HANNAH PECK**, daughter of Amiel and Hepsibah (Camp) Peck of Brookfield, Conn.

Children by first wife, born in New Milford

332 *Orange Warner*, b. Jan. 23, 1799; m. Apphia Edwards.

Miranda Warner, b. Dec. 17, 1800; d. Nov. 11, 1888; m. Asa Winton Camp. Children: Mary; Asa; Susan; William.

Alonzo Warner, b. Jan. 15, 1803; d. June 1, 1870; m. in New Milford, Nov. 16, 1831, Elizabeth Ann French of Brookfield, Conn. Children · i. ———, d. in infancy. ii. Henry A., d. of consumption at the age of 41.

Lyman Warner, b. Nov. 26, 1805; d. Nov. 26, 1871; resided in the west. He gathered a troup of dwarfs and disfigured people and travelled with them, exhibiting in various places. They later became the "Wild men of Borneo" with Barnum's Circus. Married (1) Nov. 13, 1827, Amanda Peck, b. Nov. 24, 1806; d. Mar. 29, 1832, daughter of Julius and Sarah (Dunning) Peck of Sharon, Conn.; m. (2) ———. Child by first wife: Fred, a physician. Children by second wife: i. Mary Amanda, m. Ezra Adams of Lowell, Mass. ii. Josie, d. aged 6.

333 *Alva Wright Warner*, b. Nov. 21, 1807; m. Frances A. Babbitt.

Polly Warner, b. Sept. 28, 1815; d. Apr. 2, 1903; m. Edson Corning. Children: William O.; Anna Eliza; Gilbert.

SIXTH GENERATION

198 Capt. JOHN[6] WARNER, son of Hezekiah[5] and Lois
(Penfield) Warner, born in Middletown, Conn., April 17, 1761;
died September 30, 1808, in Westfield Society, Middletown,
where he had resided. He was a farmer. He served in the
Revolution in Wadsworth's brigade under Capt. Joseph Churchill, enlisted from Middletown, was at the battles of Long Island
and White Plains, and was a captain. He is listed in the
1790 census in Middletown, with two boys under 16 and four
women and girls in the family. He was master of Harmony
Lodge, No. 20, F. & A. M., from 1802 to 1806, inclusive. This
lodge is now located in New Britain. His estate was admin-
istered November 28, 1808, by the widow, Lament Warner, and
his son, William H. Warner. In a long inventory there is mention of land, furniture, cattle, several books, and other articles.
William H. Warner was appointed guardian for David P. Warner, minor son of John, October 30, 1809. Ebenezer Roberts
was appointed guardian for Lucy and Mary Warner, minors, and
Samuel Galpin, for John Warner (Middletown probate records,
9:158). The estate was distributed September 24, 1810, to the
following: eldest son William; heir of Abigail Hough, late wife
of Samuel H. Hough; Patience, wife of Asa Roberts; Dolley;
Mary and Lucy; John; David (9:261).

Married (1) November 11 or 22, 1781, **PATIENCE HALL,**
born about 1761; died May 7, 1796, aged 35, "buried in West
field with a child in her arms" (Middletown records).

Married (2) May 9, 1797, **POLLY PLUMB,** who died Febru
ary 11, 1803, aged 27 or 28.

Married (3) **LAMENT** ———, who survived him and was
one of the administrators of his estate. She died about 1810, as
her estate was settled March 6, 1810.

Children of John and Patience (Hall) Warner, born in Middletown

Abigail Warner, b. Sept. 1, 1782; d. in Middletown, Feb. 17, 1810; m.
Samuel Hall Hough of Westfield. She left an heir, mentioned in the
distribution of her father's estate.

Patience Warner, b. July 12, 1784; resided in Middletown; m. there,
Nov. 5, 1801, Asa Roberts, b. in Middletown, Mar. 1, 1776, son of
Recompense Roberts who was born 1731. Children, born in Westfield Society, Middletown: i. Julia, b. Aug. 26, 1803; m. (1) Apr. 1,
1824, Sylvester Cornwell; m. (2) July 19, 1830, William Cornwell.
ii. Darius, b. Aug. 12, 1805; m. Dec. 25, 1827, Emily Hall. iii. Enoch,

b. Apr. 5, 1808; m. Sept. 30, 1834, Martha Ives. iv. Sherman, b.
May 14, 1810; m. Apr. 15, 1840, Mary Cornwell. v. Patience, b.
May 25, 1812; m. Oct. 10, 1831, Andrew Southworth. vi. Olive,
b. Aug. 30, 1814; m. Apr. 10, 1835, Ralph Deming. vii. Harriet (1),
b. May 5, 1817; d. Oct. 12, 1821. viii. Frederick, b. Mar. 8, 1820; d.
Oct. 5, 1821. ix. Harriet (2), b. Sept. 2, 1826; m. Aug. 2, 1847,
Hiram Remington.

334 *William Hall Warner*, b. Mar. 18, 1786; m. Hannah Rose.

Dorothy Warner, b. Jan. 22, 1789; resided in Middletown; m. as second wife, Samuel Hall Hough (see above).

Mary Warner, b. Dec. 23, 1790.

Lucy A. Warner, b. Sept. 19, 1792; d. in Middletown; m. Apr. 12,
1814, Benjamin C. Bacon, Jr., son of Benjamin and Abiah (Cornwell)
Bacon. He m. (2) Mary Sturtevant. Children: i. Abiah, b. Jan. 19,
1815. ii. and iii. Caleb and Joshua (twins), b. and d. Feb. 26, 1817.
iv. Lucy Ann, b. Sept. 11, 1818; d. Apr. 23, 1872; m. Dec. 19, 1839,
Joseph Alston Wilcox, and had Benjamin C., b. Nov. 15, 1840, Charles
H., b. Jan. 28, 1843, Willys H., b. Mar. 14, 1846, and Miranda, b. Jan.
10, 1851, m. Nov. 26, 1874, Henry Gilbert of Middletown.

335 *John Plumb Warner*, b. July 19, 1794; m. Betsey Hall.

David P. Warner, d. in Durham, Conn., July 20, 1905. His oldest
brother was appointed his guardian, Oct. 30, 1809, and Aaron Plum
was appointed guardian, Dec. 27, 1813. He married and had a daughter Martha, as mentioned in the settlement of his estate (Middletown
probate records, 56:314).

Child of John and Polly (Plumb) Warner

Rhoda P. Warner, d. Apr. 10, 1801, in the second year of her age. One
account gives the name of a daughter Rachel, but it is probably an
error for Rhoda.

199 LOIS[6] WARNER, daughter of Hezekiah[5] and Lois
(Penfield) Warner, born in Middletown, Conn., November 9,
1764; died there August 13, 1847. Her will, made August 18,
1838, probated September 20, 1847, made her son-in-law, Enoch
Wilcox, executor, and mentioned the following: daughter Hepsibah, wife of Enoch Wilcox, and grandchildren, Walter W. and
Leverett L. Wilcox, not 21; children, Linus Wilcox, Hezekiah
Wilcox, Hannah Bonfoy and Lois Ward. (Middletown probate
records.)

Married in Middletown, March 7, 1782, **ELIJAH WILCOX,
JR.** (MSS. records in Conn. Hist. Soc. Library).

Children

Hepsibah Wilcox, m. Enoch Wilcox. Children: Walter W.; Leverett L.

Linus Wilcox.

Hezekiah Wilcox, b. in Connecticut, 1785; removed to Herkimer
County, N. Y., in 1806; d. 1868; m. Abiah Clark. He was a shoe-

maker and had a sawmill in Cedarville. Children: i. Hosea. ii. Hepsibah, m. as his second wife, Daniel Golden and removed to Erie County, N. Y.; no children. iii. Olive, m. ——— Bucklin and had children, Mary and Herbert E. iv. Elijah W., b. in Winfield in 1824; m. (1) in 1850, Lydia Strait, who d. in 1857, m. (2) in 1858, Tharissa P. Winchester. Elijah Wilcox had children: Herbert Hezekiah, m. Florence Babcock, resides in Yakima, Wash., and has a son; Frank C., is a furniture dealer and undertaker in West Winfield, N. Y., m. and had three sons, Herbert, Harold and E. Walter (who d. in West Winfield, Oct., 1918, aged 30, leaving a wife and child); Nellie, m. John Wholahan and resided in West Winfield until after her husband's death, when she removed to Utica, has a daughter Olive and a son John.

Hannah Wilcox, m. Sept. 25, 1806, Richard Bonfoy and removed to West Winfield, N. Y. See below for record of their children.

Lois Wilcox, m. ——— Ward, probably of Corry, Pa.

Children of Richard and Hannah (Wilcox) Bonfoy

Elijah W. Bonfoy, b. 1807; d. 1897; m. Julia A. Hay. Children: i. W. Henry, m. Ann Murphy and had three children, two died in youth, and Alice, now dead, m. James Ball (had two children, John, now in the army, and Katherine of Utica, N. Y.). ii. Ann, d. in infancy. iii. Melvin, resides at Clayville, N. Y.; m. Julia E. Townsend; had six children: Ella (m. A. J. Gardner, lives at Utica, had six children, Westley, m. Grace Evans and has one child, Walter, Myrtle, Clara, died, Elmer and Raymond); Eva (m. J. Wagner, resides in Stafford Springs, Conn., had two children, Florence, m. Fred Bartlett, lives at New Haven, has two children, Lois and Bernice, and Gilbert, m. Lulu Ide, lives at Stafford Springs, has a child, Howard); Hattie, d. young; Myrtle, d. young; Charles, d. young; and Clifford, m. Jennie Reilly and lives at Clayville, N. Y. iv. Frank, m. (1) Mary Croft, who d. in 1901; m. (2) Elva Croft; had by first wife, two children, Nettie (m. (1) Herbert Taft, (2) Edward Appleton, resides at Westmoreland, N. Y.) and Herbert (m. Daisy Jaquay and has a child, Leah). v. George N., m. Charlotte Vibbard; had two children, Lettie (m. ——— Ripperdam, and resides in Denver, Colo.) and Nellie, d. in youth. vi. Lois, m. Stephen Croft; had four children: Edwin, d. in youth, Myra (m. Lewis Leworthy, and had nine children, Edwin, Fanny, Isa, Westley, Stuart, Lois, Sarah, Ruth, and Nina), Julia (m. Fred Philips and had one child, Lewis), and Florence, d. in youth. vii. Elvira, m. Charles Baylis. viii. John, d. in youth. ix. H. Amy, died; m. De Witt Spencer. x. Myron, died; m. Carrie Franklin.

Hannah H. Bonfoy, b. 1811; m. Seymour Eggleston. Children: i. Emily, resides in Chicago; m. ——— Hoyle; had three children. ii. Josephine. iii. Ella, not married. iv. Henry, died.

Seth Bonfoy, b. 1815; d. 1887; m. (1) Eunetia Pardee of East Haven, Conn., (2) Lizzie Rudd. No children.

David Bonfoy, b. 1817; d. 1890; m. Martha Hackley. Children: i. Roxanna, resides in West Winfield, N. Y., not married. ii. Ellen, m. Charles Leach; resides at West Winfield; had two children, Martha and Harriet. iii. Hattie, d. in youth.

Benjamin Franklin Bonfoy, b. 1820; d. 1903; married. Children: i. Albert, d. in youth. ii. George, m. Alice Burke; resides at Saskatchewan, Canada; had three children, Edith, m. Leonard Harrison (see number 345), Clarence, lives at Saskatchewan, and Ernest, now in the army.

Henry Bonfoy, b. 1822; d. 1863; married Helen Gage. Children: i. Corinna, resides in Denver, Colo.; m. Mott Boss, had six children (Corinne, died, Helen, m. and has one child, Florence, Arthur, Howard, and Phoebe, the last four residing in Denver). ii. Hattie, resides at White Hall, Ill.; m. Charles Geller; had three children, Henry, m. and has a child, Grace, lives at White Hall, and Edward, m. and has a child. iii. Nellie, resides at Colorado Springs, Colo.; m. Charles Hale; had three children, Clayton, Willis, and Barbara, died.

200 HEZEKIAH[6] WARNER, JR., son of Hezekiah[5] and Lois (Penfield) Warner, born August 25, 1766, in Middletown, Conn.; removed to Mayfield, N. Y. There are recorded in Fonda, N. Y., deeds of Hezekiah and Lucy Warner, selling property in Mayfield, in 1805 and 1809. In 1806 he was captain of a military company in Montgomery Co., N. Y. (Military minutes of the council of appointment, New York, 1783-1821, p. 866). He had previously been ensign of the same company.

Married in Cromwell, Conn., April 30, 1788, LUCY STOCKING, born May 5, 1765, daughter of Captain Zebulon and Martha (Edwards) Stocking of Upper Middletown. Captain Stocking was a sea captain and served in the French and Indian War.

Children

336   *Zebulon Penn Warner,* b. about 1790; m. Lucretia Sherwood.
337   *Lucy Warner,* b. Feb. 6, 1791; m. Isaac Horton.
338   *Hezekiah Warner, 3d,* b. 1795; m. Sarah Nichols.
      Almira Warner.
      Maria Warner.
      Julia Warner, m. John Hyatt and resided in New York State.
      Lois Warner.
      Amanda Warner.
      (Daughter.)

201 EBENEZER[6] WARNER, son of Hezekiah[5] and Lois (Penfield) Warner, born July 4, 1768, in Middletown, Conn.; died February 5, 1849. He removed to Mayfield, Fulton County, N. Y., about 1800, and to Skaneateles, Onondaga County, N. Y., in 1813, where he was a farmer. His will, made September 6, 1847, probated October 8, 1849, is recorded in Syracuse, and he is described as of Sennett (Cayuga County), but residing in the town of Skaneateles. The following heirs are mentioned: sons

Junia, Eben, Eleazer Gaylord, Vine Star, and John Penfield; heirs of his daughters Maria and Sally; daughter Minerva; wife Katherine. There is on record in Fonda, a deed of 1813 by which Ebenezer and Katherine of Brutus, N. Y., convey property in Mayfield.

In 1806 he was appointed ensign of a military company in Montgomery County, N. Y., in Brig.-Gen. Abraham Veeder's brigade, succeeding his brother Hezekiah who was made captain.

In her volume, "An American Ancestry," Mrs. Anne Warner French gives interesting lights on the personality of Ebenezer Warner. The following is from a letter written by his grandson, Seth W. Houghton of Winchester, Tenn., about 1894:

"I lived with grandfather and went to school in Skaneateles. Grandfather was a man of but few words, inflexible in his purpose without being harsh. Strictly honorable in all his dealings with his fellow men, Puritanical in his religion, Saturday at sundown all secular matters were suspended until Sunday at sundown. During that time all had to read the Bible or study their Sunday School lessons, and all had to load into the farm wagon Sunday morning and go to church,—rain or snow,—hot or cold. Family prayers were as certain as the day came. To me they were an awful nuisance, as they were always long, and I generally got very hungry. Although he was a perfect autocrat, he was kind to all who tried to do right, but woe to him who stepped aside. I loved him though he kept me straight as a shingle. He was known to everybody as 'that good old Deacon Warner,' and was a thrifty, intelligent farmer."

Married (1) in Middletown, Conn., January 5, 1792, **MARY GAYLORD,** born March 12, 1770, died July 8, 1804, daughter of Eleazer and Eunice (Gilbert) Gaylord. Eunice Gilbert's ancestry is as follows: Jonathan[1] Gilbert, b. in England, 1618; Jonathan[2], b. 1648, m. Dorothy Fletcher; Nathaniel[3], b. 1689, m. Elizabeth Prout; Eunice[4], b. 1729. The Gaylord family removed to Mayfield early.

Married (2) November 8, 1804, **KATHERINE DENISON,** born March 22, 1775, died September 23 or 29, 1849, daughter of Thomas and Katherine (Starr) Denison. The Denisons were of New London, and Hartford, and after about 1790, of Mayfield, **N. Y.**

Children by first wife

Minerva (1) *Warner,* b. Oct. 11, 1792; d. Nov. 5, 1811; birth recorded in Middletown, Conn.

Maria Warner, b. July 17, 1794; d. May 23, 1845; m. (1) at Schenectady, N. Y., Apr. 8 or 16, 1813, Ebenezer Doble Roberts; m. (2) —— Fisk. Her father's will mentions "heirs of my daughter Mariah Fisk, late Mariah Roberts, decd."

339 *Junia Warner,* b. July 30, 1796; m. Lucinda Curtis.

Sally Warner, b. Feb. 25, 1799, in Middletown, Conn.; d. July 27, 1839; m. Apr. 23, 1818, Joseph W. Houghton. Her heirs were mentioned in her father's will. One son, Seth W. Houghton, resided with his grandfather in Skaneateles and attended school there. He was living in Winchester, Tenn., in 1894.

340 *Eben Warner*, b. Aug. 24, 1801; m. Hannah Fowler.
341 *Eleazer Gaylord Warner*, b. Sept. 8, 1803; m. (1) Amelia T. Parsons; (2) Eliza A. Shelp.

Children by second wife

342 *Vine Starr Warner*, b. Sept. 13, 1805; m. Clarissa M. Stewart.
343 *John Penfield Warner*, b. Feb. 23, 1809; m. Sarah Ann Hydenburg.
Fanny Warner, b. June or Jan. 5, 1811, in Mayfield, N. Y.; d. Mar. 17, or 19, 1867; m. Feb. 26, 1835, Ebenezer M. Walker.
Minerva (2) Warner, b. May 27, 1814, in Skaneateles, N. Y.; resided in Sennett, N. Y.; m. Jan. 12, 1859, William Clark Hoyt.

202 JUNIA[6] WARNER, son of Hezekiah[5] and Lois (Penfield) Warner, born in Middletown, Conn., February 1, 1773; died in Almena, Mich., November 10, 1841. He removed to Litchfield, Herkimer County, N. Y., about 1800; settled in the east part of the town of Winfield. In deeds of 1802, 1808, and 1814, he is described as of Litchfield, and sold property in Middletown to Elijah Wilcox, Jr., and others. The 1810 census records him with his family in Litchfield. In 1835 he removed to Michigan and located in Van Buren County. He was by trade a stone mason. The book of School District No. 9, comprising parts of Winfield and Litchfield, records that on December 11, 1826, Junia Warner, Junia Warner, Jr., and Hezekiah Wilcox were allowed $155 for building the stone schoolhouse. He was later trustee of the district. Miss Lizzie Harrison of West Winfield, N. Y., has an itemized account of the building of a house by Joseph Alexander in 1833, which shows that Junia Warner worked on the house "building the suller wall," laying under-pinning, building the chimney and plastering.

Married (1) in Middletown, Conn., January 17, 1797, ELIZABETH WILCOX, born in Upper Middletown, May 3 or 8, 1775, died March 30, 1815, daughter of Josiah and Elizabeth (Treat) Wilcox. Records of Immanuel Congregational Church of West Winfield, formerly 2d Congregational Church of Litchfield, give the following:

"July 16, 1809, Elizabeth Warner was received as a member of this chh. by letter from the chh. of Christ in Worthington."
"Baptized August 1810. By Mr. Southworth the children of Junia Warner."

Married (2) in Litchfield, N. Y., February 6, 1817, **Mrs. PHILURA (RAYMOND) MERRY**, who died in Almena, Mich., at an advanced age. She had children by her former marriage.

Children by first wife

344 *Olive Warner*, b. in Middletown, Conn., June 27, 1798; m. (1) Steven Hawley, (2) Charles Gray.
345 *Eliza Warner*, b. Aug. 24, 1800; m. Joseph Alexander.
346 *Junia Warner, Jr.*, b. Feb. 19, 1802; m. Arminda Merry.
347 *Huldah Wilcox Warner*, b. Dec. 19, 1803; m. Martin Heydenburk.
     Josiah Wilcox (1) *Warner*, b. Dec. 19, 1805; d. Dec. 21, 1806.
348 *Belinda A. Warner*, b. June 24, 1808; m. Enos Northrup, Jr.
     Emeline Warner, b. in Litchfield, Sept. 19, 1810; d. there Feb. 16, 1844, not married.
     Josiah Wilcox (2) *Warner*, b. in Winfield, N. Y., Mar. 1, 1813; d. in Grand Rapids, Mich., Sept. 13, 1889, buried in Winfield. He resided in West Winfield and was justice of the peace from 1854 to 1869. His will was probated in Herkimer County. Married (1) in Winfield, Jan. 4, 1838, Dolly Maria Morgan, who d. Sept. 30, 1872, aged 59 years and 6 months, daughter of Nathaniel and Dolly (Gallup) Morgan; (2) Mar. 12, 1873, Pamelia (Day) Brainerd, b. Feb. 20, 1815, d. June 2, 1889, daughter of Capt. Eli Day. No children, but adopted Eva D., d. Oct. 2, 1862, aged 11 years, 5 days.

Child by second wife

Lois Janette Warner, b. in Litchfield, Feb. 16, 1822; d. in Kalamazoo, Mich., Jan. 23, 1847; m. May 21, 1840, Philip Rowe. Child: (Daughter), still-born, Jan. 21, 1847.

203 WILLIAM[6] WARNER, son of Eliphaz[5] and Mercy (Drinkwater) Warner, born in Judea, Conn., November 12, 1770; died at Sandgate, Vt., May 24, 1856. He was a farmer in Sandgate, and the Census of 1850 records him there with property valued at a thousand dollars.

Married (1) March 20, 1780 (Connecticut marriages, I:100), **LUCY COAN** of Woodbury, Conn., who died October 2, 1815. She was a niece of Titus Coan, an early missionary to the Sandwich Islands.

Married (2) **ABIGAIL ROOT**, who lived only a short time, no children.

Married (3) **PRUDENCE NICKERSON**, born in Massachusetts, was living in 1850.

Children by first wife

Mary Warner, b. Jan. 8, 1799, in Sandgate, Vt.; d. there Nov. 12, 1859; m. Samuel Meeker. The Census of 1850 of Sandgate records Mary Meeker, Ira Warner, aged 20, and Ann Warner, aged 17, her younger brother and sister, residing with her.

349 *William Warner,* b. Nov. 6, 1801; m. Sally Safford.
350 *Joseph Warner,* b. Oct. 7, 1803; m. Mary Coville.
     Lucina Warner, b. Dec. 6, 1805, in Sandgate; m. Clark Reed and lived in Jasper, Ohio.
351 *Gaylord Coan Warner,* b. Apr. 1, 1808; m. (1) Martha Packard, (2) Mary Adams.
352 *Benjamin Stone Warner,* b. June 15, 1810; m. Hannah Malona Gleason.
353 *John Warner,* b. June 2, 1812; m. Lydia Warren.

Children by third wife

     James Warner, b. Sept. 26, 1820; resided in Manchester, Vt., later in Lind, Waupaca Co., Wis., where he died in 1902; m. (1) Sept. 25, 1845, Jane M. Walton, (2) May 29, 1856, Anne Ross. Child: James, Jr.
354 *Lucy Mercy Warner,* b. May 2, 1823; m. (1) Henry G. Stewart, (2) T. J. Albro.
     Ira N. Warner, b. May 20, 1830; resided with his oldest sister, Mary Meeker, in Sandgate, Vt., in 1850, and was designated as a pedlar in the Census for that year. He was later a farmer and died in Aurora, Ill., Mar. 6, 1877; m. Julia ———. Child: Fred, b. June 27, 1866 (Rupert, Vt., town records).
355 *Ann Warner,* b. Feb. 9, 1833; m. Peter De Voe.

204 Dr. JOHN[6] WARNER, son of Eliphaz[5] and Mercy (Drinkwater) Warner, born December, 1772, in Litchfield, Conn.; died 1839, in Starkey, Yates Co., N. Y. He was graduated from Burlington, 1803, M.D., and became a physician and surgeon. He settled in Yates County, N. Y., living at Dundee, Big Stream (now Glenora), and Rock Stream. Among the possessions of the family are silhouettes of Dr. John Warner and his son James Ward Warner; his extensive library, including volumes of law, medicine, history, and standard literature; a copy of his surgeon's commission in the War of 1812; an old ledger, bearing among its items a visit to a patient nine miles from home in the dead of winter, for which he charged 75 cents.

Married in Barrington, Yates Co., N. Y., October, 1808, **MARY DE WITT,** born at Sussex Court House, N. J., September 5, 1789, second daughter of Daniel De Witt who was born in Holland, and his wife, Eleanor Stoll, who was born in Holland or shortly after her parents arrived in this country.

Children, first four born at Big Stream, last two at Rock Stream, N. Y.

356 *Daniel De Witt Warner,* b. Sept. 25, 1809; m. Charlotte Gordon Coon.
     Eliza Ann Warner, b. Feb. 9, 1812; d. at Rock Stream, N. Y., Feb. 16, 1871; m. John Roberts, 2d, of Reading, Steuben Co., N. Y., who d. early in 1890. Child: John Warner, b. Sept. 18, 1842, d. Mar. 3, 1873, in Reading, N. Y., not married.
     James Ward Warner, b. Feb. (?), 1814; d. in New Haven, Conn., Mar., 1841, not married.

357 *Ellen Stoll Warner,* b. May 14, 1816; m. Moses Hetfield.
      Hannah Jane Warner, b. Sept. 2, 1820, at Rock Stream; d. there Feb.
      26, 1907; m. Hector Lee of Watkins, who died July 2, 1866, at Read-
      ing, N. Y. No children.
358 *John William Warner,* b. Feb. 9, 1831; m. Nancy Corbett.

205 JOHN⁶ WARNER, son of Jabez Ichabod⁵ and Ann
(Wakeley) Warner, born June 6, 1785, in Washington (Wood-
bury), Conn.; died May 24, 1834, in Newfane, Niagara Co., N. Y.
He resided in Newfane and Olcott, N. Y.
Married ABBY ACKLEY.

Children

      John Henry Warner, b. Nov. 1, 1812; d. Feb. 9, 1889; resided in
          Olcott, N. Y.
      Ann Eliza Warner, b. Nov. 22, 1814; d. Jan. 17, 1870; resided in
          Olcott, N. Y.
359 *Leman Ackley Warner,* b. May 6, 1817; m. (1) Caroline Tomlinson;
          (2) Sarah Deming Whittlesey.
360 *Clinton Warner,* b. June 17, 1826; m. Sarah Cummings.
      Chester Warner, b. Aug. 18, 1829; d. Apr., 1898; resided in Chicago;
          m. Mrs. Jennie T. Waldo; no children.

206 ABNER⁶ WARNER, son of Jabez Ichabod⁵ and Ann
(Wakeley) Warner, born 1787, in Woodbury, Conn.; died Octo-
ber 3, 1822, in Camillus, N. Y.
Married ELIZA SPICER.

Child

      Abner Spicer Warner, b. Sept. 7, 1818, in Manlius, N. Y.; d. in Weth
          ersfield, Conn., Nov. 22, 1900. He was a graduate of Dartmouth,
          M.D., 1848; a surgeon in the 16th Conn. Volunteers; practised medi-
          cine in Wethersfield, Conn. Married (1) Nov. 23, 1847, Caroline
          Celinda Kimball, daughter of William Ripley and Eliza Dresser
          (Dorr) Kimball, b. in Cornish, N. H., Dec. 6, 1821, d. Sept. 12, 1866;
          m. (2) June 7, 1869, Jane Maria Spalding, b. in Montpelier, Vt., May
          27, 1833, daughter of Dr. James and Eliza (Reed) Spalding. Chil-
          dren by first wife, born in Wethersfield: i. George Abner, b. Mar.
          11, 1849; d. Aug. 13, 1851. ii. Caroline Eliza, b. Sept. 11, 1852; m.
          May 24, 1887, Ellsworth B. Strong of Wethersfield and had a child
          Mary Elizabeth. iii. Mary Lucia, b. May 20, 1854; m. Feb. 1, 1894,
          James T. Pratt of Hartford and had a son James, b. 1895. iv. Eliza-
          beth Williams, b. June 18, 1858. v. Eliza Spicer, b. Mar. 7, 1862; d.
          in Wethersfield, Nov. 9, 1864. Child by second wife: George S.,
          b. Dec. 28, 1871, d. July 29, 1891.

207 ANDREW⁶ WARNER, son of Jabez Ichabod⁵ and
Mary (Youngs) Warner, born in Washington, Conn., March
25, 1806; removed to Jericho, Vt., and died there, February 10,

1890. He was a farmer in Jericho; representative in the state legislature in 1839-40, and assistant county court judge in 1862-3.

Married January 7, 1840, in Jericho, **EMILY GRAVES**, born in Greenfield, Mass., December 15, 1806; died in Jericho, June 19, 1881. She was the daughter of Deacon Eli and Judith (White) Graves.

Children, born in Jericho

Jane Graves Warner, b. Jan. 21, 1841; resides in Jericho Centre, Vt. She was a student at Mt. Holyoke Seminary in 1862, and was later a teacher, nurse and librarian. Married in Jericho, Sept. 28, 1871, Hiram Stanley Hart of Burlington, Vt., who died in New York City, Dec. 29, 1884, son of Jonathan and Almira (Jones) Hart. Child: Charlotte Warner, b. in Burlington, Vt., Dec. 23, 1872; d. Nov. 25, 1875, in New York City.

Mary Ann Warner, b. May 9, 1842; d. Mar. 15, 1843.

Anna Eliza Warner, b. May 25, 1845; was a student at Mt. Holyoke in 1869; clerk in the Treasury Department, Washington, D. C., 1871-82; resides in Jericho Centre, Vt.

208 ANDREW⁶ WARNER, son of Deliverance⁵ and Esther (Karr) Warner, born November 9, 1771, recorded in East Hampton, Conn.; died in Glastonbury, Conn. Records of his family are found in Eastbury Church records and in the 1800 Census of Glastonbury.

Married in Eastbury, Conn., November 11, 1792, **GILLET** (or **JEANETTE**) **GOODALE** of Glastonbury. Joseph Goodale married Ruth Fox in 1767 and their third child was Gillet, born November 10, 1772 (Glastonbury town records).

Children

361 *Warren Warner,* b. Mar. 25, 1793; m. Wealthy Post.

Arminda (or *Miranda* or *Orrenda*) *Warner,* resided in Glastonbury; m. Alfred Chapman, b. Apr. 3, 1795, son of Epaphras and Phebe (Andrus) Chapman. Children: i. Charles, b. June 30, 1823. ii. Erastus, b. Aug. 7, 1825; d. Nov. 5, 1850. iii. Andrew W., b. Feb. 10, 1827; d. Sept. 20, 1848. iv. Emory, b. Apr. 14, 1829. v. Nelson, b. June 14, 1832. vi. Lucy Ann, b. Apr. 26, 1835; d. Jan. 1, 1850. vii. John, b. Nov. 10, 1837.

Hansy Warner, m. Gilson Huxford, and had one child.

"Twin babes of Andrew Warner and wife d. unbaptized Mar. 18, 1799" (Eastbury Church record).

Lucy Warner, d. in Glastonbury. This is perhaps the Lucy Warner who m. Oct. 7, 1829, Samuel Chapman, b. Jan. 16, 1800, son of Peleg and Lucy (Benjamin) Chapman, and had a child Martha, b. Mar., 1831, d. young. Samuel Chapman, m. (2) Jan. 3, 1832, Mrs. Mary M. Davis by whom he had seven children.

"Infant babe of Andrew Warner and wife died Dec. 16, 1801" (Eastbury Church record).

362 *Elisha Warner,* b. 1803; m. Lucy Chapman.

17

Eldridge Warner, b. in Glastonbury, 1809; d. in Portland, Conn., Jan.
14' 1885, aged 77, buried in Marlborough, Conn.; m. Jan. 27, 1831,
Clarissa Hollister, b. Dec. 19, 1801, in East Glastonbury, daughter of
Samuel and Clarissa (Shipman) Hollister. They had six children,
one of whom is Mrs. Albert Hunt of Meriden, Conn.
363 *Andrew Wells Warner,* m. Phebe Chapman.

209 SARAH[6] WARNER, daughter of Deliverance[5] and
Esther (Karr) Warner, born June 9, 1778, recorded in East
Hampton, Conn., town records; resided at Rocky Hill, Conn.,
and died there.

Married (1) at Chatham (now Portland), Conn., WILLIAM
PELTON, born at Chatham (now Portland), March, 1775, died
there suddenly, October 8, 1813, son of John[5] and Abigail
(Miller) Pelton, and descended from John[1] and Susannah
(————) Pelton, Samuel[2] and Mary (Smith) Pelton, John[3]
and Jemima (Johnson) Pelton, John[4] and Elizabeth (Champion)
Pelton, of whose families extended accounts will be found in
the Pelton Genealogy, and Stiles' History of Ancient Wethers
field. William Pelton was a ship builder.

Married (2) as his third wife, JOHN PELTON, brother of
her first husband, born at Chatham (now Portland) about 1765;
died November 8, 1826. He married (1) Jerusha Sage, by whom
he had nine children, and (2) Mrs. Chapman.

Children of William and Sarah (Warner) Pelton, born at Portland

Nathan William Pelton, b. Sept. 18, 1799; lived at Wethersfield, Conn.,
and d. there Feb. 4, 1884; was a cabinet maker; m. at Wethersfield,
Dec. 2, 1818, Abigail Coleman, b. Nov. 29, 1799, d. Nov. 6, 1877,
daughter of Elisha and Hannah (Loveland) Coleman. See further.
Sarah Pelton, b. 1801; d. 1823.

Children of John and Sarah (Warner) Pelton

Catherine Pelton, b. about 1817.
Lucy Ann Pelton, b. about 1819; m. June 19, 1838, Joseph Curtiss of
Berlin, Conn.; resided in Syracuse, N. Y.
Frances Mary Pelton, b. about 1821; d. about 1860, not married; resided
in New Haven, Conn., and d. in Milwaukee at the home of her
half-brother, Halsey Pelton.

Nathan William Pelton, mentioned above, had six children, born in
Wethersfield: i. Hannah, b. Apr. 1, 1820; m. Sept. 4, 1847, Daniel P.
Bunce of Waterbury, Conn.; no children. ii. Elizabeth Ann, b. Aug.
13, 1822; m. Dec. 1, 1841, Philo Slocum[7] Newton, b. in Heath, Mass.,
Mar. 29, 1811, d. May 2, 1891 (Richard[1], Moses[2], Moses[3], Elisha[4], Solo-
mon[5], Daniel[6]); had two children, Anna Coleman, who m. July 8, 1868,
Dr. George Fuller Hawley of Hartford, and Philo Woodhouse, who is
president and treasurer of the Newton Drug Company of Hartford

(the Allyn House Drug Store), is prominent in religious, military and masonic circles, and who m. Apr. 17, 1870, his cousin Mrs. Angelia Augusta Holden Thompson, daughter of Alfred and Lucy Maynard (Newton) Holden, has no children. iii. Sarah Maria, b. April 1, 1824; m. Isaac Sheads; had two children, Charles D. and Ida E., both dead. iv. William H., b. Dec. 31, 1826; m. Apr. 24, 1851, Nancy A. Holden; had a son, William A., of Meriden, Conn. v. Harriet D., b. Oct. 20, 1828; m. Jan. 25, 1856, Stephen Williard; had a son and five daughters. vi. Mary F., b. Dec. 24, 1840; m. at Waterbury, Conn., John G. Belden, who d. May 14, 1886, aged 53 years; had one daughter, Bessie, b. Sept. 9, 1881, d. April 25, 1884.

Dr. George Fuller[8] Hawley was descended from Joseph[1] Hawley of Stratford, Conn., Samuel[2] and Ann (Thompson), Deacon Thomas[8], Captain Ezra[4], Ezra[5], Jr., Abraham[6], George Benjamin[7], founder of the Hartford Hospital. He died in Chicago, Ill., Apr. 16, 1917. His wife, Anna Coleman Newton, was born and has always lived in Hartford, is a member of Ruth Wyllis Chapter, Daughters of the American Revolution, and numbers among her ancestors thirteen of the Founders of Hartford: Elder William Goodwin, John Crow, Andrew Warner, John White, John Bidwell, John Wilcox, William Hill, George Stocking, Samuel Hale, Jeremy Adams, Richard Lyman, Matthew Marvin, and John Hopkins. She has one son, George Burton Hawley, b. in Hartford, was graduated from Massachusetts Institute of Technology as Electrical Engineer, was with the American Telegraph and Telephone Company for twenty-one years in New York, Boston, Indianapolis, and Chicago, has been, since 1916, Trust Officer of the City Bank and Trust Company of Hartford, m. Alma Wright of Boston, and had two children, Raymond Fuller, b. in Boston, Mar. 26, 1893, d. in Hartford, Sept. 15, 1914, and Newton Coleman, b. in Indianapolis, Jan. 25, 1906.

See also Stiles' History of Ancient Wethersfield, Pelton Genealogy and Newton Genealogy.

210 MARTHA[6] WARNER, daughter of Deliverance[5] and Esther (Karr) Warner, born June 28, 1782, in Connecticut; died at Fort Edwards, where she had resided.
Married SILAS HEWITT.

Child

Maria Lucina Hewitt, b. in Waterville, Oneida Co., N. Y., Apr. 8, 1808; d. Sept. 11, 1866, in Cortland, N. Y.; m. in Sangerfield, N. Y., Mar. 15, 1826, Ira Grant, b. Dec. 7, 1802; d. in Cortland, Jan. 22, 1868, son of William and Rachel (Wedge) Grant. Children: i. Julia Maria, b. in York, Livingston Co., N. Y., Feb. 7, 1827; m. in Boston, Israel Van Hoesen, b. in Rensselaer County, N. Y., son of George and Catherine (————) Van Hoesen. ii. Bradley Martin, b. in York, Jan. 12, 1829; m. Irene Crandall. iii. William Henry, b. in Caledonia, May 29, 1831; d. Jan. 26, 1860, in Cortland, not married. iv. John Hewitt, b. in Caledonia, Jan. 5, 1834; was Mayor and Postmaster of Troy, Bradford Co., Pa.; m. Sept. 16, 1857, Maria Dobbins, b. in Troy, Sept. 16, 1836, d. there, Dec. 9, 1860, daughter of William H. and Nancy (Bothwell) Dobbins; had two children, b. in Troy, Frederic Hewitt, d. young, and William Henry, b. 1860, resides in Kent,

Ohio. v. Emma Lucina, b. in Marshall, Oneida Co., N. Y., Apr. 22 1838; d. in Winchester, Mass., Apr. 2, 1870; m. in Cortland, N. Y., Sept. 14, 1858, Barna Smith Snow, b. in Orleans, Mass., Feb. 27, 1836, son of Barna Smith and Lydia (Myrick) Snow; had children, Emma Louise, b. 1860, William Henry, b. 1862, and Barna Hewitt, who d. young.

211   ROBERT[6] WARNER, son of Daniel[5] and Lucy (Stow) Warner, born in Middletown, Conn., December 30, 1745; died in Middletown, June 9, 1826, or June 10, 1824 (report from Pension Bureau). He was a cooper by trade and was recorded in the Census of 1790 in Middletown, four males over 16, three females, and one other free person in the family. There is recorded in Middletown a manumission given by Robert Warner, November 16, 1812, to Caesar, a mulatto boy, witnessed by Clarissa Warner. His estate was appraised September 10, 1826, and reported insolvent. Only personal effects were noted, including pension money, and no heirs were mentioned. He was a soldier and officer in the Revolution and an original member of the Society of the Cincinnati. His services are reported as follows: enlisted April, 1775, in Connecticut, private, sergeant, ensign; fall of 1775, lieutenant, Capt. Ebenezer Sumner, Col. Samuel Wyllys; October 11, 1776, captain, Col. Samuel Wyllys; May 29, 1782, major, Col. Thomas Grosvenor; discharged December, 1783. He was engaged in the battles of Dorchester Heights, Flatbush, Jamaica Plains, White Plains, and in the retreat from New York to Harlem Heights. He applied for a pension from Middletown, March 19, 1818.

. Married May 16, 1771, LUCY TUELS, who died April 7, 1818. The name is written Lucy Tule in Middletown vital records, Mary in some other records. She was probably Lucy Tuel, daughter of Elijah Tuel, baptized May 6, 1753 (Records of First Church in East Middletown)

Children

Daniel Warner, b. June 18, 1772; d. in Middletown, May 2, 1804, buried in Liberty Street Cemetery, Middletown. He was perhaps the father of Laura Warner who married in 1813 Parker Pelton and had a family of eight children. An account of her family is given in the Pelton Genealogy, p. 378.

Lucy Warner, b. Mar. 28, 1774; d. Oct., 1855, in New York; m. Mar. 29, 1795, William Harrington. Children: i. Mary Pierce, b. Dec. 24, 1795; m. John Spear, Jersey City. ii. Lucia Warner, b. Nov. 26, 1798; lived in Jersey City. iii. Abigail Shailer, b. Feb. 28, 1800. iv. William Abijah, b. Jan. 24, 1802. v. Nancy Stittwell, b. Feb. 18, 1804. vi. Esther Bull, b. June 18, 1806; d. in Jersey City, Feb. 26, 1858; m. in New York City, June 13, 1833, Charles Osborn, b. at Ridgefield,

Conn., Nov. 11, 1804, son of Asahel and Nancy (Keeler) Osborn, resided in New York City from 1823 to 1862, then in Chicago, where he was a manufacturer of jewelry. vii. Daniel Warner, b. Feb. 22, 1808. viii. Robert Warner, b. Sept. 8, 1811. ix. Susan Wright, b. Oct. 16, 1813; d. not married.

Robert (1) *Warner*, b. 1776; d. Sept. 11, 1785, in Middletown, buried in Liberty Street Cemetery, Middletown.

Robert (2) *Warner*, b. 1785; d. June 9, 1817, in Charleston, S. C.

Susan (1) *Warner*, d. June 13, 1789, aged 2 years, 7 months, buried in Liberty Street Cemetery.

364 *Clarissa Warner*, b. 1789; m. Henry Southmayd.

Susan (2) *Warner*, b. 1792; d. in Monticello, N. Y.; m. after Nov. 4, 1812 (when she was party to a deed in Middletown), Samuel Galpin, son of Thomas Galpin of Berlin, Conn. He m. (2) Abbie Wilcox and had children, Charles and Mary Helen. Child of Samuel and Susan (Warner) Galpin: Samuel W., b. Apr. 11, 1821; m. 1844, Amanda Skinner and resided in Fitchburg, Mass., in 1887.

212 **WILLIAM⁶ WARNER**, son of Daniel⁵ and Lucy (Stow) Warner, born in Middletown, Conn., April 1, 1747; died there October 23, 1821, buried in Liberty Street Cemetery. He is perhaps the William Warner of the 1790 Census, one male over 16, two under 16, three females; and of the 1800 Census, one male and one female over 45, one male and two females between 10 and 16, two females under 10. He was called Captain William Warner in 1805.

Married (1) **ISABEL⁶ WARNER**, born July 4, 1754, died before August 7, 1780, daughter of Joseph⁵ and Alice (Ward) Warner; see number 110.

Married (2) November 14, 1781, **SARAH DOW**, who died April 12, 1841, aged 87, buried in Liberty Street Cemetery.

Child of William and Isabel (Warner) Warner

William Warner, Jr., died Feb. 19, 1800. His father was appointed his guardian, Sept. 20, 1780.

Children of William and Sarah (Dow) Warner

Joseph Warner, bought property in Middletown in 1820; died there in 1834. David Allen and Horace Southmayd were administrators of his estate, July 24, 1835 (Middletown land records, 50:220, 63:37).

Mary Warner, b. 1786; d. Sept. 17, 1805, buried in Liberty Street Cemetery, Middletown.

Sally Warner, d. in Middletown, Nov., 1854; m. David Allen.

Huldah Warner, resided in New York; m. Horace Southmayd.

Caroline Warner, b. 1796; d. in Middletown, 1821; m. Deacon William Woodward.

William Warner, is probably the one who married, Dec. 11, 1820, Harriet Beers of Middletown and had a daughter, Harriet, b. in Middletown, Dec. 6, 1830; m. (1) May 29, 1851, Ira Holden Brainerd, (2) Joseph P. Davis (Brainerd Genealogy).

213 MARY[6] WARNER, daughter of Stephen[5] and Mary (Starr) Warner, born in Middletown, Conn., April 10, 1751; died there August 7 or 10, 1822.

Married in Middletown, November 24, 1773, **JOSIAH STARR,** son of John and Patience (Miller) Starr. He was born at South Farms, Conn., January 27, 1751-2; died in Charlestown, Portage Co., Ohio, April 12, 1837. He was a tailor and a member of the Methodist Church. He removed, October 26, 1831, to Ohio, where most of his family had preceded him. A more complete account of this family is given in the Starr Genealogy.

Children

John Starr, b. Aug. 16, 1774, at South Farms; d. May 7, 1833, in Huron, Erie Co., N. Y. He removed to Malta, Saratoga Co., in 1800, and in 1828, to Huron. Married Sarah Chandler, daughter of Joseph and Charity (Andrews) Chandler, b. Mar. 3, 1782, in Stillwater, N. Y., d. Aug. 21, 1861. Children: i. Josiah Warner, b. Aug. 22, 1811; m. twice and had children. ii. John Milton, b. Sept. 30, 1813; m. and had children. iii. Joseph, b. Dec. 10, 1815; m. and adopted two children. iv. Samuel, b. Aug. 26, 1818; m. and had children. v. Mary, b. July 15, 1822; m. and had children. vi. Harriet, b. Oct. 11, 1824; d. Apr. 16, 1832.

Mary Starr, b. Aug. 21, 1777; d. Dec. 29, 1858, in Stow, Ohio, not married.

Josiah Starr, b. July 23, 1779; d. June 29, 1780.

Stephen Warner Starr, b. June 18, 1781; d. at St. Bartholomew's, West Indies, Dec., 1797.

Joshua Starr, b. July 22, 1786; m. and had children.

Anna (Nancy) Gilbert Starr, b. Oct. 5, 1790, in Middletown, Conn.; d. Jan. 29, 1854; m. as his second wife, John Bill, and had two children.

214 LUCRETIA[6] WARNER, daughter of Stephen[5] and Mary (Starr) Warner, born in Middletown, Conn., September 23, 1752; died May 18, 1820.

Married (1) in Middletown, January 20, 1774, **JOHN SCOTT** of Palmer, who died March 14, 1787, in his 35th year.

Married (2) as his second wife, March 27, 1791, **SETH WETMORE, Jr.,** born October 9, 1743, died April 15, 1810, son of Judge Seth and Hannah (Whitmore) Wetmore. He married (1) November 14, 1760, Mary Wright, who died December 24, 1790, and had children, Seth, William, Hannah, Samuel, Mary, Willard Wright, Titus, Josiah, Lucy and Nathaniel Downing. He was a captain in the colonial volunteer service in the Revolution.

Children of John and Lucretia (Warner) Scott

Nabby Scott, b. May 8, 1776.

Lucretia Warner Scott, b. May 16, 1780.

Ascenith Dickinson Scott, b. Oct. 1, 1782; d. Nov. 19, 1782.

Children of Seth and Lucretia (Warner) Wetmore, born in Middletown

Julia Wetmore, b. Jan. 21, 1792; m. Dec. 3, 1812, John Churchill Bush of New Haven, Conn., later of Ogdensburg, N. Y. Children: i. Robert Wasson, b. in New Haven, Nov. 18, 1813; m. Oct. 29, 1846, Catharine Udall of Hartford, Vt.; had children, Julia Sophia, Robert Wallace, d. young, John James and Henry Kirk Brown. ii. Harriet Wetmore, b. Apr. 25, 1815; m. in Ogdensburg, N. Y., May 27, 1840, Elihu William Nathan Starr, son of Nathan and Grace (Townsend) Starr of New Haven, b. Aug. 10, 1812, became Adjutant-General, Connecticut militia; had children, William Edwards, Julia Wetmore, d. young, Robert Wetmore, d. young, Henry Barnard, Frank Farnsworth, the distinguished genealogist of Middletown, and Grace Townsend.

Harriet Wetmore, b. Sept. 22, 1794; d. in Middletown, Mar. 1, 1823; m. Henry S. Ward of Middletown; no children.

215 **JONATHAN⁶ WARNER, JR.,** son of Jonathan⁵ and Mary (Griffin) Warner, born in Simsbury, Conn., August 27, 1778; died in Pittsford, Vt., May 18, 1854. He removed with his parents to Pittsford at an early age, and always resided there. He was several times member of the State Legislature and held other civil and military offices, including that of captain.

Married in Pittsford, 1801, **ANNA RIPLEY,** born in Pittsford, December 11, 1781, died there March 27, 1859, daughter of Phineas and Experience (Montague) Ripley.

Children, all born in Pittsford

365 *Seth Warner,* b. Oct. 20, 1802; m. Susan Skinner.
366 *Mary Warner,* b. Oct. 4, 1804; m. Tyler Caldwell.
    Alzina Warner, b. Oct. 14, 1806; d. May 8, 1848; m. Feb., 1840, George Porter, b. June 22, 1802; d. Sept. 4, 1881. Children, born in Salem, N. Y.: i. Mary Ann, b. Apr. 14, 1842. ii. Margaret Adelaide, b. May 22, 1844; d. Nov. 6, 1845. iii. Charles Edward, b. Nov. 19, 1846; d. May 7, 1848.
367 *Jonathan Warner, 3d,* b. Apr. 12, 1810; m. Sarah M. Walton.
368 *William Warner,* b. Jan. 28, 1812; m. (1) Harriet B. Leach, (2) Frances G. Leach.
    Anna Warner, b. May 25, 1814; d. Jan. 9, 1844; m. 1842, Abram Butterfield, b. Apr. 14, 1816, in Claremont, N. H., d. Jan. 22, 1870. Child: George, b. Dec. 11, 1843, in Rutland, Vt.; d. May 10, 1873.
    Benoni Warner, b. Oct. 27, 1816; d. Apr. 4, 1841, not married.
    Franklin Warner, b. Sept. 16, 1818; died in Oakland, Calif., Jan. 14, 1901. He was educated in Middlebury College and engaged in teaching in Pennsylvania, Ohio and Mississippi. During his residence in the latter state, he enlisted upon the breaking out of the Mexican War. To the Mexican veterans it was but a step into California, which had been brought so forcibly to their minds during the struggle, and after receiving an honorable discharge, Mr. Warner went on to the Pacific Coast. Here he engaged in mining for some time with little success. He then went to Oakland and taught in the first school in Oakland from 1854-6, in the Durant Collegiate School, 1856-60,

then again in the public school. At the beginning of the movement to found the University of California, Mr. Warner devoted months in advocating the necessity of such an institution as the Durant Collegiate School, the foundation of the present institution. All of his work was of the highest standard and for the uplift of the young people. In 1857 he purchased a tract of land, called the Warner tract, and erected many houses in the hope of inducing a certain class of homeseekers to settle there. He was so successful in this line of business that he followed the real estate business until the time of his death. He was a charter member of Live Oak Lodge, No. 61, F. and A. M., of Oakland. Mr. Warner married in 1856, Sarah Hinds Walker, b. in Boston, Mass., daughter of Barzillai and Nancy French (Hinds) Walker. She came to California in 1853 with friends from Taunton, coming by way of the Isthmus. She was educated at Warren Ladies' Seminary in Rhode Island and taught school from the age of 15. After coming to Oakland she continued teaching and was the third teacher in the Oakland schools. Mrs. Warner survived her husband. They had no children.

216   LEVI[6] WARNER, son of Jonathan[5] and Mary (Griffin) Warner, born September 11, 1795, in Pittsford, Vt., twin with Judith; died May 18, 1879. At the age of 21 he started on foot on a tour of observation for the purpose of seeing the country; went as far west as Missouri, then through the southern states, on foot and alone, keeping a daily journal of where he went and what he had seen. He returned in the fall, having walked 4,000 miles. The following year he went to Bond County, Ill., then south to New Orleans. He was in Galena during the Black Hawk War. In 1832 he went to Elkhorn Grove, Ill., and made the first claim on the south side of the Grove. He surveyed the state road from Peoria to Galena, and the county road to Mt. Carroll; was the first county surveyor of Ogle County, elected April 8, 1839; was the first town clerk and served until 1866; held the office of justice of the peace and examined teachers. He lived to a good old age and was the oldest settler in the Grove if not in the county.

Married April 12, 1835, **Mrs. MARTHA (BAILEY) WINTERS**, formerly from Greenbrier County, Va. She had seven children by her first husband, Catherine J., John C., Robert, James, William K., Joshua J., and William H.

Child of Levi Warner

Martha Maria Warner, b. Feb. 15, 1837, at Elkhorn Grove, Ill.; m. Sept. 7, 1854, Lewis Reynolds, b. in Cayuga Co., N. Y., Aug. 8, 1832, went to Cayuga Co. with his parents by wagon in 1842, was a farmer in Elkhorn township, Ill., held the office of road commissioner and school offices. Children: i. Henry, b. May 9, 1859. ii. Leonard, died.

217 **LYDIA**[6] **WARNER,** daughter of Daniel[5] and Mary (Wright) Warner, born in Hardwick, Mass., August 12, 1759; removed to Hardwick, Vt., in 1799.

Married⁀in Hardwick, Mass., February 25, 1775, **SAMUEL FRENCH,** born in Weymouth, Mass., May 12, 1753; died in Hardwick, Vt., June 17, 1832. He was a corporal in Captain Samuel Dexter's Company of Massachusetts Minute Men. His ancestry was as follows: son of Dr. Daniel[4] and Mary (Lane) French of Weymouth; Stephen[3] French, b. June 18, 1664, m. Sept. 24, 1694, Abigail Beale; Stephen[2] French of Weymouth, m. Hannah Whitman; Stephen[1] French, emigrated from Dorchester, Dorset County, England, March 30, 1630, landed at Nantasket, May 30, 1630, resided in Dorchester for a short time then removed to Weymouth, was freeman in 1636 and town officer in 1645, m. (1) Mary ————, m. (2) ————, Jan. 21, 1656, and died leaving a will which was probated July 27, 1679. Dr. Samuel William French of Milwaukee, Wis., is a descendant of this family.

Children of Samuel and Lydia (Warner) French

Lydia French, b. July 12, 1775; d. Oct. 4, 1808; m. as first wife, Sept. 20, 1795, Charles Paige, b. Oct. 16, 1771, d. Apr. 21, 1853, son of James and Thankful (Raymond) Paige. Children: i. Sophronia, m. Chiron Jenney. ii. Lucius, d. young. iii. Charles. iv. Thankful, m. Col. Abialbon Carter. v. Lucinda, d. young. vi. James. vii. Lydia W., d. not married. viii. ————, d. young.

Samuel French, b. Mar. 5, 1779; d. in Hardwick, Vt., Sept. 26, 1848; m. Tabitha Dow of Coventry, Conn., who died July 6, 1848, in Hardwick, Vt., a sister of Lorenzo Dow. Sectional differences delayed the building of the church until 1820, when Mr. French built at his own expense a church to be occupied by all denominations. He would never sell or deed it to any sect although the Congregationalists made repeated efforts to buy it. His motives were of the highest, but the outcome was deleterious to the town, as for a time the building was occupied by a sect of "New Lights." They were originally organized by a Universalist minister but they became in time extremely fanatical in their worship.

Daniel French, b. Jan. 18, 1781; was a deacon in Hardwick, Vt.; m. (1) Lucy Goss, (2) Sarah Worcester.

Mary French, b. June 15, 1784; resided in Hardwick, Vt.; m. Samuel Goss.

Jonathan Warner French, b. June 28, 1787.

Justus Warner French, b. Apr. 20, 1793; d. Dec. 25, 1862; was a clergyman; m. and had four children: The third child was Edward Warner French, a clergyman, b. Aug. 23, 1829, d. Feb. 4, 1885, m. Julia Norton Day, and their fifth child was Eleanor Gifford, who resided in Montclair, N. J.

Fordyce French, b. Apr. 13, 1798; m. Abigail Ames.

218 JONATHAN⁶ WARNER, son of Daniel⁵ and Mary (Wright) Warner, born in Hardwick, Mass., September 13, 1763; died there July 1, 1838. He was a farmer and inherited his father's homestead. After his second marriage he bought a farm and built a house on the easterly road from. Hardwick to Gilbertsville. He was ensign of militia; selectman for three years; private in the Revolution.

Married (1) February 25, 1789, **SALLY PAIGE,** who died June 11, 1807, aged 38. Sally Paige's ancestry traces back to Nathaniel¹, who came from England to Roxbury, Mass., about 1685, m. Joanna ————; Nathaniel², b. about 1679, d. in Bedford, Mass., Mar. 2, 1755, m. Susannah Lane; John³, b. Oct. 11, 1704, m. Rebecca Wheeler; John⁴, b. Sept. 2, 1753, m. Mary Cutler, and removed to Hardwick; Sally⁵.

Married (2) October 18, 1807, **Mrs. ANNIS SMITH MARSH,** born November 11, 1765, died in Springfield, Mass., May 17, 1859, daughter of Hugh (or Elihu) Smith of Palmer, Mass., and widow of Joel Marsh by whom she had four children, Phila, m. Martin Mandell, Delphia, died young, Dwight, and Joel Smith. There were no children by the second marriage. Mrs. Warner received a pension as the widow of a Revolutionary soldier, dating from February 3, 1853, at the rate of $80.00 a year. She made a will, in which she left property to her daughter Delphia, son Joel Smith, and granddaughter Mary A., wife of Joel W. Fletcher of Leominster.

Children of Jonathan and Sally (Paige) Warner, born in Hardwick

    Mary Warner, b. Dec. 3, 1789; d. at Barre, Mass., Oct. 13, 1866; m. Nov. 28, 1809, William Robinson, b. Oct. 24, 1781, d. Aug. 21, 1862, son of Joseph and Lucy (Ruggles) Robinson. They resided at Barre. Child: Maria, b. Dec. 5, 1818; m. May 26, 1841, Moses Ruggles, b. Nov. 3, 1819, a farmer and town officer in Barre, son of Daniel and Lucy (Paige) Ruggles. They had a daughter Lucy Maria Ruggles, b. Oct. 13, 1845, m. July 3, 1876, Edward H. Paige, b. Jan. 6, 1849, son of David C. and Miranda (Houghton) Paige.

    ————, b. Mar. 20, 1792; d. Mar. 26, 1792.

369   *Moses Mandell Warner,* b. Mar. 30, 1793; m. Orrell Smith.
370   *Jonathan Warner, Jr.,* b. Mar. 28, 1795; m. Emily Florilla Farnum.
    Lewis (1) *Warner,* b. Jan., 1797; d. Apr. 1, 1797.
371   *Daniel Warner,* b. July 2, 1799; m. Nancy Fish.
372   *Lewis* (2) *Warner,* b. June 1, 1801; m. (1) Veronacia Anderson; (2) Susan Weeks.
373   *William Augustus Warner,* b. Jan. 8, 1804; m. Elizabeth F. Billings.
374   *Levi Whipple Warner,* b. June 7, 1806; m. Luthera Clark.

219 ALPHA⁶ WARNER, son of Daniel⁵ and Mary (Wright) Warner, born in Hardwick, Mass., December 8, 1770; died in

Chillicothe, Ohio, January, 1854. He settled in Hardwick, Vt., and spent most of his life there; removed to Chillicothe in 1853. He was inn-keeper for nearly sixty years; colonel or captain of militia; representative in the General Assembly. The Census of 1850 notes him as inn-keeper in Hardwick, Vt., with his son Alpha.

Married (1) January 14, 1796, LYDIA COBB, born in Hardwick, Mass., January 4, 1769; died in Hardwick, Vt., May 27, 1816.

Married (2) Mrs. ANNA BURTON, who died in Hardwick, Vt., March 17, 1853, aged 66 years.

Children by first wife, born in Hardwick, Vt.

Maria Warner, b. Oct. 18, 1796.

Hiram Warner, b. May 16, 1798.

Eliza Warner, b. May 12, 1800.

Everline Warner, b. July 26, 1802; d. in Hardwick, Vt., Oct. 23, 1841.

Alexander Warner, b. Nov. 5, 1804.

Caroline Warner, b. June 23, 1807; d. Mar. 14, 1882; m. Jan. 8, 1835, James Dean Bell, b. Dec. 14, 1808, d. Dec. 6, 1880, son of James and Lucy (Dean) Bell of Walden, Vt. He was a farmer and judge of the county court, represented Walden in both branches of the Legislature. Children: i. Alpha Warner, b. Feb. 16, 1836; d. May 19, 1860. ii. Caroline Maria, b. Mar. 2, 1838. iii. Jane Dean, b. Apr. 16, 1840; d. Feb. 10, 1857. iv. Eliza Warner, b. Apr. 16, 1842; d. Dec. 14, 1864. v. Charles James, b. Mar. 10, 1845; was a farmer in Walden, Vt.; m. Oct. 4, 1870, Mary L. Perry, daughter of Charles C. and Abigail W. (Walbridge) Perry. vi. Julia Agnes, b. Feb. 21, 1848. vii. Katie Calista, b. Dec. 5, 1849; d. Nov. 21, 1858.

Daniel Warner, b. June 20, 1811.

Alpha Warner, Jr., b. July 2, 1814; was an inn-keeper with his father in Hardwick, Vt., in 1850; removed to Chillicothe, Ohio; m. (1) Feb. 26, 1851, Martha Amelia Rhodes (Danville, Caledonia Co., Vt., town records), who died in Chillicothe, Ohio, May 23, 1856, aged 33 years, and was buried with her infant son there; m. (2) Jan. 19, 1866, Lucy Ann Underwood (Barnet, Caledonia Co., Vt., town records)

Children by second wife, born in Hardwick, Vt.

Pinu Burton Warner (daughter), b. Apr. 25, 1820; d. June 6, 1822.

Joel Burton Warner, b. Jan. 13, 1825; d. Aug. 3, 1825.

William Smith Warner, b. May 29, 1826.

Lydia Ann Warner, b. Oct. 12, 1829; d. Apr. 11, 1831.

220 SUSANNA⁶ WARNER, daughter of Gen. Jonathan⁵ and Hannah (Mandell) Warner, born in Hardwick, Mass., July 10, 1767; died in Bennington, Vt., April 2, 1844. Her name is recorded as "Sukey" in the New Braintree records.

Married (1) February 16, 1786, Capt. ARTEMAS HOWE,

born in Marlboro, 1753; died in Oakham, August 31, 1800. By a former marriage he had daughters Betsey and Dulcena, whose births were recorded in New Braintree, and a son Lewis who later resided on the old Warner homestead and managed both the home farm and the tavern. Artemas Howe was in October, 1786, appointed as an aide-de-camp of Gen. Jonathan Warner, his father-in-law.

Susanna Warner Howe married (2) **MOSES ROBINSON,** born in Hardwick, Mass., March 20, 1741, son of Samuel and Mercy (Leonard) Robinson; died May 26, 1813. There were no children by this marriage. Moses Robinson was educated at Dartmouth College and removed to Bennington, Vt., with his father about 1761. He was chosen the first clerk of the town in 1762, and held the office for about twenty years. In the early part of 1777, he was a colonel of militia and was at the head of his regiment on Mount Independence when Ticonderoga was evacuated. He was a member of the Council of Safety, and on the Governor's Council for eight years until 1785. Upon the organization of the state he was appointed chief justice, a position which he held, with the exception of one year, until 1789, when he was elected Governor. In 1782 he was sent to the Continental Congress as one of the agents of the states, and he was one of the commissioners that finally adjusted the controversy with New York State. He was chosen to Congress in 1791, but resigned in 1796. He also served a term in the General Assembly in 1802.

Governor Robinson was a man of profound piety and democracy, and may be called the father of the Congregational Church at Bennington. He was a deacon of that church from 1789 up to his death. It is related that when people came to Bennington in the early days to purchase land, he would invite them to his home overnight, contrive to learn their religious opinions, and, if they were not good Congregationalists, he would persuade them to settle in Shaftsbury or Pownal, where he also had land holdings. So strong a bent did he and his associates give to the religious opinion of the community, that up to 1830 there was only the one house of public worship in the town.

Governor Robinson's first wife was Mary Fay, daughter of Stephen Fay. They had six sons; the eldest, Moses, was in 1814 a member of the Council and was repeatedly a member of the General Assembly; Aaron, Samuel and Nathan were also prominent in local affairs, and Nathan's son John S. Robinson was later Governor of his state; Fay married Seraph Howe, a daughter of his step-mother.

Children of Artemas and Susanna (Warner) Howe, born in New Braintree

Isabella Howe, b. Dec. 17, 1786.
Seraph Howe, b. July 9, 1788; m. Fay Robinson, son of her stepfather, Gov. Moses Robinson, by his first wife, Mary Fay.
Polly Howe, b. June 25, 1791.

221 BATHSHEBA[6] WARNER, daughter of Gen. Jonathan[5] and Hannah (Mandell) Warner, born in Hardwick, Mass., March 25, 1769; died about 1855, in Springfield.

Married June 8, 1798, **LUKE BROWN, Jr.,** whose father was an inn-holder in Worcester. He was graduated from Harvard, 1794, was a lawyer at Hardwick until 1806, then removed; died at Enfield about 1835.

Children

Mary Brimmer Brown, b. July 6, 1799; d. in Chicago, Ill., 1863, not married.
Bathsheba Warner Brown, b. Sept. 9, 1801; resided in Amherst, Mass.; m. Luman Scott.
Harriet Warner Brown, b. Nov. 21, 1803; was living in Belchertown in 1878, not married.
Elizabeth Follett Brown, b. June 5, 1806; m. James Hill; resided in Worthington, Mass.
Luke Brown, Jr., resided in Chicago; d. Oct. 23, 1871, on board a steamer as he was returning up the Mississippi River from New Orleans. He left a wife and children.

222 HARRIET[6] WARNER, daughter of Gen. Jonathan[5] and Hannah (Ruggles) Warner, born in Hardwick, Mass., January 15, 1783. She lived to be very old, and in her ninety-seventh year was at the home of her son William Augustus Warner Holton in Crown Point, Lake Co., Ind. She became quite blind and hard of hearing before her death, but her mind remained clear. One who visited her a few years before her death was struck with her stately, dignified apearance, "tall, erect and strong, she seemed to have inherited the qualities of her renowned ancestors."

Married in Hardwick, Mass., October 12, 1806, **ALEXANDER HOLTON,** born in Westminster, Vt., January 19, 1779; died August 4, 1823, in Vernon, Marion Co., Ind. He was the son of Joel and Bethiah (Farwell) Holton and his father was one of the first settlers in Westminster, Vt., when that place was a bone of contention between New York and New Hampshire, both states claiming it. He was fitted for college at Chesterfield Academy, and graduated from Dartmouth College in 1804, studied law and practiced his profession in Hardwick, Mass., 1807, later in Hartland and Woodstock, Vt. In March, 1815, he

removed to Vevay, Ind., and, after some years, to Vernon,
Marion Co., Ind., where he died. Accounts of this family are
given in the Winslow Memorial and Farwell Ancestral Memorial.

Children

Jonathan Warner Holton, b. July 30, 1807, in Westminster, Vt.; d.
Dec. 27, 1879. Resided at Deep River, Ind., and Stevens Creek,
Ark. He was a farmer and at the organization of Lake Co., Ind.,
he was elected the first County Treasurer. He was postmaster at
the time of his death. Married in Jennings Co., Ind., Dec. 7, 1829,
Charlotte Baily Perry, b. Feb. 13, 1812, in Blount Co., Tenn., daughter of Ransom and Catherine (Martin) Perry. Children: i. Ellen
Maria, b. Nov. 15, 1830, in Jennings Co., Ind., m. at Valparaiso, Ind.,
Sept. 12, 1865, Lewis Mosier; lived at Stevens Creek, Ark., and had
children, Catherine Louisa, b. Dec. 15, 1866, in Porter Co., Ind., and
Charlotte Eugenia. ii. John, b. Feb. 18, 1833, in Jennings Co., Ind.;
d. Apr. 11, 1843, at Crown Point, Ind. iii. Martha, b. Feb. 23, 1839,
at Crown Point; d. there Jan. 19, 1840. iv. Alexander, b. July 14,
1841, at Crown Point; d. there May 3, 1843. v. Catharine, b. Jan.
12, 1845, at Crown Point; m. Apr. 7, 1863, Philip Louks, of Dutch
and English descent, b. in Canada West, Apr. 23, 1837; lived, in
1879, at Stevens Creek, White Co., Ark.; had three sons, b. in
Wheeler, Porter Co., Ind., Warren Lincoln, b. Jan. 27, 1864, Jonathan
Wilbur Augustus, b. Nov. 2, 1868, and Perry Holton, b. Mar., 1871;
vi. Charlotte, b. May 2, 1849, at Deep River, Ind.; m. 1879, ———
Channell, and had a child, Jessie Maria. vii. Perry, b. Feb. 24, 1852,
at Deep River; d. there, Apr. 18, 1855.
William Augustus Warner Holton, b. May 15, 1809, at New Hardwick,
Vt.; was living in Hopkins, Mo., in 1881. He was a farmer and
fruitgrower, was elected first Recorder of Lake Co., Ind., at its
organization. He resided also at Deep River and Crown Point, Ind.
Married Feb. 8, 1846, Bernetta Vosburgh, b. Nov. 1, 1828, daughter
of Barnet and Sarah (Ballard) Vosburgh of Crown Point, Ind.
Children: i. Harriet Ann, b. Aug. 14, 1847; d. Aug. 28, 1847. ii.
Charles Augustus Warner, b. Aug. 1, 1848; lived in Linneus, Lynn
Co., Mo.; m. Apr., 1878, Elizabeth Dyke of McComb, Hancock Co.,
Ohio; had a child, Ethel. iii. Sarah Frances, b. Feb. 7, 1850; d.
Feb. 24, 1853. iv. John Dumont, b. Nov. 25, 1851; d. in Kansas,
Sept. 17, 1875. v. Olive, b. Feb. 3, 1853; d. Sept. 23, 1853. vi.
George, b. Aug. 11, 1856; d. July 9, 1858. vii. William Augustus
Warner, b. July 3, 1859. viii. Francis Alexander, b. Dec. 13, 1868.
Harriet Holton, b. in Vevay, Ind., Nov. 1, 1818; resided in Tiskilwa,
Ill.; m. at Crown Point, Ind., Jan. 8, 1846, Asahel Albee, b. in Bar-
ton, Vt., Dec. 17, 1816, son of Benjamin and Sophia (Vance) Albee.
He settled in Wheatland, Bureau Co., Ill., and lived at Tiskilwa in
1879. Children: i. Maria, b. Nov. 19, 1846; d. Jan. 4, 1871; m. in
Wheatland, Dec. 2, 1863, Elisha P. DeMaranville, b. July 1, 1825, in
Tompkins Co., N. Y., son of Nehemiah and Phebe (Parish) DeMaran-
ville, was a machinist in a watch factory, Elgin, Ill.; had children,
Chloe, b. Dec. 25, 1865, in Tiskilwa, and Henry, b. Feb. 11, 1870. ii.
Charles, b. July 20, 1848, m. in 1883, and resided in Dallas Co., Iowa.
iii. Alma, b. May 5, 1850; m. in Princeton, Ill., Oct. 27, 1875, Alvin

Eugene Willard, b. Dec. 22, 1846, at Great Falls, N. H., son of Fabeus̅ and Hannah (————) Willard, resided in Madison, Neb. iv. Seraph, b. July 30, 1852; d. Aug. 28, 1852. v. Miriam, b. Aug. 2, 1854; d. Jan. 1, 1881; m. Mar. 11, 1875, in Princeton, Ill., James Byron Swarthout, b. July 8, 1850, in Barrington, Yates Co., N. Y., son of James W. and Maria (Wright) Swarthout; had a child, Ada Elizabeth, b. May 1, 1877, in Milo, Ill. vi. Alexander, b. Jan. 1, 1858.

223 ABEL[6] WARNER, son of Elijah[5] and Submit (Wells) Warner, born in Hardwick, Mass., April 29, 1763; died in Plainfield, Mass., February 12, 1837. His name first appears on the roll of Captain Timothy Paige's Company, Col. John Rand's Regiment, enlisting at the age of seventeen, July 5, 1780, and serving until October 10, 1780. This company was raised by act of June 22, 1780, for three months, and did duty at West Point, N. Y. (Mass. Archives). March 15, 1785, Plainfield was set off from the north part of Cummington and incorporated as the District of Plainfield. It was here that Abel Warner first settled after his marriage. He lived on the farm that was later owned by his grandson, Francis Joy, and kept a tavern there. There was no church there for a time and they attended the church in Cummington, where some of the children were baptized. He was given in the Census of 1790 and later ones. His name is found on various committees to divide the town into school districts and other public duties. On September 9, 1800, the town of Plainfield voted to make provision for training soldiers at the general muster at Northampton. Mr. Abel Warner was allowed five shillings for conveying and taking care of the provisions which were to be collected by Mr. Elijah Warner. Among the provisions allowed the company were twenty-five pounds of cheese, one hundred and twenty pounds of wheat, and one hundred pounds of mutton.

On October 1, 1828, Abel Warner, yeoman, sold to Justus Warner, yeoman, his farm in Plainfield, consisting of one hundred and sixty acres, consideration two thousand dollars. His will was dated March 31, 1836.

Abel Warner married at Kingston, Mass., February 15, 1786 (or March 2, 1786, family record of Abel P. Warner), SARAH COOK, born December 13, 1764 (or 1765, family record of Abel P. Warner); died in Plainfield, February 25, 1850, aged 85 years. She was the daughter of Sylvanus and Sarah (Barstow) Cook of Kingston, and was descended from Francis[1] Cook, b. 1577, d. April 7, 1663, m. in Holland, Hester ————, a Walloon from southern Belgium and of a Huguenot family. Their son Jacob[2] Cook, b. in Holland, d. at Eastham, July 7, 1676, m. 1646-7,

Damaris Hopkins, daughter of Stephen Hopkins of the May-flower; Jacob³ Cook, b. March 26, 1653, d. April 24, 1747, m. December 29, 1681, Lydia Miller; John⁴ Cook, b. May 23, 1703, m. in 1730, Phebe Crossman and was the father of Sylvanus⁵ Cook, b. at Kingston, Mass., May 1, 1738, d. there, November 12, 1814, m. March 22, 1764, Sarah Barstow of Pembroke. (Signers of the Mayflower, by Annie Arnoux Haxtun; Memorial of Francis Cook, by Henry Cook.)

Children of Abel and Sarah (Cook) Warner

375 *Ira Warner,* b. Dec. 24, 1786; m. Asenath Hitchcock.
    Lorenzo Warner, b. Mar. 26, 1788; bapt. in Cummington, May 18, 1788; d. Feb. 14, 1814, while teaching school near Utica, N. Y.
376 *Polly Warner,* b. Nov. 16, 1790; m. Leonard Joy.
    Theodore Warner, b. Feb. 12, 1793; d. in De Ruyter, N. Y., Mar. 25, 1876. He was a Quaker preacher and resided in De Ruyter for many years. His will was probated in Madison County, N. Y., Jan. 29, 1877. Married (1) Jan. 30, 1815, Esther Wells, b. Cheshire, Mass., Feb. 16, 1793, d. at De Ruyter, N. Y., Dec. 17, 1857. She was a party with him in a land transaction, Apr. 25, 1825, by which they deeded land in Truxton, N. Y., to Ira Warner. Married (2) Amarilla Bradley, who died June 25, 1885, aged 76, and is buried in Pompey Hill, Onondaga County, N. Y., on the Jerome lot. Dolly M. Jerome was administrator of her estate. There were no children by either marriage.
    Sylvanus Warner, b. Sept. 20 or 2, 1794; d. in Ashtabula, Ohio, Sept. 16, 1838. He was unfortunate in business and went west, settling in Ashtabula. Married in Ashtabula, Abi C. ————, who died May 22, 1860, aged 60. He is said to have left descendants in Ashtabula.
377 *Justus Warner,* b. June 13, 1796; m. Sylvia Russell Hitchcock.
378 *Sarah Warner,* b. Jan. 13, 1798; m. Edmond Taylor.
    Charles Warner (twin), b. and d. Oct. 5, 1802.
    Giles Warner (twin), b. and d. Oct. 5, 1802.
379 *Fanny Warner,* b. Aug. 26, 1805; m. Reuben Hamlin.
    Rosamond Warner, b. June 2, 1807, in Plainfield; d. in Davenport, Iowa, 1881; m. July 2, 1829, Enoch D. Townsley. They resided in New England for a time and removed to Iowa in 1852. Children: Frutella; Adeline; Maria; Salina M.

224 **DAVID⁶ WARNER,** son of Elijah⁵ and Submit (Wells) Warner, born in Hardwick, Mass., March 10, 1765; died in Palmyra, N. Y., May 22, 1840. He removed to western New York in early life and before 1795 he had accomplished the journey to Palmyra twice, first on foot, the next time on horseback. At the first town meeting held in Palmyra in April, 1796, he was elected pathmaster and fence viewer. The earmark for his stock was recorded the same year and he was also constable. His farm was in the western part of Palmyra, the district set off as Macedon in 1827. He cleared a farm there which was later occupied by his son Nahum.

Married (1) **Mrs. MARTHA (COTTLE) WHITE,** born on Martha's Vineyard, Mass., about 1755, died October 17, 1811. She was the daughter of Benjamin and Sarah (Smith) Cottle and married (1) about 1775, in Williamsburg or Chesterfield, Mass., David White, born in Weymouth, Mass., February 25, 1753, died in Palmyra, N. Y., 1793, the first funeral in the town. He was the son of Ezekiel and Abigail (Blanchard) White. David and Martha (Cottle) White had children: David, m. Berthena Clark; Benjamin, d. young; William, M.D.; James, M.D., m. Rosamond Warner (see number 235); Salome, m. Otis Turner; Martha; Orrin and Orpheus (twins).

Married (2) December 24, 1814, **Mrs. RUTH (ROGERS) PORTER,** who died December 24, 1821. She was the widow of Noah Porter, stepson of Stephen[5] Warner, number 124. He was one of the three single men who, with Webb Harwood, went from the Berkshires in Massachusetts to Palmyra, N. Y., in 1789.

Married (3) June 27, 1822, **Mrs. DULCENA (CARPENTER) STETSON,** born in Hardwick, Mass., December 28, 1785, died September 25, 1866. She was the widow of Elisha Stetson.

Children of David and Martha (Cottle-White) Warner

Laura Warner, b. 1796; m. (1) Bela Turner, who died about 1821, son of Captain Noah and Martha (Bisbee) Turner, and brother of Otis Turner, who m. Salome White (see above). Child: Laura. Laura (Warner) Turner m. (2) Samuel Beal of Cummington, Mass., by whom she had seven children: David; Dulcena; Orpheus; Harriet; Albert; Charles; Warner.

380 *Nahum Warner,* b. Oct. 12, 1799; m. Hannah Fish.

Child of David and Ruth (Rogers-Porter) Warner

Mary Warner.

225 ELIJAH[6] WARNER, JR., son of Elijah[5] and Submit (Wells) Warner, born in Hardwick, Mass., June 10, 1767; died December 29, 1844, in Plainfield. He settled in the south part of Plainfield on the farm later occupied by his sons Wells and Cushing and his daughter Janette. The Census of 1800 records him there with his family. On September 9, 1800, he was one of the committee appointed by the town to secure provisions for the soldiers at the general muster in Northampton. In October, 1798, it was voted that Elijah Warner be directed to "collect flax sufficient to purchase the town stock of led." He served the town as selectman in 1804, 1809-13, 1815-8, 1819-24, 1830-1; was representative of the town in the General Court at Boston in 1821 and 1827; was appointed Justice of the Peace in 1828 and held

18

that office until his death. He was one of the first to be buried in an early cemetery in the southeast part of the town.

Married in Cummington, Mass., October 4, 1795, **BETSEY MITCHELL**, daughter of William[4] and Elizabeth (Ward) Mitchell (Experience[1], Edward[2], Col. Edward[3]) of Cummington, and a lineal descendant of two of the signers of the Mayflower compact, Francis Cook and Gov. William Bradford.

Children, born in Plainfield, Mass.

Elizabeth (Betsey) Warner, b. Aug. 27, 1796; m. as second wife, Dec. 23, 1830, Simeon Streeter of Cummington. Children: i. Francis Dwight, b. 1832. ii. Ellen Elizabeth, b. 1835. iii. Clark Warner, b. 1837.

381 *James Warner*, b. July 23, 1798; m. Fidelia Whiton.

Melancia Warner, b. July 8, 1800; d. in Plainfield, Nov. 3, 1884; m. as his third wife, Apr. 26, 1853, Lemuel Howlett of Hartford, Conn. No children.

Cushing Warner, b. Sept. 16, 1802; d. May 2, 1882, not married. He resided on the homestead farm. The Warner brothers were engaged also in the manufacture of brick, and, about 1830, had a factory for making satinets and custom work. This enterprise was continued only a few years.

382 *William Warner*, b. Aug. 9, 1804; m. (1) Annis Crittenden, (2) Mrs. Polly Packard Whitmarsh Latham.

Elijah Warner, 3d, b. Sept. 21, 1806; d. in Plainfield, Aug. 11, 1889; m. Jan. 11, 1844, Mary Ann Shaw, b. June 22, 1811, d. Dec. 24, 1888, daughter of Josiah Jr., and Lydia (Noyes) Shaw of Plainfield. They had no children.

Wells Warner, b. Dec. 12, 1808; d. May 10, 1882; not married; resided on the homestead in Plainfield.

Roswell H. Warner, b. Jan. 30, 1812; d. in 1890; m. May 11, 1846, Maria A. Chapman, who was born Aug., 1824, and died before 1890. They resided in Dalton, Mass. Child: Ellen E., b. Aug. 22, 1851; d. Aug. 31, 1865.

Janette Warner, b. Sept. 20, 1819; never married; resided at the homestead with her brothers, and, after they died, with her nephew, Clark W. Streeter, in Plainfield.

226 GILES[6] WARNER, son of Elijah[5] and Submit (Wells) Warner, born in Hardwick, Mass., December 3, 1771; died there, November 20, 1847; buried at Hardwick Center. He was a farmer and inherited his father's homestead.

Married (1) May 4, 1809, **BETSEY SAMPSON**, born 1774, died January 18, 1823, daughter of John and Rachel (Whitcomb) Sampson.

Married (2) April 20, 1824, **MARY STAPLES** of Prescott, Mass., who died November 28, 1862, aged 66. She was the daughter of Elias Staples.

Children by first wife

383 *Rachel Whitcomb Warner,* b. May 14, 1811; m. Loring Gilbert.
(*Infant*), b. Sept. 4, 1813; d. aged one month.

Children by second wife, born in Hardwick

Mary Abigail Warner, b. Feb. 7, 1825; d. Nov. 28, 1847; m. in Hardwick, Apr. 24, 1845, Charles Hathaway, b. in Boston, son of Jeremiah, Jr., and Sally (————) Hathaway. He was a bricklayer.
Betsey Sampson Warner, b. Mar. 3, 1827; d. Sept. 11, 1828.
Francis Giles Warner, b. Apr. 13, 1829; d. in Hardwick, Sept. 12, 1863. He was a farmer and inherited his father's homestead. Married (intentions dated Dec. 20, 1851) Louisa Sturdevant, who was born in Hardwick. Children, b. in Hardwick: i. Clarence Alfred, b. Apr. 26, 1852; d. in Hardwick, Apr. 28, 1873, not married. ii. Mary (or Fanny) Louisa, b. July 9, 1861; m. C. Wyman of Orange, Mass.
Caroline Maria Warner, b. Nov. 9, 1832 (or 1831); d. Dec. 4, 1893; m. (1) in Hardwick, Dec. 13, 1848, West Paige, b. in Hardwick, Aug. 23, 1817, d. there, Sept. 4, 1853. He was a farmer and trader and kept a livery stable in Hardwick. He was son of Stephen West and Lucy (Ruggles) Paige. She m. (2) Aug. 23, 1859, Henry Paige, a merchant of Providence, R. I., b. Apr. 5, 1829, son of Martin and Mary A. (Billings) Paige. Children of Henry and Caroline (Warner) Paige: i. George Warner, b. June 2, 1860. ii. Mary Staples, b. Mar. 26, 1864. iii. Caroline Maria, b. in Providence, Oct. 26, 1865.
George Elias Warner, b. May 29, 1834; resided in Palmer, Mass., and was a conductor of the Ware River R. R.; m. Oct. 24, 1865, Delia Cowan, daughter of John Cowan of Prescott, Mass. Children: i. Mary, b. July 28, 1871, in Ware, Mass. ii. George Loring, b. Nov. 18, 1882, is a graduate of Tufts College
James Loring Warner, b. Feb. 16, 1837; d. Feb. 18, 1874, not married.

227 **ELECTA[6] WARNER,** daughter of Elijah[5] and Submit (Wells) Warner, born in Hardwick, Mass., baptized there, September 15, 1776; died in Phillipston, Mass., March 4, 1864.

Married March 25, 1798, **SIMEON H. WHITE** of Phillipston, where they later resided. He died April 24, 1854.

Children

Electa White, b. Apr. 16, 1799; m. June 11, 1823, Abel Piper, 2d.
Howard (1) *White,* b. Oct. 31, 1801; d. Sept. 5, 1803.
Howard (2) *White,* b. Dec. 27, 1803; d. Nov. 9, 1833.
Rosamond White, b. Aug. 8, 1806; m. Mar. 10, 1827, Stephen S. Maynard.
Windsor White, b. Dec. 2, 1808; m. (int.) Sept. 6, 1834, Betsy Pierce of Petersham.
Rebeccah White, b. Dec. 28, 1810; m. Mar. 1, 1838, Daniel Witt of Templeton.
Elijah White, b. May 13, 1813; m. in Barre, Dec. 12, 1843, Abigail J. Brown.
Harriet White, b. Oct. 21, 1815; d. Sept. 6, 1838.

228 PERSIS[6] WARNER, daughter of Elijah[5] and Submit (Wells) Warner, born in Hardwick, Mass., August 17, 1783, or 1784; died at Hawley, Mass., October 23 or 27, 1853, aged 70. The History of Hawley gives a record of this family.

Married January 21, 1806, Col. **NOAH JOY,** born in Plainfield, Mass., February 27, 1782. He removed to Hawley soon after his marriage and settled in the south part of the town, where he built a hotel, which was known as Joy's Tavern and was conducted by him until his death, May 23, 1843. He was postmaster of South Hawley.

Children, born in Hawley

Laura Joy, b. Oct. 29, 1806; d. Aug. 31, 1861; m. Samuel T. Grout.
Annis Joy, b. Oct. 8, 1808; d. Jan. 17, 1857; m. Levi Holden, Jr.
Eliza Joy, b. Dec. 11, 1810; d. Feb. 13, 1892; m. Calvin S. Longley.
Hannah Joy, b. Sept. 15, 1812; resided in Shelburne Falls; m. Ashbel W. Carter.
Merrick Joy, b. Dec. 27, 1814; d. June 12, 1840.
Lorenzo W. Joy, b. Dec. 15, 1817; d. Aug. 28, 1895; was postmaster of Northampton, Mass., for some years.
Nelson Joy, b. Jan. 17, 1820; d. July 5, 1896; resided in Shelburne Falls; m. Mahaleth King.
Henry C. Joy, b. Aug. 5, 1823; d. Nov. 10, 1903; resided in Shelburne Falls; m. Jerusha King.
Mariette Taylor Joy, b. Apr. 6, 1830; m. —— Smith; was living in Malden, Mass., in 1904.

229 PATTY[6] WARNER, daughter of Elijah[5] and Submit (Wells) Warner, born in Hardwick, Mass., July 21, 1782, according to one record; died in Macedon, N. Y., August 10, 1834.

Married in Macedon, as second wife, November 17, 1814, **ISAAC DURFEE,** born in Tiverton, R. I., November 21, 1785; died in Macedon, September 2, 1855. He was son of Lemuel[5] and Prudence (Hathaway) Durfee, (Gideon[4], Job[3], Thomas[2], Thomas[1]). He married (1) Polly Cole (and had children, Hiram, Phebe, Philena and Benjamin C.) and (3) Mrs. Anna (Smith) Hoag.

Children of Isaac and Patty (Warner) Durfee

Pardon W. Durfee, b. Nov. 11, 1815; d. Jan. 18, 1817.
Elijah Warner Durfee, b. in Macedon, Feb. 27, 1817; d. in Litchfield, Mich., Dec. 30, 1875; m. in Medina, Mich., July 1, 1846, Mary Jane Kennedy. Children, none of whom ever married: i. Danforth E., b. in Macedon, May 6, 1849; d. in Litchfield, Mich., Mar. 7, 1900. ii. Earl W., b. in Macedon, Aug. 24, 1850; d. in Litchfield, Sept. 9, 1917. iii. Warner A., b. in Litchfield, Mich., Jan. 14, 1857; d. Feb. 24, 1894. iv. Mary Prudence, b. in Litchfield, Feb. 10, 1863. v. Roland, b. in Litchfield, Jan. 4, 1868.
Stephen Durfee, b. in Macedon, Aug. 6, 1818; d. Dec. 19, 1880; m.

Oct. 4, 1843, Mary Jane Burton of Rochester, N. Y., who died in Macedon, Mar. 24, 1907. Child: Burton Stephen, b. in Macedon, Apr. 2, 1845; d. Oct., 1911; m. Nov. 29, 1871, Elizabeth Jane Eves; had two children: i. Charles Reuben, b. in Macedon, Apr. 27, 1873; resides in Macedon; m. Jan. 11, 1893, Grace A. Herendeen, and has three children, Byron Herendeen, b. May 8, 1896, Edwin Burton, b. Feb. 28, 1900, and Helen Elizabeth, b. May 27, 1906. ii. Mary Eves, b. in Macedon, Mar. 24, 1880; m. Mar. 24, 1903, Willard Hicks Allen, resides in Macedon; has four children, Parke Clifford, b. July 18, 1905, Edith Mary, b. Dec. 28, 1908, Burton Willard, b. May 11, 1911, and Bernice Elizabeth, b. 1913.

Mary Durfee, b. in Macedon, Jan. 25, 1820; m. Feb. 13, 1850, Lorenzo Cook[8] Warner; see number 563.

Isaac Durfee, Jr., b. in Macedon, Mar. 10, 1822; d. Sept. 17, 1885, not married.

Lemuel Durfee, b. in Macedon, July 1, 1825; d. May 30, 1874, not married.

230 RACHEL[6] WARNER, daughter of Elijah[5] and Rachel (Sampson) Warner, born in Hardwick, Mass., October 6, 1787; died October 6, 1863, buried in Hardwick.

Married April 2, 1811, **JOSEPH ROBINSON,** born June 20, 1796; died October 23, 1854, buried in Hardwick. He was the son of Joseph and Lucy (Ruggles) Robinson and was descended from Thomas Robinson who settled in Scituate in 1640. Thomas Robinson was probably the son of the celebrated Rev. John Robinson who came from Leyden to be pastor of the Pilgrims of Plymouth in 1620. Paige's History of Hardwick gives many references to this family. Joseph Robinson was a farmer, selectman for three years, cultivated the old General Warner farm in the center of town, where he also kept a tavern, and later bought a farm on the road to Ware, about two and three-quarters miles from the Common, where he spent the rest of his life.

Children, born in Hardwick

Joseph Warner Robinson, b. Sept. 1, 1814.

Elijah Warner Robinson, b. Jan. 31, 1821; m. Oct. 23, 1855, Elizabeth Eunice Clark, daughter of Asa Clark.

Jason Mixter Robinson, b. Oct. 6, 1826; resided on his father's homestead.

Harriet Jane Robinson, b. Apr. 6, 1831; d. Sept. 16, 1869; m. (1) Apr. 5, 1849, William Browning, who died Mar. 16, 1858, and (2) Apr. 5, 1866, Albert E. Knight.

Sarah Maria Robinson, b. 1834; m. June 20, 1854, Joseph R. Robinson.

Ella Frances Robinson, name given in one list, but not in History of Hardwick.

231 JOSEPH[6] WARNER, son of Joseph[5] and Mary (Whipple) Warner, born in Cummington, Mass, September 29, 1788;

died there, May 10, 1864. He was a farmer and resided on the homestead in Cummington. He is reputed a kindly and benevolent man. August 14, 1814, he was elected lieutenant of a company in a regiment of cavalry of the 2d Brigade, 4th Division, Massachusetts Militia, and on January 31, 1818, received his commission, which is still preserved in the family. On March 3, 1819, he was elected to be captain of a company in the regiment of cavalry, in the 2d Brigade, 4th Division, Militia of the Commonwealth of Massachusetts. At the organization of the village church in Cummington in 1836, Joseph Warner was on the first standing committee. His will of April 25, 1862, appointed his son, John Franklin, executor. · `

Married December, 1812, **OLIVE HOLBROOK,** born October 18, 1790, died December 22, 1874, daughter of Amos and Lydia (Owen) Holbrook of Windsor, Mass., and granddaughter of David Holbrook, a Revolutionary soldier of Sherburne (now Holden), Mass., and of Daniel Owen of Gloucester, R. I., who was at one time deputy governor of the state and prominent in its affairs during Revolutionary times. Amos Holbrook died December 15, 1820. His wife Lydia Owen was born May 27, 1764.

Children, born in Cummington

384 *Lydia Owen Warner,* b. Aug. 8, 1813; m. William Nelson Ford.
  Francis Joseph Warner, b. Sept. 11, 1815; d. in Philadelphia, Pa., July 2, 1864, not married. He was a graduate of Union College and was an Episcopal minister in Philadelphia.
385 *Franklin John Warner,* b. Mar. 12, 1818; m. Vesta Wales Reed.
386 *Sumner Holbrook Warner,* b. Mar. 12, 1821; m. (1) Delia Hubbard, (2) Sarah Elizabeth Chappell, (3) Emily Robinson, (4) Marietta Flower.
387 *Mary Ann Warner,* b. June 30, 1823; m. Luther Martin Packard.
  Lavinia Swan Warner, b. Oct. 28, 1829; d. June 7, 1868; m. (1) Dec. 25, 1853, Watson D. Shaw of Detroit, Mich., (2) June 16, 1858, William S. Pierce of Williamsburg, Mass., a widower with one child.

232 **ELIZABETH**[6] or **BETSEY WARNER,** daughter of Stephen[5] and Lois (Goss) Warner, born June 11, 1769; resided in Cummington, Mass., and Baldwinsville, N. Y. She was a woman of great personal beauty, unusual intellectual endowments and eminent piety.

Married in 1792, **JONAS CUTLER BALDWIN,** born January 3, 1769, probably in Weston, Mass., settled in Baldwinsville, N. Y., which took its name from him, and died there March, 1827. He was the son of Samuel and Millicent (Cutler) Baldwin. Jonas C. Baldwin was educated at Williams College and studied medicine. He was a man of high intelligence, indomitable

energy and liberal views and enjoyed the confidence of the whole
community. For further references, see the Baldwin Genealogy.

Children

Betsey Baldwin, resided at East Hill, Onondaga County, N. Y.; m.
John Brown. Children: i. Cutler, d. at Seneca Lake. ii. Mary, m.
——— Townsend, and had a son who was a graduate of West Point.
iii. Emmett, d. at Seneca Lake, leaving children. iv. Martha, m.
Thomas Dorwin and d. at Onondaga, leaving no children.
Stephen Warner Baldwin, d. at Baldwinsville; married. Children:
i. Isaac, resided at Baldwinsville. ii. Stephen, resided in Brooklyn.
iii. Frank, resided in Baldwinsville. iv. Mary, m. and lived in New
York City. v. Adele.
Harvey Baldwin, b. in Ovid, Onondaga County, N. Y.; intended to
study law, but, prior to the War of 1812, entered a class in military
science and was shortly after elected officer of the militia. His
regiment was a few days later called to the defence of Oswego,
where his father and elder brother had already gone in command of
a flotilla of boats that had just been completed. He was later promoted to captain. After the war he studied law and began practice
in Syracuse in 1826. His father's large property was embarrassed
from difficulties growing out of the war and Harvey and his brother
Stephen took up the care of it. This led to the real estate business
and at one time he was conducting the largest real estate business in
Central New York. Harvey Baldwin was one of the originators of
the common school system and of the state Agricultural Society. He
wrote and spoke untiringly of the acquisition of Texas, and as early
as 1840 wrote to President Van Buren urging the purchase of California. Harvey Baldwin was the first mayor of Syracuse and was
the unsuccessful candidate for Congress on the Democratic ticket.
His children were Burnett P., Irving D. and Harvey.
Harriet Baldwin, b. 1798; d. 1864; m. 1819, Silas Wallace, M.D., bapt.
July 17, 1790, d. Mar. 29, 1864, son of Ebenezer and Ann (Snow)
Wallace of Lunenburg, Mass. He was a physician and practiced in
Baldwinsville for many years. Children: i. Linneus A. ii. Jonas C.
iii. Silas W., d. young.
Horace Baldwin, b. Mar. 11, 1801, went to Galveston, Texas, in 1839,
and d. there in 1850; m. Nov. 9, 1823, Maria Wallace, b. Oct. 20, 1802,
d. in Texas, Feb. 16, 1868, daughter of Ebenezer and Anna (Snow)
Wallace. Children: i. Delia Ann, resided in Washington. ii. Julia
Elizabeth, m. (1) J. H. Brown of Houston, Texas, (2) William M.
Reed; no children. iii. Jonas Cutler, b. Oct. 10, 1829, resided in
Houston; m. E. A. Foote of Cleveland, daughter of Judge Horace
Foote; had a daughter Mary, who m. Jan. 22, 1884, William F. Hunt-
ington of Cleveland, son of John Huntington. iv. Charlotte Maria,
m. (1) John Randen of Texas and had a daughter Elizabeth; m.
(2) F. A. Rice, who went to Houston in 1850, and had children,
Joseph, William M., Baldwin, David, Frederick, Benjamin B., George,
Minnie and Lillie.
Charlotte Baldwin, m. ——— Allen and settled in Texas. Child: Eliza,
m. James Converse, who went from Ravenna, Ohio, to Houston,
Texas, and had a son Pierce.
Austin Baldwin, d. in California, not married.

233 STEPHEN⁶ WARNER, son of Stephen⁵ Warner and Mary (Norton) Porter, born in Cummington, Mass., April 18, 1778; died in Palmyra, Lenawee Co, Mich., February 23, 1850. He resided in Cummington until August, 1831, when he removed with his family to Palmyra, Michigan. In Cummington he held several minor town offices.

Married March 9, 1802, **CLARISSA MITCHELL,** born August 10, 1785; died at the home of her daughter, Mrs. Laura M. Bement, in Toledo, Ohio, December 17, 1869. She was the daughter of William Mitchell of Bridgewater and Cummington and a lineal descendant of two signers of the Mayflower Compact, Francis Cook and Gov. William Bradford. After her husband's death she resided in Toledo, with her daughter.

Children, born in Cummington

Eliza Warner, b. Apr. 27, 1803; d. Sept. 7, 1852; m. (1) Oct. 10, 1825, Dr. Cassius Robinson of Palmyra, N. Y. Child: Lucius G., m. and had two sons, Cassius G. and George, both of whom are living in Detroit, Mich. Cassius G. Robinson has two daughters, Hazel and Gladys. Eliza Warner married (2) Henry Brown Pomeroy, b. Oct. 26, 1809, d. Aug. 24, 1852, of cholera, a month before the death of his wife from the same disease.

388 *Mary Ann Warner,* b. Jan. 31, 1805; m. Lieut. Nahum Whitmarsh.

389 *Clarissa Mitchell Warner,* b. Mar. 16, 1807; m. Horace Whitmarsh.

390 *Norton Dexter Warner,* b. Sept. 2, 1809; m. Silena Shaw.

Cassius Pomeroy Warner, b. Jan. 10, 1812; d. in California, Jan. 26, 1892; m. Calista Hotchkiss. Child: Amelia.

Stephen Warner, b. Apr. 2, 1814; d. in Toledo, Ohio, Jan. 29, 1903; m. Apr., 1844, Suzanna Warren. Children: i. Clara, d. in Toledo, Ohio, about 1872; m. Charles Green, and had a son, James D. ii. Helen, d. in infancy.

391 *Laura M. Warner,* b. May 12, 1816; m. Samuel Bement.

Rosamond Pomeroy Warner, b. Sept. 21, 1818; d. May 22, 1901, in Toledo, Ohio; m. Oct. 27, 1841, James S. Dickinson, who died June 1, 1899; no children.

392 *Lucius Warner,* b. Mar. 9, 1821; m. Lydia Whitmarsh.

Lewis Warner, b. Oct. 24, 1823; d. about 1850; m. Helen Strong. Child: Helen, d. in childhood.

William M. Warner, b. Oct. 23, 1826; d. in Cleveland, Ohio, about 1898; m. Oct. 12, 1852, Celia Wadsworth. Children: Emma; Frank.

George Warner, b. June 24, 1830; d. Oct. 26, 1842.

234 NANCY⁶ WARNER, daughter of Stephen⁵ Warner and Mary (Norton) Porter, born October 16, 1781, probably in Cummington, Mass.; died October 31, 1841, in Illinois. She was a teacher in Cummington in 1799.

Married November 26, 1801, **PHILANDER FOBES,** born in

Bridgewater, Mass., September 24, 1773; died in Illinois, September 11, 1858. He was the son of. Jason and Leah (Washburn) Fobes. In 1799 he was supercargo and part owner of a merchant ship. On one of his voyages from Massachusetts to the West Indies, his vessel was boarded by pirates, and only his personal courage and ability prevented the loss of his vessel. At the time of his marriage he was in business in Windsor, Mass., but not long after this he went to Dalton, Mass., and from there to Onondaga, N. Y. Here he remained for some years, except for a residence in Albany from 1814 to 1820. In 1836 they removed to Illinois, as a change of climate seemed desirable for his wife's health. Both of them died in that state.

Children

Aurelia Fobes, b. in Dalton, Mass., Sept. 30, 1802; d. June 14, 1875; m. July 1, 1824, Rev. Luke Lyons. Children: i. Henry Martyn, b. in Esperance, N. Y., Apr. 11, 1825; d. in Chicago, Ill., Oct. 1, 1885. ii. and iii. twins, died in infancy. iv. Mary Aurelia, b. in Cortland, N. Y., Nov. 25, 1829; m. Aug. 12, 1862, Rev. George R. Moore. v. Harriet Maria, b. in Rochester, N. Y., Aug. 13, 1832; m. Oct. 11, 1859, John N. Crawford. vi. Charles Edward, b. Mar. 15, 1834; d. Jan. 20, 1837. vii. Heber Trowbridge, b. July 1, 1836; d. 1871. viii. Seward Fobes, b. Aug. 27, 1840; d. Nov. 21, 1840. ix. Edward Warner, b. Oct. 24, 1841; d. Oct. 31, 1858. x. Theodore Luke, b. May 31, 1844; d. Jan. 22, 186–.

Cordelia Fobes, b. in Onondaga, N. Y., Dec. 11, 1806; d. in Chicago, Ill., Dec. 31, 1888.

Celina Fobes, b. in Onondaga, Feb. 10, 1809; d. Oct. 2, 1843; m. Mar. 9, 1837, Andrew Alexander of Philadelphia. Child: Ellen Cordelia, b. Dec. 26, 1837, who is now (1916) in Chicago, but had lived in Philadelphia. She is a member of the D. A. R. and has furnished material regarding this branch of the family for this book.

Philena Fobes, b. in Onondaga, Sept. 10, 1811; d. in Philadelphia, Pa., Nov. 8, 1898. For more than twenty-five years she was principal of the Monticello Seminary, Godfrey, Ill.

Philander Warner Fobes, b. in Onondaga, Mar. 10, 1814; d. at Rockledge, Fla., Mar. 30, 1893. He studied law with Harvey Baldwin of Syracuse, attended lectures in Albany, was admitted to the bar, and later made his home in Syracuse, N. Y. Married 1857, Mary C. Gallagher, daughter of Rev. Joseph Gallagher of Bloomfield, N. J. Children: i. Mary Aurelia, b. in Moffat, Scotland, Mar. 27, 1858; d. Apr. 15, 1880; was a graduate of Mt. Holyoke Seminary. ii. Joseph Warner, b. Mar. 18, 1860; is a Presbyterian minister in Peacedale, R. I. iii. Susan Cordelia, b. in Syracuse, Jan. 7, 1862; d. Dec. 26, 1892; m. 1889, James Fitch. iv. Philena, b. Dec. 23, 1864; m. Sept. 1888, Prof. Henry Burchard Fine, b. in Chambersburg, Pa., Sept. 14, 1858, a graduate of Princeton, 1880, and of Leipzig, 1885, professor of mathematics at Princeton and author of several mathematical works. v. Robert Townsend, b. in Syracuse, Dec. 27, 1867; d. Nov. 23, 1872.

vi. Alan Cutler, b. in Syracuse, Sept. 9, 1869; was mayor of that
city in 1906.
Mary Elizabeth Fobes, b. in Albany, N. Y., July 3, 1820; d. Feb. 26,
1894; m. Apr. 19, 1839, Benjamin L. Yates. Child: Henry. Ward,
b. 1840.

235 ROSAMOND[6] WARNER, daughter of Stephen[5] Warner and Mary (Norton) Porter, born August 12, 1786, probably
in Cummington, Mass.; died in Buffalo, N. Y., September 22,
1859. She was a teacher in Cummington before her marriage.
Married February 16, 1812, JAMES WHITE, M.D., of Palmyra, N. Y., born 1789, son of David White, a Revolutionary
soldier, and Martha Cottle, and grandson of Ezekiel and Abigail
(Blanchard) White. (See number 224.) They made their
wedding journey to Palmyra, on horseback. A photograph of
the bride copied from a miniature painted at the time is one of
the valued possessions of the family. They resided in Palmyra
until after the births of their children, when they removed to
Black Rock, now a part of Buffalo, N. Y., and spent the
remainder of their days there.

Children

Mary Warner White, b. Nov. 24, 1813; d. in Buffalo, 1861; m. Feb.,
1832, Philo Durfee. Children: i. Maria Louise, b. Apr. 10, 1834;
d. Mar. 23, 1843. ii. Mary Sophia, b. Apr. 12, 1836; lives in Cali
fornia. iii. Fenton, b. Mar. 3, 1838. iv. Rosamond White, b. Oct. 19,
1840. v. Cynthia Lakey, b. Mar. 10, 1843. vi. Elizabeth White, b.
Feb. 11, 1845; d. about 1896. vii. Maria Townsend, b. Sept. 17, 1847;
d. about 1903. viii. Frank, b. Nov. 4, 1849. ix. Philo P., b. about
1853.
Orpheus White, b. May 20, 1815; was drowned at Palmyra, N. Y., 1828.
Rosamond Pomeroy White, b. Dec. 10, 1819; d. in Germantown, Pa.,
Jan. 5, 1855; m. Sept. 19, 1850, Dr. George Johnson of Buffalo, N. Y.
Child: Lydia Burwell, b. in Buffalo, July 22, 1851; m. Apr. 11, 1876,
William James White of Philadelphia, and had six children: Lucia
Burwell, b. May 10, 1877, d. Feb. 14, 1878; Lulu Johnson, b. Mar. 11,
1879, d. Dec. 14, 1899; Blanche Warrington, b. Sept. 8, 1881; Rosa-
mond Pomeroy, b. Dec. 24, 1884, d. Sept. 3, 1887; Florence Warren,
b. June 27, 1889; and William Richard, b. Nov. 13, 1893.
James White, Jr., b. Apr. 1, 1821; d. in Buffalo, N. Y.; m. Catherine
Callender of Buffalo. Children: i. Hattie. ii. Charles, d. about 1890.
iii. Warren Peregrine. iv. William James, who is married and has
children, Warren Goodrich, of Buffalo, N. Y., Myra S., Charles and
Lucia Virginia.
Elizabeth White, b. Sept. 17, 1823; m. John R. Kennedy and resides
in Buffalo. Children: Helen Cornelia, Elizabeth.
Stephen Warner White, b. Jan. 1, 1827.
Henry Kirk White, b. Nov., 1832; d. in childhood.

236 ORRIN⁶ WARNER, son of Moses⁵ and Molly (Ward) Warner, born in Cummington, Mass, July 3, 1791; died September 15, 1863, probably in Palmyra, N. Y., to which place he had removed before 1817.

Married (1) February 13, 1817 (intentions published at Williamsburg, Mass., January 12, 1817), **LUCINDA STARKS,** born June 23, 1791; died November 15, 1824.

Married (2) June 3, 1825, **DELIA MC LOUTH,** born August 29, 1800; died March 27, 1848.

Married (3) May 29, 1850, **MARY DAVENPORT,** born February 13, 1829; died January 12, 1860.

Children by first wife

393 *William Starks Warner,* b. Dec. 23, 1817; m. Hepsy Page.

Sarah A. Warner, b. Apr. 8, 1820; d. Dec. 27, 1886; m. John Clark Reed, son of Daniel Reed of Cummington. Children: William Warner; Maria Adella; Rozalia Gale; Emory Clinton; Jennie Luella.

Artemas W. Warner, b. in Palmyra, N. Y., May 25, 1822; d. in Kankakee, Ill., where he had resided. Married Mary Coon. It is thought that she removed to Kansas with her children after his death. Children: Sarah E.; Leora Jane; Alice; Seth; William.

Children by second wife

Lucinda Warner, b. Feb. 12, 1826; d. May 25, 1889; buried in Palmyra, N. Y.; m. (1) Thomas Joslyn, by whom she had one son, Hiram, who lived at one time in Iowa. She married (2) July 6, 1869, William Ambrose⁷ Warner of Cummington, son of Norman⁶ and Elvira (Hartwell) Warner, b. Apr. 11, 1828, d. Apr. 22, 1900; see number 237.

Orrin (1) *Warner,* b. Feb. 1, 1828; d. Feb. 17, 1828.

394 *Orrin* (2) *Warner,* b. Jan. 14, 1829; m. (1) Mary Elizabeth Eastwood, (2) Sally Ann Carter.

Wealthy Warner, b. Apr. 30, 1831; m. William Ponsonby, and resided in Chicago, Ill. Children: i. Marietta, m. George Collins and has two children, Belle and Grace. ii. Harriet, died.

Azuriah Thayer (1) *Warner,* b. June 10, 1833; d. Aug. 31, 1834.

Azuriah Thayer (2) *Warner,* b. Mar. 4, 1835; d. Apr. 2, 1842.

Polly Warner, b. Dec. 18, 1837; d. June 4, 1840.

Peletiah West Warner, b. Apr. 19, 1840; lived in Chicopee, Mass.; m. Nov. 23, 1870, Emily Maria⁷ Warner, b. May 17, 1843, daughter of Norman⁶ and Elvira (Hartwell) Warner, number 237. Children: i. Albert Hartwell, b. Jan. 17, 1872. ii. Mattie Elvira, b. Apr. 19, 1877.

George S. Warner, b. Aug. 9, 1842; d. Apr. 5, 1843.

237 NORMAN⁶ WARNER, son of Moses⁵ and Abigail (Colton) Warner, born in Cummington, Mass., April 4, 1801; died November 10, 1880. On May 31, 1826, he received a commission as ensign of a company in the Massachusetts Militia, 2d Brigade,

4th Division; was elected lieutenant, May 1, 1827; resigned January 8, 1833.

Married March 15, 1827, **ELVIRA HARTWELL,** who died July 17, 1881. She was the daughter of William Hartwell who served as captain in the War of 1812, and his wife, Deborah Shepard of Chesterfield, Mass.

Children

William Ambrose Warner, b. Apr. 11, 1828; d. Apr. 22, 1900; m. July 6, 1869, Lucinda[7] (Warner) Joslyn, b. Feb. 12, 1826, d. May 25, 1889, daughter of Orrin[6] and Delia (McLouth) Warner; see number 236.
395 *Martha Elvira Warner,* b. Jan. 22, 1831; m. Horatio A. Loud.
Emily Maria Warner, b. May 17, 1843; m. Nov. 23, 1870, Peletiah West[7] Warner, b. Apr. 19, 1840, son of Orrin[6] and Delia (McLouth) Warner (number 236); resides in Chicopee, Mass. Children: i. Albert Hartwell, b. Jan. 17, 1872. ii. Mattie Elvira, b. Apr. 19, 1877.
Orrin Hartwell Warner, b. Oct. 15, 1845; is not married.

238   LOVICE[6] WARNER, daughter of Jonathan[5] and Elizabeth (Selden) Warner, born in Hadlyme, Conn., December 26, 1751; died there, May 22, 1777.

Married in Hadlyme, February 14, 1776, **ROBERT HUNGERFORD, JR.,** born in East Haddam, January 23, 1751-2; died in Hadlyme, town of East Haddam. He was the son of Capt. Robert Hungerford who went to Boston on the Lexington Alarm, and his wife, Grace Holmes. Robert, Jr., served in the Revolution and was a lieutenant in the Continental Army. He resided in Hadlyme and married (2) Olive Ely, by whom he had seven children, one of whom, Joseph Ely Hungerford, married Nancy Anderson and had a son, Joseph William Hungerford, who married Sarah Frances[8] Warner. See number 402.

Child of Robert and Lovice (Warner) Hungerford

Robert Hungerford, 3d, b. Jan. 17, 1777.

239   JONATHAN[6] WARNER, son of Jonathan[5] and Elizabeth (Selden) Warner, born June 17, 1756, in Chester, Conn.; died there, March 14, 1828. He was a farmer and ship-builder and had an interest in coast trading vessels. The 1800 Census of Chester records him with a family consisting of one male and one female over 45, one male between 26 and 45, one male and two females between 16 and 26, two males and one female between 10 and 16, and a boy and girl under 10. Jonathan Warner, with his wife and daughter Hepsibah, joined the Congregational Church at Chester, July 3, 1803. He acted as agent for the fourth Ecclesiastical Society of Saybrook, May 5, 1825, in the sale of some property. His will mentions wife Lucy, sons Jonathan, Ely and George, daughters Anna Pratt and Louisa Warner.

Married (1) in 1778, HEPSIBAH ELY, daughter of Joseph and Rebecca (Selden) Ely of Hadlyme, born October 22, 1753 or 1754; died April 2, 1820.

Married (2) LUCY ————, who survived him and inherited a share of his property.

Children, born in Chester

 Anna Warner, b. Nov. 18, 1778; d. 1869; resided in Chester. She joined the Congregational Church in Chester, Apr. 10, 1803. Married 1817, Joel Pratt of Saybrook.

 Hepsibah Warner, b. Sept. 12, 1780; d. in Chester, Dec. 13, 1810.

396 *Jonathan Warner*, b. Dec. 11, 1782; m. Nancy Frethy.

397 *Ely Warner*, b. May 22, 1785; m. Sarah Ward[8] Warner.

 Thomas Warner, b. Aug. 22, 1787; d. in Chester, Jan. 2, 1808 (or 1811), not married.

 Phebe Warner, b. Nov. 21, 1790; d. Sept. 2, 1811.

 Louisa Warner (has been sometimes printed as Lovicie), b. July 25, 1793; resided with her brother Ely in Chester in 1860; d. in Chester, Apr. 6, 1870, not married.

 George W. Warner, b. Nov. 29, 1796; d. Dec. 27 or 29, 1824, not married.

240 **SELDEN**[6] **WARNER**, son of Jonathan[5] and Elizabeth (Selden) Warner, born October 20, 1760, in Hadlyme, Conn.; died there, March 1, 1843, of paralysis. He was a farmer in Hadlyme; graduated from Yale College in 1782; was living in New London County at the time of the 1790 Census with his wife and two sons. Mr. Warner represented his town several times in the State Legislature. He and his wife were members of the Congregational Church at Hadlyme, and he was a deacon until 1833 when he asked to be excused from further duty. He was a captain in the 33d Regiment, 3d Brigade, Connecticut Militia, about 1799.

Married June 5, 1788, **DOROTHY SELDEN**, born December 26, 1766, died August 19, 1825, daughter of Col. Samuel and Elizabeth (Ely) Selden of Hadlyme.

The record in East Haddam of the marriage of Selden Warner of Lyme to Elizabeth Spencer, January 4, 1827, may be a second marriage of this Selden.

Children, births of first six recorded in the town records of Lyme, Conn.

398 *Selden Warner, Jr.*, name changed to *Samuel Selden Warner*, b. Mar. 15, 1789; m. (1) Abby Champlin, (2) Azubah Tully.

399   *Andrew Ferdinando Warner*, b. Dec. 29, 1790; m. Lucinthia Cone.
400   *Joseph Warner*, b. Dec. 3, 1792; m. Mary Ann Holmes.
401   *Richard Warner*, b. Oct. 19, 1794; m. (1) Mary Millicent Gilbert, (2)
         Mary Gaylord.
402   *William Henry Warner*, b. Feb. 18, 1797; m. Sarah Canfield.
403   *Matthew Griswold Warner*, b. Mar. 6, 1799; m. Lucretia Hubbard
         Loomis.
      Mary Warner, b. Jan. 17, 1801; d. in Hadlyme, Aug. 10, 1825. She
         was a member of the Congregational Church in 1822.
      Elizabeth Warner, b. Apr. 20, 1803; d. in Hadlyme, Sept. 15, 1825.
404   *Jonathan Trumbull Warner*, b. Nov. 20, 1807; m. Anita Gale.

241 CHAPMAN[6] WARNER, son of Jonathan[5] and Elizabeth (Selden) Warner, born May 19, 1764, in Saybrook, Conn.;
died June 7, 1813, in Madison, Conn. He bought and sold land
in Lyme, between 1788 and 1800; fifty acres in Lyme Parish,
from his father, February 15, 1791; land in Hadlyme Society,
1792 and 1797; property in East Haddam, describing himself
as of Lyme. He joined the church in Hadlyme, June 6, 1802.
In 1803 he was proprietor of the grist mill and saw mill. In 1811
Chapman Warner of Guilford sold land to Selden Warner, indicating his removal to Guilford about that time. (Hamburg,
Lyme records.) At the time of the Embargo Act, Guilford, like
all New England, disapproved, and on September 19, 1808, a
petition, dated August 29th, presented from New Haven to the
President of the United States praying for a suspension of the
embargo, was read in town meeting at Guilford. The town
voted its approval and on February 17, 1809, the town took original action in resolutions embodying their complaints. These
were prepared by a committee of eleven men (among them
Chapman Warner) noted as composed of the prominent men of
the town. (Steiner's History of Guilford and Madison, Conn.)
     Married December 27, 1787, SARAH COMSTOCK (Lyme
town records, Hamburg, Conn.).

Children, baptized in Hadlyme Church

Elizabeth Warner, b. Oct. 26, 1788 (Lyme town record); bapt. Jan. 4,
     1789.
Sarah Warner, bapt. Aug. 15, 1790.
Chapman Warner, Jr., bapt. July 15, 1792. He was a machinist, resided
     some years in New Jersey, then in Louisville, Ky., and later in
     Easton, Pa. Chapman Warner and his wife and Benjamin Warner
     were members of the Fourth Presbyterian Church in Louisville at its
     foundation, in 1846, from the Second Presbyterian Church (History
     of Louisville). Children: i. Benjamin, b. 1821. ii. Sarah, b. 1834.
     iii. John, b. 1838. iv. William.

Alice Wilson Warner, bapt. Apr. 27, 1794.
David Warner, bapt. Mar. 19, 1797; d. aged 4 months, 23 days.
Jemima Warner, bapt. June 17, 1798.
Calvin Warner, bapt. Apr. 5, 1801, resided in Madison, Conn.; m. and
   had children, Elizabeth and Henry.

242 P H I N E A S [6] W A R N E R, son of David[5] and Sarah
(Ward) Warner, born in Saybrook (Chester), Conn., 1749; died
in Chester, 1812. He is recorded as a resident of Saybrook by
the 1790 Census, two males over 16, three males under 16, two
females in the family; in 1800, one male over 45, one female
between 26 and 45, three males between 16 and 26, one boy
under 10. His will mentions his wife Eunice; sons John,
Timothy, David and Phineas; daughter Wealthy Spencer. The
distribution of the estate mentions widow Eunice; sons John,
Samuel, Timothy and David; niece Phoebe Brooks.

Married **EUNICE CHURCH**, born in Chester, September 18,
1748, died there, January 3, 1823, daughter of Simeon and Eunice
(Warner) Church of Chester Parish, Saybrook. Her name was
on the roll of the Congregational Church in 1786, and she
received property from her father's estate in 1793.

Children

Wealthy Warner, d. in Chester; m. Oct. 30, 1791, Daniel Spencer of
   Saybrook.
405 *John Warner,* b. Aug. 4, 1772; m. (1) Mehitabel Clark, (2) Lucy Comstock.
406 *Phineas Warner, Jr.,* b. 1777; m. Lydia Clarke.
407 *David Warner,* b. Apr. 4, 1780; m. Mary Cone.
408 *Timothy Warner,* b. Apr. 1, 1782; m. Lydia Platts.
409 *Samuel Warner,* m. (1) Wealthy Clark, (2) Phoebe Brooks.
   Eunice Warner, name given in list of children in Church Genealogy.
   Mary Warner, name given in list of children in Church Genealogy.

243 LYDIA[6] WARNER, daughter of David[5] and Sarah
(Ward) Warner, born August 21, 1751, in Saybrook (Chester),
Conn.; died there, December 20, 1788.

Married in Saybrook, December 5, 1775, THOMAS SILLI
MAN, who was born in the Parish of Canaan, Norwalk, Febru-
ary 19, 1748, and died May 26, 1839, aged 91, son of Rev. Robert
Silliman, Yale, 1737, and his wife, Anna Cook, of New Canaan
and Chester, Conn. Thomas Silliman was deacon of the Con-
gregational Church at Chester for many years. He married (2)
July 7, 1791, Huldah Dunk, by whom he had Sarah, Jonathan,
Edwin and Daniel.

Children of Thomas and Lydia (Warner) Silliman

Thomas Silliman, Jr., b. Aug. 26, 1776.
William Silliman, b. Mar. 20, 1778.
Anne Silliman, b. Jan. 12, 1780.
Lydia Silliman, b. Apr. 27, 1782.
Sarah Silliman, b. Nov. 21, 1784; d. Mar. 4, 1786.
Samuel Silliman, b. July 17, 1786, or Nov. 21, 1785; d. in Chester, June
   16, 1874. He was a joiner, later a manufacturer of glass-lined
   wooden inkstands and other novelties; m. Anne Hannah Shipman,
   daughter of Col. Edward Shipman, a Revolutionary soldier. Chil-
   dren: i. Samuel Carlos. ii. Joseph Edward (1). iii. Sarah Ann. iv.
   Lydia. v. Daniel D., m. Sarah⁸ Warner, daughter of Judge Ely⁷
   Warner, see number 593. vi. Joseph E. (2). vii. Joanna. viii.
   Thomas. ix. Frederick. x. Cordelia. All of these died before 1903,
   except Thomas, who resided in New Mexico, and was engaged in
   mining. Samuel Carlos Silliman died Apr. 22, 1896, the same day
   as his brother, Daniel D., in another part of the town.

244 WILLIAM WARNER, son of David⁵ and Sarah
(Ward) Warner, born in Saybrook (Chester), Conn., probably
about 1755. "One of the Warner family," published in 1892,
says he died in Half Moon, Saratoga County, N. Y., but we find
no record of the family there; and the History of Vanderburgh
County, Indiana, mentions William as living with his sons in
Evansville. He was the fourth postmaster of the town and
owned a two-story frame building at the corner of Locust and
Second Streets.
Married **RHODA SILLIMAN**.

Children

William Warner, Jr.
Ralph Warner.
Erastus Warner.
Alanson Warner, d. in Evansville about 1853; was married three
   times but had no children who grew to maturity. He was living in
   Evansville before 1817, was known as Major Warner and was called
   a "man well and favorably known in every branch of the county's
   early history." He advanced cash for the use of the county in 1818;
   was trustee of the village in 1819 and later, and its president for several terms; was coroner in 1819 and 1825; sheriff in 1824 and 1827;
   county treasurer in 1820, 1831-3, 1836-41. He was one of the three
   trustees of the Presbyterian Church elected at a meeting held at his
   home to arrange for the building of a Presbyterian Church, and
   gave fifty dollars to the building. He kept a hotel, pretentious for
   those days, in a two-story brick building, had a livery stable and was
   the owner of stage lines. The old Warner home was standing not
   many years ago and was still a dignified and substantial residence,
   with a keystone arch over its colonial entrance. The walls were
   built over two feet in thickness, intended, it is said, as a defense
   against earthquakes as well as against hostile enemies. He had an

adopted daughter, Nellie Nevins Warner (daughter of his wife by a former marriage), who was married first to Guilford Eggleston and, after his death, to a Mr. Culbertson of New Albany.

Ann Warner, d. in Middletown, Conn.; m. David Edwards of Middletown.

Alfred O. Warner, was a voter at town election in Evansville in 1817, and was elected to an office; was granted permission to keep hotel in his house in 1819, and town meetings were held there.

245 **ANDREW**[6] **WARNER,** son of Eleazer[5] and Elizabeth (Kirtland) Warner, born November 15, 1762, in Chester, Conn.; died April 16, 1841, in Vernon, Oneida County, N. Y., where he had settled early. He may be the Andrew Warner who was recorded in Paris, N. Y., in the 1800 Census, with a family consisting of one male and one female between 26 and 45, one male and one female between 10 and 16, and four females under 10. His will, dated 1836, was probated in Oneida County in 1841, and mentioned his sons Andrew and Lucius, daughters Elizabeth May, Laura Campbell, Ann M. Ufford, Polly Ufford, Miranda Hinman and her children.
Married **RACHEL CROCKER.**

Children

410 *Andrew Warner, Jr.,* b. Jan. 23, 1791; m. Elizabeth Clark Youngs.
  Rachel Warner, probably died before 1836 as she was not mentioned in her father's will. Married ―――― Gratton. Children: Bela; Alvin; Thomas; Lydia; perhaps others.
  Elizabeth Warner, m. David May. Children: Martin; Darwin; William, a minister; De Witt; Rachel Ann.
411 *Laura Crocker Warner,* b. Aug., 18, 1796; m. (1) Lyman Baldwin Campbell, (2) Reuben Scripture.
  Maria Warner, twin with Miranda; m. ―――― Clark.
  Miranda Warner, twin with Maria; m. ―――― Hinman, and had children born before the date of her father's will, 1836. Children: Jane; Horace; Hopkins; Anna M.
  Anna M. Warner, m. John Ufford. Children: Amelia; Sarah.
  Lucius Warner, d. in Wisconsin, Nov., 1865. He was executor of his father's will, 1836; was called of Vernon in 1841, and of Kirkland in 1843, when he gave a quit-claim to his cousin Seth. Married Sarah A. Stratton, who died Apr. 2, 1890, sister of the wife of his cousin Seth. No children.
  Polly Warner, m. before 1836, Charles Ufford. Children: Andrew; Cleora; Julian; Alfred; Elizabeth; Gustavus; Maria; Helen.

246 **ELEAZER**[6] **WARNER, JR.,** son of Eleazer[5] and Elizabeth (Kirtland) Warner, born in Saybrook, now Chester, Conn., April 2 or 3, 1764; died in Kirkland, N. Y., November 16, 1851. He probably removed with his father's family to Cambridge,

Washington County, N. Y., about 1787, and eventually settled in Clinton, Oneida County, N. Y. He served in the Revolution and drew a pension until his death. It is thought by the family that he may have been a drummer boy in his father's regiment as he was in the army on his thirteenth birthday. The 1800 Census recorded him in Paris, N. Y., one male and one female between 26 and 45, one male between 10 and 16, three boys and two girls under 10. With his wife Irinda he made deeds of property to Andrew and Seth H. Warner in Oneida County in 1843.

Marr;e_d IRINDA SKIFF, born in Massachusetts, September, 1770, daughter of John Skiff; died November 17, 1852, at Kirk land, N. Y.

Children

Lovicie Warner.

Eleazer Warner, 3d, resided in Richland, N. Y. Married. Children: i. Irinda (or Nancy in one record). ii. Sally. iii. Jonathan, was superintendent of highways in district No. 5, town of Cambridge, Washington Co., N. Y., in 1827, and is probably the Jonathan who joined the United Presbyterian Church in Cambridge in 1831. iv. Eleazer, 4th. v. Hannah. vi. Esther.

Nathaniel Warner, lived in Greenfield, Ohio; d. about 1870, not married.

Eunice Warner, m. —— Chapman;. lived in Pulaski, N. Y. A granddaughter is Mrs. Jesse Lonas of Grieg, N. Y.

John A. Warner, lived in Berlin, Mich. Married. Children: Hatsil (or Hattie) H.; Ansil A. or R.; Emma; Sylvester; Charles; Abby.

412 *Israel S. or W. Warner,* m. Samantha Ballou.

Irinda Warner, m. as his second wife, Orange Dayton; had no children.

Sylvester Warner, was among the first purchasers of U. S. land in Berlin township, St. Clair Co., Mich.; was the second supervisor of the town, elected in 1843; justice of the peace in 1839 and 1841; d. in Michigan, not married.

413 *Chloe Warner,* b. Dec. 3, 1803; m. Richardson Thurman Hough.

Lavina Warner, b. 1805; d. 1885; m. in Clinton, N. Y., Benjamin Snow, b. near Springfield, Mass., 1800, d. 1848, was a gunsmith and removed to Pulaski, N. Y. Children: i. Charles O., died. ii. Norman Guito, b. in Pulaski, Oswego Co., N. Y., Feb. 3, 1828; m. in Kirkland, N. Y., Apr. 17, 1850, Charlotte D.[8] Warner, see number 621. iii. Charles, b. 1831. iv. Benjamin, b. 1834; m. Mary Watson and had children, Norman W. and John B. v. Emily L., b. 1837; d. 1912; m. (1) James W. Fenton, b. 1832, d. 1889; m. (2) Sylvanus Convers Huntington, whose first wife was Hannah M.[8] Warner (see number 618). vi. George, b. 1841; left children. James W. and Emily L. (Snow) Fenton (see above) had children: Emily C., b. 1859, m. James T. Hoyt, b. 1851, and had two daughters, Jessie F. and Sarah F., a minister; Jessie, b. 1862; George, b. 1866, d. 1881; Benjamin, b. 1871, d. 1876; Grace, b. 1875, d. 1876.

Levi (1) Warner, d. young.

Levi (2) Warner, d. young.

Azubah Warner, m. Proctor Taft. Miss Emma Taft of Clinton, N. Y., is a descendant.

Seth H. Warner, was living in Kirkland, N. Y., in 1841; made deeds in Oneida Co., N. Y., in 1850; d. after 1865; m. Roxey L. Stratton, who- d. April 2, 1890, the same day as her sister who married Lucius Warner, his cousin. They had no children.

247 PHILIP⁶ WARNER, son of Eleazer⁵ and Elizabeth (Kirtland) Warner, born February 16, 1766, in Chester, Conn.; died in Cambridge, Washington Co., N. Y., April 15, 1848. He was one of the early settlers in Washington County and was active in public affairs; was on the committee for highways in 1803; fence-viewer and appraiser, 1808-10; one of the constables chosen at the first town meeting of Jackson, 1816, part of which was taken from Cambridge.

Married **SARAH WOODS**, who died in Oxford, N. Y., January 24, 1853, and was buried on the lot of her son Abner in Norwich. She joined the First United Presbyterian Church, Cambridge, July 17, 1796.

Children, order not known

414   *Philip Kirtland Warner*, b. April 18, 1791; m. Lovina Ackley.
415   *Sarah Warner*, b. Mar. 23, 1792; m. Abijah Pratt.
416   *Prudence Warner*, b. about 1794; m. Hiram Ackley.
     Lydia Warner, d. young.
417   *Abner Warren Warner*, m. Freelóve Goodsell.
418   *Wealthy Warner*, b. May 6, 1800; m. Alanson Hull.
     Elizabeth Warner, perhaps the Elizabeth who died in Jackson, N. Y., Feb. 3, 1832, aged 39. One record gives her as first wife of Joseph Edwin Cutler, see below.
     Phebe Warner, lived and died in West Brookfield, Mass.; m. Sept. 3, 1832, Joseph Edwin Cutler, b. July 16, 1805, son of Joseph and Phebe (Ward) Cutler. He resided in West Brookfield in 1851. Children: i. William, resided in Oakland, Cal. ii. Edwin, resided in Oakland. iii. Phebe. iv. Joseph.
     Jonathan Warner, married. Both he and his wife are buried in Cambridge.
     Clark Warner, lived near Rochester, N. Y. Married and had two sons, Edwin and Rollin.

248 SYLVESTER⁶ WARNER, son of Eleazer⁵ and Elizabeth (Kirtland) Warner, born in Chester, Conn., February 21, 1768; died in Cambridge, Washington Co., N. Y., February 18, 1841 (or January 27, 1841). He was an elder in the original White Church at Cambridge in 1794, and was a trustee of the First United Presbyterian Church of Cambridge in 1832. His name appears on a list of subscribers to the Cambridge Academy in 1814. The probate record of Washington County states that he died in Jackson (town formed from Cambridge), February 18,

1841, and the heirs were: widow Elizabeth; Azubah Cleveland of Cambridge; William S. Warner of Jackson; Lydia McGeoch of Jackson; Ann Horton of Michigan; Elizabeth Cleveland of Michigan; Abner K. Warner of Jackson; John **R**. Warner of Jackson; grandchildren, Sylvester and Martha Warner, children of his son Eleazer Warner, deceased, of Ogden, **N. Y.**

Married **ELIZABETH REED,** who died May 6, 1849, aged 80.

Children

John Warner, d. young.

Azubah Warner, m. —— Cleveland; lived in Michigan.

Elizabeth Warner, m. —— Cleveland; lived in Michigan.

Eleazer Warner, resided in Ogden, Monroe Co., N. Y.; d. before **1841,** leaving two children, Sylvester and Martha.

Ann Warner, m. —— Horton; lived in Michigan.

419 *William Sylvester Warner,* b. Dec. 24, 1807; m. Sarah Coulter.

Mary Warner, b. about 1809; d. Aug. 14, 1828, aged 19.

Lydia Warner, m. —— McGeoch, lived in Jackson, N. Y.

Abner K. Warner, d. Mar. 23, 1845, in the town of Granville, N. Y. He was living in Jackson in 1841. Married Esther —— who survived him. No children.

John R. Warner, b. about 1816; d. Jan. 6, 1852, aged 36; resided in Jackson, N. Y.; m. Mary A. ——, who survived him. Children: i. Sylvester K., b. about 1848; d. Aug. 8, 1867, aged 19 years. ii. Fanny Elizabeth, b. 1851; d. Nov. 7, 1851, aged three months.

249 KIRTLAND[6] **WARNER,** son of Eleazer[5] and Elizabeth (Kirtland) Warner, born in Chester, Conn., February 8, 1770; died April 23, 1844, in the town of Jackson, Washington Co., **N. Y.** He removed to Cambridge, Washington County, and was active in public affairs. He was one. of the first ten elders of the Presbyterian Church at Cambridge, the sixth elected. He was overseer of the poor in Cambridge, 1806-14; overseer of highways, 1809; in list of subscribers to Cambridge, Washington Co., Academy, 1814. About this time the town of Jackson was formed from Cambridge, and Kirtland Warner was elected school inspector at the first town meeting in 1815; town clerk in 1816, and 1823-31; inspector of election, 1816. In 1832 he was in the list of elders of the First United Presbyterian Church of Cambridge.

Married (1) **ELIZABETH ——,** who died November 21, 1802, aged 34. It is not known if she had children.

Married (2) in Gilead, Conn., September, 1804, **SARAH TRUMBULL,** who died January 15, 1845, aged 70. She joined the First United Presbyterian Church in Cambridge, April 17, 1808.

Children, order not known

· *Kirtland Trumbull Warner,* d. about 1858. He was inspector of schools in Cambridge, 1836; joined the First United Presbyterian Church of Cambridge, Mar. 10, 1843; resided at White Creek, 1844. His will, probated Jan., 1859, mentions only his brothers Asaph E. and Garret W. Warner, and sister Rebecca Ashton.

Asaph Edwards Warner, bapt. Sept. 27, 1807, Cambridge, N. Y. He joined the First United Presbyterian Church in Cambridge, June 19, 1831, and was an elder in the old white meeting house, served in the session twenty-one years (some time before 1892). He was justice of the peace in the town of Jackson in 1861 and 1865. Married Jane Elizabeth Warner, b. about 1813, d. May 2, 1847, aged 34; see number 252. Children: i. William K., b. 1837; d. June 21, 1847, aged 10 years, one month, one day. ii. Jane Elizabeth, b. Feb. 27, 1841.

Sarah Elizabeth Warner, bapt. Apr. 8, 1810; d. Mar. 3, 1830, aged 20. Some accounts mention a daughter Sarah M., who died before 1844, but it is probably an error for this.

Garret W. Warner, resided in White Creek, N. Y., 1844; mentioned in his brother's will.

Rebecca V. V. Warner, resided in Greenwich, N. Y.; m. before 1844, ——— Ashton.

Esther F. Warner, probably d. before 1844.

250 **JAMES⁶ WARNER,** son of James⁵ and Abigail (———) Warner, born in Saybrook, Conn., 1767 (or March 4, 1768); died December 26, 1837, in Smithville, Chenango Co., **N. Y.** He removed with his father to Cambridge, Washington Co., **N. Y.**, in 1780 and settled later in Smithville, where he died.

Married ———. He is perhaps the James Warner who married **REBECCA HATCH,** born August 21, 1783. James and Rebecca Warner are known to have had at least two daughters, Lucinda H. and Abigail Frances, while James⁶ Warner is known to have had children, Lucy, Loa, Abigail, Prudence, and Smith B.

Children

Lucy Warner.

Loa Warner.

Abigail Warner. She is possibly the Abigail Frances, daughter of James and Rebecca (Hatch) Warner, b., Dec. 4, 1805, d. Nov. 19, 1833, who m. Aug. 8, 1827, Edward Kellogg, b. Aug. 19, 1800, near Great Barrington, Mass., son of Aaron and Amelia (Noyes) Kellogg, d. June 13, 1881, in Canaan Center, N. Y. He was educated as a lawyer but was engaged in the iron foundry business in Binghamton, N. Y., and returned later to his former home in Canaan, N. Y. For further records see Kelloggs in the Old World and New, p. 538. He married (2) Lucinda Warner, his first wife's sister. Children of Abigail: i. George. ii. John Stower. iii. Mary Ann, m. George Grenville Benedict.

Prudence Warner.

Smith B. Warner, d. in Michigan, Sept. 24, 1846.

251 ARNOLD⁶ WARNER, son of James⁵ and Abigail
(————) Warner, born in Saybrook (Chester), Conn., 1772;
died about 1854, near North East, Pa., buried there. He went
with his father to Cambridge, Washington Co., N. Y., in 1780,
then to Rome, N. Y., where he kept a hotel for several years,
and later to North East, Erie Co., Pa., about 1820. He was one
of the first settlers there and took up land by purchase of the
Holland Company, a farm located about two and one-half miles
south of North East Village. He was a man of herculean
frame, six feet three inches in height. During his prime he car
ried with ease a weight of nine hundred pounds. He enlisted as
farrier in the War of 1812 and served till the close of the war.
Married March 16, 1797, **POLLY CUTLER.**

Children

420 *Walter W. Warner,* b. 1798; m. (1) ———— Bird, (2) ———— Bird, (3)
Clarissa Potter.
421 *Beulah Warner,* b. June, 1800; m. Daniel Palmer.
Prudence Warner, b. Jan. 24, 1803; d. 1836, in Erie, Pa., buried in the
cemetery at Oak Station, Greenfield, Pa.; m. June 11, 1826, John T.
Atkins. Children: i. Almira, b. Mar. 9, 1829; m. Nov. 15, 1859,
Horace Orteway. ii. Wayne, d. in infancy, buried in the abandoned
cemetery at Colt's Station, Pa.
422 *Henry C. Warner,* b. 1808; m. (1) ————————, (2) ———— Bird.
James A. Warner, b. Apr. 26, 1810; d. 1891-2; m. (1) Nov. 9, 1835,
Elizabeth Sturgeon, (2) ————————. Child by first wife: Jane, b.
Nov. 9, 1836; m. Oct., 1861, Edwin Mills of Elmira, N. Y. Children
by second wife: i. Mary, b. Nov. 10, 1844; m. Oct. 7, 1866, at Fair-
view, Pa., Rudolph Pettit; resided in Chatham, Canada, in 1894. ii.
Montgomery, b. Dec. 6, 1847; resided in Mercer, Pa., 1894; m. (1)
Susan Bixler, (2) ————————, who died a year after marriage.
423 *William C. Warner,* b. May 5, 1815; m. (1) Bothilda Atkins, (2) Susan
P. Partridge.
Mary (or *Polly*) *Warner,* b. 1821, at North East, Pa.; resided in 1894
at Findley's Lake, Chautauqua Co., N. Y.; m. (1) Sept. 23, 1842,
James Fuller, (2) June 2, 1858, Sewell Shattuck. Children: i.
Ophelia, m. John Atkins; resided at Findley's Lake. ii. Ida V., prob-
ably a child by the second husband, resided with her mother in 1894.
Sally Warner, probably the same as Mary or Polly.

252 SOLOMON⁶ WARNER, son of James⁵ and Abigail
(————) Warner, born in Saybrook (Chester), Conn., 1778;
died June 30, 1853, in the town of Jackson, Washington Co.,
N. Y. He removed when a child to Washington County with
his father, and resided later on the farm where his father settled.
He was a tanner, currier, and shoemaker as well as farmer. He
served in the War of 1812. In 1809, he was overseer of high-

ways; in 1816, overseer of the poor, fence-viewer and appraiser; in 1821, commissioner of highways, town of White Creek. He was one of the trustees of the First United Presbyterian Church, in a list of 1832. His death was accidental, killed by the cars on the railroad near his home.

Married **ELIZABETH WOODWORTH**, who died October 31, 1851, aged 69 (tombstone record).

Children

424 *Jonathan Warner,* b. Aug. 4, 1802; m. Maria Simpson.

William W. Warner, joined the First United Presbyterian Church in Cambridge, Apr. 17, 1831; was commissioner of highways in district number one, White Creek, Washington Co., in 1833; resided in Pennsylvania at the time of his father's death in 1853, perhaps in North East, Erie County.

Maria Warner, m. Henry Austin of Mexico, N. Y., and resided there.

Rosannah Warner, joined the church in Cambridge, Oct. 15, 1837; d. Oct. 5, 1852, aged 43, not married.

Solomon W. Warner, d. in the town of White Creek, Washington Co., July 6, 1868. He was director of the Cambridge Valley National Bank at its organization, 1855, one of the first trustees at the incorporation of the village of Cambridge in 1866. In 1840 with Levi Tilton he erected a small furnace which was later enlarged so that some twenty men were employed, making a specialty of the manufacture of sawmill machinery which was shipped to all parts of the world. His son Charles Dillon was later associated with the firm. Married Eliza T. ———, who survived him. Children: i. William N., was mentioned in his father's will. ii. Charles Dillon, b. July 18, 1840, was engaged in business with his father.

Jane Elizabeth Warner, b. about 1813; d. May 2, 1847, aged 34; m. Asaph Edwards[7] Warner, son of Kirtland[6] Warner; see number 249.

Abigail Warner, joined the church at Cambridge, 1836.

Freelove Warner, joined the church at Cambridge, 1831; resided at White Creek, N. Y., 1853; m. William Curtis. A son, John H. Curtis, formerly lived at Benton Station, St. Louis, Mo., but is now dead.

Cynthia Ann Warner, resided in Jackson, N. Y., 1853. She is probably the Cynthia A. Warner who resided in the town of White Creek and died May 5, 1905.

253 **HANNAH[6] WARNER,** daughter of Seth[5] and Hannah (Le Moyne-De Angelis) Warner, born August 26, 1775, probably in Saybrook, Conn.; died November 19, 1805.

Married **CHARLES DEMING,** born August 28, 1768, in Saybrook, Conn., died April 16, 1815, at Watkins Glen, N. Y., son of Charles and Ruth[5] (Warner) Deming; see number 128. He is also recorded as born October 3, 1769, died April 25, 1816. He resided in Watkins Glen, where he was a lawyer, notary public and justice of the peace, and owned a warehouse at the end of

Seneca Lake. He married (2) Judith Boardman, and (3) Clarissa Brundage, daughter of Ebenezer and Mehitable (Smith) Brundage. By his third wife he had children: Orrin Erastus, Harriet, James Silas, and Daniel Brundage. For further details of this family see the Genealogy of the descendants of John Deming, by Judson Keith Deming, Dubuque, Iowa, 1904.

Children of Charles and Hannah (Warner) Deming

Charles Seth Deming, b. Feb. 15, 1796, in Saratoga Co., N. Y.; d. Feb. 21, 1862, in Lyndon, Ill. He resided on a small farm near the head of Seneca Lake, and owned a stone quarry from which he shipped stone by schooner to Geneva. He removed about 1838 to Illinois. He was school commissioner for 14 successive years, to 1860, and was a deacon in the Congregational Church. Married (1) July 19, 1816, Betsey Corbett, who died Apr. 25, 1827, daughter of Asaph and ———— (Reed) Corbett, (2) Feb., 1828, Hannah Amanda Smith, daughter of Harry and Melinda⁶ (Warner) Smith, b. Apr. 10, 1807, d. Jan. 10, 1886. See number 254. Children by first wife: i. Charles William, b. May 1, 1817, in Reading, N. Y.; d. 1900, in Berwyn, Ill.; m. Sabrina Gibbs Chamberlain, and had seven children. ii. Asaph Corbett, b. July 24, 1819; d. June 20, 1863, in the military hospital near Murfreesboro, Tenn.; m. Harriet Barlow and had eight children. iii. George Alanson, b. Oct. 26, 1821; d. Mar. 9, 1863, in the army. iv. Louisa M., b. Mar. 26, 1824; d. Oct. 24, 1847; m. Oct. 26, 1844, Jehiel B. Smith of Lyndon, Ill. v. Hiram Dorman, b. Apr. 18, 1827; lived in Wellsboro, Pa.; m. (1) Lucinda Kennedy, (2) Julia Colton; had six children; was a soldier in the Civil War.

Samuel Warner Deming, b. Feb. 15, 1798, in Saratoga Co., N. Y.; d. Feb. 18, 1881, in Jackson, Pa.; m. (1) Aug. 22, 1817, Margaret Diven, daughter of John and Margaret (Baskin) Diven, who died 1834, (2) Sept. 17, 1834, Electa Dickinson, b. July 26, 1816, daughter of Walter and Mary (————) Dickinson. Children by first wife: i. Charlotte, b. Dec. 1, 1820; d. Apr. 2, 1821. ii. John, b. June 29, 1822; d. Feb. 15, 1823. iii. Maria Louisa, b. Nov. 28, 1825; m. Charles Tillinghast; lived in Millerton, Pa. iv. Charles F., b. Dec. 28, 1829; d. Sept. 1, 1830. Children by second wife: i. Mary Amelia, b. Aug. 6, 1835; m. Apr. 9, 1852, Albert Mitchell; lived in Millerton. ii. Matilda Clara, or Clara Matilda, b. Nov. 16, 1837, in Southport, N. Y.; m. Aug. 22, 1855, DeWitt C. Kinsman; lived in Roseburg, Ore. iii. Charles Warner, b. June 10, 1840; m. Oct. 7, 1863, Emma Gridley; no children; d. in Confederate prison at Belle Isle. iv. Alva Marion, b. June 27, 1842; d. Dec. 16, 1848. v. William Eugene, b. Sept. 7, 1844; a farmer in Somers Lane, Tioga Co., Pa.; a sergeant in the Civil War; m. July 4, 1866, Helen J. Andrews; had six children. vi. Marion Samuel, b. Nov. 21, 1853, in Jackson, Pa.; carpenter and contractor in Tioga, Pa.; m. (1) May 1, 1874, Mary Jane Wright, who d. Oct. 1, 1896, (2) Oct. 19, 1897, Ella M. Gee; had seven children. vii. Lucian Bird, b. Aug. 8, 1856, in Jackson; lived at Somers Lane, Pa.; m. Mar. 14, 1878, Ursula Montgomery; has six children.

Hiram Alanson Deming, b. Nov. 17, 1799, or Apr. 9, 1800; d. Apr. 9, 1882; settled in Syracuse, N. Y., in 1818; was schoolmaster, clerk in drygoods business, and later bookkeeper. In 1828 his name was famous throughout the country as the holder of a lottery ticket that won $10,000. Married (1) Apr. 15, 1830, Sophronia Hickox, b. Jan. 27, 1810; d. May 19, 1850, (2) June 19, 1851, Lodelia J. Benjamin, b. June 20, 1819, d. Oct. 30, 1884, daughter of Amos P. and Sarah (Bacon) Benjamin. Children, born in Syracuse, by first wife: i. Charles, b. Jan. 30, 1831; d. Sept. 3, 1849. ii. Mary Louise, b. Jan. 20, 1833; d. Aug. 15, 1834. iii. Hiram, b. June 20, 1844; d. Feb. 28, 1865. By second wife: i. Clarinda G., b. Apr. 23, 1852; d. July 27, 1852. ii. Frank Benjamin, b. Sept. 11, 1853; lived in Oswego, N. Y.; m. Elizabeth Bell Armstrong and had one son who died young. iii. Ella Rebecca, b. July 12, 1855; lived in Syracuse; m. (1) Feb. 6, 1875, George S. Coe, (2) June 18, 1885, John M. Dunlap. iv. William Charles, b. July 6, 1857; d. Nov. 3, 1862.

Hannah Maria Deming, b. Apr. 9, 1803; d. Oct. 5, 1886; m. Sept. 1, 1821, Daniel Tompkins. A daughter is Mrs. H. M. Cotey of Columbus, Wis.

254 MELINDA[6] WARNER, daughter of Seth[5] and Hannah (Le Moyne-De Angelis) Warner, born in Saybrook, Conn.; died January 27, 1854.

Married **HARRY SMITH,** son of Reuben Smith. Reuben Smith, with his two sons Harry and Jabez, went from Salisbury, Conn., to a locality now known as Peach Orchard, town of Hector, Schuyler Co., N. Y., arriving there June 1, 1793, almost the first in the section of the country. They commenced a clearing, built a temporary hut, and raised a crop of corn and wheat. After harvest they returned to Connecticut, and the following spring with their families removed to the new settlement, travelling in sleighs drawn by oxen, two of the men going on foot to drive the cattle. The whole family removed west at a later date and resided in Lyndon, Ill., and Ames, Iowa.

Children

Hannah Amanda Smith, b. Apr. 10, 1807; d. Jan. 10, 1886; m. as second wife, Feb. 21, 1828, Charles Seth Deming, b. Feb. 15, 1796, in Saratoga County, N. Y., d. in Lyndon, Ill., Feb. 21, 1862, son of Charles and Hannah[6] Warner) Deming, see number 253. See further for their children's records.

Jabez Smith, d. in the late seventies; m. Adeline ———, who resides in Lyndon, Ill. Children: i. Eleanor, b. 1858; m. John Slater, and had four children, Alma, b. 1838, m. R. J. Strahl (has two children, John, b. 1901, and Eleanor Minerva, b. 1908); Roscoe John, m. Hazel ——— (has two children, Dorothy and George Roswell); Edna Adell, m. Nov. 26, 1908, Ernest Leslie Lowell (has three children); Loretta Adeline, b. 1890, m. Aug. 24, 1915, Jackson Burton Chase. ii. Martha Electa, resides in Lyndon, m. A. E. Parmenter and had three children (Sophia, m. and has a child; Harriet Adeline, m. and has two children; Elbert).

Charlotte Smith, m. John Aljoe and died in the early eighties. She had no children who lived beyond infancy.

Hiram Smith, d. at Ames, Iowa, after 1870; m. Elizabeth ————. Children: i. Linda, m. and has several children. ii. Margaret, m. and has no children. iii. George, died.

Melinda Smith, m. and has a daughter, Mrs. Julia Brooks, who resides at Lyndon, Ill.

Harry Smith, Jr., d. after 1900; m. Mary ————. Children: i. Frank. ii. Kelley, m. and d. leaving an infant child. iii. Lacey, m. and had several children. iv. Sarah, m. Andrew Cargay and d. leaving three children, Alice (who m. ———— Parkhurst and has several children), Olin, and Edna. v. Olive, m. Wilse Greenlee, and d. leaving three children, Mary Maud, who is m. and has several children, Frank, and Halford, who was an ensign in the U. S. Navy about 1915.

Children of Charles Seth and Hannah Amanda (Smith) Deming

Elizabeth Melinda Deming, b. Oct. 4, 1829; m. June 4, 1854, Henry H. Smith. Children: i. Charles, d. in infancy. ii. Kate Adele, m. John A. Aplington; no children. iii. Helen Elizabeth, m. Carl Blackert; resides in Norman, Okla., has several children. iv. Frank, is a physician at Norton, Iowa; m. and has two children. v. Bessie Lucille, b. Oct., 1868.; not married.

Samuel Adams Deming, b. Aug. 28, 1831; d. Feb. 1, 1847.

Delia Samantha Deming, b. July 6, 1833; d. Sept. 6, 1881; m. Jan. 2, 1866, William Mawer Burkitt, son of William and Eleanor (Mawer) Burkitt. They resided in Lyndon, Ill., until about 1878. Children: i. Delia Maria (twin), b. Dec. 22, 1868; resides in Whitney, Neb.; not married. ii. Eleanor Amanda (twin), b. in Lyndon, Ill., Dec. 22, 1868; resides in Chadron, Neb.; m. Aug. 29, 1893, in Whitney, Neb., William Sherman Gillam, b. in Blandinsville, Ill., July 19, 1865, son of James Perry and Lucinda Catherine (York) Gillam (has children, Eleanor, b. June 29, 1896, Katherine, b. Sept. 9, 1898, and William Sherman, Jr., b. Aug. 3, 1908). iii. William, b. Aug. 31, 1871; m. July 29, 1897, Susan Olivia Thomas (has children, Joel Le Moyne, b. Sept. 6, 1899, and Mabel Lois, b. July 5, 1911). iv. John Mawer, b. July 18, 1874; d. Sept. 21, 1882. v. Joseph Alfred, b. Sept. 12, 1876; d. Mar. 26, 1879.

Harriet Emeline Deming, b. Apr. 16, 1835; d. Dec. 15, 1863.

Lucy Ann Deming, b. Aug. 25, 1840; d. Aug. 9, 1841.

Hannah Maria Deming, b. Apr. 8, 1842; d. Feb. 17, 1912; m. as second wife, Dec. 16, 1882, William Mawer Burkitt, see above.

Martha Electa Deming, b. Mar. 22, 1845; d. Dec. 2, 1872; m. as second wife, Andrew Wilkinson. Children: i. Charles, d. in infancy. ii. Sarah Amanda, b. Feb. 25, 1868; m. Mar., 1888, Arthur E. Fowler, and had six children, Sadie May, b. May 10, 1889, m. Aug. 23, 1916, William H. Dickinson; Lida Elizabeth, b. Jan. 19, 1894, d. 1896; Olive Deming, b. Dec. 14, 1896; Esther Marie, b. July 18, 1899; William Arthur, b. Nov. 15, 1902; Helen Lucille, b. June 17, 1905.

Seth Le Moyne Deming, b. Mar. 16, 1847; d. July 31, 1847.

255 SETH ANDREW LE MOYNE[6] WARNER, son of Seth[5] and Hannah (Le Moyne-De Angelis) Warner, born in Saybrook, Conn., February 12, 1786; died in Farmington, Mich., March 5, 1846. He resided when a youth with Paschal De Angelis in Trenton, N. Y. He joined the First United Presbyterian Church of Cambridge, N. Y., January 26, 1810. In 1817 he purchased land in Hector, at that time a part of Tompkins County, N. Y. He studied law and made his first appearance in the courts of Tompkins County in 1819. In 1825 he went to Michigan and located in what was later organized into the township of Farmington. In March, 1830, he was admitted to the practice of law in Oakland County. Although the town was not a favorable one in which to acquire an extensive law practice, he secured his share of business, and was prominent in legal and political circles. He was one of the first justices of the peace, appointed in Farmington by the Governor, and a member of the first Constitutional Convention of Michigan. Always a zealous Presbyterian, he was deacon of the church and otherwise active in its work, honored and respected by all.

During the winter of 1817-8, at a time of deep religious interest, a movement towards temperance was started in the town of Hector. On the 28th of March, 1818, the preliminary meeting was held in the bar-room of Richard Ely, Jr., and it was resolved to organize a temperance society. A committee, consisting of S. A. L. Warner, Richard Smith, and Dr. A. M. Comstock, was appointed to draw up a constitution, and the society was fully organized a few weeks later with S. A. L. Warner as its secretary. One of the clauses in the constitution reads:

"We also pledge ourselves that when called to visit our neighbors in raising buildings, or any kind of business, we will not expect to be provided with liquor to drink, nor will we furnish them ourselves when we invite our neighbors to assist us, and we will use our influence to prevent their being provided by others on similar occasions."

The first cold-water raising was an important event. The Peach Orchard Church was raised without ardent spirits, and a lunch of biscuit, pie and cake was served in place of the usual supply of whiskey. The builder hesitated to undertake it under such conditions but the trustees were firm and the task was completed without difficulties.

Seth A. L. Warner married (1) in Hector, N. Y., September 7, 1815, SALLY WIXOM, born in Hector, February 1, 1796, died in Farmington, Mich., September 4, 1837, daughter of Robert and Phebe (————) Wixom. Robert Wixom was a pioneer settler of Farmington township in 1824 and was first clerk of the township.

Married (2) in Farmington, Mich., **EMMA PALMER,** born in Montville, Conn., December 30 or 21, 1807; died January 29, 1871.

Children by first wife

425 *William Smith Warner,* b. Feb. 15, 1817; m. Polly Coomer.
426 *Robert Wixom Warner,* b. July 13 or 31, 1818; m. Caroline Amanda Murray.
427 *Paschal De Angelis Warner,* b. Aug. 12, 1822; m. Rhoda Elizabeth Botsford.

Children by second wife (one died in infancy)

Sarah Emma Warner, b. in Farmington, Oct. 8, 1838; resides there; m. in Ypsilanti, Mich., Sept. 27, 1860, James M. Wilber, b. in Collins, N. Y., 1832, d. Aug. 31, 1912, son of George and Jane W. (Lapham) Wilber. Children, born in Farmington: i. M. Eloise, b. Jan. 27, 1863; resides in Wenatchie, Wash.; m. in Farmington, Aug. 15, ——, Leroy V. Wells; no children. ii. Clinton M., b. Dec. 16, 1870; m. Dec. 27, 1904, Zayda B. Sprague; no children.
428 *Seth Andrew Le Moyne Warner, Jr.,* b. July 13, 1840; m. (1) Frances A. Phelps, (2) Emma B. Walker.
Minnie (or Ximena) Eliza Warner, b. in Farmington, Mar. 24 or Feb. 15, 1845; resides in Farmington; m. in Ypsilanti, Mich., Jan. 17 or 14, 1864, Milton R. Wilber, b. in Livonia township, Mich., son of George and Jane W. (Lapham) Wilber. No children.

256 LUCY MARIA[6] WARNER, daughter of John[5] Warner, lived in Litchfield, and Cedarville, Herkimer County, N. Y., where she died, aged over 60. She and her husband are buried in the Cedarville Cemetery.

Married **WILLIAM HADLEY,** who died in Cedarville, December, 1869. He was the son of William and Eunice Hadley who are buried in North Winfield. He was a farmer in the town of Litchfield and late in life retired to Cedarville. His grandson, Kernan J. Hadley, is now living on the homestead and remembers that his grandfather was said to have come from England with his parents when quite young, and from North Hadley to Litchfield.

Children, born in the town of Litchfield

Abram Hadley, settled in Oswego County, N. Y.; m. Jemima Townsend. Children: i. Elizabeth, died. ii. George, died.
Maria Hadley, m. Horatio Nelson and resided in Illinois. Children: Lucy; Cornelia. A grandson is Irving N. Clark of Humboldt, Iowa.
William Hadley, Jr., b. Aug. 14, 1811; d. May 26, 1886; was a farmer in Litchfield; m. Mary Ann Joslyn, b. Oct. 21, 1818, d. Nov. 2, 1893. Children: i. Romanda, b. June 30, 1842; d. Jan. 5, 1917. ii. Mary E., b. Aug. 21, 1847; d. June 7, 1915. iii. Kernan J., resides on his grandfather's homestead; m. and had children, Frank J., b. June 5,

1893, d. Jan. 18, 1907; Rice, b. Dec. 24, 1896, d. June 9, 1918; Mildred L., b. Apr. 4, 1908.

John Hadley, resided in Litchfield; m. Sarah Wilkinson. Children: i. Julia. ii. Adeline. iii. John I., b. Apr. 18, 1847; d. 1918; m. (1) Tennie Baldwin, who d. in 1887 (leaving two children, Leo, who d. in 1910, and Harry, who lives in Clayville, N. Y.); m. (2) 1893, Eva Rising.

Henry or *Harry Hadley,* twin with Harriet, b. May 18, 1815; d. Mar. 9, 1854; m. Nov. 1, 1838, Mary Elizabeth Rising. See further for their children's records.

Harriet Hadley, twin with Henry, b. May 18, 1815; m. David Cole. Children: Freeman; Rhoda; Dette; Menzo; Edward; Amelia; Albert. Of these, Albert of West Winfield, and Menzo of Bridgewater, N. Y., have families.

Elmira Hadley, twin with Alsigna; m. Benjamin Getchell and died soon after her marriage, leaving a daughter who was brought up by her grandparents, William and Lucy (Warner) Hadley, m. Eugene Huntley, and resided in Iowa.

Alsigna Hadley, twin with Elmira; d. when a small child.

Henry and Mary Elizabeth (Rising) Hadley had children, born at Cedar Lake, Herkimer Co., N. Y.

Caroline Elizabeth Hadley, b. May 27, 1841; resided in West Winfield, now in Sauquoit, N. Y.; m. at Cedar Lake, Jan. 17, 1866, Dolphus S. Marshall, b. in North Litchfield, son of Charles and Clara (Bacon) Marshall. He served three years in the Civil War. Children: i. Mary Josephine, b. in North Litchfield, Apr. 3, 1871; m. Fred Mould, resides in Sauquoit, and has a son Marshall. ii. Grace Almira, b. at Cedar Lake, Jan. 6, 1882; d. Mar. 1, 1885.

Augusta Lovina Hadley, b. Feb. 28, 1844; d. in Bristol, Ill., June 3, 1905; m. at Cedar Lake, N. Y., Mar. 22, 1865, Nelson Catlin Rider, b. at Cedar Lake, July 23, 1842, d. in Bristol, Ill., Oct. 13, 1911, son of Wakeman and Hannah E. (Bates) Rider. He was a farmer. Children, b. in Bristol: i. Carrie Augusta, b. July 21, 1872; m. Nov. 24, 1892, John Hawley Loucks, resides in Charlotte, Mich., and has children, b. in Bristol, Lawrence Jerry, b. Jan. 2, 1896; Almerin Nelson, b. Jan. 29, 1898; Charles Emmons, b. Oct. 29, 1901. ii. Jerry Wakeman, b. Feb. 25, 1875; m. in Aurora, Ill., Oct. 15, 1896, Frances Isabel Hanson, and has a son, Gerald Wakeman, b. Oct. 21, 1907, in Bristol.

Gilbert William Hadley, b. July 20, 1846; resides near West Winfield; m. (1) Jan. 27, 1875, Ellen M. Matteson, who d. Dec. 4, 1887. Child: Ona Clarissa, b. Nov. 12, 1878; m. Oct. 12, 1903, Wesley C. Dygert; resides in Calgary, Alberta; has a son Gilbert Wesley, b. Nov. 4, 1910. G. W. Hadley m. (2) May 20, 1890, Sarah A. Jones. Child: Henry Gilbert, b. Jan. 25, 1894, has the degree of M.D. from George Washington University.

Martha Jane Hadley (twin), b. Oct. 12, 1848; resides at Miller's Mills, Herkimer Co., N. Y.; m. in Bristol, Ill., Oct. 16, 1872, Israel Ira Young, b. at Miller's Mills, Dec. 8, 1848, son of Henry and Lydia (———) Young. Children: i. Harry, b. May 10, 1877; d. Oct. 2, 1902. ii. Grace Aline, b. 1887; was graduated from Syracuse University in 1910; was a teacher of German for five years;

m. Sept. 25, 1916, John Wesley Elliott, who studied for the ministry in Chicago University, A.M., 1917, resides in Haddonfield, N. J.
Mary Josephine Hadley (twin), b. Oct. 12, 1848; resides in Utica, N. Y.; m. at Cedar Lake, about Sept. 30, 1872, Orange Brainerd Holmes, b. in North Winfield, Apr. 26, 1847, son of Orange and Henrietta (———) Holmes, d. June, 1916. Children: i. Mabel Martha, b. Oct. 31, 1875; resides in Auburn, N. Y.; m. in North Winfield, Jan. 21, 1901, Maurice Richards, and has three children, Mary, b. Feb. 11, 1902; Ruth, b. Apr. 21, 1906; Jean, b. Aug. 28, 1912. ii. Harold Brainard, b. Sept. 18, 1888; is a dentist, practicing in New York City; m. in West Winfield, N. Y., Dec. 25, 1912, Millie E. Stebbins.
Lucy Maria Hadley, b. Apr. 21, 1851; resides in Hoosick Falls, N. Y.; m. Jonathan Cottrell. Children: Irving; Charles.

257 DANIEL BRAINERD⁶ WARNER, son of Daniel⁵ and Nancy (Brainerd) Warner, born in East Haddam, Conn., March 24, 1807; died there, February 25, 1891. When a young man he went to Clinton, Mich., and for a few years carried on a mercantile business there. Returning to East Haddam he engaged in the business of ship-building, and, in his later years, in the lumber business. Many of the largest ships of his day were constructed in his yard. He resided at East Haddam Landing and took a prominent part in the life of the community. He was a member and for several years vestryman of St. Stephen's Episcopal Church. In 1849 (and again in 1880) he was elected to the State Legislature; in 1852, to the State Senate, and became its President pro tem.; was county commissioner, town clerk and registrar, postmaster, and director and president of the East Haddam Bank. In military circles he was also well known, as a member of the Staff of Gen. Oliver Warner, Brigade Major and Inspector of Artillery. (Commemorative biographical record of Middlesex Co., Conn., p. 436.)

Married in East Haddam, April 28, 1835, MARY ANNA GREEN, born in East Haddam, November 11, 1816, died February 23, 1896, daughter of Oliver and Damaris (Howe) Green. Her grandfather, James Green, manufactured muskets for the government during the Revolution.

Children, all but first born in East Haddam

Nancy Lucretia Warner, b. in Clinton, Mich., May 17, 1837; bapt. at St. Stephen's Church, East Haddam, Oct. 26, 1837; d. in East Haddam, Jan. 19, 1838.
429 *Charles Belden Warner*, b. July 28, 1839; m. (1) Georgiana Goodspeed, (2) Winifred (Plumstead) Gibboney.
430 *Mary Green Warner*, b. Aug. 7, 1842; m. Norman L. Boardman.

431 *Sidney Brainerd Warner*, b. Dec. 6, 1849; m. Cassie Hillar Post.
Georgian Lucretia Warner, b. Apr. 3, 1852; resides in East Haddam and has travelled extensively; is a member of the D. A. R.
Jennett or *Antoinette Louisa Warner*, known as Nettie L., b. Sept. 22, 1854; resides in East Haddam; m. Sept. 9, 1890, Henry Martyn Morgan, b. at Bristol, England; no children.

258 SELDEN JEWETT[6] WARNER, son of Selden[5] and Betsey (Brockway) Warner, born in East Haddam, Conn., September 9, 1787; died in Lyme, October 16, 1862. He was a farmer in Lyme.

Married in Lyme, January 23, 1819 (Hamburgh Church Record), **MARY BROCKWAY**, born in Lyme, daughter of Zebulon and Abigail (Banning) Brockway, and granddaughter of Ebenezer and Mary (Butler) Brockway. She died June 10, 1854, in her 81st year.

Children

432 *Abby E. Warner*, b. June 26, 1820; m. George Nelson Phelps.
433 *Zebulon Brockway Warner*, b. Dec. 29, 1824; m. Harriet Miranda La Place.
434 *Mary Matilda Warner*, b. Apr. 30, 1829; m. Roswell Phelps La Place.
Caroline L. Warner, b. Aug. 28, 1831; d. Mar. 9, 1916; m. in Lyme, 1860, Nathan Reynolds, son of George and Polly (Miller) Reynolds of Lyme. They had no children.
John S. Warner, b. Feb. 7, 1838; d. of typhoid fever, Nov. 6, 1866, not married; was a farmer.

259 EBENEZER BROCKWAY[6] WARNER, son of Selden[5] and Betsey (Brockway) Warner, born in East Haddam, Conn., February 8, 1791; resided in Lyme, where he was a farmer and fisherman.

Married (1) in Lyme, **LUCINDA M. BANNING**, born 1795, died December 4, 1867, daughter of Joseph and Susannah[5] (Warner) Banning.

Married (2) in Lyme, **NANCY (BANNING) LAY**, born 1790, died December 1, 1871, daughter of Joseph and Susannah[5] (Warner) Banning. She had no children by this marriage. See number 138.

Children of Lucinda M. Banning

Susan M. Warner, b. Aug. 25, 1815; d. Dec. 10, 1899; m. ——— Francis.
435 *Joseph Brockway Warner*, b. Aug. 1, 1823; m. (1) Tirza A. Hurd, (2) Lydia A. Connick.
Jane Elizabeth Warner, b. Jan. 27, 1826; d. June 23, 1854.
Lucinda M. Warner, b. June 4, 1829; d. July 7, 1866.
Ebenezer Warner, b. Feb., 1833; died.

260   DAVID[6] WARNER, son of Selden[5] and Betsey (Brockway) Warner, born in East Haddam, Conn., March 7, 1798; died August 9, 1871. He resided in Lyme, Conn.
Married ELIZABETH PARKER JOHNSON, born 1801; died March 20, 1888.

Children

436   David Carlos Warner, b. 1826; m. Angeline (Tooker) Warner.
George Warner, b. 1828; d. May 20, 1894; m. 186-,. Ella Jones, b. Mar., 1847, d. Dec. 25, 1905, daughter of Henry and Phebe (Sill) Jones. Children: i. Catherine. ii. William. iii. George, m. Selina Price and had two daughters. iv. Mary. v. Louis H., b. 1874. vi. Gertie. vii. Grace.
437   Ulysses Southworth Warner, b. Sept. 27, 1833; m. Angelina Tooker.
438   Betsey Ann Warner, b. July 17, 1835; m. (1) John Russell Beebe; (2) Joseph Henry Alvord.
439   Timothy Parker Warner, b. Sept. 17, 1837; m. Caroline Maria La Place.

261   THOMAS JEFFERSON[6] WARNER, son of Selden[5] and Betsey (Brockway) Warner, born in East Haddam, Conn., January 17, 1805; died April 22, 1858. He resided in the town of Lyme, Conn.
Married August 20, 1837, SARAH BUCKINGHAM LAY, born July 17, 1810, died May 14, 1893, daughter of Erastus and Nancy (Banning) Lay, and granddaughter of Joseph and Susannah[5] (Warner) Banning. See number 138.
She married (2) as second wife, Jonathan Loring[3] La Place (Francis[2] and Abigail (Wood), Jonathan[1] and Caroline (Brockway) La Place). His first wife was Czarina Cobb.

Children

Emma Lemira Warner, b. May 20, 1838; d. Apr. 25, 1889; m. Sept. 4, 1872, Henry T. Kollock, son of —— and Polly (Cleaveland) Kollock. Child: Lemuel, b. Dec. 28, 1873, resides in West Lynn, Mass.
Helen L. Warner, b. June 25, 1841; d. Sept. 28, 1849.
Jane Elizabeth Warner, b. Mar. 14, 1844; d. July 25, 1889; m. Nov. 12, 1867, George Benjamin Jones, b. Jan. 2, 1840, in Hebron, Conn., son of Timothy Fitch and Maryette (Strong) Jones. Children: i. Emmogene Elizabeth, b. Oct. 31, 1868; m. at Westchester, Conn., Oct. 3, 1889, Thomas H. Smith of Colchester, Conn., and Denver, Colo., where they now reside; has one son, Horace Malcolm Root, b. in Denver, Apr. 27, 1897. ii. Gertrude Helen, b. in Hebron, Conn., June 19, 1870; resides in East Hampton, Conn.
Thomas Jefferson Warner, b. Aug. 8, 1846; d. Oct. 8, 1849.
Nancy Annie Warner, b. Oct. 4, 1848; m. Oct. 15, 1868, Stephen Parker Sterling, b. Oct. 15, 1842, son of Stephen Sterling of Lyme, and his wife, Sarah Marvin, daughter of Asahel[4] Marvin (Timothy[3], Elisha[2], Captain Reinold[1] or Reginald). Child: Sarah Marvin, b. Nov. 19, 1870; m. —— Meeks.

Erastus Selden Warner, b. July 21, 1852; d. Oct. 7, 1915. He was born and lived in the town of Lyme. Married Nov. 25, 1880, Kate Louisa Mather, b. in East Haddam, Conn., Nov. 20, 1852, resides in East Haddam, Conn. They had no children. She is the daughter of Eleazer Watrous and Elisabeth Louisa (Foster) Mather. Elisabeth Foster was a descendant of Reginald Foster, the emigrant, of Ipswich, Mass., and a lineal descendant of Miles Standish through the marriage of his granddaughter Hannah Standish to Nathan Foster of Stafford, Conn. Eleazer Mather was a descendant of Rev. Richard[1] Mather of Dorchester, Mass., through his son Timothy[2] (who was a brother of Increase Mather), Richard[3], Lieutenant Joseph[4], Dr. Eleazer[5], Dr. Augustus[6], Eleazer Watrous[7]. He was also a descendant of Hannah Ransom and Robert Ransom of Colchester.

Lillian Evelyn Warner, b. June 27, 1854; d. Apr. 6, 1915; m. June 3, 1890, Henry T. Kollock; no children.

262 AGUR[6] WARNER, son of Noadiah[5] and Polly (Curtis) Warner, born at Bennett's Bridge, South Britain, Conn., March 23, 1789; died March 3, 1871. He was a farmer and resided on his father's homestead a quarter of a mile southeast of Bennett's Bridge. He was a member of the Methodist Church of South Britain. Buried in Warner Cemetery.

Married **POLLY BASSETT,** born about 1790, died January 10, 1866, aged 76. It is said that she came from the western part of the state and was one-fourth Pequot Indian blood. She was a sister of Philo Bassett. Keziah Bassett, who died May 6, 1842, aged 77, and was buried in the Warner Cemetery, was doubtless a relative.

Children

Jane Ann Warner, b. Dec. 5, 1810, in South Britain; m. there, Sept. 14, 1839, Agur Treat Curtis of Stratford, and removed to Stratford. Child: Helen.

440 *Samuel Curtis Warner,* b. June 21, 1813; m. Eliza Sherman.

Mary A. Warner, b. Oct. 5, 1815, in South Britain; d. Oct. 11, 1888; m. Nov. 12, 1838 (Southbury records), Theophilus Curtis of Newtown; had two sons and a daughter.

441 *Noadiah Warner,* b. Oct. 10, 1817; m. (1) Laura J. Hinman, (2) Alice E. Beardsley.

263 JUDSON[6] WARNER, son of Harvey De Forest[5] and Elizabeth (Clark) Warner, born in Southbury, Conn., February 28, 1798; died February, 1880. He was a merchant in Bethlehem, Conn., and removed to Newtown in 1839. His sons were all farmers with the exception of Mark L.

Married in Woodbury, Conn., September 27, 1826, **ABIGAIL LEAVENWORTH,** born in Woodbury, June 4, 1804; died February 28, 1866, or March, 1867. She was the daughter of Russell and Althea (De Forest) Leavenworth. (Leavenworth Gene alogy.)

Children

Mark Warner, b. Oct. 18, 1827; d. July 15, 1828, in Bethlehem, Conn.

John Warner, b. July 23, 1829, in Bethlehem; d. 1908; buried in Stepney Cemetery; m. Dec. 4, 1862, Mariette Hull of (Stepney) Monroe, Conn.; no children.

Charles Warner, b. Feb. 17, 1831, in Bethlehem; d. in Newtown, Jan. 24, 1899; was a farmer and mill owner in Newtown; m. there, Dec. 28, 1857, Samantha Bemis, b. in Salisbury, Conn., Aug. 1, 1837, d. in Newtown, June 4, 1909, daughter of William and Sally (Blodgett) Bemis. Child: Clare B., b. July 7, 1859; d. Feb. 12, 1891; m. Dec. 26, 1877, Charles H. Botsford, b. Nov. 28, 1852, son of Sherman and Cornelia W. Botsford. He is a contractor and builder in Bridgeport. They had two children, Frederick Warner, b. Mar. 3, 1879 (resides in Stratford, Conn., m. July 8, 1903, Helma Sherman of Newtown, b. Apr. 30, 1871, and has a child, Dorothy Claire, b. in Bridgeport, May 27, 1905), and Jessie Ruth, b. Jan. 8, 1889 (resides in Stratford, m. Sept. 4, 1912, in Milford, Louis N. Harris, b. in Chattanooga, Tenn., Mar. 1, 1889, has a child, Ruth Clare, b. Jan. 14, 1914).

Jane Warner, b. Mar. 10, 1833, in Southbury; m. May, 1855, George Clark, a farmer of Newtown, and had four children, three daughters and a son, Homer G., of Sandy Hook, Conn.

Mark Leavenworth Warner, twin with Margaret, b. Mar. 25, 1835, in Southbury, Conn.; was a merchant in Unionville, Lake County, Ohio; m. Apr., 1860, and had one son, Augustus G., of Barberton, Ohio.

Margaret Warner, twin with Mark L., b. Mar. 25, 1835, in Southbury; m. Charles Curtis, a farmer and shoemaker of Newtown, and died in childbirth, May 4, 1870.

Jennette Warner, b. July 17, 1837, in Newtown; resided in Bridgeport, now in Devon, Milford, Conn.; m. in Newtown, Jan. 18, 1866, Edward Rogers of Sheffield, Mass., son of R. J. Rogers. Child: Frederick S., b. in Bridgeport, July 4, 1869; d. Aug. 22, 1872.

Russell Leavenworth Warner, b. Mar. 10, 1840, in Newtown; is a farmer there; m. (1) Feb. 1, 1862, Eliza Plumb of Newtown; m. (2) May 3, 1869, Mary E. Bennett, daughter of John C. S. and Sarah Maria (Curtis) Bennett of Trumbull, Conn.; m. (3) Emma Underhill, July 1, 1885. Child of Russell L. and Eliza (Plumb) Warner: Lester Eugene, b. in Newtown, Oct. 22, 1863; resided at Bridgeport and New Milford, where he conducted a meat business and died Jan. 18, 1913; m. in Bridgeport, Oct. 29, 1890, Annie Steer, b. in Croydon, Surrey, England, daughter of Henry and Esther (Walsh) Steer; had a son, Russell H., b. in Bridgeport, Oct. 30, 1892, is an electrical truck foreman in Waterbury, Conn., member of I. O. O. F., m. in New Milford, Jan. 26, 1914, Mabel M. Spaulding, daughter of William and Vesta (Lyons) Spaulding of Washington, Conn. They had a son, Wilbur Hawley, b. in New Milford, Nov. 25, 1914, d. May 28, 1918. Children of Russell L. and Mary E. (Bennett) Warner: i. Eliza Marie, b. Nov. 12, 1871; d. in Devon, Milford, Conn., June 28, 1916; buried in Corinth, N. Y.; m. Sept. 4, 1905, Wilbur Benjamin Griffin, son of Jeremiah and Lucy (White) Griffin of Corinth. ii. Susie May, b. 1878; d. Feb. 21, 1880, aged 1 year, 9 months.

Polly L. Warner, b. July 22, 1842, in Newtown; d. Sept. 11, 1855.

Harvey De Forest Warner, b. Nov. 20, 1846, in Newtown; removed in 1868 to Bridgeport, and in 1910 to Milford, Conn.; is a carpenter; m. in Bridgeport, Nov. 12, 1873, Mary M. Smith, b. in Norwalk, Conn., May 20, 1849, daughter of Charles Lewis and Armenda (Weed) Smith. Child: Edith Grace, b. in Newtown, Mar. 6, 1880; d. Mar. 20, 1880.

264 NOADIAH[6] WARNER, son of Harvey De Forest[5] and Elizabeth (Clark) Warner, born in Salisbury, Conn., December 12, 1809; died February 2, 1894. He resided at Ore Hill, Salisbury, and was a farmer and the owner of an iron mine. He is remembered as a great story teller.

Married in Lakeville, Conn., September 13, 1836, ADALINE JONES, born in Southeast, N. Y., January 24, 1816, died May 20, 1881, a descendant of Caleb Jones who came to this country from Wales. She was the daughter of Horace Jones and his wife, Clarissa Foster, whose mother was Lydia Crosby, a relative of the blind poetess, Fanny Crosby. The Crosbys were people of culture, ability and means.

Children, born in Salisbury

Olive J. Warner, b. Aug. 26, 1837; d. June 7, 1842; buried in Town Hill Cemetery, Salisbury.

Darwin De Forest Warner, b. June, 1838; d. Apr. 29, 1907. He was graduated from boarding school with the valedictory and entered Troy University, intending to be a lawyer, but was obliged to give it up on account of ill health. Married Mar. 6, 1886, Lydia Irene Bates, b. June 6, 1841, d. Mar. 11, 1912, at Waterbury, Conn., daughter of Nathaniel H. Bates, b. Oct. 2, 1817, d. Jan. 6, 1846, in Wolcottville, Conn., and his wife Rowania Jane Thorpe, b. Dec. 14, 1818, d. Mar. 31, 1851, in Winsted, Conn.

Elizabeth Clark Warner, b. Jan. 24, 1841. She was an exquisite singer and pianist, an inheritance from the Jones family.

442 *Milton Jones Warner,* b. Oct. 16, 1842; m. Maria Birch Coffing.

Mary Jennette Warner, b. July 3, 1844, resides in Lakeville, Conn., on the old farm on Lake Wononscopomuc (Indian for "The Smile of God") which was owned by her father and grandfather, and is now owned by her nephew, George Coffing Warner.

265 JENNETTE[6] WARNER, daughter of Harvey De Forest[5] and Elizabeth (Clark) Warner, born in Salisbury, Conn., July 15, 1817.

Married in Salisbury, October 28, 1846, JAMES ELISHA KELLOGG, born July 21, 1818, in Sheffield, Mass., died in Galesburg, Ill., July 9, 1899, son of Captain Elisha and Jane

(Saxton) Kellogg. He was a farmer and resided at the homestead in Sheffield until 1864, when he removed to Woodhull, Ill.,
and in 1890 to Galesburg to spend the remainder of his life with
his son and daughter. He was an earnest member of the
Methodist Church, superintendent of the Sunday School and
leader of the choir.

Children, born in Sheffield

Jennie Elizabeth Kellogg, b. Nov. 8, 1847; d. Apr. 27, 1849.
Harvey Elisha Kellogg, b. Feb. 6, 1849; was for thirty years in the
   dry goods business, is now a traveling salesman; resides in Gales-
   burg; not married.
Alice Jennette Kellogg, b. Feb. 10, 1851; d. Dec. 1, 1901; m. in Wood-
   hull, Ill., Dec. 23, 1879, Oscar Booth Chamberlain of Bridgeport,
   Conn., b. May 11, 1844, son of Willis and Caroline (Hall) Chamber-
   lain. He was a teacher in Galesburg. Children, born in New Canaan,
   Conn.: i. Ralph Kellogg, b. June 1, 1881; d. Dec. 18, 1881. ii. Alice
   Carolyn, b. Mar. 29, 1883; resides in Galesburg, Ill. iii. Frank
   Kellogg (twin), b. Oct. 17, 1885; d. Jan. 13, 1886. iv. Warner
   Kellogg (twin), b. and d. Oct. 17, 1885.
Mary Jane Kellogg, b. Mar. 26, 1854; d. Sept. 8, 1856.

266 DONALD JUDSON[6] WARNER, son of Harvey De
Forest[5] and Elizabeth (Clark) Warner, born in Salisbury, Conn.,
September 15, 1819; died there, May 31, 1904. He was admitted
to the Bar in 1842 and settled in Salisbury where he practised
his profession through a long, successful and honorable career;
he was Judge of the District Court and of the Court of Common
Pleas for eight years, retiring at the age limit; represented his
town several times in the General Assembly; was a warm
friend of the War Governor Buckingham, who appointed him
Quartermaster General; this was offered him unexpectedly and
he never qualified.

Married in Salisbury, November 16, 1847, **LOIS CAMP
TICKNOR BALL,** born in Salisbury, March 27, 1829, died January 13, 1880, daughter of Robert and Sophia Bingham (Ticknor) Ball.

Children, born in Salisbury

443 *Donald Ticknor Warner,* b. Dec. 15, 1850; m. Harriet Electa Wells.
   Grace Warner, b. Mar. 20, 1856; is a teacher in Salisbury; not married.
   Adéle de Forest Warner, b. Aug. 8, 1859; resides in Salisbury; not
      married.
   Lois Warner, b. Feb. 7, 1863; resides in Salisbury; not married.
   Malcolm Clark Warner, b. June 26, 1866; is in business in San Antonio,
      Texas; m. Nov. 24, 1894, Charlotte J. Marsh Shepard. No children.

267 DEFOREST[6] WARNER, son of Augustus[5] and Maria
(Cande) Warner, born February 27, 1814, in Southbury, Conn.;

died October 25, 1874, in Orchard Grove, Ind., where he had resided as a farmer for some time. He lived in Otsego County, N. Y., for a time, in the town of Otego, and his name occurs on land papers of 1839, 1840, and 1847, recorded in Cooperstown, N. Y.

Married in Connecticut, February 25, 1838, **LOVICY CURTIS**, born in Connecticut, February 23, 1821, died in Stanberry, Mo., July 30, 1897. Her mother was a Nettleton.

Children

Theron Nettleton Warner, b. Nov. 22, 1841; d. aged about 15.

Myron Curtis Warner, b. in Stratford, Conn., Jan. 25, 1844; d. in Monroe, Conn., Sept. 1, 1873; was a merchant and postmaster at Orchard Grove, Ind.; m. in Monroe, Conn., June 1, 1871, Sophronia Winton Sherman, daughter of Harry Burton and Mary Rebecca (Sears) Sherman, b. in Monroe, Conn., June 11, 1851, d. Apr. 2, 1901, in Newtown, Conn. Child: Myra Eva, b. Nov. 8, 1872, in Orchard Grove, Ind., resides in Newtown, Conn.

Anson Candee Warner, b. Apr. 11, 1846; resided in Lowell, Ind.; is probably living in Colorado; m. (1) Essie ———, (2) Gertrude Curtis, (3) Lizzie ———. He has one daughter living, Mrs. Essie Chandler, who resides in Colorado.

Thena Adell Warner, b. Feb. 5, 1859; resides in Santa Barbara, Calif.; m. Oct., 1876, J. C. Kenney. Children: i. Ina Maude, b. June 21, 1877; resides in Santa Barbara. ii. Floyd W., b. July 14, 1879; resides in Glendale, Calif.; m. Lora Fine and has children, Flora Thelma, b. Dec. 27, 1902, and Floyd Deforest, b. Dec. 21, 1907.

268 EMELINE[6] WARNER, daughter of Augustus[5] and Maria (Cande) Warner, born November 20, 1816, in the district of Wapping, Southbury, Conn.; died July 8, 1892, in Greencastle, Ind. She resided in Zoar, Conn., for sixteen years, and in Indiana (Lawrence), Kansas, and New Mexico, twenty-six years.

Married in Wapping, Southbury, Conn., January 8, 1838, **SALMON BEERS CURTIS**, born in Zoar, Newtown, Conn., son of John and Sarah Anne (Nettleton) Curtis. He died before 1892.

Child

Theron DeForest Curtis, b. in Zoar, Mar. 19, 1841; served in the Civil War; resides in Marion, Ind., in the Soldiers' Home. Children: i. Walter, died. ii. Nelson, whereabouts not known. iii. Wilbur, is superintendent of schools in Kenawee, Ill., married and has three children, Hazel, Vernon, and Margaret Ann.

269 DE LUZON[6] WARNER, son of Augustus[5] and Maria (Cande) Warner, born July 4, 1824, in Wapping district, Southbury, Conn.; died September 22, 1874, in Orchard Grove, Ind.,

where he had resided as a farmer, for some years. He resided in
Otego, Otsego County, N. Y., about 1847, as his name is found
as a landowner there.

Married at Walker's Farm, Conn., November 5, 1854, SUSAN
SHERMAN, born at Walker's Farm, Conn., October 29, 1827,
died May 5, 1909, at Crown Point, Ind., daughter of Carlos and
Polly (Plumb) Sherman.

Children

Evana Augusta Warner, b. Aug. 6, 1855; d. aged three weeks.

Etta Viola Warner, b. July 18, 1862; m. Sept. 24, 1891, Louis W.
Vilmer, who died leaving no children.

Ellen M. Warner, b. Oct. 11, 1864; resides in Chicago, Ill.; m. May 21,
1906, W. D. Jones, and has an adopted daughter, Faith Warner Jones.

Augustus Sherman Warner, b. Oct. 11, 1868; is a physician in Chicago;
studied medicine at the University of Michigan, 1891-4, was graduated
from Northwestern University in 1895, M.D. Married Aug. 31, 1898,
Eldora Williams. Children: i. Paul De Forest, b. Nov. 21, 1899; d.
May 1, 1901. ii. Philip De Luzon, b. Nov. 6, 1901. iii. Mildred
Christina, b. Nov. 24, 1903.

270 CLARINDA MARIA[6] WARNER, daughter of Augustus[5] and Maria (Cande) Warner, born in Wapping, town of
Southbury, New Haven County, Conn., February 1, 1828;
resides in Los Angeles, Calif. (1916), with her daughter. She
was educated at the Franklin Collegiate Institute, Franklin, N. Y.

Married at Orchard Grove, Cedar Creek, Lake County, Ind.,
December 3, 1854, JOHN J. CURTIS, born in Chesterfield,
Mass., September 23, 1820, died in Algona, Iowa, November 2,
1897, son of Nathan and Xoe (Cudworth) Curtis. He was educated at the Franklin Collegiate Institute, Franklin, N. Y.

Children, born at Cedar Creek, Ind.

Warner Augustus Curtis, b. Mar. 1, 1856; d. Feb. 17, 1863.

Clara May Curtis, b. May 28, 1861; was educated at Valparaiso University, Valparaiso, Ind.; resides in Los Angeles, Calif.; m. Jan. 20,
1886, Llewellyn Jackson Rice, b. Apr. 4, 1861, in Campton township,
Kane Co., Ill., son of James Caldwell and Maria (Bogue) Rice. He
was graduated from Valparaiso University and is an investment
broker. Children, born at Iowa Falls, Iowa: i. Marie Luella, b.
Jan. 8, 1887; is a graduate of the Occidental College in Los Angeles
and of the California State Normal School, a member of the Presbyterian Church, a teacher in Los Angeles. ii. Lulu Byrd, b. May 29,
1888; is a graduate of the Occidental College in Los Angeles and of
the University of Southern California, a member of the Presbyterian
Church, a teacher in Los Angeles. iii. Milton Curtis, b. Nov. 3, 1889;
d. May 17, 1902, in Phoenix, Ariz.; was accidentally shot by another
boy a little older.

Clarence J. Curtis, b. July 17, 1862; d. Aug. 23, 1863.

271 **CHARLES⁶ WARNER**, son of Joseph⁵ and Sarah (Osborne) Warner, born and lived in East Haddam, Conn., and died before September 18, 1854, when Joseph O. Warner was appointed administrator of his estate.

Married **FANNIE COMSTOCK**, born in East Haddam. Her will was made June 18, 1879, and probated March 8, 1881.

Children

Oliver Warner, probably d. young.
444 *Joseph Osborn Warner*, b. Mar. 3, 1817; m. Eliza Ann Strong.
   Sarah W. Warner, resided in Hadlyme at the time of her marriage, June 20, 1845, by the pastor of the Congregational Church, to Daniel Strong of Southampton, N..Y.
   Charles A. Warner, b. 1833, in East Haddam; d. Sept. (or Oct.) 22, 1895; buried in Hadlyme; m. in Hadlyme, July 20, 1856, Permelia R.- Mack of East Haddam, b. about 1835, d. Dec. 30, 1847, aged 22. He left property to his niece, Clara S. Warner, who was executor of his will.
   Elizabeth Warner, was not married. Her will was made Sept. 17, 1877, probated May 1, 1888, mentioned her mother Fannie, brothers Joseph O. and Charles A., and Eliza A., wife of Joseph O.

272 **OLIVER⁶ WARNER**, son of Oliver⁵ and Charity (Brainerd) Warner, born in East Haddam, Conn., September 26, 1795; died there, February 9, 1853. He was a farmer in East Haddam, residing near the Presbyterian meeting house; was a member of St. Stephen's Church and vestryman in 1836; was active in military affairs and received the rank of general. The rector's book of St. Stephen's Parish refers to his "funeral sermon from the text, 'We all do fade as a leaf,' containing a short sketch of Mr. Warner by Rev. George W. Nichols." His will was made May 11, 1847, probated February 21, 1853.

Married May 29, 1822, **ELIZABETH ANN BLAKESLEY**, born August 18, 1801, died January 8, 1868, in East Haddam, daughter of Rev. Solomon and Ann (Chapman) Blakesley who resided in New Lisbon, N. Y., in 1831.

Children, born in East Haddam

Frederick W. Warner, b. June 2, 1823; d. Feb. 2, 1896, buried in the Congregational Cemetery, East Haddam. He was a farmer in the town of East Haddam. Married in Hadlyme, Nov. 12, 1856, Phoebe Elizabeth Moseley, b. Apr. 2, 1830, in Hadlyme, d. in East Haddam, July 29, 1906, daughter of Thomas and Elizabeth⁶ (Warner) Moseley; see number 144. Child: Edward O., b. in East Haddam, Apr. 2, 1859; was executor of his father's will in 1886 and sole heir of his aunt in 1902.
Isabella Elizabeth Warner, b. July 27, 1826; d. in East Haddam, Dec. 2, 1902; not married; buried in Congregational Church Cemetery, East Haddam.

273 ORREN[6] WARNER, son of Oliver[5] and Charity (Brainerd) Warner, born in East Haddam, Conn., September 3, 1805; died July 27, 1876. He was a farmer and blacksmith in East Haddam; with his family belonged to St. Stephen's Church and was vestryman in 1850 and 1856; held the rank of colonel in a military company. He resided in the South School District of East Haddam.

Married December 8, '1830' MATILDA ANN WILLEY, who died November 1, 1900, daughter of Ethan Allen and Mary (Brockway) Willey, and granddaughter of Abraham Willey, who was ensign and sergeant in the Revolution.

Children, born in East Haddam

Harriette Street Warner, b. Oct. 24, 1833; d. in Norwalk, Conn., Nov. 26, 1887; m. Oct. 24, 1856, Edward K. Lockwood of Norwalk; no children.

Amelia Warner, b. Nov. 8, 1836; d. Oct. 22, 1903, in Portland, Conn.; m. as third wife, June 12, 1875, Henry Gildersleeve, b. Apr. 7, 1817, d. Apr. 9, 1894, in Gildersleeve, Conn., son of Sylvester and Rebecca (Dixon) Gildersleeve. He was a member of a firm of commission merchants in New York City, and, after his retirement, was connected with the ship-building interests of Portland. He m. (1) Nancy Buckingham, and had two children, (2) Emily Finette Northam, and had seven children. Child of Amelia Warner: Orren Warner, b. Nov. 26, 1878, in Gildersleeve, was graduated from Portland High School and studied at Trinity College; was in the brokerage business in Hartford and Middletown until 1903, when he returned to Gildersleeve and is extensively engaged in dairying and stock raising.

Allen Willey Warner, b. Sept. 12, 1838; d. Mar. 20, 1892, in Hartford, Conn., where he had resided for some years. Children: i. Alice Louise. ii. Thomas Benton. iii. Grace Marie. iv. ————, d. in infancy. v. Mary Lockwood. vi. Carrie. vii. Henrietta. viii. Louise.

Catherine Jeannette Warner, b. June 10, 1841.

Mary (1) Warner, b. June 10, 1842; d. June, 1845.

Matilda Warner, b. July 16, 1845; resides in Gildersleeve.

Orrin Warner, Jr., b. Oct. 27, 1847; d. in New York City, Mar. 1, 1897, where he had resided for some time.

Mary (2) Warner, b. July 17, 1850; resided in New York City; d. in Portland, Conn., Oct. 12, 1887; m. Oct. 24, 1873, Aaron Neff. Child: Mary, b. July, 1875; d. in infancy.

274 EPHRAIM[6] WARNER, son of Ephraim[5] and Elizabeth (Brainerd) Warner, born in East Haddam, Conn.; is said to have resided in Newfield, N. Y.; died in Marlborough, Conn.

Married in Millington, Conn., May 12, 1822, MARY SPENCER MINER.

Children (three)

Lucius Bolls Warner, b. in Millington, Mar. 3, 1828; went to Jamestown, Chautauqua County, N. Y., in 1850 and started a furniture and chair business, with a planing mill and lumber yard, which became one of the most important industries in Jamestown, and enjoyed a high reputation and popularity. The business was destroyed by fire in 1867 but was rebuilt on a larger scale on a new site and eventually covered over three acres. In 1887, Mr. Warner built a five-story brick building known as the Warner block. He was known as a public-spirited citizen although he never took an active part in politics. He died in Jamestown, Feb. 14, 1905. Married there, Dec. 14, 1854, Mary Minerva Henry, daughter of Rev. William D. and Minerva (Densmore) Henry. As a permanent memorial to her husband, Mrs. Warner, after his death, presented his home to the Agnes Association to be used as a home for the old people of Chautauqua County. They had two children living in 1911: Frederick Henry, b. May 13, 1863, and Mary Elizabeth, b. Nov. 30, 1866. The latter married Feb. 6, 1890, Robert Newland Marvin, b. in Jamestown, Oct. 13, 1845, d. Feb. 6, 1909, son of Judge Richard Pratt and Isabella (Newland) Marvin. Upon coming of age he assumed control of his father's large business interests and estates and was highly esteemed as a public official and an officer in many banks, railways and other organizations.

275 **WILLIAM**[6] **WARNER**, son of Ephraim[5] and Elizabeth (Brainerd) Warner, born in East Haddam, Conn., June 25, 1800; resided there and died October 15, 1877.

Married in East Haddam, January 21, 1833, **LYDIA RAY**, born in Haddam, died in East Haddam, April 26, 1873, aged 73.

Children (four)

Hannah Elizabeth Warner, b. in East Haddam; m. June, 1858, Charles Franklin Shepard, b. June 19, 1829, son of Henry and Sally (Payne) Shepard; resided in Chatham, Conn. He was in business for a few years as maker of coffin trimmings and electro-plater of bells, at Cobalt, Conn.; then was part owner of three schooners engaged in the carrying trade between New York and New Haven; in 1859 returned to the homestead and was engaged in dairying and tobacco raising. Children: i. Edgar Eugene, b. Dec. 17, 1859; d. aged two years, eight months, thirteen days. ii. Harry Addison, b. July 17, 1863; d. Oct. 4, 1863. iii. Charles Franklin, Jr., b. Nov., 1864, is a molder by trade, with Union Works at New Britain, Conn.; member of the Legislature in 1897. iv. Dwight Hamlin, b. Oct. 7, 1866; is overseer of the Corbin Shops in New Britain; m. Mary Ellen Hunt of New Britain. v. Sarah Ellen, b. Jan. 20, 1871; d. Jan. 24, 1871. vi. Mary Elizabeth Davenport, b. Apr. 30, 1872; m. Oct. 24, 1894, Charles Arnold of New Britain. vii. Hannah Ethel, b. June 25, 1874.

276 **BETSEY ANN**[6] **WARNER**, daughter of Ephraim[5] and Elizabeth (Brainerd) Warner, born May 31, 1805, in Millington, Conn.; died April 25, 1880.

Married April 8, 1827, **GUY DAVENPORT** of Canterbury, Conn.

Children

Charles Davenport, b. Oct. 14, 1830, in Norwich, Conn.; d. Aug. 14, 1832.

Betsey Jane Davenport, b. Sept. 9, 1833; d. Sept. 11, 1868; m. in Chicopee Falls, Mass., Charles A. Taylor. Children: i. Charles Davenport, d. young. ii. Carrie Mabel, d. young. iii. Elizabeth Davenport, d. aged 20. iv. Jane Davenport.

Elizabeth Ann Davenport, b. May 18, 1836, in Kinsman, Ohio; m. in Chicopee Falls, Nov. 27, 1857, James K. Lombard of Springfield, Mass., who was in 1890 rector emeritus of St. Paul's Church, Fairfield, and resided in Darien, Conn. Children: i. Jane, d. young. ii. Guy Davenport.

277 ELIJAH[6] WARNER, son of Jesse[5], Jr., and Sarah (Warriner) Warner, born in Springfield (Longmeadow), Mass., February 25, 1770; died April 10, 1841. He removed to the town of Phelps, Ontario County, N. Y., and settled on a farm near that of his father at Warner Hill, east of the village of Orleans.

Married **RELIEF MARBLE,** who died February 20, 1849, aged 74 years, 2 months, 15 days.

Children, born in the town of Phelps

Dency Warner, d. in Barre, Orleans Co., N. Y.; m. James Storms. Children: Josephine; Charles; John; Warriner; Willard.

445 *Leonard Warner*, b. 1800; m. Lavina Thurston.

446 *Chester Warner*, b. Mar. 1, 1802; m. (1) Charlotte Rosanna Brooks, (2) Phoebe Jane Swan.

Sarah Warner, d. at Albion, N. Y.; m. Orrin Crane.

447 *Houghton Warner*, b. Apr. 19, 1806; m. (1) Mary Frary, (2) Mary M. Agard.

Josephine Warner, d. at Union Springs, N. Y.; m. William Crise.

Chauncey Warner, m. Axey Holden.

278 LEWIS[6] WARNER, son of Jesse[5], Jr., and Sarah (Warriner) Warner, born in Springfield (Longmeadow), Mass., November 11, 1772; died in the town of Phelps, Ontario County, N. Y., February 26, 1813, of the prevailing epidemic of cholera. He was recorded in the 1800 Census of Phelps with two sons under ten years of age. His farm was south of and adjacent to that of his father, and was south of Warner Hill.

Married in the town of Phelps, April 21, 1796, **MERCY RICE,** born in Conway, Mass., December 4, 1775; died in the town of Phelps, December 14, 1831. She was the daughter of Caleb[5] and Lucy (Leland) Rice, descended from Edmund[1] Rice, Joseph[2] and Mary (Beers), Phineas[3] and Elizabeth (Willard), Joseph[4] and Sarah (————) Rice. For further Rice records see Ward's Rice Genealogy, published in 1857.

Children, born in Phelps

448 *Rice Warner*, b. July 8, 1797; m. Rebecca Carson.

·*Dennis Warner*, b. July 13, 1799; removed to Olean and died there, Apr. 21, 1826; m. Jan., 1820, Clarissa Andrews.

Charles Warner, b. Aug. 30, 1801; was a tanner by trade, removed to Medina, N. Y., and died there; m. Dec. 4, 1823, Adeline Jerome of Phelps.

449 *Lewis Warner, Jr.*, b. Nov. 2, 1803; m. (1) Polly Gilson; (2) Margaret Baker.

450 *De Witt Clinton Warner*, b. June 5, 1806; m. Polly Scott.

Sophia Warner, b. Sept. 18, 1808; m. in Phelps, Aug. 3, 1826, Schuyler B. Paine. They removed to York, Mich., where both died.

Delilah Warner, b. Mar. 20, 1811; d. in Jackson, Mich.; m. in Phelps, Sept. 1, 1831, Horace Garlick, who died at Mt. Clemens, Mich. They had children.

Mercy Warner, b. Oct. 7, 1813; resided in Michigan, and died Dec. 14, 1834, at York, Mich.; m. Thomas Shaw; no children.

279 RUFUS⁶ WARNER, son of Jesse⁵, Jr., and Sarah (Warriner) Warner, born in Conway, Mass., February 25, 1775; died March 12, 1873, or February 7, 1869, in Hopewell, Ontario Co., N. Y. He came with his father to Ontario County in 1796 and settled later in the town of Hopewell where he engaged in farming. He was overseer of the poor in 1822, when the town was formed from Gorham, and held other offices of trust in the community.

Married May 1, 1800, HAZEL ELPONI RICE, born May 28, 1777, died July 3, 1862, daughter of Caleb⁵ and Lucy (Leland) Rice, and a descendant of Edmund¹ Rice of Sudbury, Joseph² and Mary (Beers), Phineas³ and Elizabeth (Willard), Joseph⁴ and Sarah (————), Caleb⁵. Her name is also recorded as Hazelpony Rice. For details of Rice family see the genealogy published in 1857 by Andrew H. Ward.

Children, born in Ontario County

451 *Lucy Warner*, b. Feb. 18, 1801; m. Aaron Ward.

452 *Gustavus Warner*, b. May 3, 1802; m. (1) Velura Darling, (2) Maria ————.

William Warner, b. Dec. 4, 1803; resided in Parma, N. Y.; removed to Albion, Mich.; m. Polly Carson (or Clara ————). Children: i. Mary, not married. ii. Helen, m. ———— Royston, and died leaving two daughters, Emma and Clara. iii. Willard, married; resides in Albion, Mich. iv. Marvin, married; died.

453 *Rosanna Warner*, b. Oct. 13, 1806; m. Gaylord Kellogg.

454 *Hiram Warner*, b. May 13, 1808; m. Mary Jane Knapp.

455 *Tirzah Warner*, b. Feb. 28, 1812; m. Samuel C. Gerow.
    Morris Warner, b. May 17, 1815; d. Oct. 4, 1849, at Parma Corners,
    N. Y.; m. Margaret Marks. Children: i. Edgar, of Salt Lake City.
    ii. Morris, Jr., who d. young.
456 *Lydia Ann Warner*, b. July 19, 1818; m. Charles Darling.
    Charles Warner, removed to Albion, Mich.

280 JOHN⁶ WARNER, son of Jesse⁵ and Sarah (Warriner)
Warner, born in Conway, Mass., January 2, 1781; died in
Phelps, Ontario County, N. Y., February 9, 1872. He removed
to the town of Phelps, Ontario County, soon after his father's
family in early youth, having remained in Massachusetts to
finish learning the harness-maker's trade. He also learned the
tanner's trade. He had a tannery in Phelps and manufactured
boots and shoes for people for miles around. He settled on the
northeast corner of the four corners on Warner Hill, opposite
his father's place, and after his father ceased the business of
keeping a tavern, he kept one on his corner for the accommodation of teamsters passing through with their teams of six or
eight horses, engaged in the transportation of freight between
Buffalo and Albany. In religion he was a Universalist.
    Married SUSAN ANN POST, born 1784; died 1868. She
was from Southampton, L. I. Her sister married Henry Jessup,
an early settler of Orleans.

Children

Jesse Post Warner, b. Dec. 13, 1806; d. 1850; m. Isabella K. Finch.
    Children: i. John Finch, b. 1842; d. 1845. ii. Elizabeth, b. Nov. 19,
    1846, in Saline, Washtenaw Co., Mich.; resides in Albion, Mich., and
    is Librarian of the Albion Public Library; m. in Ypsilanti, Mich.,
    May 1, 1872, William C. Farnham, b. in Ann Arbor, Mich., Nov.,
    1846, d. Feb. 10, 1884, son of Henry and Mary (————) Farnham.
    He was a soldier in the Civil War, Company K, 27th Michigan
    Infantry. Mr. and Mrs. Farnham had two children, born in Ypsi-
    lanti: Jane Isabella, b. June 24, 1874, m. Dr. George A. Geist, and d.
    in 1904, leaving no family, and Elizabeth Warner, b. Sept. 16, 1876,
    d. Oct. 14, 1886.
457 *Edwin Warner*, b. Nov. 17, 1809; m. Polly Ann Moore.
458 *Ulysses Warner*, b. May 7, 1812; m. (1) Mary Ann Rice, (2) Eliza
    Ann Jones.
    Maria Louisa Warner, b. Mar. 15, 1814, in Ontario County, N. Y.; d.
    July 1, 1902, in Warsaw, Ind.; m. in Ontario County, Nov. 19, 1835,
    Rev. William Cool, b. in Ontario County, Mar. 27, 1814, son of
    Christopher and Mary (Wheat) Cool. Children, born in Warsaw,
    Ind.: i. Harriet Warner, m. Dr. Wright, had six children, Bertha
    O'Brian, William (who m. and had one child), Fred, Alma, and two
    others. ii. Louisa Maria, resides in Denver, Colo.; m. Anson Wil-
    liams; has two sons, Anson and Byron.
459 *Orson Warner*, b. Dec. 4, 1816; m. Eliza Jane Sanford.

George Warner, b. July 13, 1819; d. 1885, not married. Removed to California.

John Warner, b. Nov. 13, 1821; m. Jane Van Buskirk; went to California in 1849. About a year after he first went west he came back for his wife and family. One child died on the journey. Children (nine in all): i. Effie. ii. Gertrude. iii. Ella. iv. Ora, m. —— Stone, resides in Petaluma, Cal. v. John.

Susan A. Warner, b. Sept. 6, 1827, in Orleans, N. Y.; d. 1896, in Chicago, Ill.; m. in Orleans, 1846, Hezekiah Begooley Edmonston, b. in Palmyra, N. Y., 1822, d. in Quincy, Mich., 1875. Children: i. Jessie F., b. 1848, in Orleans, N. Y.; resides in Brightwood Park, Washington, D. C.; m. 1876, Romain Dalley; has three children, Bessie, b. 1879, Hezzie, b. 1883, Clyde, b. 1890. ii. Lillie B., b. 1856, in Quincy, Mich.; resides in Chicago; m. 1879, William H. Wheeler; has two children, Edgar E., b. 1883, and Harold E., b. 1893.

460 *Harriet Elizabeth Warner,* b. Sept. 13, 1831; m. Clark Crosby Sears.

281 OLIVER[6] WARNER, son of Jesse[5], Jr., and Sarah (Warriner) Warner, born in Conway, Mass., December 28, 1782; died May 29, 1829. When a young man he settled in Hopewell, Ontario County, N. Y., located on three hundred acres of land, a mile or so west of the village of Orleans, and was one of the prominent farmers of the community. He was drafted and served in the War of 1812. Oliver Warner was killed by lightning. He had made a visit to Conway, his birthplace, and was returning home. A violent thunderstorm came, and while he and the others in the stage were hastening to shelter, he was struck and killed by lightning. This was in warm weather. There was no way of keeping the body, so he was buried, and the next winter two of his sons went by sleigh to the place where he was buried, and brought his body home. He was then buried in the little cemetery in the village of Orleans, Ontario County.

Married **LUCINDA RICE,** born in Conway, Mass., October 7, 1783; died in Phelps, N. Y., September 23, 1869. She was the daughter of Caleb[5] and Lucy (Leland) Rice, descended from Edmund[1] Rice of Sudbury, Joseph[2] and Mary (Beers), Phineas[3] and Elizabeth (Willard), Joseph[4] and Sarah (————). She resided with her son Milton after her husband's death.

Children, born in Hopewell, Ontario Co., N. Y.

Louisa Warner, b. Apr. 9, 1806; resided in Hopewell and Phelps, N. Y.; d. Sept. 13, 1888; m. Apr. 26, 1824, John Knapp. Children: i. Lucinda, m. Alexander Pardee and d. leaving two children, Edgar of Phelps and Minnie of Syracuse, N. Y. ii. Malvina A., m. Nov. 16, 1856, Stalham Crittenden, b. Apr. 30, 1827, son of Cotton and Esther (Rice) Crittenden who came to Phelps, N. Y., from Conway, Mass.; was assessor of the town for twelve years; had a son, Clarence E., who m. in 1879, Grace Van Auken, daughter of George

W. and Adaline (Humphrey) Van Auken, and had three children, Alice W., Mark C., and Ross. iii. Mary Elizabeth, m. —— Wells and removed to Ada, near Grand Rapids, Mich.

Morris Warner, b. Feb. 24, 1808; d. Feb. 1, 1809.

Daniel D. Tompkins Warner, b. Jan. 20, 1810; d. Mar. 24, 1889; lived and d. at Hopewell, N. Y.; m. (1) Mary Ann Freshour, who had no children; m. (2) Rebecca Witters. Children: i. Mary Ann, d. young. ii. Mark A., resides in Connecticut; is engaged with the Conn. Bridge Co. iii. Oliver M., removed to Philadelphia. iv. Dudley M., resides in the town of Hopewell.

Myron Halley Warner, b. Mar. 25, 1812; resided for a time in Phelps, N. Y., and east of Albion; d. in Albion; m. Julia Crane. Children: i. Arvilla, m. —— Balcom of Murray, N. Y. ii. Eugenia, m. —— Wright; removed to Rochester, N. Y. iii. George, removed to New York.

Oliver Lester Warner, b. July 1, 1814; lived near Saline, Mich.; d. Nov. 2, 1891; m. Oct. 9, 1834, Mary Ann Phelps, b. Jan. 5, 1817, in Ontario County. Children, four of whom were living in 1881: i. Cone C., b. in Ontario Co., N. Y., Aug. 28, 1835; removed to Lodi Township, Washtenaw Co., Mich., and was a farmer near Saline; m. Dec. 29, 1859, Armina Sheldon, b. in Washtenaw Co., Aug. 15, 1838, daughter of Newton and Susannah (——) Sheldon, who were natives of Cayuga County, N. Y. ii. Clark, d. near Ann Arbor, Mich., aged about 18 years, not married. iii. William P., resided in Pittsford Township, Washtenaw Co. iv. Oliver Lester, Jr., m. and d. leaving no children. v. Eva, m. —— Sperry, lives about two miles from Ann Arbor. vi. Mary L., m. —— Hill; resides near her sister.

Marietta Warner, b. Nov. 20, 1816; lived and d. in Hopewell, N. Y.; m. Jared Knapp. Children: i. Oliver, lives at Hopewell Center. ii. Henrietta, m. George Phelps, and both d. leaving one child, Ellsworth of Massachusetts.

Warren Warner, b. June 15, 1819; m. Jeanette Topliff; removed to Madison, Wis.; no children.

Caleb R. Warner, b. Sept. 14, 1821; d. Mar. 23, 1844; m. Jane Hutchinson; lived and died in the town of Hopewell, N. Y.; no children.

Milton Warner, b. Nov. 21, 1824; was educated at Canandaigua Academy; resided in Hopewell; was a member of the Grange and took an active part in public affairs. Married Oct. 19, 1848, Margaret Knapp, b. in Hopewell, May 28, 1830, daughter of Halstead Knapp, whose father, David Knapp, came from Harveston, Rockland County, and settled in Hopewell. Mr. and Mrs. Warner had no children.

282 JESSE⁶ WARNER, 3d, son of Jesse⁵ and Sarah (Warriner) Warner, born in Conway, Mass., January 23, 1786 (or December 23, 1785); died in York Township, Washtenaw County, Mich., April 5, 1861. He removed with his parents to the town of Phelps, Ontario County, N. Y., in 1796, and settled on the first hill east of the village of Orleans. About 1833 he removed to Michigan and settled in York. His standing in the

new community was high, as he was a delegate to the Second
Convention of Assent (Constitutional Convention) in 1836.

The following account of his thrilling adventures in the army
was written by his youngest daughter, Margaret Warner
Kellogg:

"When my father grew to manhood he joined the 71st Regiment, New
York Militia (Philetus Swift's). He was married and had two children
when the War of 1812 began and his regiment was called to the front. He
shouldered his gun and on December 24th, 1813, marched to Buffalo, or
Black Rock, as it was then called. On December 30th a battle took place
and, owing to some mistake, they were surrounded in a woods by hostile
Indians, defeated, and forced to retreat. The woods were full of Indians
hiding behind the trees and many of our brave men were killed or wounded.
Father was wounded in the hip and, as the bullet could not be removed, he
carried it as long as he lived.

"As he was painfully limping along, the blood filling his boot, he came
suddenly into a small clearing and there he saw to his horror, his brave
commander, Col. Broughton, breathing his last; the Indians had shot him
and were just scalping him. Father was seen by the Indians before he
could escape, and being so badly wounded he knew escape was impossible.
An Indian approached him and said, 'Me no hurt you,' and took his gun
and uniform from him, giving him in place a tattered old Indian coat. He
picked up an old hat which was shaped like a sugar loaf. This hat was worn
by him when he afterward escaped and was kept as a souvenir for many
years.

"After a long and painful trip he and a fellow prisoner, Mr. Barker,
arrived at a Canadian block house not far from the Niagara River on the
Canadian side. Here they were confined in a small cell in the upper story.
They decided that they would die from the wretched treatment and food
if they waited to be exchanged or sent around by Quebec, as others were
sent, for the cold was intense and there was no heat and little clothing.

"They made a rope of a blanket and when the guard had passed on his
hourly inspection, they let themselves down from the window and ran to
the river. Here they tore the other blanket into strips and tied some rails
together making a raft which they soon got into the water. Large cakes of
ice were floating down the great Niagara River and it was a very dangerous
undertaking. But, after many narrow escapes and perilous moments, they
were near the shore, and by getting on the ice near the bank, were able to
reach land. I think the crossing was made at a point about eight miles
below the falls, and in crossing they drifted down stream over two miles.

"It seems that the guards soon discovered their escape and the Indians
were told to take them, dead or alive. No one thought they would attempt
to cross the river, and so the Indians searched the woods first, then went
to the river, where they saw the men afloat not very far down the stream.
Father heard their yells of disappointment and, if I remember rightly, the
Indians fired their guns at them, but none had the courage to try to follow
them on the river. Had the Indians captured them, they would have been
tortured and killed, as escaped prisoners were given up to the Indians.

"They reached home and found they had been given up as dead. My
father's brother, Oliver, was in the same battle, but escaped unhurt. He
heard from his comrades that his brother Jesse was wounded and so he

and all the family believed the Indians had scalped and killed him. When he got home, a man got on a horse and rode up and down the village streets shouting, 'Glory to God, Jess has got home,' and all the neighbors gathered together to hear his story."

A descendant says that the Warners as a family were all Democrats and Universalists, except two sisters who married into Orthodox families and were even then noted for their liberality in thought.

Jesse Warner married **MARGARET HUTCHISON**, born in Phelps, Ontario County, N. Y., December 15, 1792; died in York, Mich., September 19, 1849. Mrs. Kellogg writes:

"My mother was much beloved by all who knew her and I well remember the old home in the Michigan woods, the big fireplace with brick oven, the dozens of loaves of bread, pies and cakes that came out of it, and my mother's sweet face. The deer often ran across the clearing and one day a little spotted fawn jumped into my sister Elizabeth's arms for protection from the dogs."

Children, last born in York, Mich., others in the town of Phelps, N. Y.

461 *Jefferson Warner*, b. June 7, 1809; m. Susan Burnett.

Asenath Warner, b. Jan. 11 (or 19), 1811; d. in York, Mich., May 11, 1874; m. Milton Moore, b. Feb. 16, 1810, d. Dec. 9, 1851, in York. Children: i. Melissa Warner, m. Milo Clark and had one son, John, who m. Lizzie Parker and has one child. ii. Vean, m. George Harmon. iii. Lottie, m. ———— Merrill.

Almira Warner, b. Nov. 27 (or 29), 1813; d. in York, Mich., Feb. 27, 1839; m. Elijah Ellis. Her daughter m. John Jenness and had three children. Carl Coe, a great-grandson, was born in Ypsilanti, Mich., was graduated from the State Normal and University of Michigan, taught there two years and went to Harvard.

462 *Harrison Warner*, b. Oct. 8, 1815; m. Emily E. Davenport.

463 *Mary Warner*, b. Jan. 15, 1818, or Nov. 15, 1817; m. Parlia Phillips.

Caroline Warner, b. May 7, 1820; d. Jan. 18, 1904, in Saline, Washtenaw County, Mich.; m. Joseph Hand, who was born in New York. Children: i. Darwin, resided in Ann Arbor and was a soldier in the Civil War. ii. Jesse. iii. Emma.

464 *Lyman Warner*, b. May 23, 1822; m. Azuba Near.

465 *Sarah A. Warner*, b. Apr. 14, 1825; m. (1) Curtis Harmon, (2) Ezra O. Parker.

466 *Jesse Warner, 4th*, b. Apr. 30, 1827; m. Mary Eliza Kelsey.

William Oliver Warner, b. July 13, 1829; d. in York, Mich., 1901; served in Company C, 5th Michigan Cavalry, in the Civil War; m. Catherine Berry; no children.

Elizabeth Warner, b. May 1, 1832; d. in Saline, Mich., Feb. 15, 1905; m. in Adrian, Mich., Nov. 1, 1852, Wilson Hoag Berdan, b. in New York State, d. in Saline, Mich., Mar. 8, 1882, son of David and Harriet (————) Berdan. Children: i. Dwight Warner, b. in Lenawee County, Mich., Nov. 17, 1853; d. in Cheboygan, Mich., July 11, 1904;

was a physician. ii. Edward Grant, b. in Lenawee County, July 16, 1864; is depot master at the Lasalle Street Station, Rock Island Lines, Chicago.

467 *Albert Warner*, b. Dec. 13, 1834; m. Sarah A. Waugh.
468 *Margaret Warner*, b. Aug. 11, 1837; m. Elijah Ellis Kellogg.

283 **LUCINDA**[6] **WARNER**, daughter of Jesse[5] and Sarah (Warriner) Warner, born in Orleans, Ontario County, N. Y., November 21, 1796; resided after her marriage at Phelps, N. Y. Married July 4, 1813, probably in Orleans, **ELISHA PECK**, born in Phelps, April 11, 1789, died in Phelps, May 6, 1868, son of Darius and Lydia (Mack?) Peck. He married (2) Percy Scott, and (3) Sarah L. Crouch. The Peck Genealogy gives an account of this family.

Children, born at the Peck homestead in Phelps

Alvira Peck, b. Mar. 11 (or 24), 1814; m. Apr. 10, 1834, Richard Hallett; was living in Hillsdale, Mich., in 1869.

Lewis Peck, b. May 13, 1816; m. Oct. 27, 1854, Sarah Long; was graduated from Madison University in 1844; purchased his father's homestead in Phelps and resided there. He was the founder, in 1846, of the Union School which became the Phelps Union and Classical School; was supervisor of the town for several years; member of the New York State Legislature in 1860 and Assessor of Internal Revenue for some years, receiving his appointment from President Lincoln. Children: i. Cora, m. Charles Cheney of Cleveland, Ohio. ii. Nellie, m. H. C. Burdick of Claremont, Iowa. iii. Charles, present owner of the homestead in Phelps; m. Lillie Gifford, and had three children, Lewis, b. Oct. 17, ——, d. Sept. 20, 1914, m. Apr. 12, 1911, Olive Seager (and had two children, Lewis Seager and George Seager); Lillian, b. Mar. 24, 1893, m. Jan. 1, 1914, Benjamin Hale Austin; Charles Gifford, b. Oct. 20, 1898.

Lydia Peck, b. Feb. 6, 1818; d. at Phelps, Aug. 11, 1850; m. Oct., 1844, Daniel Crouch.

John Peck, b. Nov. 29, 1819; m. 1841, Amanda Gates; resided in Hillsdale, Mich.

Ira Peck, b. Nov. 18, 1821; m. Dec. 18, 1845, Marcia B. Dixon; resided in Port Byron, N. Y., in 1869.

Jesse Peck, b. Feb. 29, 1824; m. July, 1861, Hattie Walthart; resided in Brownsville, Pa.

Sarah Janet Peck, b. Dec. 13, 1825 or 1826; d. Sept. 14, 1853; m. Jan., 1846, Luther Worden.

284 **NATHAN**[6] **WARNER**, son of Nathan[5] and Jerusha (Webb) Warner, born in Hinsdale, Mass., January 31, 1785; died in Unionville, Ohio, September 8, 1841. He removed to Unionville, in the Western Reserve, in 1812, and took up five hundred acres of land near his father's claim.

Married July 4, 1810, SARAH (SALLY) COOK, born in Preston, Conn., a daughter of his father's second wife; died August 23, 1870.

Children, born in Unionville, Ohio

469 *Elbridge Oliver Warner*, b. Dec. 15, 1811; m. (1) Nancy Nellis, (2) Mrs. Minerva Shears, (3) Mrs. Sheaveral.
Sally Almira Warner, b. May 3, 1813.
Stephen S. Warner, b. Aug. 6, 1816; d. Jan. 16, 1892.
Amy J. Warner, b. July 23, 1822; d. Feb. 28, 1823.
Nathan W. Warner, b. Aug. 18, 1824; d. Mar. 14, 1825.
Emeline W. Warner, b. Apr. 13, 1827.

284a DAVID[6] WARNER, son of David C.[5] and Mary (Russell) Warner, born July 1, 1788; is said to have resided in Parma and Elba, N. Y., also at Mason and near Alaska, Mich., where he died in 1876. He was a soldier in the War of 1812 and in the Mexican War of 1847.

Married OLIVE RAWSON, born July 1, 1788, daughter of Silas and Rebecca (Fellows) Rawson of Conway, Mass., and Palmyra, N. Y.

Children

William Warner, d. in infancy.
Evaline B. Warner, b. in Parma, N. Y., 1812; d. in Alto, Mich., Feb. 20, 1895, not married.
Laura Warner, m. Eugene Smith, a merchant of Medina, N. Y. He was among the early gold-seekers who went to California. Two of their four children were: Hiram, m. and had children, Laurel and Julia, all deceased; Augusta, died.
469a *Charles C. Warner*, m. Eliza Foote.
469b *Rebecca Warner*, b. in Parma, Sept. 24, 1817; m. John McWhinney.
469c *Mary Warner*, m. Rev. John Fairchild.
469d *Jane Warner*, b. in Parma, N. Y., Nov. 26, 1821; m. Horace Sears.
469e *Lewis Warner*, b. June 2, 1823; m. Rosa A. Harris.
George Valorus Warner, was among the first pioneers to go to California in 1847; resided at Litchfield, Mich.; m. (1) Maletta Barrett, who died in 1867; m. (2) at Litchfield, Emma Lewis. Children: i. George. ii. Eliza, m. George Murdock. iii. Lillian.
Cordelia Warner, d. Oct., 1913; m. (1) Charles Bailes, (2) ———— Dennison, (3) David Slawson. Children by first husband: i. Eugene (Bailes), m. and had two children, Bertie and Allie. ii. Allie, m. and had four children; resides in Greenville, Mich. Child by second husband: John (Denison). Child by third husband: Wade (Slawson), m. and had three children, Boyd, Wadena and Donald.
Amanda Warner, m. Henry Donnelly and resided at Mason, Ingham County, Mich., where he owned the Hotel Donnelly for many years. Both are dead.
Mabelia Warner, lived near Batavia, N. Y.; d. many years ago; m. William Barton and had three children, all of whom d. in infancy.

284b WARHAM[6] WARNER, son of David C.[5] and Mary (Russell) Warner, born in Connecticut, August 21, 1779; died in Albion, Mich., in 1854. He was captain of a company in the War of 1812. In 1832 he sold his farm in western New York and removed to Michigan where he invested in some of the finest farming lands in the vicinity of Albion, then a mere nucleus of a village. His family moved there in 1834. He built the first frame house and later the first brick house in the village. With him Peabody built the first dam for water power. Mr. Warner was kind-hearted, generous, social, original in thought, prompt in action, liberal in religion, a democrat in politics, and devoted to the interests of his children. He was identified with all movements toward the improvement of the new town of Albion and also contributed largely toward building Albion College. He was a member of the Masonic fraternity.

Married (1) CYNTHIA ADAMS, born April 30, 1782, died in Albion, Mich., in 1847 or 1849, daughter of Darius and —— (White) Adams. She was an industrious, religious woman and a member of the Baptist Church.

Married (2) Mrs. EVA PHELPS, who died in 1890.

Children of Warham and Cynthia (Adams) Warner

469f *Lydia Warner,* b. Mar. 4, 1802; m. Levi Murray.

469g *Lucretia Warner,* b. Nov. 25, 1803; m. Samuel Douglas.

Ann M. Warner, b. Dec. 12, 1805; m. William Pearl. They went over the plains together in 1849 and she died there of consumption. Children: i. Augusta, b. David Peabody (children, Hermine and Pearl). ii. Lura, m. Orvis Robertson (children, William, George and Charles). iii. Ella, m. Charles Williams.

Lura Warner, b. Aug. 26, 1807; m. Chandler Church. They went to California in 1848 and lived there until his death, when she returned to Albion and bought the old Warner House. Children: i. Munson, m. Jennie Arthur and had a child, Carrie. ii. Mary, m. B. C. Whitman (their son Crosby is a physician in Paris, France). iii. J. Frank, m. Ida McCormack, had children, Mary, resides at Albion, Mich., m. Byron Jucket (had three children, Ida Lucile, d. aged 15 months, Helen and Reta), Frank E., resides in Duluth, Minn., m. Jessie Campbell (has children, Reuben and J. Frank), Chandler, was killed when a small boy by a fall from a horse, and George, d. at Albion.

Ashael Warner, b. Apr. 8, 1810; resided on a farm two miles from Albion, Mich., until his death; m. Mary Moon. Children (after their mother's death they removed to Faulkton, S. Dak., where they are prosperous farmers): i. Adelbert, m. Desla Coonrad. ii. Estella, m. Charles Oaks. iii. Myron. iv. Ernest.

Electa Warner, b. Mar. 5, 1812; m. Amos Finch.

Julia Warner, b. Feb. 27, 1814; died.

469h *William Adams Warner,* b. Jan. 30, 1816; m. Maria J. Finch.
    Elisha Warner, m. (1) Belinda Eggleston, (2) Carlinda Henry, (3) Martha Comstock. He resided in Albion all his life and died at the age of 84.
    Darius Warner, b. Apr. 7, 1823; m. Mandana G. Markham, who resides in Albion (1918) aged over 90, but well and active. ·
    Eliza Warner, b. Apr. 7, 1824; died.

285 TITUS[6] WARNER, son of Seth[5] and Mary (Clark) Warner, born January 26, 1767, probably in Belchertown, Mass.; died in Amherst, Mass., April 12, 1818; buried in Amherst. With his wife and two children he was recorded by the 1800 Census as a resident of Belchertown, and it is probable that he removed to Amherst about 1808-10. At a town meeting in Belchertown, March 5, 1792, he was chosen constable and collector for the north part of the town, and was to have four pence on the pound as a collection fee. He was also chosen one of the four hog-reeves of the town, and again in 1794 held this office. In 1795 he was again constable and in 1796 surveyor of highways. The appraisal of his estate, in 1819, mentions the following lands: home farm at Amherst, 80 acres; wood-lot, Pelham, 25 acres; home farm, Belchertown, 82 acres; Fairweather lot; Tucker farm; Rockwell place; and one-half of a pew in the Belchertown meeting house. The valuation shows him to have been a well-to-do man for those days. In the distribution of his estate, the widow received a share in the Amherst farm, while Park received land in Belchertown.

Titus Warner married December 26, 1793, **MARY** or **POLLY BAGGS,** born September 18, 1773, died November 15, 1843, buried in Amherst.

Children, first seven born in Belchertown, last two not recorded there but names found on probate court record of their grandfather's heirs

470 *Alonzo Elijah Warner,* b. Oct. 13, 1794; m. Ruth Cooke.
    Fanny Warner, b. Dec. 9, 1796; d. in Granby, Mass.; m., as recorded in Amherst, Cyrus Parker, b. Oct., 1791, son of Eli and Salome (Dickinson) Parker. Children, born in Amherst: i. Henry, b. Aug., 1824. ii. Francis, b. Oct., 1826. iii. George, b. Oct., 1829. iv. Mary Rebecca, b. June 1, 1831.
    Park (1) *Warner,* b. Aug. 11, 1798; d. Oct. 29, 180- (record torn).
    Mary (1) *Warner,* b. July 8, 1801; d. Nov. 5, 1802.
471 *Park* (2) *Warner,* b. Sept. 29, 1803; m. Joanna Adams.
    Mary (2) *Warner,* b. May 18, 1807; m. Noah Yale, recorded in Amherst. Their daughter, Harriet, m. —— Orton and resided in Bay City, Mich. (1916).
    Bathsheba Warner, b. Dec. 16, 1808; d. Dec. 17, 1809.
    Seth Porter Warner, birth not recorded in· Belchertown with other children, but given in Amherst town records as having been born in

Belchertown, although no date is given. He was mentioned in his mother's will in 1831. The historical sketch of the Belchertown Church notes that he moved away from Belchertown. He may be the Seth Warner of Belchertown who bought land in Amherst on the road leading from the east meeting house to Pelham, Feb. 18, 1833. Seth Warner of Easthampton bought land in 1846. Married in Whately, recorded in Amherst, Stetira R. Frary of Whately.

George Warner, birth recorded in Amherst but no date given; m. in Amherst, Oct. 13 or 14, 1836, Martha Smith Belding or Belden, b. Apr. 27, 1808, d. Feb. 16, 1868, recorded in Amherst, daughter of Elihu and Sarah (Clapp) Belding or Belden. Children, born in Amherst: i. Edward P., b. Mar. 16, 1838. ii. Mary E., b. Oct. 13, 1846; resides in Hinsdale, N. H.; m. —— Davison.

286 LUCRETIA⁶ WARNER, daughter of Jonathan⁵ and Mary (————) Warner, born in Belchertown, Mass., about 1774; died October 13, 1814, aged 40.

Married (intentions recorded May 13, 1796) THEODORE BRIDGEMAN, son of Joseph and Ruth (Wright) Bridgeman. He married (2) Abigail Strong, by whom he had Ann Elizabeth, and (3) Nancy Dwight, by whom he had Abigail Strong. He resided at the homestead of his father and grandfather in Belchertown and was a Lieutenant in 1815.

Children of Theodore and Lucretia (Warner) Bridgeman

Henry Augustus Bridgeman, b. Apr. 21, 1797; was a farmer at Belchertown, then insurance agent at Amherst, 1851-62, at Northampton, 1862-7, removed to Paxton, Ill.; was a member of the Massachusetts Legislature in 1844; justice of the peace in both states; m. May 6, 1821, Mary Strong, b. Oct. 25, 1795, daughter of Captain Phineas and Ann (Filer) Strong. Children: i. Phineas, b. Apr. 22, 1822; m. (1) Viann Jerusha Kendall, by whom he had five children; m. (2) Sylvia Louisa Lavinia Sherman, by whom he had six children. ii. Albert, b. July 17, 1825; d. Sept. 19, 1826. iii. Cornelia, b. July 7, 1827; d. Dec. 8, 1830. iv. Mary Strong, b. Dec. 19, 1829; m. Rev. Israel Brundage, a Congregational minister. v. Albert Henry, b. Jan. 6, 1832. For further details of these families see the Strong Genealogy.

Mary Bridgeman, b. Mar. 5, 1799; d. 1829; m. 1817, Benjamin Howe, who died in 1844, aged 50, son of Benjamin and Margaret (————) Howe.

Elijah Coleman Bridgeman, b. Apr. 22, 1801; d. 1861. He was converted at the age of 11, at the time of the great revival in Hampshire County, and was one of the class of 106 who united with the Belchertown Church. He was graduated from Amherst in 1826 and from Andover in 1829, was ordained and sent as a missionary to China in 1829, spending the four months of the journey by sailing vessel in studying the Chinese language. His letters, which came after an interval of eight months, were claimed as public property, and the profound impression made by the example of this brilliant scholar, joyfully leaving home and friends for a life among unknown heathen, created increased interest in the cause of missions throughout western Massachusetts. He joined Dr. Morrison in Canton and acquired the language so that he became interpreter for the Imperial Commissioner, and, in 1849, acted in a similar capacity for the U. S. minister. In 1847 he printed his version of the Bible at Shanghai, where he had established his station. He also produced his Chinese *Chrestomathy*, the first really useful manual of Cantonese, and founded the *Chinese Repository*.

Theodore Bridgeman, Jr., b. Oct. 3, 1803; removed to Michigan; m. before 1833, Polly ———.

Sophia Bridgeman, b. July 2, 1806; d. July 29, 1869; m. Dec. 2, 1824, George Filer, b. Mar. 25, 1799, son of Gurdon and Hannah (Barber) Filer. He was a merchant in Belchertown, removed to Albany, N. Y. Children: i. Jane Sophia, b. Nov. 28, 1825; m. William Selden George, state printer in Lansing, Mich., and had two children. ii. Augusta, b. May 6, 1840; m. De Witt Clinton Packard, a dealer in carriages, horses, and harnesses in Providence, R. I.; had two children.

Lucretia Bridgeman, b. July 17, 1808; d. 1840, aged 32.

Joseph Bridgeman, b. Mar. 16, 1812; d. Aug. 26, 1813.

Charlotte Bridgeman, b. Sept. 21, 1814; d. Sept. 15, 1815.

Ann Bridgeman, b. 1816; d. 1840; m. 1838, John S. Gould of Albany, N. Y.

287 JONATHAN COLEMAN[6] WARNER, son of Jonathan[5] and Mary (————) Warner, born about 1780, probably in Belchertown, Mass.; died February 6, 1850, in Amherst; buried there. His will, made June 15, 1842, probated April 21, 1850, mentions his wife, Achsah D., and children, Sarah Ann, Jeremy Dickinson and Sophronia.

Married in Amherst, January 20, 1807, **ACHSAH DICKINSON,** born in Amherst, December 25, 1786, died there 1850, daughter of Jonathan and Azubah (Coleman) Dickinson, who came from Belchertown to Amherst.

Children, first five baptized in Amherst

Almira Warner, bapt. July 17, 1808.

Sophronia Warner, bapt. Jan. 20, 1811.

472 *Jeremy Dickinson Warner,* b. May 23, 1813; m. Emily Rathbone.

Josiah J. Warner, bapt. Dec. 19, 1813. This may be an error for Jeremy Dickinson Warner.

Lucretia Warner, bapt. Nov. 16, 1817.

Elijah Coleman Warner, bapt. Sept. 9, 1820; was mentioned in his father's will in 1842.

Sarah Ann Warner, mentioned in her father's will, 1842.

288 JOHN[6] WARNER, son of Moses[5] and Mary (King) Warner, born in Hatfield, Mass., November 7, 1781; died there November 24, 1833. He was a farmer in Hatfield most of his life and resided in a brick house across the road from his father's residence. By his father's will he inherited the homestead farm. During the latter part of his life he drove the stage to Boston. One day when ready to start on his trip to Boston, a terrific thunder shower came up. Both horses were killed and he was stunned by the same bolt and thrown to the ground. At the time he appeared to have suffered no serious injury, but his health rapidly declined and his death in a few months was attributed by attending physicians to the shock from the stroke of lightning.

In early days a fine kind of sand was an important article for housekeepers and a bank of it was located a few feet below the surface near John Warner's farm. It is said that the town reserved this tract for the benefit of the housekeepers and the present widening of the road for some distance near the old Warner house is due to this early transaction.

John Warner married December, 1806, **C A R O L I N E WHITON**, born December 6, 1786, died March 23, 1863, daughter of Ebenezer Whiton of Lee, Mass.

Children, born in Hatfield

Mary Warner, b. Aug. 23, 1807; d. Oct., 1899; m. Oct. 23, 1828, Benjamin Maltby of Waterloo, N. Y.

473 *James Whiton Warner*, b. May 11, 1809; m. Louisa Bardwell.

John Seward Warner, b. Jan. 29, 1813; d. July 22, 1830.

Jonathan D. Warner, b. July 16, 1816; d. Feb. 16, 1903, at Hatfield; was a member of Company K, 10th Regiment, Mass. Volunteers in the Civil War.

Caroline R. Warner, b. Dec. 16, 1821; m. June 1, 1851, Rev. E. D. Holt of Rock Island, Ill.

474 *Eliza Ann Warner*, b. July 27, 1827; m. Solyman Ward Grant.

Lydia A. Warner, b. Nov. 16, 1830; d. Sept., 1858; m. Sept. 1, 1851, Leonidas Sexton.

Amanda Warner, was a minor in 1835 and probably died young.

289 **THOMAS**[6] **WARNER**, son of Eleazer[5] and Joanna (Hale) Warner, born in Ashford, Conn., February 28, 1764; baptized March 7, 1770; died in Otsego County, N. Y., October 2, 1833. He removed from Mansfield, Conn., and settled in New Lisbon, Otsego Co., N. Y., among the early settlers there.

Married **RHODA HOPKINS**, born in Mansfield, Conn., February 27, 1769, died July 29, 1841, daughter of Elisha Hopkins, a Revolutionary soldier, and his wife, Drusilla Conant, daughter of Malachi Conant. Elisha Hopkins was the son of Nathaniel and Abigail (————) Hopkins.

Children

475 *Eleazer Warner,* m. Rebecca C. Barnes.
Nelson Warner, m. Mary Ann Barnes, sister of Rebecca Barnes who
m. his brother Eleazer. Children: i. Horatio. ii. Nelson. iii.
Amanda. iv. Mary, m. Major Z. C. Rennie, and resided in Oakland,
Cal.
476 *Orrin Warner,* b. May 14, 1800; m. Susan Gardner.
477 *Joanna Warner,* b. May 6, 1804; m. Naaman Cone.
478 *Horace Warner,* b. May 13, 1808; m. Laura Hale.
Fannie Warner, d. about 1851, not married.
Eliphalet Warner, left home and was not heard of by the family.
William Warner, d. young.

290 SAMUEL[6] WARNER, son of Eleazer[5] and Joanna
(Hale) Warner, born in Ashford, Conn., January 26 (or Decem-
ber 6), 1769; baptized March 7, 1770; died in Windsor, Dane
Co., Wis., November 20, 1854. He removed to New Lisbon,
Otsego Co., N. Y., about 1792, then to Sherburne, Madison
Co. (where he and his wife were members of the West Hill
Church), later, about 1817, to Batavia, N. Y., and in 1852, to
Dane County, Wis. He was a member of the Presbyterian
Church and an elder in that church. His name occurs fre-
quently on the records of the towns in which he resided; path-
master in Burlington, N. Y., at the first town-meeting, April 2,
1793; juror in Pittsfield, July 3, 1798; assessor in New Lisbon,
March 3, 1807. The territory known as New Lisbon was at
first in the town of Otsego, in 1792 became a part of Burlington,
in 1797, of Pittsfield, in 1806, of Lisbon, and in 1808 was made
a separate town under the name of New Lisbon.
Married in Mansfield, Conn., January, 1792, IRENE ALLEN,
born in Mansfield, February 22, 1768, died in Batavia, N. Y.,
December 13, 1838. She was the daughter of Hezekiah[5] and
Sarah (Cushman) Allen, granddaughter of Timothy[4] and
Rachel (Bushnell) Allen, great-granddaughter of Timothy[3] and
Rebeckah (Cary) Allen. They were descendants of Samuel[1]
Allen, who, with his wife Ann, of Bridgewater, Somerset Co.,
England, located at Braintree, Mass., about 1630. Their son
Samuel[2], b. 1632, settled in East Bridgewater, Mass., was dea-
con, town clerk in 1660, and married Sarah Partridge.

Children

Elisha Warner, b. Sept. 14, 1793, in New Lisbon, N. Y.; d. May 25,
1826, not married.
Loring (1) *Warner,* b. May 28, 1795; d. Aug. 21, 1795, in New Lisbon.
Betsey Warner, b. Dec. 28, 1796, in New Lisbon, N. Y.; died Sept.,

1886, in Brockport, N. Y.; m. Apr. 3, 1833, in Batavia, N. Y.,
Chauncey Staples, a farmer who lived at Sweden Center, near Brockport, and died there in 1862. Children: i. Mary, b. Apr. 7, 1834; d.
July 22, 1905; lived in Brockport; was not married. ii. Grace Irene,
b. Apr. 20, 1837; d. May 14, 1872, not married.

Allen Warner, b. Mar. 28, 1799; d. Apr. 21, 1799, in New Lisbon.

Loring (2) *Warner*, b. June 1, 1801, in New Lisbon; d. Aug. 18, 1813.

Hiel Warner, b. Apr. 4, 1804, in New Lisbon; d. Nov. 4, 1832. He was
a druggist in Canandaigua, N. Y.; m. about 1827, Frances Shephard.
Child: William Shephard, b. June, 1828; d. about 1853; was graduated from Williams College 1850, then took a law course under Mr.
Hubbell in Canandaigua. He was very tall, and presented a Com-
mencement oration on "The Advantages and disadvantages of being
tall."

Irene Warner, b. May 6, 1807, in New Lisbon, N. Y.; d. Apr. 23,
1882; m. (1) in Norwich, N. Y., July, 1824, Justin Foote, a farmer
and miller, who was killed by an accident in a sawmill, 1834; m. (2)
at Alexander, Genesee Co., N. Y., Hervey J. Seymour. Children by
first husband: i. Harriet, b. July, 1826; d. 1845. ii. Daniel, b. Apr. 7,
1828; resided in Belvedere, Ill., and d. there Feb. 22, 1916; m. in
Newark, N. J., Martha Updegraff. iii. Francis, b. Apr., 1830; died.
iv. Justin, b. July, 1832. v. Samuel Isaac, b. Sept., 1834; resided in
Scranton, Pa., and d. there 1895; m. (1) Electa Sutphin, (2) Laura
Reddington. Child of Hervey and Irene (Warner) Seymour: Hervey, b. 1848; d. 1850.

479 *Samuel Allen Warner*, b. Dec. 28, 1810; m. Martha Elizabeth Brintnall
Simonds.

291 ZACHARIAH[6] WARNER, son of Eleazer[5] and Joanna
(Hale) Warner, born December 3, 1778, in Ashford, Conn.;
died February 26, 1848, in Garrettsville, Otsego Co., N. Y. He
was a comb-maker and farmer; removed from Mansfield, Conn.,
to Otsego County, N. Y., as early as 1813, as deeds of that date
are recorded in Otsego County.

Married (1) LAURA HALE, born in Ashford, May 16, 1788,
daughter of John[5] and Mehitabel (Knowlton) Hale; died in
Garrettsville, N. Y., December 16, 1825, buried, as is her husband, in New Lisbon, N. Y. John[5] Hale (James[4], Rev. James[3],
Rev. John[2], Robert[1]) was the brother of Joanna[5] Hale who
married Eleazer[5] Warner, and their brother Zachariah[5] Hale
was the father of Delos[6] Hale who married Delight[7] Warner,
and of Laura[6] Hale, who married Horace[7] Warner. See numbers 155 and 478.

Zachariah Warner married (2) Sept. 27, 1827, ANNA or
NANCY STORRS, of Mansfield, Conn., daughter of Ebenezer
and Lois (Southworth) Storrs. The marriage is recorded in
Mansfield, and his residence is given as Burlington, N. Y. She
had at one time resided in Burlington.

Children of Zachariah and Laura (Hale) Warner

480 *Truman Warner,* b. 1812; m. (1) Eliza Lee, (2) Myra Cordelia McAlmont.

Orlando Warner, d. Sept. 23, 1818.

Leander Warner, b. June 11, 1818; d. Sept. 23, 1826.

John Warner, b. Feb. 7, 1820, in Otsego Co., N. Y. He learned dentistry in Cincinnati, Ohio; began its practice in Kentucky in 1840; was at Leavenworth, Kan., from 1865 to 1877, engaged in wholesale business of queensware and plated ware. In 1877 he removed to Oakland, Cal., and practiced dentistry for seven years. He then removed to Garden Grove, Cal., where he practiced to some extent, but most of his time was devoted to the cultivation of his fruit and ornamental trees and to the beautifying of his home. He was a member of the F. and A. M., and I. O. O. F. Married in Estill Co., Ky., in 1853, Harriet Wilber, b. in New York State, daughter of Church and Hannah Seva (Gambel) Wilber, natives of Barnard, Windsor Co., Vt., who removed from New York to Michigan when Mrs. Warner was but four years of age, and later to Indiana.

481 *Horatio H. Warner,* b. Nov. 2, 1823; m. Jane Northrop.

Eliza Warner, b. Apr. 3, 1825; m. ———— Capin. He was a relative of her stepmother.

Laura Warner, d. Aug. 25, 1864; m. Eli Howe. Children: William; Lillie.

Delight Warner, m. Delos Hale, son of Zachariah Hale, see above.

Edmund Warner, went to Wisconsin; m. Mary Adams of Utica, N. Y. Children: i. Lizzie, m. J. F. Brazelton, son of J. B. Brazelton of Chicago, and resided in Fairmont, Neb. ii. William. Two others who died young. Mrs. Brazelton died about 1896, leaving children: Edmund, b. about 1886, resided in Beatrice, Neb., in 1901; Charles, b. about 1887, resided in Beatrice, Neb.; Margaret, b. about 1888; Mary, b. about 1891, was adopted by Mrs. Hancock at Fairfield, Clay Co., Neb.; Dorothea, b. about 1892, was adopted by Rev. Mr. Williams, a Baptist minister of Lincoln, Neb.; and a son, who d. shortly after his mother.

Adelbert Edwin Warner.

292 **JOSIAH[6] WARNER,** son of Josiah[5] and Deborah (Hall) Warner, born June 18, 1784, in Amherst, Mass.; died July, 1839. He may have removed to Vernon, N. Y., as there is a deed of June 9, 1813, given by Josiah and Achsah Warner.

Married in Amherst, April 15, 1805, **ACHSAH EASTMAN,** born in Amherst, October 19, 1786, daughter of Ebenezer and Mary (Dickinson) Eastman.

Children, from family record of Foster Y. Warner

Elizabeth Warner, b. Mar. 15, 1806; d. July 21, 1832.
Cordelia Warner, b. Aug. 11, 1807; d. Dec. 20, 1807.
Ebenezer E. Warner, b. Oct. 9, 1808.

482 *Foster Y. Warner,* b. July 17, 1810; m. Achsah Morton.
Joseph Warner, b. Apr. 12, 1812.
Clarissa Warner, b. Feb. 13, 1814.
Benjamin Warner, b. Dec. 25, 1815.
Josiah Warner, 3d, b. June 30, 1818 (date as given in family record).
Deborah H. Warner, b. Apr. 23, 1817 (date as given in family record).
Samuel Warner, b. Aug. 17, 1819; d. Sept. 22, 1819.
Elisha Warner, b. July 18, 1820; d. June 26, 1879.
Mary D. Warner, b. June 28, 1822.
Sumner Warner, b. May 29, 1824; was lost at sea on a whale ship about 1871.

293 MARTHA⁶ WARNER, daughter of Dr. Ichabod⁵ and Mary (Lazell) Warner, born January 24, 1761, in Bolton, Conn.; died August 14, 1846.

Married in Bolton (recorded also in Hebron town record), May 20, 1784, DAVID POST, born November 20, 1752, son of Jedediah and Deborah (Brown) Post of Hebron, Conn. He died October 5, 1840, aged 88. He was a farmer in Hebron.

Children, births found in Hebron town records

David Warner Post, b. Mar. 4, 1785; d. Feb. 10, 1824, aged 39, not married.
Diodate Post, b. Aug. 31, 1786; d. Apr. 11, 1860; m. May 29, 1810, his cousin, Pamelia Birge, daughter of Isaac and Pamelia⁶ (Warner) Birge. Child: William Alfred, b. July 7, 1814.
Jedediah Post.
Elijah Post, b. July 31, 1792; d. Apr. 20, 1869; m. Anna Bissell.
John Henry Post, b. July 14, 1794; d. Oct. 17, 1825; m. (1) June 2, 1819, Sally Sumner, by whom he had Sarah Sumner, b. Apr. 29, 1821; m. (2) May 12, 1824, Louisa West.
Ichabod Post, b. Mar. 4, 1798; d. Feb. 11, 1813, aged 15.

294 MARY⁶ or POLLY WARNER, daughter of Dr. Ichabod⁵ and Mary (Lazell) Warner, born September 7, 1762, in Bolton, Conn.; resided in Bolton and New Hartford, Conn.

Married in Bolton, April 12, 1781, BENJAMIN WELLES, JR., son of Benjamin and Lucy (Talcott) Welles.

Children

Elijah Gardner Welles, b. in Bolton, Feb. 3, 1782; d. 1855. He was a clergyman.
Polly Welles, baptized Dec. 21, 1783.
Henry Welles.
Sophia Welles, b. 1794; d. Aug., 1851; m. Anslun Abernethy.
Benjamin Welles, b. 1797; d. Oct., 1838, at La Fayette, Ind.

295 LUCY[6] WARNER, daughter of Dr. Ichabod[5] and Mary (Lazell) Warner, born in Bolton, Conn., May 11, 1764; died there May 19, 1841. She was considered a woman of superior ability and intelligence. The Strong Genealogy, published some years ago, gives a very complete account of her family.

Married in Bolton, October 25, 1781, **LEVI STRONG,** born in Bolton, August 24, 1762, died there July 24, 1823, son of Nathan and Anne (Olcott) Strong. He was a farmer and resided in Bolton.

Children, born in Bolton

Octa Strong, b. July 23, 1783; d. Oct. 14, 1816; m. Sept. 23, 1801, Jabez Backus, b. in Franklin, Conn., June 3, 1777, d. in Hebron, Conn., June 1, 1855, son of Ezra and Mercy (Lay) Backus. He was a tanner and saddler in Hebron, resided later in Attica, N. Y., 1834-54, and in Omaha City. Children: i. Levi Strong, b. June 23, 1803; d. Mar. 17, 1869; was teacher of deaf mutes at Canajoharie, N. Y., proprietor and editor for 33 years of New York Radii Weekly, a newspaper for deaf mutes; m. Anna Raymond Ormsby, one of his former pupils. ii. Ezra Lay, b. Sept. 3, 1808. iii. Lucy Ann (1), b. June 22, 1810; d. Nov. 26, 1810; was a deaf mute. iv. Lucy Ann (2), b. Dec. 6, 1811; m. Taylor G. Goodwill. v. Jamin Russell, b. Sept. 28, 1814. vi. Jabez Lewis, b. July 23, 1816.
Russell Strong, b. Aug. 29, 1785; d. Feb. 25, 1864. Farmer at Bolton, Conn., and, after 1814, at Berlin, Vt. Married June 25, 1811, Susannah Webster, b. Oct. 10, 1787, d. after 1870, daughter of Thomas and Susannah (Skinner) Webster of Hebron. Children: i. Electa Matilda, b. Jan. 18, 1812; m. Daniel Chandler, Jr. ii. Octa Lucina, b. Mar. 12, 1818; m. Theodore Strong, her cousin. iii. Russell Warner, b. June 7, 1823. iv. Lucy Ann, b. July 11, 1826. v. George Martin, b. Apr. 8, 1830; m. Nov. 24, 1853, Rebecca Campbell.
Levi Strong, Jr., b. Dec. 12, 1787; d. Oct. 6, 1859; farmer at Bolton; m. Nov. 10, 1818, Laura Newcomb of Columbia, Conn., b. 1796; d. at Ellington, Conn., Sept. 15, 1870, daughter of Joseph Newcomb. Children: i. Octa, b. Dec. 17, 1819; m. (1) Dr. Calvin Pease, (2) Erastus Olmstead. ii. Jamin, b. July 9, 1822. iii: Russell L., b. Aug., 1824; d. Apr., 1827. iv. Julius Levi, b. Nov. 8, 1828. v. Julia H., b. Mar. 6, 1833; d. 1844. vi. Elizabeth Newcomb, b. Mar. 24, 1840; m. (1) Julius Randolph Strong, son of Judah and Jerusha (Warner) Strong, b. May 1, 1802, d. Nov. 5, 1867; had a daughter, Ella Jerusha, b. Dec. 11, 1860; m. (2) Feb. 25, 1869, Samuel Cady Carpenter. vii. Emily H., b. 1844; d. aged 6 months.
Jamin Strong, b. Sept. 7, 1791; d. after 1870; m. in Parma, N. Y., Mar. 26, 1817, Belsora Tillotson, b. in Marlboro, Conn., Dec. 26, 1787, d. at Elyria, Ohio, Sept. 12, 1860, daughter of Elijah and Patience (Freeland) Tillotson. He was a blacksmith in the U. S. Armory at Springfield, Mass., 1812-3; at Parma, N. Y., 1814-37; then at Sheffield, Lorain Co., Ohio. Children: i. Octa Backus, b. Apr. 26, 1817; d. Mar. 2, 1850; m. as second wife, Mar. 15, 1841, William Harrison Adams and had three children. ii. Harvey Backus, b. Nov. 22, 1820; m. 1841, Cordelia Dutcher of Seneca Falls; had a daugh-

ter; lived in Rochester. iii. Jamin, Jr., b. Nov. 27, 1825; once professor of materia medica and therapeutics in Charity Hospital, Medical College, Cleveland, Ohio, member of the Ohio Legislature; resided at Oberlin; m. Mar. 21, 1853, Mary H. Woodruff of Buffalo, b. Oct. 16, 1832; d. Nov. 7, 1854; m. (2) Feb. 8, 1858, Nettie Louisa Lincoln, b. Mar. 16, 1836, daughter of Stillman W. and Ann (Whitney) Lincoln.

296 PAMELIA[6] WARNER, daughter of Dr. Ichabod[5] and Mary (Lazell) Warner, born February 26, 1768, in Bolton, Conn. After her husband's death she removed to Ohio with some of her children.

Married in Bolton, April 8, 1787, ISAAC BIRGE, born March, 1764, in Bolton, died there November 14, 1830. He was the son of Captain Jonathan and Priscilla (Hammond) Birge. He was a farmer in Bolton and was called Captain in records of 1807. Captain Jonathan Birge was a Revolutionary soldier, was wounded at the battle of White Plains and died in Stamford, Conn., as he was being brought home to Bolton.

Children, born in Bolton

Marvin Birge, b. Aug. 13, 1788.
Jonathan Birge, b. Aug. 1, 1790.
Pamelia Birge, b. Sept. 3, 1792; d. in Gilead, Conn., July 3, 1860; m. May 29, 1810, her cousin, Diodate Post of Hebron, son of David and Martha[6] (Warner) Post.
Simeon Birge, b. Aug. 23, 1794; was a physician.
Chester Birge, b. Sept. 20, 1796; was graduated at Yale, 1825; was a clergyman.
Alfred Birge, b. Sept. 5, 1798; d. July 13, 1826.
Elethea Birge, b. Nov. 5, 1800; m. ——— Kellogg.
Julia Birge, b. Jan. 11, 1803; m. Benjamin Sprague of Andover, Conn.
Aurelia Birge, b. Mar. 29, 1805; m. (1) ——— Atwater, (2) ——— Wood.
Mary Ann Birge, b. Sept. 8, 1807; d. July 6, 1871; m. Thomas Leverett Brown of Gilead, Conn.
Lazell Birge, b. Sept. 24, 1810.

297 ICHABOD MAPE[6] WARNER, son of Dr. Ichabod[5] and Mary (Lazell) Warner, born February 14, 1770, in Bolton, Conn.; died there, February 8, 1835. In church records he is most frequently called "Mape Warner." His father fitted him for the medical profession but he practiced for a short time only. He resided on the old Warner homestead, a mile and a quarter southwest of Bolton Center, and was a farmer the greater part of his life.

Married in Hebron, May 19, 1791, recorded also in Bolton,

MARY TALCOTT, daughter of William and Mary (Carter) Talcott. She was born in Hebron, August 28, 1771, and died September 24, 1857, in Bolton. William Talcott was an officer in the Revolutionary army.

Children, born in Bolton

Mary Warner, b. Apr. 9, 1792; d. in Gilead, Conn., Sept. 19, 1878; m. Mar. 4, 1812, Israel Ele Hutchinson, b. Aug. 16, 1786; d. in Gilead, Sept. 17, 1869. He was a farmer in Gilead. Child: Israel Champion, b. Dec. 9, 1815, in Gilead; d. in California, Sept. 22, 1884; m. Feb. 15, 1844, Katherine Hatch.

483 *Elijah Warner,* b. June or Jan. 19, 1794; m. (1) Abigail Buel, (2) Martha Hammond.

Harriet W. Warner, b. Feb. 1, 1796; d. in Gilead, May 22, 1820; m. Apr. 14, 1819, Samuel Talcott, b. in Hebron, Nov. 28, 1787, son of Gad and Abigail (Root) Talcott. He was a farmer in Gilead and married (2) in 1826, Hester Reynolds, (3) Asenath Morgan. Child of Samuel and Harriet (Warner) Talcott: Henry Wait, b. May 22, 1820, in Gilead; d. Apr. 10, 1847, in Rockton, Ill.

484 *Ashbel Warner,* b. Dec. 30, 1797; m. (1) Abigail Lyman, (2) Hannah Morgan.

Martha Warner, b. Oct. 10, 1799; d. in Vernon, Conn., Aug. 11, 1827; m. June 6, 1821, Royal Talcott, b. in North Bolton, Mar. 18, 1797, son of Jacob and Anna (Carpenter) Talcott. He died in Vernon, Oct. 9, 1823. He was a farmer in Vernon. Child: Martha, b. July, 1823; d. Mar. 10, 1826.

485 *Ichabod Warner,* b. Apr. 5, 1801; m. Lucy Foster.

486 *Sally Warner,* b. Feb. 18, 1803; m. Capt. Russel Talcott Loomis.

487 *Mariah Warner,* b. Mar. 12, 1805; m. Capt. Russel Talcott Loomis.

Jerusha Carter Warner, b. Dec. 27, 1806; d. in Gilead, Nov. 19, 1866; not married.

William Talcott Warner, b. Aug. 19, 1808. When a young man he left home, wrote once from Philadelphia, was never heard from again.

488 *Albert Francis Warner,* b. Jan. 19, 1810; m. Eunice Gager.

298 JERUSHA[6] WARNER, daughter of Dr. Ichabod[5] and Mary (Lazell) Warner, born in Bolton, Conn., February 18, 1772; died November 23, 1843, in Bolton. Married in Bolton, November 29, 1792, JUDAH STRONG, JR., son of Judah and Martha (Alvord) Strong, born July 25, 1771, died April 29, 1829. He was a farmer in Hebron, Conn. A more complete account of their family will be found in the Strong Genealogy.

Children, born in Bolton

Judah Strong, 3d, b. Sept. 8, 1793; d. in Bolton, Nov. 14, 1860; m. (1) Sept. 8, 1818, Sarah Loomis, b. 1799, d. Oct. 4, 1825, daughter of Jerijah and Abigail (Risley) Loomis of Bolton; m. (2) Sept. 7, 1826, her sister, Sophronia Loomis, b. 1805. Children by first wife:

William Gardiner; Walter L. Children by second wife: i. George Washington, a physician in San Francisco. ii. Juliette, m. —— Cooley. iii. Henry. iv. Robert N., m. (1) Hester A. Coventry, (2) Donizetta Johnson. v. Sarah, not married. vi. Cornelia, not married.

Salmon Strong, b. Mar. 21, 1795; d. Oct. 14, 1848, at Clinton, N. C., where he was a physician; m. Eliza Jane Samson of Clinton, who died Apr., 1848. They had six sons and a daughter.

Jerusha Strong, b. Jan. 27, 1796 or 1797; m. Oct. 6, 1825, Deacon Eleazer Andrus, a farmer at Bolton; no children.

Horace Strong, b. Jan. 29, 1799; d. June 18, 1840, at Lebanon, Conn.; m. (1) May 26, 1825, Hope Hale of Glastonbury, b. July, 1798, d. Sept. 2, 1834, daughter of David and Ruth (——) Hale; m. (2) Dec. 22, 1835, Emily Huntington, b. in Lebanon, Feb. 8, 1796, daughter of William and Mary (Gray) Huntington. Children: i. Martha Colton, b. Apr. 20, 1826; m. Franklin Goodrich Hollister. ii. Mary Warner, b. July 22, 1827; m. Dudley Webster. iii. Sarah Hale, b. Nov. 18, 1829; m. Lyman T. Hollister. iv. Elizabeth, b. Dec. 20, 1832; m. Richard Sparrow Clarke.

Rachel Strong, b. June 30, 1800; m. Apr. 14, 1831, Chester Holbrook, a farmer of Lebanon; no children.

Julius Randolph Strong, b. May 1, 1802; d. in Bolton, Nov. 5, 1867; m. Oct. 8, 1857, his cousin, Elizabeth Strong, b. Mar. 24, 1840, daughter of Levi and Laura (Newcomb) Strong. Child: Ella Jerusha, b. Dec. 11, 1860.

Martha Strong, b. Feb. 27, 1804; buried in East Hartford, Conn.; m. —— McCracken.

George Washington Strong, b. Jan. 18, 1806; d. Sept. 7, 1829. He was a graduate of Yale College, 1826.

Tirzah Strong, b. Aug. 10, 1809; d. Aug. 25, 1864, at South Windsor, Conn.; m. Dec. 2, 1832, Uriah Palmer of Vernon, Conn., a farmer in South Windsor. Children, Churchill and Tirzah.

William Gardner Strong, b. Sept. 7, 1811; d. in Bolton, Sept. 27, 1817.

Walter Strong, b. Mar. 20, 1816; d. Mar. 22, 1816.

299 SARAH[6] or **SALLY WARNER**, daughter of Dr. Ichabod[5] and Mary (Lazell) Warner, born April 28, 1775, in Bolton, Conn.; died in East Windsor, Conn., April 21, 1855, where she had resided.

Married in Bolton, May 8, 1794, as second wife, JONATHAN BIRGE, JR., born in Bolton, June 21, 1768, died in East Windsor, December 12, 1820, son of Captain Jonathan and Priscilla (Hammond) Birge, and brother of Isaac who married Pamelia[6] Warner; see number 296. He married (1) December, 1791, Mary Bailey, who died October 25, 1793, leaving a child, Bailey, born August 4, 1793.

Children of Jonathan and Sarah (Warner) Birge

Backus W. Birge, b. Feb. 8, 1795; d. July 29, 1832; m. —— Ripley.
Julius Birge, b. Sept. 24, 1796; m. Nov. 5, 1824, Mary A. Stoughton.

Edwin Birge, b. June 8, 1798; d. 1845; m. Dec. 23, 1823, Huldah Elmer.

Mary Bailey Birge, b. Apr. 12, 1800; buried at South Windsor, Conn.; m. Nov. 23 or 24, 1824, Wyllys Stoughton, b. Dec. 2, 1796, in East Windsor, son of Timothy and Eunice (Drake) Stoughton. Children: i. Elizabeth Warner, b. Aug. 30, 1825; d. May 10, 1847; m. Feb. 21, 1844, Henry King of South Windsor. ii. Alfred Birge, b. Aug. 5, 1827; d. Sept. 25, 1857; buried in South Windsor; m. Dec. 12, 1850, Mary Pratt, daughter of John and —— (Butler) Pratt of Middletown; had two daughters, Alice, who m. Rev. Beverly Ellison Warner, D.D., b. in Jersey City, N. J., Oct. 14, 1855, son of James and Anna (Carscallen) Warner, and Carrie, who m. William Patten of Meriden, Conn. iii. Katherine Mary, b. Aug. 15, 1831; d. Jan. 2, 1872, in Scarborough, Me.; m. Dec. 19, 1851, Rev. James Brown Thornton; had children: Eliza Gookin, d. young; Wyllys Stoughton, d. young; James Brown, b. 1861; Mary Stoughton, b. 1865.

Francis Birge, b. Dec. 22, 1803; d. 1865; m. Apr. 17, 1834, Charlotte Flint, of Hartford. Children: i. George F., b. Sept. 8, 1835. ii. Irene C., b. Oct. 27, 1838; d. Mar. 29, 1841. iii. James F., b. Dec. 24, 1843; d. July 26, 1844. iv. Walter F., b. Apr. 7, 1846.

Sarah W. Birge, b. Mar. 28, 1807.

Henry Birge, b. Feb. 22, 1808; d. 1865; m. May 9, 1836, Jane E. Filley, of Hartford. Children: i. William Henry, b. Jan. 7, 1838. ii. Mary Ann, b. Oct. 26, 1839. iii. Charles Warner, b. Mar. 23, 1841.

300 NATHAN[6] WARNER, son of Nathan[5] and Mary (Silvernail) Warner, born in Hopewell, Dutchess County, N. Y., October 31, 1765; died in Wooster township, Wayne Co., Ohio, May 12, 1844. When a 'child his parents removed to the Moravian settlement at Gnadenhütten, Northampton Co., Pa., where he resided until 1799. His name was in the census of 1790 in Penn township, with his wife and two children. He arrived at Gnadenhütten, the Moravian mission on the Tuscarawas, in Ohio, November 6, 1799, probably travelling with the family of his uncle Jonathan. He assisted in the building of the Beersheba Moravian church in 1805. In the church record it is stated that Nathan Warner completed the chimney October 15th and built the bake oven. Although a member of the Moravian church in early life, he joined the Methodists sometime after his removal to Wayne County, about 1811, and for twenty years his house was a preaching place. The first Methodist Society in Wayne County was formed there in 1812, and meetings were kept up until the old log church was built.

At the time of his location in Ohio the nearest mill was seventy-five miles distant, but by learning the use of the hominy block, and with the wild meat procured by hunting or from the Indians, the family were kept fed. In 1810 he entered on lands three miles west of Wooster, built a cabin and made some improvements, and the family was established there in the fall of 1811. The following spring came the war with England, and when the news of Hull's surrender came, he packed his goods and with his family started for their old settlement in Tuscarawas. After stopping for a night and consulting with those in the block house at Wooster he decided to return to his cabin and prepare to meet the situation.

The cabin, a solid structure of hewed logs 24 x 30 feet, was easily converted into a fort or block-house by cutting port holes for the guns and splitting heavy puncheons for the door and window shutters. All the farm implements were gathered in for weapons, and a large quantity of stones were taken upstairs to be used in case of an attack. There were but nine guns in the neighborhood, of which four belonged to Mr. Warner and his sons. They never had occasion to make a test of their equipment, although alarms were numerous and the neighbors gathered there at night. Later Beall's army camped on the farm and were met with every courtesy by the owner. The old block house was remodelled and used for years as a resi dence by the family. The Pioneer Cemetery was located on a part of this farm donated by Nathan Warner, and is now under the control of the Oak Chapel Methodist Church.

Nathan Warner married in Penn township, Pa., August 10, 1784, ANN ADELIA DAVIS, born April 22, 1761, died 1850, aged 88. A family record states that she was born in "Franklin, Danbury County, New York." It is also said that her sister married Ebenezer[6] Warner, number 302.

Children

Lydia Warner, b. June 26, 1785, in Pennsylvania; d. aged one year.
Anna Warner, b. Jan. 24, 1787, in Pennsylvania; resided in Wayne County; was not married and died at an advanced age at the home of her brother Jesse.
489 Amasa Warner, b. Nov. 29, 1788; m. (1) Lettice Foreman, (2) Cynthia Ann Walton, (3) Mary Lowery, (4) Elsyanne Lowery.
490 Nathan Warner, b. Oct. 12, 1790; m. Mary Rathbun.
491 Peter Warner, b. Aug. 11, 1792; m. (1) ——— Williams, (2) Mrs. Bett.
John Warner, b. Feb. 11, 1794.
492 Moses Warner, b. May 24, 1796; m. Mary Sheridan.
493 Joshua Warner, b. July 29, 1799; m. (1) Margaret Smith, (2) Rosanna Edmunds.
494 Susanna Warner, b. Apr. 1, 1800, in Gnadenhütten, Ohio, the first white child born in that town; m. Ernest Reatus Fox.
495 Jesse Warner, b. Nov. 22, 1802; m. (1) Jane Goodfellow, (2) Ann Oldroyd.

22

301 PETER⁶ WARNER, son of Nathan⁵ and Mary (Silvernail) Warner, born July 26, 1767, in Northampton County, Pa.;
died November 14, 1824 (?).   He went from Gnadenhütten,
Pa., to Gnadenhütten, Ohio, in 1799, and returned for his
family, reaching their new home in Ohio with his wife Grace
and three children about November 15, 1799. They later
removed to Wayne County, Ohio, and probably lived north of
Wooster.   He left the Moravian church and joined the Methodists in 1810, and took an active part in the organization of a
Methodist Society which was later united with the one at
Wooster.
Married in Pennsylvania, GRACE ————

Children, first three born in Pennsylvania
496 *Peter Warner*, m. Elizabeth ————.
   Mary Warner, was living with her brother Jonathan in 1870.
   Jonathan, b. Aug. 27, 1798, in Northampton County, Pa.; resided in
      Wayne County, Ohio; m. Loraine Pettit of Washington County,
      Ohio. They had ten children, all living in 1878. One son was Jona-
      than, Jr., who lives in West Salem, Ohio.
   Martha Warner, m. James Reed.
   David Warner.
   Salome Warner.
   Solomon Warner, b. Dec. 6, 1807, in Tuscarawas County, Ohio; lived
      in Congress, Ohio. He was a soldier in the Civil War, Co. F, 16th
      Ohio Volunteers; was in the Charge of Chickasaw, was captured
      Sept. 29, 1862, held a prisoner for 75 days, then exchanged and sent
      to Camp Chase, whence he was ordered to New Orleans and dis-
      charged Feb. 2, 1864.

302 EBENEZER⁶ WARNER, son of Nathan⁵ and Mary
(Silvernail) Warner, born September 2, 1769, in Northampton
County, Pa.; removed to Wayne County, Ohio, where he was
one of the early settlers.   He was head of a family in the census of 1810; resided about three miles from Wooster. He was
buried on the old Benjamin Jones farm in Wooster township,
as was his son Nathan.
Married ———— DAVIS, sister of the wife of his brother
Nathan.   One account says his wife was Ann Smith, daughter
of Alanson Smith.

Children
   Alanson Warner.
   Daniel Warner, was perhaps the Daniel Warner who m. Sophia Smith,
      in Harrison County, Ohio, Feb. 23, 1837.
   David Warner.
   Hannah Warner, m. in 1817, Robert Rathbone, b. Mar. 16, 1798, d. Apr.
      14, 1856, son of Robert and Anna (Allen) Rathbone. He was a

Baptist minister at the age of 19, in 1830 became an elder in the Latter Day Saints. Children: i. Enoch, b. 1818; d. near Elk Grove, Mo., 1821. ii. Hiram, b. Apr. 3, 1820; m. Mar. 20, 1842, Rosanna Edmunds. iii. and iv. (twins) Almira, b. Nov. 28, 1822, m. —— Ellsbury, and Lucretia, d. young. v. Aurelia, b. July 4, 1824; m. Michael H. Tedrow. vi. Eleanor, b. July 5, 1826; d. 1882. vii. Mary, b. 1828; d. young. viii. Ann, b. Nov. 8, 1830; d. 1837. ix. Allen, b. Nov. 8, 1834; d. young. x. Lydia, b. Mar. 30, 1836; m. Hiram Nixon. xi. William.

Lorenzo Warner.
William Warner.
Catherine Warner.
Ruth Warner.
Isabella Warner.
Nathan Warner, was killed at the age of 15 by skids falling upon him at the raising of a barn on the old Benjamin Jones farm in Wooster township, Wayne Co., and was buried in the old burying ground on that farm.

303 **MARY ANN**[6] (or ANNA MARY) WARNER, daughter of Nathan[5] and Mary (Silvernail) Warner, born April 30, 1776, at Gnadenhütten, Pa.; died September 3, 1832.

Married 1803, Rev. CHARLES GOTTLIEB BLECK, born 1755, in Somnitz, Silesia, Germany; died September 6, 1832. He was a Moravian minister in Graceham, Md., Lebanon, Hebron, Bethel, and Bethlehem, Pa.

Children

Charles A. Bleck, was a preacher in the Moravian church, and was stationed at Gnadenhütten, where he died.
Ernst Bleck, was administrator of the estate of his aunt Elizabeth Warner, 1848.
Caroline S. Bleck, was a teacher in Bethlehem for twenty successive years.
Phoebe A. Bleck, m. —— Brown; resided at Canal Dover, Ohio.
Maria E. Bleck, m. —— Rickshaw.

304 **CATHERINE**[6] WARNER, daughter of Nathan[5] and Mary (Silvernail) Warner, born March 10, 1780; removed to Ohio with the families of her brother Nathan and uncle Jonathan before 1799.

Married before 1799, ASA WALTON.

Children

Mary Walton, m. William Simmers.
Joel Walton, m. —— Petticoast.
Sarah Walton, m. Michael Rupert.
Stephen Walton, m. —— Thornburg.
Catherine Walton, m. David Metzgar.

305 DANIEL[6] WARNER, son of Nathan[5] and Mary (Sil-vernail) Warner, born in East Penn township, Northampton Co., Pa., November 6, 1782; died in Tuscarawas County, Ohio, August 8, 1835; buried in Yankeetown. When a young man of about twenty he removed to Gnadenhütten, Ohio, having crossed the mountains on foot. He and his mother kept house there together until her death in 1817. He was a day laborer working at any kind of work that offered itself, although his principal occupation was shingle making. In 1805, with a Mr. Tracy, he sawed logs with a whip-saw for the flooring of the Beersheba Moravian Church at Gnadenhütten. This was a slow and arduous task. In the first place posts were set in the ground on the hillside, then skids were laid out from the hill upon these posts making them level. A log was then rolled upon these skids and with one man standing on the log, the other below on the ground, the saw was pulled up and down, cutting one way only. The saw had a handle on each end resembling an auger handle.

In 1810 Daniel Warner united with the Methodist church. During the War of 1812 he was drafted to go to the Maumee in the defense of Ft. Meigs. He borrowed of his mother the $60.00 to pay a substitute, who, by the way, never arrived at the fort. The siege was broken before the recruits arrived at the fort and they were sent home.

After his marriage he resided in Gnadenhütten, Fry's Valley, Wooster, and again in Fry's Valley, where he was living, at the time of his death, in a cabin on a small farm which he had cleared some years before and built upon. He was buried in Yankeetown Graveyard, one and one-half miles from Gnaden-hütten, but no stone marks his grave.

Daniel Warner married in Fry's Valley, February 26, 1818, MARY ANN SIMMERS, born at Painted Post, N. Y., July 28, 1798; died at the residence of her son Jonas, in Tuscarawas County, Ohio, August 5, 1876, buried in Trenton Cemetery. After his death she married a stroller named Jackson. She was the daughter of William and Esther Simmers. Her parents moved in 1800 to Canada and settled near Dover on Lake Erie opposite Long Point, across the lake from Erie. Many stories are told in the family of their experience with the Indians, espe-cially during the War of 1812. William Simmers was born in the United States and was hostile to the British Crown. Hav-ing harbored a British spy and being summoned for trial, he thought best to return to the United States, left his land with no one to care for it, and never received a cent for it. They spent ten weeks making the trip from Canada, led only by the search for some relatives whom they knew lived somewhere on the Muskingum. They travelled in a boat which he had built himself, taking it by portage from Lake Erie to Lake Chautauqua,· then through that to one of the head waters of the Allegany River, down that river to the Ohio at Pittsburg, then to the Marietta and up the Muskingum to Coshocton, and finally to a point below Gnadenhütten where their relatives were located.

Children of Daniel and Mary (Simmers) Warner

497 · *Joel Warner,* b. Dec. 14, 1818, near New Philadelphia, Tuscarawas Co., Ohio; m. Delilah Everett.
498 *Jonas Warner,* b. Feb. 12, 1821; m. Catherine Lister.
499 *Simon Peter Warner,* b. June 17, 1823; m. Sarah Johnson.
500 *Elias Warner,* b. Jan. 27, 1826; m. (1) Lorana M. Poland, (2) Mrs. Mary Smith, (3) Mrs. Mary E.· Lenhart.
501 *William Warner,* b. June 13, 1829; m. Elizabeth Rupert.
    Esther Warner, b. Dec. 16, 1831; d. Mar. 17, 1845.
    Daniel Warner, b. Mar. 8, 1836 (posthumous); went to Rockford, Ill., where he worked at the carpenter's trade, and to Nebraska. Married in Ohio, Lucy Sponsler. Children: i. Eugene, lived in Roscoe township, Winnebago Co., Ill. ii. Ella. iii. Luther.

306 BENJAMIN[6] WARNER, son of Massa[5] and Maria Dorothea (Miksch) Warner, born in Bethlehem, Pa., November 6, 1794; died at Winston-Salem, N. C., October 30, 1854. "Born November 6, baptized November 7, 1794, Benjamin the little son of the married Brother and Sister Massa Warner, manager of the sawmill here, and Dorothea, m. n. Miksch. The sponsors were the Married Brother and Sister August & Elisabeth Klingsohr and the Married Brother and Sister Johann Christian and Elisabeth Reich, the Single Brother Paul Miksch. The baptism was performed by Br. August Klingsohr." (Transcription from Bethlehem records.) He was a member of the Moravian church, removed to Salem, N. C., kept the inn for a time, and was later a tobacco manufacturer.

Married ANNA LOUISA STOTZ, born August 17, 1795, in Salem, N. C., died there, April 21, 1851. She was the daughter of Samuel Stotz, born December 20, 1752, at Gnadenthal, near Nazareth, Pa., died at Salem, N. C., September 5, 1820, where he was Gemein Vorsteher, and his wife, Susannah Fetter, born April 30, 1770, at Lancaster, Pa.,·died October 13, 1818, at Salem, the daughter of Christian Peter and Christine (Reim) Fetter.

Children, born at Salem, N. C.

Olivia Susanna Warner, b. Aug. 19, 1826; d. in Bethlehem, Pa., July 5, 1901. She received her early education at Salem, and served twenty years as teacher in the Young Ladies' Academy. At the close of the Civil War she entered the Seminary at Hope, Ind., as teacher. After several years she removed to Bethlehem, Pa., and made her home in the Sisters' House until her death. She made the teaching of music her profession until about a year before her death. (Moravian Historical Society.)

Samuel Stotz Warner, b. June 21, 1832; d. in Bethlehem, Pa., Jan. 2, 1912. He was for many years a missionary of the Moravian church in the West Indies. Married Josephine Fenner, b. Nov. 24, 1834; d. Dec. 24, 1909, in Bethlehem, Pa. She was a teacher in the Moravian Parochial School in Bethlehem before her marriage. They had no children.

502 *Massah Miksch Warner*, b. Jan. 9, 1836; m. Celestine Victoria Reinke.

307 SAMUEL ETTWINE[6] WARNER, son of Ezra[5] and Maria Magdalina (Laner) Warner, born May 10, 1799, probably in Pennsylvania; died April 28, 1845. He was a farmer residing near Jeromeville, Ashland County, Ohio.
Married **MARY WARNER** (?).

Children, born in Jeromeville

503 *Ezra Billing Warner*, b. Dec. 6, 1829; m. Mary Catharine Ewing.

Mary Jane Warner, b. Dec. 29, 1831; d. Jan. 13, 1853, at Jeromeville, not married.

James Newton Warner, b. Jan. 30, 1834; d. in Jeromeville, May 7, 1860.

William Milton Warner, b. Sept. 12, 1836; d. 1871; m. Margaret Jane[9] Warner, b. Jan. 7, 1836, d. Nov. 19, 1898, see number 495. Children: i. ———, d. in infancy. ii. Jesse. iii. Daisy. iv. Jane L., b. in Wooster, Feb. 13, 1863; is a teacher. These three reside in Wooster and are not married.

Stephen Warner, b. July 8, 1839; was a soldier in the Civil War and died in 1862.

Samuel Warner, b. Aug. 15, 1841; d. not married. He was a soldier and probably died during the Civil War.

David Ettwine Warner, b. June 10, 1845; d. in Kansas in 1881, not married.

308 MILAN[6] WARNER, son of Matthew[5] and Eunice (Stoel) Warner, born in Windham, Conn., died before 1823. He was a sailor and was drowned by a fall from the masthead of a ship sailing from Boston. He died before his father and his children were mentioned in the will of the latter.
Married April 2, 1792, recorded in Worthington, Mass., **POLLY WATT.**

Children, recorded in Worthington

504 *Harriet Warner,* b. Apr. 12, 1792; m. Silas Marble.
   Henry Warner, baptized May 18, 1800, in Worthington, at the same
   time as his sister Harriet; d. 1865. He was mentioned in the will
   of his grandfather in 1821, and is said to have settled in Chautauqua
   County, N. Y.

309 **BELA⁶ WARNER,** son of Matthew⁵ and Eunice (Stoel)
Warner, born in Windham, Conn., October 25, 1771; died October 7, 1867. He removed with his parents to Worthington,
Mass., about 1780, and in 1841 to Meadville, Pa. There was a
Bela Warner in Colesville, Broome County, N. Y., as early as
1829, but it is probable that he was of another line of Warners.
   Married in Worthington, January 16, 1811(?), S A L L Y
KINGMAN.

Children

Charles Warner, d. Nov. 26, 1811, aged 6 months, 26 days (Worthington town records).
   ————, d. Dec. 1814, aged 7 months (Worthington town records).
William Warner, b. Sept. 19, 1815, in Worthington; d. in 1898, in a
   hospital in Meadville, Pa. The remains were cremated in Pittsburg
   and the ashes interred in Meadville. He was a farmer, dairyman
   and stock raiser, justice of the peace five years. Married (1) Mar.
   22, 1838, Amy Prentice, who d. Jan. 27, 1879, (2) Oct. 5, 1880, Mrs.
   Mary A. Elder.

310 **STOEL⁶ WARNER,** son of Matthew⁵ and Eunice
(Stoel) Warner, born March 7, 1774, in Mansfield, Conn.; died
September 5, 1828. He received land in Worthington, Mass.,
by the will of his father in 1823, but had removed to Champion,
N. Y., as early as 1803. He was a carpenter and wagon maker;
justice of the peace; supervisor of the town in 1818-20; one of
the incorporators of the Le Ray de Chaumont Agricultural
Society in 1828.
   Married in Champion, N. Y., October 3, 1803, ANNA CRAN-
DALL, born November 25, 1783, in Thetford, Orange Co., Vt.,
daughter of Abel and Elizabeth (————) Crandall.

Children, born in Champion

Fannie Warner, b. Oct. 21, 1808; m. Apr. 1, 1829, Joel A. Hubbard.
   Children: i. Stoel Warner, b. June 7, 1830; d. Mar. 7, 1848. ii.
   J. Austin, Jr., b. Oct. 19, 1853; m. Nov. 20, 1878, Marian J. Vebber;
   has a child, Verah Almira, b. Jan., 1893, at Black River, N .Y.
Edna Sawin Warner, b. Mar. 17, 1811; m. Jan. 1, 1835, Elizur Canfield;
   resided in Copenhagen, N. Y.
505 *Matthew S. Warner,* b. May 23, 1814; m. Charlotte Loomis.

311   ANDREW[6] WARNER, son of Matthew[5] and Eunice (Stoel) Warner, born July 16, 1778, at Mansfield, Conn.; died in Ontario, N. Y., January 27, 1871. He removed with his family to Worthington, Mass.; then in 1803, to Champion, Jefferson Co., N. Y., and in 1816, to Ontario, N. Y. He was a teamster in the War of 1812, and was the inheritor of the powder horn that had been made for his uncle Andrew, a Revolutionary soldier. He was mentioned in his father's will of 1823.

Married in Worthington, Mass., March 10, 1801, CHLOE FAIRMAN, born October 21, 1779, died in Ontario, N. Y., November 13, 1867, at the residence of her daughter Laura. She was the daughter of Jared and Chloe (————) Fairman of Worthington, Mass.

Children

506   *Alanson Warner,* b. Mar. 19, 1802, in Worthington, Mass.; m. Catharine Albright.

507   *Orpha Warner,* b. Oct. 25, 1804, in Champion, N. Y.; m. Philander Billson Roys.

508   *Eunice Warner,* b. Aug. 8, 1808, in Champion, N. Y.; m. George Owen.
      Emeline Warner, b. Nov. 27, 1811, in Worthington, Mass.; d. in Ontario, N. Y., Sept. 29, 1828.

509   *Laura Warner,* b. Aug. 16, 1816, in Webster, N. Y.; m. (1) Johnson Cottrel, (2) Weston Winslow.

312   ELIZABETH[6] WARNER, daughter of Elnathan[5] and Lydia (Beaumont) Warner, born April 9, 1782, in Windham, Conn.; resided later in Blandford, Mass.

Married JOSEPH EELLS, born May 12, 1781, in Coventry, Conn.; died at Norwalk, Ohio, January 1, 1861. He married (2) Abigail Green by whom he had one daughter. His ancestry is given as follows: John[1], resided in Dorchester from 1630 to about 1640, when he returned to England, taking with him his infant son Samuel[2], born in Dorchester, June 23, 1639. Samuel became a major in Cromwell's army and remained in England until 1661, when he returned to America, settled in Milford, Conn., and died April 21, 1709. He was a lawyer and a man of wealth. He was in command of a garrison in King Philip's war and was perhaps the earliest to oppose the government in selling Indian captives as slaves (1675). His wife was the daughter of Rev. Robert Linthal, the first minister of Weymouth, Mass. Their youngest son, Nathaniel[3], born February 4, 1710, was graduated from Harvard in 1728, settled as pastor in Stonington, Conn., and remained there until his death in 1786. He was appointed chaplain of a regiment raised and stationed at New London. He married Mercy Cushing, daughter of Hon. John

Cushing. Their son Nathaniel[4], born July 16, 1749, resided at North Coventry and died at Bolton, Conn., December 20, 1799, married Hannah North, was father of Joseph[5].

Children of Joseph and Elizabeth (Warner) Eells, nine in number and lived to the average age of 58 years

(*Daughter.*)
(*Daughter.*)
Cushing Eells, b. in Blandford, Mass., Feb. 16, 1810, see further.
Charles Eells, d. in Mar., 1891, aged nearly 72. He was on a visit to his brother Cushing at the time of his death. He had resided in Illinois.
John Ells, was a man of fine education, one of the founders and first superintendent of the Western Female Academy at Oxford, Ohio, over which he presided many years; d. in Oxford; m. in Dayton, Ohio, Julia A. Boal, who died in Oxford. Children, born in Oxford: i. Eleanor, d. aged 48. ii. Julia F., resided with her brother Charles. iii. Charles J., resided in Clinton County, Ohio. iv. J. Cushing, was traveling salesman for the Stoddard Mfg. Co., at Dayton, Ohio. v. H. Warner, New York City representative of the firm of Proctor & Gamble of Cincinnati; m. Natalie, daughter of Nathaniel Briggs of New York City. vi. Edward H., b. Dec. 13, 1856; learned the drug business and conducted a store with his brother for some years; removed to Highland County, but returned after three years to Oxford as manager of the Gath undertaking and wall paper firm; m. April 4, 1889, Florence M. Gath, daughter of Samuel Gath; has a son, E. Gath, b. Oct. 9, 1891. vii. Harriet B., studied under Dr. Sargent of Cambridge and became a teacher of physical culture in Vassar College.

Cushing Eells is one of the heroic characters of American missions. He was educated at East Granville, Monson Academy, and Williams College, graduating in 1834. While at college he usually walked the forty-five miles between his home and the college on the occasions of his rare vacations, many of which were spent in teaching in Holden. He then took a course in the East Windsor Theological Seminary (later the Hartford Seminary) and was a member of the second class. There he became interested in missions and in 1838 was designated by the American Board as a missionary to the Zulus of Africa. The need of workers in Oregon was so great, however, that he was sent there as one of the followers of Marcus Whitman. He was married Mar. 5, 1838, to Myra Fairbank, born in Holden, Mass., May 26, 1805, daughter of Deacon Joshua and Sally H. Fairbank. The young couple immediately started on a wedding trip across the continent and a year later completed it. The little party of missionaries traveled much of the way with representatives of the Hudson Bay Fur Company and encountered obstacles sufficient to discourage many a man, but the women of the party accomplished the journey to Walla Walla in three hundred and six days. The story of his long and useful life is well told in the volume written by his son Myron Eells (Boston and Chicago, 1894), "Father Eells or the results of fifty five years of missionary labors in Washington and Oregon." He assisted in the organization of many of the early churches of Washington and Oregon, and was a general missionary teacher. In 1866 he founded Whitman Seminary near the Columbia River in Washington Territory, at the mission station where Dr. Whitman had been massacred in 1847. The seminary was soon moved to Walla Walla, six miles distant, and in 1882 a college charter was granted. Dr. Eells put into its endowment much money and an untold amount of labor without salary. He left but few writings, mainly reports to the missionary organizations, but his name remains, beside those of Whitman and Walker, as the founders of great communities, influences that preserved Oregon to the United States, and factors whose efforts among the Indians saw rich fruit in later years.

Dr. Eells died Feb. 16, 1893, on his 83d birthday. His wife died in Skokomish, Aug. 9, 1878. They had two sons: Edwin and Myron. Edwin Eells was born July 27, 1841, in Tshimakain Mission Station, Walker's Prairie, Wash. He was Indian Agent in charge of the Puyallup Indian Agency in Washington for twenty years until it was abolished in 1894, and was known as the model agent. He married July 3, 1871, Abigail A. Foster, and had seven children: Ida Myra, Eva Alice, Gertie Fairbank, Grace Foster, Abbie May, Edna and Edwin.

Myron Eells was born at Tshimakain Station, Oct. 7, 1843; died in 1907. He was graduated from Pacific University, Oregon, in 1866; Hartford Seminary, 1871; was ordained in Hartford and preached in Boisé City, Idaho, 1871-4; was then called to Skokomish, Wash., as missionary to the Indians and made that the scene of his life work, organizing various churches. He was a trustee of Pacific University and of Whitman College, which conferred upon him the degree of D.D. in 1890, and the following year extended an invitation to become its president, which, however, he declined. Dr. Eells was well known as an authority upon ethnology and anthropology and was a member of many learned societies. He was the author of several books on the Twana, Chinook and other Indian languages, the biography of his father, and many works of historical and missionary interest, among which is the History of Indian missions on the Pacific Coast (Philadelphia, 1882). Myron Eells married Jan. 18, 1874, Sarah Maria Crosby, and had five children: Edwin Fayette, Arthur Heman, Chester Cushing, Walter Crosby, and Roy Whitman.

312a LUCY⁶ WARNER, daughter of Elnathan⁵ and Lydia (Beaumont) Warner, born March 26, 1788; resided in Lebanon, Conn.

Married (1) November 8, 1812, **SAMUEL POTTER,** born Sept. 27, 1780; died November 29, 1820.

Married (2) **BENJAMIN SEGAR.**

Children by first husband

Lucy A. Potter, b. Aug. 11, 1813; d. Apr. 17, 1860; m. Apr. 15, 1832, James Perry, b. Feb. 20, 1798, d. July 25, 1853, son of William and Elizabeth (Segar) Perry. Children: i. James N., b. June 23, 1833; m, Dec. 10, 1856, Frances A. Herrick of Norwich. ii. Henrietta M.,

b. May 1, 1835; m. May 22, 1863, Henry Potter. iii. Edwin, b. Jan. 15, 1839; d. Aug. 13, 1842. iv. Abby, b. Jan. 10, 1842; d. Dec. 20, 1883.

Lydia Maria Potter, b. May 1, 1815; d. Jan. 27, 1882; m. Sept. 29, 1840, as his second wife, Joseph Potter, b. Nov. 8, 1799, d. Feb. 27, 1885, in Lebanon, son of Governor Samuel Potter. Children: i. Mary Ellen, b. Sept. 1, 1841; d. Jan. 23, 1867; m. (1) Fred Schalk, (2) Joshua Bradley Card, Jr. (who m. (2) Jane Lillie, who was living as his widow in Lebanon, 1917). ii. Lydia, b. Sept. 21, 1844; d. Jan. 28, 1865. iii. George A., b. Sept. 23, 1854; d. Apr. 20, 1855.

Samuel W. Potter, b. Aug. 16, 1817; d. Apr. 21, 1845.

Abby Potter, b. Mar. 17, 1820; d. Dec. 20, 1849; m. (1) Dan C. Scoville, (2) Jasper Murdock. The first husband appears to have been Dan Carpenter Scovel, b. Oct. 16, 1816, in Lebanon, d. Dec. 9, 1842, in Chicago, Ill., son of Amherst and Sarah (Little) Scovel, although the Scovell Genealogy indicates that he was unmarried.

(This record is chiefly from the manuscript of Lebanon families compiled by Walter Kingsley, former town clerk, and was evidently secured by a visitation of the family.)

313 CHARLES[6] WARNER, son of Elnathan[5] and Lydia (Beaumont) Warner, born in Windham, Conn., August 2, 1798; died there October 23, 1855. He was a farmer, school teacher, surveyor and civil engineer, in Windham. Inventory of his estate was taken May 20, 1856, and his wife and Andrew Frink, Jr., were administrators.

Married in Windham, April 11, 1827, MARGARET W. HALL, born in East Haddam, Conn., December 27, 1802, died in Windham, April 25, 1890. She joined the church at Windham in 1830. George D. Wells was administrator of her estate (Windham Probate records, 22:276, 26:31).

Children, born in Windham

George Hall Warner, b. May 23, 1828; d. Mar. 18, 1850, not married, buried in Windham Cemetery. He was a student at Amherst College in 1847-8, and died of consumption.

Ann Elizabeth Warner, b. Mar. 31, 1831; resides in Windham (1917); m. there Mar. 31, 1858, Daniel Wells, b. in Charlemont, Mass., d. Apr. 28, 1884, in Waterbury, Conn. Child: George Dexter, b. in Windham, June 28, 1859; is a farmer there; m. May 19, 1885, Delia A. Mansfield. They have had five children, born in Windham: Florence Margaret, b. Mar. 13, 1886; Herbert Charles, b. Apr. 21, 1888; Daniel William, b. Sept. 7, 1890, d. Dec. 21, 1890; Belle Elizabeth, b. Jan. 4, 1892, m. in Willimantic, Conn., Aug. 12, 1913, Arnold F. Glover of East Walpole, Mass., and has a child, Christine Wells, b. Apr. 26, 1916, in Walpole; Mildred Elbertine, b. Feb. 3, 1898. This is said to be the only surviving line of descendants from Nathaniel Warner, b. 1722.

314 MARIA[6] WARNER, daughter of Jared[5] and Mary (Ripley) Warner, born October 1, 1789, in Pomfret, Conn.; died May 25, 1860.
Married in Abington, Conn., SAMUEL HUNTINGTON LYON, son of Rev. Walter and Mary (Huntington) Lyon. Rev. Walter Lyon was graduated from Dartmouth College in 1777 and was pastor of the church at Abington from 1783 to 1826.

Children

Samuel Lyon.
Eliza Fitch Lyon, b. Oct. 14, 1817; d. June 24, 1892; m. Sept. 20, 1837, Theophilus Parsons Huntington, b. in Hadley, Mass., July 11, 1811, d. July 20, 1862. Children: i. Walter Eliot, b. Mar. 27, 1842; d. Jan. 5, 1910, resided in Springfield, Mass., served nine months in the Civil War and was honorably discharged. ii. Maria Whiting, b. Mar. 9, 1845, in Hadley, m. there Sept. 10, 1870, John Duryea Elwell; resides in Schenectady, N. Y. (see below). iii. Edward Dwight, b. June 1, 1857, in Hadley; resides in Amherst; m. in Northampton, Sept. 6, 1882, Mrs. Lucy Hills. John Duryea and Maria Whiting (Huntington) Elwell had three children: i. Theodora, b. in Brooklyn, N. Y., Jan. 18, 1872; d. June 17, 1910. ii. Elizabeth Huntington, b. in Brooklyn, June 19, 1873; resides in Schenectady; m. Jan. 30, 1894, Arthur Winslow Jones; has two children, b. in Melbourne, Australia, Alfred Winslow, b. Feb. 9, 1900, and Duryea Huntington, b. May 8, 1904. iii. Cecilia, b. Feb. 19, 1881; d. Feb. 10, 1882, in Brooklyn.

315 JARED ELIOT[6] WARNER, son of Dr. Jared[5] and Mary (Ripley) Warner, born in Pomfret, Conn., March 31, 1796; died in Utica, N. Y., February 24, 1878. At the age of 14 he went to reside with an uncle, Dr. Fitch, in Clinton, Oneida Co., N. Y. About 1812 he started in the drug business in Utica and was a well-known druggist there for many years. He was an active official in the First Presbyterian Church of that city, treasurer of the County Bible Society, agent of the American Board of Foreign Missions and the American Tract Society, and was the second president of the Utica City Bank. His store was the place of deposit and distribution of numerous religious publications.
Married (1) May 15, 1821, ALATHEA R. LORD of Abington, who died in Utica, May 27, 1836.
Married (2) December 27, 1837, JULIA W. JAMES of Utica, who died in Utica, October, 1847.
Married (3) October 8, 1850, JANE HELEN RYLEY of Schenectady, born November 23, 1807, died in Utica, June 30, 1889, daughter of James Van Slyck and Jane (Swits) Ryley of Schenectady.

Children by first wife

510 *Samuel Eliot Warner*, b. May 29, 1823; m. Helen Potter.
William Lord Warner, b. June 17, 1826; d. Apr. 30, 1827.
Alathea Maria (1) *Warner*, b. Sept. 27, 1828; d. Aug. 1, 1829.

Children by second wife

Alathea Maria (2) *Warner*, b. Sept. 3, 1840; d. May 27, 1844.
Lucy Wells Warner, b. Sept. 15, 1841; d. Dec. 13, 1868.
Julia Adelphia Warner, b. Mar. 11, 1844; d. Sept. 17, 1893, not married.
Martha Warner, b. July 5, 1846; d. July 5, 1846.
Daniel James Warner, b. Aug. 20, 1847; d. Aug. 21, 1847.

Child by third wife

Anna Maria Warner, b. Aug. 17, 1851; resides in Utica (1917).

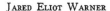

JARED ELIOT WARNER   SAMUEL ELIOT WARNER

316 **GEORGE TROWBRIDGE**[6] **WARNER,** son of Wil
liam[5] and Mary (Trowbridge) Warner, born in Hartford, Conn.,
March 5, 1802; died in Warsaw, Pa., Sept. 5, 1850. He was
always known as "Doctor Warner," was also a furrier, trapping,
curing and sewing the skins himself. He resided in Smithfield,
R. I., Uxbridge, Mass., Webster, Mass., Thompson and Eastford,
Conn.; removed between 1836 and 1839 to New York State and
bought land from ——— Swartwart on East Canada Creek,
where he lived near some "second cousins," John and Clarissa

Warner, probably John, son of Timothy[5]; see number 87. He lived in Oppenheim, Fulton Co., N. Y., and St. Johnsville, N. Y., then removed about 1848 to Williamsville, Jones township, Pa.

Married in Smithfield, R. I., April 28, 1825, **TAMZEN SMITH ROGERS,** born in Yarmouth, Mass., July 27, 1805, died in Providence, R. I., June 12, 1881.

Children

William Rogers Warner, b. in Smithfield, R. I., Mar. 31, 1826; d. at Pawtucket, R. I.; m. in Clermontville, McKean Co., Pa., Feb. 8, 1851, Catherine L. Martin, who d. at Lorraine, N. Y., Dec. 2, 1882. He was an ordained minister in the Baptist Church, preached in Detroit, Mich., for several years, and at the Taunton Ave. Church, East Providence; removed to Pawtucket about 1890, later to Providence. They had at least three sons and two daughters, of whom were: i. John Blain, an expert electrician residing in Milford, Mass.; m. and has a daughter. ii. Lucretia Lucinda (called Edith), d. 1902, not married. iii. Adam Peter (called Charles), resides in New England.

George Pearsons Warner, b. Mar. 8, 1828, in Uxbridge, Mass.; d. there, Sept. 5, 1830.

511 *James Trowbridge Warner,* b. Apr. 6, 1830, in Uxbridge; m. Martha Vesta Ditson.

Mary Rosamond Warner, b. Jan. 7, 1832, in Uxbridge; d. in Houston, Tex., Nov. 18, 1890; m. in Warsaw, Pa., Dec. 25, 1850, Joseph C. Barnes. Sylvester Barnes is a descendant.

512 *Albert Loomis Warner,* b. July 28, 1834, in Webster, Mass.; m. (1) Henrietta Rogers, (2) Emma Jane Peck.

513 *Laura Parmelia Warner,* b. Dec. 19, 1836, in Thompson, Conn.; m. (1) George H. Newell, (2) George Freeth Smith.

Victoria Augusta Warner, b. June 15, 1839, in Eastford, Conn.; m. in Portsmouth, R. I., Sept. 14, 1862, Charles C. Cailloux.

Elvira Isabella Warner, b. Sept. 19, 1842, in Oppenheim, N. Y.; m. in Pawtucket, R. I., Mar. 13, 1861, Albert F. Smith.

Tamzen Jane Warner, b. June 20, 1845, in St. Johnsville, N. Y.; resides at Arnold's Mills, R. I.; m. at Arnold's Mills, Cumberland, R. I., June 7, 1869, Rufus Clark, b. Nov. 30, 1822, d. Aug. 1, 1910. Children: i. Evelina Whipple, b. Apr. 8, 1870; d. Aug. 4, 1886. ii. Ross Rufus, b. Feb. 13, 1879; resides at Arnold's Mills, R. I.

514 *Charles Francis Pearl Warner,* b. Nov. 5, 1848, in Williamsville, Jones township, Pa.; m. (1) Emma Willard Chace, (2) Janette Augusta Lyon.

317 EARL[6] WARNER, son of Ichabod[5] and Hannah (Collins) Warner, born August 15, 1806 (Windham, Conn., town record); died in Brooklyn, Conn., November, 1881. He was a manufacturer of leather belting and dealer in leather goods, hose and belting, a tanner by trade.

Married (1) June 5, 1833, **HARRIET S. GILBERT** of Brooklyn, Conn.

Married (2) **ADELINE LESTER**, born 1809, in Groton, Conn., daughter of Nicholas Street and Elizabeth Starr (Avery) Lester.

Married (3) November 11, 1869 (Windham record), **MARY ELIZA FITCH**, born in Willimantic, Conn., March 31, 1843, died there, May 2, 1913, daughter of Harden H. Fitch who was born in Windham, and his wife, Julia Russ, who was born in Mansfield, Conn.

Child by first wife

Juliet Augusta Warner, b. Mar. 20, 1834; d. 1875; m. Edmund Perkins of Norwich, Conn. Children: i. Robert W., president of the Consolidated Trolley lines of Connecticut. ii. Donald G., a leading lawyer in Norwich.

Children by second wife

Adeline Elizabeth Warner, b. May 2, 1836; d. 1911, not married; resided in Norwich.

Earl Warner, Jr., b. in Brooklyn, Conn., Feb. 8, 1838; d. in New London, Conn., Apr. 28, 1909. He was once judge of probate for New London County but was incapacitated by ill health for some years before his death. Married in New London, June 19, 1872, Harriet Jackson Champlain, b. July 10, 1846, at New London, daughter of Henry and Ann Brown (Jackson) Champlain. Children, born in New London: i. Jewell, b. Jan. 7, 1876, is a member of the D. A. R.; resides with her brother in Norristown, Pa. ii. Henry Champlain, b. Dec. 28, 1878; served two enlistments as a member of the Conn. National Guard, and received honorable discharge. He owns and conducts a large department store in Norristown.

Frances Lester Warner, b. May 16, 1840; d. Jan. 19, 1918; m. (1) George A. Robinson of Norwich, librarian of Otis Library, 1875-1892; m. (2) Oct. 28, 1905, Benjamin E. Sibley of Rialto, Cal. By the first marriage she had two children: i. Frank Tyler, b. in Norwich, Oct. 5, 1860; married and is engaged in business in Los Angeles, Cal.; has a son Thomas Tyler, b. Mar., 1892, a lawyer in Los Angeles, enlisted in the artillery (1918). ii. Juliet Warner, b. in Norwich, Dec. 7, 1863; was teacher of art in Norwich Free Academy; has for years held a position in the Metropolitan Museum of Art, New York City.

Sarah Belton Warner, b. Apr. 23, 1842; d. Dec. 14, 1843.

Louis Belton Warner, b. Mar. 30, 1845; not married; is engaged in business in St. Joseph, Mo.

515 *Edgar Morris Warner*, b. June 16, 1850; m. Jane Elizabeth Carpenter.

Children of Earl and Mary Eliza (Fitch) Warner

William Fitch Warner, b. Aug. 11, 1870, in Brooklyn, Conn.; is a dealer in men's furnishings in Boston, Mass.; resides in Newtonville; m. at Newton Highlands, Emeline Curtis, daughter of Charles and Naomi (————) Curtis. Child: Alma De Forest, b. Mar. 22, 1913.

Minnie Celeste Warner, b. May 16, 1873, in Brooklyn, Conn.; resides

in East Hampton, Conn.; m. in Willimantic, Oct. 10, 1905, Louis
Wright Little, b. in Columbia, Conn., Apr. 29, 1873, son of Myron
Winslow and Emily (Wright) Little.

318   MARY FIELD[6] or MARY ANN FIELD[6] WARNER,
daughter of Moses[5], Jr., and Sarah (Selden) Warner, born in
Amherst, Mass., June 17, 1779.
Married in Amherst, March 6, 1800, Capt. DAVID DICKIN-
SON, born in Amherst, April 27, 1778, son of Enos and Lois
(Dickinson) Dickinson; died in Petersham, Mass. He was a
farmer and received a commission as captain in 1815 from Caleb
Strong, Governor of Massachusetts, for services in the War of
1812.

Children (daughters and one son)

Moses Field Dickinson b. in Petersham, Sept. 18, 1800, the only son of
his parents; d. in Detroit, Mich., Apr. 7, 1871. He was educated at
the famous old Amherst Academy, before the College was founded
in 1821. He was a clerk in Enfield for a time, then taught at
Petersham. He invented a system of stenography which he taught
there and in neighboring towns. He was later clerk in Boston and
in Hardwick, where he married, Sept. 27, 1831, Maria Loraine Wesson, only daughter of the Rev. William B. Wesson, Congregational
pastor at Hardwick. They set out by stage for Albany, travelled
by the canal to Buffalo, then by boat to Detroit, arriving October,
1831. Mr. Dickinson soon set up in business for himself as a copper-
smith and hardware merchant, and remained at the old store for
twenty years, retiring in 1852. He had a large trade; a large portion
was for copper work for the steamboats. In early days Mr. Dickinson was fire warden and always kept his staff of office and his black
leather hat-band with "fire-warden" in white letters, near his bed.
He was a careful, punctilious business man, square and honest in all
his engagements, bought property and improved it until he acquired
a comfortable fortune. He was punctual in collecting rents but was
far from being a hard landlord, kind and accommodating to his
friends; his two-wheeled cart, and later his carriage were always
in use, picking up neighbors and, in inclement weather, looking after
the welfare of the teachers in the school near his home. He was
a regular attendant of St. Paul's Episcopal Church, and, for a time,
vestryman in St. Peter's Church. In 1850 he built a fine country
home in what was then Springwell township, and removed there.
He was justice of the peace, took an active interest in school affairs,
was one of the promoters of the street car lines, served on the board
of commissioners on the plan of the city, 1869-71. His wife, who
died June 17, 1887, was a devout woman and for many years trustee
of St. Luke's Hospital. She was survived by five of their thirteen
children: William Cutler, proprietor of the Ft. Wyman Stock Farm,
Rolla, Mo.; Horace Hills, hardware merchant, Detroit; Maria L.,
m. Thomas McGraw, lived in Detroit; Harriet Holden, m. Edward
T. Baker of Detroit; Emily Hills, resided at the homestead, not
married.

319 AARON[6] WARNER, son of Jonathan[5] and Margaret Elizabeth (Sewall) Warner, born in Amherst, Mass., probably in 1781, baptized there, October 2, 1783; bought one-half his father's home farm in Amherst in 1807, and the following year with his brother Jonathan bought other land from his father, the home farm, and a lot in Hadley on "Mount Hollock." He removed to Andover, Windsor County, Vt., as his children's births were recorded there.

Married in Brattleboro, Vt., November 24, 1805, **REBECCA SMITH** of Brattleboro.

Children, recorded in Andover, Vt.

Jesse Warner, b. Nov. 14, 1806. He is probably the Jesse Warner recorded in the 1850 Census of Wallingford, Vt., a farmer aged 43, farm valued at $3,000, wife Susannah, aged 40, born in Vt., and four children, born in Vt.: i. Elisha, b. about 1834. ii. Christiana, b. about 1837. iii. Aaron, b. about 1839. iv. Janette, b. about 1846.

Lucinda Warner, b. Dec. 9, 1808.

Eliza Warner, b. Jan. 16, 1811.

320 **DOROTHY**[6] **WARNER,** daughter of Lemuel[5] and Dorothy (Phelps) Warner, born in Hadley, Mass., March 19, 1777. She was mentioned in her father's will, 1824.

Married November 15, 1795 (Hadley town records), Deacon **WILLIAM DICKINSON,** born January, 1765; died May 15, 1859, in Hadley, where he had settled. He was the son of Josiah Dickinson.

Children, born in Hadley

Maria Partridge Dickinson, b. Oct. 15, 1799; d. in Templeton, Vt.; m. Lewis Sabin.

William Dickinson, b. Dec. 17, 1800; d. Dec. 10, 1817, not married.

Roswell (1) *Dickinson*, b. Mar. 11, 1802; d. Jan. 13, 1803.

Dorothy (1) *Dickinson*, b. July 13, 1804; d. Sept. 27, 1810.

Roswell (2) *Dickinson*, b. Dec. 29, 1806; d. Sept. 18, 1807.

Elizabeth Dickinson, b. Aug. 20, 1808; m. Horace Goodrich.

Caroline Dickinson, b. Mar. 19, 1811.

Dorothy (2) *Dickinson*, b. Mar. 6, 1813; m. Lucius B. Shea of Boston.

George Dickinson, b. Aug. 24, 1815.

Harriet Newell Dickinson, b. Mar. 18, 1818; m. Rev. Ebenezer W. Ballard.

William Phelps Dickinson, b. Oct. 17, 1820; m. Emeline Woodbridge.

321 **OLIVER**[6] **WARNER,** son of Lemuel[5] and Dorothy (Phelps) Warner, born in Hadley, Mass., June 27, 1789; died there, January 1, 1851. His will was dated April 27, 1850, probated July 2, 1851; heirs were wife Jemima and son William P.

23

Married JEMIMA SEVERANCE, born in Greenfield, Mass.; died in Hadley, February 21, 1851, aged 63 years.

Children

Phelps Warner, b. Dec., 1816; d. Feb. 2, 1817, aged one month, 13 days.
516 William Phelps Warner, b. Mar. 6, 1818; m. Betsey Rich Abbe.
(Son), b. and d. Sept. 27, 1820, buried in Hadley.
Edward Warner, b. about 1824, was a farmer in Hadley and d. there, Aug. 15, 1843, aged 18 years, 8 months, not married.

322 MARTHA (PATTY) HUNT[6] WARNER, daughter of Noadiah[5] and Martha (Hunt) Warner, born in Hadley, Mass., October 9, 1787; died in Hadley, October 30, 1870. Married GILES CROUCH KELLOGG, born in Hadley, August 12, 1781, died there, June 19, 1861, son of Dr. Giles Crouch Kellogg of Hadley. He was a graduate of Yale, 1800; lawyer for many years in Hadley; town clerk and treasurer of Hadley, and Register of Deeds for Hampshire County; served as adjutant in a Massachusetts regiment in the War of 1812. For further records of this family see Dexter's Yale Biographies and Kelloggs in the New World, p. 1787.

Children, born in Hadley

Giles Crouch Kellogg, Jr., b. Feb. 4, 1819; d. in Hadley, Apr. 6, 1897, not married.
Mary C. Kellogg, b. 1821; d. Apr. 13, 1842; m. Sept. 24, 1841, Stephen Stone Montague, see below; no children.
Martha Hunt Kellogg, b. Oct. 25, 1823; m. in Hadley, July 5, 1854, Daniel Kellogg, b. in Amherst, Aug. 9, 1820, d. in Hadley, Jan. 27, 1899, son of Rufus and Esther (Mayo) Kellogg. He was a farmer in Hadley. Children: i. Henry Martin, b. Oct. 2, 1855, a farmer in Hadley. ii. Charles Daniel, b. May 20, 1857; d. Jan. 15, 1864. iii. Edward Hunt, b. Mar. 29, 1859; d. Apr. 10, 1874. iv. Giles Melcher, b. Aug. 16, 1863; m. Frances Angeline Crafts, and had a son, Howard Fletcher.
Lucy W. Kellogg, b. 1826; m. Stephen Stone Montague, who had first married her sister Mary. He was born Dec. 8, 1818, d. June 6, 1885, son of Stephen and Grace Grant (White) Montague. He was a merchant in Hadley and removed to Kalamazoo, Mich., in 1858. Their son, William Francis Montague, has been deputy sheriff of Kalamazoo County, is married and has children.
Ann M. Kellogg, b. Aug. 3, 1828; d. in Hadley, Oct. 3, 1892, not married.

323 HARRIET[6] WARNER, daughter of Elihu[5] and Elizabeth (Freeman) Warner, born in Hadley, Mass., July, 1793; died there, September 24, 1864.

Married October 25, 1821, JONATHAN MARSH, born January 19, 1793, son of Timothy and Mercy (Smith) Marsh; died May 5, 1843. His father died when he was three years old and in 1806 his mother married Josiah Cowles and removed to Leverett. He was apprenticed to a shoemaker, but disliked the trade and later learned the carpenter's trade. He worked in Westfield and there joined a military company, the only one in that section that was not called out for duty in Boston in 1814. He also spent a season in Pompey, N. Y., but later made his home in Leverett or Hadley, and in 1820, bought land of Elihu Warner and built a house. He resided on West Street, Hadley, where the main highway now passes out toward Northampton. A more complete account of this family will be found in "John Marsh of Hartford."

Children

John Warner Marsh, b. Feb. 1, 1824; m. Oct. 29, 1845, Harriet Elizabeth Cook. Children: i. William Dwight, m. Bertha Belle Bryant. ii. Mary Lester, m. George Perkins Metcalf. iii. Lucy Russell. iv. John Warner, Jr., m. Mrs. Lilla Frances Smith Wilson. v. George Cook. vi. Henry Rindge. vii. Fred Smith.

Timothy Smith Marsh, b. Sept. 18, 1826; was a farmer in Hadley; m. (1) Apr. 25, 1855, Maria Pomeroy Bartlett, daughter of Captain Lewis Bartlett; (2) June 8, 1870, Eliza Ann Cook, daughter of Samuel P. Cook. Children by first wife: i. Nellie Smith, m. Thomas A. Palmer. ii. Hattie Maria, d. young. iii. Jennie Maria, d. young. iv. Edward Smith.

Josiah Dwight Marsh, b. Mar. 6, 1829; was a carpenter; m. (1) Sarah Lucretia Ingram, who died Dec. 14, 1888, daughter of Peter Ingram; (2) Nov. 9, 1889, Lucy Ann Hayward. Children by first wife: i. Charles Dwight, was graduated from Amherst College, is a teacher in Ripon, Wis.; m. F. L. Wilder. ii. Carrie Barnard, d. young. iii. Emily Roberts, was graduated from Mt. Holyoke and has taught in Canada and the West.

Harriet Sophia Marsh, b. Sept. 4, 1832.

Sarah Elizabeth Marsh, b. Oct. 12, 1835.

324 HORACE[6] WARNER, son of Reuben[5] and Eunice (Carrington) Warner, born in New Milford, Conn., August 29, 1790; died in Stamford, Conn., March 6, 1866. Married in Bethel, Conn., November 20, 1823, EMELINE STEVENS, born in Derby, Conn., July 20, 1805, daughter of Oliver and Huldah (Clark) Stevens.

Children, born in New Milford

Frederick Reuben Warner, b. Oct. 28, 1827; d. in New York City, Nov. 28, 1876; m. in Newark, N. J., June 2, 1852, Angelina Durand, b. Dec. 7, 1833, in New York City, d. in Nashua, N. H., Mar. 10, 1874.

Children: i. Clara Celia, b. Apr. 27, 1853; d. Aug. 1, 1855. ii. Thomas Howard, b. July 13, 1854, in Brooklyn, N. Y.; m. in Danbury, Conn., Nov. 26, 1882, Delia Campbell, b. May 23, 1852, in Pawling, N. Y., and had three children, Josephine Maud, b. Aug. 30, 1883, Thomas Harold, b. Nov. 8, 1885, and Ethel Trowbridge, b. Nov. 27, 1887. iii. Caroline Rose, b. Nov. 3, 1857, in Newark, N. J.; m. (1) in New York City, July 13, 1878, Wirt G. Harmon, b. in Antwerp, N. Y., Oct. 5, 1857, (divorced), by whom she had two children, Annie Belle, b. Dec. 27, 1879, and Frederick Warner, b. Aug. 7, 1882; m. (2) in New York City, May 18, 1892, Leonard S. Knox, b. in Brewster, N. Y., Dec. 16, 1852, by whom she had one child, Beatrice Grace, b. May 25, 1895. iv. Alice, d. young.

James Carrington Warner, b. Mar. 11, 1832; m. (1) in Newark, N. J., Dec. 22, 1853, Caroline Adams, b. in New York, Apr. 9, 1833, (divorced); m. (2) July 2, 1893, Rebecca F. Croliss, b. Sept. 11, 1847, in Ridgefield, Conn. Children by first wife: i. Horace Adams, b. Oct. 22, 1854; d. May 31, 1890; m. Dec. 25, 1878, Florence R. Raymond. ii. Kate Weir, b. Nov. 2, 1857. iii. Isabella Thomas, b. Aug. 11, 1860; m. June 3, 1880, George W. Hallock. iv. Harriet Jane, b. Sept. 20, 1862; d. May 15, 1865.

325 DEBBY AURELIA[6] WARNER, daughter of Benjamin Ruggles[5] and Mercy (Ruggles) Warner, born in Brookfield, Conn., February 10, 1789; died April 8, 1856.

Married September 19, 1815, **WILLIAM AGUR HAWLEY**, born in Huntington, April 23, 1788, son of Agur and Anna (Hinman) Hawley; died May 20, 1854. He was graduated from Williams College in 1816, was ordained and installed as pastor of the church at Hinsdale, Mass., in 1817. He held this pastorate for twenty-three years, then took the one at Plainfield for six years. After that time he supplied, as his health permitted, in East Hawley and elsewhere. Shortly before his death he removed to Sunderland and was living with his daughter, Mrs. Nancy Smith, at the time of his death. The volume published in commemoration of the centennial of the Hinsdale Church contains an appreciation of the Rev. Mr. Hawley, and his portrait.

Children, born in Hinsdale, Mass.

Ruggles Warner Hawley, b. Nov. 8, 1816; d. Dec. 3, 1816.

Flora Minerva Hawley, b. Apr. 24, 1818; resided in Rosemond, Ill.; m. July 6, 1837, John Putnam of Hinsdale, b. Apr. 21, 1813, son of John and Philura (Curtis) Putnam. Children: i. Ophelia Mariam, b. Nov. 7, 1838; m. Nov. 7, 1861, Eugene B. Read, b. Apr. 18, 1837, son of Edwin C. and Catharine (Day) Read. ii. Flora Miranda, b. Oct. 13, 1841; m. Oct. 21, 1857, Milan J. Beckwith, b. June 7, 1830, son of Jared and Lucy (Bingham) Beckwith. iii. Walter, b. Oct. 9, 1846; is a merchant in Missouri; m. Oct. 14, 1875, Sarah E. Harrison, b. Feb. 13, 1851, daughter of Alexander and Elizabeth (Williams) Harrison of Dixon, Ill. iv. James, b. May 22, 1848; is a farmer in Rosemond; m. Oct. 12, 1871, Emma J. Payne, b. Feb. 24, 1851, daughter of John Grosvenor and Ann (Culver) Payne. v. Henry Dwight, b. Sept. 30, 1852; d. July 22, 1862. vi. Mary Sophia, b. Apr. 10, 1855; resides in Rosemond; m. Dec. 24, 1874, Daniel C. Bess, a farmer, b. Jan. 1, 1851, son of Henry and Nancy (Denbo) Bess.

William Agur Hawley, Jr., b. Aug. 28, 1820; was graduated from Williams College in 1842, and became a physician in Syracuse, N. Y.; m. Sept. 24, 1851, Elizabeth Sophia Willard, b. June 2, 1820, daughter of Benjamin and Sally (Conant) Willard of Lancaster, Mass. Children: i. Mary Elizabeth, b. June 8, 1852; resided in Lyons, N. Y. ii. William Augustus, b. Jan. 29, 1856; resided in Lyons. iii. Nora Cornelia, b. Feb. 26, 1860; resided in Lyons; m. Feb. 26, 1881, Micajah J. Howes, b. Dec. 28, 1849, son of Jonathan and Betsey L. (Williams) Howes of Holyoke, Mass.

Nancy Ophelia Hawley, b. June 17, 1822; resided in Sunderland, Mass., and in Harmal, Ill.; m. Sept. 4, 1844, Brainerd Smith, b. May 28, 1818, d. Aug. 21, 1877, son of Quartus and Abigail (Clark) Smith of Sunderland. Children: i. William Hawley, b. Oct. 7, 1845; was a teacher in Bloomington and Peoria, Ill.; m. July 19, 1870, Nellie Galusha, b. Oct. 24, 1849, daughter of Orson B. and Jane (Hinsdale) Galusha of Morris, Ill. ii. Ella Abigail, b. July 15, 1847; resided at Normal and Winona; m. Apr. 3, 1877, Jerome Chipman, a merchant of Normal, b. Apr. 12, 1843, son of John and Mary (Shaw) Chipman. iii. Flora Matilda, b. Apr. 27, 1849; d. Oct. 10, 1850. iv. Leona Aurelia, b. Aug. 19, 1851; d. Dec. 10, 1853. v. Nancy Ophelia, b. Jan. 28, 1854. vi. Hattie Canfield, b. July 18, 1857; m. Aug. 6, 1878, Adam Hoffman, school principal in Sheaton, Ill., b. in Chambersburg, Pa., son of Adam and Earnestina (Foulhater) Hoffman. vii. James Brainerd, b. Oct. 19, 1859; resides in Gardner, Ill.; m. Dec. 15, 1880, Lucy Ann Armitage, b. Nov. 20, 1859, daughter of Scott and Mary J. (Freeman) Armitage of Gardner. viii. George Kimball.

Deborah Aurelia Hawley, b. Mar. 19, 1824; resided in Rosemond, Ill.; m. Sept. 1, 1846, Orlando M. Hawks, a farmer, b. Nov. 14, 1824, son of Horace and Rachel (Smedley) Hawks. Children: i. Emma Aurelia, b. June 9, 1847; resides in Rosemond; m. Oct. 24, 1872, William Osborn Wilcox, a farmer, son of Fergus and Sally (Osborn) Wilcox. ii. Nellie Cornelia, b. Nov. 24, 1849; d. Sept. 26, 1861. iii. Herbert Handel, b. July 2, 1851. iv. Henry Martyn, b. Apr. 28, 1854. v. Lelia Ada, b. Nov. 1, 1855; m. May 8, 1879, Wellington J. Walker of Belchertown, Mass. vi. and vii. Martha Ophelia and Mary Aurelia, twins, b. Jan. 25, 1858. viii. Flora Adelia, b. Feb. 25, 1862. ix. Edwin Augustus, b. Nov. 28, 1864. x. Joseph Baxton, b. Aug. 21, 1866.

Benjamin Ruggles Hawley, b. July 30, 1826; m. Nov. 13, 1851, H. Rosamond` Hall. Children: i. Mary Aurelia, b. Feb. 24, 1853; m. Aug. 5, 1880, Wade H. Richardson, a teacher, of Milwaukee, Wis., b. Dec. 9, 1846, son of George D. and Bethany Paulina (Hill) Richardson, and had son, Walter Hawley, b. Aug. 28, 1881. ii. Kate, b. Sept. 16, 1854; m. Nov. 29, 1888, John C. Hennessey of Chicago. iii. Agnes, b. Feb. 29, 1856. iv. Julia, b. Nov. 26, 1858; m. Dec. 8, 1881, John Jackson Coon, an editor, of Gilman, Ill., b. May 6, 1861,

son of R. Runyon and Emeline (McCowan)' Coon. v. William Cary,
b. May 3, 1862. vi. Helen Rosamond, b. July 22, 1865; d. July 27,
1866. vii. Charles Gilbert, b. June 20, 1868.
Minerva Kittredge Hawley, b. Jan. 23, 1829; m. Apr. 29, 1856, John
A. L. Marvin, a planter, of New Iberia, La., b. Feb. 2, 1825, d. Apr.
15, 1878, son of William Matthew and Mary (Pettit) Marvin.
Child: Kate R., b. Aug. 16, 1859; d. Aug. 25, 1870.

(Records of the above family were taken from the Hawley Record,
published in Buffalo, 1890, by Elias Hawley.)

326 ASHBEL RUGGLES[6] WARNER, son of Benjamin
Ruggles[5] and Mercy (Ruggles) Warner, born March 20, 1794, in
Brookfield, Conn.; died at Mt. Carmel, Conn., October 12 or 13,
1867; buried in Centerville, Conn.

Married February 22, 1820, AVIS ELIZA WOODWORTH,
born April 25, 1798, died October 12, 1880, daughter of Jonathan
and Sarah (Culver) Woodworth.

Children

Almon Warner, b. Jan. 8, 1821; d. Aug., 1890.
Lyman Warner, b. Apr. 10, 1823, in Brookfield, Conn.; d. Aug. 18, 1881;
served through the Civil War; m. Apr. 19, 1855, Mary R. Williams,
b. Jan. 19, 1828, d. Dec. 5, 1877. She was a descendant of Ethan
Allen. Children, b. in Brookfield: i. Frank Ashbel, b. Mar. 15, 1856;
d. July 22, 1856. ii. Lyman Allen, b. Apr. 7, 1857; d. Feb. 28, 1861.
iii. Agnes Eliza, b. Aug. 23, 1861; d. Nov. 24, 1909. iv. Cora Allen,
b. June 27, 1864.
Helen Warner, b. in Brookfield, Oct. 14, 1825; d. Dec. 14, 1865; m.
Apr. 19, 1846, Frederick Keeler, b. Mar. 19, 1824, son of Ira Keeler
of Brookfield. Child: Helen Frances, b. 1853; d. 1857.
Sarah Jane Warner, b. Jan. 9, 1828, in Brookfield; was a teacher;
resided in Danbury, Conn., in 1916; m. in New York City, Jan. 13,
1862, Nathan Platt Gillette, b. Jan. 27, 1831, in Danbury, son of
Nehemiah and Drusilla (Platt) Gillette. Children: i. Helen War-
ner, b. Aug. 1, 1863; resides in New Haven, Conn. ii. Theodore
Wallace, b. Sept. 12, 1864; m. Dec. 31, 1893. iii. Charles Keeler, b.
Nov. 19, 1868; m. Aug. 9, 1899.
Caroline Warner, b. Nov. 28, 1831; d. Jan. 23, 1903; m. Oct. 24, 1855,
at North Haven, Conn., Elmon Pierrepont, b. Dec. 3, 1828, d. Mar.
29, 1902. They removed to Wichita, Kans. Children: i. Elbert
Wallace, b. Feb. 6, 1859; d. Sept. 6, 1872. ii. Nathan Dudley, b.
Sept. 29, 1860. iii. Charles Guy, b. Sept. 3, 1869.
Charlotte Somers Warner, b. May 15, 1834; d. Nov. 15, 1859; m.
Nov. 28, 1855.
Wallace Ruggles Warner, b. Apr. 4, 1837; d. Mar. 31, 1863, at Baton
Rouge, La. He enlisted in the 28th Conn. Regt. and died in service.

327 DANIEL NICHOLS[6] WARNER, son of Benjamin
Ruggles[5] and Hannah (Nichols) Warner, born August 8, 1803,

probably in New Milford, Conn.; died December 14, 1852. He resided for a time in Hinsdale, Mass., was a member of the church there and treasurer of the First Congregational Society at its organization in 1834. He and his wife Dorothy received letters of dismission from that church, February, 1838.

Married (1) in Amherst, Mass. (intentions recorded in Hinsdale, April 9, 1829), **DOROTHY BAKER**, born in Enfield, Conn., died in Suffield, Conn., daughter of Enos and Dorothy (————) Baker.

Married (2) **AMY KEELER**.

Married (3) **BETSEY FRY**, sister of Deacon John Fry of Danbury, Conn.

Children by first wife

Wallace Warner, b. in Hinsdale, Mar. 10, 1830; d. there Sept. 13, 1833.
Ellen Warner, b. in Hinsdale, Feb. 14, 1833.
Alfred Baker Warner, b. in Hinsdale, July 25, 1835.
Dorothea Warner.
Amelia D. Warner, b. 1840; d. in New York, Jan. 5, 1845, aged 4 years, 1 month, 6 days. She was adopted by her uncle Hiram Warner.

Children by second wife

Alice Warner.
Henry Warner.

.328 HARMON[6] **WARNER**, son of John[5] 3d, and Abigail (Stevens) Warner, born in New Milford, Conn., July 2, 1798; died in Leraysville, Pa., in 1882. He removed from Connecticut with several others of his family and settled about two miles west of Leraysville, in Pike township, Bradford County, Pa. He was a stone mason and a farmer. He was a soldier in the Mexican War in 1847.

Married in New Milford, November 25 or 26, 1817, **SALLY MAROXA JOYCE**, born in New Milford, March 21, 1800; died in Leraysville, May 25, 1886. She was the daughter of ———- and Tamar Joyce. Mrs. Tamar Joyce went to Pennsylvania and married a Deacon Wells, whose funeral was the first service held in the Methodist Church in Leraysville, before the church was quite completed or dedicated.

Children, first two born in New Milford, others in Leraysville

517   *Harriett Ann Warner*, b. Oct. 8, 1819; m. Edwin W. Taylor.
518   *Emeline Elmira Warner*, b. June 4, 1822; m. Rev. Corrington Taylor.
519   *Oliver John Warner*, b. July 20, 1827; m. Ruth Sophia Chaffee.
520   *Tamar Ann Warner*, b. Mar. 24, 1832; m. (1) Comfort Bliss Chaffee, (2) Ira Brink.
521   *Marcus Elliott Warner*, b. Feb. 23, 1835; m. Docia Ann Chaffee.

522 *Covington Harmon Warner*, b. Feb. 7, 1837; m. (1) Emeline M.
Barnes, (2) Amelia M. Brister.
523 *George Franklin Warner*, b. Dec. 29, 1839; m. Martha S. Towner.

329 ELIZUR⁶ WARNER, son of John⁵ and Abigail (Stevens) Warner, born in New Milford, Conn., March 6, 1807; died there, November 12, 1877. He was baptized and joined the church in New Milford, January 4, 1829, was dismissed to the church in Pike, Pa., April 5, 1830. He resided there some years in a locality where several other relatives had settled, then returned to New Milford and passed the remainder of his life there.

Married in New Milford, September 30, 1828, **LYRA ANN TOTMAN** of New Milford.

Children (said to have been four girls and two boys, one of the boys went west. The girls at one time returned to New Milford to live with their grandfather, but he proved to be too cross and uncomfortable to live with, so they dressed in men's clothes and returned to Pennsylvania)

524 *William S. Warner*, m. Rachel Edwards.
(*Daughter*), m. Harvey Birchard and lived in Brushville, Pa.

330 SAMUEL HORACE⁶ WARNER, usually known as Horace, son of Orange⁵, Jr., and Lucy (Sanford) Warner, born in New Milford, Conn., 1795; died there, August 13, 1822, aged 27, buried in Gallows Hill Cemetery. He was a member of St. Peter's Lodge, F. and A. M., as early as 1810.

Married **SALLY JULIA KNAPP**, born December 31, 1800, daughter of Joshua and Lodemia⁵ (Warner) Knapp; see number 95.

Children, born in New Milford

Hiram Le Grand Warner, b. Feb. 14(?), 1820; d. June 5, 1879; was in the shoe business in New Haven, later removed to Cromwell; m. Sarah Ann Rhoades, b. Nov. 9, 1828, d. Jan. 1, 1904, daughter of James and ———— (Drake) Rhoades of Wethersfield or Griswold ville, Conn. Children, born in New Haven: i. Samuel, d. aged 3 years and 11 months. ii. Frances Adelia, died. iii. Edward H., b. June 8, 1854, resides in Cromwell, Conn.; m. Mary L. Ralph, b. Apr. 1, 1853, daughter of Tilla and Margaret (Nugent) Ralph, and had two children, b. in Cromwell, Hiram Tilla, b. June 3, 1885, and Arthur L., b. Aug. 10, 1888, d. Oct. 15, 1908, at Cromwell. Hiram Tilla Warner is a foreman in a foundry in Cromwell, m. in New Haven, Dec. 21, 1909, Louisa L. Brush, b. in Flushing, N. Y., Aug. 21, 1891, daughter of Charles A. and Edith (Copp) Brush; has children, b. in Cromwell: i. Harold Nathan, b. June 18, 1910; ii. Arthur Edward, b. Feb. 1, 1912; iii. Evelyn Louisa, b. July 29, 1915.
Julia Warner, b. about 1822. Hiram T. Warner has a poem which she wrote to her brother upon the death of his child about 1850.

331 HENRY (called HARRY) SANFORD[6] WARNER, son of Orange[5], Jr., and Lucy (Sanford) Warner, born in New Milford, Conn., 1796; died there, May 6, 1856, aged 59, buried in Gallows Hill Cemetery. He was a farmer, sheep and cattle drover, bridge-builder. In his will, dated March 21, 1856, probated May 28, 1856, he gave a life interest in his estate to his father and provided schooling for his daughter Mary who was not yet of age.

Married by John Lovejoy, minister of the Methodist Church, January 7, 1829, **ELIZA ANN HILL**, born June 8, 1806, died December 27, 1890, daughter of Ebenezer and Philotheta (Lacey) Hill of New Milford.

Children, born in New Milford

525 *Stanley Le Grand Warner*, b. Feb. 23, 1831; m. Eunice P. Wanzer.
526 *Henry Orange Warner*, b. Aug. 18, 1834; m. (1) Mary J. Briggs, (2) Sarah W. Briggs.
    Mary Eliza Warner, b. May 24, 1841; resided in Newton; m. Joseph Albert Blackman. Children: Mamie; Stanley; Frank; Henry; Eva.

332 **O R A N G E** [6] **W A R N E R**, son of Cyrus[5] and Polly (Weller) Warner, born in New Milford, Conn., January 23, 1799; died there, January 11, 1871, buried in Gallows Hill Cemetery. He was an expert shoemaker by trade, a member of the Protestant Episcopal Church and a Republican in politics.

Married by the Episcopal rector in New Milford, December 19, 1822, **APPHIA EDWARDS**, born in Bridgewater, Conn., August 12, 1804, died September 28, 1855, daughter of Hanford Edwards, who was born September 12, 1784, died March 17. 1867, and his wife, Sarah Bennett, who was born May 2, 1783, died November 13, 1855. She is buried in Gallows Hill Cemetery.

Children, born in New Milford

Edwin E. Warner, b. Nov. 12, 1823; d. in Bridgeport, Conn., May 31, 1898. He was a mason by trade, a contractor and builder of masonry in Bridgeport; m. Katherine Weed of Westport, Conn. Children: Ida; Effie.
Emeline E. Warner, b. Dec. 27, 1825; d. in Waltham, Mass., Aug. 8, 1903; m. in New Milford, Sept. 17, 1850, Franklin B. Stevens of Woodstock, Conn., b. Oct. 21, 1825. He was a member of Company B, 2d Conn. Heavy Artillery, and was shot through the heart at Cold Spring Harbor, Va., June 1, 1864, and buried on the field. Children: i. Charles Lester, b. in Waterbury, Conn., Apr. 21, 1852; resides in Still River, Conn.; m. in New Milford, Dec. 28, 1892, Emogene E. Chase, b. in Fairfield, Conn., June 20, 1858. Child: Mary E., b. in New Milford, June 12, 1894. ii. Leverett Alonzo,

b. in New Milford, Jan. 3, 1855; m. in Bridgeport, July 17, 1873, Julia A. Tuttle, b. in Bridgeport, Oct. 17, 1856, and has a son, Charlie Lyon, b. in Bridgeport, July 1, 1874.

Hanford A. Warner, b. Feb. 2, 1828; d. in Waltham, Mass., Feb. 15, 1910; was in the show business for nearly fifty years; m. Mary E. Goddard of Cambridge, Mass. Children: Ernest; Henry. They are in the canoe business in Waltham.

527 *Cyrus Alonzo Warner,* b. Oct. 26, 1829; m. Angeline Elizabeth Sullivan.

Lyman F. Warner, b. July 16, 1832; d. Aug. 26, 1907, in Bridgeport, Conn. He was a mechanic and was for many years connected with the Wheeler and Wilson Sewing Machine Company. He was a member of Company K, 10th Connecticut Volunteers. Married (1) Emily Todd of New York State, b. Apr. 20, 1831; d. in Bridgeport, May 10, 1860; m. (2) Almira Merrils, who resides in Bridgeport. Children by first wife: i. Frederick A. ii. Algernon F., resides in Bridgeport.

Sarah Jane Warner, b. June 25, 1834; d. Dec. 22, 1904, in Ventura, Cal.; m. in New Milford, Nov. 15, 1856, James A. Day, b. in New York State, July 3, 1828, d. in Ventura, Jan. 2, 1915; was for many years extensively interested in fruit growing in California. Children: Alice; Bera (or Rena); Lillian; Mark.

Samuel O. Warner, b. Mar. 6, 1837; m. Fannie Hayes of New Haven; no children. He resided in New Haven, where he was for many years interested in the Winchester Arms Company.

Henry E. Warner, b. Sept. 1, 1839; d. Sept. 30, 1913, in New Preston, Conn.; m. (1) Cornelia Wildman of Brookfield, Conn.; m. (2) May 6, 1882, Estella J. Moore, b. in Washington, Conn., about 1857. Children by first wife only: i. Laura, d. in childhood. ii. Nellia, resides in Nebraska.

Franklin J. Warner, b. May 12, 1843; d. in Bridgeport, Conn., July 24, 1899; m. Emma Bassett of Bridgeport; no children. He served in the Civil War as Corporal in Company H, 2d Conn. Heavy Artillery and was wounded at Cold Spring Harbor, Va., June 1, 1864. He was a hatter by trade, and for several years before his death was manager of a hat store in Bridgeport.

333 ALVA WRIGHT[6] **WARNER,** son of Cyrus[5] and Polly (Weller) Warner, born in New Milford, Conn., November 21, 1807; died in Bridgewater, Conn., March 2, 1888. He was a blacksmith, and resided in Bridgewater, Litchfield County.

Married in Brookfield, Conn., January 27, 1827, **FRANCES A. BABBITT,** born March 7, 1808, in Brookfield, died there, December 5, 1886, daughter of Isaac and Mary (Dunning) Babbitt.

Children

Jane E. Warner, b. Nov. 16, 1829, in Brookfield, Conn.; resides in South Norwalk, Conn.; m. in Bridgewater, Aug. 5, 1838, Charles Gregory, b. in Ridgefield, Conn., Sept. 5, 1825, d. June 4, 1871, son of Lewis and Mary (Northrop) Gregory. He was a tanner and currier; served three years in the Civil War in the 2d Conn. Heavy Artillery. Children: i. Rebecca Elizabeth, b. Oct. 20, 1839; d. May 4, 1874. ii. Lucy Matilda, b. July 13, 1842; d. Dec. 16, 1844. iii. William Beach, b. Aug. 16, 1861.

Isaac E. Warner, b. July 4, 1832, in Brookfield, Conn.; d. in Bridgewater, Conn., Oct. 13, 1878; was a farmer; served in the 5th U. S. Artillery over five years; was in fifteen battles of the Civil War, including the Battle of Gettysburg, where nearly all the men of his company were killed; m. (1) in New Milford, Apr. 2, 1854, Fanny E. Ford, b. in New Milford, Jan. 15, 1834, d. there, Apr. 5, 1859, daughter of Charles and Mary (Egleston) Ford; m. (2) Mary A. Smith, b. in Southbury. Child by first wife: Laura Matilda, b. in New Milford, Dec. 12, 1855; d. Apr. 25, 1897. Children by second wife: i. Edward Isaac, b. in Bridgeport, Conn., about 1871; a farmer; m. in New Milford, Dec. 25, 1898, Mary A. Ryan, b. in Stratford, Conn., resided in Bridgeport, daughter of Michael and Julia (———) Ryan of Ireland. ii. Charles Herbert, b. July 30, 1876, in Bridgewater. iii. Lena, b. Aug. 16, 1878, in Bridgewater; d. there, Oct. 1, 1881.

Ellen Augusta Warner, b. in New Milford, Dec. 21, 1834; resides in Bridgeport, Conn.; m. in Bridgewater, Conn., Apr. 15, 1861, William Wilmot, b. in Bridgewater, Feb. 8, 1833, d. Apr. 8, 1901, son of Chauncey and Mary (———) Wilmot. Children: i. Alva F., b. Apr. 5, 1863. ii. Frank L., b. Feb. 6, 1865. iii. Wallace E., b. Jan. 26, 1869. iv. Robert L., b. July 4, 1872; d. Aug. 4, 1873. v. Cyrus Edwin, b. Sept. 4, 1874; d. Apr. 12, 1875. vi. Almira Ann, b. Aug. 19, 1876. vii. William A., b. Oct. 9, 1878.

Susan Eveline Warner, d. aged two years.

Susan Amelia Warner, b. in Bridgewater, Dec. 29, 1843; d. Aug. 16, 1894; m. in Bridgewater, May 11, 1866, Julius A. Manchester, b. in Colebrook, Conn., 1844, son of William Nelson and Content (Beach) Manchester. He resides with his daughter Elsie in Bridgeport and has taken care of the South Church for a number of years. Children: i. Ernest Beach, b. Mar. 23, 1868; m. Dec. 21, 1910, Jessie A. Whitney. ii. Walter Archie, b. June 30, 1870; d. June 13, 1907. iii. Fannie Content, b. June 15, 1873; m. (1) Aug. 16, 1892, George Bennett, who was badly injured in a fire and died soon after, leaving a son Eddie, aged three; m. (2) July 3, 1907, Harry L. Jones. iv. Freddie Lincoln, b. Nov. 9, 1871; d. Aug. 10, 1872. v. Freddie W., b. ——— 31, 1874; d. Dec. 8, 1875. vi. Grace Ellen, b. Apr. 4, 1877; d. Oct. 17, 1877. vii. Elsie May, b. Apr. 16, 1882; resides in Bridgeport; m. Nov. 4, 1909, William H. Ayrault. viii. Bertie C., b. Mar. 21, 1885; d. Aug. 2, 1885.

SEVENTH GENERATION

334 WILLIAM HALL[7] WARNER, son of Captain John[6] and Patience (Hall) Warner, born in Middletown, Conn., March 18, 1786; died August 23, 1830, aged 44. He was a farmer residing in the village of Westfield, Middletown, Conn. His name is found on land papers of 1812. Samuel H. Hough was appointed guardian to his four oldest children, March 11, 1826. Married in Westfield, HANNAH ROSE, born 1786; died in Westfield, November 7, 1838.

Children, born in Westfield

John R. Warner, d. in Tremont, Ill., about 1877; m. (1) —————— by whom he had a son Wilson, who was married twice and had by the second wife a daughter who d. unmarried about 1905; m. (2) Mary Hodges, daughter of James and Elizabeth (Prior) Hodges. There were no children by the second marriage.

Frederick Warner, b. about 1822; d. in Middletown, Oct. 20, 1875, aged 53. He was never married.

Wilson Warner, was a wanderer and left home about 1849, has only been heard from a few times since, the last time many years ago. He was never married. Asa Roberts was appointed his guardian in 1838 for the disposal of property in Westfield.

Harley Warner, d. May 4, 1833, aged 14.

528 *Sherman Roberts Warner*, b. Sept. 1, 1828; m. Delia Caroline Hodges.

335 JOHN PLUMB[7] WARNER, son of Capt. John[6] and Patience (Hall) Warner, born in Middletown, Conn., July 19, 1794; died in Meriden, Conn., March 27, 1868. He was a carpenter, resided in Meriden, and for a time in Trenton, N. Y. His name is found on the land records of Middletown in 1829.

Married October 12, 1815, BETSEY HALL, born December 7, 1793; died December 16, 1861, in Durham, Conn. She is buried with her husband in Meriden.

Children

Mary Warner, b. Mar. 24, 1817; resided in Meriden; d. Jan. 24, 1866; m. Jan. 1, 1836, George Couch. Children: i. Katie, b. Oct. 6, 1840; d. June 7, 1859. ii. George Winchell, b. Nov. 21, 1842; m. Nov. 13, 1867, Emily Southmayd; no children. iii. Martha C., b. Aug. 9, 1845; d. Aug. 13, ——; m. Edgar J. Doolittle. iv. Mary Ann, b. May 31, 1850. v. Lilla, b. Mar. 11, 1852; d. Jan., 1853. vi. James, b. Dec., 1853; d. Mar., 1854. vii. Anna, b. Mar. 15, 1857; d. Mar., 1859.

Lucy Maria Warner, b. in Trenton, N. Y., Feb. 29, 1820; d. Apr. 20,

1906; resided in Meriden and Durham, Conn.; m. in Meriden, May
22, 1839, Elim Loper Johnson, b. at Meriden, Feb. 20, 1816, d. May
8, 1895, son of Titus and Beulah (Wing) Johnson. Children:
i. John W., b. May 24, 1841; d. May 8, 1911; m. Sarah Pyncheon;
no children. ii. Charles E., b. Oct. 25, 1843; d. Aug. 13, 1851. iii.
Ella Louise, b. Aug. 25, 1845; d. Mar. 8, 1912;. m. (1) Elbridge
Maltby, (2) Frederick Conant; no children. iv. Elim William, b.
June 16, 1848; d. Jan. 17, 1861. v. Frank La Grove, b. Mar. 18, 1851;
d. Apr. 23, 1910; m. Helen Elizabeth Robinson, and had two children, William E., b. Nov. 2, 1873, m. Apr. 25, 1894, Eliza Holmes
Dudley, and Hattie Nina, b. Jan. 3, 1875.

Harriet Warner, b. Mar. 15, 1822; d. Mar. 26, 1900; resided in Meriden; m. Oct. 1, 1840, Oliver Blakeslee. Children: i. Aaron Chat-
terton, b. July 26, 1841; m. Emma Langdon. ii. Oliver D., b. June
7, 1843; d. June 10, 1909; m. Carrie Butler, had a child, Mildred,
who died. iii. Charles W., b. Apr. 5, 1848; m. Lovina Kelly, had a
son George W., b. Nov. 10, 1874; d. Nov. 2, 1914.

Martha Warner, b. Mar. 20, 1823; d. June 4, 1845; m. George D.
Winchell.

David Warner, b. Dec. 3, 1824; d. July 12, 1905. He was an ornamental painter in Meriden. Married Feb. 9, 1851, Olive Blodgett.
Child: Martha Eva, b. Oct. 13, 1852; d. Jan. 5, 1899.

529 *Charles Hough Warner*, b. Sept. 1, 1826; m. Annetta M. Stiles.

Ann J. (or *Betsey Ann*) *Warner*, b. July 5, 1828, at Westfield, Mass.;
d. Nov. 1, 1905; m. in Meriden, May 23, 1850, Dorus A. Stiles, b.
June 17, 1824, son of Henry and Sally (Avery) Stiles. He was a
tinplate and iron-worker, retired before 1886. They resided in
Durham and had no children.

Emma J. Warner, b. Aug. 16, 1834; d. Jan. 19, 1906; m. in Durham,
Conn., Cevincent Kellogg, b. in Kensington, Conn., June 8, 1832, d.
there, Apr. 24, 1862, son of William and Lydia (Graham) Kellogg.
No children.

336 ZEBULON PENN[7] WARNER, son of Hezekiah[6], Jr.,
and Lucy (Stocking) Warner, born probably in Cromwell, Conn.,
about 1790; removed to Fonda, N. Y., and then to Caledonia,
Pa., where he was a lumberman and a well-known citizen of
Elk County. A man named Boyd of Schoharie County, New
York, owned a large tract of land in the vicinity of Caledonia,
which he offered to trade for farms in Schoharie and Montgomery Counties, New York. The Warners were among the
families to take advantage of this offer. Zebulon Warner followed his brother Hezekiah to Caledonia about 1821 and
engaged with him in keeping store and running a lumber mill.
After 1828 he became postmaster at Caledonia, which had previously been known as "Bennett's Branch."

Married **LUCRETIA SHERWOOD,** born in Stratford, N. Y.
She was a sister of Sarah Sherwood who married Isaac Horton,
Jr., son of Isaac and Lucy (Warner) Horton; see number 337.

Children

Mary Warner, b. in Caledonia, Pa.; m. in Elk County, Pa., about 1860,
Frederick Schoening, by whom she had one child who died in its
infancy. She died a few years later and he married (2) Lucy M.
Horton, daughter of Isaac and Lucy⁷ (Warner) Horton; see number
337.

530 Helen Warner, b. July 10, 1829; m. Byron F. Ely.

337 **LUCY⁷ WARNER**, daughter of Hezekiah⁶, Jr., and
Lucy (Stocking) Warner, born in Hartford, Conn., February 6,
1791; died at Brandy Camp, Pa., February 2, 1845. She was
an exceptionally talented woman for the times; was a contributor to one of the early magazines, "The Ladies' Repository."
Her writings were of a religious character.

Married in Salisbury, N. Y., by the Rev. Jonathan Nichols,
September 20, 1812, **ISAAC HORTON**, born in Cheshire, Berkshire Co., Mass., September 18, 1788; died in Ridgway, Pa.,
April 2, 1873. He exchanged his farm near Salisbury or Stratford, N. Y., for Pennsylvania wild lands some time in 1818.
When he went to Pennsylvania to look over the property he
was not pleased with the trade and decided to go back to his
home farm. About this time he received word from his wife
that she was on her way and had reached a place known as
"Jersey Shore," Pa., where her son Charles was born. A
neighbor's family was moving to the same locality in Pennsylvania, and she had thought this was a good opportunity to pack
up and move, thus saving her husband a trip back. He had
not money enough to move back then so they settled in the
new lands at Brandy Camp, later removing to Ridgway. There
were no roads at that time, and only part of the way had trails
been cut through the forests. The household goods, with the
mother and her two little daughters and the new baby, were
taken in canoes as far as they could go, then she rode on horseback, carrying the baby in her arms, while the men carried the
other two children and the goods were hauled in a two-wheeled
cart through the dense woods. Their granddaughter remembers there was a few years ago on the Horton farm an old
gnarled apple orchard that the children proudly pointed out as
"the orchard that grandpa carried miles and miles on his back."

At one time Isaac Horton had the government contract for
carrying the mail, and most of the traveling was done by his
sons, with thrilling experiences, meeting wild animals and
Indians, heroic work for little fellows. The father became one
of the foremost residents of Elk County, was Judge for a number of years and was highly honored and respected.

SEVENTH GENERATION 367

Children of Isaac and Lucy (Warner) Horton

Minerva Horton, b. in Salisbury, N. Y., Mar. 14, 1814; d. in Ridgway, Pa.; m. at Brandy Camp, Joseph Taylor, who d. at Ridgway. Children, born at Brandy Camp: i. Lucy M., m. at Brandy Camp, Horace Little; both d. at Ridgway; had children, b. there, Arthur, is with the Westinghouse Company at Wilmerding, Pa., not m.; May M., is a music teacher at Ridgway, not m.; Helen, m. William Barber, an attorney of Ridgway (has children, Richard, Dana, Lucy Elizabeth, and "Teddy"); Louise, d. at Ridgway; and Benjamin, who m. Bessie Scribner, and has a son Horace, resides at Vancouver, B. C. ii. Bradford I., d. at Tarport, Pa.; m. at Wilcox, Pa., Delia Conklin, who d. at Bradford, Pa.;, had children, b. at Limeston, N. Y., Ida, resides in Toronto, Canada (m. and has children), Edna, m. Dr. Frank Stewart, resides in Bradford, Pa. (has children), and Frank, m. and wife d., no children. iii. Addie P., resides at Ridgway, not married. iv. (twin with Addie), d. young. v. Horace, d. at Clarendon, Pa.; m. (1) Sarah ———, who d. leaving children, Lorena of Ridgway, and Harry; m. (2) Mary ———, who lives in Ridgway, had one child, Belle, who lives in Erie, Pa., m. Joseph Young and has children, Lysle, David and Richard.

Lovisa Horton, b. in Salisbury, N. Y., Apr. 26, 1816; d. in Bradford, Pa.; m. (1) in Brandy Camp, William J. Andrews, who d. Feb. 26, 1845, leaving no children; m. (2) Alonzo I. Wilcox, who d. at Hackensack, N. J. Children of Alonzo and Lovisa (Horton) Wilcox, b. at Wilcox, Pa.; i. Clara, d. at Wilcox, Pa. ii. Ida A., b. 1857; resides in Hackensack, N. J.; m. at Bradford, Pa., Ernest H. Koester, who d. at Hackensack; had children, Frederick and Nina, b. in Bradford, reside in Hackensack.

Charles Horton, b. at Jersey Shore, Pa., Oct. 25, 1818; d. at North East, Pa., July 30, 1873; m. (1) in Houston Township, Pa., May 22, 1842, Phoebe W. Morey, b. Nov. 15, 1822, d. May 18, 1843, had one son who d. in infancy; m. (2) June 13, 1847, Elvira C. Jenney, b. Nov. 13, 1830, d. at North East, Pa. Children: i. Phoebe E., b. at Brockwayville, Pa., July 5, 1850; d. at Ridgway, Feb. 2, 1854. ii. William B., b. at Ridgway, Mar. 12, 1855; d. at North East, Feb. 19, 1867. iii. Harriet A., b. at Ridgway, May 30, 1864; resides at North East; m. in Erie, Pa., 1881, Earl M. Ketcham, and has two children, Lorena (b. at North East, Mar. 1, 1883, d. there, May 30, 1901, m. in Erie, Feb. 2, 1901, Robert Whitney, who d. in California, leaving a child, Harriet, b. at North East, May 23, 1901) and Stewart (b. at North East, Oct. 17, 1886, d. there, May 16, 1912, m. Belle ———).

Isaac Horton, b. at Brandy Camp, Pa., Dec. 14, 1822; d. at Erie, Pa., Aug. 26, 1887; m. at Caledonia, Pa., Feb. 23, 1843, Sarah Sherwood, b. in Stratford, Fulton Co., N. Y., Oct. 13, 1825, d. in North East, Pa., Oct. 6, 1906. She was the sister of Lucretia Sherwood, who m. Zebulon Penn Warner, see number 336. Isaac Horton was Postmaster of North East at the time of his death. For their family record see further.

Hezekiah Horton, b. at Brandy Camp, Mar. 1, 1824; d. at Helen Mills, Pa., Nov. 2, 1892; m. at Helen Mills, Hetty Eyster, who was born and died there. Children, born at Helen Mills: i. Warren H.,

m. Clara ————, b. and d. at Brockport, Pa., and had a son Ernest, b. there.   ii. Ella A., resides at Helen Mills, not married.   iii. Alonzo E., resides at Brockport; m. Nora Rogers, who d. leaving one son.   iv. Minnie, m. ———— Moyer; has a son, Burr H., and five other children.

Almira Horton, b. at Brandy Camp, Dec. 13, 1828; d. at Hackensack, N. J., not married.

Horace Horton (twin, the other d. at birth), b. at Brandy Camp, May 12, 1831; d. May 23, 1833.

Amanda Horton, b. at Brandy Camp, Sept. 11, 1833; d. at Ridgway; m. at Brandy Camp, Jerome Powell who d. at Ridgway. Children, born at Ridgway: i. Ida, d. in infancy.   ii. Walter, d. at Ridgway.   iii. Lorena, d. at Ridgway.   iv. Edgar C., resides in Ridgway; m. there, Ella Grant; has children, Grant, Jerome and Norman, of whom the first two are now in the army, the other in college.   v. Robert.

Lucy M. Horton, b. at Brandy Camp, Jan. 8, 1836; d. at Ridgway; m. Frederick Schoening, who first wife was Mary[6] Warner, daughter of Zebulon Penn[7] Warner, see number 336. Children, born in Ridgway: i. Anna, d. in Ridgway.   ii. Bertha, d. in Ridgway.   iii. Mary, m. in Ridgway, William Brew; had a daughter Lucy, and a son; resides in Hackensack.   iv. Leo, resides at Ridgway; m. Sarah ————; has two sons, Eugene and ————.

Children of Isaac, Jr., and Sarah (Sherwood) Horton

William A. Horton, b. at Stratford, N. Y., Mar. 30, 1844; d. at Brandy Camp, Pa., May 26, 1845.

Loren C. Horton, b. at Brandy Camp, Pa., Aug. 18, 1846; d. at Eldred, Pa., Oct. 26, 1897; m. at Warren, Pa., Feb., 1874, Amanda Patmore, who d. in Buffalo, N. Y., Oct. 14, 1905. They had no children, but adopted Georgianna E., who m. Harry K. Wing and resides in New York City.

M. Emma Horton, b. at Brandy Camp, Oct. 24, 1848; d. in Erie, Pa., Dec. 18, 1898; m. Nov. 9, 1870, John H. Collins, b. at Whistletown, Pa., d. at Portland Mills, Pa. Children: i. Maude S., b. at Cameron, Pa., Apr. 15, 1872; is now assistant city treasurer in Erie, Pa.; m. Feb. 2, 1898, William H. Millar, b. in Erie, June 2, 1870, d. in Joliet, Ill., July 19, 1904; had one son, Ward Horton, b. Dec., 1902, d. Mar., 1904. ii. Helen M., b. at Corry, Pa., June 12, 1886; is a trained nurse in Erie; not married.

Helen A. Horton, b. at Brandy Camp, June 22, 1850; m. Jan. 1, 1872, Alfred Short, b. at East Sharon, Jan. 1, 1847, d. at Tallahassee, Fla., Oct., 1914. Children, born at North East, Pa.: i. Ida O., b. June 10, 1873; resides in Ithaca, N. Y.; m. in North East, Jan. 10, 1898, Ralph E. Heard, b. at Ripley, N. Y.; has two children, b. in Buffalo, N. Y., Randolph A., b. Dec. 10, 1898, now in Cornell University, and Helen H., b. July 5, 1902. ii. A. Lee, b. July 17, 1875; resides in Westfield, N. Y.; m. at North East, Jan. 3, 1899, Florence Loop, b. at North East, Jan. 23, 1872; has three children, b. at North East, Marjory E., b. July 3, 1902, Sarah S., b. Aug. 13, 1907, and Alice E., b. Aug. 22, 1911. iii. Alice L., b. Sept. 18, 1882; d. at Lumber City, Pa., Apr. 26, 1904;

m. at Lumber City, June, 1903, Thomas Day, who resides in
Savannah, Ga.; had a son, John Alfred, b. in Lumber City, Apr.
18, 1904, resides in Erie. iv. Gladys E., b. Jan. 18, 1892; is a
teacher in the High School in Erie, Pa.

William S. Horton, b. at Brandy Camp, Dec. 7, 1852; d. at Ridgway, Nov. 1, 1892; was prothonotary of Elk County at the time
of his death; m. at Warren, Pa., 1880, Ella Bennett of Johnson-
burg, Pa., b. at Standing Stone, Pa., resides at Battle Creek, Mich.
Children, born in Ridgway: i. Isaac W., b. 1881; resides in
Detroit, Mich.; m., no children. ii. Ralph W., b. June, 1884; is a
Corporal in Field Artillery, West Point; not married. iii. Clara I.,
b. June, 1886; m. at Colombo, Ceylon, 1910, John P. Hocha, a
dentist in Battle Creek; no children. iv. Robert, d. at Ridgway,
aged about one year. v. Elwell, b. Feb., 1893; is Sergeant in the
army camp at Battle Creek.

Lucy M. Horton, b. at Buenavista, now Wilcox, Pa., Apr. 25, 1855;
is a grape farmer and china painter at North East, Pa.

Milton C. Horton, b. at Whistletown, Elk Co., Pa., Aug. 6, 1857; is
a banker at Poplar Bluff, Mo.; m. July, 1889, Anna Mehaffey of
Poplar Bluff, who was b. at McKeesport, Pa. Children: i. Lucy S.,
b. at North East, Pa., July 23, 1890; is Librarian at Poplar Bluff.
ii. Will W., b. at Poplar Bluff, Sept. 24, 1893; is in the insurance
business there; m. June, 1916, Pauline Harrington; has a son, Will
W., Jr., b. at Poplar Bluff, Dec. 24, 1917. iii. Ruth S., b. at Poplar Bluff, Nov. 24, 1895; m. there, Apr. 12, 1917, George B. Reed,
a jeweler; has a child, Dorothy Anna, b. at Poplar Bluff, Apr. 6,
1918. iv. Dorothy E., b. at Poplar Bluff, Oct. 13, 1897.

Ida L. Horton, b. at Whistletown, Pa., Feb. 18, 1860; m. at North
East, Nov. 9, 1880, Lester J. Chase, b. at Waterford, Pa., June 14,
1856; is in the real estate business at Erie, Pa. Child: Carl L., b.
at North East, Nov. 3, 1881; is with a construction company at
Erie; not married.

Walter E. Horton, b. at Whistletown, May 30, 1862; is with the
Metric Metal Works at Erie, Pa.; not married.

338 HEZEKIAH[7] WARNER, 3d, son of Hezekiah[6], Jr., and
Lucy (Stocking) Warner, born probably in Cromwell, Conn.,
about 1795; died in Wilmington, Ill., 1862. He removed with
his parents to Montgomery County, N. Y., and resided in Mayfield for a few years. In March, 1818, he removed to Elk
County, Pennsylvania, with his father-in-law, Jonathan Nichols,
and family, where he engaged with his brother Zebulon Warner
in store keeping and the lumber business; also conducted a
hotel. Courts were held at his home in 1843 and he is on the
list of early juries. He was on the tax list of Jay Township,
Elk County, in 1844, and was a man of some distinction, as he
was designated as the owner of a silver watch. They settled
first at Brandy Camp, and later removed to Caledonia.

Married in Caledonia, about 1817, **SARAH NICHOLS**, born

24

1800, died 1886, daughter of Elder Jonathan and Hannah
(————) Nichols, who removed from Mayfield, Montgomery
Co., N. Y., to Elk County, Pennsylvania, in 1818. He was a
Baptist minister and a physician, and, with the exception of Dr.
Rogers, he was the first of each profession in the new territory
to which he removed. In 1821 he removed to Horton Town-
ship, Brandy Camp, and died there, May, 1846.

Children

Jonathan Warner, b. in Elk Co., Pa., Oct. 4, 1818; d. Mar. 17, 1902;
   m. (1) in 1841, Julia A. Meade, who d. in the fall of 1855; m. (2)
   in 1861, Lucy Palmer. Children by first wife, first three born in
   Elk Co., Pa., others in Florence Township, Will Co., Ill.: Byron G.;
   Foster M.; Jacob H.; Charles H.; John M.; Ada; Adeline. Chil-
   dren by second wife: Lura; Julia; Delphine; Jerome.
Hannah Warner, b. 1821; d. 1903; m. Leonard Morey. Children: i.
   Phoebe. ii. Flora, m. John Casey and resides in Indianapolis, Ind.
   iii. Jennie. iv. William.
Lucy Warner, b. in Clearfield Co., Pa., Sept. 5, 1823; d. Aug. 10,
   1900; m. Sept. 11, 1844, Dr. E. H. Strong. Children: Warner P.;
   Caroline; Sarah; Mary.
Hezekiah Warner, 4th, b. 1825; m. Isabelle Vander Bogart. Child:
   Erwin, d. in infancy.
Adelbert Warner, b. 1827; d. about 1890; m. (1) Emily Hand; (2)
   Martha Storey.
Jerome Warner, b. Dec. 26, 1833; d. Aug. 19, 1871; m. Helen Ladd.
   Children: Sumner; Adelbert; Jay.
Hortense Warner, b. 1835; m. Oscar Hall. Children: Herbert;
   Edward; Jennie; Jay; Sarah.
Adeline Warner, b. July 13, 1840; m. (1) Jay Fuller, who died;
   m. (2) June 28, 1894, Chris W. Barnhart. Children by first husband,
   all d. young: Jennie; George; Jessie.

339 JUNIA[7] WARNER, son of Ebenezer[6] and Mary (Gaylord) Warner, born in Middletown, Conn., July 30, 1796; died
August 15, 1884. He was a shoemaker by trade and is perhaps
the Junia Warner who owned 64 acres of land in Machias,
Cattaraugus Co., N. Y., in 1834, only two acres of which had
been improved.
Married March 20 or 13, 1820, **LUCINDA CURTIS.**

Children

Ebenezer Warner.
Daniel Warner.
Minerva Warner, m. ———— Mixer.
Cornelia Warner, d. aged 40, "at her brother Curtis' in Michigan."
Curtis Warner, only mention of him is the foregoing reference.

340 Dr. EBEN[7] WARNER, son of Ebenezer[6] and Mary (Gaylord) Warner, born August 24, 1801, in Mayfield, N. Y.; died September 6, 1852, at Nunda, N. Y. He was a physician, removed to western New York and practiced medicine in Covington where he married and resided until about 1844. He then removed to Nunda, Livingston Co., where his death occurred. His character seems to have been drawn on much the same line as that of his father and, although he was in Nunda only eight years, he was long remembered as pre-emi nent in his profession and unsparing of himself in his ministra tions to both high and low.

His nephew, Seth W. Houghton, wrote of him:

"I have heard mother speak of Uncle Eben. She said after he had aspirations above driving oxen, he spoke to grandfather of wishing to study a profession. Upon which grandfather objected and told him to go and hang the scythe and cut the meadow. Uncle Eben hung the scythe on an apple tree, packed his grip and went to Skaneateles, where he entered the office of a prominent physician and taught school through the winter to pay expenses. After he completed his studies he went to Western N. Y., and practiced his profession with success which made grandfather very proud."

Married in Covington, N. Y., July 5, 1830, HANNAH FOWLER, born January 15, 1809, died November 28, 1892, daughter of David Isaac and Jemima (Elting) Fowler of Newburgh, Fowlerville and Nunda, N. Y. David Fowler died September 6, 1852, the same night as his son-in-law, the one from an illness, the other from exhaustion and over-fatigue, combined with a slight attack of the same illness. Mrs. War ner was descended from William Fowler of Flushing, N. Y.; Jan Elten of Flatbush, N. Y., 1663; Chrétien Deyo, a Huguenot who came to America in 1675, and other colonial families.

Children

531 *Charles Fowler Warner*, b: Aug. 20, 1832; m. Esther S. Town.
532 *Eltinge Fowler Warner*, b. Apr. 9, 1836; m. Josephine Bourne Thompson.
533 *William Penn Warner*, b. July 5, 1837; m. Anna Elizabeth Richmond.
534 *George Washington Warner*, b. May 10, 1840; m. (1) Fanny Estelle, (2) Elizabeth Battells.
Mary Cornelia Warner, b. July 2, 1843; d. Jan. 5, 1847.
Helen Warner, b. Oct. 9, 1846; d. Feb. 7, 1865.
Cornelia H. Warner, b. Oct. 6, 1849; d. Sept. 7, 1851.
Octavia W. Warner, b. Aug. 3, 1852; d. Nov. 5, 1852.

341 ELEAZER GAYLORD[7] WARNER, son of Ebenezer[6] and Mary (Gaylord) Warner, born September 8, 1803, in Mav

field, N. Y.; died October 21, 1879 or 1877. He was a farmer. Married (1) September 25, 1827, **AMELIA T. PARSONS.** Married (2) April 30, 1872, **ELIZA A. SHELP**

Children by first wife

(*Daughter*), d. in infancy.
Salina Elizabeth (*Alexander*), adopted, b. Apr. 22, 1833; d. Apr. 12, 1872.
John Parsons Warner, b. Aug. 17, 1837; d. Sept. 21, 1838.
Eleazer Gaylord Warner, Jr., b. Oct. 3, 1841; d. Apr. 19, 1843.

342   **VINE STARR⁷ WARNER**, son of Ebenezer⁶ and Kath erine (Denison) Warner, born September 13, 1805, in Mayfield, N. Y.; died October 30, 1885. He was a farmer residing in Skaneateles, N. Y. By the will of his father in 1847, he received "six volumes of Scott's Commentaries on the Bible." His own will, made May 4, 1872, probated November 25, 1885, is recorded in Syracuse, N. Y., and mentions only his wife Clarissa and son Harvey Stewart.
Married January 19, 1842, **CLARISSA M. STEWART.** She was living in Skaneateles, N. Y., about 1894. She had in her possession a large number of letters written by different members of his family to Ebenezer⁶ Warner. One, from a brother-in-law in 1804, condoles with him on losing so good a wife, and winds up with the naïve question, "Are you settled yet with Miss Denison?" Mrs. Warner also had the Concordance which was the only memento Deacon Warner had of his father. Across the back runs the large bold signature "Hezekiah Warner," and on a leaf is the sad inscription, "Minerva Warner, my first born died A. D. November 5, 1811, in the twentieth year of her age."

Children

Mary Katherine Warner, b. Nov. 19, 1842; d. May 6, 1870.
Harvey Stewart Warner, b. May 4, 1844; has been an engineer in Syracuse, N. Y.; m. Feb. 28, 1871, Etta Schooa. Children: i. Burton, b. June 21, 1873. ii. Millard, b. Jan. 30, 1875. iii. Stewart, b. Oct. 21, 1876. iv. Kate, b. Jan. 31, 1880.

343   **JOHN PENFIELD⁷ WARNER**, son of Ebenezer⁶ and Katherine (Denison) Warner, born in Mayfield, N. Y., February 23, 1809; resided later in or near Skaneateles, N. Y.; farmer.
Married March 27 or 29, 1839, **SARAH ANN HYDENBURG**, or **HEYDENBURK.**

Children

Louisa Warner, b. 1839; d. 1846.
Edward A. Warner, b. May, 1841; resided in Nebraska.
Sarah Rebecca Warner, resided in Concord, Mich.; m. Lot F. Keeler.
George H. Warner, b. May 16, 1846; was a mechanic at Grand Rapids, Mich.; m. Sept. 21, 1881, Angie Jenne. Child: Fred C., b. Apr. 8, 1886.
Ebenezer Gaylord Warner, b. July 8, 1849; m. Nov. 14, 1872, Lillian J. Tuttle. Child: William Robbins, b. June 14, 1880; d. July 26, 1889.
Fannie J. Warner, d. aged 15.

344 OLIVE[7] WARNER, daughter of Junia[6] and Elizabeth (Wilcox) Warner, born in Middletown, Conn., June 27, 1798; died September 9, 1839, in Mason, Mich., buried there. She removed with her family to Lenawee County, Michigan, in 1834, and after 1836 to Vevay, where they secured a half section of government land. The history of Ingham and Eaton Counties (1880) gives an account of this family, particularly of Henry A. Hawley.

Married (1) on her seventeenth birthday, June 27, 1815, **STEVEN HAWLEY,** a native of Amsterdam, of Scottish ancestry, who died in Herkimer Co., and is buried at Meeting House Green, Winfield, N. Y.

Married (2) **CHARLES GRAY,** who died August 1, 1846.

Children ⬛⬛⬛⬛ and Olive (Warner) Hawley

Henry A. Hawl⬛⬛⬛⬛ Mason, Ingham Co., Mich., and was a farmer on a larg⬛⬛⬛. (1) June 2, 1841, Lucy Ann Hicks, b. in Homer, N. Y., Aug. ⬛⬛, 1818, d. Nov. 18, 1853, daughter of Deacon Zephaniah Hicks, a pioneer of Ingham County; m. (2) Oct. 18, 1854, Charlotte (Chapin) Rolfe, b. in Cammillus, N. Y., May 17, 1820, d. Mar. 8, 1868, daughter of Levi and Achsah (Smith) Chapin. Children, by first wife: i. Olive Lucy, b. Mar. 11, 1842; resided in Mason; m. Dec. 24, 1863, John L. Diamond, who d. Aug. 10, 1870, and had three children, Charlotte Isabel, b. Nov. 19, 1864, d. July 25, 1898, not married, Henry, d. not married, and William A., b. July 4, 1868, d. 1911 (m. Sept. 25, 1895, Selona Dunsmore, who resides on a farm near Mason, with her son Gerald Ludlow, b. Sept. 29, 1898). ii. Calvin A., b. Nov. 3, 1843; d. May 27, 1862, while a sophomore in Michigan Agricultural College. iii. Eleanora, b. Aug. 21, 1845; d. in infancy. iv. Delora B., b. Oct. 22, 1847; d. Jan. 24, 1868, not married. v. Adelbert Stephen, b. May 23, 1851; d. Sept. 7, 1894; resided on the Hawley homestead near Mason; m. Edna Moore Gunnison (who m. (2) 1911, L. H. Ives); had children, Frances and Mary (twins), Alice Moore, m. Charles Wyman Perry, and Lucy Warner. vi. Anna E., b. Mar. 25, 1853; resides at Grass Lake, Mich.; m. Oct. 16, 1876, Marcus K. Preston and has six daughters. Child of Henry A. and Charlotte (Rolfe) Hawley: Claribel, b. Mar. 26, 1857; m. July 28, 1878, Orr Schurz, a graduate of University of Michigan, 1878, superintendent of schools at Negaunee, Mich.

Calvin Hawley, m. Ophelia ———, who d. Aug., 1891. Children: i. Olive, m. Jared Loveland. ii. Henry. iii. ———.

Children of Charles and Olive (Warner) Gray

Eliza Gray, m. Daniel Potter. Children: Olive; Warner.
Manley Gray, m. Mary Holt, who m. (2) ——— Spencer and resides in Mason, Mich. Children: Jesse; Nellie; Medora.
Emeline Gray.

345 ELIZA⁷ WARNER, daughter of Junia⁶ and Elizabeth (Wilcox) Warner, born August 24, 1800, probably in Middletown, Conn., about the time the family removed to Litchfield, N. Y.; died in Litchfield, January 29, 1860.

Married probably in Litchfield, February 6, 1820, **JOSEPH ALEXANDER,** born October 21, 1797; died November 2, 1861, at his home in Litchfield. He was probably born at or near the same place, son of Joseph Alexander, b. Apr. 30, 1769, d. Apr. 20, 1798, and Esther Bushnell, b. Dec. 9, 1766, d. Sept. 14, 1845. Joseph Alexander was the son of James Alexander who was born on the ocean in 1728 on the passage from Londonderry, Ireland, to America. The family is said to have been Scotch-Irish.

Children

Esther Jane Alexander, b. Jan. 30, 182█████████, 1883, not married.
Olive Elizabeth Alexander, b. July 15, ████████itchfield; d. Sept. 13, 1893, two and one half miles north of █████llage of West Winfield; m. in Stockbridge, N. Y., May 24, 1865, Thomas Ellis Harrison, b. in Winfield, N. Y., Feb. 25, 1836, son of Stephen and Mary (Watson) Harrison who were natives of Yorkshire, England. He resides, with his daughter, in West Winfield (1918). Children: i. Mary Eliza (Lizzie), b. Aug. 13, 1867; has taken an active part in securing records of this branch of the family. ii. Herbert Alexander, b. Apr. 11, 1871; d. May 13, 1915; was graduated from the New York Homeopathic Medical College in 1895; from 1895 to 1897, was interne in National Homeopathic Hospital, Washington, D. C.; practiced medicine in Cooperstown, N. Y., 1897 to 1902; studied at the New York Ophthalmic Hospital during 1902-3, was house surgeon there until the fall of 1903; practiced medicine in Utica, N. Y., from 1905 until his death; m. in Utica, Apr. 15, 1903, Delia De Ette Ellison, b. in Newport, N. Y., Sept. 15, 1867, daughter of Henry Duane and Elnora J. (Arnold) Ellison; had two children, b. in Utica, Thomas Duane, b. Oct. 11, 1904, and Leonard Arnold, b. July 28, 1910. iii. Leonard Ernest, b. Aug. 24, 1876, in Winfield; is a farmer there; m. in West Winfield, Apr. 4, 1908, Edith Derenda Bonfoy, b. in West

Winfield, Mar. 23, 1885, daughter of George A. and Alice (Burke) Bonfoy. George Bonfoy's line runs back to Hezekiah Warner thus: Lois (Warner) Wilcox, Hannah (Wilcox) Bonfoy, Franklin Bonfoy, George A. Bonfoy; see number 199.

346 Rev. JUNIA⁷ WARNER, JR., son of Junia⁶ and Elizabeth (Wilcox) Warner, born in Litchfield, N. Y., February 19, 1802; died in Paw Paw, Mich., December 31, 1846. The following account of his life was written by his youngest son, Wilbur Fisk Warner:

At your request I will give you a brief history of my father's, Junia Warner, Jr., short life as well as the hardships he and his family had to endure after moving into a new country.

He was a Methodist minister at Litchfield, N. Y., and in those days ministers were very poorly paid; thinking to better his condition, he decided to go West, consequently in the year 1833 he, together with his father, Junia Warner, Sr. (my grandfather), started for Kalamazoo, Mich. (then a territory), where his sister, Mrs. Martin Heydenburk, lived. After a brief rest there, they started on foot westward through the wilderness, to locate on land suitable for dairy purposes; 18 miles west, in Almena township, they found land with a spring of pure water with a brook flowing through it. They bought from the government ¼ section at $1.25 per acre and on a rise of ground up from that brook, they at once built a shanty and named it Shanty Knoll and had as their neighbors, Indians, wolves, bears, deer and other wild animals. The following year they planted on land cleared by themselves and commenced the erection of a double log house, with nothing to heat or light it except a monstrous fireplace that would take in logs six feet long. All of their cooking and baking was done there. They returned to New York state and the following spring, 1835, the two families left Utica, N. Y., via canal to Buffalo, N. Y., thence by boat to Detroit. There they purchased an ox team and covered lumber wagon and put their belongings and four grown persons and four children into it and started through the woods with no road, the only guide being blazed trees occasionally where some one had preceded them. Thus they journeyed, sleeping, eating in the wagon for the long distance of 165 miles to their new home in Almena, which you can imagine would look mighty good to them. .

Then the struggle of clearing timber land for crops began. Two and a half miles away was a little hamlet called Paw Paw. There my father started the first Methodist church, which before his death (11 years later) had become quite a good sized congregation. He, being the only minister for miles each way, was called for weddings and funerals for long distances. It was at one of these funerals, 18 miles away, that he attended on a cold December day in 1846, that he contracted pneumonia and drove home that distance and only lived three days.

One other instance of the hardships they had to endure: they hewed shingles from pine trees and with an ox team took them to Little Prairie Round, 20 miles, and exchanged them for wheat, then drove 30 miles in another direction to Comstock to have the wheat ground into flour and then home another 24 miles. It took him four days to make the trip. My grandfather died 6 years after they came and my father only lived 11 years. Thus you see my mother was left with 6 children, the oldest 20 and the youngest (myself) 3½ years old. She kept the family together. We all struggled to clear the land and build a new frame house. The old log house was used for a school house where I first attended school. The hardships we endured there would fill a book. I will relate a few of my own experiences which are still vivid in my memory. Rattlesnakes were very plentiful. On one occasion, when I was about 10 and my brother 2½ years older, we were gathering hay that had been cut with a scythe and raked by hand, I was loading and he pitching up to me. In the hay was a big rattler and when he landed on top of that load of hay, he at once notified me with his rattle. I, being barefoot, at once leaped to the ground. We captured him and found 10 rattles on him. Also many a day did this brother and I break up land with a span of horses hitched ahead of one or more yoke of oxen and attached to a big breaking plow that would cut off roots 3 to 4 inches in diameter and all this when we were mere lads—I cite these to show how different our early life was then to what most of the sons have it now.

Gradually, as the children grew to womanhood and manhood, they left the old home and made homes of their own. Out of the two families, 4 grown ups and 9 children, I am the only one now living (1916).

Junia Warner, Jr., married in Litchfield, N. Y., February 20, 1825, **ARMINDA MERRY,** born in Litchfield, April 12, 1804, died in Paw Paw, Mich., November 21, 1883, daughter of Epaphroditus Merry and Philura Raymond, who married, as her second husband, Junia Warner, Sr.

Children, first four born in Litchfield

Philura Lorette Warner, b. July 31, 1826; d. Dec. 31, 1890, in Paw Paw, Mich.; m. (1) in Paw Paw, Mar. 19, 1856, Henry Barnum, (2) in Paw Paw, May 1, 1866, Jared Palmer.

535   Elam Locke Warner, b. May 29, 1828; m. Charlotte Maria Bangs.

Mary Eliza Warner, b. Jan. 12, 1831; d. Sept. 4, 1838, in Paw Paw.

Frances Elizabeth Warner, b. Mar. 12, 1833; resided in Janesville, Wis.; was a member of the D. A. R.; m. (1) in Paw Paw, Mar. 31, 1859, Benjamin Franklin Hoyt, b. in Craftsbury, Vt., Nov. 23, 1837, d. in Paw Paw, Mar. 27, 1866, son of Asa and Mary (Gilman) Hoyt. He was a merchant, served a year and a half in the 13th Regiment, Michigan Volunteers. Mrs. Hoyt m. (2) in Grand Rapids, Mich., Sept. 4, 1888, Frederick Starr Eldred. Children by first marriage: i. Lucius Warner, b. in Hartford, Mich., Dec. 31, 1860. ii. Wilbur Fish, b. Jan. 25, 1866, in Battle Creek, Mich. Lucius Warner Hoyt was greatly interested in the genealogy of the family and about 1894 made extensive collections that have been of great benefit to workers in this history. Had it not been for his early death, he would doubtless have been able to complete at least the genealogy of his own line from Andrew[2] Warner. He was educated in Paw Paw and Grand Rapids, Mich.; Michigan Agricultural College; B.S., 1882; Columbia University Law School, 1889; A.M., University of Denver, 1901; admitted to the bar in 1889; associate professor, 1892-3, professor of law, after 1893; dean of the law department of Denver University, after 1902. Lucius W. Hoyt was married in Elora, Ont., Aug. 27, 1889, to Catharine Connal Potter.

Susan Warner, b. in Paw Paw, July, 1836; d. the same day.

Mary Ann Warner, b. Mar. 7, 1838, near Paw Paw; d. there, Apr. 2, 1905; m. in Paw Paw, Nov. 11, 1858, William Reid Sirrine.

536 *Jerome Clark Warner*, b. Dec. 14, 1840; m. (1) Antoinette Randall, (2) Jenny Kelly.

537 *Wilbur Fisk Warner*, b. June 27, 1843; m. Sarah Jenette Eldred.

Janette Warner, b. Jan. 27, 1847, near Paw Paw; d. there, Oct. 8, 1847.

347 HULDAH WILCOX[7] WARNER, daughter of Junia[6] and Elizabeth (Wilcox) Warner, born December 19, 1803, in Litchfield, N. Y.; died April 21, 1867, in Kalamazoo, Mich., where she resided at the time.

Married in Skaneateles, N. Y., November 22, 1827, MARTIN HEYDENBURK, born September 19, 1798, in Hempstead, L. I., second son of John and Hannah (————) Heydenburk. John Heydenburk was seized by the German authorities for the British service against the North American colonies during the Revolution, in the contingent known as the Hessian troops. At the close of the war, when the time came for the survivors to return to Germany, John Heydenburk deserted in order to remain in this country and was always the implacable enemy of both Germany and Great Britain. The latter country paid the German government ten pounds a head for all the missing Hessians at the final muster.

The family migrated to Spencer, Columbia County, N. Y., in 1802, and in 1816 Martin went to Skaneateles, Onondaga County, where he completed his education, and was in 1824 appointed teacher to the mission at Mackinac, Mich. After three years' service he returned to marry, and took his bride back ·to Mackinac and to six years more service among the Indians. The school was under the American Board of Commissioners for Foreign Missions and had from 70 to 100 boarding pupils and from 30 to 50 day pupils. The only remuneration he received or expected was his selection from the barrels of second-hand clothing sent by friends of the Mission, and whatever food he and his Indian boys could raise or secure from the surrounding country. As he had in boyhood been indentured to a carpenter, he was able to build the church and schoolhouse at the mission himself.

In 1833, leaving his wife and two children to follow him later, he proceeded to White Pigeon. For three years he worked as a carpenter here and at Kalamazoo, building the

Presbyterian Church at White Pigeon, one at Gull River, the Receiver's office at Kalamazoo and other buildings. He purchased a farm at Kalamazoo which he conducted until 1864, when he again took up religious work in Sabbath school and Bible classes. He united with the Presbyterian Church in Skaneateles in 1820, and was ever devoted to the work of God and the helping of his fellow-men. The latter part of his life was spent in Marshall. He married (2) Mrs. Lucy (Whittlesey) Chisholm, widow of Peter Chisholm of Marshall. In Michigan Pioneer and Historical Society Publications of 1879 may be found interesting articles by Mr. Heydenburk on the Mackinac Mission and the early days. Miss Lizzie Harrison of West Winfield has some most interesting letters written to her family by Huldah Warner Heydenburk, portraying the severity of life in pioneer davs and showing the beautiful Christian spirit with which they met their problems.

Children

Minerva W. Heydenburk, never married.
Henry Heydenburk, d. young.
Mary Belinda Heydenburk, b. July 7, 1834; d. Feb. 27, 1903; m. Henry Marhoff. Children: i. Edward. ii. Charles. iii. Alfred. iv. Herbert, d. in childhood. v. Walter. vi. Jesse. Jesse Marhoff became a Presbyterian minister, was a graduate of Olivet. College and McCormick Theological Seminary and did graduate work at Yale.
Frederick Heydenburk, d. young.

348 BELINDA A.[7] WARNER, daughter of Junia[6] and Elizabeth (Wilcox) Warner, born in Litchfield, N. Y., June 24, 1808; died November 29, 1842, in Mason, Ingham Co., Mich., buried there.

Married in Kalamazoo, Mich., November 30, 1837, ENOS NORTHRUP, Jr., born in Windham, Greene Co., N. Y., January 13, 1813. He married (2) Julia A. Monroe by whom he had children, Enos H., William M., Mary A. and Martha.

Children of Enos and Belinda A. (Warner) Northrup

Henry Irving Northrup, b. in Vevay, Mich., Sept. 9, 1840; resides in Mason, Mich.; m. July 3, 1884, Lelah Price. Children: i. Belinda Warner, b. Apr. 2, 1885; d. May 17, 1911; m. John Noxon, had a child who died and a son James. ii. Charles H., b. May 31, 1888.
Edward N. Northrup, b. Nov. 29, 1842; d. Feb., 1902, not married.

349 WILLIAM[7] WARNER, JR., son of William[6] and Lucy (Coan) Warner, born November 6, 1801, in Sandgate, Vt.; died

in 1892. He was a farmer and removed from Vermont to Ohio in 1831, traveling by carriage. He settled in Munson, Geauga County.

Married, 1825, **SALLY SAFFORD,** who died in 1864.

Children

DeWitt Clinton Warner, resided in Munson, Ohio; m. Ann Pugsley. Children: i. Eugene Leslie, b. in Munson, Oct. 31, 1863; resided in Mantua, Ohio, in 1916; m. in Chardon, Ohio, Dec. 11, 1889, Edna Hazen, b. May 11, 1864, in Munson, daughter of Livingston and Harriet (Downing) Hazen. Their daughter Ethel Mae, b. in Munson, Apr. 21, 1892, m. in Ravenna, Ohio, Jan. 19, 1910, James Ishee, resides in Huntsburg, Ohio (had a son Vaughn, b. there, Oct. 12, 1910). ii. Cyrus C., d. in Cleveland, Ohio, Feb., 1913, married and had children, Nelson and another son.

Irwin Warner, married. Children: i. Effie, m. —— Kinney, resided in Westfield, N. Y. ii. Clifford. iii. Pearl, m. —— Overton, resided in Interlaken, N. Y.

Amos Warner.
Abner Warner.
Elizabeth Warner.
Annette Warner
Lucy Warner.

350 JOSEPH⁷ WARNER, son of William⁶ and Lucy (Coan) Warner, born in Sandgate, Vt., October 7, 1803; was a farmer in Chesterland, Ohio, where he died February 4, 1890.

Married October 16, 1825, **MARY COVILLE,** who died January 28, 1890.

Children

Adelbert Warner, married. Children: i. Elmer. ii. Wilbur, m. and had two daughters. iii. Harold.

Sarah L. Warner, b. Apr. 30, 1830; resided in Fullertown, Ohio; m. Apr., 1845, Granville Nichols. Children: i. Victor, resides in Fullertown; m., has children, Hazel and Vera. ii. Nellie, resides in Chagrin Falls, Ohio; m. —— Robinson and has daughter Florence (who m. Clyde Hoopes and has a daughter Lucile). iii. Florence, resides in Geneva, Ohio; m. —— Pelton, has children, Forest and Gladys. iv. Ernest, resides in Chagrin Falls; m., has daughter Muriel and a son.

Jane Ann Warner, b. Nov. 5, 1832, in Chester, Ohio; resided in Russell, Ohio, and died there, July 2, 1900; m. June 20, 1851, Daniel Nutt, a farmer. Children: i. Daniel, resides in Chagrin Falls; m. and has children, Raymond (m. and d. leaving a son Raymond, Jr.), Blanche (m. Herbert Winchell and has a son Lawrence), and Ethel. ii. Edna, m. and d., leaving children. iii. Nellie, m. and had a son.

Benjamin Silas Warner, b. Dec. 24, 1834, in Chester, Ohio; farmer; m. Oct., 1866, Angeline Hawkins. Children: i. Olga, m. and had children, Ellen and John. ii. Gabbard. iii. Florida. iv. Delray.

538   *Andrew James Warner*, b. Jan. 13, 1837; m. Cynthia Rodgers Bartlett.
     Edwin Eugene Warner, b. Sept. 14, 1843, in Chester, Ohio; d. Jan. 19,
        1863; was a teacher.

351 GAYLORD COAN[7] WARNER, son of William[6] and
Lucy (Coan) Warner, born in Sandgate, Vt., April 1, 1808;
died June 6, 1886. , He was a farmer residing at Chardon, Ohio.
He was present at the first town meeting held at the organiza-
tion of the town of Chatham, December 5, 1833, and was one
of the eleven voters.
   Married (1) February 4, 1833, **MARTHA PACKARD**.
   Married (2) **MARY ADAMS**.

Children

539   *Darius John Warner*, b. June 30, 1834; m. Annette Elizabeth Hazen.
     Emma Warner.
     Delphia Warner.
     Julia Warner.

352 BENJAMIN STONE[7] WARNER, son of William[6] and
Lucy (Coan) Warner, born in Sandgate, Vt., June 15, 1810;
died in Munson, Ohio, March 19, 1893. He removed to Ohio
in 1831, was a farmer in Munson; justice of the peace from
1869 to 1875.
   Married January 8, 1839, **HANNAH MALONA GLEASON**.

Children, born in Munson, Geauga Co., Ohio

540   *Davis William Warner*, m. Martha Gilbert.
541   *Jane Viola Warner*, b. Dec. 3, 1842; m. David Rodgers Bartlett.
542   *John Barton Warner*, b. May 26, 1846; m. Almeda Jerusha Cole.
543   *Clarence Fremont Warner*, b. Aug. 7, 1855; m. Lavina Jane Hodges.

353 JOHN[7] WARNER, son of William[6] and Lucy (Coan)
Warner, born in Sandgate, Vt., June 2, 1812; died February
19, 1889, in Munson, Ohio. He resided in Sandgate as late as
1850, as he was recorded in the Census of that year with farm
property worth a thousand dollars. Later he was an inn-keeper
in Munson, Ohio.
   Married November 1, 1838, **LYDIA WARREN**, born about
1815.

Children, born in Sandgate

   John Henry Warner, b. Sept. 8, 1839; was justice of the peace in
      Munson, Ohio, from 1900 to 1910; m. Amelia Pratt. Children: i.
      Harriet Lucy, b. June 23, 1867, in Munson; d. there, 1907; m. there,
      Sept. 23, 1887, Benjamin Franklin Hazen, b. in Munson, Feb. 18, 1861,

son of Winchester and Laura Amanda (Perry) Hazen, resided in Munson and had a son, Charles Clarence, b. in Munson, June 21, 1893 (B. F. Hazen m. (2) Jan. 1, 1909, Mrs. Ethia Taylor). ii. Emma, m. ——— Babcock, son of Levi Babcock, and had children, Glenn, Milton, and Rosetta.

Eliza Ann Warner, b. Mar. 30, 1841; m. (1) ——— La Dow, (2) ——— Hodges. Children by first husband: i. Cora, m. George Hodges, had children, Mona and George Henry. ii. Earl, m. and had children, Claude and Maria. iii. Amy, m. James Zethmayr and had children, Gordon and Willard.

Daniel D. Warner, Denis in 1850 Census, b. June 30, 1843.

Joel B. Warner, b. July 10, 1844; recorded in 1850 Census.

Mary L. Warner, b. Oct. 22, 1848; m. Perry Parker. Children: i. Eva, m. ——— Hendricks and had children, Gladden, Arleigh, and Perry. ii. Willis, died, leaving no family.

Sarah Warner, m. Brighten Tanner. Children: i. Cecelia, m. William Franklin and had children, Harry and Leona. ii. Harvey, m. and had children. iii. Elsie, m. ——— Weaver, resided in Westfield, N. Y., had child, Persis. iv. John, m. and had children. v. Alberta, m. ——— Wightman and had a daughter.

354 LUCY MERCY[7] WARNER, daughter of William[6] and Prudence (Nickerson) Warner, born May 2, 1823, in Sandgate, Vt.; died November 14, 1879. She resided in Bennington, Vt., where she kept a boarding house.

Married (1) **HENRY G. STEWART,** born September 6, 1806, in Bloomfield, Maine.

Married (2) T. J. **ALBRO,** born November 30, 1803, in Pownal, Vt., son of Wate and Wealthy (———) Albro.

Child by first husband

Ellen Stewart, b. in Sandgate, Vt., Apr. 5, 1845; resides in Troy, N. Y.; m. in Bennington, Vt., Aug. 6, 1867, Alexander Chapman, Jr., b. in Troy, N. Y., May 4, 1844, son of Alexander and Marion (———) Chapman. Children: i. George Alexander, b. Oct. 16, 1873. ii. John Stewart, b. June 25, 1878, in Troy.

Child by second husband

Theresa Albro, b. Nov. 28, 1860, in Bennington, Vt.; m. Frank H. Crawford, b. June 26, 1861. Children: i. Randall, died. ii. Buel, resides in Brooklyn, N. Y. iii. Lida Lucy.

355 ANN[7] (or MARY ANN) WARNER, daughter of William[6] and Prudence (Nickerson) Warner, born February 9, 1833, probably in Sandgate, Vt.; died 1899. She resided in Russell, Ohio.

Married February 2, 1856, **PETER DE VOE,** a farmer.

Children

Clinton DeVoe, resides in Russell, Ohio; married. Children: i.
George, m. and has three children, Jessie, Carl and Ralph. ii. Lulu,
m. Harley Gore and has two children, Leland and Elwyn. iii. Anna,
m. John Rufiner and has two children, Dora and Wayne. iv. Lena,
m. William Danforth and has daughters, Wilena and ———— v.
Peter, died. vi. Nellie, m. Frank Schute, no children.
Charles De Voe, resides in Russell, Ohio; married. Children: i.
Theressa Prudence, m. Martin Becker, resides in Painesville, Ohio;
has children, Ruth and Glenn. ii. Lida Edith, m. Charles Graham,
no children.

356 DANIEL DE WITT[7] WARNER, son of Dr. John[6] and
Mary (De Witt) Warner, born in Big Stream (now Glenora),
N. Y., September 25, 1809; died April 19, 1888, in Rock
Stream, N. Y. He resided at each of these places and was
engaged in a general land and mercantile business.
Married in Salem, Washington Co., N. Y., September 11,
1850, CHARLOTTE GORDON COON, born in Salem, N. Y.,
1831, died at Rock Stream, N. Y., March 25, 1890, daughter of
John and Eunice (Taft) Coon.

Children

544 *John De Witt Warner*, b. Oct. 30, 1851; m. Lilian A. Hudson.
    Charlotte Elizabeth Warner, b. Aug. 22, 1853, at Glenora, N. Y.; resides
    at Rock Stream, N. Y.; not married. She is prominent in church,
    literary, and war work.
    Hector Lee Warner, b. Sept. 12, 1855, at Glenora; d. Mar. 9, 1859.
    James Ward Warner, b. Mar. 15, 1858, at Glenora, N. Y.; resides in
    New York City; is a member of the firm of J. G. Hagemeyer & Co.,
    shipping merchants; ex-President of the New York Produce
    Exchange, where he also served for a number of years as a member
    of the Board of Managers, Chairman of the Grain Committee, and
    Vice-president; member of the New York Chamber of Commerce.
    Mr. Warner is a member of the D. K. E. fraternity; has been
    President of the New York Shakespeare Club. His published
    addresses include one on *Irregular bills of lading*, delivered before
    the Council of North American Grain Exchanges, Sept., 1910.
    James Ward Warner married in New York City, June 3, 1906,
    Lilian Houghton Mills, b. in Rahway, N. J., daughter of John P. and
    Phebe Josephine (Houghton) Mills. She is descended from the
    Yorkshire Mills family; from Sir Thomas Houghton of Lanca-
    shire, England, through John Houghton, Puritan, one of the founders
    of Lancaster, Mass.; from Robert Kitchell, Treasurer of the New
    Haven Colony; from Hon. Jasper Crane, Governor Treat and other
    Newark founders. She is a member of and has held office in many
    literary, patriotic, religious and social organizations; has been chair-
    man of Young People's Work in the New York City Presbyterian
    Home Missionary Society; compiled the New England Calendar

published by the National Society of New England Women, 1911; has given many papers and readings before clubs. Mr. and Mrs. Warner are both members of the Barnard Club and the Shakespeare Club of New York City. They have no children.

Mary Eunice Warner, b. Nov. 16, 1860, at Rock Stream, N. Y.; d. Sept. 2, 1864.

Cynthia Jane Warner, b. Mar. 30, 1863, at Rock Stream; d. Sept. 3, 1864.

357 **ELLEN STOLL**[7] **WARNER,** daughter of Dr. John[6] and Mary (De Witt) Warner, born May 14, 1816, at Big Stream (now Glenora), N. Y.; died November 24, 1886, at Rock Stream, N. Y.

Married 1844, **MOSES HETFIELD** of Rock Stream.

Children

Eliza Jane Hetfield, b. Feb. 12, 1845; m. Francis Marion De Munn. Children: i. Ella, b. Dec. 13, 1868; not married. ii. Edward, b. Feb., 1873; m. (1) Mary Porter, who d. 1896, leaving a son, John Marion; m. (2) Mary Parr, and resides in Geneseo, N. Y. iii. Frank Livingston, b. at Rock Stream, Nov. 24, 1887; m. in Binghamton, N. Y., Oct. 15, 1915, Norma Soulé.

Mary Ellen Hetfield, b. Oct. 28, 1850, at Rock Stream; resides there, not married.

Hannah Angeline Hetfield, d. in infancy.

Warner Moses Hetfield, b. July 13, 1855; resides at Rock Stream; m. June. 1901, Minnie Collum of Dundee, N. Y. Child: Charles War ner Paul, b. Aug. 29, 1902.

Charlotte Eugenie Hetfield, b. Sept. 5, 1857; not married; resides with her sister Ella in the house in which they were born.

358 **JOHN WILLIAM**[7] **WARNER,** son of Dr. John[6] and Mary (De Witt) Warner, born at Rock Stream, N. Y., February 9, 1831; died at Watkins, N. Y., June 19, 1913.

Married **NANCY CORBETT.**

Children

James Ward Warner, b. Dec., 1853; d. Aug., 1857.

Ada Maria Warner, b. July 18, 1856; m. John R. Linzey. Children: i. Bessie, b. about 1880; d. 1892, aged 12. ii. Edith Maude, resides in Watkins; m. August Klube; had three children, Gladys, who d. Jan., 1913, Herman and Max.

Indianola Warner, b. Feb. 15, 1863; resides in Watkins, N. Y.; m. Henry Vosburgh, who d. May, 1907.

359 **LEMAN ACKLEY**[7] **WARNER,** son of John[6] and Abby (Ackley) Warner, born May 6, 1817, in Olcott, N. Y.; died

October 17, 1894, in Freeport, Ill. He resided in early life in Washington, Conn., where the record of his first marriage and the births of the first two children is found; in New Preston, Conn.; and after 1855 in Freeport, Ill. He was a carpenter and builder, later a woodworker, and then devoted himself to the manufacture of his patent, the "Warner Doorspring," a well known device.

Married (1) April 10, 1844, in Washington, Conn., **CARO LINE TOMLINSON,** who died May 12, 1845, leaving no children.

Married (2) March 7, 1847, **SARAH DEMING WHITTLESEY,** born in New Preston, Conn., May 25, 1822, daughter of David and Matilda Patience (Averill) Whittlesey of New Preston; died in Freeport, Ill., June 26, 1893.

Children by second wife

545 *Caroline Tomlinson Warner,* b. Oct. 5, 1848; m. Rev. Marvin B. Harrison.
546 *Andrew Clinton Warner,* b. Apr. 3, 1850; m. Myra O. Brookner.
   John Chester Warner, b. Feb. 18, 1852, in New Preston, Conn.; d. May 27, 1873, in Freeport, Ill., not married.
547 *Charles Campbell Warner,* b. Sept. 19, 1857; m. Margaret Lewis McNair.
548 *George Wilberforce Warner,* b. Mar. 27, 1859; m. Ida Mary Buckley.
   Emma Lincoln Warner, b. Oct. 23, 1866, in Freeport, Ill.; d. there, Dec. 22, 1897, not married.

360 **CLINTON⁷ WARNER,** son of John⁶ and Abby (Ackley) Warner, born June 17, 1826, in Newfane, Niagara Co., N. Y.; died August 5, 1870, at Westminster, Mass. He studied medicine and was graduated from Dartmouth in 1852; practiced medicine in Westminster after 1854. For some years he was the only physician in town, and had a large and successful practice for sixteen years, enjoying the utmost confidence of the people.

Married May 23, 1858, **SARAH CUMMINGS,** born September 16, 1827, died October 23, 1900, daughter of Rev. Henry and Mary Ann (Beaman) Cummings. Rev. Henry Cummings was pastor at Newport, N. H., Rutland, Mass., and Stafford, Vt., and some of his children were engaged in mission work. Mrs. Warner took an active interest in the affairs of the town, particularly of the First Congregational Church and of the Public Library, of which she was a trustee and librarian.

Children, born in Westminster

Chester Cummings Warner, b. June 30, 1859; d. July 7, 1867.
Mary Abbie Warner, b. Mar. 22, 1861; was graduated from Mt. Holyoke Seminary, 1883; advanced course, 1886; studied abroad a year; was a teacher of French and German at Houghton Seminary, Clinton, N. Y.
Adelaide Sarah Warner, b. Sept. 12, 1863; was graduated from Mt. Holyoke Seminary, 1886; teacher in advanced grades of public schools in Woonsocket, R. I., and Salem, Mass.; m. Dec. 2, 1902, Walter Thomas Berry, b. Mar. 23, 1871, son of Leander and Tempy (Snowman) Berry; resides in Salem, Mass. Child: Eleanor Warner, b. in Boston, Apr. 10, 1907.
Clinton Hale (or *Cummings*) *Warner*, b. Dec. 19, 1866; d. Aug. 10, 1867.
Eleanor Cummings (or *Hale*) *Warner*, b. Oct. 16, 1868; d. July 20, 1869.

361 WARREN[7] WARNER, son of Andrew[6] and Gillet (Goodale) Warner, born in Glastonbury, Conn., March 25, 1793; died in Marlborough, Conn., November 20, 1882, buried in the old cemetery near the Congregational Church at Marlborough. He resided at Eastbury. The 1850 Census recorded him as a resident of Glastonbury, a laborer, with his wife and three daughters at home.

Married December, 1814 (Gilead church record), WEALTHY or WELTHA POST of Hebron, born in Marlborough, August 31, 1786; died October 20, 1857, aged 71, buried at Marlborough. She was the daughter of Joseph, Jr., and Hannah (————) Post.

Children, born at Marlborough

549 *Norman Post Warner*, b. Aug. 24, 1815; m. (1) Eliza Carter; (2) Lydia Ann (Norton) Taylor.
Hannah Louisa Warner, b. May 10, 1817; d. Aug. 24, 18—; m. Aug. 9, 1835, David Brown. Children: i. Ellen, d. aged 5 years. ii. George, d. in infancy.
Edwin Charles Warner, b. Nov. 17, 1820; d. in Marlborough, Aug. 20, 1881. He was for many years postmaster at Marlborough, was a deacon in the Congregational Church, and was highly respected by all; m. (1) Nov. 30, 1843, Mary Elizabeth Bowen, who died May 14, 1862, aged 40, buried in Marlborough; m. (2) Jan. 7, 1863, Harriet R. Buell, b. 1827, d. Jan. 28, 1894, buried in Marlborough. Children by first wife, buried in Marlborough: i. Gertrude, b. May 8, 1852; d. young. ii. John J., b. 1853; d. Dec. 28, 1872. iii. Mary Annie, b. Aug. 23, 1858; d. Jan. 15, 1878.
Hansy Sophia Warner, b. Mar. 22, 1823; m. Chester Bidwell. Children: Arthur Edwin, d. young. ii. Clarence, d. young.

25

Celecta Ann Warner, b. Mar. 9, 1827; d. June 17, 1864, in East
Glastonbury, Conn., at the home of her sister Weltha, not married.
550 *Weltha Jane Warner,* b. Apr. 9, 1830; m. George Selden House.

362 **ELISHA⁷ WARNER**, son of Andrew⁶ and Gillet
(Goodale) Warner, born in Glastonbury, Conn., 1803; died
May 17, 1841, aged 38 years, buried in Marlborough, Conn., in
the old cemetery near the Congregational Church.
Married **LUCY CHAPMAN**, born in Berlin, Conn., 1802, died
in Marlborough, Conn., June 5, 1846, buried in the cemetery by
her husband.

Children, all dead before January, 1916, except Esther

551 *John B. Warner,* m. Elizabeth F. White.
Sarah Ann Warner, m. June 7, 1847, William Carrier.
William H. Warner, b. in Glastonbury or Marlborough, Conn., July
27, 1827; d. in Hartford, Conn., Aug. 23, 1907; was an iron worker;
m. in Glastonbury, Oct. 25, 1854, Jane Hart, b. in Farmington, Conn.,
Mar. 4, 1837, daughter of Henry and Electa Jane (Taylor) Hart.
She resides in Portland, Conn. (1916). Children: i. Wilbur Henry,
b. in Rocky Hill, Conn., Nov. 4, 1855. ii. Charles Nelson, b. in
Manchester, Conn., July 25, 1857; d. Aug. 23, 1858.
Andrew Warner, served in the Civil War from western New York;
m. (1) Amanda Watrous of Hebron, Conn.; m. (2) Sarah Tefft or
Tufts of Canandaigua, N. Y.; m. (3) Mrs. Josephine Peabody of
Canandaigua, N. Y., who resided there later. He had one son,
perhaps named Oliver.
Mariva Warner, m. Thomas Powe or Poe of Black Bend, Ala. They
had four sons and one daughter, Willie or Willemine, who resides
at Lower Peach Tree Plantation, Wilcox Co., Ala.
Oliver Warner, d. in Southington, Conn., buried in Newington; m. in
the early seventies, Belle Robbins of Newington, who died in Waterbury, Conn., a few years later. They had no children. He was a
conductor on the Hartford, Providence and Fishkill Railroad.
Esther Jane Warner, b. in Glastonbury, May 22, 1837; resides in
Meriden, Conn.; m. in Manchester, Conn., Nov. 26, 1857, Daniel C.
Pease, Jr., b. in Somers, Conn., Feb. 16, 1833, son of Daniel Cone
and Matilda (Collins) Pease. Children, b. in Springfield, Mass.:
i. Frank Walter, b. Sept. 3, 1860. ii. Clara Louise, b. Dec. 30, 1865.
552 *Hannah Louisa Warner,* b. Mar. 6, 1839; m. (1) George Eaton, (2)
Augustus Westcott Randall, (3) Jonathan Gleason Davenport
Newton.
553 *Lodica Warner,* m. Nathan Willard Babbitt.

363 **ANDREW WELLS⁷** (or **WELLS**) Warner, son of
Andrew⁶ and Gillet (Goodale) Warner, born in Glastonbury,
Conn., and died there before 1850.
Married **PHEBE CHAPMAN**, who was recorded in Glas-
tonbury with her children, in the Census of 1850. She was
born in Connecticut about 1821.

Children

Philander Warner, b. about 1831; was a butcher, residing with his mother in Glastonbury in 1850; m. before 1850, Henrietta Webber, b. about 1832.

George Warner, b. about 1832; was a stone cutter, residing with his mother in Glastonbury in 1850.

Jairus Warner, b. about 1834; was a sailor, residing with his mother in Glastonbury in 1850.

Alice Warner, b. about 1836.

Betsey Ann Warner, b. about 1838.

Mary Warner, b. about 1840.

Augusta Warner, b. about 1842.

Alonzo Warner, b. about 1845; m. Abby J. Nichols, daughter of John K. and Abby J. (———) Nichols, who died Oct. 5, 1873, aged 24 years (Glastonbury Cemetery records).

Adelaide Warner, b. about 1846.

Andrew Wells Warner, Jr., b. about 1849.

364 **CLARISSA**[7] **WARNER,** daughter of Major Robert[6] and Lucy (Tuels) Warner, born 1789, probably in Middletown, Conn.; died in Jersey City, N. J., August 18, 1873, aged 84.

Married January 3, 1814, **HENRY SOUTHMAYD,** born January 14, 1789, in Middletown, died at Jersey City, March 8, 1854, son of William and Desire (Clay) Southmayd. He was a large manufacturer of saddles and harness, especially for the market of Atlanta, Ga., where he resided for six years. He later removed to Jersey City and became agent of the "Jersey Association," proprietors of a large portion of the unsold land of the town. He was also connected with the Jersey Transportation Company; was appointed by President Taylor as Deputy Collector of the United States Customs at Jersey City.

Children, first three born in Middletown, Conn.

Henry Jared Southmayd, b. Feb. 5, 1815; was for nearly thirty years treasurer of the New Jersey Transportation Company at Jersey City.

Robert Warner Southmayd, b. Jan. 22, 1818; was a manufacturer of hats; resided in Philadelphia, Pa.

William Shailor Southmayd, b. July 7, 1819; was proprietor of a jewelry store in New York City; m. in Hoboken, N. J., Harriet Johnson of Norwalk, Conn. Children: i. Charles Allen, b. Feb. 5, 1858. ii. and iii. Twin sons who died young. iv. Elizabeth, b. May 7, 1860.

Charles Allyn Southmayd, b. in Atlanta, Ga., Sept. 9, 1823; was for some years a merchant in McGregor, Iowa, then removed to Jersey City.

John Adams Southmayd, b. in Atlanta, Ga., Apr. 29, 1825; was a manufacturer of hats in Elizabeth, N. J.; m. May 3, 1864, Eleanor Dayton, daughter of James W. Dayton of Elizabeth. Children: i. Eleanor, b. Feb. 5, 1865. ii. (Daughter), b. Aug., 1866.

Eliza Green Southmayd, b. in New York City, Feb. 16, 1828; m. Oct. 28, 1852, James Morgan, a flour merchant of New York City, son of Minot Morgan of Jersey City. Children: i. Henry Southmayd, b. Nov., 1853. ii. Jennie, b. Feb., 1861; d. Apr. 19, 1861. iii. Elizabeth Southmayd, b. Feb., 1863.

Clarissa Warner Southmayd, b. in New York City, Aug. 21, 1830; resided in Jersey City; m. June 14, 1855, Gustavus Francis Pendexter of Dover, N. H. Children: i. Clara Southmayd, b. July 12, 1856; m. Spencer De Hart. ii. Eliza Adéle, b. July 4, 1858. iii. Frank Gustavus, b. Nov. 23, 1861. iv. Mary Augusta, b. Nov. 6, 1863. v. Lucia Harrington, b. Nov., 1865.

Henrietta Clay Southmayd, b. in Jersey City, Apr. 9, 1836.

365 SETH[7] WARNER, son of Jonathan[6], Jr., and Anna (Ripley) Warner, born October 20, 1802, in Pittsford, Vt.; died in Lind, Waupaca Co., Wis., February 5, 1881. He was a farmer

Married September 13, 1832, at Charlotte, Chautauqua Co., N. Y., SUSAN SKINNER, born April 3, 1813, died in Lind, August 9, 1865.

Children

Harriet Warner, b. in Fredonia, N. Y., Apr., 1833; d. Apr. 13, 1835.

William Franklin Warner, b. in Fredonia, Jan. 5, 1836; d. Jan. 15, 1918. He was a gunsmith and resided at Lebanon, Kans. Married Dec. 30, 1860, Hannah Lamphear, who was born in Middlebury, Vt., daughter of Zebulon Lamphear. Children: i. Lyman Arthur, b. in Lind, Wis., May, 1864; d. Mar. 17, 1888. ii. Francis Adelbert, b. at Minnesota Lake, Minn., Mar. 21, 1866. iii. Ella May, b. at Alma City, Minn., Sept. 25, 1871; resides in Lebanon, Kans.; m. Luther G. Trueblood, b. Oct. 27, 1855; has a daughter, Minnie M., b. Oct. 13, 1892. iv. John, b. at Alma City, Jan. 1, 1874; d. Jan. 17, 1902. v. Estella N., b. in Lebanon, Kans., Dec. 15, 1878; m. Arthur B. Miller, b. Aug. 8, 1877; has five children, Lovie M. and Charles Lovis (twins), b. Nov. 8, 1901, Bessie Gertrude, b. Feb. 10, 1905, Louise Beatrice, b. Sept. 11, 1911, and Harley Lycurgus, b. Apr. 26, 1913.

Henry Clay Warner, b. in Rochester, Wis., July 20, 1837; d. at Lind, Wis., May 2, 1893, where he had resided. He was in a printing office, and later was a farmer. He served in the Civil War in Co. B, 14th Wisconsin Regiment; was in the battle of Shiloh, the Vicksburg and Atlanta campaigns; at Nashville, Mobile, at the capture of the Spanish Fort; was clerk of the Freedmen's Bureau in the summer of 1865; mustered out, Oct., 1865. Married in East Troy, Wis., Mar. 21, 1868, Annie Brownley, b. Sept. 25, 1843, in Spencerville, Ont., Canada, daughter of James and Ann (Stitt) Brownley. She resides in Madison, Wis. Children, b. in Lind: i. Marian Howard, b. June 6, 1869; d. Apr. 2, 1898. ii. Winnie Susan, b. June 4, 1871; is statistical clerk in the office of the State Board of Health in Madison (1916).

Charles Francis Warner, b. in Rochester, Jan. 14, 1844. He has resided at Villa Grove, Saguache Co., Colo. He enlisted as private in Co. M, 1st Wisconsin Cavalry, Dec. 18, 1861; was promoted in turn to corporal, sergeant and lieutenant; served a year in Missouri, then went to Tennessee, Kentucky, North Carolina, Georgia, Alabama, and Mississippi; was in the Wilson raid; honorably discharged, July 19, 1865. Married July 11, 1869, Amy Brown of North East, Pa., and moved to near Fort Dodge, Iowa. Children: i. Maud M., b. Jan. 21, 1871. ii. Edrick H., b. Aug. 14, 1872. iii. Charles J., b. Sept. 27, 1876.

Helen Marion Warner, b. in Lind, May 5, 1853; resides near Stevens Point, Wis.; m. William Dakin, who died before 1916. Children: Jessie; Hattie; Mary; Winnie; Elmer; Ethel; Mabel; Merle.

366 **MARY**[7] **WARNER**, daughter of Jonathan[6], Jr., and Anna (Ripley) Warner, born in Pittsford, Vt., October 4, 1804. Married November, 1826, **TYLER CALDWELL**, born July 14, 1798; died January 17, 1861. They resided in Hubbardton, Vt., Charlotte, N. Y., later in Kenosha Co., and Lind, Wis.

Children

Columbia Caldwell, b. in Hubbardton, Vt., July 11, 1828; d. 1881; resided in California; m. 1852, Stephen P. Thresher, b. in Haverhill, N. H. They had five children.
Columbus Caldwell, b. in Charlotte, N. Y., Sept. 25, 1830; was a soldier in the Civil War; m. (1) Nov., 1861, Mary L. Taggart, who died at Lind, Wis., Jan. 6, 1867; m. (2) May 15, 1868, Ida Taggart. He had two children by the first wife and one by the second.
Maryette Caldwell, b. in Charlotte, N. Y., Oct. 8, 1833; m. Nov. 26, 1865, Harvey Bowers, b. in Cayuga Co., N. Y.; one child.
Sophia Caldwell, b. in Kenosha Co., Wis., Nov. 1, 1836; d. 1858.
Harriet Emily Caldwell, b. in Kenosha Co., Wis., Feb. 13, 1839; d. in Lind, Wis., Apr. 1, 1869.
William Harrison Caldwell (twin), b. in Lind, Wis., Aug., 1840; d. Jan., 1848.
John Tyler Caldwell (twin), b. Aug., 1840; d. Dec., 1844.

367 **JONATHAN**[7] **WARNER**, 3d, son of Jonathan[6], Jr., and Anna (Ripley) Warner, born in Pittsford, Vt., April 12, 1810; died there, May 19, 1885. He was a farmer on his father's farm, one of the few places that had never passed out of the family of the first occupant.

Married June 27, 1842, **SARAH M. WALTON** of Brandon, Vt., born August 22, 1815; died July 2, 1885.

Children, born in Pittsford

Clara Walton Warner, b. June 19, 1843; resides in Lewis, Iowa.
Horace Green Warner, b. Sept. 20, 1845; died.
Mary Leach Warner, b. Sept. 5, 1849; d. in Pittsford, Jan. 2, 1869.

Sarah Manley Warner, b. June 27, 1851; d. Aug. 11, 1883; m. Sept. 22, 1880, Charles Patch.
Anna Frances Warner, b. Nov. 14, 1852; resides in Rutland, Vt.; m. in Pittsford, June 27, 1883, Hiram Francis Eggleston, b. in West Rutland, Nov. 1, 1855, son of John and Emma (———) Eggleston.
Jonathan Warner, 4th, b. Oct. 28, 1857; d. June 6, 1887. He was a farmer in Pittsford.
Harriet Warner, b. Aug. 27, 1859; d. Jan. 26, 1860.

368 WILLIAM[7] WARNER, son of Jonathan[6], Jr., and Anna (Ripley) Warner, born in Pittsford, Vt., January 28, 1812; died in Quincy, Ill., July 29, 1869. He was an active, companionable boy and when he was about twelve years of age, the boys of the town organized a military company and elected him their captain, an office which he conducted in such a way as to gain the approval of even older men. He was graduated from Middlebury College in 1837 and studied for two years at Andover Theological Seminary, but left to go into business. He resided first in Burlington, Vt., removing to Detroit, Mich., in 1855. He was treasurer of the University of Vermont for six years; financial agent of the Vermont Central Railroad; president of the Sullivan Railroad Company. In Detroit he engaged first in the lumber business, then in the iron business. He was president and leading stockholder in the Detroit Bridge and Iron Works Company, and, at the time of his death, was superintending the construction of an iron bridge across the Mississippi at Quincy, Ill. He united with the Congregational Church in 1830, and was a deacon in the Detroit church. He served as a school inspector in Detroit for a number of years, and was a member of the state Legislature in 1863 and 1867.

Married (1) in Pittsford, Vt., February 2, 1842, HARRIET B. LEACH, born in Pittsford, March 3, 1814; died in Detroit, August 22, 1859. She was the daughter of Andrew and Deborah Spooner (Bowman) Leach. She was graduated from Ipswich Female Seminary, 1836, taught there and at Abbott Academy, Andover, Mass.

Married (2) in Clinton, N. Y., FRANCES G. LEACH, born in Pittsford, August 1, 1824; died in Detroit, October 6, 1893. She was the daughter of Andrew and Olivia Safford (Moulton) Leach. She was a graduate of Mt. Holyoke Seminary, 1845.

Children by first wife

Helen Frances Warner, b. in Pittsford, Dec. 15, 1842; d. in Detroit, Mich., Oct. 23, 1905. She was graduated from Vassar College in

1868; from the medical department of University of Michigan in 1872; attended medical lectures in Vienna and Paris, 1872-4; practiced medicine in Detroit from 1874 until her health failed in 1900.

554 *Harriette .Anna Warner*, b. Aug. 7, 1845; m. William Melancthon Bishop.

Martha Spooner Warner, b. in Burlington, Vt., July 15, 1847; has resided in Detroit, Mich., since 1855; was graduated from Vassar College in 1868. Miss Warner has been most helpful in collecting records of this branch of the family.

555 *William Andrew Warner*, b. June 27, 1849; m. Maria Virginia Bishop.

Child by second wife

Fannie Leach Warner, b. in Detroit, Mich., Feb. 3, 1865; d. July 31, 1865.

369 MOSES MANDELL⁷ WARNER, son of Jonathan⁶ and Sally (Paige) Warner, born in Hardwick, Mass., March 30, 1793; died in Lyndon, Ill., January 31, 1876, buried in Prairieville, Ill. He was a farmer residing on the road between the roads from Hardwick to Gilbertsville and Ware, two miles from the Common in Ware; moved from there to Barre, Mass., in 1825. In 1838 he removed to Illinois and settled in Palmyra township, Lee County. His sons Henry, Moses and George were with him among the early settlers of that section.

Married June 1, 1816, **ORREL SMITH** of Palmer, Mass., who survived him and resided with her sons at Sterling, Ill.; buried in Prairieville, Ill.

Children, first four born in Hardwick; others in Barre, Mass.

Sarah Ann Warner, b. Nov. 1, 1817; d. Feb. 18, 1853, in Dixon, Ill.
Henry S. Warner, b. July 22, 1819. Mrs. Sarah Rich of Sterling, Ill., is his daughter.
Clarissa S. Warner, b. Aug. 2, 1821.
Moses M. Warner, Jr., b. Mar. 1, 1824. Mrs. Nettie Underwood of Kelly Lake, Wis., is his daughter.
Orrel M. Warner, b. Apr. 22, 1826; m. (1) Jared Conyne, (2) Michael Fellows of Sterling, Ill. Child by first husband: Orrel, m. Truman Wilder, had six children, most of whom were living in Battle Creek, Mich., about 1912.
Mary L. Warner, b. Apr. 1, 1828; d. Oct. 4, 1830.
556 *Mary Louisa Warner*, b. June 16, 1830; m. John Lewis Lord.
557 *Delphia M. Warner*, b. June 30, 1832; m. (1) Calvin W. Mann, (2) George⁸ Warner.
George P. Warner, b. July 22, 1834; married and has a son, Mandell, residing at Prophetstown, Ill.

370 JONATHAN⁷ WARNER, JR., son of Jonathan⁶ and Sally (Paige) Warner, born in Hardwick, Mass., March 28,

1795; died in Hardwick, Vt., September 12, 1867. He was brought up on the farm in Hardwick and attended the district schools, most of the time riding four miles on horseback each way every day. When he became of age his father gave him a tract of some three hundred acres of wild land in Hardwick, Vt., whither many of the family and neighbors from Hardwick had earlier migrated. He cleared the land and settled there, becoming one of the most reliable men of the community. He was a faithful member of the Baptist Church and an active advocate of the temperance movement. Jovial in disposition, he made friends everywhere he went. At the age of eighteen he went from Hardwick, Mass., to serve in the War of 1812; was on coast guard duty six months in Boston Harbor under Captain Gass. His widow received a pension, dated March 4, 1879.

Married in Hardwick, Vt., February 25, 1819, E M I L Y FLORILLA FARNUM, born January 16, 1801, daughter of Aaron and Florilla (Strong) Farnum; died at Hanover Center, N. H., April 6, 1889.

Children, born in Hardwick, Vt.

Adeline Florilla Warner, b. Dec. 23, 1819; d. Nov., 1914, in Arlington, Mass.; m. (1) July 1, 1850, probably as second wife, Zacharias Shedd of Franklin, Vt. (wrongly given in Hardwick, Vt., town records as Reed); m. (2) Nov. 25, 1858, David Camp of Hanover, N. H. Child by first husband: Emma (Shedd), b. June 4, 1851; d. May 30, 1883; m. in 1880, Otto Wilde.

Eliza Ann Warner, b. June 3, 1822; d. July 4, 1879; m. in Hardwick, Vt., Nov. 6, 1854, Dr. Harrison W. Brockway of St. Johnsbury, Vt. Child: Edward Augustus, b. Sept. 10, 1856; m. June 1, 1880, Lizzie A. Emmons.

Mary Jane Robinson Warner, b. Sept. 14, 1824; m. (1) Oct. 6, 1859, Garret Van Riper, who died in 1866; m. (2) Nov. 9, 1866, Alfred Taber of Franklin, N. H.

Ariadne Tilton Warner, b. Apr. 3, 1827; resided in Franklin, N. H.; m. June 12, 1855, Asa Burton Closson, b. May 21, 1806, in Thetford, Vt., d. Feb. 12, 1884, son of Simon Closson. Children: i. Jessie F., b. in Hanover, N. H., Feb. 28, 1856; resides in Franklin. ii. Elsie Y., b. Nov. 18, 1857, in Hanover. iii. Carlos Farnham, b. Mar. 1, 1868, in Franklin; m. Aug. 20, 1898, Susan A. Stevens of Franklin.

Levi Whipple Warner, b. Oct. 26, 1829; was a farmer in Hardwick in 1860; m. (1) Anna Mann, (2) Adeline Dennison, (3) Julia Griffin.

Jonathan Augustus Warner (or *Augustus Jonathan*), b. Nov. 3, 1833; m. (1) June 3, 1869, Margaret Sherry of Elmira, N. Y., who died Jan. 7, 1874; m. (2) Aug. 19, 1879, Anna T. Hoag, b. Aug. 12, 1847, d. Oct. 13, 1884; m. (3) Ora Ella De Ved. Child by first wife: Sherry A., b. Jan. 7, 1874. Child by second wife: William C., b. Oct. 13, 1884. Child by third wife: Doris E., b. Mar. 10, 1889.

558 *Charles Davenport Warner*, b. Oct. 28, 1835; m. (1) Elizabeth Westgate Johnson, (2) Marion Henderson, (3) Fannie Isabell Finlay.

559 *Laura Annette* (or *Laura Farrell*) *Warner*, b. Apr. 6, 1837, or Apr. 20, 1837; m. George Sherman.
Sidney Smith Warner, b. June 14, 1839; m. Mary ———; no children.
Louis Alfred Warner, b. May 1, 1841; d. May 27, 1870.

371 **DANIEL**[7] **WARNER,** son of Jonathan[6] and Sally (Paige) Warner, born in Hardwick, Mass., July 2, 1799; died there, September 23, 1876, buried in Hardwick. He was a farmer residing near the central bridge over the Ware River in Hardwick, later bought an estate on the easterly road to Gilbertsville, two miles from the Hardwick Common.

Married May 29, 1821, **NANCY FISH,** daughter of Deacon Henry Fish and Elizabeth (Holmes) Warner. She died February 2, 1875, aged 77 years, buried in Hardwick.

Children, born in Hardwick

Henry Fish Warner, b. Feb. 28, 1822; d. Sept. 22, 1868, not married.
(Twins), b. and d. 1825.
Elizabeth Ann Warner, b. Sept. 6, 1826; d. Nov. 19, 1850, not married; buried in Prairieville, Ill., but recorded on tombstone in Hardwick, Mass.
560 *George Warner*, b. Apr. 14, 1830; m. (1) Mary A. Walker, (2) Harriet S. Wheeler, (3) Mrs. Delphia Warner Mann.
Lucy Jane Warner, b. June 15, 1835; d. in Barre, Mass., Oct. 18, 1887; m. in Hardwick, Dec. 29, 1858, Samuel Austin Howe, b. in Barre, May 6, 1834, d. Feb. 12, 1905, son of Eliphalet and Keziah (Kinsman) Howe of Barre. Children: i. Ella Jane, m. in 1879, William Andrew Reed of Westboro, and died leaving two children, William Childs and Vera, now living in New York. ii. Daniel Austin, a merchant of Worcester, Mass., m. there in 1899, Florence Gray Tenney and has eight children, Mildred G., Frank Warner, Daniel Austin, Jr., Florence Ella, Roger B., Ruth E., Hartwell, Goddard, and Kenneth Emery. iii. Walter Eliphalet, m. May Ballou who died leaving two children, Daniel W. and Maud Bernice. iv. James Weston, m. Carrie Delano and has one child, Madeline.

372 **LEWIS**[7] **WARNER,** son of Jonathan[6] and Sally (Paige) Warner, born in Hardwick, Mass., June 1, 1801; died there, September 11, 1875. He was a farmer in Hardwick nearly all his life, was away for a short time, then returned and settled near "Taylor's Mills."

Married (1) (intentions published April 2, 1827) **VERONACIA ANDERSON,** born in New Braintree, April 29, 1806, died in Hardwick, July 6, 1853, daughter of John and Phebe (Barr) Anderson of New Braintree.

Married (2) (intentions published June 21, 1856), **SUSAN WEEKS** of Oakham.

Children by first wife

Jonathan Warner, b. in Hardwick, Jan. 26, 1828. He was an artist with a studio in New York City, but returned to live in Hardwick in later life. He died unmarried.

Charles L. Warner, b. in Hardwick, June 27, 1831; was a farmer residing on the easterly road to Gilbertsville, in Hardwick; deacon; m. (intentions published Jan. 24, 1861) Caroline Wallace, who was born in Barre. Child: Lewis, b. in Hardwick, Sept. 13, 1865; resides in Holyoke, Mass.; m. Oct. 5, 1886, Addie Pierce, b. in Buckland, about 1868, daughter of Julius F. and Mary A. (———) Pierce. They have a son.

Susan A. Warner, b. Mar. 4, 1834, in Hardwick; m. there, Apr. 7, 1885, as his second wife, Charles W. Davenport, b. about 1826, in Petersham, son of Jeremy and Polly (———) Davenport. They resided in Athol.

373 WILLIAM AUGUSTUS⁷ WARNÉR, son of Jonathan⁶ and Sally (Paige) Warner, born in Hardwick, Mass., January 8, 1804; died there, August 30, 1878, buried in Hardwick Cemetery. He was a farmer, inherited the homestead at Hardwick and was considered one of the best farmers in the town. Married May 24, 1832, **ELIZABETH F. BILLINGS,** daughter of Silas Billings. She died May 11, 1878, aged 65 years, 5 months, 9 days, buried in Hardwick Cemetery.

Children, born in Hardwick

Harriet Elizabeth Warner, b. July 7, 1834; m. Jan. 16, 1862, Harmon C. Spooner, b. in Hardwick about 1829, son of Bradford and Arethusa (———) Spooner. He was a cabinet maker and resided in Hardwick.

William Augustus Warner, Jr., b. Apr. 15, 1837; d. Sept. 22, 1894, buried in Hardwick Cemetery. He was a farmer; member of the School Committee for many years; member of the Mass. Board of Agriculture; deacon of the Hardwick Church. Married Nov. 15, 1860, Caroline Amelia Sibley, b. in Dana, Mass., adopted daughter of ——— Paige of Hardwick. After her husband's death she removed to Worcester where she now resides with an adopted son, Harry, who is married and has a son. The only child of William Augustus Warner was William Paige, b. Feb. 6, 1871, d. July 2, 1872, buried in Hardwick Cemetery.

Silas Franklin Warner, b. July 21, 1843; d. Nov. 21, 1845, buried in Hardwick Cemetery.

Mary Ann Warner, b. July 28, 1846; d. Dec. 22, 1895; m. Jan. 1, 1872, Henry Gould Towne, b. May 14, 1843, in Sturbridge, son of Solomon Gould and Sally W. (Thayer) Towne. He was a carpenter, resided at North Dana and Warren. Child: George Henry, b. Jan. 29, 1880.

Julia Maria Warner, b. Jan. 11, 1851; d. Nov. 22, 1888, in Hardwick.

374 LEVI WHIPPLE⁷ WARNER, son of Jonathan⁶ and Sally (Paige) Warner, born in Hardwick, Mass., June 7, 1806;

died July 28, 1844, buried in Hardwick Cemetery. He was a farmer.

Married April 10, 1832, **LUTHERA CLARK**, born in Hardwick, Feb. 21, 1810, daughter of Ezra and Betsey (Webb) Clark. She married (2) December 25, 1851, William Erastus Bassett and resided in Belchertown.

Children, born in Hardwick

William B. Warner, b. Dec. 10, 1832; d. Jan. 1, 1833.
Caroline Maria Warner, b. Oct. 12, 1835; m. Aug. 2, 1854, Eleazer Damon of Ware, b. in Chesterfield, Mass., Feb. 3, 1830, son of Robert Damon of Westhampton, Mass., and his wife, Sally Torry of Chesterfield. Children: i. Emma Lutheria, b. Oct. 2, 1856, d. Oct. 31, 1865. ii. Hattie Mary, b. May 4, 1864.
Emeline Frances Warner, b. Aug. 3, 1837.

375 IRA[7] **WARNER**, son of Abel[6] and Sarah (Cook) Warner, born December 25, 1786, in Plainfield, Mass.; died at Cuyler, N. Y., March 30, 1840.

Soon after his marriage in 1810, he removed to Cuyler, Cortland Co., N. Y., at that time a part of Truxton, and in 1817 he bought a farm of about 300 acres, situated three miles south of the village of Cuyler on the road to Lincklaen. He was a successful and enterprising farmer and was in advance of most other farmers of that region, in adopting improved methods of farming, stock-raising and butter-making. His death was caused by the kick of a young horse which he was breaking, and occurred eight days after the injury and four days after the birth of his oldest grandson, Ira DeVer Warner.

Married February 10, 1810, **ASENATH HITCHCOCK**, born October 15, 1784, died January 15, 1838, daughter of Captain Samuel and Thankful (Hawks) Hitchcock of Hawley, Mass. Her father was born in Springfield, Mass., the son of Samuel[4] (John[3], John[2], Luke[1]) and Ruth (Stebbins) Hitchcock, and, with his family, was one of the first three families to settle in Hawley, Mass., in 1770. He served as a private in the Revolutionary army, July 1, 1777, in Col. John Brewer's regiment; was in Col. David Wells's regiment and in 1782 was in Col. Gideon Burt's regiment. He was made Captain of the Militia, July 7, 1789, receiving his commission from John Hancock.

Children, born in Cuyler

561 *Alonzo Franklin Warner,* b. Nov. 18, 1810; m. Lydia Ann Converse.
Asenath Hitchcock Warner, b. Nov. 15, 1811; d. in DeRuyter, N. Y., Mar. 12, 1874; m. (1) Oct. 15, 1840, Weston Payne, who died a

few years later; m. (2) about 1850, Jonathan Vail of DeRuyter, who was born in 1802, and died at Marion, N. Y., in 1897. He owned a grist mill about half way between DeRuyter and Quaker Basin. By this second marriage there was a daughter, Esther, who was not of sound mind.

Abel W. Warner, b. May 11, 1814; d. Mar. 11, 1816.

562 *Harriet Newell Warner,* b. Oct. 2, 1815; m. Lewis Nash.

Esther Wells Warner, b. Apr. 15, 1818; d. Sept. 20, 1847; m. Sept., 1841, Lorenzo Samson of DeRuyter, N. Y. They had one son who died when about fourteen years old.

563 *Lorenzo Cook Warner,* b. July 11, 1819; m. Mary Durfee.

ABEL P. WARNER   MRS. ABEL P. WARNER

564 *Eliza Ann Warner,* b. Feb. 15, 1821; m. Titus Beech Davidson.

565 *Horace Horatio Warner,* b. Apr. 25, 1822; m. Ursula J. Hitchcock.

Mary Ann Warner, b. Jan. 16, 1824; d. at Homer, N. Y., Apr. 18, 1863; m. Dec. 6, 1842, Isaac Marshall Samson, who resided at Cincinnatus, N. Y., and later at Homer, where he kept the temperance hotel formerly conducted by his father. He married, as his second wife, Zelia Nash, daughter of Lewis and Harriet Newell (Warner) Nash, see number 562. Child of Mary Ann Warner: Francis, who resides in or near Cortland, N. Y.

566 *Roswell Knowlton Warner,* b. July 19, 1825; m. Remonia Vail.

Abel Parker Warner, b. in Cuyler, N. Y., Jan. 6, 1827; d. at Wilson, Kans., Oct. 12, 1892. He resided for a time at Rome, Ind., later in Chicago. He married Mar. 20, 1856, Selina May Young, b. Mar. 8, 1833, d. in Chicago, May 9, 1870, leaving no children. He returned east after her death and remained two years, then went to Kansas and settled near James Crofoot, his nephew, see number 567.

567   *Sarah Jane Warner*, b. Apr. 9, 1829; m. (1) Franklin Crofoot, (2) John Abbott.

376   **POLLY⁷ WARNER**, daughter of Abel⁶ and Sarah (Cook) Warner, born in Plainfield, Mass., November 16, 1790, baptized in Cummington, March 5, 1791; died in 1869. Married November 19, 1811 or 1812, **LEONARD JOY**, born in Plainfield, March 14, 1790; died there, January 15, 1881. He was the son of Captain Joseph and Molly (Porter) Joy, was a farmer and kept the tavern known as the Hampshire House.

Children, born in Plainfield

Lucretia Joy, b. Aug. 19, 1813; d. Mar. 17, 1818.
Cordelia Joy, b. May 27, 1815; m. as second wife, about 1839, Rush Gurney of Cummington, Mass. A son, Justus Warner, was a soldier in the Civil War and resided later in Palmyra, N. Y.
Sarah Joy, b. Mar. 28, 1817; m. Sept. 19, 1838, John M. Crane of Washington, Mass.
Emeline Joy (twin), b. June 15, 1819.
Caroline Joy (twin), b. June 15, 1819; m. May 10, 1841, Jonas Holden of Hawley, Mass.
Francis W. Joy, b. May 13, 1822; was a blacksmith and resided on the farm once owned by his grandfather Abel Warner; m. Apr., 1845, Rachel Chapel of Washington, Mass.
Charles Joy, b. Oct. 16, 1824; d. Aug. 12, 1850; m. Nov., 1848, Julia M. Sanderson.
Electa P. Joy, b. 1827; m. June 3, 1847, Reuben Scott, Jr., of Hawley.
Lorenzo W. Joy, b. in Worthington, Mass., 1832; m. Jan., 1855, Delia R. Colburn.

377   **JUSTUS⁷ WARNER**, son of Abel⁶ and Sarah (Cook) Warner, born in Plainfield, Mass., June 13, 1796; died there, September 11, 1834. He was a farmer and resided on the homestead at Plainfield, one mile north of the village. In 1825 he was elected selectman and filled that office for two years. In 1828 he was chosen town clerk. The inventory of his estate, filed in Northampton, gives a valuation of over four thousand dollars for the farm and its equipment, and among its items are forty books, a possession which, in those days, would indicate a man of more than ordinary interests.

Married in September, 1828, **SYLVIA RUSSELL HITCH-COCK**, born in Hawley, Mass., January 13, 1799; died June 3, 1866, in Cincinnati, Ohio, at the home of her son George. She was the daughter of Samuel and Thirza (Cooley) Hitchcock, and was a descendant of the pioneer Luke Hitchcock. Her grandfather Capt. Samuel[5] Hitchcock (Samuel[4], John[3], John[2], Luke[1]) was one of the first three settlers of Hawley in 1770; enlisted July 1, 1777, in Col. John Brewer's Regiment, was later under Col. David Wells and, in 1782, under Col. Gideon Burt. He received a commission from John Hancock, July 7, 1789, as captain of the militia.

Mrs. Warner married (2) Josiah Ballard of Charlemont.

Children of Justus Warner

568   Charles Dudley Warner, b. Sept. 12, 1829; m. Susan Sophia Lee.
569   George Henry Warner, b. Dec. 21, 1833; m. Elizabeth Hooker Gillette.

378 SARAH[7] WARNER, daughter of Abel[6] and Sarah (Cook) Warner, born in Plainfield, Mass., January 13, 1798; died in Ohio, July 29, 1868.

Married November 22, 1819, EDMOND TAYLOR, born August 27, 1787; died March 9, 1859. He was of Buckland, Mass., and had been previously married. They removed to Ballston Spa, N. Y., and, in 1837, to Bennington, Licking Co., Ohio, traveling by canal boat.

Children

Stoughton Lawrence Taylor, b. Mar. 6, 1822; d. 1893. He resided in Mt. Vernon, Ohio, and had several children.
Marietta Haskell Taylor, b. Apr. 13, 1824.
Justus Warner Taylor, b. Sept. 1, 1827.
James Henry Taylor, b. Jan. 3, 1829; was a Presbyterian minister and resided for some years at Rome, N. Y.
Annis Jay Taylor, b. Mar. 4, 1832.
Olive Orlinda Taylor, b. Aug. 10, 1838; m. Nov. 28, 1861, Joseph Harper Pollock. They had a son, Edwin Taylor Pollock, a Captain in the U. S. Navy, and a member of the Sons of the Revolution. Captain Pollock was the commanding officer for the first seven trips of the U. S. S. George Washington as a transport during the war, 1917-8.

379 FANNY[7] WARNER, daughter of Abel[6] and Sarah (Cook) Warner, born August 26, 1805, in Plainfield, Mass.; died in Hawley, Mass., July 22, 1839.

Married as second wife, April 17, 1828, REUBEN HAMLIN, born May 19, 1795, son of John and Sally (Town) Hamlin. He settled in Plainfield where he built a factory for making satinets, broadcloths and custom work. He was married five times: (1) Feb. 15, 1816, to Rhoda Richards, who died Dec. 29, 1826; (2) to Fanny Warner; (3) Nov. 3, 1839, to Elizabeth Jones, who died Dec. 11, 1851; (4) to Mrs. Eunice Tirrell; (5) to Mrs. Pamela Little. He had children by the first wife.

Children of Reuben and Fanny (Warner) Hamlin.

Laura B. Hamlin, b. Apr. 27, 1829; m. Dec. 22, 1853, James C. Bellman of Cincinnati.
Rosamond W. Hamlin, b. June 1, 1831; d. Aug. 29, 1844.
Alfred W. Hamlin, b. June 17, 1834; d. June 6, 1872; m. Nov. 19, 1863; Harriet N. Stratton of Jeffersonville, Ind.
Albert Wallace Hamlin, b. Mar. 13, 1839; m. Oct. 27, 1870, Rachel Mercer of Princeton, Ill.

380 N A H U M⁷ W A R N E R, son of David⁶ and Martha (Cottle-White) Warner, born in Palmyra, N. Y., October 12, 1799; died in 1881. He resided in Macedon, N. Y., on the farm which his father had cleared at an early day, but the interests of the family, social, religious and financial, have always been in Palmyra. He was president of the Union Agricultural Society for two years.

Married in Palmyra, N. Y., February 14, 1821, HANNAH FISH, born in Palmyra, 1797 or 1798; died February, 1879.

Children, born in Macedon

570 *Martha Warner,* b. Apr. 7, 1823; m. Miles B. Riggs.
571 *Mary Ann Warner,* b. Dec. 25, 1825; m. Ira Benedict.
572 *Giles Warner,* b. Nov. 29, 1830; m. Maria M. Shoemaker.

381 J A M E S⁷ W A R N E R, son of Elijah⁶ and Betsey (Mitchell) Warner, born in Plainfield, Mass., July 23, 1798; died there, April 7, 1890. He was one of a company who built a factory about 1820 for the manufacture of satinets. They also did custom work as a clothing establishment, operated several looms and employed about a dozen hands. The mill was abandoned about 1855 and the buildings were taken down.

Married September 23, 1824, FIDELIA WHITON, born December 27, 1799, died August 11, 1887, daughter of David and Rachel (Randall) Whiton who came from Abingdon to Cummington about 1790 and thence to Plainfield. Her grandmother Lucy (Bruce) Randall is said to have been a descendant of the famous Robert Bruce.

Children, born in Plainfield

James Emerson Warner, b. Sept. 24, 1825; was graduated from the Medical College in Pittsfield, Mass., in 1853, and was for some years a practicing physician in California, later in Sterling, Va. Married in Barre, Orleans Co., N. Y., Sept., 1854, Hannah E. Hanford of Barre Center, who died Feb., 1875, leaving no children.
Fidelia Loraine Warner, b. Sept. 4, 1827; d. Oct. 18, 1854; m. Oct. 30, 1849, Elijah Selden Clark, b. in Plainfield, May 12, 1827, son of Elijah and Waity (Jenks) Clark. He m. (2) Dec. 3, 1856, Hannah

L. Lyman by whom he had two children, Charles L. and Alice L. Children of Fidelia L. Warner: i. Willis Alden, b. Nov. 14, 1850; resides in Albany, N. Y. ii. George W., b. Aug. 1, 1854; resides in Acton, Mass.

Florilla D. Warner, b. Feb. 11, 1830; resided in Claridon, Ohio; m. (1) Jan. 1, 1852, Alberto C. Shattuck, who d. Oct. 15, 1852; m. (2) Feb., 1857, Rev. S. D. Taylor of South New Lyme, Ohio. Child by first marriage: Alberto C. (Shattuck), b. Dec. 22, 1852, a lawyer in Cleveland, Ohio.

Sarah W. Warner, b. Sept. 8, 1834; was a teacher in the schools of Hampshire County, Mass., for over fifty terms; resided in Claridon, Ohio, with her sister's family after the death of her parents.

573 *Almon Mitchell Warner*, b. Mar. 6, 1843; m. Elizabeth Huldah Densmore.

382 WILLIAM⁷ WARNER, son of Elijah⁶ and Betsey (Mitchell) Warner, born in Plainfield, Mass., August 9, 1804; died there, October 6, 1865. He was a farmer in Plainfield.

Married (1) in Plainfield, April 23, 1835,. **ANNIS CRITTENDEN**, born at Plainfield, April 23, 1819, died October 30, 1852, daughter of Azariah and Polly (White) Crittenden.

Married (2) in Plainfield, January 23, 1855, **Mrs. POLLY PACKARD (WHITMARSH) LATHAM**, born November 19, 1815, died February 10, 1885. She was the daughter of Jacob and Polly (Packard) Whitmarsh of Plainfield and was first married to Robert Alvord Latham, by whom she had seven children. After Mr. Warner's death she married, about 1870, Riley Westcott of Cheshire, Mass.

Children of William and Annis (Crittenden) Warner, born in Plainfield

William Edwards Warner, b. Apr. 1, 1836; enlisted Sept. 26, 1862, in Company F, 46th Mass. Volunteers, which was stationed near Newbern, N. C., where he died in service, June 28, 1863, of typhoid fever, and was buried there.

Eliza A. Warner, b. Sept. 11, 1837; d. Sept. 27, 1903; resided in Covert, Mich.; m. in Florence, Mass., Nov. 7, 1875, as second wife, William J. Shattuck, b. in Hamilton, N. Y., Aug. 31, 1822, d. Apr. 2, 1905. They had no children.

Flora C. Warner, b. Jan. 29, 1840; d. Dec. 14, 1841.

574 *Flora Mary* (or *Mary Flora*) *Warner*, b. Sept. 24, 1842; m. (1) Edward A. Rood, (2) T. H. Rood.

Laura E. Warner, b. Mar. 15, 1848; resides in Northampton, Mass.; m. in Plainfield, Nov. 27, 1867, George L. Campbell, b. July 28, 1846, son of Levi N. and Ruth (Hall) Campbell. No children.

Children of William and Polly P. (Whitmarsh-Latham) Warner

Frank Alvord Warner (twin), b. Oct. 22, 1855; d. Apr. 26, 1863.

Fannie Adelaide Warner (twin), b. Oct. 22, 1855; resides in South

Hampton, Mass.; m. in Florence, Mass., Dec. 21, 1876, Hiram M. Rood, b. in Plainfield, son of Josiah and Rosina (Beals) Rood. They adopted Edward Rood Stone, son of her husband's sister, taking him when fifteen days old. They also have one son, Frank Warner, b. Mar. 14, 1892, in Northampton.

383   RACHEL WHITCOMB[7] WARNER, daughter of Giles[6] and Betsey (Sampson) Warner, born in Hardwick, Mass., May 14, 1811; died January 6, 1894. She resided in Hardwick and Ware, Mass. Married May 6, 1831, **LORING GILBERT**, born May 22, 1802, a descendant of John Gilbert, second son of Giles Gilbert of Bridgewater, Somerset, England. John Gilbert came to America and settled in Taunton, Mass., in 1634 and was in command of troops who fought against the Indians.

Child

Joseph Loring Gilbert, b. in Ware, July 7, 1832; d. in New York City, Feb. 28, 1895; m. Feb. 19, 1855, Caroline Clementine Etchebery, b. in New York City, Mar. 17, 1838. Children: i. George, d. in infancy. ii. Charles Pierrepont Henry, b. in New York City, Aug. 29, 1863; m. Sept. 14, 1896, Florence Cecil Moss of New York and has a son Dudley. iii. Carolyn Rachel, b. June 20, 1868, in New York City; m. there June 16, 1892, Marcus M. Benjamin, b. in San Francisco, Jan. 17, 1857, son of Edmund Burke and Sarah (Mitchell) Benjamin; resides in Washington.

Charles P. H. Gilbert took special college courses in civil engineering and architecture and studied painting, sculpture and fine arts abroad. He has been an architect in New York City since 1888. He has designed many public buildings, factories and residences; is a Fellow of the American Institute of Architects; member of the Architectural League, Fine Arts Society, Municipal Arts Society, Society of the Colonial Wars, New England Society, Society of the War of 1812, Chamber of Commerce; Charter member of Squadron A, N. G. S. N. Y., formerly known as the New York Hussars; member of several social and athletic clubs; director and stockholder in several manufacturing concerns.

Carolyn Rachel Gilbert Benjamin was educated in New York City at Mlle. Tardival's School, and has taken an active part in social, philanthropic and religious affairs. She was a member of the Jury of Awards at the Omaha Exposition in 1898 and at Jamestown in 1907; member of D. A. R., Children of the American Revolution, Society of Colonial Governors, Mary Washington Monument Association, Colonial Dames, and other clubs, and has held important offices in most of them. Dr. Benjamin is an editor and scientist. He removed to New York City in early life and was a graduate of Columbia, School of Mines, 1878; A.M., Lafayette, 1888; Ph.D., Univ. of Nashville, 1889; Sc.D., Univ. of Pittsburgh, 1905; LL.D., St. John's College, Md., 1910; editor of American Pharmacist in 1882,

26

and its successor, Weekly Drug News; chemist in U. S. Appraiser's Store, New York City, 1883-5; sanitary engineer New York Board of Health, 1885; editor U. S. National Museum since 1896; has contributed many articles to cyclopedias and leading magazines and published several hand-books and guides; is a member and officer of many scientific and patriotic orders in this country and in England.

384 **LYDIA OWEN**[7] **WARNER,** daughter of Joseph[6] and Olive (Holbrook) Warner, born in Cummington, Mass., August 8, 1813; died in Grinnell, Iowa, July, 1866, to which place she had removed in 1855.
Married September 21, 1837, Deacon **WILLIAM NELSON FORD** of Plainfield, Mass.

Children

Martha Holbrook Ford, b. July 13, 1838; resides in Dakota City, Neb.; m. Nov. 11, 1857, William Adair, b. Apr. 19, 1832, a postal clerk, after 1881, on the route from Sioux City, Iowa, to Omaha, Neb. Children: i. Clara Belle, b. Sept. 17, 1858; d. Oct. 7, 1880. ii. Edward Nelson, b. June 5, 1860; lives in Seattle, Wash. iii. Sarah Lavinia, b. Sept. 8, 1862; m. June 11, 1891, John E. Duschl, a merchant of Mapleton, Iowa, where they now reside; has two children, Clara Maria, b. May 30, 1892, and John Adair, b. Aug. 10, 1894. iv. William Rollin, b. June 24, 1864, resides in Omaha, Neb., and has been connected with the National Bank for many years; m. in St. Louis, Jan. 9, 1898, Alice Chambers. v. Mary Lydia (twin), b. Jan. 24, 1867; d. July 18, 1898; was a teacher. vi. Martha Eveline (twin), b. Jan. 24, 1867; is a teacher, a graduate of the training school in Sioux City. vii. Charles Warner, b. Feb. 14, 1869; is a conductor on the Sioux City and Omaha R. R.; resides in Sioux City; m. June 19, 1895, Mabel V. Nichols; has two children, Ivan Nichols, b. Mar. 17, 1897, and Helen Margaret, b. Dec. 20, 1898. viii. Francis Ford, b. Dec. 23, 1871; is connected with the Bank of the Republic, in Chicago. ix. Alfred Cookman, b. May 13, 1873; d. Sept. 1, 1902; m. in Pocahontas, Ark., Jan. 12, 1902, Josie Smith. x. Helen Ethel, b. Apr. 19, 1875; was a graduate of the Sioux City High School; d. Mar. 19, 1897. xi. Harry Holbrook, b. Oct. 5, 1879; was graduated from the Sioux City High School and Morningside College, Sioux City, became assistant principal of a school in Dakota City, Neb., directly after graduation.
William Rollin Ford, b. Mar. 26, 1844; d. Mar. 14, 1861.
Francis Ford, b. Oct. 30, 1847; served in the Civil War in an Iowa company and died from disease contracted in the war.
Charles Ford, b. Jan. 16, 1850; d. Apr. 24, 1872.

385 **FRANKLIN JOHN**[7] **WARNER,** son of Joseph[6] and Olive (Holbrook) Warner, born in Cummington, Mass., March 12, 1818; died there, July 5, 1888. He was educated in the district and high schools of the vicinity and became a farmer and dealer in agricultural implements, residing in Cummington, on

a fine farm not far from the birthplace and home of William Cullen Bryant. Both Mr. and Mrs. Warner took an active part in the affairs of the Congregational Church and Society. Married January 1, 1843, **VESTA WALES REED,** born in Plainfield, Mass., December 15, 1820, died January 21, 1909, daughter of Joshua and Susanna (Noyes) Reed. Joshua Reed served in the commissary department of the War of 1812, carrying supplies to various points.

Children, born in Cummington

575 *Edward Franklin Warner,* b. Nov. 16, 1844; m. (1) Susie Woods Robinson, (2) Ellen A. Lovell.
576 *Worcester Reed Warner,* b. May 16, 1846; m. Cornelia Fraley Blakemore.
  Delia Holbrook Warner, b. Jan. 18, 1852; d. Aug. 15, 1879. She was graduated from Mount Holyoke Seminary and taught there until her death.
577 *Susan Lavinia Warner,* b. June 18, 1854; m. Charles D. Seely.
  Charles Francis Warner, b. June 14, 1859; d. Feb. 8, 1870.

386 SUMNER HOLBROOK[7] WARNER, son of Joseph[6] and Olive (Holbrook) Warner, born in Cummington, Mass., March 12, 1821; died April 4, 1905, in Springfield, Mass. Mr. Warner was a carpenter and house builder. In 1854 he went west in company with a partner, W. N. Fay, intending to settle in Minneapolis. They were delayed in La Crosse, Wis., by an accident to Mr. Fay, and Mr. Warner decided to settle there. They bought several house lots there and moved their families the following year. After the death of his third wife, Mr. Warner became discouraged with the location and returned east to enter the employ of the Boston and Albany Railroad as general repairer and inspector of the wood work on engines. He held this position for twenty-nine years and retired a number of years before his death.

Married (1) 1849, **DELIA HUBBARD** of Brimfield, Mass., who died December 31, 1850.

Married (2) in Plainfield, Mass., **SARAH ELIZABETH CHAPPELL,** born in Lebanon, Conn., March 14, 1832; died in La Crosse, Wis., December 23, 1856.

Married (3) April 18, 1858, **EMILY ROBINSON,** daughter of James and Adeline (———) Robinson of Cummington, Mass., and step-sister of his second wife. She died in La Crosse, Wis., October 8, 1859, of typhoid fever.

Married (4) July 14, 1864, **MARIETTA FLOWER** of Feeding Hill, Mass., who died June 2, 1913.

Child of Sumner H. and Sarah E. (Chappell) Warner

578 Walter Holbrook *Warner*, b. in Meriden, Conn., Aug. 20, 1855; m. Harriet Ashley Cooley.

387 **MARY ANN⁷ WARNER,** daughter of Joseph⁶ and Olive (Holbrook) Warner, born in Cummington, Mass., June 30, 1823; died in Shelburne Falls, Mass., August 16, 1877. Married October 4, 1843, **LUTHER MARTIN PACKARD,** born September 29, 1819; died May 4, 1899.

Children

Luther *Watson Packard,* d. in infancy.
Mary Lavinia *Packard,* b. in Cummington, Feb., 1850; resides in Rutland, Vt.; m. Oct. 6, 1869, John C. Temple. Children: i. Ethel Florence, b. Dec. 26, 1870; m. Oct. 5, 1891, Wesley E. Jones and has four children, Hammond, b. June 29, 1893, Roger, b. Aug. 13, 1894, Elvah, b. Dec., 1897, and Ethel, b. July 6, 1902. ii. Edith Lavinia, b. Oct. 22, 1873. iii. Mary White, b. Sept. 29, 1877. iv. Jenny Lind, b. Aug. 20, 1879. v. John Raymond, b. May 9, 1885. vi. Dorothy Coleman, b. Jan. 8, 1891.
Miriam *or* Marion Holbrook *Packard,* b. in Shelburne Falls, Mass., Mar. 12, 1857; resides there; m. June 15, 1881, Dr. Joseph C. Perry, a dentist. Children: i. Luther Packard, b. June 24, 1882; is a college graduate. ii. Joseph Earl, b. Dec. 30, 1884. iii. Randolph Warner, b. Oct. 9, 1892; d. Feb. 26, 1897.

388 **MARY ANN⁷ WARNER,** daughter of Stephen⁶ and Clarissa (Mitchell) Warner, born in Cummington, Mass., January 31, 1805; died October, 1878. She resided after her marriage near Lenawee Junction, Mich.
Married November 13, 1828, Lieutenant **NAHUM WHIT-MARSH,** born in Cummington, October 20, 1794, died February 7, 1857, son of Jacob Whitmarsh, who was a deacon of the Cummington Congregational Church, and his wife, Anna Pool.

Children

Charles Carroll *Whitmarsh,* b. Mar. 13, 1830; d. Jan. 16, 1914; resided at Lenawee Junction; m. Adaline Mann. Children: i. Jennie, b. Apr. 16, 1859; m. ——— Archer. ii. Emma, b. Jan. 23, 1861; m. ——— Weter. iii. George, b. Nov. 24, 1862; m. ——— Doty. iv. Franklin, b. July 31, 1867; m. ——— Colvin.
Clarissa Warner *Whitmarsh,* b. Sept. 28, 1832; m. ——— Benedict. Children: Lilla; Herma.
Lewis *Whitmarsh,* b. Dec. 6, 1834; d. aged 6 months.
Lewis W. *Whitmarsh,* b. July 10, 1838; m. and had children, George, Frank, Ada, Lilla, Effie, and Fred.

389 **CLARISSA MITCHELL**[7] **WARNER**, daughter of Stephen[6] and Clarissa (Mitchell) Warner, born in Cummington, Mass., March 16, 1807; died January 23, 1839.

Married August 9, or September 16, 1831, **HORACE WHITMARSH**, born January 5, 1801, in Cummington, died April 10, 1896, son of Jacob and Anna (Pool) Whitmarsh. He resided at Palmyra and Quincy, Mich.; Hiawatha, Kans.; and Bluff Point, N. Y. His second wife was Louisa Lewis, by whom he had two daughters, Mary Louise and Alice E.

Children of Horace and Clarissa Mitchell (Warner) Whitmarsh

Ellen Augusta Whitmarsh, b. Oct. 30, 1832; d. Mar. 17, 1855; resided at Palmyra, Mich.; m. Almon Whitman. Child: Edward.

Horace P. Whitmarsh, b. May 18, 1834, at Palmyra, Mich.; resides at Dundee, N. Y.; m. at Jericho, Ill., Oct. 28, 1857, Philena S. Johnson, daughter of Reuben and Silvia (————) Johnson, b. Jan. 2, 1835, at Mayville, Chautauqua Co., N. Y., d. Oct. 7, 1906, at Bluff Point, Yates Co., N. Y. Children: i. Mary Locelia, b. Aug. 8, 1860; d. Apr. 4, 1879. ii. Clara Philena, b. Aug. 18, 1862; d. Mar. 19, 1903. iii. Lillian Emma, b. Aug. 8, 1865; resides in Dundee, N. Y.; m. (1) Feb. 15, 1899, Daniel Budd, who died; m. (2) May 22, 1904, Oliver Disbrow.

Laura Whitmarsh, b. Oct. 12, 1836; d. Feb. 27, 1873; resides near Hiawatha, Kans.; m. James Miller and had children, Lizzie, Lulu and Emma.

Clarissa Whitmarsh, b. Jan. 5, 1839; d. Dec. 25, 1903; resided at Lenawee Junction, Mich.; m. W. H. Colvin and had daughters, Gertrude and Lulu.

390 **NORTON DEXTER**[7] **WARNER**, son of Stephen[6] and Clarissa (Mitchell) Warner, born in Cummington, Mass., September 2, 1809; died in Palmyra, Mich., May 11, 1868. He removed with his father to Palmyra in 1831.

Married in Cummington, May 10, 1833, **SILENA SHAW**, born in Worthington, Mass., January 12, 1811; died in Palmyra, Mich., June 6, 1881. She was the daughter of John and Polly (Whitmarsh) Shaw.

Children, born in Palmyra, Mich.

579 *Almon Warner*, b. Jan. 31, 1834; m. Phebe J. Gould.
580 *George Shaw Warner*, b. June 17, 1846; m. Lillian Miller.

391 **LAURA M.**[7] **WARNER**, daughter of Stephen[6] and Clarissa (Mitchell) Warner, born in Cummington, Mass., May 12, 1816; died.

Married October 27, 1841, **SAMUEL BEMENT**, born about

1810; died. He was a civil engineer, and, at the age of 93, was still well and active in his profession. He and his wife resided in Toledo, Ohio.

Children

Ella M. Bement, b. Aug. 11, 1851; m. Apr. 13, 1875, Charles H. Norris. Children: i. Charles B., b. Feb. 23, 1877; m. June, 1902, Zilla Smith. ii. Bessie, b. Feb. 2, 1879; m. Feb. 14, 1900, Easton Ferguson.
Lizzie S. Bement, b. May 19, 1856; resides in Toledo, Ohio; m. Oct. 25, 1887, Rowland J. Tappan. Child: Helen B., b. July 14, 1897.
Frank W. Bement, b. Oct. 4, 1857; m. Nov. 16, 1887, Hattie Stratton. Child: Austin B., b. Oct. 22, 1891.

392 LUCIUS[7] WARNER, son of Stephen[6] and Clarissa (Mitchell) Warner, born in Cummington, Mass., March 9, 1821 Resided in Palmyra, Lenawee Co., Mich.

Married December 31, 1849, L Y D I A C L A R K W H I T - MARSH, daughter of Alvan and Lydia (Clark) Whitmarsh of Cummington.

Children

581 *William C. Warner*, b. Nov. 30, 1851; m. Mary E. Ellis.
Edward Alvah Warner, b. Mar., 1854; d. Aug., 1860.
Frederick A. Warner, b. July, 1861.

393 WILLIAM STARKS[7] WARNER, son of Orrin[6] and Lucinda (Starks) Warner, born in Palmyra, N. Y., December 23, 1817; died at Jefferson, Ill., 1879.

Married in Chicago, Ill., June 17, 1846, **HEPSY PAGE**, who died in Chicago, April 25, 1871.

Children, all but first born in Chicago

Sarah W. Warner, b. in Madison, Wis., Mar. 22, 1847; resides in Chicago.
Charles D. Warner, b. Oct. 14, 1848; resides in Chicago; m. Apr. 10, 1883, Maud P. Bigden. Child: George H., b. June 3, 1884.
Major Lewis Warner, b. Nov. 19, 1853; resides in Chicago. He furnished a large part of the data for this branch of the family.
Mary Sophia Warner, b. Nov. 19, 1853; resides in Ripon, Wis.; m. Dec. 28, 1873, William T. Runals of Ripon. Children, all but two born in Ripon: i. Dora Edmonia, b. Oct. 16, 1878. ii. Edmund Lucien, b. Apr. 17, 1881; d. at Ripon, Sept. 26, 1895. iii. Clara Louise, b. at Green Lake, Wis., Sept. 21, 1883; m. Nov. 19, 1914, Marvin Fox of Pomona, Cal. iv. Guy Warner, b. at Green Lake, Feb. 8, 1886; m. June 24, 1914, Laura D. Cunningham of Berlin, Wis., and has a daughter, Helen Elizabeth, who was born in Ripon, Feb. 12, 1916. v. Irene Margaret, b. Apr. 16, 1891. vi. William Theodore, b. June 17, 1893.
Julia Adelaide Warner, b. June 4, 1858; d. at Indianapolis, Ind., Nov. 15, 1893; m. Feb. 15, 1882, William B. Palmer. Child: Jay R., b. Dec. 16, 1887.

394 ORRIN⁷ WARNER, son of Orrin⁶ and Delia (McLouth) Warner, born in Palmyra, N. Y., January 14, 1829. He removed to Hillsdale, Mich., January 1, 1855, and died near Hillsdale, July 10, 1884, buried in New York State. Married (1) in Macedon, N. Y., October 20, 1852, MARY ELIZABETH EASTWOOD of Macedon, born October 20, 1831; died in Hillsdale, December 20, 1873. She was a woman of many lovable traits of character. Her parents were Nathaniel Eastwood, born October 12, 1805, and Phebe Ann Shearman, born November 10, 1809, married November 4, 1826, died December 10, 1865. The marriage certificate of Orrin and Mary Warner is one of the valued treasures of his youngest son.

Married (2) November 21, 1877, SALLY ANN CARTER, who died August 2, 1886.

Children by first wife

Bleaker Lansing Warner, b. in Palmyra, N. Y., July 8, 1854; removed with his father to Hillsdale, Mich., when he was eleven years old, and resided there after that time; m. Alvira Cordelia Coryell. Children: i. Howard C., b. Jan. 7, 1882; was graduated from Hillsdale High School, resides in Jackson, Mich.; m. June 7, 1905, Clara Maul, and has a child, Royce. ii. Arlo T., b. Nov. 7, 1894; was graduated from Hillsdale High School and studied at Hillsdale College; m. and has a daughter.

Delia Ann Warner, b. Mar. 21, 1856; d. Sept. 19, 1884; m. 1871, George Schmitt. Children: i. William Henry, b. Aug. 7, 1874; d. Mar. 28, 1875. ii. George A., b. Apr. 3, 1876; is a merchant in Hillsdale; m. May 23, 1900, Clara E. La Fleur and has three children, Gertrude, b. Mar. 12, 1902, Asher La Fleur, b. July 22, 1903, and George A., b. July 22, 1908. iii. Fayette E., b. Jan. 6, 1882; d. July 23, 1899.

582 *William Arthur Lewis Warner,* b. Aug. 7, 1869; m. Lettie W. Graber.

395 MARTHA ELVIRA⁷ WARNER, daughter of Norman⁶ and Elvira (Hartwell) Warner, born January 22, 1831, probably in Cummington, Mass.; died October 16, 1875. Married September 6, 1849, HORATIO A. LOUD of Plainfield, Mass. He died April 8, 1901.

Children

Ida Josephine Loud, b. June 18, 1850; m. Dec. 23, 1893, George Devol.
Eva Adeline Loud, b. Apr. 17, 1852; m. Feb. 3, 1876, William H. Sibley. Children: i. Mabel E., b. Apr. 22, 1877. ii. Amy M., b. Sept. 4, 1878. iii. Charles H., b. Dec. 29, 1880. iv. Guy Warner.
Waldo Allen Loud, b. May 19, 1854; m. Clara Isabelle Wakefield. Children: i. Ralph Waldo, b. Jan. 20, 1879. ii. Harold Owen, b. Oct. 16, 1881. iii. Roy E., b. Mar. 16, 1883. iv. Stanley Dunham.
Henry Loud, b. Oct., 1857; d. Sept. 5, 1863.

Hattie Maria Loud, b. Jan. 12, 1860; m. Feb. 24, 1883, Henry Huck.
    Children: Raymond Herman and Karl Henry.
Bessie Elvira Loud, b. Mar. 7, 1867; m. Nov. 14, 1895, George Lamb
    Snow. Children: Martha Gladys and Hattie Josephine.
Jennie May Loud, b. Jan. 16, 1872; died the same year.

· 396 JONATHAN[7] WARNER, 3d, son of Jonathan[6], Jr., and
Hepsibah (Ely) Warner, born December 11, 1782, in Chester
parish, Old Saybrook, Conn.; died April 12, 1862, in Jefferson,
Ohio. He spent his early life as a farmer and sailor in Connecticut and made a cruise to the West Indies. In the fall of 1804
he went west on horseback and located in Jefferson, Ohio,
bringing his goods later by boat. In 1815 he became register
of deeds for the county and held the office for seven years. In
1825 he was elected treasurer of the county; representative in
the State Legislature in 1831; associate judge of the Court of
Common Pleas from 1839 to 1847; mayor of the village of
Jefferson. He is recorded in the 1830 Census of Jefferson
Borough, District No. 8, Ashtabula Co., Ohio, as a farmer with
property of considerable value. He built first a log house, then
a frame house called "Warner's Inn," and in 1834 a large
colonial house which is still standing in good condition and is
owned by his granddaughter Mrs. Marion Stafford.

Married in Jefferson, May, 1807, **NANCY FRETHY,** born
September 21, 1789, in Northampton, Mass.; died July 20, 1881,
in Jefferson, Ohio. She was the daughter of Edward and
Deborah (Pratt) Frethy. Edward Frethy came from Washington, D. C., to Jefferson and was the first merchant, first
justice of the peace, and first postmaster there.

Children, born in Jefferson

583 *Nancy Warner,* b. Apr. 18, 1808; · m. Archibald Holman.
    ————————, died in infancy.
584 *Jonathan Warner, 4th,* b. Sept. 7, 1812; m. (1) Lydia Allen, (2)
    Katherine Krum.
585 *Phebe Warner,* b. Mar. 3, 1815; m. John B. King.
586 *Adeline Warner,* b. Jan. 20, 1818; m. Rufus Percival Ranney.
587 *Jane Warner,* b. July 8, 1820; m. George Starr.
588 *Louisa Warner,* b. Jan. 4, 1823; m. Charles S. Simonds.
589 *George W. Warner,* b. Apr. 24, 1825; m. Matilda Burdett.
590 *Isabelle Warner,* b. June 5, 1827; m. (1) Monroe C. Moore, (2) John
    Ducro.
591 *Francis H. Warner,* b. May 27, 1831; m. Jane Mitchell.
592 *Charles Ely Warner,* b. May 21, 1834; m. Elizabeth Mary Butcher.

397 ELY[7] WARNER, son of Jonathan[6], Jr., and Hepsibah
(Ely) Warner, born May 22, 1785, in Chester, Conn., which

was at that time a parish of Saybrook; died there, October 21, 1872. He was the fifth generation to own and live upon the homestead his great-great-grandfather bought in 1697. The following is copied from the account of Judge Warner published in the "Commemorative biographical record of Middlesex County, Conn.":

Hon. Ely Warner, one of the most prominent and able representatives of the Bar in Middlesex County, was a native of Chester. After graduating from Yale in 1807 he taught school for a year or more, then entered a law school at Litchfield, Conn., and was admitted to the bar at Middletown, Conn., about 1811. So untiring was his industry while pursuing his professional studies, he wrote from his notes the entire course of lectures, in three manuscript volumes, said to be the only correct copy of the lectures of Judges Reeves and Gould now extant. Settling in Haddam in 1816, he represented the town in the State Legislature for two sessions, in 1825 and 1831; and in 1828, he was appointed Chief Judge of Middlesex County Court, being reappointed for several terms. Subsequently he became cashier of the East Haddam Bank. In 1837 he removed to his farm in Chester and there resided during the remainder of his life. In 1855 he was appointed county commissioner and held the office for two terms. For more than fifty years he was actively engaged as county surveyor. His death, due to paralysis, occurred at his home, Oct. 23, 1872, when in his eighty-eighth year, and at that time he was the oldest lawyer in the state.

Married at Chester, November 11, 1817, SARAH WARD[8] WARNER, born in Chester, April 5, 1798, died there, January 22, 1886. She was the daughter of John[7] and Mehitabel (Clark) Warner. See number 405.

Children

Jonathan (1) *Warner*, b. Sept. 6, 1818, in Haddam; d. Aug. 4, 1820, "aged 1 11/12" (Haddam Congregational Church records).

593 *Sarah Warner*, b. July 27, 1820; m. Daniel D. Silliman.

Jonathan Warner, b. in Haddam, July 26, 1823; d. in Chester, Mar. 26, 1905; not married.

594 *George Washington Warner*, b. Feb. 8, 1827; m. Clara Drusilla Wilcox.

Jared Clark Warner, b. in Haddam, Dec. 1, 1829; d. in East Saginaw, Mich., Aug. 9, 1855, not married. He was graduated from Yale in 1854.

595 *Hepsibah Ely Warner*, b. May 16, 1832; m. Henry Squire Russell.

Andrew Ely Warner (twin), b. May 20, 1838, in Chester; resides there, not married. He owns and lives on the farm purchased by his ancestor, Andrew[4] Warner in 1697, the sixth generation of successive owners. The house, which is illustrated on page 182, was built in 1798 by Jonathan[5] Warner, and has been handed down by inheritance to the present owner.

596 *Annie Louise Warner* (twin), b. May 20, 1838; m. Jarvis V. Smith.

398 **SAMUEL SELDEN[7] WARNER,** son of Selden[6] and Dorothy (Selden) Warner, born March 15, 1789, in Hadlyme,

Conn.; died April 1, 1868, in Toledo, Ohio. He was named
Selden and this was changed to Samuel Selden by an act of the
Legislature. In early life he was a teacher, and was later a
farmer at Hadlyme. He was a member of the Congregational
Church at Hadlyme in 1816.

Married (1) as recorded in the town records of Lyme, Conn.,
February 23, 1819, ABIGAIL CHAMPLIN of Lyme, born
1793; died April 26, 1823, aged 30 years, 15 days, buried in
Lyme. She was the daughter of Silas and Elizabeth (Lay)
Champlin.

Married (2) March 17, 1825, AZUBAH TULLY of Saybrook,
born March 20, 1789, died October 29, 1863, daughter of Elias
and Azubah (Kirtland) Tully. She was a member of the Hadlyme Congregational Church in 1828.

Children by first wife

597 *Amelia Champlin Warner,* b. Aug. 24, 1820; m. Morrison Remick
     Waite.

     Abby Elizabeth Warner, b. Aug. 23, or Sept. 22, 1822; d. July 15,
     1850, in Brooklyn, N. Y.; m. July 30, 1846, Captain Edward Green-
     field Tinker of Brooklyn. Children: i. Edward, b. Jan. 14, 1847;
     d. 1858. ii. Henry Champlin, b. Sept. 20, 1849.

Children by second wife

     Mary Eliza Warner, b. Aug. 23, 1826; d. Sept. 4, 1899; m. Sept. 1,
     1850, Joel M. Gloyd of Maumee, Ohio. No children. They resided
     in Toledo, Ohio.

598 *Samuel Selden Warner, Jr.,* b. Dec. 17, 1827; m. Harriette Newell
     Gaylord.

     Margaret Warner, b. Nov. 30, 1831; d. Dec. 23, 1833, in Hadlyme,
     Conn.

399 ANDREW FERDINANDO[7] WARNER, son of Selden[6]
and Dorothy (Selden) Warner, born in Hadlyme, Conn.,
December 29, 1790 (or December 1, 1791, according to Cone
Genealogy); died June 23, 1825, in Haddam, Conn. He was
graduated from Yale in 1812, A.B.; A.M., 1815; studied medicine in Middletown and New Haven; practiced medicine in
the west parish of Colchester and the north parish of Saybrook;
removed to Haddam in 1820. He died after an illness of only
about a week from fever, leaving a son only a week old. There
was published a sermon by the Rev. Mr. Marsh, entitled, "The
Beloved Physician," occasioned by the death of Dr. Warner,
in which are fittingly expressed the affection and high esteem
in which he was held by his community.

Married in Westchester, Conn., November 4, 1817, LUCIN-

THIA CONE, who died in Haddam, October 1, 1846, aged 50 years. She was the daughter of Deacon Cephas and Sarah (Gates) Cone of Colchester and married (2) March 16, 1826, Ira C. Hutchinson, M.D., by whom she had seven children: Lucinthia C., Leverett, Eveline (who married Cephas Brainerd, Jr., of Haddam, a prominent lawyer, greatly interested in Sunday School and Y. M. C. A. work, and in the Prison Association), John Ira, Sarah Ann, Augustus C., and Frances M. Mrs. Warner joined the Congregational Church at Haddam by letter from the Westchester Church, May 5, 1821, and the three younger Warner children were baptized there.

Children of Andrew Ferdinando and Lucinthia (Cone) Warner

Selden Cone Warner, b. Nov. 7, 1818, in Haddam, Conn.; bapt. in Westchester, Conn., May 30, 1819; d. Nov. 24, 1871, in London, England, not married. He was connected for more than 35 years with the London line of packets, as captain of the Toronto, the Westminster, the Hendrick Hudson, the Margaret Evans, and the Plymouth Rock.

Andrew Ferdinando Warner, Jr., b. Dec. 26, 1820, in Haddam; d. July 26, 1857, in Cromwell, Conn., not married. He resided for some years with his uncle, Dr. Richard Warner. His health was so poor as to prevent his engaging actively in business and he took up the collection of historical records, with particular reference to the genealogy of his family. His notes on the family were brought together in 1878 and copied systematically in a large note book, which is now in the possession of Mr. Selden Waite Warner of Orange, N. J. This book was used in 1892 for the pamphlet on the Warner family which was published in Hartford. These records, while incomplete in many places, have been of invaluable assistance in the preparation of this volume and have been largely used as a foundation from which to start. Mr. Warner was a member of the New England Genealogical and Historical Society, which said of him (Register, 12: 186), "a gentleman much respected for his intelligence, enterprise and public spirit, qualities which led him to enter warmly into plans for the improvement, material, moral and intellectual."

Lucinthia Cone Warner, b. Mar. 6, 1823; d. May 26, 1824, in Haddam.

599 William Henry Warner, b. June 16, 1825; m. Anna Pamela Conger.

400 JOSEPH[7] WARNER, son of Selden[6] and Dorothy (Selden) Warner, born December 3,. 1792, in Hadlyme, Conn.; died there, June 13, 1861. He was a farmer in the Hadlyme Society of the town of Lyme. In 1851 he was a member of the State Legislature. He was a member of the Hadlyme Congregational Church and in 1832 he and his wife were members of the choir of that church which had a reputation in those days for the high character of its music.

Married November 8, 1829, **MARY ANN HOLMES,** born February 4, 1801, in Hadlyme, died there, April 24, 1900, daughter of Ozias and Betsey (Tully) Holmes of Hadlyme.

Children, born in the town of Lyme

Nancy Holmes Warner, b. Sept. 12, 1830; d. in Hadlyme, Oct. 17, 1904. She was a school teacher. Married in New York City, Mar. 1, 1866, John Elliott Ely, b. in Hamburg, Conn., May 3, 1830, d. there, Jan. 7, 1869, son of Similias Brockway and Mary Anne (Niles) Ely. Children, b. at Hamburg: i. Elliott Warner, b. June 21, 1867; resides in Hadlyme; m. Aug. 3, 1895, Adelaide B. Hall of Hadlyme; has children, Reginald E., b. July 11, 1896, m. Dec. 25, 1914, Ida Whitmore of Chester (and had a son, Roger N., b. in Chester, Nov. 7, 1916), Gertrude A., b. June 14, 1898, Harvey H., b. Oct. 2, 1902, d. July 7, 1903, Hazel M., b. Feb. 27, 1904, and Ethel D., b. Aug. 29, 1906. ii. Joseph Niles, b. June 5, 1869, resides in Hadlyme.

Elizabeth Ann Warner, b. Mar. 21, 1834; d. Apr. 6, 1906, in Glastonbury, Conn.; m. in Hadlyme, Sept. 7, 1868, Captain Enoch Howard. Children: i. Harry D., was drowned about 1911; m. Mamie ————, who resides in Niantic, Conn. (1916), with her children, Lawrence, aged 22, Maurice, aged 20, Melville, aged 18, Thelma, aged 17, and Marion, aged 14. ii. Ozias, d. at Niantic, about 1910; m. Mamie Darrow, who has remarried and lives in Montville, Conn. (1916), has two sons aged 15 and 10. iii. Mary W., m. George · Scott; resides in Hartford (1916); has sons, Howard, aged 14, and George, aged 5.

Joseph Selden Warner, b. Feb. 22, 1837; resides in Glastonbury, Conn.; m. Nov. 28, 1867 (East Haddam Congregational Church records), Louise E. Squires, b. about 1846. They have no children.

401 **DR. RICHARD[7] WARNER,** son of Selden[6] and Dorothy (Selden) Warner of Hadlyme, Conn., was born October 19, 1794. He entered Yale College in 1813, and was graduated "with a good reputation for scholarship" in 1817. In 1821, he received the degree of M.D. from Yale Medical College. For several years he practiced medicine in his native place and adjoining towns, removing in 1823 to East Haddam. In 1825, on the death of his brother Dr. Andrew Warner of Haddam, "he received an invitation signed by over one hundred citizens of that place to remove there and another in 1829 from Lyme, numerously signed," but he declined both. In 1831, however, he removed to Cromwell where he settled permanently and practiced until his death, September 29, 1853.

The following quotation from the Proceedings of the Connecticut Medical Society, May, 1854, by William B. Casey, one of the committee to nominate professors in the Medical Institute of Yale College, gives some insight into his life and interests:

"At college Dr. Warner was in the classics a fair scholar but the natural sciences, botany, geology, mineralogy, and conchology were his favorite pursuits and he devoted much time to them. . . . His power of observation was strong, his name is mentioned several times in Silliman's Scientific Publications as a discoverer of the localities of different minerals. . . . He was intensely interested in the early discovery of propagating fish and so confident was he of its· success that he made application to congress for the appointment of a committee to visit Europe to obtain such information as would be necessary to establish fish-breeding in this country."

In the Biographical Sketches of Eminent Members of the Middlesex County Medical Society of Fifty Years Ago, by

RICHARD WARNER HOUSE IN HADLYME

Rufus W. Mathewson, in the ·Proceedings of the Connecticut Medical Society, 1882, we find the following account of Dr. Warner:

"A good citizen he gave his time and effort to the advancement of the place in which he lived. . . . He held successively all the offices of the church society and the town. He was a prime mover in setting the town of Cromwell off from Middletown.   . He *selected the name of the new town,* the ·fine elms of which bear testimony to his interest in village improvement. . . . In the movement for an academy and a new church edifice he was persistently successful. With the anti-slavery and temperance movements he was early and warmly engaged. . . . In 1829, during his clerkship to the Middlesex County Medical Society he ordered the decanters from the table at the annual dinner . . . where on motion of Dr. Woodward it was resolved that the thanks of the society be presented for his compliment to their good sense."   ·

DR. RICHARD WARNER   MRS. MARY GAYLORD WARNER

SAMUEL G. WARNER   CHARLES C. WARNER

"Dr. Warner was a man of strong character and on that account had warm friends and bitter enemies. . . . He was born a quarter of a century too early for his own comfort and gained ridicule and the title of a visionary for pushing innovations which have since become established successes. That he practiced his profession acceptably and successfully is attested by the number of offices of trust and honor which he filled in his town and in the medical societies to which he belonged. He was often Fellow of the Middlesex County Society, at one time its president. At one time, he delivered the Annual Address to the Medical Institute of Yale College and at the time of his death was President of the Connecticut State Medical Society."

Dr. Richard Warner married (1) in Mansfield, Conn., Novem ber 6, 1826, **MARY MILLICENT GILBERT**, born in Mans field, September 27, 1803, died December 13, 1836, daughter of John and Cynthia (Hyde) Gilbert.

Dr. Warner married (2) in Middletown, July 17, 1844, **MARY GAYLORD**, born April 8, 1808, died in Virginia, June 21, 1887 daughter of Captain Samuel and Polly Pons (Starr) Gaylord. She was residing in Cromwell in 1860.

Children by first wife

600 *Richard Selden Warner,* b. Mar. 27, 1828; m. Emma Amelia Craw.
Mary Gilbert Warner, b. 1829; d. Dec. 26, 1829.

Children by second wife

601 *Samuel Gaylord Warner,* b. Sept. 12, 1848; m. Anna Porter Lozier.
602 *Charles Crocker Warner,* b. Aug. 6, 1850; m. Katherine Waring Hoskins.

402 **WILLIAM HENRY[7] WARNER**, son of Selden[6] and Dorothy (Selden) Warner, born February 18, 1797, in Hadlyme, Conn.; died at Mount Clemens, McComb Co., Mich., October 6, 1849. He was a farmer, was living in Hadlyme in 1832, but before 1839 removed to Michigan.

Married 1826, **SARAH CANFIELD**, born March 1, 1799, daughter of Joel and Sarah (Peters) Canfield of Chester.

Children

Elizabeth Canfield Warner, b. Nov. 12, 1828; d. July 19, 1895; resided in Hadlyme; m. there, Dec. 28, 1859, William E. Selden of Hadlyme. Child: Maria, resides in Hadlyme.
Sarah Marilla Warner, b. Feb. 9, 1831; d. Apr. 26, 1833, in Hadlyme.
William Henry Warner, b. Jan. 10, 1833; d. Aug. 6, 1833, in Hadlyme.
Sarah Frances Warner, b. Mar. 22, 1835; resided in Hadlyme; m. at Mt. Clemens, Mich., Nov. 29, 1864, Joseph William Hungerford, b. Sept. 21, 1829, in Hadlyme, d. in Westerly, R. I., Feb. 6, 1916, son of Joseph Ely and Nancy (Anderson) Hungerford and grandson of

Robert and Lovice[6] (Warner) Hungerford. See number 238. He was educated at Williston Seminary, after which he returned to Hadlyme and was extensively engaged in farming there. He served on the board of relief for several years and represented the town in the State Legislature in 1882. He was a committeeman of the Hadlyme Congregational Church for 12 years and a deacon after 1889. They had no children.

Harriet Marilla Warner, b. Mar. 29, 1837; d. Aug., 1839 (or 1838), at Mt. Clemens, Mich.

Mary Selden Warner, b. Sept. 17, 1839; resides at Mt. Clemens or Marquette, Mich.

Henry Elfred Warner, b. Jan. 1845; d. Nov. 6, 1891, at Mt. Clemens, Mich., not married.

403   MATTHEW GRISWOLD[7] WARNER, son of Selden[6] and Dorothy (Selden) Warner, born March 6, 1799, in Hadlyme, Conn.; died in Rochester, N. Y., Dec. 29, 1884. He joined the church in Westchester, Conn., in 1824. He was a merchant in Westchester and East Haddam, removed to Rochester, N. Y. He was always active in public affairs; in East Haddam was constable and collector of the school district, and after his removal to Rochester, became city treasurer in 1847; was defeated Jackson candidate for presidential elector in 1828.

Married in Colchester, Conn., November 30, 1825, **LUCRETIA HUBBARD LOOMIS,** of the Westchester Society of Colchester, born March 5, 1804 or 5, died May 4, 1876, daughter of David and Clarissa (Williams) Loomis.

Children, births of the first three recorded at East Haddam

Matthew Griswold Warner, b. Jan. (or June) 1, 1827; resided in Rochester, N. Y.; d. in Westchester, Conn., Mar. 4, 1880, not married.

Lucretia Loomis Warner, b. July 6, 1828; d. in Rochester, Oct. 25, 1847.

Emeline Eliza Warner, b. June 4, 1830; d. in East Haddam, Sept. 16, 1831, buried in River View Cemetery, East Haddam.

Edwin Cass Warner, b. Nov. 27, 1831; d. in Rochester, May 5, 1853, not married.

Ellen Champion Warner, b. Jan. 3, 1834; d. Feb. 23, 1847.

Mary Eliza Warner, b. June 16, 1835; d. Jan. 27, 1843.

Clarissa Jane Warner, b. 1837 or 1838; d. 1875; m. Horton Sabin; resided in Rochester.

Mary Amelia Warner, b. 1842; d. Oct. 5, 1875.

404   JONATHAN TRUMBULL[7] WARNER, son of Selden[6] and Dorothy (Selden) Warner, born in Hadlyme, Conn., November 20, 1807; died in Los Angeles, Cal., April 11, 1895.

He was better known in later life as Colonel JUAN JOSE
WARNER, a name which he adopted during his residence
among Spanish-speaking people who had no equivalent in their
language for Jonathan or Trumbull. By his physician's advice
in 1830 he decided to seek a milder climate and went west,
reaching St. Louis in November. While he was in that town,
the arrival of a wagon train of furs from the Yellowstone country caused quite a sensation and gave an impetus to fur trapping
and trading. The following spring he joined an expedition to
Santa Fe, consisting of 85 men and 23 wagons, under the employ
of the famous hunter and trapper, Captain Jedediah S. Smith,
who was killed by the Indians on this expedition. He reached
Santa Fe, July 4, 1831. In September he left for California, in
the employ of Jackson, Sublette and Ewing Young, who, with a
party of eleven men, were going there to buy mules for the
St. Louis market. They had with them five pack mules laden
with Mexican silver dollars, and reached Los Angeles, December 5, 1831. Here Mr. Warner remained with one other man,
while the others went on to make their purchases of mules.
The speculation proved a failure. Jackson returned in March
with 500 horses and only 100 mules. Mr. Warner assisted in
driving the stock to the Colorado River where they experienced
considerable difficulty and no little loss in forcing the stock to
swim across the high water.

With three of the party Mr. Warner returned to Los Angeles,
and, during 1832-33, with a party of fourteen under Young, he
trapped and hunted in northern California and Oregon. In 1834
he settled in Los Angeles and engaged in merchandise. In
1840-1 he visited the Atlantic states and delivered a lecture at
Rochester, N. Y., in which he urged the building of a railroad
to the Pacific, the first time the project was presented to the
public. He spoke on the same topic at other places, during this
visit.

In 1843 he moved to San Diego, on what has since been
known as Warner's ranch, a large and valuable tract of some
26,600 acres, devoted almost exclusively to sheep and cattle
raising, with a yearly wool-clip larger than that of any other
single section of the county. At the eastern end of the valley
is the pass known as Warner's Pass, leading through the mountains to the Colorado desert. The ranch was the scene of an
exciting Indian raid in 1851. Mr. Warner had been warned
that the Calmilla Indians from nearby villages were planning
the attack, and, although discrediting the report, took the pre-

27

caution to send his family under safe escort to San Diego. Early the second morning after their departure he was awakened by cries of Indians who had surrounded the house. As was customary at the Mexican ranchos, several horses were standing near, saddled and ready for instant mounting, and loaded weapons were in profusion. As Colonel Warner stepped to the door to look for his horses, he was greeted bv a shower of arrows from some 200 Indians; all of his horses were gone save one, and that was just being untethered by an Indian. With three skilful shots the marauder and two of his companions were killed. During the temporary panic that ensued and in which the Indians withdrew to some outbuildings, Colonel Warner escaped with the single horse, carrying with him a mulatto boy, servant of an army officer at San Diego, a helpless cripple from rheumatism who had been sent to the ranch to try the beneficial waters of a spring there. With this boy he reached a friendly village of Indians, gathered a few of his own herdsmen and went back to the rancho. The party was so outnumbered by the Indians that the men fled precipitately and Colonel Warner was obliged to go back to San Diego, and abandon to the Indians the stock of merchandise, which, as was customary, was kept at large ranches. The family later returned under military escort from San Diego and were unmolested as long as they made their home there, until 1857.

After the American occupancy of California, Colonel Warner took an active part in politics and public affairs. He was Senator from San Diego County, 1851-2. From March, 1858, to June, 1860, he published the "Los Angeles Southern Vineyard." In 1860, he was elected to the Assembly from Los Angeles. In 1876 he was appointed U. S. register in bankruptcy for the southern district, an office he held until his eyes failed him. He was joint author of the "Centennial Historical Sketch of Los Angeles County," treating the part from 1771 to 1847. In 1883 he was the first president of the newly organized Historical Society of Southern California.

His home for many years was in Los Angeles, after 1887 in the university district southwest of the city, with his daughter and grandchildren.

Colonel Warner married at the Mission of San Luis Key, February, 1837, ANITA GALE, who died April 22, 1859. She was the daughter of William A. Gale of Boston and had been brought to California by her father when she was five years old. Until her marriage she lived in the home of Mrs. Eustaquia Pico, mother of Don Pio Pico, last Spanish governor of California, as daughter and sister. Close relations between the two families were maintained and in his later years Don Pio Pico was befriended by Colonel Warner who maintained him in a house adjacent to his own.

Much interesting information about Colonel Warner is found in the "Historical and biographical record of Los Angeles and vicinity," and "Illustrated history of Southern California."

Children

William Gale Warner, b. Feb. 20, 1838; d. Mar. 19, 1838, in Los Angeles.

Mary Ann or *Maria Anita Warner,* b. Nov. 19, 1839, in Los Angeles. At the age of 30 she was placed in the Stockton Asylum for the Insane.

William Henry Warner, b. 1842; d. Apr., 1847, in Los Angeles.

Elizabeth Mary Warner, b. 1844; d. in Los Angeles.

Andrew Ferdinando Warner, b. 1846, on the Warner Ranch, San Diego Co.; d. in Los Angeles, 1880; m. Chona Alaniz. Child: Artemiza.

Isabella Warner, b. 1848, on the Warner Ranch; d. 1873; m. in Los Angeles, Jesus Cruz. Child: Jane Artemiza, m. in 1889, S. Mendoza and died Apr. 27, 1891, no children.

Juan Bautiste Warner, b. 1851, on the Warner Ranch; m. in San Francisco, Annie Cross. Children: i. John Francis, b. 1877. ii. May Belle, b. 1878. iii. Oscar, b. 1880.

Amanda Conception Warner, b. Sept. 13, 1855; d. in Los Angeles, Cal., Dec. 4, 1908; m. in 1874, Manuel Rubio. Children: i. Albert, b. Aug. 5, 1875. ii. Jane D., b. Aug. 17, 1877. iii. Reginald, b. July 7, 1879. iv. Annie Mabel, b. Nov. 2, 1881. v. Viola Margaret, b. Aug. 13, 1884.

405   J O H N ⁷ W A R N E R, son of Phineas⁶ and Eunice (Church) Warner, born in Saybrook (Chester), Conn.; resided in Chester and died there, May 25, 1850, aged 77. He was recorded in the 1800 Census in Saybrook, aged over 26, wife under 26, a boy between 10 and 16, and a boy and a girl under 10. A record of this family is given in the Church Genealogy.

Married (1) October 3, 1797, **MEHITABEL CLARK** of Chester, born July 14, 1777; died December 1, 1826. She is mentioned in the distribution of the estate of Jared Clark of Saybrook in 1804.

Married (2) October 8, 1827, recorded in East Haddam, **LUCY COMSTOCK.**

Children, probably all born in Chester

Sarah Ward Warner, b. Apr. 5, 1798; m. Ely⁷ Warner. See number
397.

John Phineas Warner, b. Oct. 29, 1799; d. in Chester, July 4, 1819·
Hannah Warner, b. May 18, 1802; d. 1857; resided in Colchester; m.
Aug. 25, 1824, Benjamin Adams. Children: i. Laura Jane, b. Aug.
27, 1826. ii. Mehitabel, b. Jan. 2, 1830. iii. Benjamin, b. July 9,
1834. iv. Mary Williams, b. Jan. 23, 1840.

Jared Clark Warner, b. Dec. 9, 1804; d. in Detroit, Mich., July 18,
1887; m. Oct. 1, 1836, Sarah Finney, b. in Delaware, N. Y.; May 15,
1815, d. after 1887, daughter of Thomas and Harriet (Beatty)
Finney. A daughter married H. H. James. Mr. Warner went to
Detroit in 1831 and was in the hotel business until 1856, when he
retired and was a dealer in real estate with extensive investments.
He was proprietor of the old Eagle Hotel on Woodbridge Street,
in 1837 of the Franklin House on the corner of Bates and Larned
Streets, and later of the Yankee Boarding House. In 1843 he
created quite a stir by his decision to have no bar in his hotel, as
a bar was at that time considered an indispensable adjunct to a hotel.
He was Constable in 1837; member of the Board of Education from
1856 to 1861; member of the Board of Review from 1866 to 1872;
was one of the earliest members of the Baptist Church of Detroit.
He was always affable and courteous, highly esteemed and was
known as "Uncle Warner" by his associates.

Ariadna Warner, b. Dec. 15, 1806; d. in Texas in 1863. She was one
of the scholars at the organization of the Chester Congregational
Sunday School in 1819. Married Aug., 1832, Samuel Arnold.

Mehitabel Warner, b. Nov. 7, 1808; d. in Chester, Oct. 27, 1826, aged
18 (Haddam Church Record).

Rhoda Ann Warner, b. July 20, 1811; d. in Texas, 1876, where she
had resided. She was one of the scholars at the organization of
the Sunday School in the Chester Congregational Church in 1819.
Married Mar. 28, 1835, Epaphras J. Arnold, M.D., both of Haddam
(Haddam Church record). Children: i. Frances Annie, b. Feb. 20,
1840. ii. Evelyn Pratt, b. Jan. 8, 1842. iii. Epaphras, Jr., and Louise
(twins), b. Oct. 13, 1844.

Harriett L. Warner, b. July 6, 1815; d. Sept. 18, 1834, in Chester.
603 *Gustavus A. Warner*, b. Aug. 26, 1817; m. Clarissa Eliza Towall.

Mary Rebecca Warner, b. Nov. 12, 1819; d. in Montgomery, Texas,
in 1898; m. June 6, 1843, Robert B. Martin. Children: i. Mary
Eugene, b. Feb. 15, 1845. ii. Clara Ann, b. July 20, 1846. iii. John
Samuel, b. Oct. 28, 1848. iv. Harriet Warner, b. Apr. 11, 1851.
v. Frances Eva, b. Apr. 24, 1853; d. 1901. vi. Robert Ball, b. July
3, 1855. vii. Jared Clark, b. Feb. 20, 1858. viii. Clarence E., b. Nov.
12, 1861; d. 1881.

406 PHINEAS⁷ WARNER, JR., son of Phineas⁶ and Eunice
(Church) Warner, born in Saybrook (Chester), Conn., 1777;
died in 1824, in Montrose, Pa. In 1809 he removed with his
own family and his brothers Samuel and Timothy and their
families to Susquehanna County, Pennsylvania, traveling with

their ox-teams, droves of cattle and household goods, through the primeval wilderness. The first night in their new neighborhood was spent at the hospitable home of Elder Davis Dimock, a famous Baptist preacher, in Bridgewater township. The next day the brothers set to work to clear up farms adjacent to the Dimock farm. These are still in the possession of their descendants. Phineas Warner's home was on what is called the North Road, Montrose. He was a member of the Congregational-Presbyterian Church which was established at the house of Jehiel Warner in Rush township, Susquehanna County, December 12, 1811. His name occurs on an early tax list of Bridgewater, 1823.

Married in Chester, Conn., October 7 (or 17, Conn. marriage records), 1799, **LYDIA CLARKE** of Chester, who died 1840, aged 56, buried in Montrose Cemetery. She received property at the distribution of the estate of Jared Clarke of Saybrook in 1804.

Children, first four born in Connecticut, others in Bridgewater, Pa.

Jared C. Warner, went to Pennsylvania with his father and was on the tax list of Bridgewater in 1823.

604 *Davis Dimock Warner,* b. Feb. 1, 1802; m. (1) Mary Ann Raynsford, (2) Alzina (Trowbridge) Smith.

605 *Nelson Clarke Warner,* b. 1804; m. Eliza D. Baldwin.

606 *Sidney Haswell Warner,* b. Jan. 26, 1806; m. (1) Hannah Loomis, (2) Cornelia Machette.

Ann Warner, resided in Red Wing, Minn., in 1894; m. Dr. Ezra Sidney Park, who removed with his family to Minnesota about 1860. Children: i. Hiram Asa, b. in Montrose, Pa., 1840; m. Theodosia" Warner, see number 693. ii. Lorana, m. Silas B. Foote, a manufacturer and dealer in shoes in St. Paul for many years, and resided at Red Wing. iii. Sydney. iv. Betty. v. Jessie.

Elizabeth M. Warner, resided in Binghamton, N. Y., about 1894; died; m. —— Angell.

John P. Warner, resided in Scranton, Pa., about 1894; died.

407 **D A V I D** [7] **W A R N E R ,** son of Phineas[6] and Eunice (Church) Warner, born April 4, 1780, in Chester, Conn.; resided there and died August 12, 1864, aged 84. The Census of 1800 records him with his wife and son.

Married in East Haddam, Conn., September 10, 1799, **MARY CONE**, born 1779; died January 7, 1851.

Children

Orison C. Warner, b. 1800; resided in New Haven, Conn., and died there.

607 Roxana Warner, b. Oct. 17, 1802; m. Ely Dickinson.
    Julia Warner, resided in Chester.
    Clarissa Warner, d. in Chester, Jan. 30, 1828, aged 21.
608 Lucy Webb Warner, b. Apr. 10, 1809; m. John Tracy.
609 Azubah Warner, b. Apr. 27, 1816; m. Gideon Parker.

408 TIMOTHY[7] WARNER, son of Phineas[6] and Eunice
(Church) Warner, born in Chester, Conn., April 1, 1782; died
January 7, 1859, in Bridgewater, Susquehanna Co., Pa. He
removed with his family to Pennsylvania in 1809, and was living
in Dundaff about 1817. He was a farmer and his home was a
mile and a half from Montrose.
Married **LYDIA PLATTS** of Westbrook, Conn., born July
2, 1789; died March 26, 1860.

Children

610 Albert Oscar Warner, b. in Chester, Conn., Oct. 24, 1806; m. (1)
    Mary Ann Austin, (2) Mary Buscort Bogart.
611 Eliada Blakeslee Warner, b. May 4, 1808; m. Fidelia Luce.
    David Ely Warner, b. Sept. 6, 1809; d. Mar. 2, 1872, in Wisconsin;
    m. Nancy ————, who died May 2, 1872. No children.
    William Wilson Warner, b. Aug. 1, 1811; d. Jan. 25, 1853; was killed
    by a tree falling on him in the woods at Bridgewater, Pa. He was
    not married and lived at home with his father.
    Lerinda Marinda Warner, b. Mar. 30, 1813; d. in Monticello, N. Y.;
    m. George Cantrell of Monticello. Children: i. David. ii. Mary, m.
    Jared Barrett of New Milford, Pa. iii. Edward. iv. Minerva, m.
    Morris Allen of Monticello. v. Wealthy, m. ———— Bishop of New
    Milford, Pa.
    Juliaette Matilda Warner, b. Aug. 16, 1814; d. May 30, 1875, in Mont-
    rose, Pa.; m. Levi Marsh, from whom she separated long before
    she died. Children: Samantha; Avaline.
612 Elisha Platts Warner, b. Aug. 7, 1816; m. Margaret Bogard.
    John Ward Warner, b. Oct. 10, 1818; d. Mar. 13, 1873, near Owego,
    N. Y.; m. Jane Tupper from Le Raysville, Pa. No children.
    Lydia Maria Warner, b. Mar. 22, 1820; d. in Jackson, Pa.; m. Louis
    Benson of Jackson. Children: i. Minerva. ii. William. iii. Adelia.
    iv. George, resides in Binghamton, N. Y. v. Warner. vi. Frederick.
    Minerva Amelia Warner, b. Aug. 18, 1822; d. Nov. 19, 1904 or 1909,
    at Lake View, Pa.; m. 1861, Orren Barrett, who died Sept. 4, 1890.
    Child: John W., b. Aug. 30, 1866; d. Apr. 25, 1909, at Lake View;
    m. Sept. 21, 1887, Jennie B. Collum, b. May 30, 1868, daughter of
    William H. Collum of Smiley. She resides at Lake View and has
    a son, George H., b. Feb. 17, 1889, resides in Scranton, m. Feb. 19,
    1912, Ethel H. Steele, b. May 19, 1890, daughter of John H. Steele
    of Taylor, Pa., and has a child, Phyllis S., b. June 2, 1913.
613 George Dickinson Warner, b. Oct. 3, 1824; m. Octavia Brewster.
    Samuel Warner, b. Jan. 18, 1827; d. Jan. 21, 1827.
614 Ansel Lockman Warner, b. Feb. 28, 1828; m. Mary Jane Cook.

409 SAMUEL⁷ WARNER, son of Phineas⁶ and Eunice (Church) Warner, born in Saybrook (Chester), Conn., about 1784; died September, 1848, in Montrose, Pa. He went with his family to Susquehanna County, Pa., about 1809; was on the tax list of Bridgewater township, 1823. He was an earnest temperance advocate and an anti-slavery supporter. He was a trustee of the Susquehanna County Academy in 1828.

Married (1) **WEALTHY CLARK,** born in Connecticut; died in Montrose, Pa.

Married (2) in Saybrook, Conn., November 4, 1821, **PHOEBE BROOKS,** born in Saybrook, daughter of Simeon and Lois (Church) Brooks of Chester; died in Montrose, Pa., September, 1866.

Children of Samuel and Wealthy (Clark) Warner, first five born in Connecticut, others in Pennsylvania

615   *Wealthy Warner,* m. Simeon Tyler.
    Eunice Warner, m. ———— Payne, and had a daughter, Augusta, who married and died, leaving no children.
    Mary Warner, d. in Montrose; m. Hanzy Patrick. Child: Albert.
    Phineas Warner, d. in a hospital in New York City; m. ————.
      Children: Hetty; William; Augusta; Samuel.
    De Witt Clinton Warner, moved to Chicago; m. ———— Helm.
    Uberto O. Warner (twin), b. Dec. 26, 1815, in Montrose, Pa., went to California in 1849; married.
616   *Gilbert Warner* (twin), b. Dec. 26, 1815; m. Therese Park French.

Child of Samuel and Phoebe (Brooks) Warner

Samuel Warner, Jr., b. in Montrose; d. in Susquehanna Co., Pa.; m. Nancy ————. Children: i. Wallace, d. not married. ii. Harriet, m. Paul Miller and d. leaving no children. iii. Coralyn. iv. Julius, was killed at Petersburg, Va., 1864, not married. v. (Son.)

410 ANDREW⁷ WARNER, JR., son of Andrew⁶ and Rachel (Crocker) Warner, born January 23, 1791, probably in Vernon, Oneida Co., N. Y.; died January 19, 1842, at Sandy Creek, Oswego Co., N. Y. He resided in Vernon until about 1836 when he removed to Sandy Creek, his home for the remainder of his life. His name is found on deeds of 1829 and later, and he was mentioned in his father's will.

Married January 1, 1817, **ELIZABETH CLARK YOUNG,** who died at Sandy Creek in 1865, daughter of Israel and Hannah (Beadle) Young.

Children

Angeline L. Warner, m. Anson Maltby Duncan. Children: i. Eunice Rebecca (called Nina), b. in Beloit, Wis., 1851; d. in New York

City, Oct. 14, 1916, buried in Arlington, N. J.; m. (1) in Rockport, Mo., 1874, her cousin, Randolph Ranney, b. July 30, 1847, d. Feb. 10, 1889, son of Daniel Wells and Rachel Lavina (Warner) Ranney, see number 620; m. (2) Aug. 24, 1891, Cecil Edward D'Averon, b. in San Francisco, Oct. 2, 1859, of a French father and English mother, a civil engineer in Los Angeles, in Johannesburg, South Africa, after 1894, then in Tananarive, Madagascar, returning to New York in 1915, died in Arlington, N. J., Dec. 22, 1915. ii. Ellen Byron, d. 1892; m. 1879, Jesse Manley of Elgin, Ill. iii. Henry. iv. Rosamond (?). v. Mary, d. about 1872, not married. There were no grandchildren in this family.

617　*Andrew Sylvester Warner*, b. Jan. 12, 1819; m. (1) Mary Elizabeth Greene, (2) Chloe Monroe.

618　*Hannah Maria Warner*, b. Sept. 18, 1820; m. Sylvanus Convers Huntington.

619　*Warren William Warner*, b. Nov. 9, 1824; m. Anna Gates Lewis.
　　Elizabeth Warner, d. young.

620　*Rachel Lavina Warner*, b. 1825; m. Daniel Wells Ranney.
　　Jane Warner, d. young.
　　Jennie E. Warner, m. Dr. James Tillapaugh.
　　Mary Ann Warner, d. not married.
　　Ellen Warner, d. not married.
　　Adelaide Adersa Warner, resided at Pulaski, N. Y., for several years, then removed to Alhambra, Los Angeles Co., Cal., where she now resides; m. Newton M. Thompson of Sandy Creek, N. Y. Children: i. Newton ·Warner, is in the abstract of title business at Los Angeles. ii. Ada Belle, d. several years ago, married but had no children.

411　LAURA CROCKER[7] WARNER, daughter of Andrew[6] and Rachel (Crocker) Warner, born August 18, 1796; died January 24, 1868.

Married (1) LYMAN BALDWIN CAMPBELL, born November 4, 1790; died March 13, 1843.

Married (2) REUBEN SCRIPTURE of Sandy Creek. He was a widower with seven sons and two daughters, while she had two sons and seven daughters.

Children, born at Sandy Creek, N. Y.

Franklin Lyman Campbell, b. June 19, 1818; d.; m. Emily Trumbull. Child: Lyman, d. in childhood. After the death of Mr. Campbell's sister Rosina, they took her youngest child, Arthur Plaistead of Sandy Creek.

Laura Lavina Campbell, b. Oct. 6, 1819; d. Feb. 27, 1881; m. Thomas Cail. No children. They adopted Jennie Rickerson.

James Campbell, d. aged 14 months.

James Warner Campbell, b. at Kirkland, Oneida Co., N. Y., May 23, 1822; d. June 23, 1894; m. Dec. 31, 1849, Rosette Trumbull. No children. They adopted children, Frank and Anna.

Cornelia Rosette Campbell, b. Mar. 5, 1824; d. Apr. 4, 1896; m. Melvin Trumbull. Children: i. Henry, m. and has a daughter who m.

William H. Taylor of Pulaski, N. Y. ii. Azelia, m. ——— Cooper of Pulaski.

Rachael Ann Campbell, b. Feb. 20, 1826; d. Sept. 17, 1894; m. Nathan Averill. Child: William E., resides in Pulaski.

Marcia Isabel Campbell, b. Nov. 10, 1827; d. Mar. 8, 1894, in Pulaski; m. May 22, 1845, Charles Rollin Maltby, b. Feb. 24, 1824, d. in Richland, N. Y., Sept. 18, 1903. Children, born in Richland: i. Alta Jane, b. May 13, 1846; m. in Pulaski, Oct. 12, 1882, William H. Austin, had one child, Ruth Maltby, b. in Pulaski, Aug. 23, 1883, m. in Pulaski, June 24, 1903, Frank Earle McChesney, b. in Scriba, N. Y., Sept. 2, 1881 (has five children, first four b. in Avon, Hartford Co., Conn., Catherine Elsie, b. Aug. 27, 1904, Frances Edith, b. Aug. 29, 1905, Lillian Isabel, b. Jan. 2, 1909, William Frank, b. Jan. 8, 1910, and Lois Natalie, b. in Syracuse, N. Y., Jan. 30, 1916). ii. Ellen Lovina, b. Sept. 12, 1847; m. Oct. 1, 1873, Sidney T. Doane, b. Dec. 9, 1847, d. Dec. 19, 1900. iii. Edna Lorette, b. Jan. 8, 1850; d. in Eldora, Iowa, Dec. 22, 1909; m. at Sandy Creek, N. Y., Mar. 14, 1870, Eugene J. Upton, of Hardin County, Iowa, b. June 23, 1847. iv. Charles Rollin, Jr., b. Feb. 11, 1854; d. in Richland, N. Y., Feb. 22, 1862. v. Kate Shepherd, b. Nov. 17, 1861; m. July 16, 1889, Charles D. Edwards, b. in England, Jan. 3, 1863. vi. Mary Campbell, b. Nov. 4, 1864; m. Sept., 1889, Frank B. Rickard of Pulaski, b. Mar. 5, 1854.

Mary Elenora Campbell, b. Nov. 11, 1830; d. Aug. 28, 1866; m. Hiram Trumbull. Children: i. Phineas. ii. Frank. iii. and iv. Herbert and Henry, twins. v. and vi. Twins, stillborn. vii. (Daughter) who m. Henry L. Clark of Pulaski.

Rosina Lorette Campbell, b. Jan. 18, 1833; d. Mar. 13, 1871; m. Ford Plaistead. Children: i. Son, d. in infancy. ii. Ella Carol. iii. Clarence. iv. Jennie. v. Arthur, resides at Sandy Creek, N. Y.

Ellen Luzette Campbell, b. July 14, 1836; d. Apr. 25, 1875, not married.

412 ISRAEL S.[7] WARNER, son of Eleazer[6], Jr., and Irinda (Skiff) Warner, born May 13, 1799, in the town of Kirkland, Oneida County, N. Y., previously called Paris; died in Grundy Centre, Iowa. He was a farmer.

Married near Clinton, N. Y., December 8, 1828, **SAMANTHA BALLOU,** born June 27, 1806, in Fenner, Madison County, N. Y., daughter of Silas and Phoebe (Pray) Ballou.

Children, born in the town of Kirkland, Oneida County, N. Y.

Emogene Warner, b. Dec. 18, 1829; resides in Oriskany Falls, N. Y.; m. Elam Griggs, Children: i. Anna J., b. 1856, resides in Oriskany. ii. Katherine W., b. 1862, is a teacher in New York City and resides in Yonkers. iii. Emma J., b. Aug. 30, 1872; m. Charles William Carey; see number 622.

621 *Charlotte D. Warner,* b. Aug. 2, 1831; m. Norman Guito Snow.

Lavina S. Warner, b. Jan. 16, 1833; d. 1883; m. Charles Bragdon of Pulaski, N. Y. Children: i. Warner, b. about 1858, was drowned about Sept., 1863. ii. Bele, b. June 16, 1862.

George W. Warner, b. 1834; resides in Milwaukee, Ore.; m. in Clinton, N. Y., Cornelia Parmalee. Children: i. Rosalie, b. 1861. ii. Nellie. iii. Anna. iv. Katie. v. Fred. vi. Louis.
622 *Celestia Alvira Warner,* b. Aug. 1, 1845; m. Abram F. Carey.

413 CHLOE[7] **WARNER,** daughter of Eleazer[6], Jr., and Irinda (Skiff) Warner, born in Kirkland, Oneida Co., N. Y., December 3, 1803; died in West Leyden, N. Y., August 12, 1876. Married in the part of Paris now known as Kirkland, N. Y., May 10, 1827, **RICHARDSON THURMAN HOUGH,** born in Warrensburg, N. Y., July 15, 1806; died in West Leyden, August 26, 1871. He was the son of William Hough, Jr., who was born in Saybrook, Conn., April 24, 1767, died in West Leyden, August 29, 1854, and his wife, Eunice Skiff, daughter of John Skiff. She was born in Massachusetts, September 10, 1772, and died in New York State, May 25, 1845.

Children, first five born in the part of Boonville now called Ava; others, in West Leyden, N. Y.

Myron Beach (or *Beecker*) *Hough,* b. July 20, 1829; d. in Washington, D. C., Sept. 27, 1884, not married.
Delia Hough, b. Jan. 12, 1831; d. Jan. 19, 1889, in Cedar Falls, Iowa; m. Sept. 24, 1850, Selden Dewey, son of Abraham Dewey, b. Oct. 7, 1824, at West Leyden, N. Y., d. Dec. 29, 1915, at Ruthven, Iowa. Children, born at Lee, N. Y.: i. Charlotte Helen, b. Aug. 1, 1851; m. Jan. 31, 1883, Cyrus J. Tripp, b. at Chestertown, N. Y., May 7, 1848; had a daughter, Eva Dimmis, b. at Ruthven, Sept. 12, 1889, who m. July 3, 1911, Guy W. Monsell, b. in Wisconsin, July 20, 1885 (they have two children, b. in Ruthven, Marland Winfield, b. Mar. 15, 1913, and Ramona Charlotte, b. Sept. 10, 1914). ii. Myron Hough, b. July 17, 1854; m. Sept. 3, 1890, Isadore A. McClure, b. in Canada, Nov. 12, 1866. iii. Edwin Abram, b. Aug. 8, 1857; m. Oct. 20, 1892, Flora M. Morling, b. at Boonville, N. Y., Jan. 21, 1868; had children, b. at Boonville, Ray Morling, b. June 19, 1894, and Halsey Edwin, b. Dec. 7, 1895.
Boardman Sylvester Hough, b. Dec. 12, 1832; d. in Los Angeles, Cal., Mar. 7, 1918, not married.
Mary Sophila Hough, b. June 18, 1836; d. in West Leyden, Feb. 25, 1842.
Henry Hennessey Hough, b. Oct. 28, 1838; m. at Creek Center, N. Y., Jan. 1, 1876, Mary E. Tripp. Child: Ella Chloe, b. May 15, 1878, in Corinth, N. Y.; m. in Emmetsburg, Iowa, Oct. 30, 1907, Frederick Charles Aldinger (has a son, John Hough, b. in Lansing, Mich., July 18, 1912).
Helen Marie Hough, b. in West Leyden, N. Y., Sept. 16, 1841; resides in Washington, D. C., where she is a clerk in the Geological Survey.
Charles Hough, b. Mar., 1843; d. Mar. 31, 1843.
William Washington Hough, b. Sept. 14, 1845; m. in West Leyden, Feb. 2, 1875, Nancy M. Douglass, daughter of Thomas P. Douglass.

Children, b. in Boonville: i. Clinton Wallace, b. July 26, 1877; resides in London, England; m. Feb. 28, 1901, Cora Belle Shattuck. ii. William Douglass, b. Mar. 16, 1879, resides in Boonville; m. Aug. 2, 1905, Cora Belle Mitchell. iii. John Homer, b. Feb. 26, 1890; resides in Alhambra, Cal.; m. Sept. 27, 1913, Margaret H. Cummings, b. May 6, 1893.

414 PHILIP KIRTLAND[7] WARNER, son of Philip[6] and Sarah (Woods) Warner, born April 18, 1791; died in Norwich, N. Y., May 21, 1885, aged 94 years. He resided early in Cambridge, Washington Co., N. Y., then removed to Norwich, where he was a farmer.

Married May 20, 1813, LOVINA ACKLEY of Cambridge, N. Y., born June 29, 1794; died in Norwich, July 12, 1889, aged 96.

One of the descendants estimates that there are about one hundred and fifty or sixty of this line living in 1917.

Children

Jonathan Wood Warner, was a machinist in Norwich, N. Y., where he died May 17, 1898; m. Mar. 13, 1838, Lucy Cady, who died in Norwich before 1898 and was buried in Mount Hope Cemetery. Children: i. Sarah Jane, b. Jan. 8, 1840; d. Feb. 22, 1898; m. Charles[6] Warner, son of Abner Warren[7] and Freelove (Goodsell) Warner; see number 625. ii. Clarissa Ellen, resided in Norwich; died in 1914, aged 72, not married. iii. Ernestine, resided in Norwich; m. Willington Monroe, and had a son Jonathan.

623   Sarah Warner, b. Nov. 26, 1815; m. Reuben Burlingame.

624   Lovina Warner, b. Feb. 4, 1820; m. Alvah Snow.

Oren Warner, b. Oct. 27, 1824; d. Dec. 18, 1873. Clerk and musician. For a number of years he was in poor health and resided in Norwich with his parents. Married Mary Johnson, who died in Norwich, 1904, daughter of Homer and Roxana (Skinner) Johnson. No children.

415 SARAH[7] WARNER, daughter of Philip[6] and Sarah (Woods) Warner, born March 23, 1792; died April 8, 1833. She removed from Cambridge, N. Y., to Owego, N. Y., in 1824.

Married January 11, 1811, ABIJAH PRATT, who died July 3, 1861, aged 71. Both he and his wife are buried in Owego near their home.

Children

Mary Watrous Pratt, b. in Cambridge, Feb. 16, 1817; d. Sept. 16, 1892; m. June 18, 1838, Nelson Brown Hale of Norwich, N. Y., who died June 16, 1877, aged 70. Both are buried in Norwich. Children: i. Charles Nelson, b. Oct. 4, 1841; m. (1) Harriet Davis of Chicago, Ill., who d. May 14, 1874; m. (2) June 20, 1876, Mary Sher-

wood of Greene, N. Y., resides in Chicago. ii. Julia Frances, b.
July 2, 1844; m. Oct. 16, 1866, Eugene Eastman, resides in Syracuse, N. Y. iii. Ellen Augusta, b. July 6, 1847; m. Sept. 10, 1868,
William Breese of West Burlington, N. Y., resides in Norwich,
N. Y., where he is head of a large furniture and undertaking business. iv. Mary Eliza, b. Aug. 27, 1849; d. Jan. 5, 1886; m. Feb.
14, 1877, Charles Barnard of Chicago, who d. 1915; had two sons,
Charles Hale, who lives in Montreal, Canada, and Henry, who was
drowned in Morro Bay, Cal., July 10, 1915. v. Edwin Pratt, b. Aug.
29, 1853; d. Apr. 16, 1882, not married. vi. Samuel Sidney, b. Jan.
13, 1857; m. June 8, 1898, Annie Anison of Oxford, N. Y.
Martha Pratt, b. in Cambridge, Nov. 18, 1819; d. June 8, 1886; m. May
30, 1838, Sidney Calkins, who d. Dec. 6, 1873. Both are buried in
Missouri. Children: i. Sarah, b. John Maloney. ii. George, m. and
d. in 1862. iii. Mary, d. 1912; m. Charles Perry of Binghamton. iv.
Sidney, resides in Memphis; m. Henrietta ———. v. Frances
Rebecca, d. 1900; m. Joseph Dalrymple of Indiana, Ill.

Mr. and Mrs. Breese (above) had two children: i. Annie Augusta,
b. July 17, 1871; resides in Seneca Falls, N. Y.; m. June 7, 1893, Byron
H. Delevan of Guilford, N. Y., and has three children, Nathan Hale,
b. June 10, 1894, Nelson Breese, b. Mar. 26, 1897, and William Henry,
b. Sept. 26, 1900. ii. Harriet Davis, b. Apr. 15, 1874; resides in Norwich; m. Feb. 20, 1900, Harry B. Smith of Norwich; has three children, Harry Breese, b. May 1, 1903, Anna Augusta, b. July 6, 1906, and
Albert Benjamin, b. May 30, 1911.

416 PRUDENCE⁷ WARNER, daughter of Philip⁶ and
Sarah (Woods) Warner, born about 1794; died in Cambridge,
N. Y., 1882, aged 88.
Married HIRAM ACKLEY. Both are buried in Cambridge.

Children

Julia Ackley, m. ——— Parker.
Maria Ackley, m. ——— Deane.
Elizabeth Ackley, m. ——— Conkey.
Phebe Ackley, resided in Norwich, N. Y.; m. Van Buren Cram.
Children: i. George, m. Jennie Tanner. ii. Kittie, m. Ralph Gladding.
William Ackley.
Edwin C. Ackley, b. in Cambridge, June 14, 1828; d. there, Jan. 10, 1892.
He was a moulder and resided in Cambridge; m. in Camden, N. Y.,
Sept. 23, 1857, Susan M. West, b. Oct. 1, 1829, in Salem, N. Y.,
daughter of Aaron and Mary (Sharp) West. Child: Nettie M., b.
Jan. 6, 1867, in Cambridge.
Charlotte Ackley.
Charles Ackley, m. Susan ———.
Andrew Ackley.

417 ABNER WARREN⁷ WARNER, son of Philip⁶ and
Sarah (Woods) Warner, died in the town of North Norwich,

N. Y., April 20, 1872. He joined the First United Presbyterian Church of Cambridge, N. Y., in 1816, and in 1819, took his church letter to the Congregational Church of Norwich, N. Y. He was in the carriage business in Norwich to which his son Charles succeeded. He was president of the village in 1844 and again in 1854.

Married **FREELOVE GOODSELL** of Cambridge, who joined the Congregational Church of Norwich by letter in 1817.

Children

Clark Warner, was baptized in Norwich about 1818; d. young.

625 *Charles Warner*, b. July 2, 1829; m. (1) Serua Snow, (2) Sarah Jane" Warner.

418 WEALTHY[7] WARNER, daughter of Philip[6] and Sarah (Woods) Warner, born May 6, 1800, in Cambridge, N. Y.; died December 28, 1863.

Married May 26, 1828, **ALANSON HULL** of Oxford, N. Y., born May 6, 1806, died in Oxford, February 3, 1905, aged 98, son of Ebenezer and Bede (Jacobs) Hull.

Children, born in Oxford and educated in Oxford Academy

Edwin Alanson Hull, b. May 2, 1829; d. Nov. 18, 1910; m. (1) Nov. 29, 1854, Martha B. Merrill of Oxford; m. (2) ———. He had one son who grew up: Jesse M., died in Kansas City, Mo., leaving a wife, and three children.

Joseph Jacobs Hull, b. May 10, 1835; resides in Oxford; m. Dec. 31, 1857, Sarah M. Mead of Oxford. No children.

Sarah Elizabeth Hull, b. Mar. 30, 1838; d. Apr. 11, 1916 (or 1917); resided in Oxford on the farm where she was born; m. (1) in Oxford, Sept. 15, 1859, Israel Jacobs, who died Nov. 6, 1871, aged 40; m. (2) Aug. 16, 1876, Andrew Ackley, who died Dec. 14, 1913 (or 1912) ; no children.

Martha Warner Hull, b. July 30, 1841; resides in Coventry, N. Y.; m. in Oxford, May 9, 1866, John Waters Manning, b. in Coventry, N. Y., May 20, 1837, d. Oct. 20, 1911, son of Ira and Mary A. (Treadway) Manning. Children, b. in Coventry: i. Frank Maurice, b. Aug. 27, 1867; is a retired farmer residing in the village of Coventry, N. Y., justice of the peace; m. Sept. 18, 1901, Lucy Wilson of Coventry. ii. Sarah Elizabeth, b. Nov. 30, 1869; m. Sept. 8, 1898, Clark Smith, a farmer of Coventry; has two sons, Edward Clark, b. Nov. 29, 1901, and Russel Manning, b. Mar. 30, 1903. iii. William Alanson, b. Jan. 4, 1872, is a farmer in Coventry; m. Apr. 15, 1906; , m. Eugenia Donegan of Coventry. iv. Mary Wealthy, b. Oct. 2, 1874; d. July 31, 1889.

419 WILLIAM SYLVESTER[7] WARNER, son of Sylvester[6] and Elizabeth (Reed) Warner, born December 24, 1807, in Jackson, Washington Co., N. Y.; died June 22, 1866. He resided in Coila and Cambridge, N. Y., where he was a shoe merchant. He was justice of the peace in 1841 and 1845; supervisor of the town of Jackson in 1845-6. Married in Cambridge, N. Y., SARAH COULTER, born September 3, 1806, died May 28, 1875, daughter of James Coulter, who was born April 8, 1775, and died April 15, 1864, and his wife, Agnes Ferguson, who died February 13, 1815, aged 33 years.

Children, born in Coila

Mary E. Warner, b. Dec. 18, 1831; resides in Troy, N. Y.; m. in Coila, N. Y., May 11, 1854, Allen R. Williams, b. in Jackson, N. Y., Oct. 25, 1828. Child: James Henry, b. Oct. 27, 1856.

626 *James Warner*, b. Aug. 7, 1833; m. Charlotte Bliss Townsend.

Elizabeth Reed Warner, b. Feb. 12, 1835; d. Dec. 25, 1915, in Cambridge, N. Y., where she had resided; m. in Cambridge, in the fall of 1854, James Stewart Robertson. Children: i. Charles Stewart, who d. Aug., 1887; m. Lorraine C. Messer and had a daughter, Florence, b. in Hoosick Falls, N. Y., resides in Portland, Ore. (she m. in New York City, Nov. 1, 1902, Raymond D. Hoyt, b. in Cambridge, N. Y., son of William and Almira (————) Hoyt, and has a son, William Stewart (Hoyt), b. in Montrose, N. Y., Oct. 6, 1905). ii. Anna, d. in infancy.

Sarah Maria Warner, b. Oct. 19, 1838; d. Mar. 16, 1916, in Cambridge, where she had resided; m. in Cambridge, Jan. 24, 1861, William John Stevenson, b. in Cambridge, July 16, 1832, d. Jan. 25, 1895, son of John and Sarah (Culver) Stevenson. Children: i. Mary Ellen, b. Nov. 13, 1861; d. Feb. 3, 1890; m. ———— Balch. ii. Lily Frances, b. July 29, 1867; d. May 12, 1868. iii. Frederick Barton, b. Nov. 23, 1873.

William Sylvester Warner, Jr., b. July 21, 1840; d. June 19, 1908, in the Soldiers' Home at Bath, N. Y. He was a salesman and lived in Cambridge, not married. He served in the Civil War as 1st lieutenant, Company G, 123d N. Y. Infantry, enlisted Aug. 6, 1862, honorably discharged July, 1865.

Henry Warner, b. June 5, 1842; d. 1851, aged 9 years, 6 months.

627 *Fannie Stevenson Warner*, b. Aug. 5, 1844; m. Charles Townsend Hawley.

Lydia Ann Warner, usually called Lillie, b. Feb. 10, 1847; resides in Cambridge; m. in Troy, N. Y., Nov. 25, 1874, Henry Elisha Billings, b. in Jackson, N. Y., Sept. 22, 1844, son of Albert and Almira M. (Clapp) Billings. Children: i. Frances Louise, b. Apr. 7, 1876, in Arlington, Vt.; resides in Cambridge. ii. Grace Warner, b. May 21, 1879, in Center Cambridge, N. Y. iii. Warner Elisha, b. Mar. 28, 1885, in Cambridge; d. May 31, 1913.

420 **WALTER W.[7] WARNER**, son of Arnold[6] and Polly (Cutler) Warner, born 1798; died at Baraboo, Wis., 1859. He was inn-keeper at Erie, Pa., and also engaged in a mercantile

business, then kept hotel at Fairview, Pa. He was at Erie as late as 1853 or thereabouts. He was universally respected and was known as "Honest Walter Warner."

Married (1) ———— BIRD.

Married (2) ———— BIRD, sister of his first wife, and also of the wife of his brother Henry C.

Married (3) **CLARISSA POTTER.**

Children by first wife

Henry Warner, d. aged 8 or 9 years.

Byron Warner, resided in Oshkosh, Wis.; d. from wounds received in the Civil War. He was married and had two small children in 1854.

Child by second wife

Wallace Warner, resided in Erie, Pa.; was an officer in the Civil War.

Children by third wife

Alfred Warner, d. aged 20.

Martha Warner, was married and living in Chicago, 1894.

Josephine Warner, resided in Chicago, 1894.

Charles Warner, resided in Chicago, 1894.

421 BEULAH[7] WARNER, daughter of Arnold[6] and Polly (Cutler) Warner, born June, 1800; died 1867, in Oregon, Wis. "A woman of sterling worth and superior mind." Married November 12, 1818, **DANIEL PALMER.**

Children

Polly A. Palmer, b. 1816; m. ———— Goodnough; resided in Brooklyn, Iowa, 1894.

Benjamin F. Palmer, b. Aug. 12, 1819; m. ———— Hopkins, a granddaughter of one of the signers of the Declaration of Independence.

O. Mandeville Palmer, b. 1821; m. Huldah Hull; resided in Oregon, Wis., in 1894.

John Y. Palmer, m. Cornelia Church; resided near Brooklyn, Iowa, in 1894.

James A. Palmer, d. in the Mexican War; was 2d Lieutenant under Capt. (later Gen.) Grant.

Edward W. Palmer, m. 1856, Helen Pritchard; resided in Winona, Minn., 1894.

Edwin Palmer, m. L. Jay.

Esther Palmer, m. ———— Underwood.

Betsey Palmer, m. ———— Douglas; resided in Hampton, Iowa, 1894.

Walter Palmer, m. (1) ———— Ellsworth, (2) Mrs. Watson; resided in Baraboo, Wis., 1894.

William Palmer, m. Caroline Muelguard.

Prudence Palmer, m. C. Rowley; resided in Appleton, Wis., 1894.

Henry Palmer, m. Rebecca Pierce.

Francis Palmer, b. Jan. 14, 1844; m. ———— Pritchard.

422 HENRY C.[7] **WARNER,** son of Arnold[6] and Polly (Cutler) Warner, born 1808; · died June 2, 1844, in Lincolnville, Crawford Co., Pa. He was colonel in the state militia in the days of general training, and was for a long time hotel keeper at Fairview and Craneville, Pa.

Married (1) ————.

Married (2) ———— **BIRD,** sister to the wives of his brother Walter W.

Children by first wife

William N. Warner, d. 1889, at Lincolnville, Pa.
Edwin Warner, was killed at the Battle of the Wilderness.

Children by second wife

Amelia Warner, d. aged 20.
Rogene Warner, d. Jan. 22, 1879; m. Enoch Shrieve.
Arvilla Warner, b. 1849; d. Mar. 4, 1877; m. at Union City, Pa., E. G. Shrieve.
Ammarilla Warner, m. ———— Johnson.
Henry C. Warner, Jr., m. Sept. 18, 1889, Carrie Baker.
Francis I. Warner, b. 1852; m. J. H. Shrieve.
Mary Warner, d. in infancy.

423 WILLIAM C.[7] **WARNER,** son of Arnold[6] and Polly (Cutler) Warner, born May 5, 1815, in Rome, N. Y.; died July 23, 1892, in Baraboo, Wis., buried there. He was postmaster at Baraboo during Buchanan's administration and was for many years identified with the business interests of that place. In early days he went by wagon train to Colorado and was a successful miner there.

Married (1) **BOTHILDA ATKINS.**

Married (2) **SUSAN P. PARTRIDGE,** born at Le Grave or Luton, Bedfordshire, England.

Children by second wife

John Albert Warner, b. May 5, 1849; d. Jan. 15, 1854.
628 *Wilber William Warner,* b. Dec. 20, 1850; m. Madora A. Finster.
Robert Henry Warner, b. Aug. 2, 1852; d. Jan. 18, 1854.
Annie Rothilda Warner, b. Apr. 7, 1855; resides at Mather, Juneau Co., Wis.; m. Dec. 4, 1873, Elmer Dano, a cranberry grower.
Ellen Elizabeth Warner, b. at Baraboo, Wis., May 10, 1857; resides at Auburn, King Co., Wash.; m. at Baraboo, Oct. 31, 1878, Charles Alexander Ryan, b. in Portage, Wis., Aug. 26, 1854, son of H. R. and Abby G. (————) Ryan. He is a fruit raiser and market gardener. Children: i. Roger W., b. Sept. 26, 1893. ii. Annie Lucile, b. May 6, 1895; m. Oct. 18, 1917, Walter A. Spindler of Portland, Ore.
George W. Warner, b. July 29, 1859; d. Aug. 13, 1860, at Baraboo, Wis.

Susie W. Warner, b. in Colorado, June 25, 1862; died on the plains near Fort Kearney, where she is buried.
629 *Edwin Sherman Warner*, b. Jan. 9, 1866; m. Mable F. Ayars.
630 *Frank Seth Warner*, b. Dec. 25, 1867; m. Maud E. Wilson.

424 JONATHAN[7] WARNER, son of Solomon[6] and Elizabeth (Woodworth) Warner, born in Jackson, Washington Co., N. Y., August 4, 1802; died August 3, 1882 (August 5, on tombstone). He was a farmer of means and influence in Jackson; member of the Presbyterian Church of Cambridge, and director of the Cambridge National Bank.

Married in 1825, MARIA SIMPSON, born November 15, 1801; died June 6, 1883. She was the daughter of David Simpson, who came with his parents from Ireland to New Hampshire, then to Jackson, and engaged in the manufacture of potash, and in mercantile business. His wife, Rachel Reid, was born in Colerain, Ireland.

Children

Henry Warner, d. young.
Freelove Warner, d. young.
Anna Elizabeth Warner, b. in Jackson, Aug. 10, 1834; d. in Cambridge, N. Y., Sept. 29, 1895; m. in Cambridge, Oct. 3, 1861, Rev. William Melancthon Johnson, D.D., b. May 1, 1834, at Cambridge, son of Thias and Sarah (MacDougall) Johnson. He was pastor of the Stillwater Presbyterian Church for six years, and of the First Presbyterian Church of Cohoes for forty years. Children: i. Sarah M., b. at Stillwater, Oct. 2, 1862; resides in Troy; m. at Cohoes, Nov. 11, 1886, Stephen Viele Lewis, b. in New York City, Jan. 11, 1859, son of John and Jennie (Viele) Lewis, has two children, Margaret MacDougall, b. in Cohoes, Sept. 30, 1888, m. June 15, 1915, Henry E. Holmes, and William Johnson, b. Aug. 24, 1890, a Civil Engineer. ii. Helen J., b. in Stillwater, Oct. 2, 1864; d. in Troy, Dec. 2, 1913, not married. iii. Henry Warner, b. Jan. 10, 1867; is a physician in Hudson, N. Y.; m. Oct. 5, 1898, Anna Elizabeth Groat, b. Feb. 25, 1864, daughter of Robert Franklin and Sarah Jane (Faland) Groat, had two sons, b. in Hudson, Robert Groat, b. July 21, 1899, a student at Phillips Exeter Academy (1916), and William Warner, b. Aug. 10, 1901, a student at Loomis Institute (1916). iv. Grace Anna, b. Sept. 27, 1874; d. Sept. 21, 1875, at Cohoes.

425 WILLIAM SMITH[7] WARNER, son of Seth Andrew Le Moyne[6] and Sally (Wixom) Warner, born in Hector, now Schuyler Co., N. Y., February 15, 1817; died in Jacksonville, Fla., Feb. 7, 1895. He was eight years old when his father removed to Michigan and settled in Farmington. From 1832 to 1837 the boy was clerk in a country store, teaching school winters. He then established himself in the mercantile busi-

28

ness in Farmington. His goods were bought in New York and he traveled thither by boat from Detroit to Buffalo, by canal to Utica, by rail to Albany, then by boat again down the Hudson to New York, the trip occupying about three weeks. After some three years he sold the store and bought a grist mill at Northville, Wayne Co., Mich. He disposed of this two years later and studied law in his father's office until 1844, when he removed with his wife and two daughters to Wisconsin. They traveled by team, using the route through Chicago and Milwaukee which were then only frontier villages. He first settled in Watertown, but found no opening there for a lawyer, so engaged in business. In 1846 he removed to Sheboygan, and in 1849 to Appleton, where he bought a stock of goods and conducted a store until 1857, when he began the practice of law. He was prominently identified with the beginnings of Appleton, bought the first town lots, as overseer of the roads helped cut the trees along what is now its finest business street, and was on the committee to nominate the first officers of the town of Grand Chute. In 1851 he removed to Kankakee, where he spent two years and filled the office of justice of the peace, postmaster, town superintendent of schools and deputy town clerk. In 1853 he returned to Appleton. He many times held public offices, town clerk, police justice of the city of Appleton, alderman, city attorney, and in 1877 was elected to the State Legislature and became chairman of the Judiciary Committee. He was largely interested in real estate dealings.

Married in Farmington, Mich., April 12, 1837, POLLY COOMER, born March 1, 1819, in Canandaigua, N. Y.; died in Appleton, Wis., August 14, 1884. She was the daughter of David and Betsey (Cole) Coomer.

Children

Charles Warner, b. Mar. 13, 1838; d. Mar. 15, 1838.
Fordyce Le Moyne Warner, b. July 3, 1839; d. Jan. 24, 1841.
Amelia Victoria Warner, b. Aug. 1, 1841; d. Oct. 16, 1846.
Emily Celestine Warner, b. Apr. 11, 1844, in Farmington; resides in
  Appleton, Wis.; m. at Appleton, Dec. 25, 1862, Henry D. Ryan, b.
  Oct. 7, 1837, in Ft. Howard, Wis., a lawyer, son of Samuel and
  Martha (Johnson) Ryan. Children: i. Charlotte Amelia, b. Sept.,
  1863; d. Dec. 2, 1865. ii. Lura Warner, b. Mar., 1867; m. June 11,
  1890, William E. Stoppenbach who is assistant manager of a paper
  mill at Stevens Point, Wis.; had three children, Margaret Helen, b.
  Oct. 23, 1891, at Fern Hill, Wash., Theodore Lummis, b. May 15,
  1897, in Chicago, d. Feb. 13, 1899, and Katherine Emily, b. Mar. 3,
  1900, in Appleton, Wis. iii. Willie Dean, b. July, 1870; d. Aug. 24,

1870. iv. William Henry, b. Feb. 28, 1878; is business manager of a paper mill at Niagara, Wis.; m. at Appleton, Aug. 12, 1902, Agnes Preville. iv. Edith Millicent, b. Apr. 1, 1879.

426 ROBERT WIXOM[7] WARNER, son of Seth Andrew Le Moyne[6] and Sally (Wixom) Warner, born July 13 or 31, 1818; died in Detroit, Mich., July 25, 1849. He was a carpenter and contractor; went to Detroit at an early day; was a member of the first I. O. O. F. lodge formed there. He gave his life as a sacrifice caring for the sick, and was himself stricken with cholera.
Married in Hopewell, Ontario Co., N. Y., April 22, 1841, CAROLINE AMANDA MURRAY.

Children

Frances Robbins Warner, b. July 10, 1843, in Farmington, Mich.; resides at Fairhope, Ala.; m. (1) at Farmington, Dec. 5, 1861, Ray Hazelton Thrasher, who went out in 1863 as a member of the Mechanics and Engineers Corps of the 22d Michigan Volunteers and died June 29, 1865; m. (2) at Farmington, Sept. 19, 1867, William Riley, who died near Walled Lake, Mich., May 28, 1891. There were no children by the second marriage. Children of Ray H. Thrasher: i. Dean Warner, b. Nov. 3, 1862, in Farmington. ii. Caroline Elizabeth, b. Sept. 7, 1864, at Lakeside, N. Y.
James Gillespie Birney Warner, b. May 17, 1845, in Detroit, Mich.; d. at the National Soldiers' Home, Johnson City, Tenn., Dec. 11, 1914; was a carpenter and contractor; m. in Butler, Bates Co., Mo., May 5, 1867, Flora Braggins, b. Nov. 6, 1844, in Newton Falls, Trumbull Co., Ohio. Children: i. Robert Lyon, b. in Kansas City, Mo., May 19, 1869; was graduated from the Portland, Ore., High School and from Cornell University, 1892; is an electrical engineer, manager of the Boston office of the Westinghouse Electrical Company; resides in Brookline; m. in 1893, Anne R. Pearson of Ithaca, N. Y., B.L., Cornell University, 1892; has two children. ii. Charles Emory, b. Jan. 26, 1871, near Butler, Mo.; attended Cornell University, 1888-90; is a member of the Sons of the Revolution; resides near Boston. iii. Ethel, b. Oct. 21, 1872, near Butler; died. iv. Lucille Eva, b. May 20, 1874, in Dunkirk, N. Y.; died. v. Olive Pearl, b. Jan. 2, 1877, near Butler. vi. Ruby Fay, b. July 16, 1878, near Butler. vii. William Smith, b. Feb. 7, 1881, in Colorado Springs, Colo.; died. viii. Helen Elizabeth, b. Nov. 24, 1885, in Portland, Ore.; died.
Edney Salathiel Warner, b. in Detroit, Mich.; died.
Robert Wixom Warner, Jr., b. in Detroit; died.

427 PASCHAL DE ANGELIS[7] WARNER, usually known as P. Dean Warner, son of Seth Andrew Le Moyne[6] and Sally (Wixom) Warner, born in Hector, Schuyler Co., N. Y., August 12, 1822; died in Farmington, Mich., August 28, 1910. His

parents removed to Michigan when he was about three years old and settled about two miles north of the present Farmington village. At the age of 15 he began his long and honorable mercantile career by clerking in a country store. For six years he served in the general store in Farmington with the exception of two or three months in each year spent in school, and part of a year in the Northville school. He spent one year in Detroit as a clerk, otherwise his life was passed in Farmington. He served his community in many official capacities, as Justice of the Peace, Clerk, and Supervisor. In 1846 he purchased one half interest in a stock of goods and established the firm of Botsford and Warner. In 1850 he was a member of the Legislature from Oakland County, elected by the Democrats; again in 1864 was elected and served two terms, acting as Speaker in the second term. In 1867 he was an active member of the Constitutional Convention, and in 1869, was chosen to the State Senate. He was a man of deep religious convictions, a member of the Presbyterian Church for many years, a friend of the University and Agricultural College, and devoted to the cause of church and school.

Married in Ann Arbor, Mich., November 8, 1845, RHODA ELIZABETH BOTSFORD, who died August 11, 1911.

They had no children but adopted

Fred Maltby Warner, who was b. in Hicklings, Nottinghamshire, England, July 21, 1865, and was brought to this country by his parents at the age of three months. His mother died soon after and he was adopted by Mr. and Mrs. Warner. He was graduated from the Farmington High School and attended the State Agricultural College for a term. He then engaged as a clerk in his father's store and in a few years the business was turned over to him and successfully conducted for twenty years. In 1889 he established a cheese factory at Farmington, the success of which led to the establishment of others until he controlled a chain of twelve factories in Oakland and adjoining counties, with an annual output of some forty thousand boxes of cheese, nearly all of which is sold in Michigan. He was elected Republican State Senator for 1895-8, the youngest member at each session; in 1900 was elected Secretary of State, re-elected in 1902; was elected Governor in 1904, 1906 and 1908, the youngest man to act in that capacity since the adoption of the state constitution in 1850, and the first to receive three consecutive terms. Mr. Warner was married in 1888, to Martha M. Davis of Farmington, and has four children: i. Edessa, b. about 1891. ii. Howard, b. about 1893. iii. Harley, b. about 1895. iv. Helen, b. about 1899.

428 SETH ANDREW LE MOYNE[7] WARNER, JR., son of Seth Andrew Le Moyne[6] and Emma (Palmer) Warner, born in Farmington, Mich., July 13, 1840; resides in Alpena, Mich. He is one of the leading business men of Alpena County, carries on an extensive lumber business, and stands high in business circles and community life. He has held many public offices, as treasurer of the Fire Company, County Agent of the State Board of Correction. He is agent for the Illinois Surety Company and has a general insurance business.

Married (1) at Farmington, September 17, 1863, **FRANCES A. PHELPS.**

Married (2) March 21, 1872, **EMMA B. WALKER.**

Children by first wife

Frances Nina Warner, b. in Farmington, Feb. 25, 1865, is principal of a Kindergarten School in Detroit.

William Seth Warner, b. Mar. 30, 1867; is a fruit grower in Wenatchie, Wash.; m. in 1895, Minerva Pearsons.

Child by second wife

Ethel L. Warner, b. Aug. 18, 1874, in Alpena, Mich.; is a member of the faculty of the Thomas Normal Training School in Detroit.

429 **CHARLES BELDEN[7] WARNER,** son of Daniel Brainerd[6] and Mary Anna (Green) Warner, born in East Haddam, Conn., July 28, 1839; resides there and is a dealer in lumber, coal, and building materials. At an early age he was induced by a friend, who had gone from East Haddam to China and engaged in business there for a number of years, to make the voyage to China. He left home on Christmas, 1863, and on January 4, 1864, was a passenger in a sailing ship bound for Shanghai. He located in Swatow, and was engaged in business there from June 1, 1864, until June, 1871. He returned home by way of San Francisco, reaching there, September, 1871. While in China he took trips to Peking, Tientsin, and Hong Kong, and had many interesting experiences. The firms with which he was connected handled cotton, cotton goods and opium, with England. There were many difficulties in trading with Chinese at that time. The only coins they would accept were Mexican trade dollars that had to be weighed and taken to the two banks in Hong Kong. Mr. Warner has specimens of some coins that were issued in 1867 in the hope that they would take the place of the Mexican dollars. They are Chinese coins with "Mexican dollar" stamped across the face with a hand die. Mr. Warner is treasurer of St. Stephen's Episcopal Church.

Married (1) November 3, 1887, **GEORGIANA GOOD-SPEED**, born July 21, 1848, died April 5, 1889, daughter of George Edward and Nancy (Green) Goodspeed.

Married (2) January 1, 1903, **WINIFRED PLUMSTEAD GIBBONEY**, born October 7, 1869, daughter of Matthew and Maria Josephine (Woodbury) Plumstead, and widow of John Gibboney.

Child by first wife

George G., b. Apr. 5, 1889; d. Apr. 17, 1889.

Children by second wife

(*Twins*), b. Mar. 16, 1905. The son died March 17, and the daughter, March 18.

Damaris Warner, b. June 5, 1906, in East Haddam.

430 **MARY GREEN[7] WARNER**, daughter of Daniel Brainerd[6] and Mary Anna (Green) Warner, born in East Haddam, Conn., August 7, 1842; resides in East Haddam; is a member of the D. A. R.

Married December 25, 1863, **NORMAN BOARDMAN**, born in Chester, Conn., August 7, 1840, only child of Luther and Lydia (Frary) Boardman, and descended from Samuel Boreman or Boardman, born in Banbury, Oxfordshire, England, son of Christopher and Julian (Carter) Boreman. Samuel Boardman came to America, settling first in Ipswich, Mass., and removing later to Wethersfield, Conn. He was Deputy to the General Assembly for eighteen terms. Norman Boardman was educated in East Haddam, Hamden, Middletown and New Haven, and became head of the silver plating business established by his father. He is a member of the F. and A. M., I. O. O. F., vestryman in St. Stephen's Episcopal Church, and bank director. The Commemorative Biographical Record of Middlesex County contains an article about Mr. Boardman and his family, p. 434.

Children, born in East Haddam

Eugene Boardman, b. May 15, 1865; was educated at the Seabury Institute, Saybrook, Conn., and Cheshire Military Academy; entered the silver plating business with his father; is a member of F. and A. M., and I. O. O. F.; m. Nov. 11, 1891, Gertrude Douglas of Savannah, Ga., only child of Charles and Abbie (Keney) Douglas. Children: i. Norman Douglas, b. Sept. 20, 1893. ii. Lydia Douglas, b. Jan. 19, 1896.

Grace Warner Boardman, b. Jan. 21, 1874; m. Nov. 18, 1897, Burton Leonard Lawton, a telephone manufacturer of Meriden, Conn. Children: i. Mary Boardman, b. Oct. 31, 1898. ii. Dorothy, b. Oct. 18, 1900.

431 SIDNEY BRAINERD[7] WARNER, son of Daniel Brainerd[6] and Mary Anna (Green) Warner, born in East Haddam, Conn., December 5, 1849; resides in East Haddam, and is a merchant there.
Married May 12, 1875, **CASSIE HILLAR POST,** born in Essex, Conn., daughter of Charles and Eliza (————) Post.

Child

Daniel B. *Warner,* b. May 3, 1876, in East Haddam; m. Jan. 28, 1911, Gertrude Gyndelyn Harris. Child: Brainerd Post, b. Apr. 10, 1916.

432 ABBY E.[7] WARNER, daughter of Selden Jewett[6] and Mary (Brockway) Warner, born in Lyme, Conn., June 26, 1820; died in Hadlyme, January 12, 1907.
Married in Colchester, Conn., October 23, 1847, **GEORGE NELSON PHELPS,** born October 7, 1812, in Lyme; died there, January 26, 1865. He was a farmer in Lyme and was the son of Roswell C. and Mary (Wood) Phelps.

Children, born in Lyme

Mary Elizabeth Phelps, b. Apr. 19, 1849; m. in Lyme, William S. Hall, b. May 9, 1840, in Lyme, d. there, May 23, 1894, son of Harvey Hall. Children: i. George W., b. Feb. 10, 1867, m. May 31, 1894, Helen Isabel[8] Warner, b. Mar. 31, 1869, daughter of David Carlos[7] and Mary Angeline (Tooker) Warner, resides in Lawrence, Mass., and has a son, Horton Warner, b. May 18, 1895; see number 436. ii. John S., b. Sept. 7, 1868; resides in Hadlyme; m. Edna Wilcox.
Caroline Phelps, b. Jan. 10, 1851; resides in Hadlyme.
Isabelle Phelps, b. Mar. 9, 1856; m. in Lyme, Nov. 28, 1872, Lee L. Brockway, b. in Lyme, Oct. 27, 1852, son of Harlem and Amira (Luther) Brockway. Children, b. in Lyme: i. George Lee, b. Nov. 10, 1875; d. Dec. 3, 1875. ii. Carrie Belle, b. Sept. 13, 1877; resides in Hadlyme; m. in Lyme, Sept. 14, 1895, William Hawthorne, b. in Belfast, Ireland, June 4, 1867, d. in Hadlyme, June 30, 1908, son of William and Martha (————) Hawthorne. Mr. and Mrs. Hawthorne had two children, b. in Lyme: Martha Belle, b. Oct. 10, 1896, d. July 31, 1906, and Harold Luther, b. Jan. 24, 1905.

433 ZEBULON BROCKWAY[7] WARNER, son of Selden Jewett[6] and Mary (Brockway) Warner, born in Lyme, Conn., December 29, 1824; died there, August 1, 1905. He was a farmer and lived at Brockway's Ferry, Lyme.
Married in Lyme, January 4, 1858, **HARRIET MIRANDA LA PLACE,** born in Lyme, September 3, 1838, daughter of Jonathan Loring and Czarina (Cobb) La Place.

Children

Hattie Florence Warner, b. Dec. 13, 1858; resides in Hamburg, Conn. She was a teacher for several years before her marriage; m. Oct. 3, 1882, Hayden L. Reynolds, b. in Lyme, Jan. 13, ——, son of Ephraim O. and Aurelia (Hayden) Reynolds. Children: i. Harold, b. Aug. 13, 1884. ii. Lawrence, b. Sept. 25, 1886. iii. Donald, b. Dec. 9, 1888. iv. Dora, b. Sept. 10, 1892. v. Paul, b. July 8, 1895. vi. Harriet, b. July 20, 1897.

Hester Czarina Warner, b. June 29, 1863; was a teacher for 25 years; resides in Lyme.

May Belle Warner, b. July 14, 1867; was a teacher for several years before her marriage; m. Sept. 27, 1888, Wilson Reynolds, b. June 10, 1864, son of Ephraim O. and Aurelia (Hayden) Reynolds. They reside in Middletown, Conn. Children: i. Hester, b. Feb. 26, 1890. ii. Helen, b. Jan. 4, 1910.

Dora L. Warner, b. Nov. 4, 1870; m. Aug., 1906, Robert Huey, b. 1869, in Greystone, Ireland, son of Joseph and Mary (Dunmore) Huey. Children: i. Mary, b. Feb. 17, 1908. ii. Elizabeth, b. Oct. 22, 1912.

Musa Warner, b. July 15, 1873; is a teacher.

434 MARY MATILDA⁷ WARNER, daughter of Selden Jewett⁶ and Mary (Brockway) Warner, born in Lyme, Conn., April 30, 1829; died May 16, 1880; resided in Hartford. Married September, 1849, **ROSWELL PHELPS LA PLACE,** born September 4, 1828, died April, 1907(?). He was the son of Francis and Abigail (Wood) La Place of Joshuatown, Conn., and grandson of Jonathan and Caroline (Brockway) La Place of Southold, L. I., and Hamburgh, Essex and East Haddam, Conn.

Children

Adelaide La Place, b. May 31, 1850.

Albert La Place, b. Jan. 31, 1852; m. Feb. 19, 1880, Nancy Brown of Sag Harbor.

Ida G. La Place, b. Jan. 13, 1854; m. Sept. 28, 1882, James Ely Harding, b. Apr. 14, 1849, d. 1908; resided in Lyme, Conn. Children: i. Lee, b. Nov. 21, 1883, m. Leona ————, has two children. ii. Ray, b. June 23, 1885; m. Helen Jewett, has a son, James E. iii. James Ely, b. Jan. 15, 1887; m. and has a son. iv. Ida, b. Mar. 14, 1889. v. Ada, b. Feb. 21, 1891. vi. Ora, b. Oct. 16, 1896.

Frank Almer La Place, b. Dec. 10, 1855; m. Oct., 1881, Kate Sisson, b. Mar. 7, 1864, daughter of John and Kate (Sluman) Sisson. Child: Edward, b. 1882.

George La Place, b. Feb. 18, 1858; d. Dec. 3, 1858.

Bertha Lee La Place, b. Nov. 30, 1859.

435 JOSEPH BROCKWAY⁷ WARNER, son of Ebenezer Brockway⁶ and Lucinda M. (Banning) Warner, born in East

Haddam, Conn., August 1, 1823; died. He was a farmer in East Haddam, and sold property there as late as 1877. In his later years he became incapable of managing his estate and his wife Lydia A. was appointed conservator in 1903. Married (1) February 10, 1850, in Stamford, Vt., TIRZA A. HURD, born June 24, 1829, died January 27, 1859, daughter of Franklin and Zilpha (Potter) Hurd. Married (2) in Bennington, Vt., LYDIA A. CONNICK, born June 24, 1836, daughter of John and Julia (Allen) Connick. She resides in Hadlyme, Conn.

Children by first wife

Edgar A. Warner, b. June 26, 1850; m. in East Haddam, July 6, 1873, Ida E. Banning, b. about 1855, granddaughter of Selden Warner Banning and great-granddaughter of Joseph and Susannah[6] (Warner) Banning; see number 138. Children: i. Walter. ii. Charles Ellsworth, b. about 1882, in Lyme; is a mechanic and engineer residing in East Haddam; m. there, Sept. 5, 1913, Catherine Mary Raftery, a nurse of New York City, who was born about 1883, daughter of Patrick and Jenny (Ansbro) Raftery, one child, Mary Teressa, b. June 13, 1914, in Middletown, Conn. iii. Netta.

Zilpha Warner, b. Apr. 16, 1852; m. (1) James Hubbard, and had a daughter, Rena; m. (2) Leonard Bailey, and had a daughter, Elva.

Children by second wife

Franklin B. Warner, b. in East Haddam, July 28, 1862; resided in Brooklyn in 1890; m. in Hadlyme, July 9, 1890, Olivia I. Chester of East Haddam, b. about 1860. Child: Chester, b. Dec. 20, 1897.

Marvin Warner, b. Jan. 10, 1864; m. (1) Lucy Hall, and had a daughter, Lucy E., b. Sept. 23, 1893; m. (2) Martha Van Allen.

John H. Warner, b. in East Haddam, July 8, 1867; is a farmer in Millington, Conn.; m. Gertrude E. Gates, b. in East Haddam about 1877. Children, last three recorded in East Haddam: i. J. Leroy, b. Dec. 28, 1899. ii. Earl Stevens, b. June 21, 1903. iii. Joseph E., b. Jan. 30, 1905. iv. Malcolm G., b. Mar. 3, 1915.

Mattie Warner, b. Jan. 3, 1871; is a trained nurse.

436 DAVID CARLOS[7] WARNER, son of David[6] and Elizabeth (Johnson) Warner, born 1826; died in Hamburgh, Conn., January 22, 1895. He was a farmer and soldier, a captain in the Civil War, and went through the war from beginning to end without a scratch.

Married in Hamburgh, April 17, 1867, MARY ANGELINE (TOOKER) WARNER, widow of his brother Ulysses, and daughter of Captain Adin and Mary A. (Miller) Tooker. She was born October 1, 1832, and died September 23, 1885.

Children, born in Lyme, Conn.

Dwight Carlos Warner, b. Oct. 31, 1867; is an engineer, residing in Middlefield, Conn.; m. there, June 27, 1894, Rose Hall Terrill, b. in Middlefield, Feb. 10, 1873, daughter of Carlos B. and Mary (Hall) Terrill. Children, b. in Middlefield: i. Isaac Lawrence, b. Mar. 2, 1896. ii. Lucy May, b. May 30, 1899. iii. Ethel Julia, b. Apr. 16, 1901. iv. Gladys Rose, b. Feb. 6, 1906. v. David Elmer, b. July 12, 1907.

Helen Isabel Warner, b. Mar. 31, 1869; resides in Lawrence, Mass.; m. in Lyme, Conn., May 31, 1894, George William Hall, b. in Lyme, Feb. 10, 1867, son of William S. and Elizabeth (Phelps) Hall, and grandson of George Nelson and Abby E.⁷ (Warner) Phelps; see number 432. Child: Horton Warner, b. in Lyme, May 18, 1895.

437   **ULYSSES SOUTHWORTH⁷ WARNER**, son of David⁶ and Elizabeth (Johnson) Warner, born September 27, 1833, at Hamburgh, Conn.; died in the Civil War, July 2, 1863. He was wounded in the battle of Port Hudson, June 14, 1863; erysipelas and fever induced by the wound resulted in his death in a hospital in Baton Rouge and he was buried in the South. He was a member of Company F, 26th Regiment, Connecticut Volunteers.

Married in Sing Sing, N. Y., September 3, 1854, **MARY ANGELINE TOOKER**, born in Hamburgh, October 1, 1832, daughter of Captain Adin and Mary A. (Miller) Tooker; died September 23, 1885. She married (2) his brother David Carlos Warner.

Children

631   *Hattie Inez Warner,* b. Feb. 14, 1855; m. Fred A. Bernhardt.
      Willie S. Warner, b. Mar. 14, 1857; d. June 16, 1864.
632   *Ulysses Aden Warner,* b. Dec. 20, 1858; m. Mary Ann Finn.
633   *David Dennis Warner,* b. Feb. 27, 1861; m. Florence M. Stone.

438   **BETSEY ANN⁷ WARNER**, daughter of David⁶ and Elizabeth Parker (Johnson) Warner, born in Lyme, Conn., July 17 (or 9), 1835; died in Hartford, April (or Dec.) 12, 1899. Married (1) in Lyme, July 17, 1853, **JOHN RUSSELL BEEBE**, who died May 23, 18—. He was the son of Guy and Maria (Russell) Beebe.

Married (2) in Hartford, Conn., in 1872, **JOSEPH HENRY ALVORD**, born in Goshen, Conn., December 1, 1830, son of Chauncey Hart and Harriet Elizabeth (Lobdell) Alvord; died in West Hartford (Elmwood), Conn., July 16, 1907. He was a wagonmaker and blacksmith in Goshen, East Hampton, Glastonbury, Bloomfield, and, after 1890, in West Hartford. He married (1) in Marlborough, Betsey Matilda Latham, by whom he had two children.

Children of John Russell and Betsey Ann (Warner) Beebe

Lizzie Maria Beebe, b. Aug. 5, 1854; resides at Lyme; m. in the summer of 1872, Lodowick Bill, son of James Bill. Children: i. John Russell, b. Jan., 1873; d. aged 4 years. ii. Melville Clarence, b. Oct. 9, 1874; d. July 9, 1911.

Emma Ellen Beebe, b. Mar. 18, 1857; resides at Deep River, Conn.

Carlos Timothy Beebe, b. Mar. 9, 1863; m. in the summer of 1889, Antoinette Griffin. Child: Arthur Griffin, b. Feb., 1890.

John Roscoe Beebe, b. Jan. 19, 1867; m. in the summer of 1894, Mary Margaret Storer. No children.

Grace Darling Beebe, b. Oct. 23, 1868; m. June 11, 1889, Charles Brown. Child: Charles Warner, b. Mar. 21, 1890.

439 TIMOTHY PARKER[7] WARNER, son of David[6] and Elizabeth (Johnson) Warner, born September 17, 1837, in Lyme, Conn. He is a retired pilot and moved from Lyme to East Haddam in 1895.

Married in Montville, Conn., December 20, 1861, CAROLINE MARIA LA PLACE, born July 10, 1840, in Lyme, daughter of Jonathan Loring[3] and Czarina (Cobb) La Place (Francis[2] and Abigail (Wood) La Place, Jonathan[1] and Caroline (Brockway) La Place).

Children, born in Lyme

George Eugene Warner, b. Oct. 3, 1862; d. Apr. 13, 1894, in Lyme; m. Carrie Miner. No children.

Illione Warner, b. Nov. 28, 1864; resides in East Haddam.

Harry B. Warner, b. 1868; d. June 20, 1889.

Mildred E. Warner, b. Jan. 8, 1873; resides in Essex, Conn.; m. in Hartford, Conn., Jan. 23, 1897, Archie Lord, son of Henry and Elizabeth (Ely) Lord. Children: i. Hamilton Warner, b. Dec. 18, 1900, in Waterbury. ii. Rossiter Ely, b. May 26, 1907, in Waterbury.

Isaac R. Warner, b. Feb. 8, 1875; d. Jan. 12, 1895, in Lyme.

440 SAMUEL CURTIS[7] WARNER, son of Agur[6] and Polly (Bassett) Warner, born in South Britain, Conn., June 21, 1813; died July 18, 1872. He was a farmer and resided in the first house west of Bennett's Bridge, South Britain.

Married February 25, 1833, ELIZA SHERMAN, daughter of Carlos and Polly (Plumb) Sherman of Monroe, Conn.

Children

634 *Carlos Sherman Warner,* b. Apr. 4, 1841; m. Ellen Seeley.

635 *Lucius Curtis Warner,* b. July 10, 1844; m. Mary M. Kenney.

441 NOADIAH[7] **WARNER,** son of Agur[6] and Polly (Bassett) Warner, born at Bennett's Bridge, South Britain, Conn., October 10, 1817; died March 3, 1871. He was a farmer and resided on the old homestead near Bennett's Bridge. Married (1) **LAURA J. HINMAN,** who died May 23, 1861, aged 38, buried in Warner Cemetery, South Britain. She was the daughter of Lewis and Laura (Smith) Hinman. Married (2) **ALICE E. BEARDSLEY** of Newtown.

Children by first wife, born in South Britain

Mary Warner, b. June 24, 1843; d. June 30, 1845, buried in Warner Cemetery.

Allen L. Warner, b. July 30, 1844; was killed by the cars at Bedford, N. Y., June 10, 1868, buried in Warner Cemetery with Masonic emblem on the stone; not married.

Mary A. Warner, b. Feb. 9, 1846; d. Jan. 22, 1870, buried in Warner Cemetery; not married.

Harriet A. Warner, b. Sept. 4, 1849; m. Charles E. Hall of Derby.

Frank Warner, b. Feb. 13, 1853; d. Sept. 14, 1876, not married. He was killed by an ox team.

Ella Warner, b. Aug. 7, 1856; m. Thomas Jenner; resides in Denver.

Lottie Warner, b. Nov. 9, 1857; m. Sherman Baldwin of Milford, Conn.

Donald Warner, b. May 23, 1861; m. Viola White of Stepney; resides in Shelton.

Children by second wife, born in South Britain

Herbert N. Warner, b. Jan. 2, 1876.

(Twin daughters), b. May 11, 1878; d. May 13, 1878.

Lulu A. Warner, b. Sept. 28, 1881; resides in Fishkill-on-Hudson, N. Y.

442 MILTON JONES[7] **WARNER,** son of Noadiah[6] and Adaline (Jones) Warner, born October 16, 1842, in Salisbury, Conn.; died March 1, 1882, in Santa Fé, N. Mex. He was graduated from Williams College in 1865, from the Albany Law School, and read law with Donald J. Warner of Salisbury. He was admitted to the bar in September, 1867, and practiced in Waverly, N. Y., for some years, acting as Judge of the District Court. He was a member of Phi Beta Kappa, and was a man of an unusual variety of talents.

Married in Salisbury, September 21, 1870, **MARIA BIRCH COFFING,** daughter of George and Fanny (Williams) Coffing of Salisbury, and a descendant of Tristram Coffin, Esq., of Brixton, England, who settled at Newbury, Mass., in 1650. George Coffing was of the firm of Holley and Coffing, founded by his father John Churchill Coffing and John Milton Holley. This firm made the well-known Salisbury and Richmond brands of iron, which, for over one hundred years, have been quoted in the markets of the world as irons combining tensile strength and elasticity in the highest degee. George Coffing's grandfather was Governor of Connecticut in 1756, and opened the Fitch mine in the town of Salisbury about 1762. The furnaces of Coffing and Holley made iron for the young American navy, including the Constitution ("Old Ironsides"), and the Chesapeake; also for the War of 1812, the Greek War of 1821, the Mexican and Civil Wars. This iron was used for making the guns of the Monitor which defeated the Merrimac in the Civil War. Alexander Holley, a cousin and associate of George Coffing, aided Sir Henry Bessemer in perfecting the Bessemer process. Mr. Holley owned the Bessemer patents for the United States and built the early Bessemer plants, at Troy, Bethlehem, Youngstown, and other places.

Children

636 *George Coffing Warner*, b. July 13, 1871; m. (1) Maud Marshall Kelley, (2) Florence Ruth Loring.

Milton Jones Warner, Jr., b. Jan. 9, 1873; was graduated from Yale in 1894; resides in Pine Orchard, Conn., but is now (May, 1918) in Washington, D. C., acting as Captain in the Signal Corps. Married in Pine Orchard, Oct. 19, 1899, Olive Warner, b. June 24, 1875, daughter of Alden M. and Nellie A. (Shepardson) Young. Children: i. Olive Birch, b. Dec. 10, 1903. ii. Alden Young, b. June 24, 1906. iii. Milton Pierrepont, b. Jan. 8, 1910. iv. Elizabeth, b. Jan. 9, 1912.

Percy De Forest Warner, b. Jan. 15, 1874, in Waverly, N. Y.; resides in Waterbury, Conn., where he is with the Scovill Manufacturing Company. Married in London, England, Sept. 4, 1902, Brenda Tweed, b. in Lowell, Mass., Nov. 4, 1873, daughter of Timothy and Mary (Carleton) Tweed. They have an adopted daughter Mary, b. Feb. 23, 1916.

Elizabeth Warner, b. in Salisbury, Conn., Aug. 11, 1875; resides in Phœnix, Ariz. She was graduated from Rye Seminary at Rye, N. Y., in 1895, and from Smith College in 1899; studied Home Economics at Simmons College, Boston, in the winter of 1903-4. Married in Salisbury, Conn., Sept. 14, 1905, J. Spencer Voorhees, b. at Rocky Hill, N. J., May 14, 1858, son of Joseph Hageman and Sarah Catherine (Westbrook) Voorhees. He was graduated from Princeton University and Andover Theological Seminary; has held pastorates in Winsted, Conn., Boston, Mass., and Adams, Mass.; organized 1st Congregational Church in Huron, S. Dak., and the Congregational Church in Telluride, Colo. Latterly he has served churches in La Jolla, Cal., and Phœnix, Ariz. He was chaplain of the 3d Conn. Volunteer Infantry during the Spanish American War. Mr. and Mrs. Voorhees have a daughter, Katherine Birch van Voorhees, b. Oct. 14, 1911, in Pittsfield, Mass.

443 DONALD TICKNOR[7] WARNER, son of Donald Judson[6] and Lois Camp Ticknor (Ball) Warner, born in Salisbury, Conn., December 15, 1850; resides there. He was fitted for college at the Academy of Salisbury and entered Trinity College in the class of 1872, but did not complete the course because of illness. Later, however, he received the degree of Master of Arts from his college. He studied law with his father, was admitted to the bar in 1873, and began practising in Salisbury. He was States Attorney for Litchfield County from June, 1896, to March, 1917, when he resigned upon his appointment as Judge of the Superior Court of Connecticut. He was Judge of Probate for the Salisbury Probate District from 1885 to March, 1917; State Senator in 1895 and 1897, and Chairman of the Judiciary Committee both sessions. In 1902 he was Chairman of the Committee on the revision of the Statutes. He has been president of the Litchfield Bar Association, Lakeville Water Company, and treasurer and director of the Salisbury Cutlery Handles Company.

Married October 4, 1882, HARRIET ELECTA WELLS, born November 14, 1857, daughter of Philip Wells, born December 20, 1823, died January 28, 1872, and his wife, Elizabeth Emily Harrison, born December 25, 1831, died February 8, 1861.

Children

Donald Judson Warner, b. July 24, 1885; was graduated from Yale, LL.B., 1906; is an attorney at law in Salisbury.

Elizabeth Harrison Warner, b. Nov. 27, 1886, in Salisbury; m. Oct. 11, 1910, Irving Kent Fulton, b. Dec. 17, 1882, son of William Edwards and Ida Eleana (Lewis) Fulton of Waterbury. He is a graduate of Yale, 1906, and resides on a large farm of his father's at Salisbury. Child: Wells, b. Dec. 4, 1911, at Salisbury.

Lois Caroline Warner, b. June 30, 1888.

Mary Virginia Warner, b. Feb. 5, 1891.

Philip Wells Warner, b. Nov. 2, 1893; is sergeant at Base Hospital, Camp Hancock, Augusta, Ga.

Jeannette de Forest Warner, b. Dec. 3, 1896.

444 JOSEPH OSBORN[7] WARNER, son of Charles[6] and Fannie (Comstock) Warner, born in Hadlyme, Conn., March 3, 1817; died there, October 16, 1894. He was a farmer in Hadlyme and took an active part in public affairs; was member of the Legislature in 1884.

Married in Bridgehampton, L. I., May 22, 1844, ELIZA ANN STRONG, born in Bridgehampton, April 21, 1825, died in Hadlyme, April 30, 1896, daughter of James Rodgers and Clarissa (Sanford) Strong.

Children born in Hadlyme

Sarah Eliza Warner, b. Aug. 17, 1845; d. May 22, 1866; m. May 4, 1865, Caleb F. Rose, a builder, who resided in Hadlyme. He m. (2) her sister Josephine. Child of Sarah: Joseph Howard, b. Feb. 14, 1866, in Hadlyme; is a real estate dealer, residing in Hartford, m. in New Britain, June 15, 1898, Augusta Fenton, b. in New Britain, Jan. 27, 1863, and has a daughter, Priscilla Eliza, b. in Hartford, Feb. 26, 1902.

Josephine Warner, b. June 20, 1848; resides in Hadlyme; m. as second wife, Nov. 28, 1867, Caleb F. Rose, b. Aug. 2, 1838, son of Silas and Eliza (Fordham) Rose who lived in New York City until 1838, then in Hadlyme.

Clarissa Strong Warner, b. Sept. 13, 1851; not married.

Joseph Hart Warner, b. May 28, 1855; not married.

Rollo Frank Warner, b. Oct. 1, 1856; d. May 18, 1910, in Redlands, Cal.

James Rodgers Warner, b. Dec. 18, 1858; is a sales manager, residing in Hartford and Hadlyme. He was a member of the Legislature in 1901 and has held various town offices. Married in Hartford, Dec. 12, 1887, Bertha Jane Rich, b. Sept. 6, 1865, daughter of Charles H. and Nancy Jane (Cone) Rich of Hadlyme. They have no children.

445 LEONARD[7] WARNER, son of Elijah[6] and Relief (Marble) Warner, born in the town of Phelps, N. Y., in 1800; removed to the town of Barre, now Albion, N. Y., and settled on the farm south of and adjoining that of his brother Houghton Warner, on Mosher's Hill, in what is now the town of Albion, N. Y.

Married **LAVINIA THURSTON,** daughter of Caleb Thurston.

Children

Elizabeth Warner, m. Halsey Ross. Children: i. ———, d. young. ii. Flora, d. at Eagle Harbor, N. Y., in 1914; m. Bennett Wilson and had four children: Ross, m. Fanny Wyman of Millville, N. Y.; Rose, m. Roy Wyman; Florence, m. George Howitt of Millville; Randall, m. and has a son.

Nelson Warner, m. Lydia Green. No children.

Elijah Warner, m. Frances Phipps; both died leaving no children.

Mary Ann Warner, m. Augustus G. Swan. Child: Frankie, lives at Dayton, Cattaraugus Co., N. Y.; m. (1) Rollin Noble, (2) ——— Hall.

William H. Warner, m. Sarah Post, who married, after his death, Thomas Barnett and resides in Niagara Falls, N. Y. Children: i. Leonard, was killed by the cars at Albion, N. Y. ii. Chester, was drowned in the Erie Canal at Albion. iii. William, resides at Medina, N. Y., married and has a son, William, living there also.

Chester Warner, b. Oct. 23, 1833, in the town of Barre, now Albion; d. there, September 23, 1896; was a farmer; m. Mar. 10, 1863, Melvina Mosher, daughter of Harvey and Rebecca (West) Mosher. Child: Fred E., b. Dec. 22, 1869; resides in Albion, N. Y.; m. Clara Stevens, daughter of George and Louisa (———) Stevens.

Janette Warner, m. Amos Gannon and died leaving a daughter, Hattie, who m. ——— Tripp and resides in Medina, N. Y.
Cornelia Warner, resides at Medina, N. Y.; m. Samuel White. Children: i. William, resides at Medicine Hat, Canada; m. Grace Stanton, and has a child, Clark.
Morris L. Warner, m. Sarah Bowen, who d. in Albion, N. Y., leaving no children.

446 CHESTER⁷ WARNER, son of Elijah⁶ and Relief (Marble) Warner, born March 1, 1802, in the town of Phelps, Ontario County, N. Y., on the farm settled by his father, Elijah; lived and died there, December 8, 1865. He was a farmer. He was noted for his physical strength.

Married (1) in 1824, **CHARLOTTE ROSANNA BROOKS**, born February 6, 1808, died February 4, 1835, in the town of Phelps, daughter of Nathaniel and Margaret (Gordon) Brooks.

Married (2) October, 1836, **PHOEBE JANE SWAN**.

Children by first wife

637 *Edward Brooks Warner,* b. July 28, 1826; m. (1) Aurelia Nichols, (2) Anna Warner.
638 *Henry Wells Warner,* b. July 13, 1828; m. Esther Elizabeth Holmes.
      Charlotte Warner, b. June 5, 1830; d. Jan. 20, 1853, not married. '
639 *Sheldon E. Warner,* b. Oct. 8, 1832; m. Sarah Porter.
640 *Margaret Rosanna Warner,* b. Feb. 4, 1835; m. Albert Granger.

Children by second wife

Warren Warner, b. 1837; d. Feb. 2, 1838, aged 3 months, 16 days.
Caroline A. Warner, b. Oct. 10, 1839; m. Dwight D. Severance. He owns the Elijah Warner farm in Phelps. Children: Zillah; Ralph.
Warren L. Warner, b. May 31, 1842; m. Lucretia Boise. Child: Henry.
Sarah Warner, b. Sept. 18, 1847; m. Dec. 6, 1866, Milton Ottley; resides in Phelps, N. Y. Child: Ray.

447 HOUGHTON⁷ WARNER, son of Elijah⁶ and Relief (Marble) Warner, born April 19, 1806, in the town of Phelps, N. Y.; removed to the town of Barre (now Albion), and died there. His home was on what was then called Warner Hill, later called Mosher's Hill.

Married (1) September 29, 1828, **MARY FRARY**, born July 30, 1807; died February 9, 1849.

Married (2) August 5, 1850, **MARY M. AGARD**, born May 9, 1829.

Children, born on Warner Hill, town of Barre

Torrance Frary Warner, b. Sept. 28, 1829; d. Mar. 30, 1853, aged 23 years, 6 months, 2 days; not married.

Marvin Warner, b. Aug. 13, 1831; d. at Albion, N. Y., Apr. 14, 1899; m. Feb. 17, 1859, Mary Jane[8] Warner, daughter of De Witt Clinton[7] and Polly (Scott) Warner; see number 450. They had no children. He was a hotel keeper.

Eugenia Maria Warner, b. Sept. 11, 1834; d. Dec. 6, 1852, not married.

Judson Philonzo Warner, b. Nov. 4, 1837; m. Emma Noviatt. Children: i. Hannah, m. (1) —— Rosencrantz and had a daughter, Blanche, who resides in Kansas City; m. (2) William Blades. ii. Marvin, m. twice and has four children, living in Denver, Colo. iii. (Infant son), d. young.

Mary Louisa Warner, b. Sept. 24, 1840; d. in Denver, Colo.; m. (1) Burnam Lampson, (2) Robert Ellingham, a miner. By the second marriage she had a daughter, Georgia, who has been married twice.

Andrew Deman Warner, b. June 17, 1843; d. in Denver, Colo.; no children.

Jerome H. Warner, b. Jan. 14, 1846; resides near Albion, N. Y.; m. (1) Mary Paine, (2) Amanda Wells, a widow.

448 RICE[7] WARNER, son of Lewis[6] and Mercy (Rice) Warner, born in the town of Phelps, Ontario County, N. Y., July 8, 1797; died September 12, 1885. He was a shoe dealer and resided in Albion, N. Y.

Married September 10, 1818, **REBECCA CARSON,** born in Phelps, April 25, 1799; died in Albion, November 13, 1879. She was the daughter of —— and Ann (Scott) Carson.

Children, first six born in Phelps, last two in Albion

641 *Eliza Ann Warner*, b. Sept. 6, 1819; m. Clark Baker.

Harriet Jane Warner, b. Jan. 31, 1821; d. in Brockport, N. Y., Jan. 3, 1849; m. Dec. 21, 1846, George Benson, b. July 28, 1808, in Northumberland, England, d. in Brockport, July 5, 1891.

Lucetta Warner, b. Jan. 14, 1823; was killed by a trolley car in Chicago, Ill., Dec. 23, 1896; m. Frederick E. Parmele, b. 1818, d. in Chicago, Aug. 18, 1864, aged 46.

Marvin Lewis Warner, b. Feb. 9, 1825; d. at Pilot Hill, Cal., Dec. 21, 1896; m. Sept. 12, 1849, Nancy Ann Harmon, b. Dec. 3, 1832, daughter of Sylvester and Letitia (————) Harmon. Children: i. Clara Jane, b. July 28, 1850; d. Mar. 1, 1851. ii. Emma Marie, b. Jan. 4, 1852; m. Finley P. Brownell, resided in West Orange, N. J., in 1915. iii. Howard Ransom, b. Oct. 7, 1856; d. Apr. 13, 1858. iv. Kate, b. Jan. 3, 1859.

Alphonzo Charles Warner, b. Nov. 8, 1827; removed to Chicago and thence to California and died there; married. Children: i. Mary, married and died in Sanborn, Niagara County. ii. Jerome, resides in New York City with his daughter.

Dennis J. Warner, b. Dec. 14, 1829; d. Nov. 1, 1881, at Walla Walla, not married.

Mary Melissa Warner, b. Mar. 24, 1832; m. Sept. 15, 1865, Irving M. Thompson, b. Mar. 15, 1831, at Vernon, N, Y.. d. Mar. 22, 1905, at Albion, N. Y. Children: i. Edith, b. July 28, 1866, in Albion; mar-

29

ried and resides in Albion. ii. Warner, b. Dec. 23, 1867, in Albion. iii. Fred Meade, b. Nov. 20, 1869, in Albion.
Judson Warner, b. July 8, 1834, in Albion; removed to Chicago. He married and had four sons and four daughters.

449 LEWIS⁷ WARNER, JR., son of Lewis⁶ and Mercy (Rice) Warner, born in the town of Phelps, N. Y., November 2, 1803; removed to Albion, N. Y., and died there, March 25, 1887.

Married (1) February 1, 1826, **POLLY GILSON**, born January 4, 1805; died at Albion, August 28, 1842.

Married (2) April 26, 1843, **MARGARET BAKER** of Albion, born March 4, 1817; died at Albion, June 25, 1873.

Children

Albert Warner, removed to Inwood, Canada, died; m. Jennie Pratt, daughter of Paul and Betsey (Parker) Pratt. Child: Roswell.
Frank Warner, married and had a daughter who m. in Albion, N. Y., —— Elliott, resides in Kansas City and has children.
Henrietta Warner, resided in Kansas City; never married.

450 DEWITT CLINTON⁷ WARNER, son of Lewis⁶ and Mercy (Rice) Warner, born June 5, 1806, in Phelps, N. Y.; died December 3, 1867, in the town of Barre, N. Y. He removed to Allegany County, then to Ridgeway, Orleans County, about 1835, and to the town of Barre in 1838. He was a farmer.

Married September 25, 1827, **POLLY SCOTT**, daughter of Justin Scott of Phelps. She died December 11, 1867

Children

America Warner, b. Mar. 25, 1829, at Olean, N. Y.; d. Sept. 26, 1889; m. Dec. ——, Alphonzo W. Starkweather, a harness maker, and removed to Eagle Harbor, N. Y. Children: i. Ida, d. young. ii. Adda, d. aged 22, not m. iii. Nellie, d. aged 5 years.
Justin Warner, b. Mar. 21, 1831; d. Apr. 13, 1900; m. Apr. 13, 1860, Esther M. Whiting, who d. Jan. 1, 1911, aged 72 years, daughter of Thomas and Polly (Crane) Whiting. Children: i. Hattie Jane, b. Jan. 14, 1862, resides in Rochester, N. Y.; m. Nov. 9, 1881, Frederick Raymond, son of Alfred and Miranda (Bradner) Raymond, and had a daughter, Harriet Loraine, b. Sept. 14, 1891, m. Clifford William Marlin of Rochester, N. Y. (has a son, Raymond B., b. May 28, 1915). ii. Electa, b. Feb. 7, ——; d. aged 7 months. iii. Dewitt C., d. in infancy.
Mary Jane Warner, b. Aug. 25, 1832; m. Feb. 17, 1859, Marvin Warner, b. Aug. 13, 1831, d. in Albion, N. Y., Apr. 14, 1899, where he was hotel keeper. He was son of Houghton and Mary (Frary) Warner; see number 447. No children.

Austin Warner, b. Feb. 21, 1834; resides in Barre Center, N. Y.; m. Jane Barker, who died. Child: Mary Filena, b. Feb. 1867(?); m. Joseph Mann of Barre and d. there, about 1912, aged 45 years.

William Addison Warner, b. in the town of Barre, N. Y., July 14, 1836; farmer and harness maker; resides in Clark, Clark Co., So. Dak.; m. in Albion, N. Y., Feb. 20, 1861, Fanny Briggs, b. in Eagle Harbor, N. Y., July 11, 1840, daughter of Alvin and Sally A. (Woodward) Briggs. Child: Alvin Dewitt, b. in Eagle Harbor, N. Y., Oct. 4, 1865; resides in Vinita, Okla.; m. in Clark, So. Dak., Sept. 15, 1899, Eva E. Baker, b. in Morrison, Ill., and has two children, b. in Clark, Catherine F., b. Nov. 24, 1906, and Muriel Joyce, b. Mar. 28, 1908.

Dewitt Clinton Warner, b. Jan. 4, 1840; is a farmer in Saline, Mich.; m. in Wheatland, Mich., Apr. 26, 1869, Helen Billings, b. Feb. 19, 1846, in New York State, daughter of Dr. Dexter and Jane (Eaton) Billings of Hudson, Mich. Children: i. Marvin, b. June 16, 1870; resides at home with his father; m. (1) Verda ——— (divorced); m. (2) ———. ii. Nellie, b. Nov. 12, 1872; resides in Sharon, Pa.; m. Percy Wareham. iii. Lewis C., b. Dec. 20, 1875. iv. Harry S., b. Apr. 7, 1881.

Electa Warner, b. Sept. 30, 1841, in town of Barre, N. Y.; d. Feb. 4, 1898, in town of Albion, N. Y.; m. William Phipps. Child: Frank, b. 1870; resides near Albion; m. (1) Marietta Grinnell, divorced, (2) Winifred Riley, had a daughter, Electa Jane, who m. (1) George Main of Buffalo, N. Y., by whom she has a son, b. about 1913, (2) Millard Comstock of Rochester, N. Y.

Charles Warner, b. Nov. 14, 1859; resides in or near Adrian, Mich.; m. Amy Billings, daughter of Dr. Dexter and Jane (Eaton) Billings of Eagle Harbor, N. Y. Children: i. William, resides with his father in Adrian. ii. Morris, resides in Adrian; m. and has one child.

451 LUCY[7] WARNER, daughter of Rufus[6] and Hazel (Rice) Warner, born in Hopewell, Ontario Co., N. Y., February 18, 1801; resided in Parma, N. Y.; died March 8, 1879. Married AARON WARD.

Children

Jane Ward, m. Henry Veazie. Children: i. Lorenzo, died. ii. George, resides at Maple View, N. Y.; m. and has several children.

Lorenzo Ward, m. Lucy Doty. His son Andrew m. Olive Parmele and had two children: i. George, m. Amy Horton. ii. Ina, m. Adolph Hamman and has a daughter, Olive, b. about 1915.

452 GUSTAVUS[7] WARNER, son of Rufus[6] and Hazel (Rice) Warner, born in Hopewell, Ontario Co., N. Y., May 3, 1802; died in Albion, Mich., April 14, 1873. He owned a farm in the town of Leon, Cattaraugus Co., N. Y., in 1833, and was a member of the Baptist Church in 1839. He resided in Phelps and Parma, N. Y., and removed to Michigan; bought

a place three miles from Jackson, which he later sold and bought a place in Jackson. His sons George and William took him to Albion in his last sickness and it was there he died. Married (1) **VELURA DARLING**, who died in Albion, Mich. Married (2) **MARIA** ————. There were no children by this marriage

Children of first wife

George W. Warner, b. Dec. 23, 1822; d. Feb. 6, 1824.

Mary Ann Warner, b. July 18, 1824; d. Feb. 4, 1861; removed to Concord, Mich.

Wellington Warner, b. Jan. 14, 1826; d. Oct. 2, 1838; resided in Olean (or Leon), N. Y.

Marcellus Warner, b. Aug. 16, 1827; removed to Albion, Mich.; married and had a daughter, Nellie, b. Aug. 23, 1860, who resides in Albion, Mich., m. Aldee Torrey, and has a son, Edwin, b. Mar. 13, 1886.

Elizabeth Warner, b. Oct. 8, 1830; d. Apr. 1, 1897; m. John Darling and resided in Concord, Mich.

Dennis Warner, b. Sept. 18, 1832; d. May 31, 1848; resided in Ogden, N. Y.

Minerva Warner, b. Dec. 18, 1834; m. G. W. Stone of Albion, N. Y.

William H. Warner, b. July 13, 1836; m. Jennie Richards and resided in Cincinnati, Ohio.

George Warner, b. July 12, 1840; m. Susan Driscoll; resided in Battle Creek, Mich.

Charles D. Warner, b. June 29, 1842; d. Apr. 29, 1865; resided in Albion, Mich.

453 .**ROSANNA**[7] **WARNER**, daughter of Rufus[6] and Hazel (Rice) Warner, born in Ontario County, N. Y., probably in Phelps or Hopewell, October 13, 1806; resided in Cattaraugus County; died July 12 or 28, 1872.
Married **GAYLORD KELLOGG**, born in Brookfield, N. Y., July 31, 1797; died in Leon, N. Y., March 12, 1873. He was the son of Ashbel and Martha Bacon (Ward) Kellogg and was a farmer in Leon for many years. A more complete record of this family is found in the Kellogg Genealogy.

Children, born in Leon, N. Y.:

Delight Kellogg, b. Oct. 3, 1824; d. in Glencoe, Ill., Jan. 14, 1891; m. in Leon, Nathaniel Fry Cooper, b. in Leon, Feb. 21, 1820, d. Jan. 7, 1867, son of Nathaniel and Phebe (Barton) Cooper. He was a teacher and farmer in Glencoe. Lieutenant, Co. K, 164th Ill. Volunteers. Children, b. in Leon: i. Christiana Genett, m. William Thompson. ii. Gaylord Kellogg, m. Emma Ross. iii. Edgar Adellmer, m. Josephine Dye. iv. Lucy Jane, d. young. v. John Fry, m. Jemima Smith. vi. Flora Dell, m. Benjamin Newhall.

Richard Darling Kellogg, b. Sept. 25, 1825; was a farmer in Leon;

m. Oct. 17, 1849, Mary Elizabeth Groves, b. Sept. 28, 1829, daughter of David and Dorcas (Meacham) Groves. Child (adopted) : Mary Nina.

Rufus Ashbel Kellogg, b. Nov. 2, 1827; was a farmer in Leon until 1867, removed to Collins, N. Y., and in 1898 to Gowanda. He was postmaster in Leon and held several town offices. Married in Fredonia, Oct. 11, 1855, Alzina Eastwood, b. in Pomfret, Chautauqua Co., N. Y., Feb. 20, 1829, daughter of Martin and Harriet L. (Ward) Eastwood. Children: i. Martin Parke, m. Edith May Hurd. ii. Caroline Rosannah, m. Rev. James Calvin Rhodes.

Austin Luke Kellogg, b. Feb. 2, 1831. He was a Methodist minister in Wattsburg, Pa., Sinclairville, Busti, and East Randolph, N. Y., and Petrolia, Pa.; removed to Santa Clara, Cal., on account of his wife's health and became a gardener there. Married in Turin, N. Y., Oct. 7, 1856, Lucina Bush Sackett, daughter of Gad Sheldon and Elmira (Miller) Sackett. Child: Sheldon Gaylord, m. Annie Grant Sheppard.

Lucy Kellogg, b. May 11, 1833; m. Mar. 12, 1856, Charles Henry Evarts, b. in Bath, N. Y., Jan. 2, 1824, son of Renaldo Melville and Eliza (Morley) Evarts. They lived in Leon and Irving, N. Y. Children: i. Julia Rosanna, d. young. ii. Raymond Morley, a physician in Irving; m. Anna E. Tully. iii. George William. iv. Estelle Eliza, d. young. v. Grant Kellogg. vi. Charles Henry, d. young.

454 HIRAM[7] **WARNER,** son of Rufus[6] and Hazel (Rice) Warner, born in Hopewell, Ontario Co., N. Y., May 13, 1808; died October 11, 1884, in the town of Phelps. He settled in Phelps, N. Y., in 1836, purchased land and built the residence still occupied by the family. He was a Republican in politics and held many town offices. The family were members of the Methodist Church.

Married **MARY JANE KNAPP,** born 1809; died April, 1889.

Children, born in Hopewell, N. Y.

Maria Warner, m. Robert B. Ferguson. Children: i. Sumner, resides in the town of Phelps, N. Y. ii. Everett. iii. Alice. iv. Belle. v. Clara. vi. Margaret.

Mary Jane Warner, m. Edward Aldrich and had two daughters; resided in Manchester, N. Y.

Rufus Warner, b. Feb. 26, 1833; was a farmer residing in Phelps after 1863; m. Feb., 1863, Charlotte W. Rice of Michigan, daughter of Horace and Julia (Wheat) Rice. Children, b. in Phelps: Henry Rice; Elmer Everett; Frank Wheat; Morris E.

642 *Henry D. Warner,* b. June 17, 1844; m. Frances Belle Spear.

455 TIRZAH[7] **WARNER,** daughter of Rufus[6] and Hazel (Rice) Warner, born in Hopewell, Ontario Co., N. Y., February 28, 1812; died December 3, 1863.

Married March 8, 1832, **SAMUEL C. GEROW,** son of Daniel

and Ann (————) Gerow, born probably in Yorktown, West-
chester Co., N. Y.; died in Marysville, Cal., whither he had
gone after his wife's death. He resided in Clifton Springs and
Leon, N. Y., and removed to Fort Atkinson, Wis., in 1854.
Daniel Gerow was of Huguenot ancestry and performed active
service in the Revolution as a private in the Westchester
County militia, enlisting April 21, 1779. His wife, Ann, was of
Dutch ancestry.

Children

Mary Elizabeth Gerow, b. Feb. 10, 1833; d. in Marysville, Cal., July
19, 1874; m. in Ft. Atkinson, Wis., Apr. 1, 1856, Abner Pratt. Children, b. in Ft. Atkinson: i. Frank, died. ii. Cora, died. iii. Ardelle,
resides in California.

Lydia Jane Gerow, resides in Ft. Atkinson, Wis.; m. Mar. 6, 1854,
Charles Howard Converse, b. Feb. 6, 1830, probably in Burlington,
Vt., d. in Ft. Atkinson, Wis., Sept. 3, 1896, son of Calvin and Sally
(Thomas) Converse. He was a teacher, later farmer, fruit grower
and stock buyer; assessor of the town for several years; member
of the M. E. Church. For record of children, see below.

Sarah Ann Gerow, b. Apr. 1, 1839; d. July 28, 1857; m. Aug. 16, 1855,
John Brigham. Child: Samuel G., d. Dec. 6, 1859.

Royal B. Gerow, b. Sept. 15, 1841; d. Apr. 13, 1842, in Leon, Cattaraugus Co., N. Y.

Nelson Burleigh Gerow, b. June 3, 1844; d. Aug. 15, 1844, in Leon.

Francelia Adelia Gerow, b. May 4, 1849, in Leon; d. in Marysville,
Cal., May 7, 1876.

Children of Charles H. and Lydia J. (Gerow) Converse (for further
records see the Converse Genealogy)

Lenna Eliza Converse, b. Sept. 7, 1855, in Ft. Atkinson, Wis.;
resides there; was a teacher before her marriage in Ft. Atkinson,
Dec. 21, 1874, to Rensselaer Jay Coe, b. in Stockbridge, N. Y., July
6, 1849, son of Rensselaer and Sarah (Powers) Coe. He was
educated at Oneida Seminary, engaged in business in Pennsylvania,
located in Ft. Atkinson in 1874 and founded a nursery business,
the Coe, Converse and Edwards Company, of which he is still
president. He is one of the best informed horticulturists in the
state, is a life member and has been treasurer and president of the
State Horticultural Society, and has been interested in the development of cherry and apple orchards on a large scale in the state.
He is a member of the S. A. R., a descendant of Robert Coe who
came to Boston in 1632, of John Foreman, and of David Powers,
Sr., David Powers, Jr., and Oliver Coe, Revolutionary soldiers.
Children: i. Gertrude Zella, b. Feb. 10, 1882. ii. Sara Converse,
b. May 30, 1884. Gertrude Coe was graduated from Ft. Atkin-
son High School, State Normal School at Whitewater, attended
University of Wisconsin, and taught in Beloit and Ft. Atkinson.
She is a member of the D. A. R. and of Delta Delta Delta
Sorority. Married Dec. 31, 1908, William Thaw Clark, M.D., of
Beloit, b. May 15, 1882, son of Dr. Hiram Rufus and Sadie B.

(Johns) Clark, graduate of Beloit College and of Chicago Hahne-
man Medical School. They have resided in Woodstock, Ill., and
Ft. Atkinson, now at Junction City, Kans., where Dr.
Clark is
Captain in the Medical Officers' Reserve Corps and is instructor at
Fort Riley in the Medical Officers' Training Camp. They have
one son, Robert Coe Clark, b. Aug. 17, 1912. Sara Converse Coe
was educated at High School, business college in Janesville, Wis.,
and Sacred Heart Academy in Madison; is a member of the
D. A. R.; m. June 30, 1908, Charles Joseph Telfer, b. Jan. 31,
1885, son of George Dickson and Charlotte (Morrison) Telfer,
was educated at Ft. Atkinson High School, University of Wisconsin and Cornell University; has charge of the Landscape
Department of the Coe, Converse and Edwards Nursery Company.
Children: i. Margaret Jean, b. Apr. 1, 1911. ii. Catherine Barbara, b. June 22, 1913.
Sarah Anna Converse, b. July 1, 1859; resided at Ft. Atkinson, Wis.,
after 1901; m. Nov. 25, 1880, Frederick Helmer Turner. Children: Bernard Gerow; Warner Jess.
Darwin Clarence Converse, b. Jan. 18, 1862; is in the nursery busi-
ness with Mr. Coe; m. (1) Mar., 1893, Medora Pease, (2) June
19, 1895, Helen Asenath Powers. Children: Darwin Wilber;
Helen Louise.
Nettie Adell Converse, b. Jan. 3, 1865; m. Sept. 29, 1889, Frank Cutting Edwards. Children: Frank Merle; Lillian Marguerite.
Daisy Armeda Converse, b. Aug. 17, 1874; is a graduate of a school
of oratory, and teaches.
Della Gerow Converse, b. Jan. 23, 1877; is a graduate of Normal
School, and teaches.

456 LYDIA ANN[7] WARNER, daughter of Rufus[6] and
Hazel (Rice) Warner, born July 19, 1818, in Hopewell, Ontario
Co., N. Y,; resided in Parma, N. Y.; died February 2, 1885.
Married **CHARLES DARLING.**

Children

Ann Darling, m. Amos Coe. Children: i. Charles, m. and has five
children, Charles, Jr. (m. Ruby Loce and has sons, Lawrence and
Davis), Amos (m. Altha Furney and has one son, Avery), Everett
(m. Lillian Avery in 1917), Susan (m. Harold Adams in 1918), Earle
(m. Emma Castle in 1917). ii. William, m. and has a son, Alonzo,
who m. ——— Heffner of Parma in 1916. iii. Fred, m. and has four
children, Frances, Stanley, Olive and Mildred.
Louise Darling, resides in Rochester, N. Y.; m. W. O. Marshall. Children: i. Ida, not married. ii. Belle, m. N. W. Baldwin and has a
son, Nathan. iii. Alice, m. C. H. Gallup and has a daughter, Irma,
who m. Aug. 22, 1916, M. F. Neff Stroup (and has a daughter, Margaret Alice, b. in Palmyra, N. Y., Dec. 7, 1917). iv. Louise, m.
Harry Patterson and has a daughter, Arline, who m. in Rochester,
1916, Lewis Smith.
Mary Jane Darling, resides, at Adams Basin, N. Y.; m. Frank Nichols.
Children: i. Sadie, m. Louis Arnold of Adams Basin and has chil-

dren, Lawrence and Willis. ii. Clara, m. John Chapman of Spencer-
port, and has eleven children, Ruth, Helen, Frances, John, George,
Elsie, Florence, Charles, Marjorie, Sarah, and Donald. iii. Louis.
iv. Fred, resides in Buffalo; m. Mary Brisbane, and has a daughter,
Marian. v. Burr, m. Clara Wood and has two children, Dorothy
and Charles.
Everett Darling, not married.
Sarah Darling, resides at Adams Basin, N. Y.; m. George Gallup.
Cora Darling, not married.

457 **EDWIN⁷ WARNER,** son of John⁶ and Susan Ann
(Post) Warner, born in Orleans (then Phelps), Ontario Co.,
N. Y., November 17, 1809; died in Boston, Mass., December
18, 1887.
Married in Phelps, N. Y., September 20, 1832, **POLLY ANN
MOORE,** born in Orleans (then Phelps), Ontario Co., N. Y.,
May 24, 1813, daughter of Washington and Suzanne (Rice)
Moore.

Children, born in Orleans, N. Y.

Helen Warner, b. Sept. 29, 1833; d. Apr. 7, 1881, in Jersey City, N. J.;
    m. Feb. 25, 1855, James Turner Hough of Phelps, N. Y. Children:
    i. Fred Eugene, b. Nov. 29, 1855; d. Apr. 2, 1889; m. Ida Louisa
    Wood, and had three children, Fred Eugene, b. Oct. 30, 1880, resides
    in Jersey City, not married, Lewis, b. Apr. 29, 1882, resides in the
    West, not married, and Ida Louise, b. Jan. 9, 1884, resides in Jersey
    City, m. Dec. 10, 1913, Reginald Frye. ii. Edward Warner, b. Jan.
    2, 1859; resides in Grand Forks, N. Dak.; m. Helen Louise Hall;
    no children.
Marian Warner, b. July 13, 1835; d. Nov. 3, 1881.
George Washington Warner, b. Dec. 19, 1839; d. Mar. 19, 1895, in
    Jersey City, N. J.; not married.
Flora Warner, b. Dec. 27, 1847; d. Feb. 15, 1917; resided in Peters-
    burg, Va., and Greenfield, Mass.; m. in Jersey City, N. J., Sept. 19,
    1866, John Sylvester Devlin, b. in New York City, Dec. 26, 1840,
    son of Daniel and Mary Ann (Goodwin) Devlin. Children:
    i. Daniel, b. in Richmond, Va., Dec. 28, 1867; d. Aug. 30, 1874, in
    Jersey City, N. J. ii. Helen, b. in Richmond, July 22, 1869; d. there,
    June 10, 1870. iii. Elizabeth Marian, b. in Richmond, June 16, 1871;
    m. Mar. 18, 1896, Willis H. Weissbrod of Greenfield, Mass. iv.
    Flora Hough, b. in Jersey City, Apr. 3, 1876; m. Jan. 12, 1904,
    William H. Willcox of Petersburg, Va., and has two children.

458 **ULYSSES⁷ WARNER,** son of John⁶ and Susan Ann
(Post) Warner, born in Orleans, town of Phelps, Ontario Co.,
N. Y., May 7, 1812, and resided there; died in 1896. He learned
the tanner's trade and ran a shoe shop and tannery for some
years, also conducted a dry goods and grocery store for some
time. He was justice of the peace for over thirty years and

was a member of the Legislature in 1859. He was a Universalist in religion.

Married (1) December 10, 1835, MARY ANN RICE, born in Phelps, N. Y., died July 6, 1842, daughter of Elder Caleb Rice and granddaughter of Caleb and Lucy (Leland) Rice.

Married (2) March 23, 1843, ELIZA ANN JONES, daughter of Thomas C. and Elizabeth (Derr) Jones of Hopewell, N. Y.

Child by first wife

John C. Warner, d. about 1895; was a farmer and jeweller; m. Mary A. Petty. Child: Ulysses, died.

Children by second wife

Thomas Eugene Warner, b. in Orleans, N. Y.; resides in North Tonawanda, N. Y., where he is a printer, newspaper man and editor. As a young compositor on the staff of the New York Herald he put in type the first dispatch received over the second Atlantic cable, congratulations from Queen Victoria to President Buchanan. Mr. Warner has worked in several cities at his vocation, has been village and city clerk for twenty years, alderman, fire commissioner, and has held other offices. Married in Jersey City, N. J., Sept. 29, 1876, Florence Elizabeth Hanaford, b. in Nantucket, Mar. 19, 1854, d. 1902, daughter of Rev. P. A. Hanaford, who was born in Nantucket, May 6, 1829. Child: Dionis Coffyn, b. Nov. 24, 1881; m. July 30, 1910, E. H. Santee; no children.

Achilles Warner, b. Oct. 28, 1845, in Orleans, N. Y.; is a farmer there; m. at Clifton Springs, N. Y., Jan. 20, 1869, Alice Collins, b. at East Bloomfield, N. Y., Apr. 11, 1847, daughter of Montgomery Collins. Children: i. Grace Marie, b. July 15, 1871, in Orleans; m. Dec. 16, 1896, Rollin L. Wheat; has two children, Marion and Alice. ii. Delevan Smiley, b. Feb. 10, 1883, at Jersey City, N. J., d. July 27, 1897.

643 *Carlos E. Warner,* b. Oct. 5, 1847; m. Alice Burr Van Husan.

Clara E. Warner, b. Mar. 20, 1848; m. (1) George H. Page, who died; m. (2) James T. Hough, who died.

Adelaide E. Warner, d. about 1905; m. George H. Cramer. Children: i. Harley U., a physician, m. Vera or Sara Bowen. ii. Clara, m. Herbert Pease, and has a child, Mary Adelaide. iii. Stuart L., m. Haidee Oelkers, and has two children, Stuart and Haidee. iv. Willard, died. v. Dorothy, d. about 1905. vi. Alice Janet, not married.

Jesse Post Warner, b. Jan. 16, 1851, in Orleans, N. Y.; resides there, not married; was a stenographer, now a farmer.

Alice Mary Warner, resides in Ann Arbor, Mich.; m. Rev. W. S. Jerome, a librarian at University of Michigan. He is a descendant of Andrew Warner through Andrew's granddaughter Ruth. Child: Anne Warner.

Franklin Pierce Warner, b. Nov. 11, 1852, in Orleans, N. Y.; is a physician and surgeon in Canandaigua, N. Y.; m. at Clifton Springs, N. Y., July 11, 1881, Mrs. Harriet Elizabeth Shekell Huke, daughter of Richard Henry and Lucretia (Cast) Shekell. She was born May

12, 1848, at Hopewell, N. Y., died May 17, 1912. Children: i. Anna
Laura, b. Sept. 26, 1883; d. Feb. 9, 1887. ii. Ethel May, b. May 18,
1885; d. Nov. 26, 1900. iii. Arthur Shekell, b. Aug. 28, 1886; is a
farmer.
Willard Ellis Warner, b. Oct. 14, 1860, in Orleans, N. Y.; has been an
attorney; is now a horticulturist in Ann Arbor, Mich. He was
educated in Canandaigua and taught there; took a law course at the
University of Michigan and studied law in the office of his brother
Carlos in Detroit; was admitted to the State bar in 1885 and later
to the Federal Court; was connected with his brother's firm through
its changes in partners and in 1893 became a member of the firm of
Griffin and Warner, then, in 1895, of Warner, Codd, and Warner.
Married July 26, 1904, Gertrude Agnes Friedman, b. in Buffalo,
N. Y., daughter of Charles and Alice Josephine (Smith) Friedman,
and descended from the Sackett family whose genealogy is published.
She is a member of the D. A. R.
Louis Ulysses Warner, is a minister and has resided in Sedan, Kans.
He was graduated from the University of Chicago, 1889, Bachelor
of Theology; m. Louise Garland. Children: Louise Garland;
Anna L.
Jenny Lind Warner, m. George H. Cramer. No children.

459 ORSON[7] WARNER, son of John[6] and Susan Ann
(Post) Warner, born December 4, 1816, in Orleans, N. Y.; died
there, May 27, 1852. He was a farmer in Orleans, and resided
for a time in Miami County, Ind. One of the family relates that
Orson Warner lived on the southwest of the four corners on
Warner Hill in Phelps, where his grandfather Jesse had lived.
He went to California and was gone three years. While there
he was taken sick and lost his mind. A lady wrote his destination and he was sent home in this condition, by way of the
Isthmus of Panama and New York City. From New York he
was put on a train with the directions serving as a guide, and
was put off the train at Phelps. On arriving there someone
took him up to the home of Chester Warner who recognized
him, where he stayed for several days, they meanwhile taking
care of him. He never recovered consciousness of his surroundings and died in a short time.
     Married in Orleans, April 22, 1841, ELIZA JANE SAN-
FORD, born July 14, 1819, in Redding, Conn., died in Quincy,
Mich., August 7, 1888, daughter of Seth and Esther (Couch)
Sanford of Redding.

Children, born in Miami Couunty, Ind.

Maria L. Warner, b. July 24, 1842; resides in Quincy, Mich.
Albert J. Warner, b. Sept. 26, 1844; m. Mar. 23, 1881, in Quincy,
Adella Newton. Children: i. Ethelyn J., b. Feb. 2, 1882, in Quincy;

resides there. ii. Marie N., b. Dec. 7, 1889, in Quincy; resides there; m. Aug. 16, 1912, Chauncey Reynolds.

Elliston Warner, b. Dec. 28, 1846; resided in Quincy, Mich., and now in St. Petersburg, Fla.; m. Dec. 3, 1879, Mary Culver. Children: i. Eliza, b. Sept. 3, 1880; is a teacher in North Carolina. ii. Orson, b. Mar. 18, 1882; resides in Melrose, Mass.

460 HARRIET ELIZABETH⁷ WARNER, daughter of John⁶ and Susan Ann (Post) Warner, born in Orleans, Ontario Co., N. Y., September 13, 1831; died in Quincy, Branch Co., Mich., December 13, 1913.
Married in Orleans, N. Y., April 10, 1851, **CLARK CROSBY SEARS,** born at Millplain, Conn., October 23, 1827, son of James and Deborah (Crosby) Sears. He was a farmer at Quincy, Mich.

Children

Charles Sumner Sears, b. at Seneca Castle, N. Y., Nov. 1, 1853; is a physician at Quincy, Mich.; m. in Auburn, Ind., Sept. 14, 1881, Nettie S. Shaffer, b. in Ashland Co., Ohio, Aug. 6, 1860, daughter of Christopher C. and Martha (Ciphers) Shaffer. Child: Carl C., b. in Auburn, Ind., Nov. 7, 1883; is a physician in Quincy, Mich.; m. Elsie E. McKinstry, who was born in Wayne Co., Mich.; no children.

Florence Marian Sears, b. at Seneca Castle, N. Y., Dec. 10, 1855; resides at Coldwater, Mich.; m. in Quincy, Mich., Oct. 18, 1876, Milo D. Campbell, a lawyer. Child: Jessie M.

Helen Augusta Sears, b. at Seneca Castle, N. Y., Dec. 18, 1859; resides near Quincy, Mich.; m. in Quincy, June 20, 1883, Sereno R. Mansell. Child: Ruth Belle, b. Aug. 6, 1884; m. and has a child.

George Warner Sears, b. Nov. 7, 1863, at Quincy, Mich.; resides there.

461 JEFFERSON⁷ WARNER, son of Jesse⁶ and Margaret (Hutchison) Warner, born in Phelps, Ontario Co., N. Y., June 7, 1809; died in York, Washtenaw Co., Mich., April 7, 1878.
Married in Orleans, N. Y., **SUSAN BURNETT,** born May 8, 1816; died April 15, 1880, in Moorsville, Nash Co., Mich.

Children, born in York, Mich.

644 *Anna Giuletta Warner*, b. Oct. 20, 1836; m. Otis Adams Critchett.

Isadore Warner, b. Mar. 1, 1838; d. Dec. 26, 1901; resided in Clint, Texas; m. in Ashley, Ill., 1861, William Stanfield, b. in Evansville, Ind., 1831, son of Ashley and Mary (————) Stanfield. He was a merchant. Children: i. Clyde, b. 1865; d. 1888. ii. Jessie, b. 1867; m. John W. Bubank; resides in El Paso, Texas; has a daughter, Eleanor, who m. Judge Ballard Coldwell of El Paso.

Almira Amelia Warner, b. Sept. 10, 1839 or 1840; d. Dec. 26, 1902, at Clint, Texas, buried in Monroe, Mich., where she had resided; m. Sept., 1883, in Monroe, as second wife, Otis Adams Critchett, whose first wife was her sister Giuletta; see number 644. There were no children by this marriage.

Harriet Warner, b. Sept. 20, 1841; resides near Milan, Mich.; m. in Saline, Mich., Feb. 22, 1861, Samuel Clark, a farmer, b. in Orleans, N. Y., Aug. 24, 1836, d. in York, Mich., Mar. 8, 1899, son of John and Maria (———) Clark. Children: i. Sprague S., b. Dec. 7, 1861; d. Sept. 7, 1863. ii. Vena M., b. Jan. 28, 1866; m. Sept. 23, 1885, Herbert Gilman, and has three children, Frank C., b. June 11, 1894, a student at State Normal, Mary, b. July 27, 1897, a teacher, and Doris, b. June 15, 1903.

Prudence Warner, b. May 4, 1847; resides on a fruit farm at Shaw, Ore.; m. in Ypsilanti, Mich., Oct. 25, 1871, William Dansingburg, b. at Stony Creek, Mich., May 6, 1846, son of Peter and Elizabeth (Wilson) Dansingburg. Children: i. Fred J., b. May 11, ———, at Stony Creek; is in the automobile business in New York City. ii. Lee W., b. June 24, 1891, at Stony Creek; is in the steam-fitting and plumbing business at Minot, N. Dak.

Eugene A. Warner, b. Dec. 4, 1849; d. Apr. 17, 1903.

Louisa Warner, b. Feb. 4, 1851, at Ann Arbor, Mich.; resides in Clint, Texas; m. at Saline, Mich., Jan. 2, 1881, John J. Schairer, b. in Ann Arbor, Sept. 15, 1848, son of John George and Christiana (Ruhle) Schairer. He has an alfalfa ranch.

462   HARRISON[7] WARNER, son of Jesse[6] and Margaret (Hutchison) Warner, born in Phelps, N. Y., October 8, 1815; died in Saline, Mich., January 30, 1895.

Married **EMILY E. DAVENPORT**, born 1823; died in Saline, in 1900.

Children

Oliver M. Warner, b. in York, Mich., 1841; d. 1864. He was a member of Company C, 5th Michigan Cavalry Sharpshooters, and was shot by Colonel Mosby's guerillas.

Jane Warner, b. in York, Mich.; m. Anson Harmon, who died a few years ago. Children: i. Charles, m. Anna Cregg; has three children, Harry, in service in France (May, 1918), Cecil, and Jay. ii. Maggie, m. ——— Burkhart, lives in Saline, Mich.; no children. iii. Lulu, lives with her mother in Detroit, Mich.; m. Fred Gillon and has one child. iv. Carl, d. several years ago.

John H. Warner, b. in York, Mich., 1854; d. there, 1891.

463   MARY[7] WARNER, daughter of Jesse[6] and Margaret (Hutchison) Warner. born January 15, 1818 (or November 15, 1817), in Phelps, Ontario Co., N. Y.; died in York, Mich., March 20, 1884.

Married **PARLIA PHILLIPS**, born in Phelps, July 11, 1812; died in York, Mich., October 27, 1874. He was a farmer and the children were all born on the old farm in York township which is now owned by Millard Phillips.

Children

Henriette Phillips, b. May 26, 1840; d. Oct. 19, 1899, in Bay City, Mich.; m. Apr., 1861, Ben H. Martin, who died in Bay City, Mar. 22, 1915. Child: Will L., resides in Cheboygan, Mich.

Sarah E. Phillips, b. Nov. 25, 1842; d. Oct. 1, 1909, in Milan, at the home of her brother Millard; m. Oct. 8, 1883, John W. Fuller, who died Aug. 11, 1893, in Northville, Mich.

Ellen L. Phillips, b. Mar. 22, 1844; resides at Williamsburg, Mich.; m. William T. Cook. Children: Florence; Clifton.

William E. Phillips, b. Aug. 12, 1846; d. Apr. 11, 1852.

——————, b. Feb. 16, 1849; d. Mar. 4, 1849.

Milton E. Phillips, b. Dec. 27, 1851; d. Mar. 8, 1915, at Lake Ridge, Mich.; m. Julia Carter. Children: i. Louella, died. ii. Will C., resides on his father's farm at Lake Ridge.

Millard P. Phillips, b. Oct. 11, 1855; owns the homestead farm four miles from Milan, in York township; m. Oct. 8, 1884, Clara B. Wilcox. Children: i. Lucy M., b. May 9, 1888. ii. Millard P., Jr., b. Oct. 6, 1893.

464 LYMAN[7] WARNER, son of Jesse[6] and Margaret (Hutchison) Warner, born in Phelps, N. Y., May 23, 1822; died June 3, 1893, at his home in Milan, Monroe Co., Mich., where he had been a farmer.

Married AZUBA NEAR, born September 30, 1827; died March 6, 1908.

Children

Elizabeth Warner, d. in infancy.

Ulysses J. Warner, b. in Milan, Mich., Mar. 19, 1850; is a retired farmer residing in Milan. Married in Milan, Estella Barnum, b. in Milan, daughter of Hanson Barnum, d. Mar. 6, 1908. Child: Maud, d. Jan. 13, 1912; m. Allie Montague and had one child.

645 *June Lyman Warner,* b. in Milan, Mar. 19, 1855; m. Emogene Vescelius.

465 SARAH A.[7] WARNER, daughter of Jesse[6] and Margaret (Hutchison) Warner, born in Phelps, N. Y., April 14, 1825; died in York, Mich., February 2, 1890.

Married (1) **CURTIS HARMON.**

Married (2) **EZRA O. PARKER,** a farmer.

Children of Curtis and Sarah A. (Warner) Harmon

Estella Harmon, m. Marvin Dillon; lives at Milan, Mich. Five children.

Flora Harmon, died several years ago.

Children of Ezra O. and Sarah A. (Warner) Parker

Helen Parker.

Lizzie Parker, m. John Clark.

Clark Parker.

466 JESSE[7] WARNER, 4th, son of Jesse[6] and Margaret (Hutchison) Warner, born in Phelps, Ontario County, N. Y., April 30, 1827; died September 3, 1895, in York township, Washtenaw Co., Mich., on the farm purchased from the U. S. Government by his oldest brother, Jefferson, and adjoining the homestead farm of his father. He was supervisor of York township for many years. Married April 12, 1853, **MARY ELIZA KELSEY,** born September 17, 1835, daughter of Daniel and Mary E. (Wilcox) Kelsey who settled in Washtenaw County about 1835.

Children

Helen E. Warner, b. Dec. 30, 1854; m. William Gauntlett. Children: i. Jessie, b. in Monroe County, Mich., Dec. 12, 1879; resides in Milan; m. in York, Mich., Nov. 21, 1900, Edgar J. Forsyth, b. in York, son of James and Jennie (Dings) Forsyth, and had three children, Mary Helen, b. Aug. 21, 1901, d. Oct. 10, 1901, Adadell Gauntlett, b. Aug. 11, 1903, and Wiltrud Diantha, b. Dec. 18, 1905. ii. Clyde Warner, b. July 9, 1882, in Milan township, Monroe County, Mich.; is a farmer there; m. in Saline, Mich., Apr. 22, 1903, Blanche E. Gordon, b. in Saline township, Sept. 25, 1881, daughter of David and Almeda (Collins) Gordon. Clyde Warner Gauntlett has two children, b. in Milan, Helen M., b. July 12, 1904, and William David, b. Jan. 24, 1909.

Della Warner, b. Feb. 8, 1861, in York township; d. there, Jan. 3, 1915. She was educated at Ypsilanti Normal and Business College and was a teacher before her marriage. Married Mar. 31, 1891, Theodore Josenhans, born in Leonberg, Württemberg, Germany, Sept. 27, 1852, son of Jonathan and Charlotte (————) Josenhans. He is a farmer near Milan, Mich.

Ada Louise Warner, b. Mar. 31, 1865; resides in Saline, Mich.; m. Nov. 24, 1885, Everett A. Davenport; no children.

467 ALBERT[7] WARNER, son of Jesse[6] and Margaret (Hutchison) Warner, born in Phelps, Ontario Co., N. Y., December 13, 1834; died in York township, Washtenaw Co., Mich., September 20, 1913. Married September 5, 1860, **SARAH A. WAUGH,** born in York township, September 30, 1839, resides in Milan, Mich. She was a daughter of James Wood Waugh, a mechanic, born in Bradford, Orange Co., Vt., died in York, Mich., and his wife, Abigail Phillips, who was born in Albany, N. Y. Her grandfather was Nathaniel Waugh, one of the Green Mountain Boys from Vermont in the War of 1812.

Children, born in York, Mich.

Myrtie E. Warner, b. Oct. 3, 1862; resides in Ypsilanti, Mich.; m. Oct. 17, 1883, George H. Olds, a carpenter. She attended Normal College

SEVENTH GENERATION 463

and Normal Conservatory, taught school and music. She has three children who are graduates of Normal College, two daughters and a son who is teaching in Normal College.

Ernest D. Warner, b. July 14, 1866; is a graduate of Cleary Business College, Ypsilanti, Mich.; taught school for several years; is now in real estate business in Detroit; m. June 6, 1894, Maude R. Shoulters, who died Jan. 3, 1909.

Frank J. Warner, b. Apr. 24, 1870; is a graduate of Cleary Business College, Ypsilanti, Mich.; book-keeper in Newberry, Mich.; m. (1) Aug. 12, 1894, Julia L. Hall, who died Apr. 30, 1895; m. (2) Aug. 21, 1897, Mollie Litchard, by whom he has six children. Child by Julia L. Hall: Jesse F., b. about 1895; resides with his grandmother in Milan, Mich.

468 MARGARET[7] WARNER, daughter of Jesse[6] and Margaret (Hutchison) Warner, born in York, Mich., August 11, 1837; resides in El Paso, Texas. An account of her family will be found in the Kellogg Genealogy and also in the Winslow Memorial.

Married as his second wife, in Ypsilanti, Mich., June 3, 1858, ELIJAH ELLIS KELLOGG, born in Geneseo, N. Y., June 23, 1830, son of Erastus and Elizabeth (Ellis) Kellogg, died in Clint, El Paso Co., Texas, January 28, 1893. His first wife, Katherine Redner, died in 1856, and their son, Spencer Eddy, died young. Elijah Kellogg was a farmer in Ypsilanti township until about 1871, when he removed to Ann Arbor to educate his children, and later went to Clint, Texas.

Children of Margaret Warner

Ada Louise Kellogg, b. in Ypsilanti, Mich., May 31, 1860, resides in El Paso; m. in Ann Arbor, July 15, 1884, James Clyde Critchett, b. in Ann Arbor, Oct. 25, 1862, son of Judge Otis Adams Critchett and Anna Giuletta[8] Warner. See number 644.

Courtland Ellis Kellogg, b. in Augusta, Mich., Feb. 13, 1863; is an alfalfa grower in Clint, Texas; m. in Lima, Ohio, Nov. 9, 1897, Laura Fink, b. in Wilmington, Ohio, Mar. 21, 1864, daughter of Jacob Howard and Mary Louisa (James) Fink.

Jessie Margaret Kellogg, b. in Ann Arbor, Sept. 28, 1872; resides at Mine Le Motte, Madison Co., Mo.; m. in Clint, Texas, July 14, 1890, William H. Kinnon, b. in Winona, Minn., Nov. 29, 1865, son of William Matthew Kinnon, who was born in France, 1836, and Margaret Anna Wohlwend, who was born in Switzerland in 1843. Mr. Kinnon is a mining engineer and metallurgist, general manager of the Missouri Metals Corporation. Children: i. Margaret Anna, b. in Laredo, Texas, June 8, 1892, is a graduate of Sargent's School of Physical Training in Cambridge, Mass., and now has charge of the physical training in the El Paso (Texas) High School. ii. Louise Kellogg, b. in Denver, Colo., Feb. 5, 1903. iii. William Courtland, b. in Denver, Nov. 18, 1904.

469 ELBRIDGE. OLIVER[7] **WARNER,** son of Nathan[6] and Sarah (Cook) Warner, born in Hinsdale, Mass., December 15, 1811; died in Unionville, Ohio, March 11, 1884. He removed to Ohio with his father's family when a child, and was a farmer, stock raiser and business man of Unionville.
Married (1) **NANCY NELLIS.**
Married (2) **Mrs. MINERVA SHEARS.**
Married (3) **Mrs. SHEAVERAL.**

Children by first wife, born in Unionville

Cassious Warner, b. Jan. 4, 1844; d. aged 7.
646 *Eugene Nellis Warner,* b. Jan. 10, 1847; m. Kate Augusta Hutchins.
Josephine Warner, b. Aug. 7, 1849; died; m. Nov. 3, 1868, Wilbur Cleveland.
Arthur E. Warner, b. Dec. 22, 1851; married.
Isadore Warner, b. Jan. 22, 1856; d. Jan. 21, 1862.

469a CHARLES C.[7] **WARNER,** son of David[6] and Olive (Rawson) Warner, born March 29, 1816, in New York State; died October 30, 1885. He was a baker by trade and resided in Ridgeway, Orleans County, N. Y., about 1840.
Married September 23, 1838, **ELIZA FOOTE,** born April 6, 1822; died September 18, 1904.

Children

Calista E. Warner, b. Dec. 19, 1839; d. Aug. 16, 1841.
646a *George Edward Warner,* b. Nov. 28, 1841; m. (1) Hattie Lozier, (2) Mary Louise Hooker.
Olive Warner, b. July 20, 1843; d. Apr. 1, 1913; m. Horace Stevens. Children: i. Edward, m. and had two children, Etta and ———. ii. Frank.
Charles Warner, b. Aug. 20, 1845; d. Feb. 17, 1913; m. Sabra ——— Children: i. Lavern, m. and has two children. ii. Eva, m. Ernest Lawton and d. leaving four children. ⁻
Frank Warner, b. Mar. 28, 1847; d. June 14, 1894; m. Lottie Croninger. He served in the Civil War. Children: i. Otis, m. Ellen Lane, and had children, Lester and Marion. ii. Don, m. Hattie Hodge, and had five children, Frank, Ray, Floyd, Charlie and Nellie. iii. John, m. Minnie Johnson, and had four children, Fred, Roy, Russell and Irma. iv. Myra, m. Charles Schuskaskie, and had three children, Eva, ———, and Rosemary. v. Henry D., m. Elsie Jones, and had a child, Nahoma.
Francelia A. Warner, b. Aug. 2, 1849; d. Mar. 8, 1851.
Ella Warner, b. Aug. 12, 1851; d. Oct. 23, 1912; m. (1) Adelbert Caswell, (2) Frank Cole. Children by first husband: i. Luella, m. James Welsh, and had children, Michael (m. Jean Banker, and had Edmond and Versal), Ruth (m. Samuel Emerling), Norman, Ray, and Roland. ii. George, m. Lettie Canfield, and had a son, Roy.

Addie Warner, b. Dec. 5, 1853; d. Apr. 25, 1897; m. (1) Hiram Ellison, (2) Frank Cole. Child by first husband: Clarence, m. Mabel Grover, and had three children. Child by second husband: Herbert, m. Maude Weller, and had one child.
Carl Warner, b. Sept. 7, 1856; d. July 1, 1911.
O. B. Warner, b. Dec. 23, 1858; m. Emma Pamment. Children: i. Anna, m. R. D. Williams, and has a child, Wayne. ii. Ione.
Elmer Warner, b. June 12, 1861; m. Nancy Reasoner, and has one child.
Gladys Warner, b. Aug. 8, 1864; d. Feb. 17, 1909; m. William Davey. Child: Alma, m. Lester Tripp, and has two children, Gladys and Wayne.

469b REBECCA[7] WARNER, daughter of David C.[6] and Olive (Rawson) Warner, born in Parma, N. Y., September 24, 1817; died February 7, 1894, at the home of her son David in Caledonia, Mich. She removed with her husband from New York in 1853 and settled on a farm in Oakland County, Mich., where they resided about thirty years, then retired to Lowell, Kent Co., Mich.

Married in Parma, N. Y., October 3, 1838, JOHN MC WHINNEY.

Children

Thomas McWhinney, died; was a soldier in the Civil War.
Mary McWhinney, m. in Holley, Mich., Alex Downey. Children: i. Frank, m. Eliza Gracie; has children, Russell and Francis. ii. Rena, m. Chauncey Merwin, and has four children, Gladys, Clare, Hazel and Clyde. iii. Martha, m. John Algoe; has a son, James. iv. Lafayette, m. Emma Algoe; no children. v. Mary, m. John Smith; has five children. vi. Nettie, m. Lee Hoag.
William McWhinney, m. Mary Coppens. Children: i. Frank, m. and has children, Louis and Stanley. ii. Edna, m. Joseph Parker; has children, Gladys, Bernice, Floyd and June. iii. George, m. Vesta Parker; has two children. iv. Anna, m. Fred Kidd.
Annie McWhinney, m. William Lind. Children: i. Edwin, m. Carrie Shrouder; has children, Ruth, Olive, Annie, Emerson, Donald, William and Lillian. ii. Lillian, m. Will Jackson; had children, Audrey and Elgin (who died). iii. Elmer, d. not married. iv. Abbey Bell, died. v. Emma, m. Joseph Peet; had children, Wendell, Joseph, Paul and Edward.
David McWhinney, resides in Caledonia, Mich.; m. Emma Smith. Children: i. Bertha, m. Charles Tape; has children, Bernice and Warren. ii. Blaine, m. Edna ———; no children. iii. Boyd, m. and has three children, one of whom is Margaret.
Andrew McWhinney, m. Ella Lewis and had a son, Lewis, who died.
Olive McWhinney, m. Walter Heimer. Children: i. Norman, m. Ruth Pratt and d. leaving two children. ii. Jennie, died. iii. Nettie. iv. Earl. v. Pearl, died.
Eveline McWhinney, b. July 1, 1859; m. (1) in 1874, Chauncey Holdridge; m. (2) Mar. 12, 1881, William Henry Pinckney. Children by

30

first husband: i. Anna, b. Aug. 28, 1875; m. Feb. 21, 1914, Frank
Fairchild, and had children, William, Harold and Richard.   ii.
Chauncey, b. Aug. 14, 1879; m. Adeline Grody, and had children,
Gleason and Realdus. Children by second husband: i. Fred, m.
Alva Sayles; had children, Carlyle, Phoebe and Tilden. ii. Earl.
iii. Fay, m. (1) Zulie Witt, (2) Minnie Mayo. iv. Truly, m. Mil-
dred Patton; had children, Evelyn, Arthur and Robert. v. Dewey,
m. Mary Brooks.

469c MARY[7] WARNER, daughter of David[6] and Olive
(Rawson) Warner, born probably in Parma, N. Y.; died January 12, 1903.
Married Rev. JOHN FAIRCHILD, who died March 7, 1879,
aged 75 years, 6 months. He was a mechanic by trade, but
became a teacher and Baptist minister. They removed from
Carryville, N. Y., to Michigan in May, 1852, locating in Cascade
township, Kent County. He organized the first Baptist church
in that part of the country and, with his wife as Sunday School
superintendent, helped to bring a greater uplift of spirituality
into the community of which they were pioneers. During the
week he worked at clearing his farm, and on Sundays would
preach at two or three places. The churches at Whitneyville,
Stone School House, and Alto were established through his
influence.

Children

Horace Rawson Fairchild, b. in Oakfield, N. Y., May 6, 1840; resides
   in Grand Rapids, Mich.; is a retired farmer; m. in Caledonia town-
   ship, Kent Co., Mich., Oct. 29, 1867, Charlotte Sweet, b. in Allegany
   Co., N. Y., Dec. 1, 1849, daughter of George ' P. and Amanda
   (————) Sweet. Mr. Fairchild served in the Civil War from
   August, 1862. Children, all b. in Kent Co., Mich.: i. George H.,
   b. 1869; d. Sept. 22, 1904, not married. ii. John, m. Oct. 29, 1889,
   May Chatterdo, and has a son, Emmett, b. about 1894, now in the
   A. E. F. in France (1918); and a daughter Eva, b. about 1907. iii.
   Nettie, m. May 19, 1896, Harvey Lewis; has children, Muriel, b.
   about 1898, and Floyd, b. about 1908. iv. Mary, m. Nov. 13, 1898,
   Charles Drake; has a child, Ora, b. about 1907. v. Dwight, m.
   Oct. 17, 1901, Ida Lewis. vi. Minnie, m. Jan. 4, 1905, Charles
   Hughes.
Nellie J. Fairchild, b. in Batavia, N. Y., Sept. 4, 1843; resides in Grand
   Rapids, Mich. (St. Petersburg, Fla., winter of 1918-9); m. in Lowell,
   Mich., Sept. 6, 1868, Nathaniel L. McCarty, b. in Dumfries, Canada,
   May 6, 1838, d. Nov. 7, 1878, son of John and Sarah (————)
   McCarty. Children, b. in Lowell: i. Loyal N., b. Aug. 22, 1870.
   ii. Mary Alice, b. Mar. 6, 1873; d. Nov. 10, 1873. iii. Ernest Joy,
   b. Jan. 3, 1875. iv. Nellie Almeda, b. Jan. 17, 1877; m. in Lowell,
   July 15, 1896, Dr. Glenn G. Towsley, and has children, b. in Lowell,
   Paul G., b. Sept. 27, 1897, now in the U. S. service, and Catherine E.,
   b. May 5, 1901.

George D. Boardman Fairchild, served in the Civil War and died Dec. 12, 1891, aged 45 years, leaving no children; m. Marian Kent.
Laura F. Fairchild, m. at McCord, in 1896, William Baker. She died May 17, 1904, aged 56 years, leaving no children.

469d JANE⁷ WARNER, daughter of David⁶ and Olive (Rawson) Warner, born in Parma, N. Y., November 26, 1821; resided in Cascade, Alaska, Kent Co., Mich. Married in Carryville, N. Y., November 22, 1840, HORACE SEARS, born in New Durham, N. Y., May 3, 1819, son of Chauncey and Sally (Shufeldt) Sears. His grandfather was in the Revolutionary War. Horace Sears was a farmer in Greene County, N. Y., until 1843, when he removed to Kent County, Mich. The family are Baptists.

Children, born at the homestead in Kent County, Mich.

Alice C. Sears, b. Aug. 19, 1847; resides in Caledonia, Mich.; m. Charles Dunham, a farmer and breeder of imported horses. Children: i. George, m. Mamie Cavanaugh, and has three children. ii. Fred, m. and lives in Oregon.
Levant C. Sears, b. Mar. 3, 1853; is a farmer in Michigan; m. Julia Hall. Children: i. William, m. and has three children. ii. Nellie, m. and has three children. iii. Horace, died. iv. Charles. v. Addie, m. and has one child. vi. Harley, m. and has a child.
Walter Sears, b. Mar. 7, 1856; d. Apr. 7, 1856.
William W. Sears, b. Dec. 25, 1857; is a farmer and stock raiser in Alaska, Mich.; m. in Caledonia, Apr. 10, 1882, Lizzie McGregor, b. in New York City, July 15, 1859. Children: i. Roy, died. ii. Percy, m. Ethel Thompson, and has three children. iii. ———. iv. Genevieve, m. G. Hoppough of Belding, Mich., and has a child. v. Arlo.
Mary Addie·Sears, b. Aug. 29, 1859; resided at Mt. Pisgah, Ind., later at McCord, Mich.; m. Samuel Snyder, a farmer. Children: i. ———, died. ii. Alma. iii. Glenn, b. at McCord, Mich.; m. and had children, Thelma, B. Melba, and Ora. iv. Lena, m. John Campbell. v. Wilma, died.

469e LEWIS⁷ WARNER, son of David⁶ and Olive (Rawson) Warner, born June 2, 1823, in Parma, N.˙Y.; died in Lowell, Mich., November 14, 1906. The first twenty-four years of his life were spent on his father's farm at Parma and Carryville, N. Y. He was educated in the common schools and at Carryville Seminary. In the early forties he went to Michigan and helped clear the forest all around the little town of Lowell. He was a friend of the Indians as well as of the white men. He bought his first farm near Hillsdale, where he was married in 1856. In 1858 he returned to the old Carryville homestead to care for his aged parents. About 1861 his father sold this and went to Michigan to live with a daughter and Lewis bought a farm at Albion, Mich., where he was living when the Civil War broke out. Leaving his wife and four small children, he enlisted and remained until the close of the war. In 1868 he purchased a farm near Grand Rapids and, seven years later, one in Keene township. He and his wife spent their last years in the home of their daughter, Mrs. Curtiss of Lowell. Mr. War·ner was a well-informed man, kept pace with all the great issues of the day, was interested in public welfare, was a member of the Baptist Church of Alto, and an ardent advocate of temperance.

Married in Hillsdale, Mich., February 20, 1856, **ROSA A HARRIS,** born January 5, 1830, died March 19, 1910, in Lowell, Mich., daughter of Stephen and Mary (Halit) Harris. Her father and his brother Benjamin were among the first settlers near Chicago and bought homes on the present site of the city. In company with other pioneer settlers her mother, carrying Rosa in her arms, ran to Fort Dearborn, where they escaped the Indian massacre. At the age of eighteen she traveled alone to New Bedford, Mass., where she made her home with Edreck Clark and wife, receiving her education and learning the tailor's trade. Upon her return to Hillsdale she taught until her marriage. She was a lover of music and wrote many poems. A volume entitled "Here and there" was published in 1886, and others were published in papers. The last was written after she was eighty years old and appeared in her obituary. Never of strong health, in her later years she became almost totally deaf and blind, but she retained her beautiful Christian spirit throughout her whole life with its ·many trials and hardships.

Children

Wilbur Lea Warner, b. Dec. 4, 1856, near Hillsdale, Mich.; m. Jan. 1, 1895, Alice Middaugh. Children: i. Marjory, m. June 22, 1917, Eugene Phillips, and has a child, Mary Evaline, b. Oct. 22, 1918. ii. Gladys, m. June 22, 1917, David Phillips, has a son, David, Jr. (or Howard), b. June 12, 1918. iii. Genevieve. iv. Wilma Lea.

Mark Warner, b. in Oakfield, N. Y., Apr. 1, 1858; m. Dec. 22, 1881, Olive Sayles, who d. Sept. 25, 1911. Children: i. Ray, m. Vera Brown, and has children, Mark, Judd and Ralph. ii. Emma, m. Robert Gorden, resides at Bremerton, Wash. iii. Edith, m. John Van den Bosh, Oct. 15, 1912, and had children, Jason, Emily and ———. iv. Ethel, d. in infancy.

Judson Rawson Warner, b. Oct. 8, 1860, in Oakfield, N. Y.; d. Dec. 23, 1911; m. Dec. 23, 1891, Dora Jepson, Clarksville, Mich. Children: i. Max, b. Oct. 27, 1892. ii. ———, d. in infancy. iii. Clifford, b. in Alto, Mar., 1896. iv. Geneva, b. in Alto, May 22, 1902.

646b *Mary Evelyne Warner*, b. Apr. 9, 1862; m. Earl Custer Curtiss. (*Twins*), d. in infancy.
Grant Warner, m. (1) in 1890, Maude Cogswell, and had a child, Cecil, b. June 13, 1892; m. (2) Winnie Yates; resides in Lowell, Mich.
Mabelia Warner, m. at Lowell, Mich., Nov. 10, 1886, J. O. Scott. Children: i. Lewis, b. Aug. 16, 1887. ii. Joseph, b. in Keene, May 12, 1892; m. in Apr., 1917, Mable Gardner, and had a son, Bertram. iii. Harold. iv. Daisy, died. v. John Linwood, b. Mar. 18, 1901. vi. Beatrice, b. in Lowell, June 7, 1911. vii. Elmo, b. 1912.
Newton Warner, b. Aug. 7, 1870, in Grand Rapids, Mich.; m. Nov. 26, 1890, Mary Bourough. Children: i. Claude, b. Sept. 25, 1892; m. Lela Hurley in 1913, and has children, Eva and Mary. ii. Royden, b. Dec. 4, 1895. iii. Lewis Alva, b. 1897.
Maude Warner, b. Aug. 1, 1872, in Grand Rapids; m. June 2, 1895, in Alto, Mich., Charles Oberley. Children: i. Rose Mildred, b. Nov. 12, 1896, in Keene. ii. Charles Henry, b. at Kalkaska, Mich., Feb. 1, 1898; died. iii. Ila Margaret, b. at Kalkaska, Sept., 1900. iv. Ruby, b. at Alto, Apr., 1902. v. Warner, b. at Grand Rapids, 1903. vi. Richard, b. at Grand Rapids, Dec. 4, 1904.
Captain Joe Warner, b. Oct. 12, 1874, in Grand Rapids; d. May 8, 1881.
Rosa Warner, b. Oct. 16, 1876, at Lowell, Mich.; d. May 18, 1881.

469f **LYDIA⁷ WARNER**, daughter of Warham⁶ and Cyn thia (Adams) Warner, born March 4, 1802, in Gorham, N. Y.; died in 1873, buried in Albion, Mich.

Married **LEVI MURRAY**, who died in 1852. They removed to Michigan in 1833 and purchased a farm in South Albion. He died while on a trip to California to better his finances, and she resided on the farm until her children were grown.

Children

Julia Ann Murray, m. ——— Finley.
Loretta Murray, m. ——— Crykendall.
Walter Murray, d. leaving four children: i. Freeborn, resides in Colorado, not married. ii. Levi, resides in California, not married. iii. Ella, m. J. Hughes and died leaving two children. iv. Mary, lives in Homer, Mich.
Cynthia Murray, m. John Mount. Children: i. Lena, m. (1) Byron Angevine and had two children, Harry (m. Eleanor Dart, had four children, Byron, Rachel, d. young, Lottie and Louise) and Lottie (m. Burt Kibbe and d. two or three years later, leaving no children); m. (2) Lafayette Crandall, who d. leaving a son, Mason, who resides with his mother on her farm in Albion township. ii. Frank, d. leaving a son, Leslie, who resides with his mother in Homer, Mich. iii. Rose, m. and lives near Litchfield, Mich.
Chandler Murray, m. and has children: i. Burt, resides in the state of Washington, not married. ii. Madalina, resides in California, not married.
Mary Murray, m. Bert Reynolds of Concord, Mich., where they resided. Child: Hattie, m. Leo Parsons and resides in Union City, Mich.

469g LUCRETIA⁷ WARNER, daughter of Warham⁶ and
Cynthia (Adams) Warner, born November 25, 1803.
Married in Albion, Mich., **SAMUEL DOUGLAS.**

Children

Warham Douglas, m. Lydia Cady. Child: Lena.
Lee Douglas, m. Mary Murphy. Children: Mary; Sarah; Louise.
Almyra Douglas, b. in Sheridan, Calhoun Co., Mich., Nov. 25, 1848;
resides in Albion, Mich.; m. there, Sept. 4, 1865, James J. Earl, b.
in Steuben Co., N. Y., Mar. 16, 1836, d. Apr. 21, 1897, son of John
and Mariah Earl. Children: i. Frank, b. Mar. 2, 1867, at Kinzua,
Pa.; d. aged 7 weeks. ii. Hettie E., b. May 30, 1869, in Sheridan,
Mich.; m. —— Benjamin; had four children, b. in Nelson, Kent
Co., Mich., Earl, b. June 13, 1891, Fay E., b. Aug. 28, 1892, Berma D.,
b. July 8, 1894 (m. —— Wall, and has children, Virginia, Donald
and Margaret), and Beulah L., b. Apr. 24, 1896. iii. L. Orrena, b.
Sept. 28, 1871; d. at Evans, Kent Co., Mich., July 6, 1913; m. ——
Porter; had a son, John Martilles, b. at Evans, Oct. 14, 1911. iv.
Lucretia M., b. June 23, 1874, at Sheridan, Mich.; m. —— Cowles;
had a child, Joy Lucretia, b. Oct. 5, 1911, at Nelson, Mich. v. John
Samuel, b. Feb. 11, 1876, in Sheridan; m. and has nine children, b.
in Nelson: Winnafreda, b. July 4, 1897, Wareham ·Douglas, b. Mar.
28, 1899, Thelma M., b. Aug. 22, 1900, Harvey J., b. Sept. 27, 1902,
Elwyn, b. Feb. 1, 1905, Archie W., b. Feb. 28, 1906, Octa N., b. June
7, 1910, Elma May, b. July 27, 1912, and John Samuel, b. June 14,
1917. vi. Myra E., b. in Nelson, Oct. 7, 1882; m. —— Wetherell
and has a child, Bernard Earl, b. in Albion, May 7, 1907.

469h WILLIAM ADAMS⁷ WARNER, son of Warham⁶
and Cynthia (Adams) Warner, born January 30, 1816, in Gorham, Ontario Co., N. Y.; died October 1, 1884; resided in
Albion, Mich. When he was but six weeks old his parents
moved to Parma, N. Y., and in 1834 to Michigan. They
traveled through Canada with horses and wagon and settled in
Albion, Calhoun Co., Mich., where William bought his first
location for himself in 1840. The same year he bought the
farm of 300 acres on which he lived for the remainder of his
life. He was a non-commissioned officer in the patriot army
of General Sam Houston in the war of independence in Texas
for two years. He was one of those who crossed the plains to
California in 1849. He remained there for two years and was
moderately successful financially. He was generous almost to
a fault, kind and indulgent to his family and especially kind
to the poor. He joined the Masonic fraternity when about
thirty-five years of age and soon after, the Knights Templar.
He was a zealous Mason all his life and his funeral services

were conducted by the lodge to which he belonged. He died
suddenly of neuralgia of the heart while driving in his buggy
to Albion.
Married April 9, 1839, **MARIA J. FINCH**, born in Monroe
County, N. Y., August 8, 1820.

Children

Warham Warner, b. Feb. 3, 1845.
Julia Maria Warner, b. July 28, 1846; m. Adam Clark Green. Children: i. Rosa. ii. Bell. iii. Adeline. iv. Grace. v. Hettie, d.
aged 18.
Martha Harriet Warner, b. July 10, 1848, at Albion, Mich.; d. in
Concord, Mich., Mar. 1, 1892. She spent several years in Albion
College when a young woman, and in later life was an active Christian woman in her community. Married June 19, 1867, Philip Weit-
zel. Children: i. Edward Warner, b. in Albion, Mar. 7, 1878; m.
(1) Etta Kellogg, by whom he had a child, Edna Caroline, b. Dec.
11, 1899; m. (2) Lavina Johnston of Battle Creek, and had a child,
Philip, b. July 5, 1910, in Battle Creek. ii. Lura Adella, b. in Brown-
ington, Mo.; m. Ernest Van Wormer of Concord, Mich., and has
five children, Clarence (now in Signal Corps, A. E. F.), Andrew
(now in Auto Mechanics Division, A. E. F.), Robert, Dana and
Arthur. iii. Stanley Joy, b. in Marengo, Mich.; m. Lenna Krauseur;
has two children, Otto and Richard. iv. Arthur, b. in Marengo, Mich.
v. Clara Louise, b. Feb. 20, 1884, in Concord, Mich.; d. there, Sept.
12, 1894. vi. Dana Bell, b. Dec. 25, 1885.
Hettie Electa Warner, b. Nov. 5, 1851; m. Henry Bradley. Children:
i. Mary, m. Ray Haight; had children, Edna and Hester. ii. Herbert, m. Laura Holt, and had three children. iii. Bertha, m. (1) Lee
Marsh, and had two children, Bradley and Janina; m. (2) Charles
Yoder, and has a son, Charles, Jr. iv. Will, not married. v. Eugene,
m. Maude Mulvaney, and has children, Leland and Thomas. vi.
Roy, m. Louise Wallisdorfs, and has a child, Hettie Louise.
Lura Adella Warner, b. Oct. 21, 1853; m. Colley B. Wisner. Chil-
dren: i. Warham, d. in infancy. ii. Marion, d. in Detroit. iii.
Roxy, d. in Flint, Mich., Aug., 1918.
Mandana Gracia Warner, b. Sept. 24,'1855; m. Charles H. Cook, M.D.
After her husband's death she studied medicine at Indiana Univer-
sity and carried on a most successful practice for more than twenty
years.
George F. Warner, adopted.
William Robert Warner, b. Aug. 19, 1857; m. Jennie Crittenden.
Children: i. Harry, m. May Boughton; had children, Marjorie,
Ruth and Harold. ii. Medora Eloise, m. Joseph Cavanaugh; had
children, Mary (m. Lee Stiegelmaier and lives in Jackson, Mich.),
Leo and Harry. iii. Charles Robert, resides in Albion, Mich.; m.
Edna Gale; has a son, William R. iv. Bessie M., d. in 1909; m.
Charles Ely.
Mary Theresa Warner, b. Aug. 14, 1859; resides in Clarendon; m.
John Blue. Children: i. William, is an officer in the U. S. A. ii.
Florence.

Rosa Belle Warner, b. Mar. 4, 1862; m. Millard Fillmore Stowe; no children.
James Darius Warner, b. Oct. 21, 1863; resides in Albion, Mich.; m. (1) Eliza Lynch, (2) Diana Wright. Child: Marie, d. young.

470 ALONZO ELIJAH[7] WARNER, son of Titus[6] and Mary (Baggs) Warner, born October 13, 1794, in Belchertown, Mass.; died there, August 11, 1850. He was a successful farmer in Belchertown and his name occurs in town records and deeds, as the owner of considerable property.

Married (1) in Amherst, Mass., October 14, 1819 (intention recorded in Belchertown, September 12, 1819), SARAH STETSON, born in Amherst, Mass., July 22, 1797, daughter of Gideon and Mary (or Nancy) (Warner) Stetson.

Married (2) December 27, 1821, recorded in Belchertown, RUTH COOKE, born about 1802, died March 25, 1862, aged 60, died and buried at Belchertown. She was the sister of David S. Cooke, and of Sylvester Cooke, a Presbyterian minister. She was a woman of fine character and an earnest Christian worker in the Congregational Church at Belchertown. She was said to be, in her youth, the most beautiful woman in Hampshire County.

Children, born in Belchertown

Luman or *Charles Luman Warner,* b. about 1823; d. in Belchertown, Oct. 11, 1905, aged 82, buried in South Hadley. He was a farmer in Belchertown and joined the Congregational Church there in 1850. Married Mar. 31, 1846, Sarah A. Thompson, b. in Palmer, Mass., Feb. 28, 1829, daughter of Estus Thompson, d. May 1, 1915, buried in.South Hadley. Children: i. George Stetson, b. in Granby, Apr. 14, 1848; d. Sept. 13, 1915, in Belchertown, where he had spent the later part of his life, active in the welfare of the community; buried in South Hadley; was not married. ii. Ella, m. Arthur Chapin, lived in South Hadley Falls where both were valued members of the Congregational Church and sang in the choir for many years. iii. Edward, d. about 1885; was married and had a daughter who is teaching in the public schools of Northampton, Mass.

647 *John Warner,* b. about 1826; m. (1) Margaret M. Shumway, (2) Arminda C. Leach.
648 *Stetson Titus Warner,* b. July 25, 1828; m. Hannah Coy Richardson.
649 *George Lemuel Warner,* b. 1832; m. (1) Harriet L. Williams, (2) Helen Levantia Bogue.
Sarah Warner, b. about 1833; d. about 1906; m. Sept. 26, 1865, as second wife, John Truesdall, b. in Eastford, about 1830, son of Artemas and Floretta (————) Truesdall. He died about 1885-90. He was a mechanic and resided in Chicopee during the early years of their married -life. In the seventies they removed to Granby "Hollow" where he operated the Aldrich grist mill. Both died in Granby.

650 *Mary Elizabeth Warner*, b. Apr. 4, 1834; m. Martin M. Pulver.
Ellen Warner, b. about 1836; m. in Belchertown, Mass., Mar. 23, 1852, Willard Shumway, b. in Belchertown, about 1829, a farmer, son of Elijah Shumway. They spent their married life in South Hadley Falls, Holyoke and Springfield. Both died about 1903-8. Children: i. Clara, d. about 1913; m. Henry Moody, an expert mechanic who survived her and resides in Springfield, Mass. (had an adopted son, Frank Moody, who served in the Spanish War and was killed in Cuba). ii. Elizabeth. iii. Frank. iv. Fred.
651 *Lydia Ann Warner*, b. Nov. 30, 1839; m. Martin Sanford Arnold.
———, b. about 1841; d. May 2, 1850, aged 9 years.
652 *Celia Gertrude Warner*, b. Sept. 24, 1847; m. Marland Smith Hewes.
Osman Warner, d. young.
Elliott Warner, d. young.
Frank Warner, d. young.

471 PARK[7] WARNER, son of Titus[6] and Mary (Baggs) Warner, born September 29, 1803, in Belchertown, Mass.; died November 15, 1871, in Hadley, Mass. He resided in Granby, South Hadley and Amherst; was a selectman of Granby for several years between 1851 and 1861; representative in 1853.

Married October 6, 1825, intention recorded in Belchertown, September 17, 1825, JOANNA ADAMS, born in Shutesbury, Mass., March 30, 1805, died in Springfield, Mass., February 8, 1887, daughter of Asa, Jr., and Clarissa (Eastman) Adams. The line comes from Henry[1] Adams of Braintree, Edward[2], b. in England, 1630, John[3], Thomas[4], Asa[5], Asa[6]. The Adams family in England traces back many generations to one Ap Adam who came out of the marches of Wales and had a son, Sir John ap Adam, baron of the realm from 1296 to 1307. See Genealogy of the family of Henry Adams.

Children

Austin Warner, b. in Belchertown, Aug. 13, 1826; d. in Granby, Oct. 19, 1844.
Sarah Warner, b. in Amherst, Mar. 2, 1828; d. Mar. 3 or 5, 1828, buried in Amherst.
653 *Charles Adams Warner*, b. in Amherst, Sept. 5, 1829; m. Catharine Knight.
George Warner, b. in Granby, Jan. 22, 1835; d. Feb. 19, 1895, not married. He resided in Springfield, Mass.
654 *Lucien Warner*, b. in Granby, Feb. 22 or 23, 1837; m. (1) Adelia F. Silvey, (2) Mrs. Sadie K. Jónes.
Mary Jane Warner, b. in Granby, Dec. 8, 1841; d. Mar. 13, 1868, at Columbus, Ohio; m. in Granby, Oct. 2, 1866, Clinton W. Stebbins, b. in Granby about 1843, son of Cyrus and Mary Ann (———) Stebbins. He was a publisher. Child: Mary, b. 1868; d. about 1873.
Ella Maria Warner, b. Jan. 10, 1846; d. Mar. 12, 1846.
Milan Park Warner, b. Aug. 5, 1848; d. Aug. 29, 1903, not married. He was a landscape photographer in Springfield, Mass.

472 JEREMY DICKINSON⁷ WARNER, son of Jonathan Coleman⁶ and Achsah (Dickinson) Warner, birth not recorded in Amherst, Mass., where several of his brothers and sisters were baptized, but date given as May 23, 1813, in the Rathbone Genealogy, p. 288. He resided in Waukesha, Wis., and, after March, 1859, in Lewiston, Mo. He was mentioned in his father's will, 1842.

Married at Wauwatosa, Wis., May 5, 1841, **EMILY RATHBONE,** born August 14, 1814, died April 8, 1874, daughter of Benjamin Bagnal and Eliza Abigail (Smith) Rathbone of Springport, Cayuga Co., N. Y.

Children, born in Waukesha County, Wis.

Theodore Bridgeman Warner, b. Mar. 12, 1842; served in the Civil War in the 50th Ill. Vol. Inf.

Charles Rathbone Warner, b. Sept. 18, 1843; served in the 50th Ill. Vol. Inf.

Frederick Denison Warner, b. Dec. 1, 1846; served in the 50th Ill. Vol. Inf.; d. Dec. 1, 1864, in the Army Hospital at Nashville, Tenn.; not married.

Benjamin Franklin Warner, b. Aug. 23, 1848; served in the 14th Missouri Cavalry from Apr. 8, 1865, to Nov. 17, 1865; m. Apr. 28, 1880, Emily Blackman. Children: i. Ida Bell, b. Nov. 8, 1881. ii. Mary Myrtle, b. Jan. 26, 1885.

George Washington Warner, b. Apr. 2, 1851; resided on the old homestead farm in Lewiston, Mo.; m. Jan. 24, 1877, Celia A. Perjine. Children: i. Emily Albertie, b. Feb. 2, 1878. ii. Carlotta Elizabeth, b. Jan. 25, 1880. iii. Charles Leonard, b. Oct. 13, 1881. iv. Howard Denton, b. Feb. 24, 1884. v. Lester Vernon, b. Feb. 16, 1886. vi. Henry Earle, b. Dec. 13, 1887. vii. Orval, b. Nov. 28, 1889. viii. Cecil, b. Apr. 19, 1892. ix. Hugh, b. Mar. 8, 1895.

Sarah Augusta Warner, b. Mar. 3, 1855; d. Aug. 10, 1855, in Lewiston, Mo.

473 JAMES WHITON⁷ WARNER, son of John⁶ and Caroline (Whiton) Warner, born in Hatfield, Mass., May 11, 1809; died November, 1895. He was a farmer in Hatfield and also did auctioneering. He was active in town matters and held the offices of constable selectman, school committee and others.

Married March 30, 1836, **LOUISA BARDWELL LONGLEY,** born in Hatfield, January 14, 1816, died January 10, 1890, daughter of Alpheus and Louisa Sarah (Bardwell) Longley of Hatfield.

Children, born in Hatfield

Charles Longley Warner, b. Apr. 11, 1837; a farmer and tobacco grower in Hatfield; m. Nov. 23, 1864, Maria L. Fitch, b. Aug. 29, 1844, daughter of John T. and Julia (White) Fitch of Hatfield. Children, b. in Hatfield: i. Harvey or Harry F., b. Aug. 13, 1867; d. Oct. 13 or 31, 1873. ii. Charles Edward, b. Aug. 16, 1872; resides in Hatfield; m. Oct. 30, 1894, Myra Josephine Field, b. Mar. 19, 1871, daughter of Henry W. and Marietta (Wade) Field of North Hatfield; had children, Harold Fitch, b. July 9, 1895, d. May 14, 1896, and twins, Donald Fitch and Dorothy Field, b. Sept. 27, 1899 (Donald died June 17, 1907). iii. Luda Fitch, b. Jan. 27, 1877; d. Oct. 28, 1900.

Mary Louisa Warner, b. Nov. 26, 1838; m. William D. Billings, who was town clerk of Hatfield from 1858 to 1905. They resided for some years in the house that was the birthplace of Sophia Smith, the founder of Smith College.

Sarah Ann Warner, b. Mar. 26, 1841; m. Sept. 28, 1870, Caleb D. Bardwell, b. Sept. 28, 1840, son of Elijah and Cynthia (Field) Bardwell. He was a soldier in the Civil War from Hatfield, in Company K, 52d Regiment, Mass. Volunteers.

Moses Edward Warner, b. Feb. 3, 1843; d. Jan. 11, 1902.

Egbert Seward Warner, b. Feb. 25, 1845; resides in Hatfield. He was educated there and began work in the general store at Hatfield. He later became a successful tobacco raiser. About 1873 he took up veterinary surgery and practiced in connection with his farm. He was local agent of the S. P. C. A. and State Inspector of cattle. For over thirty years he acted as auctioneer. In town offices he was at various times constable, selectman and on the school committee and was also a member of the Hatfield sinking fund commission. Married Nov. 19, 1874, Mary Julia Hunt, b. May 16, 1852, d. May 30, 1880. Children: i. Cora Hunt, b. June 27, 1876. ii. Caroline Holt, b. Mar. 12, 1879, was graduated from the Hartford Academy and has taught there and on Cape Cod.

John Alpheus Warner, b. Oct. 10, 1846; m. Mrs. Elizabeth Bacon, who d. Apr., 1891; no children.

James Dickinson Warner, b. Apr. 24, 1849; was graduated from the University of Michigan, Ph.B., 1874; is a cement manufacturer of Long Beach, Cal.; m. Oct. 20, 1875, Hannah Bach of Ann Arbor, Mich. Children: Mosco and Clive.

Benjamin Maltby Warner, b. Jan. 14, 1853; d. Jan. 21, 1917; resided in Hatfield and was a farmer and owned several houses there; m. in Hatfield, Feb. 20, 1877, Ella Elizabeth Fitch, b. in Hatfield, Mar. 5, 1854, daughter of George Clinton and Sarah Root (Kingsley) Fitch. Children, b. in Hatfield: i. Mariam Ella, b. Aug. 1, 1878. ii. Maude Fitch, b. Jan. 13, 1885. iii. Isabel Sara, b. Jan. 9, 1889; m. in Hatfield, July 2, 1912, Richard Hughes of Greene, N. Y., son of Edward and Anna (Harvey) Hughes. He is a professor in the High School in Torrington, Conn., and they have a child, Elizabeth Anna, b. in Brattleboro, Vt., July 7, 1913.

George Whiton Warner, b. July 5, 1855; m. Oct. 3, 1883, Nellie M.

Fisher, daughter of Samuel Fisher of South Deerfield. Children:
i. Ray Fisher, b. June 14, 1885. ii. Hazel Louisa, b. Mar. 26, 1887.
iii. Gladys Martiel, b. Sept. 18, 1888. iv. Dorothy Osborn, b. Dec.
31, 1894.
Caroline Lydia Warner, b. Feb. 15, 1858; m. Oct. 11, 1893, Arthur G.
Holt of Minnesota.
Louis Ward Warner, b. Oct. 25, 1860; d. Jan. 23, 1864.

474 ELIZA ANN[7] WARNER, daughter of John[6] and Caroline (Whiton) Warner, born in Hatfield, Mass., July 27, 1827;
died in Prescott, Ont., December 22, 1858.

Married in Hatfield, March 30, 1848, as his second wife,
SOLYMAN WARD GRANT, born October 8, 1806, at East
Windsor Hill, Conn., died at Waverley, Mass., December 19,
1882. He was the son of Epaphras and Lydia (King) Grant.
He resided in New York City; Prescott, Ontario, Canada;
Ogdensburg, N. Y.; Waverley, Mass. For many years he was
a fur trader for Cronin, Hurxthal and Sears, going west by
wagon train and trading beads and trinkets with the Indians.
He was also in the employ of Grant and Barton of New York
City. In Prescott he owned a sawmill. After 1862 he resided
on a farm. He married (1) September, 1836, Lucinda F.
Rollo, who died in 1846, leaving children: Lucy Amelia;
Arthur Morris; Ralph Rollo; Lucinda Frances, d. young.
After the death of Eliza Ann Warner he married (3) December
2, 1861, Maria Carter, no children. (Grant Genealogy.)

Children of Solyman and Eliza Ann (Warner) Grant

Luda Warner Grant, b. in Brooklyn, N. Y., Aug. 14, 1850; resides in
Dorchester, Mass.; m. in Waverley, Mass., Jan. 4, 1872, Benjamin
Turner Stephenson, b. in Boston, Mar. 27, 1849, son of Benjamin
Turner and Nancy Kelleran (Hall) Stephenson. Children: i.
Frederick Howe, d. young. ii. Harris Grant. iii. Edith Alice. iv.
Barton Kingman. v. Benjamin Turner. vi. Luda Marguerite. vii.
Helen Claire.
Esther Parsons Grant, b. in East Windsor, Conn., Aug. 21, 1853; d. in
Prescott, Ont., Dec. 28, 1858.
Ellen Augusta Grant, b. in Ogdensburg, N. Y., July 7, 1855; m. in
Charlestown, Mass., Nov. 1, 1886, Joseph Waldo Wardner, b. in
Boston, Sept. 21, 1857, son of George Waldo and Mary Elizabeth
(Jones) Wardner. They reside in Charlestown.
Sears Hurxthal Grant, b. in Prescott, Ont., Nov. 29, 1858; resides in
Dorchester, Mass., where he is constable and auctioneer; m. in
Ogdensburg, Dec. 1, 1886, Harriet Edsall Seely, b. in Ogdensburg,
Mar. 30, 1860, daughter of John Fine and Hannah (Edsall) Seely.
Child: John Seely, b. in Ogdensburg, Feb. 27, 1888.

475 ELEAZER⁷ WARNER, son of Thomas⁶ and Rhoda (Hopkins) Warner, born in New Lisbon, N. Y.; died in North Haven, Conn., July 5, 1854, aged 67 (or in his 75th year). He was known as Colonel. He resided in New York State until he was about twenty, then removed to North Haven. He was a member of the State Senate, and a Deacon in the church. Married (recorded in North Haven) January 14, 1818 **REBECCA C. BARNES,** born April 5, 1791, died August 13, 1863.

Children

Amanda Louise Warner, b. Nov., 1820; d. Mar. 18, 1835.
Mary Elizabeth Warner, b. Sept. 10, 1821; d. May 10, 1822.
Rebecca Warner, d. Oct. 6, 1859; m. June 1, 1848, Dr. Roswell Stillman of Burlington, N. Y., and North Haven, Conn. He m. (2) after her death. Children: i. Catherine. ii. Mary K., m. —— Bacon, and resides in Derby, Conn. iii. Emma, d. young.

476 ORRIN⁷ WARNER, son of Thomas⁶ and Rhoda (Hopkins) Warner, born May 14, 1800; resided in Garrettsville, N. Y., and later in Vineland, N. J., where he died May 14, 1870. Married **SUSAN GARDNER.**

Children

Fidelia Warner, b. Jan. 9, 1832; d. Dec. 15, 1864, not married.
William Warner, b. Apr. 7, 1834; d. 1884; m. Apr. 2, 1868, Alzina Burtch. Child: William Leon, b. July 15, 1871; was residing in Portland, Ore., some years ago.
Andrew Gardner Warner, b. June 30, 1836; d. Dec. 15, 1871. He served in the Civil War as Sergeant and was promoted to Lieutenant of Company K, 4th Minnesota Volunteer Infantry. Married Aug. 17, 1868, Augusta Merriam. Child: Sopha May, b. May 15, 1869; d. Feb., 1870.
Orrin Delos Warner, b. Mar. 23, 1839; d. Aug., 1898; m. Dec. 25, 1872, Helen S. Jawley. Child: Ruth, b. 1877; m. A. M. Judd, and resides in Bristol, Conn.
Susan Elizabeth Warner, b. Nov. 24, 1841; d. Feb. 25, 1868; married, but left no children.
Eleazer Homer (or *Horner*) *Warner,* b. Oct. 25, 1844; d. Mar. 29, 1868, not married.
Sidney Herbert Warner, b. July 22, 1847; resides in Leslie, Mich.; m. 1883, Elma Landfurr. Children: i. Ray. ii. Iva, b. about 1890. iii. Dewitt, b. about 1894.
Dwight M. Warner, b. 1850; resides in Sparta, Mich.; m. 1871, Flora Hammond. Children: i. Edward, b. about 1876; m. and has a child, Coila, b. about 1901. ii. Bertha May, b. about 1880; m. and has two children, Warner, b. about 1903, and Mary C., b. about June, 1906. iii. William Homer, b. about 1883.

477 **J O A N N A** [7] **W A R N E R**, daughter of Thomas[6] and Rhoda (Hopkins) Warner, born May 6, 1804, in New Lisbon, N. Y.; died in Hornellsville, N. Y., October 24, 1858. Married November 17, 1825, NAAMAN CONE, born September 11, 1804, in Laurens, Otsego Co., N. Y., died in Hornellsville, October 29, 1855, son of Ira and Lydia (Hayes) Cone. He was a school official for more than twenty-five years and was postmaster at the time of his death.

Children, all but third born in New Lisbon, N. Y.

William Warner Cone, b. Oct. 18, 1827; d. Mar. 21, 1904; resided in Masonville, N. Y., and was a maker of artificial flies for catching fish; m. (1) Nov. 30, 1854, Eliza H. Utley, who died in Guilford, N. Y., June 21, 1865, daughter of Philip and Harriet (Pratt) Utley; m. (2) Dec. 6, 1867, Hannah M. Utley, b. in Burlington, N. Y., June 1, 1843, sister of his first wife. Children by first wife: i. Flora Maria, b. Feb. 7, 1856; resides in East Smithfield, Pa.; not married. ii. Frederick Naaman, b. Mar. 29, 1859; resides in Mapleton, Utah; m. Martha Newton, and had two children. Child by second wife: Harriet J., b. June 16, 1871; m. Rev. Walter S. Percey and resides in East Smithfield.

Ira Cone, b. Sept. 8, 1831; m. June 17, 1863, Isabella Thayer of Waverly, N. Y., b. Feb. 16, 1835, d. 1900. In Apr., 1861, Ira Cone raised a company under the first call for troops and was commissioned lieutenant of Company G, 23d N. Y. Volunteers, served two years. He was engaged in lumbering near Grand Rapids, Mich., for twenty years, removed to Livonia, N. Y., then to Maple Hill, Mich., and after his wife's death resided with his brother Eleazur in Hornell. He had no children.

Elijah Cone, b. Mar. 3, 1833, in Garrettsville, N. Y.; d. in Hornell, May, 1902; m. Sept. 5, 1864, Mary Jane Ormsby. Children: i. Joanna, b. Aug. 2, 1866; resides in Hornell; m. Nov. 8, 1886, William Henry Smith, and had a daughter, Bertha, b. July 26, 1887, in Red Cloud, Neb. ii. Alice, b. Nov. 8, 1868; m. Lyman A. Best of Brooklyn, N. Y. iii. Isabel, b. Nov. 28, 1871; m. ——— Simonton of Brooklyn.

Eleazur Thomas Cone, b. June 24, 1835; resides in Hornell; m. Sept. 15, 1862, Mary Elizabeth Goff. Children: i. Nellie A., b. June 14, 1863; m. ——— McIntosh; resides in Hornell. ii. Burton E., b. Nov. 23, 1865; resides in Hornell. iii. Clara Dunham, b. July 25, 1869; d. Aug. 1, 1870. iv. Nelson Warner, b. Dec. 30, 1870. v. Willard Ray, b. Apr. 10, 1874. vi. Fanny Fay, b. Dec. 5, 1877; m. ——— Larkin; resides in Perry, N. Y.

Mary A. Cone, b. July 19, 1840; resides in Hornell; m. (1) June 12, 1861, John Latham, b. July 18, 1832; m. (2) Nov. 17, 1877, William N. Burr. Children by first husband: i. George Brooks, b. June 4, 1863; d. Feb. 6, 1866. ii. Mary Eleanor, b. Aug. 13, 1866. iii. John, b. Aug. 7, 1868; d. Oct. 1, 1868.

478 HORACE[7] WARNER, son of Thomas[6] and Rhoda (Hopkins) Warner, born May 13, 1808; died March 27, 1881, buried in Evergreen Cemetery, New Haven, Conn.

Married LAURA HALE, daughter of Zachariah Hale; see number 291.

Children

Horatio Nelson Warner, resided in Hornell, N. Y., and died leaving no family.

Thomas Warner, was living in 1902; married, and had a son, residing in New Haven, and a daughter, residing in Oneonta, N. Y.

Elizabeth Warner, m. William Miller of Howard, N. Y. Children: i. Kate, was a teacher in San Francisco, Cal. ii. Fannie, died.

Rhoda Warner, resided in Centerville, N. Y., in 1870; m. ——— Sherman.

Emma J. Warner, d. before 1906; m. Apr. 24, 1854, Julius Green Bassett, b. July 31, 1831, son of Bela and Lois J. (Munson) Bassett of North Haven, Conn. He resides in New Haven, Conn., was foreman in the boiler shop of the N. Y., N. H., and H. R. R. for many years. Child: Frances Emma, b. May 3, 1855; d. July 4, 1879.

Sarah Warner, d. young of diphtheria.

Matthew Warner.

Mary Jane Warner, m. ——— Brown, and resides in Fair Haven, Conn.

479 SAMUEL ALLEN[7] WARNER, son of Samuel[6] and Irene (Allen) Warner, born December 28, 1810, in New Lisbon, Otsego Co., N. Y.; died March 27, 1883, in Windsor, Dane Co., Wis. After his marriage he settled upon the old homestead near Batavia, N. Y., and cared for his parents during their last days. After the marriage of his oldest daughter, Harriet, and her settlement in the southern part of Wisconsin (then the far west), the family decided to join her family there, and removed to Dane County, Wis. About two years later the family was visited by a scourge of typhoid fever from which a son and daughter died. Six years later the daughter, Mrs. Mann and her husband, passed away, only a few months apart, and the grandparents assumed the care of two of the four orphan children.

Mr. Warner was an active member of the Presbyterian Church in Batavia, N. Y., and with the advancing age of his father, succeeded him as elder and was invariably present at the weekly prayer meeting, walking three miles to reach it. After his removal to Dane County, he was one of those who organized the first church in that locality, later known as the Union Congregational Church, and he became one of its deacons. He was a farmer, took an active interest in the welfare of his community, and was an ardent advocate of temperance. Deacon Warner considered the interests of religion most important in his life at the regular hours of prayer and Sabbath services, never allowing other duties or plans to interfere with these hours. Married in Alexander, N. Y., January 2, 1832, **MARTHA ELIZA BRINTNALL SIMONDS,** born July 18, 1810, in Brownville, Jefferson Co., N. Y.; died August 19, 1907, on the homestead in Windsor, Wis., where she had resided for fifty-five years. She was the daughter of John Simonds, a surveyor and farmer, formerly of Pawlet, Vt., and his wife, Sabra Cole. She was descended from William[1] Simonds, who settled at Woburn in 1639, m. (1) Sarah ————, (2) Judith (Phippin) Hayward; Joseph[2] Simonds, b. 1852, m. Mary Tidd; Joseph[3], Jr., Simonds, b. 1689, at Lexington, Mass., m. (1) Rachel ————, (2) Margaret ————, (3) in 1738, Hannah Abbe of Killingly, Conn., resided in Londonderry, N. H., Killingly, Conn., and was one of the founders of Williamstown, Mass.; Joel[4] Simonds, b. 1744, m. Patience Hall; John[5]

Children of Samuel Allen and Martha Eliza Brintnall (Simonds) Warner

655   *Harriet Newell Warner,* b. Nov. 28, 1832; m. Robert Mann.
       Julius Hiel Warner, b. June 4, 1834; d. at Windsor, Wis., May 13, 1854.
656   *Clement Edson Warner,* b. Feb. 23, 1836; m. Eliza Irene Noble.
       Martha Eliza Warner, b. Oct. 30, 1838; d. at Windsor, Wis., Feb. 20, 1854.
657   *Sabra Irene Warner,* b. June 2, 1844; m. (1) Herbert Alanson Lewis; (2) Lathrop Ezra Smith.
       Frances Elizabeth Warner, b. May 26, 1846; was graduated from Fox Lake, now Milwaukee Downer College, in 1865; resides in Windsor, Wis. She was a teacher in Madison, Wis., for some time.

480   TRUMAN[7] WARNER, son of Zachariah[6] and Laura (Hale) Warner, born in 1812, in Burlington, N. Y.; died in 1876, in Little Rock, Ark. He was a lawyer and banker and was a large real estate owner in Hornell, Steuben County, N. Y., where he resided for some years. After his removal to Arkansas he took an active part in politics and was a member of the Legislature and president of the Senate in 1864. He was considered the most brilliant speaker in that legislature. On his mother's side he was descended from the famous Hale family that produced Rev. John Hale, who wrote the treatise on witchcraft that had much to do with stopping that delusion; Nathan

Hale the patriot; and Edward Everett Hale. Through the marriage of his great-grandfather to Delight Metcalf he was a direct descendant of Governor William Bradford and his son William.

Married (1) ELIZA LEE, born in 1820, in Edmiston, N. Y.; died.

Married (2) in Bath, N. Y., May 20, 1859, MYRA COR DELIA MC ALMONT, born in Hornell, N. Y., July 1, 1832, daughter of Daniel and Semantha (Dunham) McAlmont, and granddaughter of John McAlmont, Lieutenant of 3d Battalion, Bucks County Associates in the Revolution, and his wife, Jane Jamison. She is living in 1917.

Children by first wife

Caroline S. Warner, b. Feb. 20, 1845, in Edmiston, N. Y.; resides in Canisteo, N. Y.; is a member of the Presbyterian Church, and active in Red Cross work.

Mary Emily Warner, b. Feb. 7, 1848, in Hornell, N. Y.; resides in Canisteo; m. there, Aug. 28, 1865, Dr. George Riddell. Children: i. Carrie Lee, b. Jan. 2, 1868; m. June 27, 1889, Charles W. Shaut. ii. Frank C., b. Aug. 13, 1871; m. Apr., 1904, Clara Lafler; has children, Mary Elizabeth, b. Jan. 25, 1906, and Edmund H., b. Feb. 4, 1908. iii. William George, b. Nov. 9, 1876. iv. Helen Eliza, b. July 8, 1883; m. Jan. 14, 1905, Lucius A. Waldo; has children, Charles Merrel, b. Feb. 24, 1906, and Cornelia Jane, b. July 23, 1907.

Eliza Lee Warner, b. Dec. 26, 1850, in Hornell, N. Y.; m. there, Smith Langley. She resides in Canisteo, N. Y., is a member of the Presbyterian Church and active in the Red Cross. Child: George Lee, b. Aug. 16, 1876, in Canisteo, N. Y.

Child by second wife

Julia McAlmont Warner, b. Sept. 1, 1860, in Hornell, N. Y.; is a teacher, residing in Little Rock, Arkansas. Miss Warner joined the D. A. R. in 1893; the Colonial Dames in Arkansas in 1913; the Society of Colonial Governors in 1917.

481 HORATIO H.[7] WARNER, son of Zachariah[6] and Laura (Hale) Warner, born November 2, 1823, in Otsego County, N. Y.; died September, 1893, in Burlingame, Kans., where he had been a farmer.

Married in Bath, N. Y., December 30, 1853, JANE NORTH-RUP, who died in Pierceville, Kans., November 2, 1908, aged about 80. After her husband's death she resided with her son Alva in Garden City.

31

Children

658 *Alva Henry Warner*, b. July 23, 1858; m. Jennie Logue.
Adelbert Edwin Warner, b. Jan. 31, 1863, is in business in Pierceville, Kans.; m. there, 1910, Harriet White.
Clarence A. Warner, b. Sept. 7, 1868; is in business in Pierceville; m. there, 1915, Nellie Bardon.

482 FOSTER Y.[7] WARNER, son of Josiah[6], Jr., and Achsah (Eastman) Warner, born July 17, 1810; died May 22, 1879, in Whately, Mass., where he had resided and conducted a sawmill and grist mill.

Married March 2, 1837, **ACHSAH MORTON**, born November 19, 1812, died October 9, 1898, daughter of Sylvester and Lydia (Frary) Morton of Whately.

Children, born in Whately

Emerson Clark Warner, b. Aug. 26, 1839; was a farmer, dairyman and tobacco grower on the homestead in Whately, then retired to live in Northampton, Mass.; m. in West Springfield, Nov. 11, 1860, Amanda Hunter, b. in Chester, Mass., May 13, 1842, daughter of Abram and Julia (Bigelow) Hunter of Chester. Children, b. in Whately: i. Elizabeth Ann, b. Oct. 27, 1863; resided in Pasadena, Cal., now in Ontario, Cal.; m. in San Bernardino, Cal., Oct. 16, 1888, George Rufus Graves, b. Feb. 2, 1860, son of Rufus and Julia (Nutting-Dane) Graves; was killed by an electric car July 27, 1907, leaving three children, Lillian Emily, b. Sept. 3, 1889, Lemuel Arthur, b. Aug. 9, 1892, and Emerson W., b. Nov. 19, 1895. ii. Minnie Bell, b. May 16, 1870.
Harriet Emma Warner, b. May 12, 1842; d. Feb. 28, 1846.
Osmyn Erwin Warner, b. Mar. 24, 1844; d. Nov. 6, 1882, not married.
Melvin Eastman Warner, b. Jan. 11, 1847; d. Sept. 4, 1849.

483 ELIJAH[7] WARNER, son of Ichabod Mape[6] and Mary (Talcott) Warner, born June 19, 1794, in Bolton, Conn. (family record, January in town record); died there, August 21, 1837. He was a farmer in Bolton all his life.

Married (1) March 21, 1821, **ABIGAIL BUEL**, born in Hebron, Conn., died in Bolton, June 17, 1833, daughter of Benjamin and Lucy (Wells) Buel.

Married (2) June 2, 1834, **MARTHA HAMMOND** of Vernon, born September 2, 1795, died February 9, 1845, daughter of Elijah and Martha (Strong) Hammond.

Children of Elijah and Abigail (Buel) Warner, born in Bolton

Sarah Jane Warner, b. Dec. 25, 1826; d. Sept. 4, 1831.
659 *William Talcott Warner*, b. Sept. 16, 1830; m. Olive Maria Hutchinson.
Abigail Buel Warner, b. Mar. 4, 1833; d. Aug. 23, 1834.

Child of Elijah and Martha (Hammond) Warner

Josiah Hammond Warner, b. June 24, 1836; d. Jan. 17, 1858, not married. He resided in Illinois.

484 ASHBEL⁷ WARNER, son of Ichabod Mape⁶ and Mary (Talcott) Warner, born December 30, 1797, in Bolton, Conn.; died there, February 27, 1872. He was a farmer in Bolton; deacon of the Congregational Church for forty-three years and a man of great integrity, sense of justice and uprightness.

Married (1) October 2, 1825, in Salisbury, Conn., ABIGAIL LYMAN, born in Salisbury, November 24, 1800, died in Bolton, January 7, 1828, daughter of David and Flavia (Collins) Lyman.

Married (2) in Bolton, December 4, 1828, HANNAH MORGAN, born February 29, 1804, in Canterbury, Conn., died in Bolton, August 30, 1889, daughter of Shubael and Cynthia (Bellows) Morgan.

Children of Ashbel and Abigail (Lyman) Warner, born in Bolton

660 *Lyman Warner*, b. July 4, 1826; m. (1) Elizabeth Sophia Olmsted, (2) Harriet Maria Hutchinson.
    John Warner, b. Dec. 23, 1827; d. Dec., 1831.

Children of Ashbel and Hannah (Morgan) Warner, born in Bolton

661 *Cynthia Ann Warner*, b. Jan. 26, 1830; m. Elijah Anson Alvord.
    Austin Warner, b. Feb. 2, 1832; was drowned in the St. Joseph River, Mich., May 22, 1855.
662 *Morgan Warner*, b. Jan. 27, 1834; m. Sarah Briner.
663 *Dwight Warner*, b. Jan. 6, 1837; m. Mary Ann Loomis.

485 ICHABOD⁷ WARNER, son of Ichabod Mape⁶ and Mary (Talcott) Warner, born April 6, 1801, in Bolton, Conn.; died January 5, 1835, in Gilead, Conn. He was a farmer in Gilead.

Married October 7, 1829, LUCY FOSTER, born July 25, 1804, died September 23, 1900, daughter of Phineas and Hannah (Kilbourne) Foster of Hartland and Barkhamstead, Conn. She married (2) August 26, 1841, Ebenezer Elon Strong.

Children

Harriet Elizabeth Warner, b. June, 1830, in Gilead; m. in Atlanta, Ill., July 2, 1856, Charles Cochran, b. Feb. 10, 1832, in Windham, N. H., d. July 30, 1916, son of Isaac and Annie (Dinsmore) Cochran. He was a farmer in Olivet, Osage Co., Kans. Children: i. Rosalie Warner, b. June 12, 1858; d. 186–. ii. Lincoln Foster, b. Aug. 26, 1860;

d. July 2, 1914. iii. Lucy Annis, b. July 30, 1867; m. ——— Schreck; resides in Redlands, Cal. iv. Mary Louise, b. May 16, 1869; resides in Olivet, Kans. v. Harriet L., b. Mar. 13, 1871; m. ——— Keller; resides in Emporia, Kans. vi. Charles Benjamin, b. May 5, 1874; resides in Olivet.

Lemuel Foster Warner, b. in Bolton, Sept. 14, 1832; d. Apr. 10, 1905, in Melvern, Kans. He was a farmer. Married in Chicopee, Mass., Nov. 27, 1855, Sedana A. Bean, who was born in Maine. Child: Chester Mills, b. in Atlanta, Ill., May 3, 1858; resides in San Juan, Texas; a farmer; m. (1) Eliza ———, (2) Minnie Hollenbeck, and had children, Chester, b. in Kent, Wash., and Harry, b. in Melvern, Kans.

Lucy Ann Warner, b. in Gilead, Conn., May, 1835; died; resided in Lincoln, Neb.; m. May 3, 1858, in McLean, Ill., Cyrus McFarland, b. in Rhode Island, 1833. Children, b. in Fairbury, Neb.: i. Ida, b. 1859; m. ——— Chenneworth. ii. William. iii. Elmer.

486 SALLY[7] WARNER, daughter of Ichabod Mape[6] and Mary (Talcott) Warner, born in Bolton, Conn., February 18, 1803; died there, April 7, 1834.

Married in Bolton, August 9, 1826, Captain **RUSSEL TALCOTT LOOMIS,** born in Bolton, November 27, 1793, died in Gilead, Conn., December 26, 1873, son of Matthew and Ruth (White) Loomis. He was a sea captain engaged in the West India trade. He married as his second wife Mariah[7] Warner; see further. Details of the Loomis ancestry will be found in the published genealogy of that family.

Children of Russel T. and Sally (Warner) Loomis, born in Bolton

Sarah Ann Loomis, b. July 9, 1827; d. in Gilead, Dec. 14, 1872, not married.

Mary Theresa Loomis, b. May 17, 1829; d. in East Glastonbury, Nov. 26, 1908; m. in Gilead, May 12, 1850, George Champion Hutchinson, b. in Gilead, Apr. 22, 1827, d. there, Apr. 14, 1904, son of John Bissell and Lauretta (Jewett) Hutchinson. He was a farmer, and a Representative in the State Legislature in 1885. Children, b. in Gilead: i. Millard Fillmore, b. Feb. 16, 1851; is a farmer and truckman residing in Manchester, Conn.; m. in East Windsor, Mar. 31, 1885, Clara Adella Hayes, b. Jan. 12, 1864, in East Windsor, daughter of Frank and ——— (Gilman) Hayes, and has three children, b. in Manchester, Wallace Melvin, b. Apr. 17, 1887, Maude Adella and Mildred Clara (twins), b. Sept. 6, 1889. ii. Ele Warner, b. Nov. 15, 1853; d. Mar. 26, 1892, in Glastonbury, where he was a farmer; m. in New York, Nov. 12, 1875, Ida Belle Strickland, b. in Gilead, Aug. 5, 1855, daughter of Thompson and Matilda (Dickinson) Strickland, had four children; see further. iii. Mary Lauretta, b. Aug. 14, 1863; d. Dec. 23, 1902, in Gilead where she had resided; m. in Hartford, Feb. 3, 1902, Michael Carey, b. 1859; had one son, George Hutchinson, b. Dec. 8, 1902, d. Dec. 26, 1902. iv. Ruth, b. Nov. 15,

1865; resides in East Glastonbury; m. in Gilead, Mar. 4, 1890, Fred Carl Fisher, b. Nov. 14, 1864, in East Glastonbury, son of Frederick and Katherine (Smith) Fisher, has two children, Clair Hutchinson, b. July 17, 1892, now a 1st Class Private in the U. S. A., and Howard Clarke, b. Feb. 20, 1897. (Son), b. and d. May 1, 1833.

Children of Ele Warner Hutchinson (above) were: i. Russel Loomis, b. in Gilead, Sept. 27, 1876; is a duck raiser in North Raynham, Mass.; m. in Hillstown, Conn., Dec. 27, 1905, Bertha May Hills, b. in Hillstown, June 9, 1877, daughter of Edward Francis and Ellen Minerva (Johnson) Hills, and had three children, Ruth Velma, b. Jan. 3, 1907, in North Raynham, Melvin Ward, b. Jan. 14, 1908, d. June 29, 1913, and Edward Warner, b. Aug. 8, 1913. ii. Nellie Frances, b. in Glastonbury, June 30, 1878; resides in Saybrook; m. in Hartford, Jan. 1, 1900, Walter Francis Shults, b. May 12, 1874; had three children, b. in Hartford, Ernest Kenwill, b. Dec. 18, 1900, Russel Warner, b. Feb. 27, 1911, d. Apr. 19, 1911, and Richard Frederick (twin), b. Feb. 27, 1911, d. Apr. 26, 1911. iii. George Thompson, b. in East Windsor, Mar. 12, 1882; has a men's furnishing store in Wollaston, Mass.; m. in Brockton, Mass., Sept. 7, 1908, Inez Josephine Howes, daughter of George Porter and Caroline (————) Howes; has two children, Carolyn Hutchinson, b. Mar. 27, 1913, in Dorchester, Mass., and Warner Howes, b. July 6, 1916, in Wollaston. iv. Rhoda Jewett, b. Mar. 1, 1885, in Glastonbury; resides in Florence, Mass.; m. in Westfield, Mass., Oct. 6, 1908, Harold Johnson Campbell, b. Mar. 11, 1883, and has a daughter, Florence Hutchinson, b. Sept. 24, 1909, in Brockton, Mass.

487 MARIAH[7] WARNER, daughter of Ichabod Mape[6] and Mary (Talcott) Warner, born in Bolton, Conn., March 12, 1805; died June 26, 1844. She resided in Bolton and Gilead.

Married in Bolton, November 19, 1834, Captain **RUSSEL TALCOTT LOOMIS**, whose first wife was her sister Sally; see above.

Children of Russel T. and Mariah (Warner) Loomis

Jane Elizabeth Loomis b. Aug. 23, 1835; resided in Gilead, where she died Sept. 22, 1917, not married.

John Loomis, b. in Bolton, Dec. 25, 1836; is a farmer residing in South Manchester, Conn. He served three years during the Civil War in the First Light Battery, Connecticut Volunteers, is a member of the G. A. R., and of the Methodist Episcopal Church. Married in South Manchester, Oct. 16, 1865, Catherine Eliza Keeney, b. in South Manchester, June 8, 1840, daughter of Nathaniel and Clemenza (Strong) Keeney. Children, all but first b. in South Manchester: i. Keeney Bradley, b. in Hebron, Nov. 27, 1866; is a farmer in South Manchester; m. (1) June 4, 1895, Isabella Smith, b. in Dundee, Scotland, June 4, 1870, d. July 29, 1899, leaving three children, Jane Myrtle, b. in South Manchester, July 22, 1896, Isabella Evangeline, b. in Glastonbury, Mar. 4, 1898, and Adella Maie, b. in Glastonbury, July 14, 1899; m. (2) Dec. 3, 1903, Jessie Isabelle Cone, b. Jan. 24, 1874, by whom he has two children, Marian Estelle, b. July 4, 1906, and Flora June, b. June 10, 1908. ii. Clara Eva, b. Aug. 29, 1869; resides in South Manchester, not married. iii. Minnie Lucretia, b. Apr. 12, 1871; d. Aug. 31, 1888. iv. Burdette Frank, b. Nov. 16, 1872; d. May 16, 1881. v. Elvie May, b. Oct. 12, 1874; resides in Cheshire, Conn.; m. Oct. 19, 1898, John Osgood Prescott, b. July 2, 1871; had three children, Marian, b. Aug. 13, 1899, d. Aug. 15, 1899, John Herman, b. June 28, 1900, and Mabel Ruth, b. Feb. 17, 1907. vi. Arthur Emory, b. Nov. 22, 1876; is a farmer in South Manchester. vii. Warner Morton, b. Mar. 15, 1880; d. Apr. 25, 1881. viii. Maro Alden, b. July 2, 1882; resides in Longmeadow, Mass.; is a munition worker; m. Oct. 2, 1909, Myrtie May Wheeler, b. Sept. 2, 1885; no children. ix. Mabel Jane, b. July 24, 1884; resides in Summit, N. J.; m. Oct. 28, 1909, Robert Mason Cadman, has two children, Robert Loomis, b. Sept. 16, 1912, and Arthur Hills, b. May 31, 1914.

488   ALBERT FRANCIS[7] WARNER, son of Ichabod Mape[6] and Mary (Talcott) Warner, born January 19, 1810, in Bolton, Conn.; died there, October 7, 1895. He lived and died on the original Warner place in Bolton where his grandfather settled in 1761. He was a man of unusual size, six feet four in height, and at one time weighing nearly three hundred pounds. His daughters still reside on the old homestead (1916).

Married in Bolton, March 26, 1844, **EUNICE GAGER**, born' in Tolland, Conn., 1818, daughter of Andrew and Lois (Webb) Gager.

Children, born in Bolton

Albert Jerome Warner, b. Feb. 17, 1845; d. Dec. 15, 1867, not married.
Mary Talcott Warner, b. Dec. 8, 1846; resides in Bolton; m. Gustavus Hellberg, a farmer, who d. in Bolton about 1912; no children.
Katherine Hutchinson Warner, b. Jan. 20, 1849; resides in Bolton; not married.

489   AMASA[7] WARNER, son of Nathan[6] and Ann Adelia (Davis) Warner, born November 29, 1788, in Northampton County, Pa.; died in Cedar Valley, Ohio, June 25, 1850. Removed with his father to Ohio in 1799. He was a farmer and miller, held the office of constable in Wooster township, Wayne County, Ohio, in 1814, and was justice of the peace. His children were born in Wooster.

Married (1) **LETTICE FOREMAN**, who died May 8, 1817, and with her child was buried in the burying ground on the farm of Nathan Warner, the first burials there.

Married (2) **CYNTHIA ANN WALTON**, who died May 18, 1833, aged 37 years, 9 months, 8 days.

Married (3) **MARY LOWERY,** who died November 20, 1845, aged 32 years, 10 months, 18 days.

Married (4) **ELSYANNE LOWERY,** daughter of James Alexander Lowery, a soldier of the War of 1812, and his wife, Mary.

Children by second wife

664 *Joseph Warner,* b. May 30, 1820; m. Ruth S. Tillottson.
665 *Margaret Warner,* b. May 12, 1826; m. Abner Goff Chacey.
666 *Hiram Warner,* b. about 1829; m. Mary Sechrist.
667 *Eunice Ellen Warner,* m. Jacob Sechrist.
     Susannah Warner.
     Valentine Warner.

Children by third wife

Nathan Warner, d. in the army during the Civil War.
Elisha Warner, m. and had two children: Edward, who is said to have lived in Redlands, Cal.; and Alice.
668 *Ichabod Warner,* b. Oct. 16, 1841; m. Arminda Gummere.

Children by fourth wife

Maria Warner.
Delia Warner, b. Feb. 19, 1850, in Wooster, Ohio; resides at Ridgeway, Mo. Married in Urbana, Ill., Jan. 22, 1868, George W. Brewer, b. May 10, 1840, in Zanesville, Ohio, son of William and Nancy (Haynes) Brewer. Children: i. Lake (daughter), b. Jan. 4, 1882, Missouri State University, A.B. and M.D.; is a physician at Ridgeway. ii. ———, b. Jan. 13, 1883; d. in infancy. iii. Leaf (daughter), b. Nov. 24, 1886; d. Jan. 3, 1893.

490 NATHAN⁷ **WARNER,** son of Nathan⁶ and Ann Adelia (Davis) Warner, born in Penn township, Northampton Co., Pa., October 12, 1790; died in Wayne County, Ohio, September 12, 1870. He removed when a child with his parents to Wayne County in 1799 and was identified with the best interests of the community during a long life. He settled in Plain township, north of the residence of his brother Jesse, and after seven years removed to a place east of Jefferson, where he remained from 1826 to 1843. From there he went to the farm south of Jefferson where he spent the remainder of his life, and which was later owned by his son Joshua. In 1871 he built a new frame house in the same yard as the log-house and moved into that, leaving Joshua in the old house.

Nathan Warner was a born mechanic and could make anything he undertook, from a leather boot-jack to a threshing machine. He designed from his own conceptions and manufactured the first fanning mill for winnowing wheat that was ever made or used in Wayne County, and after half a century of use it was still in service and pronounced in no way inferior to many of the more improved mills of later date. His son preserved many mementos of his father's pioneer days: a copper-mounted powder horn over a foot long, on which was carved N. Warner and the date 1800, probably made for his father; a pouch of coonskin with the hair all worn off; a fine silver-mounted rifle; a coat belonging to his great-grandfather and descending to him as the third Nathan Warner in succession; a flax heckle which he made for his wife; books, all inscribed, "Nathan Warner, his book," with the date.

. In public affairs he took an active part; was one of the earliest tax-collectors; the receiver of public funds to make material improvements; one of the trustees of the township in 1835; on the first jury impanelled in Wayne County.

Nathan Warner married in Wayne County, Ohio, May 4, 1815, **MARY RATHBUN**, born April 4, 1794, in Saratoga County, N. Y., died November 26, 1893, daughter of Robert and Anna (Allen) Rathbun of Cayuga County, N. Y., and a granddaughter of Ethan Allen. Robert Rathbun was born in Rhode Island, and was a pioneer settler of Chester township, Wayne County, Ohio, in 1814. Mrs. Warner survived all her immediate relatives, brothers, sisters, husband and children. She was the mother of nine children, yet never weighed more than eighty-five pounds in her life. She removed to Wayne County, Ohio, a year after her marriage.

Children, all but first born in Plain township, Wayne Co., Ohio

Nancy Warner, b. in Wooster township, Wayne Co., Ohio, May 18, 1817; m. in Wayne County, Mar. 20, 1845, Charles H. Palmer. Children: i. Maranda Delia, m. Dean Coe, and resides in Chicago, Ill. ii. Sanford, resides in Valencia or Topeka, Kans. iii. Mary, m. —— Hines and resides in Denver, Colo. iv. Newton, d. several years ago.

Mary Warner, b. Sept. 7, 1819, in Plain township; d. June 18, 1855; m. in Wayne·County, Oct. 17, 1839, David Yarnell. Children: i. Margaret, d. in 1908. ii. Agnes, m. (1) —— Eberhard, (2) —— Cole; resides in Barberton, Ohio; has a daughter and two sons residing there. iii. Theressa D., m. ——, and resides in Lindenville, Ohio. iv. Rachel Ann, d. in infancy. v. Lovema A., b. in Wayne County, May 27, 1850; resides in Shreve, Ohio; m. there, Jan. 9, 1883, Michael Booth, b. in New York City; had a child, Mary Ann, b. May 14, 1884, d. Aug. 14, 1884.

Joel Warner, b. Sept. 22, 1821; d. May 8, 1822.

Lucinda Warner, b. Apr. 12, 1823; d. July 16, 1842; not married.

Hannah Warner, b. Feb. 18, 1825; d. Feb. 3, 1851; m. in Wayne County, Oct. 14,·1847, Jacob Heffelfinger. He married again and had children by the second marriage who always called the Warners grandparents, although not related to them.

669 *Joshua Warner*, b. July 22, 1827; m. Rebecca Jane Baker.

Samuel Warner, b. Jan. 7, 1830; d. Jan. 25, 1835.

670 *Amelia Ann* or *Anna Warner*, b. Feb. 28, 1832; m. Michael Lantz.

Nathan Warner, b. Nov. 3, 1834; d. Apr. 11, 1836.

491 PETER⁷ WARNER, son of Nathan⁶ and Ann Adelia (Davis) Warner, born August 11, 1792, in Northampton County, Pa.; died November 14, 1824. He was a traveling Methodist preacher with his field in the Muskingum Valley. He later moved to Indiana and further west but did not preach in the traveling connection.

Married (1) in Muskingum County, Ohio, ——— WIL LIAMS, who died in Indiana.

Married (2) Mrs. ——— BETT.

A list of his children has not been obtained although there are said to be descendants living in Wayne County, Ohio. Among his descendants are Washington Warner, and Mrs. S. I. Hart of Allen, Neb.

492 MOSES⁷ WARNER, son of Nathan⁶ and Ann Adelia (Davis) Warner, born in Pennsylvania, May 24, 1796; removed to Wooster, Ohio, and from there to Richland, Iowa, where he died. He was a Methodist minister.

Married (1) **MARY SHERIDAN**, who died about 1864.

Married (2) about 1866, Mrs. ——— **JAY**, who had two daughters and four sons. One of the sons is Will S. Jay, a prominent citizen of Lincoln, Neb.

Children of Moses and Mary (Sheridan) Warner

671 *Gideon Warner*, b. July 13, 1823; m. (1) Nancy Jane Charlton, (2) Matilda Brubaker.

672 *Jesse F. Warner*, b. Sept. 24, 1824; m. Hannah M. Woodward.

Delia Warner, b. in Wooster, Ohio, Oct., 1825; d. at Dakota City, Neb., Mar. 6, 1875; m. at Richland, Iowa, Jacob Harden; had seven children, one of whom, Fatima, m. Horatio Braunt and resides in Los Angeles, Cal.

Elizabeth Warner, m. Nelson Green. Some of the family live at Richland or Fairfield, Iowa. A son is L. H. Green of Hynes, Cal.

493 JOSHUA⁷ WARNER, son of Nathan⁶ and Ann Adelia (Davis) Warner, born July 29, 1799, in Northampton County, Pa.; died December 18, 1877, in Wooster, Wayne Co., Ohio, where he had resided on a farm for many years. He removed to Ohio with his father when a baby, and in 1810, to Wooster township. He was a deeply religious man and a class leader in the Oak Chapel Methodist Church for sixty years. The Methodists organized a society at his father's house as early as 1812 and quarterly meetings were also held there by noted divines. His house was the nucleus for gatherings of ministers and was never too full to accommodate all who came.

Married (1) April 24, 1828, **MARGARET SMITH**, who died about 1834.

Married (2) April 12, 1842, **ROSANNA EDMUNDS**, born in Chester township, Wayne Co., November 21, 1818, daughter of Nathaniel and Mary (Smith) Edmunds.

Children by second wife, all born in Wooster, Ohio

Mary Delia Warner, b. Feb. 28, 1843; m. Aug. 15, 1878, Rev. Isaac Beebe and resided near Warsaw, Ind.; no children.

John B. Warner, b. Aug. 23, 1845; d. Apr. 14, 1901; attended Wooster University, 1873-4, was graduated from Fort Wayne College, scientific course, 1876; was professor of mathematics there for some time, then returned to Wayne County on account of his father's health. He settled on a farm in the western part of Wayne County in 1879. He was a member of the Methodist Church and was formerly one of its exhorters. Married Dec. 25, 1876, Ida P. Wagner, b. Mar. 14, 1858, in Elkhart County, Ind., daughter of Joseph and Sarah E. (————) Wagner of Milford, Ind. Children: i. Talmadge Joshua, b. Nov. 16, 1877. ii. Joseph O., b. Sept. 23, 1881; m. Feb. 26, 1908, Helen Shepherd; has a son, Joseph Onis, b. Jan. 20, 1910. iii. Adola, b. Dec. 16, 1884; m. Mar. 15, 1909, William H. Duncan. •

Phebe Warner, b. Oct. 2, 1847; resided in Wooster and died June 13, 1914, not married.

673 *Wesley Warner*, b. Mar. 18, 1850; m. Anna E. Yost.

Eunice Warner, b. Nov. 24, 1852; m. Jan. 24, 1894, S. M. Dennis; no children.

Lizzie Warner, b. Mar. 28, 1855; m. Mar. 28, 1887, William J. Woodward; resides in Warsaw, Ind. Children: i. Joyce, b. June 11, 1888. ii. Edgar, b. Dec. 22, 1890. iii. Glenn, b. June 10, 1893.

Emma L. Warner, b. Oct. 2, 1857; m. Sept. 26, 1891, Levi H. Becker; no children.

Francis A. Warner, b. Apr. 2, 1860; m. Dec. 25, 1888, Mary Bahl, daughter of Solomon Bahl. Children: i. Zella, b. Apr. 18, 1892. ii. Lloyd, b. June 30, 1894. iii. Hattie, b. Feb. 16, 1899.

Edgar H. Warner, b. Aug. 28, 1862; resides in Wooster, Ohio; m. Feb. 23, 1888, Joanna France, b. in Wooster, Ohio, Jan. 9, 1865, daughter of John and Sarah (Lehman) France; no children. He was educated for the ministry at the University of Wooster but was compelled to give up his literary work on account of ill health. While in college he led his classes in all branches of study. He then spent four years on a ranch in Kansas to regain his health. After returning from the west he purchased a farm in Medina

EDGAR H. WARNER

County, Ohio, which he improved to such an extent that his country home was the marvel of his friends and neighbors for its beauty and grandeur. In early life Mr. Warner was chosen to many positions of trust both in church and state, but in recent years he has refused to accept any position in politics saying that "there is too much graft in politics for a Christian." "He is loved by all those who know him best, and especially by those who have had a hard struggle to gain their livelihood in this selfish world. Entirely devoid of a selfish spirit, he always considers the interests and feelings of others in preference to his own. To lose a friend from any cause whatsoever is a great shock to his affectionate disposition." At the present time, Mr. Warner is a General Agent for the Wooster Preserving Company, a position which he has held with great success as a salesman for seventeen years.

494 SUSANNAH[7] WARNER, daughter of Nathan[6] and Ann Adelia (Davis) Warner, born April 1, 1800, in Gnadenhütten, Tuscarawas Co., Ohio, the first white child born in the town; died December 18, 1888, at the home of her son, three miles west of Wooster, Ohio.

Married about 1832, ERNEST REATUS FOX, born in Bethlehem, Pa.; died in Tuscarawas County, December 18, 1852. He was a shoemaker by trade.

Child

Cyrus Wesley Fox, b. May 24, 1842, near Wooster, Ohio, and resides there. He has been engaged in various occupations, mostly selling medicines and notions. Married near Wooster, Dec. 27, 1872, Sarah Jane Miller, b. Mar. 5, 1844, near Green Castle, Ind., daughter of Levi and Susan (———) Miller. Children: i. Son, d. in infancy. ii. Herbert Roy, b. Oct. 6, 1875; is a carpenter in Charlevoix, Mich.; m. (1) ———, by whom he had a child, Clifford Wayne, b. about 1903; m. (2) Florence Swailes of Charlevoix. iii. Ernest Carl, b. Sept. 13, 1878; is a farmer in Midland, Mich.; m. Elsie Ogilvie of Wellington, Ohio, and has a daughter, Ethel, b. about 1906. iv. Foster Deforest, b. Aug. 14, 1885; has been in the far west since about 1913.

495 JESSE[7] WARNER, son of Nathan[6] and Ann Adelia (Davis) Warner, born November 22, 1802, in Tuscarawas County, Ohio; died August 6, 1872, in Wooster, Ohio. He removed with his parents to Wayne County about 1811, and spent much of his life in that vicinity. He was a Methodist preacher, began as an exhorter about 1832, was received on trial in the Michigan Conference in 1837, and held appointments at Dalton, Millersburgh, Waynesburgh, Ashland, Wooster, Keene, Shanesville, Bolivar, Newcomerstown, Roscoe, Mount Eaton, and Jeromeville. Late in life he retired to a farm at Wooster.

Married (1) in 1830, **JANE GOODFELLOW,** who died in 1843, daughter of William and Jane (Allison) Goodfellow of Plain township, Wayne Co., Ohio.
Married (2) **ANN OLDROYD,** born October 17, 1818, in Huddersfield, Yorkshire County, England.

Children by first wife, born in Wayne County

Malinda Spear Warner, b. Mar. 3, 1832; d. Nov. 26, 1898, in Wayne County; m. Dr. M. A. Frost. Child: Florence, F., b. July 22, 1872; is a Methodist deaconess.
674   *Elmore Yocum Warner,* b. July 7, 1833; m. ————.
Margaret Jane Warner, b. Jan. 7, 1836; d. Nov. 19, 1898; m. William Milton[7] Warner, son of Samuel E.[6] and Mary Warner. See number 307.
Lemuel Warner, b. Aug. 3, 1838; d. Aug., 1854.
Clara Ellen Warner, b. June 3, 1840; d. Dec. 19, 1893; m. Wm. H. Robison. Children: i. Nina, b. in Wooster, Ohio, Apr. 15, 1866; d. Dec. 27, 1887. ii. J. Walter, b. July 22, 1870.

Children by second wife, born in Wayne County, Ohio

675   *Edwin Lambert Warner,* b. Oct. 20, 1847; m. Marietta Virginia Silver.
Melville Leonidas Warner, b. Oct. 2, 1849; resides in Wooster, Ohio; m. (1) in Bellevue, Ohio, Sept. 27, 1871, Rosa Williams, b. in Bellevue, Mar. 14, 1851, d. in Cleveland, Ohio, Mar. 15, 1895, daughter of David and Rebecca (————) Williams; m. (2) Dec. 9, 1895, Imogene Markel Troutman, who d. Apr. 19, 1917, in Wooster, Ohio. Children by first wife: i. Ralph M., b. in Wayne County, Ohio, Feb. 10, 1881; is a mechanical engineer, residing in Pennsylvania; m. a Southern lady and has a son. ii. Bertha R., b. Jan. 18, 1886; d. Jan. 19, 1891. iii. Nina Ann, b. Dec. 13, 1887; d. Dec. 26, 1891.
Alice Euphemia Warner, b. Oct. 7, 1851; resides in Wooster, Ohio, with her brother Melville.
Lyman Simpson Warner, b. Apr. 11, 1854; resides in Wooster, Ohio; m. near Wooster, Oct. 25, 1882, Mary Bucher, b. in Wayne County, Ohio, Apr. 11, 1854, daughter of John and Mary (————) Bucher. Children, b. in Wayne County: i. David M., b. Jan. 22, 1885; is a mechanic. ii. Ross O., b. Apr. 13, 1886; is a builder and contractor. iii. Alice Dale, b. May 26, 1892.
Charles Ellis Warner, b. Feb. 19, 1856; is a farmer residing in Wooster, Ohio; m. there, Nov. 28, 1883, Nettie Snyder, b. in Shreve, Ohio, Dec. 22, 1859, daughter of George and Elizabeth (————) Snyder. Child: Gertrude A., b. May 27, 1887; d. Feb. 19, 1910.
Mary Ada Warner, b. Mar. 12, 1858; d. in Wayne County, Nov. 3, 1889; m. near Wooster, Oct. 25, 1882, D. Robison Houser, b. in Wayne County, May 2, 1854, son of Jacob and Elizabeth (————) Houser. Children, b. near Wooster: i. Edith Dale, b. July 1, 1884; is a bookkeeper. ii. J. Earl, b. Aug. 17, 1886; is a photographer, now in Signal Service. iii. George Victor, b. Nov. 19, 1888; is in postal service.
Ann Luella Warner, b. June 1, 1860; m. near Wooster, as second wife,

Apr. 1, 1892, D. Robison Houser. Children, b. in Wayne County:
i. Nona, b. Feb. 27, 1893. ii. Mary F., b. Feb. 26, 1895; d. July 14,
1898. iii. Fred, b. June 9, 1900. iv. Helen, b. Jan. 29, 1903.

496 PETER⁷ WARNER, JR., son of Peter⁶ and Grace
(————) Warner, born in Pennsylvania; died in Iowa,
November 12, 1878. He was a member of the Methodist Episcopal Church for over fifty years, was engaged in ministerial
work as an itinerant. He was twice married and had ten children.
Married ELIZABETH ————, born in Ohio.

Children

Marion Warner, b. in Wayne County, Ohio, Mar. 1, 1830; removed
with his parents in 1834 to Wayne township, Ind., on the Tippe-
canoe River; resided after 1879 on a farm in Kosciusko County,
Ind., and owned a sawmill and grist mill. Married Jan. 6, 1853,
Virginia Bowling, daughter of Thomas and Susan (————)
Bowling. (History of Kosciusko County.)

Charles J. Warner, b. Jan. 1, 1836, in Wayne township, Wayne Co.,
Ohio. He was educated in the public schools, taught winters and
attended school summers for five years, then studied medicine with
Dr. W. C. Moore of Congress for four years; removed to Home-
ville, Medina Co., Ohio, for two years and studied at Cleveland
Medical College, graduating in 1862, then returned to Congress.
He was a man of fine physique, six feet tall; attained considerable
eminence in his profession; was an earnest advocate of more and
better schools, and made and published addresses on that subject.
Married Sept. 15, 1859, Mary E. Pancoast of Congress, Ohio, who
died Dec. 8, 1866. Children: i. A. C. ii. Ellsworth, died Dec. 8,
1866. (History of Wayne County, Ohio.)

Ordine Warner.

William Warner.

497 JOEL⁷ WARNER, son of Daniel⁶ and Mary (Simmers)
Warner, born December 14, 1818, near New Philadelphia, Tuscarawas Co., Ohio; died in New Philadelphia, February 2, 1897.
He began clerking in a store at Newcomerstown early in life
and later was engaged in both lumber and mercantile business.
He was county recorder in 1846 and held other offices of trust
and public interest. His granddaughter, Mrs. Agnes McClelland Daulton, writes of him:

We all so love his memory. I always love to think of the moment when
death was seen as a fact. He was seventy-eight and he said, "I do not
want to die, but a man who does not face the inevitable bravely is a fool."
My first memory of him is sitting on his knee while he recited Bobby
Burns and Tom Moore by the yard for me; in girlhood listening to him

recite Milton or splendid sentences his rich memory held as treasures. He taught me as a child never to tear a book or paper, for he said, "A precious word—a thought—may be there," and though that seems far-fetched to me now, then it planted a seed in my mind that has done much in my life. In those early days in Ohio he used to go miles to borrow a book and would then sit reading by candle light until far into the morning. He was a hero worshipper, a lover of all that was strong and beautiful in life and literature, a splendid thinker, a great talker, honorable, upright, inspiring. He filled us all with a love for study, for books, for great and beautiful things, and so, as his daughters went out of his house, they brought to their own homes the same love.

Married in Zoar, Ohio, March 5, 1846, DELILAH EVER-ETT, born near New Philadelphia, October 19, 1824; died August 12, 1875, in New Philadelphia. She was the daughter of Moses and Mary (Burroway) Everett.

Children, born in New Philadelphia

676 *Lucy Warner,* b. Dec. 16, 1846; m. Lewis Robert McClelland.
Agnes Warner, d. aged two years.
Alice Warner, d. aged two years.
Alma Warner, b. Jan. 2, 1855. She resides in Barnard, N. C.; has been doing missionary work among the mountain people of that section for a number of years.
Blanche Warner, b. June 10, 1857; resides in Ouray, Colo.; m. in Pueblo, Colo., Feb. 11, 1892, Thomas Downer, b. at Kirdford, near Petworth, Sussex, England, Mar. 14, 1844, son of John and Mary Downer. Mrs. Downer was a teacher for six years before her marriage. She has no children. Mr. Downer had by his first wife, Elizabeth Deborah Pritchard of England, the following children, b. in Colorado: i. Malcolm Holbrook, an assayer in Goldfield, Nev. ii. Roger Holbrook, an assayer in Goldfield. iii. Phyllis Margaret, m. —— De Cou, and lives at Camp Bird Mills, Ouray Co., Colo.
Omega Warner, b. Dec. 22, 1860; resides in Cleveland, Ohio; m. in New Philadelphia, Apr. 10, 1881, Chester B. Campbell, b. in Quincy, Ind., Nov. 2, 1859, son of John L. Campbell, who was born in Boston, Mass., May 17, 1830, and his wife, Elizabeth Benjamin, who was born in New York, Jan. 29, 1836. Child: Helen Alice, b. Dec. 23, 1881; m. 1909, John Philip Hartman and resides in Cleveland; has three children, Alma Louise, b. 1910, Joel Warner, b. 1913, and John Philip, b. 1916.
Horace Greeley Warner, b. July 4, 1870; d. Aug., 1870.

498 JONAS[7] WARNER, son of Daniel[6] and Mary (Sim-mers) Warner, born February 12, 1821, on Fry's Creek, township of Warwick, now Clay, Tuscarawas Co., Ohio; died in New Philadelphia, Ohio, June 15, 1905. In 1828 his father moved to Wayne County, Ohio, where he remained for two years, then moved back to Fry's Valley. Upon his father's

death, when Jonas was but fourteen years of age, he was thrown
upon his own resources and was sent away to work. After a
short and unpleasant experience near Trenton, he ran away
from this first place, and went to live, on the first of January,
1836, with Benjamin Walton, where he remained for some
years. In 1844 he made a trip to Indiana and bought some land
there, but returned to Ohio the following year to take charge
of a sawmill which he later rented and ran for himself, with
considerable success. In 1850 he made a prospecting trip west,
and later removed to near Warsaw, Kosciusko Co., Ind. This
proved most unsatisfactory, and they returned almost at once
to the old home. In 1856 he bought the farm which he made
his home for many years, although he was also engaged in the
coal business, and late in life he removed to New Philadelphia
where he died. He joined the Lutheran Church in 1845, as his
wife was already a member of that church, but in 1865 he united
with the Methodists, the rest of his family having joined the
year before, and was class leader for a number of years.

Married in Uhrichsville, Tuscarawas Co., Ohio, October 26,
1845, CATHERINE LISTER, born in Mill township, Tuscarawas Co., February 29, 1828, oldest of the family of Alfred and
Sarah (Haga) Lister, the former of Irish and Scotch descent,
the latter of German; died at Tuscarawas (formerly called
Trenton), Ohio, September 12, 1891.

Children, born in Tuscarawas County, Ohio

Jesse Taylor Warner, b. Jan. 5, 1847; d. in Tuscarawas County, Ohio,
June 11, 1882. He was a Methodist minister, a member of the North
Ohio Conference. Married Sept. 9, 1874, Clara Andrews of Canal
Dover, Ohio. Child: Myrtle, b. in Tuscarawas, Ohio, July 1, 1875.
Millard Fillmore Warner, b. Oct. 15, 1848; d. Aug. 29, 1908, in Cleveland, Ohio. He was a Methodist minister, left the pastorate and
became professor, vice-president, and president (1892-8), successively, of Baldwin University, Berea, Ohio. He was for one term a
member of the Senate of Ohio from Cuyahoga County. Married
at Harmony, N. J., Jan. 5, 1876, Mabel Gray De Witt of New
Jersey. Children: i. Faith, b. Apr. 28, 1877, in Monsey, N. Y.; was
graduated from Baldwin University; m. in Berea, Ohio, Sept. 1,
1898, Robert Burton Newcomb, who is a lawyer in Cleveland, b. in
New York City, son of Gilbert Leroy and Elizabeth (Sunderland)
Newcomb, and has two children, Millard Warner, b. in Berea, Nov.
20, 1899, and Robert Burton, b. in Cleveland, Mar. 9, 1904. ii. Carl
Norman, b. Dec. 6, 1879, in Jeromeville, Ohio; was graduated from
Baldwin University; married and has children, Kathryn, Adelaide
and Carl N.
Louis Kossuth Warner, b. Aug. 4, 1850; d. in Delaware, Ohio, Mar.
25, 1904. He was a Methodist minister and was district superin-

tendent of Mansfield district at the time of his death. Married at Ft. Pembina, N. Dak., Aug. 25, 1880, Ellen J. Collier, who died May 20, 1915. Child: Eleanor Frances, b. Aug. 10, 1890, in Clyde, Ohio; student in Illinois State University, Urbana, Ill.

Martha Warner, b. Nov. 17, 1853; d. Oct. 17, 1875.

Anna Mary Warner, b. Dec. 7, 1855; d. Apr. 16, 1864.

Allie Warner, b. Jan. 31, 1858; d. Sept. 15, 1863.

Minnie Warner (twin), b. Oct. 12, 1861; resides in Akron, Ohio; m. Dec. 5, 1883, John L. Hoagland, b. near Newcomerstown, Ohio, son of Nicholas and Adeline (Lowe) Hoagland. Children, b. in Akron: i. May Catherine, b. Sept. 23, 1884; m. Oct. 9, 1907, Cecil C. Welker. ii. Elmer Millard, b. Feb. 22, 1888; resides in Akron, Ohio; m. Margaret Hoy, who died Sept. 27, 1917, in Akron, Ohio.

May Warner (twin), b. Oct. 12, 1861; resides in New Philadelphia, Ohio; not married.

Bingham Warner, b. Aug. 30, 1864; d. May 18, 1866.

Edgar Haga Warner, b. Sept. 22, 1868; is pastor of the First Methodist Church, Barberton, Ohio. He was graduated from Baldwin University in 1892 and from Harvard University in 1893; has been pastor at Birmingham, Penfield, Rocky River, Oberlin, Massillon, Cleveland, East Liverpool and Barberton. Married in Axtel, Ohio, May 1, 1895, Louie Sperry, b. in Axtel, Feb. 19, 1876, daughter of Calvin and Mary (Hull) Sperry. She was a student of Oberlin Conservatory of Music. Children: i. Edgar Gordon, b. Feb. 20, 1907, in Oberlin. ii. Lilan Ruth, b. July 6, 1911, in Cleveland.

499 SIMON PETER[7] WARNER, son of Daniel[6] and Mary (Simmers) Warner, born June 17, 1823, near New Philadelphia, Ohio; removed to Rockford, Ill., where he was a millwright and resided on the south side of the town.

Married in Ohio, **SARAH JOHNSON.**

Children

Charles Warner, d. in Cleveland, Ohio, Aug. 26, 1917, aged 60; m. Mary E. Barnes, who resides in Cleveland. Children: Florence, b. 1879; m. in 1910, Roy Rodebaugh; resides in Cleveland; has two children, Robert and Sue. ii. Clarence, b. 1880; resides in Texahoma, Texas. iii. Cora, b. 1887; m. Walter John Brant; has one son, John.

Almeda Warner, died.

Frank E. Warner, died.

Albert S. Warner, died. He was a physician in Nebraska.

Nettie Warner, lives in Rockford, Ill.

Mabel Warner, lives in Rockford, Ill.

500 ELIAS[7] WARNER, son of Daniel[6] and Mary (Simmers) Warner, born January 27, 1826, on Fry's Creek, Ohio, in the cabin his father built. After his father's death when he was but a child, he was bound out and resided in various fam-

32

ilies until he was of an age when he could go to work with his older brothers. He lived in several places in Tuscarawas County, for some time after his marriage at Wave Mills, then north of Trenton. On May 2, 1864, he was ordered on a 100 day service, and was discharged at Camp Chase, Ohio, 1864, from the 161st Regiment, Ohio Volunteers. He was with General Hunter on a raid up the Shenandoah Valley and helped guard a provision train up to him. During their stay up the valley they were cut off by General Breckenridge. General Hunter took them within sixteen miles of Lynchburg, then sent them to Union lines with but four days' rations. They were twelve days on the march and the last eight days they lived on parched corn stolen from the mules' rations.

The following December, 1864, Elias Warner moved to Iowa, and there his youngest child was born, but after a year he returned to Ohio, and resided in Trenton and vicinity, and later in New Philadelphia.

Married (1) in Ohio, 1851, **LURANA M. POLAND**, who died May 29, 1866, buried in New Philadelphia, Ohio, new cemetery.

Married (2) August 21, 1866, **Mrs. MARY SMITH,** widow of Thomas J. Smith. After their marriage they resided on her farm north of Trenton for a year, and after 1876, in New Philadelphia. She died April 29, 1886, and was buried on Goshen Hill.

Married (3) May 30, 1887, **Mrs. MARY E. LENHART,** widow of Daniel Lenhart.

> *Children by first wife, first three born in Ohio*
>
> *Mary Ellen Warner*, b. Mar. 14, 1852; d. Sept. 21, 1863.
> *Lelia Josephine Warner*, b. July 14, 1854; resides in Alliance, Ohio; m. July 17, 1879, T. Joseph Moore, who was born 1843, and is a contractor and cabinet maker, retired on account of ill health. He served three years in the Civil War. Child: Lulu May, b. 1880; resides in Alliance; m. J. P. Hoops.
> *Jessie May Warner*, b. Feb. 20, 1857; d. Feb. 27, 1857.
> *Sarah Olive Warner*, b. Mar. 24, 1858; resides in New Philadelphia, Ohio; m. William Fickes.
> *Ida Catherine Warner*, b. Sept. 21, 1860; d. Mar. 24, 1864.
> *Wesley Ellsworth Warner*, b. 1863; d. Mar. 23, 1864, aged 7 months, 24 days.
> *Elias Grant Warner*, b. May 29, 1865, in Iowa; resides in New Philadelphia, Ohio; m. —— Wolfe.

501   **WILLIAM⁷ WARNER**, son of Daniel⁶ and Mary (Simmers) Warner, born June 13, 1829, in Wayne County, Ohio;

died February 2, 1904, in Warwick township, Tuscarawas Co., Ohio, where he had lived most of his life. When he was but six months of age his parents returned from Wayne County to their old home in Fry's Valley, Tuscarawas County. After his father's death, when William was about six years old, he resided with his mother and the younger children at their grandfather's until the following spring, when he went to live with a neighbor. While there he had a long sickness with ague, followed by dropsy, and his mother took him home with her. He was never strong after this illness, and somewhat later became so deaf he was unable to attend school for some time. His childhood was spent living with and working for several farmers, and in 1845 he went to New Philadelphia to learn the tailor's trade. He worked at this in Leesburg and Trenton also, and after his marriage commenced keeping house in Mud Run Valley, then moved to Gnadenhütten, and in 1854 to Oldtown Valley where he worked at the cooper's trade, and on the farm. He lived in Oldtown Valley for seventeen years, then moved to Warwick township, and built the house in Trenton where they lived afterward. He was out of the state only once in his life, on a trip to Pennsylvania in 1849. He joined the Methodist Church in New Philadelphia in 1846.

Married in Oldtown Valley, November 21, 1850, CATHERINE ELIZABETH RUPERT, born April 25, 1831; died April 4, 1912.

Children

Amanda Warner, b. in Gnadenhütten, Ohio, Aug. 17, 1851; m. Oct. 24, 1872, James Nargney; resides in Uhrichsville, Ohio.

Sarah Melissa Warner, b. Sept. 11, 1853; m. Apr. 15, 1874, James Wilson.

James S. Warner, b. Aug. 6, 1855; resides in New Philadelphia, Ohio; m. Mar. 25, 1884, Mary Giogan. Children: i. Dean, 2d Lieutenant, Heavy Field Artillery, Camp Sherman, Mar., 1918; ii. Elton, died.

Mary Warner, b. Mar. 8, 1858; m. Dec. 22, 1885, George McIlraine; resides in New Philadelphia.

Clara Warner, b. Mar. 4, 1860; d. Dec. 24, 1915; m. Sept. 6, 1881, Jesse Gram.

Florence Warner, b. Sept. 3, 1862; m. (1) 1884, Ervin Stucker, (2) 1894, Edward Todd.

Wesley Wilbur Warner, b. July 21, 1865; d. of diphtheria, Oct. 24, 1866.

Charles Warner, b. Aug. 7, 1867; m. (1) May 14, 1888, Ollie Wilcox, (2) Dec. 8, 1892, Etta Demuth.

Catherine Nora Warner, called Nora, b. Sept. 25, 1870; m. Sept. 17, 1891, Gideon Renwick.

Ida Alice Warner, b. Feb. 2, 1874; d. Aug. 22, 1883.

502 MASSAH MIKSCH[7] WARNER, son of Benjamin[6] and
Anna Louisa (Stotz) Warner, born in Salem, N. C., January 9,
1836; died in Philadelphia, Pa., December 21, 1900. He served
a year in Salem as apprentice to the printing trade, then took up
the study of music, especially the piano. He spent a year in
Philadelphia, then three years in Leipzig, Germany, studying
under Hans von Bülow and other German masters. Returning
to Philadelphia, he took up music as a profession, was organist
at St. Luke's Episcopal Church, Germantown, and later of the
Woodland Church. As a man he was universally esteemed, as
a teacher much beloved, and as a member of the Moravian
Church, faithful and devoted. On the occasion of his death an
article appeared in "City and State," written by Philip H.
Goepp, a Philadelphia composer and teacher of wide reputation,
who is still active in the musical life of that city, and from that
the following appreciation is taken:

Massah M. Warner was one of those men who represent the highest
aim, without any pretense, without the talent for earning applause which
so many lesser men have, in all phases of life. So when he goes those
who knew him feel a certain fault in not having acclaimed his worth while
he was here. Now it seems almost too late to say that he was the best
teacher of the piano in Philadelphia. He was not recognized sufficiently,
because in these days technical instruction is valued beyond true musical
teaching. The real teaching of music to the heart and mind is surprisingly
rare. It was here that Massah Warner was eminent, and herein lay the
charm of his teaching—and more, it earned the affection of his pupils, so
that he probably taught no one who was not his friend. But with it all
he had the most thorough grasp of finger technique. Like many of the
best musicians of the world he was not fitted for public playing, being hin-
dered by his very anxiety for excellence. But at home with his friends his
playing seemed all the greater delight in the absolute perfection of its clearness, together with the warm musical feeling. . . . One of the greatest
of his traits was a pervading simplicity, as well of character as of manner.
With strong and deep religious convictions, he led the most quietly regular
life, and thus stood opposed to the false notion that a good musician must
be a Bohemian. In a sense he was musically a conservative, that is, one
of the brave figures who must stand out of the fashion, for the great principles of clearness, thoroughness and sincerity. . . . In few cases does
death seem so hard and inexplicable—not of the author who leaves his
books, or the composer of songs, as of the man whose personal equipment
and personal character and influence which make for the best equally with
books and songs, are suddenly snatched and lost from our midst.

Massah M. Warner married in Bethlehem, Pa., March 30,
1869, CELESTINE VICTORIA REINKE, born December 2,
1839, in Nazareth, Pa., daughter of Rev. Samuel Reinke and
Charlotte Sophia Hueffel, whose father was the Moravian

MASSAH M. WARNER

bishop, Christian Gottlieb Hueffel. She resides in Philadelphia, with her children.

Children, born in Philadelphia

Sophia Louisa Warner, b. Oct. 5, 1871. She is now the home-keeper and is also much interested in church and charitable work.

Paul Theodore Warner, b. Sept. 7, 1879. He has been in the employ of the Baldwin Locomotive Works since 1901, and is now Assistant Advertising Manager of the company.

503 EZRA BILLING[7] **WARNER**, son of Samuel Ettwine[6] and Mary (Warner?) Warner, born in Jeromeville, Ashland Co., Ohio, December 6, 1829; died in McComb, Ohio, November 28, 1900. About 1859 he moved to a farm north of McComb, and later to Arcadia, Ohio, where he managed a flour mill for a number of years. Later in life he became a stationary engineer. In Arcadia he was justice of the peace, and in McComb, a member of the council.

Married near Jeromeville, Ohio, **MARY CATHARINE EWING**, born near Jeromeville, October 8, 1829, died in Findlay, Ohio, April 4, 1914, daughter of James and Annamaria (Long) Ewing. In early life Mr. and Mrs. Warner were members of the Moravian Church but at the time of her death Mrs. Warner was a member of the Presbyterian Church.

Children, first three born near Jeromeville, three near McComb, and others in Arcadia, Ohio

Sarah Alvira Warner, b. Nov. 25, 1850; resides in McComb; m. John W. Ebersole. Children: i. James E., m. and d., leaving no children. ii. Lettie M., died; m. (1) ——— Wolford and had a child, Clem, who resides at Middletown, Ohio; m. (2) ——— Frankfather, and had a child, Boyd. iii. Ara. iv. John.

Mary Selena Warner, b. June 8, 1852; resides with her son in Toledo, Ohio; m. (1) Robert Locy, (2) Pline Jones, who died about 1915. Children by first husband: i. John E. ii. Lankford. iii. Zettie. iv. Milton, resides in Toledo. v. James E., resides in Detroit, Mich.; m. and has children, Howard, Helen and Mary. vi. Rolland.

John Philip Warner, b. June 19, 1854; resides in Fostoria, Ohio; is an evangelist in the Methodist Episcopal Church; m. in Fostoria, May 18, 1876, Ellen Amanda Johnson, b. in Seneca County, Kans., daughter of Thomas and Eliza (———) Johnson. Child: Lida E., b. in Fostoria, Feb., 1877; m. Wiley W. Weaver.

Annamaria Warner, b. Oct. 8, 1856; d. Nov. 1, 1861.

James Ewing Warner, b. Apr. 24, 1859; is a real estate dealer in San Antonio, Texas; m. Mina Marshall. No children.

Milton Warner, b. July 3, 1861; is a farmer, conducts a real estate and insurance business, and is notary public in Carr, Weld County, Colo. He is an elder in the Presbyterian Church. Married Sept.

18, 1890, Celestia I. Metz, b. in New Waterford, Ohio, Dec. 3, 1862, daughter of Hiram and Emeline (Lingenfelter) Metz. Children, b. in McComb, Ohio: i. Karl M., b. July 9, 1891; is a book-keeper in Greeley, Colo.; married. ii. Arthur H., b. Aug. 26, 1893; was graduated from the University of Colorado in 1917, attended officers' training camp at Fort Riley, Kans., and later at Fortress Monroe, Va., was made 2d Lieutenant in U. S. Heavy Artillery, stationed at Fort Adams, Newport, R. I., Nov. 13, 1917. iii. Walter, d. in childhood.

Ellora Warner, b. Apr. 11, 1864; resides in Findlay, Ohio; m. Tobias Holsinger. Child: Verna, m. Joseph Peffley; resides in Findlay, and has two children, Mary and Ruth.

Lucretia May Warner, b. May 31, 1866; d. May 7, 1904.

(Son), b. Dec. 13, 1868; d. Feb. 23, 1869.

Ezra Jay Warner, b. Mar. 15, 1870; resides in Findlay, Ohio, and is principal of the Public School; not married.

Jeston Warner, b. Jan. 8, 1873; resides in Findlay, Ohio; is notary public and conducts a loan and real estate business; m. Florence McClure. No children.

504 HARRIET[7] WARNER, daughter of Milan[6] and Polly (Watt) Warner, born April 12, 1792, baptized May 18, 1800, in Worthington, Mass.; received property from her grandfather's estate in 1823.

Married in Worthington, December 15, 1808, **S I L A S MARBLE**, born January 5, 1786.

Children, born in Worthington

Mary Marble, b. Oct. 26, 1809; m. Jan. 23, 1840, David P. Eno of Granby, Conn.

————, b. Mar. 4, 1811; d. Mar. 5, 1811.

Huldah Marble, b. Jan. 8, 1812, date so given in Worthington town records.

Joseph Barnard Marble, b. Apr. 26, 1812, date so given in Worthington records; m. June 11, 1846, Jerutia Ann Morgan.

Pamelia Marble, b. Aug. 9, 1814; m. Apr. 5, 1837, Jonathan Prentice.

Amelia or *Aurelia Brewster Marble*, b. Dec. 20, 1816; m. Apr. 5, 1837, Nathan C. Brewer.

Sarah W. Marble, b. Feb. 24, 1821; m. Oct. 28, 1847, Charles F. Moor, aged 29, a farmer, and son of John and Anna (————) Moor.

Eunice W. Marble, b. May 5, 1823; m. Oct. 28, 1847, Abner W. Witt, aged 29, a farmer and son of William and Beulah (————) Witt of Easthampton. They lived to celebrate their golden wedding in 1897.

Alvah B. Marble, b. Apr. 3, 1825; m. Oct. 11, 1849, Jane M. White.

Lucy A. Marble, b. Oct. 27, 1827; m. June 22, 1848, William R. Searl aged 25, a carpenter of Southampton, son of Samuel and Zeruah (————) Searl.

Silas M. Marble, b. Dec. 29, 1829.

Maria H. Marble, b. Feb. 25, 1832.

Henry Marble, b. July 8, 1834.

505 MATTHEW S.[7] WARNER, son of Stoel[6] and Anna (Crandall) Warner, born May 23, 1814, in Champion, N. Y.; died there, November 26, 1854. He was a farmer in Champion. Married in Champion, April 30, 1837, CHARLOTTE LOOMIS, born in Champion, December 22, 1815, daughter of Alvin and Nancy (————) Loomis.

Children, born in Champion

Laura A. Warner, b. July 30, 1838; d. Jan. 18, 1873; m. Nov. 24, 1858, Joshua Colvin. Children: i. Cora Anna, b. May 31, 1867; d. Mar. 11, 1890. ii. (Son), b. July 31, 1872; d. Aug. 28, 1872.
Matthew S. Warner, Jr., b. Aug. 6, 1842; d. Aug. 28, 1843.
Elizur C. Warner, b. Sept. 15, 1853; resides in Carthage, N. Y.; m. in Champion, Nov. 13, 1878, Bessie E. Merrill, b. Apr. 4, 1859, daughter of Allen and Huldah (————) Merrill. Children: i. Merrill Stoel, b. July 11, 1880; d. July 12, 1880. ii. Minnie, b. Nov. 22, 1882; m. Apr. 23, 1903, William J. Perry.

506 ALANSON[7] WARNER, son of Andrew[6] and Chloé (Fairman) Warner, born in Worthington, Mass., March 19, 1802; died in Ontario, N. Y., November 3, 1883. He went with his parents to Ontario, N. Y., in 1816, and was a farmer there. He was the inventor of the Differential Gear universally used on automobiles and road engines, patented November 13, 1865. He was also inventor of the Hand Corn Sheller, a machine considered of much merit at the time.
Married in Williamson, N. Y., September 29, 1830, CATH-ERINE ALBRIGHT, born in Holland, daughter of John and Penelope (Lewis) Albright, and came to America at the age of five years. She was residing in ·Ontario about 1895, aged 83.

Children, born in Ontario, N. Y.

Chloe Warner, b. Sept. 11, 1831; m. June 4, 1851, David B. Reed, a farmer in Ontario.
Lamyra Warner, d. in infancy.
677 *John Albright Warner*, b. Aug. 12, 1835; m. Harriet Ann Morris.
Edna Ann Warner, b. Dec. 26, 1837; d. in Ulah, Ill., May 30, 1917; m. Mar., 1863, Charles Atherton Morris, son of Lyman and Anna (Millet) Morris of Springwater, N. Y. They settled in Ulah, Ill., and the family are Methodists. Mr. Morris gave land from their farm for the church building. Children: i. Anna Frances, d. in infancy in Ulah. ii. Helen Charlotte, b. May 24, 1868, in Ulah; m. Feb. 3, 1890, William S. Johnston, a farmer and grain dealer of Ulah, and had five children, b. in Ulah: Harry, b. Nov. 13, 1890, Elmer, b. July 5, 1895, d. in infancy, Clyde, b. Dec. 27, 1897, Bertha, b. Dec. 17, 1901, and May, b. Mar. 25, 1904.
Mary Maria Warner, b. Nov. 17, 1840; m. Mar. 15, 1869, John Thomas

Bradshaw, who was b. Nov. 23, 1842, d. in Ontario, Aug. 30, 1906, son of James and Phebe H. (————) Bradshaw of Gloversville, N. Y. He was a farmer. Child: Chloe Luella, b. in Sodus, N. Y., Aug. 15, 1876; d. Dec. 29, 1893.
Emeline Frances Warner, b. Mar. 22, 1844; d. Apr. 14, 1913, in Fort Collins, Colo.; m. Edward Eugene Sheffield, b. in Ontario County, N. Y., son of Edward and Belinda (Smith) Sheffield of Ontario. They settled in Ulah, Ill., went later to Iowa, then to Fort Collins, Colo. Children: i. Nelson Jerome, b. Sept. 16, 1866, in Henry County, Ill. ii. Edward Ulysses, b. Sept. 25, 1868, in Henry County. iii. Frances Alvira, b. Apr. 8, 1871, in Guthrie County, Iowa. iv. Nellie Elizabeth, b. Mar. 23, 1880, in Perry, Iowa.
678 *Albert Eldoras Warner*, b. Mar. 27, 1854; m. Martha Louise Granger.

507 ORPHA[7] WARNER, daughter of Andrew[6] and Chloe (Fairman) Warner, born October 25, 1804, in Champion, N. Y.; died July 5, 1905, in David City, Neb., at the residence of her son.
Married in Ontario, N. Y., January 28, 1838, PHILANDER BILLSON ROYS, who was a successful farmer living at Pultneyville, Wayne Co., N. Y., where he died in 1869.

Children, born in Pultneyville

Laura Saloma Roys, d. in Pultneyville, aged 18.
Andrew Billson Roys, b. Apr. 21, 1841. In his early life he was a sailor and made several voyages as captain of a whale ship. After his marriage he settled in David City, Neb., and was engaged in the undertaking business for a number of years, is now retired. He married Julia King, who died Dec. 20, 1917, in Dakota City. Child: Albert E., b. Feb. 19, 1872; d. Oct. 18, 1875, in David City.
Ellen Aurelia Roys, b. June 29, 1849; d. Aug. 29, 1906; m. Philander B. Royce of Connecticut, a veteran of the Civil War. They settled in Bellwood, Neb., and kept a hotel for several years, then engaged in farming until his wife's death. Children, first two b. in Pultneyville, others in Bellwood: i. Charles, b. Nov. 30, 1869. ii. Alice Lenore, b. Dec. 6, 1871. iii. Edward, b. Sept. 10, 1881. iv. Winifred, b. May 4, 1888; m. Renwix Hanner of David City, a farmer, and has a son, Richard Lee, b. in David City, in 1915.

508 EUNICE[7] WARNER, daughter of Andrew[6] and Chloe (Fairman) Warner, born August 8, 1808, in Champion, N. Y.; died March 10, 1865, in Wilna, N. Y.
Married in Wilna, February 21, 1830, GEORGE OWEN, a farmer of Wilna.

Children, born in Wilna

William Owen, m. Lovissa Armstrong of Wilna, and has children, Laura and Maynard.
Myron Owen, b. Apr. 10, 1834; settled in Jefferson County, N. Y.;

506 THE DESCENDANTS OF ANDREW WARNER

m. Cynthia Carpenter. Children: i. Mamie, m. George Gates, and had five children. ii. Jesse, m. Minnie Maurer of Beaver Falls, N. Y., and d. there, in 1909; had a daughter, Gladys, b. in Beaver Falls.

509 LAURA[7] WARNER, daughter of Andrew[6] and Chloe (Fairman) Warner, born August 16, 1816, in Webster, N. Y.; died February 27, 1897, in Ontario, N. Y., at the residence of her nephew, John Albright Warner.

Married (1) November 8, 1843, **JOHNSON COTTREL,** born January 5, 1817, son of John and Phebe (————) Cottrel of Williamson, N. Y., died in Williamson, July 13, 1849.

Married (2) 1868, **WESTON WINSLOW,** a farmer of Web ster, who died there in 1869.

Children of Johnson and Laura (Warner) Cottrel

Harriet E. Cottrel, b. in Williamson, Aug. 15, 1846; resides in Penfield, N. Y.; m. Apr. 20, 1887, James H. Braman, a farmer of Penfield, who died Oct. 5, 1905.

Helen J. Cottrel, b. in Williamson, Aug. 29, 1849; d. Dec. 8, 1884, at the residence of her mother in Ontario, N. Y.

510 SAMUEL ELIOT[7] WARNER, son of Jared Eliot[6] and Alathea R. (Lord) Warner, born in Utica, N. Y., May 29, 1823; died in Brooklyn, N. Y., July 6, 1887. He was educated at Black River Institute and was graduated from Williams College in 1843. He went to New York and was for over forty years connected with the American Tract Society as secretary and editor of the Illustrated Christian Weekly. He resided in Brooklyn, early united with the Clinton Avenue Congregational Church of that city and was deeply interested in the work of its Atlantic Avenue Chapel, acting as secretary and superintendent of its Sunday School. He was deacon for several terms of four years each. Mr. Warner was an ardent advocate of temperance. A memorial volume, "In remembrance," published after his death, contains eloquent tributes to his character in the sermon delivered by his pastor, Dr. Thomas B. McLeod, October 2, 1887. Mr. Warner's portrait appears, with that of his father, on page 349.

Married August 20, 1850, **HELEN POTTER,** born in Utica, August 10, 1825, died in Brooklyn, January 11, 1893, daughter of William Frederick Potter, who was born in Branford, Conn., October 28, 1786, died in Utica, N. Y., 1850, and his wife, Eunice Camp, who was born in Glastonbury, Conn., March 16, 1795, died in Utica, 1851.

Child

Sophia Alathea Warner, resides in Brooklyñ, N. Y.; m. Mar. 12, 1884, Samuel Theodore Dauchy, son of Samuel and Clarissa H. (Kellogg) Dauchy. No children. His first wife was Margaret Clements.

511 JAMES TROWBRIDGE⁷ WARNER, son of George Trowbridge⁶ and Tamzen Smith (Rogers) Warner, born in Uxbridge, Mass., April 6, 1830; died in Milford, Mass., December 13, 1901.
Married in Pawtucket, R. I., December 9, 1856, MARTHA VESTA DITSON, born April 1, 1841; died August 28, 1900.

Children

James Henry Warner, b. July 12, 1857; resides in Brooklyn, N. Y.; m. Aug. 28, 1880, Alice Maria Fairbanks, b. Sept. 21, 1861, died. Children: i. Bertha Fairbanks, b. July 1, 1881; married. ii. Blanche Alice, b. Aug. 8, 1883; married.
Benjamin Trowbridge Warner, b. July 14, 1861; d. Oct. 22, 1911; m. Aug., 1885, Etta Ells Hollis, who resides in Brockton, Mass. No children.
Frank Augustus Warner, b. May 22, 1866; resides in Marlboro, Mass.; is employed in the shoe manufacturing business; m. Oct. 30, 1895, Lucy Newell Baker, b. June 21, 1868. Children: i. Newell Francis, b. Aug. 23, 1896; is at present (Apr., 1918) a musician on board the U. S. S. *Charleston,* somewhere on the Atlantic Ocean. ii. Ralph Baker, b. Feb. 28, 1900; is in school. iii. Warren Stebbens, b. Sept. 24, 1901, is in school. "The boys all have the same love of music that most of the Warners have, and I try to encourage it," writes the father.
Charles Frederick Warner, b. June 8, 1868; resides in Matteawan, Dutchess Co., N. Y.; m. Carrie ————. Child: Helen, b. about 1913.
Nelson Dwight Warner, b. June 13, 1872; resides in Milford, Mass.; m. Bertha Whipple. They have had two children who died young.
Laura Violetta Evelyn Warner, b. June 1, 1874; resides in Uxbridge, Mass.; m. Frank A. Dewolf. Child: Lillian, m. May 7, 1917, Adolph Lee.
Samuel Asa Warner, b. Aug. 28, 1875; resides in Matteawan; not married.
Davy Crockett Warner, b. Nov., 1878; d. aged 3 months.

512 ALBERT LOOMIS⁷ WARNER, son of George Trowbridge⁶ and Tamzen Smith (Rogers) Warner, born in Webster, Mass., July 28, 1834; resides in Pawtucket, R. I. (1918). He is a member of the Sons of the Revolution.
. Married. (1) at Cotuit Port, Mass., September 1, 1859, HENRIETTA ROGERS, who died at Cotuit Port, February 19, 1865.
Married (2) in Pawtucket, August 26, 1866, EMMA JANE

PECK, born in Smithfield, R. I., October 22, 1847; died in Pawtucket, August 22 (or 23), 1916.

Child by first wife

George Newell Warner, who died in Darlington, S. C., in 1886; m.
Leila ————, who died about 1887; no children.

Children by second wife

Olive Henrietta Warner, b. at Central Falls, R. I., Aug. 9, 1867;
resides in Pueblo, Colo. She is a member of the D. A. R. and has
been State Regent. Married in Pawtucket, R. I., June 5, 1889,
Freeman Cudworth Rogers, b. in Webster, Mass., Oct. 16, 1868, son
of Edwin and Annie (McKensie) Rogers. They have no children.
Albert Russell Warner, b. in Pawtucket, R. I., May 5, 1876; resides
in Pawtucket; m. Hattie Sayball; no children.
Grace Ethelyn Warner, d. in infancy.

513 LAURA PARMELIA[7] WARNER, daughter of George
Trowbridge[6] and Tamzen Smith (Rogers) Warner, born in
Thompson, Conn., December 19, 1836; died in Nayatt, R. I.,
February 18, 1914.
M a r r i e d (1) in Cambridgeport, Mass., May 21, 1860,
GEORGE H. NEWELL, who died in Attleboro, Mass., Sep-
tember 2, 1860.
Married (2) in Providence, R. I., January 17, 1870, GEORGE
FREETH SMITH, born in Birmingham, England, February 1,
1844. He resides in Nayatt, R. I.

Children by second husband

Edward Pearl Smith, b. at Nayatt, R. I., Nov. 29, 1871, and resides
there; m. at Nayatt, Apr. 5, 1894, Isabella Grant. Children: i.
George Grant, b. Dec. 29, 1894; d. Sept. 21, 1895. ii. Laura Grant,
b. Dec. 18, 1896; a student at Rhode Island Normal School. iii.
John Gray, b. Feb. 8, 1899; d. July 9, 1914. iv. Marion Pearl, b.
Dec. 25, 1900; a student at Barrington High School. v. Edward
Albert, b. Jan. 23, 1903.
Laura May Smith, b. in South Scituate, R. I., June 12, 1873; resides
in Lexington, near Concord Junction, Mass.; m. Dec. 7, 1904, Dr.
Ernest Mayell, b. in Newton, Mass., Dec. 4, 1876. Children: Ruth
Curtis; Laura Smith.
Sarah Rosamond Smith, b. Nov. 24, 1874; resides in Nayatt, R. I.; is
a teacher in Pawtucket, R. I.
George Warner Smith, b. in Nayatt, Dec. 26, 1877; lives near Fort
Smith, Ark.; m. Sept. 19, 1912, Ada Frances Ingram, b. Sept. 11,
1884. Child: George Francis, b. Sept. 1, 1913.

514 CHARLES FRANCIS PEARL[7] WARNER, son of
George Trowbridge[6] and Tamzen Smith (Rogers) Warner, born
in Williamsville, Jones township, Pa., November 5, 1848.

Married (1) at Pawtucket, R. I., December 25, 1871, **EMMA WILLARD CHACE**, born October 20, 1845; died at Pawtucket, March 19, 1876.

Married (2) at Pawtucket, November 27, 1879, **JANETTE AUGUSTA LYON**, born July 14, 1851; died February 5, 1918.

Children by first wife

Grace Pearl Warner, b. July 20, 1873; m. June 15, 1893, Adolphus Daniels. Children: i. Emma Lillian, b. Feb. 20, 1895. ii. William Ellis, b. Sept. 22, 1896. iii. Dorothea Fuller, b. Dec. 12, 1898. iv. Charles Winthrop, b. May 21, 1900. v. Adolphus, Jr., b. July 8, 1902; d. Mar. 24, 1905. vi. Grace Jeanette, b. Mar. 28, 1904. vii. Ruth Pearl, b. June 12, 1909.

Edith Carrie Warner, b. Oct. 6, 1875; d. 1876.

Child by second wife

Carrie Edith Warner, b. Sept. 2, 1880; d. Sept. 23, 1880.

515 EDGAR MORRIS[7] WARNER, son of Earl[6] and Ade line (Lester) Warner, born June 16, 1850, in Worcester, Mass.; resides in Putnam, Conn. He attended Bartlett High School in New London, studied law with Hiram Willey of New London and George Pratt of Norwich, was graduated from the Harvard Law School with the degree of LL.B. in 1872, and admitted to the Bar of New London County in September, 1872. After practicing law in Norwich for three years he located in Central Village in 1875. In 1885 he extended his practice by opening an office in Putnam and subsequently removed there. He was Clerk of the House, State Legislature, 1877, 1879, and Clerk of the Senate in 1880; Representative from the Town of Putnam in 1895; First Judge of the City Court of Putnam, 1896-1901; in 1901 was appointed Clerk of the Superior Court for Windham County. He is a member of the S. A. R. and for more than twenty years, as Chairman of the committee on Prison and Jail Work of the State Y. P. S. C. E., has spoken and labored for Probation and Prison Reform.

Married in Putnam, August 3, 1887, **JANE ELIZABETH CARPENTER**, who was born in Putnam, daughter of Judge John A. and Marcia (Chandler) Carpenter. She is a member of the D. A. R. as a descendant of Joseph Bailey (1756-1841) of Coventry and West Greenwich, R. I., also as descendant of Robert Carpenter, born in East Greenwich, R. I., a soldier in the Continental army, and of David Lillibridge of Willington, Conn., who was a Lieutenant in the Militia and a Justice of the Peace during Revolutionary times.

EDGAR MORRIS WARNER

Children, born in Putnam

Frances Lester Warner, b. July 19, 1888; was graduated from Mt. Holyoke College in 1911, and in 1917 became a teacher of English in the college. She has contributed articles for many publications. Among them are: "Endicott and I conduct an Orchestra," The Atlantic Monthly, Dec., 1916; "Endicott and I go Sketching," Century, June, 1917; and "Preserving the Past," Atlantic Monthly, Nov., 1917.

Gertrude Chandler Warner, b. Apr. 16, 1890. She has had published two books for children, "The House of Delight" and "Star Stories for Little Folks"; she is a regular contributor to well-known children's magazines and her work has occasionally appeared in the standard periodicals.

John A. Carpenter Warner, b. July 12, 1893; was graduated from Worcester Polytechnic Institute, June, 1917; enlisted in the Aviation Service and went to France as a member of the Research Division of the 201st Squadron, Dec., 1918.

516 WILLIAM PHELPS⁷ WARNER, son of Oliver⁶ and Jemima (Severance) Warner, born in Hadley, Mass., March 6, 1818; died there, July 6, 1872. He was a farmer and resided in Hadley.

Married December 14, 1852, **BETSEY RICH ABBE,** born in Enfield, Conn., November 18 (or 13), 1830, died May 24, 1906, daughter of Henry Augustus and Elizabeth (Allen) Abbe of Enfield. For ancestry see "The Families of Abbe and Abbey." She was a member of the D. A. R.

Children

Edward Allen Warner, b. Dec. 14, 1853; d. Oct. 14, 1906, not married.
Helen Abbe Warner, b. Aug. 31, 1858; d. at Ardmore, Pa., Dec. 12, 1912; m. Elisha Dickinson of Hadley, who d. ——.
Isabel Huntington Warner, b. Mar. 1, 1867; resides in Philadelphia, Pa.; m. (1) Dana Bartholomew of Ansonia, Conn., b. in Wolcottville (now Torrington), Conn., Apr. 8, 1847, d. at Saratoga, N. Y., Sept. 1, 1900; m. (2) in New York, Feb. 3, 1909, Peter Boyd of Philadelphia, who died there, Dec. 11, 1911. Children by first husband: i. Pauline Warner, b. at Ansonia, Sept. 25, 1889; d. there, Jan. 14, 1890. ii. Helen Gertrude, b. at Ansonia, Nov. 25, 1890; resides with her mother in Philadelphia.

517 HARRIETT ANN⁷ WARNER, daughter of Harmon⁶ and Sally Maroxa (Joyce) Warner, born October 8, 1819, in New Milford, Conn.; died August 1, 1900, in Rome, Pa.

Married in Pike, Pa., **EDWIN M. TAYLOR,** born March 8, 1812, in Connecticut; died in Rome, Pa., 1892. He was a farmer and was the son of Benjamin and Abisha (————) Taylor.

Children, born in Rome

Mortimer K. Taylor, b. Sept. 25, 1835; d. Dec. 20, 1893, in Cleveland, Ohio. He was general agent for the New Automatic Sewing Machine Company, with offices in many cities. He was at the Cleveland office when he died suddenly from blood poisoning in the hand. Married in Herrick, Pa., Nov. 7, 1861, Martha Hale Maynard, b. in Rome, Aug. 3, 1843, daughter of William and Nancy (Cranmer) Maynard. Children: i. N. Viola, b. May 28, 1864, in Orwell, Pa.; m. in Scranton, Dec. 24, 1894, George W. Chase. ii. Minnie E., b. in Rome, Oct. 5, 1868; m. there, June 24, 1897, Rev. S. W. Trousdale, Ph.D. iii. Isabelle, b. in Peekskill, N. Y., Aug. 16, 1872; d. there, Feb. 19, 1873. iv. Eva L., b. Feb. 21, 1876, in Peekskill; m. in Rome, Pa., July 28, 1898, Emery G. Moore.

Orville H. Taylor, b. Aug. 1, 1844; d. Aug. 19, 1910, in Rome, where he had lived all his life. He was choir leader of the Methodist Church in Rome for thirty years. Married in Orwell, Pa., June 9, 1876, Olivia Lung, daughter of Alanson and Maria (———) Lung. She resides in Brooklyn, N. Y., with her son. Children, born in Rome: i. Lillian, b. 1880; was a teacher in the public schools of Pennsylvania and New Jersey, also a music teacher; m. July 20, 1915, Albion U. Jenkins, principal of a school in Paterson, N. J. ii. Harold, b. 1890; is a graduate of Pratt Institute and a teacher in Brooklyn.

518 EMELINE ELMIRA[7] WARNER, daughter of Harmon[6] and Sally Maroxa (Joyce) Warner, born June 4, 1823, in New Milford, Conn.; died at Whitney's Point, N. Y., October 5, 1884.

Married July 9, 1845, Rev. **CORRINGTON E. TAYLOR,** born at Taylor Hill, near Pike, Pa., son of Benjamin and Abisha (———) Taylor; died at Whitney's Point, N. Y. He was a Methodist minister and held pastorates in many places.

Children

Hedding Taylor, d. in infancy.
Frank Taylor, b. at Little Meadows, Pa., June 11, 1846; was graduated from a medical college in Cleveland, Ohio, and was a successful physician in Castle Creek, N. Y., where he died Nov. 9, 1900. He married (1) Louisa Stevens, of Stevensville, Pa., daughter of Cyrus and Lydia Ann (Lacey) Stevens, and granddaughter of Aden and Annice[6] (Warner) Stevens; see number 190. His second wife and a daughter, Teressa, survived him.

519 OLIVER JOHN[7] WARNER, son of Harmon[6] and Sally Maroxa (Joyce) Warner, born in Leraysville, Pa., July 20, 1827; died in New York City, March 12, 1896. He 'was a cattle drover, and after 1872 was in the butter and milk business in New York City.

Married in Orwell, Pa., September 19, 1848, **RUTH SOPHIA CHAFFEE**, born in Pike township, Bradford County, Pa., June 15, 1830, at the old Chaffee homestead on Chaffee Hill; died in New York City, January 6, 1896. She was the daughter of Comfort Bliss and Docia (Sexton) Chaffee.

Children

Phoebe Rosabelle Warner, b. Aug. 10, 1849; d. in Union, N. Y., Jan. 27, 1906; m. Melsa Wilson, who was engaged in a butter and milk store in New York City, and died there. Child: Clarence, b. in Windham, Bradford Co., Pa.

Melville Bliss Warner, b. 1853; d. Sept. 19, 1871.

Elwyn Heading Warner, d. young.

Merton Harmon Warner, d. young.

Jessie Flora Warner, d. Dec. 7, 1870.

Oliver Fremont Warner, b. Sept., 1863; d. Sept. 23, 1884; was in milk business in New York City; m. there, Annie Richards. Child: Mabel Lillian, b. Jan. 30, 1884.

Minnie Sophia Warner, b. Mar. 13, 1864; resides in Union, N. Y.; m. in New York City, Sept. 2, 1886, Frederick De Witt Brown, b. in Apalachin, Tioga Co., N. Y., May 4, 1854. He was a druggist in New York City at the time of his marriage, later in the same business in Union; retired from business a few years ago and built a brick block in Union, known as the Brown Block. Child: Leila Rosabelle, a High School student (1916).

520 **TAMAR ABIGAIL[7] WARNER**, daughter of Harmon[6] and Sally Maroxa (Joyce) Warner, born in Le Raysville, Pa., March 24, 1832; died November 17, 1906, at Orwell Hill, Pa. She was a member of the Methodist Church.

Married (1) at Orwell, Pa., September 20, 1848, **NATHANIEL BLISS CHAFFEE**, born April 1, 1826, in Warren, Pa., died near Petersburg, Va., January 22, 1865, son of Comfort Bliss and Docia (Sexton) Chaffee. He was a farmer and dealer in live stock; resided at Orwell, Pa. He was a corporal in the Civil War and died in a field hospital near Petersburg. Congregationalist.

Married (2) **IRA BRINK.**

Children of Nathaniel B. and Tamar A. (Warner) Chaffee

Olive Rosetta Chaffee, b. Nov. 6, 1849; resides at Orwell, Pa.; m. there, Feb. 8, 1866, Robert Arnold, a farmer, b. in Warren, Pa., soldier in the Civil War. Children: i. Edward Bliss, b. Jan. 8, 1867; m. Carrie Aurelia Beers. ii. Tamar Antoinette, b. Sept. 7, 1869; m. John Curtis Pettes. iii. Clara Syrena, b. Dec. 18, 1874.

Myron William Chaffee, b. Apr. 8, 1855; resides in Stevensville, Pa.; m. Carrie Northrop.

33

George Mervin Chaffee, b. Mar. 3, 1857; resides in Lincoln, Kans.; m. Lucretia Titus.
Phoebe Gertrude Chaffee, b. Aug. 1, 1860; resides in Herrick, Pa.; m. James R. Titus.
Lincoln Elliott Chaffee, b. May 13, 1863; resides at Camptown, Pa.; m. Sarah Titus.

521 MARCUS ELLIOTT[7] WARNER, son of Harmon[6] and Sally Maroxa (Joyce) Warner, born February 23, 1835, in Le Raysville, Pa.; died there, November 30, 1905. He was a farmer and resided with his father and mother, caring for them in their old age. He served in the Civil War in the 141st Regiment, a three-year regiment, was captain of Company D, and present in 32 battles and at the surrender of General Lee. Married in Orwell, Pa., November 21, 1855, DOCIA ANN CHAFFEE, born in Orwell, Pa., November 16, 1833, daughter of Comfort Bliss and Docia (Sexton) Chaffee.

Children, born in Orwell

Edwin Fremont Warner, b. Aug. 30, 1857; is a commercial traveler; resides in Brooklyn, N. Y.; m. in Herricksville, Pa., Dec. 19, 1880, Emma A. Doolittle, b. in Wyalusing, Pa., May 28, 1863, daughter of James Weston and Amanda (Overpeck) Doolittle. Child: Grace May, b. June 12, 1894, in Brooklyn.
Etta May Warner, b. May 13, 1866, in Pike, Pa.; is a nurse, but owns and keeps a home in Raymond, N. H., when she is not nursing; has been active in church and missionary societies and clubs, and in W. C. T. U. work. Married (1) in Brooklyn, N. Y., Sept. 6, 1894, Rev. Charles Norris Tilton, b. in Raymond, N. H., Apr. 4, 1868, d. of pneumonia, in Wadena, Minn., Feb. 19, 1905, after being there only four months. He was a son of Belknap and Emma (Foster) Tilton, was graduated from Philips Exeter Academy, 1890, and Boston University, 1894. She married (2) in Le Raysville, Pa., Dec. 23, 1911, Jonah Norris Tilton, b. in Concord, N. H., June 29, 1840, d. Nov. 21, 1915. Children by first husband: i. Beulah Naomi, b. July 6, 1895; a teacher. ii. Warner Belknap, b. Oct. 11, 1896; is in college. iii. Paul Josiah, b. Oct. 13, 1897; is in college. iv. Charles Norris, b. June 16, 1904.

522 COVINGTON HARMON[7] WARNER, son of Harmon[6] and Sally Maroxa (Joyce) Warner, born in Pike, Bradford Co., Pa. (or in Le .Raysville?), February 7, 1837; died in Rushville, Susquehanna Co., September 29, 1901. In 1858 he began reading medicine with Dr. Benjamin De Witt of Le Raysville, Pa. He attended a course of lectures at the University of Michigan and another at Georgetown, where he was graduated in 1861. After practicing medicine at Bellefontaine, for two years, he returned to Bradford County and enlisted, March,

1864, as private in the 141st Pennsylvania Volunteers, in service with the Army of the Potomac until November, 1864, when he was detailed as assistant surgeon to the Emery Hospital in Washington. He remained on duty in the hospital until March, 1865, when he returned to the front and continued there until the end of the war. He practiced medicine at Stevensville, Pa., until 1869, then removed to Le Raysville, and from there to Rushville, Susquehanna County, in 1883. His genial nature, uniform courtesy, and open hospitality won him many friends, and his successful treatment commanded the confidence of his patients, thus winning him a large practice.

Married (1) February 23, 1862, **EMELINE** or **EMMA M. BARNES** of Orwell, Pa., who died March 12, 1872.

Married (2) about 1873, **AMELIA M. BRISTER.**

Children by first wife

Marion Harmon Warner, b. at South Hill, Pa., July 21, 1863; resides at North Branch, Minn., where he is a farmer, and fruit and vegetable inspector. Married in Sunrise, Minn., Nov. 24, 1885, Isabell C. Clover, born in Sunrise, daughter of Daniel and Sarah Clover. Children: i. Emma Adelle, b. Nov. 30, 1886, in Sunrise; d. Jan. 27, 1903. ii. George Leroy, b. July 29, 1889, in Sunrise; is agent for the N. P. R. R. at Stacy, Minn.
Carrie Warner, d. in infancy.

523 GEORGE FRANKLIN[7] WARNER, son of Harmon[6] and Sally Maroxa (Joyce) Warner, born in Le Raysville, Pa., December 29, 1839; died in Stevensville, Pa., December 6, 1906. He was a blacksmith and was quite a musician, taught vocal music.

Married at Taylor Hill, Rome, Pa., February 28, 1860, **MARTHA S. TOWNER.**

Children

Flora Warner, resides in Pottersville, Pa.; m. F. L. Worden.
Jessie Warner, m. ―― Leighton.

524 WILLIAM S.[7] WARNER, son of Elizur[6] and Lyra Ann (Totman) Warner, born in New Milford, Conn.; died there, October 3, 1879, aged 44 years, 4 months, 15 days, buried in Gallows Hill Cemetery.

Married **RACHEL EDWARDS,** who was living in 1897.

Children

Hannah Eliza Warner, b. 1862; d. Feb. 3, 1863, aged 5 months, 12 days.
William Hanford Warner, b. Mar. 20, 1868, in Bridgewater, Conn.;

was accidentally drowned June 15, 1913. He was a carpenter. Married (1) Addie S. Gardner, b. in Sherman, Conn., daughter of Franklin Gardner, d. in Lanesville district, New Milford, Feb. 27, 1896, aged 27 years, 9 months; m. (2) Apr. 9, 1898, Mrs. Mary Jane Daskam, b. in Michigan, d. in New Milford, Nov. 7, 1904, aged 49, daughter of Peter and Maria (Caterell) Knapp. Children by first wife: i. Minnie R., b. in New Milford, Feb. 21, 1887. ii. Stanley H., b. in New Milford, Feb. 4, 1893.

525 STANLEY LE GRAND[7] WARNER, son of Henry Sanford[6] and Eliza Ann (Hill) Warner, born in New Milford, Conn., February 23, 1831; was a farmer in the Lanesville section of New Milford until his retirement a few years ago. While in his eighty-fifth year, Mr. Warner took an active interest in the family history and from his remarkable memory helped build up many of the fragmentary records of the earlier Warner families of New Milford.

Married November 7, 1853, **EUNICE P. WANZER**, born April 19, 1833; died in New Milford, August 8, 1911. She was the daughter of Daniel and Hannah (Briggs) Wanzer of Sherman, Conn.

Children, born in New Milford

679 *Henry Daniel Warner*, b. Nov. 14, 1857; m. Harriet Aminta Sabin.

Harriet Louisa Warner, b. Nov. 30, 1861; resides in New Milford; m. Sept. 21, 1887, John Frederic Addis, son of John W. and Jane E. (Terrill) Addis, and a descendant of a sister of Roger Sherman. Mr. Addis came from Litchfield to New Milford when eleven years of age. Children: i. John Stanley, b. Apr. 4, 1889; resides in New Milford; m. Nov. 18, 1915, Dorothy Lawson Crowell of Perth Amboy, N. J. ii. Doris E., b. Jan. 18, 1901. iii. Mary Stewart, b. Mar. 7, 1902.

Edith M. Warner, b. Sept. 23, 1870; was graduated from Ingleside Academy and taught there; resides in Mt. Vernon, N. Y.; m. Nov. 26, 1907, Franklin B. Dailey, b. in Warren, Conn., about 1866, is a salesman, son of Lewis and Hannah (Bates) Dailey. Children: Franklin Bates and Harry Warner (twins), b. Aug. 14, 1909.

526 HENRY ORANGE[7] WARNER, son of Henry Sanford[6] and Eliza Ann (Hill) Warner, born in New Milford, Conn., August 18, 1834; died there, May 8, 1909. He was a farmer and tobacco dealer of New Milford. He was educated in New Milford and at Nine Partners, Dutchess Co., N. Y., and at the High School in New Britain, Conn. At his father's death he became proprietor of one of his farms, and took up tobacco culture. In 1869 he built a large warehouse and engaged in the business of buying and packing tobacco, conducting a warehouse in Hartford also. He was extensively engaged in stock raising, breeding full-blooded Holstein cattle and some of the finest trotting horses in the country. He was Master of St. Peter's Lodge, F. and A. M., in New Milford for a number of years, Most Worshipful Grand Master of the state for two terms; County Commissioner in 1892-3, and held other minor public offices.

Married (1) November 13, 1854, MARY J. BRIGGS, born September 6, 1832, died abut 1855, in her 23d year, daughter of Willis Briggs of Sherman, Conn.

Married (2) July 14, 1856, SARAH W. BRIGGS, born March 15, 1838, daughter of Willis Briggs of Sherman. She resides in New Milford.

Children by second wife, born in New Milford

Willie Warner, d. Jan. 15, 1860, aged 15 days (town record).

Fred H. Warner, b. Sept. 21, 1861; is a farmer, residing on his father's stock farm; m. Feb. 4, 1885, Minerva L. Irwin, b. in New Milford, about 1863. Children, b. in New Milford: i. Harry Beardsley, b. Nov. 16, 1889. ii. Josephine Maria, b. Sept. 18, 1892.

Charles Briggs Warner, b. May 1, 1866; resides in New Milford; not married.

Mary J. Warner, b. Feb. 20, 1868; resides in New Milford; m. Carl F. Schoverling. Children: Caroline W.; Matilda D.

527 CYRUS ALONZO[7] WARNER, son of Orange[6] and Apphia (Edwards) Warner, born in New Milford, Conn., October 26, 1829; died July 10, 1912, in Bristol, Conn. He was a clock maker by trade.

Married February 12, 1854, ANGELINE ELIZABETH SULLIVAN, born in New Milford, May 24, 1833, died October 17, 1912, daughter of Henry and Maria (Mead) Sullivan.

Children, born in Bristol, Conn.

Carrie Maria Warner, b. Dec. 29, 1855; resides in Bristol; was graduated from Bates College, Lewiston, Maine, 1877; m. Nov. 27, 1879, Henry Sanford Morehouse, b. Nov. 14, 1856, in Washington, Conn., son of Hobart and Paulona (Titus) Morehouse, d. Nov. 5, 1882. Child: Harry Warner, b. Sept. 29, 1881, in Washington, Conn.; was graduated from Worcester Polytechnic Institute, 1903; is an engineer with the Western Union Telegraph Company in New York City; m. Oct. 30, 1909, Edith Louise Torres, b. Jan. 22, 1890, daughter of Charles and Emma (Dayton) Torres of Brooklyn, N. Y.

Minnie Apphia Warner, b. Feb. 12, 1859; m. Nov. 9, 1881, Edward Minor Dailey, son of Edward and Emily (Minor) Dailey of Terryville, Conn. Children, b. in Bristol, Conn.: i. Georgia Emily, b. Mar. 28, 1883; d. Oct. 8, 1884. ii. May Warner, b. Nov. 5, 1885; is children's Librarian in Bristol, Conn. iii. Edward Cyrus, b. Dec. 12, 1887; d. Dec. 31, 1889.

EIGHTH GENERATION

528 SHERMAN ROBERTS[8] **WARNER,** son of William Hall[7] and Hannah (Rose) Warner, born in Middletown, Conn., September 1, 1828; died in New Haven, Conn., December 27, 1877. As shown by the records, his father died when he was less than two years old and his mother before he was eight. He continued to live in Westfield, in the family of a farmer by the name of Roberts for whom he worked for his board and keep until he was sixteen years old, at which time he walked to New Haven with less than three dollars in his pocket, hired out to Lyman Treadway, a tinsmith on State Street in that city, for whom his oldest brother, John, was at that time working. He stayed with Lyman Treadway until he learned his trade and for a short time thereafter.

He joined the volunteer Fire Department of New Haven and became Captain of old Number 5, a company noted for its activity and valor. Later on he became assistant Chief of the New Haven Volunteer Fire Department. He was prominently identified with everything pertaining to the growth and improvement of New Haven, and could always be counted on to do his share when called on. A silver trumpet and chief's fire hat with silver plate attached to same, both of which were presented him at different times by admiring associates of the Fire Department, are now in possession of the New Haven Colony Historical Society. He retired from the New Haven Fire Department at the time it became a pay department.

After leaving the employ of Lyman Treadway, he engaged in the same line of business in New Haven with his brother John. Sometime after that his brother John went West and Sherman eventually went into company with Lyman Treadway, from whom he learned his trade, furnishing most of the capital necessary to start the business, Mr. Treadway having met with some reverses in business prior to that. He remained in company with Mr. Treadway under the name of Treadway and Warner until within a few years of his death.

He was an inventor and held valuable patents on various steamfitting appliances, and the firm of Treadway and Warner equipped many factories throughout the eastern and southern part of the United States with Sherman R. Warner's patent steam heating system, which was a system well ahead of the time in which it was invented and installed by Sherman R. Warner and Treadway & Warner.

Mr. Warner died very suddenly at the age of forty-nine, being engaged at that time in the same line of business under his own name without partner.

Married in New Haven, Conn., October 9, 1850, DELIA CAROLINE HODGES, born in New Haven, October 26, 1831, died there, August 17, 1887, daughter of James and Elizabeth (Prior) Hodges.

Children, born in New Haven

Sherman Wilson Warner, b. Aug. 12, 1853; d. Apr. 16, 1854.
Margaret Hodges Warner, b. Aug. 2, 1856; d. Oct. 31, 1889, not married.
James Hodges Warner, b. June 16, 1858; d. Dec. 12, 1859.
Hannah Rose Warner, b. Oct. 21, 1859; not married.
680 *William Alling Warner*, b. May 6, 1861; m. (1) Nettie Clark Ensign, (2) Hannah Minerva Granniss.
Elizabeth Wood Warner, b. Jan. 20, 1863, not married.
681 *Roland Treadway Warner*, b. Sept. 14, 1866; m. Agnes Day Henderson.

529 CHARLES HOUGH[8] WARNER, son of John Plumb[7] and Betsey (Hall) Warner, born in Trenton, N. Y., September 1, 1826; died January 5, 1899. He was a machinist and resided in Meriden, Conn.

Married at Feeding Hills, Mass., May 23, 1850, ANNETTA M. STILES, born in Southwick, Mass., January 14, 1829, daughter of Henry and Sally (Avery) Stiles.

Children

Henry Stiles Warner, b. Feb. 18, 1851, in Meriden, Conn.; d. May 4, 1856, at Feeding Hills, Mass.
Sara Annette Warner, b. Nov. 23, 1855, in Meriden; resides there; m. in Meriden, Mar. 25, 1884, Charles A. Hickox, b. in Durham, Conn., Oct. 15, 1851. Child: Mildred, b. July 10, 1888; d. July 10, 1888. Mrs. Hickox is a member of the D. A. R.
Harry Ellsworth Warner, b. May 18, 1863; d. June 23, 1863, in Meriden.

530 HELEN[8] WARNER, daughter of Zebulon Penn[7] and Lucretia (Sherwood) Warner, born at Brandy Camp, Pa., July 10, 1829; resided later in Ridgway, Elk Co., Pa.

Married at Brandy Camp, Feb. 28, 1847, BYRON F. ELY, born July 7, 1821, in Rushford, N. Y., son of La Fayette and Isabel (Harvey) Ely. In 1835 he started out alone to make his way in the world. He went first to Olean, N. Y., and was engaged to assist in running a lumber raft down the Allegheny River to Pittsburgh. From this experience he was attracted to lumbering and worked at that and similar lines of work until 1848 when he formed a partnership and engaged actively in the lumber business. After this his interests were in mills and lumbering at Balltown, Whistletown, Portland, and Ridgway. In 1878 he built an extensive sawmill just outside the town of Ridgway and carried on a large business, with a capacity for turning out some eighty thousand feet of lumber a day. He was a prominent man of the community along various lines of activity, was one of the organizers of Elk Lodge, No. 379, F. and A. M., in 1867, and was its treasurer for over twenty-one years, also R. A. M. In 1890 he was treasurer of the township.

Children

Mary Ely, b. at Ridgway, Pa., June 2, 1849; m. Henry S. Thayer, b. at Ridgway, Jan. 13, 1847, son of David and Sarah (Stewart) Thayer. Children, b. at Ridgway: i. Harry Edwin, b. Feb. 23, 1875; m. Grace McClelland, and has a son, Harry S., b. at Ridgway. ii. Helen Sarah, b. Apr. 4, 1889; m. at Ridgway, Earl Overholtzer, and resides in Ridgway.

Frank Charles Ely, b. at Ridgway, Apr. 21, 1853; lumberman at Ridgway; m. June 18, 1874, Ida Antoinett Garrett, b. in Liberty, N. Y., Nov. 13, 1853, daughter of Louis S. and Abbey Jane (Lawrence) Garrett. Children, b. at Ridgway: i. Maud May, b. May 15, 1879. ii. Roy Byron, b. Oct. 23, 1882; m. ——— May of Ridgway and has two children.

Louis Warner Ely, b. at Ridgway, Mar. 26, 1859; resides in Spokane, Wash.; m. twice and had children.

Fred H. Ely, b. in Elk County, Pa., July 20, 1863; is an attorney at law in Philadelphia, Pa.; m. in York, Pa., Sept. 27, 1887, Olive Horton Ross, b. in McVeytown, Mifflin County, Pa., Oct. 30, 1864, daughter of James H. and Martha (Kime) Ross. Child: Byron F., b. in Ridgway, Pa., July 10, 1888; m. Aug. 15, 1911, Alice Marrett of Louisville, Ky.

Carrie R. Ely, b. at Ridgway, Aug. 9, 1867; resides at St. Mary's, Pa.; m. at Ridgway, Jan. 21, 1891, Burket Turner Darr. Children, b. at St. Mary's, Pa.: i. Marjory Helen, b. Jan. 27, 1893. ii. Fred Ely, b. Apr. 5, 1908.

531 CHARLES FOWLER[8] WARNER, son of Dr. Eben[7] and Hannah (Fowler) Warner, born in Covington, N. Y., August 30, 1832. He removed when a boy to Nunda with his father; was educated at Wesleyan Seminary, Lima, N. Y.; studied medicine with his father until his death, then entered Jefferson Medical College and was graduated in 1854. He

began practice in Nunda, but soon removed to Mankato, Minn. During the Civil War he was assistant surgeon of the 136th N. Y. Volunteers and was later surgeon of the 58th N. Y. National Guards. In Mankato he was alderman in 1873; president of the Common Council; health officer of the city several years; county physician two terms. He was one of the prime movers in getting the city to establish a system of water works and to purchase Sibley Park. Dr. Warner was president of the Mankato Driving Park Association; one of the founders of the Minnesota Valley Medical Association and its president; member of the American Medical Association and of the International Railway Surgeons' Association; local surgeon for several important railway lines.

Married in Nunda, N. Y., June, 1854, ESTHER S. TOWN of Nunda, born there February 26, 1832, died June 8, 1913, daughter of Ira and Rebecca (Baker) Town.

Children

————————, d. young.

Clayton E. Warner, b. Mar. 14, 1857, in Nunda; d. Feb. 8, 1902, in Billings, Mont.

Lillaette Warner, b. Apr. 17, 1859, in Nunda; resides in Mankato, Minn.; m. in Mankato, May 31, 1882, H. E. Baker. Child: Warner, b. in St. Paul, Minn.

532 ELTINGE FOWLER[8] WARNER, son of Dr. Eben[7] and Hannah (Fowler) Warner, born in Covington, N. Y., April 9, 1836; died in Seattle, Wash., December 16, 1911. He was educated at Genesee College, and in 1857 located in St. Paul, Minn., where he was employed by the Northwestern Express Company, running between St. Paul and Prairie du Chien. He later passed into the service of the American Express Company as agent at St. Paul, became superintendent of a division in 1879, resigning in 1882. Few expressmen saw such varied changes in the business as did Mr. Warner. During his experience dog-trains, Red River carts, stages, steamboats, and railroads were the means of transportation. During the Civil War General Fremont made a requisition on General Pope, then stationed in St. Paul, for three million dollars, and the funds were forwarded to him by express, with seventeen hundred dollars charges. During the time that Mr. Warner was manager of the Northwestern Express Company not a package was lost. Some money was missed but was recovered.

In 1882 he commenced dealing in furs, but the following year entered largely into the lumbering trade. He also commenced the buying of buffalo horns on the prairie, and in one year shipped a hundred car loads to be used as fertilizer. At one time he was manager of the Rock County Farming Company, which owned 73,000 acres. He was very fond of hunting, was president of the Sportsmen's Club, and active in the legislation to protect game.

Married in Boston, Mass., 1864, **JOSEPHINE BOURNE THOMPSON**, born in Boston, January 8, 1842; died in St. Paul, December 29, 1881. Among her ancestors are Zachariah Hicks, Marshal of the day when Washington entered Boston, and his son John Hicks of Cambridge, b. 1749, of whom Longfellow wrote in Paul Revere's ride:

> "And one was safe and asleep in his bed
> Who at the bridge would be first to fall,
> Who that day would be lying dead,
> Pierced by a British musket-ball."

Children, born in St. Paul

Amos Thompson Warner, b. Jan. 2, 1872; m. Bernice Howard. Child: Josephine Audrey.

Helen Josephine Warner, b. Feb. 18, 1874; resides in Newton Center, Mass.; m. in St. Paul, Oct. 7, 1902, John Franklin McKey. Children: i. Josephine Elizabeth, b. May 24, 1906. ii. Katherine Eltinge, b. Apr. 28, 1911; d. May 28, 1911. iii. Helen Marjorie, b. Dec. 17, 1912.

Eltinge Fowler Warner, Jr., b. Nov. 25, 1878; was graduated at Princeton University, B.S., 1901; resided for a time in Seattle, now in New York City; president of Field and Stream Publishing Company, publisher of Smart Set Magazine, Field and Stream, The Parisienne, Clever Stories, Fascinating Fiction. Married in New York City, May 2, 1908, Ruth Lois Eaton, b. in Calais, Maine, 1886, daughter of Bradley Eaton.

533 WILLIAM PENN[8] WARNER, son of Dr. Eben[7] and Hannah (Fowler) Warner, born in Covington, N. Y., July 5, 1837. He was educated at Union College, graduating in 1858; settled first in Winchester, Tenn., later went to St. Paul, Minn., in 1860. He was admitted to the bar in Tennessee in 1859, and after his removal to St. Paul, formed a partnership with John B. Brisbin, later with M. J. Severance, who became judge of the sixth municipal district. In 1890 he was senior member of the firm Warner and Lawrence.

Married in Nunda, N. Y., June 29, 1865, **ANNA ELIZABETH RICHMOND**, born December 11, 1842, daughter of Bradford and Anne (Whitwell) Richmond. Her ancestry goes back to John and Priscilla (Molines) Alden, through their daughter Elizabeth, m. William Pabodie, Elizabeth Pabodie, m. John Rogers, Elizabeth Rogers, m. Sylvester Richmond, Perez Richmond, Perez Richmond, Bradford Richmond, Bradford Richmond, Anna Elizabeth Richmond.

Children

Anne Richmond Warner, b. in St. Paul, Minn., Oct. 14, 1869; d. Feb. 1, 1913; m. in St. Paul, Sept. 12, 1888, Charles E. French, son of George Reade and Susan Caroline (Weeks) French of Fall River, Mass., and Wilmington, N. C. In 1889 Mr. French removed from Wilmington to St. Paul. Children: i. Charles Elting, b. Sept. 19, 1889. ii. Anna Hathaway; b. Apr. 6, 1892; d. Dec. 17, 1892. Anne Warner attained considerable fame by her published works, among which were: "A Woman's Will," 1904; "Susan Clegg and Her Friend, Mrs. Lathrop," 1904; "The Rejuvenation of Aunt Mary," 1905; "Susan Clegg and Her Neighbor's Affairs," 1906; "Seeing France with Uncle John," 1906; "An American Ancestry," 1894. This last, a volume of 186 pages, takes up all the ancestral lines of Mrs. French's son, and gives many personal items about the Warner ancestors as well as others. Among the colonial ancestors of Charles Elting French are: John Hathaway of Taunton, John Tripp, William Chase, John Reade, Richard Pearce, Peter Tallman, William Freeborn, Thomas Brownell, George Parker, Clement Weaver, Thomas Rogers, John Pabodie, John Alden, Nathaniel Potter, Francis Purdy, Nicholas Theall, William Fowler, Louis du Bois, Chrétien Deyo, Matthys Slecht, Jan Van Leyden, Matthys Blançsan, Francis Cooke, Anthony Paine, William Molines, and others.
Richmond Perez Warner, b. in St. Paul, Aug. 26, 1871; resides in St. Paul; is treasurer of Griggs, Cooper & Company.

534 GEORGE WASHINGTON⁸ WARNER, son of Dr. Eben⁷ and Hannah (Fowler) Warner, born May 10, 1840, in Covington, N. Y.; died June 5, 1897. He removed with his father's family to Nunda, N. Y., in 1844; resided later in Mankato, Minn., where he was a druggist, then express messenger. Married (1) at Winchester, Tenn., 1866, FANNY ESTELLE. Married (2) at Mankato, Minn., ELIZABETH BATTELLS.

Children

Dudley Warner.
Nora Warner.

535 ELAM LOCKE⁸ WARNER, son of Rev. Junia⁷ and Arminda (Merry) Warner, born in Litchfield, N. Y., May 29, 1828; died December 5, 1902, in Paw Paw, Mich., where he had resided. He was president of the Van Buren County Agricultural Society in 1887.

Married in Paw Paw, October 5, 1854, **CHARLOTTE MARIA BANGS.**

Children

Frank Allene Warner, b. Mar. 24, 1856; resides in Paw Paw.
Bangs Fremont Warner, b. June 24, 1858; is a stock raiser at Paw Paw; m. Nov. 2, 1882, Clara Terissa Bray. Child: Leo, b. June 6, 1883.
Junia Joshua Warner, b. Aug. 2, 1860; ·is a passenger and freight agent at Oakland, Cal.; m. June 24, 1889, Ethel M. King.
Roy Warner, b. Dec. 26, 1871; d. July 16, 1872.

536 **JEROME CLARK[8] WARNER,** son of Rev. Junia[7] and Arminda (Merry) Warner, born December 14, 1840, near Paw Paw, Mich.; was a merchant in Paw Paw. He enlisted in February, 1864, in Company H, 13th Michigan Regiment, and served till the close of the war. He was wounded at Bentonville.
Married (1) in Paw Paw, October 20, 1868, **ANTOINETTE RANDALL.**
Married (2) in Paw Paw, May 10, 1876, **JENNY KELLY.**

Children by second wife, born in Paw Paw

Wilbur Jerome Warner, b. Jan. 25, 1879; resides in Paw Paw; m. Vivian ———, and had a child, b. before Sept., 1907.
Glenn Elam Warner, b. Sept. 15, 1882; was graduated from the law school of the University of Michigan in 1904, and is an attorney in Paw Paw.
Guy Frank Warner, twin with Glenn Elam, b. Sept. 15, 1882.
Leland Raymond Warner, b. Dec. 14, 1884.
Elaine Warner, b. Nov. 6, 1889.

537 **WILBUR FISK[8] WARNER,** son of Rev. Junia[7] and Arminda (Merry) Warner, born June 27, 1843, at Almena, Mich.; resided there till 1873, then removed to Grand Rapids, Mich.; traveling salesman. For an account of his early life, see Rev. Junia[7] Warner, number 346.
Married in Winfield, N. Y., **SARAH JENETTE ELDRED,** born in Winfield, September 5, 1846, daughter of Zenas and Hannah (———) Eldred of East Winfield.

Children, last three born in Grand Rapids

Lucy Warner, b. and d. July 14, 1871, at Paw Paw.
Fisher Devere Warner, b. Nov. 30, 1874; d. in Denver, Colo., July 16, 1896.
Josiah Wilbur Warner, b. Dec. 16, 1878; resides in Grand Rapids; m. June 12, 1906, Beatrice Eva Logan. Children: i. Ruth Beatrice,

b. Mar. 1, 1907. ii. Wilbur Logan, b. and d. Oct. 12, 1908. iii. Gail
Barbara, b. Nov. 22, 1910.
Starr Eldred Warner, b. Aug. 10, 1880; d. Oct. 24, 1903.

538 ANDREW JAMES[8] WARNER, son of Joseph[7] and
Mary (Coville) Warner, born January 13, 1837, in Chester,
Geauga Co., Ohio; died in Chardon, Ohio, December 30, 1908.
He was mayor, feed merchant and general manager of the
telephone company in Chardon. Until the time of his death
he was ever interested in all public affairs. It was mainly
through his efforts that the Cleveland and Eastern Railroad
trolley line, ran its tracks into Chardon. He was also active
in promoting an electric light plant to be owned and operated
by the village.
Married in Newbury, Geauga County, January 17, 1860,
CYNTHIA RODGERS BARTLETT, born in Danby, Vt.,
November 2, 1840, daughter of Daniel and Ruth (Rodgers)
Bartlett.

Children

Lillian Eveline Warner, b. in Newbury, Geauga Co., Ohio, Feb. 21,
1862; resides in Chardon, Ohio; m. in Chesterland, Geauga Co.,
1883, Emory Augustine Cook, b. in Chardon, Jan. 21, 1859, son of
Alpheus and Laura Grosvenor (Anderson) Cook. Children, b. in
Chardon: i. Warner Doyle, b. Mar. 27, 1890. ii. Andre Bartlett, b.
Mar. 6, 1893. Both these sons were graduated from Howe Military
School and Kenyon College, became pharmacists, and were in the
U. S. A. in training at Fort Benjamin Harrison, Ind., July, 1917.
Elmie Lydia Warner, b. Aug. 1, 1873, in Chester, Ohio; m. Prof.
Mallory.

539 DARIUS JOHN[8] WARNER, son of Gaylord Coan[7] and
Martha (Packard) Warner, born June 30, 1834, in Chatham,
Ohio; died August 10, 1910, in Chardon, Ohio. He was a stu-
dent at Oberlin, 1854-5; resided at Munson, Ohio, most of his
life; held various offices, constable, school director and the like.
Married in Munson, December 25, 1858, ANNETTE ELIZA-
BETH HAZEN, born March 5, 1840, in Munson, daughter of
La Fayette and Sarah Jane (Bond) Hazen; died in Cleveland,
April 23, 1911.

Children, born in Munson

Fred Clare Warner, b. July 31, 1864; d. in Munson, Feb. 11, 1913; m.
in Middlefield, Ohio, Feb. 23, 1892, Carrie Adelle Stratton, b. in
Middlefield, Sept. 28, 1869, daughter of Justin and Hannah
(Clement) Stratton. She resided in Chardon, Ohio, in 1914. Chil-
dren, first three b. in Munson, fourth in Cleveland: i. Franz
Packard, b. Nov. 18, 1892; resides in Burton, Ohio; m. in Chardon,

Oct. 2, 1910, Anna Helen Bailey, b. in Cleveland, Feb. 15, 1893, daughter of John and Anna (Levy) Bailey, and has children, Marjorie Velda, b. Mar. 20, 1912, and Fred John, b. Jan. 15, 1914. ii. Reid Bernard, b. Mar. 24, 1894. iii. Jay Dexter, b. Jan. 23, 1899. iv. Hildagrace Laura, b. Feb. 18, 1901.

Grace Anna Warner, b. Dec. 18, 1869; resides in Greenacres, Wash. (1916); m. (1) in Burton, Ohio, Sept. 17, 1885, Walter William Honeywell, b. in Munson, Apr. 29, 1868, son of William Alexander and Elizabeth (Langhorn) Honeywell; m. (2) in Spokane, Wash., July 11, 1911, Lester Leon Bower, b. in Berwick, Pa., Dec. 12, 1882, son of Alfred and Martha (Seybert) Bower. Children by first husband: i. Lloyd Elroy, b. Apr. 1, 1887, in Chardon; m. in Cleveland, Sept. 11, 1913, Alexine Patti Steffan, b. in Hannibal, Mo., Oct. 29, 1890, daughter of Rudolph Emil and Ida May (Eichelberger) Steffan; resided in Cleveland in 1916 and had a son, Jack Steffan, b. there Aug. 5, 1914. ii. Hellene, b. Sept. 6, 1900. Child by second husband: Mary Elsie, b. in Spokane, Aug. 6, 1912.

540 DAVIS WILLIAM[8] WARNER, son of Benjamin Stone[7] and Hannah Malona (Gleason) Warner, born in Munson, Geauga Co., Ohio.
Married **MARTHA GILBERT**.

Children

Bertha Evalena Warner, b. in Munson, Sept. 16, 1867; resides in Painesville, Ohio; m. Jan. 3, 1889, Will H. Savage, b. in Russell, Ohio, Jan. 8, 1863, son of Henry and Jane (Ladow) Savage. Child: Flora Abbie, b. at Burton Station, Oct. 13, 1890; m. in Painesville, July 26, 1911, Enos J. Houghkirk, and has a son, Howard Davis.
Charlotte Warner, died.
Blanche Warner.

541 JANE VIOLA[8] WARNER, daughter of Benjamin Stone[7] and Hannah Malona (Gleason) Warner, born in Munson, Geauga Co., Ohio, December 3, 1842; resides in Chardon, Ohio. Married in Munson, January 27, 1864, **DAVID RODGERS BARTLETT**, born in Danby, Vt., August 26, 1841, died November 30, 1910, son of David and Ruth (Rodgers) Bartlett. He was a soldier in the Civil War.

Children, born in Munson

Mildred Jane Bartlett, b. July 20, 1867; m. in Thompson, Geauga Co., Ohio, Dec. 22, 1886, William Henry Zimmerman, b. in Milton township, Wayne Co., Ohio, Jan. 1, 1869, d. May 26, 1909, son of Thomas and Margaret (————) Zimmerman. Children: i. Howard Lee, b. Nov. 10, 1887, in Montville, Geauga County. ii. Gleason Lloyd, b. at Fowler's Mills, Geauga County.
Walter B. Bartlett, b. Sept. 9, 1871, killed by an accident, Nov. 18, 1873.
Norman G. Bartlett, b. May 12, 1879; m. Dec. 4, 1907, Clara B. Mummery.

542 JOHN BARTON[8] **WARNER,** son of Benjamin Strong[7] and Hannah Malona (Gleason) Warner, born in Munson, Geauga Co., Ohio, May 26, 1846; is a farmer residing in Munson. He is justice of the peace (1916) and has been an elder in the Disciple Church in Munson about forty years. Married in Munson, March 18, 1875, by his father, who was justice of the peace at that time, to **ALMEDA JERUSHA COLE,** born in Brecksville, Cuyahoga Co., Ohio, October 8, 1854, daughter of Jesse and Nancy Maria (Judd) Cole.

Children, born in Munson

Bernice Estelle Warner, b. May 15, 1876; resides in Burton, Ohio; m. Dr. A. D. Warner.
Harmon Benjamin Warner, b. Feb. 18, 1880; resides in Sand Springs, Mont.; not married.
Horace Jesse Warner, b. July 20, 1883; resides in Warren, Ohio; not married.
Veron John Warner, b. June 1, 1891; resides in Munson; not married.

543 **CHARLES FREMONT**[8] **WARNER,** son of Benjamin Stone[7] and Hannah Malona (Gleason) Warner, born in Munson, Geauga Co., Ohio, August 7, 1855; resides at Chardon, Ohio. Mr. Warner resided for a time in Pauline, Neb., where he was engaged in railroading in various capacities and was justice of the peace. In 1888 he returned to Cleveland, and in 1902 to Chardon to engage in mercantile business. He is a member of F. and A. M.; K. of P.; Captain of the Geauga County Uniform Rank in the latter; author of "Sketches along the St. Joe Trail."

Married in Newbury, Geauga Co., Ohio, November 6, 1878, **LAVINA JANE HODGES,** born in Newbury, April 20, 1860, daughter of Benjamin Franklin and Christiana Hunter (Zethmayr) Hodges, and granddaughter of John and Jane (Murray) Zethmayr of Edinburgh, Scotland.

Children

Clara Elnora Warner, b. in Newbury, Ohio, Dec. 14, 1880; was graduated from Cleveland High School and is now engaged in merchandise and millinery in Chardon; m. in Cleveland, July 22, 1899, William James Fleet, b. in Cleveland, June 18, 1878, son of William D. and Sarah J. (Forbes) Fleet. Mr. Fleet is with Company C, 25th U. S. Engineers, American Expeditionary Forces in France, April, 1918. Children: i. Clarence Darius, b. Nov. 27, 1900, at Newbury. ii. Eugene Erastus, b. Feb. 9, 1903, at Chardon.
Frank Worthy Warner, b. Nov. 9, 1883, at Munson; d. June 13, 1886, at Pauline, Adams Co., Neb.

544 JOHN DE WITT[8] WARNER, son of Daniel De Witt[7] and Charlotte Gordon (Coon) Warner, born October 30, 1851, in Schuyler County, N. Y.; is a lawyer and publicist in New York City. He was fitted for college at Starkey Seminary, Eddytown, N. Y.; was graduated in the first class to enter Cornell University, Ph.B., 1872; Albany Law School, LL.B., 1876. He taught in the Ithaca (N. Y.) Academy from 1872 to 1874; was admitted to the bar in 1876; member of law firms, Iselin and Warner, 1877-83; Warner and Frayer, 1883-95; Peckham, Warner and Strong, 1895-1904; Warner, Wells and Korb, 1905-10; Warner and Korb, 1910 to date. He was editor of the Ithaca Daily Leader in 1871; tariff reform editor

JOHN DeWITT WARNER

of the New York Weekly World in 1891-2; Democratic member of the 52d Congress from the 11th New York District, and of the 53d Congress from the 13th New York District. In Congress he served on the House committees on Banking and Currency—in which he was Chairman of its sub-committee to draft bill for elastic bank note currency; Manufactures—in which he was Chairman of its sub-committee that investigated the sweating system; and Public Buildings—in which he was Chairman of its sub-committee on the eastern and middle states; was active for the repeal of the Sherman Act, Silver

Purchase and "Force" Bill, and in House passage of the Wilson Tariff Bill, to which he secured free sugar amendment; advocated Torrey Bankruptcy Act; opposed Bland Seniorage Bill, Anti-option Bills and pension frauds, and secured investigation of public buildings in New York City. He was active for free trade; led the fight for free sugar and compiled pamphlets exposing the sugar trust. After leaving Congress he successfully fought Ship Subsidy legislation pending in the 55th, 56th and 57th Congresses. From 1906 to 1908 he was President of the American Free Trade League; 1908-1910, one of the organizers of International Free Trade Congress, London, 1908, and Antwerp, 1910; has been a member of the general committee, Church Congress, since 1907; President of the New York City Art Commission, 1902-5.

Mr. Warner is a speaker and writer on tariff, finance, social and political economy, church polity, municipal art, university development, the drama, and many other subjects. In religion he is an Episcopalian. He was Counsel for the Mutual Life Policy Holders' Association, 1907-8; of New York City Dock Department, 1911-13, and of Commission to revise New York Banking Law, 1913-4; Trustee of Cornell University, 1882-7, 1894-9, 1903-8; member of New York City, New York State and American Bar Associations, National Sculpture Society, Scenic Preservation Society, Municipal Art Society, Central Council Delta Kappa Epsilon Fraternity, American Playgoers (incorporator, vice-president and governor), National Arts (a founder and director), Shakespeare, Reform and Cornell University (a founder and ex-president of the last three), American Humane Society (director and treasurer). He was Vice-Chairman of the Mayor's Committee for the celebration of the 550th anniversary of Shakespeare's birth in 1914.

John De Witt Warner married June 14, 1877, LILIAN AUGUSTA HUDSON of Ithaca, born in Oneonta, N. Y., September 26, 1855, daughter of Joseph and Harriet C. (Phelps) Hudson. Mrs. Warner is prominent in social organization and literary—especially Shakespeare—study.

Children

Joseph De Witt Warner, b. Aug. 17, 1880, in New York City; was graduated from Cornell University, A.B., 1903; University of Michigan, B.S. (Forestry), 1905; is U. S. Supervisor of Flathead Forest Reserves at Kalispell, Mont. Married June 3, 1907, Edith Saunders of Belfast, Allegany Co., N. Y. Children: i. John De Witt, 2d, b. Nov. 9, 1909. ii. Newland Saunders, b. Aug. 1, 1917.

34

Charlotte Lilian Warner, b. Mar. 8, 1883; m. Oct. 17, 1910, William
Joshua Barney of New York City, where they now reside. Mr.
Barney was the son of Joshua C. and May Florence (Kelly) Barney and a direct descendant of Commodore Joshua Barney of Baltimore. Child: William Joshua, Jr., b. Aug. 17, 1911.

545 CAROLINE TOMLINSON[8] WARNER, daughter of
Leman Ackley[7] and Sarah Deming (Whittlesey) Warner, born
October 5, 1848, in New Preston, Conn.; died in Scribner, Neb.,
December 12, 1910. She was graduated from the Rockford
Female Seminary in 1869; removed to Scribner in 1881 and
resided there until her death.

Married February 26, 1880, Rev. **MARVIN B. HARRISON,**
son of ———— and Grace Ann (Bradley) Harrison. He was
ordained in 1881, and was pastor of the First Congregational
Church in Scribner, Neb., from 1881 to 1918, when he retired.

Children, all but first born in Scribner

John Leman Harrison, b. in Freeport, Ill., Dec. 10, 1880; is a grad-
uate of Doane College and the University of Nebraska; U. S.
engineer in the Philippines; resides at Iloilo, P. I.; m. Nov. 2, 1911,
Florence Bonell. Child: Florence Elizabeth, b. Oct. 2, 1915.
Paul Wilberforce Harrison, b. Jan. 12, 1883; is a graduate of Doane
College and Johns Hopkins University; is a medical missionary in
Arabia, at Bohrain.
Grace Harrison, b. Mar. 28, 1886; is a graduate of Doane College;
m. Aug. 27, 1913, Professor Percy E. Swift of Doane College, and
resides in Crete, Neb. Child: Altheda Muriel, b. Aug. 15, 1914.
Henry Charles Harrison, b. Oct. 31, 1888; is a graduate of Colorado
College; m. Sept. 7, 1915, Ida Johnson; resides in New York City.
Marvin Clinton Harrison, b. July 13, 1890; is a student in Harvard
University (1916).

546 ANDREW CLINTON[8] WARNER, son of Leman
Ackley[7] and Sarah Deming (Whittlesey) Warner, born April 3,
1850, in New Preston, Conn., removed in 1855 with his father's
family to Freeport, Ill., where he received his education. For
three years he was deputy in the County Clerk's office in Freeport, and in 1871 took a similar position in Dixon, Ill., where
he now resides. He was Deputy County Treasurer for fifteen
years, since then has been a member of the bar and has attained
considerable success as a legal counsellor and confidential
administrator, and in the handling of mortgage investments;
was Mayor of Dixon in 1886 and 1887; Supervisor for two
years; director of the North Dixon School District for eleven
years. Almost ultra-conservative, he has the confidence of a

large clientele and, through making wise and somewhat extensive investments in western lands, he has secured a considerable competency.
Married at Dixon, Ill., December 16, 1875, **M Y R A O BROOKNER**, daughter of Christopher Brookner, who was born at Osnabrock, Germany, and Jane Robins, who was born in Athens, Maine. Both her parents died in Dixon, Ill.

Children

Henry Chester Warner, b. Dec. 19, 1876; was graduated from the University of Wisconsin, and was admitted to the bar; resides in Dixon, where he practises law and handles investments. He was a delegate to the National Republican Convention in Chicago, 1916; chairman of the Republican County Central Committee for Lee County. Married Sept. 19, 1913, Lucile Mertz of Burnette Creek, Ind. Children: i. Myra Alice, b. Sept. 30, 1914. ii. Louise, b. Aug. 14, 1916.

Edward Clinton Warner, b. Sept. 18, 1878; resides in Chicago and is at the head of an extensive accountant business, manager of a school of instruction for operators of the Comptometer Machine for rapid calculation and handles contracts for computation work of all kinds; m. Apr. 30, 1917, Edith Saxton.

James Christopher Warner, b. Oct. 12, 1881; died on shipboard off the coast of Durban, Africa, Jan., 1902.

William Herbert Warner, b. Dec. 17, 1882; was graduated from Illinois State University as Civil Engineer, and is engaged in his profession in Chicago; resides in North Evanston, Ill.; m. Dec. 22, 1906, Elsie Emmitt.

John Francis Warner, b. Nov. 13, 1885; d. Sept. 4, 1891.

Frederick Milton Warner, b. Aug. 9, 1890; resides in Waterloo, Iowa, and is salesmanager of the Inter-State Tractor Company of Waterloo, manufacturers of farm tractors; m. June 24, 1916, Marguerite Burchell of Erie, Ill.

Robert Leman Warner, b. Aug. 23, 1894; was graduated from the Law School of the University of Illinois and admitted to the bar, 1917; was called for enlistment in September, 1917, and appointed sergeant of his company. He is now (March, 1918) at the Officers' Training Camp at Rockford, Ill.

547 Rev. CHARLES CAMPBELL[8] WARNER, son of Leman Ackley[7] and Sarah Deming (Whittlesey) Warner, born September 19, 1857, in Freeport, Ill.; died suddenly in Mobridge, S. D., December 26, 1916. He was a graduate of Beloit College, 1881, A.M., 1884; Chicago Theological Seminary, 1884; D.D., Fargo College, 1912. He held pastorates at the Congregational Church in Lasalle, 1884-8; Alton, Ill., 1888-91; Morris, Ill., 1891-5; Presbyterian Church, Florence, Colo., 1895-8; Congregational Church, Monticello, Iowa, 1898-1903;

Eldora, Iowa, 1903-8; Crookston, Minn., 1908-11; Grand Forks, N. D., 1911-13; Mobridge, S. D., 1913-6. He was trustee of Thrall Academy at Sorum, S. D., and at the time of his sudden death, had just resigned his pastorate to become the financial agent for the academy and was looking forward to giving the best years of his life to the new work. He was a director of the S. D. Congregational Conference, and had been moderator of the Northwestern Association of Congregational Churches. Only a short time before his death, Dr. Warner had been interested in furnishing records for this book.

Married at Ottawa, Ill., June 20, 1889, **MARGARET LEWIS MC NAIR**, born in Ottawa, September 8, 1862, daughter of David and Harriet (Waldo) McNair, and a descendant of Jonathan Edwards. She is now in Grinnell, Iowa, with her daughter.

Children, born in Morris, Ill.

Chester McNair Warner, b. July 15, 1892; was a graduate of the Crookston (Minn.) High School and studied law at the University of North Dakota; resides in Grand Forks, N. D., and is a traveling salesman for the Stone Piano Company of Grand Forks; m. in Grand Forks, Apr. 19, 1916, Winifred Streetes. Child: Rogene Annette, b. Apr. 3, 1917.

Margaret Whitney Warner, b. Feb. 4, 1895; graduate of Grinnell College, 1918; librarian in the Library of the School of Music at Grinnell, Iowa.

548   **GEORGE WILBERFORCE[8] WARNER**, son of Leman Ackley[7] and Sarah Deming (Whittlesey) Warner, born March 27, 1859, in Freeport, Ill.; resides in Topeka, Kans. He was educated at the University of Wisconsin; engaged in the manufacture of hardware novelties and the Warner Doorspring, and is now manufacturing electrical therapeutic devices, X-Ray apparatus and supplies. He resided in Freeport until 1899, when, on account of ill-health, he removed to Beatrice, Neb., and in 1909, to Topeka.

Married in Carbondale, Ill., June 22, 1886, **IDA MARY BUCKLEY**, born July 20, 1859, in Freeport, Ill., daughter of William Musson and Anna M. (Burrell) Buckley.

Children, born in Freeport

Robert Wilberforce Warner, b. Aug. 20, 1889; is a graduate of Washburn College and Kansas State University; is now (May, 1918) in U. S. A. service at Pittsburgh, Pa., in the ordnance department, as an Electrical Engineer.

Florence Halford Warner, b. Aug. 23, 1892; was graduated from

Washburn College and is a Y. W. C. A. Secretary in Wichita, Kans. *John Chester Warner*, b. Feb. 14, 1896; is a member of the 1916 class of Washburn College; enlisted in the Kansas National Guards, Aug., 1917; became Lieutenant in Company A, 110th Field Signal Battalion, 35th Division, U. S. N. G., now on the way to France (Apr., 1918).

549 NORMAN POST[8] WARNER, son of Warren[7] and Weltha (Post) Warner, born in Marlborough, Conn., August 24, 1815; died November 12, 1890. He was a carpenter, residing in Hebron, Conn., and Chicopee Falls, Mass.

Married (1) in Marlborough, January 1, 1844, **ELIZA CARTER**, born September 17, 1819; died September 24, 1846, buried in the old cemetery near the Congregational Church in Marlborough. No children. She was the daughter of Charles and Laura (Washburn) Carter.

Married (2) in Hartford, Conn., October 8, 1850, **Mrs. LYDIA ANN (NORTON) TAYLOR**, born in Hebron, Conn., July 20, 1818, died June 23, 1884, daughter of Davis and Laura (White) Norton.

Children of Norman Post and Lydia Ann (Norton) Warner

Charles Henry Warner, b. July 23, 1851; d. Aug. 2, 1853.

Norton Post Warner, b. Mar. 17, 1853; d. June 19, 1884; m. July 17, 1875, Ellen Frances Barrett, b. Jan. 17, 1858, d. Apr. 1, 1884. Children: i. George Norton, b. Aug. 28, 1876; d. May 27, 1897. ii. Charles Post, b. Jan. 1, 1878; m. Feb. 12, 1908, Margaret Davidson.

Ella Carter Warner, b. July 14, 1861, in Chicopee Falls, Mass.; m. in Hebron, Conn., June 8, 1886, William Jewett[9] Warner, son of William Talcott[8] and Olive Maria (Hutchinson) Warner; see number 659.

550 WELTHA JANE[8] WARNER, daughter of Warren[7] and Weltha (Post) Warner, born in Marlborough, Conn., April 9, 1830; died June 24, 1893, at East Glastonbury, Conn.

Married in Eastbury, Conn., November 23, 1851, **GEORGE SELDEN HOUSE**, born in Eastbury, May 28, 1827, died January 5, 1892, in East Glastonbury, son of Sylvester and Eunice (Ackley) House.

Children, born at East Glastonbury

Herbert Burdette House, b. Oct. 31, 1852; resides in Hartford, Conn.; m. at East Glastonbury, Nov. 26, 1873, Mary Miner, b. Jan. 17, 1855, daughter of William and Susan (Hills) Miner. Children: i. Lewis Ezra, b. at East Glastonbury, Mar. 25, 1875; d. at East Hartford, June 24, 1894. ii. Eugene Herbert, b. Mar. 1, 1877, at Gilead. iii. Alice, b. Mar. 30, 1881, at Gilead. iv. Walter Selden, b. Sept. 17, 1888, at East Hartford.

Ellen A. House, b. Mar. 15, 1854; resides at East Glastonbury; m. there, Apr. 24, 1899, Alpheus D. Clark, b. in Middletown, Conn., Feb. 7, 1836, son of Alfred and Christina S. (―――) Clark of Middletown. After the age of 16 he farmed in summer and taught school in winter. He served two years in the Civil War as a private from Middletown, was promoted to Captain and served till the close of the war. He then settled in East Glastonbury and engaged in farming and business; has been town officer and member of the Legislature, is a member of the M. E. Church. Mr. Clark's first wife was Mary Hentze, who died in 1897, leaving two children, Flora M. and Elisha P.

Wilbur Warner House, b. Jan. 26, 1857; d. Feb. 22, 1884; studied for the ministry; m. at East Glastonbury, Aug. 14, 1883, Mary J. Hunt, b. Apr. 18, 1853, at Glastonbury, daughter of Robert and Mary (―――) Hunt.

Lillian Weltha House, b. Dec. 3, 1859; d. at East Glastonbury, Oct. 19, 1883.

551 JOHN B.[8] WARNER, son of Elisha[7] and Lucy (Chapman) Warner, born in Marlborough, Conn.; died in Stamford, Conn., January 30, 1894, aged 71.

Married June 7, 1847, ELIZABETH F. WHITE of Marlborough, born in Hebron, Conn.; died in New Britain, Conn., November 23, 1887. She was the adopted daughter of James and Lucinda (―――) White.

Children

Augusta Lucina Warner, b. in Marlborough, Conn., July 4, 1848; d. in Portland, Conn., Dec. 16, 1912; resided in New Britain; m. in Marlborough, Sept. 29, 1868, Evelyn U. Thompson, b. in Portland, July 29, 1843, d. Jan. 18, 1912, son of John Loomis and Marietta (Case) Thompson. Children, b. in New Britain: i. Edith Augusta, b. Apr. 25, 1871; has been a contralto soloist in various churches in the city for thirty years, for the past twelve years in Trinity M. E. Church; m. May 7, 1891, Dudley T. Holmes, eldest son of Joseph and Fannie (Morgan) Holmes of Norwich, Conn., secretary of W. L. Damon Lumber and Coal Co.; one child, Fannie Evelyn, b. Apr. 24, 1893, in New Britain. ii. Harry Ulysses, b. Aug. 18, 1878; is proprietor of a decorating company; m. Dec. 11, 1906, Marion Holsapple; has one son, Harry Ulysses, b. June 13, 19―, in New Britain. iii. Alfred Newton, b. Feb. 16, 1882; is a member of the firm, Nelson and Thompson, merchant tailors; m. Dec. 2, 1913, Florence Shaylor.

Sarah E. Warner, b. in Hebron, Conn., Sept., 1851; d. in Marlborough, July 17, 1889; m. in Marlborough, Sept., 1871, John H. Fuller, b. in Pomfret, Conn., Mar. 22, 1844, son of Joel and Emeline (―――) Fuller; resides in Marlborough. Children, b. in Marlborough: i. Frank, b. Nov. 28, 1872; resides in East Hampton. ii. Emma, b. Jan. 28, 1874; d. Apr. 17, 1906, at Manchester, Conn. iii. Mabel, b. Mar. 20, 1884.

Frank Warner, b. and d. in Meriden, in infancy.
Elizabeth Warner, d. in Sacramento, Cal.; m. in Berlin, Conn., Monroe
Dudley of Berlin. They removed to California after their marriage.
Child: Bessie M., m. —— Hoskins, and resided in Meridian,
Sutter Co., Cal.

552 HANNAH LOUISA[8] WARNER, daughter of Elisha[7]
and Lucy (Chapman) Warner, born March 6, 1839, in Marlborough, Conn.; died in Hartford, Conn., October 12, 1912.
Married (1) **GEORGE EATON** of Coventry, Conn., who died
in New York City.
Married (2) **AUGUSTUS WESTCOTT RANDALL,** born
in Johnson, R. I., March 27, 1825; died in Hartford, Conn. His
mother was a descendant of Roger Williams.
Married (3) December 31, 1896, at Hartford, **JONATHAN
GLEASON DAVENPORT NEWTON,** born in Gloucester
County, N. J., January 19, 1840, son of Dan and Sybil Rosana
(Davenport) Newton. He married (1) at Portsmouth, Va.,
1868, Missouri Elizabeth Hudgins who died in Hartford in
1894. He had seven children by this first marriage, none by the
second. He was a market gardener and florist near Hartford.

Childen of Augustus W. and Hannah Louisa (Warner) Randall
Arthur M. Randall, b. in New York, Nov. 30, 1867; resides in Hartford.
Burt W. Randall, b. in Hartford, Oct. 30, 1872; resides there.
Roger Williams Randall, b. in Hartford, Mar., 1876; d. 1876.

553 LODICA[8] WARNER, daughter of Elisha[7] and Lucy
(Chapman) Warner, born probably in Glastonbury or Marlborough, Conn., about 1841; resided in Fitchburg, Mass.
Married in 1861, **NATHAN WILLARD BABBITT,** born
May 22, 1839, died December 2, 1899, son of Isaac Thompson
and Ann P. (Lewis) Babbitt. He married (2) Fannie J. Griggs.

Children of Nathan W. and Lodica (Warner) Babbitt
Herman Babbitt, b. in Fitchburg, Mass., May 7, 1862 or 1864; resides
in East Oakland, Cal.; m. (1) in Fitchburg, Sept. 8, 1887, Lilla
Estelle Carlton, who d. Jan. 19, 1900; m. (2) in Gardner, Mass.,
Aug. 8, 1900, Lizzie Sweet Proctor, daughter of Isaac D. and Carrie
(——) Proctor. Children by first wife: i. Leon Carlton, b.
Aug. 9, 1888, in Fitchburg. ii. Leslie Warner, b. Aug. 17, 1889, in
Fitchburg. iii. Lucy Luella, b. Aug. 12, 1893, in Gardner.
Herbert Leon Babbitt, d. in infancy.
Annie M. Babbitt, b. 1870, in Fitchburg; d. Sept., 1908, in South
Framingham, Mass.; m. Sept. 6, 1888, Winifred H. Fay, son of
John Fay, and had three children, Rodney, Lawrence, and Arlton.

554 HARRIETTE ANNA[8] WARNER, daughter of William[7] and Harriet B. (Leach) Warner, born in Burlington, Vt., August 7, 1845; resided in Hannibal, Mo., then in Detroit, Mich. She was graduated from Vassar College in 1867; taught in the Detroit Central High School from 1878 until 1914 when she retired. She is a Congregationalist, a member of the Phi Beta Kappa Society, Association of Collegiate Alumnæ, and College Club of Detroit.

Married in Detroit, October 13, 1870, **WILLIAM MELANCTHON BISHOP**, born in Indiana, Pa., March 28, 1846; died April 25, 1878. He was the son of Rev. Henry and Elizabeth (Humrickhouse) Bishop, and resided in Hannibal, Mo.

Children, born in Hannibal

William Warner Bishop, b. July 20, 1871; was graduated from the University of Michigan, 1892, A.M., 1893; taught in Missouri, Evanston, Ill., and Brooklyn, N. Y.; was head of the cataloguing department of Princeton University for five years; superintendent reading rooms, Library of Congress, seven years; now librarian of the University of Michigan; resides in Ann Arbor. Married in Louisville, Ky., June 28, 1905, Finie Murfree Burton, daughter of Dr. George W. and Anna (Bennett) Burton. Child: William Warner, Jr., b. at Princeton, N. J., June 10, 1906.

Helen Louise Bishop, b. Nov. 7, 1873; was graduated from Detroit High School; Vassar College, A.B., 1897; University of Michigan, A.M., 1904; American School of Classical Studies in Rome, 1900-1; teacher in High School, Covington, Ind., 1898-9; Rockford College, 1902-3; Meredith College, Raleigh, N. C., 1905-7; Detroit Central High School since 1908. Author of "The Fountain of Juturna in the Roman Forum." Miss Bishop is a member of the Congregational Church, Phi Beta Kappa, College Club of Detroit, and Association of Collegiate Alumnæ.

Elizabeth Lorraine Bishop, b. Nov. 1, 1875; was graduated from Vassar College, 1897, A.M., 1898; took graduate work at the University of Chicago; is professor of Latin in the Western College for Women, Oxford, Ohio. Miss Bishop is a member of the Congregational Church, Phi Beta Kappa Society, Association of Collegiate Alumnæ, Archæological Institute of America, Classical Association of Middle West and South.

555 WILLIAM ANDREW[8] WARNER, son of William[7] and Harriet B. (Leach) Warner, born in Burlington, Vt., June 27, 1849; resides in Detroit, Mich., where he is a broker in merchandise. He studied at the University of Michigan from 1868 to 1871.

Married in Elvira, Iowa, May 16, 1872, **MARIA VIRGINIA BISHOP**, born in Indiana, Pa., November 5, 1848, daughter of Rev. Henry and Elizabeth (Humrickhouse) Bishop.

Children

Edward Lothrop Warner, b. in Hannibal, Mo., Dec. 12, 1872; is in the insurance business in Detroit, Mich.; m. in Detroit, June 11, 1907, Bessie Louise De Graff, b. in Detroit, Mar., 1877, daughter of William and Annie (Hutchins) De Graff. Child: Edward Lothrop, b. in Detroit, July 12, 1908.

William Bishop Warner, b. in Hannibal, Mo., Dec. 20, 1874; is in the dry goods business at Brookline, Mass.; m. in Chicago, Ill., Apr. 17, 1909, Sibyl Moore Carson, b. in Toledo, Ohio, Sept. 8, 1883, daughter of Edward D. and Zoe (Compton) Moore. Child: Zoe Compton, b. in Brookline, July 26, 1910.

Frances Leach Warner, b. in Hannibal, Mo., Oct. 21, 1876; was graduated from the Detroit Normal School in 1897; is first assistant in the Grammar School, Detroit, Mich.

Ernest Humrickhouse Warner, b. in Detroit, Oct. 11, 1881; is in the dry goods business in Detroit; m. in Windsor, Ont., Jan. 21, 1902, Helene Bernadetta Rickard, b. in Detroit, Jan. 1, 1884, daughter of John J. and Ellen M. (O'Hara) Rickard. Children: i. William Rickard, b. Dec. 21, 1902; d. July 16, 1903. ii. Edward John, b. in Detroit, Aug. 2, 1904. iii. Stanley Bishop, b. in Detroit, Nov. 28, 1905.

Henry Laurence Warner, b. in Detroit, Apr. 6, 1886; was a student in engineering at the University of Michigan for three years, from 1905 to 1908; is now in the dry goods business at Minneapolis, Minn.

556 MARY LOUISA[8] WARNER, daughter of Moses Mandell[7] and Orrel (Smith) Warner, born in Barre, Mass., June 16, 1830; resides in Dixon, Ill. She has been a resident of Lee County since 1838. After her marriage she lived on a farm two and a half miles west of Dixon until 1902.

Married at her parents' home between Dixon and Sterling, Ill., June 17, 1851, JOHN LEWIS LORD, born in Hopkinton, N. H., June 10, 1829, son of John and Achsah (Cary) Lord.

Children

Augustus Warner Lord, b. Mar. 3, 1852; resides in Dixon; m. Mary Crowell. Children: John S.; Frank.

Paul G. Lord, b. Dec. 31, 1853; resides in Dixon; m. Jessie Manny. Children: i. Merritt M., who is an aviator. ii. Pauline, m. —— Bischoff.

John Prentiss Lord, b. Apr. 17, 1860; is a surgeon of Omaha, Neb., at present a Major in the Medical Reserve Corps at Ft. Riley, Kans.; m. Minnie Swingley. Children: i. Louise, m. —— Vaughan. ii. Upton Prentiss.

Mary Elizabeth Lord, b. Dec. 18, 1863; is not married; resides with her mother in Dixon.

Fred L. Lord, b. Feb. 19, 1869; resides in Dixon; m. Lena Hyde. Children: Nolan L.; Arvene H.

Grace Eva Lord, b. Sept. 26, 1871; resides in Los Angeles, Cal.; m. George H. Johnson.

557   DELPHIA M.[8] WARNER, daughter of Moses Mandell[7] and Orrel (Smith) Warner, born in Barre, Mass., June 30, 1832; resides with her step-daughter, Mrs. Tuttle, at the homestead on the road from Hardwick to Gilbertsville (1917). Married (1) April 2, 1856, CALVIN W. MANN, born in Hardwick, April 2, 1831, died there, May 25, 1883, son of South worth Julius and Isabel (Whiting) Mann.

Married (2) November 20, 1901, as his third wife, GEORGE[8] WARNER, born in Hardwick, April 14, 1830; died there, February 23, 1908; see number 560.

Children of Calvin and Delphia (Warner) Mann, born in Hardwick

Jennie Eliza Mann, b. Jan. 15, 1857; resides in Worcester, Mass.; m. in Hardwick, Dec. 5, 1883, Albert Billings Haskell, b. in Wethersfield, Vt., May 31, 1858, d. in Worcester, Mass., Mar. 29, 1895, son of Jacob Reed and Marietta (Thrasher) Haskell. Children, b. in Hardwick: i. Edna Mann, b. Apr. 7, 1885; m. Feb. 19, 1917, Charles F. Hitchcock, son of Frederic A. and Clara (Packard) Hitchcock of Hardwick, Mass. ii. Stanley Reed, b. June 5, 1887; d. May 21, 1904, in Worcester. iii. Katherine, b. Oct. 6, 1892.

Lucius Calvin Mann, b. Apr. 17, 1870; m. July, 1893, Annie J. Bartlett of Springfield, Mass., daughter of Homer and Josephine (————) Bartlett. She died in Worcester, Mass., June 3, 1899.

558   CHARLES DAVENPORT[8] WARNER, son of Jona than[7], Jr., and Emily Florilla (Farnum) Warner, born in Hard wick, Vt., October 30, 1835 (or October 28, town records); resides in Arlington, Mass. He was educated in the common schools and at Colby Academy, Meriden, N. H. At the age of 22 he and his brother Levi entered into a partnership to carry the homestead farm which they later bought. This was located in the south part of the village of East Hardwick about a mile from the center, and contained about 150 acres. In 1872 he removed to Arlington, Mass., in order to be near a market and the following year he sold the Hardwick farm and devoted himself to market gardening. After a few years he started an express route from Arlington to Boston and built up a large business in the twenty-five years before he retired. He is a member of the Baptist Church.

Married (1) in Enfield, N. H., June 11, 1866, ELIZABETH WESTGATE JOHNSON, born 1833, died June 24, 1873, daughter of John and Elizabeth (Westgate) Johnson.

Married (2) in Cambridge, Mass., June 23, 1884, MARION HENDERSON of North Cambridge, born November 20, 1843, died February 14, 1914, daughter of Robert and Marion (Johnston) Henderson.

Married (3) in Arlington, Mass., December 31, 1914, **FANNIE ISABELL FINLAY**, born in Charlottetown, Prince Edward's Island, daughter of William and Mary Jane (————) Finlay of that place.

Children by first wife

Alice Elvira Warner, b. Mar. 9, 1867, in Hardwick, Vt.; d. in Arlington, Mass., May 27, 1894; m. in Arlington, Nov., 1889, William Alanson Spaulding of Hanover Center, N. H. Child: Charles Jackson, b. Aug. 30, 1890, in Hanover Center.

Gertrude Elsie Warner, b. in Hardwick, Vt., Oct. 30, 1868; resides in Roxbury, Mass.; m. in Arlington, May 25, 1899, Charles Roscoe Houston, b. in Thornton, N. H., Dec. 17, 1866, son of Henry C. Houston, b. in Thornton, 1809, and Sally Packard, b. in Merrimac, N. H., 1823. Child: Elizabeth Marion, b. in Roxbury, May 2, 1900; is a sophomore in Radcliffe College (Mar., 1918).

Wallace Warner, b. June 22, 1870; d. in Arlington, May 22, 1872.

559 **LAURA ANNETTE**[8] **WARNER**, daughter of Jonathan[7], Jr., and Emily Florilla (Farnum) Warner, born in Hardwick, Vt., April 20, 1837 (or Laura Farrell, born April 6, 1836, town records).

Married January 8, 1862, **GEORGE SHERMAN** of Tioga County, N. Y., born May 27, 1825; died October 10, 1883.

Children

Guy Warner Sherman, b. Oct. 21, 1862; m. 1885, Henrietta Withington. Child: Clifford Withington, b. Oct. 10, 1887.

William Tecumseh Sherman, b. Sept. 29, 1865; m. Nov. 29, 1890, Nellie Clark. Children: i. Rhoda May, b. Oct. 20, 1891. ii. Ruth Belle, b. Apr. 14, 1893. iii. George Clark, b. 1895.

Mary Maud Sherman, b. Oct. 29, 1867; m. Jan. 20, 1892, Irving Farrant. Child: Stanley Sherman, b. Sept. 18, 1893.

Louis Alfred Sherman, b. July 3, 1870; m. Nov., 1893, Carrie Cogswell.

Levi Whipple Sherman, b. Jan. 28, 1875; m. Mar., 1897, Almira Pinney. Children: i. Phillis, b. Apr. 14, 1898. ii. Vera S., b. Apr. 12, 1900. iii. Alfred C.

560 **GEORGE**[8] **WARNER**, son of Daniel[7] and Nancy (Fish) Warner, born in Hardwick, Mass., April 14, 1830; died there, February 23, 1908, buried in Hardwick Cemetery. He was a farmer, inherited his father's homestead; was town assessor for seven years, selectman from 1876 to 1883 and later.

Married (1) October 17, 1855, **MARY A. WALKER**, born in Barre, Mass., daughter of Arad and Avalina (Powers) Walker. She died November 24, 1856, aged 21 years, buried in Hardwick Cemetery.

Married (2) October 21, 1858, HARRIET S. WHEELER, born in Rutland, Mass., February 16, 1830, daughter of John and Sophia (Wheeler) Wheeler. She died September 17, 1898, buried in Hardwick Cemetery.
Married (3) November 20, 1901, Mrs. DELPHIA M.[8] (War-NER) MANN, daughter of Moses Mandell[7] and Orrel (Smith) Warner; see number 557.

Child by first wife

682 *Mary Elizabeth Warner*, b. Sept. 22, 1856; m. Arthur Birks Wilkes.

Children by second wife, born in Hardwick

Sarah Esther Warner, b. Dec. 16, 1859; d. Dec. 31, 1859, buried in Hardwick.
George Franklin Warner, b. June 11, 1862; d. Jan. 25, 1863, buried in Hardwick.
Hattie Sophia Warner, b. Nov. 6, 1865; resides on her father's homestead between Ware and Hardwick; m. in Hardwick, Aug. 19, 1896, Olie A. Tuttle, b. in Lee, N. H., Mar. 17, 1870. He was a teacher and the son of William B. and Martha (Langley) Tuttle. They have one son, Warner Benjamin, b. in Nahant, Mass., June 12, 1899.
George Daniel Warner, b. Nov. 5, 1867; m. Mary Richardson, who was born in Hardwick. He has been the keeper of the hotel in Hardwick for several years. Child: George Wheeler, b. in Hardwick, Jan. 6, 1900.

561 ALONZO FRANKLIN[8] WARNER, son of Ira[7] and Asenath (Hitchcock) Warner, born November 18, 1810, at Cuyler, N. Y.; died December 31, 1846, at Union, N. Y.

Alonzo Franklin Warner spent his childhood and early manhood at home, attending the district school and assisting in the work of the farm. After reaching manhood, he taught school for one or more terms. He remained at home helping on the farm for several years after he was of age, and in return for his services, his father gave him a farm of about 100 acres situated in the town of Lincklaen, one mile south of the old homestead. This he occupied from the time of his marriage until a few months after his father's death, when he and his uncle, Theodore Warner, were appointed executors of his father's estate, and he removed to the old homestead that he might keep up the home for his younger brothers and sisters.

About three years later, he removed to Macedon, N. Y., and took charge of a farm owned by his great-aunt, the widow of David Warner. Here he remained until the spring of 1846, when he bought a farm in the town of Union, very near the shores of

Lake Ontario, and about ten miles north of Spencerport, N. Y. This was a new, undeveloped country filled with malaria, from which the whole family suffered, so that at times they were all sick together. He accepted it all bravely, as he was happy to again have a home of his own. The following winter he was taken with pneumonia, and died after a few days' sickness.

Mr. Warner was an upright, hard-working and thrifty man. He was so conscientious himself that it was difficult for him to realize that others were not the same, and for this reason he was not always successful in dealing with other men. He was a strong abolitionist and was one of the first two to vote the abolition ticket in the town where he resided. The same sturdy principles made him a strictly temperate man, and an earnest supporter of the temperance movement which first swept over the country during the early part of the nineteenth century. He was a man of medium height, weighed 160 pounds, and stooped a little, the result, probably, of hard work.

Married at Lincklaen, N. Y., December 24, 1838, LYDIA ANN **CONVERSE**, born at Butternuts, N. Y., December 25, 1815; died at Union Valley, N. Y., March 5, 1886. She was the daughter of Calvin and Harriet (Fuller) Converse, and a descendant of Deacon Edward[1] Converse, who was born in England, came to Massachusetts in 1630, died in Woburn, Mass., August 10, 1663. The line of descent from Deacon Edward Converse is as follows:—Samuel[2], Samuel[3], Ensign Edward[4], Captain Edward[5], Sergeant Edward[6], Calvin[7]. (For further particulars, see "The Converse Family," published in 1905 by Chas. Allen Converse.) Mrs. Warner's mother, Harriet (Fuller) Converse, born April 14, 1790, died August 20, 1831, was a descendant of Captain Matthew Fuller, the first regular physician to settle in Barnstable, Mass.

Mrs. Warner was a woman of marked ability and strong personality; self-reliant and a natural leader among her associates. She possessed a good education for her time, and taught school for several years before her marriage. She was industrious and thrifty, a good manager, and devoted to the care of her family. She also found time for public service and was ever ready to support any good cause, to nurse the sick, to help the poor and tó comfort the distressed. After her husband's death, she removed to Lincklaen, N. Y., where she resided during the childhood of her two sons. Mrs. Warner was married (2) in 1861 to William Breed of DeRuyter, N. Y. Soon after this marriage, she removed to Union Valley, N. Y., where she afterwards resided.

Children

683 Ira DeVer Warner, b. at Lincklaen, N. Y., Mar. 26, 1840; m. (1)
     Lucetta M. Greenman, (2) Eva Follett.
684 Lucien Calvin Warner, b. at Cuyler, N. Y., Oct. 26, 1841; m. Keren
     Sarah Osborne.

562 HARRIET NEWELL[8] WARNER, daughter of Ira[7]
and Asenath (Hitchcock) Warner, born October 2, 1815; died
at Homer, N. Y., Sept. 30, 1887.
Married December 25, 1838, LEWIS NASH, who died in
De Ruyter, N. Y., about 1894. He resided for many years on a
farm immediately south of the Ira Warner farm, later in
De Ruyter and Homer.

Children

Zelia Asenath Nash, who d. in 1875. She married in 1864, Isaac
     Marshall Samson, whose first wife was her aunt, Mary Ann Warner.
     Children of Zelia Nash: i. Lewis. ii. Ira, d. 1892. iii. Mary. iv.
     Gertrude.
Ira Warner Nash, b. in De Ruyter, 1844; d. Sept., 1890; m. (1) Oct.
     18, 1870, Ella M. Hitchcock, b. in Albion, Ind., Sept. 4, 1852, d. in
     Union City, Mich., Feb. 1, 1872, daughter of Henry H. Hitchcock
     of Goshen, Ind., who was a grandson of Samuel Hitchcock and a
     descendant of Luke Hitchcock; m. (2) Ella Williams of Lima, Ind.
     By the first wife he had a daughter, Ella Hitchcock, who died in
     1887. By the second wife he had a daughter, Katherine Williams,
     who resides with her mother in Lima, Ind.

563 LORENZO COOK[8] WARNER, son of Ira[7] and Ase
nath (Hitchcock) Warner, born in Truxton (now Cuyler),
N. Y., July 11, 1819; died at Palmyra, N. Y., June 6, 1881. He
moved to Palmyra when a young man, bought a large farm and
conducted it with great success.
Married February 13, 1850, MARY DURFEE, daughter of
Isaac and Patty[6] (Warner) Durfee; see number 229. She was
born in Macedon, N. Y., January 25, 1820; died in Palmyra,
September 7, 1888.

Child

Lorenzo Durfee Warner, b. Apr. 17, 1862; is a farmer residing in
     Palmyra, N. Y.; m. in Macedon, N. Y., Mar. 3, 1897, Ida E. Baumer,
     b. in Rochester, N. Y., July 6, 1870, daughter of Jacob and Eva
     (Neff) Baumer. Children: i. Prudence M., b. Mar. 2, 1898, in
     Macedon, N. Y. ii. Lorene Durfee, b. May 26, 1910, in Palmyra,
     N. Y.

564 ELIZA ANN[8] WARNER, daughter of Ira[7] and Asenath
(Hitchcock) Warner, born in Truxton, N. Y., February 15, 1821;
died in Richburg, Allegany Co., N. Y., May 8, 1867.

TITUS B. DAVIDSON   ELIZA WARNER DAVIDSON

CHARLES DEVER DAVIDSON AND FAMILY

Married in Homer, Cortland Co., N. Y., March 25, 1851, Dr.
TITUS BEECH DAVIDSON, born in Lisle, Broome Co.,
N. Y., April 5, 1822; died in Richburg, aged 59 years. He was
the son of Daniel J. and Huldah (Peck) Davidson. He became
a member of the Cortland County Medical Society at Homer,
June 16, 1847, and was later a physician in Richburg.

Children

Marshall Sampson Davidson, b. in Spafford, Onondaga Co., N. Y.,
June 14, 1852; resides in Dorrance, Kans. (1918); m. Charity
Van Velzor. Child: Maud Adelle, who was born at Eldred, McKean
Co., Pa., May 30, 1883, and married Thadd McNeil.
Mary Eliza Davidson, b. in Richburg, N. Y., Dec. 24, 1856; d. Sept.
6, 1906; m. Samuel Withey.
Charles Dever Davidson, b. in Richburg, N. Y., Dec. 6, 1862; is
engaged in farming and ranching at Dorrance, Kans.; m. at
Ellenwood, Barton Co., Kans., ·Dec. 18, 1884, Annie B. Houska.
Children, b. in Barton Co., Kans.: i. Blanche A., b. Aug. 24, 1889;
m. Nov. 18, 1907, Charles R. Allen. ii. Mary Eliza, b. Dec. 11,
1893; m. Dec. 26, 1915, Roy Huston. iii. Annie May, b. Jan. 10,
1896; m. July 7, 1914, Ralph Foster. iv. Marshall Frank, b. Apr. 15,
1898. v. Frank Charlie, b. May 14, 1900.

565 HORACE HORATIO[8] WARNER, son of Ira[7] and
Asenath (Hitchcock) Warner, born near Truxton, Cortland
Co., N. Y., April 25, 1822; died at Rome City, Ind., November
28, 1896. In 1849 he went to western Indiana, and, having relatives already located in Orange Township, he settled there on
the place where he spent the remainder of his life. He owned
a farm of some five hundred acres which he* conducted with
much success, and was one of the prominent and substantial
men of the community.
Married in Parma, N. Y., April 25, 1847, U R S U L A J.
HITCHCOCK, born in Barre, N. Y., September 15, 1823; died
at Rome City, Ind., February 6, 1895. She was the daughter
of Pliny and Millicent (Howe) Hitchcock, and was descended
from the pioneer, Luke Hitchcock.

Child

Margaret Warner, b. at Parma, N. Y., Aug. 22, 1848; d. at Rome City,
Ind., Apr. 12, 1895; m. at Rome City, Jan. 21, 1869, George Broth-
well, b. at Bridgeport, Conn., Jan. 25, 1841, d. at Rome City, Ind.,
Jan. 28, 1908, leaving no children. He was the son of Emery and
Polina (Treadwell) Brothwell. He went to Noble County, Ind., in
1858 and resided with his uncle until the Civil War. He enlisted
Aug. 12, 1862, in Company B, 12th Indiana Volunteers, 15th Army
Corps, and was honorably discharged June 20, 1865. His first battle

was at Richmond, Ky., where he was taken prisoner, paroled, came home on a furlough, was exchanged and rejoined his regiment. He took an active part in the battles of Chattanooga, Mission Ridge, Kenesaw, Lookout Mountain and Vicksburg, was all through the Atlantic Campaign, with Sherman on his march to the sea and with him went to Washington. After the war he took a business course and was at South Bend, Ind., for two years. After his marriage he became a farmer with his wife's father. He and his wife were active members of the Methodist Church.

566 **ROSWELL KNOWLTON**[8] **WARNER,** son of Ira[7] and Asenath (Hitchcock) Warner, born near Cuyler, Cortland Co., N. Y., July 19, 1825; died February 19, 1900, at Marion, N. Y., where he had resided for many years. He was educated in the public schools and was a farmer in Cortland County until 1858, when he removed to Palmyra, and in 1865, to Marion. He continued farming until 1884, after which time he lived in Marion, retired.

Married at De Ruyter, N. Y., December 27, 1848, **REMONIA VAIL,** born in Cortland County, October 25, 1829, daughter of Henry Vail.

Children

685 *Erotus Warner,* b. Sept. 12, 1850; m. Ellen Marietta Wake.
686 *Lewis N. Warner,* b. Nov. 5, 1855; m. Amelia E. Allen.
Mary E. Warner, b. June 7, 1857, in Truxton, N. Y.; resided after marriage at Marion, N. Y., since 1913 at Winter Park, Fla.; m. at Marion, June 14, 1883, George Eldredge, b. Jan. 18, 1854, at Little York, Cortland Co., N. Y., son of George W. and Polly (White) Eldredge. He was a farmer. Child: Marion Ramonia, b. Mar. 1, 1894; attended business college and was a bookkeeper and typewriter at Homer, N. Y.; m. Mar. 15, 1918, William H. Grant of Sennett, Cayuga Co., N. Y., where they now reside.
Horace A. Warner, b. Jan. 23, 1859, at Palmyra, N. Y.; d. Jan. 25, 1891; was a merchant in Marion, N. Y.; m. Minnie Potter. Children: i. Harry Ross, b. Jan. 26, 1882. ii. Myrtle S., b. July 23, 1883.
George S. Warner, b. Feb. 1, 1863, at Palmyra; was a merchant in Marion, N. Y., after his marriage; now resides in Rochester, N. Y., where he is a salesman; m. in Marion, Oct. 22, 1885, Clella W. Martin, b. in Marion, Apr. 12, 1862, daughter of Henry A. and Jane (Baker) Martin, who were born in England. Child: Lee H., b. in Marion, May 12, 1892; is a salesman; was educated at the High School and in engraving.

567 **SARAH JANE**[8] **WARNER,** daughter of Ira[7] and Asenath (Hitchcock) Warner, born in Truxton, Cortland Co., N. Y., April 9, 1829; died in La Fayette, N. Y., November 28, 1888. Married (1) in Lincklaen, N. Y., June 5, 1850, FRANKLIN

35

CROFOOT, born at Preble, N. Y., March 24, 1822; died there, April 18, 1855.
Married (2) JOHN ABBOTT of La Fayette, N. Y.

Children by first husband

James F. Crofoot, b. in Preble, Cortland Co., N. Y., Mar. 19, 1851; d. Apr. 10, 1912, at Wilson, Kans., where he had been a farmer; m. in Bunker Hill, Kans., Sept. 26, 1877, Ida E. Davis, b. in Pensville, Ohio, daughter of Harvey and Leanah (————) Davis. Children, b. in Wilson, Kans.: i. Ira D., b. May 17, 1880; m. May 17, 1908, Eva A. Corson. ii. Frank L., b. May 11, 1882; d. Nov. 11, 1884. iii. Sarah L., b. Apr. 10, 1884; m. Nov. 6, 1907, Andy Austin. iv. Grace C., b. May 25, 1887; m. Oct. 27, 1909, George A. Perrill.

Jennie Crofoot, b. in Preble, Jan. 23, 1855; d. at Richburg, N. Y., Oct. 18, 1862.

568   **CHARLES DUDLEY**[8] **WARNER**, son of Justus[7] and Sylvia Russell (Hitchcock) Warner, born September 12, 1829, in Plainfield, Franklin Co., Mass.; died in Hartford, Conn., October 20, 1900.

Married in Syracuse, N. Y., October 8, 1856, SUSAN SOPHIA LEE, daughter of William Elliott and Susan (Smythe) Lee. She resides in Hartford, Conn. They had no children.

The early years of one who was destined to become a conspicuous figure in the annals of American literature, were spent at the ancestral Warner homestead in the hills of Plainfield, Mass. His father died when he was but five years of age, and his brother, three. The mother kept her little family together for three years more, then, at the death of the grandfather, Abel Warner, she removed to the neighboring village of Charlemont, where Charles was to reside with his relative and guardian, Jonas K. Patch. The latter was a man of prominence in the community and the owner of a large farm, upon which his ward lived and worked until he was about twelve years of age. It was here that he experienced the incidents and lived among the scenes that he afterward depicted in "Being a Boy."

When he was about twelve years of age, his mother removed with her children to Cazenovia, N. Y., where her father, Samuel Hitchcock, resided. During the next seven years he attended school in Cazenovia at the Oneida Conference Seminary, except that for about a year he lived in De Ruyter, N. Y., with a Quaker uncle, Theodore Warner, and attended the De Ruyter Academy. In 1848 he entered the Sophomore class of Hamilton College, graduating in 1851 with the highest honors of his

CHARLES DUDLEY WARNER

class. After graduating he was undecided as to his career. He was always fond of reading, and while still in college he contributed to "Putnam's" and "The Knickerbocker" magazines. He prepared a "Book of Eloquence" which was published in Cazenovia in 1853, and spent some time in New York and in Detroit as the editor of a Detroit magazine. His health was not very good at this time, and having secured a position as a member of a surveying party engaged on a railway in Missouri, he spent the years 1853-4 with them, returning fully restored to health.

THE BIRTHPLACE OF CHARLES DUDLEY WARNER, PLAINFIELD, MASS.

Still with no definite profession in mind, but with an inclination towards the law, he lived for some time with his uncle, Hon. Simeon Cooley Hitchcock of Binghamton, N. Y., and commenced the study of law. Later he went to Philadelphia and entered the law department of the University of Pennsylvania, where he was graduated in 1858 with the degree of LL.B. After that he settled in Chicago and spent two years in the practice of law.

Fortunately for the world, the legal profession was not to be his life work. Among his classmates and intimate friends in Hamilton College was Joseph R. Hawley, who had now settled in Hartford, Conn. In 1860 he induced Mr. Warner to become the associate editor of the Hartford Press. A little later the Press and the Hartford Courant were united, and he became a co-editor, with General Hawley, of this important paper. Here he found his permanent work and at the time of his death he was still one of the editors and owners. About this time the civil war broke out, General Hawley entered the military service of the country, and during all the period of the war, the management of the paper, was left largely in Mr. Warner's hands. He edited it with indefatigable energy, and gave it the reputation it has maintained as an exponent of affairs and as a moulder of opinion. Its literary fame is largely due to his connection with it.

In 1868-9 Mr. Warner spent fourteen months abroad and gained considerable reputation by a series of foreign letters to the "Courant" that were widely copied. During 1870 he decided to divert his readers from the grim topics of the day and published a series of articles on his amateur gardening experiences. Henry Ward Beecher was visiting his sister, Harriet Beecher Stowe, in Hartford, and was so much impressed by these articles that he urged their publication by James T. Fields, who consented on the condition that Mr. Beecher should write the introduction. This was done and the volume "My Summer in a Garden" was published. Its instantaneous success made it evident that a new American writer of distinction had appeared.

From this start, book after book was given to the public from his pen; essays, travel sketches, papers on important questions of social and political reform, novels, etc. In them all Charles Dudley Warner maintained and steadily developed the brilliant name he had made by his first volume.

In his early literary career he contributed largely to the Atlantic Monthly, but later became associated with Harper's Monthly. In 1884, he became the editor of "The Editor's Drawer," and in 1894 he succeeded William Dean Howells as editor of "The Editor's Study." His last contribution to that department appeared in the number for July, 1898.

As a traveller and in describing travel, Mr. Warner especially excelled. Among his travel works are these: "Saunterings," 1872; "Baddeck, and That Sort of Thing," 1874; "My Winter on the Nile," 1876; "In the Levant," 1878; "A Roundabout Journey," 1883; "Their Pilgrimage," 1886, and numerous articles in magazines.

Some of his most important work in "Harper's" was in a

series of papers, beginning with "Studies in the South," followed by "Mexican Papers" and "Studies in the Great West." In these he discussed the educational, political and social conditions of these regions. Indeed, one of the most marked features of Mr. Warner's career was his warm interest in philanthropic, educational and sociological questions. He was for many years a member of the State Commission on Prisons of Connecticut and of the National Prison Association. He spent many weeks in the study of the State Reformatory School at Elmira, N. Y., and both by his voice and pen he contributed largely to the introduction of reform methods in the construction of prisons and the treatment of prisoners.

He delivered many lectures before educational and other societies, which have for the most part been pleas for higher individual and national culture, for an enlargement of our collegiate courses and for an improvement in their methods. He was an ardent Abolitionist during the anti-slavery agitation, and was a Republican from the formation of that party, though not a strong partisan. He was frequently called to perform civic duties and his pen and voice were untiring in efforts to better the conditions of the negro, to elevate the standards of schools and hospitals, and to improve the conditions of society.

Mr. Warner was active in the municipal and social life of Hartford, and as a member of the Park Commission had a large share in developing the fine park system of that city. The part that he bore in his civic and social duties in Hartford, as a citizen, a neighbor and a friend was a very great matter in his life. The foundation of the Home and Training School for Nurses in connection with the city hospital was chiefly due to his labors. His own private charities, beneficence, and kindly offices were constant.

Mr. Warner was one of the best members of the distinguished literary circle in Hartford. Mrs. Harriet Beecher Stowe lived next door on one side of his home, while his brother George lived on the other, with Mark Twain just around the corner. At the back of the generous grounds of all these homes is the stream known to the children of Hartford as "Mark Twain's River." His home was within easy walking distance of the "Courant" office. Mr. Warner loved out-of-door life and spent as much of his time as he could gain from his literary duties about his grounds, and in walking in all seasons and in all kinds of weather. He used to take prolonged summer vacations in the Adirondacks and other mountain resorts, and one of his most delightful books, "In the Wilderness," was the outcome of such experiences.

Mr. Warner·was a fine-looking man. He was tall, spare and erect in frame, with a face indicative of thought and refinement. His head was large, his forehead high, his eyes clear and kindly. He would be marked anywhere as a person of striking appearance. He was a man of great personal as well as literary charm, loyal to his friends, generous in recognition, kindly and broad-minded, courteous in manner to all. Three years after his death, his old paper, the "Courant," said in an editorial:

> "His life was a full and helpful and happy life. He went through this world with an alert interest in everything to be seen in the journey— observing, comprehending, and interpreting. He did what he could, and not by any means in his books alone, to make the world a saner, wholesomer world for men, even the most unfortunate of them, to live in."

Mr. Warner belonged to many organizations of all kinds. He was a member of the Players, the Authors, the University and the Century Clubs of New York and whether at Hartford, New York or elsewhere, he was a favorite social figure. As early as 1872 he received the honorary degree of A.M. from Yale, and Dartmouth paid him the same honor in 1884.

Mr. Warner was the general editor of "The American Men of Letters" series, and in 1895 undertook the managing editorship of "A Library of the World's Best Literature," published in thirty volumes. His writings, in addition to those already mentioned, are as follows: "Backlog Studies" (1872), "Being a Boy" (1877), "In the Wilderness" (1878), "The American Newspaper; An Essay" (1881), "Captain John Smith" (1881), "Washington Irving" (1881), "On Horseback; A Tour of Virginia, North Carolina and Tennessee" (1888), "A Little Journey in the World" (1889), "Our Italy" (1891)—relates to Southern California,—"As We Were Saying" (1891), "The Work of Washington Irving" (1893), "The Golden House" (1894), "As We Go" (1894), "The Relation of Life to Literature" (1896), "The People for Whom Shakespeare Wrote" (1897). He also wrote in collaboration with Mark Twain, "The Gilded Age," published in 1873. With William Cullen Bryant and George P. Putnam he published in 1880, "Studies of Washington Irving."

His last work was a novel, "That Fortune," of which he was revising the proofs at the time of his fatal illness.

The finest appreciations of his life and works are to be found in the little volume by Mrs. James T. Fields, "Charles Dudley Warner," New York, 1904; and the introduction to the uniform edition of his collected works, written by Thomas R. Lounsbury, Hartford, 1905.

569 GEORGE HENRY[8] WARNER, son of Justus[7] and Sylvia Russell (Hitchcock) Warner, born in Plainfield, Mass., December 21, 1833; resides in Hartford, Conn. He was educated at the Cazenovia Seminary, and in early manhood was engaged in mercantile business in Nunda, N. Y., and in gas lighting companies in Rochester, N. Y., and Cincinnati, Ohio. In 1866 he removed from Cincinnati to Hartford and has since resided there. Until 1892 he was in a law corporation, but since then has been in literary occupations, notably with his brother, Charles Dudley Warner, on the "Library of the World's best literature." Among his published works are, "The Jewish Spectre," 1905, and essays and reviews on various subjects. Mr. Warner is a member of the Players' Club of New York City.

Married in Hartford, Conn., September 20, 1864, ELIZABETH HOOKER GILLETTE, born in Bloomfield, Conn., December 7, 1835; died September, 1915, buried in Farmington. She was the daughter of Hon. Francis and Eliza (Hooker) Gillette, and granddaughter of Rev. Ashbel and Achsah (Francis) Gillette of Hartford, and of Edward and Elizabeth (Daggett) Hooker. Mrs. Warner was a lineal descendant of Rev. Thomas Hooker, one of the founders of Hartford, and of John Doggett, of Martha's Vineyard, who came to America with Winthrop.

Children, born in Hartford

Francis Gillette Warner, b. May 21, 1867; resides at El Dorado Ranch, Placerville, ·Cal. He is a stock raiser. Married in Oakland, Cal., Nov. 27, 1909, Amy Louise Phelan, b. in Oakland, June 17, 1876, daughter of William Seymour and Louise Maria (Putnam) Phelan. They have no children.

Angelica Warner, b. Sept. 7, 1869; d. the same day.

Sylvia Warner, b. Sept. 26, 1871; d. Dec. 3, 1874.

Margaret Warner, b. Dec. 23, 1872; resides in Hartford; is a graduate of Bryn Mawr College.

570 MARTHA[8] WARNER, daughter of Nahum[7] and Hannah (Fish) Warner, born in Palmyra, N. Y., April 7, 1823; died 1898.

Married June 17, 1847, MILES BRADLEY RIGGS. They resided in Macedon, Wayne Co., N. Y.

Children, born in Macedon

Warner Bradley Riggs, b. Nov. 26, 1849; d. in Austin, Texas, Mar. 2, 1905. He was graduated from Phillips Andover Academy in 1867; Yale College, 1871; Auburn Theological Seminary, 1876; taught school in the winters of 1867-8, 1871-2, and in Canandaigua Academy, 1872-3; went to Texas, October, 1876, and preached in Brenham, 1876-86; settled in Dallas in 1886, and was a Presbyterian preacher until his death. Married (1) 1878, Lilla Graham of Austin, Texas, b. Feb. 14, 1851, d. July 15, 1879, by whom he had one child, Lilla Graham, b. July 2, 1879, d. Oct. 5, 1879. Married (2) in Houston, Texas, Mar. 11, 1884, Julia Winne, b. in Galveston, Dec. 21, 1857, daughter of Gilbert and Charlotte Jane (————) Winne. Children: i. Charlotte Louise, b. Dec. 17, 1886; is a teacher. ii. Arthur Bradley, b. Feb. 7, 1891; d. Oct. 3, 1894. iii. Ruth Warner, b. June 30, 1895; d. Aug. 12, 1896. iv. Mary Shepard, b. Mar. 6, 1898.

Herman L. Riggs, b. July 14, 1853; d. in Palmyra, July 13, 1911; m. in Palmyra, Oct. 4, 1876, Margaret Turner Sexton, b. Feb. 1, 1854, in Palmyra, and lives there. Children, first four b. in Macedon, last in Palmyra: i. Pliny Sexton, b. Aug. 28, 1877; m. Helen Manning; has two children, Caroline, b. Sept. 7, 1907, in Pelham, N. Y., and Helen, b. Sept. 23, 1910, in White Plains, N. Y. ii. Sarah Middlebrook, b. Nov. 18, 1878; m. in Palmyra, June 17, 1909, Richard Porter Bloom, and has a child, Martha Middlebrook, b. May 11, 1910. iii. Martha Warner, b. May 15, 1882; m. (1) in New York City, Nov. 24, 1903, Arthur D. Truax, son of Justice Charles H. Truax; had a child, Margaret Eva; m. (2) Aug. 3, 1918, Frederick W. Griffith of Palmyra. iv. Miles Bradley, b. Sept. 4, 1883; lives in Palmyra. v. Hermione, b. Sept. 15, 1889; m. in Palmyra, July 5, 1910, Russell Lord Tarbox, and has a son, Henry Fisk, 2d.

Frank H. Riggs, b. Sept. 20, 1856; resides in Rochester, N. Y., where he is a bookkeeper; m. in Rochester, Aug. 31, 1881, Katie Beard, b. in Rochester, Nov. 1, 1855, daughter of Fred and Mary (Blake) Beard. They have no children.

571 MARY ANN⁸ WARNER, daughter of Nahum⁷ and Hannah (Fish) Warner, born in Macedon, N. Y., December 25, 1825; died in New York City, June 22, 1910. Married in Macedon, September 4, 1848, **IRA BENEDICT,** born July 8, 1817, in Saratoga County, N. Y. (East Line); died April 13, 1895. He was the son of Bushnell and Cynthia (Landon) Benedict.

Children, born in Macedon, N. Y.

Cynthia Adella Benedict, b. July 18, 1849; d. in Troy, N. Y., Oct. 17, 1879; m. Jan. 1, 1870, Murray Channing Aspinwall, b. in Saratoga Springs, N. Y., Feb. 25, 1848, son of a Universalist minister. Child: Warner Howard, b. in Palmyra, Aug. 11, 1874; m. Lucille Sturgis of New York City, and has a son, Howard Channing, b. in Piermont, N. Y., Mar. 19, 1908.

Harriette Sewell Benedict, b. Dec. 4, 1852; resides in New York City;

m. in 1876, Sherman Williams, b. in Harmony, Chautauqua Co., N. Y., Mar. 10, 1842; served three years during the Civil War in the 49th N. Y. Volunteers; was twice elected treasurer of Chautauqua County, in 1869, and again in 1872; member of the State Assembly in 1876, and re-elected in 1877 from Chautauqua County; appraiser of merchandise in the New York Customs House. Child: Elsie Adele, b. in Troy, N. Y., Aug. 24, 1882; is teacher of Physical Training in the Manhattan Trade School for Girls, New York City.

572 GILES[8] WARNER, son of Nahum[7] and Hannah (Fish) Warner, born in Macedon, N. Y., November 29, 1830; died at the Soldiers' and Sailors' Home in Bath, N. Y., October 18, 1900. He served in the Civil War, mustered in at Macedon, August 30, 1862, as a private in Company C, New York Cavalry for three years; transferred January 6, 1864, to 7th Company, 2d Battalion, Veteran Reserve Corps; honorably discharged July 21, 1865. He spent most of his life on his father's farm in Macedon.

Married January (or June) 2, 1850, MARIA M. SHOE-MAKER, born October 29, 1829; died at Wymore, Neb., October 20, 1904.

Children

Hattie T. Warner, b. 1853; lived only a few months.
David Rollo Warner, b. Sept. 10, 1855; d. in Philadelphia, Pa., Jan. 21, 1902; m. in Butler, N. Y., Oct. 29, 1879, Hattie Hamilton, who died in Rochester, N. Y., Aug. 3, 1904. They had no children.

573 ALMON MITCHELL[8] WARNER, son of James[7] and Fidelia (Whiton) Warner, born in Plainfield, Mass., March 6, 1843; is a lawyer in Cincinnati, Ohio. He served during the Civil War, first enlistment, August 30, 1862, 2d sergeant, 37th Massachusetts Infantry, Company H; transferred to Company E and promoted to 1st Sergeant at Battle of Sailor's Creek, Va.; promoted to 2d Lieutenant, June 7, 1865; was severely wounded while attempting to capture a flag, and received an honorable discharge, August 28, 1865. His regiment formed part of the 6th Army Corps and participated in eighteen battles. Mr. Warner graduated from Williston Seminary in 1862, and, after his return from the war, took up the study of law in the offices of Church and Sawyer at Albion, N. Y., with Sanford E. Church, who was later Chief Justice of the Court of Appeals of New York, and John G. Sawyer, who was County Judge of Orleans County and member of Congress for eight years. Mr. Warner was admitted to the bar in Buffalo, N. Y., in May, 1869. He practiced in Albion until 1870, then in Leesburg, Va., for

two years, in Huntington, W. Va., two years, and in 1874 located in Cincinnati, where he has since practiced. He was for eight years Judge of the Court of Insolvency for Hamilton County, and is now Judge of the Court of Common Pleas, First Judicial District of Ohio. He has been prominent in fraternal circles, F. and A. M., I. O. O. F., and G. A. R., Past Commander of the Department of Ohio in the latter organization. The family have always been Congregationalists.

Married in Albion, N. Y., October 12, 1870, ELIZABETH HULDAH DENSMORE, born in Kendall, Orleans Co:, N. Y., June 23, 1850, daughter of Dennis and Christina (———) Densmore.

Children

Maude Loraine Warner, b. Sept. 15, 1873, in Huntington, W. Va.; was graduated from the Cincinnati schools; Vassar, 1896; Kirksville (Mo.) Osteopathic College; is a practitioner in Cincinnati.

Carrie Elizabeth Warner, b. Nov. 16, 1880, in Cincinnati; is a graduate of Cincinnati schools and of Vassar, 1903.

574 FLORA MARY[8] WARNER, daughter of William[7] and Annis (Crittenden) Warner, born in Plainfield, Mass., September 24, 1842; resides in South Haven, Mich., with her son.

Married (1) in Plainfield, October 25, 1863, EDWARD A. ROOD, born in Plainfield, May 18, 1840; died February 9, 1897, on his way home from Florida where he had spent six weeks for his health. He was the son of Josiah and Abigail (———) Rood.

Married (2) January 12, 1904, T. H. ROOD, brother of her first husband.

Children of Edward A. Rood

Frank E. Rood, b. Oct. 27, 1864; resides in South Haven, Mich.; m. and has six children: i. Edward A., b. Dec. 7, 1890; m. May 23, 1912, Glendora L. Enlow; resides on a large fruit and stock farm; has one child, Enlow Arlton, b. Oct. 6, 1913. ii. Paul J., b. Jan. 29, 1893; is a graduate of the Michigan Agricultural College; m. Jan. 1, 1915, Alice M. Enlow. iii. Edith L., b. Nov. 29, 1895; is a student at Kalamazoo College. iv. Clare A., b. Feb. 13, 1898; was graduated from the High School in 1916. v. Josephine F., b. Jan. 23, 1900; is in High School. vi. Genevieve, b. Feb. 6, 1906.

Lillian A. Rood, b. Oct. 7, 1868; d. Nov. 15, 1899, not married.

575 EDWARD FRANKLIN[8] WARNER, son of Franklin John[7] and Vesta Wales (Reed) Warner, born in Cummington, Mass., November 16, 1844; died in Cummington, March 27, 1911. He was a farmer and a dealer in agricultural implements.

Married (1) January 1, 1867, **SUSIE WOODS ROBINSON** of Cummington, born in Plainfield, Mass., January 1, 1849, daughter of William and Caleina (————) Robinson; died March 20, 1867.
Married (2) July 4, 1869, **ELLEN A. LOVELL,** born in Cummington, October 5, 1851, daughter of Jacob and Laura Ann (Barrus) Lovell. On her mother's side she is a lineal descendant of Thomas Hinckley, governor of Plymouth Colony.

Child

Ethel Susie Warner, b. in Cummington, Apr. 9, 1875; was graduated from Northampton High School, 1893; Smith College, A.B., 1897; m. in Cummington, Aug. 30, 1905, Charles Merton Phinney, b. in Chester Center, Mass., Oct. 4, 1872, son of Charles T. and Julia (Crowe) Phinney of Chester, Mass. They have resided in Chester until her father's death, since which time they have resided on the home-stead in Cummington, the fifth generation of Warners in direct line to occupy the old home that has been in the Warner family since the settlement of the town. The farm was bought Sept. 5, 1771, by Stephen Warner of number five in the County of Hampshire and Province of the Massachusetts Bay—"Stephen Warner Yeoman and Lois his wife." The present house was built in 1779 (see illus-tration page 174), the family living prior to that time in a log cabin. Mr. Phinney is engaged in raising live stock. Mrs. Phinney is active in church and social work; a member of the Congregational Church and of the Highland Congregational Club of Cummington; secretary and treasurer of the Chester Center Library Association, 1907-11.

576 **WORCESTER REED**[8] **WARNER,** son of Franklin John[7] and Vesta Wales (Reed) Warner, born in Cummington, Mass., May 16, 1846; resides in Cleveland, Ohio, and at "Hill-holm," Tarrytown, N. Y.
He is a well-known mechanical engineer and manufacturer, of The Warner & Swasey Company, Cleveland.
After learning the machinist's trade in Boston and Exeter, N. H., he was with the Pratt and Whitney Company of Hart-ford from 1870 to 1880, at the same time prosecuting his studies in astronomy and other scientific lines and experimenting in telescope building as a recreation.
In 1881 Mr. Warner formed a partnership with Ambrose Swasey for the manufacture of machine-tools, wherein they quickly achieved a reputation second to none in America.
Later his interest in such matters led the firm into the making, also, of instruments of precision, including range-finders, gun-sights, field-telescopes, binoculars, etc., for the government, as well as astronomical instruments. In this latter field The

WORCESTER REED WARNER

Warner & Swasey Company stands pre-eminent, having designed
and constructed the mountings for the largest refracting tele-
scopes in the world, including those at the Washington Naval,
the Lick and Yerkes Observatories, others as notable for the
Canadian government and many lesser equipments for college
observatories generally.

Mr. Warner is a leading figure in the business, financial and general community life of Cleveland. In that connection he is vice-president of the Society for Savings, director of the Guardian Trust Company, member of the Advisory Board of the Citizens Savings & Loan Company, trustee of Case School of Applied Science, Adelbert College, Western Reserve University and the Cleveland School of Art; member of the Advisory Board of the Art Museum and past president of the Cleveland Chamber of Commerce. Also he is a charter member and past president of the American Society of Mechanical Engineers, member of the British Astronomical Society and the American Astronomical and Astro-physical Society and Fellow of the Royal Astronomical Society and the American Association for the Advancement of Science. He has received the unusual degree of Doctor of Mechanical Science, is a Republican in politics and an elder in the Second Presbyterian Church of Cleveland. His clubs are the Union, University, Rowfant and Engineers', of Cleveland, and the Engineers' and Sleepy Hollow Country, of New York.

Mr. Warner has traveled extensively and, in 1916, endowed the Worcester R. Warner Collection of Oriental Art in the Art Museum of Cleveland.

He inherited the tall stature, large physique and sturdy health typical of the descendants of Andrew Warner. His birthplace in Cummington, still owned by the family, was built by his great-great-grandfather in 1779 and contains interesting relics of Revolutionary days. Also he can claim direct descent, in several lines, from Mayflower ancestry.

Mr. Warner married in Cleveland, June 26, 1890, **CORNELIA FRALEY BLAKEMORE,** born in Philadelphia, July 27, 1859, daughter of Thomas Fayette and Susan Payne (Bayly) Blakemore, originally of Virginia. She was graduated from the Chestnut Street Seminary *(now Ogonz School), Philadelphia, in 1887, prepared for Harvard Examinations under private tutors, was teacher in and, later, associate principal of a well-known private school for girls, in Cleveland. Before her marriage Mrs. Warner was active in the Episcopal and, later, in the Presbyterian Church, and has always been deeply interested in educational and philanthropic movements, both local and national.

Children

Worcester Reed Warner, b. Mar. 21, 1892; d. Feb. 12, 1897.
Helen Blakemore Warner, b. Aug. 2, 1894.
Marion Holbrook Warner, b. Sept. 16, 1898; d. Feb. 21, 1900.

577 SUSAN LAVINIA[8] WARNER, daughter of Franklin John[7] and Vesta ·Wales (Reed) Warner, born in Cummington, Mass., June 18, 1854; resided in Brockport, N. Y., later in Montclair, N. J.
Married November 28, 1882, CHARLES D. SEELY, born at Warsaw, N. Y., July 20, 1853, son of George Washington and Mary Jane (Munger) Seely; died at Brockport, N. Y., May 22, 1915. He was professor of Latin and Greek in the State Normal School at Brockport, N. Y., from 1885 until his death.

Children

Bertha Warner Seely, b. in Cummington, Mass., Sept. 19, 1883; m. May 18, 1916, at Montclair, N. J., George Quincy Dunlop, b. Jan. 31, 1869, at Ventnor, Ontario, Canada, son of James and Jane (Henderson) Dunlop. Bertha W. Seely was educated at the Brockport Normal School and at Bryn Mawr College, A.B., 1905; was private secretary at Bryn Mawr College, 1905-07; secretary of Horace Mann School, New York City, 1907-12; secretary, Department of Conventions and Conferences, National Board of Y. W. C. A., New York City, 1912-16; resided in New York City and Montclair, N. J., now in Indianapolis, Ind.; member of the Congregational Church. Child: Evelyn Cornelia, b. Apr. 14, 1917, in Williams Bay, Wis.
Evelyn Elizabeth Seely, b. in Brockport, N. Y., June 9, 1888; m. June 29, 1911, at Brockport, N. Y., Lambert Lincoln Jackson, b. Apr. 14, 1870, at Binghamton, N. Y., son of Benjamin and Evaline (Bunker) Jackson. They reside in Montclair, N. J. Child: Alan Seely, b. June 1, 1918. Evelyn E. Seely was educated at the Brockport Normal School and at Bryn Mawr College, A.B., 1910. Member of Baptist Church.
Charles Warner Seely, b. Nov. 25, 1893, in Brockport, N. Y.; m. July 30, 1918, at New York City, Emma Pennington Lester, daughter of William Christie and Agnes (Pennington) Lester. Charles Warner Seely was educated at the Horace Mann School, New York City, and at Amherst College. He entered business with the Warner and Swasey Company, manufacturers of machine tools, Cleveland, Ohio, in Jan., 1913, remaining until Apr., 1917, when he accepted a position with the War Industries Board, in Washington, D. C. In Oct., 1917, he was commissioned as First Lieutenant in the Ordnance Reserve Corps, United States Army, and sailed for overseas service in Aug., 1918. Member of Presbyterian Church.

578 WALTER HOLBROOK[8] WARNER, son of Sumner Holbrook[7] and Sarah Elizabeth (Chappell)) Warner, born in Meriden, Conn., August 20, 1855; resides in Springfield, Mass., where Mr. Warner was engaged in the business of engraving and die-sinking until 1913, when he was succeeded by his son.
Married in Springfield, February 27, 1878, HARRIET JEANNETTE COOLEY, daughter of R. M. Cooley of Springfield.

Children

Raymond Cooley Warner, b. Aug. 30, 1880; resides in Springfield; m. June 15, 1905, Sarah Beatrice Welch of West Granville, Mass. Children: i. Beatrice Fayoline, b. Apr. 24, 1906. ii. Raymond Cooley, b. Nov. 6, 1907. iii. Harriet Welch, b. Nov. 7, 1909; d. Nov. 21, 1910.
Fayoline Jeannette Warner, b. July 1, 1885; d. Oct. 21, 1887.
Sarah Madeleine Warner, b. Sept. 17, 1888; m. Apr. 15, 1916, Archibald Gardner Fletcher.

579 ALMON[8] WARNER, son of Norton Dexter[7] and Silena (Shaw) Warner, born in Palmyra, Mich., January 31, 1834; died March 1, 1886.
Married January 17, 1866, PHEBE J. GOULD. She resides with her son in Adrian, Mich.

Children

Julia A. Warner, b. Dec. 9, 1866; m. June 23, 1892, Merrett A. Lemm. Children: i. Kenneth Almon, b. Oct. 2, 1893. ii. Maud Adell, b. June 9, 1895. iii. Myrle Silena, b. Oct. 2, 1897. iv. Forest Warner, b. Nov. 10, 1900.
James Norton Warner, b. Mar. 31, 1868; m. Feb. 20, 1890, Jennie Soper; resides in Adrian, Mich. Children: i. Leonard Almon, b. Dec. 24, 1892. ii. James Guy, b. June 20, 1894. iii. Burrell Hulsey, b. Feb. 17, 1896. iv. Charles Lowell, b. July 6, 1899. v. Cassius Merril, b. Apr. 14, 1901; d. Oct. 5, 1901.
Silena A. Warner, b. May 23, 1875; d. Aug. 16, 1895, not married.

580 GEORGE SHAW[8] WARNER, son of Norton Dexter[7] and Silena (Shaw) Warner, born in Palmyra, Mich., June 17, 1846; died at Alum Springs, Va., August 23, 1880.
Married in 1873, LILLIAN MILLER.

Children

Blanche E. Warner, b. Jan. 30, 1874; m. Edwin C. Hague, son of S. M. Hague. Children: i. Grace Lillian. ii. Sinclair Miller, b. May 7, 1896. iii. Clive, b. Mar. 21, 1897.
Grace Mary Warner, b. Jan. 30, 1876; m. Jan. 30, 1901, Charles A. North, son of William C. North. Child: Anna Dix, b. Apr. 24, 1902.
George Shaw Warner, Jr., b. Sept. 10, 1878.

581 WILLIAM C.[8] WARNER, son of Lucius[7] and Lydia (Whitmarsh) Warner, born in Palmyra, Mich., November 30, 1851; died in Fort Scott, Kans., April 9, 1916. After 1891, he resided in Fort Scott, where he was cashier and chief clerk of the Missouri Pacific Railway, and, until recently, of the St. Louis and San Francisco Railroad. He was a member of

the United Workmen, Modern Woodmen, and Knights and Ladies of Security. For many years he was a director of the Y. M. C. A., and a deacon in the Baptist Church. At the time of his death he was senior deacon. "His life in private and in public was that of a consistent Christian, sensitive to all his obligations to society and government and his God." Married May 22, 1873, **MARY E. ELLIS,** daughter of Hiram and Hester (————) Ellis of Blissfield, Mich.

Children

Cassius E. Warner, b. Mar. 22, 1874; m. Sept. 17, 1902, Ada B. Cormany of Fort Scott, Kans., daughter of William and Susan (————) Cormany. Children: i. Richard C., b. July 30, 1903. ii. Grace, b. May 4, 1906.

Clarence S. Warner, b. Feb. 23, 1876; d. Aug. 12, 1876.

Lorena E. Warner, b. Feb. 20, 1879.

582 WILLIAM ARTHUR LEWIS[8] WARNER, son of Orrin[7] and Mary Elizabeth (Eastwood) Warner, born in Hillsdale, Mich., August 7, 1869; resides in New Decatur, Ala., the name of which was changed to Albany in 1912. Mr. Warner is a member of the Masonic order, has been Postmaster, Fire Chief, and Chairman of the Republican County Committee. Married in New Decatur, February 28, 1889, **LETTIE W. GRABER** of Indiana. Mrs. Warner is Worthy Matron of Mizpah Chapter, Order of the Eastern Star at Albany and takes an active part in the affairs of that organization.

Children

Grace Eastwood Warner, b. Jan. 8, 1890; resides in Albany, Ala. She was educated at Athens (Ala.) Female College, Martin College in Pulaski, Tenn., and was graduated from Wheeler Business College in Birmingham, Ala.

Gladys Davenport Warner, b. Mar. 3, 1893; d. of typhoid fever in Riverside Hospital, Charleston, S. C., Aug. 6, 1914. She was educated at New Decatur High School and Martin College, and was considered a very beautiful girl. She had a most winning personality and won hosts of friends, although quiet in manner. She was married Sept. 18, 1913, to Carl Brimhall of Indiana.

Harold William Warner, b. Jan. 21, 1895; d. Dec. 28, 1904.

Fay Orrin Warner, b. Nov. 10, 1899; d. Dec. 9, 1899.

Waldo Cecil Warner, b. and d. June 14, 1902.

583 NANCY[8] WARNER, daughter of Jonathan[7], 3d, and Nancy (Frethy) Warner, born April 18, 1808, in Jefferson, Ohio; died January 30, 1885, in Lenox, Ashtabula Co., Ohio. She had resided in Lenox and Ashtabula.

36

Married in Jefferson, April 27, 1825, **ARCHIBALD HOL-MAN,** born April 5, 1801, in Sandisfield, Mass.; died in Lenox, Ohio, July 6, 1877. He was the son of Thomas Holman, a Revolutionary soldier, and his wife, Huldah.

Children, born in Lenox

Andrew S. Holman, b. Aug. 26, 1826; was a volunteer in the Union army, 29th Regiment, from New Lyme, Ashtabula County; m. Kezia Gleason. A daughter is Ellen J. White of Sugar Creek, Pa.

Theodore E. Holman, b. May 18, 1828; d. in Thompson, Geauga Co., Ohio; m. in Lenox, Jan. 29, 1849, Maria H. Woodruff. A son, Stanley A. Holman, resides in Collinwood, Ohio.

Edward O. Holman, b. Apr. 21, 1831.

Phebe E. Holman, b. Mar. 7, 1833; d. in Fowler, Oto Co., Colo.; m. James F. Outt.

Almeda F. Holman, b. Oct. 27, 1836.

Ellen J. Holman, b. July 13, 1838; was a member of the D. A. R.; d. in Washington, D. C.; m. Morris Julius Foote of Washington.

Ruth N. Holman, b. Aug. 5, 1840; d. in Lenox, Apr. 21, 1880.

Jasper Orland Holman, b. May 10, 1842; m. (1) in Lenox, Sept. 5, 1872, Lydia Rebecca Bailey, b. in Lenox, Oct. 20, 1846, d. Dec. 12, 1903, daughter of David L. and Almira (Woodruff) Bailey; m. (2) in Rock Creek, Ohio, Dec. 25, 1904, Emma A. Clark. Children by first wife, b. in Lenox: i. David Archibald, b. Nov. 21, 1873; resides in East Cleveland, Ohio; m. in Jefferson, May 6, 1901, Althea May Aten, b. in Williamsfield, Ohio, Mar. 1, 1877, daughter of John G. and Mary Louise (Belknap) Aten. ii. Howard Bailey, b. June 24, 1875; is a machinist; resides in Cleveland, Ohio; m. there, Sept. 12, 1906, Lottie Edna Martin, b. in Cleveland, Oct. 4, 1881, daughter of Joseph Francis and Emily Hepsibah (Young) Martin; has a son Ford Martin, b. in Cleveland, Nov. 12, 1907. iii. Ruth, b. Aug. 24, 1882.

Lydia S. Holman, b. Dec. 31, 1843; d. in Independence, Kans., June 28, 1914; m. —— Juett, who resides in Independence.

584 JONATHAN[8] **WARNER, 4th,** son of Jonathan[7], 3d, and Nancy (Frethy) Warner, born September 7, 1812, in Jefferson, Ohio; died there, March 3, 1888. He was a farmer in Jefferson.

Married (1) in Kinsman, Trumbull Co., Ohio, November 13, 1839, **LYDIA ALLEN,** born in Kinsman; died November 2, 1843.

Married (2) in Cherry Valley, Ashtabula Co., Ohio, January 15, 1848, **KATHERINE KRUM,** born February 22, 1821, in Manheim, Herkimer Co., N. Y., died December 23, 1885, daughter of John Peter and Sarah (Trowbridge) Krum.

Children by second wife, born in Jefferson

Flora Isabel Warner, b. Dec. 19, 1850; resides in Jefferson; m. there, Jan. 8, 1895, Frank P. Ives, b. Apr. 3, 1852, in Geneva, Ashtabula

Co., Ohio, son of Edmund E. and Margaret (Turck) Ives. No children.

Lena Evelyn Warner, b. Mar. 13, 1858; resides in Jefferson; m. there, Mar. 17, 1885, John Clark Pritchard, b. June 5, 1858, in Nelson, Portage Co., Ohio, son of John and Eliza (Linzee) Pritchard. Children, b. in Jefferson: i. Emma Catherine, b. July 13, 1889. ii. Herbert Warner, b. July 17, 1892; resides in Ashtabula, Ohio; m. in Jefferson, Sept. 16, 1914, Edna Lyle Chapin. iii. John Harold, b. Sept. 26, 1895. iv. Mary Eliza, b. July 5, 1900; d. Sept. 7, 1900.

Howard Jonathan Warner, b. Feb. 28, 1860; resides in Jefferson; m. (1) in Jefferson, Oct. 22, 1885, Nettie Frances Ryder, b. in Jefferson, Nov. 7, 1863, d. Jan. 19, 1889, daughter of Cecil S. and Almeda (Sherman) Ryder; m. (2) in Jefferson, Oct. 12, 1893, Lizzie Armenta Wilder, b. in Jefferson, June 18, 1861, daughter of Edward J. and Mary (Henry) Wilder. Child of first wife: Alice Catherine, b. in Jefferson, Oct. 26, 1886. She is assistant to the official stenographer of Jefferson.

585 PHEBE[8] WARNER, daughter of Jonathan[7], 3d, and Nancy (Frethy) Warner, born March 3, 1815, in Jefferson, Ohio; resided in Ravenna, Ohio, and died there, December 20, 1903.

Married in Jefferson, September 19, 1855, **JOHN B. KING,** born March 30, 1807, in Blandford, Mass., died in Ravenna, Ohio, 1864, son of William and Betsey (————) King.

Child

Flora Louisa King, b. Jan. 26, 1858; resides in Ravenna; m. in Cleveland, July 27, 1887, Thomas B. Alcorn. Children: i. William Brayton, b. Aug. 3, 1890, in Ravenna; m. there, June 30, 1915, Perlina Lucy White. ii. Harold King, b. in Pittsburgh, Pa., Nov. 22, 1892.

586 ADELINE[8] WARNER, daughter of Jonathan[7], 3d, and Nancy (Frethy) Warner, born January 20, 1818, in Jefferson, Ohio; died in Cleveland, Ohio, June 3, 1900. She was interested in the family history and furnished the records for her branch as given in the Ely Ancestry; a good account of this family is also published in Middletown Upper Houses. The family are members of the Episcopal Church.

Married in Jefferson, Ohio, May 1, 1839, **RUFUS PERCIVAL RANNEY,** born October 30, 1813, in Blandford, Mass.; died in Cleveland, December 6, 1891. He was the son of Rufus and Dolly D. (Blair) Ranney of Blandford; removed in 1824 to Freedom, Ohio; in 1836 to Jefferson; in 1845 to Warren; in 1856 to Cleveland. He was a lawyer and took an active part in political affairs. He was delegate to the Constitutional Convention of 1850; judge of the Supreme Court from 1851 to 1856, and from 1862 to 1864; was a candidate for member of Congress and governor of Ohio on the minority ticket but not elected.

Children

Richard W. Ranney, b. Mar. 5, 1840; d. July 26, 1840.
Howard Ranney, b. Sept. 7, 1841; d. Oct. 14, 1846.
Cornelia Ranney, b. Nov. 30, 1842; d. May 1, 1873; resided in New York City; m. T. Kelly Bolton and had two sons.
Charles Percival Ranney, b. Oct. 7, 1847; is an attorney in Cleveland; m. there, Feb. 12, 1873, Alice Gregory Benedict, b. in Cleveland, Dec. 12, 1851, daughter of Edwin G. and Philena (Osborn) Benedict. Children: i. Rufus Percival, b. May 24, 1874; resides in Cleveland; m. ——— Sawyer. ii. Cornelia Alice, b. July 6, 1875; m. Jan. 2, 1902, John Nelson Stockwell, Jr., b. in Cleveland, Apr. 11, 1872, son of John Nelson Stockwell, the astronomer, and his wife, Sarah Healey (see below). iii. Constance Ethel, b. Mar. 6, 1882, d. 1882. iv. Alice Elizabeth, b. Jan. 23, 1894. John Nelson Stockwell, Jr. (see above), was educated at Western Reserve University and Cornell University, 1895-7; is a lawyer in Cleveland; was member of the Legislature, 1906 to 1909. They have three children, Alice Kean, b. Feb. 18, 1903, Katherine Ranney, b. May 25, 1904, and John Nelson, 3d, b. Oct. 8, 1906, d. Dec. 2, 1906.
John Rufus Ranney, b. Oct. 5, 1851; d. in Cleveland, June 4, 1901, where he was a lawyer; m. in Cleveland, Nov. 17, 1881, Mary Luggett, b. in Cuyahoga Falls, Ohio, daughter of David Luggett who was born in Scarborough, England, and his wife, Sarah Elizabeth Page. They had no children.
Harriet L. Ranney, b. Aug. 20, 1859; d. May 18, 1868.

587 JANE[8] WARNER, daughter of Jonathan[7], 3d, and Nancy (Frethy) Warner, born July 8, 1820, in Jefferson, Ohio; died September, 1892. Resided in Canfield, Hudson and Morgan, Ashtabula County, and later in Lenox with her sister.
Married October 20, 1841, GEORGE STARR, born September 21, 1816, in Danbury, Conn.; died May 27, 1875. He was the son of Comfort and Abigail (Barnum) Starr. He is described as "a tailor by trade, a farmer by practice, and a constable by election; class leader and steward in the Meth odist Church."

Children

Ellen Louise Starr, b. Apr. 19, 1843; d. Feb. 28, 1862.
Mary Jane Starr, b. July 6, 1845; d. Feb. 15, 1862.
Ann Eliza Starr, b. Aug. 25, 1847; resides at Hart's Grove, Ashtabula County; m. Oct. 1, 1868, Austin J. Hyde, b. Sept., 1847, in Bristol, Ohio. Children: i. Arthur Henry, b. Mar. 29, 1870. ii. Minnie Belle, b. Mar. 14, 1873; d. same day. iii. Flora May, b. Feb. 12, 1875.
Orlando Comfort Starr, b. May 26, 1850, in Morgan, Ohio; resides there, near East Trumbull; farmer and teacher of penmanship; m.

Apr. 18, 1872, Mary J. Scouton, b. in Cazenovia, N. Y., Nov. 24, 1852, daughter of Elias O. and Mary J. (Hubbard) Scouton. Children: i. Ethel Lamont, b. Oct. 14, 1873. ii. George William, b. Feb. 9, 1876. *Alice Isabelle Starr*, b. Apr. 20, 1853; d. Jan. 27, 1854.

588 LOUISA[8] **WARNER**, daughter of Jonathan[7], 3d, and Nancy (Frethy) Warner, born January 4, 1823, in Jefferson, Ohio; died January 1, 1899.
Married February 6, 1844, **CHARLES S. SIMONDS** of Jefferson.

Children, born in Jefferson

Charles Henry Simonds, b. Nov. 19, 1844; m. Feb. 11, 1915, Kathleen Willard.

Albert Gallatin Simonds, b. Nov. 20, 1846; m. May, 1887, Mary Carnahan. Children, b. in Minneapolis, Minn.: i. Sarah Louise, b. Sept. 13, 1888. ii. Charles Albert, b. Nov., 1889; d. 1891. iii. Albert Carnahan, b. Apr., 1892. iv. James Warner, b. Jan., 1894.

Louisa Maria Simonds, b. Feb. 18, 1849; m. Aug. 12, 1869, Edward C. Wade. Children, b. in Jefferson: i. Alice Louise, b. Sept. 3, 1870; m. Oct. 23, 1899, Dorland W. McBride, and had three children, b. in Conneaut, Ohio: Margaret Louise, b. Aug. 27, 1900, Emily Cadwell, b. Oct. 15, 1901, and Mary Ranney, b. July 5, 1903, d. Oct., 1905. ii. Grace Emily, b. June 4, 1877. iii. Charles Simonds, b. Dec. 8, 1882.

Adaline Warner Simonds, b. Dec. 23, 1851; resides in Ravenna, Ohio; m. Sept. 22, 1904, Clinton C. Canfield.

William Rufus Simonds, b. Dec. 22, 1853; d. Jan. 27, 1854.

Phebe Amelia Simonds, b. Apr. 21, 1862; m. Feb. 19, 1889, B. F. Beardsley.

589 GEORGE W.[8] **WARNER**, son of Jonathan[7], 3d, and Nancy (Frethy) Warner, born April 24, 1825, in Jefferson, Ohio; was killed in an accident in Wallula, Wash., March 22 or 25, 1877. He was a farmer and stock raiser.
Married in Lenox, Ashtabula Co., Ohio, November 7, 1872, **MATILDA BURDETT**, born in Austinburg, Ashtabula Co., Ohio, daughter of Thomas and Jane (————) Burdett, who were born in England. She resides in Wallula.

Children, born in Wallula

Jessie Louise Warner, b. Oct. 15, 1873; resides in Wallula; m. in Ashtabula, Ohio, Nov. 30, 1899, Gustav A. Kuhlenkamp, b. in Germany, Jan. 15, 1876, son of John and Doris (————) Kuhlenkamp. He is a farmer in Wallula. Children: i. Mabel Martha, b. Apr. 2, 1902. ii. Cathrina Wilhelmina, b. Jan. 31, 1906. iii. Henry George, b. Nov. 6, 1908. iv. Alma Isabelle, b. June 22, 1912.

George Warner, b. Dec. 9, 1875; is a farmer in Wallula; m. in Wallula, Nov. 9, 1898, Velida Gertrude Lambdin, b. July 4, 1873, in

Milton, Ore., daughter of Samuel and Mary Elizabeth (————)
Lambdin. Children, b. in Wallula: i. Elsie Pearl, b. Oct. 15, 1899.
ii. Verna Lucile, b. Aug. 7, 1901. iii. Evangeline, b. Jan. 6, 1904.
iv. Lila Rowenna, b. Apr. 7, 1906. v. Ada Elaine, b. Jan. 3, 1908. vi.
Ruth Louise, b. Dec. 4, 1910. vii. George L., b. June 27, 1913. viii.
Blanche (twin), b. Dec. 25, 1914; d. Jan. 1, 1915. ix. Beatrice
(twin), b. Dec. 25, 1914; d. Jan. 25, 1915.

590 ISABELLE⁸ WARNER, daughter of Jonathan⁷, 3d,
and Nancy (Frethy) Warner, born June 5, 1827, in Jefferson,
Ohio; died in Cleveland, May 23, 1913.
Married (1) November 14, 1848, MONROE C. MOORE of
Greenville, Pa., who died October 5, 1850.
Married (2) October 10, 1855, JOHN DUCRO, born March
22, 1824, in St. Wendel, Germany; died in Ashtabula, Ohio,
December 4, 1904.

Children by second husband

Carolyn Ducro, b. 1856; d. 1877.
Willie Ducro, b. 1858; d. 1865.
Katherine Ducro, b. 1861; m. Aug. 20, 1879, Lucien Seymour. Child:
Carrie, b. July 28, 1881; m. Mar. 23, 1901, James de Nio, and has
two children, Virginia, b. Apr. 19, 1902, and Isabel, b. Dec. 14, 1903.
Anna L. Ducro, b. 1863; m. Jan. 22, 1885, John C. Crosby; resides in
Pittsburgh, Pa. Children: i. Flora Isabel, b. Apr. 20, 1886. ii.
Edward Lewis, b. Apr. 6, 1888; is Captain in the Ordnance Department, U. S. R., located at Washington, D. C. (Apr., 1918); m. Oct.
2, 1916, Louise McGonigle Nelson. iii. Lily Catherine, b. Apr. 14,
1890; m. in Pittsburgh, Oct. 1, 1913, James Oliver Challinor of Pittsburgh, and has a daughter, Anne, b. Sept. 30, 1915. iv. Marian, b.
Jan. 22, 1898.
John P. Ducro, b. Dec. 20, 1865; m. (1) Oct., 1890, Mary Niles, who
d. Sept., 1892; m. (2) 1897, Carrie Butz. Children by second wife:
i. Genevra, b. Aug. 1, 1900. ii. John, b. Nov. 22, 1902; iii. Frederick,
b. Nov. 24, 1904.
Edward G. Ducro, b. 1867; m. (1) Sept. 1888, Gertrude Fish, who
d. Feb., 1893; m. (2) Oct. 15, 1895, Mary Eames. Children by
second wife: i. Isabel, b. Aug. 5, 1896. ii. George, b. Feb., 1899.
Albert Ducro (twin), b. Dec. 24, 1869; d. aged 9 months.
Ferdinand Ducro (twin), b. Dec. 24, 1869; d. aged 5 years.
Ellen Ducro, b. 1871; d. aged 9 months.

591 FRANCIS H.⁸ WARNER, son of Jonathan⁷, 3d, and
Nancy (Frethy) Warner, born May 27, 1831, in Jefferson, Ohio;
died January 20, 1904; resided in Carver, Carver Co., Minn.
He attended Jefferson Academy and Grand River Institute;
was admitted to the bar at Warren, Trumbull Co., Ohio, in
1854; went to St. Paul the following year but removed soon
to Shakopee and practiced four years; settled in Carver in

1859. He was a member of the Constitutional Convention from Scott County; county attorney, 1862-8; elected judge of probate, 1877.
Married June 18, 1859, JANE MITCHELL.

Children (one died young)

Adaline C. Warner, b. 1860.
Francis H. Warner, Jr., b. 1862; resides at Valley City, N. D.
Phebe J. Warner, b. 1869.
Jane S. Warner, b. 1877.

592 CHARLES ELY⁸ WARNER, son of Jonathan⁷, 3d, and Nancy (Frethy) Warner, born May 21, 1834, in Jefferson, Ohio; died there, February 6, 1906. He was a farmer in Jefferson Borough.
Married at Rock Creek, Ohio, October 23, 1867, ELIZABETH MARY BUTCHER, born March 5, 1847, in Ashburton, Devonshire, England, daughter of Thomas and Betsey (Kerton) Butcher.

Children, born in Jefferson

Marion Elizabeth Warner, b. Oct. 16, 1868, in Jefferson; resides in Lawrence, Mich.; m. in Jefferson, May 14, 1891, John Chester Stafford, B.S. (Michigan Agricultural College), 1888; b. in Ashtabula, Ohio, June 11, 1866, son of Jonathan and Henrietta (McNutt) Stafford. Children, first three b. in Lawrence, Mich.: i. Charles Warner, b. Oct. 23, 1892; was graduated from Ohio State University with the degree of mining engineer; member of Sigma Xi; is now assistant superintendent of mines at Stone, Ky.; m. at Columbus, Ohio, July 20, 1916, Mae Jeannette Whipp; has a daughter, Ruth Jeannette, b. at Columbus, Nov. 20, 1917. ii. James McNutt, b. Oct. 2, 1894; was educated at Michigan Agricultural College. iii. Elizabeth May, b. June 6, 1896; graduate of Ypsilanti Normal; teacher at East Tawas, Mich. iv. Henrietta Maude, b. Jan. 9, 1899, in Keeler, Mich.; graduate of Lawrence High School.
Cornelia A. Warner, b. Dec. 20, 1869; is an attorney at law and deputy clerk of Ashtabula County, Ohio; resides in Jefferson.

593 SARAH C.⁸ WARNER, daughter of Ely⁷ and Sarah Ward⁸ (Warner) Warner, born July 27, 1820, in Haddam, Conn.; died in Chester, Conn., March 27, 1892.
Married November 12, 1848, DANIEL DAVIS SILLIMAN, born July 10, 1816, died April 22, 1898, son of Samuel and Anne Hannah (Shipman) Silliman, and grandson of Thomas and Lydia⁶ (Warner) Silliman; see number 243. He was engaged with his father and brothers in the manufacture of glass-lined wooden inkstands for counting houses and schools, an invention

of their own which had an extensive sale all over the United States. During the Civil War they manufactured pocket inkstands that were purchased by the soldiers. So numerous were the orders that they were obliged to run day and night. In later years, as customs changed, their business became less brisk.

Mr. Silliman was first selectman for many years; member of the Legislature in 1877; a member of the school board from 1872 to 1875; led the choir in the Congregational Church for several years; organized the Chester Drum Corps in 1868 and remained a member until his strength failed; taught several bands and led them with his favorite instrument, the bugle. Of him it was said, "Loved and respected by all who knew him, in his death Chester lost a valuable citizen, and its people, a good friend."

Children, born in Chester

Frederick William Silliman, b. May 7, 1850; resides in Chester; m. Sept. 26, 1877, Mary Elizabeth Fargo, b. June 29, 1855, daughter of Asa Fargo of Chester. Children: i. Kate Lucinda, b. Jan. 27, 1879. ii. Vinnie Elizabeth, b. Aug. 1, 1880; resides in Chester; m. Apr. 9, 1902, Arthur A. Devoe, b. Feb. 1, 1877, in New York City, and has three children, Joseph Stanbury, b. Feb. 11, 1904, Bernell Frederick, b. Feb. 4, 1907, and Ellis Arthur, b. Aug. 16, 1915. iii. Sarah Fargo, b. Sept. 21, 1881; resides in Chester; m. Frederick C. Buckingham; has a child, Mary Frederica, b. May 3, 1915. iv. Louise Adele, b. Mar. 23, 1883; resides in Chester; m. George Bole; has two children, Adele Silliman, b. June 17, 1908, and Norma Elizabeth, b. Feb. 11, 1911. v. William F., b. Nov. 22, 1884. vi. Thomas C. d. young. vii. Louis Ayer, b. June 14, 1887; resides in Chester; m. Emma Harris of New York; has five children, Horace Frederick, b. Sept. 16, 1905, Helen Marguerite, b. May 18, 1907, Thelma Jessie, b. May 21, 1909, Dorothy Ruth, b. Dec. 12, 1911, and Edith Claire, b. Mar. 20, 1913. viii. Benjamin Harrison, b. Nov. 15, 1888; m. Apr. 27, Janette Taylor of Poquonock, Conn.; resides in Poquonock. ix. Leda Ruth, b. Nov. 23, 1889; m. at Deep River, Sept. 15, 1915, William Joseph Messenger; resides in New Haven. x. Raymond Davis, b. July 13, 1892; m. May 27, 1916, Susan Avis of New Haven; resides in New Haven.

Bessie (or *Sarah Anna*) *Silliman,* b. Apr. 11, 1852; d. Oct. 6, 1873; m. Nov. 13, 1872, Samuel Smith Webb, b. at Whig Hill, Chester, son of Philip S. Webb. No children. He m. (2) Mrs. Hattie (Fox) Smith. Mr. Webb is an extensive farmer and has held many public offices, including those of constable and deputy sheriff.

Kate Warner Silliman, b. Sept. 12, 1856; m. Dec. 11, 1877, R. Clifford Tyler, b. in Chester, Dec. 11, 1853. Children: i. Carrie Silliman, m. Edward W. Clark of Chester. ii. Mildred J., m. Robert W. Abbey of Chester. iii. Franklin Warner, m. Elizabeth M. Crouch of Chester. iv. Frederick C. v. Bessie F.

Carrie Roberta Silliman, b. Aug. 15, 1858; d. Jan. 31, 1907, not married.

594 GEORGE WASHINGTON[8] WARNER, son of Ely[7] and Sarah Ward[8] (Warner) Warner, born February 8, 1827, in Haddam, Conn.; resides in Chester, Conn. He served in the Civil War as a musician in the 24th Connecticut Volunteers. He has been a teacher and is still living (1918) in Chester, Conn. Married in Middletown, Conn., November 9, 1860, **CLARA DRUSILLA WILCOX,** born November 9, 1840, in Haddam, daughter of Ebenezer and Alma Eliza (Hubbard) Wilcox; died March 2, 1913.

Children

Nellie Eudoria Warner, b. Aug. 2, 1861; d. Oct. 20, 1882, in Chester.
William Andrew Warner, b. Mar. 4, 1863, in Chester, and resides there; m. Sept. 29, 1899, Lillian B. Helwig, b. Mar. 5, 1876, d. Jan. 4, 1903. Child: Stanley Miller, b. Oct. 5, 1900.
Agnes Fidelia Warner, b. Jan. 12, 1865, in Chester; resides in Chester.
Lillian Alida Warner, b. in Chester, Feb. 23, 1867; resides in Rochester, N. Y.; m. (1) May 12, 1886, Isaiah Vars, b. July 20, 1858, d. Sept. 8, 1889, formerly of Niantic, R. I.; m. (2) in Cambridge, Mass., June 23, 1906, Harry Jeremiah Potter, b. in Bath, Maine, May 17, 1869, son of Jeremiah Pattee and Lettice Zoraida (Sanford) Potter. Child of Isaiah and Lillian (Warner) Vars: Ethel Dorothea, b. in Middletown, Conn., Apr. 15, 1887; m. Nov. 9, 1914, Andrew B. Potter of Newton, Mass., b. May 12, 1887, son of Charles S. and —— (Page) Potter, and has a son, Andrew B., b. Aug. 2, 1916.
Louis Ely Warner, b. June 19, 1870; resides in South Framingham, Mass.; m. June 5, 1902, Jessica Evelyn Knapp, b. Mar. 28, 1875. Child: Charles Deniston, b. Aug. 4, 1911.
Edith Adele Warner, b. May 30, 1872, in Chester; resides there; m. in Chester, Oct. 7, 1891, Edgar Wallace Smith, b. Apr. 19, 1858, in Chester, son of Julius and Lucinda (Dolph) Smith. Children, b. in Chester: i. Helen Warner, b. Aug. 30, 1892; d. Aug. 20, 1907. ii. Warner Gifford, b. May 6, 1894. iii. Norwood Stanley, b. Mar. 3, 1897.
Elsie Wilcox Warner, b. Nov. 24, 1884, in Chester; m. there, Oct. 7, 1913, Ernst Domansky Moore, b. in Boston, Mass., Jan. 18, 1884; resides in Chester, Conn. Children: i. Ely Warner, b. Sept. 29, 1914. ii. Edith Crawford, b. Feb. 22, 1916. iii. Richard Henry, b. Jan. 23, 1918.

595 HEPSIBAH ELY[8] WARNER, daughter of Ely[7] and Sarah Ward[8] (Warner) Warner, born in Haddam, Conn., May 16, 1832; died April 26, 1907, in Chester, Conn., where she had resided.
Married December 3, 1851, **HENRY SQUIRE RUSSELL,** born February 7, 1830, son of Samuel and Emerance (Squire) Russell of Chester.

Children

Frances Gertrude Russell, b. in Chester, Feb. 13, 1853; resides in Providence, R. I.; m. (1) June 2, 1875, Josiah Emerson Westcott,

b. Dec. 29, 1828, d. Mar. 23, 1891; m. (2) Apr. 28, 1903, James B. Phetteplace of Providence, b. Apr. 22, 1832. Children by first husband: i. Harrison Russell, b. Apr. 24, 1876; m. (1) Oct. 8, 1903, Eileen Perry Sammis of Providence, b. Aug. 28, 1875, d. Dec. 28, 1907; m. (2) Mar. 5, 1912, Mary Garfield Smith of Providence, b. June 20, 1881; resides in Hyde Park, Mass. ii. Leslie Peckham, b. June 2, 1880; resides in Pawtucket, R. I.; m. Sept. 5, 1906, Carrie Adams of Pawtucket, b. Dec. 7, 1881; has children, Olive Harrison, b. May 29, 1907, Geneva, b. June 11, 1910, and Robert Adams, b. Feb. 11, 1914.

Caroline Squire Russell, b. in Chester, July 10, 1854. Miss Russell resides in the old Judge Warner house in Chester.

596 ANNIE LOUISE[8] **WARNER**, daughter of Ely[7] and Sarah Ward[8] (Warner) Warner, born in Chester, May 30, 1838; died April 25 or 27, 1905, in Chester, Conn., where she had resided.

Married February 20, 1869, **JARVIS V. SMITH**, born April 22, 1840, died February 20, 1907, son of Joseph and Charlotte (Ray) Smith.

Children

Jared Ely Smith, b. in Chester, Oct. 3, 1871; resides in New Haven, Conn.; m. Phoebe Gladding.

Susie Smith, b. in Chester, June 11, 1872; m. Oct. 27, 1897, George Wilcox of Chester, b. Sept. 4, 1872. Child: Vernon Smith, b. Aug. 21, 1908.

Jonathan Warner Smith, b. Jan. 25, 1875; resides in Chester; m. Sept. 9, 1907, Annie Bott of Gloucester, Mass.

Amy Smith, b. Apr. 15, 1877.

Jasper Andrew Smith, b. Sept. 15, 1880; resides in Chester; m. May 25, 1910, Lillie Belle Holden of Chester, b. Oct. 30, 1892; has children, Louise Holden, b. Mar. 26, 1911, and Jarvis Elmer, b. Apr. 4, 1913.

Jerome V. Smith, b. Jan. 9, 1883; d. Sept. 4, 1885.

597 AMELIA CHAMPLIN[8] **WARNER**, daughter of Sam uel Selden[7] and Abigail (Champlin)) Warner, born August 24, 1820, in Hadlyme, Conn.; died February 21, 1896, in Washington, D. C.

Married September 21, 1840, **MORRISON REMICK WAITE**, born in Lyme, Conn., November 9, 1816; died March 23, 1888, during a term of his court. He was the son of Henry Matson and Maria (Selden) Waite, and was descended from Thomas Waite, Jr., who was born in Watertown, Mass., in 1677, and married Mary Bronson, a granddaughter of the first Matthew Griswold. Henry Matson Waite was the son of Colonel Richard Waite, and the grandson of Colonel Samuel Waite. Morrison R. Waite was graduated from Yale

College in 1837, and studied law with his father who was at the time Judge of the Supreme Court of Errors. In 1838 he removed to Ohio and was admitted to the bar in 1839. He practiced law in Maumee City, 1839 to 1850, and Toledo from 1800 to 1874. In 1849 he was elected to the State Legislature. In 1871 he was one of the Counsel of the United States before the Tribunal of Arbitration at Geneva, under the treaty of Washington for the settlement of claims for depredations by the Confederate cruiser "Alabama"; in 1873 was unanimously elected by both parties as a member of the Convention to amend the Constitution of Ohio, and was made its president; in January, 1874, was nominated and confirmed as Chief Justice of the Supreme Court of the United States, taking the oath of office on March 4th. In 1875, when some of his friends in Ohio proposed that he should consent to be a candidate for the Presidency, he wrote a letter declining the honor and his opinions on the subject were universally applauded throughout the country. He was distinguished during his whole career for his strict probity and integrity of character.

Children

Henry Selden Waite, b. July 18, 1841; d. Apr. 10, 1873; m. Aug. 10, 1865, Ione Brown. Children: i. Morrison Remick, b. Dec. 13, 1866. ii. Henry Matson, b. May 15, 1869. iii. Amelia Champlin, b. Feb. 2, 1872; d. July 31, 1875.

Christopher Champlin Waite, b. Sept. 24, 1843; m. Oct. 22, 1868, Lillie P. Guthrie. Children: i. Henry Selden, b. May 4, 1874. ii. Ellison, b. Mar. 8, 1880.

George Francis Waite, b. Apr. 27, 1845; d. Jan. 20, 1846.

Edward Tinker Waite, b. Oct. 16, 1846, in Toledo, Ohio; d. Dec. 23, 1889, in Washington, D. C. He was a lawyer in Toledo. Married Oct. 29, 1873, Anna Chadwick Brainerd, b. Aug. 30, 1848, in Lyme, Conn., daughter of Davis Smith and Ann Maria (Chadwick) Brainerd. Children: i. (Daughter), b. and d. July 31, 1874. ii. Mary Gloyd, b. Jan. 27, 1877. iii. Brainerd, b. May 22, 1881.

Mary Frances Waite, b. 1847.

598 SAMUEL SELDEN⁸ WARNER, JR., son of Samuel Selden⁷ and Azubah (Tully) Warner, born December 17, 1827, in Hadlyme, Conn.; died November 3, 1887, in Toledo, Ohio. He went to sea as a young man, was first mate, then captain on the line of packets which crossed the ocean to Liverpool and Havre before the days of steamships. About 1860 he went into the United States Revenue Marine Service and was a captain in that service from the early sixties until his death in 1887.

Married in Cuyahoga Falls, Ohio, January 5, 1853, **HARRI-ETTE NEWELL GAYLORD,** born in Middletown, Conn.,

June 13, 1829, daughter of Samuel and Fanny (Starr) Gaylord. After his death she resided in North Brookfield, Mass., with her daughter, Mary.

Children

Samuel Selden Warner, 3d, b. July 12, 1854, recorded in Middletown, Conn., parents living in Lyme, Conn.; d. Sept. 3, 1854, in Cromwell, Conn.

Fannie Azubah Warner, b. Sept. 3, 1855, in Brooklyn, N. Y.; d. June 5, 1857, in Cromwell, Conn.

Frank Herbert Warner, b. Apr. 22, 1858, in Brooklyn, Eastern District; m. at Yalesville, Conn., Mar. 27, 1883, Mary Jane Pilkington, b. in Middletown, May 14, 1858. Children: i. Fannie Ione, b. Dec. 10, 1885, in Detroit, Mich. ii. Dorothy Jennie, b. Apr. 28, 1888, in Dayton, Ohio. iii. Bessie Marion, b. Apr. 1, 1890, in Toledo, Ohio.

Mary Gloyd Warner, b. Dec. 19, 1861, in Cromwell; resides in North Brookfield, Mass.

William Howard Warner, b. May 21, 1866, in Brooklyn, N. Y.; has resided in Lima, Ohio; m. in Ottawa, Ohio, Oct. 24, 1892, Mary Matilda Schreiber, b. in Napoleon, Ohio, May 25, 1868. Children, b. in Lima, Ohio: i. Lillian Maynard, b. Dec. 4, 1893. ii. Helen Grace, b. Aug. 5, 1897.

Clarence Devereaux Warner, b. May 4, 1870, in Castine, Maine; d. there, Sept. 26, 1870.

599 WILLIAM HENRY[8] WARNER, son of Andrew Ferdinando[7] and Lucinthia (Cone) Warner, born June 16, 1825, in East Haddam, Conn.; died in Seattle, Washington, September 1, 1897. He was a merchant, residing in Haddam, Hartford and New York City, and removed to Seattle, where he died. He was a member of the Union League Club and New England Society.

Married in New York City, November 2, 1852, ANNA PAMELA CONGER, born November 25, 1830, in Montgomery, Orange Co., N. Y., daughter of Joshua and Maria (Luqueer) Conger.

Children

Selden Waite Warner, b. Feb. 2, 1854, in New York City; is a travelling salesman in New York City; resides in Orange, N. J. He is the possessor of the manuscript book of Warner records collected by his uncle, Andrew Ferdinando Warner, which, with his own corrections and additions, he has allowed us to use in compiling this volume. Mr. Warner was married in Toledo, Ohio, Dec. 4, 1883, to Harriet Eliza Brown. Children: i. Selden Gloyd, b. Dec. 8, 1884. ii. Josephine, b. Nov. 11, 1891.

Kate Schuyler Warner, b. Oct. 21, 1855; resides in Brooklyn, N. Y.; m. Oct. 11, 1877, Charles F. Guyon. Children: Ethel Warner; Kate Rich.

Edwin Hall Warner, b. Feb. 21, 1858. He is a civil engineer, was connected with the Seattle, Lake Shore and Eastern Railway 'n

Seattle, is now in Los Angeles, Cal. Married in Seattle, Aug. 21, 1890, Frances Beatrice Genevieve Ferguson, b. at Tepic, State of Jalisco, Mexico, Aug. 10, 1868. No children.

Joseph Lowrey Warner, b. in Brooklyn, Eastern District, May 28, 1866; was graduated from the Columbia School of Mines, in 1887; was a mining engineer in Baker City, Ore.; is located in Seattle, Wash. (1916). Married (1) in Brooklyn, N. Y., Mar. 19, 1891, Marguerite Hayes of White River, Wash., who died Dec. 2, 1891; m. (2) in Oakland, Cal., July 25, 1896, Adelaide Amelia Coulpe, b. in Chicago, Apr. 3, 1874, from whom he was divorced; m. (3) Sept. 10, 1913, Catherine Livingston Catlin. He has no children.

Annie Kissam Warner, b. Dec. 28, 1867; resided at Short Hills, N. J.; m. Dec. 12, 1887, Parker D. Handy of New York City. Children: Cortlandt; Truman; Ruth.

RICHARD SELDEN WARNER

600 **RICHARD SELDEN**[8] **WARNER,** son of Richard[7] and Mary Millicent (Gilbert) Warner, born March 27, 1828, in East Haddam, Conn.; died in Springfield, Mass., November 16, 1908, buried with his wife in South Norwalk, Conn. He was living in Cromwell in 1858, and resided later in Meriden and Deep River, Conn.

Married in Norwalk, Conn., February 22, 1865, **EMMA AMELIA CRAW,** born June 14, 1835, in Minnepaw (South Norwalk), Conn., died in Norwich, Conn., March 13, 1915, daughter of Martin Street and Laura Ann (Bishop) Craw.

Children

Mary Gilbert Warner, b. Aug. 30, 1868, in Meriden, Conn.; m. in New Haven, Conn., Jan. 15, 1900, Robert I. Couch, who died in New Haven, July 6, 1902. No children. Mrs. Couch took up the study of osteopathy after her husband's death and practised in Philadelphia for several years; is now living in New York City.

Helen Amelia Warner, b. Feb. 5, 1871, in Deep River, Conn.; resides in Norwich, Conn.; m. in New Haven, Apr. 19, 1897, John G. Lyman. Children: i. John, b. Mar. 2, 1898. ii. Merton, b. Oct. 6, 1901. iii. Helen, b. Oct. 1, 1902. iv. Edward, b. Feb. 22, 1905.

Martin Richard Warner, b. Oct. 30, 1873, in Deep River, Conn.; resides in Springfield, Mass., where he is a die sinker in the United States Armory; m. in New Haven, June 20, 1900, Alice Isabelle Elkins, b. July 23, 1870, in New Haven, daughter of William Henry Harrison and Marietta Josephine (Steele) Elkins. Children, b. in Springfield: i. Dorothy, b. Oct. 22, 1907; d. June 13, 1913. ii. Elmer Elkins, b. Sept. 2, 1909. iii. Ralph Selden, b. Apr. 1, 1916.

601 SAMUEL GAYLORD[8] WARNER, son of Richard[7] and Mary (Gaylord) Warner, born September 12, 1848, in Cromwell, Conn.; resides in Kansas City, Mo., where he is general passenger and ticket agent for the Kansas City Southern Railway. His portrait will be found on page 414. Married April 1, 1875, in Aurora, Ind., ANNA PORTER LOZIER, born June 6, 1854, in Manchester, Ind., daughter of Abram and Lucinda (Pierce) Lozier.

Children

Helen Lozier Warner, b. Jan. 7, 1876, in Brooklyn, N. Y.; d. at South Hill, Essex Co., Va., Dec. 17, 1878.

Gaylord Warner, b. July 31, 1877, in Middletown, Conn.; resides in Minneapolis, Minn., where he is assistant general passenger agent for the Chicago, Rock Island and Pacific Railway; m. in Belton, Texas, Oct. 31, 1897, Letitia Stokes Brown of that place, b. Oct. 31, 1880, daughter of Richard Henry and Margaret (Friou) Brown. Children: i. Richard Gaylord, b. Oct. 23, 1898, in Tyler, Texas; enlisted as a volunteer Apr. 22, 1917, in the First Minnesota Field Artillery, which later became the 151st U. S. Field Artillery, a unit in the "Rainbow," or 42d Division. He was just completing his four years course in the West High School of Minneapolis at the time of his enlistment, and was presented with a diploma by the school on account of his voluntary enlistment and satisfactory standing. He went overseas in the middle of October, 1917, celebrating his nineteenth birthday on the way over. His battery landed October 30th. ii. Flo Lozier, b. Dec. 18, 1901, in Little Rock, Ark. The family are members of the Episcopal Church.

Anna Warner, b. Oct. 24, 1881, in Dunnsville, Va.; d. in Kansas City, Mo., Jan. 15, 1913; m. in 1907, Paul J. Leidigh. No children.

602 CHARLES CROCKER⁸ WARNER, son of Richard⁷ and Mary (Gaylord) Warner, born August 6, 1850, in Cromwell, Conn.; resides at Ware's Wharf, Essex Co., Va., where he is a farmer. His portrait appears on page 414.
Married in Midway, Essex Co., Va., April 13, 1882, KATHERINE WARING HOSKINS, born July 18, 1854, daughter of Captain John Thomas and Hannah E. (Ware) Hoskins of Virginia.

Children

Susie Ware Warner, b. at Belleview, Essex Co., Va., May 7, 1883; m. Dec. 15, 1909, William Arthur Maddox of Washington, D. C.; resides in New York City. Professor Maddox took the degree of B.A. at William and Mary College, Va., M.A. and Ph.D., at Columbia University, and is now assistant professor in the Department of Education at Teachers College, Columbia University. He is the author of "The Free School Idea in Virginia Before the Civil War," published in 1918.
Selden Richard Warner, b. Jan. 27, 1885; was graduated from William and Mary College, B.S., 1908; A.M., Cornell University; has been professor of biology in Sam Houston Normal Institute, Huntsville, Texas, since 1912; m. Aug 5, 1915, Grace Christian Miller, a graduate of the University of Tennessee. Child: Mary Gaylord, b. at Ithaca, N. Y., July 11, 1916.
John Thomas Warner, b. Apr. 13, 1887; d. Aug. 17, 1887.
Charles Andrew Warner, b. Apr. 20, 1888; was graduated from the Medical College of Virginia with the degree of D.D.S. in 1912; is a dentist and practises his profession at Tappahannock, Essex Co., Va.
Thomas Hoskins Warner, b. June 20, 1890; was graduated from Bethany College, W. Va., and was, for a time, a minister in the Christian Church; is now at Officers' Training Camp (October, 1918).

603 GUSTAVUS A.⁸ WARNER, son of John⁷ and Mehitabel (Clark) Warner, born August 26, 1817, in Chester, Conn.; died in Saybrook, 1863. He resided in Saybrook.
Married October 28, 1839, CLARISSA ELIZA TOWALL.

Child

John Jared Warner, b. Oct. 3, 1846; resided in Boston, Mass.; m. (1) 1872, Flora S. Leland of Oak Point, Maine, who died Oct. 3, 1888; m. (2) 1894, Emily Loverew, who died Feb., 1903. Children by first wife: i. Albert Leland, b. May 16, 1874; resides in Wollaston, Mass.; m. July 28, 1904, Elnora Blanche Taylor of Bridgewater, N. S., b. Sept. 16, 1885. ii. Daisy Ella, b. Nov. 24, 1876; has resided in Yonkers, N. Y.; m. June 25, 1902, Rev. Frederic Charles Harding of Fording Bridge, England, b. Feb. 28, 1873, and has a child, Frederic Warner, b. May 16, 1903. Child by second wife: Muriel Marian, b. July 19, 1897.

604 **DAVIS DIMOCK**[8] **WARNER,** son of Phineas[7] and Lydia (Clarke) Warner, born in Connecticut, February 1, 1802; died March 29, 1879, in Montrose, Pa. He removed with his father's family to Susquehanna County about 1810, and played an active part in the development of his community. He was for many years proprietor of the Franklin House. He was elected associate judge in 1851, and twice represented the district in the state legislature. While associate judge he attended the inauguration of President Buchanan and was one of those affected by the "National Hotel poisoning sickness," from which some of his friends from the same county died. Mr. Warner was in the state military service for some time and received the title of brigadier-general by which he was usually known. He was in command of the militia at the hanging of Treadwell, an occasion memorable in the history of Susquehanna County. General Warner was a communicant of St. Paul's Episcopal Church, a trustee of the Montrose Academy, and a member of the I. O. O. F.

Married (1) **MARY ANN RAYNSFORD,** daughter of Joshua W. Raynsford, who came from Windham County, Conn., in 1801, to Bridgewater township, Susquehanna County, and his wife, Hannah Lathrop, daughter of Walter Lathrop. She was a teacher in the Susquehanna County Academy before her marriage.

Married (2) **ALZINA (TROWBRIDGE) SMITH,** born in Great Bend, Pa., February 25, 1811, daughter of Lyman and Asenath (Blair) Trowbridge, and widow of Charles Smith of Great Bend.

Children, born in Montrose

Jared C. Warner, b. June 28, 1831; d. in Scranton, Pa., Aug. 25, 1910, where he had been a coal inspector and liveryman; m. Achsah Kingsley, who d. Nov. 19, 1891. Children: i. Fred, b. in Montrose, May 31, 1856. ii. Davis Dimock, b. in Montrose, June 1, 1860. iii. Harry, b. in Scranton, died.

687 *Ellen Warner,* b. Aug. 9, 1833; m. Henry Stark Searle.

688 *Ann Eliza Warner,* b. Dec. 5, 1834; m. Jerome Richards Lyons.

Edward Raynsford Warner, b. about 1836; was not married; d. in New York City, Jan. 2, 1905, buried in Montrose. He was appointed to the U. S. Military Academy in 1853 and was graduated as Second Lieutenant of Artillery four years later. During the Civil War he was Lieutenant Colonel of the 1st New York Artillery, was mustered out of the service in 1865, and soon after was assigned as a Captain to the 3d Artillery of the regular army. During the Civil War he distinguished himself by gallant conduct in the battles of the Wilderness and Gettysburg, and for his valor in the Petersburg operations he was brevetted a brigadier-general.

After military service of over thirty years he retired to his old home in Montrose. He left a large sum of money to found a public library and to erect a public building in Montrose.

Henry D. Warner, was a broker and member of the Produce Exchange in Chicago and d. there; m. Ellen Irene ————. Children: i. Charles, d. in Chicago. ii. Ellen. iii. Lillie. iv. Fannie. v. Irene. vi. Russell, d. in Chicago.

689 *Frederic Raynsford Warner*, b. Mar. 7, 1839; m. Euzelia McCollum. *Salome Warner*, was a teacher in Montrose before her marriage to Addison Watrous; died abroad, perhaps in Lucerne. *Delphine Warner*, b. Nov. 1, ————; resides in Denver, Colo.; m. Nov. 1, 1864, Edward J. Rogers. Child: Edith, b. Mar., 1867, in Montrose; m. C. Stuart Wallace and resides in Melbourne, Australia.

690 *Mary Frances Warner*, b. Apr. 7, 1848; m. Benjamin Franklin Stark.

605 NELSON CLARKE[8] WARNER, son of Phineas[7] and Lydia (Clarke) Warner, born in Deep River, Conn., 1804; died in Montrose, Pa., 1888. When four years of age he removed from Connecticut with his father's family to Susquehanna County, and spent most of his life as a farmer in Montrose. When a youth of sixteen he walked back to his native place, accomplishing the journey entirely on foot. He was sheriff of Susquehanna County from 1845 to 1848.

Married in 1831, **ELIZA D. BALDWIN** of Bridgewater, Pa., who died in 1884.

Children

Lydia F. Warner, b. about 1832; was mentioned in her father's will; m. Charles N. Stoddard, a merchant; resides in Montrose (1918); had six children, five of whom are dead.

Edson Scott Warner, b. May 27, 1834; resides in Montrose; was a captain in the Civil War from Montrose, Company K, 56th Pennsylvania Infantry; director in the First National Bank, Montrose, 1866; postmaster two terms; m. (1) Alice Burritt, divorced; m. (2) 1878, Frances M. Thompson of Owego, N. Y. Children: i. Charlotte Emily, b. 1879; m. 1906, Daniel Searle; has son, Daniel Warner, b. 1909. ii. Charles Thompson, b. 1881; not married. iii. Harold Edson, b. 1888; m. 1911, Lelia Italca Smith.

691 *Fletcher Gustavus Warner*, b. Jan. 25, 1837; m. (1) Martha M. Backus, (2) Mary Emily Bushnell.

692 *Charles Nelson Warner*, b. Apr. 19, 1839; m. Eliza Brown Houston. *Mary A. Warner*, died; m. George P. Little, who is now dead. Children: i. Ralph B., died in Montrose, June 16, 1916, aged 51; was appointed President Judge of the Court of Susquehanna County about 1908. ii. George, d. not married. iii. Anna, m. ———— Jeffus, and is divorced.

Emily A. Warner, b. 1845; d. 1914, not married.

Helen E. Warner, resides in Montrose; m. F. I. Lott, a lawyer; Child: Emily, m. Dr. Albert Earle Ainey, a dentist, and has two children, Helen Louise and Dorothy.

Sidney Warner, died.

37

NELSON CLARKE WARNER (NO. 605)

606 SIDNEY HASWELL⁸ WARNER, son of Phineas⁷ and Lydia (Clarke) Warner, born in Saybrook (Chester), Conn., January 26, 1806; died January 19, 1881. He removed to Bridgewater township, Susquehanna Co., Pa., with his parents in 1809. In his boyhood he helped his father clear his farm in the new country, early became a teacher and, among those fortunate enough to be his pupils, he had a lasting reputation for his learning and literary ability. While teaching he began the study of medicine and in 1836 he was licensed as a practitioner of medicine at Lenox, Mass. He soon removed to Huntington township, Lucerne Co., Pa., and took up his practice. The family have a commission from the Governor of Pennsylvania appointing him assistant surgeon in the militia, July 11, 1843. He spent most of his life in Huntington township and was prominent in his profession. The family were Baptists.

Married (1) October 1, 1835, **HANNAH LOOMIS** of Springfield, Pa., born in Claremont, N. H., July 8, 1808; died April 13, 1844, buried in Pine Grove Cemetery, Huntington township. She was the daughter of Horatio Porter Loomis.

Married (2) in Philadelphia, Pa., January 3, 1845, **CORNELIA MACHETTE,** born June 10, 1810; died May 9, 1897, buried in Pine Grove Cemetery. She was of French ancestry, the daughter of Samuel T. Machette, and his wife, Susan Nice, whose father was the founder of Nicetown, a suburb of Trenton, N. J.

Children by first wife

Geraldine Warner.
693 *Theodosia Warner,* m. Hiram Asa Park.
694 *Adelaide Warner,* b. May 2, 1839; m. Mark Lafayette Koons.
Hannah Warner, m. Dr. H. C. Bacon.
Jared Dimock Warner, resides in Shickshinny, Luzerne Co., Pa.

Child by second wife

695 *James Nelson Warner,* b. Dec. 5, 1845; m. Jennie Edith Stark.

607 ROXANA⁸ WARNER, daughter of David⁷ and Mary (Cone) Warner, born in Chester, Conn., October 17, 1802; died there, October 16, 1879.

Married September 24, 1822, **ELY DICKINSON,** born March 12, 1800; died March 18, 1880. He resided in Chester, but was of Haddam at the time of his marriage.

Children, born in Chester

Roxana Azubah Dickinson, b. Nov. 9, 1823; d. Aug. 30, 1900; m. Charles Benjamin Hanson. Children: i. Frederick Augustus, was of the 15th Conn. Volunteers; d. in Andersonville Prison. ii. Charles Dickinson, was of the 1st Conn. Heavy Artillery; d. in Salisbury Prison. iii. Jennie Evalena, b. Aug. 27, 1856, in New Haven; resides there. iv. Lizzie M., b. June 28, 1858; resides in New Haven; m. there, Nov. 10, 1881, William Hubbard Smith, b. in New Haven, Apr. 21, 1855, son of Jeremiah and Hannah (Sampson) Smith; has two children, Jennie Louise, b. Nov. 14, 1883, m. Benjamin F. Runges of New Haven (has a child, Elinor, b. Dec. 11, 1910), and Edna Estella, b. Aug. 18, 1886, m. Oct., 1913, Frederick Jewell Dawless of New Haven (has a child, Jeanette, b. June 27, 1916).

David W. Dickinson, b. Mar. 29, 1826; drowned in the Connecticut River, June 1, 1843.

Clarissa M. Dickinson, b. Apr. 9, 1828; d. Feb. 15, 1847; m. Apr. 26, 1846, William Parker of Chester; no children.

Calista M. Dickinson, b. June 29, 1830; d. in Ravenna, Ohio, Jan. 1, 1913; m. (1) Samuel Parker of Chester, and had two children; m. (2) Sept. 18, 1857, Edward Knapp, b. 1820, d. Dec. 3, 1903.

Eunice Cordelia Dickinson, b. Apr. 30, 1833; d. Feb. 5, 1905, in Bridgeport, Conn.; m. Feb. 18, 1855, William Henry Frisbie of Branford, Conn., b. May 11, 1826, d. Dec. 31, 1906. Child: Samuel Ely, resides in Milford, Conn.

John E. Dickinson, b. June 15, 1835; d. Sept. 25, 1912, at Deep River, Conn.; m. Jan. 30, 1876, Catherine Cramer, b. Mar. 18, 1851, of Baden, Germany. Children: i. Ella Gertrude, m. William James Ralston and lives in Deep River. ii. Walter S., lives in Deep River. iii. Leon A., lives in Deep River.

Emma Dickinson, b. Nov. 2, 1837; d. Apr. 3, 1892, in Garretsville, Ohio; m. Nov. 28, 1860, Edwin Holden. Members of her family are: Mrs. Gelston L. Holden of Charlestown, Ohio; Mrs. Lura Holden Wadsworth of Warren, Ohio; Louis Wadsworth of Cavett, Ohio; Mrs. Charles G. Seltzer of Dayton, Ohio; Volney E. Baldwin of Youngstown, Ohio; Frank M. Holden of Cripple Creek, Colo.

George E. Dickinson, b. Nov. 16, 1840.

Mary Jane Dickinson, b. Mar. 2, 1844; d. May 10, 1876; m. Dec. 16, 1860, James Cone of Chester.

608 LUCY WEBB[8] WARNER, daughter of David[7] and Mary (Cone) Warner, born April 10, 1809; resided in Chester, Conn.; died in Guilford, Conn., April 27, 1861.

Married November 28, 1826, **JOHN TRACY** of Colchester, Conn., born August 20, 1802; died March 14, 1859.

Children

Sarah Warner Tracy, b. Apr. 3, 1833; d. Apr. 6, 1893, in New Haven, Conn.; m. Sept. 7, 1853, Rufus Chapman of Lyme, Conn., b. Sept.,

1826, d. July 3, 1875. Children: i. Grace L., m. George P. Otis of New Haven. ii. Charles L., m. Isabella Davidson of New Haven. Both have large families and more of the record will be found in the Church Genealogy.

Mary E. Tracy, b. Apr. 18, 1835; d. Nov. 25, 1842.

John Isham Tracy, b. Feb. 27, 1837; resided in East Haddam; m. Mar. 14, 1867, Mary A. Bingham, b. Feb. 22, 1839, d. July 18, 1911.

Daniel O. Tracy, b. Jan. 26, 1839; d. in Bridgeport, Conn., Mar. 7, 1904; m. Mar. 8, 1870, Louise M. Late of South Windsor, Conn., who died Apr. 13, 1907. Child: George Everett.

Susan A. Tracy, b. May 12, 1842; resides in Chester, Conn.; m. (1) Nov. 24, 1864, William H. Leete of Guilford, b. June 11, 1828, d. Feb. 7, 1866; (2) Jan. 1, 1871, George A. Bogart of Chester, b. July 14, 1836, d. May 26, 1905. Child by first husband: Annette, b. Sept. 1, 1865; d. Feb. 20, 1866. Children by second husband: i. Bessie S., b. May 29, 1875. ii. Fred H., b. Jan. 16, 1877; m. Oct. 15, 1902, Florence Rogers Powers of Salem, Mass.; has resided in Hartford and Lancaster, Pa.

William E. Tracy, b. Sept. 14, 1846; resides in Chester.

Jane Annette Tracy, b. Aug. 16, 1848; d. Oct. 17, 1864.

609 AZUBAH[8] WARNER, daughter of David[7] and Mary (Cone) Warner, born in Whig Hill District, Chester, Conn., April 27, 1816; died in Deep River, Conn., Feb. 25, 1905. Married April 22, 1835, GIDEON PARKER of Chester, born December 3, 1817, died April 14, 1889, son of John Parker, Jr. He learned the mercantile business in what is remembered as the "Stone Store" in Chester, removed to Vermont for a time, but returned to Chester in 1849 as cashier of the Deep River Bank, a position he held until his death. He was a member of the Deep River Baptist Church, held the office of town clerk and other public offices.

Children

John Judson Parker, b. Sept. 19, 1836; d. Feb. 29, 1872; m. July 4, 1862, Mary Drinker of New York City; no children.

Sarah Jane Parker, b. Feb. 26, 1840; resides in Deep River.

Rosamond Clarissa Parker, b. Jan. 30, 1847; resides in Deep River; m. Jan. 25, 1878, Lewis Le Vaughn of Rocky Hill, Conn., b. Apr. 14, 1846. Children: i. William P., b. Nov. 18, 1878; resides in New York City; m. Lucy E. Malone, b. 1876, daughter of Edgar Malone of Ithaca, N. Y. ii. John D., b. July 17, 1883; m. May 11, 1904, Agnes Loomis of Farmington, Conn.; resides in St. Paul, Minn.

Isabelle Frances Parker, b. Sept. 10, 1848; resides in Deep River.

Genio S. Parker, b. Jan. 6, 1851; resides in Hartford, Conn.; m. Jan. 1, 1874, Ida B. Fuller, b. Feb. 28, 1851, daughter of Stephen Fuller of Deep River. Child: Frank J., b. Aug. 5, 1876; m. Jan. 10, 1899, Lillian Mack, b. Aug. 27, 1882, daughter of Myron J. Mack of Hartford; resides in Hartford.

Louis P. Parker, b. in Deep River, Aug. 7, 1858; m. (1) Dec. 9, 1887, Florence Morley, b. Oct. 23, 1859, d. Dec. 3, 1888, daughter of Samuel Morley of Essex, Conn. Child: Florine Margaret, b. Nov. 25, 1888. He married (2) Oct. 28, 1891, Margaret A. Minke, b. Sept. 8, 1859, daughter of Jacob Minke of Essex. Mr. Parker was connected with the bank from the age of sixteen; in 1885 went to Essex as cashier of the Essex National Bank. He was deacon of the Baptist Church after 1896, a trustee of the church and superintendent of the Sunday School.

Gideon Parker, b. Apr. 24, 1863; d. Apr. 29, 1863.

610 ALBERT OSCAR[8] WARNER, son of Timothy[7] and Lydia (Platts) Warner, born October 24, 1806, in Saybrook (Chester), Conn.; died March 13, 1899, in Bridgewater, Pa., where he had resided, a mile and a quarter from Montrose. He was a millwright and wagon maker.

Married (1) at Silver Lake, Pa., January 9, 1833, MARY ANN AUSTIN, born at Silver Lake; died December 3 or 4, 1833.

Married (2) at Pittston, Pa., January 22, 1835, MARY BUS-CORT BOGART, born in Plainfield, Pa., June 1, 1814; died November 22, 1891, in Bridgewater.

Children by second wife

Amzy Merritt Warner, b. Nov. 2, 1835, in Nicholson, Pa.; d. Jan. 9, 1853, in Montrose, Pa.

Sophia Madeline Warner, b. June 25, 1839, in Montrose, Pa.; resides in Higganum, Conn.; m. Nov. 4, 1874, Thomas J. Clark, b. in Haddam, Conn., Sept. 21, 1831, d. May 4, 1910. He was the son of George W. and Cynthia (Selden) Clark. After his father's death when he was fifteen, he learned the stone-cutting trade, then made a trip to Apalachicola, Fla., where he learned the business of engineer in a factory for the compression of cotton for foreign shipments. For a few years he alternated at these two trades in the north and south. For several years he was engaged in the construction of buildings, then went into partnership with his brother in large contracts for erecting mills, taking the stone and mason work under his supervision. He was vice-president of the Cutaway Harrow Company, a large business in which he was an important factor in the development of the town. Mr. Clark m. (1) in 1855, Elizabeth Quick, by whom he had Arthur Franklin, Effie Elizabeth, Elwyn Thomas and Ada Selden. Children of Thomas and Sophia (Warner) Clark: i. Nina Gertrude, b. Feb. 2, 1876; m. Aug. 19, 1903, Ephraim P. Arnold, Jr., of Haddam, Conn., b. Oct. 25, 1876; resides in Higganum. ii. (Daughter), b. about 1881.

Mary Letitia Warner, b. June 25, 1845, in Montrose; d. there, Sept. 26, 1847.

Frank Albert Warner, b. Nov. 30, 1852, in Montrose; resides in Binghamton, N. Y.; is a master plumber and proprietor of the Warner

Plumbing Company. Married in Montrose, Nov. 28, 1877, Alice I. Foster, b. June 16, 1852, in Greene, N. Y., daughter of Francis C. and Matilda A. (Slauson) Foster. No children.

611 ELIADA BLAKESLEE⁸ WARNER, son of Timothy⁷ and Lydia (Platts) Warner, born May 4, 1808; died in Bridgewater, Pa., January 4, 1888.

Married September 27, 1832, **FIDELIA LUCE**, born May 19, 1813, died August 26, 1875, daughter of Captain Asa C. Luce of Bridgewater, Pa.

Children

Mary E. Warner, b. Jan. 2, 1834; d. Feb. 16, 1883.
Martha A. Warner, b. Jan. 31, 1836; d. Jan. 1, 1860, at Table Rock, Neb.; m. Nov. 14, 1857, Luther Mumford of Thompson, Pa.
696 Charles A. Warner, b. Oct. 2, 1837; m. (1) Margaret Fay, (2) Ruth A. Cooper.
Asa W. Warner, b. Nov. 4, 1846; d. Oct., 1912; m. Jan. 16, 1884, Hattie S. Harris, b. Jan. 29, 1859, daughter of Washington·Harris of Greene, N. Y. She resides in Baldwinsville, N. Y. Child: Earl, b. May 16, 1885; d. July 27, 1885.

612 ELISHA PLATTS⁸ Warner, son of Timothy⁷ and Lydia (Platts) Warner, born August 7, 1816, in Bridgewater, Susquehanna Co., Pa.; died May 12, or February 18, 1893, in Bucklin, Mo. He was a farmer and carpenter.

Married **MARGARET BOGARD**, born near Wilkesbarre, Pa., February 19, 1820; died in Bucklin, Mo., December 30, 1897.

Children

Leander S. Warner, b. Jan. 11, 1841.
696a Erastus H. Warner, b. Apr. 22, 1842; m. Lettie Jane Ackerson.
Betsey M. Warner, b. July 28, 1843; m. George W. Griffin.
Lydia Malvina Warner, b. May 27, 1845, in Montrose, Susquehanna Co., Pa.; d. Mar. 3, 1912, in Bucklin, Mo.; m. Sept. 19, 1865, Edward S. Fitzgerald. Children, three sons and nine daughters, seven of whom died before 1912: i. Frank. ii. Billie, d. about 1916 in Bucklin. iii. Stella. iv. Daisy, m. ——— Davolt and resided in Bucklin. v. Rebecca, m. ——— Sage and resided at Pacific Junction, Iowa.
Sarah L. Warner, b. Nov. 5, 1847; d. Nov. 21, 1908, at La Grange, Pa.; m. in Overfield township, May 22, 1868, Edmund Dailey, b. in Overfield township, Jan. 9, 1848, son of Harrison and Rachel (Williams) Dailey. Children: i. John B., b. July 20, 1870, in Bucklin, Mo. ii. Allen E., b. July 25, 1873, in Overfield township; resides in Osterhout, Pa. iii. Cynthia L., b. in Overfield township, Nov. 29, 1875.
John B. Warner, b. Dec. 22, 1849.
Mary Jane Warner, b. in Overfield Township, Pa., Dec. 22, 1851; d. in Carterville, Mo.; m. in St. Catherine, Mo., James Willson, who d.

in Leavenworth, Kans.   Children, all of Carterville, Mo.: i. Minnie. ii.
George, now in France. iii. Edward. iv. Ella. v. Jessie. vi. Alice.
Davis D. Warner, b. Feb. 25, 1854.
Cynthia A. Warner, b. Feb. 2, 1856, in Factoryville, Pa.; m. in Atchi-
son, Kans., Feb., 1883, John F. Gregory, b. in Baltimore, Md., Mar.
7, 1846, d. in St. Louis, Mo., 1895, son of Henry M. and Susan Gregory
of Baltimore. He was a house painter. Child: Cynthia Irene, b.
in Atchison, Oct. 29, 1885; m. in Bucklin, Mo., Jan. 6, 1904, Henry
L. Wright, a poultry packer, b. in Bucklin, June 19, 1882, son of
Hira L. Wright. They have six children, Opal Maud, b. Oct. 9,
1904, Rachel Mae, b. Mar. 17, 1906, Warner Hira, b. Nov. 29, 1908,
George Harold, b. Sept. 6, 1910, Francis Scott, b. Aug. 9, 1913, and
Jessie Arvilla, b. July 30, 1916.
Nancy A. Warner, b. Sept. 8, 1858.
Florence A. Warner, b. Nov. 27, 1861; m. Emerson Merritt Severance.
Jessie B. Warner, b. Mar. 11, 1863.
George F. Warner, b. Jan. 28, 1866.

613 GEORGE DICKINSON[8] WARNER, son of Timothy[7,]
and Lydia (Platts) Warner, born in Bridgewater, Susquehanna
Co., Pa., October 3, 1824; died May 13, 1863, in the South,
while a soldier in the Civil War.
Married **OCTAVIA BREWSTER** of Bridgewater, Pa. She
died in Johnstown, Pa., 1898.

Children

697 *Addie Alice Warner*, b. Jan. 3, 1849; m. Avery Whitmore Barrett.
698 *Gustavus J. Warner*, b. about 1851; m. Susan Rice.
699 *Fanny Warner*, b. July 20, 1853; m. Ernest F. Eifert.
700 *Adelpha A. Warner*, b. June 11, 1854; m. George W. Edmiston.
Victoria Warner, resides in Hendricks, W. Va.; m. P. J. Reid.

614 ANSEL LOCKMAN[8] WARNER, son of Timothy[7] and
Lydia (Platts) Warner, born February 28, 1828, in Bridgewater,
Pa.; died in New Milford, Pa., March 21, 1893.
Married September 6, 1853, **MARY JANE COOK** of Jack-
son, Pa., born November 24, 1833; died October 7, 1889.

Children

701 *Eliza G. Warner*, b. Aug. 26, 1854; m. Charles Wirth.
702 *Lillice E. Warner*, b. Apr. 7, 1857; m. Bennett B. Freeman.
Edson M. Warner, b. Oct. 16, 1859; d. Oct. 12, 1887.
703 *Gordon D. Warner*, b. Sept. 17, 1861; m. (1) Icie Bell, (2) Ella
Gifford.

615 WEALTHY[8] WARNER, daughter of Samuel[7] and
Wealthy (Clark) Warner, born in Connecticut; died in Mont-

rose, Pa., March, 1837 or 1838. She resided in Montrose and Dimock, Pa.

Married October 30, 1822, **SIMEON TYLER**, son of Simeon and Betsey (Brewster) Tyler, born in Westhampton, Mass., December 6, 1797; died in Brooklyn, Pa., 1857.

Children, born in Dimock, Pa.

Amanda R. Tyler, b. Feb. 10, 1823; m. John Foster. Children: i. Eliza, m. Dr. E. B. Hinds, and had children, Carrie, who m. ——— Sawyer and resides in Calicoon, N. Y., Lillian, Daisy and James. ii. Frank. iii. John. iv. Josephine, m. Benjamin Glidden; no children.

Eliza O. Tyler, b. July 9, 1825; d. Dec. 4, 1893, in Philadelphia; m. Orlando G. Hempstead. Children: i. Delos B., resides in Philadelphia; m. Ida McFadden; no children. ii. Frederick, d. in infancy. iii. Ernest Alexis, b. 1851; m. Annie Mary[9] Warner (see number 616). iv. William O., resides in Philadelphia; m. Vinie Patton; had children, Florence, who m. and d. without children, and William O., Jr., resides in Philadelphia, m. and has two children. v. Minnie E., d. June 10, 1902, not married. vi. Harry Newton, resides in New York City; m. and has children, Gordon and John Brush.

Casper William Tyler, b. Mar. 6, 1837; m. Lucy Therese[9] Warner; see number 616.

616 GILBERT[8] WARNER, son of Samuel[7] and Wealthy (Clark) Warner, born in Montrose, Pa., December 26, 1815; died in Meadville, Pa., March 27, 1893.

Married, probably in Auburn, N. Y., 1840 or 1841, **THERESE PARK FRENCH,** born November 5, 1818, died at Montrose, Pa., September 6, 1866, daughter of Luther French of Stonington, Conn., and his wife, Lucy Park of Connecticut.

Children, born in Montrose

Lucy Therese Warner, b. Apr. 27, 1842; d. in Meadville, Pa., Aug. 28, 1901; m. in Montrose, Mar. 24, 1864, Colonel Casper William Tyler, b. in Montrose, Mar. 6, 1837, resides in Meadville, son of Simeon and Wealthy[8] (Warner) Tyler; see number 615. Colonel Tyler served in the 141st Regiment, Pennsylvania Volunteers, in the Army of the Potomac. Children: i. Elizabeth Reed, b. in Montrose, Aug., 1866; resides ·in Chicago. ii. Mabel Louise, b. in Meadville, Oct., 1868; m. ——— Hughes; resides in Long Beach, Cal.; no children. iii. Grace, b. Aug., 1873; d. 1876. iv. Dorothea, b. in Meadville, Aug., 1887; resides in Chicago with her sister.

Theodore F. Warner, b. 1844; was killed at the battle of the Wilderness, May 6, 1864; not married.

Willie Romeyne Warner, b. Oct. 3, 1846; d. June 27, 1848.

Annie Mary Warner, resides in Meadville; m. in Detroit, Mich., Aug. 5, 1875, Ernest Alexis Hempstead, b. in Dimock, Pa., 1851, son of

Orlando G. and Eliza O. (Tyler) Hempstead. Children, b. in Meadville: i. Marguerite, Ph.B., Cornell University, 1900; member of Sigma Xi and Kappa Alpha Theta; resides in Ithaca, N. Y.; m. in Meadville, June 22, 1904, Benjamin Freeman Kingsbury, b. in St. Charles, Mo., Nov. 18, 1872, son of B. B. and Sarah R. (Freeman) Kingsbury, was graduated from Buchtel College (Akron, Ohio), A.B., 1893, Cornell University, Ph.D., 1895, University of Freiburg, Baden, Germany, M.D., 1903, was assistant professor of histology and embryology at Cornell, 1898-1902, professor of physiology there since 1902; has children, Marguerite, b. Oct. 8, 1905, Ernest Hempstead, b. Nov. 9, 1907, and Robert Freeman, b. June 26, 1912. ii. Louise, was educated at Allegheny College, 1896-8, Cornell University, 1898-1900, B.S., Columbia University, 1902-3; member of Phi Beta Kappa, Sigma Xi, and Kappa Kappa Gamma; has been a teacher in Oil City High School, Miss Knox's School, Briarcliff Manor, and at the Mount Vernon Seminary, Washington, D. C., since 1911. iii. Helen, is a physician in Cleveland, Ohio; was educated at Allegheny College, A.B., Cornell University, and Johns Hopkins Medical School, M.D.; has written many medical papers; is a member of the American Medical Association, Cleveland Medical Society and the Society for the Study and Prevention of Infant Mortality.

Harry Gilbert Warner, b. Aug., 1857; d. in Battle Creek, Mich., Sept., 1874.

617 COL. ANDREW SYLVESTER[8] WARNER, son of Andrew[7], Jr., and Elizabeth Clark (Young) Warner, born in Vernon, Oneida Co., N. Y., January 12, 1819; died at Sandy Creek, Oswego Co., N. Y., December 26, 1887.

In April, 1837, he went with his father's family from Vernon and settled on the "Warner cross road" in the western part of the town of Sandy Creek, Oswego County on the farm which later he owned and tilled during the rest of his lifetime.

He was a student at Mexico Academy, and for a time was teacher in the public schools. As he was the oldest son he assumed the responsibility of caring for the large family after the death of his father in 1843, and through his self-denial and assistance a brother and sister were enabled to complete their college education. In those early days much of the land was still covered with a dense forest and with tireless energy he cleared the land, built many farm buildings and increased the acreage of the large homestead.

Andrew S. Warner was a progressive farmer. He had the first mowing machine in his section. His large orchards were noted for the variety of fruit. His live stock and the products of the loom were awarded many prizes at the local fairs. In politics he was originally a Whig and was one of the organizers

COL. ANDREW SYLVESTER WARNER

of the Republican party in Oswego County. He was a member
of the New York State Assembly in the years 1855 and 1856
and was State Senator in 1860 and 1861. During the Civil
War he was active in recruiting several regiments and served
as Colonel of the 147th Regiment, New York State Volunteers.
It is related that as this newly organized regiment was about
to entrain for the front, several of the volunteers decided they
would not go, whereupon Colonel Warner quickly drew his
sword and firmly enforced discipline. While Colonel Warner
was a strict disciplinarian he was indefatigable in his efforts
to provide the necessary comforts for his men and was popular
with the soldiers of his command. Due to his arduous work
under unfavorable conditions his health failed and he received
an honorable discharge. He held many other offices of trust
and "enjoyed the distinction of wielding a greater political
influence for twenty years than any other Republican in his
district. Few men in Oswego county led a more active life
and none were more closely identified with all interests which
conserve the prosperity of a community. He was a man of
large and powerful physique, untiring energy, exceedingly
good judgment and jovial nature." He never used liquor or
tobacco in any form. He was a member of the F. & A. M. and
attended the Congregational Church. He died December 26,
1887, and lies in the cemetery at Sandy Creek, N. Y. A. S.
Warner Camp S. of V. of Pulaski, N. Y., was named in memory
of him.

Andrew S. Warner married (1) October 19, 1842, **MARY
ELIZABETH GREENE,** who died June 22, 1859, daughter of
Henry K. Greene of New Haven, Oswego County.

He married (2) October 3, 1861, **CHLOE MONROE,** born
in Sandy Creek, May 22, 1840, died February 14, 1916, second
daughter of Barnabas and Avis (Mallory) Monroe. Barnabas
Monroe was born 1809, died at Sandy Creek, 1875, married
1837, Avis Mallory, born 1815, died at Sandy Creek, 1892. They
came from Shaftsbury, Vt., among the early settlers of Sandy
Creek, living for many years in the large colonial mansion on
the Ridge Road near Lacona. From early youth she was an
active member of the Congregational Church and for many years
a member of the Monday Historical Club of Pulaski. She was
a woman with "a perfect Christian character," of fine intellectual taste, an affectionate mother, devoted wife and kind
neighbor.

Children of Andrew S. and Mary E. (Greene) Warner

704 *Adelbert Andrew Warner*, b. July 8, 1846; m. Catherine Henrietta
Bettinger.
Arthur Warner.
705 *Gerrit Smith Warner*, b. Oct. 4, 1855; m. Anna Lloyd.

*Children of Andrew S. and Chloe (Monroe) Warner, born at
Sandy Creek*

Wilbert Charles Warner, b. Feb. 16, 1863; was a student at Cornell
University (1883-4) and at Syracuse University; was graduated
from Dartmouth College, M.D., 1887; studied at the University of
Vienna, 1891-2; has practiced medicine in Cleveland, Ohio, since
1893. He is a member of the American Medical Society, Cleveland
Medical Academy, Ohio State Medical Society, F. and A. M., and
Sons of Veterans. Dr. Warner is not married.
Monroe Warner, b. Nov. 23, 1865; was graduated from Cornell Uni-
versity, C.E., 1888; is a civil engineer, residing in Cleveland, Ohio;
not married; manager of the Warner Manufacturing Company,
successors to A. E. Francis, sole manufacturers of the Francis
Engravers. In 1890 Mr. Warner was Deputy U. S. Surveyor in South
Dakota; Assistant Engineer, State of New York, 1895-1898. He
is a member of the Cleveland Engineering Society, Cornell Club,
F. and A. M., Phi Gamma Delta, and Sons of Veterans.
Warren William Warner, b. June 27, 1869; attended Cornell Univer-
sity; is president of the Bryant Park Bank, New York City, and has
served as assistant bank examiner for New York City; is a Royal
Arch Mason; resides in Pelham, N. Y.; m. June 24, 1903, Frances
L. Whitman.
Mary T. F. Warner, b. Oct. 30, 1876; d. Oct. 28, 1877.

618 HANNAH MARIA[8] WARNER, daughter of Andrew[7],
Jr., and Elizabeth Clark (Young) Warner, born September 18,
1820, in Vernon Center, Oneida Co., N. Y.; died May 23, 1887,
in Pulaski, Oswego Co., N. Y. She was a graduate from Ober-
lin, Classical course, in 1845, and resided in Pulaski after 1849.
Married in the town of Sandy Creek, Oswego Co., N. Y.,
February 12, 1846, **SYLVANUS CONVERS HUNTINGTON**,
born April 14, 1820, at East Charleston, Vt., son of Joseph and
Eliza (Convers) Huntington. He was county judge of Oswego
County from 1856 to 1859. He married (2) Mrs. Emily (Snow)
Fenton; see number 246.

Children

Hannah Metelill Huntington, b. May 6, 1853, in Pulaski; d. Oct. 18,
1912, not married.
Sylvanus Convers Huntington, Jr., b. June 12, 1857, at Glen. Castle,
Broome Co., N. Y.; resides in Oswego, N. Y. He was graduated
from Oberlin in 1876 and became a tutor of Greek there. He is a

lawyer and is now in the abstract of title business at Oswego. Married at Pulaski, Nov. 1, 1883, Mary Ellen Douglas, b. Dec. 22, 1861, at Rutland, Jefferson Co., N. Y., daughter of Rev. James and Mary (Burt) Douglas. Children, b. in Pulaski: i. Carl Douglas, b. Jan. 26, 1885; is assistant examiner in the U. S. Patent Office, Washington, D. C.; not married. ii. George Warner, b. July 8, 1887; is a bookkeeper in New York City; m. in New York City, June 2, 1915, Marie Rerrick, b. at Roda, Va., Nov. 11, 1888, daughter of Leonard and Clara (Wagner) Rerrick. iii. James Douglas, b. May 1, 1892; d. Jan. 26, 1893. iv. Maurice Burt, b. July 19, 1894; graduated from Cornell University, 1917. v. Ralph Isham, b. July 2, 1898; d. Sept. 29, 1914, in Oswego.

619 WARREN WILLIAM[8] WARNER, son of Andrew[7], Jr., and Elizabeth Clark (Young) Warner, born in Vernon, Oneida Co., N. Y., November 9, 1824; died at Clifton Springs, N. Y., April 15, 1889. He was brought up near Pulaski, N. Y., was graduated from Hamilton College and Auburn Theological Seminary, and became a Congregational minister. He was pastor of Congregational churches in northern and central New York, and retired after over thirty years of ministry, taking up his residence in Clifton Springs.

Married December 2, 1858, ANNA GATES LEWIS, born October 2, 1833, in Pulaski, N. Y., daughter of Hiram and Anna M. (Gates) Lewis.

Child

Mary Warner, b. Sept. 25, 1867; resides in Arlington, N. J. She is a member of the Presbyterian Church. Married July 4, 1894, Wallace Pfleger, b. Feb. 6, 1866; d. Sept. 10, 1915. He was a member of the Ferguson Bros. Manufacturing Company, Hoboken, N. J. Child: Kenneth Warner, b. July 22, 1899; resides with his mother in Arlington.

620 RACHEL LAVINA[8] WARNER, daughter of Andrew[7], Jr., and Elizabeth Clark (Young) Warner, born in 1825, in Vernon, Oneida Co., N. Y.; died in Missouri, 1879. Married at Sandy Creek, N. Y., July 16, 1845, DANIEL WELLS RANNEY, born October 4, 1819, at Knoxboro, N. Y., died in Florida, April 10, 1866, son of Oliver and Sally (Reynolds) Ranney. He studied medicine and established a water cure in Knoxboro in 1850.

Children, born in Knoxboro

Rudolph Ranney, b. July 30, 1847; d. Feb. 10, 1889, in Los Angeles, Cal., where he was judge of the Criminal Court for some years; m. in Rockport, Mo., 1874, Eunice Rebecca (Nina) Duncan of Beloit,

Wis., daughter of Anson Maltby and Angeline L. (Warner) Duncan; see number 410. They had no children.
Frank W. Ranney, b. Feb. 8, 1850; d. May 10, 1902, in Keswick, Cal.; m. in Tarkio, Mo., Feb. 7, 1876, Lucy Carney, b. July 9, 1859, d. Jan. 14, 1888, at Tarkio, daughter of Thomas and Phebe Elizabeth (Baxter) Carney. Children: i. Mabel, m. William E. Edmondson; resides in Springfield, Mo.; had two children, William Warner, b. June 14, 1909, d. 1913, and Ruth, b. Apr. 25, 1911. ii. Warren W., resides in Alhambra, Cal.

621 **CHARLOTTE D.**[8] **WARNER**, daughter of Israel S.[7] and Samantha (Ballou) Warner, born in the town of Kirkland, Oneida Co., N. Y., August 2, 1831; resides in Northampton, Mass.
Married in Kirkland, N. Y., April 17, 1850, **NORMAN GUITO SNOW**, born in Pulaski, N. Y., February 3, 1828, son of Benjamin and Lavina[7] (Warner) Snow; see number 246.

Children

Emma Snow, b. Apr. 19, 1857; d. 1860.
Benjamin Warner Snow, b. in Henry, Ill., Aug. 15, 1860; is head of the department of physics at the University of Wisconsin, Madison, Wis. He was educated at Cornell University, B.S., 1885; University of Göttingen, 1887; University of Strassburg, 1888; University of Berlin, 1890-1892, Ph.D., 1892. He was fellow in physics at Cornell, 1885-6; instructor in physics at Ohio State University, 1888-90; professor of physics at Indiana University, 1892-3; professor at University of Wisconsin since 1893. Professor Snow is a member of the American Academy for the Advancement of Science, secretary of one section in 1894; American Physical Society; Delta Upsilon; Sigma Xi. He has published several scientific books. Married Sept. 22, 1896, Agnes Campbell Butler of Madison, Wis.
Julia Warner Snow, b. in La Salle, Ill., Aug. 30, 1863; is associate professor of botany at Smith College, Northampton, Mass. She was graduated from Cornell University, B.S., 1888; fellow at Cornell, 1888-9; M.S., 1889; fellow, Association of Collegiate Alumnæ, 1891-2; Ph.D., Zurich, 1893; University of Basle, 1896; Assistant, U. S. Fish Commission Biological Survey of Lake Erie, summers, 1898-1901; teacher of science in American College for girls, Constantinople, 1894-6, assistant in botany, 1897; instructor in botany, University of Michigan, 1898-1900; instructor in biology, Rockford College, 1900-1, assistant in botany, 1901-2; instructor in botany, 1902-6; at Smith College since 1906. Professor Snow is a member of the Botanical Society of America, Kappa Alpha Theta, and Sigma Xi, and is the author of several scientific works.

622 **CELESTIA ALVIRA**[8] **WARNER**, daughter of Israel S.[7] and Samantha (Ballou) Warner, born in Oneida County, N. Y., August 1, 1845; resides in Lidgerwood, N. D. She was first named Alice Antoinette, but the name was later changed.

Married in Cedar Falls, Iowa, June 26, 1867, **ABRAM F. CAREY,** born in Randolph County, Ind., August 20, 1846, son of John N. and Amelia (Wallace) Carey. He is a farmer.

Children, reside in Lidgerwood ·

George Warner Carey, b. in Black Hawk County, Iowa, July 8, 1869; m. Nov. 24, 1897, Rosalie Henslick, b. Sept. 10, 1872, at Lowrie, Minn., daughter of Casper and Anna (————) Henslick. Children: i. Maude K., b. Sept. 1, 1898. ii. Nellie J., b. Sept. 9, 1900; died. iii. Warner G., b. Nov. 20, 1902. iv. Lester F., b. Sept. 8, 1904. v. Leonard O., b. Apr. 21, 1908.

Charles William Carey, b. in Black Hawk County, Iowa, May 26, 1871. He has served three terms in the lower house of the North Dakota Legislature and is at present in the upper house; m. Sept. 8, 1897, Emma J. Griggs, b. in Oneida County, N. Y., Aug. 30, 1872, daughter of Elam and Emogene[8] (Warner) Griggs; see number 412. Children: i. Elam G., b. June 12, 1898. ii. Victor M., b. Jan. 22, 1901. iii. Clinton C., b. Apr. 26, 1904. iv. Helen A., b. Mar. 25, 1906.

Eugene Walter Carey, b. in Russell County, Kans., Sept. 22, 1873; m. Feb. 25, 1903, Nellie E. Stonehocker, b. at Axtel, Kans., Sept. 16, 1881, daughter of Joseph Stonehocker, who was born in Ohio, Aug. 18, 1846, and his wife, Mary A. R. Woodring, who was born in Pennsylvania, Mar. 24, 1850. Children: i. Lloyd Joseph, b. Dec. 27, 1903. ii. Elwyn Arville, b. Mar. 26, 1911. iii. Claude Eugene, b. Oct. 23, 1913.

623 SARAH[8] WARNER, daughter of Philip Kirtland[7] and Lovina (Ackley) Warner, born in Cambridge, Washington Co., N. Y., November 26, 1815; died January 4, 1897, in Springvale, near Norwich, N. Y. She came with her parents to Norwich in 1825 and with the exception of five years in South New Berlin, she spent her whole life in the same neighborhood. "A· faithful home maker, her children rise up to call her blessed." Married June 18, 1831, **REUBEN BURLINGAME,** born in South New Berlin, N.·Y., July 8, 1805, died August 10, 1871, son of Josiah Burlingame, a Methodist preacher and a root doctor.

Children

Philip J. Burlingame, b. in Norwich, N. Y., Apr. 18, 1836; d. at Addison, N. Y., 1885. He was a soldier in the Civil War, a cavalryman with the first company that marched into Richmond. Married Amy Barton, had four children; two daughters died unmarried about 1900, the other two daughters and three grandchildren are living in Steuben County, N. Y. (1917).

Mary F. Burlingame, b. in Norwich, Aug. 26, 1839; resides there; m. there, July 4, 1860, George H. Johnson, b. in Norwich, July 8, 1834, son of Homer and Roxy (Skinner) Johnson. For record of their children see further.

Freeman Burlingame, farmer in Springvale, N. Y.; m. Helen Jackson. Children: i. Anna, m. Ben Macclagin, and has a son, Lawrence. ii. Arthur. iii. and iv. Twin babies, d. young.

Lovina Burlingame, b. May 27, 1844; d. Apr. 2, 1917; m. Nov. 26, 1861, William Curnalia, who d. Oct. 11, 1911. They resided at Springvale, N. Y. Children: i. Addie, m. Chester Morehouse, and has seven children. ii. Melville E., m. and has one child. iii. Clarence E., m. and has four children. iv. William J., m. and has four children. v. Devillo H., m. Mary Cole. vi. Ella, m. Edwin J. Elliott, and has two sons. vii. Howard J., not married.

Helen D. Burlingame, d. May 5, 1906; m. Herman Lewis.

Sarah A. Burlingame (Addie), b. Mar. 23, 1849; m. Feb. 1, 1872, Peter Bates. Children: i. Walter, b. Dec. 23, 1874; is a machinist; m. in 1905. ii. Eugene, b. Dec. 30, 1882; is a mechanic; m. in 1907. iii. Bertha B., b. May 14, 1884; m. in 1904, ———— Wheeler, and has children, Eleanor, b. Dec. 6, 1905, and Ruth, b. Feb. 15, 1909. Other grandchildren of Peter and Sarah Bates are: Hulda Bates, b. Feb. 7, 1908, Dorothy Bates, b. Dec. 24, 1911, and Earl and Elsa Bates, b. Aug. 28, 1913.

Lucy A. Burlingame, b. in Norwich, May 23, 1850; resides there; m. there, in 1868, Harris Lewis, b. in Norwich, 1844, son of ———— and Mary A. (Smith) Lewis. Children: i. Willard A., b. in Norwich, May 30, 1870. ii. Harris H., b. in Norwich, Sept. 12, 1873. iii. Robert O., b. in Portage, Livingston Co., N. Y., Aug. 23, 1879. iv. Alta M., b. in Portage, June 15, 1881; d. Oct. 17, 1916. v. Finch E., b. in Urbana, Steuben Co., N. Y., Aug. 25, 1889.

Elbert Burlingame, m. Matilda Main; resides in Springvale, N. Y.

Alice Burlingame, b. June 23, 1861; d. 1909; m. Peter Elliott.

Mrs. Mary F. Burlingame Johnson of Norwich, mentioned above, has been a member of the First Baptist Church of Norwich for the last forty years; deaconess for many years; director of the Woman's American Baptist Home Mission Society for Chenango County, for twenty-six years; president of the local missionary society and interested in all Sunday School and Church work. Her children are:

Henry Homer Johnson, b. Apr. 25, 1861; was a merchant in Norwich for some years; is now engaged in agriculture; m. Lizzie R. Johnson, who d. in Apr., 1901. Children: i. Homer C., a merchant. ii. Mable E., graduate of a Normal School and now a teacher. iii. Grace R., graduate of Denison College in 1917; now teaching. iv. George L., a salesman; is now (June, 1918) in his country's service in France.

George Francis Johnson, b. Oct. 9, 1863; Baptist minister, graduate of Colgate University and Theological Seminary; is working in connection with the Baptist State Convention as evangelist and missionary; m. June, 1893, Lillian Whitney of Triangle, N. Y. Children: i. Evangel, b. 1896. ii. Paul, d. in infancy. iii. Ruth. iv. George F., Jr. v. Esther. vi. Paul Charles.

Charles E. Johnson, b. in Norwich, Oct. 25, 1867; d. July 31, 1910, after an illness of a year. He was a member of the First Baptist Church in Norwich and took an active part in Church and Sunday School work and the county organizations.

38

Frederick Leslie Johnson, b. Nov. 20, 1874; is a merchant in Norwich and a deacon in the First Baptist Church; m. in 1906, Nellie
Willard, who is a graduate of the Albany Normal College and
a teacher in the High School in Norwich. They have no children.

624 LOVINA[8] WARNER, daughter of Philip Kirtland[7]
and Lovina (Ackley) Warner, born February 4, 1820; died in
Norwich, N. Y., September 27, 1871.
Married **ALVAH SNOW.**

Children, born in Norwich

Nelson Snow, b. 1843; d. Feb. 28, 1879; m. (1) Jean Cady, divorced;
m. (2) Hattie Johnson.
Cornelia Snow, b. Dec. 18, 1844; d. at Holmesville, N. Y., Dec. 25,
1900; m. Dec. 18, 1865, Elias Belden. Children: i. Orrin, b. in
Norwich, June 7, 1868; is a Presbyterian minister in Ohio; m. Jan.
30, 1889, Adeline Rogers, and had two children, Charles, b. July 17,
1890, m. Apr. 16, 1911, Zepha Adams (and has two children, Omer,
b. Mar. 28, 1912, and Marion, b. Feb. 4, 1914), and Aletha Beatrice,
b. May 27, 1907. ii. George, b. Apr. 22, 1871; m. Mar. 5, 1893, Rose
Carr, and had three children, Carrie May, b. Dec. 20, 1893, d. Dec.
28, 1893, Nina Pearl, b. Apr. 18, 1899, m. May 19, 1915, Lewis
Goodspeed, and Orrin M., b. Apr. 6, 1903. iii. Lois M., b. Sept. 13,
1875; d. May, 1902; m. Aug., 1894, Albert Lampher.
Frank Snow, b. Jan. 22, 1846; d. at Peoria, Ill., in 1916; m. Lottie
Bowles. Child: Charles B., b. July 12, 1872; d. in Peoria, Ill., June
24, 1917; m. June 6, 1895, Mary Hessler, and had a son, Earl F.,
b. in Peoria, Jan. 13, 1897.
Clara Lamira Snow, b. Oct., 1851, in Norwich; resided there, and d.
July 16, 1909; m. in Poolville, N. Y., Mar., 1868, George Hazard
Burdick, b. in Norwich, Nov. 6, 1842, son of Samuel and Polly
(Beale) Burdick. His grandfather was a Revolutionary soldier
and a Free Baptist minister. Children, b. in Norwich: i. Calvin G.,
b. Sept. 21, 1869; m. in New Britain, Conn., July 14, 1891, Hattie
Tryon, a descendant of the Massachusetts Colonial Governor Tryon,
has a daughter, Viola, b. in New Britain, July 26, 1892. ii. Herbert
J., b. Jan. 18, 1873; is a trustee of the M. E. Church and a
member of the Masonic Lodge in Norwich; m. Phoebe Frink;
has two children, b. in Norwich, Stanley, b. Mar. 30, 1901, and
Lewis B., b. Oct. 20, 1910. iii. Clara E., b. June 14, 1878; was a
graduate of the Albany Business College and an expert stenog-
rapher; d. in Norwich, Apr., 1906. iv. Charles, b. 1885; d. 1886.
v. Walter E., b. May 19, 1887; d. Sept. 27, 1917; m. in Binghamton,
N. Y., May 30, 1917, Mary Irving; had a son, Walter Irving, b. in
Norwich, Mar. 21, 1918. vi. Harriett M., b. Aug. 30, 1890; m. in
Norwich, Nov. 9, 1915, Rufus Wells, owner of Norwich Stock Farm
(Holstein-Friesian thoroughbred cattle); has a son, Lawrence, b. in
Norwich, Nov. 16, 1916. vii. Paul Alvah, b. Feb. 12, 1894; student
in engineering at Syracuse University; member of Theta Alpha;
left on May 29, 1918, with Chenango County's drafted men for
military service.

Sarah Lodisca Snow, b. Mar. 19, 1854; resides in Norwich; m. there, Nov. 16, 1869, David Wicks, b. in Norfolk, England, Aug. 31, 1845, d. July 20, 1912, son of John Wicks. Children, b. in Norwich: i. Grace Belle, b. June 8, 1870; m. in Norwich, Sept., 1896, Allen La Mott Roe, who d. Nov., 1902, leaving a child, Grace W., b. in Albany, N. Y., Feb. 26, 1900. ii. Anna May, b. Sept. 10, 1871; m. in Norwich, Mar. 21, 1892, George Henry Smith; had three children, b. in Poolville, Gordon Henry, b. Feb. 7, 1894, Wesley Newton, b. May 2, 1895, and Grace, b. Nov. 27, 1898. iii. David, b. Oct. 5, 1873; d. Mar. 11, 1881. iv. Florence Lilly, b. Nov. 5, 1875; m. (1) in Sherburne, N. Y., Sept. 4, 1897, Virgil Cain; had one child, Adrian, b. Dec. 11, 1899; m. (2) in Norwich, Feb. 1, 1901, L. Gilbert Sanford. v. Bessie Maud, b. Mar. 24, 1879; m. in Norwich, Oct. 21, 1903, William Blossom; had six children, all but last b. in Norwich, Paul E., b. Aug. 28, 1904, d. June 2, 1909, Pauline I., b. Apr. 7, 1906, Prudence, b. Dec. 7, 1908, Stewart, b. Mar. 14, 1911, Florence Lilly, b. Feb. 21, 1916, and Wilfred, b. in Syracuse, N. Y., Apr. 20, 1917. vi. Bertha Ellen, b. Mar. 22, 1881; m. in Norwich, Mar. 21, 1905, Charles Hemingway; had two children, b. in Ilion, N. Y., George H., b. Dec. 5, 1908, and June Delight, b. Feb. 17, 1915. vii. Robert Nelson, b. Sept. 11, 1884; m. in Cohoes, N. Y., Aug. 23, 1905, Corrine De Marsh; had four children, Hazel, b. June 8, 1906, d. May 29, 1908, Edward, b. Feb. 3, 1908, Robert, b. May 30, 1910, and Kenneth, J., b. July 13, 1913. viii. Hazel D., b. Mar. 15, 1887; m. in Binghamton, May 5, 1918, Arthur Meade. ix. Edward R., b. May 1, 1890; m. July 20, 1911, Hazel Philpott; had three children, David, b. June 24, 1912, Richard J., b. Feb. 3, 1914, and Corrine H., b. Feb. 23, 1917. x. Joseph Alvah, b. Jan. 30, 1893; m. in Rome, N. Y., Nov. 17, 1915, Ruth Wolcott; had one child, Iona L., b. May 21, 1917.

Lily Snow, b. Jan. 2, 1852; d. at South New Berlin; m. Herbert Sargent. Children: i. Bertha, b. Apr. 3, 1875; m. at South New Berlin, June 7, 1893, Benjamin Wightman; has a son, Guy, b. June 2, 1896. ii. Blanche, b. Sept. 1, 1881, at South New Berlin; m. at Kings Park, L. I., Jan. 6, 1907, John James Lyman; has four children, b. at Kings Park, Lily Maria, b. Feb. 19, 1909, Agnes Bertha, b. July 19, 1911, John Herbert, b. Jan. 7, 1914, and Stanley Ambrose, b. Mar. 16, 1917.

Walter Mirvil Snow, b. Aug. 22, 1858; m. at Norwich, Apr. 4, 1895, Jennie B. Arnold.

625 CHARLES[8] **WARNER,** son of Abner Warren[7] and Freelove (Goodsell) Warner, born July 2, 1829, in Norwich, N. Y., where he is now living (1916). He was engaged in the carriage business with his father and later conducted it alone. Married (1) September 19, 1853, **SERUA SNOW,** born June 7, 1829, died February 19, 1863, daughter of Thomas and Phebe (———) Snow.

Married (2) May 16, 1865, **SARAH JANE**[9] **WARNER,** born January 8, 1840, died February 22, 1899, daughter of Jonathan Wood[8] and Lucy (Cady) Warner; see number 414.

Children by first wife

Edith Augusta Warner, b. Nov. 9, 1855, in Norwich; resides in the town of Norwich; m. May 8, 1879, Charles Titus, b. in North Norwich, Apr. 19, 1854, son of Smith and Lucinda (————) Titus. He is a farmer. No children.

Warren S. Warner, b. 1858, in Norwich, where he now resides. He is a foreman on the D. L. and W. Railroad. Married at South New Berlin, 1881, Helen I. Sargent, b. in South New Berlin, 1861, daughter of Charles and Margaret (————) Sargent. Child: Charles Starr, b. at South New Berlin, 1885; is a poultry man residing there; m. there, 1910, Millicent Payne.

Florence May Warner, b. Feb. 14, 1863, in Norwich; d. Mar. 25, 1885; m. Jan. 1, 1885, William Joler.

Child by second wife

Nellie Warner, b. June 16, 1872; m. Aug. 19, 1890, Frank Brown. Children, b. in Binghamton, N. Y.: i. N. Pauline, b. July 3, 1891. ii. F. Marthena, b. Nov. 25, 1895.

626 **JAMES**[8] **WARNER,** son of William Sylvester[7] and Sarah (Coulter) Warner, born August 7, 1833, in Coila, N. Y.; died July 10, 1913, in Sandwich, Ill. He removed to Illinois about 1855, was at first a teacher, then engaged in the clothing business, retired in 1889.

Married in Sandwich, Ill., July 4, 1859, **CHARLOTTE BLISS TOWNSEND,** born July 29, 1838, in Somonauk, Ill., daughter of Avery and Nancy (Dennis) Townsend.

Children, born in Sandwich

Mary Frances Warner, b. Nov. 6, 1860.

James Le Roy Warner, b. May 19, 1863; is a dealer in dry goods and general merchandise in Sandwich.

Lois Estelle Warner, b. Mar. 30, 1866; d. Aug. 28, 1888.

Sarah Bessie Warner, b. Nov. 2, 1872; m. Charles Howison. Children, b. in Sandwich: i. Charlotte, b. Mar. 9, 1900. ii. Charles, Jr., b. Apr. 25, 1909.

Henry Sylvester Warner, b. May 24, 1882; m. Blanche Brisbie. Children, b. in Sandwich: i. Robert, b. Feb. 5, 1908. ii. James, b. June 29, 1909.

627 **FANNIE STEVENSON**[8] **WARNER,** daughter of William Sylvester[7] and Sarah (Coulter) Warner, born in Coila, N. Y., August 5, 1844; resided in Cambridge, N. Y., and died there, May 23, 1875.

Married in Cambridge, December 9, 1863, **C H A R L E S TOWNSEND HAWLEY,** born in Cambridge, February 15, 1841, son of Ransom and Margaret (Tice) Hawley. He was a railroad agent and coal merchant.

Children

William Chauncey Hawley, b. in Cambridge, N. Y., Aug. 31, 1865; is Chief Engineer and General Superintendent of the Pennsylvania Water Company at Wilkinsburg, Pa., residing at Edgewood, Pittsburg, Pa. He was graduated from Washington Academy at Salem, N. Y., in 1881; from Rensselaer Polytechnic Institute, Troy, N. Y., June, 1886, with the degree of Civil Engineer; has since followed hydraulic and sanitary engineering, doing work in New York, Illinois, Wisconsin, Iowa, New Jersey, West Virginia, and Pennsylvania. From February, 1896, to June, 1902, he was engineer and superintendent of the Water Department, Atlantic City, N. J.; since that date in his present position. Mr. Hawley is a member of the Episcopal Church. He was married in Ferguson, Mo., Dec. 25, 1890, to Susan Cornelia (Nellie) Newton, b. Feb. 6, 1871, in Chetopa, Kans., daughter of Edmund B. and Harriet (Hitchcock) Newton. Children: i. Margaret, b. in Chicago, Mar. 2, 1892; was graduated from Smith College, 1913; resides in Mifflintown, Pa.; m. Mar. 23, 1914, Rev. John C. Ely, Jr., a Presbyterian minister, son of Rev. John C. and Flora A. (Brooks) Ely of Oakland, Md.; has two children, Hawley Brooks, b. in Wilkinsburg, Pa., Jan. 2, 1915, and Warner Chenowith, b. in Mifflintown, Pa., Apr. 29, 1916. ii. William Chauncey, Jr., b. in Wilkinsburg, Feb. 24, 1904.

Charles Hawley, Jr., b. Aug. 15, 1867; d. July 7, 1906.

Irving Gardner Hawley, b. Dec. 21, 1871; d. Aug. 25, 1872.

Francis Edwin Hawley, b. Apr. 24, 1875; d. May 30, 1875.

628 WILBER WILLIAM⁸ WARNER, son of William C.⁷ and Susan P. (Partridge) Warner, born in Lockport, Erie Co., Pa., December 20, 1850; died in San Diego, Cal., April 11, 1916, while on a trip for his health. With his father's family he went to Baraboo, Wis., at an early age and prepared for the University of Wisconsin at the collegiate institute of Baraboo. In his sophomore year he left college and became a clerk and traveling salesman for H. N. Clark, music dealer of Madison. In 1875 Mr. Warner succeeded to the business which he re-organized and conducted, as wholesale and retail dealer in musical instruments, with uninterrupted success until his retirement about 1913. At one time he was a member of the city water board and rendered valuable service to the city. He was president of the organization that undertook and carried out the dredging of the Yahara River from Lake Monona to Lake Waubesa, and in all public improvements and civic affairs he took an active interest. His business was managed with scientific precision, and his energy and industry were without limit. He was fond of the finest in literature and had travelled extensively in this country and abroad, with an observant eye and phenomenal memory. "He seemed to have forgotten nothing ever seen, read, or heard; and he was a graceful and gracious conversationalist. His morality was exemplary; a truer friend there scarcely could be."

Married at Pulaski, N. Y., May 13, 1875, **MADORA A. FIN STER**, born in Dugway, Oswego Co., N. Y., daughter of Sherman W. and M. B. Finster.

Child

Paul Sherman Warner, b. in Baraboo, Wis., Aug. 25, 1876; resides in Madison, Wis., where he conducts a general insurance, bond and mortgage business; m. in St. Paul, Minn., Oct. 7, 1902, Luella Hughson, b. in St. Paul, Dec. 10, 1876, daughter of E. E. and Anna May (Nutting) Hughson of St. Paul. Children: Dorothy, b. in Madison, June 29, 1905, and William Hughson, b. in Madison, Nov. 27, 1910.

629 **EDWIN SHERMAN**[8] **WARNER,** son of William C.[7] and Susan (Partridge) Warner, born January 9, 1866, at Bara boo, Wis.; resided formerly in Madison, Wis., now in Seattle, Wash., where he is engaged in the business of decorative paint ing and paper hanging.

Married at Baraboo, Wis., October 22, 1880, **MABLE F. AYARS,** born at Baraboo, April 2, 1871, adopted daughter of John Ayars of Baraboo.

Children, all but last born in Madison, Wis.

Howard E. Warner, b. Mar. 15, 1893; m. May 25, 1914, Ann Hughes of Seattle, Wash., from whom he is divorced.
Esther Warner, b. Nov. 14, 1894; m. July 24, 1915, George Nelson of Seattle.
Wilber V. Warner, b. Dec. 5, 1895; resides in Seattle.
Arthur L. Warner, b. Aug. 1, 1900; resides in Seattle.
Robert W. Warner, b. in Seattle, May 23, 1910.

630 **FRANK SETH**[8] **WARNER,** son of William C.[7] and Susan (Partridge) Warner, born December 25, 1867, in Bara boo, Wis.; resides in Seattle, Wash. He was formerly a farmer and hop-raiser at O'Brien, King Co., Wash., and is now a whole sale dealer in hay and grain in Seattle, with a warehouse at Wapato.

Married in O'Brien, Wash., August 13, 1891, **MAUD E. WILSON,** who had resided in Carthage, Mo.

Children

Wayne W. Warner, b. Sept. 22, 1892; m. in Tacoma, Wash., Apr. 15, 1916, Marie Meyers.

Ruth E. Warner, b. Oct. 24, 1893, in O'Brien, Wash.; died; m. at Seattle, Wash., Nov. 3, 1913, Walter R. McCurdy.

631   HATTIE INEZ[8] WARNER, daughter of Ulysses Southworth[7] and Mary Angeline (Tooker) Warner, born February 14, 1855, in Hamburg, Conn.; resides at Ft. McCoy, Fla.
Married January 1, 1879, FRED A. BERNHARDT, a merchant, born at Shelburne Falls, Mass., June 2, 1854, son of Gustavus Reinhold and Althea (————) Bernhardt.

Children

Florence Winona Bernhardt, b. Feb. 28, 1880; m. July 3, 1901, Frederick Ames.
Della Warner Bernhardt, b. Aug. 5, 1881; m. Aug. 26, 1914, Cornelius Gast.
David Frederick Bernhardt, b. Dec. 11, 1885; is a successful electrician; was electrical engineer for the J. B. King Company; later, power sales engineer for the electric light and power company on Staten Island; was a member of the N. Y. N. G. for three years. Married July, 1910, Bessie Ludi.
Helen Isabel Bernhardt, b. Nov. 28, 1889; m. Feb. 14, 1916, William Bohmann.

632   ULYSSES ADEN[8] WARNER, son of Ulysses Southworth[7] and Mary Angeline (Tooker) Warner, born December 20, 1858, in Lyme, Conn.; died January 17, 1911, in Waterbury, Conn. He was a letter carrier and had been in the postoffice for nineteen and a half years. He was a member of Company A, Connecticut National Guard, and, at the time of receiving his honorable discharge, he was first sergeant.
Married in Waterbury, Conn., October 30, 1889, MARY ANN FINN, born in Baltimore, Md., October 8, 1859, died in Waterbury, Conn., May 15, 1916, daughter of James Thomas and Mary Ann (Bowes) Finn.

Children

Helen Illione Warner, b. May 6, 1891, in Waterbury; resides there; m. there, Feb. 10, 1913, Harrie Avelyn Loomis, b. June 12, 1890, in Norwalk, Conn., son of Charles Fitch, Jr., and Nettie T. (Rice) Loomis. Children: i. Charles Alvin, b. Jan. 19, 1915. ii. Nettie Ruhamah, b. Jan. 1, 1918.
Ulysses Horton Warner, b. June 12, 1896, in Waterbury; stenographer and bookkeeper. Enlisted in the Quartermaster's Department, U. S. A., Oct. 26, 1917, was called for active service, Dec. 15, 1917, and sent to Camp Johnston, Jacksonville, Fla., transferred from there to Camp McArthur, Waco, Texas.

633   DAVID DENNIS⁸ WARNER, son of Ulysses Southworth⁷ and Mary Angeline (Tooker) Warner, born February
27, 1861, in Lyme, Conn.; resides in Moravia, N. Y., where he
is engaged as a clerk.

Married in Moravia, February 17, 1892, **FLORENCE M.
STONE**, born in Moravia, May 30, 1872, daughter of ·George
and Mary (————) Stone.

Children, born in Middletown, Conn.

Ruby Mae Warner, b. May 23, 1893; resides in Moravia.
Pearl Angeline Warner, b. May 24, 1898.
Wesley Stone Warner, b. Aug. 16, 1901; is a student in Moravia.

634   CARLOS SHERMAN⁸ WARNER, son of Samuel Cur
tis⁷ and Eliza (Sherman) Warner, born in Newtown, Conn.,
April 4, 1841; resides in Brooklyn, N. Y. In early life Mr.
Warner left the farm for a career of work in construction lines,
his first position being with a civil engineering corps on the
Boston, Hartford and Erie Railway. ·He was next engaged
with Smith and Ripley in the building of the Connecticut Western Railway, as paymaster, bookkeeper and superintendent of
construction, and was with the same firm while building the
Holyoke branch of the New Haven and Northampton Railway.
He was paymaster for Sidney Dillon on the tunnel under West
Point during the early part of that work. He served as paymaster and purchasing agent for Dillon, Clyde, & Company,
during the construction of the Fourth Avenue improvement in
New York City from 47th Street to the Harlem River, a work
costing several millions and covering a period of two years.
From that time until about 1878, Mr. Warner was with Smith
and Ripley as superintendent of construction, in extending the
railroad from Northampton to Turners Falls, from South Deerfield to Bardwell's Ferry, and from Wayland, N. Y., to Buffalo.
The firm of Warner and Madigan was .then formed and has
successfully carried on extensive contracts for building railroads, waterworks and mill construction, notable among which
are: the building of the Northern Adirondack Railroad; the
extension of the Wheeling and Lake Erie in Ohio; the grading
and masonry at the Vanderbilt Mausoleum Grounds on Staten
Island; the Akron branch of the Baltimore and Ohio Railroad;
the Pennsylvania, Poughkeepsie and Boston, from Slatington,
Pa., to Middletown, N. Y.; two railroads near Scranton, Pa.;
the Rumford Falls and Rangeley Lakes Railway in Maine, and

several small roads in northern New Hampshire and Maine; mills in the Hudson and Androscoggin Rivers.

Carlos Sherman Warner married in Monroe, Conn., June 26, 1866, **ELLEN A. SEELEY**, born in Monroe, Conn., March 31, 1845, daughter of Nathan W. and Julia (Taylor) Seeley, and a descendant of Captain Nathaniel Seeley, an early settler of Fairfield, Conn. An account of her lineage will be found in the Commemorative biographical record of Fairfield County, Conn., page 994.

Children

Elma Luola Warner, b. Oct. 1, 1873, in New York City; is a teacher of physical culture in Erasmus Hall High School, Brooklyn, N. Y.
Ethel Julia Warner, b. Nov. 5, 1886, in Brooklyn; is a kindergarten teacher in Brooklyn.

635 LUCIUS CURTIS⁸ WARNER, son of Samuel Curtis⁷ and Eliza (Sherman) Warner, born July 10, 1844, in Newtown, Conn. He is a physician, has resided in Chicago, now in Shawnee, Okla., where he and his family are connected with the Balneal Remedy Company and are also interested in real estate and oil business.

Married April 27, 1870, in Indiana, near Chicago, **MARY M. KENNEY**, born in Orchard Grove, Ind., March 14, 1850, daughter of Charles and Hannah (Woodruff) Kenney.

Children

Bertrand A. Warner, b. Oct. 17, 1872, at Kankakee City, Ill.; is a physician in Shawnee, Okla.; not married.
Elmer Warner, b. Dec. 23, 1873, at Orchard Grove, Ind.; is a physician in Shawnee, Okla.; not married.
Charles V. Warner, b. May 9, 1877, at Alvin, Ill.; resides at Tampico, Mexico, where he is engaged in the real estate and oil business; m. in Shawnee, Okla., Nellie Lahn.

636 GEORGE COFFING⁸ WARNER, son of Milton Jones⁷ and Maria Birch (Coffing) Warner, born in Salisbury, Conn., July 13, 1871. He was educated at Reid's Classical School, Lakeville, Conn., the University of Virginia, and was graduated from Columbia University with the degree of LL.B. in 1891. He is a lawyer in New York City and is also interested in banking and the steel business. Since he became of age he has looked after the iron interests of the family and is now probably the largest single individual owner of iron ore bed rights in the town of Salisbury. Mr. Warner is chairman of the Board and of the Executive Committee of the Fulton Steel Corporation, maker of high speed steels and alloy steels by the electric furnace process at Fulton, where he has been associated with his brother for some sixteen years in some of the hydro-electric developments on the Oswego River.

George C. Warner was married (1) in Chicago, Ill., May 9, 1900, to **MAUD MARSHALL KELLEY,** born in Denver, Colo., March 2, 1876, daughter of Walter Jacob and Caroline (Marshall) Kelley; died in New York City, February 3, 1903. She was the granddaughter of Jacob and Abbie (Case) Kelley of Lowell, Mass., and of Seth Marshall of Painesville, Ohio.

Mr. Warner married (2) December 28, 1905, **FLORENCE RUTH LORING,** daughter of Sanford and Stella (Dyer) Loring of Chicago, formerly of Boston. Stella Dyer Loring was daughter of Dr. Charles Volney Dyer, one of the pioneer settlers of Chicago, and a descendant of Mary Dyer who was burned as a Quaker on Boston Common, and also of Roger Williams. Dr. Dyer was a surgeon in Fort Dearborn when there was no one living at Chicago except those within the stockade of the fort. He was one of the large landowners of Chicago, one of the leaders of the Abolition Party in Illinois, and a friend of Abraham Lincoln, by whom he was sent to Europe in 1863, as one of the judges of the International Court on the Abolition of the African Slave Trade. Dr. Dyer had two other children, Louis Dyer, professor of Greek at Harvard and Cornell, and later at Baliol College, Oxford, England, and Charles Gifford Dyer, the well-known artist.

Children of George C. and Maud M. (Kelley) Warner

Maud Marshall Warner, b. Mar. 15, 1901.
George Coffing Warner, Jr., b. Feb. 3, 1903; d. Feb. 5, 1903, in New York City.

Children of George C. and Florence R. (Loring) Warner

Percy De Forest Warner, b. Oct. 5, 1906.
Ruth Loring Warner, b. June 8, 1909.
Gifford Dyer Warner, b. Jan. 19, 1912.

637 EDWARD BROOKS[8] WARNER, son of Chester[7] and Charlotte Rosanna (Brooks) Warner, born in the town of Phelps, Ontario Co., N. Y., July 28, 1826; died in Michigan, March 31, 1907. He removed to Baltimore, Barry Co., Mich., in 1853, and bought a piece of timber land. He was by trade a carpenter and he settled near Barney's Mill, where he worked while his brother Henry Wells Warner was engaged in clearing the farm. Their nearest neighbor was four miles away on the road to Battle Creek, which was at that time a small village seventeen miles away. The lumber from the mill was hauled to Battle Creek by ox teams.

Married (1) in 1853, AURELIA NICHOLS of Orleans, Ontario County, N. Y. She was of delicate health when they removed to Michigan, and after a few years became worse. They returned to their old home in Orleans, but she lived only a few months and died in 1854.

He married (2) May 12, 1856, ANNA WARNER, daughter of Alanson and Sarah (Hymer) Warner. Her people removed from Ohio to Michigan about 1855. She died January 21, 1908.

Children of second wife, born in Baltimore, Barry County, Mich.

Sarah J. Warner, b. Mar. 5, 1857; resides in Hastings, Barry County; m. (1) in Hastings, Dec. 24, 1873, Frank E. Smith, who died in 1889; m. (2) June 19, 1902, Charles E. Lunn, b. in Michigan, Dec. 8, 1863, son of Joseph W. and Eliza (Bird) Lunn of England.

Sheldon E. Warner, b. May 5, 1868; d. June, 1912. He resided on his father's farm in Baltimore. Married Mar. 17, 1895, Blanche Traxel of Nashville, Mich. Children: i. Carl T., b. Dec. 17, 1895; is now at Camp Custer (Mar., 1918); m. in 1917. ii. Nellie, b. Sept., 1902.

Nelson Burdett Warner, b. Feb. 20, 1875; d. aged 3 weeks.

638 HENRY WELLS[8] WARNER (or WELLS HENRY), son of Chester[7] and Charlotte Rosanna (Brooks) Warner, born in the town of Phelps, N. Y., July 13, 1828. He went west with his brother Edward and for several years worked with him at farming in the Michigan wilderness. He later studied medicine at Ann Arbor and settled in Gaylord, Mich., where he practiced until his death.

Married at Maple Grove, Mich., April 7, 1854, ESTHER ELIZABETH HOLMES, who was born near Lockport, N. Y., daughter of Matthew and Martha (Baker) Holmes.

Children

Chester Matthew Warner, b. Feb. 27, 1855; d. Apr. 11, 1856.

Martha Alice Warner, b. May 5, 1857, in Dowling, Mich.; resides in Detroit, Mich.; is a nurse; m. in Gaylord, Mich., Aug. 6, 1882, Edwin Francis Queenette, b. in Olean, N. Y., son of George and Sophia (————) Queenette. Children: i. Grace May, b. June 14, 1883; m. ———— Morrow. ii. Edward, b. Oct. 18, 1887; d. July 9, 1888.

Edward Brooks Warner, b. Apr. 14, 1859, in Dowling, Mich.; is a taxidermist and farmer, residing in Gaylord, Mich.; m. in Vanderbilt, Jan. 1, 1889, Mary Ann Combs, b. in Seaforth, Ontario, Canada, daughter of James and Elizabeth (———) Combs. Children, b. in Gaylord: i. Elmer Elijah, b. Dec. 28, 1889. ii. Mabel Elizabeth, b. Apr. 17, 1891; d. Aug. 21, 1891, at Petoskey, Mich. iii. Sadie May, b. Feb. 20, 1893.

Marian Lillis Warner, b. in Dowling, Mich., Nov. 6, 1863; resides in Detroit, Mich.; m. in Gaylord, Mich., Oct. 21, 1882, Rev. Elmer Elsworth Carpenter, b. in Hinckley, Ohio, May 2, 1862, son of Otis Harrison and Adelia (———) Carpenter; no children.

Elijah Nelson Warner, b. May 11, 1869; d. Nov. 2, 1892.

639 SHELDON E.[8] WARNER, son of Chester[7] and Charlotte Rosanna (Brooks) Warner, born October 8, 1832, in the town of Phelps, on the place settled by his grandfather, Elijah, on the hill to the east and just above the village of Orleans, Ontario Co., N. Y. When twenty-one years of age he removed to the town of Barre, now Albion, Orleans County, where he was married and settled at Porters Corners. Here he resided until 1886 when his residence on the northwest corner was destroyed by fire. The same year he removed to Albion and established his home on the northwest corner of Main and Park Streets, where he resided until his death on May 14, 1906, which resulted from an attempt to bury a large stone. He was a farmer, a man of strong practical sense, sound judgment and keen business intelligence.

Married in Barre, December 22, 1853, SARAH J. PORTER, born April 25, 1853, at Porters Corners in the town of Barre; died March 9, 1910, at Albion, N. Y. She was the daughter of Allen and Electa (Scott) Porter.

Children

    Charlotte Warner, b. Jan. 23, 1855; d. Feb. 12, 1855.
706 *George Porter Warner*, b. May 3, 1856; m. Ellen P. Culver.
707 *Electa Jane Warner*, b. Apr. 28, 1859; m. Eugene D. Peirson.
708 *Henry Eugene Warner*, b. May 20, 1864; m. Catherine E. McCarthy.

640 MARGARET ROSANNA[8] WARNER, daughter of Chester[7] and Charlotte (Brooks) Warner, born in Phelps, N. Y., February 4, 1835; resides in Dowling, Mich. She attained by home study and experience much ability in writing sketches and composing poetry and songs, but all her writings were destroyed in a fire and little has been published. Among published articles were essays upon farming. She held the highest offices in Baltimore Grange, Number 472, and gave several public addresses through that medium. She was actively

interested in the Sabbath school, and she composed and taught the children many songs. Married in Phelps, N. Y., April 13, 1853, A L B E R T GRANGER, born in Sodus, N. Y., December 25, 1825, son of Rhesa and Phoebe (Bartlett) Granger. He was a farmer in Dowling, Mich.

Children

Philo Adelbert Granger, b. Oct. 9, 1856, in Maple Grove Township, Mich.; d. Oct. 9, 1907; was a first class brick mason and general contractor, residing at Dowling, Mich.; was educated in rural schools and at Battle Creek High School; trained and sold many valuable hunting dogs and horses outside of his trade, and was a good mechanic; m. at Hastings, Mich., May 14, 1881, Clara G. Sanborn, b. in Baltimore Township, Mich., Oct. 21, 1862, d. June 13, 1890, daughter of D. C. and Frances (Jennings) Sanborn. Children: i. Frances Rosanna, b. Mar. 30, 1882; d. Mar. 11, 1905; was a teacher before her marriage. ii. Maude Sanborn, b. Mar. 1, 1885; resides in Hastings, Mich. iii. Grace, b. Dec. 25, 1887; d. Jan. 16, 1889.

Lottie Josephine Granger, b. June 5, 1858, in Maple Grove Township, Mich.; resides in Quimby, Mich.; was educated in rural schools and at Battle Creek High School; m. in Dowling, Mich., Mar. 2, 1879, Marquis Elizer Crowfoot Segur, a farmer, b. July 13, 1856, son of Clement and Emeline (Kemerling) Segur, and a descendant of Marquis Segur, a noted French author who died in Paris in 1918. Children, all but first two reside in Quimby, Mich.: i. Granger Albert, b. Feb. 5, 1880; resides in Benson, Ariz. ii. Nellie Margaret, b. May 4, 1885; resides in Dowling, Mich. iii. Clara Emeline, b. July 28, 1887. iv. Elsie Marian, b. Apr. 1, 1890. v. Franklin Benjamin, b. June 21, 1893; is now in military service. vi. Helen Rosanna, b. June 27, 1897. vii. Reginald Marquis, b. Mar. 13, 1900. Granger, Clara, Franklin, and Helen received their education at the Michigan Business and Normal College in Battle Creek, Mich. Reginald is now in High School.

Chester Warner Granger, b. in Phelps, N. Y., June 3, 1860. He went to Alaska at the time of the opening of the Klondike gold fields in 1894, and is now settled on a beautiful farm near Dowling, Mich., near his son Frank. Married in Dowling, Jan. 16, 1880, Nellie Captolia Pritchard, b. in Wassion, Ohio, Nov. 10, 1862, daughter of Solomon and Wealthy (Emmons) Pritchard. Children: i. Belle, b. Nov. 20, 1885; d. July 9, 1886. ii. Frank, b. Aug. 17, 1893; was educated at the Michigan Business and Normal College in Battle Creek and resides near Dowling. iii. Charlie, b. Aug. 11, 1903; d. May 15, 1916.

Alberta Rosanna Granger, b. July 15, 1877, in Dowling, Mich.

641 ELIZA ANN[8] WARNER, daughter of Rice[7] and Rebecca (Carson) Warner, born in the town of Phelps, Ontario Co., N. Y., September 6, 1819; died in Albion, N. Y., February 20, 1900.

Married as his second wife, in Albion, August 27, 1840.
EDWARD CLARK BAKER, born August 24, 1812, at Sand
Lake, Rensselaer Co., N. Y.; died in Albion, N. Y., March 7,
1887.

Children

Helen Augusta Baker, b. Feb. 17, 1842, at Carlton, N. Y.; d. Sept. 16,
1910; m. at Albion, N. Y., Nov. 8, 1878, Robert Campbell, b. Mar.
4, 1843, d. June 30, 1886, at Carlisle, Canada. Child: Donald
Edward, b. Mar. 18, 1880; m. at Albion, N. Y., June 28, 1904, Maude
Virginia Butler, b. Oct. 3, 1883.
Clark Rice Baker, b. Nov. 12, 1843, at Carlton, N. Y.; d. Sept. 24,
1913, at Easton, Md.; m. at Ellisburg, N. Y., Apr. 3, 1876, Rosemund
Ersuline Russell, b. Feb. 9, 1846. Children: i. Lewis Russell, b.
Apr. 12, 1877, at Albion; m. at Passaic, N. J., Nov. 13, 1904, Cath-
leen Graham Leeson, b. in Paterson, N. J., Nov. 9, 1885; had two
children, Edward Clark, b. July 4, 1906, at St. Michaels, Md., and
a son who d. Feb. 16, 1910. ii. Grace Eliza, b. Apr. 23, 1880, at
Suspension Bridge, N. Y.; m. at Ossining, N. Y., Sept. 18, 1902,
Walter Classman; has two children, Delrain Warner, b. Oct. 23,
1903, at Ossining, and Elwood Walter, b. Aug. 1, 1910, at Yonkers,
N. Y. iii. Bessie Frances, b. Dec. 31, 1881, at Vassar, Mich.; m.
Oct. 2, 1898, Fred E. Purdy; had four children, Allene Louise, b.
July 28, 1899, at Sing Sing, N. Y., Russell Clark, b. Dec. 17, 1900,
at Sing Sing, Le Roy Reed, b. July 1, 1903, at Ossining, and Edna,
b. Jan. 30, 1910, in New York City, in an ambulance on the
way to the hospital, d. in Bellevue Hospital, Jan. 31, 1910.
Frederick Henry Baker, b. June 20, 1847, at Albion, N. Y.; was accidentally shot by Mr. Gibson and d. at Pocahontas, Va., Sept. 17,
1891; m. at Midlothian, Va., Nov. 26, 1873, Emma Virginia Marri-
sett. Children, first five b. at Midlothian, Va.: i. Roswell Edward,
b. Apr. 13, 1875; accidentally drowned at Chesapeake Beach, Md.,
Sept. 17, 1910; m. Sept. 21, 1904, in Washington, D. C., Florence
Mabel Szegedy, b. Sept. 5, 1882; had one child who d. before 1915.
ii. Helen Louise, b. July 29, 1877; m. at Pocahontas, Va., Nov. 17,
1897, Daniel Frazier; had four children, Gladys, b. about 1899, Virginia, b. about 1901, Louise, b. about 1905, and Lillian, b. 1907. iii.
Walter Frederick, b. Mar. 2, 1879. iv. Gertrude Lovinia, b. Aug. 2,
1881; m. in Washington, D. C., Feb. 3, 1904, Elmer Ellsworth Ship-
ley. v. Arthur Lee, b. Mar. 18, 1884; m. in Washington, D. C., Jan.
12, 1909, Marie Taylor. vi. Ernest Izard, b. June 30, 1886; d. June
3, 1887. vii. Ellwood George, b. Sept. 20, 1888; d. Oct. 22, 1888,
at Pocahontas, Va. viii. Lestille Virginia, b. Feb. 4, 1891, at Pocahontas, Va.
Caroline Rebecca Baker, b. May 14, 1852, at Albion; d. there, Feb. 18,
1913; was a teacher for forty-three years.

642 HENRY D.[8] WARNER, son of Hiram[7] and Mary Jane
(Knapp) Warner, born in Hopewell, Ontario Co., N. Y., June
17, 1844; died June 4, 1908. He was a prosperous farmer and
fruit grower in the town of Phelps, N. Y., a Republican in
politics and a Universalist in religion.

Married January, 1875, **FRANCES BELLE SPEAR**, daughter of James Allen and Mary (Baggerly) Spear of Clifton Springs, N. Y., and of Maryland ancestry.

Children

Belle W. Warner, m. Charles J. Carr of Dayton, Ohio.
Earl Spear Warner, b. Aug. 12, 1880, in Phelps; was graduated from Hobart College, B.L., 1902, Cornell University, LL.B., 1905; admitted to the bar in 1905, and opened an office in Phelps, Jan., 1906, where he still continues. In 1908 and later he was village attorney; President of the Phelps Business Men's Club; in 1910 was treasurer of the Cayuga, Ontario, Seneca, Yates, Schuyler and Honeoye Falls Firemen's Association; is a Republican in politics; member of F. and A. M., R. A. M., Commandery, Knights Templar, Mystic Shrine; Theta Delta Chi and Phi Delta Phi; Universalist. Married in Phelps, N. Y., Nov. 26, 1907, Selma Louise Holbrook, b. in Phelps, Aug. 22, 1884, daughter of Charles Hartman and Lucretia (Dillingham) Holbrook.
Theodore Henry Warner, b. May 16, 1889.

643 CARLOS E.^{8} WARNER, son of Ulysses^7 and Eliza Ann (Jones) Warner, born October 5, 1847, in Orleans, Ontario Co., N. Y.; has been an attorney in Detroit, Mich., since 1872. He was educated at the Canandaigua Academy, and, after a year of teaching, began the study of law at Canandaigua in 1867, was admitted to the bar two years later and practiced in Canandaigua until 1872 when he removed to Detroit, which has since been his home. He was a member of various law firms: Moore and Griffin; Moore, Canfield and Warner; Griffin and Warner; after 1896, Warner, Codd and Warner, of which he was the senior member. He was attorney for the Detroit Chamber of Commerce; one of the incorporators of the Sandwich, Windsor, and Walkerville Street Railway at Windsor, Ontario, in 1880; member of the Board of Education of Detroit for four years and its president for two; Chairman of the Democratic Congressional Committee, First Michigan District, 1894-5, and a member of the Democratic State Central Committee in 1896; member of the Woodward Avenue Baptist Church.

Married June 5, 1873, **ALICE BURR VAN HUSAN**, daughter of Caleb Van Husan of Detroit.

Children

Kathleen Elsie Warner, resides in Detroit; m. in 1894, George P. Codd, b. in Detroit, Dec. 7, 1869, son of George C. Codd. He is a lawyer. Children: John W.; George C.; Kathleen.

Emily Corwin Warner, m. Jonathan Palmer. Children: Jonathan; Carlos.
Carlos E. Warner, Jr.
John Sill Warner, died aged about 6 years.

644 ANNA GIULETTA[8] WARNER, daughter of Jefferson[7] and Susan (Burnett) Warner, born in York township, Washtenaw Co., Mich., October 20, 1836; died July 31, 1882, in Bay View, Mich., where she had been taken for her health. Married in Ann Arbor, Mich., November 23, 1861, OTIS ADAMS CRITCHETT, born in London township, Monroe Co., Mich., November 30, 1838, son of James and Abigail (Winslow) Critchett; died in Monroe, Mich., June 8, 1894 or 5. After attending the district school until 17 years old, he engaged in teaching and subsequently entered Lodi Academy. He was graduated from the University of Michigan in 1862, A.B.; LL.B., 1864; A.M., 1865. He was admitted to the bar in 1865 and practiced law until his health failed a few years before his death. He was elected prosecuting attorney in 1866, and judge of the probate in 1872; was the Republican candidate for judge in the 22d circuit in 1881. He was appointed postmaster by President Garfield and held the office for four years. He married (2) September, 1883, in Monroe, Almira Amelia[8] Warner, sister of his first wife, born September 10, 1839 or 1840, died December 26, 1902.

Children

James Clyde Critchett, b. in Ann Arbor, Oct. 25, 1862; m. there, July 15, 1884, Ada Louise[6] Kellogg, daughter of Elijah Ellis and Margaret[7] (Warner) Kellogg; see number 468. He was a student at the University of Michigan for three years and in the law school one year; was admitted to the bar in 1886; spent a year in Mexico in the employ of his uncle, who was a contractor engaged in building the Mexico Central Railroad; was a teacher, then in the employ of the Express Company at El Paso, Texas, and Mexico City, later became customs inspector in Clint, Texas. Children: i. Ruth Anne, b. in Juarez, Mexico, Dec. 25, 1891. ii. Helen Louise, b. in Clint, Texas, Feb. 4, 1895; d. there, Dec. 18, 1898. iii. Ethel May, b. in Clint, Nov. 27, 1896. iv. Marion, b. in Clint, June 10, 1899; d. in El Paso, Sept. 14, 1899.

John Fremont Critchett, b. in Monroe, Mich., Nov. 1, 1866.

Mary Abigail Critchett, b. in Monroe, Sept. 1, 1869; d. there, Aug. 25, 1870.

Otis Adams Critchett, b. in Monroe, Aug. 17, 1875.

One of these sons resided in Nova Scotia in 1902.

645 JUNE LYMAN[8] WARNER, son of Lyman[7] and Azuba (Near) Warner, born in Milan, Mich., March 19, 1855; is a

salesman, residing in Elk Rapids, Mich. He removed from Milan, Monroe County, to Grand Traverse County, August, 1881, and bought eighty acres of land in Williamsburg, only fifteen acres of which were then cleared. He was Treasurer of Whitewater Township for six years and Supervisor for four years. Since 1899 he has resided in Elk Rapids, and was Mayor, 1916-8. The family are Spiritualists in religion, and are all members of the Red Cross.

Married at Stony Creek, December 31, 1874, **EMOGENE VESCELIUS**, born in Milan, Mich., September 14, 1857, daughter of Jacob R. and Lury (Harmon) Vescelius.

Children

Claud H. Warner, b. at Milan, Sept. 5, 1876; resides on a farm near Williamsburg, Mich.; m. (1) Feb. 18, 1897, Martha Hamilton, who died May 1, 1904; m. (2) Hattie Langcaval. Children by first wife: i. Dewey E., b. Sept. 16, 1898; d. Feb. 1, 1912. ii. Gordon J., b. Mar. 19, 1902. Children by second wife: i. Normagene, b. in Williamsburg, Feb. 23, 1908. ii. Josephine Louise, b. Mar. 21, 1918.

Vida Lury Warner, b. at Williamsburg, Feb. 27, 1888; resides on a farm near Williamsburg; m. (1) Lowell Morrison, who died Jan. 27, 1912; m. (2) Apr. 5, 1913, Bert J. Hedgler. Child by first husband: Marjorie Azuba, b. at Elk Rapids, Mar. 27, 1908. Child by second husband: June Claudia, b. at Williamsburg, Oct. 9, 1917.

646 EUGENE NELLIS[8] WARNER, son of Elbridge Oliver[7] and Nancy (Nellis) Warner, born in Unionville, Ohio, January 10, 1847; died in 1914. He was a prosperous farmer in Unionville, a leader in all things good, and one of the most highly respected citizens of Northeastern Ohio.

Married in Unionville, April 17, 1872, KATE AUGUSTA HUTCHINS, born August 15, 1853, in Unionville, daughter of Calvin and Emeline (Crosby) Hutchins.

Children

Dorr Eugene Warner, b. Dec. 6, 1873; is an attorney in Cleveland, Ohio; was graduated from Princeton, A.B., 1896; LL.B., Western Reserve University, 1899.

Otto Nellis Warner, b. Dec. 21, 1874; is a physician in Conneaut, Ohio; was graduated from Western Reserve University, M.D., 1898; is an officer in the Medical Reserve Corps.

Josephine C. Warner, b. Sept. 26, 1877; resides in Madison, Ohio; m. —— Lyons.

George Elbridge Warner, b. June 21, 1880; is a farmer in Unionville, Ohio.

Nettie Nancy Warner, b. Aug. 26, 1881; d. May 2, 1907.

Mary E. Warner, b. Nov. 17, 1885; resides in Perry, Ohio; m. —— Salkeld.

39

Elbridge Stephen Warner, b. Feb. 15, 1896; was graduated from Cor
nell University, B.S., 1917; resides in Unionville; is a member of
the U. S. Naval Reserves.

646a **GEORGE EDWARD**[8] **WARNER,** son of Charles C.[7]
and Eliza (Foote) Warner, born November 28, 1841, in Ridge
way, Orleans Co., N. Y.; resides in Williamston, Mich. He is
by trade a carpenter and mason, also a baker and confectioner.
He saw three years' service in the Civil War, and is a member
of Eli P. Alexander Post, 96, G. A. R. of Williamston.
Married (1) February 18, 1861, HATTIE LOZIER, born in
Medina, N. Y., February 18, 1843; died February 6, 1866.
Married (2) in Oak Orchard, N. Y., April 21, 1869, MARY
LOUISE HOOKER, born in Ridgeway, N. Y., February 26,
1851, daughter of Chauncey David and Sarah Louise (Reynolds)
Hooker.

Child of George E. and Hattie (Lozier) Warner

Lena Warner, b. Feb. 3, 1863; m. June 9, 1878, Charles Felter. Children: Bertha; Alma; George; Earl.

Children of George E. and Mary L. (Hooker) Warner

Charles Warner, b. in Ridgeway, N. Y., Apr. 7, 1871; d. same day.
Carrie C. Warner, b. Nov. 24, 1872, at Ridgeway, N. Y.; m. Nov. 17,
1909, Charles Retter. She is a member of the Woodman Circle,
auxiliary of the Woodmen of the World.
Mattie Warner, b. Apr. 21, 1877; d. May 12, 1877, at Wheatfield,
Ingham Co., Mich.
Emma Maude Warner, b. May 28, 1880; resides in Williamston; is
a member of the Woodmen Circle and of the Women's Relief Corps,
Eli P. Alexander Post, of Williamston; m. Dec. 25, 1900, George H.
Landenberger, b. in Watertown, Clinton Co., Mich., May 14, 1873,
son of Jacob and Lizzie Landenberger. Children: i. George, Jr., b.
Apr. 19, 1902; d. same day. ii. Jean H., b. Mar. 17, 1904, at Leroy,
Ingham Co., Mich. iii. Ilah I., b. Sept. 28, 1915, at Williamston,
Mich.
Mabel May Warner, b. Aug. 3, 1887, at Wheatfield, Mich.; is a mem-
ber of the Women's Relief Corps, Eli P. Alexander Post, of Wil-
liamston; m. July 20, 1904, Sylvester Torrance. Children: i. Glenn,
b. Mar. 9, 1908. ii. Eldred, b. Nov. 6, 1913.

646b **MARY EVELYNE**[8] **WARNER,** daughter of Lewis[7]
and Rosa A. (Harris) Warner, born in Albion, Calhoun Co.,
Mich., April 9, 1862; resides in Lowell, Mich. Before her
marriage she was a teacher in the public schools. She has
taken great interest in art and literature and has written for
the press. For nine years she was lecturer of the Grange, of the
County Grange for four years, and was Master of the Grange

for two years. She belongs to the Methodist Church and was an active worker until ill health compelled her to remain at home. Married in Lowell, Mich., November 9, 1886, E A R L CUSTER CURTISS, born in Vergennes, Kent Co., Mich., October 8, 1862, son of S. P. and Lucy (Vinton) Curtiss. He is a farmer in Lowell township; studied medicine but has been more interested in agricultural pursuits. He is an active community builder and has held many public offices. He is a member of the Methodist Church.

Children born in Lowell

Rosella Curtiss, b. Nov. 22, 1887; was graduated from High School and taught music; m. June 21, 1910, O. J. Yeiter who is in the furniture business in Lowell. Children: i. Evelyn, b. Feb. 26, 1912, in Metolis, Ore. ii. Gerald Samuel, b. June 2, 1918, in Lowell, Mich.

Elizabeth Curtiss, b. May 22, 1889; was a High School graduate and taught several years at the I. O. O. F. Home Orphanage in Jackson; is also a dressmaker; m. June 26, 1917, W. K. Lusk of Rustburg, Va.

Sessions Paul Curtiss, b. June 19, 1892; is living on a farm near The Dalles, Ore.; m. June 22, 1915, Ellen Schantz. Child: Sessions Paul, Jr., b. Feb. 17, 1918, near The Dalles.

Dale Custer Curtiss, b. Nov. 23, 1893; resides in Lowell; m. June 12, 1917, Laura M. Vanderhill.

Marie Amanda Curtiss, b. Nov. 12, 1895; was a High School graduate and teacher; m. June 12, 1915, Charles H. Smith of Ypsilanti, Mich. Child: Adrian, b. at Osseo, Mich., July 18, 1917.

Lennah Maud Curtiss, b. Feb. 7, 1898, was graduated from Lowell High School, 1917, took up Civil Service and a business course in Grand Rapids and in May, 1918, went to Washington in the War Department.

Evelyn Gertrude Curtiss, b. Sept. 6, 1901.

647 JOHN[8] WARNER, son of Alonzo Elijah[7] and Ruth (Cooke) Warner, born in Belchertown, Mass., about 1826; was living in Granby, Mass., in 1882; died about 1898. He was a farmer and a veteran of the Civil War.

Married (1) in Belchertown, October 4, 1848, MARGARET M. SHUMWAY, born in Belchertown about 1822, daughter of Henry Shumway of that place.

Married (2) in Granby, Mass., September 4, 1882 (Granby town records), ARMINDA C. (LEACH) DOMKLEY, born in Burke, Vt., about 1830, daughter of George and Sarah (————) Leach. She was living in South Hadley at the time of her marriage.

Children by first wife

Minnie M. Warner, b. in Belchertown about 1851; m. May 23, 1880, recorded in Belchertown and Granby, Alphonzo J. Whitmarsh, b. in

South Hadley, about 1851, son of James and Lucy H. (Davison) Whitmarsh. She was a teacher before her marriage and was for some years superintendent of schools in Granby, an unusual honor for a woman at that time. He was a farmer in Granby for some years, but they spent their later life in South Hadley Falls, where both died about 1910.

Clarence Duane Warner, b. in Granby, about 1852; d. Oct. 16, 1905 (college record), in Kimmswick, a suburb of St. Louis, Mo., where he was engaged in farming on a small scale, hoping to regain his health. He was a graduate of Massachusetts Agricultural College at Amherst, B.Sc., 1881; taught in Providence, R. I.; was a student of mathematics at Johns Hopkins University, Baltimore, 1885-6; professor of mathematics and physics at Massachusetts Agricultural College from 1886 to 1896, when he was obliged to give up his work on account of ill health. He was a man of wonderful personality and had a host of friends; a Christian of high standing, he was, while a professor at Massachusetts Agricultural College, active in directing the morals of the boys. Professor Warner married in Willimantic, Conn., Aug. 26, 1886, Nellie Marion Malkin, b. in New Canaan, d. in Amherst, Aug. 22, 1888, aged 29 years, 3 months, 2 days, daughter of William Malkin, who was born in Cheshire, England, and Marion Malkin, who was born in London, England.

Henry A. Warner, b. in Belchertown, 1854; d. there, Aug. 4, 1858, aged 4.

Edna O. Warner, b. in Belchertown, Sept. 21, 1855; was a teacher before her marriage; resides in Fitchburg, Mass.; m. in Belchertown, June 15, 1885, as his second wife, Clarence Merrett Pratt, b. in Pelham, Mass., Oct. 24, 1847, son of Warner and Sophronia (Arnold) Pratt. He is a building contractor in Fitchburg. No children.

Nella Warner, b. Jan. 27, 1857, in Granby; d. there, about 1882; m. May 8, 1877, recorded in Granby, Varnum T. S. Keith, b. in Springfield, Mass., about 1853, son of Arad and Abigail (Frost) Keith. He was a farmer in Granby. Children: i. Nella, m. —— Rumrill; resides in Chicopee Falls, Mass. ii. Grace, d. in infancy.

Herbert Warner, b. in Granby, June 1, 1860, recorded in Granby as Claron Herbert; is a farmer in Granby.

648 STETSON TITUS[8] WARNER, son of Alonzo Elijah[7] and **Ruth** (Cooke) Warner, born in Belchertown, Mass., July 25, 1828; died in Springfield, Mass., February 19, 1902. He was a farmer in Belchertown in early life; in 1849 went in a sailing vessel "around the Horn" to California, where he remained for four years, mining some and cooking on a boat part of the time. He then returned to Massachusetts and spent most of his life farming. His name was sometimes recorded Titus S. on deeds.

Married about 1857, **HANNAH COY RICHARDSON,** born in Harford, Pa., June 17, 1829; died in Agawam, Mass., April 21, 1901. Both Mr. and Mrs. Warner are buried in Oak Grove

Cemetery, Springfield. They were both much interested in missionary work and gave liberally to that cause.

Child

Lillian M. Warner, b. in Belchertown, Mass., Jan. 21, 1860; resides in Springfield, Mass.; m. there, Oct. 7, 1886, Willie Lemuel Chandler, b. in Neemaha, Neb., Dec. 1, 1858, son of William and Loraine (Goodale) Chandler. Children: i. Alice Warner, b. Aug. 17, 1893; m. Jan. 15, 1916, Joseph Proctor Stimson, a tool maker, and has two children, Miriam Elizabeth, b. Dec. 18, 1916, and Marjorie Alice, b. Dec. 31, 1917. ii. Ruth Warner, b. Nov. 3, 1895; m. Aug. 27, 1917, Samuel Lester Stimson, brother of Joseph. Samuel Lester Stimson was drafted in 1917, was sent to Camp Devens, Ayer, Mass., then to Camp Gordon, Atlanta, Ga.; is now, May, 1918, a member of Company F, 307th Supply Train.

649 GEORGE LEMUEL[8] WARNER, son of Alonzo Elijah[7] and Ruth (Cooke) Warner, born in Granby, Mass., 1832; died in Springfield, Mass., April 26, 1897. He was a farmer and lived in Springfield. He was a veteran of the Civil War and saw much service in the New Orleans campaign.
Married (1) June 12, 1850, HARRIET L. WILLIAMS.
Married (2) February 6, 1867, HELEN LEVANTIA BOGUE, born in St. Charles, Ill., October 31, 1842; died March 17, 1910.

Children by first wife

Harriet Warner, b. in Granby, Mass., Mar. 18, 1861.
Eugene Warner, b. in Granby. Belchertown records give a son born to George Warner, Apr. 23, 1863, and another Dec. 25, 1864, names not given.

Children by second wife

Frank Dayton Warner, b. in Piper City, Ill., Dec. 17, 1867; was in the real estate business in Springfield for many years; m. Aug. 27, 1889, Rosetta M. Richards. Child: Mabel, b. in Springfield, Mass., 1894.
Fred George Warner, b. in Piper City, Ill., Nov. 10, 1869; was for many years a successful contractor and builder in Springfield; m. in Springfield, June 28, 1899, Mabel F. Parmelee. Children: i. Doris Helen, b. Oct. 5, 1901. ii. Donald, b. June, 1914; d. aged six weeks.
Minnie Ella Warner, b. in Piper City, Ill., July 31, 1872; m. (1) in Chicago, Ill., Lewis Lee Gleason of Granby, Mass., who died in Jacksonville, Fla., Mar., 1911; m. (2) May, 1915, Edward F. Werden of Pittsfield, Mass. Children by first husband, b. in Springfield, Mass.: i. Leon Warner, b. Jan. 29, 1893. ii. Ethel Helen, b. Oct. 18, 1896. iii. Stanley Lewis, b. Feb. 7, 1897.
Marland Hewes Warner, b. in Montgomery, Mass., Sept. 27, 1875; was a mason by trade; m. in 1896, Marcia Richards of Franklin, Vt. Child: Donald, d. in infancy.

Willa Henrietta Warner, b. in Montgomery, Mass., June 5, 1877; resides in Longmeadow, Mass.; m. in Weehawken, N. J., July 7, 1914, Samuel Thompson Ball, who has been a successful real estate man in Springfield for many years.

Wilbur C. Warner, b. at Dwight, Mass., Mar. 11, 1882; is serving in the war in France, Apr., 1918; m. in Portsmouth, England, Nov. 20, 1916.

Grace Estella Warner, b. in Winchendon, Mass., Apr. 9, 1884; m. in 1912, Leonard Herbert of Lynn, Mass.

650 MARY ELIZABETH[8] WARNER, daughter of Alonzo Elijah[7] and Ruth (Cooke) Warner, born in Belchertown, Mass., April 4, 1834; died in Montpelier, Ind., July 16, 1916. She spent most of her married life in Piper City, Ind., and Benton Harbor, Mich., where her husband died, and she then went to live with her son in Montpelier, Ind., where she died. She paid periodic visits to her brothers and sisters in the east, which were occasions for celebrations and great rejoicing. She was a very brilliant woman, sparkling with wit and humor and captivated everyone who knew her. For over sixty years she was an active member and worker in the Presbyterian Church; was also a member of the W. R. C. and Ladies' Circle, and took a great interest in the work.

Married in Belchertown, Mass., September 1, 1853, MARTIN M. PULVER, born January 21, 1831, in Copake, N. Y., died in Benton Harbor, Mich., February 11, 1914, son of Peter I. and Sally (Maxfield) Pulver. He enlisted December 5, 1861, in Company F, 31st Regiment, Massachusetts Infantry, 19th Army Corps; served as private, Sergeant, 2d Lieutenant, and was finally mustered out of service at the end of the war as Major of the 91st Colored Infantry.

Children

Edward F. Pulver, b. Aug. 19, 1854, in Princeton, Ill.; is an accountant and resides in Montpelier, Ind.; m. at Piper City, Ill., May 26, 1881, Ohio Estella Snider, b. at El Paso, Ill., May 26, 1860, daughter of Jacob F. and Melissa P. (———) Snider. Children: i. Mary Melissa, b. June 22, 1883, at Piper City; m. Oct. 9, 1909, at Benton Harbor, Mich., Robert E. Stevenson, b. in North Salem, Ind., son of Wesley and Mary C. (Dodd) Stevenson, a manufacturer of automobiles; resides in Indianapolis, Ind.; no children. ii. Willard F., b. June 8, 1888, at Minneapolis, Minn.; d. there, Aug. 12, 1888.

Wilson B. Pulver, b. Jan. 30, 1860, at Springfield, Mass.; d. Sept. 10, 1878, at Piper City, Ill.

Freddy B. Pulver, b. Aug. 20, 1866, at Piper City; d. there, Dec. 24, 1867.

651 LYDIA ANN[8] WARNER, daughter of Alonzo Elijah[7] and Ruth (Cooke) Warner, born in Belchertown, Mass., November 30, 1839; died January 25, 1915, at Dwight, Belchertown, buried there. Married in Belchertown, November 17, 1859, MARTIN SANFORD ARNOLD, born in Pelham, Mass., February 12, 1837; died in 1899. He was the son of Savannah and Emeline (———) Arnold. They resided in Granby until 1881, when they removed to Dwight, Belchertown, Mass. They will be long remembered for their helpful Christian lives in the town of Dwight, where all were welcome at their pleasant country home.

Children

Osman Savannah Arnold, b. June 26, 1862; d. Jan., 1903; m. 1896, Mattie Jewett. He was a farmer living in South Amherst, Mass. They had one daughter who died when about six years old.

Edith Gertrude Arnold, b. July 20, 1867; m. in Belchertown, Aug. 25, 1893, Arthur Jenks, a farmer, b. in Ludlow, Mass., Mar. 22, 1869, son of Lucian and Alameda (———) Jenks. She resides on the old place at Dwight, where her mother spent the last years of her life under her watchful, tender care, and patient nursing. Children: i. Raymond Warner, b. in South Amherst, Aug. 18, 1896; m. Apr. 29, 1916, Edith S. Marsh, daughter of Charles and Grace (Jones) Marsh; has a son, Sanford Lewis, b. in Dwight, Feb. 25, 1917. ii. Leo Arnold, b. Sept. 29, 1900, at Dwight. iii. Merwin Arthur, b. Nov. 19, 1912, at Dwight.

Frank Luman Arnold, b. June 27, 1871; was graduated from Massachusetts Agricultural College in 1891, B.Sc.; Boston University, B.Sc.; Chemist, Massachusetts Experiment Station, 1891-5; Chief Chemist, Bowker Fertilizer Company, Elizabeth, N. J., and Cincinnati, Ohio, 1895-1904; Superintendent of Sulphuric Acid plants, Merrimac Chemical Company, Woburn, Mass., since 1904; resides in Woburn; m. at Gloucester, Mass., Apr. 21, 1896, Bertha May Kimball, daughter of Joseph W. and Mary (Blaisdell) Kimball of Gloucester. Children: i. Mildred Irene, b. Apr. 3, 1897; a member of the class of 1919, Smith College. ii. Elliott Frank, b. June 25, 1907. iii. Eleanor Kimball, b. Mar. 13, 1910.

Maud Adella Arnold, b. in Granby, Mass., May 23, 1873; was a graduate of Belchertown High School and was a teacher for several years before her marriage; m. in Belchertown, Apr. 5, 1899, Charles Eugene Page, a farmer of Claremont, N. H. He was born in Nelson, N. H., Nov. 21, 1865, son of Sewell Willard and Nancy A. (Jenkins) Page. Child: Katherine Lydia, b. Aug. 27, 1900, in Stoddard, N. H.

652 CELIA GERTRUDE[8] WARNER, daughter of Alonzo Elijah[7] and Ruth (Cooke) Warner, born in Belchertown, Mass., September 24, 1847; resides in Berkeley, Cal. She was a teacher in the schools of Chicago for several years.

Married in Piper City, Ill., June 22, 1870, **MARLAND SMITH HEWES,** born in Boston, Mass., September 16, 1847, son of Aaron Tapley and Louisa (Smith) Hewes. He died January 21, 1915. He was a nephew of David Hewes, a California pioneer who gave the gold spike which was driven in the Central Pacific Railroad to celebrate the connection of the two great oceans of the world. Marland Hewes removed to Chicago when a young man; after the fire of 1871, he went to St. Louis, later to Los Angeles and Berkeley. He was a successful business man in the wholesale boot and shoe trade in San Francisco. He was a genial, happy man, earnest in church work, a blessing to his family and to all with whom he was associated. He was a member of the Sons of the American Revolution.

Child

Mabel Warner Hewes, b. Feb. 13, 1877; was graduated from Mills College in 1897 with high honors, and was for a time president of the Alumnæ Association; has travelled extensively in many parts of the world; m. June 29, 1910, Henry Edmonds Chandler, who is in the real estate business. They reside in Berkeley, Cal. They have two children, Edmond Hewes, b. July 26, 1912, a member of the Junior Red Cross of Berkeley, and Marland Hewes, b. Apr. 16, 1917. Both Mr. and Mrs. Chandler are active in church and club circles in Berkeley.

653 CHARLES ADAMS[8] WARNER, son of Park[7] and Joanna (Adams) Warner, born in Amherst, Mass., September 5, 1829; died in Chaska, Minn., October 27, 1867. He sailed for California from Boston on March 1, 1849, with a party of over a hundred men from New England who had formed a company and purchased the vessel Regulus and equipment. After a voyage of about seven months they landed at San Francisco on September 29th. Mr. Warner spent the winter near Benicia making shingles and in the spring went to Salmon Falls on the south fork of the American River thirty-five miles from Sacramento City to engage in mining.

In 1856 Mr. Warner went to Minnesota and located at Chaska the following year. There he kept a frontier store; was postmaster; took an important part in territorial politics and the establishment of state government; was Senator for Carver County in 1860; established the Chaska Herald in 1860; was a Mason of high degree. In the History of the Minnesota Valley it is stated, "It is due to the memory of T. D. .Smith and Charles A. Warner to state that much of the business prosperity

CHARLES ADAMS WARNER

of Chaska was due to their enterprise, when in the early days of competition the weight of one man's character often decides the prestige of a town."

We have here reproduced some of the letters written by Mr. Warner to his father in 1849, feeling that they will be of interest to many of our readers for the light they throw upon the early days of gold mining.

Charles A. Warner was married in Easthampton, Mass., September 5, 1851, to **CATHERINE KNIGHT**, born in Stafford, Conn., April 25, 1829, died in South Hadley, Mass., February 19, 1902, daughter of Milo and Mary (Ingalls) Knight. She was descended from David[1] and Sarah (Backus) Knight, who were married March 17, 1691-2 and resided in Norwich, Conn.; Benjamin[2] Knight, who was wounded at the falling of a bridge across the Shetucket in 1728, an accident in which many lives were lost, and his wife, Mary Adams; Asher[3] and Mary (Clark) Knight; Milo[4] Knight and his wife, Mary Ingalls, the daughter of Calvin and Mary (Horton) Ingalls.

Children

709 *William Austin Warner,* b. in South Hadley, Mass., Dec. 12, 1853; m. Julia Anna Burnette.

Alice Kate Warner, b. in Chaska, Minn., Apr. 11, 1858; d. there, Feb. 20, 1862.

Clinton James Warner, b. in Chaska, Jan. 5, 1865; d. there, Apr. 25, 1866.

SHIP REGULUS AT SEA LAT 2, 20 SOUTH LON 29, 40
April 5th 1849

Dear Father,

As business is not very driving at present I thought I would sit down & let you know how we get along we hauled out into the Stream from Tea Wharf the first day of March same day sailed down to Nantasket roads about 10 miles below Boston where we laid waiting for the wind the Pilot came on board the S about 9 oclock in the morning we sailed out with a fair wind which did(not) leave us until we crossed the Gulf stream when we was becalmed about 2 hours when we took the South East Trade wind which carried to within 7 degrees of the line in 3 weeks since then we have calms & light bafling winds until this morning when a fine breeze sprang up which promices to carry us into Rio in a few days We expect to be in Rio but 3 days long enough to get what vegitables & water we want each one has 2 days on shore 2/3 on shore at time the other third having to stay on board to do duty & carry those that go on ashore off & bring them back, there is no sickness on board nor has there been any for 3 weeks we have had but 3 cases besides sea Sickness one of the mumps & 2 of the measles since we came out we clean out between Decks evry day have a wind sail at evry hatch which makes it very airy & comfortable It has been very pleasant most of the time we had one gale which carried away the main sail but it did not last long we have spoke 2 ships both foreign one French man from Havere, to St Domingo there was but one man who speak English at all & he but little the Other was a Swede's ship she lay becalmed about 10 miles off the Captain went on board in one of the boats he started about 3, oclock P M soon after he started a squall came up the ship was hove aback to wait for him we waited until evening the boat did not come it was very dark. we began to feel very much alarmed for her safty we burnt torches hoisted lights to the mast head fired guns rung the bells anything to make a noise until about 11 when they got back they had heard us & seen our lights but they was very buisy drinking wine &c with the jolly old Scotch captin as they called him that they could not leave. . . . 18th Spoke the ship Morrison from N. Y. with 130 passengers had been out 70 days the 2nd day out she was in a gale that carried the Fore Main & Mizen Top Masts stove her bulworks & washed off all the water they had on deck so that they was put on allowance they gambled drinked one man had 40 barrells of brandy on board they had one man in irons for drawing a knife upon a person who he was playing cards with for money quite a. number was going back from Rio 20th spoke the Bark Lenark for California she sailed 2 or 3 weeks before we did April 25th We arrived in Rio yesterday having made the passage 50 days we lay off Cape Frio 60 miles from Rio 6 days there is 19 California ships here . . . There is between 2 & 3000 Californin on shore now Oranges 5,00,00 for 1,00,00 Limes 125 a bushell Watermelons Pine Apples & all kinds of Tropical fruits in abundance.

Californin are all the go here you go on shore & the natives although they cannot speak english they have learnt to say Californyans & it is the only thing that you can here that you can understand several ships put into St Catherines they had some trouble with the natives & went on shore & took the island the Briy Perey left here yesterday morning to quell the riot the store ship Lexington left here a few days ago for Boston she had 300,000 in gold dust a rumor reached here yesterday that the Ship Florida from New Orleans was lost off the river La Platte & 201 lives lost out of 205 she had on board I should write more but a vessel sails tomorrow for Baltimore.

C A WARNER

SAN FRANCISCO Sept. 29, 49

Dear Father

We anchored here about an hour ago 4, oclock this afternoon the Mail Steamer leaves here in the morning for Panama, all letters must be aboard by 9 tonight the news is very good gold a plenty to be had by digging for it it is very healthy here there is over 300 sail here now, & more scattered along up the river, labourers get here common $5 to 8 per day machanics from 12 to 18, cotton goods & provisions about as cheap as at home Woolen goods very high building lots one was sold a day or two ago 40 feet square for 10,000 all kinds of lumber very high Board from 10 to 15 dollars per day a great many vessels are deserted & all hands gone to the mine the Ed Everett which cost 40,000 at home was sold for 12,000, what we shall do I do not know but the company will never work together but they will break up & form in small companies if I can get good wages this winter here or at Stockton about 3 miles father up the river I think that I shall not go to the mines till spring . . . there is nearly 300 sail here and 200 more scattered along up the river and bay Flour will not bring but 7 to 8 dollars per barrell here but if you want to buy you have to give a good price for it   pork 25   beef 15 to 20, Potatoes very scarce and worth 50c per lb   Onions from 60 to 70c per lb   eggs 25c apiece   hens $25, each   Meats & game plenty   good beef 12c per lb   all kinds of lumber very high   Most of the people here live in tents   property is safe anywhere   Chests Trunks & boxes of goods are piled up along the shore & nobuddy touches them   Judge Lynch presides if anything is stolen & if a person is caught stealing no matter how trifling he loses one ear if any amount over 300 dollar he is strung up at once & there is not the least disturbanc of any kind   I was on shore last night & this fornoon & have not seen a drunken man   all kinds of Liqur & beer 25c a glass   there is a great deal of gambling here & risk it all at one throw of the dice if they lose go back and get some more

but little attention is paid the Sabbath   I saw a man to day just from the mines   he showed me 90,00 of gold which he had been 7 weeks getting   he had one lot of 9,00 which he got out of one hole in about 2 hours with nothing to wash the earth in but a tin pail   he says says that tin pans and Cradles (such as you have read about) are used more than anything else to wash gold   it is healthy at the mines   now people go in small companies the smaller the better no one will molest them no one goes armed

MARTENEZ. RED WOODS. Dec 6th 49

Dear Father

Once more I take my pen to address a few lines to you hoping that you will answer them as soon as possible. I have received but one letter yet from home & that from Asa & Kate when I first arrived, last week I sent to San Francisco with 3 others bearing a persons expences down & back on purpose to get *Letters*   his expences were about $40 & I did not get any letter at that   I do not know but evry one has forgotten me but I hope that I shall have some coming along by & by   my health now is very good I have been sick about six week   we lay in San Francis harbor about 4 weeks before we came to *Benicia*   I was taken sick there the last week we lay there but kept around until we came up to *Benicia*   there was about 30 sick with the Dysentery   2 of the company had died   I took but little medicine mostly Opium & ocasionly physic but did not get any better   I had no confidence in the Doctor that came out with us   I kept around as much as I could   I could get nothing to eat but ship fare without paying an enormous price   at last I had a chance to get across the bay & I went out about 9 miles to a *Spanish Ranche* & staid a few days living on milk at 50 cts a quart & soon got better & went back on board the ship   expecting to go to the mines this fall I belonged to a company of four & had drawn my share of such things as were divided with them but I saw a great many coming down from the mines & it was so late & bad getting provisions hauled to the mines that I gave it up   I was offered $20 a thousand to come out about 20 miles from Benicia & make shingles this winter & thought that I would accept it as soon as the company affairs were settled I came out here   I have been here now about 3 weeks & shall stay until spring before I try the mines   the rainy season commenced about 4 weeks ago & rained 5 or 6 days that is all the rain we have had until yesterday it rained in the fornoon & in the afternoon snowed   this morning it is pleasant but the snow is 3 inches deep   the natives say that they

hardly ever knew it to snow before the Yankee came here last season &
that they will be the ruin of the country The Bunker Hill Co is now
among the things that was, the last kick was given about 3 weeks ago
evrything of consqence has either been divided or sold (with the exception
of the ship,) & the enormous *Thirty One Dollars & Seventy Five* ^{cts} has
been distributed among each of the lucky share holders & the Co. that
old Father Taylor praised up so much has mutually dissolved by a vote
of 105 yeas & 1, Nay most of them formed in small companies & went
to the mines`. . . . Provisions very high. Flour 50 dollars a barell Pork
about the same sugar 50 cts a lb but I do not think that they will hold
up so long you cannot get a meale of vituels any where for less than from
one to two dollars the poorest board 20 dollars a week Boots & Shoes very
high last week I was offered 50 dollars for my long Boots but would not sell
them Boots such as I could buy at home for 20.00 have rose within 2
weeks from 10,00 to 70 & 80 dollars a pair There is 5 or 6 Steamers on
the river now the principal one is the Lenaton which came around the
horn this year she goes up one day & comes back the next & hardly ever
has less than 2 or 300 passengers fare from San Francisco to Saramento
City $30, the place where I am at work is 20 miles from Benicia 12 from
San Francisco there is about 10 acres in the woods & there is 150 men
to work here among the rest is 2 Ministers & 4 Doctors all have to
work here the trees are very large there is one here that measures 21
feet across the stump 6 feet from the ground many of the trees make
from 50 to 100,000 shingles we have beef Cattle brought in to the woods
by the Spainyards for 25 dollars each deer are plenty there was 11 killed
last sunday that I know of Potatoes are 25 cts a lb and hard to get at
that price Pumpkins 50^{cts} each & very small at that our principal living
is bread & meat with rice & some other small articles that I received from
the ship I have enough now to last me until spring when I shall try the
mines

SALMON FALLS July 25th 50

    My health is very good & has been nearly all of the time since
I came into the mines in March last I am now on the south Fork of the
American River 35 miles from Sacramento City the mines here have been
very good but at present are pretty well worked out Salmon Falls is one
of the pleasantest vilages that I have seen in the mines it got its name
from the Indians who resort here in large numbers at this season of the
year to catch Salmon they catch them in nets & by spearing them their
nets are small like our scoop nets they will sit on the banks by the falls
where the water pours over some 8 or 10 feet the Salmon try to go up
through the current to get up as high as the water pours over perpin-
dicular when the force of the water will throw them out the Indians stand
by with the nets & dart it under him as he falls back into the water I
have seen them catch them that would weigh 20 lbs. The Indians here
are the most miserable beings I ever saw they go almost naked 2-3 of
them do not have more than a cotton shirt I have seen a dozen of them
sitting around gambling with one another for the shirts one of them
would win them all then they would go off home naked. There has been
but few dipredatin committed by them around here lately they begin to
find that it is no use contending with the American in the Spring there
was about 3000 at one time encamped within five miles of this place holding
Council jerking beef &c preparing themselves to fight they sent their

squaes off to the mountains some depredation were committed over on the North Fork but the miner turned out killed several wounded more & frightened the rest into a treaty, they have been pretty civil since. When I first came to Salmon Falls there was but a few tents here now the place is laid out in building lots & there is six large framed buildings and stores & 11 boarding houses & I should think a population of about 500, there is two bridges across the river within thirty rods of each other one of which cost 12,000 the other 27,000 & they are runing opposition crossing for nothing on one, & on the other they give a man a drink of Liquor to cross it is a very healthy place & I doupt not that in time it will be a large town I shall leave here to morrow & go about five miles father up the river near the mouth of the Weaver Creek

654 L U C I E N [8] W A R N E R, son of Park[7] and Joanna (Adams) Warner, born February 22, 1837, in Granby, Mass.; died November 20, 1907. He studied mathematics at Amherst and Nashua, N. H., and practiced as civil engineer in Nashua. In 1857 he went to Chicago, and later to Davenport, Iowa, where he was for some time assistant city engineer. In February, 1865, he located in Minnesota where his older brother, Charles Adams Warner, had already located at Chaska. Lucien Warner became editor and proprietor of the Valley Herald, the official and only paper published in the county. After his brother's death in 1867 he continued his business in the store and post-office. He later began the manufacture of bricks and removed to St. Paul, where he entered the contracting business. He was a perpetual member of the Chamber of Commerce, director of the St. Paul National Bank, member of the executive committee of the Relief Society, director of the American Home Missionary Society for Minnesota, and a member and senior deacon of Plymouth Congregational Church.

Married (1) in Granby, Mass., November 18, 1858, ADELIA F. SILVEY, born February 27, 1834, at Sandy Hill, N. Y., died in St. Paul, Minn., July 24, 1884, daughter of Thomas Augustus and Lydia (Eggleston) Silvey.

Married (2) in St. Paul, July 28, 1886, SADIE K. JONES, born December 4, 1849, widow of General Fielder A. Jones, U. S. A.

Children by first wife

710 *Lily Maria Warner*, b. June 21, 1860, in Granby, Mass.; m. Frank W. Noyes.

Alice Emma Warner, b. July 19, 1862, in Granby, Mass.; resides in St. Paul; m. in St. Paul, June 6, 1889, Dr. B. H. Ogden, son of Benjamin Ogden, who was b. July 10, 1827, in Pennington, N. J., d. in St. Paul, Apr. 27, 1898, and his wife, Arletta Jane Skinner, b. about 1836, d. in Northfield, Minn., Oct. 10, 1863. Children of

B. H. and Alice Emma (Warner) Ogden, b. in St. Paul: i. Warner, b. Oct. 27, 1894. ii. Arletta Adelia, b. Oct. 20, 1902.

711 *Arthur Churchill Warner*, b. Oct. 31, 1864; m. Edith Randolph.

Mary Jane (Minnie) Warner, b. Aug. 21, 1869, in Chaska, Minn.; resides in Seattle, Wash.; m. in St. Paul, Dec. 23, 1890, Joel Robb Gay, son of Thomas William Gay, who was b. in Gamarville, Iowa, Oct. 31, 1835, d. in Evanston, Ill., Jan. 11, 1893, and his wife, Priscilla Robb, b. in McConnellsville, Ohio, 1840, d. Dec., 1885, in Gay's Mills, Wis. Children of Joel Robb and Minnie (Warner) Gay: i. Donald Warner, b. Dec. 13, 1892, in Martinez, Cal.; d. Oct. 12, 1915, in San Francisco, not married. ii. Gladys Adelia, b. Oct. 29, 1894, in Minneapolis. iii. Gordon Lucien, b. Feb. 22, 1896, in Grand Rapids, Mich.

Grace Jessie Warner, b. Sept. 14, 1874, in Chaska, Minn.; resides in St. Paul.

Bess Silvey Warner, b. Feb. 7, 1878, in St. Paul; resides in Minneapolis; m. in St. Paul, Feb. 7, 1900, Arthur William Selover, son of Peter Selover, who was b. in New Jersey, Nov. 10, 1830, d. in Minneapolis, Apr. 22, 1910, and his wife, Jennie Howard, b. in southern Ireland, Apr. 4, 1845; is living in Minneapolis. Children of Arthur William and Bess S. (Warner) Selover, last three b. in Minneapolis: i. Arthur Lucien, b. Oct. 14, 1901, in St. Paul. ii. Harvey William, b. Aug. 23, 1904. iii. Robert, b. Sept. 15, 1907. iv. William, b. Dec. 10, 1912; d. Dec. 28, 1912.

Child of Lucien and Sadie K. (Jones) Warner

Lucia Clayton Warner, b. May 26, 1887, in St. Paul; d. there, Mar. 5, 1910; m. in St. Paul, Apr. 6, 1909, Andrew J. Lee, son of Andrew James Lee, who was b. July 10, 1853, in Norwood, Ill., d. Oct. 17, 1881, at Cannon Falls, Minn., and his wife, Isabell Tretten, who was b. in Hallingdal, Norway, Nov. 26, 1853, resides in Cannon Falls. Children of Andrew J. and Lucia C. (Warner) Lee, b. in St. Paul: Twins, Richard Gretton and Ralph Ogden, b. Feb. 28, 1910. The latter died Mar. 8, 1910.

655 HARRIET NEWELL[8] **WARNER,** daughter of Samuel Allen[7] and Martha Eliza Brintnall (Simonds) Warner, born November 28, 1832, in Batavia, N. Y.; died in Vienna, Dane County, Wis., March 29, 1860.

Married September 24, 1850, **ROBERT MANN,** who died in October, 1860. He was a farmer and removed soon after their marriage to Wisconsin, where other members of his wife's family joined them later.

Children

Edgar Warner Mann, b. Nov. 28, 1851; d. Dec. 7, 1904. After the death of his parents he resided with his mother's parents; was educated at Beloit College and the University of Wisconsin; was an attorney at Cheyenne, Wyo.; member of the Wyoming Legislature, 1879; Register of U. S. Land Office, 1881-5; county attorney,

1885-7; city attorney from 1896 until his death; m. at St. Joseph,
Mo., 1881, Emma Corlett, who survived him only a few years.
Children: i. Walter, was graduated from Crete College and resides
in Omaha, Neb. ii. Mary, m. John Imerslun and resides in Kersey,
Colo.

Eliza Jane Mann, b. Mar. 23, 1854; resides in Omaha, Neb.; m. Feb.
19, 1880, Charles J. Caswell. Child: Gertrude, was graduated from
Lewis Institute and Chicago University; m. Dr. William Spaulding;
resides in Greeley, Colo., and has three children, Charlotte, b. Dec.
20, 1905, Caswell, b. July 27, 1908, and William, Jr., b. Apr. 24, 1911.

Martha E. Mann, b. July 6, 1857; d. at Park Rapids, Minn., Jan. 23,
1917, buried at Windsor, Wis. She was graduated from the University of Wisconsin, B.S., 1878; m. June 28, 1883, William T.
Stone, M.D. Children: Allen Warner and Herbert, both of whom
reside in Park Rapids.

Harriet Newell Mann, b. Mar. 7, 1860; m. Nov. 2, 1882, Rev. Carl
Luse; resides at Amboy, Ind., temporarily at Windsor, Wis. She
has an adopted daughter, Irene, now Mrs. Charles Pond of Kokomo,
Ind.

656 CLEMENT EDSON[8] WARNER, son of Samuel Allen[7]
and Martha Eliza Brintnall (Simonds) Warner, born near
Batavia, N. Y., February 23, 1836; died May 22, 1916, at his
home in Windsor, Wis. With his parents he came to Windsor
in 1852; was educated in the public schools and at the Sun
Prairie Seminary and the University of Wisconsin; taught
school for a number of terms, but loved farm life and turned
to that as his life vocation. He assisted his father on the old
homestead until his marriage, when he settled on an adjacent
farm. Here all of his children were born and both he and his
wife died. The farm is still in the possession of his children.

In March, 1864, he raised a company for the 36th Regiment,
Wisconsin Infantry, and was mustered in as a captain. This
regiment joined the army of the Potomac in May and within one
hundred days was nearly annihilated in the battles around Richmond and Petersburg. During this time Captain Warner was
rapidly promoted to major and to lieutenant-colonel, then to
colonel. He lost an arm August 14, 1864, while in command of
the regiment at Deep Bottom, Va., but returned to his regiment
in November and was in command until the close of the war.
His regiment participated in various battles in Virginia, was in
the final charge at Petersburg, was present at the surrender of
Lee at Appomattox Court House, April 9, 1865, and, under
command of Colonel Warner, was in the final Grand Review at
Washington, May 22 and 23, 1865. The regiment then returned
to Wisconsin and was disbanded, July 12, 1865. Of all the

COL. CLEMENT EDSON WARNER

regiments in the war, only five suffered more in battle than the
36th Wisconsin, and considering the length of its service, its
loss was greater than any other.

Colonel Warner was a member of the Lucius Fairchild Post
of Madison, Wis., and of the Military Order of the Loyal Legion
of the United States, Commandery of the State of Wisconsin.
Upon nomination by the Republican party he was elected in
1866 to the state senate where he served in 1867-8, and again, in
1882, to the assembly where he served in 1883. He held many
positions of trust and honor in church, town and county, as
well as state affairs. After his death the numerous tributes to
his character were gathered and published by Fanny Warner
and Lathrop Ezra Smith, together with a genealogical account
of the family by his son, Ernest Noble Warner (Madison, Wis.,
1917, 71 pp.).

Clement E. Warner married in the town of Turtle, near
Beloit, Wis., February 7, 1867, ELIZA IRENE NOBLE, born
June 19, 1842; died in Windsor, Wis., March 30, 1916. She was
educated at Rockford Seminary and Fox Lake (now the Mil-
waukee-Downer) College, graduating with the first class in
1865. Her ancestry is traced to Thomas[1] Noble, born in Eng-
land about 1633, removed to America 1655, to Boston, Spring-
field, finally settled in Westfield, married Elizabeth Dewey;
Mark[2] and Mary (Marshall) Noble; Noah[3] and Sarah (Bar-
ber) Noble; Zenas[4] and Hannah (Jones) Noble, Zenas a
Revolutionary soldier and delegate to the first Massachusetts
Constitutional Convention; Saul[5] and Margaret Lee, Saul a
Revolutionary soldier, born in Pittsfield, Mass., removed to
Paris, Rome and Floyd, N. Y.; Alanson[6] and Eliza (Hannahs)
Noble, removed to Beloit, Wis.; Eliza Irene.[7] See Noble Gene-
alogy by Boltwood for further details of this family.

*Children of Clement E. and Eliza Irene (Noble) Warner,
born in Windsor, Wis.*

Ernest Noble Warner, b. July 23, 1868; was graduated from the University of Wisconsin, B.L., 1889, LL.B., 1892; is practising law in
Madison, Wis. He resides at Merrill Springs Farm a few miles
out of Madison, where he operates his home farm and an adjoining
one which he owns. Here his children have been reared; he has
been a leader in the movement for better country living, better
country schools and community undertakings. He has served as
Clerk of the District School Board and is a member of the Committee on Common Schools for Dane County; president of the Wisconsin Country Life Conference Association since 1914; president
of the Madison Park and Pleasure Drive Association since 1912;
life member of the State Historical Society of Wisconsin; presi-

dent, director and chairman of the finance committee of the Northwestern Securities Company and director of the Windsor State Bank. He is a member of the Madison Club and Madison Association of Commerce. In political affairs Mr. Warner is a Republican and a leader in the Wisconsin progressive program. He was law examiner in the office of the Attorney General from 1899 to 1903; member of Assembly in 1905, and author of the Wisconsin Civil Service Act passed at that session; member of the publication committee of the Wisconsin State Bar Association from 1899 to 1909 and had personal supervision of volumes 1 to 8 of its reports; has written articles for newspapers and magazines and is in much demand as a speaker on public occasions. He is a member of the Dane County Council of Defense and is an active participant in all the current war drives and activities. He is a deacon in the First Congregational Church; member of the Board of Directors and Ministerial Relief Committee of the Wisconsin Congregational Association; moderator of the Madison District Congregational Convention, 1917; delegate to the National Congregational Council, 1917-1921; president of the Wisconsin Congregational Club of Madison.

Mr. Warner married July 5, 1894, Lillian Dale Baker, daughter of Rev. John Uglow and Elizabeth (Dale) Baker of Edmund, Iowa County, Wis. Both Mr. and Mrs. Baker were born in Cornwall, England. Mrs. Warner was a classmate of her husband at the Madison High School and at the University of Wisconsin, B.A., 1889, and a member of Phi Beta Kappa (honorary). Children, b. in Madison: i. John Clement, b. July 9, 1896; was graduated from the Madison High School and the University of Wisconsin, B.S. Agriculture, 1918, attained special distinction in public speaking and debating, was awarded the William F. Vilas Medal, member of the intercollegiate debating team, elected member of Delta Sigma Rho (honorary), president of the Agricultural Literary Society, advertising manager and contributing editor of the Country Magazine, University of Wisconsin; enlisted May 17, 1918, in U. S. Coast Artillery, reported at Jefferson Barracks, St. Louis, May 23d, transferred to Fort Totten, Long Island, N. Y., June 15th, where he became sergeant and was sent to Officers' Training Camp; received his commission as Second Lieutenant the last of November, was honorably discharged and placed on the officers' reserve list. ii. Elizabeth Dale, b. June 23, 1900; was graduated from the Madison High School in 1917; taught a country school one year; attended (July, 1918) the University of Wisconsin. iii. Ernest Noble, Jr., b. Dec. 2, 1905.

Edith Marie Warner, b. Feb. 19, 1871; was educated at Oberlin College; m. in Windsor, Feb. 21, 1912, Charles Jesse Dodge; resides in Windsor.

Bessie Irene Warner, b. Feb. 27, 1873; resides in Windsor; was educated at Oberlin; m. in Windsor, Feb. 7, 1895, George Edgar Haswell, b. in Nicolaus, Cal., Feb. 16, 1862, son of Edwin L. and Jane (Dodge) Haswell. Mr. Haswell is a farmer. Children, b. in Windsor: i. Clement Dodge, b. Sept. 8, 1899; was graduated from DeForest High School, 1918. ii. Marion Noble, b. Nov. 1, 1901. iii. Alfred Warner, b. July 25, 1913; d. Nov. 24, 1913.

Arthur Warner, b. Dec. 4, 1874; d. Dec. 16, 1874.

Fanny Warner, b. Dec. 25, 1875; was graduated from the University of Wisconsin, B.L., 1900, and taught for a number of years in graded and High schools; then cared for her parents until their death. She resides in Windsor.

Florence Maurine Warner, b. Oct. 14, 1877; resides in Kenosha, Wis.; was graduated from the University of Wisconsin, B.S., 1900; University of Minnesota, M.A., 1904; m. in Windsor, Wis., June 30, 1908, Victor E. Thompson, b. in Elmwood, Wis., Aug. 19, 1881, son of Christopher and Sarah (Fishbyrne) Thompson. He is a graduate of Stout Institute, Menominee, 1904, University of Wisconsin, Ph.B., 1916; has had charge of manual training in the Grand Rapids schools; is now director of Continuation Schools at Kenosha, Wis. Children, b. in Grand Rapids, Wis.: i. Herbert Warner, b. Apr. 12, 1909. ii. Arthur William, b. May 17, 1912.

Julius Herbert Warner, b. Dec. 2, 1882; was graduated from the University of Wisconsin, B.A., 1904; is a mining geologist in Butte, Mont.

657 SABRA IRENE[8] **WARNER,** daughter of Samuel Allen[7] and Martha Eliza Brintnall (Simonds) Warner, born June 2, 1844, in Batavia, N. Y.; resides in Madison, Wis. She was educated at Rockford Seminary and was one of the first women who attended the University of Wisconsin. She has been prominently identified with the work of the Congregational Church in Madison.

Married (1) in Windsor, Wis., September 17, 1867, **HERBERT A. LEWIS,** who died January 4, 1884. He was born in New Haven, Addison Co., Vt., son of Newton L. and Almira Lewis. He was clerk of the Court at Madison, 1866-70, later studied law and practiced his profession until his death; served in the Civil War in Company D, 40th Regiment, Wisconsin Volunteer Infantry; for many years he was an active member and officer in the First Congregational Church of Madison.

Sabra I. Warner married (2) at Madison, Wis., June 21, 1894, **LATHROP EZRA SMITH,** formerly of Cresco, Iowa, now of Madison, Wis. He was born in Newtonville, Ontario, Canada, son of Ezra Colburn and Sarah (White) Smith.

Children of Herbert and Sabra (Warner) Lewis

May Miller Lewis, b. in Madison, July 19, 1868; resides in Cresco, Iowa; m. in Cresco, Iowa, Nov. 16, 1897, Joseph Henry Howe. Children: i. Joseph Warner, b. Jan. 19, 1902. ii. Herbert Lewis, b. Sept. 21, 1904.

Clement Newton Lewis, b. July 5, 1871; d. Feb. 23, 1888.

Arthur Warner Lewis, b. in Madison, Wis., Nov. 5, 1877; d. in Galena, June 28, 1910. He was graduated from the University of Wisconsin,

B.A., 1904; became a geologist and mining engineer engaged in developing the lead and zinc fields of southwestern Wisconsin. He did valuable work for the U. S. Coast and Geodetic Survey in Colorado and Kansas, and made interesting geological explorations in several states and Canada, for the government, for the U. S. Steel Company and as confidential agent for capitalists. He spent some time in Canada, locating iron ore bodies and compiled numerous maps of unexplored territory.

658 ALVA HENRY[8] WARNER, son of Horatio H.[7] and Jane (Northrup) Warner, born in Douglas County, Kans., July 23, 1858; resides in Garden City, Kans., where he is cashier of the National Bank. He was formerly in the hardware and farm machinery business.

Married in Burlingame, Kans., August 16, 1882, JENNIE LOGUE, born in Bureau County, Ill., November 18, 1860, daughter of Maurice Reeves and Ann Eliza (Hilton) Logue.

Children

Edna Warner, b. in Wabaunsee County, Kans., Nov. 2, 1884; attended Kansas State University and the Boston Conservatory of Music; is a member of Betty Washington Chapter, D. A. R., Lawrence, Kans.

Grace Warner, b. at Pierceville, Kans., Aug. 28, 1887; was graduated from the School of Fine Arts, Kansas State University, 1909; married Carl William Abercrombie, son of William Nelson Abercrombie, b. in Ontario, Canada, and his wife, Elizabeth Pemberton, who was born in Missouri. They reside in Wichita, Kans., where he is in the automobile business. Child: William Warner, b. 1914, at Oak Lodge, Medford, Ore.

Orville Hilton Warner, b. at Pierceville, May 16, 1890; was graduated from Kansas State University, A.B., 1912; is a flying cadet, Squadron 44, Aviation Barracks, Berkeley, Cal. (1917); m. Mar. 19, 1914, Gretchen Augusta Rankin, daughter of John Knox and Augusta (Ficher) Rankin. She was graduated from Kansas State University in 1912, and is a member of Betty Washington Chapter, D. A. R., Lawrence, Kans.

Vivian Warner, b. July 16, 1892; was educated at the Central College for Women, Lexington, Mo., and at National Park Seminary, Washington, D. C.; m. Nov. 17, 1917, Lieutenant Dudley Andrus Ward of New Rochelle, N. Y., son of William Ward, b. in New York City, and his wife, Minnie Dudley, who was b. in Boston, Mass. Lieutenant Ward is now (1917) in Camp Funston, Kans., 340th F. A.

659 WILLIAM TALCOTT[8] WARNER, son of Elijah[7] and Abigail (Buel) Warner, born September 16, 1830, in Bolton, Conn.: died December 19, 1913 (or 1914), in Gilead, Conn. He was a farmer in Gilead and justice of the peace for many years He represented the town of Hebron in the state Legislature.

Mr. Warner was a deacon in the Congregational Church at Gilead for many years.

Married in Gilead, September 14, 1853, **OLIVE MARIA HUTCHINSON**, born December 9, 1833, in Gilead, died there; daughter of Capt. John Bissell and Lauretta (Jewett) Hutchin son.

Children, born in Gilead

Charles Hutchinson Warner, b. Sept. 23, 1854; is an insurance adjuster in San Francisco, Cal.; m. in San Francisco, Apr. 23, 1887, Isabel Whitney, b. Nov. 6, 1850, in New Orleans, La., d. in San Francisco, Jan. 1, 1913, daughter of George Otis and Abigail Taylor (Fitch) Whitney. Child: Helen Whitney, b. in San Francisco, Feb. 12, 1888; d. Apr. 14, 1888. Mr. Warner is a member of the Sons of the American Revolution.

Josiah Buell Warner, b. Dec. 14, 1857; resides in Alameda, Cal.; member of the Sons of the American Revolution; m. in San Francisco, Sept. 16' 1886, Helen Gray Dix, b. Sept. 16, 1866. Child: Olive Frances, b. Nov. 14, 1890, in San Francisco; m. in Alameda, Nov. 15, 1914, Henry Lester Dow, and lives in Alameda.

William Jewett Warner, b. Mar. 1, 1864; resides in Gilead, Conn., town of Hebron; farmer and dairy inspector. He was representative of his town in the state legislature in 1895. Married in Hebron, June 8, 1886, Ella Carter⁹ Warner, b. in Chicopee Falls, Mass., July 14, 1861, daughter of Norman Post⁸ and Lydia Ann (Norton-Taylor) Warner; see number 549. Mrs. Warner is much interested in family history and has gathered much genealogical data regarding her ancestral families. Child: Norman Jewett, b. Aug. 26, 1887, in Gilead; m. May 24, 1912, Mabel Hortense Perry, b. Sept. 28, 1890, daughter of William Childs and Iva Allene (Brown) Perry, and has two children, Norton Perry, b. Apr. 17, 1913, and William Hutchinson, b. June 1, 1915.

660 LYMAN⁸ WARNER, son of Ashbel⁷ and Abigail (Lyman) Warner, born July 4, 1826, in Bolton, Conn.; resides in Salisbury, Conn. (1917). He was educated at Williams College, 1854, and Hartford Theological Seminary and entered the ministry as a Congregational clergyman preaching at Rockford, Iowa, East Hartland and Burlington, Conn., and West Granville, Mass. He was a Home Missionary for eight years from 1863-1871. After his retirement he made his home at Salisbury, at first on the old Lyman homestead, later moved into the village where he still lives, in remarkable health at the age of ninety (1917).

Married (1) in East Hartford, Conn., October 15, 1857, **ELIZABETH SOPHIA OLMSTED**, born October 13, 1828, in East Hartford, daughter of Ashbel and Delia (Belden) Olmsted; died January 16, 1892.

Married (2) in Salisbury, Conn., June 14, 1894, HARRIET MARIA HUTCHINSON, born in Salisbury, July 26, 1843, daughter of Myron and Mary (Smith) Hutchinson and granddaughter of Asa and Lydia (Galusha) Hutchinson and of Gideon and Eunice (Hurd) Smith. No children.

Children of Lyman and Elizabeth S. (Olmsted) Warner

William Lyman Warner, b. 1858; d. Dec. 3, 1858, in Ashfield, Mass.

Elizabeth Belden Warner, b. Jan. 20, 1860; d. Apr. 27, 1881, in Burlington, Conn.

Katherine Lyman Warner, b. Aug. 4, 1861; d. June 9, 1875, in East Hartland, Conn.

Charles Lyman Warner, b. Oct. 27, 1868, at Rockford, Iowa; resides in Salisbury, Conn. He was graduated from Williams College in 1891, and was a teacher for some time. He is now (1916) state supervisor of schools for Salisbury and South Canaan, Conn. Mr. Warner is a member of the Connecticut Historical Society and of the Salisbury Association. He is also a member of the Society's Committee of the Congregational Church. Married in Salisbury, Aug. 29, 1910, Bessie Tryphena Everts, b. Sept. 11, 1884, in Michigaume, Mich., daughter of William P. and Sara J. (Knox) Everts. Children: i. Elizabeth, b. Aug. 3, 1911, in Bridgeport, Conn. ii. Edward Everts, b. Sept. 20, 1914, in Sharon, Conn.

Edward Olmsted Warner, b. Dec. 21, 1870, in Rockford, Iowa; resides in Haverford, Pa. (1916). He was graduated from Lehigh University in 1894; is an engineer; was connected with street railway work on inspection work for the Japanese government; then in iron and steel business. He has lived principally in Hartford, Conn., Chicago, and Philadelphia. Married in Schenectady, N. Y., Oct. 27, 1904, Louie Darling, b. in Toronto, Ontario, Canada, Dec. 2, 1877, daughter of Henry W. and Helen Ritchie (Christie) Darling. She is a graduate of Toronto University, 1901, and has lived principally in Toronto, Boston, Mass., Albany and Schenectady, N. Y. Children: i. Lyman Darling, b. June 15, 1906, in Haverford. ii. Elinore Stanley, b. Feb. 20, 1911, in Haverford.

661 CYNTHIA ANN[8] WARNER, daughter of Ashbel[7] and Hannah (Morgan) Warner, born January 26, 1830, in Bolton, Conn.; died December 1, 1910, in Bolton. A woman by nature modest and retiring, after her husband's death she brought up her large family on slender resources, keeping the children together and giving them good educations, and also taking into her home and caring for four aged members of the family. She was a member of the Bolton Congregational Church for fifty years.

Married in Bolton, October 12, 1856, ELIJAH ANSON ALVORD, born April 10, 1825, in Bolton, died there, October

4, 1870, son of Martin and Martha Burleigh (Clark) Alvord. An account of his family will be found in the Alvord Genealogy. He was educated in the public schools of Bolton and East Hartford, Conn.; became a farmer and dealt largely in wood and charcoal, displaying a wonderful amount of energy and power to accomplish work.

Children, born in Bolton

Joseph Clark Alvord, b. Oct. 1, 1858; d. May 1, 1894, in Manchester, Conn.; was graduated from the Hartford High School; was selectman at the age of 22 and the following year was elected to the State Senate; m. Feb. 17, 1886, in Hartford, Carrie Lou Smith, b. in Hartford, Dec. 27, 1858, d. there, Mar. 4, 1899, daughter of Franklin and Lydia H. (Champlin) Smith. Child: Raymond Smith, b. in Hartford, June 14, 1889.

John Austin Alvord, b. Dec. 3, 1859; is a grocer and postmaster at Manchester, Conn.; m. in Pomfret, Apr. 16, 1889, Ada Louisa Clark, b. in Pomfret, Jan. 26, 1861, daughter of Abiel Lafayette and Harriet (May) Clark. Child: Harold Clark, b. Feb. 14, 1892, in Manchester.

Anna Maria Alvord, b. Aug. 11, 1861; was graduated from the Rockville High School, then resided on the homestead with her mother; has taken an active part in the life of the community, especially in connection with the church and the Grange.

William Elijah Alvòrd, b. Dec. 16, 1863; resides in Manchester; is a manufacturer of soap; has been selectman of the town and was representative in 1895; m. in Bolton, June 19, 1895, Elulia Josephine Martin, b. in Bolton, Sept. 15, 1867, daughter of Joel Wales and Josephine (Loomis) Martin. Child: Martin Earl, b. in Manchester, Nov. 9, 1901.

George Warner Alvord, b. Sept. 27, 1865; resides in Bolton (1916); is a farmer; not married.

Samuel Morgan Alvord, b. Nov. 19, 1869; resides in Hartford; m. in Pennington, N. J., Dec. 27, 1900, Mary A. O'Hanlon, b. in Lambertville, N. J., Feb. 13, 1865, daughter of Rev. Thomas O'Hanlon, a Methodist minister, president of Pennington Seminary for many years, and his wife, Maria Maps. Child: Morgan Hanlon, b. in Hartford, Mar. 31, 1902. Mr. Alvord was educated at the Hartford High School; Yale, 1896; Phi Beta Kappa, and Alpha Delta Phi· took honors in Latin and Greek; has been instructor in Latin at the Hartford High School for some years. He is a deacon in the Farmington Ave. Congregational Church. He is the editor of the Alvord Genealogy.

662 MORGAN⁸ WARNER, son of Ashbel⁷ and Hannah (Morgan) Warner, born January 27, 1834, in Bolton, Conn.; died April 27, 1899, in Chicago, Ill. He left his home in Bolton in early life for the west; was engaged in construction work on the railroad for many years, and was also a farmer in

Kansas. He resided in Fort Wayne, Ind.; Wilson, Bunker Hill and Topeka, Kans.

Married in 1860, **SARAH BRINER** of Indiana, who died in 1894. She was the daughter of Jesse and Mary Ann (————) Briner.

Children

Dwight Warner, d. in infancy.

712 *Persis Ann Warner*, b. Jan. 20, 1862; m. Philip Howell.

George Albert Warner, b. July 31, 1863, in Fort Wayne.

William Warren Warner, b. Feb. 13, 1866; d. Dec. 22, 1880.

Lillian Alida Warner, b. Apr. 10, 1868, in Fort Wayne.

Mary Elizabeth Warner, b. June 26, 1870, at Fort Wayne; resides in Hattiesburg, Miss.; m. in Topeka, Kans., Mar. 14, 1894, William James Haynen, b. in Montreal, Canada, son of William J. Haynen. Children: i. Joseph Reily, b. Dec. 2, 1899. ii. William James, b. Aug. 25, 1901. iii. Marvin Francis, b. Apr. 29, 1905. iv. Mary Edna, b. July 18, 1909. v. John Franklin.

Alma T. Warner, b. Sept. 28, 1872, in Fort Wayne; resides in Topeka, Kans.; m. in Kansas City, Mo., Nov. 10, 1893, Edward Ellsworth McFadden, b. in Salem, Ind., June 1, 1861, son of Adam and Sarah (Mobley) McFadden. Children: i. Carrie Grace, b. Sept. 19, 1894; m. Nov. 19, 1915, Willis Leroy Kirk. ii. Lillie May, b. Feb. 27, 1896. iii. Ray Edward, b. Mar. 13, 1900. iv. Harold Warner, b. Oct. 15, 1902.

Frank E. Warner, b. July 20, 1874; d. young.

Jessie J. Warner, b. 1875; resides in Eland, Wis.

663 **DWIGHT[8] WARNER**, son of Ashbel[7] and Hannah (Morgan) Warner, born January 6, 1837, in Bolton, Conn.; died in Hartford, June 1, 1905. He served in the Civil War in the 16th Connecticut Volunteers; contracted rheumatism at the battle of Antietam and was assigned to hospital duty during the remainder of the war. He held various town offices in Bolton and was esteemed as a man of generous and kindly disposition. He was a farmer.

Married in Bolton, January 2, 1866, **MARY ANN LOOMIS**, born July 25, 1840, daughter of Jerijah and Mary Ann (Rice) Loomis. She resides in Bolton (1917).

Children, born in Bolton

Dwight Delos Warner, b. May 21, 1868; killed by an accident, Mar. 30, 1875.

Robert Loomis Warner, resides in Manchester, Conn.; is a motorman on the trolley line; m. Harriet Howard, daughter of George and Minnie (Maine) Howard of Bolton. Children, b. in Bolton: i. Ruth, b. Aug. 5, 1894. ii. Louise, b. Mar. 31, 1896; d. Aug. 8, 1896. iii. Mary, b. June 1, 1897.

Charles Royal Warner.

664 JOSEPH[8] **WARNER,** son of Amasa[7] and Cynthia Ann (Walton) Warner, born May 30, 1820, in Wayne Co., Ohio; died April 19, 1895. He was a farmer and settled in 1848 on 160 acres of land near Pierceton, Washington township, Kosciusko Co., Ind., which he purchased from his father. Married in Ohio, January 1, 1846, **RUTH S. TILLOTTSON,** born near Rochester, N. Y., August 30, 1825, daughter of Asa and Ruth (Beebe) Tillottson.

They had no children of their own but adopted seven, of whom were

Isaac Harrison Warner, was a soldier in the Civil War and died.
Clarissa Madden Warner, m. William Clover and d. leaving two children, Eva and Chester.
Tillie Warner, m. Seward Crosby, and resided, before her death, in Larwell, Ind.
Marion Galbraith Warner, a farmer in Washington township, Kosciusko Co., Ind.
Francis Moore Warner, resides in Washington township.
Blanche Wilt Warner, resides in North Dakota; m. (1) Edward Pocock, (2) Joel Perkins.

665 MARGARET[8] **WARNER,** daughter of Amasa[7] and Cynthia Ann (Walton) Warner, born May 12, 1826, near Wooster, Ohio; died December 27, 1899, at Richland, Iowa. Married at Wooster, April 11, 1850, **A B N E R G O F F CHACEY,** who died in Richland at the home of his son John.

Children

John Chacey, b. May 5, 1851, in Wayne Co., Ohio; d. May 1, 1913, in Richland, Iowa; m. Fannie ———, who resides in Richland. Children: D. H. (son), b. Feb. 15, 1877. ii. George, b. June 25, 1881; d. Oct. 7, 1882. iii. Chalmer, b. Oct. 18, 1884. iv. Orla E., b. Oct. 27, 1886.
Hiram B. Chacey, resides in Meriden, Kans.
Alice Salome Chacey, b. Oct. 13, 1854, in Wooster, Ohio; resides in Richland, Iowa; m. Dec. 17, 1879, Orlane Worley, b. Dec. 21, 1855, son of William and Jane (———) Worley. Children: i. Dorothy, b. Sept. 28, 1882, in Richland; m. ——— Liblin. ii. Ethel, b. Jan. 20, 1884, in Richland; m. ——— Bordner. iii. Chase, b. Apr. 13, 1885, in Ollie, Iowa. iv. Blanche, b. Feb. 23, 1887, in Richland; m. ——— Bragg. v. Margaret, b. Dec. 8, 1893, in Ollie; m. ——— Davis. vi. Ruth, b. Dec. 30, 1899, in Ollie.
Cynthia Ann Chacey, b. Feb. 2, 1858, in Richland, Iowa; resides in Eddyville, Iowa; m. in Ottumna, Iowa, Mar. 4, 1903, C. H. Stuber, b. in Chillicothe, Ohio, son of Abram and Mary (———) Stuber.
Samuel Edwin Chacey, b. Feb. 15, 1860, in Richland, Iowa; was a teacher; now in insurance business in Richland; m. in Sigourney, Iowa, Dec. 31, 1889, Dora Halferty, b. in Richland, July 11, 1865, daughter of David and Mary (———) Halferty. Children, b. in

Richland: i. Inez M., b. Nov. 18, 1890; graduate of the Battle Creek (Mich.) Sanitarium as a registered nurse. ii. Richard H., graduate of Richland High School, now a farmer. *Leilla Chacey*, m. Sherman Wade; resided in Cody, Wyo., at the time of her death. He lives in Opportunity, Wash. *Eunice Ellen Chacey*, b. Sept. 10, 1866, in Richland; resides in Ollie, Iowa; m. Nov. 1, 1894, Charles F. McCarty, b. in Brighton, Iowa; son of Robert and Rebecca (Hyde) McCarty. He is a mechanic. Mrs. McCarty studied elocution in Iowa State University and at Iowa Wesleyan University two years. Child: Robert D., b. May 2, 1898, in Ollie, Iowa; attended Central College at Pella, Iowa, for a year; is now in the U. S. Surveying Co., at Winslow, Ariz. *Frank Chacey*, resides in Richland.

666 HIRAM⁸ WARNER, son of Amasa⁷ and Cynthia Ann (Walton) Warner, born about 1829, in Cedar Valley, Ohio; died in 1903, aged 74 years, 2 months, 11 days. Married August 18, 1853, **MARY SECHRIST**, who died in 1910, aged 75 years, 5 months, 25 days.

Child

McKendree Winfield Warner, b. Jan. 23. 1855, in Cedar Valley, Ohio; is a farmer and resides near Wooster, Ohio (R. F. D. 9); m. in Wooster, May 14, 1890, Agnes L. Hinish, b. in Wooster, daughter of George W. and Mary A. (————) Hinish. Children, b. in Wooster, all residing with their father (1917): i. Mary Garman, b. Feb. 18, 1891. ii. Winfield Hiram, b. Oct. 16, 1893. iii. George Hinish, b. Mar. 29, 1896. iv. Ethel Lucile, b. Oct. 1, 1904. The family are all Methodists; farmers, school teachers or engaged in mercantile business.

667 EUNICE ELLEN⁸ WARNER, daughter of Amasa⁷ and Cynthia Ann (Walton) Warner, born December 19, 1830, in Wooster, Ohio; is at present (1917) with her daughter, Mrs. De Armond in Los Angeles, Cal., but has resided in Martinsburg, Iowa. Married in Wayne County, Ohio, March 30, 1855, JACOB SECHRIST, born July 12, 1829, in Fayette County, Pa., son of Jacob and Susannah (Brinneman or Brenemen) Sechrist. He has been a farmer, but is now retired.

Children

Alonzo Granville Sechrist, b. near Congress, Wayne Co., Ohio, Sept. 28, 1855; resides in Lawton, Okla.; m. in Wray, Colo., Sept. 28, 1897, Mrs. Mattie E. Taylor, b. in Maryville, Nodaway Co., Mo., daughter of Richard and Julia (————) Conway. She had a child, Bessie Taylor, b. in Maryville, Sept. 28, 1894; none by this marriage. Mr. Sechrist is a lawyer, and is the author of a book on the interpretation of the Bible.

Maurice Simpson Sechrist, b. in Keokuk Co., Iowa, Dec. 1, 1857; is
a carpenter in Hedrick, Iowa; m. (1) in Keokuk Co., Nov. 20, 1879,
Sarah L. Speirs, b. in Indiana, daughter of Robert and Sarah
(Thurston) Speirs; m. (2) Dec. 29, 1904, Maggie Braden, b. in
Iowa, daughter of Robert and Mary (Dale) Braden. Children:
i. Dora I., b. Dec. 21, 1881; resides in Pomona, Cal.; m. 1898, C. R.
May, and has a son, b. 1900. ii. Zena B., b. Nov. 28, 1883; resides
in Iowa City, Iowa; m. 1909, Ralph D. Smith; no children. iii.
Chester A., b. Feb. 20, 1888; is a mail clerk in Los Angeles; not
married.

Elmer W. Sechrist, b. May 19, 1859; d. aged 7.

Emmett L. Sechrist, b. in Jefferson Co., Iowa, Aug. 10, 1860; resides
in Ballston, Ore.

Eva Lunette (Nettie) Sechrist, b. near Wooster, Ohio, Jan. 6, 1863;
was a teacher for a time; resides in Los Angeles; m. Aug. 29, 1888,
Thomas E. De Armond, b. in Henry County, Iowa, June 26, 1861,
son of Robert and Elizabeth (Bebb) De Armond. He is a rancher.
Children: i. Zella, b. Oct. 14, 1889; was a teacher before her marriage; m. July 9, 1913, George W. Culbertson, a High School professor, son of Robert Elmore Culbertson. ii. Zolo Robert, b. June
11, 1893; is a student at the University of Southern California.

Edgar H. Sechrist, b. in Akron, Ohio, Apr. 18, 1865; resides in Wray,
Colo.; farmer and real estate agent; m. in Martinsburg, Iowa, Ida
Heninger, b. in Martinsburg, Oct. 24, 1869, d. in Denver Hospital,
Apr. 1, 1903, daughter of Henry and Sarah (———) Heninger.
Children, first two b. in Martinsburg: i. Floyd H., b. Aug. 8, 1891;
d. Aug. 13, 1892. ii. Lloyd E., b. Aug. 3, 1892; is U. S. surveyor
in Los Angeles, Cal. iii. Henry R., b. Mar. 24, 1895, in Wray, Colo.;
resides there. iv. Sadie, b. Nov. 9, 1899, in Wray, Colo.; resides in
Los Angeles.

Mertie L. Sechrist, b. in Martinsburg, Iowa, Apr. 18, 1870; m. there,
Jan. 12, 1893, Fountain Bottorff, a farmer, b. there, July 1, 1870, son of
John and Mary (———) Bottorff. They reside in Hedrick, Iowa.
Child: Deane, b. June 18, 1896; was graduated from High School;
taught two years and is now a student in Penn College, Oskaloosa,
Iowa.

Gertrude I. Sechrist, b. in Keokuk County, Iowa, Feb. 13, 1872; resides
in Pomona, Cal.; m. in Martinsburg, Iowa, Sept. 12, 1898, Schuyler
C. Sheets, b. Sept. 19, 1869, son of Leander and Ellen (McVey)
Sheets. Children, b. in Rowley, Buchanan Co., Iowa: i. Helen
Ione, b. Nov. 22, 1903. ii. Don Keith, b. Mar. 7, 1906.

668 ICHABOD[8] **WARNER,** son of Amasa[7] and Mary
(Lowery) Warner, bórn October 16, 1841, near Wooster,
Wayne Co., Ohio. He is a farmer in Goodland, Kans.
Married in Fairfield, Jefferson Co., Iowa, August 16, 1866,
ARMINDA GUMMERE, b. May 23, 1845, in Grant County,
Ind., daughter of Swithin A. and Lucinda (———) Gummere.

Children

Chase Warner, b. Oct. 4, 1867, in Birmingham, Van Buren Co., Iowa;
m. Oct. 15, 1891, Lulu Poff. Children: i. Lloyd, b. Nov. 1, 1896. ii.

Merle, b. Sept. 5, 1899. iii. Mace, b. Sept. 19, 1905. iv. Evelyn, b. Dec. 1, 1907. v. Lowell, b. Apr. 30, 1916.

Mertie Warner (son), died young.

Wade Warner, b. Sept. 28, 1884, at Libertyville, Jefferson Co., Iowa; is in the abstracts and real estate business at Goodland, Kans.; m. June 5, 1906, Mattie Sapp. Children: i. Beatrice, b. May 8, 1907. ii. Dorothy Agnes, b. Aug. 14, 1913.

669 JOSHUA[8] WARNER, son of Nathan[7] and Mary (Rathbun) Warner, born July 22, 1827, east of Jefferson, Ohio; died December 5, 1881, on his farm two and one half miles northeast of Meriden, Kans. He was born and lived on his father's farm adjoining the little town of Jefferson, Plain township, Wayne Co., Ohio, until after the births of his children. He was, for his time, an unusually well educated and well read man, with literary inclinations. He wrote many poems of real merit. On September 13, 1868, he was ordained as a minister in the Methodist Episcopal Church in the North Ohio Conference, convened at Wooster, Ohio, and from that time did much local preaching and evangelistic work in Ohio and Kansas. He removed with his family to Meriden, Kans., in September, 1879. Joshua Warner was an ardent abolitionist. During the Civil War he was repeatedly refused service in the Northern army through failure to pass physical examinations. He helped conduct the "underground railway," during the war, between Columbus and Cincinnati and Lake Erie. In his local church he was the pillar, the friend, confidant and counsellor of men and women, old and young, and the most respected man in his community. He was a firm, wise and loving father, whose children honored him in life and hold his memory the most sacred influence in their characters and lives.

Joshua Warner married in Lattisburgh, Wayne Co., Ohio, November 30, 1848, REBECCA JANE BAKER, born in New Pittsburgh, Ohio, February 4, 1831; died October 2, 1905, in San Diego, Cal. She was the daughter of James and Honor (Hull) Baker of Virginia.

Children, born in Jefferson, Wayne County, Ohio

713 *Harvey Amander Warner*, b. Nov. 9, 1849; m. Elizabeth Adelaide Mackey.
714 *Wilber Orville Warner*, b. Aug. 27, 1851; m. (1) Elma Brubaker, (2) Annie Young, (3) Jennie Crigger.
715 *Lorin Selvey Warner*, b. Oct. 23, 1853; m. Sarah Shutt.
716 *Orpha Meralda Warner*, b. Dec. 5, 1855; m. Archie McDanel.
Olin Baker Warner, b. Feb. 11, 1858; d. Nov. 26, 1881. He was educated in the Wayne schools and entered Ohio Wesleyan in 1876. In

the spring of 1879 he removed to Kansas and continued his education at Baker University. He was licensed to preach in the Methodist Episcopal Church at the Quarterly Conference of Baldwin City Station, Topeka District, Kansas Conference, Feb. 25, 1881. He died on his charge at Ivy, Wilmington Circuit, Lyon County.

717 *Lois Realura Warner*, b. Dec. 25, 1862; m. John Norman Glenn.
718 *Guy Leon Warner*, b. June 18, 1865; m. Lydia Elizabeth Shutt.
719 *Elizabeth Lucinda Warner*, b. Nov. 17, 1875; m. (1) Charles H. Mull, (2) Bruce Josserand.

670 AMELIA ANN[8] WARNER, daughter of Nathan[7] and Mary (Rathbun) Warner, born February 28, 1832, near Jefferson, Wayne Co., Ohio; resides in Jefferson.
Married at her father's home near Jefferson, in 1851, MICHAEL LANTZ, born in Berks Co., Pa., February 28, 1834.

Children

Mary Ella Lantz, b. in Wayne County, Ohio, May 19, 1856; resides in Germantown, Ohio; m. May 19, 1877, George Albert Houser, b. May 19, 1857. Children: i. Clarence True, b. in Wayne County, Apr. 19, 1879; is a graduate of Londonville High School and the Ohio State University at Columbus, Ohio; is first assistant Botanist in the Ohio State Experiment Station at Wooster, Ohio, with his field for work in the branch station at Germantown, where he resides; m. Dec. 25, 1905, Sarah Edith Weber, b. in Ada, Hardin Co., Ohio, Sept. 1, 1882; has two children, b. in Wooster, Mary Elizabeth, b. June 8, 1907, and Albert Weber, b. July 23, 1909. ii. Mary Ethel, b. Jan. 24, 1882, in New Pittsburg, Wayne Co., Ohio; resides in Wooster; m. Dec. 25, 1903, Floyd M. Specht, a teacher, b. in Jeromesville, Ohio, Aug. 23, 1879; two children, Miles Standish, b. at Reedsburg, Ohio, July 13, 1906, and Glenn Elwyn, b. at Wooster, Dec. 19, 1913. iii. Mabel, b. in New Pittsburg, Aug. 19, 1886; d. aged six weeks. iv. Beulah Independence, b. in New Pittsburg, July 4, 1889; resides in Wooster; m. 1910, at Germantown, Oscar David Kaufman, b. in Wayne County, Ohio, Oct. 12, 1873, who was a mail carrier for many years, then studied law and was admitted to the bar at Columbus in 1915; has three children, Gertrude Houser, b. in Wooster, Feb. 9, 1911, Kathryn Elizabeth, b. Nov. 19, 1912, and Mildred Grace, b. July 19, 1914. v. Alice Elizabeth, b. Jan. 24, 189–; was graduated from the Germantown High School in 1910; took the training for nurses at the Wooster Hospital; m. Apr., 1915, Jacob U. Kaufman, a farmer of Wayne County, b. there, 1881; two children, Susan Ella, b. June 2, 1916, and Dallas Albert, b. Nov. 10, 1917.
Ralph Warner Lantz, b. July 27, 1859, in Wayne County, Ohio; resides in Lawrenceburg, Tenn.; is a real estate agent; m. Ida Wagner. Children: Lela; Lloyd; Winifred; Lynn; Maybelle.
Eva Lantz, b. July 9, 1865, in Whitley County, Ind.; is not married.
Eugene Arthur Lance, b. near Columbia City, Whitley Co., Ind., Jan. 6, 1869; is a farmer near Lawrenceburg, Tenn.; has taught school, and been a contractor and painter; m. in New Pittsburg, Ohio, Dec.

22, 1898, Mary Magdaline Piper, b. in New Pittsburg, June 16, 1873, daughter of John and Elizabeth (————) Piper. Children, first three b. in Wooster, Ohio: i. Tulla Udal, b. Oct. 23, 1899. ii. Freda Aileen, b. June 8, 1901. iii. Hazel Zelma, b. Feb. 6, 1904. iv. Amelia Elizabeth, b. in Lawrenceburg, Tenn., Dec. 27, 1908; d. Nov. 15, 1909. v. Marguerite Eugenia, b. in Lawrenceburg, Oct. 12, 1910.

671 GIDEON[8] WARNER, son of Moses[7] and Mary (Sheridan) Warner, born in Wooster, Wayne Co., Ohio, July 13, 1823; died in Edmonton, Canada, February 3, 1903. He was a carpenter, farmer and millwright. He resided in Richland, Keokuk Co., Iowa, after October, 1842. In the spring of 1858 he rode up to the banks of the Missouri River at Sioux City with a herd of cows he had brought from eastern Iowa. These were sold to the settlers and in company with a number of friends he took an elk hunt on the then unsettled valleys of the Logan and Elkhorn north of the present Norfolk, not a solitary white man to be seen in the region. On some high rocks near Dakota City, Neb., is engraved "G. Warner, July 22, 1858." In the spring of 1867 he moved his family to the new country and settled on a farm on Omaha Creek, five miles directly south of Dakota City. In 1859 he went to Colorado during the gold excitement and was located where Georgetown is now situated. With his brother he was one of the surveying party that laid out the first railroad projected in Dakota County, in 1868. In 1877 he started on a two-years' journey into the far west, visiting the Black Hills Country, crossed over the Big Horn Mountains through Pryor's Pass, visited the National Park and Custer's battlefield, spent the winter at Fort Custer, prospected for gold, passed on down the Yellowstone River to Fort Keogh and Miles City.

Married (1) in Richland, Iowa, 1848, N A N C Y J A N E CHARLTON, who died about a year later as the result of a rattlesnake bite. She left a child who died soon after.

Married (2) in Eddyville, Iowa, October, 1850, MATILDA BRUBAKER, born in Lancaster County, Pa., June 22, 1832, died December 27, 1912, daughter of Daniel Brubaker.

Children by second wife, last two born in Dakota County, Neb., others in Keokuk County, Iowa

Jane Warner, b. Sept. 5, 1851; resides in Emerson, Neb.; m. in Dakota City, Neb., Feb. 2, 1878, John Ward, b. in Greenwich, Conn., Jan. 13, 1848, son of Horatio and Maria (————) Ward. He is a retired farmer. Child: Helen Grace, b. Aug. 15, 1878; m. Lyman Hutchings, b. Sept. 22, 1874, and has three children, John William, b. Nov.

17, 1901, Rubie, b. Dec. 27, 1905, and Helen Genevieve, b. July 30, 1913.

Julia Warner, b. 1852; d. 1893; m. ——— Clapp, died.

720   *Alice Warner,* b. November 13, 1854; m. Andrew Russell Bevins.

Ella Warner, b. 1856; m. ——— Corbett; resides in Long Beach, Cal. *Winfield Warner,* died.

721   *Daniel Webster Warner,* b. Oct. 1, 1857; m. Mary Jane Brubaker. *Elizabeth Warner,* b. 1859; died.

Emma Warner, b. 1862; was a teacher; m. ——— Rathbun; resides in La Crosse, Wash.

Margaret Warner, died.

U. S. Grant Warner, b. 1864; died.

722   *William P. Warner,* b. Apr. 28, 1866; m. Alice M. Graham.

George O. Warner, b. 1869, in Dakota City, Neb.; resides in McGregor, Minn.

Elmer E. Warner, b. 1871, in Dakota City; resides at Square Butte, Mont.

672   **COL. JESSE F.[8] WARNER,** son of Moses[7] and Mary (Sheridan) Warner, born in Wooster, Ohio, September 24, 1824; died in Dakota City, Neb., March 26, 1890. At an early age he removed to Richland, Iowa, where he resided until 1857. Piloting a prairie schooner, he conveyed his family to Nebraska and located May 17, 1857, on a farm one-half mile south of Logan. In the fall of 1857 he returned to Iowa for a herd of cows, and the following year brought a drove of hogs. This stock originated a large part of the stock of early days in Dakota County. Mr. Warner was admitted to the bar in 1857. From early manhood he had taken an active interest in politics, and when the Whig party was dissolved he threw all his energies into the struggle over slavery. He participated in the campaigns of 1854 and 1856, and in 1860 was a delegate to the convention at Chicago which nominated Abraham Lincoln. One of his most valued treasures, his certificate signed by John M. Thayer, chairman Republican Territorial Committee, is cherished by the family. The day the news of the fall of Fort Sumter reached him, he started for his old home in Iowa to raise men for the service, and entered the army at once as Second Lieutenant, 7th Iowa Infantry; was promoted to a captaincy, and after three years was compelled to resign on account of injuries and broken health. He commanded his company in the charge that carried the works at Fort Donaldson and there received the injury that caused him many years of suffering and finally resulted in his death. Soon after his return to Iowa he was chosen Colonel of one of the Border State Regiments for home defense, but it was never called for duty.

In 1867 Colonel Warner located in Dakota City, Neb., and was closely identified with the life of the country from that time; established a land office; surveyed and selected claims for many of the first settlers of his own and adjoining counties; practiced law from 1868 to 1878; was a presidential elector in 1868 and cast Nebraska's maiden vote; in 1869 purchased a farm eight miles from Dakota City and in connection with it raised fruit and burned the lime that was used in the construction of most of the buildings of the time, including the court house, churches and schools; represented his county in the state legislature, 1879-80; was U. S. Indian Agent of the Omaha and Winnebago agencies from 1886 to 1889, with the farming and general behavior of the Indians a credit to his administration. He held many public offices and was a leader in G. A. R. circles. As a public speaker he excelled and was in great demand for public gatherings of all kinds.

Married in Richland, Iowa, September 7, 1849, HANNAH M. WOODWARD, daughter of Samuel and Abigail (————) Woodward. She died in Lyons, Neb., February 2, 1905.

Children, all but last born in Richland, Iowa

Leander Monroe Warner, b. Jan. 23, 1851; d. in Paris, Texas, Oct. 1, 1915. He was justice of the peace for Omadi precinct in 1891; in 1893 was one of the prominent citizens of Homer, Neb., conducting a real estate and loan business, hardware and confectionery stores, and one of the publishers of the Homer Independent, while his wife had the only millinery store in the town. Married Emma Mona Willis, who d. in 1916, daughter of Britton Willis. Children: i. May, died. ii. Ethel, died. iii. Howard, resides in Chillicothe, Mo. - iv. Blanche, resides in Chillicothe. v. Helen, died.

Nellie Warner, b. July 6, 1852; d. at Lyons, Neb., Sept. 8, 1892. She was a teacher before her marriage, Jan. 9, 1873, to Dr. Egbert J. De Bell, b. in Greene County, N. Y. He studied medicine, was graduated from the Albany (N. Y.) Medical College in 1869. He went to Illinois and in 1871 to Dakota County, Neb., where he was appointed U. S. Physician at Winnebago Agency, and later held the same position at Pine Ridge Agency, Dak. In 1879 he located in Dakota City, Neb., for the practice of medicine; was in 1893 post trader at Rosebud Agency, S. Dak.; resides now at West Point, Neb. Children: i. Georgia, b. Jan. 2, 1881; m. Orville Miller of Oak Creek, S. Dak. ii. Florence, b. July 22, 1882; m. E. A. Youngquist of Carter, S. Dak. iii. Nellie, b. June 30, 1890; m. ———— Thomas, and resides in Minneapolis, Minn.

Eunice Clementine Warner, b. Nov. 27, 1853; resides in Colosse, S. Dak.; m. Aug. 18, 1887, R. C. Bauer, who had been a teacher in Dakota County, Neb.

Mary Melinda Warner, b. Apr. 9, 1857; resides at Rosebud Agency, S. Dak.; m. Nov. 25, 1883, David Parmelee.

Moses Milburn Warner, b. Aug. 20, 1855; m. at Homer, Neb., Dec. 14, 1892, Mable Clare Taylor, b. in Homer, May 1, 1870, daughter of William and Martha (Hindman) Taylor. Children: i. Jessie Marie, b. in Lyons, Neb., June 2, 1903; d. there, June 25, 1903. ii. Mary Luella, b. at Sioux City, Iowa, Feb. 12, 1915. Mr. Warner has been at different times U. S. Surveyor in the allotments for the Winnebago Indians; Indian Department Clerk; U. S. Indian Agent for the Omaha and Winnebago Indians; Census enumerator at Lyons, Neb., 1900. He has been in the newspaper business for over forty years, took charge of the Lyons Mirror in 1890 and continued its

MR. AND MRS. MOSES M. WARNER AND DAUGHTER MARY

publication until November, 1917, when the office was destroyed by fire. Mr. Warner then arranged for a consolidation with the Lyons Sun and continued the paper. He is the author of "Warner's History of Dakota County," which contains the names of some ten thousand pioneers. He is a member of the I. O. O. F., Sons of Veterans, A. O. U. W., Select Knights, Degree of Honor, Rebekahs, Good Templars; a member of the Methodist Church and a Democrat in politics. For 36 years he was historian of the Dakota County Pioneers and Old Settlers Association, and for 15 years secretary of the Burt County Pioneers and Old Settlers Association.

Ernest Jesse Warner, b. at Dakota City, Neb., June 16, 1868; d. in Anchorage, Alaska, July 26, 1917; m. in Blair, Neb., Sept. 7, 1891, Eunice A. Babbitt, who resides in Colton, Cal. Children: i. J. Victor. ii. Ernest Jesse, resides in Los Angeles, Cal. iii. Eunice, m. Horace Englen of Rosebud Agency, S. D. iv. Helen, died.

673 WESLEY[8] WARNER, son of Joshua[7] and Rosanna (Edmunds) Warner, born in Wooster, Ohio, March 18, 1850; is a farmer residing on the Lincoln Highway in Wooster. His family are all members of the Methodist Church. Married near Burbank, Ohio, October 2, 1873, ANNA E. YOST, born October 21, 1851, near Burbank, daughter of Christian and Elizabeth (Cover) Yost.

Children, born in Wooster

Henry S. Warner, b. Mar. 11, 1875. He is General Secretary of the Intercollegiate Prohibition Association, with headquarters in Chicago. He is the author of "Social Welfare and the Liquor Traffic," used as a text book in many schools and colleges in the study of civic problems. Married in St. Paul, Minn., Aug. 24, 1908, Florence Wells. No children.

Glenn Y. Warner, b. Apr. 3, 1877. He is in charge of the department of public speaking of Winona College, Winona Lake, Ind. Chautauqua work and evening entertainment are his specialties.

Clyde Wesley Warner, b. July 24, 1883. He is in charge of the department of Osteopathic technique and principles at the American School of Osteopathy, Kirksville, Mo. Married in Delaware, Ohio, Sept. 1, 1910, Harriet Wilkin. Child: Barbara Wilkin, b. May 13, 1916.

Paul J. Warner, b. Sept. 17, 1885; is science teacher in the High School at Beaver Dam, Wis.; m. Sept. 1, 1910, Emma L. Curtice. Children: i. Robert C., b. Aug. 4, 1911. ii. Alberta, b. Sept. 17, 1912.

Mary Eda Warner, b. Feb. 20, 1888.

Katherine G. Warner, b. Apr. 23, 1892. She is teacher of literature and English in the High School at Barberton, Ohio.

674 ELMORE YOCUM[8] WARNER, son of Jesse[7] and Jane (Goodfellow) Warner, born July 7, 1833, near Wooster, Wayne Co., Ohio; died July 6, 1886, in Norwalk, Huron Co., Ohio. He was a Methodist Episcopal minister; was received on trial in the North Ohio Conference in 1857; was ordained deacon in 1859; appointed to Monroeville in 1860, then in succession to Milan, Mount Eaton, Bellevue, Monroeville, Clyde, Bellevue again, and Wellington. He was then presiding elder of the Sandusky District for four years, after which he held pastorates at Galion and Berea, then became presiding elder of the Mansfield District for four years. He then asked for a supernumerary relation on account of feeble health and retired to his home in Norwalk. During the Civil War he was chaplain from the Firelands, Ohio.
Married ————.

Children

Lee L. Warner, b. July 22, 1863, at Middletown, Holmes Co., Ohio; d. Dec. 19, 1888, at Bowling Green. He was a Methodist Episcopal minister; graduated from Baldwin University about 1883; entered the itinerant ministry at Greenleaf, Kans., May, 1884; returned to Ohio in 1885 on account of his father's failing health. Married at Lakeside, Aug. 17, 1884, Laura M. Case of Bowling Green. They had two children.

Winifred Warner, b. June 19, 1866; m. —— Bushnell.
Eddy Warner, b. Dec. 23, 1873.
Joy Warner, b. Aug. 5, 1879.
Bruce Warner, b. May 20, 1884; d. May 25, 1915.

675 EDWIN LAMBERT[8] WARNER, son of Jesse[7] and Ann (Oldroyd) Warner, born October 20, 1847, near Wooster, Ohio; resides in Mansfield, Ohio, and Zephyrville, Fla. He is a Methodist Episcopal minister, North East Ohio Conference, retired.

Married near Wooster, Ohio, March 26, 1872, **MARIETTA VIRGINIA SILVER**, born July 8, 1850, daughter of John and Mary (Robison) Silver.

Children

Mary Edna Warner, b. Sept. 22, 1874, near Wooster, Ohio; m. June, 1888, T. B. Jarvis.
Florence Grace Warner, b. July 30, 1877, at Brighton, Ohio.
Jay Odell Warner, b. Oct. 17, 1883, in Wooster, Ohio. For five years he was pastor teacher in a boy's boarding school in Hilo, Hawaii; three years pastor of the Methodist Episcopal Church in New York and Massachusetts; member of the New York Conference; appointed at Conference of Apr., 1917, to special work as director of boys from 12 to 19 in Y. M. C. A. at Pittsfield, Mass.

676 LUCY[8] WARNER, daughter of Joel[7] and Delilah (Everett) Warner, born in New Philadelphia, Ohio, December 16, 1846; resides in Zena, Ulster Co., N. Y. She attended Oberlin College with her daughter.

Married in New Philadelphia, September 6, 1866, **LEWIS ROBERT MC CLELLAND**, born in Shepardstown, Ohio, October 7, 1842, son of Joseph and Hannah (Lister) McClelland. Mr. McClelland served in the Civil War for four years and was Commander of his Post.

Child

Agnes Warner McClelland, b. Apr. 29, 1867; m. Dec. 9, 1900, in Cleveland, Ohio, George Daulton, b. in Edina, Mo., Oct. 18, 1861, d. in New York City, Jan. 29, 1913; no children. Mr. Daulton was a writer of Chicago, resided later in New York City. Mrs. Daulton was a frail child and was educated largely at home, and at Oberlin College. She resides with her parents in Zena, Ulster Co., N. Y., in an old house built in 1799, purchased by her father about 1910. Here she carries on the literary work in which she has attained such distinction, particularly in writing for young people. Among her published works are: "Wings and Stings," and "The Autobiography of a Butterfly," two nature books used in public schools; "Fritzi"; "From Sioux to Susan (Century Company); "Gentle Interference of Bab"; Marooning of Peggy"; "Capers of Benjy and Barby" (Appleton's); "Uncle Davie's Children" (Macmillan's). Mrs. Daulton has written for St. Nicholas and other magazines and has also lectured in a large field of subjects. She has never been a club woman but is honorary member of Chicago Women's Club of New York, Staten Island Women's Club, and Fortnightly Club of Staten Island.

677 JOHN ALBRIGHT[8] WARNER, son of Alanson[7] and Catharine (Albright) Warner, born in Ontario, N. Y., August 12, 1835. He was educated at Macedona and Walworth Academies, became a carpenter and worked at the trade for some years, then was a farmer and resided on one farm for forty years. He and his family are members of the Second Advent Church.

Married December 25, 1860, HARRIET ANN MORRIS, born in Springwater, Livingston Co., N. Y., July 10, 1838, daughter of Lyman and Anna (Millet) Morris of Springwater.

Children, first two born in Webster, N. Y., others in Ontario

Clarence Morris Warner, b. Mar. 20, 1861; went to Illinois in 1884, bought a farm in Ulah and located there. In 1910 he sold this farm and located on a farm in Tecumseh, Shawnee Co., Kans. He and his family are members of the Methodist Church. Married Jan. 2, 1888, Anna Anderson, daughter of Hans and Christina (———) Anderson of Ulah, Ill. Children, b. in Ulah: i. Mabel Edith, b. Nov. 28, 1889. ii. Harriet Christine, b. Sept. 20, 1891. iii. Willis Anderson, b. Oct. 3, 1893. iv. Leigh Arthur, b. July 3, 1902.

Roscoe Durwood Warner, b. Feb. 20, 1863; d. in infancy.

Sarah Edith Warner, b. Dec. 2, 1866; m. in Ontario, N. Y., Mar. 27, 1889, Francis Fayette Field, who d. in Williamson, N. Y., June 5, 1917. He was a farmer in Williamson, son of Henry Daw and Elizabeth (———) Field of Williamson. They had no children, but adopted Luther Morris Warner, son of her brother, Arthur Andrew Warner.

Anna Emeline Warner, b. Oct. 15, 1868; d. in infancy.

Frances Lillian Warner, b. Jan. 10, 1876; m. Mar. 6, 1901, Howard Elias Colby, a farmer in Pultneyville, N. Y., son of Sherman and Sarah (Smith) Colby of Ontario. Children, b. in Pultneyville: i. Harold Morris, b. Jan. 28, 1902. ii. Wilbur Warner, b. Oct. 21, 1904.

Arthur Andrew Warner, b. Oct. 30, 1877; d. Jan. 2, 1910, in Ontario, N. Y.; was a farmer in Ontario; m. Feb. 18, 1904, Ella May Schirmerhorn, who died Jan. 28, 1909. She was the daughter of Rufus

and Honor (————) Schirmerhorn of Ontario. Child: Luther
Morris, b. May 6, 1907; was adopted by his aunt and uncle, Francis
Fayette and Sarah Edith (Warner) Field, and resides in William-
son, N. Y.

678 ALBERT ELDORAS[8] **WARNER,** son of Alanson[7] and
Catharine (Albright) Warner, born March 27, 1854, in Ontario,
N. Y. To him has come down the powder horn once owned by
Andrew[5] Warner, and it is a highly prized heirloom of Revolu-
tionary times.

Married July 1, 1874, **MARTHA LOUISE GRANGER,** born
in Ontario, April 22, 1854, daughter of Joseph and Sarah (Norton) Granger. The Granger family traces its maternal ancestry
back to one Admiral Warner of England, born about 1720.

Children

Orrie Andrew Warner, d. in infancy.
Manley Granger Warner, b. Nov. 11, 1881, in Ontario; m. Jan. 10,
    1907, Jessie De May, b. Mar. 25, 1883, daughter of Isaac and Cynthia
    (————) De May. Children: i. Cecil Manley, b. July 25, 1909,
    in Manchester, N. Y. ii. Earl Albert, b. May 27, 1913, in New-
    ark, N. Y.

679 H E N R Y   D A N I E L[8] **W A R N E R,** son of Stanley
Le Grand[7] and Eunice P. (Wanzer) Warner, born in New Milford, Conn., November 14, 1857; resides in Pawling, N. Y.,
where he is farm manager for John G. Dutcher, vice-president
of the Pawling Savings Bank.

Married April 6, 1881, **HARRIET AMINTA SABIN,** born in
New Milford, October 28, 1858, daughter of Charles Huram and
Laura Ann (Thorp) Sabin.

Children, born in New Milford

Mildred Sabin Warner, b. Feb. 16, 1882; resides in Newtonville,
    Mass.; m. in Pawling, N. Y., June 28, 1905, William Sherman
    Trowbridge, b. Jan. 11, 1880, in Pawling, N. Y., son of Belden
    Crane and Josephine Maria (Campbell) Trowbridge. At the age
    of sixteen, Mr. Trowbridge entered the New York Central offices,
    from there went to Boston as assistant auditor of the Boston and
    Albany Railroad, of which he is now chief auditor. Children:
    i. Marion Warner, b. June 30, 1906. ii. Marjory Annis, b. Dec. 23,
    1910. iii. Lois Sabin, b. Dec. 22, 1913.
Charles Huram Warner, b. May 20, 1884.
Amy Bostwick Warner, b. Dec. 10, 1886; m. Mar. 20, 1912, Joseph
    Paisley of Mount Vernon, N. Y. Child: Helen Warner, b. Apr. 20,
    1913.
Madeline Wanzer Warner, b. Jan. 31, 1894; is engaged in settlement
    work.

NINTH GENERATION

680 WILLIAM ALLING[9] WARNER, son of Sherman Roberts[8] and Delia Caroline (Hodges) Warner, born in New Haven, Conn., May 6, 1861. He resides in New-Haven and is a dealer in wholesale building materials.

Married (1) in New Haven, October 20, 1886, **NETTIE CLARK ENSIGN**, born in New Haven, July 6, 1861, died there, December 17, 1887, daughter of Edwin W. and Julia Maria (Mix) Ensign.

Married (2) February 28, 1894, **HANNAH MINERVA GRANNISS**, daughter of Thomas and ——— (Richardson) Granniss.

Child by first wife

Winfred Clark Warner, b. in New Haven, Dec. 12, 1887; was graduated from Yale in 1910.

Child by second wife

Sherman Roberts Warner, 2d, b. Dec. 8, 1894; is a student at Yale (1915).

681 ROLAND TREADWAY[9] WARNER, son of Sherman Roberts[8] and Delia Caroline (Hodges) Warner, born in New Haven, Conn., September 14, 1866. He is a hardware dealer in New Haven.

Married in New Haven, November 28, 1888, **AGNES DAY HENDERSON**, born in New Haven, January 9, 1866, daughter of David and Elizabeth Caroline (Chase) Henderson.

Children, born in New Haven

Donald Henderson Warner, b. Jan. 23, 1890.
Roland Emerson Warner, b. Sept. 9, 1892.
Gordon Chase Warner, b. Dec. 25, 1899.
William Alling Warner, 2d, b. July 10, 1905.

682 MARY ELIZABETH[9] WARNER, daughter of George[8] and Mary A. (Walker) Warner, born in Hardwick, Mass., September 22, 1856; was graduated from Mount Holyoke College in 1879 and became a teacher. Resides in Hamilton, Ontario, Canada.

Married in Hardwick, July 20, 1882, **ARTHUR BIRKS WILKES**, born April 21, 1847, in Montreal, Canada, son of

William Arthur and Ellen (Birks) Wilkes,   He is an iron merchant.

Children

Paul Henry Wilkes, b. in Oberlin, Ohio, Sept. 9, 1883; is an accountant residing in Chicago, Ill.; m. June 29, 1910, Georgina Hayes.
Children: i. Helen Elizabeth, b. in Hamilton, Ont., Oct. 27, 1912.
ii. Ralph Hayes, b. in Toronto, Jan. 2, 1915.

Harriet.Mary Ellen Wilkes, b. in Oberlin, Ohio, Aug. 1, 1885; d. in
Kingston, Ont., Sept. 19, 1889.

George Warner Wilkes, b. in Kingston, Ont., June 9, 1891; d. there,
Dec. 28, 1891.

Arthur Warner Wilkes, b. in Kingston, Ont., Jan. 27, 1893; d. there,
Sept. 3, 1893.

Ruth Beulah Wilkes, b. in Toronto, Oct. 3, 1895; is a graduate of
Collegiate Institute and Normal School and is a teacher.

Theodore Birks Wilkes, b. in Toronto, June 19, 1898; is a student
at the Collegiate Institute.

683   IRA DE VER[9] WARNER, son of Alonzo Franklin[8] and
Lydia Ann (Converse) Warner, born at Lincklaen, N. Y.,
March 26, 1840; died at his winter home in Augusta, Ga., Jan-
uary 11, 1913.

The father of Ira DeVer Warner died when he was six years
old, and a few months later his mother bought a farm of twenty
acres in the hamlet of Lincklaen, Chenango Co., N. Y., and here
he spent his childhood and youth.   He was educated in public
school and in a select school taught by the local minister, Rev.
Shubael Carver.   When he was sixteen years old he taught
school in the town of Lincklaen and again the following winter
in the adjoining town of Cuyler.

At the age of nineteen, he went to McGrawville (now
McGraw), N. Y., and commenced the study of medicine with
Dr. Kingman of that place.   In the fall of 1861, he entered
Geneva Medical College at Geneva, N. Y., from.which he was
graduated in 1863, and was the valedictorian of his class.   He
then commenced the practice of medicine at Nineveh, Delaware
Co., N. Y., but in 1864 he bought out the practice of Dr. Kingman and settled in McGrawville.   Here he built up a fine practice and was highly esteemed as a physician and as a citizen.

In 1867 he joined with his brother, Lucien C. Warner,
recently graduated from New York University Medical College,
in giving courses of lectures upon physiology and hygiene.
This he continued for about ten years, visiting several hundred
cities and towns in New York, Pennsylvania, Ohio, Michigan,

DR. IRA DEVER WARNER

and nearly all of the New England states. He was an easy, fluent speaker with a good fund of humor, and was very popular and successful as a lecturer.

In 1874, he forméd a partnership with his brother, who was now residing in New York City, for the manufacture of a health corset. At first the goods were made in McGrawville, but in the fall of 1876 he removed with the business to Bridgeport, Conn., where he afterwards resided. The business was very prosperous from the first and was soon extended to include a full line of all styles of corsets, waists and hose supporters. In 1894 the partnership was changed to a corporation and the "Warner Brothers Company" took its place among the leading industries of Bridgeport, their sales at this time being over two million dollars a year.

Dr. Warner was active in many enterprises outside of his immediate business interests. In 1886, in company with his brother and Hon. P. T. Barnum, he organized the Citizens Water Company of Bridgeport. This was later consolidated with the Bridgeport Hydraulic Company, and Dr. Warner became the president of the Company and a large owner of its stock. At the time of his death, he was President of The Warner Bros. Company, the Bridgeport Hydraulic Company and the Bridgeport Gas Light Company. He was also for many years a director in the New York, New Haven & Hart ford Railroad.

Dr. Warner took a prominent interest in the First Presby terian Church, of which he was a member, and in all the phil anthropic enterprises of the city. In 1883 he helped to organize the Bridgeport Y. M. C. A., and in 1888 he gave the Association the lot on the northwest corner of Main and Gilbert Streets and was active in raising the $150,000.00 used to erect a building on that spot. He was President of the Association until 1906 when he retired and was made honorary president until the time of his death. He was also for several years chairman of the State Committee of the Y. M. C. A. and frequently visited the different Associations of the State, making public addresses and assisting them in their local work.

He was a member of the Bridgeport Chamber of Commerce, of the Black Rock Yacht Club, the Brooklawn Country Club, the Seaside Club, the Union League Club of New York and the Country Club of Augusta, Ga.

In his will, he divided among the members of his family an estate valued at over three million dollars.

Dr. Warner married (1) September 24, 1862, LUCETTA MARIA GREENMAN of McGrawville, N. Y., daughter of David Waterbury and Maria (McGraw) Greenman, born January 19, 1839; died October 31, 1895, at Bridgeport, Conn. She was a woman of lovely spirit and rare personal charm. Her health was never robust, yet she was active in helping the sick and needy and in every effort to better the conditions of society. She was especially interested in Seaside Institute which was established for the girls who worked in the factory of the Warner Brothers Company.

Married (2) September 14, 1897, EVA FOLLETT of Wrentham, Mass., daughter of Alonzo and Tryphena Collins (Doane) Follett, born September 4, 1871. Mrs. Warner was a generous supporter and worker in the Red Cross and other agencies for helping the soldiers and aiding those made destitute in the late European war.

Children by first wife

723 *Annie Lucetta Warner,* b. Jan. 11, 1867; m. Nathaniel Wheeler Bishop.
724 *DeVer Howard Warner,* b. Nov. 20, 1868; m. Isabella Maude Winton Cady.
      Hugh F. Warner, b. June 6, 1876; d. May 1, 1879.

Child by second wife

Ira Follett Warner, b. Dec. 7, 1901. He is now (1918) preparing for college at the Hotchkiss Preparatory School at Lakeville, Conn.

684 LUCIEN CALVIN[9] WARNER, son of Alonzo Franklin[8] and Lydia Ann (Converse) Warner, born at his grandfather's homestead in Cuyler, N. Y., October 26, 1841; resides in New York City. Left fatherless at the age of five, he lived with his mother and brother on a small farm in Lincklaen, Chenango Co., N. Y., during his boyhood and attended district school there. In the spring of 1858, when 16 years of age, he taught his first district school at Cuyler, N. Y. He prepared for college at the De Ruyter Academy, teaching school winters. In 1860, he went to Oberlin College, graduating in 1865, with the degree of A.B., having paid the entire expenses of the course by work of various kinds during the college year, and by teaching school during the three months' winter vacation. On May 5, 1864, he enlisted in a company formed of Oberlin men, which became Company K, 150th Regiment, Ohio Volunteers, on duty at forts in and around Washington. During his service he was in Fort Stevens in command of a cannon when General Early attacked that Fort in his raid on Washington. On August 23, 1864, he was mustered out of service and returned to his college work. After graduation he entered the Medical Department of New York University, graduating with the degree of M.D. in 1867. He also received from Oberlin College A.M. for graduate work in 1870, LL.D. in 1900, and from New York University LL.D. in 1917.

For six years after completing his studies, Dr. Warner travelled and lectured throughout the country on health subjects. at first with his brother and after 1872 alone. He wrote and published two popular medical books: The Functions and Diseases of Women,· 1872, and Man in Health and Disease, in 1873. In the fall of 1873, he settled in New York City in the practice of medicine, but after one year a strong inclination for business pursuits led him to give up the practice of medicine, and in 1874 he formed a partnership with his brother in the manufacture of a newly designed health corset. This business was incorporated in 1894 under the name of the Warner Brothers Company, of which he became Vice-President until 1913, and since then President. In 1900 Dr. Warner organized the Warner Chemical Company, of which he is President, and his son Franklin, Treasurer. He is also director of the Home Insurance Company, the Warner-Klipstein Chemical Company, and the Monarch Chemical Company. He was one of the organizers and first President of the Hamilton Bank of New York, and the Woman's Hotel Company.

From 1880 to 1895, the family resided in Harlem, and the Warner home was a favorite place for public gatherings of a philanthropic and benevolent nature. Dr. Warner was deeply interested in the Harlem Y. M. C. A., of which he was President 1881-1892, during which time it erected its first building and toward which he contributed largely both in time and money.

In 1895, Dr. Warner built a beautiful residence at Irvington. where the family resided until 1902. The children having all married and settled in homes of their own, Dr. and Mrs. Warner decided to give up the care of a large establishment, and they have since resided in an apartment hotel, being free to travel at will. Always fond of travel, they have visited Europe sixteen times since their first trip in 1880, have made trips to all parts of their own country, and Canada, Mexico, South America, Australia and twice around the world.

Dr. Warner joined the Congregational Church in Lincklaen, N. Y., when he was seventeen years old, and since then he has

DR. LUCIEN C. WARNER

been active in religious work. On his removal to New York City, he joined the Broadway Tabernacle Congregational Church, in which he has been an active worker in all the church activities, and a deacon since 1892. He has also taken an active part in the national denominational societies; a corporate member of the American Board of Commissioners for Foreign Missions; President of the Congregational Church Building Society 1897-1917; member of the Executive Committee of the American Missionary Association since 1892, and its Chairman since 1913; member of the Congregational Board of Ministerial Relief and Chairman of the Finance Committee of this and other societies. He has been a leader in the affairs of the Congregational Council, as a member of the Commission of Nineteen, which was instrumental in bringing the Council into closer relations with the benevolent societies of the denomination, and has served on other important commissions and boards. In 1910 he was a delegate to the World's Missionary Conference at Edinburgh.

Dr. Warner has been especially interested in religious and philanthropic work of an interdenominational character. He was chairman of the New York State Committee of the Y. M. C. A., 1893-5, and of the International Committee, 1895-1910. During this time he travelled extensively over the country in promoting the interests of the Associations. He has been a trustee of Oberlin College for over forty years, and has given to it two large buildings, one for the Conservatory of Music and one for a gymnasium. With his brother he built the Seaside Institute at Bridgeport ' for the use of their employees.

Dr. Warner is a member of the University Club of New York, the Adirondack League Club, the Scarsdale Golf Club, the New York Chamber of Commerce, the New England Society, Society of Mayflower Descendants, Metropolitan Museum of Art, American Museum of Natural History, Congregational Club (of which he was President 1889-94) ; National Geographic Society.

In 1914 he published an autobiographical volume, The Story of My Life during Seventy Eventful Years, 1841-1911.

Lucien C. Warner married in McGrawville, N. Y., April 12, 1868, KEREN SARAH THIRZA OSBORNE, who was born October 15, 1849, at East Scott, near Homer, N. Y., the daughter of Judge Noah Humphrey Osborne, who was born at Goshen, Conn., August 26, 1802, died in New York City, July

26, 1894, and his wife, **Eliza Azubah Thompson**, born at Farmington, Conn., July 31, 1805, died at McGrawville, N. Y., July 5, 1881. Judge Osborne was descended through his mother, Sarah Marshall Humphrey, from Michael Humphrey, who settled in Windsor, Conn., about 1643. When Keren was six months old, the family removed to the hamlet of Scott, and four years later, to the village of McGrawville, which was her home until her marriage, with the exception of three years on a farm northwest of McGrawville. She was educated by her brother, at private schools, and at the New York Central Academy, later studying music at Friendship, N. Y.

Mrs. Warner has been in close sympathy and co-operation with her husband in all his benevolent and philanthropic work. She was the first President of the Woman's Auxiliary of the Harlem Young Men's Christian Association, and managed a large fair in aid of its building fund; a charter member and the first President of the Harlem Relief Society; a member of the first Board of Directors of the Harlem Young Women's Christian Association, and was elected its first President, but the pressure of other duties prevented her acceptance. In 1890 she joined Sorosis, the first chartered woman's club ever organized, and has served five times as chairman of its Executive Committee. She has been active in social matters, but she has been more interested in welfare work, especially in efforts to better the condition of women and children. She has not favored the extension of suffrage to women, as she has believed that women could accomplish more for good government without the vote than with it. During the great world war, she has devoted most of her time to work for the Red Cross. In 1902 she received from Oberlin College the honorary degree of A.M., in recognition of her services in benevolent and philanthropic work.

On April 12, 1918, Dr. and Mrs. Warner celebrated their Golden Wedding at their home in New York. There were present their four children with their wives and husbands and six of the seven grandchildren. The oldest grandson, Lucien Hynes Warner, was absent, attending Pomona College, California. Speeches were made, toasts were given, and presents exchanged, and altogether it was a rare and delightful occasion to those concerned.

Children of Lucien C. and Keren S. T. (Osborne) Warner

725 *Agnes Eliza Warner,* b. Feb. 22, 1872; m. Seabury Cone Mastick.
726 *Franklin Humphrey Warner,* b. June 6, 1875; m. Estelle Dunn Hynes.

727 *Lucien Thompson Warner*, b. Apr. 18, 1877; m. Mary Barbour Whit-
     man.
728 *Elizabeth Converse Warner*, b. May 27, 1879; m. William Gibson
     Gallowhur.

685 EROTUS[9] **WARNER**, son of Roswell Knowlton[5] and
Remonia (Vail) Warner, born September 12, 1850, at De Ruyter, **N. Y.**; resides in Marion, **N. Y.** He was educated in Palmyra, **N. Y.**, and has followed farming all his life. For some
years he has made a specialty of fruit growing and truck farming and is also a dealer in cement products and coal. He is a
member of the Grange and A. O. U. W. of Marion.

Married January 31, 1872, **ELLEN MARIETTA WAKE**,
born May 3, 1852, in Williamson, N. Y., daughter of John and
Marietta (Rice) Wake. John Wake was born in England in
1823, the youngest of a family of thirteen children. He came
to this country with his parents in 1831, crossing the ocean in
a sail boat, and coming up the St. Lawrence River, then settling
in Williamson.

MAJOR OSCAR CZAR WARNER

Children

Melville E. Warner, b. in Marion, Nov. 24, 1872. He is in business
  with his father in Marion, N. Y., manufacturing cement products,
  tile and brick.

Florence May Warner, b. in Palmyra, May 19, 1879; m. ——— Lookup.
Children, b. in Marion: i. Gertrude Ellen, b. Apr. 29, 1901. ii. George
Erotus, b. Feb. 5, 1906.   iii. Herbert Charles, b. Aug. 2, 1908.
Oscar Czar Warner, b. Nov. 5, 1883, at Marion, N. Y.; was graduated
from Marion Collegiate Institute, spent a year in Rochester Business Institute, entered Purdue University, Lafayette, Ind., in 1903,
graduating in 1907 with the degree of Bachelor of Science in Electrical Engineering; received advanced degree, E.E., from Purdue in
1917. In Apr., 1909, he was commissioned a Second Lieutenant in
the U. S. Army; promoted to First Lieutenant in 1910; Honor
Graduate from the Coast Artillery School at Fortress Monroe, Va.,
in 1914, and was then placed in command of the U. S. Army mine-
laying ship, the "General Frank"; in February, 1916, he was detailed
as head of the electrical course in the Enlisted Specialists School at
Fortress Monroe and served there until Jan., 1918; received Captain's commission, July, 1916; in Jan., 1918, received orders for duty
in France; promoted to the rank of Major, May 4, 1918. Married
Dec. 12, 1914, Mona Loraine Lovell, b. Nov. 10, 1890, daughter of
William H. and Sarah (Elliott) Lovell.

686   LEWIS N.[9] WARNER, son of Roswell Knowlton[8] and
Remonia (Vail) Warner, born November 5, 1855, at Preble,
N. Y.; resides in Marion, N. Y., where he is a carpenter.
Married **AMELIA E. ALLEN,** born April 5, 1858, at Spring-
field Center, Otsego Co., N. Y., daughter of Abram and Emma
(Hodgkins) Allen who came from England in 1844.

Children

Lillian A. Warner, b. July 2, 1879; d. June 11, 1881, in Marion.
Jessie Emma Warner, b. June 25, 1882, in Marion; m. in Marion, Aug.
19, 1903, Miles B. Dean, b. Jan. 26, 1880, son of John and Lizzie
(———) Dean of Marion. He was educated at the High School
and is now a farmer in Marion. Children, b. in Marion: i. Arthur
G., b. June 12, 1904. ii. Earl L., b. Nov. 19, 1908. iii. George Byron,
b. Dec. 7, 1910. iv. Ivan A., b. Oct. 13, 1912.
Lewis Carl Warner, b. Mar. 18, 1891, at Marion; is cost clerk with
the Reed Manufacturing Company of Newark, N. Y.; m. in Newark,
Aug. 7, 1913, Mildred Bradley, daughter of Dennis and Estella
(———) Bradley of Newark.

687   ELLEN[9] WARNER, daughter of Davis Dimock[8] and
Mary Ann (Raynsford) Warner, born in Montrose, Pa., August
9, 1833; died in Scranton, Pa., January 19, 1874.
Married about 1852, **HENRY STARK SEARLE,** born
December 25, 1828; died in Battle Creek, Mich., August 4, 1894.
He was the son of Daniel Searle and Johanna Stark.

Children, all but last born in Montrose

Carrie Catlin Searle, b. Oct. 5, 1854; d. in Trenton, N. J., Aug., 1916;
m. Oct. 5, 1876, Henry Welling of Trenton, b. in Titusville, N. J.,

42

July 4, 1847. Children, b. in Trenton: i. Jared Warner, b. July 14, 1877, is a civil engineer; resides in Greenville, Miss.; m. Aug. 14, 1912, Sadie ————. ii. Margaret Wyckoff, b. May 12, 1879; resides in Passaic, N. J.; m. July 7, 1906, George B. Willard. iii. Francis Searle, b. Apr. 9, 1881; d. in Trenton, N. J.; m. July 17, 1907, William D. Gowdy of Brooklyn, N. Y. iv. Charlotte Paul, b. Oct. 7, 1883; d. in Trenton, Dec. 7, 1892. v. Mary MacDonald, b. Jan. 17, 1886; is a teacher in Brooklyn, N. Y. vi. John Alden, b. Dec. 17, 1887; is serving in the Ordnance Department, U. S. A., at Camp McClellan. vii. Henry, b. Sept. 5, 1890; is in France, Second Lieutenant, 316th Infantry. viii. Daniel Searle, b. Sept. 25, 1894; is in France, First Lieutenant, 115th F. A.; m. Nov. 28, 1917, Bertha Fisher.

Henry Searle, b. 1856; d. young.

Edward Raynsford Warner Searle, b. June 15, 1858; is a lawyer in Montrose; m. Nov. 25, 1879, Margaret Bedell. Children: i. Johannah Stark, b. Aug. 30, 1889. ii. Clara, b. Sept. 1, 1896.

Fanny Elizabeth Searle, b. Nov. 27, 1860; resides in Scranton, Pa.; m. Oct. 8, 1884, Sidney T. Hays, b. July 26, 1850, d. Apr., 1914. Child: Warner Searle, b. Dec. 20, 1886; is commissioned Captain in the National Army, U. S. A., in charge of electrical work at Pig Point, Portsmouth, Va.

Warner Searle, b. May 21, 1867; is a salesman and resides in Philadelphia, Pa.; m. May ————.

Raynsford Searle, b. in Scranton, June 5, 1869; is a broker and resides in Buffalo; m. Margaret Gray. Children: i. Fred Warner, b. about 1894; is a First Lieutenant, U. S. A. ii. Margaret, b. about 1898.

688 ANN ELIZA[9] **WARNER,** daughter of Davis Dimock[8] and Mary Ann (Raynsford) Warner, born in Montrose, Pa., December 5, 1834; died there, December 29, 1899.

Married August 25, 1855, **JEROME RICHARDS LYONS,** born in Milford, Pa., July 30, 1828; died in Montrose, Pa., May 5, 1877. He was a man of marked genius in his profession as an architect. He enlisted in the Civil War, March, 1862, as Captain of Company A, 57th Regiment, Pennsylvania Volunteers, and was one of the four brothers for whom the "Four Brothers G. A. R. Post" is named. He was architect and builder of the Susquehanna County Soldiers Monument.

Children

Annie Lyons, b. in Scranton, Pa., Aug. 31, 1856; d. there, Oct. 21, 1856.

Ernest Warner Lyons, b. in Madison, Wis., Oct. 8, 1857; resides in Spokane, Wash.; is railway clerk for the Northern Pacific; m. in Portland, Ore., Jan. 15, 1885, Elizabeth Jean Harkness. Children: i. Harriet Huse, b. in Tacoma, Wash., Oct. 18, 1886. ii. (Daughter), b. and d. in Montrose, Pa., Oct., 1888.

Eugene Henry Lyons, b. in St. Louis, Mo., Dec. 1, 1859; d. in Montrose, Pa., Mar. 30, 1863.

Anna Lyons, b. in Montrose, Pa., Mar. 29, 1862; resides in Tacoma, Wash.; not married.
Miriam Lyons, b. in Montrose, Feb. 23, 1867; resides in Tacoma; m. Oct. 2, 1889, Harry O. Watrous, b. Aug. 26, 1865. Children: i. Irene, b. in Forest City, Pa., Aug. 18, 1890. ii. Anna, b. in Carbondale, Pa., June 8, 1894. iii. Ruth, b. in Carbondale, Jan. 31, 1899. iv. Janet, b. in Carbondale, July 18, 1905. v. Walter Harry, b. in Tacoma, Wash., Sept. 1, 1907.
(Son), b. in Montrose, Sept. 12, 1869; d. there, July 6, 1870.

689 FREDERICK RAYNSFORD[9] **WARNER,** son of Davis Dimock[8] and Mary Ann (Raynsford) Warner, born in Montrose, Pa., March 7, 1839; died in Geneva, Ill., October 19, 1912. He was a grain dealer and broker in Chicago, Ill., and a member of the Board of Trade. He served in the Civil War as First Lieutenant in Captain Telford's Company, 50th Regiment, Pennsylvania Volunteers, recruited in Bradford County.
Married October 19, 1864, **EUZELIA MC COLLUM.**

Children

Addison Raynsford Warner, b. in Montrose, Pa., Jan. 15, 1867; resides in Hyland Park, Ill.; is a member of the Board of Trade; m. Nov. 1, 1893, Estelle Diefenderfer.
Harry Dimock Warner, b. in Montrose, Aug. 12, 1869; resides in Geneva, Ill.; is paymaster for the I. C. R. R.; m. June 30, 1897, Harriette King Young.
Mabelle Warner, b. in Waverly, N. Y.,; d. in Chicago, Ill.
Robert Warner, b. in Waverly, July 9, 1873; d. July 10, 1873.

690 MARY FRANCES[9] **WARNER,** daughter of Davis Dimock[8] and Mary Ann (Raynsford) Warner, born April 7, 1848, in Montrose, Pa.; died in Wilkes-Barre, Pa., January 15, 1915.
Married October 13, 1868, **BENJAMIN FRANKLIN STARK,** born July 15, 1846; died April, 1893.

Children

Frederick Wagner Stark, b. Apr. 30, 1870; m. Oct. 27, 1897, Claire Warbrick. Children, b. in Wilkes-Barre: i. Robert Warbrick, b. Jan. 13, 1902. ii. Claire Elizabeth, b. Mar. 13, 1903.
Ellen Warner Stark, b. Feb. 22, 1872; m. Apr. 27, 1892, Frederick Merrill Chase; no children.
Jared Warner Stark, b. Dec. 7, 1875; m. Sept. 17, 1902, Helen Carhart. Children: i. Edward Carhart, b. in Kingston, Pa., Nov. 20, 1903. ii. Elizabeth Helen, b. in Kingston, Pa., Mar. 27, 1905. iii. Jared Warner, Jr., b. in Wilkes-Barre, Feb. 7, 1907.

Mary Louise Stark, b. June 20, 1879; m. Oct. 18, 1905, Edward Bow-
man Mulligan. Children, b. in Wilkes-Barre: i. Edward Bowman,
Jr., b. Sept. 26, 1906. ii. Ellen Stark, b. Apr. 30, 1909.
Harold Raynsford Stark, b. Nov. 12, 1880; was graduated from
Annapolis and is a commissioned officer in the U. S. Navy; m. at
Lake Carey, Wyoming Co., Pa., July 24, 1907, Katharine Rhoads,
b. in Wilkes-Barre, July 31, 1880, daughter of Samuel and Jessie
(Wheaton) Rhoads, and granddaughter of Thomas Jefferson and
Maria (Woodruff) Rhoads. Children: i. Mary, b. in Wilkes-
Barre, Jan. 24, 1910. ii. Katharine Rhoads, 2d, b. at Virginia
Beach, Va., July 26, 1911.

691 FLETCHER GUSTAVUS[9] WARNER, son of Nelson
Clarke[8] and Eliza D. (Baldwin) Warner, born in Bridgewater,
Pa., January 25, 1837; is a merchant at Montrose. He was
graduated from West Point in 1862, and was a captain in the
Civil War. He served thirteen months in Company G., 50th
Regiment, Pennsylvania Volunteers, was wounded in both legs
at the battle of Antietam and was not able to rejoin his regiment. He was found in an old barn by his brother Charles or
he would have died from exposure and the wound. Mr. Warner
has been court crier.

Married (1) in Bridgewater, Pa., October 19, 1859, **MARTHA
M. BACKUS**, born April 18, 1841, in Bridgewater, daughter of
George and Eliza (Crandall) Backus; died December 12, 1874,
in Montrose

Married (2) at Windsor, N. Y., May 29, 1878, **MARY EMILY
BUSHNELL**, born at Ararat, Pa., April 17, 1847, daughter of
Albert and Harriet Wadsworth (Tyler) Bushnell.

Children by first wife

Eliza Backus Warner, b. in Montrose, July 10, 1860; d. Mar. 19, 1881.
Nelson Clarke Warner, b. in Montrose, Aug. 21, 1863; is a dry goods
merchant in Montrose; m. there, Nov. 17, 1887, Harriet Emily
Rogers, b. Dec. 30, 1864, in Montrose, daughter of Samuel B. and
Marilla (Avery) Rogers. Child: Kenneth Rogers, b. Sept. 3, 1888,
in Montrose; d. at Camp Hancock, near Augusta, Ga., of pneumonia,
Feb. 10, 1918, while in his country's service.
James Carmalt Warner, b. July 7, 1874, in Montrose; d. there, Oct.
14, 1874.

Child by second wife

Louise Bushnell Warner, b. Dec. 17, 1880; m. Jan. 15, 1906, Samuel J.
Rogers, b. in Montrose, Jan. 17, 1873, son of Samuel B. and Marilla
(Avery) Rogers. Children, b. in Montrose: i. Emily Louise, b.
Sept. 13, 1908. ii. Marilla Avery, b. Feb. 20, 1913.

692 CHARLES NELSON[9] WARNER, son of Nelson
Clarke[8] and Eliza D. (Baldwin) Warner, born April 19, 1839 on

CHARLES NELSON WARNER

Antietam, Fredericksburg, Gettysburg, where he was brevetted for bravery, and was with General Wilson's force that raided the South. He later read law and was admitted to the bar in November, 1875.

Married at Leavenworth, Kans., October 25, 1866, **ELIZA BROWN HOUSTON,** born in Columbia, Pa., February 6, 1839, daughter of John Wright and Mary Bloomfield (Martin) Houston.

WILLIAM HOUSTON WARNER

a farm near Montrose, Pa.; resides in Montrose. He was educated at Montrose and at West Point, graduating there in 1862. He entered the regular army; was brevetted captain, April 2, 1865; and received an honorable discharge after fourteen years of service. He was in several of the Civil War battles: the second Battle of Bull Run, South Mountain,

Children

Charles Nelson Warner, Jr., b. Mar. 4, 1868, at Fort Washington; d. there of typhoid fever, Nov. 5, 1869.

William Houston Warner, b. at Fort Washington, Nov. 10, 1869; resides in Montrose, Pa.; not married. In his early twenties he was elected cashier of the First National Bank of Montrose, at the time the youngest cashier in the United States. He is considered a model citizen, interested actively in the affairs of the community; treasurer of various organizations; warden of the Episcopal Church; past master in Masonry and a Knight Templar; in demand as a public speaker, but, although frequently urged to take the nomination for Legislature, has refused.

Nelson Clarke Warner, 2d, b. Sept. 6, 1871, on a farm near Montrose, Pa.; is a successful merchant in Montrose. He is a past master in Masonry and a Knight Templar. Married Sept. 7, 1907, Bessie Chamberlain. Children, b. in Montrose: i. William Chamberlain, b. May 7, 1909. ii. Houston Bogley, b. Sept. 1, 1910. iii. Nelson Clarke, Jr., b. Sept. 17, 1912. iv. Robert Anthony, b. Aug. 18, 1914; d. Jan. 29, 1915. v. Philip Bryce, b. Sept. 6, 1917.

Mary Bloomfield Warner, b. Apr. 17, 1874; is a versatile business woman and artist. She taught a kindergarten in Binghamton, N. Y., for some time, took up trained nursing, and is now doing splendid work for the Associated Charities in Philadelphia.

Eliza Sarah Warner, b. Jan. 15, 1876; m. in 1907, Franklin Schuyler Sonnakolb, a famous pianist and composer; no children. She resided in Rome, Ga., and Charleston, S. C., for some time; is now in Philadelphia.

Susan Eleanor Warner, b. Sept. 14, 1879; resides in Montrose. She was graduated from the West Chester State Normal School (Pa.) in 1900, Wellesley College, 1904; taught her own private school near Pittsburg, Pa., for five years, Miss Warner's Day School for Girls; then graduated from King's School of Oratory in Pittsburg and traveled as a reader and elocutionist until her marriage, July 22, 1914, to David Finis Gaston, Jr., of Gastonburg, Ala. Child: David Finis, 3d, b. in Philadelphia, May 27, 1915.

693 THEODOSIA[9] **WARNER,** daughter of Sidney Haswell[8] and Hannah (Loomis) Warner, born in Huntington, Luzerne Co., Pa.; died in 1885. She resided in Red Wing, Minn.

Married in Huntington, Pa., 1863, HIRAM ASA PARK, born in Montrose, Pa., 1840, son of Ezra Sidney and Ann[8] (Warner) Park; see page 421.

Children

Robert Ezra Park, b. Feb. 14, 1864, in Huntington, Pa.; is a teacher of sociology at the University of Chicago; resides in Chicago; m. June 11, 1894, Clara Cahill, b. in Hubbardston, Mich., daughter of Judge Edward and Lucy (Crawford) Cahill. Mrs. Park has studied art in Chicago, New York, and abroad and paints mostly children's portraits. After her marriage she took up the work of child welfare and has been active in speaking and introducing legislation on the subject. She has also written short stories and magazine articles. Children: i. Edward Cahill, b. Apr. 24, 1895; m. 1917, Fenhiss Kerlin. ii. Theodosia Warner, b. May 1, 1896. iii. Margaret Lucy. iv. Robert Hiram.

Edward Warner Park, b. June 5, 1869; d. Nov. 17, 1869.

Asa Eugene Park, b. July 16, 1870; d. Feb. 24, 1886.

Herbert Arthur Park, b. Dec. 21, 1874; resides in Watertown, S. Dak.; m. Sept. 6, 1911, Ethel Phillips.

Augustine Hawley Park, b. Mar. 24, 1879; d. Feb. 28, 1898.

694 ADELAIDE[9] WARNER, daughter of Sidney Haswell[8] and Hannah (Loomis) Warner, born in Huntington township, Luzerne Co., Pa., May 2, 1839; resided in Shickshinny, Luzerne County, where she died May 11, 1918.

Married in Huntington township, October 14, 1858, MARK LAFAYETTE KOONS, born in New Columbus, Luzerne County, December 13, 1827, son of John and Anna Andrus (Fellows) Koons.

Children

Annie Koons, b. Sept. 12, 1859; d. July 7, 1860.

Cornelia Koons, b. June 24, 1861; resides in Shickshinny. She studied at the University of Michigan and also at the Art Students' League in New York City.

Fred Warner Koons, b. Nov. 5, 1863; d. Jan. 13, 1876.

Henry Haynes Koons, b. Jan. 14, 1867, in New Columbus, Pa.; is a physician and surgeon in Los Angeles, Cal. He received his education at Huntington Mills Academy; Ann Arbor (Mich.) High School, 1884-8; literary department of University of Michigan; University of Pennsylvania, 1893 to 1897, when he was graduated with the degree of M.D. He was Interne at the University Hospital, Philadelphia, 1897-8; Howard Hospital, 1899; Lieutenant-surgeon, 7th Pennsylvania Regiment, 1898-9. He is president of the Pacific Bond and Mortgage Company of Los Angeles; director of the Municipal Securities Company, Los Angeles; member of D. Hayes Agnew Surgical Society, County and State Medical Societies, American Medical Association, F. and A. M. and Shrine, University and Athletic Clubs of Los Angeles. Dr. Koons was commissioned Captain and stationed at Base Hospital No. 1, Fort Sam Houston, Texas (June, 1918). He was married in Los Angeles, Dec. 2, 1916, to Louise Brewer.

695 JAMES NELSON[9] WARNER, son of Sidney Haswell[8] and Cornelia (Machette) Warner, born in Huntington township, Luzerne Co., Pa., December 5, 1845; died at the German Hospital, New York City, April 28, 1905. After an academic education he was graduated with honors from the Pennsylvania College of Dental Surgery in 1873, and took up the practice of

his profession in Hazelton. Two years later he removed to Wilkes-Barre and remained there the rest of his life, attracting patients from some distance by his skill in his profession. He took an active part in the state and county dental associations; was a member of the Episcopal Church; and a member of F. and A. M., Commandery and Shrine.

Married in Wyoming, Pa., November 7, 1883, **JENNIE EDITH STARK,** born in Plaine, Luzerne Co., Pa., December 23, 1856, daughter of John Michael and Sarah (Davidson) Stark. She resides in Wilkes-Barre.

Children, born in Wilkes-Barre

Sidney Stark Warner, b. July 19, 1886; is a dentist in Wilkes-Barre; m. there, Oct. 17, 1913, Bessie Coralyn Roberts, born in Watertown, N. Y., 1885, daughter of Daniel Charles and Mary (Yeager) Roberts; no children.

Benjamin Stark Warner, b. Nov. 21, 1889; d. Jan. 25, 1891.

James Stark Warner, b. Dec. 28, 1891; is now in the United States Navy at Newport, R. I.

696   CHARLES A.[9] **WARNER,** son of Eliada Blakeslee[8] and Fidelia (Luce) Warner, born October 2, 1837, near Montrose, Pa.; died March 19, 1913, in Ceres, N. Y. When a boy he learned the trade of harness-maker in Binghamton, N. Y.; in 1857 went to Ceres and worked at his trade; in 1860 opened a harness shop in Richburg; worked at his trade in Olean, from 1862 to 1867; established himself in the harness business in Ceres where he spent the remainder of his life, also conducting a grocery in addition. He was justice of the peace in 1863. The family belong to the Methodist Church.

Married (1) in Montrose, 1863, **MARGARET FAY,** born April 8, 1840, died September 9, 1869, daughter of Patrick Fay of Bolivar, N. Y.

Married (2) April 16, 1871, **RUTH A. COOPER,** born July 23 or 25, 1841, died October 5, 1913, daughter of Cyrus and Harriet (Fitch) Cooper.

Children by first wife

Mabel A. Warner, b. Nov. 2, 1863; resides in Cleveland, Ohio; m. May 25, 1882, Jewett B. Almy, b. May 10, 1861. Children: i. Margaret M., b. Mar. 8, 1883; resides in Beechnew, Pittsburg, Pa.; m. June 19, 1906, Thomas Kearns, b. Oct. 25, 1876, in Pittsburg and has children, Thomas Almy, b. June 1, 1908, and John, b. Sept. 15, 1912. ii. Hazel D., b. Nov. 1, 1884; m. Jan. 10, 1914, J. Fred Wolfersherger of Cleveland, Ohio, b. May 25, 1876, and has children, Mary Elizabeth, b. Feb. 10, 1915, and a daughter, b. July, 1916.

729 *Anna R. Warner*, b. July 19, 1865; m. Irvin Horatio Stevens.
Clarence F. Warner, b. Dec. 8, 1866; d. Nov. 25, 1906; m. Sept., 1884,
Myrtie Hanks. One child, d. young.
Ella M. Warner, b. Oct. 31, 1868; resides near Bolivar, N. Y.; m. Dec.
1, 1886, James Anderson, b. Aug. 9, 1859. Child: Agnes E., b. Apr.
1, 1888; d. May 13, 1916; m. Sept. 9, 1908, Chester Corbin, b. Apr.
9, 1886, resides near Bolivar; had three children, James Ward, b.
July 1, 1909, E. Louise, b. Oct. 5, 1910, and Donald H., b. Aug. 31,
1913.

Children by second wife

Leona H. Warner, b. Oct. 8, 1872; resides in Wellsville, N. Y.; m.
May 23, 1894, John W. Miller, b. Aug. 11, 1870. He is special agent
for the Provident Life and Trust Company of Philadelphia. Chil-
dren: i. Ruth, b. July 17, 1895. ii. David, b. Apr. 26, 1904.
Reanard Warner, b. Sept. 7, 1874.
Ethel Warner, b. Aug. 26, 1876; resides in Webster, N. Y.; m. June
6, 1899, Alexander B. McMillen, b. 1874. Children: i. Donald C,
b. Mar. 19, 1900. ii. Kenith, b. Dec. 23, 1903. iii. Hugh A., b. Aug.
24, 1915.
Bessie Warner, b. Aug. 2, 1879; d. Aug. 17, 1906; m. Feb. 11, 1904,
Charles A. Herrick of Shingle House, Pa., b. Jan. 4, 1871.
Ralph W. Warner, b. May 14, 1884; d. May 21, 1885.

696a ERASTUS H.[9] WARNER, son of Elisha Platts[8] and
Margaret (Bogard) Warner, born April 22, 1842; died September 1, 1909, in Marceline, Linn Co., Mo. He was a soldier in
the Civil War.

Married **LETTIE JANE ACKERSON**, who died in Marceline, aged 75. They were both born in Pennsylvania and went
to Missouri in 1876.

Children

Leander A. Warner, b. in Pennsylvania, Aug. 22, 1865; m. Jan. 20,
1901, Laura Lawson, b. Oct. 20, 1880, and has adopted son, Raymond
B. Warner, b. in Missouri, Aug. 22, 1897, who enlisted in the U. S.
Army Apr. 21, 1917, and is in France (Jan., 1919) in Co. J, 308th
Infantry, 77th Division, U. S. Infantry.
Elisha P. Warner, b. in Wyoming County, Pa., July 15, 1867; resides
in Bucklin, Mo., and is working for the Prairie Pipe Line Company;
m. and has children: i. John D., b. Aug. 18, 1879, in Baker town-
ship, Linn Co., Mo.; is engineer for the A. T. and S. F. R. R.;
resides in Marceline, Mo.; m. at Quincy, Ill., Oct. 15, 1908, Myrtle
Jacquette Harris; has a son, John D., Jr., b. at Fort Madison, Iowa,
Mar. 10, 1917. ii. Andy, b. in Bucklin, May 27, 1881; is employed
by the A. T. and S. F. R. R.; m. in Bucklin, Mar. 14, 1905, Ethel
Millsap; has five children, Georgia, b. Feb. 1, 1906, Mable, b. Jan.
3, 1909, Willie, b. Apr. 17, 1911, John R., b. July 13, 1915, and Arthur
Lee, b. Mar. 18, 1918; members of the M. E. Church South.
Jennie Warner, b. in Lackawanna County, Pa., Jan. 31, 1870; m. at
Bucklin, Mo., June 26, 1892, Thomas J. Sportsman, and had six
children, b. in Marceline, Mo.: i. Della M., b. Feb. 6, 1895; was

graduated from the Marceline High School in 1912. ii. Andy M., b. May 12, 1897; after a year in the High School enlisted in the U. S. Army, Apr. 21, 1917, and the following November went overseas with Co. K, 168th Infantry Regiment, 42d (Rainbow) Division. iii. Gerald W., b. Jan. 17, 1903; is freight and baggage clerk for the A. T. and S. F. R. R. iv. Elmer O., b. Sept. 28, 1904. v. Ira T., b. Aug. 2, 1912; d. Mar. 14, 1913. vi. Infant, b. and d. Aug. 2, 1912. *Evert M. Warner*, b. June 11, 1874; m. Dec. 20, 1897, Viola Dowell, b. Aug. 17, 1880; had seven children: i. Beulah Mae, b. in Linn County, Mo., Mar. 18, 1899; is a teacher. ii. Albert Herman, b. June 27, 1901; is a farmer and railroad man. iii. Theodore Evert, b. May 14, 1903. iv. Lettie Jane, b. Mar. 28, 1905. v. George Franklin, b. Feb. 22, 1907. vi. Viola Grace, b. Jan. 19, 1909. vii. Ruby Ellen, b. Aug. 24, 1911.

697   ADDIE ALICE[9] WARNER, daughter of George Dickinson[8] and Octavia (Brewster) Warner, born January 3, 1849, in Bridgewater, Pa.; died June 1, 1904, in Jackson, Susquehanna Co., Pa.

Married in Jackson, November 14, 1868, AVERY WHITMORE BARRETT, born August 14, 1827, in Brattleboro, Vt., son of Levi and Fanny (————) Barrett; died December 19, 1894, in Philadelphia, Pa.   He was a farmer.

Children, born in Jackson

Grace F. Barrett, b. Aug. 9, 1869; d. Feb. 27, 1871.
Alice M. Barrett, b. May 12, 1871; m. (1) in Jackson, Everett P. Payne, who d. June 24, 1904; m. (2) in Binghamton, N. Y., Dec. 27, 1905, Edward H. Woodward. Children by first husband: i. (Son), b. and d. Apr. 12, 1892. ii. Mark, b. Apr. 23, 1896; d. Dec. 22, 1900.
Ernest A. Barrett, b. May 1, 1873; m. in Hornell, N. Y., June 10, 1903, Leona M. Miller. Child: Kenneth Edward, b. Feb. 9, 1911.
Newell G. Barrett, b. Apr. 22, 1875; d. Jan. 31, 1879.
William C. Barrett, b. Apr. 16, 1877; m. in Union, N. Y., Jan. 22, 1897, Bertha L. Norton. Children: i. Clifton A., b. July 31, 1898. ii. Marguerite, b. July 22, 1900.
Ada V. Barrett, b. Aug. 30, 1880; m. in Binghamton, N. Y., Mar. 21, 1903, Ray L. Brown.
Myrtie M. Barrett, b. May 22, 1887; d. Aug. 22, 1889.
Harry M. Barrett, b. May 1, 1889; m. in Jackson, Apr. 6, 1912, Bertha Conrad. Child: (Son), b. in Binghamton, N. Y., June 12, 1913; d. June 14, 1913.
Mildred O. Barrett, b. Sept. 24, 1891.

698   GUSTAVUS J.[9] WARNER, son of George Dickinson[8] and Octavia (Brewster) Warner, born in Bridgewater, Susquehanna Co., Pa., about 1851; died January 11, 1892, aged 41 years, 6 months.
Married in Clarion County, Pa., SUSAN RICE.

Children, first four born in Clarion County, last four in Warren County, Pa.
Adelpha M. (or Della A.) Warner, b. May 11, 1872.
George D. Warner, b. Aug. 16, 1874.
Ernest R. Warner, b. Feb. 6, 1876.
Charles Warner, b. Feb. 2, 1878.
John D. Warner, b. May 12, 1881.
Fannie Warner, b. 1883.
Etta Warner, b. 1885; died.
Timothy Warner, b. 1887.

699 **FANNY**[8] **WARNER,** daughter of George Dickinson[9] and Octavia (Brewster) Warner, born July 20, 1853, in Bridgewater, Susquehanna Co., Pa.; resides in Orosi, Cal. Married in Fryburg, Clarion Co., Pa., May 2, 1882, **ERNEST F. EIFERT,** born in Germany, April 25, 1855.

Children

Newell E. Eifert, b. in Warren Co., Pa., Sept. 26, 1884; is a worker in oil-wells, Coalinga, Cal.; m. June, 1908, Nina Naugent.
Clemons G. Eifert, b. in Warren Co., Pa., Feb. 17, 1886; served three years in the engineers' corps, U. S. A.; is a worker in oil-wells, Yenangyaung, India; m. in St. Louis, Mo., June, 1911, Mae McClusky.
Dorthea E. Eifert, b. in Barnes, Pa., Feb. 10, 1888; m. at Tionesta, Pa., Dec. 3, 1909, Elton G. Jaguay, a merchant in Cutter, Cal.
Clide A. Eifert, b. in Elk County, Pa., Oct. 23, 1889; d. Aug. 7, 1891.
Earl W. Eifert, b. at Corduroy, Elk Co., Pa., Aug. 13, 1892.
Florence M. Eifert, b. at Corduroy, June 7, 1894; m. at Visalia, Cal., Sept. 18, 1914, John W. Cummings, a farmer at St. Barnidoro, Cal.

700 **ADELPHA A.**[9] **WARNER,** daughter of George Dickinson[8] and Octavia (Brewster) Warner, born June 11, 1854, in Bridgewater, Susquehanna Co., Pa. Married in Fryburg, Clarion Co., Pa., August 18, 1870, **GEORGE W. EDMISTON,** born in Fryburg, March, 1853.

Children

Elizabeth May Edmiston, b. Mar. 7, 1871.
Jessie A. Edmiston, b. Mar. 24, 1872; d. Feb. 12, 1893; m. —— Neely.
Flora O. Edmiston, b. Apr. 21, 1874.
Fannie B. Edmiston, b. Nov. 4, 1875.
John D. Edmiston, b. Mar. 13, 1878.
Webster D. Edmiston, b. Sept. 25, 1881.
Ethel M. Edmiston, b. Aug. 30, 1885; d. Jan. 21, 1893.
Guy W. Edmiston, b. Dec. 12, 1886.
Myrtle P. Edmiston, b. Dec. 8, 1889.
Roy Edmiston, b. May 16, 1891; d. Jan. 28, 1893.
Lester Edmiston, b. Sept. 5, 1892.

701 ELIZA G.[9] WARNER, daughter of Ansel Lockman[8] and Mary Jane (Cook) Warner, born August 26, 1854; resides in New Milford, Pa.

Married March 18, 1880, CHARLES WIRTH, born September 12, 1855, in Karlsruhe, Germany.

Children

Jennie K. Wirth, b. Jan. 27, 1881; d. Feb. 18, 1909; m. 1907, George Kern of New Milford, b. 1878.

George P. Wirth, b. July 20, 1884; d. July 21, 1911; m. Mar. 6, 1907, Lulie Decker, b. Dec. 21, 1883. She resides in New Milford.

Louise M. Wirth, b. July 11, 1893; resides in Syracuse, N. Y.; m. June 27, 1912, J. Ceylon Jackson of Syracuse. Child: Donald Wirth, b. June 8, 1913.

702 LILLICE E.[9] WARNER, daughter of Ansel Lockman[8] and Mary Jane (Cook) Warner, born April 7, 1857; resides near Montrose, Pa.

Married July 5, 1874, BENNETT B. FREEMAN of Montrose, b. July 7, 1852.

Children

Grace M. Freeman, b. May 21, 1875; d. Sept. 26, 1909; m. Jan. 16, 1895, A. J. Tingley of Dimock, Pa., b. June 18, 1865. Children: i Bryant A., b. Nov. 5, 1895. ii. Freeman T., b. Oct. 29, 1898.

Nettie May Freeman, b. Oct. 29, 1876; resides near Halstead, Pa.; m. Jan. 16, 1894, Mark D. Reynolds of Lanesville, Pa., b. June 30, 1872. Children: i. Edna Ruth, b. Aug. 7, 1898. ii. Olive Jane, b. Jan. 2, 1906. iii. Bernice Irene, b. Oct. 16, 1911.

Arthur L. Freeman, b. Dec. 22, 1878; resides near Montrose, Pa.; m. Jan. 18, 1905, Coral Lillian Birtch of West Brooklyn, Pa., b. Mar. 2, 1889. Children: i. Edgar La Verne, b. Jan. 11, 1906. ii. Orrin Bennett, b. Apr. 21, 1908. iii. Agnes Philathea, b. Oct. 1, 1911.

Gordon W. Freeman, b. July 29, 1880; resides at Heart Lake, Pa. m. (1) Nov. 5, 1902, Fanny Pearl Darrow, b. July 8, 1883, d. May 12, 1907; m. (2) Sept., 1908, Mea Richardson. Children by second wife: i. Helene, b. Oct. 3, 1909. ii. Hazel Mae, b. Jan. 24, 1911. iii. Lillian Catherine, b. Nov. 2, 1912..

703 GORDON D.[9] WARNER, son of Ansel Lockman[8] and Mary Jane (Cook) Warner, born September 17, 1861; resides in Lancaster, Pa.

Married (1) January 25, 1886, ICIE BELL, born September 29, 1860; died May 18, 1895.

Married (2) June 1, 1897, ELLA GIFFORD of Clifford, Pa born December 18, 1870.

Children by first wife

Charles Warner, b. Apr. 4, 1888.
Blanche Warner, b. Jan. 21, 1890; d. July 15, 1899.
Paul Warner, b. Aug. 16, 1894.

Child by second wife

Ruth Warner, b. Sept. 21, 1901.

704 ADELBERT ANDREW⁹ WARNER, son of Andrew Sylvester⁸ and Mary Elizabeth (Greene) Warner, born July 8, 1846; resides in Rockport, Mo.; is a gardener. He was educated at Mexico, Belleville and Pulaski Academies, and was graduated from Eastman College in 1867. He accompanied his father to the War and was with him to care for him while sick at the White House in Washington. He then enlisted in Company E, 189th New York Volunteers, 5th Army Corps, 2d Brigade, 1st Division. He was in service nine months when the war closed. He was in the battles at Five Forks, Appomattox and others in which his regiment took part, was at the surrender of Lee, and in the Grand Review at the close of the war. Married in Belleville, Jefferson Co., N. Y., 1868, CATHARINE HENRIETTA BETTINGER, born in Richland, N. Y., daughter of Daniel and Ann (Kiblin) Bettinger.

Children

730 Mary Ann Warner, b. Dec. 30, 1868; m. Cyrus Grant McMillen.
731 Lillian B. Warner, b. July 8, 1871; m. Tracy Andrew Evans.

705 GERRIT SMITH⁹ WARNER, son of Andrew Sylvester⁸ and Mary Elizabeth (Greene) Warner, born at Sandy Creek, N. Y., October 4, 1855; died at Pulaski, N. Y., July 18, 1907. He was a traveling salesman.
Married at Sandy Creek, May 3, 1874, ANNA LLOYD, born in Pulaski, August 28, 1856, daughter of Robert and Anna (Burr) Lloyd.

Children

Andrew Robert Warner, b. in Pulaski, N. Y.; resides at Mentor; Ohio. He is a physician, superintendent of the Lakeside Hospital, Cleveland; A.M.; M.D. Married at St. Thomas, Ontario, Canada, Aug. 30, 1911, Athel Axford, b. at St. Thomas, Dec. 27, 1885, daughter of John H. and Ann (Hepburn) Axford. Children: i. Anne, b. Dec. 31, 1912, in Cleveland, Ohio. ii. Jane, b. Oct. 12, 1915, in Mentor, Ohio.
Arthur Lloyd Warner, b. Apr. 14, 1877; is a mail clerk; m. Jan. 15, 1907, Winnifred Bartlett Tapley, daughter of Frederick C. Tapley,

who was b. at Amesbury, Mass., Nov. 25, 1835, d. at Potsdam,
N. Y., Sept. 8, 1896, and was married at Clarkson, N. Y., Oct. 31,
1867, to Mary Gilbert Clark, b. Sept. 6, 1841, at Clarkson and d. there,
Apr. 18, 1880. Children: i. Beatrice Clark, b. Nov. 25, 1907, at
Clarkson. ii. Andrew Garrett, b. Oct. 6, 1909, at Clarkson. iii.
Arthur Lloyd, b. Nov. 19, 1916, at Cleveland.
Mary Elizabeth Warner, b. May 31, 1879, in Pulaski, N. Y., where she
now resides.
Jessie Anna Warner, b. Dec. 20, 1881, in Pulaski, N. Y.; resides in
Lacona, N. Y.; m. in Pulaski, July 29, 1908, Floyd Harlow Stevens,
b. in Lacona, Mar. 17, 1880, son of Henry and Caroline (Streeter)
Stevens. Children: Floyd Harlow, Jr., b. Nov. 14, 1911. ii. Henry
Warner, b. Feb. 23, 1913; d. Feb. 25, 1913. iii. Margaret Anna, b.
Nov. 18, 1916.
Edwin Ryan Warner, b. Aug. 20, 1884, in Pulaski, N. Y.; resides in
Syracuse, N. Y.; is engaged in commercial business; m. in Pulaski,
Dec. 20, 1911, Helen Jeannette Woods, b. in Pulaski, Feb. 26, 1887,
daughter of Charles Franklin and Helen (Ingersoll) Woods. Child:
Edwin Woods, b. Jan. 2, 1915.

706 **GEORGE PORTER**[9] **WARNER,** son of Sheldon E.[8]
and Sarah (Porter) Warner, born in the town of Barre, now
Albion, N. Y., May 3, 1856. He resides in Albion, N. Y., and is
a dealer in real estate.

Married in the town of Albion, March 8, 1882, **ELLEN POR-
TER CULVER,** born in the town of Barre, January 15, 1857,
daughter of Orange A. Culver who was born August 1, 1817,
and his wife, Sarah W. Stevens.

Children, born in Albion

Inez Emilie Warner, b. Dec. 20, 1886; was graduated from the Albion
High School, 1905; resides in Albion; not married.
Howard Sheldon Warner, b. Oct. 30, 1893; was graduated from the
Albion High School in 1912 and attended Cornell University two
and one-half years; has enlisted in the Engineering Corps (Avia-
tion Branch) of the Signal Corps; not married.
Lowell Culver Warner, b. May 7, 1896; d. in Albion, Feb. 15, 1897.

707 **ELECTA JANE**[9] **WARNER,** daughter of Sheldon E.[8]
and Sarah (Porter) Warner, born April 28, 1859, at Porters
Corners, in the town of Barre, now Albion, N. Y.; resides at
Hudson, Mich.

Married January 12, 1881, **EUGENE D. PEIRSON** of Hud
son, Mich., to which place they then removed. In May, 1898,
they removed to Albion, N. Y., and again in 1906, located at
Hudson, Mich. Mr. Peirson was a farmer, and is now deceased.

Children, born at Hudson, Mich.

Warner D. Peirson, b. Jan. 28, 1882; was graduated from the Hudson High School and d. there, Feb. 17, 1904, not married.
Harry Peirson, b. Apr. 4, 1886; d. Aug. 27, 1886.
Robert Peirson, b. Oct. 2, 1887; was graduated from the Hudson High School, 1908; is now a member of the National Army, Corporal, Statistical Department; not married.
Sheldon E. Peirson, b. Apr. 2, 1894; was graduated from the Hudson High School, 1912; resides there; not married.

708 HENRY EUGENE[9] WARNER, son of Sheldon E.[8] and Sarah Jane (Porter) Warner, born in the town of Barre, now Albion, N. Y., May 20, 1864; is a lawyer; resided in New Rochelle, N. Y.; removed to Elizabethtown, N. Y., in the fall of 1918. Mr. Warner was graduated from the Albion High School, 1882; Albany Law School, 1885; was located at Holley for six months, in Albion two years, in North Tonawanda after 1888. In the latter place he was village attorney, 1892-6; Member of Assembly, 1896-7. In 1908 he removed to New York City and in 1910 to New Rochelle; was Court and Trust Fund Examiner, 1900-1912. Since 1915 he has been Title Examiner, Attorney General's Office of New York State. Mr. Warner has published several legal works. He has made extensive collections of genealogical data regarding the Warner family and has investigated the records at many of the original homes of the family in Massachusetts. These records he has very generously placed at the disposal of the present editors and they have been freely used in compiling this Genealogy, adding greatly to the accuracy and completeness of many parts of it.

Henry E. Warner married in the town of Barre, N. Y., June 29, 1886, CATHERINE ELIZABETH MC CARTHY, born in the town of Barre, January 31, 1864, daughter of Michael and Margaret (McCarthy) McCarthy.

Children, born at North Tonawanda, N. Y.

Paul Charles Warner, b. Mar. 30, 1890; removed with his father to New York City in 1908 and to New Rochelle in 1910. He was graduated from the North Tonawanda High School in 1908 and from the Massachusetts Institute of Technology in 1913. He immediately entered upon the practice of his profession as an architect in New York City, and was lecturer at Cooper Union. Since war has been declared he has entered the service and holds the commission of Ensign in the Naval Flying Corps. He is not married.
Margaret Ellen Warner, b. June 11, 1891; removed to New York City in 1909 and to New Rochelle in 1910. She was graduated from the North Tonawanda High School in 1909 and from New Rochelle College in 1914; not married.

Mary Eugenie Warner, b. Jan. 10, 1896; removed to New York City in 1908 and to New Rochelle in 1910; was graduated from the New Rochelle High School in 1914, and is now attending New Rochelle College.

Constance Elizabeth Warner, b. May 10, 1905; removed to New York City in 1908, and to New Rochelle in 1910.

709 **WILLIAM AUSTIN**[9] **WARNER,** son of Charles Adams[8] and Catherine (Knight) Warner, born in South Hadley, Mass., December 12, 1853. He resides in Northampton and New York City, where he is Sales Manager and Director of the American Lithographic Company. He removed with his parents to Minnesota in 1857, where he remained until after the death of his father; served as Page in the Minnesota State Senate in 1862; returned to Massachusetts in 1868 and attended Williston Seminary the following year; was graduated from Highland Military Academy, Worcester, Mass., in 1872. Mr. Warner is a member of Jerusalem Lodge, F. and A. M. of Northampton, also the Commandery and Chapter of Northampton, and of Aleppo Temple, Mystic Shrine. He is a member of the Salmagundi Club of New York City, Country clubs of Englewood, N. J., and Northampton, Mass., and of the Boston City Club.

Married in South Hadley, December 16, 1874, **JULIA ANNA BURNETTE,** born in South Hadley, December 10, 1853, daughter of Nelson Warner and Ruth Cordelia (Kellogg) Burnette and granddaughter of Stoughton W. and Flora (Dennison) Burnette, and John and Laura (Chapin) Kellogg.

Children, born in South Hadley

Charles Nelson Warner, b. Apr. 30, 1876; resides in Toms River, N. J.; m. in Chicago, Ill., Jan. 2, 1905, Maud Estell Staring, b. Feb. 16, 1879, daughter of Peter and Elizabeth Irene (Garlock) Staring of Ludington, Mich. Child: William Austin, 2d, b. Aug. 7, 1913, in Toms River.

Alice Ethelberta Warner, b. Apr. 22, 1879; resides in Northampton, Mass.; m. there, May 6, 1903, Philip Witherell, b. Nov. 20, 1877, in Northampton, son of Alphonse and Esther (Hoxie) Witherell. He is general manager for the Williams Manufacturing Company. Children: i. Catherine Knight, b. Oct. 1, 1904. ii. Julia Esther, b. Apr. 16, 1907. iii. Warner, b. Feb. 18, 1909. iv. Margery Edwards, b. Dec. 19, 1910.

710 **LILY MARIA**[9] **WARNER,** daughter of Lucien[8] and Adelia F. (Silvey) Warner, born in Granby, Mass., June 21, 1860; resides in St. Paul, Minn.

Married in St. Paul, September 1, 1881, **FRANK W. NOYES**, son of James Amos Carver Noyes, who was born in Albion, Maine, December 25, 1823, died in St. Paul, July 12, 1859, and his wife, Eliza A. Jeans, who was born in Kentucky, March 25, 1826, and died in St. Paul, June 20, 1884. The Noyes family comes from Nicholas Noyes who arrived in Newburyport, Mass., in 1634, the son of Rev. William Noyes of Chalderton, County Wilts, England.

Children, born in St. Paul

Albert Lucien Noyes, b. July 9, 1882; is a clerk for the Northern Express Company in St. Paul; m. there, Mar. 16, 1905, Sarah Frances Hess, b. in St. Paul, Aug. 29, 1881, daughter of Samuel L. and Sarah (Boxell) Hess. Children, b. in St. Paul: i. Holly Frances, b. Nov. 7, 1907. ii. Gordon Carver and Howard Lucien (twins), b. Feb. 16, 1912.
Arthur Vincent Noyes, b. July 8, 1888; is a letter carrier in St. Paul; m. there, Oct. 28, 1909, Lillian Averil Williams, b. in St. Paul, daughter of James and Mary Ann (Job) Williams. Children, b. in St. Paul: i. Lucia Mae, b. Sept. 10, 1910. ii. Grace Wright, b. Aug. 13, 1912. iii. James Roswell, b. July 27, 1915.
Clarence Silvey Noyes, b. Nov. 9, 1890; m. at Henning, Minn., Nov. 26, 1912, Blanche Mathew. Child: Russell Mathew, b. Oct. 7, 1913.

711 **ARTHUR CHURCHILL[9] WARNER**, son of Lucien[8] and Adelia F. (Silvey) Warner, born October 31, 1864, in Granby, Mass.; resides in St. Paul, Minn.
Married in Seattle, Wash., April 22, 1890, **EDITH RANDOLPH**, daughter of Captain Simon Peter Randolph, who was born January 10, 1835, in Lincoln, Ill., died in Seattle, January 15, 1909, and his wife, Catherine Breckenridge, who was born in Springfield, Ill., June 19, 1838; resides in Seattle.

Children

Adelia Randolph Warner, b. Mar. 12, 1891, in Seattle; d. Mar. 13, 1891.
Ralph Randolph Warner, b. Mar. 30, 1892, in St. Paul; d. Apr. 5, 1892.
Arthur Lucien Warner, b. Jan. 12, 1895, in Minneapolis; d. July 8, 1895.
Alice Warner, b. Dec. 26, 1896, in Minneapolis.
Ruth Warner, b. Sept. 20, 1898, in Seattle.
William Randolph Warner, b. June 23, 1904, in Seattle.

712 **PERSIS ANN[9] WARNER**, daughter of Morgan[8] and Sarah (Briner) Warner, born January 20, 1862, in Fort Wayne, Ind.; resides in Frank, Pa., postoffice, Scott Haven.

43

Married at Bunker Hill, Kans., June 2, 1881, PHILIP
HOWELL, who died in Frank, Pa., March 18, 1915. He was
the son of John and Susannah (Swanger) Howell, and was by
trade a carpenter.

Children

Bertha Mabel Howell, b. Mar. 14, 1882; m. Apr. 18, 1901, Albert Cecil
Rodibanger.
Susan Alma Howell, b. Dec. 19, 1883; m. Feb. 20, 1906, Thomas
Mains of Boston, Pa.
Lillie Mae Howell, b. May 13, 1886; d. June 14, 1886.
Sarah Ellen Howell, b. Dec. 1, 1887; became a missionary, Oct. 14,
1908.
Frank Lloyd Howell, b. July 20, 1890.
Victor Warner Howell, b. Nov. 15, 1892; d. July 26, 1905.
Crete Marie Howell, b. July 22, 1895; became a missionary, Mar. 5,
1912.
Mary Esther Howell, b. Aug. 20, 1898.
Philip Earl Howell, b. Aug. 5, 1901.

713 HARVEY AMANDER[9] WÁRNER, son of Joshua[8]
and Rebecca Jane (Baker) Warner, born near Jefferson, Wayne
Co., Ohio, November 9, 1849; died June 9, 1911, in Kansas
City, Mo. His boyhood was spent on his father's farm and
attending school in the neighboring village. With the idea of
teaching he took a course at the Normal School in Smithville,
Ohio, then decided to take up the study of medicine. He was
graduated from the Medical Department of the University of
Wooster at Cleveland, Ohio, and in 1873 commenced practice in
Wooster. In September, 1878, he removed to Kansas and established himself in the town of Meriden, Jefferson County, where
he followed his profession for ten years, building up a large
practice and making a high reputation among the physicians
of the state. In 1888 he removed to Topeka, Kans., and soon
became interested in the subject of fraternal insurance. To this
topic he gave his best thought and attention. He was the founder
of the "Knights and Ladies of Security" in 1892; the lodge
was organized in the Warner home on Klein Street and its
first meeting was held in the room where the doctor had written out the fundamental working plan of the organization. He
was the originator of the reserve fund idea. under which the
society began its work and under which it continues. He had
the plan copyrighted and through his generosity and interest
in the order, all benefits that accrued from the copyright were
given to the Knights and Ladies of Security Lodge. Dr.
Warner was the medical director of the lodge for over eighteen

years; was chairman of the medical section of the National
Fraternal Congress for many years; was elected vice-president
of the Congress in Boston; president of the same in Detroit;
was founder of Home Mutual Life Insurance Company in
Topeka in 1909 and secretary of the company. He was a natural leader among men, a splendid and magnetic public speaker
and of generous and kindly disposition. He was a 32d degree
Mason.

Dr. Harvey A. Warner married February 8, 1872, **ELIZA-
BETH ADELAIDE MACKEY,** born in Wayne County, Ohio,
daughter of David Mackey, who was born in Ireland in 1796,
and Margaret McKee, who was born in Mifflin, Pa. Mrs.
Warner resides in Topeka, Kans.

Children

Harvey Scott Warner, b. in Wooster, Ohio, May 13, 1874; was edu-
cated in the public schools of Meriden and Topeka and in Strickler's
Business College in Topeka; was employed in the offices of the
Knights and Ladies of Security from 1896 to 1907; is a printer in
the State Printing Plant at Topeka; m. June 28, 1898, Janeta
Dudding of Warrensburg, Mo.

Frederick Warner, b. Mar. 3, 1878, at Lattisburg, Ohio; d. in Meriden,
Kans., 1880.

Maud Mackey Warner, b. Apr. 6, 1880, in Meriden, Kans.; d. 1880.

714 **WILBER ORVILLE**[9] **WARNER,** son of Joshua[8] and
Rebecca Jane (Baker) Warner, born near Jefferson, Wayne
Co., Ohio, August 27, 1851; resides in Meriden, Kans. He
received a common school education and has been a farmer, railroad man, and stationary engineer.

Married (1) in Wayne County, Ohio, January, 1870, **ELMA
BRUBAKER,** born in Congress, Ohio, January, 1852, died in
Jefferson, Ohio, May 26, 1874, daughter of Ephraham Brubaker,
who was born in France.

Married (2) September, 1876, **ANNIE YOUNG,** who died at
Marceline, Mo., July, 1889.

Married (3) at Cumberland Gap, Va., June, 1890, **JENNIE
CRIGGER,** who died at Meriden, Kans., January 24, 1908.

*Children of Wilber O. and Elma (Brubaker) Warner, born in
Jefferson, Ohio*

Effie May Warner, b. Nov., 1870; m. (1) in Lecompton, Kans., 1885,
Abner Todd, who died in Colorado about 1890; m. (2) in Topeka,
Kans., June, 1892, Lawrence Johnson, and resides in Los Angeles,
Cal. Child by first husband: Leona Elma, b. in Lecompton, Sept.,

1886; m. and resides near Grand Junction, Colo. Children by second husband: i. Daisy, b. in Topeka, May, 1893. ii. (Son), b. in Corona, Cal., in 1904 or 1905.

Martha Elma Warner, b. May 13, 1874; m. (1) at Mulhall, Okla., 1889, Theodore Bishop; m. (2) —— Lane, and resides in Long Beach, Cal. Children by first husband: i. Effie, m. Louis Leaderly of Los Angeles, Cal. ii. Vernon. iii. Jesse, now in A. E. F. in France, June, 1918.

Children of Wilber O. and Annie (Young) Warner

Jennie Warner, b. Sept., 1877, at Jefferson, Ohio; d. June, 1881, at Kilmer, Kans.

Marybe Beatrice Warner, b. in Meriden, Kans., 1880; d. there, Aug., 1898.

Wilber Coates Warner, b. at Lecompton, Kans., June, 1883; d. at Meriden, Kans., Apr., 1914, not married.

Olin Warner, b. 1885, at Marceline, Mo.; d. there, Apr., 1889.

Children of Wilber O. and Jennie (Crigger) Warner

Alva Warner, b. 1893, in Marceline, Mo.; resides in Topeka, Kans.; married.

Lorin D. Warner, b. 1896, in Marceline; is Corporal in Battery A, 130th Field Artillery, 35th Division, A. E. F., June, 1918.

Ernest Warner, b. 1906; resides in Meriden, Kans.

715 LORIN SELVEY⁹ WARNER, son of Joshua⁸ and Rebecca Jane (Baker) Warner, born October 23, 1853, in Jefferson, Wayne Co., Ohio. He received his education in Wayne County and removed to Meriden, Kans., in the spring of 1879. He has been a farmer all his life. In March, 1897, he removed to Valle Vista, near Hemet, Cal., and is still residing there.

Married in Jefferson, Ohio, September 12, 1876, **SARAH SHUTT,** daughter of Rev. George and Sarah (Martin) Shutt.

Children

George Elvin Warner, b. in Jefferson, Ohio, Sept. 13, 1877; died at Valle Vista, Cal., Dec. 10, 1899.

Lorin Le Roy Warner, b. at Meriden, Kans., May 23, 1879; resides in Los Angeles, Cal.; m. there, July 28, 1903, Jessie Rutledge. Children: i. Robert, b. 1904. ii. Katherine. iii. Frances.

Ossian Roscoe Warner, b. at Meriden, Kans., Sept. 17, 1880; is a farmer and teamster; m. at Valle Vista, Cal., Apr. 14, 1904, Callie Copley. Child: Ossian Scott, b. in Los Angeles, 1906.

716 ORPHA MERALDA⁹ WARNER, daughter of Joshua⁸ and Rebecca Jane (Baker) Warner, born December 5, 1855, in Jefferson, Wayne Co., Ohio; died at Meriden, Kans., September 29, 1888. She was educated in the public schools and Wooster

University, and removed to Meriden, Kans., immediately after her marriage, in September, 1878.

Married August 29, 1878, **ARCHIE MC DANEL** of Ashland, Ohio, born in New Brighton, Pa., September 2, 1851, son of Uriah McDanel, who was born at New Brighton, August 5, 1822, died at Ashland, Ohio, May 12, 1912, married June 5, 1845, his cousin, Sarah Ann McDanel, born in New Brighton, August 12, 1825, died in Ashland, April 5, 1877. Archie McDanel was a farmer, carpenter and civil engineer.

Children

Orlin Elvero McDanel, b. Dec. 29, 1879, in Meriden, Kans.; is an electrical engineer at Pleasant Hill, Mo.; removed to Ashland, Ohio, in 1889; m. (1) at Mansfield, Ohio, Feb. 20, 1902, Sylvia M. Gipe, b. near Oliverburgh, Ohio, Nov. 10, 1881, d. at Ashland, Ohio, Mar. 28, 1907, leaving two children, Alfred Edward, b. at Ashland, Jan. 20, 1903, and Frances, b. at Ashland, Apr. 29, 1905. Orlin E. McDanel m. (2) at Harrisonville, Mo., Mar. 28, 1911, Mrs. Roxie Lee (Jones) Richardson, b. at Harrisonville, July 12, 1888. Child: Orlin Edgar, b. at Marion, Ohio, Aug. 20, 1912.

Abbie S. McDanel, b. and d. Aug. 26, 1881, at Meriden, Kans.

Zilla Mabel McDanel, b. at Meriden, Kans., Dec. 24, 1887; removed to Ashland, Ohio, in 1889; married and now resides, a widow with two children, with her father in Ashland.

717 **LOIS REALURA**[9] **WARNER**, daughter of Joshua[8] and Rebecca Jane (Baker) Warner, born December 25, 1862, in Jefferson, Wayne Co., Ohio; was educated at the school in Jefferson and at Ashland High School; removed with her parents to Meriden, Kans., in September, 1878, and entered Baker University at Baldwin, Kans., in the autumn of 1881. She was prominent in literary circles, was a brilliant student and represented her society in an oratorical contest against a men's society which was represented by W. A. (now Bishop) Quayle. In September, 1888, she removed to Lincoln, Neb.; to Colorado in June, 1892; to Hemet, Cal., March, 1896; to San Diego, Cal., in 1897, and is now residing there.

Married December 28, 1885, **JOHN NORMAN GLENN**, born in Jeromeville, Ashland Co., Ohio, September 29, 1857, son of Nathan and Lucretia (Ebbert) Glenn, both of whom died in Meriden, Kans. John Norman Glenn was a railroad clerk to 1902; assayer to 1904; is now landscape gardener at San Diego Public Park.

Children

John Paul Glenn, b. at Plattsmouth, Neb., Dec. 30, 1886.

Helen Glenn, b. at Lincoln, Neb., Nov. 28, 1888; m. at San Diego, Cal., Mar. 14, 1912, Frank Green, b. in St. Louis, Mo., Nov. 27, 1882. Children: i. Helen Lois, b. Feb. 18, 1913, at San Diego. ii. Franklin Thomas, b. Apr. 20, 1915, at Los Angeles, Cal.
Frances Glenn, b. at Fulford, Eagle County, Colo., Aug. 1, 1892; m. in Los Angeles, Dec. 14, 1911, James Preston Cutler, b. in McPherson, Kans., July 9, 1885. Children: i. Robert Glenn, b. Aug. 19, 1913, in San Diego. ii. Josephine, b. May 1, 1915, in Los Angeles.
Warner Scott Glenn, b. in San Diego, Cal., June 23, 1905; d. there, Mar. 12, 1908.

718   GUY LEON[9] WARNER, son of Joshua[8] and Rebecca Jane (Baker) Warner, born in Jefferson, Wayne Co., Ohio, June 18, 1865. He was educated in the schools of Jefferson, Ashland High School and spent three years in Baker University at Baldwin, Kans. He is a farmer, carpenter and butcher. The family are all members of the Methodist Episcopal Church. Mr. Warner is active in church work and community betterment.

Married in Meriden, Kans., September 5, 1888, LYDIA ELIZABETH SHUTT, daughter of Rev. George Shutt, born October 5, 1818, died October 25, 1897, married May 3, 1849, Sarah Martin, born February 8, 1830, died February, 1864.

Children, first four born in Meriden, Kans.

Edna Parilla Warner, b. Dec. 16, 1890; m. in Topeka, Kans., Dec. 27, 1911, Ernest Amon Janeway, son of Enoch and Ruth (Heston) Janeway.
Maurice Silvester Warner, b. Aug. 30, 1893; is at Camp Doniphan, a member of Company B, 110th Field Signal Battalion, N. G., U. S. A., June, 1918.
Martin Baker Warner, b. Mar. 2, 1896; is at Camp Kearney, Headquarters Company, 160th Infantry, N. G., U. S. A., June, 1918.
Edith Marilla Warner, b. Aug. 3, 1898.
Erminna Elma Warner, b. Oct. 12, 1900, in Kilmer, Kans.

719   ELIZABETH LUCINDA[9] (or BETH) WARNER, daughter of Joshua[8] and Rebecca Jane (Baker) Warner, born November 17, 1875, near Jefferson, Wayne Co., Ohio; resides in Cimarron, Kans. She removed with her parents to Ashland, Ohio, in 1876, and in September, 1878, to Meriden, Kans. In June, 1886, she went with her married sister Lois to Plattsmouth, Neb., and attended school there in the winter of 1886-7. From 1888 to 1891 she resided with her sister in Lincoln, Neb., and attended school; was at the Topeka High School in 1891. In the spring of 1892 she removed with her sister's family to Colorado and taught in Eagle County, 1892-3. In 1893-4 she entered Colorado State Normal at Greeley; taught summer

school in Eagle County, 1894; entered Kansas State Normal at
Emporia, 1894, and was graduated from the academic course in
1897, having represented her society in both oratory and dra-
matic art; taught in the primary department of Meriden (Kans.)
schools, 1897-8; in Topeka, 1898-1902; was graduated from the
Life Diploma course, Kansas State Normal, June, 1903, having
done work in summer schools; taught in San Diego, 1902-4, and
was married there, July 12, 1904, to Charles H. Mull of Wakeeney,
Kans. She was widowed in March, 1906. She began teaching
in the Kansas State Normal College, taking courses in summer
in the Universities of Illinois and Chicago, and a one year's
residence at the University of Illinois, receiving the degree of
A.B. in Education, June, 1912. She established the Department
of Home Economics at Kansas State Normal College in 1911,
and was Professor of Home Economics there, 1911-1914; held
the same position in Extension Division, Oklahoma A. and M.
College, January to August, 1914; was elected to position at
Kansas State Agricultural College in the spring of 1914. The
first edition of her "Laboratory Guide and Note-book in Food
Preparation," published in September, 1914, has been extensively used by classes in home economics in many schools all
over the United States. She represented the Government and
State Agricultural College in the Food Drive and Home Economics Lectures in the summer of 1917

Married (2) August 15, 1914, **BRUCE JOSSERAND**, superintendent of schools at Cimarron, Kans., born in Gray County,
Kans., Oct. 23, 1888, son of John Franklin Josserand, a farmer,
who was born in Newman, Ill., December 31, 1857, removed to
Gray County in 1884, married at Garden City, Kans., March
9, 1887, Anna Dulin, born at Paris, Ill., July 28, 1865. Bruce
Josserand was educated in the public schools of Gray County,
at Baker University and Kansas State Normal College. He
is at present a tractor farmer and wheat grower.

Children of Bruce and Elizabeth L. (Warner) Josserand

Jean Warner Josserand, b. and d. Sept. 1, 1915.
Jane Josserand, b. Aug. 17, 1918.

720 **ALICE A.**[9] **WARNER**, daughter of Gideon[8] and Matilda
(Brubaker) Warner, born in Richland, Keokuk Co., Iowa,
November 13, 1854; resides in Beatrice, Neb.

Married at Dakota City, Neb., August 30, 1876, **ANDREW
RUSSELL BEVINS**, born in Potsdam, St. Lawrence Co.,
N. Y., son of Ira and Mary (Russell) Bevins.

Children, born at Omaha, Neb.

Ira Jesse Bevins, b. Jan. 18, 1879; m. at Hastings, Neb., Jan. 16, 1901, Corinne Althen. Children: i. Althen, b. about 1902. ii. Arline, b. about 1904. iii. Marjorie, b. about 1906.

Elmer Russell Bevins, b. Aug. 4, 1881; m. at Hamakapoko, Maui, Hawaii, Apr. 2, 1910, Ethel Taylor. Children: i. Alice Emily, b. about 1911. ii. Mildred, b. about 1913. iii. Barbara, b. 1916.

Warner Earle Bevins, b. Sept. 14, 1883; m. at Minneapolis, Minn., July 22, 1907, Maude ———. Child: Billy Earle, b. 1916.

Mildred Lauretta Bevins, b. May 22, 1890; m. in Chicago, Ill., June 24, 1916, John Charles Haley of Beatrice, Neb. They reside in Beatrice.

721 **DANIEL WEBSTER**[9] **WARNER,** son of Gideon[8] and Matilda (Brubaker) Warner, born in Richland, Keokuk Co., Iowa, October 1, 1857; resides in Edmonton, Alberta, Canada, where he is a farmer and breeder, making a specialty of Shorthorn cattle and Berkshire swine. In May, 1882, he removed from his old home in Dakota County, Neb., to Wakefield, Dixon Co., Neb., living there until March 2, 1899, when he removed to his present home in Canada. He has always preferred and lived in a new country, has taken an interest in its improvement and directed his energies towards building up any locality in which he has lived. He is a lover of hunting and a good marksman with both shotgun and rifle. He was nominated on the Liberal ticket, February 18, 1914, for the Federal Parliament of Canada, to represent the local constituency of Battle River in Alberta, but was defeated although he ran far ahead of his ticket. He is general manager of the Gold Bar Stock Farm, of which his son Huron D. Warner is manager; of the Beaver Meadows Stock Farm, of which his son-in-law, Agnew Compton Dodds, is manager; and of the Sunnyside Stock Farm in Tofield, of which his son John B. Warner is manager.

Married in Wakefield, Neb., December 31, 1885, **MARY JANE BRUBAKER,** born in Cedar, Mahaska Co., Iowa, November 26, 1868, daughter of John and Adeline (Dunlap) Brubaker.

Children, all but last born in Wakefield, Neb.

Gideon Warner, b. Apr. 3, 1887; d. Apr. 21, 1892.

John B. Warner, b. Jan. 17, 1889; had college business training; resides in Tofield, Alberta, Canada; manager of Sunnyside Stock Farm, a five hundred acre farm well stocked with pure bred Shorthorns and Berkshire hogs; m. Oct. 19, 1915, Pearl A. Richardson, who d. July 23, 1917.

Rosella May Warner, b. June 14, 1892; had training in college in music and painting; m. Dec. 9, 1914, Agnew Compton Dodds, of Scotch descent, b. in U. S. A. He is manager of the Beaver Meadows Stock Farm.
Huron Donnelly Warner, b. Sept. 27, 1895; had college business training and is manager of the Gold Bar Stock Farm in Edmonton.
Duane Webster Warner, b. June 24, 1902; d. Nov. 2, 1908.

DANIEL W. AND WILLIAM P. WARNER

722 **WILLIAM P.⁹ WARNER**, son of Gideon⁸ and Matilda (Brubaker) Warner, born in Keokuk, Iowa, April 28, 1866; is a lawyer and farmer residing in Dakota City, Neb. He was elected County Judge in 1889; has been State Senator; was U. S. Marshal for the district of Nebraska for ten years, from 1905 to 1915. At the last election he was designated as the Republican candidate for Congress from his district. At the same time his brother, Daniel W. Warner, was the candidate for his national Parliament in Canada. Both the brothers were popular candidates personally and ran ahead of their respective tickets, but the cause of defeat was the same in both cases, the determination of the people to sustain their respective governments by re-electing the party in power and take no chances. Under war conditions the party odds were too strong to overcome by popular personality of the candidates.

Married in Sioux City, Iowa, **ALICE M. GRAHAM,** born in Faribault, Minn., April 5, 1869, daughter of Robert Graham.

Children, first four born in Dakota City, Neb.

Margaret Warner, b. June 30, 1895.
Graham Warner, b. Apr. 7, 1899; is now serving in the U. S. Navy.
Herbert Warner, b. June 30, 1901.
Kathryn Warner, b. July 6, 1903.
W. Philip Warner, b. in Omaha, Neb., Sept. 9, 1910.
David R. Warner, b. in McGregor, Minn., Aug. 19, 1912.

723 ANNIE LUCETTA[10] WARNER, daughter of Ira
DeVer[9] and Lucetta (Greenman) Warner, born at McGrawville,
N. Y., January 11, 1867. At the age of nine, she removed with

MRS. ANNIE WARNER BISHOP AND FAMILY

her parents to Bridgeport, Conn., and has since resided there.
She was educated at private schools in Bridgeport and at Miss
Brown's School in New York City. Mrs. Bishop has for many
years been active in the church and philanthropic work in
Bridgeport. She has been president of the Thursday Reading
Club since its organization 25 years ago. She is also a mem-

ber of the Cosmopolitan Club, the War Work Council of the Y. W. C. A. and the Bridgeport chapter of the Red Cross.

Married October 31, 1889, NATHANIEL WHEELER BISHOP, son of William D. and Julia Tomlinson Bishop. Mr. W. D. Bishop was prominent as a lawyer and business man

LIEUT. NATHANIEL W. BISHOP

in Bridgeport and throughout the state. He was a director of the New York, New Haven and Hartford Railroad and for several years he was its President.

Nathaniel Wheeler Bishop received his early education in Bridgeport, and studied at Yale for about two years. After leaving college, he entered the law department of Yale, from which he was graduated in 1889. Since then he has been engaged in the general contracting business in Bridgeport and vicinity. During the Spanish-American war, he served as Lieutenant of the Naval Reserve. At the outbreak of the war with Germany, he again offered his services to the Government and was assigned to duty first at Black Rock, Conn., and later as liaison officer in New York Harbor, in charge of the embarkation of troops.

Children

Warner Bishop, b. at Bridgeport, Conn., Dec. 16, 1892; educated at private schools in Bridgeport; prepared for college at Taft School, Watertown, and spent three years at Yale. In 1917, he volunteered in the United States Navy and is serving as a Yeoman at Headquarters of the 3d Naval District, New York.

Alfred Bishop, b. Apr. 8, 1897; educated in private schools of Bridgeport and at Choate School at Wallingford, Conn; entered Yale in 1916; enlisted in the Naval Reserve in Apr., 1918.

Nathaniel Bishop, b. November 26, 1903; now studying at Choate School, Wallingford, Conn.

724 DE VER HOWARD[10] WARNER, son of Ira DeVer[9] and Lucetta (Greenman) Warner; born at McGrawville, N. Y., November 20, 1868. At the age of eight he removed with his parents to Bridgeport, Conn., where he has since resided. He was educated in the private schools of Bridgeport, and later studied with a tutor. At the age of nineteen, he entered the corset business conducted by his father and uncle and spent several years in close application to the details until he had thoroughly mastered every department. After a few years, he was made superintendent of the factory and, later, manager of the business. Under his able management, the business has steadily increased until it is now the largest of its kind in the world with sales of over $7,000,000.00 annually. The business extends to all parts of America and to nearly every foreign country.

In addition to managing the large interests of the Warner Bros. Company, he is the president of the Bridgeport Hydraulic Co., the Bridgeport Gas Light Company and the mercantile business of the D. M. Read Company. He is also a director of the Bridgeport National Bank, president of the Mountain Grove Cemetery Association and vice-president of the Bridgeport Hospital. He has taken a great interest in the hospital, and has contributed to it largely both in services and in money. He has also been very active in promoting a "housing company" to provide for the 50,000 extra population suddenly brought to Bridgeport by the great munitions plants of that city.

DeVer Howard Warner

He is a member of the Brooklawn Country Club, the Algonquin Club and the Seaside Club of Bridgeport and of the Union League Club of New York City. He resides in Fairfield, Conn., in the beautiful old home once the residence of Aaron Burr. He also has a large summer home on Greenfield Hill about four miles back from Fairfield, Conn.

Married May 13, 1888, ISABELLA MAUDE WINTON CADY, born July 15, 1867, daughter of Robert and Frances Augusta (Cady) Winton, and adopted by her mother's brother, Hon. Hiram Torrey Cady, and his wife, Harriet Elizabeth Cook. Mrs. Warner is descended through her mother from six of the original Mayflower settlers, as follows:

Gov. Wm. Bradford[1], Wm. Bradford[2], Israel Bradford[3], Abner Bradford[4], Elisha Bradford[5], Jane Bradford[6] (married Elansan Cady), Frances Augusta Cady[7], Isabella Maude Cady[8].

Richard Warren[1], Mary Warren[2] (m. Robert Bartlett), Benjamin Bartlett[3], Benjamin Bartlett, Jr.[4], Sarah Bartlett[5] (m. Israel Bradford[3]).

Elder William Brewster[1], Love Brewster[2], Sarah Brewster[3] (m. Benjamin Bartlett[3]).

William Mullins[1], Priscilla Mullins[2], who married John Alden, a fellow passenger on the Mayflower, Elizabeth Alden[3] (m. William Paybodie), Ruth Paybodie[4] (m. Benjamin Bartlett, Jr.[4]).

Francis Cooke[1], Mary Cooke[2] (m. John Thompson), Esther Thompson[3] (m. Wm. Reed), Bathesda Reed[4] (m. Nicholas Porter), Suzannah Porter[5] (m. Abner Bradford[4]).

Mrs. Warner is also descended in the fifth generation through her father, Robert Winton, from George Seton, the 5th Earl of Winton.

Mrs. Warner is interested in the philanthropic and social activities of Bridgeport and vicinity. She is President of the Wednesday Afternoon Musical Club, Vice-President of the Associated Charities, Director of the Bridgeport Hospital, of the Bridgeport Orphan Asylum and of the Connecticut George Jr. Republic, a Trustee of Y. W. C. A., member of the Finance Committee of Fairfield War Bureau, of the Executive Committee of Fairfield Red Cross and a member of Farmington Club.

Children

DeVer Cady Warner, b. in Bridgeport, Conn., Mar. 14, 1889. His early education was in private schools in Bridgeport. He prepared for college at the Taft School at Watertown, Conn., and was graduated from Yale in 1912. After graduation he entered the factory of the

COM. SEABURY CONE MASTICK AND MRS. AGNES WARNER MASTICK

Warner Brothers Company of Bridgeport, working in several different departments. In July, 1917, he entered the government service and on December 18, 1917, he received a commission as Second Lieutenant. He served first in the Ordnance Department in charge of the inspection of materials made for the Army. Later he was transferred to the Quartermaster's Department and in October, 1918, he was sent to France. Mr. Warner married at Bridgeport, June 26, 1912, Julia Wilcox Smith, b. Dec. 19, 1888, daughter of Friend William and Harriet Merritt (Knowlton) Smith. Children: i. DeVer Knowlton, b. at Bridgeport, Mar. 11, 1913. ii. Stuart Todd, b. Oct. 5, 1915. DeVer Knowlton Warner was "class boy" in his father's class at Yale. As such he appeared at the first triennial reunion in June, 1915, dressed in costume like the rest of the class, and started the baseball game by throwing the first ball.

Margaret Lucetta Warner, b. at Bridgeport, Oct. 15, 1891. She received her early education in private schools in Bridgeport and later studied for two years at the Misses Master's School at Dobbs Ferry, N. Y. Married at Greenfield Hill, Conn., Sept. 23, 1913, John Field, b. at Niagara, Wis., Sept. 26, 1886, son of Walter and Emma (Tourget) Field. Mr. Field prepared for college in the public schools of Washington, D. C., and was graduated from Yale College with the degree of A.M. in 1910. After graduation he entered the business of the Warner Brothers Company at Bridgeport, and, after a few months' experience, was made superintendent of the corset department. At the outbreak of the war with Germany, he entered the government service, receiving a commission as First Lieutenant in the Ordnance Reserve Corps, Gun Division. Children: i. John Warner, b. Sept. 15, 1914. ii. William Warner, b. July 1, 1917.

Bradford Greenman Warner, b. Jan. 12, 1901. Educated in private schools of Bridgeport. In the fall of 1918, he entered the New York office of the Warner Brothers Company.

725 AGNES ELIZA[10] WARNER, daughter of Lucien Calvin[9] and Keren (Osborne) Warner, born February 22, 1872, at McGrawville, N. Y. Mrs. Mastick prepared for college at the Classical School for Girls in New York, and was graduated from Oberlin College in 1892. She has been active in Christian and philanthropic work ever since her graduation. She was president of the Harlem Young Women's Christian Association from 1903-1905 and again from 1909-1916, and a director of the New York City Association from 1911 to 1916. In 1909 she was elected a member of the National Board of the Young Women's Christian Association and is chairman of its Office Department.

She is a member of Sorosis, The Women's University Club, the Association of Collegiate Alumnæ, The Congregational Club of New York and Vicinity, the Society of Mayflower

44

Descendants, and the Fortnightly Club of Pleasantville, N. Y. The line of Mayflower descent is from Francis Cook (or Cooke) and Stephen Hopkins as follows: Francis[1] Cook; Isaac[2] Cook, m. Damaris Hopkins, daughter of Stephen Hopkins; Isaac[3]; John[4]; Sylvanus[5]; Sarah[6], m. Abel[6] Warner.

Married at Irvington-on-Hudson, N. Y., October 1, 1896, SEABURY CONE MASTICK, born July 19, 1871, at San Francisco, Cal., son of William Henry and Laura Jeannette (Mastick) Cone. On the death of his mother in 1873, he was. legally adopted by his mother's brother, Seabury L. Mastick, and took his mother's maiden name. Mr. Mastick was graduated from Oberlin College in 1891 and from the Hastings College of Law, University of California, in 1894. After practising a short time in San Francisco, he removed to New York in 1896 and took up the practice of patent law. In 1916 he was given the honorary degree of Master of Arts from Oberlin College. He has been a member of the Faculty of the Department of Chemical Engineering in Columbia University since 1914.

In July, 1904, Mr. and Mrs. Mastick bought an abandoned farm in Westchester County near Pleasantville, N. Y., which they named "Bear Ridge Farm" and where they have since made their home. Both Mr. and Mrs. Mastick have taken an active interest in the community life. They have no children.

Mr. Mastick is senior warden of the local Protestant Episcopal Church and has been Republican leader of the town of Mt. Pleasant since 1913. At the break of diplomatic relations between the United States and Germany in 1917, he immediately offered his services to the Government and on February 20th received a commission as Lieutenant, Junior Grade, of the Naval Reserve. He was called to the colors in May and was promoted to the rank of Lieutenant on November 3, 1917, and to Lieutenant-Commander on November 2, 1918. He was first assigned to duty with the Bureau of Ordnance, United States Navy, and served as Assistant Naval Inspector of Ordnance for New England with headquarters at Bridgeport, Conn. In November, 1918, he was placed in command of a new plant being erected by the navy at Baldwin, Long Island, for the manufacture of star shells.

Commander Mastick is a member of the following societies and clubs: Association of the Bar of the City of New York, University Club of New York, Columbia University Club, Chemical Club, Palestine Commandery, Knights Templar, Cos-

mos Club of Washington, D. C., American Chemical Society,
Military Order of Foreign Wars, and Sons of the American
Revolution.

726 FRANKLIN HUMPHREY[10] WARNER, son of Lucien
Calvin[9] and Keren (Osborne) Warner, born in New York City,
June 6, 1875. He received his early education in the private
schools in New York City except for two periods of about five
months each spent at Lausanne, Switzerland, in the study of
French. He entered Oberlin College in 1894, graduating in
1898. During his college course he gave especial attention to
chemistry and other scientific studies. After graduating, he
entered the chemical business, which his father had established
a short time before, working first in the factory and later in
the office, until he became thoroughly trained in the business.
The factory was first located in Mott Haven, but in 1900 a new
factory was erected at Carteret, N. J., fronting on Staten Island
Sound. The business was later incorporated under the name
of "The Warner Chemical Company" and was steadily developed and extended until the factory now covers seven acres and
the yearly sales exceed two million dollars. The chief chem-
icals manufactured are the compounds of phosphoric acid,
especially the different phosphates of soda, and the various
compounds of chlorine. In 1916, he was active with others in
organizing the Warner-Klipstein Chemical Company which
erected a large chemical plant at South Charleston, W. Va.,
devoted entirely to the making of chlorine gas from salt, and
the manufacture of this gas into chlorine compounds. Mr.
Warner is Treasurer of the Warner Chemical Company and of
the Warner-Klipstein Chemical Company and is a director of
the Monarch Chemical Company.

In 1901, Mr. Warner settled in White Plains, N. Y., and
has since resided there. He has taken an interest in many
activities outside of his business, both in White Plains and New
York City. He is President of the White Plains Young Men's
Christian Association, and has been very active in promoting
its interests. He is a member of the Congregational Church
of White Plains, and an active worker and leader in it. For
many years he has been Chairman of the Army Branch of the
Metropolitan Organization of the Young Men's Christian Association which conducts work in the different forts and camps
for soldiers in Greater New York. During the German war
he was a volunteer worker under the War Work Council of

FRANKLIN HUMPHREY WARNER

the Y. M. C. A., and assisted in the selection of secretaries for overseas work. He is also a Trustee of the Home Mission Boards of the Congregational Church, Trustee and Treasurer of the American College of Madura, India, and Trustee and Treasurer of Talladega College, Alabama.

Amateur photography has also claimed considerable of his attention, and he has made many fine autochrome plates for use with the lantern. He is active in all sports, is fond of hunting and is a member of the Scarsdale Golf and Country Club, of the Chamber of Commerce of the State of New York, of the New York Chemical Club, and of the Congregational Club of New York and Vicinity.

Married April 25, 1899, at Los Angeles, Cal., **ESTELLE DUNN HYNES,** daughter of Samuel Burke and Ellen Magelen (Anderson) Hynes (Samuel Burke[5], Rev. Thomas Woodruff[4], William Rose[3], Thomas[2], William[1]). William Hynes came from Londonderry, in the extreme North of Ireland, sometime before December 7, 1745, as a record left by him shows that on that date he entered the service of Benjamin Franklin of Philadelphia for one year. His son, Thomas, lived in Maryland and was a Captain in the war of the Revolution. Later he removed to Kentucky.

On her mother's side, Mrs. Warner is descended from the Andersons of Kentucky and the Finleys of Virginia. Her great-grandfather, John Finley, lived near the Natural Bridge in Virginia where he was the owner of slaves, probably inherited through his wife. He was strongly opposed to slavery, and so removed to Ohio about 1833, where he freed his slaves and gave to each a small allotment of land. His wife was Ann Letcher, the aunt of John Letcher, war Governor of Virginia, 1861-65.

Mrs. Warner is an active worker in the church and in various philanthropic societies. For several years she was Secretary of the Woman's National Home Missionary Union. She is a member of the National Board of the Y. W. C. A., a Trustee, of the Home Mission Boards of the Congregational Church and a member of Sorosis, the first woman's club organized in America.

In 1916, Mr. and Mrs. Warner made a trip of seven months in Japan, China, Ceylon and India, visiting the mission stations as members of a deputation sent out by the American Board. On this trip they made a careful study of the field, taking a large number of autochrome photographs. Since their return, both Mr. and Mrs. Warner have spent a large amount of time

LUCIEN THOMPSON WARNER

in lecturing before churches and societies around New York and throughout the country.

Children

Lucien Hynes Warner, b. at Irvington, N. Y., Sept. 9, 1900; educated at White Plains, partly in private schools and partly in the public school. In Sept., 1918, when eighteen years old, he joined the Students Army Training Corps at Oberlin College, Ohio, and continued with it until after the. armistice, when the Corps was disbanded, and he was honorably discharged on December 21, 1918. After his discharge he resumed his college studies in the Sophomore class.

Douglas Calvin Warner, b. Sept. 28, 1904, at White Plains, N. Y. Now a student in the White Plains public school.

727 **LUCIEN THOMPSON**[10] **WARNER,** son of Lucien Calvin[9] and Keren (Osborne) Warner, was born in New York City, April 18, 1877. His early education and preparation for college were in private schools in New York City, except for two winters in Switzerland spent chiefly in the study of French and German. He received the degree of A.B. from Oberlin College in June, 1898, and the degree of LL.B. from the Law Department of Columbia University in 1901. After graduation, he was admitted to the New York Bar, but did not take up the practice of law. In the fall of 1901, he removed to Bridgeport, Conn., and entered the business of The Warner Brothers Company, established by his father and uncle in 1874. At first he was employed in the advertising department, but in 1903 he was made secretary of the company, and his responsibilities were enlarged to include the export business, and still later to include the entire selling organization. In addition to his duties with the Warner Brothers Company he is a director of the Bridgeport Hydraulic Co., and the Bridgeport Gas Light Company, and trustee of the Bridgeport Savings Bank.

Mr. Warner has taken an active part in the religious, social and philanthropic interests of Bridgeport. He is a director of the Bridgeport Young Men's Christian Association, and served four years as its President. He was active in bringing about the union of the two oldest Congregational churches, under the name of The United Church. He was a member of the original committee that founded the Boy Scouts of America of the United States, and was President of the Bridgeport Council from its formation until 1917. In 1915-1916 he served on the Vice Commission appointed by the Mayor of Bridgeport, which spent many weeks in investigating the moral conditions and brought in a report which did much to clean up the city. In 1916 and 1917 he served on two commissions that prepared commission and commission manager forms of City Government for Bridgeport, which were later defeated at the polls. He is a member of Phi Gamma Delta, Phi Delta Phi, and Phi Beta Kappa fraternities; The University Club of New York, the Bridgeport University Club, the Brooklawn Country Club, the Seaside Club of Bridgeport, the Phi Gamma Delta Club, the Columbia University Club, and the Chicago University Club.

He is a trustee of Oberlin College and a member of the International Committee of the Young Men's Christian Association. At the breaking out of the war with Germany, he was appointed a member of the Executive Committee of the National War Work Council of the Y. M. C. A., and as a volunteer worker, he was made Chairman of the War Personnel Board for the selection and training of secretaries for service overseas and for the cantonments of America. Up to December 10, 1918, the Council had sent overseas 7,989 men and 1,659 women, besides nearly 10,000 who had been placed in the cantonments of America.

Married April 29, 1903, at Groton, Conn., **MARY BARBOUR WHITMAN**, daughter of Arthur Train and Mary Helen (Howland) Whitman, born November 22, 1878, at Sacramento, Cal. Mrs. Warner is descended from John Whitman, who came to America and settled in Weymouth, Mass., before 1638. He was appointed Ensign by Governor Winthrop in 1645. The line of descent from John[1] Whitman is as follows:—Thomas[2], Nicholas[3], Thomas[4], William[5], Oakes[6], Alphonzo Loring[7], Arthur Train[8], Mary Barbour[9] Whitman. Alphonzo Loring Whitman was a graduate of Bangor Theological Seminary, and held pastorates in Holden, Mass., and Westerly, R. I., where he remained nearly 20 years. He married Mary Elizabeth Barbour of Groton, Conn., daughter of Honorable Noyes Barbour, a member of Congress for 14 years, and a descendant of Elder William Brewster of the Mayflower.

Mrs. Warner is descended on her mother's side from Henry Howland who arrived at Plymouth, Mass., before 1625. The line of her descent from Henry[1] Howland is as follows:—Isaac[2], Benjamin[3], Zoeth[4], Benjamin[5], Isaac[6], Elery Almy[7], Isaac[8], Mary Helen[9], Mary Barbour[10] Whitman. The Friends' Record of Newport, R. I., has the following entry:

"Zoar Howland of Dartmouth in plimoth Colony was married to Abigail his wife in the tenth month of the year one thousand six hundred and fifty six."

Also:

"Zoar Howland was killed by the Indians at Pocasset, 21st Day of 1st month, 1676."

Elery Almy Howland moved to Janesville, Wis., in 1850, where he was Mayor of the city. (For further particulars see "History of Descendants of John Whitman of Weymouth, Mass.," by Charles H. Farnham, The Tuttle, Morehouse & Taylor Company, New Haven, 1889. Also "Genealogy of the Howland Family in America," by Franklyn Howland, New Bedford, Mass., 1885.)

Mrs. Warner received her early education at the Englewood High School, Chicago, and entered Vassar College in 1897, graduating with honor in 1901. She is prominent in the church and philanthropic work of Bridgeport, a Director of the Bridgeport Young Women's Christian Association, and during the German was has been especially active in the Red Cross, devoting a large part of her time to this work. She is a member of the Wednesday Afternoon Musical Club, the College Club of Bridgeport, the Association of Collegiate Alumnae, the Society of Mayflower Descendants, and Phi Beta Kappa Fraternity.

Children

Arthur Warner, b. Feb. 8, 1904; now attending the Hotchkiss School at Lakeville, Conn.
Agnes Howland Warner, b. Feb. 29, 1908.

728 ELIZABETH CONVERSE[10] WARNER, daughter of Lucien Calvin[9] and Keren (Osborne) Warner, born in New York City, May 27, 1879. Prepared for college at the Classical School for Girls in New York City, except for two winters in Switzerland, spent mostly in the study of French and German. Entered Oberlin College in 1896 and spent one year. Traveled with her parents for one year in Japan, China and India; entered Vassar College in 1898 and was graduated in 1901.

She resides at Scarsdale, N. Y., and is a leader in the philanthropic and social activities of the community. She organized the Scarsdale Chapter of the Red Cross in 1914 and was its chairman for one year and since then a member of the board. She is a director of the Country Branch of the New York Ortho-

ELIZABETH WARNER GALLOWHUR   COL. WILLIAM GIBSON GALLOWHUR

ELIZABETH WARNER GALLOWHUR AND FAMILY

pedic Hospital, President of the Scarsdale Nursing Association, a member of the Women's University Club of New York, a member of Sorosis, and of the Society of Mayflower Descendants. Married at Irvington-on-Hudson, N. Y., October 15, 1902, **WILLIAM GIBSON GALLOWHUR**, son of George and Sarah (Powell) Gallowhur, born August 25, 1873, at Girard, Pa. Mr. Gallowhur took special studies at Oberlin College for four years and soon after engaged in business in New York City where he has for several years been Secretary of the Monarch Chemical Company. In January, 1918, he enlisted in the army, receiving a commission as Captain. He served first in the Ordnance Department in the construction of Edgewood Arsenal, Maryland, which was built for the manufacture of poison gases. Later he was transferred to the Chemical Warfare Section, U. S. Army, promoted to the rank of Major, and then to Lieutenant Colonel and appointed Executive Officer in command of Edgewood plant, Edgewood Arsenal.

Mr. Gallowhur is a member of the Union League Club and the Whitehall Club of New York City, the Adirondack League Club, the Scarsdale Gun Club, and the Manursing Island Club at Rye, N. Y.

Children

George Gallowhur, b. at Bronxville, N. Y., Sept. 4, 1904; now attending the Hackley School at Tarrytown-on-Hudson, New York.
Keren Warner Gallowhur, b. at White Plains, N. Y., Mar. 26, 1907.
Elizabeth Gallowhur, b. at Scarsdale, N. Y., Nov. 11, 1909.

729 **ANNA R.**[10] **WARNER**, daughter of Charles A.[9] and Margaret (Fay) Warner, born in Olean, N. Y., July 19, 1865; resides in Coudersport, Potter Co., Pa.

Married in Ceres, N. Y., October 15, 1884, **IRVIN HORATIO STEVENS**, born in Cuba, N. Y., April 13, 1863, son of Albertus A. and Emily (Richardson) Stevens.

Children

Mildred Stevens, b. in Ceres, N. Y., July 25, 1885; resides in Coudersport; m. there, Mar. 4, 1905, Franklin Dickinson Knox, b. in Coudersport, July 12, 1880, son of Franklin William and Elizabeth (Dickman) Knox. Children: i. Phyllis Elizabeth, b. Dec. 10, 1905. ii. Rachael Stevens, b. Mar. 27, 1908. iii. Gretchen Louise, b. Oct. 12, 1916.
Margaret Stevens, b. in Coudersport, Feb. 16, 1890; resides in Scio,

N. Y.; m. Jan. 1, 1916, Lewis F. Potter of Genesee, Pa., b. Dec., 1890. Child: Virginia Marion, b. in Scio, Jan. 13, 1917.
Grace W. Stevens, b. Aug. 22, 1892; resides in Coudersport; m. Oct. 28, 1915, William D. Fish, b. June 6, 1875. Child: Marion Winifred, b. at Coudersport, Aug. 16, 1916.
Fay W. Stevens, b. Aug. 17, 1894; resides in South Bethlehem, Pa.
Charles A. Stevens, b. Aug. 18, 1898.

730 **M A R Y   A N N** [10] **W A R N E R,** daughter of Adelbert Andrew[9] and Catherine Henrietta (Bettinger) Warner, born in Richland, N. Y., December 30, 1868; died in Pickering, Mo., July 23, 1901.
Married March 15, 1885, **CYRUS GRANT MC MILLEN,** born in Burnside, Hancock Co., Ill., July 30, 1864, son of James B. and Margaret McMillen.

Children

Ora Mae McMillen, b. near Marysville, Mo., Feb. 24, 1887; was graduated from Kansas State Agricultural College, B.S., 1916; instructor in Home Economics since 1916 at Topeka High School, Topeka, Kans.
James Adelbert McMillen, b. near Marysville, Mo., Jan. 23, 1889; A.B., University of Missouri, 1913; B.L.S., New York State Library School, 1915; Librarian at University of Rochester (N. Y.), since 1915. He enlisted as a Chief Quartermaster, Naval Aviation, Naval Reserve Flying Corps, was assigned to Massachusetts Institute of Technology for a three months' course, Aug. 19, 1918.
Audrey Arvilla McMillen, b. at Wilcox, Mo., Sept. 19, 1891; m. at Pickering, Mo., Nov. 30, 1916, Walter Thomas Chaney, b. in Topeka, Kans., July 20, 1891, son of John Thomas and Anna (Johnstone) Chaney. Child: Mary Anna, b. Jan. 21, 1918. Mr. Chaney was graduated from High School in 1910, entered Washburn College, Topeka, Kans., the same fall, and, after two and a half years' academic work and three years of law, received the degree of LL.B. in 1915; is now assistant prosecuting attorney for Shawnee County.
Edith Margaret McMillen, b. at Wilcox, Mo., Jan. 14, 1895; m. in 1914, Byron M. Hanna, b. July 5, 1893. Children: i. Mary Beatrice, b. Feb. 1, 1915. ii. Alice Margaret, b. Sept. 19, 1916.

731 **LILLIAN B.**[10] **WARNER,** daughter of Adelbert Andrew[9] and Catherine Henrietta (Bettinger) Warner, born in Tarkio township, Mo., July 8, 1871; resides in Oakdale, Neb. Married near Rock Port, Mo., March 19, 1890, **TRACY ANDREW EVANS,** born in Rock Port, February 11, 1870, son of Andrew and Rachel Diana (Haught) Evans. He is a farmer

Children

Merle Benjamin Evans, b. in Tarkio, Mo., Dec. 8, 1890; m. in Oak-dale, Neb., Feb. 25, 1914, Vera Beer, daughter of Charles Bernard and Esther (Simmonds) Beer. Child.: Arline Mildred, b. Aug. 28, 1917.

Cecil Lillian Evans, b. at Rock Port, Mo., Jan. 19, 1893; m. in Oak-dale, Neb., Feb. 12, 1913, George William Stanton, a farmer, son of Lawson Jay and Lissa Ann (Van Hoosen) Stanton, and a direct descendant of the Van Hoosens of New York.

ADDITIONS AND CORRECTIONS

DAVID C.⁵ WARNER, see page 200. Additional data regarding children.

Lucinda⁶ Warner, resided in Gorham, N. Y.; m. Enos Pembrook, who removed to Illinois with his children after his wife's death. Children: Thomas; Ursula; Richard; Elihu; Celinda; Mary Ann.

Polly⁶ Warner, m. in Gorham, N. Y., Asa Adams, a farmer. After some years they removed to Parma, N. Y., and in 1833 to Oakland County, Mich., where both of them died. They were faithful members of the Baptist Church of which he was a deacon the greater part of his life. Children: i. Eber, m. Freelove Durham. ii. Clarissa, m. William Hildreth. iii. Fidelia, m. Zenas Phelps. iv. Madison, m. Marcia Spencer. v. David, m. (1) Catherine Cole, (2) Ellie Cogswell. vi. Darius, d. in infancy. vii. Lucretia, d. in infancy.

Anna⁶ Warner, m. Richard Church. Children: i. Darling, m. Annis Rockwell; had children, Edwin, Philetus, Harvey, Sarah, Caroline, Leonard and Darling. ii. Valowa, m. Leonard Cutler. iii. Austin, m. Melinda Billings; had children, Mary Louise (m. Jairus Raub, resides in Marshall, Mich.); Jennie (m. J. B. Braman, resides in Marshall); Georgia (m. G. E. Howe, resides in Kalamazoo, Mich., has children, Daisy, Austin and Rosa); Birdie (m. George Willsbrands, resides in Detroit and has a son Keith); and Minnie (m. Charles Myler and has a child Margaret). iv. Alonzo, m. Mary Fellows; had children, Francis, Eleda, Sarah and Richard. v. Hannah, m. Samuel Jennings; had children, Melvina and Matilda. vi. Charles, m. Mary Bentley; had children, Herbert, Ida, Sarah and Eli. vii. John, m. Ann Cogshall. viii. Sarah, m. Alonzo Cutler, resided in La Porte, Ind.; had children, Austin, Lewis and George. ix. Munson, m. (1) Amanda Clark, (2) Amelia Eldrogh. x. Eli, m. Sarah Holley. xi. Lydia, m. Professor Hand.

Russell⁶ Warner, m. Ora Phelps. Children: i. Asenath, m. Lyman Baker. ii. Nancy, m. Simon Piper. iii. Lucinda, m. Edward Piper. iv. Silas, m. Nancy Rogers. v. Luther, m. Martha Wilson. vi. Anitis, m. Walsten Childs of Adrian, Mich. vii. Isaiah, m. Lovina Jennings, d. 1872, in Homer, Mich.; had children, Ida, d. 1880, m. Henry Minor; Jay, d. aged 16; Guy, m. Etta Witham; Fred, m. Elitha Smith; Emma, d. Mar., 1887, m. William Witham; Kate, m. Jay Cool; and Benjamin, m. Harriet Carey.

Stephen⁶ Warner, m. Betsey Rice, who m. (2) —— Hard. Children: i. Calvin, married. ii. William, committed suicide by hanging. iii. Byron, d. young. iv. Ursula.

Betsey⁶ Warner, b. Sept., 1791; d. 1857; m. David Johnson. They went from Parma, N. Y., to Homer, Mich., in 1833, among the first settlers there, while it was still a wilderness.

Children of David and Betsey (Warner) Johnson

Caroline Johnson, m. John Drury. Children: i. Jerome. ii. George, m. and had a son Charles. iii. Cordelia. iv. Caroline, m. —— Tinger and has a son Fred.

Angeline Johnson, m. (1) Nathan Hall. Children: i. Edgar, m. and has a child May. ii. Alfred, m. and has Eugene and Flora. iii. Marie, m. —— Rose and has children, Warren (m. and has a child Elsa) and May (m. —— Farwell and has a son Starr). Angeline Johnson m. (2) Shepard Ostrom. Child: Lemuel, m. and has son Maynard who is married and has a son.
Belinda Johnson, died.
Marietta Johnson, m. David Burt and had six children of whom only two grew up: Charles D., m. and had children, Frank and Edwin, and James, m. and had children, Mary and John.
Pamelia Johnson, m. Ellery P. Potter. Children: i. Charles H., d. in Savannah, a prisoner of war; had children, E. P., Leila, m. William Hannon, and Sue (m. George Feigner and had children, Allen, Ellery and George E.). ii. Mary E., m. Stephen R. Allen and had a daughter Ina. iii. Harvey H., had a son Charles H. (m. and has Russell, Estella, Elida and Kermit). iv. Ellery J. v. Elida. vi. Edwin.
Eliza Johnson, m. Allen Card. Child: Emily, m. Seth King and had four children, Edith (m. —— Adams, two children, Marion and King); Edwin (has children, Lester, Edna and Ellery); Myron (has Ernest and Bertie); and Myrtle (m. and has three children).
Marie Johnson, m. Laban Barnhardt. Children: i. Nellie, m. Enos Hinkley; has children, Claude, Ada, Fred and Laurel. ii. Luman, has a daughter. iii. Heman, has a daughter.
Delsina Johnson, m. George Daniels. Child: Edward.

Harriet[6] Warner, m. Sylvester Rice. Children: i. Philetus, m. Sarah Clark.[--] ii. David, m. Barbara Harris. iii. Samuel, m. Lovina Kilborn. iv. Eber, m. Rachel Lewis. v. Russell, m. Addie Lovejoy. vi. Amanda, m. James Atwater. vii. Imogene, not married. viii. Sylvester, m. Amanda Duncan. ix. Lucinda, m. Leander Smith.

Elihu[6] Warner, removed from Sharon, N. Y., when six years of age, to Walworth, N. Y., and from there to Reading, Mich., where he died at the age of 88 years; m. Lucina Clarke, who died four years later aged 88 also. Children: i. Mary Ann, m. Samuel Taggart. ii. John, m. Elsie Barry; resided at Reading, Mich. iii. Olive, resided at Reading, m. Albert Bigelow. iv. Lewis, m. Viola Bowers. v. Susan, resided at Reading; m. Henry Barnes. vi. Emily, m. Samuel Craig. vii. Sarah Ann, resided at Coldwater, m. Henry McKenzie. viii. Clattantomis, m. (1) Julia St.John, (2) Josephine Brown.

John[6] Warner, b. Jan. 1, 1798; d. in Coldwater, Mich., Jan. 24, 1871; m. June 12, 1821, Hannah Brown, b. Nov. 3, 1794, d. in Adrian, Mich., Nov. 7, 1873. Children: i. Samuel Milo, b. Mar. 24, 1822; d. Apr. 12, 1881; m. Jane Hinkle. ii. Ursula or Aussula, b. Mar. 30, 1824; d. Sept. 29, 1893; m. V. J. Osborn. iii. Dexie A., b. May 14, 1826; d. Apr. 26, 1875; m. John Hughes of Grand Rapids. iv. Eliza C., b. June 4, 1829; d. July 30, 1882; m. Apr. 2, 1851, Riley Cole and had one daughter, Sada A., b. June 27, 1854, m. Apr. 19, 1875, George O. Cole, no blood relative. They had four children, Don H., b. Feb. 13, 1876, d. Sept. 29, 1879; C. Leon, b. Feb. 19, 1878, d. June 6, 1882; George R., b. Aug. 23, 1879, m. Sept. 26, 1910, Adeline Reid, no children; Grayce E., b. Dec. 8, 1884, m. Nov. 9, 1904, Edward E. Beecher and had a daughter, Virginia Cole, b. Aug. 31, 1910. v. John, Jr.,

704 THE DESCENDANTS OF ANDREW WARNER

b. Sept. 5, 1831; d. Nov. 9, 1877, at Bismarck, N. Dak., not married. vi. Charles C., b. Mar. 25, 1834; d. Aug. 30, 1876, not married. vii. Horace H., b. Mar. 17, 1837; .d. Apr. 3, 1847. viii. and ix. Caroline C. and Emeline E. (twins), b. Feb. 11, 1841. Caroline C. Warner m. Jan. 8, 1860, Albert N. Codner of Grand Rapids, and had a child, Clara A., b. Feb. 28, 1863 (m. Feb. 1, 1882, Frank Button and has a child, Mae, b. Mar. 27, 1890). Emeline E. Warner m. (1) Mar. 14, 1866, Harry Bowen, and had children, i. Ada M., b. Feb. 24, 1867; m. Nov. 5, 1890, Charlie Waters; had two sons, Milan, b. Sept. 2, 1891 (m. Sept. 12, 1911, Cora Morris and had two children, Donald Washington, b. Feb. 22, 1913, and Ada Aurele, b. Jan. 29, 1916), and Roy, b. Feb. 6, 1897. ii. Bertha E., b. May 17, 1868; m. Sept. 25, 1887, Isaac Eldridge; had children, Laurence, b. Mar. 15, 1891, Harry, b. June 10, 1892, and Inez, b. Feb. 8, 1898. Emeline E. Warner m. (2) June 21, 1880, Jerome Seger.

Luther⁶ Warner, d. Apr. 21, 1850, of cholera, while on his way to Utah, where his children all went; m. Pamilla Stanton. Children: i. Elnora, b. June, 1822; m. (1) Robert Barry, (2) in Michigan, —— Dalton. ii. Betsey, m. —— Dalton. iii. Stanton, died, not married. iv. Adeline, m. —— Founteir of California. v. Laura Ann, d. 1852, not married. vi. Tirza, m. Rila Howard and lived in Anthony, Idaho, had nine children. vii. Charles A,. resides in Sanford, Ariz.

JUDSON PHILONZO⁸ WARNER, son of Houghton⁷ and Mary (Frary) Warner, page 449, was born November 4, 1837, and resided later in Kansas City, Mo. He was connected with the American Steel and Wire Company. He sold the first foot of barbed wire in the United States, made by the Glidden Company. Statistics in trade journals state that he sold more barbed wire than any other man in the United States up to the time of his death.
Married at Rockford, Ill., January 24, 1861, EMMA E. OVIATT, born at Hudson, Summit Co., Ohio, November 14, 1843, daughter of Steven T. and Hannah (Downs) Oviatt.

Children

Hannah Warner, b. Apr. 14, 1862, at Rockford, Ill.; m. (1) Henry J. Rosencrans, b. in Walworth Co., Wis., May 2, 1842; d. Nov. 16, 1903, in Kansas City, Mo.; m. (2) William H. Blades, b. Oct. 2, 1852, in Grand Rapids, Mich., no children. Child by first husband: Blanche (Rosencrans), b. July 15, 1887, in Kansas City, where she now resides; m. there, Apr. 10, 1913, Dr. Otto Leslie Castle, b. Mar. 22, 1884, in Pleasant Hill, Mo., d. in Kansas City, Apr. 25, 1917. Mrs. Castle has two children, b. in Kansas City, Dorothy Blanche, b. Apr. 21, 1914, and Eula Leslie, b. June 26, 1917, two months after her father's death from typhoid fever. Mrs. Castle is recording secretary of the Kansas City Chapter, D. A. R.
Marve Earl Warner, b. July 14, 1869, in Lorimer Co., Colo.; is manager of the Shields-Metzler Grocery Company in Colorado Springs; m. and has four children.
Clay Warner, b. in Denver, 1872; d. aged 22 days.

· **BETSEY M:[9] WARNER**, see page 583, daughter of Elisha Platts[8] and Margaret (Bogard) Warner, born July 28, 1843, in Montrose, Pa.; died in Bucklin, Mo., August 1, 1910. Married in Pennsylvania, September 15, 1860, **GEORGE W. GRIFFIN**, who died in Kansas City, June 15, 1917.

Children, born in Pennsylvania

Eudora Ann Griffin, d. in infancy.
Jerome E. Griffin, resides in Bucklin, Mo.; m. (1) Annie Davolt, (2) Sarah Ellen Nickerson. Children by first wife (one d. in infancy) · i. John, m. Sadie Durbin; is a farmer near Ethel, Mo.; had two children, one of whom d. in infancy. ii. Myrtle, m. Claud Hix, a telephone operator of Bucklin; resides now near Meadville, Mo.; has eight children. iii. Lillie, m. Frank Griggs, a farmer of Bucklin; resides now near Ethel; has nine children. iv. Simon, m. Emma Hair; is a farmer in Oklahoma; has a son and daughter. v. Charles, m. Flora Fodare; is a farmer in Iowa. vi. Bettie, m. Elmer Bailey of Hybrid, Mo., has a son Elmer Ray. vii. Dora, m. John Downing; resides in Iowa; has two children. viii. George, m. Lena Mather; is a farmer near New Boston, Mo. ix. Arvilla, m. George Nickerson; resides in New Boston; has a daughter. x. Robert. xi. Albert. Child by second wife: Viola.

LYDIA MELVINA[9] WARNER, see page 583, daughter of Elisha Platts[8] and Margaret (Bogard) Warner, born in Montrose, Pa., May 27, 1845; died in Bucklin, Mo., March 3, 1912. Married **EDWARD L. FITZGERALD**.

Children

Billie Fitzgerald, b. in Pittston, Pa., Mar. 8, 1874; d. in Bucklin, Mo., Mar. 20, 1916.
Daisy Fitzgerald, b. Jan. 26, 1884, in Macon Co., Mo.; m. Feb. 11, 1902, James P. Davolt, b. in Macon Co., Apr. 9, 1882, farmer. Children, first b. in Macon Co., others in Linn Co.; i. Mabel, b. Feb. 9, 1903. ii. Orvle, b. June 18, 1905. iii. George, b. June 15, 1907. iv. Lydia, b. Sept. 1, 1911.

GEORGE F.[9] WARNER, son of Elisha Platts[8] and Margaret (Bogard) Warner, born January 28, 1866. Married in Bucklin, Mo., Dec. 15, 1891, **NELLIE REYNOLDS**, born July 1, 1870. Children: i. Jessie, b. Sept. 9, 1892. ii. Edith, b. March 22, 1894. iii. Ruth, b. May 27, 1896, d. Nov. 14, 1899. iv. William D., b. April 17, 1898. v. Laura, b. Feb. 6, 1902. vi. Clarence M., b. Aug. 21, 1904. vii. Ralph E., b. Oct. 26, 1906. viii. Davis V., b. Sept. 12, 1908. ix. Nellie, b. Aug. 12, 1914.

45

FLORENCE ARVILLA⁹ WARNER, see page 584, daughter of Elisha Platts⁸ and Margaret (Bogard) Warner, born March 27, 1861, in Wyoming County, Pa.; resides in Kansas City, Mo. Married in Kansas City, October 29, 1889, EMERSON MERRITT SEVERANCE, born in Vermont, May 12, 1848; died in Kansas City, Mo., October 19, 1909. He was employed in the Fort Scott and Gulf local freight office.

Children, born in Kansas City

Albert Leslie Severance, b. Aug. 20, 1891.
Ray Eugene Severance (twin), b. Jan. 15, 1899.
Roy Clarence Severance (twin), b. Jan. 15, 1899; is a yeoman in the United States Navy; enlisted August, 1918; sailed for France on the U. S. Transport Arizonian, Feb. 5, 1919.

CORRECTION FOR PAGE 293

250 JAMES⁶ WARNER, son of James⁵ and Abigail (————) Warner, born in Saybrook, Conn., March 20, 1768; resided after his marriage in Greene, Chenango Co., N. Y.; married in 1794, Polly Norton of Easton, Washington Co., N. Y., formerly of Connecticut, probably New London. She was the daughter of John⁴ Norton, b. 1740, and Jean Smith (Joseph¹ Norton, Marshal of Martha's Vineyard, 1692, and Mary Bayes, John² and Mary (————) Norton, John³ and Hepsibah (Coffin) Norton, John⁴). Children, b. at Easton, N. Y.: i. Lucy, b. Mar. 5, 1795, d. Sept. 28, 1879, m. at Smithville, N. Y., Oct. 20, 1819, Ezek King Carpenter. Her granddaughter is Ellen M., wife of I. H. Light, Bloomington, Ill. ii. Loa, b. 1796, m. Thomas Wells. Her granddaughter is Mrs. George Race of Greene, Chenango Co., N. Y. iii. Abigail, b. 1798, m. John H. Smith. iv. Prudence, m. Feb., 1830, at Smithville, N. Y., William Tilton and d. within a year. iv. Polly, d. aged about 6 years. v. Smith B., m. Hannah Smith of Smithville, N. Y., and removed to Michigan in 1843. His family lived in Shiawassee County.

LINES WHOSE CONNECTION IS UNCERTAIN

CHARLES WARNER is believed to have been a descendant of Andrew Warner, although his connection with recorded branches of the family is not established. He was born in Windham, Conn., November, 1762; resided for a time in Coventry; died in Geddes, Onondaga County, N. Y., November 26, 1837, buried in Geddes, now a part of Syracuse. He enlisted at Windham, Conn., July 15, 1779, in Captain Williams' Company of Colonel Durkee's Regiment, Connecticut Troops, and remained in service until January 10, 1780, when he was honorably discharged. He again enlisted at Windham in the early part of July, 1781, in Captain Williams' Company of Colonel Webb's Regiment, Connecticut Troops, and was discharged in January, 1782. He applied for a pension, September 11, 1832, from Salina, N. Y., and it was allowed in April, 1835. Charles Warner was a member of the Presbyterian Church, a man of gentle and amiable disposition, honest and upright in all his dealings with his fellow men.

Charles Warner married October 5, 1789, SARAH STOCKWELL, who applied for a widow's pension from Salina, September, 1843. It was granted September, 1844. She was buried in Geddes.

Children

Esther Warner, b. Aug. 13, 1790.

Lucy Warner, b. Aug. 13, 1792; d. Apr. 8, 1831; m. ——— Van Dezen.

Charity Warner, b. Apr. 9, 1795; d. Sept. 2, 1895, aged over a hundred years. She was born in New York State and married Elias Eliot, Dec. 12, 1813. They settled in the little village of Geddes, near the site of Syracuse. N. Y. Elias Eliot was born Mar. 1, 1794, son of Andrew and Jennie (Ayres) Eliot, died May 11, 1841. After his death his wife lived in Louisville, Ky., with her youngest daughter until the latter's death, then went to Yankton, S. Dak., to reside with her daughter Helen Eliot Moody, and with her removed to Deadwood, S. Dak., where she died. Mr. and Mrs. Eliot had children: i. Sarah Jane, b. Mar. 1, 1815; d. July 7, 1890; m. Feb. 8, 1835, David Ripley and had eight children, Sarah Jane, Frances Ann, Charles Elias, Helen Maria, George Warner, Wesley, Lucy Cornelia (b. Dec. 20, 1847, m. Mar. 19, 1864, Frederick C. Hills and had five children, Kate (b. Jan. 7, 1868, m. May 20, 1891, Dixon S. Elliott), Fred A., Charles S., Stanley Eliot, and Louis Brown), and James Wesley. ii. Andrew J., b. Feb. 11, 1817; d. Sept. 27, 1886. iii. Lucy Ann, b. Feb. 17, 1819. iv. Charles, b. Dec. 1, 1821. v. Elias, b. July 28, 1822. vi. Wesley, b. Jan. 5, 1824. vii. Lewis, b. Feb. 13, 1826. viii. James, b.

Oct. 11, 1828.   ix. George W., b. Nov. 11, 1831.   x. Warner, b. Jan.
31, 1833.   xi. Helen C., b. Apr. 9, 1836;   m. Gideon L. Moody and
resides in Los Angeles, Cal.   xii. Mary Elizabeth, b. Apr. 5, 1838;
m. Thomas Calvin Chandoin and had a daughter Mary Alice who m.
William Selbie of Deadwood, S. Dak., b. in Aberdeen, Scotland, Mar.
20, 1851, son of Rev. William Selbie, a highly esteemed minister who
preached for over forty years at Maryculture near Aberdeen.   William Selbie came to America and to Minnesota in 1871; resided in
Deadwood after 1877.

Zerena Sophia Warner, b. Apr. 11, 1797.

Betsey Warner, b. July 27, 1799.

Mary (Polly) Warner, b. Dec. 6, 1801, in Cherry Valley, N. Y.; m.
Ferris Hubbell.

Sarah or Rhoda Warner, b. May 17, 1805.   The family Bible from
which dates were taken does not give the name Sarah but Rhoda
in this order.

Charles Eldridge Warner, b. June 6, 1807; d. Dec. 29, 1835.

Israel Warner, name not on list taken from Bible.

ELY or **ELI WARNER** of Hartford, Conn.   Many of his
descendants believe that he was descended from Andrew Warner,
but we have no definite records of his ancestry.   This brief
account of his family is here included in the hope that the missing connection may be found and the exact relationship established.   He died in Hartford, January, 1813.   He was married
December 15, 1752, to **AZUBA ALLYN**, born 1731, died January,
1774, aged 43, daughter of Capt. Thomas and Elizabeth Allyn of
Windsor.   Her gravestone was standing in the Ancient burying
ground in Hartford in 1838.   (Sexton's burials for 1774; Conn.
Quarterly.)

        Children of Ely and Azuba (Allyn) Warner

Azuba Warner, b. Oct. 27, 1755; m. —— Williams.

Eunice Warner, b. Jan. 24, 1757; m. Loomis Warner.

Ely Warner, Jr. b. Nov. 13, 1758; d. Aug. 15, 1782.

Lovisa Warner, b. June 23, 1760; d. July 31, 1798; m. Joseph Whiting
Seymour, b. 1763, d. at Hartford, Sept. 7, 1815, son of Capt. Zebulon
and Ann (Marsh) Seymour of Hartford.   He m. (2) Dec. 22, 1799,
Lucy Sharp, widow of Jacob Baldwin.   He had eleven children.

Henry Allyn (1) Warner, b. June 27, 1762; d. Apr. 28, 1763.

Lucretia Warner, b. Oct. 15, 1763; m. Simeon Griswold.

Charlotte Warner, b. Jan. 23, 1765; m. Salmon Gunn.

Clarissa Warner, b. Aug. 10, 1766; m. William Davey.

Henry Allyn (2) Warner, b. Feb. 23, 1768; d. Jan. 14, 1813; m. Mrs.
Elizabeth Ostrander Warner, widow of his brother Jonah Whiting
Warner.   Children: Henry A.; Eli W.; Lucy; Ann Eliza, m.
—— Hurlburt.   Miss Georgianna Hurlburt of Racine, Wis., is a
descendant.

Jonah Whiting Warner, b. Sept. 23, 1769; d. Mar. 11, 1802, in Hartford; m. in Windsor, Conn., Apr. 13, 1799, Elizabeth Ostrander, b. in Albany, N. Y., d. in Racine, Wis., Oct. 8, 1885, daughter of John, Jr., and Catherine (Witzell) Ostrander. See further.
Lucy Warner, b. Nov. 4, 1776; d. Mar. 5, 1797.

Jonah Whiting and Elizabeth (Ostrander) Warner had two daughters, Cornelia, b. May 5, 1800, in Hartford, Conn., d. Nov. 30, 1868, in New Albany, Ind., and Catherine, who m. ———— Phelps and d. leaving no children. Cornelia Warner married in Hartford, May 17, 1826, George Stephen Butler, b. in Hartford, July 8, 1795, d. in Louisville, Ky., Aug. 6, 1831, of yellow fever which he contracted while on a visit to New Orleans. He was the son of Richard and Lucy (Ranney) Butler and was himself a descendant of Andrew[1] Warner through Andrew[2] and Rebecca (Fletcher) Warner, John[3] and Anna (Ward) Warner, Abigail[4] and Joseph Ranney (see page 96). Children of George Stephen and Cornelia (Warner) Butler: i. Mary Elizabeth, b. Feb. 19, 1827; d. Aug. 20, 1905; m. Oct. 7, 1847, Walter Mann, b. Sept. 16, 1827, d. Aug. 16, 1892, son of Asa and Freelove (Clark) Mann (see further). ii. Charles Henry, b. Oct. 19, 1829, in Louisville; d. Oct. 8, 1905, in Oswego, N. Y.; m. Oct. 9, 1860, Catherine Slocum, b. June 27, 1836, d. July 14, 1902, in Oswego, daughter of Matthew Barnard and Mary (Ostrander) Slocum (see further). iii. Georgiana, b. Feb. 21, 1831; d. Nov. 19, 1881; m. Dr. Charles Bowman and had a daughter Cornelia, b. 1856.

Children of Walter and Mary Elizabeth (Butler) Mann: i. Cornelia, b. Apr. 23, 1849; d. Mar. 20, 1876. ii. Walter Butler, b. Sept. 26, 1851; d. Sept. 6, 1865. iii. Eliza Stewart, b. Sept. 23, 1859, in New Albany, Ind.; is a member of the D. A. R., Colonial Dames and Descendants of Colonial Governors; resides in St Paul; m. there, Aug. 5, 1880, Dr. Charles Eastwick Smith, son of Franklin R. and Mary (Guest) Smith of Philadelphia (have children, Mary Guest, b. Oct. 7, 1881, and Charles Eastwick, Jr., b. Jan. 14, 1883, Yale 1904, and Penn. Med. Univ. 1908). iv. Catherine Phelps, b. June 28, 1861; d. Feb. 19, 1897. v. Frederick Clark, b. Apr. 28, 1868; resides in St. Paul; m. Jan. 29, 1896, Carrie Agnes Hill; no children. vi. Charles Edward, b. July 9, 1870; resides in Minneapolis; m. Oct. 15, 1895, Annie Harrison Comstock (have children, Stewart Harrison, b. Dec. 26, 1903, and George Comstock, b. Aug. 30, 1906).

Children of Charles Henry and Catherine (Slocum) Butler: i. Georgiana, b. Feb. 18, 1862; resides in Sapulpa, Okla., m. in Miles City, Mont., May 31, 1906, Dr. Edward A. Mattoon. ii. Charles Warner, b. Dec. 24, 1863, in Oswego, N. Y.; is a banker in Miles City, Mont.; m. in Lisbon, N. Dak., June 6, 1900, Jessie Rawson, b. in Northfield, Minn., Apr. 10, 1879, daughter of Willis and Sarah Alice (Converse) Rawson. They have children, b. in Miles City, Charles Willis, b. Mar. 31, 1901, Walter Rawson, b. Aug. 17, 1904, and Richard Slocum, b. June 1, 1907.

Descendants of the following family have the tradition that they spring from Andrew Warner of Cambridge.

NATHAN[1] **WARNER**, born about 1720; died January 16, 1802, aged 82 years. He had a son Oliver[2] Warner who removed after the Revolution to Warren, Herkimer Co., N. Y., and died May 8, 1813.

OLIVER[2] **WARNER** married **RACHEL LOOMIS**, born May 15, 1765, died April 25, 1851, daughter of John and Rachel (Harris) Loomis of Salem, Conn.

Children of Oliver Warner

Collins Warner, b. Feb. 3, 1787; d. Mar. 11, 1848, in Warren, N. Y.; m. Sally Isham. Children: i. Oliver, d. in New York City, 1860. ii. Sophia, b. 1824; m. (1) Lorenzo Ludden, (2) Merrick Ludden; resided in Columbia, Herkimer Co., N. Y. iii. Horace, d. aged 12. iv. Melinda, b. 1832; m. John Northrup; resided in Red Wing, Minn. v. Malvina, d. 1863, resided in Warren, N. Y.; m. Rolden Wightman; no children.

Nathan Warner, b. Apr. 3, 1788; d. May 16, 1841, in Cato, N. Y.; m. Hannah De Long. Children: i. Eliza, b. 1817; d. 1868, in Meridian, N. Y.; m. Garret V. Peak. ii. Angeline, b. 1819; m (1) Ransom Hunt, who d. June 10, 1841, (2) Elijah Peak.

Owen Warner, b. Mar. 6, 1790; d. June 9, 1846, in Albany, N. Y.; m. Eliza Freeman Loomis, b. Oct. 4, 1796, daughter of Dudley and Olive (Jones) Loomis of Warren, N. Y. They resided in Buffalo and Albany. Children: i. Howard, d. 1839, not married. ii. (Daughter).

Olcutt Warner, b. Sept. 17, 1792; d. July, 1815, not married.

Selinda Warner, b. Aug. 18, 1794; d. June 14, 1861; m. Job Bronson, who d. July 28, 1864; resided at Crain's Corners, N. Y. Children: i. Jane Melvina, b. Sept. 5, 1816; resided in Illinois; m. Jan. 18, 1851, William Lloyd, who d. Mar. 6, 1877; no children. ii. Olcutt Warner, b. Apr. 12, 1818; m. Apr. 24, 1851, Elizabeth G. Harter; resided in Mohawk, N. Y., and had children, Ferris Howard, b. Jan. 24, 1853, d. Dec. 22, 1864, Arthur Warner, b. June 3, 1855, Lydia Jane, b. Feb. 28, 1859, d. Jan. 15, 1865, and Alida Selinda, b. Aug. 24, 1861.

Oliver Warner, Jr., b. Nov. 8, 1796; d. May, 1879, in Paw Paw, Mich.; m. Avis Warren. Children: i. Otis, m. and lived in Paw Paw. ii. (Daughter) m. ———— Richmond and lived in Paw Paw.

Elias Warner, b. Oct. 4, 1798; resided in Albany, N. Y.; m. Sarah Smith who d. Sept. 2, 1856. Child: Elizabeth L., b. Apr. 12, 1828; resided in Castleton, N. Y.; m. Feb. 1, 1849, John J. D. Witbeck and had six children, Joel D., d. young, Mary S., m. Alpha W. Briggs, Charles E., m. Ella F. Regua, Annie A., Lizzie S. and Jennie O.

Hubbel Warner, b. Aug. 18, 1800; resided at Little Prairie, Mich.; m. Catherine Hughes. Children: i. Hubbel Loomis, b. 1824; m. and resided in Volinia, Mich. ii. Francis E., m. and resided in Dowagiac, Mich. iii. Harvey S. iv. Maria, d. 1874. v. Angeline, b. 1840; resided in Dowagiac.

Sophia Warner, b. Sept. 9, 1802; d. May 27, 1869; resided in Castleton, N. Y; m. Ezekiel McKannan. Children: i. Hugh, b. 1826; m. Hattie Smith. ii. Rachel, d. 1869; m. Albert Backus. iii. Oliver.

iv. Sophia, m. George Clark. v. Sarah, m. ——— Berry. vi. George.
vii. James, d. aged 16. viii. Jemima, not married. ix. Mary, b.
1844.
Loomis Warner, b. Dec. 9, 1804; d. Dec. 26, 1888, buried in West Winfield, Herkimer Co., N. Y., where he had been a practicing physician. He was graduated from the Fairfield Medical College, M.D.,
1826. Married Oct. 15, 1827, Mary Ann Root. Children: i. (Son),
b. Mar. 1, 1829; d. Mar. 4, 1829. ii. Sarah Florett, b. Nov. 1, 1830;
resides in West Winfield and Albany, N. Y.; m. May 6, 1868, Henry
W. Joslyn, b. May 20, 1829, d. Feb. 15, 1891, buried in West Winfield.
iii. Hannah Maria, b. July 24, 1832; d. Mar. 26, 1851. iv. Frances
Louisa, b. May 9, 1847; d. Aug. 28, 1900, buried in West Winfield;
m. Sept. 14, 1869, Haines D. Cunningham, b. Apr. 16, 1841, d. Sept.
23, 1899. He was a graduate of Union College in 1866, resided in
Saratoga, N. Y.

It is believed that **SAMUEL WARNER**, born June 10, 1779,
may have been connected with the family of Samuel[3] Warner,
see page 63. No record of the place of his birth or of his
parents' names has been found. He was married in Chesterfield, N. H., March 20, 1804, to Relief Crossfield. Their son
Albert Warner, born 1809, married October 2, 1831, Lucina
Snow and had a son Horace Everett Warner, born in Kirkland,
Ohio, January 10, 1839. He served as private in Company E,
22d Wisconsin Infantry, in the Civil War and lost an arm at
the battle of Resaca, Ga. He was graduated from Beloit College, Wisconsin, in 1867 and married there, October 14, 1870,
Anna J. Riggs, born in Lacquiparle, Minn., April 13, 1845,
daughter of Rev. Stephen Return Riggs and Mary A. Longley.
Mr. Warner practiced law at Vinton, Iowa, from 1873 to 1885;
was in the U. S. Civil Service from 1887 to 1904. He is a writer
and resides in Groton, N. H. Among his publications are: The
Ethics of Force, 1905; The Cricket's Song and Other Melodies,
1907. The family are Congregationalists. Horace E. Warner
has three children: i. Marjorie Fleming, b. Sept. 29, 1871; ii.
Arthur Hallam, b. Oct. 28, 1875; iii. Everett Longley, b. in
Vinton, Iowa, July 16, 1877.

Everett L. Warner is a painter and etcher, residing in New
York City. He was a pupil at the Art Students' League, New
York, and Julian Academy, Paris. He has won many awards
for his pictures: 1st Corcoran prize, Washington Water Color
Club, 1902; Sesnan gold medal, Pennsylvania Academy of Fine
Arts, 1908; silver medal, International Exposition, Buenos
Aires, 1910; 2d Hallgarten prize, Salmagundi Club, 1913;
bronze medal, Society of Washington Artists, 1913; silver and
bronze medals, Panama Pacific Exposition. He is represented

in the permanent collections at the Corcoran Gallery, Washington, the Pennsylvania Academy of Fine Arts, Boston Museum of Fine Arts, Museums of Toledo, Ohio, and Syracuse, N. Y., City Art Museum, St. Louis, Art Institute, Chicago, and New York Public Library. Since 1917 Mr. Warner has been engaged in ship camouflage and is the originator of one of the five systems of camouflage approved by the ship protection committee of War Risks. He was elected Associate National Academician in 1913 and is a member of the following clubs: Society of Washington Artists; Washington Water Color Club; New York Water Color Club; American Water Color Society; Society of New York Etchers; National Arts; Salmagundi.

INDEX

46

Mrs. Lura Holden, 580
WAGNER, Clara, 590
  Florence, 250
  Gilbert, 250
  Howard, 250
  Ida, 638
  Ida P., 490
  J., 250
  Joseph, 490
  Martin, 217
  Mrs. Sarah E., 490
WAIT, Albert, 234
  Elijah, 64
  Jeremiah, 234
  John, 70
  Jonathan, 68
  Joseph, 234
  Josiah, 129
  Lydia, 142
  Warner, 234
WAITE, Amelia Champlin, 571
  Benjamin, 105
  Brainerd, 571
  Christopher Champlin, 571
  David, 105
  Edward Tinker, 571
  Ellison, 571
  George Francis, 571
  Hannah, 105
  Henry Matson, 570, 571
  Henry Selden, 571(2)
  Joseph, 105
  Lucy, 105
  Martha, 105
  Mary, 105
  Mary Francis, 571
  Mary Gloyd, 571
  Morrison Remick, 570, 571
  Moses, 105
  Rhoda, 105
  Richard, 570
  Samuel, 570
  Thomas, 570
WAKE, Ellen Marietta, 656
  John, 656
WAKEFIELD, Clara Isabella, 407
WAKELEY, Abner, 155
  Ann, 155
  Mrs. Sarah, 155
WAKEMAN, Ebenezer, 103
  Esther, 26
  Francis, 26
  Hester, 26
  Samuel, 18
  Mrs. Sarah Hanford, 103

WALBRIDGE, Abigail W., 267
WALCUT, Sarah, 71
WALDEN, Jane, 3
  John, 3
WALDO, Charles Merrel, 481
  Cornélia Jane, 481
  Harriet, 532
  Mrs. Jennie T., 256
  Lucius A., 481
  Nancy, 138
  Zacheus, 138
WALES, Nathaniel, 125, 126
WALKER, Arad, 539
  Barzillai, 264
  Ebenezer M., 253
  Emma B., 437
  George Leon, 22
  Henry J., 234
  Mary A., 539
  Sarah Hinds, 264
  Wellington J., 357
WALL, ——, 470
  Donald, 470
  Margaret, 470
  Virginia, 470
WALLACE, Amelia, 592
  C. Stuart, 577
  Caroline, 394
  Ebenezer, 279(2)
  Jonas, 279
  Linneus A., 279
  Maria, 279
  Silas, 279
  Silas W., 279
WALLASTON, Captain, 15
WALLER, Eunice, 149
WALLISDORFS, Louise, 471
WALNER, see WARNER
WALSH, Esther, 306
WALTHART, Hattie, 321
WALTON, Asa, 216, 339
  Benjamin, 496
  Boaz, 133, 217
  Catherine, 339
  Mrs. Catherine, 216
  Cynthia Ann, 486
  Jane M., 255
  Joel, 339
  Mary, 339
  Sarah, 339
  Sarah M., 389
  Stephen, 339
WANZER, Daniel, 516
  Eunice P., 516
WARBRICK, Claire, 659
WARBURTON, John, 96
WARD, ——, 250
  Aaron, 451

Abigail, 53, 100
Alice, 158
Andrew, 451
Anna, 52
Dudley Andrus, 629
Elizabeth, 274
George, 451
Harriet L., 453
Helen Grace, 639
Henry S., 263
Horatio, 639
Ina, 451
Jane, 451
Mrs. Lois, 249, 250
Lorenzo, 451
Mrs. Maria, 639
Martha Bacon, 452
Mary, 53, 180
Molly, 180
Nathaniel, 18, 22
Patience, 96
Phebe, 291
Mrs. Phoebe, 52
Samuel, 53, 96
Sarah, 70, 183
Mrs. Sarah, 31
William, 52, 180, 629
WARDNER, George Wa⁣
476
  Joseph Waldo, 476
WARE, Hannah E., 575
WAREHAM, Percy, 451
WARNARD, see WARNER
WARNER, A. C., 494
  Dr. A. D., 527
  Aaron, 92, 139, 141(2), 229, 353(2)
  Abby, 113, 195, 290
  Abby E., 303, 439, 44
  Abby Elizabeth, 410
  Abel, 172, 231, 233, 397, 546, 690
  Abel Parker, 396
  Abel W., 396
  Mrs. Abi C., 272
  Abigail, 33, 34, 50, 52, 96, 98, 99, 114, 127, 141, 150, 158, 185, 209, 233, 246, 248, 295, 706
  Mrs. Abigail, 185
  Abigail Buel, 482
  Abigail Francis, 293
  Abner, 155, 256, 379
  Abner K., 292
  Abner Spicer, 256
  Abner Warren, 291,
  Abraham, 42, 44, 63, 6
  Achilles, 457

Frederick Milton, 531
Frederick Reuben, 355
Frederick W., 195, 311
Freelove, 295, 433
Gabbard, 379
Gail Barbara, 525
Garret W., 293
Gaylord, 574
Gaylord Coan, 255, 380
Geneva, 468
Genevieve, 468
George, 163, 192, 194,
    196(2), 203, 225, 245,
    280, 304(2), 317, 318,
    322, 325, 387, 393, 452,
    473, 538, 539, 565
George Abner, 256
George Albert, 633
George Coffing, 307, 445,
    601, 602
George D., 667
George Daniel, 540
George Dickinson, 422,
    584
George Edward, 464, 610
George Elbridge, 609
George Elias, 275
George Elvin, 676
George Erastus, 225
George Eugene, 443
George F., 471, 584, 705
George Franklin, 360, 515,
    540, 666
George G., 438
George H., 373, 406
George Hall, 347
George Henry, 398, 552
George Hinish, 635
George L., 566
George Lemuel, 472, 613
George Leroy, 515
George Loring, 275
George Newell, 508
George Norton, 533
George O., 196, 640
George P., 391
George Pearsons, 350
George Porter, 604, 670
George S., 256, 283, 545
George Shaw, 405, 560(2)
George Stetson, 472
George Trowbridge, 224,
    349
George Valorus, 322
George W., 164, 237, 285,
    408, 426, 432, 452, 565
George Washington, 237,
    371, 409, 456, 474, 523,
    569

George Wheeler, 540
George Whiton, 475
George Wilberforce, 384,
    532
Georgia, 665
Georgian Lucretia, 303
Geraldine, 579
Gerrit Smith, 589, 669
Gertie, 304
Gertrude, 317, 385
Gertrude A., 493
Gertrude Chandler, 511
Gertrude Elsie, 539
Mrs. Gezier, 230
Gideon, 92( )2, 130, 143(2),
    489, 639, 680
Gifford Dyer, 602
Gilbert, 423, 585
Giles, 172, 233, 272, 274,
    399, 554
Giuletta, see Alma Giu-
    letta
Gladys, 465, 468
Gladys Davenport, 561
Gladys Martiel, 476
Gladys Rose, 442
Glenn Elam, 524
Glenn Y., 643
Gordon Chase, 647
Gordon D., 584, 668
Gordon J., 609
Grace, 238, 304, 308, 561,
    629
Mrs. Grace, 338
Grace Anna, 526
Grace Eastwood, 561
Grace Estella, 614
Grace Ethelyn, 508
Grace Jessie, 623
Grace Marie, 312, 457
Grace Mary, 560
Grace May, 514
Grace Pearl, 509
Graham, 682
Grant, 469
Graves, 185
Grisil, 113, 114
Gustavus, 315, 451
Gustavus A., 420, 575
Gustavus J., 584, 666
Guy, 702
Guy Carlton, 118, 119
Guy Frank, 524
Guy Leon, 638, 678
Hanford A., 362
Hannah, 28, 30, 33, 34, 35,
    37, 38, 39, 42, 44, 47(2),
    58, 59, 64, 84, 85, 98(2),
    106, 109, 113, 116, 133,

136, 137, 141, 149, 1[
    170, 178, 181, 186, 1[
    214, 217, 219, 227, 2[
    241(2), 244, 290, 2[
    338, 370, 420, 449, 4[
    579, 704
Mrs. Hannah, 34, 118, 1
Hannah Eliza, 515
Hannah Elizabeth, 313
Hannah Jane, 256
Hannah Louisa, 385, 3
    535
Hannah M., 290
Hannah Maria, 424, 5
    711
Hannah Rose, 519
Hansy, 257
Hansy Sophia, 385
Harley, 364, 436
Harmon, 240, 241, 359
Harmon Benjamin, 527
Harold, 379, 471
Harold Edson, 577
Harold Fitch, 475
Harold Nathan, 360
Harold William, 561
Harriet, 163, 169, 170, 1
    192, 200, 202, 233, 2
    246, 261, 269, 343, 3
    365, 388, 390, 423, 4
    503, 613, 703
Harriet A., 444
Harriett Ann, 359, 511
Harriette Anna, 391, 53
Harriet Christine, 645
Harriet Elizabeth, 3:
    394, 459, 483
Harriet Emma, 482
Harriet Jane, 356, 449
Harriett L., 420
Harriet Louisa, 516
Harriet Lucy, 380
Harriet Marilla, 416
Harriet Newell, 396, 4
    542, 622
Harriette Street, 312
Harriet W., 334
Harriet Welch, 560
Harrison, 320, 460
Harry, 221, 246, 394, 4
    484, 576
Harry B., 443
Harry Beardsley, 517
Harry Dimock, 659
Harry Ellsworth, 519
Harry F., 475
Harry Gilbert, 586
Harry Ross, 545
Harry S., 451

CPSIA information can be obtained
at www.ICGtesting.com
Printed in the USA
LVOW04s2253020516

486389LV00035B/895/P